Berlin Transit

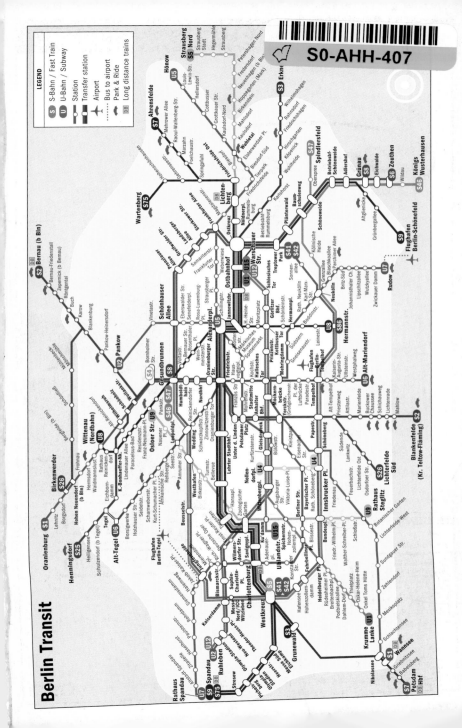

LEGEND

S3	S-Bahn / Fast Train
U	U-Bahn / Subway
	Station
	Transfer station
	Airport
·········	Bus to airport
	Park & Ride
DB	Long distance trains

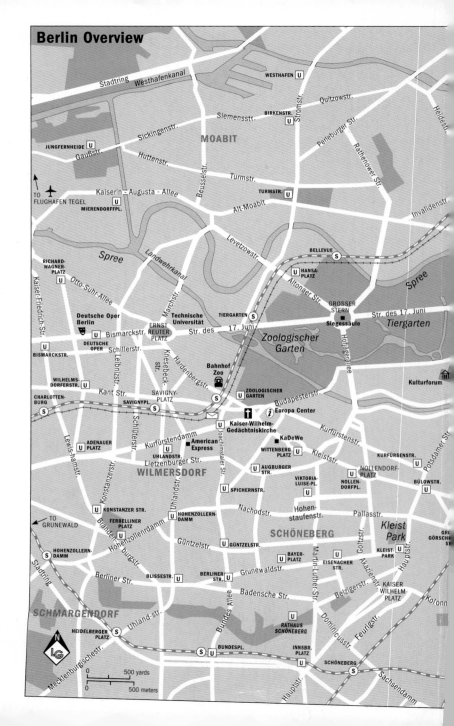

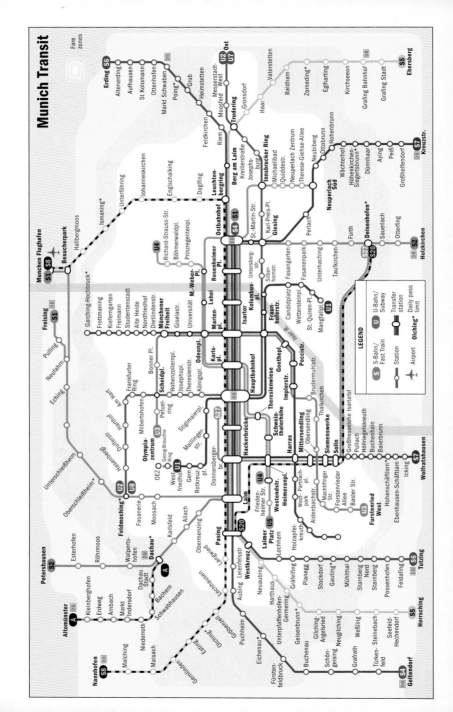

Munich Transit

LET'S GO

■ THE RESOURCE FOR THE INDEPENDENT TRAVELER

"The guides are aimed not only at young budget travelers but at the independent traveler; a sort of streetwise cookbook for traveling alone."

—The New York Times

"Unbeatable; good sight-seeing advice; up-to-date info on restaurants, hotels, and inns; a commitment to money-saving travel; and a wry style that brightens nearly every page."

—The Washington Post

"Lighthearted and sophisticated, informative and fun to read. [Let's Go] helps the novice traveler navigate like a knowledgeable old hand."

—Atlanta Journal-Constitution

"A world-wise traveling companion—always ready with friendly advice and helpful hints, all sprinkled with a bit of wit."

—The Philadelphia Inquirer

■ THE BEST TRAVEL BARGAINS IN YOUR PRICE RANGE

"All the dirt, dirt cheap."

—People

"Anything you need to know about budget traveling is detailed in this book."

—The Chicago Sun-Times

"Let's Go follows the creed that you don't have to toss your life's savings to the wind to travel—unless you want to."

—The Salt Lake Tribune

■ REAL ADVICE FOR REAL EXPERIENCES

"The writers seem to have experienced every rooster-packed bus and lunar-surfaced mattress about which they write."

—The New York Times

"Value-packed, unbeatable, accurate, and comprehensive."

—The Los Angeles Times

"[Let's Go's] devoted updaters really walk the walk (and thumb the ride, and trek the trail). Learn how to fish, haggle, find work—anywhere."

—Food & Wine

LET'S GO PUBLICATIONS

TRAVEL GUIDES

Australia 8th Edition
Austria & Switzerland 12th edition
Brazil 1st edition
Britain & Ireland 2005
California 10th edition
Central America 9th edition
Chile 2nd edition
China 5th edition
Costa Rica 2nd edition
Eastern Europe 2005
Ecuador 1st edition **NEW TITLE**
Egypt 2nd edition
Europe 2005
France 2005
Germany 12th edition
Greece 2005
Hawaii 3rd edition
India & Nepal 8th edition
Ireland 2005
Israel 4th edition
Italy 2005
Japan 1st edition
Mexico 20th edition
Middle East 4th edition
Peru 1st edition **NEW TITLE**
Puerto Rico 1st edition
South Africa 5th edition
Southeast Asia 9th edition
Spain & Portugal 2005
Thailand 2nd edition
Turkey 5th edition
USA 2005
Vietnam 1st edition **NEW TITLE**
Western Europe 2005

ROADTRIP GUIDE

Roadtripping USA **NEW TITLE**

ADVENTURE GUIDES

Alaska 1st edition
New Zealand **NEW TITLE**
Pacific Northwest **NEW TITLE**
Southwest USA 3rd edition

CITY GUIDES

Amsterdam 3rd edition
Barcelona 3rd edition
Boston 4th edition
London 2005
New York City 15th edition
Paris 13th edition
Rome 12th edition
San Francisco 4th edition
Washington, D.C. 13th edition

POCKET CITY GUIDES

Amsterdam
Berlin
Boston
Chicago
London
New York City
Paris
San Francisco
Venice
Washington, D.C.

LET'S GO

GERMANY

KATHERINE J. THOMPSON EDITOR
WILL B. PAYNE ASSOCIATE EDITOR

RESEARCHER-WRITERS
ROSS AUDET
HEATHER BARCLAY
ALEXANDER BEVILACQUA
INGRID GUSTAFSON
MELISSA MUCH
VENU AARRE NADELLA

GENEVIEVE CADWALADER MAP EDITOR
LEIGH PASCAVAGE MANAGING EDITOR

ST. MARTIN'S PRESS ⚓ NEW YORK

Maps by David Lindroth copyright © 2005 by St. Martin's Press.

Let's Go: Germany Copyright © 2005 by Let's Go, Inc. All rights reserved. Printed in the United States of America. No part of this book may be used or reproduced in any manner whatsoever without written permission except in the case of brief quotations embodied in critical articles or reviews. Let's Go is available for purchase in bulk by institutions and authorized resellers. For information, address St. Martin's Press, 175 Fifth Avenue, New York, NY 10010, USA. www.stmartins.com.

Distributed outside the USA and Canada by Macmillan, an imprint of Pan Macmillan Ltd. 20 New Wharf Road, London N1 9RR
Basingstoke and Oxford
Associated companies throughout the world
www.panmacmillan.com

ISBN: 0-312-33548-2
EAN: 978-0312-33548-9
First edition
10 9 8 7 6 5 4 3 2 1

Let's Go: Germany is written by Let's Go Publications, 67 Mount Auburn Street, Cambridge, MA 02138, USA.

Let's Go® and the LG logo are trademarks of Let's Go, Inc.
Printed in the USA.

ABOUT LET'S GO

GUIDES FOR THE INDEPENDENT TRAVELER

At Let's Go, we see every trip as the chance of a lifetime. If your dream is to grab a machete and forge through the jungles of Brazil, we can take you there. If you'd rather bask in the Riviera sun at a beachside cafe, we'll set you a table. We write for readers who know that there's more to travel than sharing double deckers with tourists and who believe that travel can change both themselves and the world—whether they plan to spend six days in London or six months in Latin America. We'll show you just how far your money can go, and prove that the greatest limitation on your adventures is not your wallet, but your imagination. After all, traveling close to the ground lets you interact more directly with the places and people you've gone to see, making for the most authentic experience.

BEYOND THE TOURIST EXPERIENCE

To help you gain a deeper connection with the places you travel, our researchers give you the heads-up on both world-renowned and off-the-beaten-track attractions, sights, and destinations. They engage with the local culture, writing features on regional cuisine, local festivals, and hot political issues. We've also opened our pages to respected writers and scholars to hear their takes on the countries and regions we cover, and asked travelers who have worked, studied, or volunteered abroad to contribute first-person accounts of their experiences. We've also increased our coverage of responsible travel and expanded each guide's Alternatives to Tourism chapter to share more ideas about how to give back to local communities and learn about the places you travel.

FORTY-FIVE YEARS OF WISDOM

Let's Go got its start in 1960, when a group of creative and well-traveled students compiled their experience and advice into a 20-page mimeographed pamphlet, which they gave to travelers on charter flights to Europe. Four and a half decades later, we've expanded to cover six continents and all kinds of travel—while retaining our founders' adventurous attitude toward the world. Our guides are still researched and written entirely by students on shoestring budgets, experienced travelers who know that train strikes, stolen luggage, food poisoning, and marriage proposals are all part of a day's work. This year, we're expanding our coverage of South America and Southeast Asia, with brand-new *Let's Go: Ecuador*, *Let's Go: Peru*, and *Let's Go: Vietnam*. Our adventure guide series is growing, too, with the addition of *Let's Go: Pacific Northwest Adventure* and *Let's Go: New Zealand Adventure*. And we're immensely excited about our new *Let's Go: Roadtripping USA*—two years, eight routes, and sixteen researchers and editors have put together a travel guide like none other.

THE LET'S GO COMMUNITY

More than just a travel guide company, Let's Go is a community. Our small staff comes together because of our shared passion for travel and our desire to help other travelers see the world. We love it when our readers become part of the Let's Go community as well—when you travel, drop us a postcard (67 Mt. Auburn St., Cambridge, MA 02138, USA) or send us an e-mail (feedback@letsgo.com) to tell us about your adventures and discoveries.

For more information, visit us online: www.letsgo.com.

CONTENTS

RESEARCHER-WRITERS

Ross Audet *Schleswig-Holstein, Mecklenburg Vorpommern, Hamburg*

A hiker, mountain biker, and fan of classical music and German hip-hop, Ross took a break from studying electrical engineering to put his stamp of approval on German *Bier* and German beaches. All across the northern coast, he faced sunburnt German tourists and rickety church towers with the same unshakable smile, using his German skills and California smarts to stay alert for potential dangers like quicksand, nude beaches, and wild Hamburg nightlife.

Heather Barclay *Baden-Württemberg, Rheinland-Pfalz, Hessen*

A Divinity School student who has studied her share of saints, Heather overcame enough challenges to earn her own place in the canon; through a mid-lake hailstorm, food poisoning and sunstroke, three broken computers, and logistical nightmares, she found a way to get everything done (and done well), always with unbelievable optimism. Even when covered in mud, Heather managed to make friends with nice German men and backpackers of all nationalities.

Alexander Bevilacqua *Bayern*

Alex, who attended German school in Milan from the tender age of four, passed under many guises during his journey without anyone ever guessing that he was an Australian/Italian researcher currently living in the US. He made interesting new friends on his way through the cities and forests of Bavaria. Alex hopes eventually to hold "some fabulous pan-European job," and in the meantime enjoys studying literature, intellectual history, and philosophy.

Ingrid Gustafson *Sachsen, Sachsen-Anhalt, Thüringen, Niedersachsen*

Though her job (asking touchy Leipzigers about their failed Olympic bid) earned her the occasional (not unexpected) frosty glare, Ingrid's warm Kansas smile thawed the Eastern Germans right out. She stumbled across a wedding deep in the forest, ran a 2½hr. trail in an amazing 70min., and generally had a great time in the wooded hills and vibrant cities of the former East, all the while making acquaintances and receiving advice she never knew she needed.

Melissa Much *Nordrhein-Westfalen, Rheinland-Pfalz, Niedersachsen*

Melissa sped fearlessly from town to town on Germany's western borders, passing enough cornfields to keep her from missing her Iowa hometown (pop. 854), and staying focused despite the lure of the Dutch cities she loves and the siren song of Herbert Grönemeyer concerts. Her graduate studies in environmental science didn't help much in the tiny Frisian Islands, but her German and Dutch skills were as valuable as her loves of hiking, journalism, and travel.

Venu Aarre Nadella *Berlin and Brandenburg*

No single person could embody the spirit that is Berlin, but Venu comes very close. This aggressively outgoing, genuinely sweet, septalingual (yes, *septa*) gospel singer and tennis player charmed and clubbed his way across the city, making friends and breaking hearts as he went. This fall, he'll be taking his degree in Sociology and Swedish to his other favorite city (Helsinki) on a Fulbright scholarship before moving to London to become a consultant.

CONTRIBUTING WRITERS

Mattias Frey was a Researcher-Writer for *Let's Go: Austria & Switzerland 2002*. He is now a freelance film critic and protests from his home in the Kreuzberg neighborhood of Berlin.

Sameer ud Dowla Khan is a graduate student of Linguistics at the University of California, Los Angeles. He is a fan of German in particular, though he's also studied Spanish, Bengali, Chinese, and Arabic, and his current focus is on phonology.

Barbara Richter was a Researcher-Writer for *Let's Go: Austria & Switzerland*. A native Austrian, then New Jersian, she'll be continuing her studies in chemistry and physics at graduate school.

ACKNOWLEDGMENTS

Team Germany thanks: Our RWs, for 24hr. days and unbelievable stories; calm, cool, patient Leigh; ever-unruffled Anne and Prod, for laptops and packages; Genevieve; Joanna's mad proofing skillz; B&I: cutely small but fiercely sexy; A&S, the basement's breath of sanity; EIRE, for teaching us to live *and* to love; Ella for tranquility; Chris, for all the answers; Jesse, für Rat u. Musik; wankery; mochas; HARIBO; Deutsche Post (...just kidding. Our vengeance will be swift. You sure weren't.)

Katherine thanks: Will, you crazy freshman—you stole all my pens but you did a hell of a job with every single thing I threw at you; little Laura, for making sure I ate, big Laura for frozen pencils, both for balconies and sanity; my posse—aesh, bex, jim, zoe—I love you all; coffee runs; Jeremy, who is secretly cut; HRST for parties and painting; kev, drewsef, smeary, whom I love but neglect; molls, mydzi, scotty; G&G and Mimi for understanding why I can't call more; Jaxie, my best friend and swister; Mom and Dad for dragging me to Europe, for teaching me Deutsch, and for everything else.

Will thanks: Katherine, for putting up with my antics; the basement, for being nice to the freshman; Jeremy, for all the times we humiliated Katherine; Laura, for calling me your favorite; Julia, for being silly; Lindsay, for playing the fiddle; Max, for living; Kim, for living through Max's alarm clock; Jimbo, Lowell roomie!; the whole 51 gang; all my C-town buddies; Maura, for everything; Campbell, crazy little bro, for seeing the Cure with me; Mom and Dad for moving us to *Deutschland* and my entire family. Also, Klaus.

Genevieve thanks: GER; the RWs for their hard work and impeccable sense of direction; Elizabeth and mapland for an excellent summer.

Editor
Katherine J. Thompson
Associate Editor
Will B. Payne
Managing Editor
Leigh Pascavage
Map Editor
Genevieve Cadwalader
Typesetter
Christine Yokoyama

LET'S GO

Publishing Director
Emma Nothmann
Editor-in-Chief
Teresa Elsey
Production Manager
Adam R. Perlman
Cartography Manager
Elizabeth Halbert Peterson
Design Manager
Amelia Aos Showalter
Editorial Managers
Briana Cummings, Charlotte Douglas,
Ella M. Steim, Joel August Steinhaus,
Lauren Truesdell, Christina Zaroulis
Financial Manager
R. Kirkie Maswoswe
Marketing and Publicity Managers
Stef Levner, Leigh Pascavage
Personnel Manager
Jeremy Todd
Low-Season Manager
Clay H. Kaminsky
Production Associate
Victoria Esquivel-Korsiak
IT Director
Matthew DePetro
Web Manager
Rob Dubbin
Associate Web Manager
Patrick Swieskowski
Web Content Manager
Tor Krever
Research and Development Consultant
Jennifer O'Brien
Office Coordinators
Stephanie Brown, Elizabeth Peterson

Director of Advertising Sales
Elizabeth S. Sabin
Senior Advertising Associates
Jesse R. Loffler, Francisco A. Robles, Zoe
M. Savitsky
Advertising Graphic Designer
Christa Lee-Chuvala

President
Ryan M. Geraghty
General Manager
Robert B. Rombauer
Assistant General Manager
Anne E. Chisholm

HOW TO USE THIS BOOK

COVERAGE. Welcome to *Let's Go: Germany!* We'll be your guide to all things German, from Aachen to Zittau, from Berlin's throbbing clubs to Munich's leafy *Biergärten*. In this book, each German *Land* (province) has its own chapter, starting with Berlin and moving counterclockwise around the map. Within each *Land*, we begin coverage at the major transportation hub and move outward toward smaller cities, towns, and villages.

PLANNING YOUR TRIP. Our **Discover** section is packed with **suggested itineraries** and must-see cities, sights, and castles to ensure you get the most out of every mile on your trip. Take a look at **Life and Times** to educate yourself on Germany's history and culture, or at **Essentials** to find invaluable tips on planning, packing, and what to do when disaster strikes on the road.

LISTINGS. We list establishments in order of value starting with the best, and awarding our absolute favorites the ▪*Let's Go* **thumbpick.** We know there are days when even the most budget of budget-travelers just want to eat in a nice restaurant or sleep in a hotel with their own shower, so we now offer a **wider range of food and accommodations** options. Rest assured that whether you want to spend €10 or €100 per day, you'll get the best possible value (see xiii for more information).

FEATURE ARTICLES. In addition to up-to-date coverage, this book gives you all the insider information and hidden deals you need to be a traveler instead of a tourist. With our **in-depth features,** learn how to *Prost* with pride (p. 491), discover where you can dine in pitch darkness in Berlin (p. 120), and find out how to save serious money on train tickets (p. 531); plus interviews with locals, the low-down on regional legends and festivals, and **extended articles** on protests in the capital (p. 85), and why the German "Language" is so crazy (p. 60).

LANGUAGE. English may be plenty to get you through large cities like Berlin, Hamburg, and Munich, but in smaller towns, German is still the language of choice. If you're ever at a loss for words, check out the **Appendix** (p. 649) for a guide to speaking *Deutsch* and lists of **useful phrases.** So you won't miss your train to *München* while you're looking for the one to Munich, we list the German name of each city and *Land* first, followed by its English version.

ALTERNATIVES TO TOURISM. Increased tourism has adversely affected many of Germany's cities. To help encourage responsible travel sensitive to the culture, environment, and economy of the destination, this book includes information on volunteer, study, and work options abroad, including a first-hand account of research in a German science lab and advice on how to do that yourself (p. 79).

SOLO TRAVELERS. Information in this guide is presented with the solo traveler in mind. Transportation prices, unless otherwise noted, are one-way, and lodging and food prices are based on the amount one person would spend. Wherever possible, we also list accommodations, discounts, and activities for larger groups.

A NOTE TO OUR READERS. The information for this book was gathered by *Let's Go* researchers from May through August of 2004. Each listing is based on one researcher's opinion, formed during his or her visit at a particular time. Those traveling at other times may have different experiences since prices, dates, hours, and conditions are always subject to change. You are urged to check the facts presented in this book beforehand to avoid inconvenience and surprises.

① ② ③ ④ ⑤

PRICE RANGES>>GERMANY

Our researchers list establishments in order of value from best to worst, with our favorites denoted by the ☒ Let's Go thumbs-up. Since the best value is not always the cheapest price, however, we have also incorporated a system of price ranges, based on a rough expectation of what you will spend. For **accommodations,** we base our range on the cheapest price for which a single traveler can stay for one night. For **restaurants** and other dining establishments, we estimate the average amount a traveler will spend for a meal. The table below tells you what you will *typically* find in Germany at the corresponding price range; keep in mind that no system can allow for every individual establishment's quirks, and that typical prices in Germany vary as much from town to town as they do between regions.

ACCOMMODATIONS	RANGE	WHAT YOU'RE *LIKELY* TO FIND
❶	under €12	Campgrounds, dorm rooms, or dorm-style rooms. Expect bunk beds and a communal bath; you may have to provide or rent towels and sheets.
❷	€12-20	Upper-end hostels or small hotels. You may have a private bathroom, or there may be a sink in your room and communal shower in the hall.
❸	€20-30	A small room with a private bath. Should have decent amenities, such as phone and TV. Breakfast may be included in the price of the room.
❹	€30-50	Similar to 3, but may have more amenities or be in a more highly-touristed or conveniently-located area.
❺	above €50	Large hotels or upscale chains. If it's a 5 and it doesn't have the perks you want, you've paid too much.
FOOD	**RANGE**	**WHAT YOU'RE *LIKELY* TO FIND**
❶	under €4	Probably a fast-food stand, *Imbiß*, university cafeteria, or bakery. Rarely ever a sit-down meal.
❷	€4-8	Some sandwich shops, pizzerias, and take-out options, but also quite a few ethnic restaurants. May be take-out or sit-down.
❸	€8-12	Entrees are more expensive, but chances are, you're paying for decor and ambience. You'll probably have a waiter or waitress, so the tip will bump you up a few euro.
❹	€12-20	As in 3, the higher prices are probably related to better service, but in these restaurants, the food will tend to be a little fancier or more elaborate, or the location will be especially convenient or historical.
❺	above €20	Your meal might cost more than your room, but there's a reason—it's something fabulous or famous, or both, and you'll probably need to wear something other than sandals and a t-shirt.

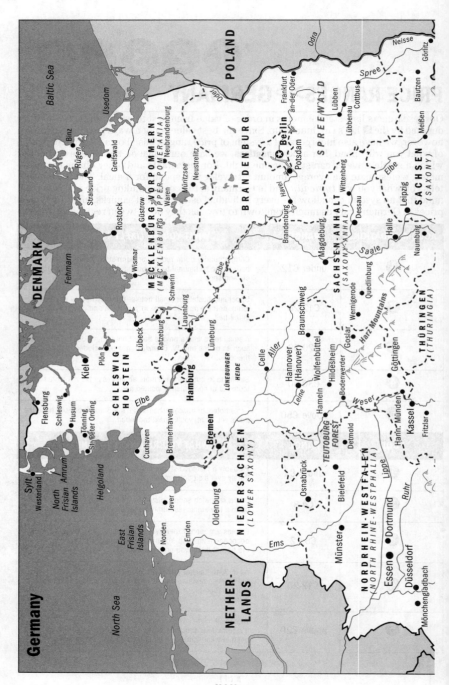

Germany

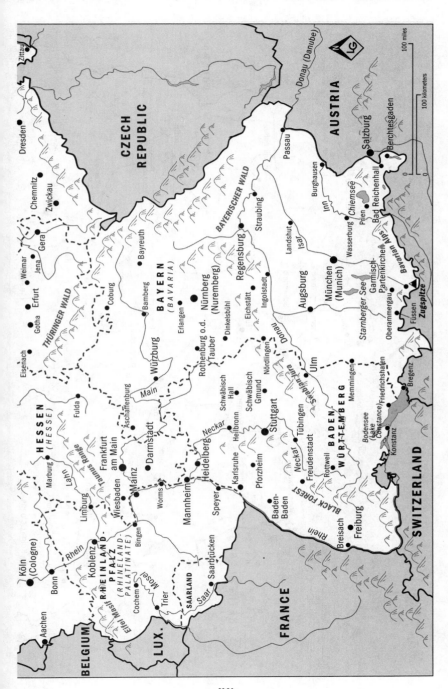

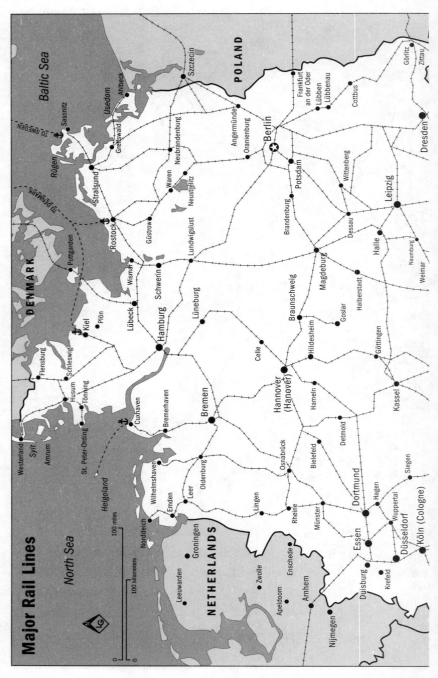

Major Rail Lines

XVI

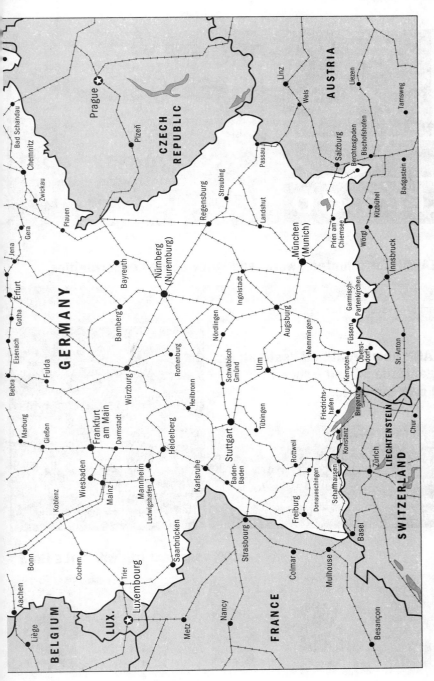

DISCOVER
GERMANY

In the town of Rottweil, deep in the Black Forest of Baden-Württemburg, stands one of the strangest churches in Europe. The Kreuz-Münster Cathedral was built over a span of 700 years in four distinct architectural styles, and should be a monstrosity. But somehow the pieces blend together seamlessly; and that, in a nutshell, is Germany. Forged from dozens of squabbling principalities in the 19th century and rebuilt after two World Wars and 50 years of political division, Germany is a nation where thousands of different mindsets peacefully coexist. The country is 34% Catholic and 34% Protestant. Roman ruins share the horizon with glass-and-steel corporate headquarters. While grim-faced, punctual businessmen and traditional country-folk are going to sleep, purple-haired ecstasy enthusiasts, proudly assertive gay populations, and party-happy youths begin to stumble out of bed. In this land of meat and potatoes, 20% of Germans are vegetarians, and falafel is well on its way to being the most popular type of fast food. Nor does the landscape offer consistency: snow-capped Alps in the south balance sandy beaches and mud flats in the north, with windswept heaths, sprawling lake plains, and castle-dotted river valleys falling in between. Bach and Beethoven have no more of a monopoly on the German psyche than do Kraftwerk or Herbert Grönemeyer, and the average German is more likely to be wearing an American football jersey than a pair of *Lederhosen*. So throw out whatever stereotypes you have and discover Germany.

FACTS AND FIGURES

Only **unified since 1871,** the German nation is younger than the United States.

Germany has the world's **third largest economy,** behind the US and Japan.

At 2.4% of the population, **Turks** form the largest ethnic minority.

Germany's **total population** is approximately 83 million, 10.5% of which is **unemployed.** This rate is around twice as high in the former DDR.

The meat and potatoes diet takes a toll— **68% of German men are overweight.**

Germans drink about **120L of beer per person per year.** German breweries produce **10% of the world's beer.**

The national soccer team holds 3 **World Cups** and 3 **European Championships.** Germany will host **World Cup 2006.**

The **total land area** of Germany is half the size of Montana.

WHEN TO GO

Temperatures and airfares rise with the number of tourists in July and August. May, June, and September have fewer vacationers and cooler, rainier days. Cold and wet weather should never be unexpected in Germany, however: between one-third and one-half of the days each year bring some amount of precipitation, and even in July, hailstorms can blow in to blue skies with little warning. In June and July, school groups overrun the more popular youth hostels, bringing noise, confusion, and hallway-soccer in their wake—don't say we didn't warn you. In the winter months, some German hostels hibernate and museum hours may be shortened. Winter sports gear up in November and continue through April; high season for skiing is mid-December to March. For a temperature chart, see **Climate**, p. 649. For a chart detailing holidays in Germany, see **Holidays,** p. 649.

THINGS TO DO

Germany's alpine wonderlands, seaside resorts, medieval relics and cosmopolitan metropolises form one of the most richly diverse regions in all of Europe. Each of the country's historically distinct cities and regions pulls Germany in its own direction, but the unifying trademark of any German effort is its intensity. Lively modern cities are intensely active; droll storybook villages are intensely provincial; scenic wilderness preserves are intensely natural. For regional attractions, see the **Highlights of the Region** section at the beginning of each chapter.

UNDISCOVERED NATIONAL PARKS

Germany's national parks are gorgeous, fantastically varied, and surprisingly lightly-touristed. The National Parks route in the **Suggested Itineraries** section below will give you an idea of what's available; see each park's section later in the book for a more extensive description.

CATHEDRALS AND CASTLES

Early examples of fine German engineering can be seen in the magnificent castles and cathedrals scattered across the country. Set in a meticulously contrived (but beautiful) park in Potsdam, **Schloß Sanssouci** (p. 153) sports a frilly French Rococo style. In the cliffs over the Rhein River, the romantic half-ruins of **Burg Rheinfels** (p. 359) have underground passages that you can tour by candlelight. Two hundred years after castles went out of style, Mad King Ludwig II commissioned **Neuschwanstein,** the unfinished gem of the **Bavarian Royal Castles,** (p. 472) whose lofty spires inspired Disney's Cinderella's Castle. For our list of the top-ten Teutonic palaces see p. 53. The powerful architectural statements of German secular rulers are divinely answered by the magnificent churches and cathedrals that have been erected across Germany. The epitome of Roman-Catholic extravagance, Cologne's über-big **Dom** (p. 291), the largest High Gothic cathedral in the world, was built sporadically between 1288-1880. Other important cathedrals include the imposing **Münster** (p. 414) in Freiburg, which rings the oldest bells in Germany; the **Frauenkirche** (p. 453) in Munich, whose two distinctive towers dominate the city skyline; and the **Münster** (p. 406) in Ulm, where the largest spire in the world peaks at 161m. Protestant worship houses stake a claim to German skylines as well. Wittenberg is home to the **Schloß-kirche** (p. 586), upon which Martin Luther nailed his *95 Theses* in 1517, sparking the Protestant Revolution. Hamburg's **Große Michaeliskirche** (p. 223) has a famous copper tower which is the city's distinctive symbol. The **Nikolaikirche** in Leipzig (p. 645) is doubly famous as the church in which Bach composed his *St. John's Passion* and as the rallying point for the demonstrations in early October 1989 that hastened the fall of communist East Germany.

FESTIVALS AND HOLIDAYS

If Germany works hard, it plays even harder—time things right, and you can hit a festival in every town you visit. Themes range from the humble (local produce) to the lofty (high culture) to the downright gratuitous (sex-and-drugs-

and-techno-and-pancakes). A few even claim international renown: Munich's **Oktoberfest** (Sept. 17-Oct. 2, 2005), began as a wedding celebration centuries ago, and continues to fill the city with reveling beer drinkers every year. Berlin's **Love Parade,** (which may not take place in 2005 due to financial problems—see **All You Need is $$,** p. 107) reverberates all weekend without sleeping. Famous DJs are imported, bodies are bared, and general hullaballoo ensues. In the spring, Cologne hosts the yearly **Karneval** celebration, where extravagantly costumed fools traipse in parades and general revelry for the week before Ash Wednesday, the wildest day being Rose Monday (Feb. 7, 2005). During Advent, traditional **Christmas Markets** spring up all over Germany, serving *Glühwein* and other holiday spirits. Nürnberg's *Christkindlmarkt* with its glorious *Lebkuchen* (gingerbread) is the most famous. Finally, for film fanatics, Berlin hosts the young but prestigious **Berlinale Film Festival** (Feb. 12-17, 2005) every year.

■ LET'S GO PICKS

BEST ACCOMMODATIONS: Dessau's **Bauhaus** architectural school (p. 588); and a medieval castle among the vineyards of **Bacharach** (p. 360).

BEST BATHROOMS: The **Schwarzes Café** (p. 110) in Berlin's Charlottenburg is home to bathroom "art." It's like peeing in a Prince video. And the **Old Commercial Room** in Hamburg has a throne that's actually...a throne (p. 223).

BEST PLACE TO GET SLOSHED: Riverside beer garden **Zum Flaucher** (p. 460) has yet to be swamped by Munich's tourists; **Andechs** monastery serves the holiest—and at 12%, most potent—brew in Bayern (p. 465); and **Hansens Brauerei** in Flensburg sells its suds by the meter (p. 212).

BEST PLACE TO GET SCHLOß-ED: Mad King Lugwig's fairy-tale Königsschlößer (royal castles) in Bavaria (p. 472), or the ancient relics along the meandering Rhein (p. 358).

BEST PLACE TO WEIN: Nothing to complain about in **Neustadt** (p. 378), where a 2hr. sampling of *Reisinger* runs €6.

BEST PLACE TO DANCE: Try the eclectic **SO36** (p. 144) in Berlin, the house-heavy **U Bar** (p. 335) in Frankfurt, or the industrial **Docks** (p. 232) in Hamburg.

BEST CHANCE FOR *KULTUR*: It doesn't get more grandiose than the opera house at **Bayreuth** (p. 551), which hosts a yearly festival of performances (tickets start at €5 and climb sky-high) in honor of its founder, Richard Wagner.

BEST BEACHES: Sunbathe with the stars on **Sylt** (p. 203), avoid the crowds on nearby **Amrum** (p. 207), or dip into the Baltic Sea from **Rügen Island** (p. 179). The **Bodensee** (p. 427) on the Swiss border is a tropical respite from Germany's wet, gray climate.

BEST SOVIET LEGACIES: Socialist edifices line **Straße der Nationen** (p. 634) in Chemnitz (formerly Karl-Marx-Stadt). In Hamburg, Russia's former **U-434** (p. 226) is the world's largest non-nuclear sub.

BEST SECLUDED SPOT: For pristine beauty in the mountains of Bavaria, visit the town of **Ramsau** (p. 488). **Bad Langensalza** provides a picturesque base for forays into Hainich Nationalpark (p. 582).

***SÄCHS*-IEST SCHWEIZ:** The **Basteiaussicht** (p. 624) in the Sächsische Schweiz looks out over the lush Elbe River Valley.

DIRTIEST FUN: Run across the quicksand-dotted **Wattenmeer** mudflats between the islands of Sylt and Amrum (p. 201) at low tide.

SUGGESTED ITINERARIES

BEST OF GERMANY

THE BEST OF GERMANY (3 WEEKS)
Enter Germany at its center, **Berlin** (p. 83). The capital's enormous cultural and historical treasures, not to mention its chaotic nightlife, sprawl over an area eight times the size of Paris. Save time for a daytrip to the Neoclassical splendors of nearby **Potsdam** (p. 151). The jumping nightlife, exquisite palaces, and museums of **Dresden** (p. 606) are no less intense, but nearby **Leipzig** (p. 640) eases the burn with a laid-back college crowd and museums and monuments galore. **Weimar** (p. 558), the most thoroughly rebuilt city in Eastern Germany, rests solidly on the cultural heritage of Goethe, the *Bauhaus* architectural movement, and Germany's first liberal constitution. Continue your trip into Germany's past in **Rothenburg** (p. 530), a medieval city that deserves to be as kitschy as it wants to be. As the capital of Bavaria, **Munich** (p. 435), takes merriment and *Gemütlichkeit* seriously; its excellent museums and jovial beer halls both bear witness to its prosperity. Continuing south, the castles of **Neuschwanstein, Hohenschwangau,** and **Linderhof** make up the fairy-tale triumvirate of Mad King

Ludwig's **royal castles** (p. 472). Head west into Baden-Württemberg to live out your favorite Brothers' Grimm fairy tale in the **Black Forest** (p. 418); from the winding alleys of **Freiburg** (p. 411) to the mountain-top lakes at **Titisee** and **Schluchsee** (p. 421), magic fills the air. To the north, **Heidelberg** (p. 388) is home to Germany's oldest, most prestigious, and most scenic university and the brooding ruins of the city's castle. Next stop: **Koblenz** (p. 353), gateway to the Rhein and Mosel. Daytrip to the **Lorelei** cliffs of the **Rhein Valley** (p. 359) and embark on a side-trip to the wine-growing **Mosel Valley** (p. 365). Next, saunter northward to **Cologne** (p. 285), site of Germany's largest cathedral, the magnificent Gothic **Kölner Dom,** and home to a driving nightlife. Then head north to **Bremen,** a storybook town that is surprisingly cosmopolitan. A skip to the northeast, reckless **Hamburg** (p. 213), Germany's second largest city, fuses the burliness of a port town with city flair, while the stolid townhouses of **Lübeck** (p. 190) recall an earlier age when the town was capital of the Hanseatic league.

THE RHEIN AND WINE (1 WEEK) The famous valleys of Rheinland-Pfalz and Baden-Württemberg are tightly grouped, making an excellent bike or bus tour. Trains are less convenient, but travel to the area's major towns, permitting excursions into the valleys below. Start off in **Stuttgart** (p. 380) and spend a day walking the nearby fountains of the Schloßgarten or partying on Königstraße. Then move on to Germany's most popular Unitown, **Heidelberg** (p. 388), taking time to look at the city's famed castle from the *Philosophenweg* trail across the Neckar. Heidelberg is a perfect base for daytrips down the **Neckar Valley** (p. 393), a miraculously untouristed stretch of the river that weaves between lookout castles and thickly forested hills. Ferry across the Rhein to touristy **Rüdesheim** (p. 361), then stop off for a visit to the famed wineries of **Bacharach** (p. 360), or continue

NIGHTLIFE TOUR

Hamburg

Berlin

Düsseldorf
Köln (Cologne)

Dresden

Frankfurt

München (Munich)

guardian of Germany's most respected ritual: the mass consumption of beer. The Bavarian metropolis manages to feel old-world while fostering impressive punk and gay scenes. If money is what you want, head to the fashion-conscious economic capital, **Frankfurt** (p. 325), where only the rich and the beautiful make it past the bouncer. Or head for **Cologne** (p. 285) to indulge in a few (dozen?) rounds of the local specialty-brew, *Kölsch.* Stop in **Düsseldorf** (p. 307) to pay homage to "the longest bar counter in the world:" 500 pubs stretching across the Old Town. Last stop: **Hamburg** (p. 213), where everything—yes, *everything*—is for sale along the *Reeperbahn,* Germany's most notorious red-light district. If that's not your thing, chill with the fun-loving student crowd in the Sternschanze. Whew. Tired out? Oh, hell—go back to Berlin and start over again. You can always sleep on the train.

DISCOVER

ESSENTIALS

PLANNING YOUR TRIP

ENTRANCE REQUIREMENTS
Passport (p. 9). Required of citizens of Australia, Canada, Ireland, New Zealand, the UK, and the US.
Visa (p. 10). May be required of citizens of other countries.
Work Permit (p. 10). Required of all foreigners planning to work in Germany.

EMBASSIES AND CONSULATES

GERMAN CONSULAR SERVICES ABROAD

The German embassy or consulate in your home country can supply legal information concerning your trip, arrange for visas, and direct you to a wealth of other information about tourism, education, and employment in Germany. For a listing of German embassies and consulates worldwide, visit www.auswaertiges-amt.de.

Australia: Embassy: **Canberra,** 119 Empire Circuit, Yarralumla, ACT 2600 (☎02 6270 1911; www.germanembassy.org.au). Consulates: **Melbourne,** 480 Punt Rd., South Yarra, VIC 3141 (☎03 9864 6888; meldiplo@bigpond.net.au); **Sydney,** 13 Trelawney St., Woollahra, NSW 2025 (☎02 9328 7733; info@sydney.diplo.de).

Canada: Embassy: **Ottawa,** 1 Waverly St., ON, K2P OT8 (☎613 232 1101; www.ottawa.diplo.de). Consulates: **Montréal,** Edifice Marathon Ste. 4315, 1250 Blvd. René-Lévesque Ouest, Québec, H3B 4X1 (☎514-931-2277; www.montreal.diplo.de); **Toronto,** 77 Bloor St. West Ste. 1702, Toronto ON, M5S 2T1 (☎416 925 2813; www.germanconsulatetoronto.ca); **Vancouver,** World Trade Centre Ste. 704, 999 Canada Pl., Vancouver, BC, V6C 3E1 (☎604 684 8377; germanconsulatevancouver@telus.net).

Ireland: Embassy: **Dublin,** 31 Trimleston Ave., Booterstown, Blackrock/Co (☎01 269 3011; www.germanembassy.ie).

New Zealand: Embassy: **Wellington,** 90-92 Hobson St., Thorndon (☎04 473 6063; www.deutschebotschaftwellington.co.nz).

UK: Embassy: **London,** 23 Belgrave Sq. SW1X 8PZ (☎020 7824 1300; www.germanembassy.org.uk). Consulate: **Edinburgh,** 16 Eglington Crescent, Edinburgh, EH 12 5DG, Scotland (☎0131 337 2323; fax 346 1578).

US: Embassy: **Washington, D.C.,** 4645 Reservoir Rd. N.W. 20007-1998 (☎202-298-4000; www.germany-info.org). Consulates: **New York,** 871 U.N. Plaza, NY 10017 (☎212-610-9700; fax 610-9702); **Los Angeles,** 6222 Wilshire Blvd., Ste. 500, CA 90048 (☎323-30-2703; losangeles@germanconsulate.org); other consulates in **Atlanta, Boston, Chicago, Houston, Miami,** and **San Francisco** (see embassy website for contact information).

CONSULAR SERVICES IN GERMANY

For the latest information, contact the **Auswärtiges Amt,** Wederscher Markt 1, 11013 Berlin (Federal Foreign Office; ☎030 5000 0; www.auswaertiges-amt.de). Foreign embassies in Berlin are listed on p. 95. For a complete list of foreign missions in Germany, see www.auswaertiges-amt.de/www/en/laenderinfos/vertretungen.

Australia: Frankfurt, Grüneburgweg 58-62, 60322 (☎069 90 55 80; fax 90 55 81 19).

Canada: Düsseldorf, Bernratherstr. 8, 40213 (☎0211 172 17 28; ddorf@dfait-maeci.gc.ca). **Hamburg,** Ballindamm 35, 20095 (☎040 460 02 70; hamburg@consulates-canada.de). **Munich,** Tal 29, 80331 (☎089 219 95 70; munic@dfait-maeci.gc.ca). All are listed at www.kanada-info.de.

Ireland: Frankfurt, Oberlindau 5, 60323 (☎069 97 14 21 51; fax 97 14 21 55). **Hamburg,** Feldbrunnenstr. 43, 20148 (☎040 44 18 62 13; fax 44 10 80 50). **Munich,** Denninger Str. 15, 81679 (☎089 20 80 59 90; fax 20 80 59 89).

New Zealand: Hamburg, Domstr. 19, 20095 (☎(040) 442 55 50; fax 44 25 55 49).

UK: Düsseldorf, Yorckstr. 19, 40476 (☎0211 944 80; www.british-consulate-general.de). **Frankfurt,** Trition Haus, Bockenheimer Landstr. 42, 60323 (☎069 170 00 20; fax 72 95 53). **Hamburg,** Harvestehuder Weg 8a, 20148 (☎040 448 03 20; fax 4 10 72 59). **Munich,** Bürkleinstr. 10, 80538 (☎089 21 10 90; fax 21 10 91 66). **Stuttgart,** Breite Str. 2, 70173 (☎0711 16 26 90; fax 1 62 69 30).

US: Düsseldorf, Willi-Becker-Allee 10, 40227 (☎0211 78 88 09 27; fax 788 89 38). **Frankfurt,** Siesmayerstr. 21, 60323 (☎069 753 50; fax 75 35 23 00). **Hamburg,** Alsterufer 27/28, 20354 (☎040 411 71 10; fax 411 71 12 22). **Leipzig,** Wilhelm-Seyfferth-Str. 4, 04107 (☎0341 213 84 10; fax 213 84 71). **Munich,** Königinstr. 5, 80539 (☎089 288 80; fax 28 30 47).

TOURIST OFFICES

The **German National Tourist Board** is based in Frankfurt at Beethovenstr. 69, 60325 (www.deutschland-tourismus.de).

Australia: Sydney, German National Tourist Office, G.P.O. Box 1461, Sydney, N.S.W. 2001 (☎02 82 96 04 88; gnto@germany.org.au).

Canada: Toronto, 480 University Ave. Ste. 1410, Ontario M5G 1V2 (☎416 968 1685; info@gnto.ca).

UK: London, P.O. Box 2695, W1A 3TN (☎20 7317 0908; www.germany-tourism.co.uk).

US: New York, 122 E. 42nd St., 52nd fl., New York, NY 10168-0072 (☎212 661 7200; www.cometogermany.com). **Los Angeles,** 8484 Wilshire Blvd. Ste. 440, Beverly Hills, CA 90211 (☎323 655 6085; gntolax@aol.com). **Chicago,** P.O. Box 59594, Chicago, IL 60659-9594 (☎773 539 6303; gntoch@aol.com).

DOCUMENTS AND FORMALITIES

PASSPORTS

REQUIREMENTS
Citizens of Australia, Canada, Ireland, New Zealand, the UK, and the US need valid passports to enter Germany and to re-enter their home countries. Germany does not allow entrance if the holder's passport expires in under six months; returning home with an expired passport is illegal, and may result in a fine.

NEW PASSPORTS
Citizens of Australia, Canada, Ireland, New Zealand, the UK, and the US can apply for a passport at any passport office and many post offices and courts of law. All applications must be filed well in advance of your departure, although most passport offices offer rush services (which take about 2 weeks) for a very steep fee.

ONE EUROPE. European unity has come a long way since 1958, when the European Economic Community (EEC) was created to promote European solidarity and cooperation. Since then, the EEC has become the European Union (EU), a mighty political, legal, and economic institution. On May 1, 2004, Cyprus, the Czech Republic, Estonia, Hungary, Latvia, Lithuania, Malta, Poland, Slovakia, and Slovenia—were admitted to the EU, joining Austria, Belgium, Denmark, Finland, France, Germany, Greece, Ireland, Italy, Luxembourg, the Netherlands, Portugal, Spain, Sweden, and the UK.

What does this have to do with the average non-EU tourist? The EU's policy of **freedom of movement** means that border controls between the first 15 member states (minus Ireland and the UK, but plus Norway and Iceland) have been abolished, and visa policies harmonized. While you're still required to carry a passport (or government-issued ID card for EU citizens) when crossing an internal border, once you've been admitted into one country, you're free to travel to other participating states. Britain and Ireland have also formed a **common travel area,** abolishing passport controls between the UK and the Republic of Ireland.

PASSPORT MAINTENANCE

Photocopy the page of your passport with your photo, as well as your visas, traveler's check serial numbers, and any other important documents. Carry one set of copies in a safe place, apart from the originals, and leave another set at home. Consulates also recommend that you carry an expired passport or an official copy of your birth certificate in a part of your baggage separate from other documents.

If you lose your passport, immediately notify the local police and the nearest embassy or consulate of your home government. You will need to know all information previously recorded and show ID and proof of citizenship. Any visas stamped in your old passport will be irretrievably lost. If you need to re-enter your home country right away, ask for immediate temporary traveling papers.

WORK PERMITS

Admission as a visitor does not include the right to work, which is authorized only by a work permit, obtainable after entry into Germany. Entering Germany to study requires a special student visa (see **Alternatives to Tourism,** p. 74).

IDENTIFICATION

When you travel, always carry at least two forms of identification on your person, including a photo ID; a passport and a driver's license or birth certificate is usually adequate. Never carry all of your IDs together; split them up in case of theft or loss, and keep photocopies of all of them in your luggage and at home.

STUDENT, TEACHER, AND YOUTH IDENTIFICATION

The **International Student Identity Card (ISIC),** the most widely accepted form of student ID, provides discounts on some sights, accommodations, food, and transport; access to a 24hr. emergency helpline; and insurance benefits for US cardholders (see **Insurance,** p. 19). In Germany, discounts apply to many hostels, bus tickets, museums, bike rentals, and theater tickets; check www.isic.org for an updated listing of benefits. Applicants must be full-time secondary or post-secondary school students at least 12 years of age. Because of the proliferation of fake ISICs, some services (particularly airlines) require additional proof of student status.

The **International Teacher Identity Card (ITIC)** offers teachers the same insurance coverage as the ISIC and similar but limited discounts. For travelers who are 25 years old or under but are not students, the **International Youth Travel Card (IYTC)** also offers many of the same benefits as the ISIC. Each of these cards costs US$22 or equivalent. ISIC and ITIC cards are valid for roughly one and a half academic years; IYTC cards are valid for one year from the date of issue. Many student travel agencies (p. 23) issue the cards; for a list of issuing agencies or more information, see the **International Student Travel Confederation (ISTC)** website (www.istc.org).

The **International Student Exchange Card (ISE)** is a similar identification card available to students, faculty, and youth (ages 12 to 26). The card provides a number of discounts in Germany, medical benefits, access to a 24hr. emergency helpline, and the ability to purchase student airfares. The card costs US$25; call US ☎ 800-255-8000 for more info, or visit www.isecard.com.

CUSTOMS

Upon **entering Germany,** you must declare certain items from abroad and pay a duty on values that exceed a certain allowance. (Unless you plan to import a BMW, you can probably pass right through the customs barrier with minimal to-do.)

 CUSTOMS IN THE EU. As well as freedom of movement of people within the EU (p. 10), travelers in the 15 original EU member countries (Austria, Belgium, Denmark, Finland, France, Germany, Greece, Ireland, Italy, Luxembourg, the Netherlands, Portugal, Spain, Sweden, and the UK) can also take advantage of the freedom of movement of goods. This means that there are no customs controls at internal EU borders (i.e., you can take the blue customs channel at the airport), and travelers are free to transport whatever legal substances they like as long as it is for their own personal (non-commercial) use—up to 800 cigarettes, 10L of spirits, 90L of wine (60L of sparkling wine), and 110L of beer. You should also be aware that duty-free allowances were abolished on June 30, 1999 for travel between EU member states; however, travelers between the EU and the rest of the world still get a duty-free allowance when passing through customs.

Non-EU citizens may "import" gifts and commodities for personal use into Germany according to the following limits: 200 cigarettes (or tobacco equivalent); 1L of spirits stronger than 44 proof, or 2L of weaker spirits, sparkling wines, or liqueur; 2L of table wine; 50g of perfume; and 500g of coffee. To prevent problems with transporting **prescription drugs,** bring their original bottles and a copy of your prescription. The total value of all other personal use goods cannot exceed €175, but there are no regulations on the import or export of currency. Upon **returning home,** you must declare all articles acquired abroad and pay a duty on the value of articles that exceed the allowance established by your country's customs service. Goods and gifts purchased at **duty-free** shops abroad are not exempt from duty or sales tax; "duty-free" merely means that you need not pay a tax in the country of purchase. Duty-free allowances have been abolished for travel between EU member states, but still exist for those arriving from outside the EU. In order to expedite your return, make a list of any valuables brought from home and register them with customs before traveling abroad, and keep receipts for all goods acquired abroad. Germany also levies a Value-Added Tax on all consumer purchases, but non-EU tourists are usually able to get these taxes refunded on large items (p. 15).

MONEY

CURRENCY AND EXCHANGE

The currency chart below is based on August 2004 exchange rates between local currency and Australian dollars (AUS$), Canadian dollars (CDN$), European Union euros (EUR€), New Zealand dollars (NZ$), British pounds (UK£), and US dollars (US$). Check the currency converters on websites like www.xe.com or www.bloomberg.com or in a large newspaper for the latest exchange rates.

EURO (€)		
AUS$ = €0.59		€1 = AUS$1.70
CDN$ = €0.63		€1 = CDN$1.59
NZ$ = €0.53		€1 = NZ$1.87
UK£ = €1.50		€1 = UK£0.67
US$ = €0.82		€1 = US$1.21

As a general rule, it's cheaper to convert money in Germany than at home. While currency exchange will probably be available in your arrival airport, it's wise to bring enough foreign currency to last for the first 24-72 hr. of your trip.

When changing money abroad, you lose money with every transaction, so **convert large sums** (unless the currency is depreciating rapidly), **but no more than you'll need.** If you use traveler's checks or bills, carry some in small denominations (the equivalent of US$50 or less) for times when you need to exchange money at disadvantageous rates, but bring a range of denominations since charges may be levied per check cashed. Store your money in a variety of forms; ideally, at any given time you will have some cash, traveler's checks, and an ATM and/or credit card.

TRAVELER'S CHECKS

Traveler's checks are one of the safest and least troublesome means of carrying funds, and most German banks will cash them, though very few shops, hotels, or other privately owned establishments will. American Express and Visa are the most recognized brands, but Travelex/Thomas Cook checks are also accepted by many German banks. Many banks and agencies sell them for a small commission. Check issuers provide refunds if the checks are lost or stolen, and many provide

THE EURO. The official currency of 12 members of the European Union—Austria, Belgium, Finland, France, Germany, Greece, Ireland, Italy, Luxembourg, the Netherlands, Portugal, and Spain—is the euro. The currency has some important—and positive—consequences for travelers hitting more than one euro-zone country. For one thing, money-changers across the euro-zone are obliged to exchange money at the official, fixed rate (see below), and at no commission (though they may still charge a small service fee). Second, euro-denominated traveler's checks allow you to pay for goods and services across the euro-zone, again at the official rate and commission-free. For more info on the Euro, check a currency converter (such as www.xe.com) or www.europa.eu.int.

additional services, such as toll-free refund hotlines abroad, emergency message services, and stolen credit card assistance. Ask about refund hotlines and the location of refund centers when purchasing checks, and always carry emergency cash.

American Express: Cheques available with commission at select banks, at all AmEx offices, and online (www.americanexpress.com; US residents only). Also offered are "Cheques for Two," which allow 2 people to sign and use a single set of checks. American Express cardholders can purchase checks by phone (☎800 721 9768). Cheques available in AUS$, CAN$, EUR€, JPN¥, UK£, and US$. For purchase locations or more information contact AmEx's service centers: in Germany ☎0180 22 55 222; in Australia 800 68 80 22; in New Zealand 0508 555 358; in the UK 0800 587 6023; in the US and Canada 800-221-7282; elsewhere, call the US collect at 1-801-964-6665.

Visa: Checks available (generally with commission) at banks worldwide. For the location of the nearest office, call Visa's service centers: in the UK ☎0 800 89 5078; in the US 800 227-6811; elsewhere, call the UK collect at 44 173 331 8949. Checks available in CAN$, EUR€, JPN¥, UK£, and US$.

Travelex/Thomas Cook: Issues Visa traveler's checks. Members of AAA and affiliated automobile associations receive a 25% commission discount on check purchases. In the US and Canada call ☎800-287-7362 or 800-223-7373; in the UK call 0800 62 21 01; elsewhere call the UK collect at 44 1733 31 89 50.

CREDIT, DEBIT, AND ATM CARDS

Credit cards are usually accepted by large establishments in Germany, and more rarely by private pensions or small restaurants. Where they are accepted, credit cards often offer superior exchange rates—up to 5% better than the retail rate used by banks and other currency exchange establishments. Credit cards may also offer services such as insurance or emergency help, and are sometimes required to reserve hotel rooms or rental cars. **Mastercard** (a.k.a. EuroCard or Access in Europe) and **Visa** (a.k.a. Barclaycard) are the most widely accepted; **American Express** cards work at some ATMs and at AmEx offices and major airports.

ATM cards are very popular in Germany. Depending on the system that your home bank uses, you can most likely access your personal bank account from abroad with the same four-digit PIN you use at home. ATMs get the same wholesale exchange rate as credit cards, but there is often a limit on the amount you can withdraw per day (usually around US$500). There is typically also a surcharge of US$1-5 per withdrawal. Some ATMs will only allow you to withdraw in €50 or €100 increments, and few allow you to check the balance of a foreign bank account. The two major international money networks are **Cirrus** (US ☎800-424-7787 or www.mastercard.com) and **Visa/PLUS** (US ☎800-843-7587 or www.visa.com). Most ATMs charge a transaction fee that is paid to the bank that owns the ATM.

Debit cards are a relatively new form of purchasing power that are as convenient as credit cards but have a more immediate impact on your funds. A debit card can be used wherever its associated credit card company (usually Mastercard or Visa) is accepted, but the money is withdrawn directly from the holder's checking account. Debit cards often also function as ATM cards and can be used to withdraw cash from associated banks and ATMs throughout Germany.

American Express also offers a TravelFunds® card: a reloadable, debit-type card not linked to your bank account, making theft of it less of an issue. To learn more, call ☎ 1-888-412-6945 in the US, or call collect from elsewhere 1 801 945 9450.

ATMS AND PINS. To use a cash or credit card to withdraw money from a cash machine (ATM) in Europe, you must have a 4-digit **Personal Identification Number (PIN).** If your PIN is longer than 4 digits, ask your bank whether you will need a new one, or if you can just use the first four. **Credit cards** don't usually have PINs, so if you want to hit up German ATMs with a credit card to get cash advances, call your credit card company before leaving to request one.

Travelers with alphabetic, rather than numerical, PINs may also be thrown off by the lack of letters on European cash machines. The following are the corresponding numbers to use: 1=QZ; 2=ABC; 3=DEF; 4=GHI; 5=JKL; 6=MNO; 7=PRS; 8=TUV; and 9=WXY. Note that if you mistakenly punch the wrong code into the machine 3 times, it will **swallow your card for good.**

GETTING MONEY FROM HOME

If you run out of money while traveling, the easiest and cheapest solution is to have someone back home make a deposit to the bank account linked to your credit or ATM card. Failing that, consider one of the following options. The online **International Money Transfer Consumer Guide** (http://international-money-transfer-consumer-guide.info) may also be of help.

WIRING MONEY

It is possible to arrange a **bank money transfer** *(Überweisung)*, which means asking a bank back home to wire money to a bank in Germany. This is the cheapest way to transfer cash, but it's also the slowest, usually taking several days or more. Note that some banks may only release your funds in local currency, potentially sticking you with a poor exchange rate; inquire about this in advance. Money transfer services like **Western Union** are faster and more convenient than bank transfers—but also much pricier. Western Union has many locations worldwide. To find one, visit www.westernunion.com, or call in Australia ☎ 800 501 500, in Canada 800-235-0000, in the UK 0800 83 38 33, in the US 800-325-6000, or in Germany ☎ 030 18 03 03 03 30 (Berlin) or 089 69 24 27 85 91 (Munich). Money transfer services are also available at **American Express** and **Thomas Cook** offices.

US STATE DEPARTMENT (US CITIZENS ONLY)

In serious emergencies only, the US State Department will forward money within hours to the nearest consular office, which will then disburse it according to instructions for a US$30 fee. If you wish to use this service, you must contact the Overseas Citizens Service division of the US State Department (☎ 317-472-2328; nights, Sundays, and holidays 202-647-4000).

COSTS

The cost of your trip will vary considerably depending on where you go, how you travel, and where you stay. The most significant expenses will probably be your round-trip **airfare** to Germany (see **Getting to Germany: By Plane,** p. 23) and a **railpass** or **bus pass** (p. 29). Before you go, spend some time calculating a reasonable daily **budget.**

STAYING ON A BUDGET

Though it varies by region, a bare-bones day in Germany (camping or sleeping in hostels/guesthouses, buying food at supermarkets) might cost about €30-40 (US$35-50); a slightly more comfortable day (sleeping in hostels/guesthouses or budget hotels, eating one meal per day at a restaurant, going out at night) would cost €50-70 (US$70-85); and for a luxurious day, the sky's the limit. Don't forget to factor in emergency reserve funds (at least US$200) when planning how much money you'll need.

TIPS FOR SAVING MONEY

Simpler ways to save include searching out free entertainment, splitting accommodation and food costs with trustworthy fellow travelers, and buying food in supermarkets rather than eating out. Bring a **sleepsack** (p. 15) to save on sheet charges in hostels, and do your **laundry** in the sink (unless you're explicitly prohibited from doing so). That said, don't go overboard; staying within your budget is important, but not at the expense of your health or a great travel experience.

TIPPING AND BARGAINING

Tipping is not practiced as liberally in Germany as it is elsewhere—most Germans only round up a euro or two in restaurants and bars as tip, no matter the bill, and may give a small tip when they are getting a service, like a taxi ride. Tips in Germany are not left lying on the table, but handed directly to the server when you pay. If you don't want any change, say *Das steht so* (dahs SHTAYT zo) or *Das stimmt so* (dahs SHTIMT zo). Germans rarely bargain except at flea markets.

TAXES

Most goods and services bought in Germany include a **Value-Added Tax** of 16% (7% for books) called the *Mehrwertsteuer* (MwSt). Non-EU citizens can usually get MwSt refunded for large purchases (not services). Ask for a **Tax-Free Shopping Form** at points of purchase, and present it at customs upon leaving the country, along with your receipts and the goods (which must remain unused until you leave the country). Refunds can be claimed at **Tax Free Shopping Offices,** found at most airports, road borders, and ferry stations, or by mail (Tax-Free Shopping Processing Center, Trubelg. 19, 1030 Vienna, Austria). For more information, contact the German VAT refund hotline (in English, ☎ 49 228 406 2880; vathotline@bff.bund.de).

PACKING

Pack lightly: Lay out only what you need, then take half the clothes and twice the money. The Travelite FAQ (www.travelite.org) is a good resource for tips on traveling light. If you plan to do some hiking, also consult **Camping and the Outdoors,** p. 42.

> **Luggage:** A sturdy **frame backpack** is unbeatable. (For pack-buying-basics, see p. 44.) Toting a **suitcase** or **trunk** is fine if you plan to stay in 1 or 2 cities and explore from there, but not a great idea if you plan to move around frequently. In addition to your main piece of luggage, a **daypack** (a small backpack or courier bag) is useful.

> **Clothing:** Germany is fairly temperate, but places like the northern islands and the Alps can get very cold very fast, and the weather all over Germany is unpredictable. It is always a good idea to bring a warm jacket or wool sweater, a rain jacket, sturdy shoes or hiking boots, and thick socks. Flip-flops or waterproof sandals are must-haves for grubby hostel showers. You may also want one outfit for going out, and maybe a nicer pair of shoes. Many religious or cultural sites request modest and respectful dress.

> **Sleepsack:** Some hostels require that you either provide your own linen or rent sheets from them. Save cash by making your own sleepsack: fold a full-size sheet in half the long way, then sew it closed along the long side and one of the short sides.

Converters and Adapters: In Germany, electricity is 220 volts AC, enough to fry any 120V North American appliance. Residents of Canada, the UK, and the US should buy an adapter (which changes the shape of the plug; US$5) and a converter (which changes the voltage; US$20-30). Don't make the mistake of using only an adapter (unless appliance instructions explicitly state otherwise). Australians and New Zealanders (who use 230V at home) won't need a converter, but will need a set of adapters to use anything electrical. For more on all things adaptable, check out http://kropla.com/electric.htm.

Toiletries: Toothbrushes, towels, cold-water soap, talcum powder (to keep feet dry), deodorant, razors, tampons, and condoms are often available (look for an *Apotheke*), but may be difficult to find; bring extras. **Contact lenses** are likely to be expensive and difficult to find, so bring enough extra pairs and solution for your entire trip. Also bring your glasses and a copy of your prescription in case you need emergency replacements.

First-Aid Kit: A basic first-aid kit: bandages, pain reliever, antibiotic cream, a thermometer, Swiss Army knife, tweezers, moleskin, decongestant, motion-sickness remedy, diarrhea or upset-stomach medication, antihistamines, sunscreen, insect repellent, burn ointment, a syringe for emergencies (get an explanatory letter from your doctor).

Film: Film and developing in Germany are expensive, so consider bringing along enough film for your entire trip and developing it at home. Less serious photographers may want to bring a disposable camera or two. Despite disclaimers, airport security X-rays can fog film, so buy a lead-lined pouch at a camera store or ask security to hand-inspect it. Always pack film in your carry-on luggage, since higher-intensity X-rays are used on checked luggage. A **digital camera** can save a lot of money and trouble on the road, but will need frequent recharging and is very attractive to thieves. A single memory chip may not last for your entire trip, and while some Internet cafes allow the burning of CDs, many others don't, and those who do may charge exorbitant prices.

Other Useful Items: Bring a **money belt** and small **padlock**. Basic **outdoors equipment** (plastic water bottle, compass, waterproof matches, pocketknife, sunglasses, sunscreen, hat) can also be useful. **Quick repairs** of torn clothes can be done with a needle and thread; electrical tape is also good for patching tears. If you want to do laundry by hand, bring detergent, a small rubber ball to stop up the sink, and string for a makeshift clothes line. **Other things** to pack include a rain coat or poncho; sealable **plastic bags** (for wet clothes, soap, food, or shampoo); an **alarm clock;** safety pins; rubber bands; a flashlight; earplugs; trash bags; and a small **calculator**. A **cell phone** can be a lifesaver (literally) on the road; see p. 36 for information.

Important Documents: Don't forget your passport, ATM and/or credit cards, adequate ID, and photocopies of all these documents in case they are lost or stolen (p. 10). Also useful are: traveler's checks (p. 12); a hosteling membership card (p. 39); driver's license (p. 10); travel insurance forms; ISIC card (p. 10); and rail or bus pass (p. 29).

SAFETY AND HEALTH

GENERAL ADVICE

In any type of crisis situation, the most important thing to do is **stay calm.** Your country's embassy abroad (p. 8) is usually your best resource when things go wrong; registering with that embassy upon arrival in the country is often a good idea. The government offices listed in the **Travel Advisories** box below can provide information on the services they offer their citizens in case of emergencies abroad.

LOCAL LAWS AND POLICE

DRUGS AND ALCOHOL

A meek "I didn't know it was illegal" will not fly in Germany; it is your responsibility to familiarize yourself with local laws. If you carry insulin, syringes, or any **prescription drugs,** you must have a copy of the prescriptions and a doctor's note. Avoid public drunkenness; it can jeopardize your safety and earn the disdain of locals. The (not strongly enforced) drinking age in Germany is 16 for beer and wine and 18 for spirits. The maximum blood alcohol level for drivers is 0.08%.

Needless to say, **illegal drugs** are best avoided; the average sentence for possession in Germany is seven years. In 1994, the German High Court ruled that while **possession of marijuana or hashish is still illegal,** possession of "small quantities for personal consumption" is not prosecutable. Each *Land* has interpreted "small quantities" differently. More liberal areas like Berlin and Hamburg tend toward the higher end of this range, while East Germany and more conservative states like Bavaria are less lenient. The worst thing you can possibly do is carry drugs across an international border; not only could you end up in prison, you could be stained with a "Drug Trafficker" stamp on your passport for life. If arrested, call your country's consulate. Embassies may not be willing to help those arrested on drug charges. Refuse to carry anyone's excess luggage onto a plane; it's better to look a little unchivalrous than to end up in jail for possession of a controlled substance.

SPECIFIC CONCERNS

TRAVEL ADVISORIES. The following government offices provide travel information and advisories by telephone, by fax, or via the web:

Australian Department of Foreign Affairs and Trade: ☎13 0055 5135; www.dfat.gov.au.

Canadian Department of Foreign Affairs and International Trade (DFAIT): In Canada and the US call ☎800-267-8376, elsewhere call ☎1 613 944 4000; www.dfait-maeci.gc.ca. Call for their free booklet, *Bon Voyage...But.*

New Zealand Ministry of Foreign Affairs: ☎04 439 8000; www.mft.govt.nz/travel/index.html.

United Kingdom Foreign and Commonwealth Office: ☎020 7008 0232; www.fco.gov.uk.

US Department of State: ☎202-647-5225, http://travel.state.gov. For *A Safe Trip Abroad,* call ☎202 512 1800.

ANTI-AMERICAN SENTIMENT

Anti-Americanism is almost non-existent in Germany. Even Germans who are vocally opposed to the policies of the U.S. government tend to be welcoming of American tourists. Harassment of any type is typically not tolerated in public places, so if you do experience it, head for a public area immediately.

TERRORISM

Although former DDR citizens are now fairly used to travelers' presence, right-wing groups maintain a potentially uncomfortable presence in disadvantaged areas of Germany. Many neo-Nazis sport the traditional skinhead uniform of flight jackets worn over white short-sleeved shirts and tight jeans rolled to reveal high-

ESSENTIALS

cut combat boots. Often, white supremacists and neo-Nazis will distinguish themselves with white laces, while anti-gay skinheads wear pink laces. Left-wing, anti-Nazi "S.H.A.R.P.s" (Skinheads Against Racial Prejudice) favor red laces.

International relations remain volatile in the wake of recent terrorist activities and wars. Security, beefed up after September 11th, remains tight, so be sure to always carry identification, and don't joke about bombs, illegal substances, or terrorists in public places, as officials have been instructed to arrest anyone who might pose a threat. While Germany has not been a target for international terrorism, travelers should be conscientious about protecting themselves, especially in major airports and train stations. The box on **travel advisories** lists offices to contact and webpages to visit to get the most updated list of your home country's government's advisories about travel.

PERSONAL SAFETY

EXPLORING AND TRAVELING

To avoid unwanted attention, try to blend in as much as possible. Respecting local customs (and often dressing more conservatively than you might at home) may placate would-be hecklers. Familiarize yourself with areas before setting out, and carry yourself with confidence. Check maps in shops and restaurants rather than on the street. If you are traveling alone, tell someone at home your itinerary, and never admit that you're by yourself. When walking at night, stick to busy, well-lit streets and avoid alleyways, parks, parking lots, or other dark, deserted areas. If you feel uncomfortable somewhere, leave as quickly and directly as you can.

There is no sure-fire way to avoid all the threatening situations you might encounter while traveling, but a good **self-defense course** will give you concrete ways to react to unwanted advances. **Impact, Prepare, and Model Mugging** can refer you to local self-defense courses in the US (☎800-345-5425). Visit the website at www.impactsafety.org for a list of nearby chapters. Workshops (1½-3hr.) start at US$75; full courses (20-25hr.) run US$350-400.

If you are using a **car,** learn local driving signals and wear a seatbelt. Children under 40 lbs. should ride only in carseats, available for a small fee from most car rental agencies. Study route maps before you hit the road, and if your car breaks down, wait for the police to assist you. For long drives, invest in a cellular phone and a roadside assistance program (p. 32). Park your vehicle in a garage or well traveled area, and use a steering wheel locking device in larger cities. **Sleeping in your car** is one of the most dangerous (and often illegal) ways to get your rest.

POSSESSIONS AND VALUABLES

Never leave your belongings unattended; crime can occur anywhere. Bring your own **padlock** for hostel lockers, and don't ever store valuables in any locker. Be particularly careful on **buses** and **trains;** determined thieves will sometimes wait for travelers to fall asleep. Carry your backpack in front of you where you can see it. When traveling with others, sleep in alternate shifts. When alone, select your train compartment with care: never stay in an empty one, and lock your pack to the luggage rack. Try to sleep on top bunks with your luggage stored above you (if not right with you), and keep important documents and valuables on your person.

There are a few steps you can take to minimize the financial risk associated with traveling. First, **bring as little with you as possible.** Second, buy a few combination **padlocks** to secure your belongings either in your pack or in a hostel or train station locker. Third, **carry as little cash as possible.** Keep your traveler's checks and ATM/credit cards in a **money belt**—not a "fanny pack"—along with your passport and ID cards. Fourth, **keep a small cash reserve separate from your primary stash.** This should be about US$50 (euros are best) sewn into or stored in the depths of your pack, along with your traveler's check numbers and important photocopies.

In large cities **con artists** often work in groups and may involve children. Beware of certain classics: sob stories that require money, rolls of bills "found" on the street, mustard or milk spilled (or saliva spit) onto your shoulder to distract you while they snatch your bag. **Never let your passport and your bags out of your sight.** Beware of **pickpockets** in city crowds, especially on public transportation. Also, be alert in public telephone booths: if you must say your calling card number, do so very quietly; if you punch it in, make sure no one can look over your shoulder.

If you will be traveling with electronic devices, such as a laptop computer or a PDA, check whether your homeowner's insurance covers loss, theft, or damage when you travel. If not, consider purchasing a low-cost separate insurance policy. **Safeware** (☎US 800-800-1492; www.safeware.com) specializes in computers and charges $90 for 90-day comprehensive international travel coverage up to $4000.

PRE-DEPARTURE HEALTH

In your **passport,** write the names of any people you wish to be contacted in case of a medical emergency, and list any allergies or medical conditions. Matching a prescription to a foreign equivalent is not always easy, safe, or possible, so if you take prescription drugs, bring up-to-date, legible prescriptions or a statement from your doctor stating the medication's trade name, manufacturer, chemical name, and dosage. While traveling, keep all medication with you in your carry-on luggage. For tips on packing a basic **first-aid kit** and other health essentials, see p. 16.

IMMUNIZATIONS AND PRECAUTIONS

Travelers over two years old should make sure that the following vaccines are up to date: MMR (measles, mumps, and rubella); DTaP or Td (diphtheria, tetanus, and pertussis); IPV (polio); Hib (*haemophilus* influenza B); and HepB (Hepatitis B). For recommendations on immunizations and prophylaxis, consult the CDC (p. 20) in the US or the equivalent in your home country, and check with a doctor.

INSURANCE

Travel insurance covers four basic areas: medical/health problems, property loss, trip cancellation/interruption, and emergency evacuation. Though regular insurance policies may well extend to travel-related accidents, you may consider purchasing supplemental travel insurance if the potential cost of trip cancellation, interruption, or emergency medical evacuation is greater than what is covered by a basic policy. Prices for travel insurance purchased separately generally run about US$50 per week for full coverage, while trip cancellation/interruption may be purchased separately at a rate of US$3-5 per day depending on length of stay.

Medical insurance (especially university policies) often covers costs incurred abroad; check with your provider. **US Medicare** does not cover foreign travel. **Canadian** provincial health insurance plans increasingly do not cover foreign travel; check with the provincial Ministry of Health or Health Plan Headquarters for details. **Homeowners' insurance** (or your family's coverage) often covers theft during travel and loss of travel documents (passport, tickets, etc.) up to US$500.

ISIC and **ITIC** (p. 10) provide basic insurance benefits to US cardholders, including US$100 per day of in-hospital sickness for up to 60 days and US$5000 of accident-related medical reimbursement (see www.isicus.com for details). Cardholders have access to a toll-free 24hr. helpline for medical, legal, and financial emergencies overseas. **American Express** (US ☎ 800-528-4800) grants most card-holders automatic collision and theft car rental insurance and ground travel accident coverage of US$100,000 on flight purchases made with the card.

INSURANCE PROVIDERS

STA (p. 23) offers a range of plans that can supplement your basic coverage. Other private insurance providers in the US and Canada include: Access America (☎ 800-284-8300; www.accessamerica.com); Berkely Group (☎ 800-797-4514; www.berkely.com); Globalcare Travel Insurance (☎ 800-821-2488; www.globalcare-cocco.com); Travel Assistance International (☎ 800-821-2828; www.europ-assistance.com); and Travel Guard (☎ 800-826-4919; www.travelguard.com). Columbus Direct (☎ 020 7375 0011; www.columbusdirect.co.uk) operates in the UK and AFTA (☎ 02 9264 3299; www.afta.com.au) in Australia.

USEFUL ORGANIZATIONS AND PUBLICATIONS

The US **Centers for Disease Control and Prevention** (**CDC;** ☎ 877-FYI-TRIP; www.cdc.gov/travel) maintains an international travelers' hotline and an informative website. The CDC's comprehensive booklet *Health Information for International Travel* (The Yellow Book), an annual rundown of disease, immunization, and general health advice, is free online or US$29-40 via the Public Health Foundation (☎ 877-252-1200; http://bookstore.phf.org). Consult the appropriate government agency of your home country for consular information sheets on health, entry requirements, and other issues for various countries (see the listings in the box on **Travel Advisories,** p. 17). For quick information on health and other travel warnings, call the **Overseas Citizens Services** (☎ 888-407-4747 M-F 8am-8pm; after-hours ☎ 202-647-4000; ☎ 317-472-2328 from overseas), or contact a passport agency, embassy, or consulate abroad. For information on medical evacuation services and travel insurance firms, in the UK check www.fco.gov.uk or, in the US, try http://travel.state.gov/medical.html. For general health info, contact the **American Red Cross** (☎ 800-564-1234; www.redcross.org).

STAYING HEALTHY

Common sense is the simplest prescription for good health while you travel. Drink lots of fluids to prevent dehydration and constipation, and wear sturdy, broken-in shoes and clean socks. And while giant *Krüge* of beer and soft pretzels may (for good reason) be all you want to eat, a visit once in a while to the fresh produce sections of grocery stores or farmers' markets will have your body thanking you.

ONCE IN GERMANY

ENVIRONMENTAL HAZARDS

Heat exhaustion and dehydration: Heat exhaustion leads to nausea, excessive thirst, headaches, and dizziness. Avoid it by drinking plenty of fluids, eating salty foods (e.g., crackers), avoiding dehydrating beverages (e.g., alcohol and caffeinated beverages), and always wearing sunscreen. Continuous heat stress can eventually lead to heatstroke, characterized by a rising temperature, severe headache, delirium and cessation of sweating. Victims should be cooled off with wet towels and taken to a doctor.

Sunburn: Always wear sunscreen with a high SPF when spending excessive amounts of time outdoors, even if it is cloudy. If you get sunburned, drink more fluids than usual and apply an aloe-based lotion. Severe sunburns can lead to sun poisoning, a condition that affects the entire body, causing fever, chills, nausea, and vomiting. Sun poisoning should always be treated by a doctor.

Hypothermia and frostbite: A rapid drop in body temperature is the clearest sign of overexposure to cold. Victims may also shiver, feel exhausted, have poor coordination or slurred speech, hallucinate, or suffer amnesia. *Do not let hypothermia victims fall asleep.* To avoid hypothermia, keep dry, wear layers, and stay out of the wind. When the temperature is below freezing, watch out for frostbite. If skin turns white or blue, waxy, and cold, do not rub the area. Drink warm beverages, stay dry, and slowly warm the area with dry fabric or steady body contact until a doctor can be found.

High Altitude: Allow your body a couple of days to adjust to less oxygen before exerting yourself. Note that alcohol is more potent and UV rays are stronger at high elevations.

INSECT-BORNE DISEASES

Many diseases are transmitted by insects like mosquitoes, fleas, ticks, and lice. Be aware of insects in wet or forested areas, especially while hiking and camping; wear long pants and long sleeves, tuck your pants into your socks, use insect repellents such as DEET, and soak or spray your gear with permethrin (licensed in the US only for use on clothing). **Ticks**—responsible for Lyme and other diseases— are most common in rural and forested regions, mainly in Bavaria and Baden-Württemburg. Always check your clothes and skin after returning from a hike.

Tick-borne encephalitis: A viral infection of the central nervous system transmitted during the summer by tick bites (primarily in wooded areas) or by consumption of unpasteurized dairy products. The risk of contracting the disease is relatively low, especially if precautions are taken against tick bites.

Lyme disease: A bacterial infection carried by ticks and marked by a circular bull's-eye rash of 2 in. or more. Later symptoms include fever, headache, fatigue, and aches and pains. Antibiotics are effective if administered early. Left untreated, Lyme can cause problems in joints, the heart, and the nervous system. If you find a tick attached to your skin, grasp the head with tweezers as close to your skin as possible and apply slow, steady traction. Removing a tick within 24 hours greatly reduces the risk of infection. Do not try to remove ticks with petroleum jelly, nail polish remover, or a hot match. Tick bites usually occur in moist, shaded environments and heavily wooded areas.

FOOD- AND WATER-BORNE DISEASES

Prevention is the best cure: be sure that your food is properly cooked and the water you drink is clean. German tap water is generally safe to drink except in the most polluted areas of the former DDR, though most Germans drink bottled mineral water. Peel and wash fruits and vegetables from street markets. Other culprits are raw shellfish, unpasteurized milk, and dishes with raw eggs. Always wash your hands before eating or bring an antibacterial hand cleaner. Germans' compulsive tendencies extend into the culinary realm, and most food is prepared under strictly-monitored sanitary conditions. Use your own judgment when it comes to *Imbiß* (fast food) fare and food from street vendors—some places are cleaner than others. While there has been recent concern about vCJD (the human variant of BSE, or "Mad Cow Disease") throughout Europe, cases are extremely rare.

Traveler's diarrhea: Results from drinking fecally contaminated water or eating uncooked and contaminated foods. Symptoms include nausea, bloating, and urgency. Try quick-energy, non-sugary foods with protein and carbohydrates to keep your strength up. Over-the-counter anti-diarrheals (e.g., Imodium) may help. The most dangerous side effect is dehydration; mix 8 oz. of water with ½ tsp. of sugar or honey and a pinch of salt, try uncaffeinated soft drinks, or eat salted crackers. If you develop a fever or your symptoms don't go away after 4-5 days, consult a doctor. Consult a doctor immediately for treatment of diarrhea in children.

ESSENTIALS

Hepatitis A: A viral infection of the liver acquired primarily through contaminated water, including through shellfish from contaminated water. Symptoms include fatigue, fever, loss of appetite, nausea, dark urine, jaundice, vomiting, aches and pains, and light stools. The risk is highest in rural areas and the countryside, but it is also present in urban areas. Ask your doctor about the Hepatitis A vaccine (Havrix or Vaqta) or an injection of immune globulin (IG; formerly called gamma globulin).

Giardiasis: Transmitted through parasites (microbes, tapeworms, etc. in contaminated water and food) and acquired by drinking untreated water from streams or lakes. Symptoms include diarrhea, abdominal cramps, bloating, fatigue, weight loss, and nausea. If untreated it can lead to severe dehydration. Giardiasis occurs worldwide.

OTHER INFECTIOUS DISEASES

Rabies: Transmitted through the saliva of infected animals; fatal if untreated. By the time symptoms (thirst and muscle spasms) appear, the disease is in its terminal stage. If you are bitten, wash the wound thoroughly, seek immediate medical care, and try to have the animal located. A rabies vaccine, which consists of 3 shots given over a 21-day period, is available and recommended for developing world travel, but is only semi-effective. Rabies is found all over the world, and is often transmitted through dogs.

AIDS and HIV: For information on Acquired Immune Deficiency Syndrome (AIDS) in Germany, call the US Centers for Disease Control's 24hr. hotline at ☎800 342 2437, or contact the Joint United Nations Programme on HIV/AIDS, 20, ave. Appia, CH-1211 Geneva 27, Switzerland (☎41 22 791 3666; fax 22 791 4187). Germany screens incoming travelers for AIDS, primarily those planning extended visits, and may deny entrance to those who test HIV-positive. Contact the German consulate for information.

Sexually transmitted diseases (STDs): Gonorrhea, chlamydia, genital warts, syphilis, herpes, and other STDs are more common than HIV and can cause serious complications. Though condoms may protect you from some STDs, oral or even tactile contact transmit them. If you think you may have contracted an STD, see a doctor immediately.

OTHER HEALTH CONCERNS

MEDICAL CARE ON THE ROAD

Germany has good medical care readily accessible to travelers. EU citizens in possession of an E11 form can get free first aid and emergency services. Travelers from outside the EU may visit private general practitioners and pay on a per-visit basis (US$40 for a non-specialist visit is reasonable) for non-emergency situations.

If you are concerned about obtaining medical assistance while traveling, you may employ special support services. The *MedPass* from **GlobalCare, Inc.,** 6875 Shiloh Rd. East, Alpharetta, GA 30005, USA (☎800 860 1111; www.globalcare.net), provides 24hr. international medical assistance, support, and medical evacuation resources. The **International Association for Medical Assistance to Travelers (IAMAT;** US ☎716 754 4883, Canada 519 836 0102) has free membership, lists English-speaking doctors worldwide, and offers detailed info on immunization requirements and sanitation. If your regular **insurance** policy does not cover travel abroad, you may wish to purchase additional coverage (p. 19).

Those with medical conditions (such as diabetes, allergies to antibiotics, epilepsy, heart conditions) may want to obtain a **Medic Alert** membership (first year US$35, then annually US$20), which includes a stainless steel ID tag and other benefits like a 24hr. collect-call number. Contact the Medic Alert Foundation, 2323 Colorado Ave., Turlock, CA 95382, USA (☎888-633-4298; outside the US ☎209 668 3333; www.medicalert.org).

WOMEN'S HEALTH

Women traveling in unsanitary conditions are vulnerable to **urinary tract (including bladder and kidney) infections.** Over-the-counter medicines can sometimes alleviate symptoms, but if they persist, see a doctor. **Vaginal yeast infections** may flare up in hot and humid climates. Wearing loose trousers or a skirt and cotton underwear will help, as will over-the-counter remedies like Monostat or Gynelotrimin; an *Apotheke* can provide the German equivalent. **Tampons, pads,** and **contraceptive devices** are widely available, though your favorite brand may not be stocked—bring extras of anything you can't live without. First-trimester **abortion** is legal in Germany, but a three-day wait and counselling are required; in Germany contact **PRO FAMILIA Bundesverband** (a planned parenthood group; www.profamilia.de).

GETTING TO GERMANY

BY PLANE

When it comes to airfare, a little effort can save you a bundle. If your plans are flexible enough to deal with the restrictions, courier fares are the cheapest. Tickets bought from consolidators and standby seating are also good deals, but last-minute specials, airfare wars, and charter flights often beat these fares. The key is to hunt around, be flexible, and ask persistently about discounts. Students, seniors, and those under 26 should never pay full price for a ticket.

AIRFARES

Airfares to Germany peak between June and September; holidays are also expensive. Midweek (M-Th morning) round-trip flights run US$40-50 cheaper than weekend flights, but they are generally more crowded and less likely to permit frequent-flier upgrades. Patching one-way flights together is the most expensive way to travel. Flights between Germany's capitals or regional hubs—Berlin, Frankfurt, Hamburg and Munich—will tend to be cheaper.

If Germany is only one stop on a more extensive globe-hop, consider a round-the-world (RTW) ticket. Tickets usually include at least five stops and are valid for about a year; prices range US$3400-5000. Try **Northwest Airlines/KLM** (US ☎ 800-447-4747; www.nwa.com) or **Star Alliance**, a consortium of 22 airlines including United Airlines (US ☎ 800-241-6522; www.staralliance.com).

Fares for round-trip flights to Berlin, Frankfurt, and Munich from the US or Canadian east coast cost US$1000-1500, US$500-600 in the winter; from the US or Canadian west coast US$1000-1800/US$600-800; from the UK, UK£80/UK£50; from Australia AUS$2500/AUS$2000; from New Zealand NZ$4500/NZ$5500.

BUDGET AND STUDENT TRAVEL AGENCIES

While agents specializing in flights to Germany can make your life easy, they may not spend the time to find you the lowest possible fare—they get paid on commission. Travelers holding **ISIC** and **IYTC cards** (p. 10) qualify for big discounts from student travel agencies. Most flights from budget agencies are on major airlines, but in peak season some may sell seats on less reliable chartered aircraft.

CTS Travel, 30 Rathbone Pl., London W1T 1GQ, UK (☎0207 209 0630; www.ctstravel.co.uk). A British student travel agent with offices in 39 countries including the US, Empire State Building, 350 Fifth Ave., Ste. 7813, New York, NY 10118 (☎877-287-6665; www.ctstravelusa.com).

STA Travel, 5900 Wilshire Blvd., Ste. 900, Los Angeles, CA 90036, USA (24hr. reservations and info ☎800-781-4040; www.sta-travel.com). A student and youth travel organization with over 150 offices worldwide (check their website for a listing of all their offices), including US offices in Boston, Chicago, L.A., New York, San Francisco, Seattle, and Washington, D.C. Ticket booking, travel insurance, railpasses, and more. Walk-in offices located throughout Australia (☎03 9349 4344), New Zealand (☎09 309 9723), and the UK (☎0870 1 600 599).

Travel CUTS (Canadian Universities Travel Services Limited), 187 College St., Toronto, ON M5T 1P7 (☎416-979-2406; www.travelcuts.com). Offices across Canada and the US including Los Angeles, New York, San Francisco, and Seattle.

USIT, 19-21 Aston Quay, Dublin 2 (☎01 602 1777; www.usitnow.ie), Ireland's leading student/budget travel agency has 22 offices throughout Northern Ireland and the Republic of Ireland. Offers programs to work in North America.

FLIGHT PLANNING ON THE INTERNET. The Internet may be the budget traveler's dream when it comes to finding and booking bargain fares, but the array of options can be overwhelming. Many airline sites offer special last-minute deals on the Web. Try Aer Lingus (www.aerlingus.com), British Airways (www.british-airways.com), Eurowings (www.eurowings.de), Lufthansa (www.lufthansa.de), Ryanair (www.ryanair.com), United (www.ual.com).

STA (www.sta-travel.com) and **StudentUniverse** (www.studentuniverse.com) provide quotes on student tickets, while **Orbitz** (www.orbitz.com), **Expedia** (www.expedia.com), and **Travelocity** (www.travelocity.com) offer full travel services, as well as the European **Opodo** (www.opodo.com). **Priceline** (www.priceline.com) lets you specify a price, and obligates you to buy any ticket that meets or beats it; **Hotwire** (www.hotwire.com) offers bargain fares, but won't reveal the airline or flight times until you buy. Other sites that compile deals for you include www.bestfares.com, www.flights.com, www.lowest-fare.com, www.onetravel.com, and www.travelzoo.com.

Increasingly, there are online tools available to help sift through multiple offers; **SideStep** (www.sidestep.com; download required) and **Booking Buddy** (www.bookingbuddy.com) let you enter your trip information once and search multiple sites.

An indispensable resource on the Internet is the **Air Traveler's Handbook** (www.faqs.org/faqs/travel/air/handbook), a comprehensive listing of links to everything you need to know before you board a plane.

COMMERCIAL AIRLINES

The commercial airlines' lowest regular offer is the **APEX** (Advance Purchase Excursion) fare, which provides confirmed reservations and allows "open-jaw" tickets. Generally, reservations must be made seven to 21 days ahead of departure, with seven- to 14-day minimum-stay and up to 90-day maximum-stay restrictions. These fares carry hefty cancellation and change penalties (fees rise in summer). Book peak-season APEX fares early. Use **Expedia** (www.expedia.com) or **Travelocity** (www.travelocity.com) to get an idea of the lowest published fares, then use the resources outlined here to try and beat those fares. Low-season fares should be appreciably cheaper than the **high-season** (June to Aug.) ones listed here.

TRAVELING FROM NORTH AMERICA

Basic round-trip fares to Germany range from roughly US$400-1500 to Berlin or Frankfurt, Germany's air transportation hub. Standard commercial carriers like American and United will probably offer the most convenient flights, but they may not be the cheapest, unless you manage to grab a special promotion or airfare war ticket. You will probably find flying one of the following "discount" airlines a better deal, if any of their limited departure points is convenient for you.

Finnair: ☎ 800-950-5000; www.us.finnair.com. Cheap round-trips from San Francisco, New York, and Toronto to Helsinki; connections throughout Europe.

Icelandair: ☎ 800-223-5500; www.icelandair.com. Stopovers in Iceland for no extra cost on most transatlantic flights. New York to Frankfurt flights are not significantly cheaper than other carriers, but cheap last-minute offers are available by subscribing to their Lucky Fares email list.

TRAVELING FROM THE UK AND IRELAND

Because of the many carriers flying from the British Isles to the continent, we include only discount airlines or those with cheap specials here. The **Air Travel Advisory Bureau** in London (☎ 020 7306 3000; www.atab.co.uk) provides referrals to travel agencies and consolidators that offer discounted airfares out of the UK.

Aer Lingus: Ireland ☎ 0818 365 000; www.aerlingus.ie. Return tickets as low as €40 from Dublin, Cork, Galway, Kerry, and Shannon to Düsseldorf, Frankfurt, and Munich.

British Midland Airways: UK ☎ 0870 607 05 55; www.flybmi.com. Departures from throughout the UK. London to Frankfurt UK£112 in the low season.

KLM: UK ☎ 0870 507 40 74; www.klmuk.com. Cheap return tickets from London and elsewhere to Frankfurt and Düsseldorf.

Ryanair: Ireland ☎ 0818 303 030, UK 0871 246 0000 (10p per min.); www.ryanair.com. From Dublin, London, and Glasgow to Berlin, Erfurt, Hahn (near Frankfurt), and Friedrichshafen. Deals from as low as UK£6 for flights on weekdays.

TRAVELING FROM AUSTRALIA AND NEW ZEALAND

Air New Zealand: New Zealand ☎ 0800 73 70 00; www.airnz.co.nz. Auckland to Frankfurt.

Singapore Air: Australia ☎ 13 10 11, New Zealand 0800 808 909; www.singaporeair.com. Flies from Auckland, Sydney, Melbourne, and Perth to Western Europe and offers occasional special fares.

Thai Airways: Australia ☎ 1300 65 19 60, New Zealand 09 377 02 68; www.thaiair.com. Offers a limited number of flights from Auckland, Sydney, and Melbourne to Frankfurt and Berlin.

STANDBY FLIGHTS

Traveling standby requires considerable flexibility in arrival and departure dates and cities. Companies dealing in standby flights sell vouchers rather than tickets, along with the promise to get you to your destination (or near your destination) within a certain window of time (typically 1-5 days). You call in before your specific window of time to hear your flight options and the probability that you will be able to board each flight. You can then decide which flights you want to try to make, show up at the appropriate airport at the right time, present your voucher, and board if space is available. Vouchers can usually be bought for both one-way and round-trip travel. You may receive a monetary refund only if every available flight within your date range is full; if you opt not to take an available (but perhaps less convenient) flight, you can only get credit toward future travel. Carefully read agreements with any company offering standby flights. To check on a company's service record in the US, call the Better Business Bureau (☎ 703-276-0100). Be aware that it is difficult to receive refunds, and clients' vouchers will not be honored when an airline fails to receive payment in time.

TICKET CONSOLIDATORS

Ticket consolidators, or **"bucket shops,"** buy unsold tickets in bulk from commercial airlines and sell them at discounted rates. The best place to look is in the Sunday travel section of any major newspaper (such as the *New York Times*), where many bucket shops place tiny ads. Call quickly, as availability is typically extremely limited. Not all bucket shops are reliable, so insist on a receipt that gives full details of restrictions, refunds, and tickets, and pay by credit card (in spite of the 2-5% fee) so you can stop payment if you never receive your tickets. For more info, see www.travel-library.com/air-travel/consolidators.html.

Some ticket consolidators include **Cheap Tickets** (☎ 800-652-4327; www.cheaptickets.com), **Flights.com** (www.flights.com) and **TravelHUB** (www.travelhub.com). Keep in mind that these are just suggestions to get you started in your research; *Let's Go* does not endorse any of these agencies. As always, be cautious, and research companies before you hand over your credit card number.

BY TRAIN

Trains in Germany are generally comfortable, convenient, fast, and keep rigidly to their schedules. Second-class compartments, which seat two to six, are great places to meet fellow travelers. Trains, however, are not always safe; for safety tips, see p. 18. For long trips, make sure you are on the correct car, as trains sometimes split at crossroads. Towns listed in parentheses on European train schedules require a train switch at the town listed immediately before the parenthesis.

You can either buy a **railpass,** which allows you unlimited travel within a particular region for a given period of time, or rely on buying individual **point-to-point** tickets as you go. Almost all countries give students or youths (usually defined as anyone under 26) direct discounts on regular domestic rail tickets, and many also sell a student or youth card that provides 20-50% off all fares for up to a year.

RESERVATIONS. While seat reservations are required only for selected trains (usually on major lines), you are not guaranteed a seat without one (usually US$3-10). You should strongly consider reserving a few hours ahead at the very least during peak holiday and tourist seasons. You will need a **supplement** (US$10-50) or special fare for high-speed or high quality trains such as Germany's ICE. InterRail holders must also purchase supplements (US$10-25) for trains like EuroCity and InterCity; supplements are unnecessary for Eurailpass and Europass holders.

OVERNIGHT TRAINS. On night trains, you won't waste daylight hours traveling and you can avoid the expense of a hotel. **Sleeping accommodations** on trains differ from country to country, but typically you can either sleep upright in your seat or pay for a separate space. **Couchettes** (berths) typically have four to six seats per compartment (about US$20 per person); **sleepers** (beds) in private sleeping cars offer more privacy and comfort, and run US$40-150. If you are using a railpass valid for a restricted number of days, inspect train schedules to maximize use: an overnight train or boat journey uses up only one travel day if it departs after 7pm.

SHOULD YOU BUY A RAILPASS? Railpasses were conceived to allow you to jump on any train in Europe, go wherever you want whenever you want, and change your plans at will. In practice, it's not so simple. You still must stand in line to validate your pass, pay for supplements, and fork over cash for seat and couchette reservations. More importantly, railpasses don't always pay off. If you are planning to spend extensive time on trains, hopping between big cities, a railpass will probably be worth it. But in many cases, especially if you are under 26, point-to-point tickets may prove a cheaper option.

MULTINATIONAL RAILPASSES

EURAILPASS. Eurail is **valid** in most of Western Europe: Austria, Belgium, Denmark, Finland, France, Germany, Greece, Hungary, Italy, Luxembourg, the Netherlands, Norway, Portugal, the Republic of Ireland, Romania, Spain, Sweden, and Switzerland. It is **not valid** in the UK. Standard **Eurailpasses**, valid for a consecutive given number of days, are best for those planning on spending extensive time on trains every few days. **Flexipasses**, valid for any 10 or 15 (not necessarily consecutive) days within a two-month period, are more cost-effective for those traveling longer distances less frequently. **Saverpasses** provide first-class travel for travelers in groups of two to five (prices are per person). **Youthpasses** and **Youth Flexipasses** provide parallel second-class perks for those under 26.

EURAILPASSES	15 DAYS	21 DAYS	1 MONTH	2 MONTHS	3 MONTHS
1st class Eurailpass	US$588	US$762	US$946	US$1338	US$1654
Eurail Saverpass	US$498	US$648	US$804	US$1138	US$1408
Eurail Youthpass	US$414	US$534	US$664	US$938	US$1160

EURAIL FLEXIPASSES	10 DAYS IN 2 MONTHS	15 DAYS IN 2 MONTHS
1st class Eurail Flexipass	US$694	US$914
Eurail Saver Flexipass	US$592	US$778
Eurail Youth Flexipass	US$488	US$642

Passholders receive a timetable for major routes and a map with details on possible ferry, steamer, bus, car rental, hotel, and Eurostar discounts.

EURAIL SELECT PASS. The Eurail Select Pass is a slimmed-down version of the Eurailpass: it allows five to 15 days of unlimited travel in any two-month period within three, four, or five bordering countries of the 18 Eurail network countries. **First-Class passes** (for individuals) and **Saverpasses** (for people traveling in groups of 2-5) range from US$356/$304 per person (5 days) to US$794/$674 (15 days). **Second-Class Youthpasses** for those aged 12-25 cost US$249-556. For a fee, you can add **additional zones** (including Austria/Hungary and Belgium/Luxembourg/Netherlands). You are entitled to the same **freebies** afforded by the Eurailpass, but only when they are within or between countries that you have purchased.

EURO DOMINO. The Euro Domino pass is available to anyone who has lived in Europe for at least six months; however, it is only valid in one country (which you designate when buying the pass, and can't be your country of residence). It is available for 29 European countries plus Morocco. Reservations must still be paid for separately. **Supplements** are included for many high-speed trains (e.g., French TGV, German ICE). The pass must be bought within your country of residence; for travels from three to seven days within Germany, Euro Domino passes range from €180-252, €135-187 for travelers under 26.

SHOPPING AROUND FOR A EURAIL. Eurailpasses are designed by the EU, and can be bought only by non-Europeans almost exclusively from non-European distributors. These passes must be sold at uniform prices determined by the EU. However, some travel agents tack on a US$10 handling fee, and others offer certain bonuses with purchase. If you're planning to travel early in the year, you can save cash by purchasing before January 1, when prices usually rise (you have three months from the purchase date to validate your pass in Europe).

It is best to buy your Eurail before leaving; only a few places in major European cities sell them, and at a marked-up price. You can get a replacement for a lost pass only if you have purchased insurance on it under the Pass Protection Plan

ESSENTIALS

(US$14-17). Eurailpasses are available through travel agents, student travel agencies like STA (p. 23), and **Rail Europe** (Canada ☎800-361-7245; UK 08 705 848 848; US 877-257-2887; www.raileurope.com) or **DER Travel Services,** whose services are available at several outfits across the US (☎800-782-2424; www.der.com).

DISCOUNTED TICKETS

For travelers under 26, **BIJ** tickets (Billets Internationals de Jeunesse; operated by **Wasteels**) are a great alternative to railpasses. For international trips within Europe as well as most ferry services they knock 20-40% off 1st- and 2nd-class fares. Tickets are good for two months after purchase and allow stopovers along the normal direct route of the train journey. Issued for a specific international route between two points, they must be used in a designated direction and order and must be bought in Europe. The equivalent for those over 26, **BIGT** tickets provide a 20-30% discount on 1st- and 2nd-class international tickets. Both types of tickets are available from European travel agents and many ticket counters.

FURTHER READING AND RESOURCES ON TRAIN TRAVEL.
Info on rail travel and railpasses: www.raileurope.com.
Point-to-point fares and schedules: www.raileurope.com/us/rail/
    fares_schedules/index.htm. See if a railpass would save you money.
European Railway Server: mercurio.iet.unipi.it/home.html. Links to rail servers
    throughout Europe.
Thomas Cook European Timetable, updated monthly, covers all major and most
    minor train routes in Europe. In the US, order it from Forsyth Travel Library
    (US$29; ☎800-367-7984; www.forsyth.com). In Europe, find it at any Tho-
    mas Cook Money Exchange Center.
On the Rails Around Europe: A Comprehensive Guide to Travel by Train, Melissa
    Shales. Thomas Cook Ltd. (US$19).

GETTING AROUND GERMANY

BY TRAIN OR BUS

RAILPASSES AND DISCOUNTED FARES

BASIC DISCOUNTS. Deutsche Bahn offers some terrific discounts to travelers. **Groups of up to four** people ride for half-price with the purchase of a full-price ticket, and **children** up to age 14 ride free with a parent or grandparent. Buyers who purchase tickets at least three days in advance are eligible for the **Sparpreis25** or **Sparpreis50** discounts: **Sparpreis25** offers a 25% discount, while **Sparpreis50** will give you a 50% discount on trips that leave and return on a weekend.

DEUTSCHE BAHN PASS. Designed for tourists, the German Railpass allows unlimited travel for four to 10 days within a month. Non-Europeans can purchase German Railpasses in their home countries and—with a passport—in major German train stations. A second-class Railpass costs €180 for four days of unlimited travel and €316 for 10. The **German Rail Youth Pass,** for tourists under 26, is €142 for four days and €216 for 10. The second-class **Twin Pass,** for two adults traveling together, is €270 for four days and €474 for 10.

BAHNCARD. A great option for those making frequent and extensive use of German trains for more than one month, the **Bahncard25** is valid for one year and entitles you to a 25% discount on all trains (including on already discounted tickets). Passes are available at major train stations and require a passport-sized photo and mailing address in Germany. A second-class card costs €50; children under 18 and partners of Bahncard25 holders can get their card for only €5. A newer Bahncard50, giving you 50% discounts on tickets, now costs €200 (€100 for students up to 26 years old, retirees, and partners of other Bahncard50 holders).

REGIONAL PASSES. This type of pass covers a specific area within a country or a round-trip from any border to a particular destination and back; these are useful as supplements when your main pass isn't valid. The **Prague Excursion Pass** is a common purchase for Eurailers, whose passes are not valid in the Czech Republic; it covers travel from any Czech border to Prague and back out of the country (round-trip must be completed within 7 days; 2nd-class US$40, under 26 US$35).

RAIL-AND-DRIVE PASSES. In addition to simple railpasses, many countries (as well as Eurail) offer rail-and-drive passes, which combine car rental with rail travel—a good option for travelers who wish both to visit cities accessible by rail and to make side trips into the surrounding areas. Prices range per person from $295-539, depending on the type of pass, type of car, and number of people included. Children under the age of 11 cost $123, and adding more days costs $49-95 per day (see **By Car,** below).

BUS TRAVEL

The few parts of Germany that are inaccessible by train can often be reached by bus. Service between cities and to outlying areas runs from the local main bus station, the **Zentralomnibusbahnhof (ZOB),** which is usually near the main train station. Buses can be slightly more expensive than the train for comparable distances. Railpasses are not valid on any buses other than a few run by Deutsche Bahn.

Europe's largest coach operator is **Eurolines,** Am Römerhof 17, 60486 Frankfurt (☎069 790 350; www.eurolines.com). Although Eurolines mostly offers travel between countries, its internal routes include Berlin-Hannover and Frankfurt-Munich, as well as routes covering the Romantic Road, Castle Road and Strasbourg-Reitlingen (Black Forest) all offered through its German subsidiary Deutsche Touring GmbH (www.deutsche-touring.de). **Eurolines Pass** offers unlimited 15-day (€220-285, under 26 €185-240), 30-day (€310-425/€250-345) or 60-day (€390-490/€310-380) travel between 30 major cities.

BY CAR

Cars offer speed, freedom, access to the countryside, and an escape from the town-to-town mentality of trains. Although a single traveler won't save by renting a car, four usually will. If you can't decide between train and car travel, you may benefit from a combination of the two; RailEurope and other railpass vendors offer rail-and-drive packages. Fly-and-drive packages are also often available from travel agents or airline/rental agency partnerships.

Before setting off, know the laws and driving customs of the countries in which you'll be driving (e.g., many German Autobahns have no official speed limit, but if you are traveling in the left lane you are expected to change lanes to let faster cars pass you). For an informal primer on European road signs and conventions, check out www.travlang.com/signs. The **Association for Safe International Road Travel (ASIRT),** 11769 Gainsborough Rd., Potomac, MD 20854 (US ☎301-983-5252; www.asirt.org), can provide more specific information about road conditions.

RENTING A CAR

You can rent a car from a US-based firm (Alamo, Avis, Budget, or Hertz) with European offices, from a European-based company with local representatives (Europcar), or from a tour operator (Auto Europe, Europe By Car, and Kemwel Holiday Autos) that will arrange a rental for you from a European company at its own rates. Multinationals offer greater flexibility, but tour operators often strike better deals. It is always significantly less expensive to reserve a car from the US than from Europe. Ask airlines about special fly-and-drive packages; you may get up to a week of free or discounted rental. Expect to pay at least US$40 per day, plus tax (5-25%), for a teensy car. Reserve ahead and pay in advance if at all possible. Always check if prices quoted include tax and collision insurance; some credit card companies provide insurance, allowing their customers to decline the collision damage waiver. Ask about discounts and check the terms of insurance, particularly the deductible size. Rates are generally lowest in Belgium, Germany, Holland, and the UK, and highest in Scandinavia and Eastern Europe. The minimum age in Germany is usually 21. At most agencies, all that's needed to rent a car is a license from home that you've had for 1-3 years, depending on the company.

Auto Europe: US and Canada ☎888-223-5555 or 207-842-2000; www.autoeurope.com.

Avis: Australia ☎136 333; Canada 800-272-5871; New Zealand 0800 65 51 11; UK 0870 606 0100; US 800-230-4898; www.avis.com.

Budget: Canada ☎800-268-8900; UK 1344 484 100; US 800-527-0700; www.budgetrentacar.com.

Europe by Car: US ☎800-223-1516 or 212-581-3040; www.europebycar.com.

Europcar International: 3 Avenue du Centre, 78 881 Saint Quentin en Yvelines Cedex, France (☎30 44 90 00; US 877-940-6900; www.europcar.com).

Hertz: Australia ☎9698 2555; Canada 800-263-0600; UK 0990 99 66 99; US 800-654-3131; www.hertz.com.

Kemwel: US ☎877-820-0668; www.kemwel.com.

LEASING OR BUYING A CAR

For longer than 17 days, leasing can be cheaper than renting; it is often the only option for those ages 18 to 21. The cheapest leases are agreements to buy the car and then sell it back to the manufacturer at a prearranged price. As far as you're concerned, though, it's a lease and doesn't entail enormous financial transactions. Leases generally include insurance coverage and are not taxed. The most affordable ones usually originate in Belgium, France, or Germany. Expect to pay around US$1100-1800 (depending on size of car) for 60 days. Contact **Auto Europe, Europe by Car,** or **Kemwel** (see above) before you go. If you're brave and know what you're doing, **buying** a used car or van in Germany and selling it just before you leave can provide the cheapest wheels for longer trips. You must show proof of insurance before registering or driving your car. Check with consulates for import-export laws concerning used vehicles, registration, and safety and emission standards.

ON THE ROAD

German road conditions are generally excellent, even in the former DDR. Yes, there is no set speed limit on the **Autobahn,** or German highway; only a recommendation of 130km per hour (81mph) exists. Germans drive *fast*. Watch for signs indicating right-of-way (usually designated by a yellow triangle). The Autobahn is indicated by an intuitive "A" on signs; secondary highways, where the speed limit is usually 100km per hour (60mph), are accompanied by signs bearing a "B." Germans drive on the right side of the road, and it is illegal to pass on the right, even on superhighways. If a car is coming up behind you in the left lane of the Autobahn, you are expected to change lanes to the right to let the other driver pass you safely. In cities and towns, speeds hover around 30-60kph (around 20-35mph). Wearing a **seatbelt** is the law in Germany, and children should sit in the rear seat; children under 40 lb. (17kg) should ride only in a specially-designed carseat, available from most car rental agencies. The legal cut-off for blood-alcohol levels is 0.08%. German police strictly enforce driving laws.

DRIVING PRECAUTIONS. When traveling in the summer, bring substantial amounts of water (a suggested 5L of **water** per person per day) for drinking and for the radiator. When traveling for long distances, make sure tires are in good repair and have enough air, and get good maps. A **compass** and a **car manual** can also be very useful. You should always carry a **spare tire** and **jack, jumper cables, extra oil, flares, a flashlight (torch),** and **heavy blankets** (in case your car breaks down at night or in winter). If you don't know how to **change a tire,** learn before heading out, especially if you might be in deserted areas. Blowouts on dirt roads are exceedingly common. If you do have a breakdown, **stay with your car;** if you wander off, there's less likelihood trackers will find you.

DRIVING PERMITS AND CAR INSURANCE

INTERNATIONAL DRIVING PERMIT (IDP)

If you plan to drive a car while in Gemany, you must be over 18 and have an International Driving Permit (IDP), though you can drive with a valid American or Canadian license for six months, after which a German license is required. It may be a good idea to get one anyway, in case you're in a situation (e.g., an accident or stranded in a small town) where the police do not know English; information on the IDP is printed in 10 languages, including German.

Your IDP, valid for one year, must be issued in your own country before you depart. An application for an IDP usually requires one or two photos, a current local license, an additional form of identification, and a fee. To apply, contact the national or local branch of your home country's automobile association. Be careful when purchasing an IDP online or anywhere other than your home automobile association; many vendors sell permits of dubious legitimacy for higher prices.

CAR INSURANCE

Most credit cards cover standard insurance. If you rent, lease, or borrow a car, you will need a **green card,** or **International Insurance Certificate,** to certify that you have liability insurance and that it applies abroad. Green cards can be obtained at car rental agencies, car dealers (for those leasing cars), some travel agents, and some border crossings. Rental agencies may require you to purchase theft insurance in countries that they consider to have a high risk of auto theft.

BY BICYCLE

With a mountain bike you can do some serious sightseeing. Many airlines will count your bike as your second free piece of luggage; a few charge extra (US$60-110 one-way). Bikes must be packed in a cardboard box with the pedals and front wheel detached; many airlines sell bike boxes (US$10). Most ferries let you take your bike for free or for a small fee, and you can always ship your bike on trains. Renting a bike can often be even easier; many youth hostels rent bicycles for low prices. In addition to **panniers** to hold your luggage, you'll need a good **helmet**

(US$25-50) and a **sturdy lock** (from US$30). For more country-specific books on biking through Germany, try **Mountaineers Books,** 1001 S.W. Klickitat Way, Suite 201, Seattle, WA 98134 (☎800-553-4453; www.mountaineersbooks.org).

If you are nervous about striking out on your own, **Blue Marble Travel** (Canada ☎519-624-2494; France 42 36 02 34; US 215-923-3788; www.bluemarble.org) offers bike tours for small groups of ages 20 to 49 throughout Europe. **CBT Tours,** 2506 N. Clark St. #150, Chicago, IL 60614 (☎800-736-2453; www.cbttours.com), offers full-package biking, hiking, and multisport tours (US$1500-2500) to Germany.

BY FOOT

The very best of Germany can be seen only by foot. *Let's Go* includes many day-trips, but native inhabitants, hostel proprietors, and fellow travelers are the best source for tips. Many European countries have hiking and mountaineering groups; alpine clubs in Germany provide simple accommodations in splendid settings.

BY THUMB

 Let's Go never recommends hitchhiking as a safe means of transportation, and none of the information presented here is intended to do so.

Let's Go strongly urges you to consider the risks before you choose to hitchhike. Hitching means entrusting your life to a stranger and risking assault, sexual harassment, and unsafe driving. In spite of this, some people choose to hitchhike, because it allows them to meet local people and travel in areas where public transportation is unreliable. The choice, however, remains yours. Hitchhiking at night can be particularly dangerous; experienced hitchers stand in well-lit places. For women traveling alone, hitching is far more dangerous; a man and a woman are a safer combination, two men will have a harder time, and three will get nowhere. Successful hitchers pick spots outside of built-up areas where drivers can stop, return to the road without causing an accident, and have time to look over potential passengers as they approach. Hitching (or even standing) on highways is usually illegal: one may only thumb at rest stops or at the entrance ramps to highways. Success often depends on appearance. Drivers prefer hitchers who are neat and wholesome-looking. Long-distance hitching in Germany demands close attention to expressway junctions, rest stop locations, and often a destination sign.

Germany does have a ride service, known as the **Verband der Deutschen Mitfahrzentralen,** which pairs drivers with riders; the fee varies according to destination. Not all organizations screen drivers and riders; ask in advance. **Mitfahrzentrale** offices are listed under the **Transportation** header of most large cities. The central website (in German; www.mitfahrzentrale.de) has more information.

BY PLANE

The recent emergence of no-frills airlines has made hopscotching around Europe by air increasingly affordable and convenient. Though these flights often have inconvenient hours or serve small regional airports, with one-way flights averaging about US$50, it's never been faster or easier to jet set across the Continent.

Air Berlin: UK ☎0870 738 88 80; www.airberlin.com. Serves Berlin, Bremen, Cologne/Bonn, Dortmund, Dresden, Düsseldorf, Erfurt, Frankfurt, Hamburg, Hannover, Karlsruhe/Baden-Baden, Leipzig/Halle, Münster/Osnabrück, Munich, Nürnberg, Paderborn, Rostock/Laage, and Stuttgart, and over 50 other destinations across Europe.

ESSENTIALS

easyJet: UK ☎0871 750 01 00; www.easyjet.com. Serves Berlin, Cologne/Bonn, Dortmund and Munich, as well as 40 other destinations across Europe.

Deutsche BA: Germany ☎01805 35 93 22; www.deutscheba.de. Serves Berlin, Cologne/Bonn, Düsseldorf, Hamburg, Munich, and Stuttgart; limited service to Nice and Ibiza.

Europe by Air: ☎888-387-2479; www.europebyair.com. *FlightPass* allows you to country-hop to over 150 European cities. US$99 per flight.

Germania: Germany ☎01805 73 71 00; www.gexx.de. Serves Berlin, Bremen, Cologne/Bonn, Düsseldorf, Frankfurt, Hamburg, Hannover, and Stuttgart, as well as 18 other destinations across Europe.

germanwings: Germany ☎01805 95 58 55; www.germanwings.com. Serves Berlin, Bonn, Cologne, Dresden, and Stuttgart, and 29 other destinations across Europe.

Hapag-Lloyd Express: Germany ☎0180 509 35 09; www.hlx.com. Serves Berlin, Cologne/Bonn, Hamburg, Hannover, Stuttgart, and 30 other European destinations.

Ryanair: Ireland ☎0818 303 030; UK 087 246 00 00; www.ryanair.com. Serves Berlin, Erfurt, Frankfurt, Friedrichshafen, Karlsruhe/Baden-Baden, and Niederrhein (Düsseldorf, Cologne, Essen), as well as 78 other destinations across Europe.

The **Star Alliance European Airpass** offers economy class fares as low as US$65 for travel within Europe to more than 200 destinations in 43 countries. The pass is available to transatlantic passengers on Star Alliance carriers, including Air Canada, BMI British Midland, Lufthansa, and United Airlines, as well as on certain partner airlines. See www.staralliance.com for more information. In addition, a number of European airlines offer discount coupon packets. Most are only available as tack-ons for transatlantic passengers, but some are stand-alone offers. Most must be purchased before departure, so research in advance.

KEEPING IN TOUCH

BY MAIL

SENDING MAIL HOME FROM GERMANY

Airmail is the best way to send mail from Germany. **Aerogrammes,** printed sheets that fold into airmail envelopes, are available at post offices. Write "airmail," "par avion," or "Luftpost" on the front. Most post offices will charge extra fees for (or refuse to send) aerogrammes with enclosures. **Surface mail** is the cheapest but slowest way to send mail. It takes one to two months to cross the Atlantic and one to three to cross the Pacific. These are standard rates for mail from Germany to:

Australia, Canada, New Zealand, and US: Allow 4-10 days for regular airmail home. Postcards/aerogrammes cost €1. Letters up to 20g cost €1.55; packages up to 0.5kg €12, up to 2kg €36.

Ireland and UK: Allow 3-6 days for regular airmail home. Postcards/aerogrammes and letters up to 20g cost €0.55; packages up to 0.5kg €6, up to 2kg €18.

SENDING MAIL TO GERMANY

To ensure timely delivery, mark envelopes "airmail," "par avion," or *Luftpost*. In addition to the standard postage system whose rates are listed below, **Federal Express** (Australia ☎13 26 10; Canada and US 800-463-3339; Ireland 1800 535 800; New Zealand 0800 733 339; UK 0800 123 800; www.fedex.com) handles express mail services from most countries to Germany; for example, they can get a letter from New York or London to Germany in two days for US$31.80.

Australia: Allow 3-10 days for regular airmail to Germany. Postcards and letters up to 20g cost AUS$1; packages up to 0.5kg AUS$14.50, up to 2kg AUS$50.50. EMS can get a letter to Germany in 2-3 days for AUS$35. www.auspost.com.au/pac.

Canada: Allow 4-7 days for regular airmail to Germany. Postcards and letters up to 30g cost CDN$1.40; packages up to 0.5kg CDN$11.20, up to 2kg CDN$37.35. Purolator International can get a letter to Germany in 2-3 days for CDN$56.20. www.canada-post.ca/personal/rates/default-e.asp.

Ireland: Allow 2-6 days for regular airmail to Germany. Postcards and letters up to 50g cost €0.65; packages up to 0.5kg €9.50, up to 2kg €23. Swiftpost International can get a letter to Germany in 2-6 days for €7. www.letterpost.ie.

New Zealand: Allow 4-10 days for regular airmail to Germany. Postcards and letters up to 50g cost NZ$7.09; packages up to 0.5kg NZ$17.23, up to 2kg NZ$55.25. International Express can get a letter to Germany in 2-4 days for NZ$33. www.nzpost.co.nz/nzpost/inrates.

UK: Allow 3-4 days for regular airmail to Germany. Letters up to 20g cost UK£0.40; packages up to 0.5kg UK£4.30, up to 2kg UK£16.30. Airsure delivers letters about a day faster for UK£4.00 more. www.royalmail.co.uk/calculator.

US: Allow 4-7 days for regular airmail to Germany. Letters up to 1 oz. cost US$0.80; packages up to 1 lb. US$8.70, up to 5 lb. US$38. US Express Mail takes 3-5 days and costs US$26. http://ircalc.usps.gov.

RECEIVING MAIL IN GERMANY

There are several ways to arrange pick-up of letters sent to you by friends and relatives while you are abroad. Mail can be sent via **Poste Restante** (General Delivery; Postlagernde Briefe) to almost any city or town in Germany with a post office, and is very reliable. Address *Poste Restante* letters like so: Franz-Heinrich Van BISMARCK, Postlagernde Briefe, Berlin, GERMANY. The mail will go to a special desk in the central post office, unless you specify a post office by street address or postal code. It's best to use the largest post office, since mail may be sent there regardless. It is usually safer and quicker, though more expensive, to send mail express or registered. Bring your passport (or other photo ID) for pick-up; there may be a small fee. If the clerks insist that there is nothing for you, have them check under your first name as well. Sending a postcard within Germany costs €0.45, while sending letters (up to 20g) domestically requires €0.55. *Let's Go* lists post offices in the **Practical Information** section for each city and most towns.

BY TELEPHONE

CALLING HOME FROM GERMANY

A **calling card** is usually cheapest. Calls are billed collect or to your account. You can frequently call collect without possessing a company's calling card just by calling their access number and following the instructions. **To obtain a calling card** from your national telecommunications service before leaving home, contact the appropriate company listed below at the numbers in the first column. To **call home with a calling card,** contact the operator for your service provider in Germany by dialing the appropriate toll-free access number (listed below in the second column).

COMPANY	TO OBTAIN A CARD, DIAL:	TO CALL ABROAD, DIAL:
AT&T (US)	800 364 9292	0800 225 5288
Canada Direct	800 561 8868	0800 888 0014
MCI (US)	800 777 5000	0800 888 8000
Telstra Australia	13 22 00	0800 0800 061

ESSENTIALS

You can usually make direct international calls from pay phones, but if you aren't using a calling card, you'll need a lot of coins. Prepaid cards are generally less cost-efficient. Placing a collect call through an international operator is even more expensive, but may be necessary in case of emergency.

 PLACING INTERNATIONAL CALLS. To call Germany from home or to call home from Germany, dial:

1. **The international dialing prefix.** To call from **Australia,** dial 0011; **Canada** or the **US,** 011; **Ireland, New Zealand,** or the **UK,** 00; **Germany,** 00.
2. The **country code** of the destination country. To call **Australia,** dial 61; **Canada** or the **US,** 1; **Ireland,** 353; **New Zealand,** 64; the **UK,** 44; **Germany,** 49.
3. The **city/area code.** *Let's Go* lists the city/area codes for cities and towns in Germany opposite the city or town name, next to a ☎. If the first digit is a zero (e.g., 020 for London), omit the zero when calling from abroad (e.g., dial 20 from Canada to reach London).
4. The **local number.**

CALLING WITHIN GERMANY

You can always find a **public phone** *(Telefonzelle)* in a post office. Additionally, phones are located at all train and bus stations, on ICE trains, and on nearly every other street corner. Most public phones accept only telephone cards, though restaurants and bars sometimes have coin-operated phones. Telephones in transport hubs and near major attractions sometimes give you the option of paying by **credit card.** You can pick up a **Telefonkarte** (phone card) in post offices, at a *Kiosk* (newsstand), or at selected Deutsche Bahn counters in major train stations. The cards come in €5, €10, and €25 denominations. The computerized phone will tell you how much time, in units, you have left on your card.

Another kind of prepaid telephone card comes with a Personal Identification Number (PIN) and a toll-free access number. Instead of inserting the card into the phone, call the access number and follow the directions on the card. These cards can be used to make international as well as domestic calls. Rates tend to be highest in the morning, lower in the evening, and lowest on Sunday and late at night. Before settling on a calling card plan, be sure to research your options in order to pick the one that best fits both your needs and your destination.

To place **inter-city calls,** dial the **Vorwahl** (area code), including the first zero that appears in the code, followed by the **Rufnummer** (telephone number). There is no standard length for telephone numbers. The smaller the city, the more digits in the city code, while telephone numbers tend to have three to 10 digits. The **national information number** is ☎118 33. For **international information,** call ☎118 34. **Phone rates** tend to be highest in the morning and afternoon, lower in the evening, and lowest after 9pm and on Sundays and holidays.

CELLULAR PHONES

The international standard for cell phones is **GSM,** a system that began in Europe and has spread to much of the rest of the world. To make and receive calls in Germany you will need a **GSM-compatible phone** (about €100 in Germany for a basic model) and a **SIM (subscriber identity module) card,** a country-specific, thumbnail-sized chip that gives you a local phone number and plugs you into the local network. Many SIM cards are **prepaid,** meaning that they come with calling time included and you don't need to sign up for a monthly service plan. Incoming calls are frequently free. When you use up the prepaid time, you can buy additional cards or vouchers (usually available at convenience stores) to get more. For more information on GSM phones, check out www.telestial.com, www.vodafone.com, www.orange.co.uk, www.roadpost.com, www.t-mobile.com, or www.plane-tomni.com. Companies like **Cellular Abroad** (www.cellularabroad.com) rent cell phones that work in a variety of destinations around the world, providing a simpler option than picking up a phone in-country. For more information about cell phones in Germany, go to www.german-way.com/german/handy.html.

 GSM PHONES. The majority of GSM phones sold in the United States operate on a different **frequency** (1900) than international phones (900/1800) and will not work abroad. Tri-band phones work on all three frequencies (900/1800/1900) and will operate through most of the world. As well, some GSM phones are **SIM-locked** and will only accept SIM cards from a single carrier. You'll need a **SIM-unlocked** phone to use a SIM card from a local carrier.

TIME DIFFERENCES

Germany is 1hr. ahead of **Greenwich Mean Time (GMT).** It is 6hr. ahead of New York, 9hr. ahead of Vancouver and Los Angeles, 1hr. behind Pretoria, 9hr. behind Sydney, and 11hr. behind Auckland. Germany usually switches to and from Daylight Saving Time a week earlier than the United States.

BY EMAIL AND INTERNET

Internet access is fairly widespread in Germany, and Internet cafes can be found in most large towns. Though in some places it's possible to forge a remote link with your home server, in most cases this is a much slower (and thus more expensive) option than taking advantage of free web-based email accounts (e.g., www.hotmail.com and www.yahoo.com). Internet cafes and the occasional free Internet terminal at a public library or university are listed in the Practical Information sections of major cities. For lists of additional cybercafes in Germany, check out www.cyber-star.com or www.cybercaptive.com.

Increasingly, travelers find that taking their laptop computers on the road with them can be a convenient option for staying connected. Laptop users can call an Internet service provider via a modem using long-distance phone cards specifically intended for such calls. They may also find Internet cafes that allow them to connect their laptops to the Internet. Travelers with **wireless-enabled computers** may be able to take advantage of an increasing number of Internet "hotspots," where they can get online for free or for a small fee. Larger German cities such as Berlin, Bonn, Düsseldorf, Frankfurt, Hamburg, Heidelberg, Cologne, Munich, Stuttgart, and Weimar are reported to have a number of these access points. Newer computers can detect these hotspots automatically; otherwise, websites like www.jiwire.com, www.wi-fihotspotlist.com, and www.locfinder.net can help you find them. For information on insuring your laptop while traveling, see p. 19.

ACCOMMODATIONS

HOSTELS

In 1908, a German named Richard Schirmann, believing that life in industrial cities was harmful to the physical and moral development of Germany's young people, built the **world's first youth hostel** in Altena—a budget dormitory that would bring

travel within the means of urban youth. Germany has been a leader in hostelling ever since. Hostels provide dorm-style accommodations, often in large single-sex rooms with bunk beds, although some hostels do offer private rooms for families and couples. They sometimes have kitchens and utensils, bike or moped rentals, storage, email terminals, and laundry facilities. However, there can be **drawbacks:** some hostels close during daytime "lockout" hours, have a curfew, or impose a maximum stay. There's often little privacy, and you may run into more screaming pre-teen groups than you care to remember. Sleeping bags are usually prohibited for sanitary reasons, but almost all hostels provide clean sheets and blankets for a fee (usually about €3). Whatever the locale, a bed in a hostel will average around €12-20 and a private room around €20-40.

 A HOSTELER'S BILL OF RIGHTS. There are certain standard features that we do not include in our hostel listings. Unless we state otherwise, you can expect that every hostel has no lockout, no curfew, a kitchen, free hot showers, some system of secure luggage storage, and no key deposit.

Hostelling in Germany is overseen by **Deutsches Jugendherbergswerk (DJH),** Bismarckstr. 8, 32756 Detmold, Germany (☎05231 740 10; www.jugendherberge.de). The hostels are open to members of the DJH or the International Youth Hostel Federation (see below), but travelers can join or buy guest passes at the hostels. DJH has recently initiated a growing number of **Jugendgästehäuser,** youth guest-houses that are generally more expensive, have more facilities, and attract slightly older guests. DJH has absorbed hundreds of hostels in Eastern Germany with efficiency, though some still lack the sparkling facilities of their western counterparts. Germany currently has about **600 hostels**—more than any other country. DJH's *Jugendherbergen in Deutschland,* a guide to all federated German hostels, can be purchased at German bookstores and major newsstands, by writing to DJH, or from the **DJH webpage,** which also has pictures, prices, addresses, and phone numbers for almost every hostel in Germany. Contact information can also be found on most German cities' official webpages, listed under the tourist office in the **Practical Information** section of cities in this guide. **Eurotrip** (www.eurotrip.com) has information on and reviews of budget hostels and international hostel associations. The **Internet Guide to Hostelling** (www.hostels.com) provides hostel directory in addition to hostelling and backpacking tips.

HOSTELLING INTERNATIONAL

Joining the youth hostel association in your own country automatically grants you membership privileges in **Hostelling International (HI),** a federation of national hostelling associations. Non-HI members may be allowed to stay in some hostels, but will have to pay extra to do so. HI's umbrella organization's web page (www.hihostels.com) can be a great place to begin researching hostelling in a specific region. Other comprehensive hostelling websites include www.hostels.com and www.hostelplanet.com. Most HI hostels also honor **guest memberships**—you'll get a blank card with space for six validation stamps. Each night you'll pay a nonmember supplement (one-sixth the membership fee) and earn one guest stamp; get six stamps, and you're a member. This system works well in most of Western Europe, but in some countries you may need to remind the hostel reception. A new membership benefit is the FreeNites program, which allows hostelers to gain points toward free rooms. Most student travel agencies (p. 23) sell HI cards, as do all of the national hostelling organizations listed below. All prices listed below are valid for **one-year memberships** unless otherwise noted.

Australian Youth Hostels Association (AYHA), 422 Kent St., Sydney, NSW 200 (☎02 9261 1111; www.yha.com.au). AUS$52, under 18 AUS$19.

Hostelling International-Canada (HI-C), 205 Catherine St. #400, Ottawa, ON K2P 1C3 (☎613-237-7884; www.hihostels.ca). CDN$35, under 18 free.

An Óige (Irish Youth Hostel Association), 61 Mountjoy St., Dublin 7 (☎830 4555; www.irelandyha.org). €20, under 18 €10.

Hostelling International Northern Ireland (HINI), 22 Donegall Rd., Belfast BT12 5JN (☎02890 31 54 35; www.hini.org.uk). UK£13, under 18 UK£6.

Youth Hostels Association of New Zealand (YHANZ), Level 1, Moorhouse City, 166 Moorhouse Ave., P.O. Box 436, Christchurch (☎0800 278 299 (NZ only) or 03 379 9970; www.yha.org.nz). NZ$40, under 18 free.

Scottish Youth Hostels Association (SYHA), 7 Glebe Cres., Stirling FK8 2JA (☎01786 89 14 00; www.syha.org.uk). UK£6, under 17 £2.50.

Youth Hostels Association (England and Wales), Trevelyan House, Dimple Rd., Matlock, Derbyshire DE4 3YH, UK (☎0870 770 8868; www.yha.org.uk). UK£13.50, under 18 UK£6.75.

Hostelling International-USA, 8401 Colesville Rd., Ste. 600, Silver Spring, MD 20910 (☎301-495-1240; www.hiayh.org). US$28, under 18 free.

BOOKING HOSTELS ONLINE. One of the easiest ways to ensure you've got a bed for the night is by reserving online. Click to the **Hostelworld** booking engine through **www.letsgo.com,** and you'll have access to bargain accommodations from Argentina to Zimbabwe with no added commission.

OTHER TYPES OF ACCOMMODATIONS

HOTELS, GUESTHOUSES, AND PENSIONS

Hotel singles in Germany cost about €25 (US$30) per night, doubles €40 (US$50). The cheapest hotel-style accommodations are places with **Pension, Gasthof, Gästehaus,** or **Hotel-Garni** in the name. Breakfast *(Frühstück)* is almost always included. You'll typically share a hall bathroom; a private bathroom will cost extra. Some hotels offer "full pension" (all meals) and "half pension" (no lunch). If you make reservations in writing, indicate your night of arrival and the number of nights you plan to stay. The hotel will send you a confirmation and may request payment for the first night. Often it is easiest to make reservations by phone.

HOME EXCHANGES AND HOSPITALITY CLUBS

Home exchange offers the traveler various types of homes (houses, apartments, villas, even castles in some cases), plus the opportunity to cut down on accommodation fees. For more information, contact HomeExchange.com (a number of listings in Germany, particularly Berlin), P.O. Box 787, Hermosa Beach, CA 90254 USA (☎800-877-8723; www.homeexchange.com), or Intervac International Home Exchange Germany (☎07052- 932406; www.intervac.com).

Hospitality clubs link their members with individuals or families abroad who are willing to host travelers for free or for a small fee to promote cultural exchange and general good karma. In return, members usually must be willing to host travelers in their own homes; a small membership fee may also be required. **GlobalFreeloaders.com** (over 800 members in Germany; www.globalfreeloaders.com) and **The Hospitality Club** (several thousand German members; www.hospitalityclub.org) are good places to start. **Servas** (www.servas.org) is an established, more formal, peace-based organization, and requires a fee and an interview to join. An Internet

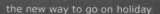

search will find many similar organizations, some of which cater to special interests (e.g., women, GLBT travelers, etc.) As always, use common sense when planning to stay with or host someone you do not know.

LONG-TERM ACCOMMODATIONS

Travelers planning to stay in Germany for extended periods of time may find it most cost-effective to rent an **apartment**. A basic one-bedroom (or studio) apartment in Berlin start at €250-350 per month. Besides the rent itself, prospective tenants usually are also required to front a security deposit (frequently one month's rent) and the last month's rent.

CAMPING AND THE OUTDOORS

The 26,000 campsites dotting Alps, forests, beaches, and even the suburbs of major cities demonstrate German enthusiasm for the outdoors. Hiking trails wind through the outskirts of every German city, and a national network of long-distance trails weaves the country together. The Black Forest, Saxon Switzerland, the Harz Mountains and the Bavarian Alps are especially well-traversed. The outdoor facilities in Germany are among the best-maintained in the world, usually accessible by public transportation and providing showers, bathrooms, and a restaurant or store. Camping costs €3-6 per person with a surcharge for tents and vehicles. Blue signs with a black tent on a white background indicate official sites.

The **Great Outdoor Recreation Pages** (www.gorp.com) provides excellent general information for travelers planning on camping or spending time in the outdoors.

> **LEAVE NO TRACE.** *Let's Go* encourages travelers to embrace the "Leave No Trace" ethic, minimizing their impact on natural environments and protecting them for future generations. Trekkers and wilderness enthusiasts should set up camp on durable surfaces, use cookstoves instead of campfires, bury human waste away from water supplies, bag trash and carry it out with them, and respect wildlife and natural objects. For more detailed information, contact the **Leave No Trace Center for Outdoor Ethics,** P.O. Box 997, Boulder, CO 80306, USA (☎800-332-4100 or 303-442-8222; www.lnt.org).

USEFUL PUBLICATIONS AND RESOURCES

A variety of publishing companies offer hiking guidebooks to meet the educational needs of novice or expert. For information about camping, hiking, and biking, write or call the publishers listed below to receive a free catalog. Campers heading to Europe should consider buying an International Camping Carnet. Similar to a hostel membership card, it's required at a few campgrounds and provides discounts at others. It is available in North America from the **Family Campers and RVers Association** and in the UK from **The Caravan Club** (see below).

Automobile Association, Contact Centre, Carr Ellison House, William Armstrong Dr., Newcastle-upon-Tyne NE4 7YA, UK (☎0870 600 0371; www.theAA.com). Publishes Caravan and Camping Europe and Britain (both UK£8) as well as *Big Road Atlases* for Europe, Britain, France, Germany, Italy, and Spain.

Camping Germany, (www.camping-germany.de), offers information and pictures for campgrounds all over the country. Site available in a sometimes amusingly flawed English translation.

The Caravan Club, East Grinstead House, East Grinstead, West Sussex, RH19 1UA, UK (☎44 01342 326 944; www.caravanclub.co.uk). For UK£30, members receive travel equipment discounts, maps, and a monthly magazine.

The Mountaineers Books, 1001 SW Klickitat Way, Ste. 201, Seattle, WA 98134, USA (☎206-223-6303; www.mountaineersbooks.org). Boasts over 600 titles on hiking, biking, mountaineering, natural history, and conservation.

Sierra Club Books, 85 Second St., 2nd fl., San Francisco, CA 94105, USA (☎415-977-5500; www.sierraclub.org). Publishes general resource books on hiking and camping.

NATIONAL PARKS

Germany's national park system is generally well-maintained and wonderfully under-crowded, frequented by vacationing German families and the lucky few tourists who venture in to explore them. The heaviest concentration of parks is in former East Germany and Bavaria. **Winter sports,** especially skiing and tobogganing, are popular in the Berchtesgaden and Bayerischer Wald (Bavarian Forest) parks; Saxon Switzerland and Harz parks in the east are popular for their magnificent **hiking opportunities** among chalk cliffs and forested peaks. Germans are predictably fastidious about their parks, placing strict limits on camping, starting fires, and all other activities that could potentially harm the environment.

There are no entrance fees for German parks, although camping is nearly always restricted to designated campgrounds, which charge around €5-10 per camper per night. Parking can also be costly. Travelers can also stay at huts in some parks, which rarely require reservations and cost €10-20. For general information, contact **Nationalpark-Service,** Informationshaus, 17192 Federow (☎03991 66 88 49; www.nationalpark-service.de). Specific listings of ranger offices in each national park can be found in their respective sections in this book.

WILDERNESS SAFETY

THE GREAT OUTDOORS

Staying **warm, dry, and well-hydrated** is key for a happy and safe wilderness experience. Prepare yourself for any length of hike by packing a first-aid kit, a reflector, a whistle, high energy food, extra water, raingear, a hat, and mittens. Wear wool or insulating synthetic materials designed for the outdoors, never cotton.

German weather is fickle; check **weather forecasts** often and pay attention to the skies when hiking. Always let someone (a friend, your hostel, a park ranger, a local hiking group) know where you will be and when you expect to be back. Know your physical limits and do not attempt a hike beyond your ability. See **Safety and Health,** p. 16, for information on outdoor ailments and medical concerns.

When setting up and breaking down camp, a bit of environmental responsibility will help keep you and the site healthy. A campstove is a safer (and more efficient) way to cook than a fire; if you must make one, keep it small and use only dead branches or brush rather than cutting vegetation. Make sure your campsite is at least 150 ft. (50m) from water supplies or bodies of water. If there are no toilet facilities, bury human waste (but not paper) at least four inches (10cm) deep and above the high-water line, and 150 ft. or more from water supplies and campsites.

WILDLIFE

Bear-bagging—hanging edibles and other fragrant objects from a tree out of reach of hungry paws—is the best way to keep your toothpaste from becoming a condiment. Bears and bugs are also attracted to any perfume, so scented toiletries should stay at home. Always pack trash in a plastic bag and carry it with you until you reach the next trash receptacle. For more information, consult *How to Stay Alive in the Woods*, by Bradford Angier (Black Dog & Leventhal Books, US$8).

CAMPING AND HIKING EQUIPMENT

WHAT TO BUY

Good camping equipment is both sturdy and light. North American suppliers tend to offer the most competitive prices.

Sleeping Bags: Most sleeping bags are rated by season; "summer" means 30-40°F (around 0°C) at night; "four-season" or "winter" often means below 0°F (-17°C). Bags are made of **down** (warm and light, but expensive, and miserable when wet) or of **synthetic** material (heavy, durable, and warm when wet). Prices range US$50-250 for a summer synthetic to US$200-300 for a good down winter bag. **Sleeping bag pads** include foam pads (US$10-30), air mattresses (US$15-50), and self-inflating mats (US$30-120). Bring a **stuff sack** to store your bag and keep it dry.

Tents: The best tents are free-standing (with their own frames and suspension systems), set up quickly, and only require staking in high winds. Low-profile dome tents are the best all-around. Worthy 2-person tents start at US$100, 4-person at US$160. Make sure your tent has a rain fly and seal its seams with waterproofer. Other useful accessories include a **battery-operated lantern**, a plastic **groundcloth**, and a nylon **tarp.**

Backpacks: Internal-frame packs mold well to your back, keep a lower center of gravity, and flex adequately to allow you to hike difficult trails, while **external-frame packs** are more comfortable for long hikes over even terrain, as they carry weight higher and distribute it more evenly. Make sure your pack has a strong, padded hip-belt to transfer weight to your legs. There are models designed specifically for women. Any serious backpacking requires a pack of at least 4000 in^3 (16,000cc), plus 500 in^3 for sleeping bags in internal-frame packs. Sturdy backpacks cost anywhere from US$125 to 420—your pack is an area where it doesn't pay to economize. On your hunt for the perfect pack, fill up prospective models with something heavy, strap it on correctly, and walk around the store to get a sense of how the model distributes weight. Either buy a **rain cover** (US$10-20) or store all of your belongings in plastic bags inside your pack.

Boots: Be sure to wear hiking boots with good **ankle support.** They should fit snugly and comfortably over 1-2 pairs of **wool socks** and a pair of thin **liner socks.** Break in boots over several weeks before you go to spare yourself blisters.

Other Necessities: Synthetic layers, like those made of polypropylene or polyester, will keep you warm even when wet. A **space blanket** (US$5-15) will help you to retain body heat and doubles as a groundcloth. Plastic **water bottles** are vital; look for shatter- and leak-resistant models. Carry **water-purification tablets** for when you can't boil water. Although most campgrounds provide campfire sites, you may want to bring a small **metal grate** or grill. For those places (including virtually every organized campground in Europe) that forbid fires, you'll need a **camp stove** (the classic Coleman starts at US$50) and a propane-filled **fuel bottle** to operate it. Also bring a **first-aid kit, pocketknife, insect repellent,** and **waterproof matches** or a **lighter.**

WHERE TO BUY IT

The companies listed below offer lower prices than many retail stores.

Campmor, 28 Parkway, P.O. Box 700, Upper Saddle River, NJ 07458 (US ☎888-226-7667; www.campmor.com).

Discount Camping, 880 Main North Rd., Pooraka, South Australia 5095 (Australia ☎08 8262 3399; www.discountcamping.com.au).

Eastern Mountain Sports (EMS), 1 Vose Farm Rd., Peterborough, NH 03458 (US ☎888-463-6367; www.ems.com).

L.L. Bean, Freeport, ME 04033 (US and Canada ☎800-441-5713; UK ☎0800 891 297; www.llbean.com).

Mountain Designs, 51 Bishop St., Kelvin Grove, Queensland 4059 (Australia ☎07 3856 2344; www.mountaindesigns.com).

Recreational Equipment, Inc. (REI), Sumner, WA 98352 (US and Canada ☎800-426-4840, elsewhere 253-891-2500; www.rei.com).

YHA Adventure Shop, 19 High St., Staines, Middlesex, TW18 4QY (UK ☎1784 458625; www.yhaadventure.com).

SPECIFIC CONCERNS

SUSTAINABLE TRAVEL

As the number of travelers on the road continues to rise, the detrimental effect they can have on natural environments becomes a concern. Realizing that through a sensitivity to issues of ecology, travelers can be a force in preserving and restoring the places they visit, *Let's Go* promotes the philosophy of **sustainable travel.**

Ecotourism, a rising trend in sustainable travel, focuses on conserving natural habitats and using them to build up the economy without exploitation or overdevelopment. Travelers can make a difference by doing advance research and by supporting organizations and establishments that pay attention to the impact on their natural surroundings and strive to be environmentally-friendly.

ECOTOURISM RESOURCES. For more information on environmentally responsible tourism, contact one of the organizations below:
The Centre for Environmentally Responsible Tourism (www.c-e-r-t.org).
Earthwatch, 3 Clock Tower Pl., Ste. 100, Box 75, Maynard, MA 01754, USA (☎800-776-0188 or 978-461-0081; www.earthwatch.org).
International Ecotourism Society, 733 15th St. NW, Washington, D.C. 20005, USA (☎202-347-9203; www.ecotourism.org).

TRAVELING ALONE

There are many benefits to solo travel, including greater interaction with locals and independence. On the other hand, any lone traveler is a more vulnerable target for harassment and street theft. Try not to stand out as a tourist, look confident, and be especially careful in deserted or very crowded areas. If questioned, never admit that you are traveling alone. Maintain regular contact with someone at home who knows your itinerary. For more tips, pick up *Traveling Solo* by Eleanor Berman (Globe Pequot Press, US$18), visit www.travelaloneandloveit.com, or subscribe to **Connecting: Solo Travel Network,** 689 Park Rd., Unit 6, Gibsons, BC V0N 1V7, Canada (☎604-886-9099; www.cstn.org; membership US$28-45).

FEMALE TRAVELERS

Women exploring on their own inevitably face some unique safety concerns, but it's easy to be adventurous without taking undue risks. German cities have services catering to women's traveling needs, from women-only taxis to **Frauenzentren**

ESSENTIALS

(women's centers); these resources are listed in the **Practical Information** for each city. German standards of public behavior are fairly reserved, and harassment is relatively uncommon. Although women are still not as politically and economically active as men, laws regarding maternity leave are very liberal, and Germany's childcare system is excellent. More information is available at *Frauenzentren*.

If you are concerned about safety, consider staying in hostels which offer single rooms that lock from the inside or in some of Germany's few women's hotels. Avoid remote locations and solitary late-night treks or metro rides. Always carry extra money for a phone call, bus, or taxi. **Hitchhiking** is never safe for lone women, or even for two women traveling together. Look confident and approach older women or couples for directions if you're lost or uncomfortable. Generally, the less you look like a tourist, the better off you'll be. Dress conservatively, especially in rural areas. Wearing a conspicuous **wedding band** sometimes helps to prevent unwanted overtures (Germans wear them on the ring finger of the *right* hand).

Your best answer to verbal harassment is no answer at all; feigning deafness, sitting motionless, and staring straight ahead at nothing in particular will do a world of good that reactions usually don't achieve. The extremely persistent can sometimes be dissuaded by a firm, loud, and very public *"Lass mich in Ruhe!"* ("Leave me alone!"; LAHSS meech in ROOH-uh). Don't hesitate to seek out a police officer or a passerby if you are being harassed. Memorize the emergency numbers in Germany—**police: ☎110** and **ambulance: ☎112,** and consider carrying a whistle on your keychain. A self-defense course will both prepare you for an attack and enhance your awareness of your surroundings (see **Self Defense**, p. 18). Also be sure you are aware of the health concerns that women face when traveling (p. 23).

GLBT TRAVELERS

Attitudes toward gay, lesbian, bisexual, and transgendered (GLBT) travelers in Germany are surprisingly accepting. While homophobia persists in rural areas and conservative Bavaria, Germans are generally more tolerant than Americans and Brits, though not quite as open-minded as the Dutch. The German word for gay is *schwul* (SHVOOL), which refers exclusively to men; lesbians are *lesbe* (LEZ-buh). *Let's Go* provides information on local bisexual, gay, and lesbian culture in **Practical Information** listings and **Entertainment and Nightlife** sections of city descriptions. The epicenter of gay life in Germany (and possibly in all of Europe) is Berlin (p. 83). Other major centers include Hamburg (p. 230), Cologne (p. 296), and Munich (p. 459). While tolerance is still a new concept in Eastern Germany, growing gay scenes have developed in Leipzig (p. 647) and, to a lesser extent, Dresden (p. 618).

To avoid hassles at airports and border crossings, transgendered travelers should make sure that all of their documents report the same gender. Many countries (including the US, the UK, Canada, Ireland, Australia, and New Zealand) will amend the passports of post-operative transsexuals to reflect their true gender, although governments are generally less willing to amend documents for pre-operative transsexuals and other transgendered individuals.

Women should look for *Frauencafés* and *Frauenkneipen*. It should be stressed that while such cafes are for women only, they are *not* exclusively for lesbians. Of the dozens of regional and national gay and lesbian organizations; two of the largest are the **Bundesverband Homosexualität (BVH),** Greifswalder Str. 224, 10405 Berlin (☎030 441 24 98), and the **Lesben- und Schwulenverband Deutschland (LSVD),** Friedrichstr. 165, 10117 Berlin (☎030 201 08 04). Listed below are contact organizations, mail-order bookstores, and publishers that offer materials addressing some specific concerns. **Out and About** (www.planetout.com)

offers a bi-weekly newsletter addressing travel concerns and a comprehensive site addressing gay travel concerns. The online newspaper **365gay.com** also has a travel section (www.365gay.com/travel/travelchannel.htm).

Gay's the Word, 66 Marchmont St., London WC1N 1AB, UK (☎+44 20 7278 7654; www.gaystheword.co.uk). The largest gay and lesbian bookshop in the UK, with both fiction and non-fiction titles. Mail-order service available.

Giovanni's Room, 1145 Pine St., Philadelphia, PA 19107, USA (☎215-923-2960; www.queerbooks.com). An international lesbian/feminist and gay bookstore with mail-order service (carries many of the publications listed below).

International Lesbian and Gay Association (ILGA), 81 rue Marché-au-Charbon, B-1000 Brussels, Belgium (☎+32 2 502 2471; www.ilga.org). Provides political information, such as homosexuality laws of individual countries.

FURTHER READING: GLBT TRAVEL.

Spartacus 2003-2004: International Gay Guide. Bruno Gmunder Verlag (US$33).

Damron Men's Travel Guide, Damron Accommodations Guide, Damron City Guide, and *Damron Women's Traveller.* Damron Travel Guides (US$11-19). For info, call ☎800-462-6654 or visit www.damron.com.

Ferrari Guides' Gay Travel A to Z, Ferrari Guides' Men's Travel in Your Pocket, Ferrari Guides' Women's Travel in Your Pocket, and *Ferrari Guides' Inn Places.* Ferrari Publications (US$16-20).

The Gay Vacation Guide: The Best Trips and How to Plan Them, Mark Chesnut. Kensington Books (US$15).

TRAVELERS WITH DISABILITIES

Germany provides services, information and accessibility to facilities for travelers with disabilities (**Behinderte** or **Schwerbehinderte**). Both national and regional tourist boards provide directories on the accessibility of various accommodations and transportation services. Germany's excellent public transportation systems make most places easily accessible for travelers with disabilities; many buses and subways are wheelchair accessible. A wheelchair icon or a large "B" indicates access. Intersections in major cities have audible crossing signals for the blind.

All ICE, EC, and IC trains are equipped for **wheelchair accessibility,** and you can request free seat reservations. Rail is probably most convenient for disabled travelers in Europe; for more information, check out www.bahn.de. **Guide dog owners** should be aware that Germany requires evidence of rabies vaccination from a licensed veterinarian at least 30 days but not more than 12 months before entering the country; a notarized German translation of this certificate is required. Those with disabilities should inform airlines and hotels of their disabilities when making reservations; some time may be needed to prepare special accommodations. Call ahead to restaurants, museums, and other facilities to find out if they are handicapped-accessible. For those who wish to rent cars, some major **car rental** agencies (Hertz, Avis, and National) offer hand-controlled vehicles.

USEFUL ORGANIZATIONS

Access Abroad, www.umabroad.umn.edu/access. A website devoted to making study abroad available to students with disabilities. The site is maintained by Disability Services Research and Training, University of Minnesota, University Gateway, Ste. 180, 200 Oak St. SE, Minneapolis, MN 55455, USA (☎612-624-6884).

Flying Wheels, 143 W. Bridge St., P.O. Box 382, Owatonna, MN 55060, USA (☎507-451-5005; www.flyingheelstravel.com). Specializes in escorted trips to Europe for people with physical disabilities; plans custom accessible trips worldwide.

Mobility International USA (MIUSA), P.O. Box 10767, Eugene, OR 97440, USA (☎541-343-1284; www.miusa.org). Provides a variety of books and other publications containing information for travelers with disabilities.

Society for Accessible Travel & Hospitality (SATH), 347 Fifth Ave., #610, New York, NY 10016, USA (☎212-447-7284; www.sath.org). An advocacy group that publishes free online travel information and the travel magazine *OPEN WORLD* (annual subscription US$13, free for members). Annual membership US$45, students and seniors US$30.

MINORITY TRAVELERS

Germany has a significant minority population composed mainly of about two million Turks. Travelers may notice that some older Germans harbor a bit of resentment towards this burgeoning population, which first arrived in Germany during the post-WWII years as *Gastarbeiter* (guest workers). Since then, many Turks have settled and prospered in Germany, becoming a powerful economic presence. In addition, there are about a million residents from the former Yugoslavia. Eastern Germany also has about 100,000 Vietnamese residents.

In certain regions, mostly large cities of former East Germany, minority tourists may feel threatened by small but vocal neo-Nazi groups. While they represent only a fraction of the population, Neo-Nazi skinheads have been known to attack foreigners, especially non-whites. In these areas, common sense will serve you best. Keeping abreast of news of attacks is the best strategy for staying safe.

DIETARY CONCERNS

Although Germany is unapologetically carnivorous, **vegetarianism** has become increasingly popular (see **Food and Drink**, p. 61) in the wake of Mad Cow disease, growing health consciousness, and a blooming alternative scene. Nearly six million Germans do not eat meat, and vegetarian restaurants have proliferated in larger cities, while health food shops, such as the well-known **Reformhaus,** provide a large selection of vegetarian and vegan products. *Let's Go: Germany* tries to list restaurants that offer vegetarian and vegan choices whenever possible. Many are ethnic restaurants; traditional German restaurants often offer very few completely vegetarian dishes. For more information about vegetarian travel, contact:

European Vegetarian Union, Hildegund Scholvien, Friedhofstr. 12, 67693 Fischbach (☎06305 272; www.european-vegetarian.org). Website includes lists of vegetarian- and vegan-friendly brands and restaurants.

Vegetarian Association of Germany, Blumenstr. 3, 30159 Hannover (☎0511 363 20 50; www.vegetarierbund.de).

North American Vegetarian Society, P.O. Box 72, Dolgeville, NY 13329, USA (☎518-568-7970; www.navs-online.org). Publishes *Transformative Adventures,* a global guide to vacations and retreats (US$15).

The travel section of the The Vegetarian Resource Group's website, at www.vrg.org/travel, has a comprehensive list of organizations and websites that are geared toward helping vegetarians and vegans traveling abroad. For more information, visit your local bookstore or health food store, and consult *The Vegetarian Traveler: Where to Stay if You're Vegetarian, Vegan, Environmentally Sensitive,* by Jed and Susan Civic (Larson Publications; US$16), or *Vegetarian Europe,* edited by Alex Bourke

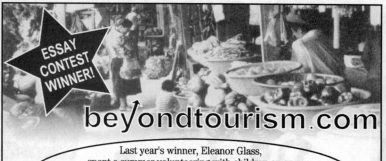
ESSENTIALS

(Vegetarian Guides; US$16.95). Vegetarians will also find numerous resources on the web; try www.vegdining.com and www.happycow.net, for starters. A list of vegetarian restaurants in Germany can be found at www.fleischlos-geniessen.de.

Travelers who keep **kosher** should contact synagogues in larger cities for information on kosher restaurants. Your own synagogue or college Hillel may have helpful lists or books, and a number of Jewish establishments in Germany can be found on the worldwide kosher restaurant database at http://shamash.org/kosher. If you are strict in your observance, you may have to prepare your own food on the road. A good resource is the *Jewish Travel Guide*, edited by Michael Zaidner (Vallentine Mitchell; US$18). Travelers looking for halal restaurants may find www.zabihah.com a useful resource.

OTHER RESOURCES

Let's Go covers many aspects of budget travel, but we can't include *everything*. Below are resources that can serve as jumping-off points for your own research.

USEFUL PUBLICATIONS

For books on Germany's culture and history, see **Additional Resources**, p. 73.

A Traveller's Wine Guide to Germany, Kerry Brady Stewart. Traveller's Wine Guides, 1997 (US$18). Exactly what it says it is, by a well-known oenophile.

Atlantik-Brücke, Magnus-Haus Am Kupfergraben 7, D-10117 Berlin-Mitte. Devoted to promoting mutual understanding (hence "Atlantic Bridge"), it publishes *These Strange German Ways*—a must for any American planning on living in Germany—as well as *Meet United Germany, German Holidays and Folk Customs,* and *Speaking Out: Jewish Voices from United Germany.* Order the books from the Hamburg office (☎(030) 20 39 830).

Culture Shock! Germany, Richard Lord. Graphic Arts Publishing Co., 1996 (US$13). A readable lowdown on living in Deutschland that isn't afraid to hold your hand.

Germany by Bike, Nadine Slavinski. Mountaineers Books, 1994 (US$15). Twenty tours throughout the *Länder,* with information on getting ready to *Tour de...Deutschland.*

Wicked German, Howard Tomb. Workman, 1992 (US$5). A little guide to everything you really didn't need to know how to say in German.

WORLD WIDE WEB

Almost every aspect of budget travel is accessible via the web. After a few minutes at the keyboard, you can make a reservation at a hostel or find out exactly how much a train from Berlin to Munich costs. Listed here are some regional and travel-related sites to start off your surfing; other relevant web sites are listed throughout the book. Because website turnover is high, use search engines (such as www.google.com) to find additional information on your own.

WWW.LETSGO.COM Our freshly redesigned website features extensive content from our guides; community forums where travelers can connect with each other and ask questions or advice—as well as share stories and tips; and expanded resources to help you plan your trip. Visit us soon to browse by destination, find information about ordering our titles, and sign up for our e-newsletter!

THE ART OF TRAVEL

Backpacker's Ultimate Guide: www.bugeurope.com. Tips on packing, transportation, and where to go. Also tons of country-specific travel information.

BootsnAll.com: www.bootsnall.com. Numerous resources for independent travelers, from planning your trip to reporting on it when you get back.

How to See the World: www.artoftravel.com. A compendium of great travel tips, from cheap flights to self defense to interacting with local culture.

Travel Intelligence: www.travelintelligence.net. Articles by distinguished travel writers.

Travel Library: www.travel-library.com. Personal travelogues and a great set of links.

World Hum: www.worldhum.com. Independently produced "travel dispatches."

INFORMATION ON GERMANY

Atevo Travel: www.atevo.com/guides/destinations. Travel tips and itineraries.

CIA World Factbook: www.odci.gov/cia/publications/factbook/geos/gm.html. Tons of vital statistics on Germany's geography, government, economy, and people.

Das Deutschland Portal: www.deutschland.de. The official German site about Germany, available in English for your convenience.

Geographia: www.geographia.com. Highlights, culture, and people of Germany.

PlanetRider: www.planetrider.com. A subjective list of links to the "best" websites covering the culture and tourist attractions of Germany.

TravelPage: www.travelpage.com. Links to official tourist office sites in Germany.

World Travel Guide: www.travel-guides.com. Helpful practical info.

Germany Tourism: www.germany-tourism.de. A rich source of information for travelers to Germany, including some stunning panoramic pictures.

LIFE AND TIMES

Germany has long been a wellspring of revolutionaries and innovators, for better or worse. One of its first heroes is **Charlemagne,** a Germanic leader who united post-Roman Europe under a relatively enlightened rule. **Martin Luther,** an ordinary German monk, became one of the most influential figures in Western history when he authored his **95 Theses** and gave birth to the Protestant Reformation. Intellectuals **Karl Marx** and **Friedrich Engels** developed the revolutionary new idea of communism, which would fuel 19th-century discontent and precipitate the major conflicts of the second half of the 20th century. One of the most brutal figures in history, **Adolf Hitler,** inextricably linked Germany to the horrors of the Holocaust and concentration camps. Today, Germans grapple with the fact that the same country that produced Goethe, Kant, and Beethoven is responsible for Hitler, Goebbels, and Mengele, while still coming to terms with the social and economic problems brought on by the country's staggeringly quick reunification nearly 15 years ago. While a clear picture of the country's future remains elusive, Germany entered the new millennium more unified and stable than ever before.

HISTORY

Few national histories are as ambiguous and rife with conflict as Germany's. Documented German history has been a roller coaster of loose alliances and fractured unions since 90 BC, when Roman author Posidonium first called Central European tribes "Germans" *(Germaniae)*. The radical swings between the enlightened absolute rulers of the 18th century and the brutal National Socialism of the first half the 20th century have so baffled historians that a few of them invented the *Sonderweg* theory: that from its earliest days, Germany has developed on a path wholly distinct from the rest of Europe.

EARLY GERMAN HISTORY: 58 BC-AD 1517. By 58 BC, the Roman Republic had expanded its borders to the Rhein, causing pagan clans of the Germanic peoples in Central Europe to join forces for defense. In AD 9, when battles erupted in the Teutoburg Forest (near present-day Osnabrück), the allied Germans scored a resounding homecourt victory, earning the nickname "Teutons" and a date to mark the first assertion of a truly Germanic culture. After five centuries of mutual antagonism and several barbarian attacks on Rome, the weakened Roman Empire fell in 476, leaving the vestiges of Christianity to take root amidst the Germans.

Without a common enemy to unify them, the disparate clans went their own ways. While southern Germanic tribes took over formerly Roman soil, the **Franks** expanded their power into the Rhein Valley, uniting nearly every Germanic kingdom of Europe three centuries later under the rule of **Charlemagne** (known in Germany as Karl der Große), crowned emperor by the pope in 800. Charlemagne initiated administrative reforms and cultural advancements; under his rule monasteries became centers of learning and European commerce was revived.

Disputes among Charlemagne's sons prompted the **Treaty of Verdun,** which split the empire into three kingdoms, foreshadowing the future border disputes of France and Germany. Although German king **Otto I "the Great"** managed to partially reunify the kingdoms in 962, earning himself the title of Holy Roman Emperor, destructive internal disputes divided the would-be German lands into a fractured feudal society. Otto I initiated a close relationship between the church and the monarchy, but in the **Investiture Crisis** of 1075 the Pope demanded autonomy, sparking conflict that ravaged Germany for nearly 50 years. Finally, the **Concordat of Worms** (1122) restored peace by setting up checks and balances between the pope and the king with respect to appointment of church officials.

War broke out time and again between the dozens of minor dukes and princes vying for power, while the **bubonic plague** of the 14th century wiped out entire villages. The **Golden Bull of 1356** declared that seven electors—three archbishops and four secular leaders—should approve all imperial selections. Under the leadership of the **House of Habsburg** (who occupied the throne for five centuries), the Empire began to define itself more clearly. Manufacturing and sea trade transformed small North Sea towns into wealthy merchant oligarchies, which banded together in 1358 to form the **Hanseatic League.** This trade federation had outposts as far away as England, Norway and Russia, and grew powerful enough to wage a successful war against Denmark. Yet while German interests focused on the wealthy towns, discontent roiled in rural regions, and outlying areas of the Holy Roman Empire slipped out of the Habsburgs' control entirely.

THE REFORMATION: 1517-1700. On All Saints' Day 1517, **Martin Luther,** a monk and professor of Biblical studies at the University of Wittenberg (p. 583), posted his **95 Theses** on the door of the city's castle church, igniting the **Protestant Reformation.** Luther objected to the Roman Catholic Church's practice of selling indulgences—gift certificates for the soul that promised to shorten the owner's stay in purgatory—insisting that salvation came through God's grace alone. While Luther's movement broke the unity of Western Christianity, his vernacular **translation of the Bible** helped crystallize the many German dialects into a standard German *(Hochdeutsch)* based on the Saxon language.

The Reformation soon grew into a political movement, as German electoral princes adopted Lutheranism as a way to stem the flow of money to Rome. Habsburg Emperor **Charles V (Karl V),** the most powerful leader since Charlemagne, who initially resolved to destroy the subversive doctrine of Lutheranism, eventually decided to sign the 1555 **Peace of Augsburg,** granting individual princes the right to choose their territory's official religion, further dividing the empire.

Charles' successors were less than thrilled with the agreement. When Archduke Ferdinand of Austria tried to impose Catholicism on Bohemia, his Protestant subjects rebelled, throwing a papal representative out a window in the 1618 **Defenestration of Prague.** The ensuing **Thirty Years' War** (1618-48) was a

TOP 10 CASTLES

Everyone's heard about **Neuschwanstein,** the "Cinderella castle" (p. 472), but a few of our other favorites include:

10. Jugendherberg Stahleck, Bacharach. Hostels don't get any better than this: stay in a 12th-century castle overlooking the Rhein for €15 per night (p. 360).

9. Schloß Gottorf, Schleswig. A former Viking stronghold now holds six museums (p. 210).

8. Moritzburg, Dresden. A huge palace full of hunting trophies on a custom-made island (p. 619).

7. Wilhelmshöhe, Kassel. Every town needs a mad prince, artificial ruins, and a 350 ft. high statue of Hercules (p. 350).

6. Heidelberger Schloß, Heidelberg. This fortress guards Germany's oldest university and largest wine barrel (p. 391).

5. Burg Rheinfels, St. Goar. Bring a candle to explore the ruined underground passages (p. 359).

4. Schloß Hohenschwangau, Füssen. The royal bedroom is inlaid with thousands of crystals to mimic the night sky (p. 472).

3. Schloß Sanssouci, Potsdam. A French-named English garden in Germany's capital (p. 153).

2. Wartburg, Eisenach. Deep in the Thuringian forest, this fortress inspired Bach, Goethe, Martin Luther, and Wagner (p. 577).

1. Schloß Linderhof, Oberommergau. The hunting lodge for a king who has everything: complete with mosque, half-ton chandeliers and a man-made grotto (p. 473).

catastrophic and bloody setback in Germany's development, killing off one-third of the population before the **Peace of Westphalia** ended the conflict. This document served as the de facto constitution of the empire until its abolition in 1806.

THE RISE OF BRANDENBURG-PRUSSIA: 1700-1870. After the Thirty Years' War, **Brandenburg-Prussia** (around Berlin) was the ascendant state in Germany, with King Friedrich II—known as **Frederick the Great**—at the reins. An enlightened despot and artistic patron, Friedrich's greatest contributions were administrative and military reforms. He snatched Silesia from the Habsburgs during the **Seven Years' War** (1756-1763), and joined forces with Russia and Austria to partition Poland in 1772. He also linked Brandenburg to Prussia for the first time, piecing together a kingdom for the Habsburgs' dynastic rivals, the **Hohenzollern.**

In 1806, **Napoleon** conquered and disbanded the remains of the Holy Roman Empire, creating a subservient **Confederation of the Rhein.** After the vertically-challenged French general incorporated hundreds of thousands of German soldiers into his armies, a rebellion known as the **Wars of Liberation** ousted him from German territory (see **Jena,** p. 566). The 1815 **Congress of Vienna** partially restored the pre-war German state system, creating the Austrian-led **German Confederation.** In 1818, Prussia sponsored the **Zollverein,** a customs union linking North German territories in a free trade zone. By 1834, most of Germany was included.

In 1848, as revolution broke out again in France and discontent spread across the rest of Europe, the German Confederation decided to let an elected assembly decide its future. The **Frankfurt National Assembly** drafted a liberal constitution and invited **Friedrich Wilhelm IV** of Prussia to be emperor. He refused to accept a crown with limited authority, and crushed the ensuing revolt with the Prussian army. In 1862, Prussian King Wilhelm I appointed a talented aristocrat named **Otto von Bismarck** as chancellor. The founder and greatest practitioner of *Realpolitik* ("realism"; taking a cue from Machiavelli's "the ends justify the means"), he exploited a remarkably complex series of alliances and compromises that were frequently dissolved in favor of more violent tactics. Blood and iron, Bismarck proclaimed, were paramount to the creation of a strong, unified German nation. To demonstrate this, he fought Denmark in 1864 and seized control of Northern Schleswig. This offensive led to the **Austro-Prussian War,** which Prussia won in 1866 at Sadowa. Bismarck made it clear that Prussia would dominate German affairs, making the current constitution null and void. In 1867, he disbanded the Confederation and replaced it with the Prussian-dominated **North German Confederation.**

SECOND REICH: 1871-1914. Realizing that France would never willingly acquiesce to a fully united Germany under Prussian rule, Bismarck suckered the nation into a misguided declaration of the **Franco-Prussian War** in 1870. The technologically superior Prussian army swept through France, capturing Emperor Napoleon III and crowning Wilhelm **Kaiser of the German Reich** at the Palace of Versailles. With France out of the way, Bismarck founded the **German Empire** on his own terms in 1871: unification for an authoritarian monarchy. The so-called conservative empire gained popular support by promoting aggressive nationalism.

Germany industrialized at breakneck speeds in the late 19th century, but the aristocratic political system could not keep up. To consolidate power, Bismarck began a series of social initiatives known as the **Kulturkampf,** including unemployment insurance for the working class, but repressed trade unions and the Social Democrats. These improvements allowed Bismarck to quell revolts, but he was forced to resign in 1890 over disputes with the new Kaiser Wilhelm II.

These rapid transitions produced tremendous social friction. To shift the focus from unrest at home, Germany accelerated its foreign adventurism—a policy derisively known as **"Flucht nach vorn"** (escape forward). Disputes over colonial issues left Germany diplomatically isolated in Europe. Though its navy did not yet compare with the British fleet, Germany kept the most powerful army in the world at the turn of the century, prompting Britain, France, and Russia to unite and form the **Triple Entente.** Meanwhile, democratic opposition began to pose a challenge within the regime itself. To the Kaiser and his supporting elite, it appeared that dramatic and militaristic action would be required for self-preservation.

WORLD WAR I: 1914-1918. On the eve of WWI, Europe was balanced in a web of alliances so complex that minor disputes threatened to disintegrate into total continental war. The first domino fell in 1914, when a Serbian nationalist assassinated **Archduke Franz-Ferdinand,** Habsburg heir to the Austrian throne. Austria marched on Serbia in immediate retaliation, and Russia ran to the aid of its Slavic ally. After Russia ignored Germany's ultimatum to retreat, Germany united with Austria to form the **Central Powers,** prompting France to mobilize. Germany declared war on France and demanded that the German army be allowed to march through Belgian territory. When Belgium refused, Britain, treaty-bound to defend Belgian neutrality, declared war on Germany. Despite this opposition, Germany advanced through Belgium and northern France, sweeping all of Europe into war.

The German offensive was stalled at the **Battle of the Marne.** Four years of agonizing **trench warfare** ensued just 50km outside of Paris. The magnitude of the slaughter was unprecedented, as were the weapons used: tanks, planes, flamethrowers, and poison gas. In 1917, Germany's policy of unrestricted submarine warfare provoked the U.S. to enter the war on the side of the Allies. A British naval blockade, coupled with the manpower of the US, let the Allies emerge victorious.

THE WEIMAR REPUBLIC: 1918-1933. In late 1918 the German army was on the brink of collapse, and riots broke out on the home front. On November 9, 1918, Social Democratic leader **Philipp Scheidemann** declared a republic in Berlin, with **Friedrich Ebert** as its first president. France insisted on a harsh peace in the **Treaty of Versailles,** which called for staggering reparation payments, reduced the German army to 100,000 men, and ascribed full blame for the war to Germany. The newborn republic was literally starved into accepting the treaty by an Allied blockade.

Feeding on popular unease, the new **Communist Party** (*Kommunistische Partei Deutschlands*—KPD), led by **Karl Liebknecht** and **Rosa Luxemburg,** launched a revolt in Berlin (p. 143). A group of right-wing army veterans known as the **Freikorps** launched their own coup d'état under **Wolfgang Kapp;** the workers, however, didn't share their revolutionary fervor, and demonstrated support for the new republic through a general strike, organizing a force of 50,000-80,000 against the coup. The republic emerged bruised but intact. Its leaders drew up a constitution in **Weimar** (p. 558), the birthplace of German Enlightenment, which now gave its name to the period of intense cultural activity between the World Wars.

By 1922-23, hyperinflation from war debts had become so severe that paying for a loaf of bread literally required a wheelbarrow full of bills. The American **Dawes Plan** staved off total economic collapse by reducing the demand for war reparations. Relative calm and remarkable artistic production ensued, though the old, reactionary order still clung to power in many areas of society. It was during the abortive 1923 **Beer Hall Putsch** uprising in Munich that frustrated artist and decorated Austrian corporal **Adolf Hitler** was arrested. He received the minimum sentence of five years—but served only 10 months. During this time in jail, Hitler wrote *Mein Kampf* ("My Struggle") and decided that his party, the **National Socialist German Workers Party** (*Nationalsozialistische deutsche Arbeiterspartei*—NSDAP, also known as the **Nazis**), should seize power by constitutional means. Two aspects of the Weimar constitution expedited this process. Proportional representation encouraged a turbulent spectrum of political parties, while the infamous **Article 48** (drafted by sociologist Max Weber) gave chancellors power to rule by decree during crises, creating the potential for a dictatorship.

LIFE AND TIMES

The Nazi party had nearly quadrupled its membership to 108,000 by 1929, but it was still a fringe party, receiving only 2.6% of the vote. Then the Great Depression struck in 1929, leaving 25% of the population unemployed, and membership in the NSDAP exploded to over a million. The **SA** *(Sturmabteilung)*, its paramilitary arm, grew to match the German army by 1930. Hitler failed in a presidential bid against the aging Franco-Prussian war-hero Paul von Hindenburg in 1932, but parliamentary elections made the Nazis the largest party, with 37% of the seats in the *Reichstag*. After intense political maneuvering, President Hindenburg reluctantly appointed Hitler chancellor of a coalition government on January 30, 1933.

THE THIRD REICH: 1933-1945. Although Hitler now held the most powerful governmental post, the Nazi party still had difficulty obtaining a majority in the *Reichstag*. Within two months of taking control, Hitler convinced the ailing Hindenburg to dissolve the *Reichstag* and hold new elections, allowing Hitler to invoke Article 48 and rule by decree for seven weeks. During this reign of terror, he curtailed freedom of the press, authorized special security arms (the Special State Police or **Gestapo**, the **SA** "Storm Troopers," and the **SS** Security Police), and brutalized opponents. Politically astute, he seized the opportunity of the mysterious *Reichstag* fire one week prior to the elections to declare a state of emergency and round up his opponents, many of whom were relocated to newly-built **concentration camps**. In the ensuing election on March 5, 1933 the Nazis got 44% of the votes, once again less than a majority. However, they arrested and browbeat enough opposing legislators to secure passage of an **Enabling Act** in 1933, making Hitler the legal dictator of Germany. Hitler proclaimed his rule the **Third Reich**, successor to the Holy Roman Empire (800-1806) and the German Empire (1871-1918).

Vilifying the Weimar government as soft and ineffectual, Hitler's platform played on post-war anxieties. Germany's failing economy encouraged a public largely receptive to ideas of anti-Semitism and German racial superiority. Aided by **Joseph Goebbels,** his propaganda chief, Hitler embarked upon a campaign of self-promotion. Nazi rallies were masterpieces of political demagoguery, and the Nazi emblem, the **swastika** (co-opted from Hindu tradition), appeared everywhere from propaganda films to the fingernails of loyal teenagers. *Heil Hitler* and the right arm salute became a legally required greeting.

The Third Reich's massive industrialization program restored full employment. This productivity, however, was hardly innocent: German business was mounting a war effort. Hitler defied the Versailles Treaty, freeing Germany from reparations and beginning rearmament. Next, he stared down the Western Allies and annexed Austria—the infamous **Anschluß**—in 1938. He demanded territorial concessions from Czechoslovakia, claiming (truthfully) that the **Sudetenland** was home to millions of ethnic Germans. British Prime Minister Neville Chamberlain assured Hitler in the 1938 **Munich Agreement** that Britain would not interfere with this hostile takeover. The Allies continued to tolerate Germany's aggressive expansionism until war was inevitable. Not everyone kept silent, though; many **resistance** movements sprang up in Germany itself. The young members of **Die Weiße Rose** (the White Rose), five Munich University students and their professor, were executed for treason in 1943 after Gestapo caught them distributing anti-Nazi leaflets.

WORLD WAR II: 1939-1945. On September 1, 1939, German tanks rolled across the eastern border into Poland. Britain and France, bound by treaty to defend Poland, declared war on Germany but did not attack. The Soviet Union likewise ignored the German invasion, having secretly divided up Eastern Europe with Germany under the **Molotov-Ribbentrop Pact.** In a month, Poland was crushed by Germany's new tactic of **Blitzkrieg** (literally, "lightning war"); Hitler and Stalin carved it up accordingly. By April 9, 1940, Hitler had overrun Denmark and Norway. A month later, the *Blitzkrieg* roared through Luxembourg and overwhelmed Belgium, the Netherlands, and France. The Nazis failed to bomb London into submission in the aerial **Battle of Britain,** despite leveling most of the city. Preparations for a cross-channel invasion were shelved as Hitler turned his attentions to the Soviet Union. The German **invasion of the USSR** in June 1941, unsurprisingly, ended the Hitler-Stalin pact, bringing the Soviets in on the side of France and Britain. Despite the Red Army's overwhelming manpower, the German invasion nearly succeeded. At his apex of power in late 1941, Hitler held an empire from the Arctic Circle to the Sahara Desert and from the Pyrenees to the Urals.

The Soviets suffered extremely high casualties, but *Blitzkrieg* faltered in the Russian winter. Hitler's stubborn refusal to allow a retreat at the bloody battle of **Stalingrad** resulted in the death or capture of over 200,000 troops and represented a crucial turning point in the East. Following the bombing of Pearl Harbor, Hitler declared war on the U.S. The Allies began their counterattack in North Africa, and soon Germany was retreating on all fronts. The Allied landings in Normandy on **D-Day** (June 6, 1944) preceded an arduous, bloody advance across Western Europe. The Third Reich's final offensive, the **Battle of the Bulge,** failed in December 1944. The following February, at least 35,000 people died in the Allied **firebombing of Dresden,** an operation of questionable necessity. Most of the casualties were civilians and many of them refugees (p. 606). In March 1945, the Allies crossed the Rhein; in April, the Red Army took Berlin. With Soviet troops overhead, Hitler killed himself in his underground bunker. The Third Reich, which Hitler had boasted would endure for 1000 years, had lasted only 12.

THE HOLOCAUST. The persecution of the Jews began years before WWII. The racial ideology that had fueled Hitler's rise to power regarded history in terms of racial confrontations with absolute winners and losers. In his mind, the German *Volk* would either triumph universally or perish; the Jews represented the antithesis of Hitler's fanatic nationalism, militarism, and belief in the infallibility of the *Führer*. In 1935 the first anti-Semitic **Racial Purity Laws** deprived Jews of German citizenship. On November 9, 1938, known as **Kristallnacht** (Night of Broken Glass), Nazis destroyed Jewish businesses, burned synagogues, killed nearly 100 Jews, and sent 20,000 more to concentration camps.

Early on, German SS troops massacred entire Jewish towns as they rolled eastward, but as the war progressed, institutions of mass execution were developed as Nazis further expanded the persecution and deportation of minorities under their control. Seven extermination camps—**Auschwitz, Buchenwald** (p. 564), **Chelmno, Treblinka, Majdanek, Sobibor, and Belzec**—and dozens of "labor" camps such as **Bergen-Belsen** (p. 263), **Dachau** (p. 464), and **Sachsenhausen** (p. 148) were operating before war's end. Nearly six million Jews (two-thirds of Europe's Jewish population), mostly from Poland and the Soviet Union, were gassed, shot, starved, worked to death, or killed by exposure, along with five million other Soviets, Slavs, Gypsies, homosexuals, the mentally disabled, and political dissenters.

OCCUPATION AND DIVISION: 1945-1949. Germans call their defeat at the end of WWII *Nullstunde*—"Zero Hour"—the moment at which everything began again. Germany had suffered an estimated 3.6 million military and 1.3 million civilian casualties, and 5.7 million more civilian deaths came after the war. The war left Germany desolate, and reconstruction under Allied occupation did not begin until 1948. In July 1945, the U.S., the U.K., France, and the Soviet Union met at **Potsdam** to partition Germany into occupation zones: German territory east of the Oder and Neisse rivers—one quarter of the nation—was confiscated and placed under Soviet and Polish administration, the coal-rich Saarland was put under French control (until 1957), and Berlin was held jointly by the U.S and the U.S.S.R.

The three-pronged Allied program of **Occupation**—demilitarization, democratization, and de-Nazification (including the 1945 trials of the Nazi war criminals in Nürnberg)—proceeded apace, but growing animosity between the Soviets and the Western allies made joint control of Germany increasingly difficult, paving the way for total division in 1949. In 1947, the Western Allies merged their occupation zones into a single economic unit, to be rebuilt as a market economy with the aid of huge cash infusions from the American **Marshall Plan.** The Soviets, who suffered immeasurably more in the war than the US or Britain, had neither the desire nor the resources to help the East rebuild and plundered it instead, permitted by the Potsdam agreement. The Western Allies ceased their contribution to the East in 1948 and effectively severed the East's economy from the West's by introducing a new currency, the **Deutschmark.** This reform resulted in a Soviet **blockade** of West Berlin and was followed shortly by the full **division of Germany** in 1949.

EAST AND WEST: 1949-1989. Upon division, West Germany established the **Bundesrepublik Deutschland (BRD),** or Federal Republic of Germany, as a provisional government. Its headquarters were seated in the sleepy university town of Bonn. Under Western supervision, the fledgling government drafted a **Basic Law** to safeguard individual rights. The document did not ratify German autonomy, however, as the Allies retained ultimate political authority over the country. The first chancellor of the new government was **Konrad Adenauer,** whose Christian Democratic Union (*Christlich Demokratische Union*—CDU) had won a small parliamentary majority over the Social Democratic Party (*Sozialdemokratische Partei Deuschlands*—SPD) in the 1949 elections. Adenauer pushed to integrate Germany with a unified Europe—a goal that anticipated the creation of the EU—and to reestablish German national self-determination, culminating in the recognition of **West German sovereignty** by the Western Allies in 1955. Reconstruction helped restore self-esteem and purpose in post-war BRD citizens. An influx of *Gastarbeiter* (guest workers) from Turkey and the guidance of economist **Ludwig Erhard** helped transform Germany into the world's fourth-largest economy by the 1960s.

Meanwhile, the Soviet Union ended free elections after their chosen **Socialist Unity Party** (*Sozialistische Einheitspartei Deutschlands*—SED) suffered a defeat at the hands of the SPD in Berlin ballot boxes. A People's Congress of pre-selected candidates from the SED was "elected" and declared the establishment of the **Deutsche Demokratische Republik (DDR),** or German Democratic Republic. Berlin housed the new government under SED leader **Wilhelm Pieck.** While the republic paid lip service to guarantees of civil liberties, the SED retained strict controls over citizens of the DDR, causing many to seek refuge in West Germany. Political conditions relaxed after Stalin's death in 1953, but nationalization of industry continued and impossibly high goals resulted in a **worker's revolt** on June 17, 1953, which was quickly crushed by Soviet tanks. In 1955, in response to the BRD's normalization of relations with the West, the DDR joined in signing the **Warsaw Pact.**

By 1961, the tally of illegal emigrants from East to West had reached three million. With SED party head **Walter Ulbricht** at the helm, the DDR decided to act; on the night of August 12, the beginnings of the **Berlin Wall** were constructed. By morning, Berliners found themselves blessed with an "anti-fascist protective wall"; needless to say, they knew which way the guns were pointed. In 1968, Ulbricht launched the DDR's second constitution, jettisoning most democratic rights.

The BRD's miraculous recovery had ground to a halt by 1967, when its first postwar recession loosened the CDU's grip on power. The Social Democrats embraced dynamic young leader **Willy Brandt,** who took control in 1969 and enacted vital reforms; more important, however, were Brandt's diplomatic achievements. His **Ostpolitik** (Eastern Policy) sought improved relations with the DDR and the rest of the Eastern Bloc. For the first time, many *Wessis* were permitted to visit their relatives in the East. Brandt won the Nobel Peace Prize in 1971. Meanwhile, East German president **Erich Honecker** maintained East German subservience to the Soviet Union. By the late 1970s, DDR citizens enjoyed the highest standard of living in the Eastern Bloc, but were still far behind the West. The secret police, or **Stasi,** held files on every citizen; one in seven East Germans was a paid informant.

Throughout the 70s, West German prosperity and economic success continued to soar. The Social Democratic star fell, however, with mounting unemployment. **Helmut Kohl** of the CDU became chancellor in 1982, enacting tight monetary policy and military cooperation with the US. In 1985, *glasnost*-minded **Mikhail Gorbachev** of the USSR sent waves of reform throughout the Eastern Bloc—except the DDR. By May 1989, the floodgates had begun to open, as Hungary dismantled its barbed-wire border with Austria. On October 6, Gorbachev attended East Germany's 40th birthday and rebuked Honecker publicly, announcing that the USSR would not interfere with the DDR's domestic affairs. Honecker resigned; chaos reigned as thousands of DDR citizens escaped to the West via Czechoslovakia. On November 8, the entire DDR *Politbüro* resigned. One day later, a Central Committee spokesperson announced the **opening of all borders to the West,** including the Berlin Wall.

REUNIFICATION AND ITS AFTERMATH: 1989-2000. The *Wende* ("change" or "turning"), as East Germans know the DDR's end, was the most significant turning point in Germany since WWII; the euphoria of those months is most evocatively expressed by images of Berliners celebrating on the Brandenburg Gate, the symbolic conduit between East and West, and destroying the concrete and barbed-wire Wall. However, joy soon gave way to disillusionment as the DDR lingered and East and West feuded over the terms of *Wiedervereinigung* (reunification). In March 1990, the CDU-backed **Alliance for Germany** won elections to preserve Kohl's hold on power. On September 12, 1990, the two Germanys and four occupying powers signed the **Four-Plus-Two** treaty, marking the **end of a divided Germany;** October 3, 1990 marks the date on which the Allies forfeited their occupation rights.

Reunification was not conducted on equal terms; the East was absorbed into the structure of the BRD, which then tried desperately to deal with the collapse of the East's inefficient industries and institutions. The BRD plunged into its worst recession in history, with unemployment skyrocketing in the East. Westerners resented the inflation and taxes required to rebuild the new federal states, while Easterners had to go without the generous social benefits afforded them by communism. Economic frustrations led to scapegoating of foreigners, punctuated by attacks on immigrants in Mölln and Rostock in 1992 and 1993.

The BRD's post-*Wende* woes led to Kohl's ouster in 1998, after a 16-year run, by **Gerhard Schröder,** who led a coalition of Social Democrats and the **Green Party.** He appointed environmental warrior **Joschka Fischer** as secretary of state, who soon announced that the government intended to shut down all of Germany's nuclear reactors, causing angry friction with France and the UK. In 1999, the government moved from Bonn to Berlin, inaugurating the much-heralded **Berlin Republic.**

TODAY

While average unemployment in Germany hovers around 10%, rates in the former DDR remain almost twice as high. Nevertheless, Germany still boasts **the world's third-largest economy** and is the European Union's industrial heavyweight, giving it tremendous clout. Many Germans believe that the nation should be more isolated, but the country's centrality in the EU keeps it in the thick of international affairs.

Exploring the dialects of everyone's favorite "language"

German is recognized as an official or national language in eight nations: Germany, Switzerland, Austria, Italy, Denmark, Belgium, Luxembourg, and Liechtenstein. It's used by over 100 million people, making it the world's 10th most widely-spoken language. But "German" is not actually a language at all. Even on a good day, a Bavarian farmer and a sailor from Bremen would probably not understand each other, despite their common citizenship. The "German language" is, in fact, a wide group of related but distinct dialects.

So what exactly do the terms "language" and "dialect" actually mean? Most linguists would say that if two people can communicate with each other fairly well, they're speaking the same language. And if those people happen to speak with the same pronunciation, grammar, and vocabulary, they're speaking the same dialect. There are three main language areas in the German-speaking part of Europe, each with countless dialects.

Oberdeutsch (Upper German) is spoken in the mountains (hence "upper") of Austria, Switzerland, Liechtenstein, northern Italy, and southern Germany. People here are fervently proud of their heritage, and hardly ever speak Standard German; you'll probably have trouble understanding their thick accent and musical intonation. Make sure you order a *Maß* (liter) of *Bock* (strong beer), *Goaßmaß* (beer, cola, and cognac), or *Schdamperl* (schnapps) at the bar; if you're a *Saufaus* (strong drinker), you might end up doing a *Schuaplattler* (drunken bar dance). Just remember to use a *Biafuizl* (beer cover) or you'll fall prey to the *Noagerlzuzla* (guy-who-drinks-up-your-beer-while-you're-not-watching). More importantly, don't *froasel* (annoy) any *Eigschnappters* (easily-insulted guys) or you'll get *aufgmischt* (thrashed) in the *Hoisl* (bathroom).

Mitteldeutsch (Middle German) is spoken from Luxembourg to Poland and the Czech Republic, across central Germany. This narrow band has spawned two national languages. *Hochdeutsch* (Standard German) is based on the 16th-century Middle German spoken around Meißen. *Lützebuergesch* (Luxembourgish) is a western Middle German dialect that is now one of the three official languages of the Grand Duchy of Luxembourg (along with Hochdeutsch and French).

In the coastal plains of southern Denmark, eastern Netherlands, and northern Germany and Poland, people speak a very different language, variously named *Niederdeutsch* (Low German), *Niedersächsisch* (Low Saxon), *Plattdeutsch* (Flat German), or just *Platt*. English speakers may breathe a sigh of relief in these lowlands; the

Platt dialects often sound and look more like English than German. The words for open, water, good, and later, for example, are spelled (but not spoken) the same in both English and Platt (compare with the Hochdeutsch *offen*, *Wasser*, *gut*, and *später*). The huge difference between Platt and Hochdeutsch (Northern Germans can converse more easily with their Dutch neighbors than with other Germans) is leading to Platt's gradual decline; speakers are so self-conscious of their distinct language that most of them prefer to speak Standard German even at home. Niederdeutsch resembles English in its refusal to participate in the softening of consonants p, t, and k to f, s, and ch, respectively, a shift that occurred in Mittel- and Oberdeutsch. Where Standard German speakers would say *Schiff* (ship), *weiß* (white), and *brechen* (breaking), northerners might prefer *Schipp*, *witt*, and *breken*.

So how did German reach this fractured state, and why doesn't everyone just speak the same language? The answer is historical: a map of medieval Europe shows that the "German-speaking area" was originally settled by dozens of distinct tribes. Distantly related through ancestry, Franks, Saxons, Burgundians, Thuringians, Alemannes, and Bavarians formed their own kingdoms and spoke their own languages. When dealing with other tribes, officials often turned to Latin: totally foreign, but universally respected.

Not until the kingdoms of central Europe were united under the Holy Roman Empire did the common people get fed up with resorting to Latin to communicate with the next city. Martin Luther picked up on this and boldly translated the Bible from Latin into a local Saxon dialect. He picked this believing it would be the easiest to understand across the whole Empire, which at that time comprised the modern-day nations of Germany, Austria, and Switzerland. His translation formed the base from which later writers slowly shaped a standard German language.

This unifying language, Hochdeutsch, is taught in all public schools, and is used in formal situations, the media, and virtually all written documents. Colloquial variations of Hochdeutsch, called *Umgangssprachen* (literally, "languages of going around"), introduce regional pronunciation and vocabulary to varying degrees. All Germans are familiar with Hochdeutsch, but few of them are ready to trade in their ancient linguistic traditions for national unity. In the past decade, more literature, news, and songs have been published in local dialects, a sign that Germans will likely remain a proudly multilingual people.

Sameer ud Dowla Khan is a graduate student in Linguistics at the University of California, Los Angeles, focusing in phonology. He's loved German in all of its forms since he first heard it spoken, and has been studying it for several years, along with Spanish, Bengali, Chinese, and Arabic.

POLITICS. Schröder narrowly triumphed in his September 2002 re-election bid against **Edmund Stoiber,** the conservative former governor of Bavaria. Schröder's popularity had waned, due mostly to widespread strikes and the persistence of unemployment, which he had promised to reduce. In a bizarre campaign twist, Schröder went to court to stop newspapers from reporting that he colored his hair, implying that a politician who colors his hair will similarly color the truth. Schröder's Social Democrat-Green alliance won control of parliament by barely 1%, leaving Stoiber to claim that the governing coalition would fall to pieces within the year. Thus far the government has proved as stable as any in the last 10 years.

FOREIGN POLICY. Germany was one of the most outspoken critics of Anglo-American foreign policy in the wake of the terrorist attack of September 11, 2001, and American officials called relations "poisoned" and refrained from sending congratulations to Schröder when he was re-elected. But recent ties have become more cordial: in February of 2004 Schröder and US President Bush issued a joint statement on "The German-American Alliance for the 21st Century," and in June Schröder attended the funeral of US President Ronald Reagan. Schröder also accepted French President Jacques Chirac's invitation to the 60th-anniversary commemoration of the Allied D-Day invasion, calling that day a victory for Germany as well as for the Allies. Showing a strong hand in working toward international safety, Germany took command of the NATO force in Afghanistan in 2003, while more recently German police have captured a high ranking member of al Qaeda and held suspects from the March, 2004 train bombings in Madrid.

LANGUAGE

Though German, or *Deutsch*, is clearly the language of choice in Germany, don't despair if your *Sprach* is sub-par. Most people in urban areas, especially younger Germans, are impressively fluent in English. Depending on your German background, you may find it easier to use English as a tourist. Dialects are distinct and disparate—it's no surprise that *Frieslanders* and Bavarians can often barely understand each other (see **Speaking of German,** p. 60).

RELIGION

Germany's legacy as a land of strong Catholic rule under the Holy Roman Empire was followed closely by a long tradition of Protestantism: it was in Wittenberg that Luther nailed his 95 Theses to the church door in 1517. Germany has developed as a Christian country (supported by the government), with the Protestant North and the Roman Catholic South each currently representing about one-third of the country's inhabitants. The total Jewish population in Germany today has risen to approximately 60,000. The largest Jewish congregations are in Berlin and Frankfurt, which together are home to over 10,000 Jews. An influx of foreign workers has brought a strong Islamic population; more than three million Muslims, most from Turkey, now live in Germany, and mosques can be found in many cities.

CULTURE

FOOD AND DRINK

German food gets bad press. Maybe it isn't as "gourmet" as French cuisine or "delicato" as Italian fare, but *deutsche Küche* has a robust charm that meat-and-potato lovers find especially satisfying. And if the local food is not to your taste,

Germany's cities offer a wide variety of quality ethnic restaurants. Be careful when ordering from a German menu; ingredients such as *Aal* (eel), *Blutwurst* (blood sausage), and *Gehirn* (brains) can occasionally be found in regional dishes. **Vegetarians** should not fear this land of carnivores. Since the 1970s, vegetarianism has steadily gained popularity in Germany, with a recent rise due to the fear of mad cow and foot-and-mouth disease. Approximately one-fifth of Germany's population now eats little or no meat. Vegetarian restaurants abound in most cities, and vegetarian and *Biokost* (health food) supermarkets are more common. As most vegetarian fare relies heavily on cheese, **vegans** may have a more difficult time finding non-dairy options. For more information, see **Dietary Concerns** (p. 48).

The typical German **Frühstück** (breakfast) consists of coffee or tea with a selection of *Brötchen* (rolls), butter, marmalade, *Wurst* (cold sausage of myriad varieties), *Schinken* (ham), *Eier* (eggs, usually soft- or hard-boiled), *Käse* (cheese), and *Müsli* (granola). **Mittagessen** (lunch) is traditionally the main meal of the day, consisting of soup, sausage or roasted meat, potatoes or dumplings, and a salad or *Gemüsebeilage* (vegetable side dish). **Abendessen** or **Abendbrot** (supper) is a reenactment of breakfast, with less *Müsli* and coffee, and more wine or beer. **Dessert** after meals is rare, but many older Germans indulge in a daily ritual of **Kaffee und Kuchen** (coffee and cakes), analogous to English "tea-time," at 3 or 4pm.

Germany's bakeries produce a delicious range of **Brot** (bread). *Vollkornbrot* is a heavy whole-wheat, *Roggenbrot* is rye, *Schwarzbrot* (black bread) is a dense, dark loaf, and *Bauernbrot* (farmers' bread) a lighter, slightly sour country recipe. Go to a *Bäckerei* (bakery) and point to whatever looks good. Bread is usually sold as a whole loaf; for half, ask for *ein Halbes*. German bread does not contain preservatives and will go stale the day after its purchase; Germans typically make the *Bäckerei* a daily stop. *Brötchen* (rolls) come in staggering varieties, starting with the simple, white *Wasserbrötchen* and extending to the hearty *Kürbiskernbrötchen* (pumpkin seed rolls). No visit to Germany would be complete without a taste of a *Bretzel*, the South German soft pretzel that puts ballpark vendors to shame, and that in larger bakeries also comes in roll and even baguette shapes.

Aside from breads, the staples of the German diet are *Wurst* (sausage, in dozens of varieties; see **The Best Wurst**, p. 342), *Schweinefleisch* (pork), *Rindfleisch* (beef), *Kalbfleisch* (veal), *Lammfleisch* (lamb), *Huhn* (chicken), and *Kartoffeln* (potatoes). Sampling the various **local specialties** around Germany gives a taste of diverse culinary traditions. In **Bavaria,** *Knödel* (potato and flour dumplings, sometimes filled with meat or jam) are popular, as is *Weißwurst*, a sausage made with milk. Thüringen and northern Bavaria are famed for their succulent grilled *Bratwurst*, a roasted sausage eaten with potatoes or bought from a street vendor clasped in a roll and bathed in mustard and *sauerkraut*. Southwestern Germany is known for its *Spätzle* (rough, twisty egg noodles), and *Maultaschen* (pasta pockets) are popular in **Swabia. Hessians** do amazing things with potatoes; fear not the delectable *grüne Soße* (green sauce). The North and Baltic seacoasts harvest *Krabben* (shrimp) and *Matjes* (herring), as well as other fresh forms of seafood.

When Turks began immigrating to West Germany in the early 1960s, the German palate was first treated to such now-ubiquitous delights as the *Döner Kebap;* thin slices of lamb mixed with cucumbers, onions, and red cabbage in a wedge of *Fladenbrot*, a round, flat, sesame-covered bread. Other well-known Turkish dishes include *Börek*, a flaky pastry filled with spinach, cheese, or meat; and *Lahmacun* (also called *türkische Pizza*), a smaller, zestier version of Italy's staple fast food. Turkish restaurants and *Imbiße*, popular and cheap fast-food stands, also proffer *Kefir* (flavored yogurt drinks) and *Baklava* for dessert.

Beer and wine (p. 63) are the meal-time **beverages.** *Saft* (juice), plain or mixed with mineral water, is an alternative. Germans do not guzzle glasses of water by the dozen as Americans do, although they will sip a (small) glass of carbonated mineral water—ask for *Wasser ohne Gas* to get the non-bubbly kind. If you ask for water in a restaurant, you'll get the expensive bottled type, so be sure to ask for *Leitungswasser* (tap water) if that's what you want.

With very few exceptions **restaurants** expect you to seat yourself. If there are no free tables, ask someone for permission to take a free seat by saying *Darf ich Platz nehmen?* (DAHRF eesh PLAHTS nay-men). In a less formal setting, just say *hallo*. It's standard practice for perfect strangers to plunk down next to you—they may or may not be interested in conversation. In traditional restaurants, address waiters as *Herr Ober*, and waitresses (but no one else) as *Fräulein* (FROY-line). At the table, Germans eat with the fork in the left hand and the knife in the right and keep their hands above or resting on the table. While eating, it is polite to keep the tines of your fork pointing down at all times. When you're finished, ask the server *Zahlen, bitte* (TSAH-len, BIT-tuh: "check, please"); it's considered rude to bring customers the bill before they have asked for it. Taxes *(Mehrwertsteuer)* and service *(Bedienung)* are always included in the price, but it is customary to leave a small tip, usually by rounding up the bill to the nearest euro.

Eating in restaurants at every meal will quickly drain your budget. One strategy is to stick to the daily fixed-price option, called the *Tagesmenü*. A cheaper option is to buy food in **grocery stores.** University students eat in cafeterias called **Mensen.** Some *Mensen* (singular *Mensa*) require a student ID (or charge higher prices for non-students), while some are open only to local students, though travelers often evade this requirement by strolling in as if they belong. In smaller towns, the best budget option is to stop by a bakery *(Bäckerei)* for bread and garnish it with sausage and cheese purchased from a butcher *(Fleischerei* or *Metzgerei)*.

BEER

> Beer brewers shall sell no beer to the citizens, unless it be three weeks old; to the foreigner, they may knowingly sell younger beer.
> —German Beer Law, 1466

Germans have brewed frothy, alcoholic malt beverages since the 8th century BC, and they've been consuming and exporting them in prodigious quantities ever since. The state of Bavaria alone contains about one-fifth of all the breweries in the world. The Germans drink more than 120L of beer per person every year. According to legend, the German king Gambrinus invented the modern beer recipe when he threw some hops into fermenting malt. During the Middle Ages, monastic orders refined the art of brewing, imbibing to stave off starvation during long fasts. It wasn't long before the monks' lucrative trade caught the eye of secular lords, who established the first *Hofbrauereien* (court breweries).

To ensure the quality of this new phenomenon, Duke Wilhelm IV of Bavaria decreed in 1516 that beer could contain only pure water, barley, and hops. As a result, German beer contains no preservatives and will spoil relatively quickly. Wilhelm's Purity Law *(Reinheitsgebot)* has endured to this day, with minor alterations to permit the cultivation of Bavaria's trademark wheat-based beers. Most German beer is **Vollbier,** containing about 4% alcohol. **Export** (5%) is also popular, and stout, tasty **Bockbier** (6.25%) is brewed in the spring. **Doppelbock** is an eye-popping concoction reserved for special occasions. *Ein Helles* gets you a light-colored beer, while *ein Dunkles* can look like anything from Coca-Cola to molasses. The average German beer is maltier and thicker than Czech, Dutch, or American beers (hence the term *"fluβiges Brot"*: liquid bread). Generalizations are difficult, however, as each region boasts its own special brew. Here are a few:

BEER	REGION	DESCRIPTION
Altbier	Düsseldorf	dark, top-fermented beer
Berliner Weiße	Berlin	light beer, often served *mit Schuß* (raspberry syrup)
Bockbier & Doppelbock	Einbeck (near Hannover)	strong, bottom-fermented, many seasonal versions
Dampfbier	Bayreuth	fruity, top-fermented
Dortmunder Export	Dortmund	mild, bottom-fermented lager
Dunkles Lagerbier	Bavaria	dark lager, strong malt, bottom-fermented
Gose	Leipzig	top-fermented wheat beer with oats
Hefeweizen	Bavaria	wheat beer, more hops than Weißbier
Kölsch	Cologne (Köln)	pale, top-fermented beer (by law, served only in Köln)
Märzen	Bavaria	amber colored lager
Pils (Pilsner)	North Germany	clear, bitter taste (extra hops)
Radler (Alster)	Hamburg	mix of half beer, half lemon-lime soda
Rauchbier	Bamberg	dark and smoky
Weißbier (Weizenbier)	Bavaria/south	wheat beer, smooth and refreshing, rich brown color

The variety of places to drink beer is almost as staggering as the variety of brews. A traditional **Biergarten** consists of outdoor tables under chestnut trees; often simple food is served as well. In the days before refrigeration, the broad leaves of the trees kept beer barrels cool—now they just shade the beer drinkers. A **Bierkeller** is a subterranean version of the *Biergarten*. To order *ein Bier*, hold up your thumb, not your index finger. Raise your glass to a *Prost* (cheers), make eye contact with your companions, and drink. Another option for beer drinking is the **Gaststätte,** a simple, local restaurant. It's considered bad form to order only drinks at a *Gaststätte* during mealtimes, but at any other time, friends linger for hours over beers. Many *Gaststätten* have a *Stammtisch* (regulars' table), marked by a flag, where interlopers should not sit. The same group of friends may meet at the *Stammtisch* every week for decades to drink and play cards. **Kneipen** are bars where hard drinks are also served.

WINE AND SPIRITS

Although overshadowed by Germany's more famous export beverage, German wines win over connoisseurs and casual drinkers alike. Over 80% of German wines are white, though they vary widely in character. Generally, German wines are sweeter and taste fresher than French, Mediterranean, or Californian wines. Because Germany is the northernmost of the wine-producing countries, the quality of a vineyard's produce can vary considerably with the climate.

Dry wines are labeled *trocken* or *halbtrocken* (literally, half dry), while mild, sweeter wines are called *lieblich*. Only wines with 45g/L of residual sugars can be labeled *süss* (sweet). Cheap wines are classified as *Tafelwein* (table wine) or *Landwein* (superior table wine), while the good stuff (which is still pretty affordable) is *Qualitätswein* (quality wine). The label *Qualitätswein bestimmter Anbaugebiete*, or *Q. b. A.*, designates quality wine from a specific cultivation region. *Qualitätswein mit Prädikat* (quality wine with distinction) denotes an even purer wine derived from a particular variety of grape. The *Prädikat* wines are further subdivided according to the ripeness of the grapes when harvested; from least to most ripe, they are *Kabinett, Spätlese, Auslese, Beerenauslese, Trockenbeerenauslese,* and *Eiswein*. The grapes that produce the *Trockenbeerenauslese* are left on the vine well into winter until they have shriveled into raisins and begun to rot—no kidding. During the *Erntefesten* (harvest festivals) of many towns in the Southwest, vintners will sometimes add alcohol to the fresh-pressed, cloudy grape juice to make the intoxicatingly spicy *Neue Süsse* (new sweet wine).

Most vineyards cluster in the Rhein and Mosel valleys, along the Main River in Franconia, and in Baden. Of the dozens of varieties, the most famous are *Riesling*, *Müller-Thurgau*, *Sylvaner*, and *Traminer* (source of *Gewürztraminer*). In wine-producing towns, thirsty travelers can stop for samples. In Hessen, the beverage of choice is **Ebbelwei** or *Äpfelwein* (apple wine), a hard cider similar in potency to beer. After a meal, many Germans aid their digestion by throwing back a shot of **Schnapps,** brandy distilled from fruit. **Kirschwasser,** a cherry liqueur from the Black Forest, is the best known and probably the easiest to stomach, but adventurous sorts can experiment with the sublime *Black Haus*, 100 proof, blackberry *Schnapps* also from the Schwarzwald. Each year, unsuspecting tourists are lured into buying little green bottles of **Jägermeister,** one of Germany's numerous (and barely palatable) herb liqueurs.

CUSTOMS AND ETIQUETTE

Although Germans may seem reserved or even unfriendly, they are not as stand-offish as they may first appear. Germans are very frank and will not hesitate to show disapproval. To the uninitiated this may come across as confrontational, but it stems mostly from honesty. Many Germans consider effusive chumminess insincere, and Americans are often perceived as disingenuous for being overly friendly.

Though the complex rules surrounding German etiquette make Miss Manners look like a gas station attendant, most apply only with older Germans and in rural areas. Even so, travelers should bear a few things in mind. In general, Germans are more formal than Americans and Australians, and incredibly big on punctuality. An invitation to a German home is a major courtesy; you should bring a gift for the hostess. Among the older generations, be careful not to use the informal *du* (you) or a first name without being invited to do so. *Du* is appropriate when addressing fellow students and friends, or when addressing children. In all other circumstances, use the formal *Sie* for "you," as in the question *Sprechen Sie Englisch?*

Addressing a woman as *Fräulein* is inappropriate in most instances; address all women as *Frau* (followed by a name). While the average German's language skills are, in general, impressively well-developed, Germans will be more receptive to a traveler who knows at least a little German; learn some before you go (see the **Appendix, p.** 649, for help). In any case, remember at least two phrases: **bitte** (both please and you're welcome; BIT-tuh) and **danke** (thank you; DAHNK-uh).

The first time you see a German standing at an intersection in the rain, no cars in sight, waiting for the "walk" signal, you'll see what a law-abiding nation Germany is. **Jaywalking** is only one of the petty offenses that will mark you as a foreigner (and subject you to fines); **littering** is another. Many tourists also do not realize that the **bike lanes** marked in red between the sidewalk and the road are strictly off-limits for pedestrians. The drinking age is 16 for beer and wine and 18 for hard liquor, although neither is strictly enforced, and it is not uncommon to see young teenagers in a store picking up a bottle of wine for the family dinner. Driving under the influence, however, is a severe offense. **Drug** use has yet to become publicly acceptable, even where penalties are more relaxed (see **Essentials,** p. 8).

THE ARTS

Germany is the land of *Dichter und Denker*—poets and philosophers. The humanities in Germany have had an enormous influence on the world, to say nothing of the pivotal role German research has had in the natural sciences.

HISTORY

ARCHITECTURE. Churches and castles around Germany manifest stunning Romanesque, Gothic, and Baroque styles, with foundations laid by Germany's unique history and geography. The **Romanesque** period, spanning the years 800 to 1300, arose from direct imitation of Roman ruins. Outstanding Romanesque cathedrals can be found along the Rhein at Speyer, Trier, Mainz, and Worms.

Gothic style, characterized by pointed rib vaulting, gradually replaced the Romanesque form between 1300 and 1500. Gothic cathedrals often take the form of a cross, facing east so that the morning sun would shine down onto the altar. The Gothic cathedral at Cologne (p. 291) is one of the most famous structures in Germany. Secular architecture at the end of the Middle Ages is best remembered through the **fachwerk** (half-timbered) houses that still dominate the Altstädte of many German cities. In the South, the **Renaissance** influence can be felt in the Augsburg Rathaus (p. 529) and the Heidelberg Schloß (p. 391).

By 1550, Lutheran reforms put a damper on the unrestrained extravagance of cathedrals in the North, while the Counter-Reformation in the Catholic South spurred the new **Baroque** style. The **Zwinger** in Dresden (p. 613) is a magnificent example of Baroque fluidity and contrast. This style eventually reached a fanciful extreme with **Rococo,** as exemplified by **Schloß Sanssouci** at Potsdam (p. 153). Versailles set a decadent precedent that influenced Bavarian castles, notably **Herrenchiemsee** (p. 495) and the **Königsschlößer** (p. 472).

Eventually this exuberance ran its course. The late 18th century saw an attempt to bring Greco-Roman prestige to Germany in the form of **Neoclassical** architecture. This style was spurred on by the pomp of **Karl Friedrich Schinkel** (p. 129), state architect of Prussia. The **Brandenburger Tor** and the buildings along **Unter den Linden** in Berlin (p. 121) were products of this new, simpler period.

The **Mathildenhöhe** buildings in Darmstadt (p. 338) are products of a much more modern movement, **Jugendstil,** which derived its name from the Munich magazine *Die Jugend.* This style, strongly influenced by *art nouveau,* spanned the decades before and after the turn of the century. In the 1920s and early 30s, **Walter Gropius** and the **Bauhaus** school of Weimar and Dessau came to the fore, seeking to unite the principles of form and function in sleek glass and concrete buildings.

Hitler disapproved of the new buildings. He named a design school reject, **Albert Speer,** as his minister of architecture, and commissioned ponderous, neoclassical buildings appropriate to the "thousand-year Reich." Many were intended for public rallies, such as the **congress hall** and **stadium** in Nürnberg (p. 546) and the **Olympic Stadium** in Berlin (p. 112). After the war, Soviet architecture began to clutter East Germany, reaching a high-point with the 365m high **Fernsehturm** (TV tower) in Berlin (p. 125). Berlin's Karl-Marx-Allee (p. 138) is rich in **Plattenbauen,** the dispassionate pre-fab apartment buildings that can be found throughout East Germany. Throughout Germany, reconstruction of war-torn Altstadt architecture fostered a revival of old forms.

FINE ARTS. German art first broke its Gothic fetters (i.e., became interesting) with Renaissance painters like **Matthias Grünewald** and **Hans Holbein the Younger,** who gave depth and realism to secular subjects. Their prolific colleague **Lucas Cranach** went beyond realistic portraits to churn out pieces with historical and mythological themes. **Albrecht Dürer's** *A Young Hare* is recognizable the world over, and his self portraits were some of the first, and most influential, in Western art.

During the tumult of the **Protestant Reformation** and the Thirty Years' War, the visual arts suffered from lack of financial encouragement in Germany, but by the 19th century German critics were advocating Romantic painters' return to traditional, divinely inspired German masterworks. This idea easily bled into the melancholy landscapes of **Philipp Otto Runge** and **Caspar David Friedrich**, who painted Rügen's chalk cliffs and the ancient ruins of Eldena.

In the 20th century, German art boomed. **German Expressionism** recalled the symbolist tendencies of Viennese **Jugendstil** (Art Nouveau) and **French Fauvism**. Its deliberately anti-realist aesthetics intensified colors and the representation of objects to project deeply personal emotions. **Die Brücke** (The Bridge) was the earliest Expressionist group, founded in Dresden in 1905. Its artists, especially the celebrated **Ernst Ludwig Kirchner**, used jarring outlines and deep color to make artwork loud and aggressively expressive. A 1911 exhibition in Munich entitled **Der Blaue Reiter** (The Blue Rider), led by Russian emigré **Wassily Kandinsky**, marked the rise of a second Expressionist school. Kandinsky's contribution was a 1910-11 series called *Improvisations*, considered to be some of the first totally abstract paintings in Western art. Other members include Swiss painter and fellow Bauhauser **Paul Klee**, whose simple style has remained influential throughout the century.

WW I and its aftermath forced politics onto German art. **Max Ernst** started a **Dadaist** group in Cologne expressing artistic nihilism with collage and composition. The grotesque, satirical works of **Otto Dix** juggled Expressionism and Dadaism; ultimately the artist embraced **Neue Sachlichkeit** (New Objectivity), an anti-fascist movement that sought to understand the rapid modernization of life through matter-of-fact representation. Perhaps its best-known proponent, **Max Beckmann** painted severely posed figures, expressing a tortured view of man's condition. The smaller German **Realist** movement devoted itself to bleak, critical works such as the social reform posters of **Käthe Kollwitz**. Sculptor **Ernst Barlach** infused realism with religious themes, inflaming Nazi censors (p. 169).

Nazism drove most artists and their work into exile. Themes of *Blut und Boden* (Blood and Soil) dominated Nazi visual arts, depicting the mythical union of folkish blood and German soil through idealized images of workers, farmers, and soldiers of the "master race." In 1937, the Nazis' infamous **Entartete Kunst** (degenerate art) exhibit ridiculed pieces by Kandinsky, Kirchner, and other masters by displaying them alongside paintings by psychotics and mental patients.

After the war, German art made a quick recovery. In **East Germany**, state-supported **Socialist Realism** dominated, particularly in Leipzig, while West German art was characterized by **abstraction**. As time went on, installations, "actions," and other new media art pieces, especially video, edged out painting, although **Sigmar Polke**, **Gerhard Richter**, and a few

TOP 10 ARTLESS MUSEUMS

Germany has amazing amounts of world-class art. You won't find any of that here:

10. Mining Museum, Freiburg. Don a whole miner's uniform and delve into the mountain (p. 415).

9. Deutsches Museum, Munich. The cold precision of this science museum challenges German stereotypes (p. 455).

8. Hanfmuseum, Berlin. An insider's look at hemp (p. 131).

7. Medieval Crime Museum, Rothenburg. Testing torture devices on rude tourists is probably against German law. Also, they have chastity belts (p. 532).

6. Wikingermuseum, Schleswig. Vikings are tall and fierce, and so are their artifacts, especially reconstructed longboats (p. 211).

5. Erotic Art Museum, Hamburg. Visitors to this risqué collection will learn that "Victorian pornography" is no oxymoron (p. 228).

4. Mercedes Museum, Stuttgart. The only thing missing is an *Autobahn* test drive (p. 385).

3. ZAM, Munich. A collection of several (bizarre) museums, ZAM brings together rabbit lovers and chamber pot enthusiasts, with surprising results (p. 456).

2. Schockeladenmuseum, Köln. Sample sweet molten chocolate from a golden fountain. Need we say more? (p. 294).

1. Checkpoint Charlie, Berlin. The most moving and fascinating display on the Berlin Wall and those who got past it (p. 142).

other masters kept the medium alive. Richter gained renown for his paintings of photos of the criminal Baader-Meinhof group, entitled *October 15, 1977.* Polke also studied with **Josef Beuys,** known for his performance art "actions," at his **Constructivist sculpture** school at Düsseldorf.

LITERATURE. German literary history begins around 800, with an epic poem describing the fatal struggle between the heroic **Hildebrand** and his son Hadubrand. The next several centuries showed an intriguing mix of Christianity and the culture of the German tribes. As chivalry took hold in Germany, a tradition of lyric poetry on the theme of unrequited love emerged, best represented by **Walther von der Vogelweide.** The medieval troubadour performed in this **Minnesang** genre until the mid-13th century, when the **lyric ballad** became popular. The epic poetry tradition continued with the 13th-century **Nibelungenlied,** describing the struggles of the hero **Siegfried.** During the **Reformation** in the late 15th century, poetry took a more serious turn, and **Martin Luther's** translation of the **Bible** in the 1530s laid the foundations for a standardized form of modern German writing.

What Luther did for language, **Martin Opitz** and **Andreas Gryphius** did for poetics a century later, insisting on strict rules for meter and stresses. The first significant German novel, **Hans J. C. von Grimmelshausen's** roguish epic *Simplicissimus,* was written during the Thirty Years' War. Literature on the whole, however, suffered during the long war, such that German writing styles were frequently imitations.

Sentimental, unusually personalized verse arose in the mid-18th century, about the time **Johann Wolfgang von Goethe** was writing his early poetry (p. 562). Goethe's lyrics possessed a revolutionary immediacy and drew on rediscovered folk songs and ballads. His novel *Die Leiden des jungen Werthers* (The Sorrows of Young Werther) drew the attention of Europe to the budding **Sturm und Drang** (Storm and Stress) movement, which would greatly influence early Romantic literature. Goethe later turned to the *Bildungsroman* (coming of age tale) and to themes of classicism and orientalism. His masterpieces are numerous; his retelling of the **Faust** legend is often considered the pinnacle of a German literature that had moved to the center of Europe's attention by the time Goethe died in 1832.

In the early 19th century, **Romanticism** began to flower, with the poetry of **Novalis,** and **J. C. Friedrich Hölderlin,** who wrote mythical poetry until he succumbed to insanity. While doing research for a German dictionary, **the Brothers Grimm** documented fairy tales for the first time. **E.T.A. Hoffmann** wrote ghost stories that were later analyzed by Freud (see **Bamberg,** p. 552). Romanticism gave way to realistic political literature around the time of the revolutions of 1848. **Heinrich Heine** was the finest of the **Junges Deutschland** (Young Germany) movement and also one of the first German Jews to achieve literary prominence (see **Düsseldorf,** p. 307). Social dramatists **Georg Büchner** and **Gerhart Hauptmann** achieved great influence around the turn of the century with characteristic *fin-de-siècle* realism.

Hermann Hesse incorporated Eastern spirituality into his writings (his 1922 novel *Siddhartha* became a paperback sensation in the 1960s), while **Thomas Mann** carried the Modernist novel to a high point with *Der Zauberberg* (The Magic Mountain), using the traditional *Bildungsroman* to criticize German culture (see **Lübeck,** p. 190). Also vital to the period were German-language writers living in Austria-Hungary, among them **Rainer Maria Rilke, Robert Musil,** and **Franz Kafka.**

In the years before WWI, Germany produced a violent strain of Expressionist poetry that mirrored developments in painting. The style was well suited to depict the horrors of war, though several of its masters were killed in battle. The **Weimar Era** was filled with lively artistic production. Its most famous novel was **Erich Maria Remarque's** bleak portrayal of the Great War, *Im Westen nichts Neues* (All Quiet on the Western Front). **Bertolt Brecht** presented mankind in its grotesque absurdity through dramas and poems (see **Berlin**, p. 127). The Third Reich burned more books than it published; the Nazi attitude toward literature was summed up by Goebbels: "Whenever I hear the word 'culture,' I reach for my gun."

While the literature of the Weimar period seemed to succeed WWI almost effortlessly, WWII left Germany's artistic consciousness in shambles. To nurse German literature back to health, several writers joined to form **Gruppe 47,** named after the year of its founding. The group included many who would become world-class authors, such as **Günter Grass** and the poet **Paul Celan.** Much of the ensuing literature dealt with the problem of Germany's Nazi past, while the poetry of **Hans Magnus Enzensberger** and the novels of Grass and **Heinrich Böll** also turned a critical eye towards post-war West Germany's repressive, overly-bureaucratic tendencies. The state of letters in the DDR, however, was largely determined by the waxing and waning of government control. Many expatriates, particularly those with Marxist leanings from before the war (such as Brecht), returned to the East with great hopes. But the communist leadership was not interested in eliciting free artistic expression, causing many talented writers to emigrate.

PHILOSOPHY. German philosophy is like German *Wurst*: thick and difficult to digest. **Immanuel Kant,** the foremost thinker of the **German Enlightenment,** built a rational argument in favor of the Golden Rule. Meanwhile **Johann Gottlieb Fichte** spearheaded the new **German Idealist** movement, which stressed the importance of a spirit or *Geist* in interpreting experience (p. 566). **G. W. F. Hegel** proposed that world history as well as the development of the individual consciousness could be understood as conflicts between thesis and antithesis, which produced synthesis—essentially the idea that from struggle comes growth. The two thinkers were laid to rest side by side in a Berlin cemetery (p. 127). Hegel's view of world history would, after some distortion, eventually provide a theoretical backing for German nationalism. Meanwhile, **Johann Gottfried Herder** pushed for romantic nationalism, asserting that the spirit of a nation could be found in its folklore and peasant traditions. **Karl Marx** turned Hegel around, asserting that class conflict was the stage on which the world was made—and the rest is history.

Similarly controversial, **Friedrich Nietzsche,** influenced by pessimist par excellence **Arthur Schopenhauer,** scorned the mediocrity of hypocritical Judeo-Christian masses and advanced the idea of the *Übermensch* (superman). Evidence suggests his works were later edited to emphasize their anti-Semitic elements.

Writing around the turn of the century, **Max Weber** announced that the world was trapped in a bureaucratic iron cage and spoke out against the archaic, retarding effect of noble **Junker** society on German agriculture. **Martin Heidegger** made his name with *Sein und Zeit* (Being and Time). This notoriously cumbersome book details the importance that man understand what it means to question the meaning of life in a world where one-sided technical development had led to a crisis of existential alienation. The most celebrated post-war exponent of this school, **Jürgen Habermas,** has criticized German re-unification, citing the danger of joining two nations that had adopted two very different cultures.

MUSIC. A tradition of secular music began in the 12th century with the **Minnesänger,** German troubadours whose technique of singing poetry passed gradually to the **Meistersänger** of the 14th and 15th centuries. Religious reformation ushered in musical reforms, with German *cantata* and *oratorio* (sacred and secular forms) becoming the first genres to be composed in the language of the people. **Johann Pachelbel** (best known for his Canon in D) worked in the new musical style of the "Passion," a piece centered on the life of a saint. **Georg Friedrich Händel's** *Messiah* (1742, think "Hallelujah!"), initially considered heretical for using religion in a theatrical setting, has become a staple of choral music (and advertising).

Johann Sebastian Bach (1685-1750) began as a composer of sacred organ music, but eventually moved into the secular world; his *Brandenburg Concerti* were written in an attempt to secure a post as a court composer. Bach's appointment as cantor to Leipzig's largest church, the Thomaskirche in 1723 (p. 644), brought him once again to Lutheran music. During his appointment, Bach composed over 200 cantatas, one for every Sunday. He wrote both the *St. Matthew* and *St. John Passions* during this time, as well as his famous Easter and Christmas Oratorios.

Ludwig van Beethoven's symphonies and piano sonatas bridged Classicism and Romanticism, driven by intense rhythm and emotion. His later string quartets and *Ninth Symphony*, a mammoth orchestral and choral masterpiece, were written in the 1820s, well after he had gone completely deaf. The ethereal nature of **Felix Mendelssohn-Bartholdy** is represented by his overture to *A Midsummer Night's Dream*. **Robert Schumann** is best known for his piano works and song cycles like the *Dichterliebe* (poet's love), which draws inspiration from poetry of Heine and Goethe. **Johannes Brahms** imbued Classical forms with rich Romantic emotion, while the highly nationalistic **Richard Wagner** revolutionized the German opera and was the most influential German composer after Beethoven. He composed many renowned operas—*Tannhäuser, Tristan und Isolde, Der Ring des Nibelungen*—as **Gesamtkunstwerken** (total works of art), unifying music and text, poetry and philosophy. Through the use of a resurfacing *Leitmotif,* Wagner gave signature sounds to certain characters or dramatic actions.

Paul Hindemith headed a group of German Neoclassicists (a school of composing inspired by Stravinsky). They embraced the older, variational forms (such as the sonata) most suited to the abstract aesthetic of the time. Yet at the same time, an anti-Romantic backlash and the unstable Weimar economy encouraged smaller, cheaper musical forms like jazz. A new movement of *Gebrauchsmusik* (utilitarian music) engendered music for amateur players and film scores. **Carl Orff,** Hitler's favorite composer, is known for his *Carmina Burana*, a resurrection of bawdy 13th-century lyrics with a bombastic score. Prior to WWII, music hall works bred the *Singspiel;* satiric operettas with songs of the political avant-garde. **Kurt Weill's** partnership with Bertolt Brecht mastered the genre with *Die Dreigroschenoper* (Three-Penny Opera) and the universally-known song *Mackie Messer* (Mack the Knife). After the immediate post-war period, largely dominated by schmaltzy *Schlagermusik* (pop music), many exiled musicians returned to Germany to try to revitalize the otherwise unremarkable music scene.

FILM. The newborn medium of film exploded onto the German art scene in the Weimar era thanks to numerous brilliant directors. *Das Cabinet des Dr. Caligari* (The Cabinet of Dr. Caligari), an early horror film directed by **Robert Wiene,** plays out a melodrama of autonomy and control against sets of painted shadows and tilted walls. **Fritz Lang** produced a remarkable succession of films, including *M.*, *Dr. Mabuse der Spieler*, and *Metropolis*, a dark and brutal vision of the techno-fascist city of the future. Meanwhile, **Josef von Sternberg** extended the tradition into sound with his satiric and pathetic *Der blaue Engel* (The Blue Angel), based on a Heinrich Mann novel and starring **Marlene Dietrich.** Relics of this era are on display at the former **UFA** studio grounds in Potsdam and Babelsberg (p. 155).

Heeding Hitler's prediction that "without motor-cars, sound films, and wireless, (there can be) no victory for National Socialism," propaganda minister **Joseph Goebbels** became a masterful manipulator. Most **Nazi films** were political propaganda and many, such as *Der Ewige Jude* (The Eternal Jew) glorified anti-Semitism. The frighteningly compelling films of **Leni Riefenstahl** functioned as propaganda, while taking the art of the documentary to new heights. Her *Triumph des Willens* (Triumph of the Will) documented a Nürnberg Party Rally (p. 546), and *Olympia* recorded the 1936 Olympic Games in Berlin (p. 454).

LIFE AND TIMES

Film continued to be a vigorous artistic medium in the latter half of the 20th century, with a flood of new cinema in West Germany in the late 60s and the 70s. The renaissance began in 1962 with the **Oberhausen Manifesto,** a declaration by independent filmmakers demanding artistic freedom and the right to create new feature films. **Rainer Werner Fassbinder** made fatalistic films about people corrupted or defeated by society, including an epic television production of Alfred Döblin's mammoth novel *Berlin Alexanderplatz.* Fassbinder's film *Die Ehe der Maria Braun* (The Marriage of Maria Braun) and **Volker Schlöndorff's** *Die Blechtrommel* (The Tin Drum, based on Günther Grass's novel) brought the new German wave to a wider, international audience. **Wolfgang Petersen** directed *Das Boot* (The Boat), one of the most famous submarine films ever made. **Wim Wenders's** "road films," such as *Alice in den Städten* (Alice in the Cities) and the award-winning *Paris, Texas*, examine unconventional relationships and freedom of life on the road.

East German film was subject to more constraints than other artistic media due to the fact that all films had to be produced under the supervision of the state-run German Film Corporation (DEFA). **Slatan Dudow** produced the first of the DEFA's films, *Unser täglich Brot* (Our Daily Bread), a paean to the nationalization of industry, as well as *Stärker als die Nacht* (Stronger than the Night), which tells the story of a communist couple persecuted by the Nazis. After a brief post-Stalinist thaw, few East German films departed from the standard format of socialist heroism or love stories. **Egon Günther's** 1965 film *Lots Weib* (Lot's Wife), an overtly feminist exploration of marital breakdown and divorce, was one notable exception. The next year saw **Frank Beyer's** politically daring *Spur der Steine* (Trace of Stones). Beyer later made the critically acclaimed *Jakob der Lügner* (Jacob the Liar), which was nominated for an Oscar. The DDR also devoted a healthy portion of its filmmaking resources to **documentaries,** with **Winfried Junge, Volker Koepp,** and **Jürgen Böttcher** making significant contributions—although most of these films shunned political critique, instead glorifying the East and vilifying the West.

CURRENT SCENE

ARCHITECTURE. New construction since the *Wende* has once again put Germany on the architectural map, although many buildings were designed by non-German architects. Berlin is home to many high-profile projects, such as Sir Norman Foster's glass dome on the **Reichstag** (p. 126) and the reconstruction of **Potsdamer Platz** (p. 123), anchored by the steel and glass Sony Center. Daniel Libeskind's highly conceptual **Jewish Museum** (p. 143) opened in 2002, and American architect Peter Eisenman's contemplative **Holocaust memorial** will be dedicated in 2005.

FINE ARTS. Germany produces and exhibits a huge range of modern art, from video and multimedia installations to avant-garde painting and sculpture. *Kunstfonds* (art funds) have supported artists since 1980, and the modern art school in Leipzig enjoys international renown. Kassel deserves special mention, as it host the acclaimed "Documenta" exhibit every five years, showcasing contemporary art in various indoor and outdoor installations throughout the town. Other museums to watch are Berlin's **Hamburger Bahnhof** (p. 129), Cologne's **Museum Ludwig** (p. 306), and Düsseldorf's **Kunstsammlung im Ständehaus** (p. 312).

LITERATURE. Since reunification, there has been a period of artistic anxiety in the former East as many authors faced scandals over *Stasi* ties. Günther Grass's receipt of the Nobel Prize for Literature in 1999 provided the newly-reunited Germany with its first literary icon and propelled German literati back into an international spotlight. However, the new world of capitalism has filled the shelves of many corner bookstores with translations of American best-sellers, pushing many works by German authors to the side. For happening German literature, look for **W. G. Sebald, Monika Maron, Peter Schneider,** and **Bernhard Schlink.**

MUSIC. Current German musical tastes dip more into the American and British pop worlds than into the tunes of fellow Teutons. Apart from **Nina Hagen's** apocalyptic 80s hit *99 Luftballons* and, more recently, **Rammstein's** frightening tune *Du Hast,* Germany is best known internationally for its hugely influential ◼**Krautrock** of the 60s and 70s (a blend of rock instrumentation and electronic textures characterized by repetition and sparse lyrics, featuring artists such as **Can, Faust, Kraftwerk,** and **Neu!**), and for having pioneered **techno,** an umbrella term for various kinds of electronic music, from dancefloor dignitaries such as Berlin's **Paul von Dyk** to more cerebral artists like Köln's ◼**Schneider TM.** Germany's techno zenith is the annual **Love Parade** in Berlin (p. 106), when DJs such as **Dr. Motte** (the parade's founder) induce hundreds of thousands of Germans to drop ecstasy and get down.

Apart from techno, Germany enjoys a vital rock scene, with such notable acts as **Die Ärtzte, Einstürzende Neubauten** (collapsing new buildings) and ◼**The Notwist** (recently signed to U.S. record label Domino). After becoming a rock sensation in the 60s, Germany's equivalent to the Boss, **Herbert Grönemeyer,** has recently enjoyed a comeback among the younger generations. Influenced by American musical trends, Germans have also begun to dabble in hip-hop and rap, ranging from the wildly popular **Die fantastischen Vier** to the cannabis-inspired tracks of the Hamburg crews **Fünf Sterne Deluxe** and **Fettes Brot.** One of the most prolific home-grown, **3p** (from Frankfurt) bills itself as the number one source of *deutsche Soulmusik.* Under its aegis, numerous hip-hop stars, among them **Sabrina Setlur, Xavier Naidoo,** and **Illmatic,** have come to the forefront of the German charts.

FILM. Since the *Wende,* German film has struggled to create a new identity. **Tom Tykwer** wowed international audiences in 1998 with stylish, high-energy *Lola Rennt* (Run Lola Run); the film is, to many, iconic of a reunified and postmodernist Germany, heartbeat set apace with furious techno and bodies relentlessly in motion. **Wim Wenders's** hugely popular documentary *Buena Vista Social Club* celebrates Cuban music and spawned a best-selling soundtrack. **Caroline Link's** dramatic *Nirgendwo in Afrika* (Nowhere in Africa), follows a Jewish family that flees to Kenya in 1938. Based on a true story, the film won the 2002 Academy Award for Best Foreign Film. The most successful German movie to date, however, is **Wolfgang Becker's** *Goodbye, Lenin!,* a nuanced and affecting (not to mention hilarious) portrait of life in the DDR after reunification.

PUBLICATIONS. British dailies, such as the *Times* and *Guardian,* are widely available at newsstands in most cities. The *International Herald Tribune* and the European edition of the *Wall Street Journal* are the most common US papers. American and British armed forces maintain English-language radio stations in Western Germany. German speakers can keep track of things with German-language papers both in print and on the web. Hamburg-based weekly *Der Spiegel* (www.spiegel.de), one of the world's leading newsmagazines, provides reliable coverage of world events. *Die Zeit* (www.zeit.de) is a left-leaning weekly newspaper. The *Frankfurter Allgemeine Zeitung* (www.faz.de) is a more conservative daily, as is the much-respected Munich-based *Süddeutsche Zeitung* (www.sueddeutsche.de); of course, the tabloid *Bild* (www.bild.de) is far more popular. Radical Berlin offers the liberal newspaper *Berliner Tagesspiegel* (www.tagesspiegel.de) and the leftist *Tageszeitung* (www.taz.de). For a far-leftist spin on the news, check out the daily *Neues Deutschland* (www.nd-online.de).

HOLIDAYS AND FESTIVALS

Stores, museums, and most tourist offices will be closed on the days listed, as the local population either sleeps late or spends the day in church.

2005	2006	HOLIDAY	ENGLISH
Jan. 1	Jan. 1	Neujahrstag	New Year's Day
Jan. 6	Jan. 6	Heilige Drei Könige	Epiphany
Mar. 25	Apr. 14	Karfreitag	Good Friday
Mar. 27	Apr. 16	Ostersonntag	Easter Sunday
Mar. 28	Apr. 17	Ostermontag	Easter Monday
May 1	May 1	Tag der Arbeit	Labor Day
May 5	May 25	Christi Himmelfahrt	Ascension Day
May 15	June 4	Pfingstsonntag	Whit Sunday (Pentecost)
May 16	June 5	Pfingstmontag	Whit Monday
May 26	June 15	Fronleichnam	Corpus Christi
Aug. 15	Aug. 15	Maria Himmelfahrt	Assumption Day
Oct. 3	Oct. 3	Tag der deutschen Einheit	Day of German Unity
Nov. 1	Nov. 1	Allerheiligen	All Saints' Day
Dec. 24	Dec. 24	Heiligabend	Christmas Eve
Dec. 25-26	Dec. 25-26	1. und 2. Weihnachtstagtage	Christmas Day and Boxing Day
Dec. 31	Dec. 31	Silvester	New Year's Eve

LIFE AND TIMES

ADDITIONAL RESOURCES

GENERAL HISTORY

Craig, Gordon. *The Germans*. An excellent picture of modern German society.

Fulbrook, Mary. *Anatomy of a Dictatorship: Inside the GDR, 1949-1989*. A retrospective of the East German state.

Peukert, Detlev. *The Weimar Republic*. Thorough examination of the trends of the interwar period, such as doing the Charleston and not getting enough to eat.

Schulze, Hagen. *Germany: A New History*. Comprehensive overview of German history from its inauspicious beginnings to the present.

GERMAN CULTURE

▨ Zeidenitz, Stefan and Ben Barkow. *Xenophobe's guide to the Germans*. Everything you ever wanted to know about the German psyche, but were afraid to ask.

▨ Lord, Richard. *Culture Shock! Germany!* An essential guide to Teutonic customs and etiquette. Required reading for anyone planning on living in Germany.

ALTERNATIVES TO TOURISM

A PHILOSOPHY FOR TRAVELERS

Let's Go believes that travelers can have a profound impact on their destinations. We know that many travelers care deeply about the communities and environments they explore—but also that even conscientious tourists can inadvertently damage natural wonders and harm cultural environments. With this "Alternatives to Tourism" chapter, *Let's Go* hopes to promote a better understanding of Germany and afford travelers the opportunity to enhance their experience.

Germany may seem quaint, cold, or simply quirky at first glance, but a longer stay and more involvement in the local culture will reveal nuances that unlock the real Germany and open you up to a wealth of new experiences and friendships. Some ways to accomplish this goal include **volunteering, studying**, or **working** for an extended period of time, all of which offer unique perspectives different from those of a tourist. Entering German society as a student or worker can also help you improve your German, which many travelers find to be the greatest boundary between them and cultural immersion. Germany can be somewhat of a bureaucratic maze to enter as anything other than a traveler, so you'll need some perseverance or enough cash to cover volunteering or study programs that take care of the paperwork for you. Unemployment remains high throughout Germany, so don't get discouraged if you come up empty-handed after your first few stabs at finding a job—German university students often take years off to do internships, and many organizations can help you piggy-back onto this practice. Whether you find yourself re-creating an ice age house on the banks of the Rhein or studying the effects of cultural integration in Berlin, you are likely to discover an experience more memorable than any that you may have had as a tourist.

 Start your search at ▓ **www.beyondtourism.com,** Let's Go's brand-new search able database of Alternatives to Tourism, where you can find exciting feature articles and helpful program listings divided by country, continent, and program type.

VOLUNTEERING

Volunteering in Germany can be an extraordinarily enriching way to engage with German culture, although (depending on the supervising program) the volunteer may feel more like a cog in a foreign machine than a truly significant contributor to German society. Most people choose to go through a parent organization that takes care of logistical details and frequently provides a group environment and support system. There are two main types of organizations—religious (often Catholic) and secular—although there are rarely restrictions on participation for either. Many of Germany's volunteering opportunities involve environmental preservation—working on farms or in forests and educating people on protecting the environment—though opportunities for civil service and community building still exist, especially in East Germany.

Fees for such organizations can be surprisingly hefty, although they often cover airfare and most, if not all, living expenses. Research your program thoroughly before committing to it. Living and working conditions vary widely, so talking to previous participants may give you a sense of whether you want to join and what to expect when you arrive.

ENVIRONMENTAL CONSERVATION

Agriventure, Servicing offices, Lerchenborg Gods, 4400 Kalunborg, Denmark (☎45 59 5115 25; www.iaea.de or www.agriventure.com). Organizes agricultural exchanges and homestays at farms throughout Europe.

Earthwatch, 3 Clocktower Pl. Ste. 100, Box 75, Maynard, MA 01754 (☎800 776 0188 or 978 461 0081; www.earthwatch.org). Arranges 1- to 3-week programs in Europe (occasionally Germany) to promote conservation of natural resources. Fees vary based on location and duration; costs average $1700 plus airfare.

Jugend Umwelt Projektwerkstaat (JUP), Turmstr. 14a, D-23843 Bad Oldesloe (☎04531 45 12; http://projektwerkstaat.de). Organizes stays at work camps in Germany geared toward protecting the environment.

Willing Workers on Organic Farms (WWOOF), Postfach 210259, 01263 Dresden, Germany (www.wwoof.de). Membership (€18) in WWOOF gives you room and board at a variety of organic farms in Germany in exchange for chores.

COMMUNITY AND CIVIL SERVICE

AFS Intercultural Programs, AFS International, 71 West 23rd St., 17th fl., New York, NY 10010 (☎212 807 8686; www.afs.org). Offers volunteer opportunities for 18+ travelers to serve local communities, with a separate education program.

AIDS Take Care, Schloßstr. 15, 82269 Getendorf/München (☎8193 930 00; fax 95 07 54). Based in Germany, this organization supports AIDS education and patient treatment throughout the world.

Amnesty International, Sektion der Bundesrepublik Deutschland e.V., 53108 Bonn (☎0228 98 37 30; www.amnesty.de). Human rights organization often has internship and volunteer positions available.

Habitat for Humanity International, 121 Habitat St., Americus, GA 31709 (☎229 924 6935, ext. 2551; www.habitat.org). Volunteers build houses in over 83 countries. Periods of involvement range from 2 wk. to 3 yr. Short-term programs run US$1200-4000.

Internationale Begegnung in Gemeinschartsdiensten, e.V., Schlosserstr. 28, D-70810 Stuttgart (☎0711 649 11 28; www.ibg-workcamps.org). Camps bring together Germans and foreigners to promote mutual understanding and tolerance.

Service Civil International Voluntary Service (SCI-IVS), SCI Deutscher Zweig e.V., Blücherstr. 14, D-53115 Bonn (☎0228 21 20 86; www.sci-d.de). In the US, SCI USA, 5474 Walnut Level Rd., Crozet, VA 22932, USA (☎/fax 206 350 6585; www.sci-ivs.org). Arranges placement for work in German civil service camps for those 18+. Program fee (including registration) US$175.

Volunteers for Peace, 1034 Tiffany Rd., Belmont., VT 05730 (☎802 259 2759; www.vfp.org). Arranges placement in German civil service camps. Membership (Annual *International Workcamp Directory* US$20) required for registration. Programs average US$200-500 for 2-3 wk.

ALTERNATIVES TO TOURISM

YOUTH AND THE ELDERLY

Big Friends for Youngsters (Biffy), German Children and Youth Foundation, Tempelhofer Ufer 11, D-10963 Berlin (☎030 25 76 76 12; www.biffy.de). The German arm of the Big Brothers Big Sisters program; provides mentoring for young kids in need of guidance on a longer term basis.

Bund Jugend, Am Köllnischer Park 1A, 10179 Berlin (☎030 275 86 50; www.bundju-gend.de). This eco-friendly group provides information and organizes events for youth in Germany, including volunteer and internship opportunities.

Elderhostel, Inc., 11 Avenue de Lafayette, Boston, MA 92111-1746 (☎877 426 8056; www.elderhostel.org). Sends volunteers over age 55 around the world to work in construction, research, teaching, and other projects. Costs around $100 per day plus airfare.

HISTORICAL RESTORATION

Archaeological Institute of America, 656 Beacon St., Boston, MA 02215 (☎617 353 9361; www.archaeological.org). The *Archaeological Fieldwork Opportunities Bulletin*, available on the organization's website, lists field sites throughout Europe.

Open Houses Network, Goetheplatz 9B, D-99423 Weimar (☎03643 502390; www.openhouses.de). A group dedicated to restoring and sharing public space (mostly in the former DDR), providing lodging for anyone who arrives, in return for work.

Pro International, Bahnhofstr. 26A, 35037 Marburg (☎06421 65277; http://www.pro-international.de/germany.htm). Since 1949, this volunteer organization has brought together youth from around the world to help reconstruct and preserve sites in Germany.

DATABASES

www.alliance-network.org. Umbrella website that brings together various international service organizations from around the world.

www.ciee.org. Offers a large database of opportunities for volunteering, searchable by country, area of interest, and months available.

www.idealist.org. Provides extensive listings of service opportunities (150+ in Germany alone), with contact info and descriptions.

www.istc.umn.edu. Run by the University of Minnesota, offers a searchable database of international programs.

www.oekojobs.de. Look for environmentally-oriented volunteer opportunities at this German-language site.

www.worldvolunteerweb.org. Offers organizations around the world a venue to advertise volunteer opportunities and events.

STUDYING

Study abroad programs range from basic language and culture courses to college-level classes, often for credit. In order to choose a program that best fits your needs, you will want to find out what kind of students participate in the program and what sort of accommodations are provided. You may feel more comfortable with large groups of students who speak the same language, but that will not give you the same opportunity to practice German. For accommodations, dorm life provides a better opportunity to mingle with fellow students, but there is less of a chance to experience the local scene. If you live with a family, there is a potential to build lifelong friendships and experience day-to-day life in more depth, but conditions can vary greatly from family to family.

VISA INFORMATION
Residence permits of the appropriate type are generally necessary for all foreign citizens to work and study in Germany; get them once in Germany at the local Aliens' Office (Ausländeramt). **Students** must have a letter of acceptance from the appropriate school, two passport-size photographs, a US$39 fee, and proof that they have sufficient means of support; citizens of the UK and Ireland must also have a student visa. Non-EU citizens must also take a medical exam and register at the local police station within a week of arrival.

UNIVERSITIES

Those relatively fluent in German may find it cheaper to enroll directly in a university abroad, although getting college credit may be more difficult. Many American schools require students to pay them for credits they obtain elsewhere. Most university-level study abroad programs are meant as language and culture enrichment opportunities and are therefore conducted in German. Still, many programs do offer classes in English as well as beginner- and lower-level language courses. The following is a list of organizations that can help place students in university programs abroad, or have their own branch in Germany.

AMERICAN PROGRAMS

International Association for the Exchange of Students for Technical Experience (IAESTE), 10400 Little Patuxent Pkwy. Suite 250, Columbia, MD 21044, USA (☎410 997 2200; www.aipt.org). Offers 8- to 12-week training programs in Germany for college students. Each program has its own specific requirements. US$30 application fee.

School for International Training, College Semester Abroad, Admissions, Kipling Rd., P.O. Box 676, Brattleboro, VT 05302, USA (☎800 257 7751 or 802 257 7751; www.sit.edu). Semester- and year-long programs in Germany, including a Berlin-based course on culture and ethnicity, run US$10,600-13,700. Also runs the **Experiment in International Living** (☎800 345 2929; www.usexperiment.org), 3- to 5-week summer programs that offer high-school students cross-cultural homestays, community service, ecological adventure, and language training in Germany and cost US$1900-5000.

GERMAN PROGRAMS

Deutscher Akademischer Austauschdienst (DAAD), 871 United Nations Plaza, New York, NY 10017, USA (☎212 758 3223; www.daad.org); in Germany, Kennedyallee 50, 53175 Bonn; mailing address Postfach 200404, 53134 Bonn. Information on language instruction, exchanges, and the wealth of scholarships for study in Germany. The place to contact if you want to enroll in a German university; distributes applications and the valuable *Academic Study in the Federal Republic of Germany.*

German American Partnership Program (GAPP), Goethe-Institut Inter Nationes New York 1014 Fifth Ave., New York, NY 10028 (☎212 439 8700; www.goethe.de/uk/ney/gapp/index.htm). For high school students and classes interested in exchanges, homestays, and study in Germany. GAPP subsidizes travel, housing, and food costs for qualified groups and individuals.

DATABASES

The following resources offer a wide range of programs and durations for students of all ages. If you are uncertain about what type of program you are most interested in, they may provide a good starting point.

www.studyabroaddirectory.com. This site lists summer and term-time study opportunities at German universities, as well as language schools throughout Germany. Searchable by academic specialty, for those looking to study a specific subject.

www.studyabroad.com. A good resource for finding programs that cater to your particular interests. Links to various semester abroad programs based on a variety of criteria, including desired location and focus of study.

LANGUAGE SCHOOLS

Language schools can be independently run international or local organizations or divisions of foreign universities. They rarely offer college credit. They are a good alternative to university study if you are looking for a deeper focus on the language or a slightly less rigorous courseload. These programs are also good for younger high school students who might not feel comfortable with older students in a university program. Some good programs include:

BWS Germalingua, Bayerstr. 13, 80335 München, Germany (☎089 599 892 00; www.germalingua.com). Part- and full-time language classes in Munich and Berlin for up to 1 yr. Full-time 2-week courses from €390; night classes from €75 per wk.

Eurocentres, 101 N. Union St. Suite 300, Alexandria, VA 22314, USA (☎703 684 1494; www.eurocentres.com). In Europe, Head Office, Seestr. 247, CH-8038 Zurich, Switzerland (☎41 1 485 50 40; fax 481 61 24). Language programs for beginning to advanced students with homestays in Germany.

Goethe-Institut, Dachauer Str. 122, 80637 München, Germany; mailing address Postfach 190419, 80604 München (☎089 15 92 10; www.goethe.de). Runs German language programs in 16 German cities and abroad; also orchestrates high school exchange programs in Germany. For information, look on the web, contact your local branch (**Australia:** Melbourne, Woollahra; **Canada:** Montreal, Ottowa, Toronto, Vancouver; **Ireland:** Dublin; **New Zealand:** Wellington; **UK:** Glasgow, London, Manchester; **US:** New York, Washington, D.C., Boston, Atlanta, San Francisco, Los Angeles) or write to the main office. 8-week intensive summer course from €1680, with room from €2200 (prices depend on city).

Language Immersion Institute, 75 South Manheim Blvd., SUNY-New Paltz, New Paltz, NY 12561, USA (☎845 257 3500; www.newpaltz.edu/lii). 2-week summer language courses and some overseas courses in German. Program fees around US$1000.

WORKING

Some travelers want long-term jobs that allow them to get to know another part of the world in depth. Other travelers seek out short-term jobs, usually in the service sector or in agriculture, working for a few weeks at a time to finance the next leg of their journey. This section discusses both short-term and long-term opportunities for working in Germany. Make sure you understand Germany's **visa requirements** for working abroad. See the box on p. 80 for more information.

The best tips on jobs for foreigners often come from other travelers; newspaper listings are another start. English speakers are occasionally a prized commodity within the tourist industry, especially at tourist offices, pubs, cafes, restaurants, and hotels. Other fields such as fast food, agriculture, and nursing (for which you will need further health certification), as well as sectors involving skilled construction labor, can also be traveler-friendly. It is critical that you be aware of your rights as an employee; make sure you have a signed agreement with your employer, and make the boundaries of your job explicit, unless you relish the prospect of non-stop toilet maintenance.

TEST TUBES AND TEUTONS
Research in Germany

During my time as an college student in the United States, I took an unforgettable semester off to work at the University of Ulm doing chemistry research. I was interested not only in learning about polypeptides and phenolphthalein, but also in discovering how Germans differ in their approaches to research, academics, and life. I wanted to get to know Germany (and Europe) more intimately than the average tourist, using the city of Ulm as the stronghold from which I would sally forth to other nations.

For centuries, Germany has been known for its rigorous intellectual tradition, especially in the physical sciences. After sitting in on a mind-blowing statistical mechanics lecture in Ulm, I learned that the professor was also deeply interested in history. In particular, he emphasized Einstein's variegate contributions to the field and the fact that Ulm was his birthplace. Germany may have lost some of its academic luster since the times of Boltzmann, Leibniz, and Hegel, but academic research there is still as vital as the flow of the mighty Rhein.

I began my search for a position in a German lab by talking to my academic advisor in the States about potential contacts in Germany. I then emailed these professors my résumé to convey to them my sincere interest. Finding professors who wanted an American protégé ended up being much easier than finding a reliable, sufficient, and legal method of financing my trip. I eventually was lucky enough to come upon a professor whose university could fund my studies, which meant I could stop trying to arrange my own funding through the **German Academic Exchange Program** (www.daad.de).

Undertaking academic research in Germany had several advantages over participating in a mere study abroad program, the best being that my trip was financed. I also appreciated the interaction afforded by eating with students in their dining hall. During my time in Germany, I lived in university housing with visiting scholars from many different countries, all of whom had very different academic and personal backgrounds, and fascinating stories to tell. The true highlight of my research experience, however, was the opportunity to get involved in intense, focused scholarship, which can be far more intellectually rewarding than the academic dabbling of broad overview classes.

To pursue academic research in Germany, you usually have to be a university student or graduate with a strong interest in pursuing a narrow research topic in a rigorous academic setting. In most fields, especially scientific ones, you do not need to speak any German at all, let alone know how to decline an unpreceded adjective in front of a feminine noun in the dative case. Everyone in my lab špoke some heartfelt variant of English, and I was actually required to give my presentations in English.

My six-month stay in Germany was ridiculously rewarding. Academically, my project succeeded beyond our wildest dreams. I worked hard, but received unending support from my labmates. I survived the student dining hall, sat in on sundry classes, and went to a few raging university parties. But even as we climbed scientific mountains together, I saw firsthand the ways in which German students differed from Americans. One day I arrived at work to find that the students had gone on strike (by refusing to attend classes, a tough move for the industrious Germans) to protest an administrative fee that the university was planning to establish.

While based in Ulm, I also had the opportunities to explore Munich and Stuttgart and spend a strenuous but rewarding weekend biking at the glorious Chiemsee in Bavaria. Since I was a wage-earning chemist instead of a starving backpacker, my quick trips to Austria, France, and England had a more generous budget than they otherwise would have, and the superb European train system and new discount airlines helped make them relatively hassle-free. Academic research was a phenomenal way for me to get to know Germany, change the shape of my life for a while, see much of Europe, and even learn a little bit of science.

Barbara Richter *was a Researcher-Writer for* Let's Go: Austria & Switzerland. *A native Austrian now based out of New Jersey, she will be continuing her studies in chemistry and physics at graduate school, though unfortunately not in Germany.*

For US college students, recent graduates, and young adults, the simplest way to get legal permission to work abroad is through **Council Exchanges Work Abroad Programs** (http://us.councilexchanges.org). Affiliated with the Council on International Educational Exchange, they can help you obtain a three- to six-month work permit/visa and provide assistance finding jobs and housing, as well as further resources for student exchanges and volunteering. (Fees run about US$300-425.)

VISA INFORMATION. To **work** in Germany, non-EU citizens will need a **work permit,** for which they may apply before or after arriving in Germany. Requirements differ based on the job type and country of origin; contact the local German consulate for more information. **Residence permits** of the appropriate type are generally necessary for all foreign citizens to work in Germany; get them once in Germany at the local Aliens' Office (Ausländeramt). Foreigners will also need two passport-size photographs, a US$39 fee, and proof that they have sufficient means of support. Non-EU citizens must also take a medical exam and register at the local police station within a week of arrival.

LONG-TERM WORK

If you're planning on spending a substantial amount of time (more than three months) working in Germany, search for a job well in advance. International placement agencies are often the easiest way to find employment abroad, especially for teaching English. **Internships,** usually for college students, are a good way to segue into working abroad; although they are often unpaid or poorly paid, many say the experience is well worth it. Be wary of advertisements or companies that claim to get you a job abroad for a fee—often the same listings are available online or in newspapers, or are even out of date. Some reputable organizations are:

Career Journal, (www.careerjournaleurope.com), is affiliated with the *Wall Street Journal*. It provides a searchable index of jobs, usually in the financial sector, for young professionals dreaming of middle-management jobs abroad.

Carl Duisberg Gesellschaft e.V. (CDG), Weyerstr. 79-83, 50676 Cologne, Germany (☎0221 209 80; www.cdg.de/english/indexz.htm). Professional training for students and young people from Germany and abroad.

International Association for the Exchange of Students for Technical Experience (IAESTE), 10400 Little Patuxent Pkwy., Ste. 250, Columbia, MD 21044-3519, USA (☎410 997 3069; http://www.aipt.org/subpages/iaeste_us/index.php). 8- to 12-week internships in Germany for college students who have completed 2 years of technical study. US$10 application fee.

International Co-operative Education, 15 Spiros Way, Menlo Park, CA 94025, USA (☎650 323 4944; www.icemenlo.com). Finds summer jobs for students in Germany. Costs include a US$200 application fee and a US$600 fee for placement.

Jobs Abroad, (www.jobsabroad.com), provides an index of jobs, searchable both by location and type. Some are teaching-oriented; many offer help finding housing.

TEACHING ENGLISH

Teaching jobs abroad are rarely well-paid, although some elite private American schools can pay somewhat competitive salaries. Volunteering as a teacher in lieu of getting paid is also a popular option, and in those cases teachers often get some sort of a daily stipend to help with living expenses. You can also get a private tutoring job by posting signs around learning centers, marketplaces, and public transportation stops stating that you are a native speaker; scan classifieds in local newspapers, too, and consider putting in your own ad. Teaching with an organization, however, is more secure (and generally more lucrative) than going it alone. Many schools require teachers to be certified in **Teaching English as a Foreign Language (TEFL)** or have a **Certificate in English Language Teaching to Adults (CELTA)**, which can be obtained in Germany or at TEFL and CELTA centers for US$400-1000. Some schools go further and necessitate the **DELTA (Diploma in English Language Teaching to Adults).** Non-certified teachers will have a more difficult time finding jobs, especially with more reputable organizations.

Native English speakers working in private schools are most often hired for English-immersion classrooms where no German is spoken. Those volunteering or teaching in public schools are more likely to be working in both English and German. Placement agencies or university fellowship programs are the best resources for finding teaching jobs in Germany, but the **Long-Term Work** resources (p. 80) can also be useful. You can try making contact directly with schools; the best time to do so is several weeks before the start of the school year. The following organizations are extremely helpful in placing teachers.

Fulbright English Teaching Assistantship, U.S. Student Programs Division, Institute of International Education, 809 United Nations Plaza, New York, NY 10017-3580, USA (☎ 212 984 5400; www.iie.org). This highly competitive program sends college graduates to teach in Germany.

International Schools Services (ISS), 15 Roszel Rd., Box 5910, Princeton, NJ 08543, USA (☎ 609 452 0990; www.iss.edu). Hires teachers for more than 200 overseas schools, including a few in Germany; candidates should have experience teaching or with international affairs. 2-year commitment expected.

AU PAIR WORK

Au pairs are typically women (although sometimes men), aged 18-27, who work as live-in nannies, caring for children and doing light housework in foreign countries in exchange for room, board, and a small spending allowance or stipend. Most former au pairs speak favorably of their experience. One perk of the job is that it allows you to really get to know the country and language without the high expenses of traveling. Drawbacks, however, often include long hours of constantly being on duty and somewhat mediocre pay. Au pairs in Germany can expect to earn a similar salary to other EU countries, roughly €50-80 per week for 25-30 hours of work. Much of the au pair experience really does depend on the family with whom you're placed. The agencies below are a good starting point for looking for employment as an au pair.

Au Pair Homestay, World Learning, Inc., 1015 15th St. NW, Suite 750, Washington, DC 20005, USA (☎ 800 287 2477; fax 202 408 5397).

Au Pair in Europe, P.O. Box 68056, Blakely Postal Outlet, Hamilton, Ontario, Canada L8M 3M7 (☎ 905 545 6305; www.princeent.com).

Childcare International, Ltd., Trafalgar House, Grenville Pl., London NW7 3SA (☎ 44 020 8906 3116; www.childint.co.uk).

InterExchange, 161 Sixth Ave., New York, NY 10013, USA (☎ 212 924 0446; www.interexchange.org).

SHORT-TERM WORK

Traveling for long periods of time can get expensive; therefore, many travelers take odd jobs for a few weeks at a time to earn extra cash to carry them through another month or two of touring. To some extent, the German tourist industry relies on students (and illegal immigrants) to provide the brawn for hotels, hostels, and resorts, so ask around. A popular option is to work several hours a day at a hostel in exchange for free or discounted room and/or board. More so than with long-term work, word of mouth is crucial; be alert and inquisitive. *Let's Go* tries to list temporary jobs like these whenever possible; check the practical information sections in larger cities, or check out the list below for some of the available short-term jobs in popular destinations.

Cafe Nöö, Große Klausstr. 11, Halle (☎0345 202 16 51; p. 591). Frank Ziegerhorn sometimes hires short-term java makers, especially June-Sept.

Mitte Backpacker Hostel, Chausseestr. 102, Berlin (☎262 51 40; www.backpacker.de; p. 119). This hostel (as well as its sister **Bax Pax** in Kreuzberg; p. 141) occasionally employs internationals. Some German-speaking ability is required. The shortest work period is 1 month. Other privately-owned hostels in Berlin may also hire short-term workers, but rarely for periods shorter than 1 month.

FOR FURTHER READING ON ALTERNATIVES TO TOURISM

Alternatives to the Peace Corps: A Directory of Third World and U.S. Volunteer Opportunities, by Joan Powell. Food First Books, 2000 (US$10).

How to Get a Job in Europe, by Sanborn and Matherly. Surrey Books, 1999 (US$22).

How to Live Your Dream of Volunteering Overseas, by Collins, DeZerega, and Heckscher. Penguin Books, 2002 (US$17).

International Directory of Voluntary Work, by Whetter and Pybus. Peterson's Guides and Vacation Work, 2000 (US$16).

International Jobs, by Kocher and Segal. Perseus Books, 1999 (US$18).

Invest Yourself: The Catalogue of Volunteer Opportunities, published by the Commission on Voluntary Service and Action (☎718-638-8487).

Overseas Summer Jobs 2002, by Collier and Woodworth. Peterson's Guides and Vacation Work, 2002 (US$18).

Work Abroad: The Complete Guide to Finding a Job Overseas, by Hubbs, Griffith, and Nolting. Transitions Abroad Publishing, 2000 ($16).

Work Your Way Around the World, by Susan Griffith. Worldview Publishing Services, 2001 (US$18).

BERLIN

Berlin is bigger than Paris, up later than New York, wilder than Amsterdam, and more diverse than London. Dizzying, electric, dynamic, the city is nearing the end of a profound transition from Newly Reunited Post-Cold War Metropolis to Geographic And Emotional Center Of An Eastward Expanding European Union. Everything in this city of 3.5 million is changing, from the demographics of the diverse population to which *Bezirk* (neighborhood) is currently "in." The long, agonizing period of division and the plunge-into-cold-water swiftness of reunification in 1989 resulted in a turbulent decade filled with euphoria, disillusionment, wild despair, and wilder optimism. In 1999 the government moved from Bonn to Berlin, throwing the new capital back into chaos as construction sites sprang up everywhere and droves of bureaucrats began looking for new homes. Amid lingering turmoil, spectacular and ambitious plans for the city's renovation are speeding toward completion. The glass and steel Potsdamer Platz now towers where the *Mauer* used to stand and the **Lehrter Hauptbahnhof**, soon to be Europe's largest train station, will open in time for Germany to host World Cup 2006. But while Berlin surges ahead as one of the most vibrant of cities, memories of the past century—both the days of the Nazi regime and the DDR—remain etched in daily life.

TO DO IN BERLIN

ABANDON MODESTY AND MODERATION while partaking in Berlin's notorious **nightlife** (p. 106) in the districts of Mitte, Kreuzberg, Prenzlauer Berg, and Friedrichshain, or while experiencing the unparalleled **gay scene** in Schöneberg.

ASCEND the sleek spiraling glass dome atop the **Reichstag** (p. 126) and wonder how many other countries have a **solar-powered parliament.**

BASK in the green serenity of the **Tiergarten** (p. 126); stop at the grandiose **Siegessäule** on your way to the broad boulevard **Unter den Linden** (p. 121), where the **Brandenburg Gate** and other historic buildings transport visitors to the regal Berlin of old.

GAWK IN ADMIRATION at Old Masters and avant garde alike in **Museumsinsel** (p. 127), **Kulturforum** (p. 128), **Dahlem** (p. 149), and **Charlottenburg** (p. 113).

MINGLE WITH HIPSTERS in **Hackescher Markt** before relaxing with a foaming *Milchkaffee* at one of the many cafes in the **Hackeshe Höfe.** (p. 127)

RELIVE THE COLD WAR at **Checkpoint Charlie** (p. 142) or at the longest surviving stretch of the **Berlin Wall,** now the canvas for the **East Side Gallery** (p. 138).

SOAR 368m up from **Alexanderplatz** (p. 124) to view Berlin from the DDR's pride and joy, the **Fernsehturm** (p. 125), or just check the time at home on the **World Clock.**

SURVEY THE "NEW BERLIN" that city planners designed over a decade ago while you are dwarfed by the ultra-modern grandeur of **Potsdamer Platz** (p. 123).

The ramifications of this transformation are profound, and Berliners are understandably ambivalent about it all. Nobel laureate **Günter Grass** goes so far as to contend that Germany shouldn't even have been allowed to reunite. The problem of *Mauer im Kopf* ("wall in the head;" still-existing feelings of division) is more prevalent here than anywhere else in the country. Westerners or *Wessies* resent having to spend so much to give a leg up to their less-affluent eastern neighbors, while Easterners or *Ossies* disdain what they consider an attitude of superiority from the West. Both sides are less than enthusiastic about sharing "their" city.

The idea of a disconnected city is familiar to Berliners. There is no "downtown" in the traditional sense; instead, the city is composed of many *Bezirke*. These neighborhoods began as individual settlements on the Spree River, growing together over hundreds of years to form a city spread out over an area eight times the size of Paris. Neighborhoods struggle to maintain their individuality, even while they are becoming more integrated. Areas that no one would have dreamed of visiting five years ago have become nightlife hotspots, and districts where everyone wanted to live last week will be passé tomorrow. The atmosphere is the most tolerant of any of Germany's cities, with a world-famous **gay and lesbian scene** and few racist crimes. The city isn't known for settling into a rut, but its very dynamism endangers the preservation of its rich history. In Friedrichshain, controversy rages over plans to tear down the DDR-era *Palast der Republik*, while the longest remaining portion of Berlin's once ubiquitous Wall is rapidly being defaced.

Come watch Berlin change before your very eyes, because, as an old German song goes, "*Es gibt nur einmal, und kommt nicht wieder*" (It will only happen once, and never again).

 HOW TO USE THIS CHAPTER. Berlin is best experienced one *Bezirk* at a time. Listings for accommodations, food, sights, museums, and nightlife are grouped together by neighborhood. More general information on these aspects of Berlin, as well as shopping, gay and lesbian offerings, and specific listings for camping and entertainment—including galleries, theater, concerts, and film—can be found after the practical information below.

HISTORY

THE BEGINNINGS: LOTS OF WAR

Berlin, now Germany's most populous city, was originally the site of small Slavic settlements in the marshlands along the Havel and Spree Rivers during the early Middle Ages; in fact Berlin takes its name from the Slavonic word *birl*, meaning "swamp." The Saxon duke **Albrecht der Bär** (Albert the Bear) came to power in Brandenburg during the 12th century and successfully removed the Slavs from the region, resettling it with immigrants from the west. By the 13th century, the trading posts Cölln and Berlin were founded, and in 1307 the two formally united. The electors of Brandenburg seized control from the merchant class in 1411 and began building a capital to match their dreams of glory. With the Edict of Potsdam (1685), **Friedrich Wilhelm** (the Great Elector) bolstered the city's population by accepting Huguenot and Jewish refugees from newly intolerant France, and in 1701 Berlin became the capital of the Kingdom of Prussia. In the following years, Berlin flourished as an intellectual hotspot thanks to the ruler **Friedrich II** (the Great), thinkers such as dramatist **Gotthold Ephraim Lessing,** and educators like the **Humboldt brothers.** Still, Berlin remained little more than an ornate garrison town, as Friedrich's penchant for martial pomp and circumstance turned the city into an assortment of broad avenues and grandiose parade grounds (**Alexanderplatz** and the **Lustgarten** were designed for the quick deployment of troops) with few civilians. Conquered by **Napoleon** in 1806 and beset by revolution in 1848, the city fell into a decline until **Otto von Bismarck** unified Germany in 1871. Though Berlin was made capital of the fledgling empire, it never became the center of the new nation in the way that Paris was to France, or London to England. Munich and Frankfurt remained cultural and commercial rivals, and most Germans felt little affection for the Prussian capital. It was not until the 1918 establishment of the first German Republic that Berlin became the undisputed center of national life.

Protest and Politics in Contemporary Berlin

The city is broke to the tune of €50 billion. The new central train station, set to become Europe's busiest upon its completion in 2006, is the subject of a heated naming battle and, because of a political compromise, will be built with a half a roof. The university professors are on strike, the mayor is gay, and the ex-vice-mayor is a communist. Greetings from Berlin!

Even after reunification and the end of the Cold War, the city on the Spree remains the hub of politics and hotbed of protest it has always been. Following news of the attacks in the United States on September 11, thousands of Berliners gathered at the Brandenburg Gate in a vigil for the victims of terrorism. In the Bundestag, Chancellor Gerhard Schröder declared the country's "unconditional solidarity" with America and the war against terrorism with the assent of all major political parties. The honeymoon ended in a hurry. Berliners welcomed US President George W. Bush in May 2002, with that year's largest demonstration and the largest police presence in the city's history. Naturally, there was a demonstration against the demonstration, entitled "Thanks, America!" Though the anti-demonstration drew only a few dozen Bush well-wishers, it was blissfully unaffected by the water cannons and tear gas that broke up the larger protest down the street. On February 15, 2003 as many as 750,000 Berliners weighed in against the war in Iraq with the largest protest in the history of the Federal Republic of Germany.

Demonstrations have become so widespread that on Saturday and Sunday mornings a local Top 40 radio station features a segment called the "Demo Report." One part news and one part traffic wrap-up, "Demo Report" summarizes the rallies and protests taking place in the city and reports on which streets will be closed in the process. For the average activist, the segment amounts a protest hit parade; more bourgeois listeners use it as a guide of where not to park the BMW that day. Besides more or less spontaneous events, there is a firmly established calendar of protest in Berlin. Christopher Street Day in June celebrates Berlin's rich gay culture and agitates for queer rights in Germany. Of course, the most passionate day of protest is May Day, when rabble rousers and the riot police alike take the train from previously unheard of villages in Bavaria and Mecklenburg-Vorpommern to the capital. Besides the usual looting and exchanges with police on Oranienplatz in Kreuzberg, the affair generally sees a major confrontation in the early morning hours in Prenzlauer Berg's Mauerpark.

The events at the Rotes Rathaus, Berlin's city hall, inspire a similar fervor. After scandal dissolved the "great coalition" between Germany's two largest parties in spring 2001, a temporary government of Social Democrats and Greens ruled the city, led by acting mayor Klaus Wowereit. When political opponents began a whispering campaign about the new mayor's sexuality in an attempt to discredit him, Wowereit publicly declared his homosexuality. "I'm gay and that's a great thing too," he famously announced, and then rode the resulting goodwill to re-election in October 2001. This time, his Social Democrats and the Democratic Socialists, the communist successors to the DDR's ruling party, teamed up to form a new coalition. The old Democratic Socialist leader, Gregor Gysi was Wowereit's vice-mayor until a frequent-flier-miles scandal ousted him. The new government has been vehemently criticized for proposed funding cuts aimed at alleviating the city's enormous debt. Every time the city tries to slash services or funding for the arts, they're met with thousands of Berliners in the streets.

This isn't to say that the whole city is looking to get in on the action. Much like Berlin's nightlife, the seat of revolutionary zeal has moved east since reunification. Whereas poorer districts like Wedding and Neukölln were once strongholds for tortured intellectuals and dissidents in West Berlin, Prenzlauer Berg and Friedrichshain now serve as the post-Wall protest axis, along with eternally rebellious Kreuzberg. Anti-capitalist and anti-gentrification graffiti ("Yuppies go home!") are ubiquitous, reflecting a fear that these working-class districts will become like posh Charlottenburg, bourgeois Zehlendorf, or, god forbid, Hamburg or Munich.

Mattias Frey was a Researcher-Writer for Let's Go: Austria & Switzerland 2002. He is now a freelance film critic in Berlin and protests from his home in Kreuzberg.

BETWEEN WARS: REBELLION AND POVERTY

WWI and the Allied blockade reduced Berlin to poverty. A popular uprising led to **Kaiser Wilhelm II's** abdication and **Karl Liebknecht's** declaration of a socialist republic with Berlin as the capital on November 9, 1918. Locally, the revolt, led by Liebknecht and **Rosa Luxemburg,** turned into a full-fledged workers' revolution that controlled the city for several days. The rival Social Democratic government, proclaimed that same day by **Philipp Scheidemann** from the window of the Reichstag, enlisted the aid of right-wing mercenaries, the **Freikorps,** who brutally suppressed the rebellion, murdering Liebknecht and Luxemburg. Chancellor Gustav Stresemann's economic plan, supplemented by generous loans from the US, countered post-war economic instability in 1923. Meanwhile, Berlin had become one of the major cultural centers of Europe. Expressionist painting flourished, **Bertolt Brecht** developed revolutionary new theater techniques, and artists and writers from all over the world flocked to the city. The city's "Golden Twenties" ended abruptly with the 1929 economic collapse. With 10% of Germany's unemployed living in Berlin, the city erupted with bloody riots, radicalization, and political chaos.

WAR AGAIN: A BROKEN CITY

With the collapse of the Germany economy, the popularity of the extremist Nazi party rose rapidly and in 1930 the Nazis became the second most powerful party in the *Reichstag* (Parliament). When Hitler took power on January 30, 1933, traditionally left-wing **"Red Berlin"** was not one of his strongholds. Furious at the radical city, Hitler famously declared: "Berliners are not fit to be German!" He finally consolidated control over the city through economic improvements and totalitarian measures, marshalling support for the savage anti-Semitic pogrom of November 9, 1938 known as **Kristallnacht.** Berlin suffered acutely during WWII; Allied bombing and the Battle of Berlin leveled one-fifth of the city, killing 80,000 citizens. With almost all the healthy men dead or gone, it was Berlin's **Trümmerfrauen** (rubble women) who literally picked up the broken pieces of the city, creating hills of the tons of rubble strewn across the defeated capital. The pre-war population of 4.3 million was reduced to a mere 2.8 million by 1945. Only 7000 members of Berlin's once-thriving Jewish community of 160,000 survived the Holocaust.

The Allies divided post-war Germany into French, British, American, and Soviet sectors controlled by a joint **Allied Command.** On June 16, 1948, the Soviets withdrew from the alliance and demanded full control of Berlin. Ten days later, they blockaded land and water routes into the non-Soviet sectors; the Allies saved the people from starvation by a massive airlift of supplies called the **Luftbrücke** (air bridge). On May 12, 1949, the Soviets ceded control of West Berlin to the Allies.

THE DDR YEARS: CONCRETE AND CHECKPOINTS

On October 5, 1949, the Soviet-controlled German Democratic Republic was formally established (p. 58), with East Berlin as its capital—the city was officially divided. East Berliners, dissatisfied with their government, staged a **workers' uprising** on June 17, 1953. Soviet tanks overwhelmed the demonstrators, and the upshot of the day's events was the renaming of a major West Berlin thoroughfare to "Straße des 17. Juni" in a gesture of solidarity between *Ossis* and *Wessis* (Eastern and Western Berliners). Another result of the Soviet repression was a rise in the number of **Republikflüchtige** (Republic-deserters) who immigrated to West Berlin—200,000 in 1960 alone. On the morning of August 13, 1961, the East German government responded to the exodus of its workforce with the overnight construction of the **Berlin Wall,** meant to cut off all interaction between the two halves of the city. The 165km-long wall, erected as an "anti-fascist protective barrier," according to the East German government, separated families and friends, in some places even running through people's homes. In the early 1970s, a second wall was erected parallel to the first; the space between them was filled with barbed wire, land mines, and glass shards and patrolled by dogs and armed East German border guards. Known as the **Todesstreifen** (death strip), this wasteland claimed hundreds of lives. The Western Allies responded to West Berlin's isolation by pouring millions into the city's reconstruction; to emphasize the glories of capitalism, the commercial center around Kurfürstendamm was created to be *das Schaufenster des Westens* (the shop-window of the West).

West Berlin remained under joint French, British, and American control. Berliners elected a mayor, but the Allies retained ultimate authority over the city until German reunification in 1990. The city adopted the resolutions of the Federal Parliament, but was not officially a part of the Federal Republic of Germany. One perk of its "special status" was West Berliners' exemption from military conscription. Thousands of German artists, punks, homosexuals, and left-wing activists moved to Berlin to escape the draft, forming an unparalleled alternative scene. The West German government, determined to make a Cold War showcase of the city, further enhanced its vitality by subsidizing Berlin's economy and cultural scene.

THE WALL COMES DOWN

On November 9, 1989—the 71st anniversary of the proclamation of the Weimar Republic, the 66th anniversary of Hitler's Beer Hall *Putsch*, and the 51st anniversary of *Kristallnacht*—a series of popular demonstrations throughout East Germany, riding on a decade of discontent and a year of rapid change in Eastern Europe, culminated in the opening of the Berlin Wall. Photos of jubilant Berliners embracing beneath the Brandenburg Gate that night provided some of the most memorable images of the century. Berlin was officially reunited (and freed from Allied control) along with the rest of Germany on October 3, 1990, to widespread celebration. Since then, the euphoria has evaporated and *Ossis und Wessis* have encountered many differences and obstacles to unity. Resignation to reconstruction has taken the place of the biting criticism and tasteless jokes that were standard just after reunification. The eastern suburbs of Berlin remain economically disadvantaged, though the situation is slowly improving. After a decade of planning, the *Bundestag* (German Parliament) finally moved from Bonn to Berlin in 1999, restoring Berlin to its pre-war status as the locus of German political power.

■ INTERCITY TRANSPORTATION

Berlin, located on the Prussian plains of northeastern Germany, is rapidly becoming the hub of the domestic and international rail networks. Three hours southeast of Hamburg by train and seven hours north of Munich, Berlin has rail and air connections to most European capitals, including those in Eastern Europe. Nearly all European airlines have frequent service to one of Berlin's airports.

Flights: For information on all 3 of Berlin's airports, call ☎0180 500 01 86. Currently, the city is transitional from three airports to one (Flughafen Schönefeld), but at least until 2008, **Flughafen Tegel** will remain Western Berlin's main international airport. Take express bus X9 from Bahnhof Zoo, bus #109 from "Jakob-Kaiser-Pl." on U7, bus #128 from "Kurt-Schumacher-Pl." on U6, or bus TXL from Potsdamer Pl. **Flughafen Schönefeld,** southeast of Berlin, is used for intercontinental flights and travel to developing countries. Take S9 or 45 to "Flughafen Berlin Schönefeld" or the Schönefeld Express train, which runs every 30min. through most major Bahn stations, including Bahnhof Zoo, Ostbahnhof, Alexanderpl., and Friedrichstr. **Flughafen Tempelhof,** Berlin's smallest airport, was slated to close in 2003 but remains open for flights within Europe. U6 to "Pl. der Luftbrücke."

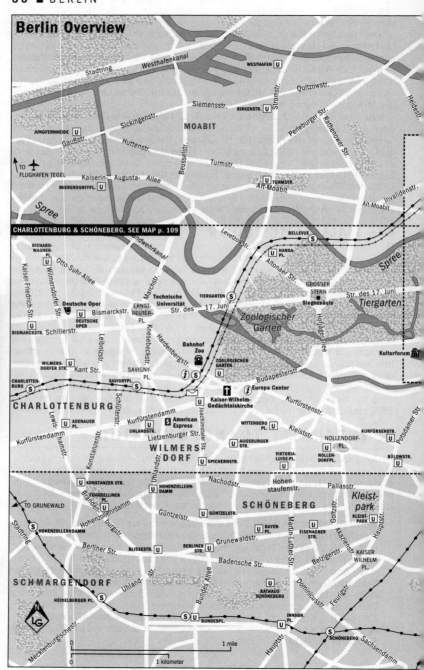

Berlin Overview

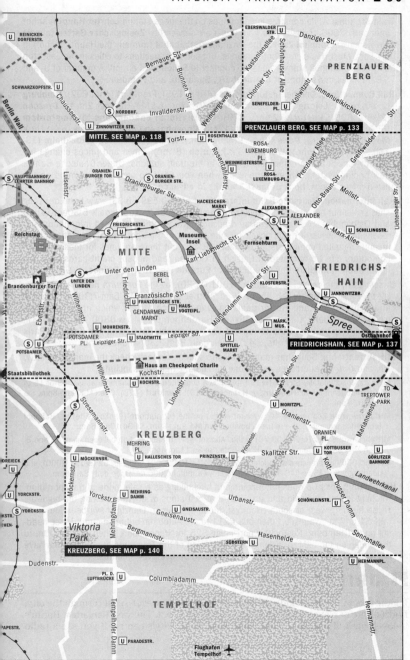

Train Stations: While construction continues on the mega-station **Lehrter Hauptbahnhof** until early 2006, trains to and from Berlin are serviced by **Zoologischer Garten** (almost always called **Bahnhof Zoo**) in the West and **Ostbahnhof** (formerly the Hauptbahnhof) in the East. Most trains go to both stations, but some connections to cities in the East stop only at Ostbahnhof. Many trains also connect to **Schönefeld** airport. A number of U- and S-Bahn lines make stops at **Oranienburg, Spandau,** and **Potsdam.**

Rail Connections: One per hr. to: **Cologne** (4¼hr., €95); **Frankfurt** (4hr., €92); **Hamburg** (2½hr., €49); **Leipzig** (2hr., €33); **Munich** (6½-7hr., €111). One per 2hr. to: **Dresden** (2¼hr., €30); **Rostock** (2¾hr., €29). **International connections** to: **Amsterdam** (6½hr.); **Brussels** (7½hr.); **Budapest** (12hr.); **Copenhagen** (7½hr.); **Kraków** (8½-11hr.); **Moscow** (27-33hr.); **Paris** (9hr.); **Prague** (5hr.); **Rome** (17½-21hr.); **Stockholm** (13-16hr.); **Vienna** (9½hr.); **Warsaw** (6hr.); **Zurich** (8½hr.). Times and prices change frequently—check at the computers located in the train stations. Under Deutsche Bahn's new pricing system, prices depend on when you book—to save 30% or more on the listed prices above, book **at least 3 weeks in advance.**

Rail Information: Deutsche Bahn Information (☎0180 599 66 33; www.bahn.de) Long lines snake out the door of the **Reisezentrum** in Bahnhof Zoo (open daily 5:30am-11pm) and Ostbahnhof. Lines are separated according to whether you need information and reservations or just a quick ticket; be sure to wait in the right line. Both stations have recently installed computers for domestic tickets, but there are lines for these, too. All computers can be operated in English or German, and accept credit cards only. For information in **English,** buy your tickets at **EurAide** (see **Tourist Offices,** p. 94).

Buses: ZOB, the central bus station (☎301 03 80), by the *Funkturm* near Kaiserdamm. U2 to "Kaiserdamm" or S4, 45, or 46 to "Witzleben." Open M-F 6am-7:30pm, Sa-Su 6-noon. Check *Zitty* and *Tip* for deals on long-distance buses, which are slower than trains, but usually cheaper. **Gullivers,** Hardenbergpl. 14 (☎0800 48 55 48 37; www.gullivers.de), is at the far end of the bus parking lot in Bahnhof Zoo. To: **Paris** (14hr., €59); **Vienna** (10½hr., €49). Open daily 9am-2:30pm and 3-7pm.

Mitfahrzentralen: Berlin has many small ride sharing centers; check the magazines *Zitty, Tip,* and *030* for addresses and phone numbers. Larger ones include:

Citynetz, Joachimstaler Str. 17 (☎194 44), has a computerized ride-share database. U9 or 15 to "Kurfürstendamm." To: **Hamburg** or **Hannover** (€19); **Frankfurt** (€29). Open M-F 9am-8pm, Sa-Su 9am-7pm.

Mitfahrzentrale Zoo (☎194 40; www.mfzoo.de) on the U2 platform (Pankow side) at "Bahnhof Zoo." Affiliated with Gullivers (see above). Open M-F 9am-8pm, Sa-Su 10am-6pm.

Mitfahrzentrale Alex (☎241 58 20) in the "Alexanderpl." U-Bahn station between lines #2 and 8. Open M-W and F 10am-6pm, Th 10am-8pm, Sa-Su 11am-4pm.

Mitfahr2000 has branches at Joachimstaler Str. 1 (☎194 2000), Yorckstr. 52 (☎194 2000), and Oderberger Str. 45 (☎440 93 92). Online at www.mitfahr2000.de. Open daily 8am-8pm.

Hitchhiking: *Let's Go* does not recommend hitchhiking as a safe mode of transportation. Hitching is rare in Berlin and also illegal at rest stops or anywhere along the highway. Those heading west or south (Hanover, Munich, Weimar, Leipzig) have been known to take S1 or 7 to "Wannsee," then bus #211 to the Autobahn entrance ramp. Those heading north (Hamburg, Rostock) report riding S25 to "Hennigsdorf," then walking 50m to the bridge on the right, or asking for the location of the *Trampenplatz*. Both spots have crowds, but it is said that someone gets picked up every few minutes.

❖ ORIENTATION

Landmarks in Berlin include the **River Spree,** snaking west to east through the city, north of the narrower **Landwehrkanal** that flows into it. The vast **Tiergarten,** Berlin's beloved park, lies between the waterways at the city's center. If you see a radio tower it's either the **Funkturm** (pointed and Eiffel-like) in the west or the **Fernseh-turm** (with the globe) in the east at **Alexanderplatz.** Major streets include **Kurfürsten-damm** (nicknamed the Ku'damm), lined with department stores and running into the **Bahnhof Zoologischer Garten** (Bahnhof Zoo for short), the transit hub of West Berlin. The eloquent wreck of the **Kaiser-Wilhelm Gedächtniskirche** is near Bahnhof Zoo, as is the **Europacenter,** one of Berlin's few real skyscrapers.

The grand, tree-lined **Strasse des 17 Juni** runs east-west through the Tiergarten, ending at the triumphant **Brandenburger Tor** at the park's eastern border. From here it becomes **Unter den Linden,** flanked by the bulk of Berlin's imperial architecture (see **Sights,** p. 121). Next to the Brandenburger Tor is the **Reichstag,** and several blocks south, **Potsdamer Platz** is shadowed by the glittering **Sony Center** and the towering Deutsche Bahn headquarters. Streets in Berlin are short and frequently change names, and street numbers often climb to the end of the street and then wrap around to the other side, conveniently making the highest- and lowest-numbered buildings across from one another. A map with an index is invaluable here.

The former West, including **Charlottenberg** and **Schöneberg,** is still the commercial heart of united Berlin. In the former East are the happening neighborhoods of **Mitte, Prenzlauer Berg,** and **Friedrichshain;** counter-culture **Kreuzberg** was part of West Berlin but falls geographically in the east. Berlin is rightly called a collection of towns, not a homogeneous city, as each *Bezirk* maintains a strong sense of individual history and identity: every year, for example, citizens of Kreuzberg and Friedrichshain battle with vegetables for possession of the **Oberbaumbrücke** on the border between them (www.oberbaumbrueckenfest.de).

 SAFETY PRECAUTION. Berlin is by far the most tolerant city in Germany, with thriving minority communities. In fact, among major cities, Berlin has the fewest hate crimes per capita and very few neo-Nazi skinheads. However, minorities, gays, and lesbians should exercise caution in the outlying eastern suburbs, especially at night. If you see people wearing dark combat boots (especially with white laces) exercise caution, but do not panic, and avoid drawing attention to yourself.

▛ LOCAL TRANSPORTATION

Berlin is eight times the size of Paris, but with a train pass and a city map it's yours. Maps are €0.50 at any tourist office or *Fahrscheine* station and include a **transit map** of S-bahn and U-bahn lines, enough to get you almost anywhere. Make sure to pick up a **night bus map** *(Nachtnetz)* if you plan to be out past midnight, as most U-bahn and several S-bahn lines shut down until about 4am.

Public Transportation: The **BVG** (*Berliner Verkehrsbetriebe*) is one of the most efficient transportation systems in the world. While virtually all of the reconstruction and expansion of the pre-war transit grid has been completed, BVG's mascot, **Max,** an affable cartoon mole, alerts travelers to disruptions in service. In most cases, the worst inconvenience is an extra 20min. wait.

Orientation and Basic Fares: It is futile to try to see all of Berlin on foot. Fortunately, the extensive **Bus, Straßenbahn** (streetcar or tram), **U-Bahn** (subway), and **S-Bahn** (surface rail) systems will get you to your destination safely and relatively quickly. Berlin is divided into 3 transit zones. **Zone A** encompasses central Berlin, including Tempelhof Airport. The rest of Berlin is in **Zone B; Zone C** consists of the outlying areas, including Potsdam and Oranienburg. An AB ticket is the best deal, as you can buy extension tickets for the outlying areas. A one-way ticket *(Einzelfahrausweis)* is good for 2hr. after val-

BERLIN

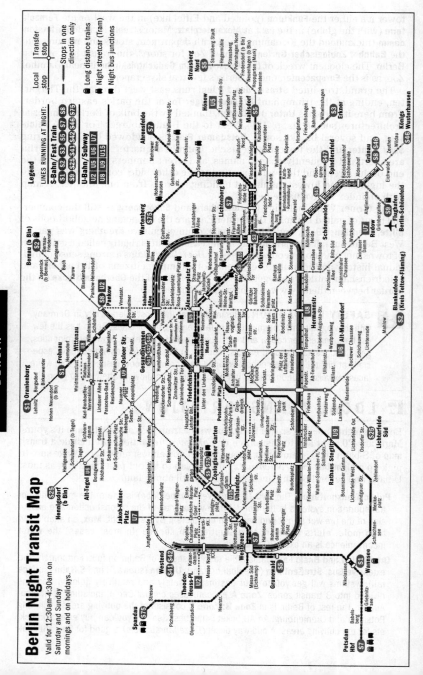

Berlin Night Transit Map

Valid for 12:30am-4:30am on Saturday and Sunday mornings and on holidays.

Legend

LINES RUNNING AT NIGHT:

S-Bahn/Fast Train
S1 S2 S3 S5 S7 S8
S9 S25 S41 S42 S46 S75

U-Bahn/Subway
U2 U5 U6 U7
U8 U9 U15

- Long distance trains
- Night streetcar (Tram)
- Night bus junctions

○ Local stop
◎ Stops in one direction only
◉ Transfer stop

idation. (Zones AB €2, BC €2.25, ABC €2.60. Children under 6 free with an adult; children under 14 pay a reduced fare.) **Within the validation period, the ticket may be used on any S-Bahn, U-Bahn, bus, or streetcar.**

Special Passes: Single tickets are seldom worth purchasing during a visit to Berlin. A **Tageskarte** (AB €5.60, BC €5.70, ABC €6) is good from the time of validation until 3am the next day. The **WelcomeCard** (€21, sold at Tourist Info centers) is valid on all lines for 72hr. and includes discounts on select tours and sites. The BVG now offers a competitive product, good only within zones AB for 48hr. (€14.50) or 72hr. (€18.90) but with discounts at over 30 local attractions. The **7-Tage-Karte** (AB €24.30, BC €25, ABC €30) is good for 7 days of travel. An **Umweltkarte Standard** (AB €64, BC €65.50, ABC €79.50) is valid for 1month. With proof of study at a Berlin university you can get the **Azubi Karte** (AB €46.50) for discounts. **Bikes** require a supplemental ticket, and are permitted on the U-Bahn and S-Bahn, but not on buses and streetcars.

Purchasing Tickets: Buy tickets, including monthly passes, from *Automaten* (machines), bus drivers, or ticket windows in the U- and S-Bahn stations. When using an Automat, make your selection before inserting money; note that machines will not give more than €10 change. Also, many machines do not take bills; you may have to save coins or use a ticket window to buy more expensive day or week passes. Some machines accept credit cards. **Time-stamp your ticket by inserting it into one of the machines marked "hier entwerfen" before boarding!**

 THERE ARE NO FREE RIDES. You may have noticed that getting on and off the U-Bahn, S-Bahn, Straßenbahn, or bus doesn't involve that ticket that you just bought. Does Berlin public transportation work on the honor system? Of course not! Every so often, plainclothes officials will board your car and ask to see your ticket once the doors close. They accept no excuses for *Schwarzfahren* (riding without paying), and if you fail to produce a validated ticket you'll be slapped with a **€40 fine,** due on the spot if you can't provide identification.

Maps and Information: The BVG's numerous **Fahrscheine und Mehr** (tickets and more) stations have tons of maps. **Liniennetz** maps of U-Bahn, S-Bahn bus lines, and night bus lines are free. BVG **information line:** ☎ 194 49, open 24hr.; www.bvg.de.

Night Transport: On weekdays, U- and S-Bahn lines generally do not run 1-4am. On F-Sa nights, S-Bahn lines run at 30min.-1hr. intervals and most U-Bahn lines run at 15min. intervals until their final runs around 12:15am. An extensive system of approximately 70 **night buses** runs every 20-30min.; pick up the free *Nachtliniennetz* map at a *Fahrscheine und Mehr* office. The letter **N** precedes night bus numbers.

Ferries: Stern und Kreis Schifffahrt, Puschkinallee 15 (☎ 536 36 00; www.sternundkreis.de), operates ferry services along the Spree Apr.-Oct. Ferries leave from locations throughout the city, including Friedrichstr., Museumsinsel, the Dom, and the Nikolaiviertel. Ferries run daily 10:30am-4:30pm; fares depend on distance traveled (€2-17). Pleasure cruises available. *Fahrscheine und Mehr* offers more information.

Taxis: (☎ 26 10 26 or 21 02 02 or 690 22.) Call at least 15min. in advance. Women may request a female driver. Trips within the city are priced up to €21.

Car Rental: Most companies have counters at the airports and around Bahnhof Zoo, Ostbahnhof, and Friedrichstr. S-Bahn stations. Offices are also clustered in the Europa Center with entrances at Budapester Str. 39-41. **Hertz** (☎ 261 10 53), open M-F 7am-8pm, Sa 8am-4pm, Su 9am-1pm; **Avis** (☎ 230 93 70), open daily 24hr.; **Comfort Cars** (☎ 263 92 99), open M-Th 7am-7pm, F 7am-8pm, Sa 9am-3pm.

Bike Rental: Fahrradstation, Friedrichstr, 141-142 (☎20 45 45 00), is centrally located in the "Friedrichstr." S-Bahn station. €15 per day. Open M-F 8am-8pm, Sa-Su 10am-4pm. **Prenzelberger Orangebikes** 37 Kollwitz Pl. (☎0160 234 88 36), U2 to "Senefelderpl." €10 per day. Open M-F 2:30-7pm, Sa 10am-7pm, Su 7-8pm. **Velomondo,** Motzstr. 12. (☎21 75 30 46), U1, 2, 4 to "Nollendorfpl." €10 per day, €37 per wk. Open M-F 10am-7pm, Sa 10am-2pm. **Deutsche Bahn Call-A-Bike** (☎0800 522 55 22; www.callabike.de), are all over the city. After signing up, call to unlock a bike. It costs 6 cents per minute (up to €15 per day) or €60 for a week. Only truly convenient with a cell phone and a decent grasp of *Deutsch,* as you must call to pick up and drop off.

◪ PRACTICAL INFORMATION

CITY CODE:	The city code for all of Berlin is ☎030.

TOURIST OFFICES

Now privately-owned, tourist offices provide a narrower range of free services and information than they once did. They still sell a useful **city map** (€0.50) on which sights and transit stations are clearly marked, and book same-day **hotel rooms** for a €3 fee—room prices start around €30 and only get higher. A free list of (expensive) hotels and pensions is often available. The monthly *Berlin Programm* (€1.60) lists museums, sights, restaurants and hotels, and opera, theater, and classical music performances. A number of mini-mag Berlin city guides are available at hotels; many are in English. German speakers should get *Tip* (€2.50) or *Zitty* (€3) for the most comprehensive listings of film, theater, concerts, clubs, and discos. *Siegessäule, Sergej,* and *Gay-yellowpages* have gay and lesbian event and club listings. English-language movie and theater reviews are in the *Ex-Berliner* (€2) and www.berlin.de has comprehensive information on all aspects of the city.

EurAide (www.euraide.com), in Bahnhof Zoo. In the *Reisezentrum* (travel center) amid the ticket windows. Sells rail tickets, maps, phone cards, and walking tour tickets, and gives away much more: general assistance in English and German and lists of recommended hostels. Arrive early–the office is often packed and doesn't accept phone calls. Open June-Oct. daily 8am-noon and 1-6pm, Nov.-May M-F 8am-noon and 1-4:45pm.

Tourist Info Centers (☎25 00 25; www.berlin-tourist-information.de), reserve rooms for a €3 fee, with friendly service in English. A list of campgrounds, pensions, transit maps (free), and city maps (€0.50) is available. From outside Germany, call (☎49 700 TO BERLIN/700 86 23 75 46) or write Berlin Tourismus Marketing GmbH, Am Karlsbad 11, 10785 Berlin. One location is at the **Europa-Center,** entrance on Budapester Str. From Bahnhof Zoo, walk along Budapester Str. past the Kaiser-Wilhelm-Gedächtniskirche; the office is on the right after about 2 blocks. Open M-Sa 10am-7pm, Su 10am-6pm. Another office is near the **Brandenburger Tor,** S1, 2, or 25 or bus #100 to "Unter den Linden," on your left as you face the pillars from the Unter den Linden side. Open daily 10am-6pm. The 3rd location is at the **Alexanderplatz Television Tower** across from the Alexanderpl. station. Open daily 10am-6pm. All locations are extend hours April-Oct.

CITY TOURS

Unless otherwise noted, the tours listed below are conducted in English.

▨ **Terry Brewer's Best of Berlin** (www.brewersberlin.com) is heavy on information and personal touches. Terry and his guides are legendary for vast knowledge and engaging personalities, making the long walk well worth it (5hr., some tours run 8hr.). Tours leave daily 10:30am from the Neue Synagoge on Oranienburger Str., near Tucholskystr. (S1, 2, or 25 to "Oranienburger Str.") The tour picks up guests at hostels **Odyssee** (p. 136) 9:15am, **Circus** (p. 119) 9:40am and 2pm, and **Clubhouse** (p. 119) 10:15am. €10, under 14 free. An abridged (4hr.) tour is offered Apr.-Oct. 12:30pm. Also offers a full day "Best of Potsdam" tour (May-Oct. T, Th, Su 9am at the World Clock at Alexanderpl.)

Insider Tour (☎ 692 31 49; www.insidertour.com) offers a variety of fun, erudite tours that hit all the major sights. More importantly, the guides are superb—their enthusiasm for Berlin is contagious and their accents span the English-speaking world. **The Famous Insider Walk** picks up daily at 9:45am and (in summer) 2:15pm at the Reisebank in the Zoo Station. Tours also pick up at Hackesher Markt 45min. later and last 4hr. from there. €12, students and under 26 €9. **Bike tours** meet at Fahrradstation (for rental) in the Friedrichstr. S-Bahn station at 10:30am and (in summer) 3pm (€22/€19). Also offers themed Red Star (Communist East Berlin), Nazi, and Bar & Club Crawl tours.

Original Berlin Walks (☎ 301 91 94; www.berlinwalks.com) offers a range of English-language walking tours, including "Infamous Third Reich Sites," "Jewish Life in Berlin," and "Discover Potsdam." Their **"Discover Berlin Walk"** (4hr.; €12, students €9) is one of the best ways to get acquainted with the city. Guides' outstanding knowledge complements their eager attitude. Tours 2½-6hr. meet at 10am ("Discover Potsdam" at 9:40am) at the taxi stand in front of Bahnhof Zoo. The "Discover Berlin Walk" also meets Apr.-Oct. at 2:30pm. Tours start at €10, under 26 €7.50. Tickets available at EurAide.

New Berlin (☎ 973 03 97; www.newberlintours.com) offers **free tours** (on a tips only basis) of Berlin's biggest sights, and special tours (Sachsenhausen; Third Reich tour, etc.) for a fee. Backpackers with little cash are encouraged to take the tour, and tell their friends about it if they have a good time. Tours leave every day from the Brandenburg Gate (10:45am and 2:30pm) and the Zoologischer Garten (10:15am and 2pm).

Bus tours are offered by various companies. **Severin + Kühn's Stadtrundfahrt** (☎ 880 41 90; www.severin-kuehn-berlin.de) hits 14 different sites (2hr.; €18). You can get on and off at any stop all day; tours are led by cassette tape in English, German, and 7 other foreign languages. Tours start at 10am at Ku'damm 216 (in front of Hotel Tempinski) or at Alexanderpl. and run every 15min. after that. Many other bus tours leave roughly every hr. from near the Europa-Center and Gedächtniskirche or from Unter den Linden near the Brandenburg Gate. Most cost about €17 for a full day of sightseeing.

TRAVEL AGENCIES

STA: Books trains (free), flights (€12) and hotels (€12, free with flight booking). Branches at: **Dorotheenstr. 30** (☎ 20 16 50 63). S3, 5, 7, 9, or 75, or U6 to "Friedrichstr." Open M-F 10am-7pm, Sa 11am-3pm. **Gleimstr. 29** (☎ 28 59 82 64). S4, 8, or 85, or U2 to "Schönhauser Allee." Open M-F 10am-7pm, Sa 11am-4pm. **Hardenbergerstr. 9** (☎ 310 00 40). S3, 5, 7, 9, or U2 to Bahnhof Zoo. Open M-F 10am-7pm, Sa 11am-3pm. **Takustr. 47** (☎ 831 10 25). Open M-F 10am-6:30pm, Sa 11am-2pm.

EMBASSIES AND CONSULATES

Berlin's construction plans include a new complex to house foreign dignitaries. Though most have moved to their new homes, the locations of some embassies and consulates remain in a state of flux. For the latest information, call the **Auswärtiges Amt Dienststelle Berlin** (☎ 20 18 60; www.auswaertiges-amt.de) or visit their office on the Werderscher Markt (U2 to "Hausvogteipl."). After a long debate over the security of proposed locations, the US Embassy is now in the process of moving to a spot next to the Brandenburg Gate, to be completed by 2008.

Australian Embassy: Wallstr. 76-79 (☎ 880 08 80; www.australian-embassy.de). U2 to "Märkisches Museum." Open M-F 8:30am-1pm and 2-5pm, closes F at 4:15pm.

Canadian Embassy: Friedrichstr. 95 (☎20 31 20; www.canada.de), 12th fl. of the Intl. Trade Center. S1, 3 or U6 to "Friedrichstr." Open M-F 8:30am-12:30pm and 1:30-5pm.

Embassy of Ireland: Friedrichstr. 200 (☎22 07 20; www.botschaft-irland.de). U2 or U6 to "Stadtmitte." Open M-F 9:30am-12:30pm and 2:30-4:45pm.

New Zealand Embassy: Friedrichstr. 60 (☎20 62 10; www.nzembassy.com). U2 or U6 to "Stadtmitte." Open M-F 9am-1pm and 2-5:30pm, F closes at 4:30pm.

British Embassy: Wilhelmstr. 70-71 (☎20 18 40; www.britischebotschaft.de). S1-3, 5, 7, 9, 25, or 75, or U6 to "Friedrichstr." Open M-F 9am-4pm.

American Citizen Services/US Consulate: Clayallee 170 (☎832 92 33; fax 83 05 12 15). U1 to "Oskar-Helene-Heim." Open M-F 8:30am-noon. Telephone advice available M-F 2-4pm; after hours, call ☎830 50 for emergency advice.

FINANCIAL SERVICES

Currency Exchange: The best rates are usually found at exchange offices with **Wechsel-stube** signs outside, at most major train stations and large squares. **ReiseBank,** at Bahnhof Zoo (☎881 71 17; open daily 7:30am-10pm) and at Ostbahnhof (☎296 43 93; open M-F 7am-10pm, Sa 8am-8pm, Su 8am-noon and 12:30-4pm), is conveniently located, but has poor rates. Traveler's checks are recommended only as emergency reserves, they can cost €5-8 to change and few businesses accept them.

Bank and ATM: ATMs are labeled "*Geldautomat.*" **Berliner Sparkasse** and **Deutsche Bank** have branches everywhere. Their ATMs usually accept MC and V, with a PIN. **Citibank** has 23 branches in Berlin with **24hr. ATMs,** including: Friedrichstr. 194-99 (U-Bahn to "Stadmitte") and Tegel Airport.

American Express: Main Office, Bayreuther Str. 37-38 (☎21 47 62 92). U1, 2, or 15 to "Wittenbergpl." Holds mail and offers banking services. No commission for cashing American Express Traveler's Cheques. Expect out-the-door lines F-Sa. Open M-F 9am-7pm, Sa 10am-1pm. **Branch office,** Friedrichstr. 172 (☎20 17 400). U6 to "Französische Str." Same services and hours.

LOCAL SERVICES

Luggage Storage: In **Bahnhof Zoo,** lockers €0.50-2 per day, depending on size. 72hr. max. If all the lockers at Zoo are full, check your luggage at the **Gepäckaufbewahrung** (€2 per piece per day). Open daily 6:15am-10:30pm. Lockers, accessible 24hr., are also at **Ostbahnhof** and **Alexanderplatz.**

Bookstores:

Marga Schöler Bücherstube, Knesebeckstr. 33 (☎881 11 12), at Mommsenstr., between Savignypl. and the Ku'damm. S3, 5, 7, 9, or 75 to "Savignypl." Off-beat and contemporary reading material in English. Open M-W 9:30am-7pm, Th-F 9:30am-8pm, Sa 9:30am-4pm.

Hugendubel has that massive-chain-store flavor. Branches at Tauentzienstr. 13 (☎21 40 60) on the Ku'damm; Friedrichstr. 83; Karl-Marx-Str. 66; Potsdamer Str. 7; Wilmersdorfer Str. 121. Open M-Sa 9:30am-8pm.

Dussman, Friedrichstr. 90 (☎20 25 11 11). S1-3, 5, 7, 9, 25, or 75, or U6 to "Friedrichstr." Another immense *Über*-bookstore, with books in English on the 2nd fl. Open M-Sa 10am-10pm.

Libraries: Staatsbibliothek Preußischer Kulturbesitz, Potsdamer Str. 33 (☎26 61). A book for every Berliner: 3.5 million in all. Lots of English-language newspapers. Built for West Berlin in the 1960s, after the Iron Curtain cut off the original **"Staabi"** at Unter den Linden 8 (☎26 60), next to the Humboldt-Universität (p. 122). Now you can choose between them. Both open M-F 9am-9pm, Sa 9am-5pm; Potsdamer Str. also Sa until 7pm. Day-pass required for entry, €0.50.

Language Instruction: Goethe-Institut, Schönhauser Str. 20 (☎ 25 90 63; www.goethe.de). S1 to "Feuerbachstr." The best known and most expensive program. All levels of German available. Office open M 9am-6pm, Tu-Th 9am-5pm, F 9am-2pm. €1015 for 4 wk., €1825-1925 for 8 wk., 24hr. of instruction per wk. *Tip* and *Zitty* have ads for schools and private tutors—check the classifieds under "Unterricht."

EMERGENCY AND COMMUNICATIONS

Police, Pl. der Luftbrücke 6. U6 to "Pl. der Luftbrücke." **Emergency** ☎ 110. **Ambulance and Fire** ☎ 112.

Crisis Lines: English spoken at most crisis lines.

American Hotline (☎ 0177 814 15 10). Crisis and referral service.

Berliner Behindertenverband, Jägerstr. 63d (☎ 204 38 47; www.bbv-ev.de). Advice for the handicapped. Open M-F 8am-4pm.

Deutsche AIDS-Hilfe, Dieffenbachstr. 33 (☎ 690 08 70; www.aidshilfe.de).

Drug Crisis (☎ 192 37). Open M-F 8am-10pm, Sa-Su 2-9:30pm.

Frauenkrisentelefon (☎ 614 22 42). Women's crisis line. Open M and W noon-2pm, Th 2-4pm.

Lesbenberatung, Kulmer Str. 20 (☎ 217 27 53). Lesbian counseling.

Schwulenberatung, Mommsenstr. 45 (☎ 194 46). Gay men's counseling.

Schwules Überfall, (☎ 216 33 36). Hotline/legal help for gay violence victims. Open daily 6-9pm.

Sexual Assault Hotline (☎ 251 28 28). Open Tu and Th 6-9pm, Su noon-2pm.

Pharmacies: Pharmacies are ubiquitous. **Europa-Apotheke,** Tauentzienstr. 9-12 (☎ 261 41 42), near Bahnhof Zoo, is conveniently located. Open M-F 6am-8pm, Sa 9am-4pm.

Medical Assistance: The American and British embassies list English-speaking doctors. **Emergency doctor** (☎ 31 00 31); **Emergency dentist** (☎ 89 00 43 33). Both 24hr.

Internet Access: Internet access points abound in Berlin. There is **free Internet** access at the **Deutsche Staatsbibliothek** (see above). Also try: **Netlounge,** Auguststr. 89 (☎ 24 34 25 97). U-Bahn to Oranienburger Str. €1.50 per hr. Open noon-midnight. **Easy Everything** has several locations throughout Berlin: Karl-Marx-Str. 78, Kurfürstendamm 224, Schloßstr. 102, Sony Center, and Rathausstr. 5. **Wireless Internet** can be found throughout Berlin, both free and charge-based services (see **Essentials,** p. 37).

Post Offices: Joachimstaler Str. 7 (☎ 88 70 86 11), down Joachimstaler Str. from Bahnhof Zoo and near the intersection with Kantstr. **Poste Restante** should be addressed: NAME, Postlagernde Briefe, Postamt in der Joachimstaler Str. 7, 10706 Berlin. Open M-Sa 8am-midnight, Su 10am-midnight. Branches: **Tegel Airport,** open M-F 8am-6pm, Sa 8am-noon; **Ostbahnhof,** open M-F 8am-8pm, Sa-Su 10am-6pm. Most neighborhood branches are open M-F 9am-6pm, Sa 9am-noon.

▙ ACCOMMODATIONS

Same-day accommodations in Berlin aren't impossible to find, but you may need to wait until late in the day when establishments have vacancies due to cancellations. If you want to stay in the same place longer than a couple of days or on weekends, reservations are essential. Watch out for the **Love Parade,** when same-day space is impossible to find; prices go up by at least €10 per night and only a few hostels (like **Circus,** p. 119) save beds for the stranded. Book at least two weeks ahead to get a room and two months ahead to have a selection.

For a €2-6 fee, **tourist offices** will find you a room in a hostel, pension, or hotel. Be prepared to pay at least €30 for a single and €52 for a double. In that price range, there are plenty of locations, comfort levels, and amenities; be sure you know what you're getting. Some tourist offices also have the pamphlet *Hotels und Pensionen* which lists hotels, pensions, and hostels across the price spectrum.

For stays of a month or more, a **Mitwohnzentrale** (homeshare company) finds rooms in *Wohngemeinschäfte*, or WG (shared apartments). Leases typically require a passport and payment up front for those without a German bank account. Rooms start at around €250 a month. Private apartments run at least €350 per month. Mitwohnzentralen charge commission on the monthly rent; the longer the stay, the lower the percentage. Some Mitwohnzentralen arrange stays shorter than a month for prices comparable to those at pensions. **Home Company Mitwohnzentrale,** Joachimstaler Str. 17, is the biggest. Commission is 20% for stays up to one month. (U9 or 15 to "Kurfürstendamm." ☎194 45; www.homecompany.de. Open M-F 9am-6pm, Sa 11am-2pm.) Located in Mitte, **City Mitwohnzentrale,** Linienstr. 111, has pictures of rooms it rents. Commission starts at 25%. (S1 to Oranienburgerstr. ☎194 30; www.city-mitwohnzentrale.de. Open M-F 10am-6pm, Sa 10am-3pm.) **Erste,** Sybelstr. 53, charges 29% commission, but has a more personal touch. (U7 to "Adenauerpl." ☎324 30 31; www.mitwohn.com. Open M-F 9am-8pm, Sa 10am-6pm.) **Fine+Mine,** Neue Schönhauser Str. 20, is on the other side of town in the Hackescher Markt. (☎235 51 20. Open M-F 10am-6pm.)

Another long-term option is to live in a **Wohnheim. Studentenwerk** (www.studentenwerk-berlin.de) manages over 40 of these apartments, limited to students studying in Berlin. For interns or youth staying long-term for other reasons, **Wohnheim Berlin Junge Politik** in Charlottenburg offers single rooms starting at €180 per month and apartments at €230 (www.junge-politik-berlin.de).

HOSTELS AND DORMITORIES

HI hostels in Berlin are state-owned, and usually clean, reliable, and filled with German school groups. Some impose a curfew or require an access code for late entry. Some also require a membership card and charge an extra €3 a night without one. Purchase an **HI card** at Tempelhofer Ufer 32, (€20, under 26 €12), where the staff reserves rooms in HI hostels for €5. (U1, 2, or 15 to "Gleisdreieck." ☎264 95 20. Open M, W, F 9am-4pm, Tu and Th 9am-6pm.)

If you're looking for a more party-ready crew, crash at one of the **private hostels,** which have a mostly non-German clientele. These centers for the young and hip are located near the train stations and major nightlife areas and have a guest turnover rate of about two days, so you'll never be bored.

HOTELS AND PENSIONS

Many small pensions and hotels are fairly cheap, particularly since most are amenable to *Mehrbettzimmer*, where extra beds are moved into a large double or triple. However, these benefits are really only for groups of three or more; hotels will not usually allow random individuals to stay together. Most affordable hotels are in western Berlin, though inexpensive hotels are beginning to appear in the east, notably around Mitte's Oranienburgerstr. The best place to find cheap rooms is in Charlottenburg, especially around Savignypl. and Wilmersdorfer Str.

CAMPING

Deutscher Camping-Club runs campgrounds in Wannsee, Spandau, and Köpenick. Reservations are recommended; write to Deutscher Camping-Club Berlin, Geisbergstr. 11, 10777 Berlin, or call in advance. (☎218 60 71; www.dccberlin.de. Sites charge €5.10 per person, €2.35 per child, €3.80 per tent.)

Dreilinden, Albrechts-Teerofen (☎805 12 01). S7 to "Griebnitzsee," turn right out of the station, follow Rudolf-Breitschied-Str., take a right on Bäkestr. and follow to campground (about 40min.). A peaceful, isolated location near the river. Open Mar.-Oct. ❶

Kladow, Krampnitzer Weg 111-117 (☎365 27 97). U7 to "Rathaus Spandau," then bus #135 (dir.: Alt-Kladow) to the end. Switch to bus #234 to "Krampnitzer Weg/ Selbitzerstr.," then follow Krampnitzer Weg 200m. A store and restaurant complement the swimmable lake in this semi-suburban locale. Open year-round. ❶

ACCOMMODATIONS BY PRICE

OVER €50 (❺)	
ART Hotel Charlottenburger Hof (110)	CB
Art Hotel Connection (115)	SB
Frauenhotel Artemisia (110)	CB
Honigmond (120)	M
Hotel-Pension Hansablick (120)	M

€50 AND UNDER (❹)	
Hotel-Pension München (114)	SB
Pension Güntzel (115)	SB
Hotel-Pension Cortina (110)	CB
Hotel Sachsenhof (115)	SB
▨ Pension Knesebeck (110)	CB
Pension Kreuzberg (141)	KB

€30 AND UNDER (❸)	
CVJM-Haus (114)	SB
Hotel-Pension Charlottenburg (110)	CB
Jugendhotel Berlincity (115)	SB
Jugendgästehaus Tegel (146)	OD
Jugendgästehaus am Zoo (110)	CB

€20 AND UNDER (❷)	
A&O Hostel (110)	CB
Alcatraz (134)	PB
Bax Pax (141)	KB
Circus (119)	M
Clubhouse Hostel (119)	M
Die Fabrik (141)	KB
Heart of Gold Hostel (119)	M
Hotel Transit (141)	KB
Jugendherberge Berlin Inter'l HI (114)	SB
Jugendgästehaus am Wannsee (146)	OD
▨ Lette'm Sleep Hostel (134)	PB
▨ Mitte's Backpacker Hostel (119)	M
Odyssee (136)	FH
Sunflower Hostel (138)	FH

€12 AND UNDER (❶)	
Backpacker's Paradise (146)	OD
Dreilinden Camping (98)	OD
Kladow Camping (99)	OD
Meininger City Hostel (114)	SB

AREA ABBREVIATIONS: CB Charlottenburg **FH** Friedrichshain **KB** Kreuzberg **M** Mitte **OD** Outer Districts **PB** Prenzlauer Berg **SB** Schöneberg

BERLIN

▣ FOOD

Food in Berlin is less German than it is cosmopolitan. The city boasts a variety of tasty local options, as well as terrific ethnic food thanks to its Turkish, Indian, Italian, and Thai populations. In early summer, expect an onslaught of the wildly popular *Spargel* (asparagus). Berlin's dearest culinary tradition, however, is breakfast, a gloriously civilized institution often served in cafes well into the afternoon. Relax over a leisurely *Milchkaffee*, a bowl of coffee foaming with milk.

Almost every street in Berlin has its own Turkish restaurant and *Imbiß* (usually open ridiculously late, some 24hr.). The *Döner Kebap* (shaved roast lamb or chicken stuffed into a toasted flatbread and topped with vegetables and garlic sauce) has cornered the fast-food market, with *Falafel* running a close second. Either makes a small meal for €1.50-3. Another budget option for travelers is to buy sandwiches (usually baguettes) at a local *Bäckerei or Konditorei*, with the average price ranging from €1.50-€2.50. Quality Indian and Italian eateries also abound, and of course the city has its fair share of *Currywurst* and bratwurst. Slightly more upscale, but still budget-friendly and relaxed, are Berlin's numerous cafes, restaurants, and *Kneipen* (bars). While some *Kneipen* serve only drinks, the lines that separate the three are otherwise blurry. Both cafes and restaurants may offer meals of many sizes, and all three invariably have lengthy drink menus. **Aldi, Plus, Edeka,** and **Penny Markt** are the cheapest supermarket chains, followed by the pricier **Bolle, Kaiser's**, and **Reichelt.** Supermarkets are usually open M-F 9am-6pm and Sa 9am-4pm, though some are open as late as 8pm on weekdays. Bahnhof Zoo's open-air market fires up Saturday mornings on Winterfeldtpl., and almost every neighborhood has its own market as well. For cheap veggies and huge wheels of *Fladenbrot*, hit the kaleidoscopic **Turkish market** in Kreuzberg, along Maybachufer on the Landwehrkanal, every Friday. (U8 to "Schönleinstr.")

FOOD BY TYPE

AFRICAN	
Blue Nile (142)	KB ❸
The Chop Bar (134)	PB ❷
ASIAN	
Bua Luang (116)	SB ❷
Fish and Vegetables (115)	SB ❷
Monsieur Vuong (120)	M ❷
Orchidee (111)	CB ❸
Sarod's Thai Restaurant (142)	KB ❷
Thai Phiset (134)	PB ❶
▨ Zab Thai Cusine (110)	CB ❹
CAFES	
Beth Café (120)	M ❷
▨ Cafe Berio (115)	SB ❷
Café Bilderbuch (115)	SB ❸
Café-Restaurantion 1900 (135)	PB ❸
▨ Café-Restaurant Miró (134)	PB ❸
Café V (141)	KB ❸
Hannibal (142)	KB ❷
Malzcafe (135)	PB ❷
Restaurant-Cafe Bleibtreu (111)	CB ❸
Schwarzes Café (110)	CB ❸
Toronto (115)	SB ❹
CONTINENTAL	
Assel (121)	M ❸
Dollinger Cafe-Restaurant (111)	CB ❸
Nosh (134)	PB ❸
▨ Unsicht Bar (p. 120)	M ❺
DESSERT	
Dolce Freddo (116)	SB ❶
Melek Backerei (141)	KB ❶

GERMAN	
Abendmahl (141)	KB ❹
▨ Die Feinbeckerei (115)	SB ❷
Weinhaus Hoff (141)	KB ❸
▨ Zur Henne (141)	KB ❷
INDIAN	
Amrit II (120)	M ❸
Yogi-Snack (138)	FH ❷
FAST FOOD	
Ali Baba (111)	CB ❶
Bagels & Bialys (120)	M ❶
Baharat Falafel (115)	SB ❶
Bella Italia (116)	SB ❶
Curry 36	KB ❶
Dada Falafel (120)	M ❶
▨ Damas Falafel (110)	CB ❶
LATIN AND SOUTH AMERICAN	
Art-Café Mirò (111)	CB ❸
La Bodeguita del Medio (134)	PB ❸
MEDITERRANEAN	
Bar Tolucci (116)	SB ❸
Bella Italia (116)	SB ❶
Cappuccino (138)	FH ❷
Intimes (138)	FH ❸
Li Do (134)	PB ❷
▨ Mario Pasta Bar (110)	CB ❸
MENSA/CAFETERIA	
Mensa der Humboldt-Universität (121)	M ❶
Mensa TU (111)	CB ❶

AREA ABBREVIATIONS: CB Charlottenburg **FH** Friedrichshain **KB** Kreuzberg **M** Mitte **OD** Outer Districts **PB** Prenzlauer Berg **SB** Schöneberg

◉ SIGHTS

Most of central Berlin's major sights are along the route of **bus #100**, which travels from Bahnhof Zoo to Alexanderpl., passing the Siegessäule, Brandenburg Gate, Unter den Linden, and the Berliner Dom among others. Tickets for individual bus rides quickly add up, but a day pass will save you money (see **Local Transportation,** p. 91). There are only a few places to see **remnants of the Berlin Wall:** a narrow band stands in Potsdamer Pl. (p. 123); the tremendously popular **Haus Am Checkpoint**

Charlie guards another piece (p. 142); the sobering Documentation Center in Prenzlauer Berg has preserved an entire city block (p. 135); and a much-embellished section of the wall in Friedrichshain has become the East Side Gallery (p. 138).

🏛 MUSEUMS

Berlin is one of the world's great museum cities, with collections of art and artifacts encompassing all subjects and eras. The **Staatliche Museen zu Berlin (Stiftung Preußischer Kulturbesitz or SPK)** runs over 20 museums in four major regions—the **Museumsinsel** (an island of historic museums in the middle of the Spree), **Kulturforum, Charlottenburg,** and **Dahlem**—as well as elsewhere in Mitte and around the Tiergarten. These museums' prices are standardized; single admission costs €6, students €3, and is valid for all SMB-PK museums on the day of purchase; the *Drei-Tage-Karte* (€12, students €6) is valid for three consecutive days. Both cards can be bought at any SMB-PK museum. Admission is free the first Sunday of every month. Non-SMB-PK-affiliated museums tend to be smaller and more specialized, dealing with everything from Käthe Kollwitz to the cultural history of marijuana. *Berlin Programm* (€1.60) lists museums and some galleries.

GALLERIES

Berlin has an extremely well-funded art scene, with many first-rate galleries. The work is as diverse as Berlin's cultural landscape and includes everything from early Christian antiques in Charlottenburg to conceptual installations in Mitte. A few good pamphlets, all with maps and available just about anywhere in the city, are: *ARTery Berlin* (€2.50), with complete show listings in English and German; *Berliner Kunst Kalender* (€2); and the free *Berliner Galerien.*

The center of Berlin's gallery world is Mitte, which has more contemporary work than classics; the *Berlin Mitte* pamphlet provides listings and a map. Five times a year, Mitte offers a *Galerienrundgang* tour of the galleries (dates are listed in the pamphlets). On nearby Sophienstr., Gipsstr., Auguststr., Linienstr., galleries pack the streets and *Hinterhöfe* (courtyards hidden behind building facades). Charlottenburg also has a large selection of galleries, many of which tend to be more upscale. Kreuzberg hosts a handful of spaces, and in recent years a scene has developed in Prenzlauer Berg off of Danziger Str. For a walking tour of galleries in Mitte, see **Galleries of Mitte,** p. 128; for more galleries, see p. 131.

🎭 ENTERTAINMENT

Berlin has one of the world's most vibrant cultural scenes, bustling with exhibitions, concerts, plays, and dance performances. The city generously subsidizes its art scene despite recent cutbacks, and tickets are usually reasonable, especially with student discounts. Numerous festivals celebrating everything from Chinese film to West African music enrich the regular offerings; posters proclaiming special events plaster the city well in advance. Reservations can be made through the box office. Most theaters and concert halls offer up to 50% off for students if you buy at the *Abendkasse* (evening box office), which generally opens 1hr. before shows. Other ticket outlets charge 15-18% commissions and do not offer student discounts. There is a ticket counter in the **KaDeWe** (p. 105. ☎217 77 54. Open M-F 10am-8pm, Sa 10am-4pm.) Theaters generally accept credit cards, but many ticket outlets do not. Most theaters and operas close from mid-July to late August.

Hekticket, Hardenbergstr. near the Cineplex. (☎23 09 93 33; www.hekticket.de). Last-minute tickets up to 50% off. Open M-Th noon-7pm, F-Sa 10am-8pm, Su 3-6pm. **Branch** at Alexanderpl., Karl-Liebknecht-Str. 12. Same hours, closed July to mid Aug.

NO MORE FREE RIDE

Higher education in Berlin is in a state of emergency. Totally broke, the city has proposed increasingly huge cuts in educational funding to take place over the next few years such that by 2009, €75 million will have been axed per year. With classrooms already overcrowded at the city's three major universities, government officials plan to make matters worse by laying off 250 of 1082 professors.

To minimize the setbacks caused by these funding cuts, conservative parties urge that Germany follow other EU countries like the Netherlands and England in introducing tuition fees for students who stay longer than the average study time. This proposal sparked massive student protests in Berlin last winter. Conservatives argue that there is currently no incentive for students to speed through their studies; the average German student graduates at 26, much later than most of the rest of the world. But students claim that tuition fees (of up to €1000) will not only deter less-well-off youth from enrolling in universities, but will also make finishing studies on time virtually impossible since students will be working even longer at the part-time jobs they already balance with coursework.

Definitive plans have yet to be made, but it seems as though the Humboldtian ideal that students should linger over their education is in danger.

Berlin Ticket, Potsdamer Str. 96 (☎23 08 82 30; www.berlin-ticket.de). By phone only. Open M-F 9am-7pm.

Theater & Konzertkasse City Center, Kurfürstendamm 16 (☎88 72 66 20), at the corner of Joachimstaler Str. Open M-F 11am-7pm, Sa 10am-4pm.

CONCERTS, OPERA, AND DANCE

Berlin reaches its musical zenith in September during the fabulous **Berliner Festwochen,** which draws the world's best orchestras and soloists. The **Berliner Jazztage** in November, featuring top jazz musicians, also brings in the crowds. For tickets (which sell out months in advance) and more information for both festivals, call or write to Berliner Festspiele (☎25 48 90; www.berlinerfestspiele.de). In mid-July, the **Bachtage** feature an intense week of classical music, while every Saturday night in August the **Sommer Festspiele** turns the Ku'damm into a multi-faceted concert hall with punk, steel-drum, and folk groups competing for attention.

The monthly pamphlets *Konzerte und Theater in Berlin und Brandenburg* (free) and *Berlin Programm* (€1.50) list concerts, as do the biweekly *Zitty* and *Tip*. The programs for many theaters and opera houses are also listed on huge posters in U-Bahn stations. Tickets for the *Philharmonie* and the *Oper* are nearly impossible to get without writing months in advance, except by standing outside before performances with a small sign saying *"Suche Karte"* (seeking ticket)—people often try to unload tickets at the last moment, usually at outrageous prices.

■ **Berliner Philharmonisches Orchester,** Herbert Von Karajanstr. 1 (☎25 48 81 32; www.berlin-philharmonic.com). S1, 2, or 25 or U2 to "Potsdamer Pl." and walk up Potsdamer Str. It may look bizarre, but this yellow building, designed by Scharoun in 1963, is acoustically perfect: every audience member hears the music exactly as it is meant to sound. The *Berliner Philharmoniker,* led by the eminent Sir Simon Rattle, is one of the world's finest orchestras. It is practically impossible to get a seat; check 1hr. before concert time or write at least 8 wk. in advance. Closed late-June to early-Sept. Box office open M-F 3-6pm, Sa-Su 11am-2pm. Tickets start at €7 for standing room, €15 for seats.

Konzerthaus (Schauspielhaus am Gendarmenmarkt), Gendarmenmarkt 2 (☎20 30 90; www.konzerthaus.de). U2 or 6 to "Stadtmitte." The opulent home of Berlin's symphony orchestra. Last-minute tickets are somewhat easier to come by. No performances mid-July to Aug. Box office open M-Sa 11am-7pm, Su noon-4pm.

Deutsche Oper Berlin, Bismarckstr. 35 (tickets ☎343 84 01; www.deutscheoperberlin.de). U2 to "Deutsche Oper." Berlin's best and youngest opera, featuring newly commissioned works as well as German and Italian classics. Box office open M-Sa 11am until 1hr. before performance, Su 10am-2pm. Evening tickets available 1hr. before performances. Closed July-Aug. Tickets €10-112. 25% student discounts.

Deutsche Staatsoper, Unter den Linden 7 (☎20 35 45 55; www.staatsoper-berlin.de). U6 to "Französische Str." or bus #100, 157, or 348 to "Deutsche Staatsoper." Eastern Berlin's leading opera company, led by Daniel Barenboim (also conductor of the Chicago Symphony Orchestra). The big budget leads to grandiose productions. Occasional ballet and classical music performances. Tours on some M and Sa-Su (call for times). Box office open M-F 11am-7pm, Sa-Su 2-7pm, and 1hr. before performances. Closed mid-July to Aug. Tickets €5-120; students €10, 1hr. before shows.

Komische Oper, Unter den Linden 14 (☎20 26 00; www.komische-oper-berlin.de). U6 to "Französische Str.," or S1, 2, 25 to "Unter den Linden." Started by zany post-war director Walter Felsenstein and now under the direction of Andreas Homoki, the 112-year-old comic opera is known for fresh versions of the classics. Program ranges from Mozart to Gilbert and Sullivan. Box office open M-Sa 11am-7pm, Su 1-4pm. Tickets €8-93. 25% student discounts almost always available 1hr. before performances.

THEATER

Theater listings, found on the yellow and blue posters in most U-Bahn stations, are available in the monthly pamphlets *Kultur!news* and *Berlin Programm*, as well as in *030*, *Zitty*, and *Tip*. In addition to the world's best German-language theater, Berlin also has a lively English-language scene; look for listings in *Zitty* or *Tip* that say "in englischer Sprache" (in English). A number of privately run companies called *Off-Theaters* also occasionally feature English-language plays. As with concert halls, virtually all theaters are closed in July and August (closings are indicated by the words *Theaterferien* or *Sommerpause*).

Deutsches Theater, Schumannstr. 13a (☎28 44 12 25; www.deutsches-theater.berlin.net). U6 or S1-3, 5, 7, or 9 to "Friedrichstr." Go north on Friedrichstr., turn left on Reinhardtstr., and then right on Albrechtstr., which curves into Schumannstr. Even western Berlin admits it: this is the best theater in Germany. Max Reinhardt made it great 100 years ago, and it now produces innovative takes on classics and newer works from Büchner to Mamet to Ibsen. The **Kammerspiel** (☎28 44 12 26) stages smaller, provocative productions. Box office for both open M-Sa 11am-6:30pm, Su 3-6:30pm. Tickets for *Deutsches Theater* €4-42, for *Kammerspiel* €8-29; students €8.

Hebbel-Theater, Stresemannstr. 29 (☎25 90 04 27; www.hebbel-theater.de). U1, 6, or 15 to "Hallesches Tor." The most avant of the avant-garde theaters in Berlin, drawing innovative talent from all over the world. Committed to producing in the original language, this venue brings in the playwrights to collaborate with the actors. Order tickets from the box office (open daily noon-7pm) on Stresemannstr., or by phone daily 4-7pm, or show up 1hr. before shows. Tickets €11-23, students €11.

Berliner Ensemble, Bertolt-Brecht-Pl. 1 (☎28 40 81 55; www.berliner-ensemble.de). U6 or S1-3, 5, 7, 9, 25, or 75 to "Friedrichstr." The theater established by Brecht is enjoying a renaissance under the eye of Claus Peymann. Hip repertoire with Heiner Müller, young American playwrights, and Brecht himself. Some premieres. Box office open M-F 8am-6pm, Sa-Su 11am-6pm, and 1hr. before shows. Tickets €2-24, students €7.

Maxim-Gorki-Theater, Am Festungsgraben 1 (☎20 22 11 15; www.gorki.de). U6 or S1-3, 5, 7, 9, 25, or 75 to "Friedrichstr.," or bus #100, 157, or 348 to "Deutsche Staatsoper." Contemporary theater with a repertoire ranging from Schiller to Albee. Box office open M-Sa noon-6:30pm, Su 4-6:30pm and 1hr. before shows. Tickets €8-30.

Die Distel, Friedrichstr. 101 (☎204 47 04; www.distel-berlin.de). U6 or S1-3, 5, 7, 9, 25, or 75 to "Friedrichstr." During DDR days, this cabaret was renowned for political satire. Now as popular as ever, the shows feature lots of snappy dialogue and German slang, making it hard for non-speakers to follow. Box office open M-F noon-6pm and 2hr. before performances. Tickets €7-21; students 25% off 2hr. before performances.

Vagantenbühne, Kantstr. 12a (☎312 45 29; www.vaganten.de). U2 or 9 or S3, 5, 7, 9, or 75 to "Zoologischer Garten." This off-beat venue in a courtyard near the Ku'damm, presents a healthy balance of contemporary German plays and clever takes on classics. Box office open M 10am-4pm, Tu-F 10am-8pm, Sa 2-8pm. Tickets €9-17, students €7.

Friends of Italian Opera, Fidicinstr. 40 (☎691 12 11; www.thefriends.de). U6 to "Pl. der Luftbrücke." The name of Berlin's leading English-language theater is a joking reference to the mafia in *Some Like It Hot*. A smaller, less well-funded venue, this stage still produces new, experimental works and old favorites like Samuel Beckett and Tennessee Williams. Box office opens at 7pm. Most shows at 8pm. Tickets €8-15.

Volksbühne, Am Rosa-Luxemburg-Pl. (☎247 67 72; www.volksbuehne-berlin.de). U2 to "Rosa-Luxemburg-Pl." Berlin's famous left-leaning "people's theater," which opened in 1890 and moved into its current building in 1914. High on shock value, low on name recognition. Box office open daily noon-6pm. Tickets €10-28, students €6. The Volksbühne also features 2 nightclubs for the proletariat: the *Roter Salon* and *Grüner Salon*.

Prater, Kastanienallee 7-9 in Prenzlauer Berg (☎247 67 72; www.praterteam.de). U2 to "Eberswalder Str." Smaller sister theater to the Volksbühne. Box office open daily noon-6pm and 1hr. before performances. There's a *Biergarten* out back (open M-F from 4pm, Sa from noon), and the theater occasionally doubles as a club. Prater also hosts the popular bar and concert venue **Bastard;** check listings to see what's playing.

Schaubühne am Lehniner Platz, Kurfürstendamm 153 (☎89 00 23; www.schaubuehne.de). U7 to "Adenauerpl.," or S3, 5, 7, 9, or 75 to "Charlottenburg." One of Berlin's most progressive theaters, formerly known as the *Schaubühne am Halleschen Ufer*, featuring a wide variety of dance and theater. Box office open M-Sa 11am-6:30pm, Su 3-6:30pm, and 1hr. before performances. Tickets €6.50-36, students €8.

FILM

On any night in Berlin you can choose from over 150 different films. *O.F.* next to a movie listing means original version (i.e., not dubbed in German); *O.m.U.* means original version with German subtitles. Check *Tip* or *Zitty* for theater schedules. Mondays through Wednesdays are *Kinotage* at most theaters, with reduced prices and further discounts for those with a student ID. The city also hosts the international **Berlinale** film festival (Feb. 12-17, 2005).

Arsenal, in the Filmhaus at Potsdamer Pl. (☎26 95 51 00). U2 or S1, 2, or 25 to "Potsdamer Pl." Run by the *Freunde der deutschen Kinemathek,* the founders of the *Berlinale,* Arsenal showcases indie films and some classics (€6). Frequent appearances by guest directors make the theater a popular meeting place for Berlin's filmmakers.

Filmkunsthaus Babylon, Rosa-Luxemburg-Str. 30 (☎242 50 76; www.fkh-babylon.de). U2 to "Rosa-Luxemburg-Pl." Shows classics like *Goodfellas* in the main theater and art films from around the world in the intellectual **Studiokino** (entrance on Hirtenstr.). Main theater €6.50, students €5.50. Studiokino €5.50.

Progress Studiokino Börse, Burgstr. 27 (☎24 00 35 00; www.kino-boerse.com). S3, 5, 7, 9, or 75 to "Hackescher Markt." Features contemporary German films, as well as frequent showings of the DDR-era *Die Legende von Paul und Paula,* a cult favorite among East Berliners for its poetic storytelling and realistic depiction of East Berlin life. €6, students €5. Tu and Th €4.

Odeon, Hauptstr. 116 (☎78 70 40 19; www.yorck.de). U4 to "Rathaus Schöneberg." One of the 1st English-language theaters in Berlin, Odeon shows mainstream American and British flicks, generally with German subtitles. €7, M-Th €4.

CineStar, in the Sony Center, Potsdamer Pl. 4 (☎20 66 62 60). S1 or 2, or U2 to "Potsdamer Pl." English-language blockbusters in a huge, glittering theater with seating so steeply raked you'll fear for your life. Open 11am-11:30pm. €7.90, Tu and Th €6.

Freiluftkino: Berlin buzzes with outdoor movies in summer: **Freiluftkino Hasenheide** (☎30 87 25 10; www.freiluftkino-hasenheide.de), at the Sputnik in Hasenheide park, screens silent films and last year's blockbusters. U7 or 8 to "Hermannpl." **Freiluftkino Kreuzberg,** Mariannenpl. 2 (☎24 31 30 30), screens all flavors of foreign films. U1, 8, or 15 to "Kottbusser Tor." **Freiluftkino Friedrichshain** (☎29 36 16 29; www.freiluft-kino-berlin.de), in Volkspark Friedrichshain, shows modern Hollywood and German films. U5 to "Straußberger Pl." €5.50 for all theaters. Reduced admission M and W.

▒ SHOPPING

When West Berlin was a lonely outpost in the consumer wilderness of the Eastern Bloc, West Berliners had no choice but to buy local. Consequently, the city amassed a mind-boggling array of things for sale: if a price tag can be put on it, you can buy it in Berlin. The high temple of consumerism is the seven-story **KaDeWe department store** on Wittenbergpl. at Tauentzienstr. 21-24, the largest department store on the continent. The name is a German abbreviation of *Kaufhaus des Westens* (Department Store of the West); for the tens of thousands of product-starved East Germans who flooded Berlin in the days following the *Wende*, KaDeWe *was* the West. (☎212 10. Open M-F 10am-8pm, Sa 9:30am-8pm.) The sidewalks of the 2-mile-long **Kurfurstendamm,** near Bahnhof Zoo, have at least one big store from every mega-chain you can name. Near Hackescher Market and Alte Schönhauser Str., the art galleries of Mitte give way to clothing galleries with similar price tags.

SECOND HAND. Zweite Hand (second-hand; €2), appears Tu, Th, and Sa, with listings for everything under the sun: plane tickets, silk dresses, cats, and terrific deals on **bikes.** Boutiques on **Kastanianallee** and **Oranienburger Straße** sell chic second-hand clothes for first-hand prices. Kreuzberg's strip for used clothing and cheap antiques is **Bergmannstraße.** *(Take U7 to "Gneisenaustr.")* Get your leather jacket at **Made in Berlin,** which has funky used stuff for cheap. *(Potsdamer Str. 106. U1 or 15 to "Kurfürstenstr."* ☎262 24 31. M-F 10:30am-7pm, Sa 11am-8pm.) **Garage,** in Nollendorf-pl., has heaps of quirky and vintage used clothing. *(Ahornstr. 3.* ☎211 27 60. Open M-W 11am-7pm, Th-Sa 11am-8pm.)* If you simply must have a new old vest to wear clubbing, get to **Humana.** *(Schönhauser Allee 45.* ☎29 00 20 10. Open M-Th 10am-9pm, F 10am-8pm.)

FLEA MARKETS. The market on **Straße des 17. Juni** probably has the best selection, but the prices are higher than those at other markets. *(S3, 5, 7, 9, or 75 to "Tiergarten." Open Sa-Su 11am-5pm.)* **Winterfeldtplatz** overflows with food, flowers, and people crooning Dylan tunes over acoustic guitars. *(Near Nollendorfpl. Open W and Sa 8am-1pm.)* The **Trödelmarkt** at Nostitzstr. 6-7, in Kreuzberg, aims to help Berlin's homeless. *(U6 or 7 to "Mehringdamm." Open Tu 5-7pm, Th 11am-1pm and 3-6pm, Sa 11am-3pm.)* Other major markets are around **Ostbahnhof** in Friedrichshain *(near Erich-Stein-furth-Str.; S3, 5, 7, 9, or 75 to "Ostbahnhof;" open Sa 9am-3pm, Su 10am-5pm),* on **Am Weidendamm** in Mitte *(S-Bahn or U6 to "Friedrichstr;" open Sa-Su 11am-5pm)* and on **John-F.-Kennedy-Platz** in Schöneberg *(U4 to "Rathaus Schöneberg;" open Sa-Su 8am-4pm).*

CDS AND MUSIC. Berlin's enormous electronics store **Saturn** has a respectable CD store in its basement level. Most CDs are €12-16. *(Alexanderpl. 8. U2, 5, or 8 or S3, 5, 7, 9, or 75 to "Alexanderpl."* ☎24 75 16. Open M-F 9am-8pm, Sa 9am-4pm.)* If you're looking for used CDs or LPs, snoop around the streets near Schlesisches Str. *(U1 or 15* to *"Schlesisches Tor.")* A variety of used CDs and records are bought and sold at **Cover,** where pop music rules the day. *(Turmstr. 52. U9 to "Turmstr." ☎ 395 87 62. Open M-F 10am-8pm, Sa 10am-4pm.)* **WOM** offers a decent selection in the Wertheim department store on the Ku'damm near Joachimstaler Str. **Freak Out** features somewhat less mainstream music, ranging from electronica to reggae. The back room contains used CDs and LPs, most around €5. *(Rykestr. 23. U2 to "Eberswald Str." Walk down Danzigerstr. ☎ 442 76 15. Open M-F 11am-6:30pm, Sa 11am-2pm.)*

🔒 NIGHTLIFE

Berlin's nightlife is world-renowned, absolute madness, a teeming cauldron of debauchery that runs around the clock. Bars typically open around 6pm and get crowded around 10pm, just as the clubs are opening their doors. Bar scenes wind down anywhere between midnight and 6am; meanwhile, around 1am, dance floors fill up and the lights begin flashing at clubs that groove until dawn, when a variety of after-parties and 24hr. cafes keep up the perpetual motion. In summer months it's only dark from 10pm to 4am, so it's easy to be unintentionally included in the early morning crowd, watching the sun rise on Berlin's landmarks and waiting for the cafes to open. From 1-4am on weekdays, 70 **night buses** operate throughout the city, and on Friday and Saturday nights the U- and S-Bahn lines run throughout the night, though on a slightly more limited schedule. The best sources of information about bands and dance venues are the bi-weekly magazines *Tip* (€2.50) and the superior *Zitty* (€2.30), available at all newsstands, or the free and comprehensive *030*, distributed in hostels, cafes, shops and bars.

In eastern Berlin, **Kreuzberg's** reputation as dance capital of Germany is challenged nightly as clubs sprout up in **Mitte, Prenzlauer Berg,** southern **Friedrichshain,** and near **Potsdamer Platz.** Berlin's largest bar scene sprawls down pricey, packed **Oranienburger Straße** in Mitte. Prenzlauer Berg, originally the edgy alternative to the trendy Mitte repertoire, has become more expensive and established, especially around **Kollwitzplatz** and Kastanianallee. Still, areas around Schönhauser Allee and Danziger Str., such as the "LSD" zone of Lychener Str., Schliemannstr., and Dunckerstr., keep the dream alive. **Friedrichshain,** despite increasing gentrification, boasts edgier venues farther east, as well as a lively bar scene along Simon-Dach-Str. and Gabriel-Max-Str. Raging dance venues aimed at young Berlin are scattered between the car dealerships and empty lots on Mühlenstr.

In western Berlin, gay life centers around **Nollendorfplatz,** where the crowds are usually mixed and establishments range from relaxed to promiscuous. **Gneisenaustraße,** on the western edge of Kreuzberg, offers a variety of ethnic restaurants and some good bars. Closer to the former Wall, a dizzying array of clubs and bars on and around **Oranienstraße** rage all night, every night with a superbly mixed crowd of partygoers: male and female, gay and straight, and everyone from punk to preppy. East Kreuzberg gets even more radical—fight the power, defy the Establishment! The Ku'damm is best avoided at night, unless you enjoy fraternizing with drunken businessmen and middle-aged tourists (or are one).

If at all possible, try to hit Berlin during the **Love Parade,** usually held the third weekend of July, when all of Berlin says "yes" to everything (though financial troubles may have changed it forever; see **All You Need Is $$,** p. 107). Prices skyrocket during this weekend of hedonism and insanity. Underground counter-movements such as the **Hate Parade** and the **Fuck Parade,** despite arrests that have hampered the fun in recent years, can be interesting, cheap party alternatives—ask around to find out what's planned. It's also worth mentioning that Berlin has **decriminalized marijuana possession** of up to 8g, though police can arrest you for any amount if they so desire. Smoking pot in public is not widely accepted, though it's becoming more common in some clubs—it's pretty easy to tell which ones.

▼ GAY AND LESBIAN BERLIN

With a virtually unparalleled cafe, club, bar and sex party scene, Berlin is one of the gay capitals of Europe. Indeed, as the popular t-shirt proudly declares, "Berlin ist schwul" (Berlin is gay). During the Cold War, thousands of homosexuals flocked to west Berlin to take part in its left-wing activist scene as well as to avoid West Germany's *Wehrpflicht* (mandatory military service). Even before the war, Berlin was known as a gay metropolis, particularly in the tumultuous 1920s. **Christopher Isherwood** lived at Nollendorfstr. 17 in legendarily gay-friendly **Nollendorfplatz** while writing his collection of stories *Goodbye to Berlin*, which later became the musical *Cabaret*. The city's reputation for tolerance was marred by Nazi persecutions of the 1930s and 40s, when thousands of gay and lesbian Berliners were deported to concentration camps. A triangular pink marble plaque outside the Nollendorfpl. U-Bahn station honors their memory. When the Wall fell, Berlin's *Szene* was revitalized by East Berlin's formerly oppressed homosexual community and the subsequent surge of new gay and lesbian clubs in the eastern half of the city. All of Nollendorfpl. is gay-friendly, with mixed bars and cafes on the main streets (Goltzstr., Akazienstr., and Winterfeldtstr.), and more flamboyant locales in the "Bermuda Triangle" of Motzstr., Fuggerstr., and Eisenacherstr.

Mann-o-Meter, Bülowstr. 106, at the corner of Else-Lasker-Schüler-Str., offers counseling and information on gay nightlife and long-term living arrangements, in addition to reasonably priced drinks and **Internet** access. (☎216 80 08; www.mann-o-meter.de. Open M-F 5-10pm, Sa-Su 4-10pm.) **Spinnboden-Lesbenarchiv,** Anklamer Str. 38, tends toward culturally hip lesbian offerings, with exhibits, films, and all kinds of information about current lesbian life. (U8 to "Bernauer Str." ☎448 58 48. Open W and F 2-7pm.) **Lesbenberatung,** Kulmer Str. 20a, has a library, movie screenings, and counseling on lesbian issues. (U7 to "Kleistpark." ☎215 20 00. Open M-Tu and Th 4-7pm, W 10am-1pm, F 2-5pm.)

For up-to-date event listings, pick up a copy of the amazing *Siegessäule* (victory column; free) at virtually any gay establishment, or visit www.siegessaeule.de. Less in-depth, but also useful, is *Sergej*, a free publication for men. The monthly *Blattgold* (€3 from women's bookstores and some natural food stores) has information and listings for women. **Eisenherz Buchladen,** Lietzenburger Str. 9a, has gay-themed books, many in English. (☎313 99 36. Open M-F 10am-8pm, Sa 10am-4pm.) Most *Frauencafes* are not exclusively lesbian, but do offer an all-female setting.

ALL YOU NEED IS $$

Berlin, long considered the world capital of techno music, has for the past 15 years strengthened this title by virtue of one event. Originally started in 1989 as a gathering of 150 peace-love-and-unity protesters, the Love Parade has rapidly become one of the biggest parties on the planet, attracting over a million people and spreading to other cities, including San Francisco and Mexico City.

Unfortunately, love now comes at a price. Ever since the Parade lost "demonstration" status in 2001, raising money to organize the festival of *Friede und Freude* (peace and joy) has been quite the obstacle. Faced with the choice of ticketing to help cover costs, the organizers cancelled Love Parade 2004 rather than destroy the event's reputation of being "open to anyone."

But the story doesn't end there. The organizers managed to put together a much smaller demonstration called "Fight the Power." The parade consisted of only five wagons and traveled a much shorter route, but over 30,000 Berliners attended. Local clubs and bars joined in the effort, creating a Love Week of festivities and special parties. Dr. Motte, the founder of the Parade, once proclaimed that "music... speaks in thousands of languages and is understood by, all." It remains to be seen whether blaring music will be heard on the streets of Berlin in July of 2005.

The second half of June is the high point of the annual queer calendar of events, when the ecstatic, champagne-soaked floats of the **Christopher Street Day (CSD)** parade (June 25, 2005, see **CSD**, p. 230) line the streets. A 6hr. street party drawing more than 250,000 revelers, CSD 2004 included a speech from Berlin's openly gay mayor. The weekend before CSD sees the smaller but no less jubilant **Lesbisch-schwules Stadtfest** (gay/lesbian city fair) at Nollendorfpl.

CHARLOTTENBURG

Originally a separate town founded around the grounds of Friedrich I's imperial palace, Charlottenburg became an affluent cultural center during the Weimar years, home to dozens of fashionable cabarets. For the most part, present-day Charlottenburg is composed of quiet, upscale residential areas and caters to an older crowd, with nightlife options few and far between. The exception to this is the lively area surrounding the **Bahnhof Zoo,** which includes Berlin's main shopping strip, the **Ku'damm,** and several notable sights. This area—where up-scale department stores, street performers, and punks happily coexist—is the life-blood of the generally tame Charlottenburg and is well worth the visit.

⚑ ACCOMMODATIONS

HOSTELS

Jugendgästehaus am Zoo, Hardenbergstr. 9a (☎312 94 10; www.jgh-zoo.de), opposite the Technical University Mensa. Bus #145 to "Steinpl.," or take the short walk from Bahnhof Zoo straight down Hardenbergstr. (not Hardenbergpl.). Tucked away on the 4th floor of this late-19th century building, Jugendgästehaus am Zoo contains 85 beds in simple rooms. The prices and location (a few minutes walk from the zoo) are hard to beat. Reception 24hr. Check-in 9am. Check-out 10am. Lockout 10am-2pm. 4- to 8-bed dorms €20, under 27 €17; singles €28/€25; doubles €47/€44. ❸

A&O Hostel, Joachimstaler Str. 1-3 (☎0800 222 57 22; www.aohostel.com), 40m from Bahnhof Zoo—turn right at the Hardenbergpl. exit and cross the street, then climb the stairs just past the *Wurst* stand. A&O owes it success to a prime location and dirt-cheap dorms. Lobby/bar is packed at night. Breakfast €2. Sheets €3. Reception 24hr. Check-out noon. 16-person "easy dorm" €10; smaller dorms €15-17, with showers €20-24; singles €70; doubles €72; prices lower in winter. ❷

Charlottenburg and Schöneberg

⚑ ACCOMMODATIONS	🍴 FOOD & DRINK	🍷 BARS	🏛 MUSEUMS
A&O Hostel, **24**	Ali Baba, **36**	& ★ NIGHTLIFE	Ägyptisches Museum, **2**
ART-Hotel Charlottenburger Hof, **13**	Art-Café Mirò, **14**	A-Trane, **18**	Akademie der Künste, **6**
Art Hotel Connection, **45**	Baharat Falafel, **57**	Abraxas, **17**	Bauhaus-Archiv, **28**
CVJM-Haus, **39**	Bar Tolucci, **49**	Connection, **44**	Bröhanmuseum, **4**
Frauenhotel Artemisia, **41**	Bella Italia, **54**	Hafen, **47**	Brücke Museum, **40**
Hotel-Pension Charlottenburg, **37**	Bua Luang, **62**	Heile Welt, **42**	Erotik Museum, **23**
Hotel-Pension Cortina, **20**	Cafe Berio, **55**	Metropol, **52**	Gemäldegalerie, **30**
Hotel-Pension Hansablick, **5**	Café Bilderbuch, **59**	Mister Hu, **60**	Käthe-Kollwitz Museum, **38**
Hotel-Pension München, **42**	Damas Falafel, **11**	Neue Ufer, **64**	Kunstgewerbemuseum, **29**
Hotel Sachsenhof, **50**	Die Feinbeckerei, **63**	Quasimodo, **22**	Neue Nationalgalerie, **31**
Jugendgästehaus am Zoo, **10**	Dolce Freddo, **53**	Slumberland, **56**	Museum Berggruen, **3**
Jugendherberge Berlin International (HI), **32**	Dollinger Cafe-Restaurant, **15**	Tom's Bar, **48**	Museum Für Fotografie, **12**
Jugendhotel Berlincity, **61**	Fish and Vegetables, **58**		Schloß Bellevue, **7**
Meininger City Hostel, **46**	Mario Pasta Bar, **34**	● SIGHTS	Schloß Charlottenburg, **1**
Pension Güntzel, **18**	Mensa TU, **9**	Aquarium, **27**	
Pension Knesebeck, **19**	Orchidee, **16**	Elefantententor, **26**	
	Restaurant-Cafe Bleibtreu, **35**	Kaiser-Wilhelm- Gedächtiskirche, **25**	
	Schwarzes Café, **21**	Siegessäule, **8**	
	Toronto, **65**		
	Zab Thai Cuisine, **33**		

BERLIN

Charlottenburg and Schöneberg

BERLIN

Tiergarten

Spree

Straße des 17. Juni

Bellevueallee

Großer Weg

Großer Stern

Hofjägerallee

Klingelhöferstr.

John-Foster-Dulles-Allee

TO MITTE & PRENZLAUER BERG

FRIEDRICHSHAIN

Stauffenbergstr.

Schöneberger Ufer

Reichpietschufer

TO KREUZBERG

Potsdamer Str.

Pohlstr.

Nelly-Sachs-Park

Kurfürstenstr.

Bülowstr.

DENNEWITZPL.

SCHÖNEBERG

Genthiner Str.

Kluckstr.

Magdeburger Str.

Lützowstr.

Derfflingerstr.

Einemstr.

Lützow-PL.

NOLLENDORF-PL.

NOLLENDORFPL.

Maaßenstr.

Gleditschstr.

Goltzstr.

Eisenacher Str.

Frobenstr.

A.d. Urania

Kleiststr.

Martin-Luther-Str.

VIKTORIA-LUISE-PL.

VIKTORIA-LUISE-PL.

Welserstr.

Fuggerstr.

Ansbacher Str.

Motzstr.

WITTEN-BERGPL.

WITTENBERGPL.

KaDeWe

AUGSBURGER STR.

Augsburger Str.

Geisbergstr.

Spichernstr.

SPICHERNSTR.

Aquarium

Elefantentor

Budapester Str.

Europa Center

Tauentzienstr.

Nürnberger Str.

Kurfürstendamm

KURFÜRSTENDAMM

Rankestr.

ANGELESPL.

Lietzenburger Str.

Joachimstaler Str.

Bundesallee

Fasanenstr.

Zoologischer Garten

BREITSCHEID-PL.

HARDENBERG-PL.

ZOOLOGISCHER GARTEN

Bahnhof Zoologischer Garten

Hardenbergstr.

Kantstr.

UHLANDSTR.

Meierottostr.

Neuer See

Landwehrkanal

Hofjägerallee

Fasanenstr.

Technische Universität

ERNST-REUTER-PL.

ERNST-REUTER-PL.

Hardenbergstr.

STEINPL.

SAVIGNY-PL.

SAVIGNYPL.

Knesebeckstr.

Grolmanstr.

Uhlandstr.

Bleibtreustr.

Wielandstr.

Leibnizstr.

GEORGE-GROSZ-PL.

Schlüterstr.

Goethestr.

Pestalozzistr.

Niebuhrstr.

Mommsenstr.

OLIVAER PL.

Pariser Str.

LUDWIGKIRCHPL.

Ludwigkirchstr.

Düsseldorfer Str.

WILMERSDORF

Württemberg.

Kol.

ADENAUERPL.

ADENAUERPL.

Brandenburgische Str.

Konstanzer Str.

Lewishamstr.

Pfalzburger Str.

Deutsche Oper

DEUTSCHE OPER

SHAKESPEARE-PL.

Bismarckstr.

BISMARCKSTR.

Schillerstr.

Krumme Str.

Krumme Str.

Pestalozzistr.

WILMERSDORFER STR.

Wilmersdorfer Str.

RICHARD-WAGNER-PL.

RICHARD-WAGNER-PL.

Richard-Wagner-Str.

Otto-Suhr-Allee

Wilmersdorfer Str.

SOPHIE-CHARL.-PL.

SOPHIE-CHARLOTTE-PL.

Kaiser-Friedrich-Str.

Goethepark

Gierkeplatz

Zillestr.

Kantstr.

Windscheidstr.

Suarezstr.

STUTTGARTER PL.

CHARLOTTENBURG

Droysenstr.

Holtzendorffstr.

TO FUNKTURM (1km)

TO AMTSGERICHT...

Kaiser-Friedrich-Str.

Fritschestr.

Fraunhoferstr.

Kohlrausch-str.

Abbestr.

Einsteinufer

Marchstr.

Salzufer

Straße des 17. Juni

Spree

Spreeweg

Bellevue

Schloßpark Bellevue

BELLEVUE

Bellevueufer

HANSA-PL.

Händelallee

Altonaer Str.

Klopstockstr.

Levetzowstr.

Flotowstr.

Bachstr.

TIERGARTEN

Lessingstr.

Guericke str.

Galvanistr.

Gaußstr.

Landwehrkanal

Spandauer Damm

Schustehrus-park

Schloßstr.

TO SPANDAU

Schöneberger Str.

TO 36 & 63 (100m)

TO 37 (500m)

TO 58 (1km)

TO 26 & 43 (500m)

TO 40 (3.5km)

Hochmeister Platz

Westfälische Str.

Joachim-

Friedrich-Str.

LEHNINER PL.

400 meters

400 yards

HOTELS

▨ **Pension Knesebeck,** Knesebeckstr. 86 (☎312 72 55; fax 313 95 07). S3, 5, 7, 9, or 75 to "Savignypl." Follow Kantstr. to Savignypl. and go clockwise around the green until Knesebeckstr. appears on your left. Guestbook entries attest to the friendliness of this cozy pension's owners and to the quality of the hearty breakfast. Each of the nine rooms has its own personality, complete with wardrobes, colorful walls and couches. Laundry €4. Reception 24hr. Check-out 10-11am. Singles €35-39, with shower €40-45; doubles €55-61/€65-72; quads and up €25-30 per person. ❹

Hotel-Pension Charlottenburg, Grolmanstr. 32/33 (☎88 03 29 60; www.pension-charlottenburg.de). S3, 5, 7, 9, or 75 to "Savignypl." All of this pension's 17 rooms has TV and telephone; more expensive ones have private showers. Breakfast included. Check-out 11am. Singles €30-48; doubles €54-78; triples and up €25 per person. ❸

Hotel-Pension Cortina, Kantstr. 140 (☎313 90 59; www.touridat.de/pension/cortina-berlin). S3, 5, 7, 9, or 75 to "Savignypl." High-ceilinged rooms with quirky furnishings. Expensive rooms have private showers. Breakfast included. Reception 24hr. Check-out 10am. Singles €31-47; doubles €47-77; triples and up €21-31 per person. ❹

ART-Hotel Charlottenburger Hof, Stuttgarter Pl. 14 (☎32 90 70; www.Charlottenburger-Hof.de). S3, 5, 7, 9, or 75 to "Charlottenburg" or U7 to "Wilmersdorfer Str." Owned by an art enthusiast, Charlottenburger Hof offers 46 rooms, each with its own unique decor as well as phone, TV, and computer with **free Internet** access. More expensive rooms have whirlpools and balconies. Breakfast in the adjoining Art-Café Miró €8 (p. 111). Laundry around €3. Reception 24hr. Singles €70-90; doubles €85-120; quads €125-160. Lower prices in low season and occasional discounts through the website. ❺

Frauenhotel Artemisia, Brandenburgische Str. 18 (☎873 89 05; www.frauenhotel-berlin.de). U7 to "Konstanzer Str." Pricey but rare—an elegant hotel for women only, the first of its kind in Germany. Outdoor terrace provides a sweeping view of Berlin. Speiseraum serves breakfast (included) and drinks (5-10pm) to a mixed all-female crowd. Reception 6:30-10pm. Singles €59, with bath €79; doubles €89/€104; extra bed €23; children under 3 free, children 3-8 €10 per night. Discounted rates for longer stays; your birthday night is free if you pay for 2 other nights. Check website for more specials. ❺

◖ FOOD

▨ **Damas Falafel,** Goethestr. 4 (☎37 59 14 50). Frequented by students and businessmen alike, this small restaurant is a vegetarian haven in a city of carnivores. The falafel (€2.50) and makali (mixed grilled vegetables, €3) are particularly popular and quite tasty. Don't forget to load up on free *Zimttee* (cinnamon tea). Open daily 11am-10pm. ❶

▨ **Zab Thai Cuisine,** Leibnizstr. 43 (☎324 35 16). Bus #149, 349 or X34 from Zoologischer Garten to "Kantstr/Leibnizstr." or #145 to "Otto-Suhr-Allee/Leibnizstr." The term *Zab* refers to food that is delicious and spicy. Scrumptious fruit cocktails (€4.50) and main courses (€12-20), made from the freshest ingredients, served in a romantic setting with friendly service. Open M-F noon-3pm and 6pm-midnight, Sa 5pm-midnight. ❹

▨ **Mario Pasta Bar,** Leibnizstr. 43 (☎324 35 16). Same building as Zab (see above) The type of cozy place where a menu is rarely offered—instead, the cook greets the guests and helps them select their meal. Delicious hand-made pasta (€6.50-7.50) or meat (€10.50-11.50) on a rotating weekly menu. Open M-Sa noon-3pm and 6:30-11pm. ❸

Schwarzes Café, Kantstr. 148 (☎313 80 38). S3, 5, 7, 9, or 75 to "Savignypl." Exposed brick walls, frescoes, and absinthe on the menu give Schwarzes a bohemian feel. Locals flood this 2-floor cafe at night, fighting for a patio spot out back or the outdoor seating at the entrance. The ground floor bathrooms must be seen to be believed. Breakfast (€6-8) served around the clock. Open 24hr. (except Tu 3am-10am). ❸

Restaurant-Cafe Bleibtreu, Bleibtreustr. 45 (☎881 47 56). S3, 5, 7, 9, or 75 to "Savignypl." Gilt mirrors, classic film posters, and a London phone booth decorate this local favorite. International food and vegetarian plates €5-6. Open daily 9:30am-1am. ❸

Orchidee, Stuttgarter Pl. 13 (☎31 99 74 67). Won ton, satay, pho, and maki all under one roof. Orchidee groups its pan-Asian menu by cuisine; so whatever you want, you'll have four countries to visit. Try the coconut juice: pure, canned, delicious (€2), or take advantage of the lunch special (11am-4pm) with half-price sushi or free appetizer/soup with any entree (€5.50-11). M-Sa 11am-midnight, Su 3pm-midnight. ❸

Ali Baba, Bleibtreustr. 45 (☎881 13 50). S3, 5, 7, 9, or 75 to "Savignypl." Under the same ownership as Restaurant-Cafe Bleibtreu, this pizzeria caters to faithful followers who crowd the outdoor seating to enjoy mountainous servings of spaghetti (€4) and crispy personal pizzas (€3-5), baked fresh every 3min. Open daily 11:30am-3am. ❶

Art-Café Mirò, Stuttgarter Pl. 14 (☎32 90 74 04). S3, 5, 7, 9, or 75 to "Charlottenburg," or U7 to "Wilmersdorfer Str." This restaurant has recently started exhibiting local artists and poets, but the creativity doesn't stop there: the international *tapas*, declared *Kunstwerke* (works of art, €2-6), tend to surprise diners with their stylish presentation. Breakfast buffet (€8) served 7-11am, entrees €4.50-14. Open 24hr. ❸

Dollinger Cafe-Restaurant, Stuttgarter Pl. 21 (☎323 87 83). S3, 5, 7, 9, or 75 to "Charlottenburg" or U7 to "Wilmersdorfer Str." Located in a quiet neighborhood setting and with plentiful outdoor seating, this laid-back spot is always packed with locals. Traditional dishes (€8-13) and all-day breakfast (€3-8). Open daily 9am-2am. ❸

Mensa TU, Hardenbergstr. 34 (☎311 22 53). U2 to "Ernst-Reuter Pl.," bus #145 to "Steinpl.," or walk 10min. from Bahnhof Zoo. The mightiest Mensa in Berlin (behold its huge neon sign), offers 3 entree choices and vegetarian options. Meals €2-4, students €2-3. Cafeteria downstairs has slightly higher prices (entrees about €3). Mensa open M-F 11am-3pm (last entrance 2:40pm). Cafeteria open M-F 9:30am-6pm. ❶

 SIGHTS

AROUND BAHNHOF ZOO

During the city's division, West Berlin centered around Bahnhof Zoo, the station that inspired U2's "Zoo TV" tour. (U-Bahn line U2 runs through the station—clever, no?) The area surrounding the station is dominated by a slew of department stores and peepshows intermingled with souvenir shops and other G-rated attractions.

ZOOLOGISCHER GARTEN. Germany's oldest zoo houses around 14,000 animal inhabitants of 1,500 species, most of which in open-air habitats. Feeding times are posted at the gate. The second entrance is the famous **Elefantentor** (across from Europa-Center), a decorated pagoda of pachyderms standing at Budapester Str. 34. *(Open daily May-Sept. 9am-6:30pm; Oct.-Feb. 9am-5pm; Mar.-Apr. 9am-5:30pm. €10, students €7.50, children €5. Combination ticket to zoo and aquarium €15/€12/€7.50.)*

AQUARIUM. Within the walls of the Zoo, but independently accessible, is the Aquarium, with three floors of fish, reptiles, amphibians, and insects. Check out the psychedelic jellyfish tanks, filled with translucent sea nettles, or the mudskipper, a fish that can live on land. *(Budapester Str. 32. Open daily 9am-6pm. €7.50, students €7, children €4.50. See above for Aquarium-Zoo combo tickets.)*

KAISER-WILHELM-GEDÄCHTNISKIRCHE. Nicknamed "the hollow tooth" *(Hohler Zahn)* by Berliners, this shattered church has been left in its jagged state as a reminder of destruction caused by WWII. Finished in 1895 in a neo-Romanesque/Byzantine style, the church has an equally striking interior, with cracked, colorful mosaics covering the ceiling, floors, and walls. Inside is a small exhibit showing what the church used to look like, as well as horrific photos of the city in the wake of WWII. In the summer, Berlin's youth, salesmen, and street performers gather in front of the church to hang out, sell their wares, and play bagpipes and sitars. (☎ 218 50 23. Exhibit open M-Sa 10am-4pm. Church open daily 9am-7pm.)

MUSEUM FÜR FOTOGRAFIE. The former Landwehr-Casino building became a museum in June 2004, featuring two permanent exhibits from Helmut Newton: one entitled "Sex and Landscapes," and an equally explicit photographic journal of his life with his wife. The third floor houses rotating exhibits. (Jebensstr. 2, directly behind the Zoo station. ☎ 20 90 55 66. Open Tu-F 10am-6pm, Sa-Su 11am-6pm. €6, students €3.)

BEATE UHSE EROTIK MUSEUM. The world's largest sex museum contains over 5,000 sex artifacts from around the world, primarily from the 17th to 20th centuries. A small exhibit describes the life of **Beate Uhse,** a pilot-turned-entrepreneur who pioneered Europe's first and largest sex shop chain. The enormous gift shop on the ground floor gives people the chance to buy a little something to remind them of their visit. (Joachimstalerstr. 4, at the corner of Kantstr. right across the street from the Zoo station. ☎ 886 06 66. Open daily 9am-midnight. €5, students €4.)

SCHLOß CHARLOTTENBURG

The broad Baroque palace, which was commissioned by Friedrich I in the 17th century for his second wife Sophie-Charlotte, stands impassively at the end of a beautiful, tree-lined esplanade in northern Charlottenburg. The Schloß's extensive grounds include the **Neringbau** (or **Altes Schloß**); the palace proper, which contains many rooms filled with historic furnishings and gratuitous gilding; the **Neuer Flügel,** which includes the marble decadence of the receiving rooms and the more sober royal chambers; the **Neuer-Pavillon,** a museum dedicated to Prussian architect Karl Friedrich Schinkel; the **Belvedere,** a small building housing the royal family's porcelain collection; and the **Mausoleum,** the final resting spot for most of the family. Stroll the **Schloßgarten** behind the main buildings, an elysium of small lakes, footbridges, fountains, and meticulously manicured trees. (Take bus #145 from Bahnhof Zoo to "Luisenpl./Schloß Charlottenburg" or U2 to Sophie-Charlotte Pl. and walk about 10-15 min. up Schloßstr. ☎ 320 92 75. **Altes Schloß** open Tu-F 9am-5pm, Sa-Su 10am-5pm. €8, students €5; accessible only with tour (in German, with written translations available in English and French). Upper floor, same hours, €2/€1.50. **Neuer Flügel** open Tu-F 10am-6pm, Sa-Su 11am-6pm. €5, students €4. **Neuer Pavillon** open Tu-Su 10am-5pm; €2/€1.50. **Belvedere** open Apr.-Oct. Tu-Su 10am-5pm; Nov.-Mar. Tu-F noon-4pm and Sa-Su noon-5pm. €2/€1.50. **Mausoleum** open Apr.-Oct. Tu-Su 10am-noon and 1-5pm. €1. **Schloßgarten** open Tu-Su 6am-10pm. Free. **Combination tickets** include admission to all parts of the Schloß except the Neringbau, €7, students €5, family card €20.

OTHER SIGHTS IN CHARLOTTENBURG

OLYMPIA-STADION. At the western edge of Charlottenburg, the Olympic Stadium is one of the most prominent legacies of the Nazi architectural aesthetic. It was erected for the 1936 Olympic Games, in which African-American Jesse Owens triumphed over Nazi racism, winning four gold medals. Hitler refused to congratulate Owens because of his color, but there's now a Jesse-Owens-Allee to the south of the stadium. Film buffs will recognize the complex from Leni Riefenstahl's controversial film *Olympia*. Primarily due to the upcoming World Cup in 2006, the stadium will be under construction until at least late 2004. The *Glockenturm* (bell tower) provides a great lookout point. (S5 or 7 to "Pichelsburg," turn left onto Schirwindter Allee and left again onto Passenheimerstr. Glockenturm open April-Oct. 9am-6pm.)

🏛 MUSEUMS

SMB-PK CHARLOTTENBURG

The Ägyptiches Museum, the Sammlung Berggruen, and the Brohanmuseum of the state-run SMB-PK are all clustered near the Schloß Charlottenburg. Take bus #145 from "Bahnhof Zoo" to "Luisenpl./Schloß Charlottenburg" or U2 to "Sophie-Charlotte Pl." and walk 10-15min. up the tree-lined Schloßstr.

🗠ÄGYPTISCHES MUSEUM. This stern Neoclassical building contains a huge array of ancient Egyptian art—hulking sarcophagi, mummified cats, a temple gateway framing a statue of Tutankamen—dramatically lit for the full Indiana Jones effect. The most popular item on display is the famous limestone bust of **Queen Nefertiti** (1340 BC) by the sculptor Tuthmosis. *(Schloßstr. 70. ☎34 35 73 11. Open M-Su 10am-6pm. Audio guide included in entrance price. €6, students €3. Th 2pm-6pm free. Day card to the State Museums of Berlin €10, students €5.)*

MUSEUM BERGGRUEN. Subtitled "Picasso and his Time," this museum contains three floors of the consummate Cubist's work. The bottom floor exhibits works that influenced the artist, including African masks and late French Impressionist paintings by Matisse; the top floor showcases paintings by Bauhaus teacher Paul Klee and Alberto Giacometti's surreally elongated sculptures. *(Schloßstr. 1. Across the street from the Ägyptisches Museum, in an identical building. ☎32 69 58 11. Open Tu-Su 10am-6pm. Audio guide included in entrance price. €6, students €3. Day card available, see above.)*

INDEPENDENT MUSEUMS

KÄTHE-KOLLWITZ-MUSEUM. Through both World Wars, Käthe Kollwitz, a member of the Berlin *Sezession* (secession) movement and one of Germany's most prominent modern artists, protested war and the condition of the working class through her harsh pen marks. Here you'll find three floors of her drawings, posters, and self-portraits, in addition to a rotating exhibit. *(Fasanenstr. 24. U15 to "Uhlandstr." ☎882 52 10. Open M, W-Su 11am-6pm. €5, students €2.50.)*

BRÖHANMUSEUM. This sleek building is full of *Jugendstil* (Art Nouveau) and Art Deco paintings, houseware, and furniture. The ground floor consists of several ensembles of furniture, complete with accompanying paintings from the same time period (1889-1939). The first floor is a small gallery dedicated to the Modernist Berlin *Sezession* painters, and the top floor houses special exhibitions. *(Schloßstr. 1a, next to the Berggruen. ☎32 69 06 00; www.broehan-museum.de. Open Tu-Su 10am-6pm. Usually €5, students €4. Prices fluctuate depending on the special exhibit.)*

BRÜCKE MUSEUM. This museum features four rooms of bright, fierce paintings from the *Brücke* school, a short-lived component of German Expressionism whose name (literally "the bridge") emphasizes its connection to other European schools of art, such as Art Nouveau. *(Bussardsteig 9. U1 or 7 to "Fehrbelliner Pl." then bus #115 (dir.: Spanische Allee/Potsdamer Chaussee) to "Pücklerstr." Follow the signs down Pücklerstr., Fohlenweg, and Bussardsteig. ☎831 20 29; www.bruecke-museum.de. Open M and W-Su 11am-5pm. €4, students €2.)*

🔲 NIGHTLIFE

Quasimodo, Kantstr. 12a (☎312 80 86; www.quasimodo.de). U2 or 12 or S3, 5, 7, 9, or 75 to "Zoologischer Garten." Beneath a huge indoor/outdoor cafe, this spacious venue showcases soul, R&B, and jazz. Cover €7-24. Concert tickets available from 5pm at the cafe upstairs or through the Kant-Kasse ticket service (☎313 45 54). Open M-F from 5pm, Sa-Su from 2pm. Concerts start at 11pm. Call or go online for a schedule.

A-Trane, Bleibtreustr. 1 (☎313 25 50; www.a-trane.de). S3, 5, 7, 9, or 75 to "Savignypl." Red curtains and dim lights create a mellow glow. There's little chatting: the jazz fans are here for the music. Cover €8-15. Doors open at 9pm, music 10pm-2am M-F, later Sa-Su. Usually closed Su-M. Tables can be reserved online in advance.

Abraxas, Kantsr. 134 (☎312 94 93). U7 to "Wilmersdorferstr." You won't find any techno in this club; instead, prepare yourself for Latin, Jazz, African, and Brazilian music. Popular since the 80s, Abraxas caters to a slightly older clientele in a relaxed and friendly atmosphere. Cover €3-7. Open Tu-Sa 10pm-late.

SCHÖNEBERG

South of the Ku'damm, Schöneberg and Wilmersdorf are pleasant, middle-class residential districts noted for their lively cafes, world-class restaurants, and entrancing shopping streets. The kind of place where breakfast is an institution rather than a meal, and locals lounge for hours in laid-back cafes, the *Bezirk* of Schöneberg has managed to retain the feel of a self-contained neighborhood while incorporating itself into the greater city. The area around Nollendorfpl., where even the military store is draped with rainbow flags, is the nexus of Berlin's gay and lesbian community, and the streets surrounding Hauptstr. are home to a sizable Turkish population. The birthplace of **Marlene Dietrich** and former stomping grounds of **Christopher Isherwood,** Schöneberg has a decidedly mellow atmosphere.

ACCOMMODATIONS

HOSTELS

Meininger City Hostel, Meininger Str. 10 (☎78 71 74 14, 666 36 100 or 0800 634 64 64; www.meininger-hostels.de). U4, bus #146 or N46 to "Rathaus Schöneberg." Walk toward the Rathaus tower on Freiherr-vom-Stein-Str., turn left onto Martin-Luther-Str., then right on Meininger Str. Free shuttle pickup at Bahnhof Zoo for groups of 5 or more. A hostel run for students, by students. Lively atmosphere and superb value. Breakfast buffet and sheets included. Locker keys €5 deposit. Towels €5 deposit. Reception 24hr. Book in advance. Co-ed dorms €12.50; 4- to 5-bed dorms €21; singles €33; doubles €46. Flash a copy of *Let's Go* for a 10% 1st night discount. ❶

CVJM-Haus, Einemstr. 10 (☎264 10 88; www.cvjm-berlin.de). U1, 2, 4, or 15 to "Nollendorfpl." Unlike most accommodations at this price and in such a prime location, guests here seldom have to sleep in a room with strangers. With 80 beds in 25 rooms, CVJM is especially popular with school groups, so reserve well ahead. Breakfast buffet included. Sheets €4. Reception M-F 8am-5pm. Quiet time 10pm-7am and 1-3pm. Keys are available for curfew-free revelry. €25 per person. ❸

Jugendherberge Berlin International (HI), Kluckstr. 3 (☎257 99 808, www.hostel.de). From Bahnhof Zoo, take bus #129 (dir: Hermannpl.) to "Gedenkstätte," or U1 to "Kurfürstenstr.," then walk up Potsdamer Str., go left on Pohlstr., and right on Kluckstr., passing Lützowstr. The ultimate *Gästehaus*, just too big to shake off that HI feeling. Bikes €10 until midnight, €15 for 24hr. **Internet** €1 per 30min. Breakfast and sheets included. Lockers, laundry facilities (€4) available. Key deposit €10. 24hr. reception and cafe. After midnight, the door opens every 30min. Lockout 11am-1pm. Dorms €12, over 26 €16; 3-5 person room €19/23.10; doubles €24/28. ❷

HOTELS

Hotel-Pension München, Güntzelstr. 62 (☎857 91 20; www.hotel-pension-muenchen-in-berlin.de). U9 to "Güntzelstr." 8 rooms with cable TV and phones; contemporary Berlin art in the foyer. Breakfast (included) is served in a charming kitchen. Garage space €5. Singles €40, with bath €55; doubles with bath €70-80; triples €95; quads €105. ❹

Pension Güntzel (☎857 90 20; www.pension-guentzel.de), right downstairs from the Hotel-Pension München, lacks the chic feel of its neighbor but also has well-furnished rooms (TV and phone). Singles €43, with bath €53; doubles €59-69/€69-79. ❹

Hotel Sachsenhof, Motzstr. 7 (☎216 20 74; Hotel-Sachsenhof@t-online.de). U1, 2, 4, or 15 to "Nollendorfpl." Near the U-Bahn and Nollendorfpl.'s bars and cafes. Small rooms with phones, TVs, and inexplicable leopard-print carpets. Expensive rooms have private showers or bathrooms. Singles €30-65; doubles €51-80; extra bed €17. ❹

Jugendhotel Berlincity, Crellestr. 22 (☎78 70 21 30; www.jugendhotel-berlin.de). U7 to "Kleistpark." Dark blue accents the blond wood furniture and floors in each of the 50 sleek little rooms. Some have a view of the TV tower over the hostel's courtyard. Popular with frenetic school groups. Lobby bar serves beer and *caipurinahs*. Breakfast included. 6-bed dorms €26-28; singles €38, with bath €55; doubles €60/€79. ❸

Art Hotel Connection, Fuggerstr. 33 (☎210 21 88 00; www.arthotel-connection.de). U1, 2, or 15 to "Wittenbergpl.," off Martin-Luther-Str. For **men only.** Located directly above the club Connection, this hotel caters to a gay crowd seeking to take advantage of all the craziness Berlin's gay scene has to offer. 16 unique rooms, all with phones, TVs, and showers; 3 even have slings and other sex toys. Singles €55-85; doubles €70-110. Cheaper in winter, with advanced booking, or for stays over 3 nights. ❺

🅕 FOOD

To experience Schöneberg's relaxed cafe culture, look no farther than the intersection of Maaßenstr. and Winterfeldstr. Large, well-established cafes line the sidewalks with outdoor seating.

Cafe Berio, Maaßenstr. 7 (☎216 19 46). U1, 2, 4, or 15 to "Nollendorfpl." Always jam-packed with locals, this 2-floor Viennese-style cafe is a pleasant place to sit outside and read the newspaper. Of special note are the breakfast menu (€3.50-8.50) and the business lunch (€4.50 for entree and drink, M-F 12pm-2pm). Open daily 8am-1am. ❷

Die Feinbeckerei, Vorbergstr. 2 (☎784 51 58). U7 to "Kleistpark." Like Die Feinbeckerei's interior, its Swabian cuisine is unassuming and cost-effective. The *Spätzle* (noodles) with cheese or herbs (€6.50) and the weekday lunch special (€4.90 for any entree, M-F 12pm-5pm) cannot be beat. Open daily noon-midnight. ❷

Baharat Falafel, Winterfeldstr. 37 (☎216 83 01). U1, 2, 4, or 15 to "Nollendorfpl." This ain't no greasy *Döner* stand—it's all about falafel. Your choice of 3 or 5 chick-pea balls in a fluffy pita, with veggies and heavenly sesame, mango, or chili sauce (€2.50/€3). Plates from €6, complete with hummus, tabuli, and aubergine pasta. Wash it down with fresh-squeezed *Gute-Laune Saft* (good mood juice) for €1.50. Open daily 8am-4am. ❶

Café Bilderbuch, Akazienstr. 28 (☎78 70 60 57). U7 to "Eisenacher Str." Fringed lamps, oak bookcases, and fat, colorful sofas give Café Bilderbuch the feel of a Venetian library. The tasty brunch baskets, served around the clock, culminate in a sumptuous Sunday buffet (€8). From Oct.-Apr. you can dance to swing and jazz music at the Su afternoon *Tantzee*. Open M-Th 9am-1am, F-Sa 9am-2am, Su 10am-1am. ❸

Toronto, Crellestr. 17 (☎781 92 30). U7 to "Kleistpark." Located at the corner of an idyllic residential block, Toronto's international cuisine appeals to locals who want to read the paper while enjoying a quiet lunch (€5.40-8.80). Try the *Tagesmenu*, a 3-course meal for €14. Open M-Th 9am-12:30am, F-Su 10am-12:30am. ❹

Fish and Vegetables, Goltzstr. 32 (☎215 74 55). U1, 2, 4, or 15 to "Nollendorfpl." Order generous portions (€4-6) from a bleak little counter in the back of this tasty Thai spot and enjoy them on the tables outside. Get anything with *Kokosmilch* (coconut milk): bad for the heart but so delicious. Open Su-Th 11am-midnight, F-Sa 11am-1am. ❷

Bella Italia, Maaßenstr. 12. U1, 2, 4, or 15 to "Nollendorfpl." Bella Italia is most known for its delicious, oven-baked pizza, served 24hr. (€1 per slice or €3 for your own little pie). Also serves pasta dishes, salads, and omelettes (€3.50-4). ❶

Dolce Freddo, Maaßenstr. 6. Top off a meal with one of 20 ice cream flavors (€0.70 per scoop; up to €4.50 for specialties). Open daily 10am-1am, later in summer. ❶

Bua Luang, Vorbergstr. 8 (☎781 83 81). U7 to "Kleistpark." Named after Buddah's lotus blossom, this relaxed Thai restaurant makes crunchy pad thai (€6.50) and other spicy noodle dishes (€5.20-8) in a quiet residential section of Schöneberg. Plentiful outdoor seating. Lunch special with soup and entree €6.50. Open daily noon-11pm. ❷

Bar Tolucci, Eisenacherstr. 86 (☎214 16 07). U7 to "Eisenacherstr." This small restaurant serves traditional Tuscan dishes (€7-13), not to mention homemade cakes and desserts. The small garden is a perfect spot to relax and enjoy a leisurely meal in the summer. Open daily 10am-late. Kitchen open until midnight. ❸

◉ SIGHTS

FEHRBELLINER PLATZ. This Wilmersdorf square was erected by the Nazis as a vision of the fascist architectural future. The gruesomely regular, prison-like blocks were meant to be model apartment houses; to get the full effect, try to imagine a city full of them. *(U1 or 7 to "Fehrbelliner Pl.")*

GRUNEWALD. In summer, clear your head in this 745-acre birch forest, the dog-walking turf of many a Berliner. About a kilometer into the wood, the **Jagdschloß,** a restored royal hunting lodge, houses paintings by German artists like Graff and Cranach. The one-room hunting museum in the same building provides an interesting contrast, featuring cabinets full of weapons, racks of antlers, mounted wild boars, and everything from goblets to tea sets adorned with hunting scenes. *(Am Grunewaldsee 29. U1 or 7 to "Fehrbelliner Pl.," or S45 or 46 to "Hohenzollerndamm," then bus #115 (dir.: Neuruppiner Str.) to "Pücklerstr." Walk west 15min. on Pücklerstr. to the lodge. ☎813 35 97. Open Tu-Su 10am-1pm and 1:30-5pm. €2, students €1.50.)*

◪ NIGHTLIFE

BARS AND CLUBS

▨ **Slumberland,** Goltzstr. 24 (☎216 53 49). U1, 2, 4, 12, or 15 to "Nollendorfpl." Palm trees, rotating art from Africa and, yes, a real sand floor, must be seen to be believed. Listen to Bob Marley while drinking a tall Hefeweizen (€3). The secret to the frappes is coffee crystals. Open M-Th 6pm-2am, F 6pm-4am, Sa 11am-4am, Su 4pm-2am.

Mister Hu, Goltzstr. 39 (☎217 21 11). U1, 2, 4, or 15 to "Nollendorfpl." Green bead lights and a rocky bar create mystique. Happy hour 5-8pm, Su all cocktails €4.50, including concoctions like "G-thang" (cachaca, guava syrup, grenadine, maracuja, and grapefruit). Open Su-Th 5pm-4am, F-Sa 5pm-5am, Sa from 11am in summer.

Metropol, Nollendorfpl. 5 (☎21 73 68 11; www.metropol-berlin.de). U1, 2, 4, or 15, or night buses N5, 19, 26, 48, 52, or 75 to "Nollendorfpl." Don't tell someone to meet you here without specifying a room and a floor. **Tanz Tempel,** the main venue of Metropol, is vast, and has the power to match—650,000 watts of light, 35,800 of sound—and DJs who aren't afraid to use it. The colossal structure also houses **West-Side Club** and **Love Lounge.** Drinks €2.50-4. Music and hours vary—check *Siegessäule* or *Sergej* for details.

BERLIN

GAY AND LESBIAN

Hafen, Motzstr. 19 (☎ 214 11 18; www.hafen-berlin.de). U1, 2, 4, or 15 to "Nollendorfpl." The 8 owners take turns at the bar, surrounded by their own art on the walls, as DJs spin their favorites. Mostly male but not restricted. "Weekly pub quiz" M at 10pm (first M of the month in English). Drinks €2.50-7.50. Open daily 8pm-late.

Heile Welt, Motzstr. 5 (☎ 21 91 75 07). U1, 2, 4, or 15 to "Nollendorfpl." Despite the recent addition of 2 enormous, quiet inner sitting rooms, Heile Welt's clientele still packs the bar and spills into the street. Mostly male crowd during "prime time," more mixed in the early evening and early morning. Open daily 6pm-4am.

Neue Ufer, Hauptstr. 157 (☎ 78 95 79 00). U7 to Kleistpark. Formerly Anderes Ufer, "the other shore," this long-running cafe has become "the new shore" and abandoned the rainbow ship that once decorated the interior. But the beer (€2.30-3.50) and coffee (€1.50-2.80) still flow and the mood is still mellow. Open daily 11am-2am.

Connection, Fuggerstr. 33 (☎ 218 14 32). U1, 2, or 15 to "Wittenbergpl." The name says it all. Find your soulmate (or 1-night stand) in the disco, then go downstairs to dimly-lit, labyrinthine **Connection Garage** to "get acquainted." First F of the month mixed, otherwise men only. Cover €7, includes 1st drink. Open F 11pm-6am, Sa 11pm-7am.

Tom's Bar, Motzstr. 19 (☎ 213 45 70; www.toms-bar.de). U1, 2, 4, or 15 to "Nollendorfpl." Gay men don't come to Tom's for a relaxed drink; they come to cruise and take advantage of the vast dark room below. Rotating DJs spin techno and house Th nights. Open Th 10pm-6am, F-Sa 10pm-late.

MITTE

Mitte, once the heart of Berlin, is home to most of the city's Imperial architecture. The district was split down the middle by the wall, and much of it languished in disrepair during the DDR days, but the wave of revitalization that swept post-wall Berlin hit Mitte first. It still boasts a first-rate nightlife, but by now the best clubs have been closed; they were the illegal ones, as every good Berliner knows. Mitte may have received a final coat of polish, but you can still find devastated war wrecks squeezed in among grandiose Prussian palaces, glittering modern constructions, swank galleries, and stores so hyper-hip they only sell one thing—messenger bags, acid-tone sweaters, or rugs with words on them.

THE LOCAL STORY

MMM... JFK

"All free men, wherever they may live, are citizens of Berlin. And therefore, as a free man, I take pride in the words: *Ich bin ein Berliner.*" Ending his speech with these now-famous words on June 26, 1963, the 15th anniversary of the Berlin Airlift, John F. Kennedy assured a crowd of 1.5 million West Berliners of the Allies' commitment to protect their city.

But JFK's final four words, the product of a last-minute decision to utter something in German, have caused some to insist that Kennedy actually called himself a jelly doughnut (in German, *ein Berliner*). The difference between a citizen of Berlin and a pastry in this case depends on the article "ein" (a) which a native German speaker would omit when expressing place of origin. Thus, a German from Hamburg would say, *"Ich bin Hamburger,"* while a hamburger, if it could talk, might tell you *"Ich bin ein Hamburger"* before you scarf it down.

Natives point out that in Berlin the pastry is called a *Pfannkuchen,* and that Kennedy's version is a grammatically valid way to emphasize the final word.

Grammar aside, JFK's speech galvanized a city afraid of losing American support. The Rathaus, site of the speech, now houses Berlin's municipal government and remains open to tourists.

(John-F.-Kennedy-Pl. U4 to "Rathaus Schöneberg." ☎ 75 60 70 20. Open daily 9am-6pm.)

BERLIN

Berlin Mitte

TO PRENZLAUER BERG

Volkspark Friedrichshain

TO KREUZBERG

TO SCHÖNEBERG

TO CHARLOTTENBURG

Berlin Mitte

ACCOMMODATIONS
Circus, 4 & 17
Clubhouse Hostel, 18
Honigmond, 3
Hotel-Pension Hansablick, 43
Jugendherberge Berlin
International (HI), 66
Mitte's Backpacker Hostel, 2

FOOD & DRINK
Amrit II, 8
Assel, 21
Bagels & Bialys, 15
Beth Café, 9
Dada Falafel, 7
Mensa der Humboldt-U, 33
Monsieur Vuong, 16

BARS & NIGHTLIFE
2BE-Club, 23
Café Silberstein, 20
Delicious Doughnuts, 12

Sage Club, 71
Strandbar Mitte, 24
Tacheles, 12
Tresor/Globus, 67
VEB-OZ, 25
WMF, 26
Zosch, 13

ENTERTAINMENT
Deutsche Staatsoper, 49
Konzerthaus, 58
Philharmonie, 62

CHURCHES
Berliner Dom, 39
Deutscher Dom, 59
Französischer Dom, 57
Marienkirche, 40
St.-Hedwigs-
Kathedrale, 54

MUSEUMS
Alte Nationalgalerie, 29
Altes Museum, 38
Bodemuseum, 27
Deutsche Guggenheim
Berlin, 47
Deutsches Hist. Museum, 36
Filmmuseum Berlin, 64
Gemäldegalerie, 63
Hamburger Bahnhof, 5
Hanfmuseum, 56
Haus am Checkpoint
Charlie, 70
Kunstgewerbemuseum, 61
Kunst-Werke Berlin, 12
Märkisches Museum, 61
Martin-Gropius-Bau, 68
Neue Nationalgalerie, 65
Neuer Berliner Kunstverein, 6
Neues Museum, 30
Pergamonmuseum, 28
Schinkelmuseum, 55
Topographie des Terrors, 69

SIGHTS
Alte Bibliothek, 48
Alter-Jüdischer Friedhof, 22
Berliner Rathaus, 53
Bertolt-Brecht-Haus, 1
Brandenburger Tor, 44
Checkpoint Charlie, 71
Deutsche Staatsbibliothek, 32
Fernsehturm, 41
Führerbunker, 59
Hotel Adlon, 44
Humboldt-Universität, 34
Jüdische Knabenschule, 14
Lustgarten, 37
Marx-Engelo-Forum, 52
Neue Wache, 35
Neue Synagoge, 19
Palast der Republik, 51
Reichstag, 31
Russian Embassy, 46
Sowjetisches Ehrenmal, 42
Staatsrat, 50

ACCOMMODATIONS

HOSTELS IN MITTE AND TIERGARTEN

Mitte's Backpacker Hostel, Chausseestr. 102 (☎28 39 09 65; www.backpacker.de). U6 to "Zinnowitzer Str." Look for the giant orange sign. The apex of hostel hipness, with a gregarious English-speaking staff and themed rooms—don't miss the chance to sleep under a huge metal spider. The staff has information on nightlife, travel, and sight-seeing. A pickup spot for **Terry Brewer's Tours** and **Insider Tours** bike tours (p. 94). Bikes €10 per day. **Internet** €6 per hr. Kitchen available. Sheets €2.50. Laundry €5. Reception 24hr. Dorms €15-18; singles €20-30; doubles €40-60; €1-2 less in winter. ❷

Circus, Rosa-Luxemburg-Str. 39-41 (☎28 39 14 33; www.circus-berlin.de). U2 to "Rosa-Luxemburg-Pl." Close to Alexanderpl., Circus was designed with the English-speaking traveler in mind, complete with laundry, **Internet** (€0.60 per 10 min.), nightlife info, and help booking your next hostel. Wheelchair-accessible. A 2nd **Circus**, at Rosenthaler Pl. on Weinbergsweg 1a, has similar facilities and prices. **Terry Brewer's Tours** stops at both locations and **Insider Tours** bike tour stops at the Rosenthaler branch, which rents bikes for €12 per day. Sheets €2. 24hr reception and bar. 4- to 8-bed dorms €15-18; singles €32, €45 with shower; doubles €48/60; triples €60. Cheaper in winter. ❷

Heart of Gold Hostel, Johannisstr. 11 (☎29 00 33 00; www.heartofgold-hostel.de). S1, 2, or 25 to "Oranienburger Str." or U6 to "Oranienburger Tor." Designed in tribute to *The Hitchhiker's Guide to the Galaxy*, this new hostel is clean, simple, and friendly. **Internet** €0.50 per 10min. Breakfast €3. Laundry €3. Reception and bar open 24hr. 6-bed dorms €17; 4-bed dorms €19; 3-bed dorms €21; singles €24-28; doubles €48-56. ❷

Clubhouse Hostel, Kalkscheunestr. 2 (☎28 09 79 79 or 0800 BOOK-A-BED; www.clubhouse-berlin.de). S1, 2, or 25 to "Oranienburger Str." or U6 to "Oranienburger Tor." Enter the courtyard from Johannisstr. 2 or Kalkscheunestr. A great location in the center of the Oranienburger Str. nightlife, plus a partnership with Club "Kalkscheune" downstairs. Terry Brewer's Tours pick up guests daily at 10:15am. **Internet** €0.50 per 5min. Breakfast buffet €3. Sheets €2. 24hr. reception and bar. Call at least 2-3 days ahead. 8- to 12-bed dorms €14; 6- to 7-bed dorms €17; singles €32; doubles €46. ❷

THE BIG SPLURGE

BLIND DINING

€44 for four meat courses; €30 for three vegetarian ones; at these prices, a meal at **Unsicht Bar** had better change your life. It will. What this restaurant offers is hard to duplicate: elegant meals served in total darkness.

Customers place their order in the dimly-lit lobby before being led by a waiter into a pitch black room with a seating capacity of 120. Once in the dark, traditional table manners are tossed aside as most diners eat with their hands, following waiters' advice as to where to find what food. The staff creates an atmosphere of professionalism without removing the priceless thrill of uncertainty. Maybe you have crumbs all over your shirt. Maybe there's dressing in your hair. Maybe you're about to eat live octopus. The 12 waiters (most blind or visually impaired) undergo intense training in order to master navigating the dining area and serving customers in the absence of vision.

Those unwilling to commit to a meal can hear spoken word plays, cabaret, or poetry at Unsicht Bar's *Dunkelbühne* (Dark Stage) on Friday and Saturday (cover €12). In the dark you are more than blind, you're completely invisible—the meaning of "unsichtbar." So come to find out what it's like to be blind and unseen.

(Gormannstr. 14. U8 to "Weinmeisterstr." ☎24 34 25 00; www.unsicht-bar-berlin.de. Reservations required. Open daily from 6pm.)

HOTELS IN MITTE AND TIERGARTEN

Honigmond, Tieckstr. 12 (☎284 45 50; www.honigmond-berlin.de). S1 or 2 to "Nordbahnhof" or U6 to "Zinnowitzer Str." Old-fashioned, well-furnished rooms distinguish this elegant *Kaffeehaus-Restaurant* with canopy beds, iron grating, and bubbling fountains. Reception 9am-6pm. Check-in 3pm-1am; call ahead if arriving after 8pm. Occasionally has same-day space. Singles €49-89; doubles €69-89, with bath €89-119. ❺

Hotel-Pension Hansablick, Flotowstr. 6 (☎390 48 00; www.hotel-hansablick.de). S3, 5, 7, 9, or 75 to "Tiergarten." Some of the rooms in this old, high-ceilinged building have balconies overlooking the Spree; all have bath, minibar, phone, and cable TV. Riverboat tours stop 200m away. Breakfast included. Reception 24hr. Singles €82; doubles €101-121; extra bed in doubles €31. Mention *Let's Go* for a 5% discount. ❺

🄵 FOOD

Monsieur Vuong, Alte Schönhauser Allee 46 (☎30 87 26 43). U2 to "Rosa Luxembourg Pl." Extremely popular among local professionals, Monsieur Vuong serves delicious Vietnamese food (glass noodle salad €6.50) to patrons in authentic, all-wood furniture. Entrees €6-9. Open M-Sa noon-midnight, Su 2pm-midnight. ❷

Amrit II, Oranienburger Str. 50 (☎28 44 44 82). S1 or 2 to "Oranienburger Str." People naturally congregate in the lively outdoor dining area at this sleek Indian restaurant. Entrees (€7-10) can be split, and vegetarians will not be disappointed. Open M-Th and Su noon-1am, F-Sa noon-2am. The original location in Kreuzberg (Oranienstr. 202-203; ☎617 55 50) has the same hours. ❸

Dada Falafel, Linienstr. 132 (☎27 59 69 27). S1 or 2 to "Oranienburgertor." Located just off of Oranienburger Str., Dada Falafel caters to executives during the day and clubgoers at night. Most popular on the menu at this takeout joint are the falafel and *schawarma* sandwiches (€3). Open daily 10am-2am; F-Sa until 4am. ❶

Bagels & Bialys, Rosenthalerstr. 46 (☎283 65 46). U8 to Rosenthaler Pl. Because even Dada closes sometimes. Takeout stand for sandwiches of the world: baguettes, falafel, and bagels, with a selection, and prices (€2.50-4) that is hard to beat. Open 24hr. ❶

Beth Café, Tucholskystr. 40 (☎281 31 35), just off Auguststr. S1, 2, or 25 to "Oranienburger Str." Popular among the local Jewish community, Beth Café serves cheap, quality kosher dishes like falafel (€3.20) or a bagel with lox and cream cheese (€2.50). Tourist posters of Jerusalem brighten the inside, and out back is a little courtyard perfect for afternoon tea. Other dishes €3-8. Open Su-Th noon-8pm. ❷

Assel, Oranienburger Str. 21 (☎281 20 56). S1, 2, or 25 to "Oranienburger Str." One of Mitte's oldest restaurants, Assel is popular with a younger crowd. Ivy-covered basement bistro and bar with a rotating menu that has everything from Tex-Mex to pasta (€3-13). Menu includes a "hangover breakfast" (espresso with lemon, free-flowing Berlin tap water, and Alka-Seltzer; €2.80). Open daily 10am-late. ❸

Mensa der Humboldt-Universität, Unter den Linden 6, in the back of the university's main building. The cheapest *Mensa* in Berlin has typical cafeteria food, and a fantastically convenient location amidst Mitte's many stellar sights. Full meals €1.80-3. Student ID required. Open M-F 11:30am-2:30pm. ❶

SIGHTS

UNTER DEN LINDEN

Unter den Linden, one of the best known boulevards in Europe, was the spine of Imperial Berlin. During the DDR days, it was known as the "idiot's mile," because it was often all that visitors saw, giving them little idea of what the eastern part of the city was really like. Beginning in Pariser Pl. in front of the Brandenburger Tor, the street runs east through Bebelpl. and the Lustgarten, punctuated by huge squares framed with dramatically beautiful buildings. *(S1, 2 or 25 to "Unter den Linden." Bus #100 runs the length of the street every 4-6min.)*

▩ **BRANDENBURGER TOR.** Berlin's only remaining gate, the Brandenburg Gate was built by Friedrich Wilhelm II in the 18th century as an image of peace. It later became the symbol of the divided city: situated in the center of the city along the Wall, it was once a barricaded gateway to nowhere. Today, it is the most powerful emblem of reunited Germany and Berlin. The **Room of Silence** in the northern end of the gate provides a non-denominational place for meditation and reflection.

PARISER PLATZ. Ringed since 1735 by impressive Hohenzollern palaces, including the *Stadtpalais*, this area suffered acutely in WWII when all but a few of the venerable buildings were destroyed. Since then, massive reconstruction has taken place, including the renovation of the **Hotel Adlon,** once the premier address for visiting dignitaries and celebrities. *(The square in front of the Brandenburger Tor.)*

RUSSIAN EMBASSY. Rebuilding the edifices of the rich and famous wasn't a big priority in the workers' state of the DDR. The exception was Berlin's largest embassy, which covers almost an entire city block.

IN RECENT NEWS

A FITTING TRIBUTE

Nearly 60 years after the end o Holocaust, what was a 19,000m wasteland opposite the Tiergarten and between Brandenburger To and Potsdamer Platz will become the "Memorial to the Murdered Jews of Europe."

Declaring that no means o remembrance could possibly dc justice to the suffering inflicted b the Nazi regime, the American architect Peter Eisenmal designed a memorial that would engage the visitor by having him wande through a grid of 2700 concrete slabs with varying heights tha constantly change senses o scale and perception. An under ground information center, tc open in Spring 2005, will provide tangible information to supple ment the abstractness of the memorial. The centerpiece of the center, a Room of Names will fea ture a never-before-released list o known victims of the Holocaus from *Yad Vashem,* Israel's centra Holocaust memorial.

Journalist Lea Rosh, now head of the foundation, proposed the memorial in 1988, but the road tc actual construction was rocky Bureaucracy and a conflicted sense of historical self-awareness kept Parliament from giving funds for the site until 1999. Located amid a slew of embassies and the German Reichstag, the memoria will serve as a constant reminde of the past in the heart of ever changing Berlin.

(www.holocaust-mahnmal.de)

While the *Palais* reverted to being just another embassy at the end of the Cold War (the huge bust of Lenin that once graced its red star-shaped topiary was quietly removed in 1994), you can still marvel at the imposing building from behind the iron fencing. *(Unter den Linden 55.)*

DEUTSCHE STAATSBIBILIOTHEK. The stately library's shady, ivy-covered courtyard, accentuated by lounging intellectuals, provides a pleasant respite from the surrounding urban bustle. *(Unter den Linden 8. ☎26 60. Library open M-F 9am-9pm, Sa 9am-5pm.* **Free Internet.** *Admission €0.50.)*

HUMBOLDT-UNIVERSITÄT. Just beyond the Staatsbibliothek lies the H-shaped main building of Humboldt University, whose hallowed halls have been paced by the likes of Hegel, Einstein, Bismarck, the Brothers Grimm, and Karl Marx. In the wake of the post-1989 internal ideological *Blitzkrieg*, in which many departments were purged of socialist leanings, international scholars have descended upon the university to take part in its dynamic renewal. Budding socialists can peruse the works of Marx and Lenin at the book vendors outside, under the statue of a triumphant **Frederick the Great.** *(Unter den Linden 6.)*

NEUE WACHE. The New Guardhouse was designed by Prussian architect **Karl Friedrich Schinkel** in unrepentant Neoclassical style. During the DDR era, it was called the "Memorial to the Victims of Fascism and Militarism," even as goose-stepping East German soldiers stood guard outside. Closed after reunification, the building reopened in 1993 as a war memorial. The remains of an unknown soldier and an unknown concentration camp victim are buried inside with earth from the camps at Buchenwald and Mauthausen and from the battlefields of Stalingrad, El Alamein, and Normandy. A copy of Käthe Kollwitz's sculpture *Mutter mit totem Sohn* (mother with dead son) conveys the solemnity of the space and serves as a memorial to victims of war of all kinds. *(Unter den Linden 4. Open daily 10am-6pm.)*

BEBELPLATZ. On May 10, 1933 Nazi students burned nearly 20,000 books here by "subversive" authors such as Heinrich Heine and Sigmund Freud—both Jews. A plaque in the center of the square is engraved with Heine's eerily prescient 1820 epigram: *Dort wo man Bücher verbrennt, verbrennt man am Ende auch Menschen.* ("Wherever they burn books, eventually they will burn people too.") The memorial is currently under wraps as a massive parking lot is built below Bebelpl., and its ultimate fate is uncertain. On the west side of the Platz, the building with the curved facade is the **Alte Bibliothek.** Once the royal library, it is now home to Humboldt's law faculty. On the other side of the square is the **Deutsche Staatsoper,** one of Berlin's three opera houses, fully rebuilt after the war from original sketches by Knobelsdorff, the architect who designed Schloß Sanssouci in Potsdam (p. 153). The distinctive blue dome at the end of the square belongs to the **St.-Hedwigs-Kathedrale.** Completed in 1773 as Berlin's first Catholic church built after the Reformation, it was destroyed by American bombers in 1943. Originally designed after the Roman Pantheon, the church was rebuilt in the 1950s in a more contemporary style. Marvel at the silent vastness of the dome, or attend an organ concert Wednesday at 3pm. *(Cathedral open M-Sa 10am-5pm, Su 1-5pm. Free.)*

ZEUGHAUS. This heavily ornamented building is the former military museum and hall of fame of the Prussian army. Now it houses the **Museum of German History,** which plans to reopen in late 2004 (p. 131). Recent renovations added a second building designed by I.M. Pei. *(Unter den Linden 2. ☎20 30 40.)*

AROUND POTSDAMER PLATZ

■ **POTSDAMER PLATZ.** Built under Friedrich Wilhelm I as an approximation of Parisian boulevards, Potsdamer Platz was designed for the primary purpose of mobilizing troops quickly. The commercial and transport hub of pre-war Berlin, the square was caught in the death strip between East and West during the Cold War. After reunification, Potsdamer Platz became the new commercial center of a united Berlin, and achieved infamy in the 1990s as the city's largest construction site. Today the cutting-edge, wildly ambitious architectural designs make for metallically spectacular sightseeing. The central complex of buildings overlooking Potsdamer Str. includes the towering **Deutsche Bahn headquarters,** the glossy ■**Sony Center,** and an off-kilter glass recreation of Mt. Fuji that covers the vast courtyard enclosed by the buildings. Take in a movie, go window-shopping, or just sit and marvel at the enormity of it all. (U2, or S1, 2, or 25 to "Potsdamer Pl.")

FÜHRERBUNKER. Near Potsdamer Pl., unmarked and inconspicuous, is the site of the bunker where Hitler married Eva Braun and then ended his life. Plans to restore the bunker were shelved for fear that the site would become a shrine for radical groups, so all there is to see now is an empty dirt expanse and the occasional lost tourists still seeking the long-destroyed building. (The bunker is now under the parking lot at the corner of In den Ministergarten and Gertrude Kolmar Str.)

GENDARMENMARKT

Several blocks south of Unter den Linden, this gorgeous Platz was considered the **French Quarter** in the 18th century, when it became the main settlement for Protestant Huguenots fleeing persecution by "Sun King" Louis XIV. During the last week of June and the first week of July, the square becomes an outdoor stage for open-air classical concerts. (U6 to "Französische Str." or U2 or 6 to "Stadtmitte." For concert tickets, go to one of the discount ticket offices for last-minute deals (p. 102) or call ☎ 69 80 75 22.)

DEUTSCHER DOM. Gracing the southern end of the square, the Dom is not currently used as a church but instead houses **Wege Irrwege Umwege** ("Milestones, Setbacks, Sidetracks"), an exhibition tracing German political history from despotism to democracy. (Gendarmenmarkt 1. ☎ 22 73 04 31. Open Sept.-May Tu 10am-10pm, W-Su 10am-6pm; June-Aug. Tu 10am-10pm, W-Su 10am-7pm. Free.)

FRANZÖSISCHER DOM. Built in the early 18th century by French Huguenots, the Dom now holds a restaurant and small museum on the Huguenot diaspora. The tower offers a 360° view of the city.

FROM THE ROAD

GOAL!!

June 23, 2004: a day that will be mourned by Germans for at least the next few years. No wars broke out and no beloved politicians died—Germany's male soccer team was eliminated from Euro Cup 2004. On this night I found myself in a crowd of 5000 fans under the screen at the Sony Center, clutching a bratwurst and a German flag and cheering "Ollie Ollie!" as Germany's famous goalkeeper thwarted Czech shots. After 21 minutes, two complete(ly drunk) strangers hugged me as Germany took the lead, 1-0. An hour later, I found myself consoling these same men, now teary-eyed, as we left the Sony Center with dashed hopes.

In Germany, *Fußball* is no merely a game, it's a way of life. Three-time winners of both the World Cup and the European Championships, the German men's team rarely falls off FIFA's top 10; and Germany's women hold the World Cup title after crushing Sweden, 1-0, in 2003. The German *Bundesliga*, founded in 1964, is composed of 18 league teams who battle from August to the end of May.

Germany is a nation where it is impossible to walk past 10 people without spotting a team jersey. You may not understand the football obsession, but if you take a seat in a local *Kneipe*, be ready to get hugged as *FC Bayern München* battles *Werder Bremen*.

- Venu Nadella, 2005

(Gendarmenmarkt 5. At the opposite end of the square from the Deutscher Dom. ☎229 17 60. Museum open Tu-Sa noon-5pm, Su 11am-5pm. Tower open daily 9am-7pm. Museum €2, students €1. Tower €2/€1.50.)

MUSEUMSINSEL

After crossing the Schloßbrücke over the Spree, Unter den Linden becomes Karl-Liebknecht-Str. and cuts through the **Museumsinsel** (museum island), home to five major museums and the **Berliner Dom.** Take S3, 5, 7, 9, or 75 to "Hackescher Markt" and walk toward the Dom. Or, pick up bus #100 along Unter den Linden and get off at "Lustgarten." For information on the **Altes Museum, Pergamon, Bodemuseum,** and **Alte Nationalgalerie,** see **Museums,** p. 127.

LUSTGARTEN. This immaculate green stretch, where students sun themselves and children splash in the fountain, is bounded by the Karl Friedrich Schinkel-designed **Altes Museum** to the north and the **Berliner Dom** to the east. The massive granite bowl in front of the museum was meant to adorn the main hall, but didn't fit through the door. Now the bowl sees daily indignities as policemen shoo away children who treat it as a playground.

BERLINER DOM. This elegantly bulky, multiple-domed cathedral, one of Berlin's most recognizable landmarks, proves that Protestants can design buildings as dramatically as Catholics. Built during the reign of Kaiser Wilhelm II in a faux-Renaissance style, the cathedral suffered severe damage in a 1944 air raid. Today's church is the result of a 20-year process of reconstruction. Look for the Protestant icons (Calvin, Zwingli, and Luther) that adorn the decadent interior, or soak in a glorious view of Berlin from the tower. *(Open M-Sa 9am-8pm, Su noon-8pm, closed during services 6:30-7:30pm. Free organ recitals W-F at 3pm. Frequent **concerts** in summer; buy tickets in the church or call ☎20 26 91 36, M-Sa 10am-8pm, Su noon-8pm. Combined admission to Dom, crypt, tower, and galleries €5, students €3.)*

SCHLOßPLATZ. Known as Marx-Engels-Pl. during the days of the DDR, this square houses the glaring, amber-colored **Palast der Republik,** where the East German parliament met, and is the former site of the **Berliner Schloß,** the Hohenzollern family palace. In 1990, city authorities discovered that the building was full of asbestos and shut it down for renovations. Remarkably, the palace survived the war, only to be demolished by DDR authorities in the 1950s in censure of its royal excess. The Platz houses a small exhibit chronicling the history of the Schloß, as well as the city's plans to rebuild the palace. The **Staatsrat,** the temporary office of the federal chancellor, currently resides on the site—its modern facade has a slice of the old palace embedded in it. The East German government preserved this section because **Karl Liebknecht** proclaimed a German socialist republic from its balcony. The final fate of the Platz probably won't be decided before 2005. *(Across the street from the Lustgarten.)*

MARX-ENGELS-FORUM. Across the river from Museumsinsel on the south side of Karl-Liebknecht-Str. stands a memorial of steel tablets dedicated to the world-wide workers' struggle against fascism and imperialism. Bulbous statues of Marx and Engels preside over the oft-graffitied tablets, while stone reliefs of struggling workers circumscribe the memorial. The park and the street opposite Karl-Liebknecht-Str. together used to be known as the Marx-Engels-Forum. The street is called Rathausstr., but rather than rename the park, the city has left it nameless.

ALEXANDERPLATZ AND NIKOLAIVIERTEL

Karl-Liebknecht-Str., which divides the Museuminsel, leads into the monolithic Alexanderplatz. Take U2, 5, or 8, or S3, 5, 7, 9, or 75 to "Alexanderpl."

FERNSEHTURM. The tremendous and bizarre TV tower, the tallest structure in Berlin at 368m, was originally intended to prove East Germany's technological capabilities (though Swedish engineers were brought in to help build it); as a result, the tower has acquired some colorful politically-infused nicknames, among them the perennial favorite "Walter Ulbricht's Last Erection" (p. 58). Look at the windows when the sun is out to see the cross-shaped glint pattern known as the *Papsts Rache* ("pope's revenge," so named because it defied the Communist government's attempt to rid the city of religious symbols). An elevator whisks tourists up and away to the magnificent view from the spherical node 203m high, and a cafe one floor up serves international meals for €9-13. (☎ 242 33 33. Open daily Mar.-Oct. 9am-1am; Nov.-Feb. 10am-midnight. €6.80, under 16 €3.50.)

ALEXANDERPLATZ. Formerly the bustling heart of Weimar Berlin, this plaza was transformed in East German times into an urban wasteland of fountains and prefab office buildings, including some concrete-block classics. In the 1970s, the grey drear was interrupted by enormous neon signs with declarations like "Medical Instruments of the DDR—Distributed In All the World!" in order to satisfy the people's need for bright lights and semblances of progress. Today chain stores like **Kaufhof** have replaced the signs and serve as a backdrop for the affairs of bourgeois German shoppers, tourists, and numerous punks with dogs.

MARIENKIRCHE. The church is Gothic, the altar and pulpit Rococo, the tower Neo-Romantic: the result of several centuries of additions to the original structure. Relatively undamaged during the war, this little church still holds relics from other nearby churches that used it as a shelter. Knowledgeable guides explain the artifacts, as well as the painting collection, mainly comprised of works from the Dürer and Cranach schools. (☎ 242 44 67. Open daily in summer 10am-6pm, in winter until 4pm.)

BERLINER RATHAUS. Called the *Rotes Rathaus* (red city hall) for its brick color, not the politics of the government that used it in the DDR days. Now the seat of Berlin's municipal government, the building is often mobbed by schoolchildren who come on field trips to watch legislation in action. (Rathausstr. 1. Open M-F 9am-6pm. Free. Call ☎ 90 26 25 23 for guided tours. Free.)

SCHEUNENVIERTEL AND ORANIENBURGER STRAßE

Northwest of Alexanderpl., near Oranienburger Str. and Große Hamburger Str., is the **Scheunenviertel,** once the center of Berlin's Orthodox Jewish community. Prior to WWII, Berlin did not have ghettos; wealthier and more assimilated Jews tended to live in Western Berlin, while Orthodox Jews from Eastern Europe settled in the Scheunenviertel. The neighborhood shows evidence of Jewish life back to the 13th century, though the Jews were expelled from the city several times before WWII, once for allegedly causing the Black Death. Today, the Scheunenviertel is known for its teeming masses of outdoor cafes than for its historical significance, but the past few years have seen the opening of several Judaica-oriented bookstores and kosher restaurants. (S1, 2, or 25 to "Oranienburger Str." or U6 to "Oranienburger Tor.")

NEUE SYNAGOGE. This huge, "oriental-style" building, modeled after the Alhambra, was designed by Berlin architect Eduard Knoblauch. The synagogue, which seated 3200, was used for worship until 1940, when the Nazis occupied it and used it for storage. Amazingly, the building survived *Kristallnacht*—the SS torched it, but a local police chief bluffed his way past SS officers to order the fire extinguished. The synagogue was later destroyed by bombing, but its restoration, largely financed by international Jewish organizations, began in 1988. The temple's beautiful, gold-laced domes were opened to the public in 1995. Too big for Berlin's remaining Jewish community, the striking building is no longer used for services and instead houses an exhibit chronicling its history as well as temporary exhibits on the history of Berlin's Jews. *(Oranienburger Str. 30. ☎88 02 83 00. Open May-Aug. Su-M 10am-8pm, Tu-Th 10am-6pm, F 10am-5pm; Sept.-Apr. Su-Th and Sa 10am-6pm, F 10am-2pm. A series of security checks is required to enter. Museum €5, students €3. Permanent exhibit only €3/€2. Dome €1.50/€1.)*

ALTER JÜDISCHER FRIEDHOF. Obliterated by the Nazis, the old Jewish cemetery now contains only the restored gravestone of the Enlightenment philosopher and scholar Moses Mendelssohn; the rest is a quiet park. In front, a prominent plaque marks the site of the **Jüdisches Altersheim,** the Jewish old-age home which after 1942 served as a holding place for Jews before their deportation to concentration camps. *(At the end of Große Hamburger Str., near Oranienburger Str.)*

JÜDISCHE KNABENSCHULE. Next to the cemetery on Große Hamburger Str. stands Berlin's oldest **Jewish school,** where Moses Mendelssohn taught. The plaque on the side of the school memorializes Mendelssohn, "the German Socrates," who translated the Hebrew Bible into German and supported interaction between Berlin's Jewish and non-Jewish communities. Corresponding with his progressive outlook, the school's enrollment was only half-Jewish. The building was reopened as a school in 1992, and its student body is still half-and-half. Across the street, between the two yellow cafes, signs on the side of a bombed-out building memorialize its former residents, listing their occupations and the years of their deaths.

TIERGARTEN

In the center of Berlin, the lush **Tiergarten** provides welcome relief from the urban chaos around it. Stretching from Bahnhof Zoo in the west to the Brandenburg Gate in the east, the vast landscaped park was formerly used by Prussian monarchs as a hunting and parade ground. Today, it's frequented by strolling families, elderly couples, and, at night, cruising gay men. **Straße des 17. Juni** bisects the park from west to east, connecting Ernst-Reuter-Pl. to the Brandenburg Gate. The street is the site of many *Demos* and parades; in early July, the park hosts the serious partying (i.e., widespread sex) of the Love Parade (see **All You Need Is $$,** p. 107).

■**THE REICHSTAG.** The current home of Germany's governing body, the *Bundestag,* the Reichstag has seen some critical moments in history. Here, Philipp Scheidemann made his 1918 proclamation *"Es lebe die Deutsche Republik"* ("Long live the German Republic"), and in 1933 Adolf Hitler used a fire here as an excuse to declare a state of emergency and seize power. Recently, a glass dome was added to the top, built around the upside-down solar cone that powers the building. A walkway spirals up the inside of the dome, leading visitors through panoramic views to the top of the cone. Throngs of tourists wait in line to get there, but the patient are well rewarded with a spectacular view of the city. *(☎22 73 21 52. Open daily 8am-midnight; last entrance 10pm. Free.)*

AROUND THE REICHSTAG. Across the construction site lies the brand-new **Chancellory.** The huge white and blue residence is reportedly a source of embarrassment to Chancellor Schröder, who wishes to keep a low profile. Tourists aren't permitted inside. The nearby **Palais am Pariser Platz,** north of the Brandenburg Gate, used to be the site of a castle; enter the courtyard now to find Stephen Balkenhol's startling 1998 statue *Großer Mann mit kleinem Mann* (Big Man with Little Man).

SIEGESSÄULE. In the heart of the Tiergarten, this slender 70m victory column commemorates Prussia's crushing victory over France in 1870. The statue at the top—Victoria, the goddess of victory—is made of melted-down French cannons. In a less-than-subtle affront to the French, the Nazis moved the monument here in 1938 from its former spot in front of the Reichstag in order to increase its height and visibility. Climb the monument's 285 steps for a panorama of the city. *(Großer*

Stern. Take bus #100 or 187 to "Großer Stern" or S5, 7, or 9 to "Tiergarten" and walk 5 minutes down Straße des 17. Juni. ☎391 29 61. Open Apr.-Nov. M-F 9:30am-6:30pm, Sa-Su 9:30am-7pm; Nov.-Mar. M-F 10am-5pm, Sa-Su 10am-5:30pm. €2.20, students €1.50.)

SOWJETISCHES EHRENMAL. At the eastern end of the Tiergarten, the Soviet Memorial rises (yes, in western Berlin) above a pair of red star-emblazoned tanks, the first two to enter Berlin in 1945. This memorial honors the Soviet soldiers who lost their lives storming the city; an estimated 2500 soldiers are buried at the end of the park. *(Bus #100 to "Pl. der Republik" and walk down Entlastungsstr. to Str. des 17. Juni.)*

OTHER SIGHTS IN MITTE

■ **HACKESCHE HÖFE.** A complex of buildings built in the early 1900s as a combination of offices, workshops, factories and apartments, these eight gorgeous connected courtyards have been heavily restored and now feature theaters, bars, restaurants, shops, and above all else, cafes. *(Rosenthaler Str. 40/41. ☎28 09 80 10; www.hackesche-hoefe.com.)*

KOPPENPLATZ. This square is home to a simple yet stunning monument to Nelly Sachs, a Jewish Berliner who shared the Nobel Prize for literature in 1966. No men on horseback, no walls of names, just an overturned chair and a line of her poetry pays tribute to her flight from Berlin in 1940. *(U8 to Rosenthaler Pl.)*

BERTOLT-BRECHT-HAUS. If any one man personifies the maelstrom of political and aesthetic contradictions that is Berlin, it is **Bertolt Brecht** (p. 68), who lived and worked in this house from 1953 to 1956. "There is a reason to prefer Berlin to other cities," the playwright once said, "because it is constantly changing. What is bad today can be improved tomorrow." The **Brechtforum** on the second floor sponsors exhibits and lectures on artistic and metropolitan subjects. *(Chausseestr. 125. U6 to "Zinnowitzer Str." ☎283 05 70 44. Obligatory German tours every 30min. Tu-F 10-11:30am, Th also 5-6:30pm, and Sa 9:30am-1:30pm; every hr. Su 11am-6pm. €3, students €1.50.)*

DOROTHEENSTÄDTISCHER FRIEDHOF. Attached to Brecht's house is the cemetery where he and his wife, Helene Weigel, are buried, their graves marked by simple stones bearing only their names. Other famous personages interred in the cemetery include Karl Friedrich Schinkel, Heinrich Mann, and Hegel and Fichte, who lie side by side in the middle of the yard. A map near the entrance points out locations of notable graves. *(Open daily Apr.-Sept. 8am-8pm and Oct.-Mar. 8am-4pm.)*

SCHLOß BELLEVUE. This *Schloß*, finished in 1786, was the first palace in Berlin to be built in the classical style. The guest house of the Third Reich government, this three-winged complex was severely damaged in WWII but reconstructed in the 1950s and now serves as the official residence of the federal president in Berlin. It is closed to the public. *(Spreeweg 1. Bus 100 to "Schloß Bellevue." ☎200 00.)*

HI-FLYER BALLOON. Tethered to the ground near Potsdamer Platz, this hot-air balloon rises 150m into the air every 15min. for a spectacular bird's-eye view of the surrounding area. *(At the corner of Voßstr. and Ebertstr. ☎226 67 88 11; www.air-service-berlin.com. Open summer M-Th and Su 10am-10pm, F-Sa 10am-12:30am; winter M-Th and Su 11am-7pm, F-Sa 11am-8pm. €19, students €10.)*

🏛 MUSEUMS

MUSEUMSINSEL (MUSEUM ISLAND)

The Museumsinsel holds the treasures of Germany in five separate museums. These Athens-esque temples of culture, built in the 19th and 20th centuries, are separated from the rest of Mitte by two arms of the Spree. Many of the museums

BERLIN

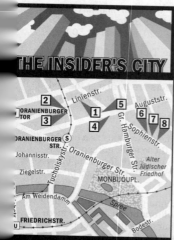

GALLERIES OF MITTE

1 Marvel at the tasteful large-scale photography of **Kicken Berlin,** Linienstr. 155. (☎28 87 78 82; www.kicken-gallery.com. Open Tu-F 11am-6pm, Sa 2-6pm.)

2 If analog art has got you down, **DAM,** Tucholskystr. 37, displays digital art installations and has showings (daily noon, 3, and 5pm) of video works on the Sony Center screen. (☎28 09 81 35; www.dam.org/berlin. Open Tu-F noon-6pm, Sa 12pm-4pm.)

3 The spartan **Wohnmaschine,** Tucholskystr. 35, founded in 1988, is Mitte's oldest gallery, and exhibits everything from American photographs to German sculpture. (☎30 87 20 15; www.wohnmaschine.de. Open Tu-Sa 11am-6pm.)

4 Next door to one another, **Oona,** Auguststr. 26 (☎28 04 59 05; www.oona-gallerie.de. Open Tu-F 2-7pm, Sa 1-6pm.), exhibits jewelry while **EIGEN+ART,** also Auguststr.

are undergoing extensive renovation: the **Bodemuseum** will be closed until 2006 and the **Neues Museum** should reopen in 2008, when it will house the collection currently in the Ägyptisches Museum (p. 113). *(S3, 5, 7, 9 or 75 to "Hackescher Markt" or bus #100 to "Lustgarten." ☎20 90 55 55. All SMB museums open Tu-Su 10am-6pm, Th until 10pm unless noted. All offer free audio tours in English. Admission to each is €6, students €3 unless noted. All sell a 3-day card good for admission to every museum; €10, students €5.)*

■ **PERGAMONMUSEUM.** One of the world's great ancient history museums, the Pergamon dates from the days when Heinrich Schliemann and other zealous 19th-century German archaeologists dismantled the remnants of collapsed empires the world over and sent them home for reassembly. Named for Pergamon, the city in present-day Turkey from which the enormous **Altar of Zeus** (180 BC) was taken, the museum features gargantuan pieces of ancient Mediterranean and Near Eastern history from as far back as the 10th century BC. The colossal blue **Ishtar Gate** of Babylon (575 BC) and the Roman **Market Gate of Miletus** are just two more massive pieces in an astounding collection that also includes Greek, Assyrian, Islamic, and Far Eastern art. *(Bodestr. 1-3. ☎20 90 55 77. Last entry 30min. before closing.)*

ALTE NATIONALGALERIE. After extensive renovations, this renowned museum is again open to hordes of eager 19th-century art-lovers. Everything from German Realism to French Impressionism; Caspar David Friedrich and Karl Friedrich Schinkel are but two names in an all-star cast. *(Am Lustgarten. ☎20 90 58 01.)*

ALTES MUSEUM. At the far end of the Lustgarten, the Altes Museum's galleries are surprisingly untouristed. The lower level contains the *Antikensammlung*, a permanent collection of ancient Greco-Roman (especially Etruscan) decorative art. Upstairs, temporary exhibits await. *(Lustgarten. ☎20 90 52 54.)*

KULTURFORUM

The **Tiergarten-Kulturforum** is a complex of museums at the eastern end of the Tiergarten, near the Staatsbibliothek and Potsdamer Pl. Students and local fine arts aficionados swarm throughout the buildings and on the multi-leveled courtyard in front. *(S1, 2, or 25 or U2 to "Potsdamer Pl." and walk down Potsdamer Str.; the museums will be on your right on Matthäikirchpl. ☎20 90 55 55. Hours and prices same as above.)*

■ **GEMÄLDEGALERIE.** One of Germany's most famous museums, and rightly so. It houses an enormous collection of 2700 13th-18th century masterpieces by Italian, German, Dutch, and Flemish masters, including works by Dürer, Rembrandt, Rubens, Vermeer, Raphael, Titian, and Botticelli. *(Stauffenbergstr. 40. ☎ 266 29 51.)*

NEUE NATIONALGALERIE. This sleek building, designed by Mies van der Rohe, contains both interesting temporary exhibits and a formidable permanent collection of 20th century art including works by Warhol, Munch, Kirchner, and Beckmann, as well as a variety of oft-grotesque and ever-interesting modern selections; never has roadkill looked so cool. *(Potsdamer Str. 50, just past the Kulturforum. ☎ 266 26 62.)*

KUNSTGEWERBEMUSEUM. The Museum of Decorative Arts highlights masterpieces of design, from spoons to tables to carpets to boxes. A crazy congregation of chairs, including a shopping-cart-turned-recliner, makes the contemporary exhibit unique. *(☎ 266 29 02. Open Tu-F 10am-6pm, Sa-Su 11am-6pm. €3, students €1.50.)*

KUNSTBIBLIOTHEK/KUPFERSTICHKABINETT. A stellar collection of lithographs and drawings by Renaissance masters, including many Dürers and Goyas, and Botticelli's fantastic illustrations for the *Divine Comedy*. *(☎ 266 29 02. Library open M 2-8pm, Tu-F 9am-8pm. Tours Su at 3pm. Free.)*

OTHER MUSEUMS IN MITTE AND TIERGARTEN

◙HAMBURGER BAHNHOF/MUSEUM FÜR GEGENWART. Berlin's foremost collection of contemporary art, with a colossal 10,000 square meters of exhibition space in this converted train station. The museum features some cheerfully amusing works by Warhol, as well as pieces by Beuys and Kiefer and some in-your-face temporary exhibits. The hugeness of the rooms allows for the display of some truly outrageous sculpture work. *(Invalidenstr. 50-51. S3, 5, 7, 9, or 75 to "Lehrter Stadtbahnhof" or U6 to "Zinnowitzer Str." ☎ 39 78 34 12. Open Tu-F 10am-6pm, Sa-Su 11am-6pm. Tours Su at 4pm. €6, students €3.)*

ANNE FRANK ZENTRUM. Tucked in an idyllic courtyard, this center is dedicated to the fight against discrimination and prejudices, particularly antisemitism. A permanent exhibition entitled "Anne Frank—a story for today" features a timeline of her short life. Several moving films about Frank and the Holocaust are screened continuously. *(Rosenthaler Str. 39. ☎ 24 04 88 64; www.annefrank.de. Open M-F noon-8pm, Sa-Su 11am-8pm. €3, students €1.50.)*

SCHINKELMUSEUM. In Berlin, if it's made of stone, Karl Friedrich Schinkel likely designed it; the lovely **Friedrichwerdersche Kirche** is no exception. It now houses 19th-century French and German sculpture

26, features large-scale paintings (☎ 280 66 05; www.eigen-art.com. Open Tu-Sa 11am-6pm.)

5 Don white gloves and rifle through drawers of great photographs at **volcker & freunde galerie,** Auguststr. 62. (☎ 28 09 61 15; www.voelcker.de. Open W-F noon-7pm, Sa 11am-5pm.)

6 Paint-splattered pieces by cutting-edge young artists from around the globe can be found at **griedervonputtkamer,** Sophienstr. 25. (☎ 28 87 93 80; griedervonputtkamer@gmx.net. Open Tu-Sa 11am-6pm.)

7 Glasswork spanning four centuries, from Baroque to Art Deco, and beyond, is displayed at **Galerie Splinter,** Sophienstr. 20-21. The owners are happy to give advice to collectors and gift-givers looking to purchase pieces. (☎ 28 59 87 37; www.glasgaleriesplinter.de. Open W-Sa 2-7pm.)

8 **Asperger Gallery Berlin** features abstract contemporary paintings, sculptures, and photographs, Sophienstr. 18. (☎ 28 04 49 04; www.asperger-gallery.de. Open W-Sa 2-7pm.)

BERLIN'S BOMBSHELL

Marlene Dietrich was "the most intriguing woman" John Wayne had ever known. A stunning actress, singer, and activist, "Lili Marlene" charmed many in her 53 year career.

Born in Schöneberg in 1901, Marlene loved her native Berlin, especially Unter den Linden, where her mother ran a jewelry shop. At 21 she debuted on Berlin's stages, and soon entered the morally permissive cabaret scene, where director Josef von Sternberg discovered her. Marlene starred in his 1929 film *The Blue Angel*, and soon became the highest paid actress of her time.

Marlene was reigning in Hollywood when Hitler requested she return to Germany. She refused, instead becoming an American citizen in 1937 and touring the European front in USO shows. She earned the Medal of Freedom and title as Knight and Officer of the *Légion d'Honneur*. After the war, Marlene toured four continents and revived Europe's cabaret scene. A fall fractured her leg, and she withdrew into seclusion in Paris for 13 years.

Dietrich had not been home in over 60 years when she was buried next to her mother in Berlin upon her death in 1992. Today, her fans can find thousands of photographs, textile items, and written documents as part of the "Marlene Dietrich Collection Berlin" in the **Filmmuseum at Potsdamer Platz** (see right).

and an exhibit on the Prussian architect's life and work. *(Werderscher Markt, on the corner of Oberwallstr., south of Unter den Linden. U2 to "Hausvogteipl." ☎208 13 23. Open Tu-Su 10am-6pm. €3, students €1.50.)*

SENATSVERWALTUNG FÜR STADTENTWICKLUNG. In the government's center for urban planning, the fascinating permanent exhibit "Urban Planning: Plans, Models, Projects" showcases two models at 1:500 and 1:1000 scales of future plans for the city, as well as a model of the way East Berlin looked in 1989 after the fall of the Wall. *(Behrenstr. 42. U6 to "Französischestr." ☎90 20 50 09; www.stadtentwicklung.berlin.de. Open daily 10am-6pm. Free.)*

INDEPENDENT MUSEUMS

DEUTSCHE GUGGENHEIM BERLIN. Located in a newly renovated building across the street from the Deutsche Staatsbibliothek, this joint venture of the Deutsche Bank and the Guggenheim Foundation features new exhibits of contemporary art every few months. *(Unter den Linden 13-15. ☎202 09 30; www.deutsche-guggenheim-berlin.de. Open daily 11am-8pm. €3, students €2.50; M free.)*

KUNST-WERKE BERLIN. Under the direction of Mitte's art world luminary Klaus Biesenbach, this former margarine factory now houses studio space, a matrix of rotating contemporary exhibitions, and a cafe in a beautiful garden. Check the website for current shows. *(Auguststr. 69. U6 to "Oranienburger Tor." ☎243 45 90; www.kw-berlin.de. Exhibitions open Tu-Su noon-6pm. €4, students €2.50.)*

FILMMUSEUM BERLIN. This museum chronicles the development of German film with a special focus on older works like Fritz Lang's *Metropolis*. The contrast between old film (whole rooms are devoted to such icons as Leni Riefenstahl and Marlene Dietrich) and new can be disconcerting at times. Still, the exhibits (with good English captions) are fascinating, and the ultra-futuristic entrance is not to be missed. *(Potsdamer Str. 2; 3rd and 4th fl. of the Sony Center. S1, 2, 25 or U2 to "Potsdamer Pl." ☎300 90 30; www.filmmuseum-berlin.de. Tickets sold on the ground fl. Open Tu-Su 10am-6pm, Th until 8pm. €6, students €4, children €2.50.)*

BAUHAUS-ARCHIV MUSEUM FÜR GESTALTUNG. A must-visit for Bauhaus fans, this building was designed by Bauhaus founder Walter Gropius and houses changing exhibits of paintings, sculptures, and—of course—that famous furniture. *(Klingelhöferstr. 14. Bus #100, 187, 200, or 341 to "Nordische Botschaften/Adenauer-Stiftg." ☎254 00 20. Open M and W-Su 10am-5pm. €4, students €2.)*

MARTIN-GROPIUS-BAU. Walter Gropius's uncle Martin designed this neo-Renaissance wedding cake as a museum for and tribute to the industrial arts. The style is anything but Bauhaus slick—the ornate fixings are absolutely decadent. The building alone is worth the price of admission, and the temporary exhibits of modern art and history are usually excellent. *(Niederkirchnerstr. 7. U2 or S1 or 2 to "Potsdamer Pl." ☎ 25 48 60. Open daily 10am-8pm. Admission depends on exhibit; around €6-8, students €4.)*

DEUTSCHES HISTORISCHES MUSEUM. Scheduled to have reopened by the end of 2004, these exhibits trace German history from Neanderthals to Nazis, while rotating exhibitions examine the last 50 years with large quantities of DDR art in the "painting-of-a-happy-faced-worker" vein. *(Unter den Linden 2. S3, 5, 7, 9, or 75 to "Hackescher Markt." ☎ 20 30 40. Open M-Tu and Th-Su 3-6pm. €2.)*

HANFMUSEUM. Catering to the curious and the devoted, this museum details the medical and textile uses of marijuana, as well as the debate over its legality. *(Mühlendamm 5. U2 to "Klosterstr." ☎ 242 48 27. Open Tu-F 10am-8pm, Sa-Su noon-8pm. €3.)*

TOPOGRAPHIE DES TERRORS. Housed in the crumbling torture bunkers discovered beneath the former Gestapo headquarters, a comprehensive exhibit of photographs and documents details the Nazi party's rise to power and the atrocities that occurred during the war. English audio guides are available, but you don't need to read the captions to be moved by the photographs. Along the outside perimeter of the exhibit stand the remaining 200m of the Berlin Wall, a graffitied memorial to the city's divided past. *(Behind the Martin-Gropius-Bau, at the corner of Niederkirchnerstr. and Wilhelmstr. S1 or 2, or U2 to "Potsdamer Pl." ☎ 25 48 67 03. Open daily 10am-6pm. Free.)*

🏛 GALLERIES

AKADEMIE DER KÜNSTE. This 300-year-old institution has been the core of Berlin's art community for years, promoting a variety of media: film, literature, painting, photography, music, architecture, performing arts, and more. The Akademie sponsors a variety of prizes and hosts exhibitions in its Hanseatenweg location. *(Hanseatenweg 10. S3, 5, 7, 9, or 75 to "Bellevue," or U9 to "Hansapl." ☎ 39 07 60; www.adk.de. Open M 2-8pm, Tu-Su 11am-8pm. Exhibits range from free to €7, students €4.)*

NEUER BERLINER KUNSTVEREIN. This organization puts art into the hands of the public. Besides hosting a gallery space, it sponsors the weekly "Treffpunkt NBK," a series of lectures, discussions with artists, performances and more. It also lends contemporary works to Berlin residents for €0.50 per month through the **Artothek,** and has myriad videos available to the public via the **Video-Forum.** *(Chausseestr. 128-129. ☎ 280 70 20; www.nbk.org. Gallery open M-F noon-6pm, Sa-Su 2-6pm.)*

📷 NIGHTLIFE (BARS AND CLUBS)

WMF, Karl-Marx-Allee 34. (☎ 288 78 89 10). U5 to Schillingstr. Newly lodged in a former East German dinner cabaret, more chic than some of its neighbors, WMF fills its dance floors with electroloungers Th and Sa. Sundays belong to GMF, a gay party for guys who can't stop shaking it, with some girls and straight men in the mix. Cover €7-13. Open Th and Sa from 11pm, Su from 10pm.

Tresor/Globus, Leipzigerstr. 126a (☎ 229 06 11 or 612 33 64). U2 or S1, 2, or 25 or night bus N5, 29, or 52 to "Potsdamer Pl." One of the most rocking techno venues in Berlin. Downstairs, former bank vaults flicker and throb in strobe lights as ravers sweat to hardcore techno; upstairs the ceilings are higher, the music is slower, and the lighting is (slightly) more subdued. Tresor provides a good mid-week option, as it opens W when many other clubs stay closed. Cover W €3, F €7, Sa €4. Open W and F-Sa 11pm-6am.

Zosch, Tucholskystr. 30 (☎280 76 64). U6 to "Oranienburger Tor." Refreshingly far from the crowded Oranienburger Str. scene and hidden behind layers of ivy, this place fills to the corners every night. Bright, laid-back bar on the ground fl. is comfy like a living room and filled with Mitte-dwellers just looking to relax. The basement has live music, fiction and poetry readings, and a darker bar. Performances (and crowds) vary widely from day to day. Dixieland jazz W. Open M-F from 4pm, Sa-Su from noon.

2BE-Club, Ziegelstr. 23. S1, 2, or 25 to Oranienburger Str. or U6 to Oranienburger Tor. Outside this huge club there's a packed bar in a tent-like courtyard; inside there's a widespread, committed dancing to deep-based reggae and hip hop. Both fl. have palm trees and summery images projected on the walls. F-Sa ladies free until midnight. Cover €7.50-8. Open F-Sa from 11pm, sometimes Su and M as well.

Strandbar Mitte, Monbijioustr. 3. S3, 5, 7, 9, or 75 to "Hackescher Markt." In Monbijoupark, across from the Bodemuseum. Filled with deep beach chairs and a huge pit of sand, this bar radiates California sunshine. The outdoor sound system blasts hits as locals enjoy beer (€2.50-3) and cocktails (€4-7). Open summer only, daily from 10pm.

Delicious Doughnuts, Rosenthaler Str. 9 (☎28 09 92 74). U8 to Rosenthaler Pl. This bar's cute, curvacious design draws you through the door and into one of the loungeable booths. Other facilities include foosball and a pocket-sized dance floor. Shades keep early-morning stragglers protected from the sun. Open daily from 10pm-7am.

Café Silberstein, Oranienburger Str. 27 (☎281 20 95). S1, 2, or 25 to "Oranienburger Str." 3 words say it all: sushi until midnight. Japanese/industrial-chic motifs, chairs with 8ft. high backs, and an intellectual 30-something crowd. Open daily after 10am-late (normally 3am); sushi (€6-15) served daily noon-midnight.

VEB-OZ, Stadtbogen 153, Monbijoupark (☎28 39 14 40). Under the S-Bahn tracks just west of Hackescher Markt. The name stands for *Verkehrsberuhigte Ost Zone,* and though it's recently moved from Oranienburger Str., it took its kitschy East German paraphernalia along for the ride. The new location may be somewhat tiny and transparent, but it still has the traditional foosball opportunities. Open daily from 6pm.

Sage Club, Kopenicker Str. 76 (☎27 59 10 82; www.sage-club.de). U8 or night bus N8 to "Heinrich-Heine-Str." This chic, well-moneyed club has a dance floor and several bars in an old U-Bahn station. The wooden patio, open F-Sa, has porch swings, couches, and a pool. Th punk/indie, F funk/disco/R&B, otherwise house. Cover €5-13. Open Th from 10pm, F-Su 11pm-9am. The packed "Sage Market" is open Su noon-10pm.

Tacheles, Oranienburger Str. 53-56 (☎282 61 85). U6 to "Oranienburger Tor" or S1, 2, or 25 to "Oranienburger Str." or night buses N6 or 84. Housed in a bombed-out department store and the adjacent courtyard, this edgy complex boasts a motif of graffiti and scrap metal artwork. A playground for artists, punks, and curious tourists, the labyrinth of rooms leads into several art galleries, movie theaters, and inexplicable balcony bars. Flickering films broadcast onto the building across the street, a metal dragon breathes fire in **Cafe Zapata,** and then there's the occasional vicious rave. Opening times for the theater and galleries vary, as do rave dates; check www.tacheles.de. For theater tickets, call ☎28 09 68 35. Cafe Zapata open daily noon-4am. **Offen Bar Konzept** on the top floor serves drinks with a view (and a breeze) starting every day at 8pm.

Kaffee Burger, Torstr. 60 (☎28 04 64 95; www.kaffeeburger.de). U2 to "Rosa-Luxemburg-Pl." This laid-back bar/club continuously packs in a diverse crowd with its wide variety of nightly parties, especially on bimonthly "Russian Disco" night. Live bands Th 10pm. Open M-Th and Su 7pm-late, F 8pm-late, Sa 9pm-late. Cover free-€5.

Kinzo Club, Karl-Liebknecht-Str. 11 (☎97 00 48 20). S3, 5, 7, 9, or 75 or U2, 5, or 8 to "Alexanderpl." Located in a spacious basement, this club caters to a younger, dance-happy crowd that loves house and neo-disco. "Chantals House of Shame" (Th), including a show (drag or musical), is a great option for gays looking to dance the night away. Cover €6-8. Open W-Sa 11pm-late.

Adagio, Marlene-Dietrich-Platz 1 (☎ 258 98 90; www.adagio.de). S1, 2, 25 or U2 to "Potsdamer Platz." Located next to the Theater am Potsdamer Platz and featuring elegant medieval decor, this gigantic club has a rather chic, slightly older clientele. Music varies by night: W house; Th latest hits; F (singles' night) and Sa party classics and R&B. Cover W-Th €5, F-Sa €10. Open W-Th 7pm-late, F-Sa 10pm-late.

PRENZLAUER BERG

Though largely overlooked during post-war reconstruction efforts, *Prenzlberg* (as locals call it) has been transformed in recent years from a heap of crumbling, graffiti-covered buildings into perhaps the hippest of Berlin's *Bezirke*. Attracted by low rents, thousands of students and artists moved into the neighborhood after reunification; today, the streets are owned by well-dressed first graders and their

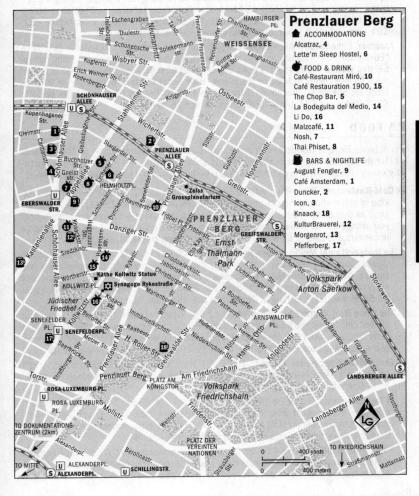

Prenzlauer Berg

🏠 ACCOMMODATIONS
Alcatraz, **4**
Lette'm Sleep Hostel, **6**

🍴 FOOD & DRINK
Café-Restaurant Miró, **10**
Café Restauration 1900, **15**
The Chop Bar, **5**
La Bodeguita del Medio, **14**
Li Do, **16**
Malzcafé, **11**
Nosh, **7**
Thai Phiset, **8**

🍸 BARS & NIGHTLIFE
August Fengler, **9**
Café Amsterdam, **1**
Duncker, **2**
Icon, **3**
Knaack, **18**
KulturBrauerei, **12**
Morgenrot, **13**
Pfefferberg, **17**

BERLIN

hip young parents, and studded with cool but costly second-hand clothing stores. Everything in Prenzlauer Berg used to be something else. Scrumptious brunches unfold every Sunday in what were once butcher shops, a former power plant stages thoughtful exhibitions about furniture, and kids cavort in breweries-turned-nightclubs. Relics of Prenzlberg's past life are disappearing, but cafe-bar owners know shabby chic when they see it: mismatched sofas and painted advertisements for cabbage remain. Rest assured, a cafe-bar is still a bar, and if you fancy a chill place to drink after dark instead of a sweaty dance floor, Prenzlberg is your spot.

ACCOMMODATIONS (HOSTELS)

Lette'm Sleep Hostel, Lettestr. 7 (☎44 73 36 23; www.backpackers.de). U2 to "Eberswalder Str." With its street-level common room and laid back staff, you could easily mistake Lette'm Sleep for one of the bars or cafes lining Helmholtzpl. The big kitchen is the social nexus of this cozy 48-bed hostel. **Free Internet** access. Wheelchair-accessible. Sheets €3. 4- to 6-bed dorms €15-16; doubles with sheets €48; triples €57. 10% discount (15% in winter) for stays over 3 nights. ❷

Alcatraz, Schönhauser Allee 133a (☎48 49 68 15; www.alcatraz-backpacker.de). U2 to "Eberswalder Str." Tucked away in a courtyard, Alcatraz offers 80 beds in small, spray-painted rooms. The TV room is quite the hang-out after dark, and the location is convenient for late nights in Mitte or Prenzlberg. Bike rental €5. **Internet** €3 per hr. Kitchen facilities. Sheets €3. Reception 24hr. Dorms €13; in winter €10; singles start at €40/€30; doubles at €44; triples at €60; quads at €76. ❷

FOOD

Prenzlauer Berg is flooded with restaurants and cafes, particularly at the borders of Hemholzpl. Eating out in the *Bezirk* is quite common; on Sundays, when virtually every restaurant serves brunch, you'll be hard-pressed to find an outdoor spot.

Café-Restaurant Miró, Raumerstr. 29 (☎44 73 30 17). U2 to "Eberswalder Str." The kind of place where generous portions of Mediterranean cuisine (€8-11) look almost as good as they taste. The main dining area makes a good date, and the back room, where you lounge on fat pillows, defines the word comfy. Breakfast €4-7. Soups €3, large appetizers and salads €4-9. Open 10am-late. Kitchen closes at midnight. ❸

La Bodeguita del Medio, Husemannstr. 10 (☎44 03 27 60). U2 to "Eberswalder Str." A Cuban *tapas* bar, decorated by multilingual customer scrawlings that cover every free surface. Aside from the *tapas* (€4-8) there's not really a menu, just new dinner specials every day. Don't forget to add your own sage advice to the closest scrap of wood. Sa-Su €9.50 dinner buffet starting at 7pm. Open M-F 4pm-2am, Sa-Su 11am-2am. ❸

The Chop Bar, Pappelallee 29 (☎44 03 62 76). Giraffe statues, wide-eyed masks, and swirled ceilings set the tone in this friendly West African restaurant. Try the *Jassa Djin*, a tasty mackerel dish (€7), the *Suppu Kanje*, lamb with white rice or tofu (€7.50), or one of the vegetarian options (€6.50-7). Open Su-Th 4-11pm, F-Sa 4pm-midnight. ❷

Thai Phiset, Pappelallee 19 (☎41 72 52 75). The cheapest lunch in Prenzlberg that still comes on a plate. Noodle dishes from €2.50, chicken €3.20-4.50. Brunch Su 11am-5pm. Open daily 11am-11pm. ❶

Li Do, Knaackstr. 30-32 (☎440 84 72). U2 to "Senefelderpl." This little restaurant obsesses over elegant food that's still less expensive than the surrounding sidewalk sprawlers. A blini burger (€8) is lox layered with blini (thin buckwheat pancakes). Or, try the more filling pasta specials (€5). Open daily 9am-late. ❷

Nosh, Pappelallee 77 (☎44 04 03 97). U2 to "Eberswalder Str." A fresh little concept restaurant amid Prenzlberg's run-down sophistication. "Borderless cooking" brings bagels topped with pesto-olive spread (€4.50), pad thai (€7.50) and the Brighton breakfast (eggs, baked beans, grilled tomatoes, bacon and toast, €6.50) together on one menu. Nosh's baked goods (€1.50-2.50) are so heavenly that other cafes sell them. Open daily 9am-late, kitchen closes at midnight. ❸

Café Restauration 1900, Husemannstr. 1 (☎442 24 94; www.restauration-1900.de), at Kollwitzpl. U2 to "Senefelderpl." The fashionable crowd is very Prenzlauer Berg at this ideally-located cafe, one of the most popular in the *Bezirk*. The salad for 2 (€18.80) challenges conventional notions of what "salad" should include. Those on a budget can take advantage of the brunch buffet on weekends (€7.80; 10am-4pm). Open daily 10am-late. Kitchen closes at midnight. ❸

Malzcafé, Knaackstr. 99 (☎44 04 72 27; www.malzcafe.de). U2 to "Eberswalder Str." Off Danziger Str. Medieval frescoes decorate the walls of this restaurant with vegetarian (€3-8) and international cuisine (€5-9). Brunch buffet (€6.10) Sa includes unlimited cake. Open daily from 10am-4am. Kitchen closes at 1am. Brunch Sa-Su 10am-4pm. ❷

 SIGHTS

▧DOKUMENTATIONSZENTRUM DER BERLINER MAUER. A museum, chapel, and an entire city block of the preserved Berlin Wall—two concrete barriers separated by the open *Todesstreife* (death strip)—combine to form a controversial memorial to "victims of the communist tyranny." The **museum** assembles a comprehensive record of all things related to the wall; exhibits include lots of historic photos, film clips, and sound bites. Climb up the spiral staircases for the full effect of the desolate scene below you. *(Bernauer Str. 111. U8 to "Bernauer Str." Open W-Su 10am-5pm. Free.)*

KOLLWITZPLATZ. This little triangle of greenery is a nexus of Prenzlauer Berg's cafe scene, populated by relaxing couples and sand-covered babies. The Platz centers on a statue of famed visual artist **Käthe Kollwitz** (p. 113). The monument has been painted a number of times in past years in acts of affectionate vandalism, most notably with big pink polka-dots. *(U2 to "Senefelderpl." Kollwitzstr. forks right off of Schönhauser Allee and runs along one side of Kollwitzpl.)*

JÜDISCHER FRIEDHOF. Prenzlauer Berg was one of the major centers of Jewish Berlin, especially during the 19th and early 20th centuries. The ivy-covered Jewish cemetery on Schönhauser Allee contains the graves of composer Giacomo Meyerbeer and painter Max Liebermann. *(Open M-Th 8am-4pm, F 8am-3pm. Men must cover their heads before entering the cemetery.)* Nearby stands the **Synagoge Rykestraße,** Rykestr. 53, one of Berlin's loveliest synagogues. It was spared on *Kristallnacht* thanks to its inconspicuous location in a courtyard.

ZEISS-GROSSPLANETARIUM. In 1987 this planetarium opened as the most modern facility of its kind in the DDR. Though compared to its peers in the West it seems about as technologically advanced as a *Trabi* (p. 638), it can still show you the stars. Call or check the web for show times. *(Prenzlauer Allee 80. S4, 8, or 85 to "Prenzlauer Allee"; it's across the bridge. ☎42 18 45 12; www.astw.de. €5, students €4.)*

 NIGHTLIFE

BARS AND CLUBS

Morgenrot, Kastanienallee 85 (☎44 31 78 44). U2 to "Eberswalder Str." Candy-print wallpaper and hip art lure young Prenzlberg dwellers off the Kastanianallee strip. By day, it's a vegetarian restaurant, by night, there are frosty vodka shots (€4) and a €4.50 *Milchkaffee* and cake deal. Th-Su vegetarian brunch buffet 11am-4pm. Open Tu-W 3pm-1am, Th-Su 11am-1am, F-Sa until 3am.

August Fengler, Lychener Str. 11 (☎44 35 66 40; www.augustfengler.de). U2 to "Eberswalder Str." Most Prenzlberg nightlife is either dirty or disposable, but this hip, homey cafe-bar with illustrated walls manages to avoid both extremes. DJs W-Th. Live music F-Sa (reggae, funk, house, jazz, Latin). Open daily from 7pm, music starts at 10pm.

Icon, Cantianstr. 15 (☎48 49 28 78; www.iconberlin.de). U2 to "Eberswalder Str." There's plenty of dancing in Icon's brick underground tunnels, and just enough light to flirt. Frequented by a generally young crowd. Cover €5-10. F hip-hop/reggae, Sa drum'n'bass, starting 11:30pm. Hours vary, check online for details.

Duncker, Dunckerstr. 64 (☎445 95 09). U2 to "Eberswalder Str." This small, dark and intense club mixes it up: Su-M goth, Tu hippie music, W parties, Th live bands, F-Sa varies. Garden with grill in back. Cover €2-4, Th often free. Partyers show up around 2am.

Knaack, Greifswalderstr. 224 (☎442 70 61; www.knaack-berlin.de). Tram #2, 3, or 4 to "Am Friedrichshain." 4-floored Knaack has an enviable infrastructure, with music ranging from disco to rock and punk—virtually everything but techno. Live music on the ground fl., billiards upstairs, occasional karaoke contests. **Internet** €1 per hr. (1hr. min.). Lots of touring bands, many foreign. Tickets available on the billiard floor; cover varies. Check schedule for details. Dance floors open F-Su and sometimes W at 11pm.

KulturBrauerei, Knaackstr. 97 (☎441 92 69; www.kulturbrauerei.de). U2 to "Eberswalder Str." Enormous party space in a former East German brewery. This expansive village of *Kultur* houses the highly popular clubs **Soda** and **Kesselhaus,** a Russian theater, upscale cafes, and an art school. Dance floors and stages abound. Music includes hardcore, *Ostrock,* disco, techno, reggae, *Schlager,* and more. Cover (like opening times) varies wildly among venues—€1.50-16 or more.

Pfefferberg, Schönhauser Allee 176 (☎44 38 33 42; www.pfefferberg.de). U2 or night bus N58 to "Senefelderpl." *Biergarten,* nightclub, cinema, and live music venue. Tango night may change your life, as could one of the after-hour parties that start around 6am. Cover free-€15. Garden open M-F from 3pm, Sa-Su from noon. Club open F-Sa.

Café Amsterdam, Gleimstr. 24 (☎448 07 92). S4, 8, or 85 or U2 to "Schönhauser Allee." Relaxed and romantic with gilt-framed paintings and sweet, creamy cocoa. Gay friendly. Pasta dishes (€6-7) until 11:30pm. Brunch Sa-Su from 10am. Open M-F from 4pm.

FRIEDRICHSHAIN

As the alternative scene follows low rents ever eastward and farther from the geographical center of the city, Friedrichshain is becoming its new temple. Relatively untouched since reunification, this *Bezirk* still retains much of its DDR atmosphere, from the pre-fab apartment houses and gray concrete to the massive remains of the Wall. The somewhat oppressive architecture is livened up by a bustling bar scene, second-hand clothing stores, and ethnic merchants. The central axis of the young populace is **Simon-Dach-Straße,** covered with sunsoaked outdoor seating and crowds of chic 20-somethings sipping elaborate cocktails. Farther north, the slightly grungier area around **Rigaerstraße** is a thriving stronghold of Berlin's legendary underground, home to squatter bars, makeshift clubs, and sidewalk punks with the inevitable assortment of excitable dogs. Lacking the laid-back cafe scene and wealth of conventional sights of which other *Bezirke* can boast, Friedrichshain embraces an individual flavor and up-and-coming atmosphere.

▌ ACCOMMODATIONS (HOSTELS)

Odyssee, Grünberger Str. 23 (☎29 00 00 81; www.hostel-berlin.de). U1 or 15, or S3, 5-7, 9, or 75 to "Warschauer Str.," or U5 to "Frankfurter Tor." A rarity: hip AND spotless. Someone sunk a lot of money into this place, but at €13 a night, it won't have been

BERLIN

Friedrichshain

▲ ACCOMMODATIONS
Odyssee, **3**
Sunflower Hostel, **10**

🍴 FOOD & DRINK
Cappuccino, **7**
Intimes, **2**
Yogi-Snack, **8**

🍸 BARS & NIGHTLIFE
Astro-Bar, **5**
Die Busche, **11**
Dachkammer Bar, **6**
Euphoria, **4**
Paule's Metal Eck, **9**

● SIGHTS
East Side Gallery, **12**
Gedenkstätte
Normannenstraße, **1**

you. Bar open until dawn. **Internet** €3 per hr. Breakfast €3. Sheets included. Reception 24hr. Reserve ahead. 8-bed dorms €13; doubles €45, with shower €52; triples €57; quads €68. 7th, 13th, and 14th nights free. Prices lower in winter. ❷

Sunflower Hostel, Helsingforser Str. 17 (☎44 04 42 50; www.sunflower-berlin.de). U1 or 15, or S3, 5-7, 9, or 75 to "Warschauer Str." Turn right out of the station and then left onto Helsingforserstr., closest to the river. Airy, relaxed, Eastern-style house, featuring a leafy lounge and 130 beds in simple, colorful rooms. The staff knows the nightlife scene unbelievably well. **Internet** €1.50 per 15min. Sheets and locks €3 deposit each. Laundry €4.50. Reception 24hr. 6- to 8-bed dorms €13-15; singles €35; doubles €45; triples €57; quads €68. 7th night free. ❷

❸ FOOD

Intimes, Boxhagener Str. 107 (☎29 66 64 57). U5 to "Frankfurter Tor." Don't be fooled by the makeshift sign—the tiled Mediterranean interior, hearty portions, numerous vegetarian options, and the lively nightlife of this Greek joint will win you over. Meals €6-11. Su brunch 10am-4pm (€8). Open daily from 10am. Kitchen open 10am-midnight. ❸

Yogi-Snack, Simon-Dach-Str. 11 (☎29 00 48 38). Friedrichshain fuels its curry addiction at this attractively dark Indian restaurant. Sizable entrees with salad and rice range €4-9. Wash it all down with a €1 spice-tinged Yogi Tea. Open daily noon-midnight. ❷

Cappuccino, Simon-Dach-Str. 7 (☎292 64 57). U5 to "Frankfurter Tor." A frantically popular hole-in-the-wall frequented by locals, serving up quality pastas and pizzas (€3-5) and gyros (€7) in an orange cave-like interior. Rinse with a flaming sambucca shot, usually free with any main dish. Open M-F 10am-1am, Sa-Su noon-1am. ❷

SIGHTS

▨ EAST SIDE GALLERY. The longest remaining portion of the Wall, this 1.3km stretch of cement slabs and asbestos also serves as the world's largest open-air art gallery, unsupervised and open at all hours. The murals are not remnants of Cold War graffiti, but rather the efforts of an international group of artists who gathered here in 1989 to celebrate the end of the city's division. It was expected that the wall would be destroyed soon after and the paintings lost, but in 2000, with this portion still standing, many of the same artists reconvened to repaint their work, covering the scrawlings of tourists; unfortunately, the new paintings are once again being rapidly eclipsed by graffitied scribblings, especially on the side toward Warschauer Str. (*Along Mühlenstr. Take U1 or 15 or S3, 5, 6, 7, 9, or 75 to "Warschauer Str." or S5, 7, 9, or 75 to "Ostbahnhof" and walk back toward the river.*)

KARL-MARX-ALLEE. The cornerstone of the East German National Construction Program, Karl-Marx-Allee became a showcase of the infant communist government in the early 1950s, when it was known as Stalinallee. Billed as Germany's "first socialist road," the broad avenue, widened in the 1960s to accommodate grandiose military parades, is flanked by scores of pre-fab gems, climaxing with the "people's palaces" at Strausberger Pl. (*U5 to "Strausberger Pl."*)

FORSCHUNGS- UND GEDENKSTÄTTE NORMANNENSTRAßE. The Lichtenberg suburb harbors perhaps the most hated and feared building of the DDR regime: the headquarters of the East German secret police, the **Staatssicherheit** or **Stasi.** During the Cold War, the Stasi kept dossiers on six million of their own citizens, in a country of only 16 million people. On January 15, 1990, a crowd of 100,000 Berliners stormed and vandalized the building to protest the police state. Since a 1991 law returned the records to the people, the "Horror Files" have rocked Germany, exposing millions of informants—and wrecking careers, marriages, and friendships—at all levels of society. Today, the building maintains its oppressive Orwellian drear and much of its worn 70s decor. The exhibit displays the offices of **Erich Mielke** (the loathed Minister for State Security from 1957 to 1989), a large collection of tiny microphones and hidden cameras used for surveillance by the Stasi, and a bizarre DDR Stasi shrine full of Lenin busts. *(Ruschestr. 103, Haus 1. U5 to "Magdalenenstr." From the station's Ruschestr. exit, walk up Ruschestr. and take a right at the sign on Normannenstr.; it's Haus #1 in the complex of office buildings. ☎553 68 54; www.stasi-museum.de. Exhibits in German. Open Tu-F 11am-6pm, Sa-Su 2-6pm. €3.50, students €2.50.)*

🔊 NIGHTLIFE

BARS AND CLUBS

Astro-Bar, Simon-Dach-Str. 40 (☎768 26 25; www.astro-bar.de). The rough edges of this retro-space locale are obscured by plenty of 70s plastic robots. Back room with many mod things to sit on and many mod things sitting on them. DJs spin anything from R&B to reggae to loud electronica. Cocktails €4.50-5.50. Open daily from 6pm.

Dachkammer Bar (DK), Simon-Dach-Str. 39 (☎296 16 73). U5 to "Frankfurter Tor." Rustic themed, with lots of brick, lots of wood, and lots of comfy places to relax. If you're lucky, someone will bring an acoustic guitar to serenade you while you enjoy snacks (from €4) and sip cocktails (€5-7). Open M-F noon-late, Sa-Su 10am-late.

Paule's Metal Eck, Krossener Str. 15 (☎291 16 24; www.paules-metal-eck.de). U5 to "Frankfurter Tor," on the corner of Simon-Dach-Str. A well-executed fake heavy metal bar—don't let the chihuahua skeletons or the hooded monk over the door scare you off. Beer €1.90-3.90, cocktails €3.50-6. Open noon until late.

Euphoria, Grünberger Str. 60 (☎29 00 46 83). U5 to "Frankfurter Tor," on the corner of Simon-Dach-Str. A bright-orange hot spot. The creatively-named cocktails (€4-8) are the way to go: bomb down an "Autobahn," replenish your "Red Power," investigate a "Monica & Bill," or float away with a "Pink Elephant." Open daily 9am-late.

GAY AND LESBIAN

☒ Die Busche, Mühlenstr. 12. U1, 12, or 15, or S3, 5-7, 9, or 75 to "Warschauer Str." East Berlin's most famous disco in the DDR days is still a color-saturated haven of dance, spinning an incongruous rotation of techno, top 40, and German *Schlager* to a mixed crowd. W night is a great midweek option for when most other gay/lesbian clubs are closed. Cover €3.50-5. Open W and F-Su from 10pm-5am, F-Sa until 6am.

KREUZBERG

Across the Spree and over the wall from Freidrichshain, Kreuzberg is West Germany's dose of counter-culture. A center of Berlin's alternative *Szene*, Kreuzberg's only certainty is unpredictability. In the 1960s and 70s, much of the area was occupied by *Hausbesetzer* (squatters) until a conservative city government forcibly evicted most of them in the early 80s. The ensuing riots threw the city into chaos; during President Reagan's 1985 visit to Berlin, authorities so feared protests from Kreuzberg that they cordoned off the whole district. Anti-government demonstrations are still frequent and intense; the most prominent is the annual May 1 demonstration, which brings out police helicopters, fire hoses, and Molotov cocktails. This *Bezirk*'s edgy anti-establishment reputation belies its incredible diversity. Home to an especially large segment of the city's immigrant and ethnic population, Kreuzberg boasts a staggering array of cheap food stands, sidewalk fruit vendors, and cafes. The atmosphere has been mixed up by recent

BERLIN

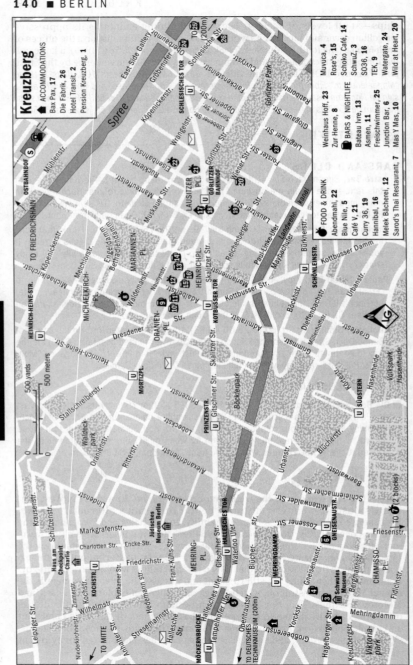

Kreuzberg

ACCOMMODATIONS
Bax Pax, **17**
Die Fabrik, **26**
Hotel Transit, **2**
Pension Kreuzberg, **1**

FOOD & DRINK
Abendmahl, **22**
Blue Nile, **5**
Café V, **21**
Curry 36, **19**
Hannibal, **16**
Melek Bäckerei, **12**
Sarod's Thai Restaurant, **7**

Weinhaus Hoff, **23**
Zur Henne, **8**

BARS & NIGHTLIFE
Bateau Ivre, **13**
Asmen, **11**
Freischwimmer, **25**
Junction Bar, **6**
Mas Y Mas, **10**

Muvuca, **4**
Rose's, **15**
Schoko Café, **14**
SchwuZ, **3**
SO36, **16**
TEK, **9**
Watergate, **24**
Wild at Heart, **20**

renovations bringing a wave of gentrification in the form of prepsters and sober government workers. Kreuzberg defiantly rejects stereotypes, presenting instead a kaleidoscopic mix of people who keep the dynamic scene perpetually grooving.

ACCOMMODATIONS

HOSTELS

Die Fabrik, Schlesische Str. 18 (☎611 71 16; www.diefabrik.com). U1 or 15 to "Schlesisches Tor" or night bus #N65 to "Taborstr." Frequented by a slightly older clientele, this classy former factory now has spacious rooms and a classy leather and glass lounge. Easy access to Kreuzberg nightlife and no curfew. Reception 24hr. Surprisingly comfortable "sleep-in" deal puts you in a 7-bed dorm for €18, €15 in winter; singles €38/€32; doubles €52-64/€42-56; triples €69/€60; quads €84/€76. ❷

Hotel Transit, Hagelberger Str. 53-54 (☎ 789 04 70; fax 78 90 47 77). U6 or 7, or night bus #N19 to "Mehringdamm." Modern rooms with bath overlooking a courtyard in this friendly (and gay-friendly) hotel. **Internet** €6 per hr. Breakfast included. Reception 24hr. 3- to 6- bed Dorms €15; singles €52; doubles €60; quads €104. ❷

Bax Pax, Skalitzer Str. 104 (☎69 51 83 22; www.baxpax.de). U1 or 15 to "Görlitzer Bahnhof," right across the street. Run by the same friendly people as Mitte's Backpacker Hostel. At the start of mighty Oranienstr., with a pool table, fuzzy blue carpets, and a bed inside a VW Bug (ask for room 3). Kitchen facilities. **Internet** €3 per hr. Sheets €2.50. Reception 24hr. Big dorms €12; 8-bed dorms €15; 6- to 7-bed dorms €16; 4- to 5-bed dorms €18; singles €30; doubles €46; triples €60. Prices lower in winter. ❷

HOTELS

Pension Kreuzberg, Großbeerenstr. 64 (☎251 13 62; www.pension-kreuzberg.de). U6 or 7 or night bus #N19 to "Mehringdamm." Gorgeous staircases, a cheery yellow breakfast room and antique iron stoves in some rooms. Neighborhood is lively, even for Kreuzberg. Breakfast included. Reception 8am-10pm. Singles €40; doubles €52. Larger rooms €22.50 per person. ❹

FOOD

■ **Zur Henne,** Leuschnerdamm 25 (☎614 77 30). U1 or 15 to "Kottbusser Tor." Though this charming, traditional German restaurant does serve other dishes (€2.50-6), virtually everyone orders the famous *Brathänchen* (fried chicken), arguably the best in Berlin. Always packed, reserve a table in advance. Open Tu-Su 7pm-late. ❷

Café V, Lausitzer Pl. 12 (☎612 45 05). U1 or 15 to "Görlitzer Bahnhof." Top-of-the-line, bottom of the food chain. Berlin's oldest vegetarian restaurant, featuring vegan and fish entrees served in a romantic yellow interior. Try the spinach balls in cheese sauce (€8.80) or any of the equally tasty specials (€6-8). Open daily 10am-late. ❸

Abendmahl, Muskauer Str. 9 (☎612 51 70; www.abendmahl-berlin.de). U1 or 15 to "Görlitzer Bahnhof." A favorite of gay and lesbian Berliners. Vegetarian and fish entrees (sorrel cream soup €6.50) are upstaged by the fabulously macabre desserts—the "Last Date" is ice cream petit-fours shaped like coffins (€8.50). If you can't afford the meal of your choice, buy a postcard of it. Open daily from 6pm. ❹

Melek Bäckerei, Oranienstr. 28 (☎614 51 86). U1, 8, or 15 to "Kottbußer Tor." Popular sweets shop has delicious Turkish pastries for pocket change. 100g baklava €0.80. Open 24hr. to accommodate the sugar-deprivation cravings of late-night partygoers. ❶

Weinhaus Hoff, Reichenberger Str. 116 (☎342 08 13; www.weinhaus-hoff.de). U1 or 15 to "Görlitzer Bahnhof." Delicious Swabian specialties in an out-of-the-way restaurant lined with wine bottles. Pork filet with mushroom cream and *Spätzle* is a house specialty (€7.50). Open M-Sa 4pm-midnight. ❸

FLEEING THE EAST

Almost 2.7 million East Germans fled the DDR from 1949-1961, so the communist regime built a wall to "protect" its citizens from the purportedly evil influences of the capitalist West. Nearly 96 miles of cement and 302 watch towers weren't enough; countless patrol dogs were trained, car-trapping trenches were dug, and endless restrictions were put on buildings near the wall.

But the government could not prevent an estimated 40,100 "barrier breakers," more than half within the first four years of the Wall's construction, from successfully leaving the communist East between 1961 and 1989. Some seeking reunions with long-lost family, others simply a better life, these East Germans went to extremes to escape: over and under ground, through air and water, often risking their lives.

Westerner Kurt Wordel smuggled over 55 people past Checkpoint Charlie from 1964-66 under the hood of his Volkswagen. Wordel and other "escape helpers" also made fake passports from places like Monaco and Andorra. Mothers dropped their babies from 4th-floor windows on Bernauer Str. into safety nets on the western side, and over 2000 East German soldiers and police used their positions of authority to flee the DDR.

For East Berliners, escape often required the help of strangers, like in the case of Tunnel 57,

Blue Nile, Tempelhofer Ufer 6 (☎25 29 46 55). U1 or 15 to "Möcknerbrücke," or U6 to "Hallesches Tor." Its location is remote and service is slow, but honey wine (€2.50) sweetens the wait. Meals come on *injera,* a spongy Ethiopian sourdough bread. Vegetarian or meat combos (€7-12) big enough to share. Open daily from 3pm. ❸

Hannibal, corner of Wienerstr. and Skalitzerstr. (☎611 23 88). U1, 12, or 15, or night bus #N29 to "Görlitzer Bahnhof." Eclectic: an alligator on the bar; turf on the ceiling; comfy sofas and hard benches. Good for a leisurely breakfast, massive Hannibal-burger (€6), or fruit smoothie (€2.90). Open M-Th 8am-3am, F-Sa 8am-4am, Su 9am-3am. ❷

Sarod's Thai Restaurant, Friesenstr. 22 (☎69 50 73 33). U7 to "Gneisenaustr." Mostly known for its €5 all-you-can-eat Thai lunch special (M-F noon-4pm), Sarod has a menu including over 150 choices. Open M-F noon-11:30pm, Sa-Su 2pm-11:30pm. ❷

Curry 36, Mehringdamm 36. U6 or 7 to "Mehringdamm." Ideally located next to several clubs, Curry 36 serves up some of the best curry sausages in Berlin as well as burgers and other fast food (€2-4). Be prepared to take your place in a long line of police officers, clubbers, and taxi drivers. Open M-F 9am-4am, Sa 10am-4am, Su 11am-3am. ❶

👁 SIGHTS

▨ HAUS AM CHECKPOINT CHARLIE. From its beginnings as a 2½-bedroom apartment, this eccentric museum at the famous border-crossing point has become one of Berlin's most popular attractions. A strange mix of earnest eastern sincerity and glossy western salesmanship, the museum is a wonderfully cluttered collection of artwork, newspaper clippings, and photographs mixed in with all types of devices used to get over, under, or through the wall. The exhibits detail how women curled up in loudspeakers, men attempted to crawl through spike-laden gates, and student groups dug tunnels with their fingers, all in an attempt to reach the West. In and surrounding the museum are a clutter of shops selling all things Wall-related, while out on the street, the unassuming station itself is overshadowed by two large photos of an American and a Russian soldier looking into "enemy" territory. *(Friedrichstr. 43-45. U6 to "Kochstr." ☎253 72 50; www.mauer-museum.com. Museum open daily 9am-10pm. German-language films every 2hr. from 9:30am. €9.50, students €5.50.)*

AROUND MEHRINGDAMM. The broad thoroughfare of Mehringdamm runs through a vibrant, quickly gentrifying area of Kreuzberg. Around Chamissopl.,

Bergmannstr. holds an especially large number of popular cafes, second-hand clothing stores, and used music shops, while the quieter Fidicinstr. is lined with some of Berlin's most graceful old facades. To the north is the nightlife hotspot Gneisenaustr., filled with lively bars and clubs. On the other side of Mehringdamm, the forested Viktoriapark contains Kreuzberg's namesake, a 66m hill featuring Berlin's only waterfall, and an artificial one at that. South of it all is the **Platz der Luftbrücke,** a flower-ringed field with a monument known as the *Hungerharke* (hunger rake) to Berliners and dedicated to the 78 pilots who lost their lives in the 328 days of the Berlin Airlift. *(U6 to "Platz der Luftbrücke" or U6 or 7 to "Mehringdamm.")*

ORANIENSTRAßE. This colorful mix of cafes, bars, and stores boast a more radical element: the May Day parades always start on Oranienpl., the site of frequent riots in the 1980s. Revolutionaries jostle shoulders with Turkish families, while an anarchist punk faction and a boisterous gay and lesbian population make things interesting after hours (see **Nightlife,** p. 144). Restaurants, clubs, and shops of staggering diversity beckon to passersby. *(U1 or 15 to "Kottbusser Tor" or "Görlitzer Bahnhof.")*

EASTERN KREUZBERG. The **Landwehrkanal,** a channel bisecting Kreuzberg, is where the Freikorps threw Rosa Luxemburg's body after murdering her in 1919 (see p. 55). The tree-dotted strip of the canal near Kottbusser Damm, **Paul-Linke-Ufer,** is pleasant and shady, popular with families and runners. *(U8 to "Schönleinstr.")* This ethnic part of town—especially near **Schlesisches Tor** and the former Wall—is rich in Balkan and Turkish restaurants. The **Oberbaumbrücke** spanning the Spree was once a border crossing into East Berlin; it now serves as an entrance to Friedrichshain's nightlife scene. *(U1 or 15 to "Schlesisches Tor.")*

🏛 MUSEUMS (INDEPENDENT)

▓ JÜDISCHES MUSEUM BERLIN. Daniel Libeskind's design for this zinc-plated museum is fascinating simply as an architectural experience. No two walls are parallel, and jagged hallways end in windows overlooking "the void" frequently enough to make any visitor uncomfortable. Wander through the labyrinthine "Garden of Exile" or experience the chill of being shut in the "Holocaust Tower," a giant, asymmetrical concrete room nearly devoid of light and sound. Exhibits feature works by contemporary artists, memorials to victims of the Holocaust, and a history of Jews in Germany. Enter through the older-looking building next door. Ticket includes entry to a

built entirely by university students who sacrificed their studies for 10 months without pay to build the longest known tunnel (145m) and facilitate the escape of 57 fellow Berliners in October 1964. Other escapes necessitated deep betrayal; in order to bring his wife into West Berlin, Peter Selle seduced a similar-looking West German girl, took her across the border, and then stole her papers. The girlfriend was held for two months and Selle was jailed for four months once he returned to West Berlin.

Escape to the West was risky to say the least. A class of East German students jumped onto the moving Moscow-Paris express train, one artist swung hand over hand along an 11,000-volt transmission line, and 28-year-old Peter Faust built an inflatable boat with hockey-stick-sails and rowed across the Baltic Sea.

Perhaps most famous is the story of the Strelzyles and Wetzels, two four-person families who together built a hot-air balloon out of 1250m^2 of fabric and squeezed into less than 2m^2 of floor space as they flew 28 minutes at 30mph from Oberlemnitz in the East to Naila in the West.

Not all escape attempts were successful; 628 East Germans have been deemed "casualties of the Wall," and over 3200 were arrested in their flight.

*For more information about the Berlin Wall and these or similar escape attempts, visit the **Haus am Checkpoint Charlie** (p. 142).*

second exhibit located near Hackescher Markt, at Rosenthalerstr. 33, which memorializes Otto Weidt, a German who tried to rescue Jews from deportation. *(Lindenstr. 9-14. U6 to "Kochstr." or U1, 6, or 15 to "Hallesches Tor." ☎ 308 78 56 81; www.jmberlin.de. Open daily 10am-8pm, M until 10pm. €5, students €2.50.)*

DEUTSCHES TECHNIKMUSEUM. Sporting an airplane on the roof, this colossal museum includes aged trains, a history of film technology, and plenty of model ships. Across the parking lot, another building features a collection of classic cars, music makers, a plethora of science experiments involving optical illusions, and, best of all, a revolving playhouse. A new aeronautical wing is under construction, slated for completion in spring 2005. Many exhibits are in English. *(Trebbiner Str. 9. U1, 2, or 15 to "Gleisdreieck" or U1, 7, or 15 to "Möckernbrücke." ☎ 90 25 40; www.dtmb.de. Open Tu-F 9am-5:30pm, Sa-Su 10am-6pm. €3, students €1.50. 1st Su of the month free.)*

MÄRKISCHES MUSEUM. Two millennia of Berlin artifacts are displayed in this museum, including a permanent exhibition entitled "Look at this city!" tracing the history and cultural history of Berlin from the Middle Ages to the present. *(Am Köllnischen Park 5. U2 to "Märkisches Museum." Take Wallstr. past Inselstr.; it's on the right. ☎ 30 86 60; www.stadtmuseum.de. Open Tu-Su 10am-6pm. €4, students €2. W free.)*

SCHWULES MUSEUM. A series of rotating exhibitions and preserved documents and objects that shed light on the past and current lifestyles of gays and lesbians. A permanent exhibit, new in December 2004, traces the history of homosexuals in Germany (and especially in Berlin) from 1800 to 1970. *(Mehringdamm 61. ☎ 69 59 90 50. Open Tu-F 2-6pm, Sa 2-7pm. €5, students €3.)*

◧ NIGHTLIFE

Although clubs are emerging throughout the rest of eastern Berlin (namely Friedrichshain) Kreuzberg is still a nightlife *Bezirk*, full of options for virtually every demographic.

BARS AND CLUBS

▨ **Freischwimmer,** vor dem Schlesischen Tor 2 (☎ 61 07 43 09). U1 or 15 to "Schlesisches Tor" or night bus #N65 to "Heckmannufer." A mess of waterside tables tangled in roses—indoors or outdoors; with chubby sofas or in boats. Food until midnight, F-Sa until 1am. F a roll of the die determines the cover charge (€1-6). M poetry reading then a party. Su brunch (€8.20, 11am-4pm). Open M-F from noon, Sa-Su from 11am.

▨ **SO36,** Oranienstr. 190 (☎ 61 40 13 06; www.SO36.de). U1, 12, or 15 to "Görlitzer Bahnhof" or night bus #N29 to "Heinrichpl." Berlin's best mixed club, where everyone grooves to a mish-mash of wild genres. Massive, dark dance fl. M is "electric ballroom," a techno party hosted by Berlin's up-and-coming DJs and big-screen anime. Th hip-hop, reggae, punk, ska, or concerts. F-Su range from techno to live concerts. Last Sa of every month is gay night. Cover for parties €4-8, concerts €7-18. Open daily from 11pm.

Wild at Heart, Wiener Str. 20 (☎ 61 07 47 01; www.wildatheartberlin.de). U1, 12, or 15 to "Görlitzer Bahnhof." A red cave of decadence: shrines to Elvis, Chinese lanterns, fuzzy hearts, flaming booths, tiki torches, and glowing tigers. Pierced and punked clientele. Live bands usually 4 times per wk., almost always Sa and Su. Open daily from 8pm.

Bateau Ivre, Oranienstr. 18 (☎ 61 40 36 59). U1, 12, or 15 to "Görlitzer Bahnhof." Locals relax over coffee or beer (€2.30-3.40) at this friendly bistro-bar before shakin' it across the street at SO36, making late night tables a hot commodity. In the morning, weary clubbers stagger in, looking for breakfast after a long night. Open daily 9am-late.

TEK, Oranienstr. 36. U1, 8, or 15 to Kotbusser Tor. Catering to a relatively young crowd, this bar offers cheap drinks (wine and Hefeweizen €2, Becks €1.60) and a down-to-earth atmosphere. Movies Su at 8pm. Open W-F and Su from 5pm.

Muvuca, Mehringhof, Gneisenaustr. 2a (☎693 01 75; www.muvuca.de). U6 or 7, or night bus #N4, 19, or 76 to "Mehringdamm." A bar, venue, Afro-Brazilian eatery, and club run by a socialist collective in a steel and concrete courtyard. Hosts political meetings, (primarily) lesbian events, and an anarchist bookstore. Open Tu-Su 3pm-late.

Mas Y Mas, Oranienstr. 167 (☎61 65 81 78). U1, 12, or 15 to "Görlitzer Bahnhof." With gold-striped walls, chandeliers, and sultry Latin music, this bar is steeped in a darkly elegant atmosphere. Fantastic drinks have names like "Income Tax" or "Wedding Bells." Happy hour (daily 6-9pm and 1-2am, and all day W) cocktails €4. Open daily 6pm-late.

Junction Bar, Gneisenaustr. 18 (☎694 66 02; www.junction-bar.de). U7 to "Gneisenaustr." or night bus #N4 or 19 to "Zossener Str." A small but jumpin' venue for American music, featuring nightly shows crowded with older partyers. Live rock, soul, funk, jazz, or blues Su-Th from 9pm, F-Sa 10pm. DJs start Su-Th 11:30pm, F-Sa 12:30am. Cover €6 for live music and DJs. Cover for DJs only Su-Th €3, F-Sa €4.50. Take a break at **Junction Cafe** upstairs (open 11am-2am).

Asmen, Oranienstr. 170 (☎81 79 73 08). U1, 12, or 15 to "Görlitzer Bahnhof." Yet another bar on Oranienstr. Wide selection of cocktails (€5-8) and other drinks (€2-4). Happy hour daily 5-10pm. Cocktails €4.50. Open M-F 5pm-2am, Sa-Su 5pm-late.

Watergate, Falckensteinstr. 49 (☎61 28 03 95; www.water-gate.de). U1 or 15 to "Schlesisches Tor." Currently one of the hippest clubs in Berlin, with 2 floors and rotating DJs. The view of the Spree from the lower-level "Water Floor" lounge is amazing. Cover €6-10. Open Th-Sa 11pm-late.

GAY AND LESBIAN

Most bars and clubs here are on and around Oranienstr. between Lausitzer Pl. and Oranienpl. Take U1, 8, 12, or 15 to "Kottbußer Tor" or U1, 12, or 15 to "Görlitzer Bahnhof." After hours, night bus #N29 runs the length of the strip.

▨ **Rose's,** Oranienstr. 187 (☎615 65 70). U1, 12, or 15 to "Görlitzer Bahnhof." Marked only by "Bar" over the door. It's Liberace meets Cupid meets Satan. A friendly, mixed gay and lesbian clientele packs this intense and claustrophobic party spot at all hours of the night. The voluptuous dark-red interior is accessorized madness, boasting hearts, glowing lips, furry ceilings, feathers, and glitter. Margaritas €4. Open daily 10pm-6am.

▨ **SchwuZ,** Mehringdamm 61 (☎62 90 880; www.schwuz.de). U6 or 7 to "Mehringdamm." Hidden behind **Sundström,** a popular gay and lesbian cafe. Features 2 small dance floors and a lounge area with

THE LOCAL STORY

WALKING MAN

The easiest way to decide if you're in East or West Berlin is not to pull out your map, but to look at the pedestrian traffic lights. When you cross the streets in most of West Berlin, you see a standard crossing light: a green walking man telling you to go, and a red standing man telling you to stop. In East Berlin, the crossing light figures are thicker and more eye-catching. The green walking man strides jauntily forward with his hat cocked back; the red standing man (still hatted) throws both arms fully to the sides.

The crossing-man of eastern Berlin, known as the *Ampel-Männchen,* or "little traffic-light guy," was created by traffic psychologist Karl Peglau in 1961 during the days of the DDR. Its simple, cheerful design was meant to appeal to children, but the Ampel-Männchen is beloved by just about everyone.

When the city was reunified, plans were made to standardize the symbols. Eastern Berliners protested, starting a "Save the Ampel-Männchen" campaign. Not only did the little man remain on traffic lights in East Berlin, but he soon showed up on t-shirts, mouse pads, key-chains, and candy sold at most souvenir shops. The Ampel-Männchen is such a popular icon that designers and artists have dedicated entire exhibits to him. Though many would like to forget the legacies of the East, this form of *Ostalgie* is fondly embraced.

its own DJ. Music varies from alternative to house depending on the night (check *Siege-ssäule*), every 2nd F of the month is for lesbians. Frequented by a relatively young, chill crowd. Cover €4-8. Open F-Sa from 11pm.

Schoko-Café, Mariannenstr. 6 (☎615 15 61; www.schoko-fabrik.de). Lesbian central; a bright and colorful cafe with billiards, Turkish baths, a cultural center, and innumerable other women-only services. Dancing every 2nd Sa of the month (from 10pm) and cultural events every weekend. Friendly and laid-back. Open daily from 5pm.

OUTER DISTRICTS

Berlin's outer districts, primarily residential neighborhoods surrounded by greenery, provide a pleasant respite from the bustle of the metropolis. The vast **Treptow** park is a relaxing locale for summer lounging, **Wannsee** is where Berlin goes to the beach, and **Oranienburg** contains the sobering former concentration camp **Sachsenhausen.** **Dahlem's** suburban streets are home to affluent professionals, the sprawling **Freie Universität,** and one of Berlin's federally controlled museum complexes. **Spandau** is one of the oldest parts of Berlin and in many ways remains a stubbornly independent city, with a lively pedestrian zone, stately archaic houses, and glitzy car dealerships. Neighboring **Steglitz** is remarkable only for its trendy shopping district (U9 to "Schloßstr.") and expansive botanical garden. All of these districts are 20-50min. by train from the heart of the city and make good daytrips.

▐ ACCOMMODATIONS (HOSTELS)

TEGEL

Jugendgästehaus Tegel, Ziekowstr. 161 (☎433 30 46; JGH-Tegel@t-online.de). S25 to "Tegel" or U6 to "Alt-Tegel," then bus #222 or night bus #N22 (dir.: Alt-Lübars) to "Titusweg." A stately red brick building with the feel of a Victorian boarding school. **Free Internet** on a single computer. Breakfast and sheets included. Reception 7:30am-11pm. Singles €27; doubles to 8-bed dorms €20 per person. Under 27 only. ❸

Backpacker's Paradise, Ziekowstr. 161 (☎433 86 40). Nightly campfires and good hot showers in a little lot behind the *Jugendgästehaus.* A hotspot on the Italian Eurail circuit. Space is nearly always available. The *Kantine* serves a breakfast buffet (€2) and cheap snacks (open 8-11am and 6-11pm). Lockers €0.50. Laundry €3. Reception 24hr. Open mid-June to Aug. €6 gets you a blanket and foam pad in a 20-person tent, €1.50 more provides a cot to put them on. Under 27 only. ❶

WANNSEE

Jugendgästehaus am Wannsee (HI), Badeweg 1 (☎803 20 34; www.jugendherberge.de). S1 or 7 to "Nikolassee." From the main exit, cross the bridge, continue through the park, and head left on Kronprinzessinweg; Badeweg will be on your right after 5min. Many German school groups frequent this pseudo-dorm with a lake view, 30min. from central Berlin. Patio chess with knee-high pieces. Breakfast and sheets included. Key deposit €10. Reservations recommended. €23.10, under 27 €19. ❷

◉ SIGHTS

For excursions to Potsdam, see **Brandenburg** (p. 151).

WANNSEE

Most Berliners think of the town of Wannsee, on a lake of the same name, as the beach. Wannsee has long stretches of sand along the Havel-Uferpromenade, and the roads behind the beaches are crowded with vacation villas. To reach the locally beloved baths, **Wannsee Strandbad,** take S1 or 7 to "Nikolassee," cross the bridge in front of the main exit, continue through the park, and follow the signs down the road in the same direction. Getting to the beach along the Uferprome-nade is more complicated: take S1 or 7 to "Wannsee," then bus #114 to "Haus der Wannsee-Konferenz." Walk along Am Großen Wannsee to Haveleck. Or, take bus #A16 from the Wannsee station to "Pfaueninsel," backtrack to Pfaueninsel-Chaus-see, and take it to Uferpromenade, which will appear on your right. On summer weekends, a special bus shuttles bathers from the train station. The beach fills up absurdly early with German families; be prepared to battle the crowds for choice spots. *(Baths open May-Aug. M-F 10am-5pm, Sa-Su 8am-8pm. €4, students €2.50.)*

HAUS DER WANNSEE-KONFERENZ. Wannsee's reputation is tarnished by the memory of the notorious **Wannsee Conference** on January 20, 1942. Leading offi-cials of the SS completed the details for the implementation of the "Final Solu-tion"—including the deportation and murder of all Europe's Jews—in the **Wannsee Villa,** formerly a Gestapo intelligence center. In January 1992, the 50th anniversary of the Nazi death-pact, the villa reopened as a museum with permanent Holocaust exhibits and a documentary film series. The villa is discomfortingly lovely, and the exhibit is gripping. *(Am Großen Wannsee 56-58. Take bus #114 from the S-Bahn station to "Haus der Wannsee-Konferenz." ☎ 805 00 10. Open M-F 10am-8pm. Free.)*

PFAUENINSEL. The banks of Peacock Island (the second largest island in Berlin) served as the perfect setting for Friedrich Wilhelm II's "ruined" castle, where he and his mistress could romp for hours. A flock of the island's namesake fowl roams about the gardens surrounding the fairy-tale castle. *(Take bus #216 or 316 from the S-Bahn station to "Pfaueninsel" and hop on the ferry. Castle open daily May-Aug. 8am-8pm; Apr. and Sept. 8am-6pm; Oct. 9am-5pm; Nov.-Feb. 10am-4pm. €1.)*

GLIENICKER BRÜCKE. At the southwestern corner of the district, this bridge crosses the Havel River into Potsdam and the former DDR. Closed to traffic in Cold War days, it was the spot where East and West once exchanged captured spies. The most famous such incident traded American U2 pilot Gary Powers for Soviet spy Ivanovich Abel. For sights on the other side of the bridge, see p. 154. *(Bus #116 from the S-Bahn station (dir.: Glienicker Brücke–Potsdam) to the end.)*

WANNSEE CRUISES. Two ferry companies run boats from the Wannsee water-front behind the park. Boats set sail once or twice an hour, though the ferries' lei-surely pace means that they're meant more as pleasure cruises than efficient transportation. *(Across Kronprinzessinweg from S-Bahn station "Wannsee." Call **Stern und Kreis** at ☎ 803 87 50 or **Reederverband** at ☎ 803 87 53 for details. Most cruises €7-10.)*

TREPTOW

SOWJETISCHES EHRENMAL. This powerful Soviet War Memorial is a mammoth promenade built with marble taken from Hitler's Chancellery. The Soviets dedi-cated the site in 1948, honoring the millions of Red Army soldiers who fell in what Russians call the "Great Patriotic War." Massive granite slabs along the walk are adorned with quotations from Stalin and depictions of terrifying war scenes, while the colossal bronze figure at the head of the promenade symbolically crushes Nazism underfoot. Even the trees are designed to bow towards this gargantuan stoic soldier; the total effect is a little grandiose, but very moving. Buried beneath the trees surrounding the monument are the bodies of 5000 unknown Soviet sol-diers who died in the Battle of Berlin in 1945. *(S4, 6, 8, 9, or 85 to "Treptower Park." Exit on the Puschkinallee side and walk into the forest, away from the station. Eventually, the path opens out onto an expansive garden; across the street to the right is a massive stone arch leading to the monument.)*

BERLIN

TREPTOWER PARK. On the banks of the Spree, this relaxed stretch of green contains more than just the Soviet Memorial. **Stern und Kreis,** which runs ferry tours all along the river, is based here, as are several shops and waterfront cafes. Berliners come to the park to picnic, throw boomerangs, or just stretch out semi-nude on the grassy expanse. Also in the park is the **Figurentheater,** where wooden puppets perform a variety of *Märchen* (fairy tales). Follow the yellow signs. *(Puschkinallee 15a. ☎ 53 69 51 50. Performances €4.30-9.)*

ORANIENBURG AND SACHSENHAUSEN

KZ SACHSENHAUSEN. The small town of Oranienburg, just north of Berlin, was home to the Nazi concentration camp Sachsenhausen, where more than 100,000 Jews, communists, intellectuals, gypsies, and homosexuals were killed between 1936 and 1945. The **Gedenkstätte Sachsenhausen,** a memorial preserving the remains of the camp and recalling those imprisoned in it, was opened by the DDR in 1961. Some of the buildings have been preserved in their original forms, including sets of cramped barracks, the cell block where particularly "dangerous" prisoners were kept in solitary confinement and tortured daily, and a pathology department where Nazis performed medical experiments on inmates both dead and alive. However, only the foundations of **Station Z** (where prisoners were methodically exterminated) remain. A stone monolith commemorating the camp's victims stands sentinel over the wind-swept grounds and several small museums. **Barracks 38 and 39,** the special "Jewish-only" barracks torched by right-wing extremists in 1992 and since reconstructed, feature displays on daily life in the camp during the Nazi period and the history of the barracks. The jail block contains a **museum** detailing its uses and the punishments inflicted there, along with rotating exhibits on individual prisoners. The museum buildings and *Industriehof* contain broader exhibits on Sachsenhausen. A DDR slant is still apparent; the main museum building features Socialist Realist stained-glass windows memorializing "German Anti-Fascist Martyrs." Even more than the exhibits, the blunt gray buildings, barbed-wire fencing, and vast, bleak spaces express the camp's brutality and despair. *(Str. der Nationen 22. S1 (dir.: Oranienburg) to the end (40min.). Then either use the infrequent bus service on lines 804/821 to "Gedenkstätte" or take a 15-20min. walk from the station. Follow the signs from Straslunderstr., turn right on Bernauer Str., left on Str. der Einheit, and right on Str. der Nationen. ☎ 03301 20 00; www.gedenkstaette-sachsenhausen.de. Open daily Mar. 15-Oct. 15 8:30am-6pm; Oct. 16-Mar. 14 8:30am-4:30pm. Last entry 30min. before closing. Museums closed M. Free. Audio tour rental €3.50.)*

SPANDAU

ZITADELLE. This is the medieval fort you dreamed of as a kid. Rising sternly from the water, accessible only by a single stone bridge, Spandau's citadel was considered impregnable in the 16th and 17th centuries. During WWII, the Nazis used the fort as a chemical weapons lab, and in 1945 the Allies employed the Zitadelle as a prison to hold war criminals before the Nuremberg Trials. Nowadays the citadel is a sort of wistful ghost town filled with old field-cannons, statues, a **medieval history museum,** and a variety of art galleries. The solid brick facade is overgrown with ivy, and the ramparts are carpeted in fields of grass. The thickly fortified **Juliusturm,** dating to circa 1200, is Spandau's unofficial symbol. *(Am Juliusturm. Take U7 to "Zitadelle." ☎ 354 94 42 00. Open Tu-F 9am-5pm, Sa-Su 10am-5pm. Last entry 30min. before closing. Museum and tower €2.50, students €1.50.)*

STEGLITZ

BOTANISCHER GARTEN. The Botanischer Garten is one of the best botanical gardens in the world, featuring everything from orderly English gardens and Japanese koi ponds to rolling meadows and vast greenhouses (lush even in winter). Put simply, the combined scent is divine. *(Königin-Luise-Str. 6. S1 to "Botanischer Garten." Follow the signs from the S-Bahn station. ☎83 85 01 00. Open daily May-July 9am-9pm; Apr. and Aug. 9am-8pm; Sept. 9am-7pm; Mar. and Oct. 9am-6pm; Feb. 9am-5pm; Nov.-Jan. 9am-4pm; Last admission 30min. before closing. Museum open daily 10am-6pm. Museum and gardens €5, students €2.50; 2hr. before closing €2/€1. Museum only €2/€1.)*

🏛 MUSEUMS

SMB-PK DAHLEM

The **Museen Dahlem** consists of the three museums, all housed in one enormous building in the center of Dahlem's Freie Universität. The **Museum Europäischer Kulturen,** also part of the complex, is located a couple of blocks away.

■ ETHNOLOGISCHES MUSEUM. The Ethnology Museum dominates the main building and richly rewards a trek to Dahlem. The exhibits are stunning, ranging from huge pieces of ancient Central American stonework to African elephant tusk statuettes to enormous, authentic boats from the South Pacific. While smaller, the **Museum für Indisches Kunst** (Museum for Indian Art), housed in the same building, is no less fascinating, featuring ornate gilded shrines and brightly painted murals. The **Museum für Ostasiatisches Kunst** (Museum for East Asian Art) also has a good collection, including many fanciful tapestries. Both the Museum for Indian Art and the Museum for East Asian Art offer computer exhibits for children. *(U1 to "Dahlem-Dorf" and follow the "Museen" signs to get to the main building. ☎830 14 38. Open Tu-F 10am-6pm, Sa-Su 11am-6pm. €3, students €1.50.)*

MUSEUM EUROPÄISCHER KULTUREN. This part of Dahlem's museum complex features the permanent exhibit "Cultural contacts in Europe," which uses pictures to show how European cultures developed through communication with one another. *(From the main building, turn right out the front door onto Lansstr. Turn left onto Takustr., right onto Königin-Luise-Str., and left onto Im Winkel. The museum is on the left where the road forks. ☎83 90 12 79. Open Tu-F 10am-6pm, Sa-Su 11am-6pm. €3, students €1.50.)*

🎭 NIGHTLIFE (TREPTOW)

▩ Insel der Jugend, Alt-Treptow 6 (☎533 71 69; www.insel-berlin.com). S4, 6, 8, or 9 to "Treptower Park," then bus #265 or N65 to "Rathaus Treptow." The name may mean "island of youth," but Pinocchio never had it this good. The club, located on an island in the Spree River, is a tower of 3 winding stories crammed with gyrating bodies, multiple bars, river-side couches, an open-air movie theater, and a sweet little cafe. Depending on the night, the top 2 floors spin reggae, hip-hop, ska, and house (sometimes all at once), while the techno scene in the basement is generally as frantic as can be. Club cover W free, Th-Sa €4-6. Club open W from 7pm, F-Sa from 10pm, sometimes Th from 9pm. Cafe open Sa-Su from 2pm. Movies M- Tu, Th, Su; €5-8.

BRANDENBURG

Completely surrounding Berlin, the *Land* of Brandenburg is a perfect escape from the sprawling urban behemoth within it. The infamous **Hohenzollern** family emerged from the province's forests to become the rulers of Prussia, leaving their mark on the region in the shape of more than 30 stunning palaces. The castles attract their share of visitors to Brandenburg, especially the sprawling **Sanssouci,** at only a 30min. train trip away, a favorite jaunt for native Berliners.

HIGHLIGHTS OF BRANDENBURG

RINSE AWAY the (figurative) grit of Berlin with a visit to the refreshingly lavish Park Sanssouci (p. 153) in regal Potsdam (p. 151).

LOUNGE IN A GONDOLA on the winding canals near tiny Lübbenau (p. 159), under the trees and among the ghosts of the swampy Spreewald (p. 157).

POTSDAM   ☎ 0331

Visitors disappointed by Berlin's distinctly unroyal demeanor can get their Kaiserly fix by taking the S-Bahn to nearby Potsdam, the glittering city of **Friedrich II** (the Great). While his father, **Friedrich Wilhelm I** ("the Soldier King"), wanted to turn Potsdam into a huge garrison of the tall, tall men he had kidnapped to serve as his toy soldiers, the more aesthetically minded Friedrich II beautified the city with **Schloß Sanssouci** and the surrounding park, and the nearby **Neues Garten** with its **Marmorpalais**. Potsdam was Germany's "Little Hollywood" in the 1920s and 30s, when the suburb of **Babelsberg** played a critical role in the early film industry. A 20min. air raid in April 1945 brought Potsdam's glory days to an end. As the site of the 1945 **Potsdam Conference**, in which the Allies divvied up the country, Potsdam's name became synonymous with German defeat. After hosting Communist Party fat cats for 45 years, the 1000-year-old city gained independence from Berlin in 1991, recovering its eminent status as capital of the *Land*. Much of the residential city has been recently renovated to create long boulevards adorned with gateways and historic buildings. Today, the city moves at a leisurely pace, its parks, palaces, and picturesque avenues swelling with curious—and mostly German—visitors.

▐▀ ▐▌ TRANSPORTATION AND PRACTICAL INFORMATION

Trains: S1 and RE1 run to Potsdam's Hauptbahnhof from Berlin's Friedrichstr. (40min. or 25min., €2.60), or take S7 from Charlottenburg and transfer to S1 at Wannsee. Trains every hr. to: **Dessau** (1½hr., €20); **Leipzig** (2½hr., €27); **Magdeburg** (1½hr., €16.20).

Public Transportation: Potsdam is in Zone C of Berlin's BVG transit network. It is also divided into its own subdivisions of A, B, and C; special Potsdam-only tickets can be purchased on any bus or streetcar (€1.40, valid 1hr.; day ticket €3.20). The **Potsdam Card** is valid for 3 consecutive days in all zones and also gives discounts at many attractions (€9.80). The **Berlin Welcome Card** (€21) is also valid in Potsdam.

Bike Rental and Tours: Potsdam is best seen by bike. **Cityrad** rents bikes right from the Hauptbahnhof (Babelsbergerstr. exit) at prices reasonable for Potsdam. (☎0331 27 06 210. €11 per day. Open M-F 9am-7pm, Sa-Su 9am-8pm). Or get off the S1 at "Griebnitzsee" and rent from **Potsdam Per Pedales**, Rudolf-Breitscheid-Str. 201. From there, pay to take your bike on the S-Bahn or get a map for the bike route that passes the Schloß Babelsberg and villas used for the Potsdam conference. 3 different bike **tours** (€10, students €8) also available, call ahead for English group tours (☎0331 748 00 57). €9 per day, students €7. Open daily Oct.-Apr. 9am-6:30pm; May-Sept. until 7pm.

Tourist Office: Friedrich-Ebert-Str. 5 (☎505 88 38). Across the street from the "Alter Markt" streetcar stop. From the station, cross Lange Brücke, which turns into Friedrich-Ebert-Str. The office sells cheap city maps and books rooms (€25-52). For accommodations information, call ☎275 58 16. Open Apr.-Oct. M-F 9am-6pm, Sa-Su 9:30am-4pm; Nov.-Mar. M-F 10am-6pm, Sa-Su 10am-2pm.

Tours: The tourist office runs 3½hr. tours of the city, inquire at the office. **Berlin Walks** has 5-6hr. walking tours that leave from the taxi stand outside Berlin's Bahnhof Zoo. May-Sept. Sa at 9:30am. €15, students €11.20. **Terry Brewer's** also offers a Potsdam tour, leaving from the World Clock at Alexanderpl. May-Oct. Tu, Th, Su at 9am. €10. **Bus tours** leave from the Filmmuseum, Breitestr. 1a. Tu-Su at 11am. €26 with admission to Sanssouci, €15 without castle. Other tours (€8) have narrower themes.

Post Office: Pl. der Einheit, 14476 Potsdam. Open M-F 9am-6:30pm, Sa 9am-1pm.

BRANDENBURG

BRANDENBURG

Potsdam

FOOD & DRINK
Casablanca, **1**
Siam, **2**

0   400 yards
0   400 meters

Marmorpalais

Neuer Garten

Heiliger See

TO SCHLOSS CECILIENHOF (800m)

TO SCHLOSPARK GLIENICKE, GLIENICKER BRÜCKE (1km)

Am Neuen Garten

TO KAPELLE ALEXANDER NEWSKI (300m)

Hebbelstr.

Kurfürstenstr.

Puschkinallee

Russische Kolonie

Am Schragen

Jägerallee

Friedrich-Ebert-Str.

HOLLÄNDISCHES VIERTEL

BASSIN-PLATZ

Französische Kirche

Franzöische Str.

Am Kanal

Altes Rathaus

Babelsberger Str.

Potsdam Hauptbahnhof

Cityrad

Am Alten Markt

Am Bassin

Lange Brücke

Nauener Tor

Jägerstr.

Kirche St. Peter und Paul

Schloßstr.

Filmmuseum

Obelisk

Nikolaikirche

AM NEUEN MARKT

PLATZ DER EINHEIT

Yorckstr.

Dortustr.

Breite Str.

TO WISSENSCHAFTSPARK ALBERT EINSTEIN (1km)

Jägertor

Hegelallee

Gutenbergstr.

Brandenburger Str.

Charlottenstr.

Brandenburger Tor

LUISEN-PLATZ

Lindenstr.

Feuerbachstr.

Zeppelinstr.

Dampfmaschinen-haus

Neustädter Havelbucht

Ribbeckstr.

Pappelallee

Gregor-Mendel-Str.

Voltaireweg

Triumphtor

Obeliskportal

Schopenhauerstr.

Friedenskirche

BRANDENBURGER VORSTADT

Lennéstr.

Bornstedter Str.

Bildergalerie

Schloß Sanssouci

Neptun-grotte

Marlygarten

Am Grünen Gitter, Alter

Weg nach Sanssouci

Maschinen-teich

Geschwister-Scholl-Str.

Ruinenbergstr.

Zur Historischen Mühle

Neue Kammern

Sizilianischer Garten

Nordischer Garten

Rosengarten

Große Fontäne

An der Orangerie

Orangerie

Maulbeerallee

Botanischer Garten

Park Sanssouci

Hauptallee

Chinesisches Teehaus

Ökonomieweg

Römische Bäder

Schloß Charlottenhof

Maschinen-teich

Eichenallee

Drachenhaus

Antikentempel

Freundschafts-tempel

Schloß Theater

Hippodrom

Fasanerie

Neues Palais

Lindstedter Weg

Lindenavenue

Am Neuen Palais

Bahnhof Park Sanssouci

Amundsenstr.

ACCOMMODATIONS AND CAMPING

Potsdam has limited budget accommodations options. **Jugendgästehaus Sieben-schläfer ❷**, Lotte-Pulewka-Str. 43, located in Babelsberg, is a hostel one S-bahn stop from the Potsdam Hauptbahnhof. (☎0331 74 11 25; www.jgh-potsdam.de. Sheets €3.30. Laundry €3.50. Reception 6am-11pm. 7- to 8-bed dorms €12; 3- to 6-bed dorms €14; singles €18.50; doubles €15.) Another option is in **Wannsee** (p. 146), 10min. away by S-Bahn. The hostels in central Berlin are also a short S-Bahn ride away. Hotels are scarce, but the tourist office finds private rooms and has a list of campgrounds in the area. **Campingplatz Sanssouci-Gaisberg ❶**, An der Pirsch-heide 41, is on the scenic banks of the Templiner See. Take regional train #94 or 95 to "Bahnhof Pirschheide" and call to get a ride over. (☎951 09 88. Phone reception 8am-1pm and 3-8pm. Wash €3.50. Dry €3.50. €8.20 per person, €1 per child.)

FOOD

Bright, renovated **Brandenburger Straße,** the local pedestrian zone, encompasses many of the city's restaurants, fast-food stands, and markets. The dozens of cafes near Brandenburger Tor are lovely but pricey, as are parts of Friedrich-Ebert-Str. and the **Holländisches Viertel** (see **Sights**, p. 153), lined with chic cafes. Head to the **flea market** on Bassinpl. for fresh produce. (Open M-F 9am-6pm.) In the Hauptbahn-nhof is a massive **Kaufland** grocery store. (Open daily 6am-8pm) **Casablanca Cafe/ Pizzeria ❷**, Jägerstr. 1 (☎270 38 33) is a comfy cafe, decorated with murals of canals, that serves pasta and pizza starting at €4.50. (Open M-F 11am-11pm, Sa-Su noon-11pm.) **Siam ❷**, Friedrich-Ebert-Str. 13 (☎200 92 92), prepare tasty Thai food (€5-8) right before your eyes in a bamboo-heavy interior. The outdoor seating is some of Potsdam's best for people watching. (Open daily noon-11pm.)

SIGHTS

A good investment for sightseeing is a **day ticket,** valid and available at all castles in Potsdam (€15, students €10, family card €25.50).

PARK AND SCHLOß SANSSOUCI

PARK SANSSOUCI. The castle's 600-acre "backyard," a testament to the size of Friedrich II's treasury and the diversity of his aesthetic tastes, has two distinct areas to explore. Half of the park is done in Baroque style—straight paths inter-secting at topiaries and statues of nude nymphs arranged in geometrically pleasing patterns—and the other half is in the rambling, rolling style of English landscape gardens. The sheer magnitude of the park—encompassing wheat fields, rose trel-lises, and lush, immaculate gardens—makes it a fascinating place to spend an afternoon. For information on the park's many attractions, from Rococo sculp-tures to beautiful fountains, head to the visitors center next to the windmill behind Schloß Sanssouci. (☎969 42 00. Open daily Mar.-Oct. 8:30am-5pm; Nov.-Feb. 9am-4pm.)

SCHLOß SANSSOUCI. The park's main attraction, the Versailles-esque Schloß, sits atop a landscaped hill. Designed by **Georg Wenzeslaus von Knobelsdorff** in 1747, the yellow palace is small and airy, adorned with rich depictions of Dionysus and other Greek gods. Tours of the castle in German leave every 20min., but the final tour (5pm) usually sells out by 2pm during the high season. An English-language tour, led by the tourist office, includes only the main Schloß. Inside the castle, the style is cloud-like French Rococo—all pinks and greens with gaudy gold trim. Friedrich, an unrepentant Francophile until his death, built the ornately tropical *Voltairezimmer*, decorated with carved reliefs of parrots and tropical fruit, in

BRANDENBURG

honor of Voltaire, though the writer never stayed here. The library reveals another of Friedrich's eccentricities: whenever he wanted to read a book, he had a copy printed for each of his palaces—*en français*, of course. In a macabre gesture, Friedrich's remains, which were spirited away to a salt mine near Tübingen in 1945 to save them from the Red Army, were returned to the grounds in 1991, and now lie under six plain flagstones next to the Schloß. *(Bus #695 runs through the park and around the western edge; the stop "Schloß Sanssouci" is closest to the castle. ☎ 969 41 90. Open Tu-Su Apr.-Oct. 9am-5pm; Nov.-Mar. 9am-4pm. Mandatory tours €8, students €5.)*

NEUES PALAIS. At the opposite end of the park, the New Palace is the largest and last of the park's four castles. Commissioned by Friedrich the Great to emphasize Prussia's power after the Seven Years' War, this 200-room ornate pink Schloß features royal apartments, festival halls, and the impressive **Grottensaal,** whose shimmering walls are literally coated with seashells. The **Schloßtheater** hosts occasional summer performances. *(☎ 969 42 55. Open Apr.-Oct. M-Th and Sa-Su 9am-5pm; Nov.-Mar. Sa-Th 9am-4pm. €5, students €4. Tours €1 extra in summer.)*

IN THE PARK. Next to the Schloß Sanssouci is the **Bildergalerie,** whose collection of Caravaggio, van Dyck, and Reubens crams a long hall of massive and elaborate canvases. *(☎ 969 41 81. Open mid-May to mid-Oct. Tu-Su 10am-5pm. €2, students €1.50.)* On the other side of Schloß Sanssouci lies the **Neue Kammern,** a former guest house and recital hall. The ball and festival rooms are lavishly decorated; check out the Hohenzollern porcelain in a huge gold-trimmed closet room. *(Open mid-May to mid-Oct. Tu-Su 10am-5pm; Apr. to mid-May Sa-Su 10am-5pm. €2, students €1.50. Tour €1 extra.)* The stunning **Sizilianischer Garten** is next door. Overlooking the park from the north, the pseudo-Italian **Orangerie** is famous for its 67 dubious Raphael imitations that replace originals swiped by Napoleon. *(Open mid-May to mid-Oct. daily 10am-12:30pm and 1-5pm. Mandatory tours €3. Tower only €1.)* Romantic **Schloß Charlottenhof,** whose park surroundings were a Christmas gift from Friedrich Wilhelm III to his son Friedrich Wilhelm IV, melts into landscaped gardens and grape arbors to the south. *(Open mid-May to mid-Oct. daily 10am-5pm.)* Nearby are the **Römische Bäder** (Roman baths). Meant to provide an exotic contrast to the Italian villas, the gold-plated **Chinesisches Teehaus** stands complete with a parasol-wielding rooftop Buddha and 18th-century *chinoiserie* porcelain inside. *(Open mid-May to mid-Oct. Tu-Su 10am-5pm. €1)* The plainer **Friedenskirche** awaits at the east entrance of the park. Friedrich Wilhelm IV and his wife Elizabeth are buried below glittering mosaics.

OTHER SIGHTS

NEUER GARTEN. Nuzzling the Heiliger See, Potsdam's second park contains several royal residences. **Schloß Cecilienhof,** built in the image of an English Tudor manor, houses exhibits documenting the **Potsdam Treaty,** which was signed at the palace in 1945. Visitors can see numerous Potsdam Conference items, including the table at which the Big Three bargained over Europe's fate. *(☎ 969 42 44. Open Tu-Su Apr.-Oct. 9am-5pm; Nov.-Mar. 9am-4pm. €4, students €3. Tours €1 extra in summer.)* The garden also contains the **Marmorpalais,** the huge marble-intensive palace that Friedrich II commissioned in 1786 as the centerpiece of the park. Many odd little buildings are scattered throughout the grounds, including a replica of an Egyptian pyramid formerly used for food storage. *(To get to the Neuer Garten, take bus #692 to "Schloß Cecilienhof." Marmorpalais open Apr.-Oct. Tu-Su 10am-5pm; Nov.-Mar. Sa-Su 10am-4pm. €2, students €1.50. Tour €1 extra in summer.)* Yet another palace-park, **Schloßpark Glienicke** contains a casino as well as its namesake, **Schloß Glienicke,** a mediocre yellow-green affair built by Schinkel in 1828 for Prince Karl of Prussia. *(Take streetcar #93 (dir.: Glienicker Brücke) to the end and continue along Berliner Str. to the bridge; the castle is on the other side. Open Apr.-Oct. Sa-Su 10am-5pm.)* A walk back on Berliner Str. leads to the **Glienicker Brücke** (a.k.a. "The James Bond Bridge"), which was swallowed up by the death strip between the DDR and West Berlin. Closed to traffic until 1989, it was instead used for the exchange of spies, and was known rather ironically as the "Bridge of Unity." Across the water you can see **Schloß Babelsberg** and the **Maschinenhaus,** and on the other side is the more distant **Heilandskirche.**

RUSSISCHE KOLONIE. In the beginning of the 19th century, General Yorck brought 500 Russian soldiers to Prussia, and Friedrich Wilhelm III, a great fan of Russian culture and handsome soldiers, discovered that many of them had singing talent. Unfortunately, only 12 of the original group were left by the 1820s. To mitigate the depressing atmosphere, Friedrich III built each soldier a small, ornate wooden house. The nearby pink onion-domed **Kapelle Alexander Newski,** designed by Karl Friedrich Schinkel, was also intended as compensation. *(Streetcar #90, 92, or 95 to "Puschkinalle" and follow the street north. www.alexandrowka.de.)*

FILMMUSEUM. Housed in an old orangerie that once held Friedrich's stables, this museum documents Potsdam's days as a film mecca, with artifacts like Marlene Dietrich's costumes, as well as a silent film archive and a small **movie theater.** *(On the corner of Breite Str. and Schloßstr. ☎271 81 12; www.filmmuseum-potsdam.de. Open daily 10am-6pm. €5, students €4. Movies from 6pm, kids movies from 2pm. Theater open daily noon-1am. €4.50, students €3.50. During "blue hour" W-Su beginning at 5pm, €3.)*

HOLLÄNDISCHES VIERTEL. Friedrich's attempt to import Dutch craftsmen to beautify the city produced the Dutch Quarter, which lies in the center of the town around Friedrich-Ebert-Str. Though it fell into disrepair during the mid-20th century, the neighborhood was revitalized when entrepreneurs converted the beautiful old buildings into a row of shops and restaurants in 1990.

NIKOLAIKIRCHE. Toward the waterfront, the impressive dome of the Nikolaikirche rises above its neighbors. On closer inspection, the dome and the granite cube it sits on don't seem to match. While the topping is light and spacious, the interior was renovated à la DDR with glass and sound-tiles that somehow dampen the aesthetic impact. In front is an **obelisk** decorated with sphinxes and ram skulls, dedicated to the great architect Karl Schinkel. *(Am Alten Markt. ☎270 86 02. Open M 2-5pm, Tu-Sa 10am-5pm, Su noon-5pm. Vesper music Su 10pm.)*

FILMPARK BABELSBERG. Back in the Golden Age of European cinema, the **UFA-Fabrik** in Babelsberg was *the* German studio, giving Marlene Dietrich, Hans Albers, and Leni Riefenstahl their first big breaks. Fritz Lang also made *Metropolis* here. That said, this amusement park has little to do with film, and little beyond the lunch-counter *Wurst* is particularly German. Still, the park is fun and very family-conscious, with rides and huge walk-through exhibits geared toward children. *(August-Bebel-Str. 26-53. Take S7 to "Babelsberg," then bus #690 or 698 to "Filmpark." ☎721 27 50; www.filmpark.de. Open Apr.-Nov. daily 10am-6pm. €17, students €15.50.)*

BRANDENBURG ☎03381

When Albert the Bear chose Brandenburg on the Havel for the site of his cathedral in 1165, the small, laid-back town had to deal with sudden prominence, reluctantly growing to assume a central political role in the region. In the end, Brandenburg's slow pace triumphed over any demands imposed by its key location. These days, the town has reverted to its idyllic state, and residents spend their time fishing by the Havel or strolling the Altstadt's cobblestone streets. The province's namesake moves at a leisurely gait and invites you to do the same along its scenic waterways.

◨◪ TRANSPORTATION AND PRACTICAL INFORMATION. Brandenburg is on the Magdeburg-Berlin regional express line, with frequent **Trains** to **Berlin** (40min., €5.70) and **Magdeburg** (1hr., €10). Visitors from Berlin should consider buying a day ticket valid on all Berlin and Brandenburg public transportation

(€11.40), or Brandenburg Ticket for up to 5 people (€23). The **tourist office**, Stein-str. 66/67, is at the streetcar stop "Neustädter Markt." From the station, cross Am Hauptbahnhof, walk along Große Gartenstr., and follow it right onto Jakobstr., which becomes Steinstr. The staff books rooms for free, distributes English maps and brochures, and runs **walking tours** (1hr., May-Sept. Sa-Su 11am, €3) and **boat tours**, which leave several times a day from near the Jahrtausendbrücke at the end of Hauptstr. (☎194 33 or 58 58 58; www.stadt-brandenburg.de. Open May-Sept. M-F 10am-7pm, Sa 9am-5pm, Su 10am-3pm; Oct.-Apr. M-F 10am-7pm, Sa 10am-2pm.)

⌂ ⌘ ACCOMMODATIONS AND FOOD. There's no youth hostel in Brandenburg, but private rooms are abundant and cheap—ask at the tourist office for a brochure or look for "Zimmer frei" signs. Hidden behind a cafe directly on Steinstr. is the **Pension Blaudruck ❷**, Steinstr. 21, with six small, charming rooms adorned with paintings and stray ivy creeping in from the window. The proprietors dress all in blue and the courtyard is full of hanging chickens and laundry. Call ahead. (☎22 57 34; fax 52 42 22. Singles €20; doubles €40-50, extra beds €5.) By a quiet canal between the Altstadt and train station, **Pension "Haus am Jungfernsteig" ❸**, Kirchhofstr. 9/Jungfernsteig 6a, run by a kindly violinist couple, has spacious rooms with TVs, skylights, and shared bathrooms. (☎25 01 70. Breakfast included. Singles €26; doubles €47; triples €64.50.) **Campingplatz Malge ❶**, in the woods 20min. from the city center, has about 40 tent sites. Take Bus B from Neustädter Markt to "Malge," cross the train tracks, and walk straight into the campground. By bike, take Steinstr. southwest out of the city, follow it straight when the main road branches off, and look for signs to turn right for Malge. (☎66 31 34. Reception 9am-1pm and 3-5pm. Open Apr.-Oct. €5 per person, €4-8 per tent.)

The main cafe and *Imbiß* scenes are on **Steinstraße** and perpendicular to **Haupt-straße**, which also features an open-air **farmer's market** behind the Katharinen-kirche. (Open M-F 7am-5pm, Sa 7am-noon.) **Nummer 31 ❷**, Steinstr. 31, offers gourmet pizzas in a good old German setting for €3-5. (☎22 44 73. Open daily 11am-11pm.) The **Kartoffelkäfer ❸**, Steinstr. 56, serves tasty meals centered around that German favorite: the potato. The outdoor cafe is a short walk from Neustädter Markt. (☎22 41 18. Entrees €6-9. Open daily 11am-midnight.)

◪ SIGHTS. Brandenburg's sights can be found along Steinstr. and its extension. Begin your tour of the **Neustadt** at the end of Steinstr. with the 14th-century **Stein-turm**, which holds a maritime history museum with displays on each level of the tower. Brave the steep, narrow spiral staircase for a view of the Havel and pedestrian Brandenburg. (☎20 02 65. Tower open Tu-F 9am-5pm and Sa-Su 10am-5pm. €3, students €1, family pass €5.) Work your way up the street through the DDR-filled **Nostalgie-Museum**, Steinstr. 52. (☎22 06 20. Open Tu-Su 10am-noon and 1-6pm. €1.50.) The 14th-century **St. Katharinenkirche**, on the corner of Neustädter Markt, is a beautiful example of North-German *Backstein* (glazed brick) Gothic, now pockmarked by war damage. It's under construction but still open. (Open M-Sa 10am-noon and 1-4pm, Su 11am-4pm.) Walking through Molkenmarkt, across the river and along St. Petri will bring you to the famed **Dom St. Peter und Paul**, Burghof 11, a cathedral currently housing a rotating exhibition. Artwork is placed in the aisles with surprising abandon. The church is also adorned with its own art; architect **Friedrich Schinkel** couldn't resist adding a few touches like the "Schinkel-Rosette" and the window over the entrance. Surprises await the intrepid explorer in the many mysterious wings. The **Dommuseum** inside displays an array of old clothing, local-history treasures, and a great stash of medieval books. (☎22 43 90. Open M-F 10am-4pm, Sa 10am-5pm, Su 11am-5pm. €3, students €2.) Across the street, the **Petrikapelle** has gone from church to contemporary art gallery. (☎20 03 25. Open M-Tu and Th-F 10am-4pm, W 10am-noon, Sa 10am-5pm, Su 11am-5pm.)

For those with time to spare, Brandenburg's **Altstadt,** across the Havel, has even more centuries-old buildings (including towers from the 12th-century walls), fewer glossy storefronts, and a quieter, more reflective feel. From St. Katharinenkirche, head down Hauptstr. across the river. For 500 years, a 6m statue of the epic hero **Roland** has stood here in front of the Rathaus. Farther afield, the modern and comically phallic **Friedenswarte,** on the Marienberg, directly uphill from Am Marienberg, provides a great view of the contrasting antiquity surrounding it. (Open Apr.-Oct. Tu-Su 10am-5pm. €2, students €1.)

SPREEWALD (SPREE FOREST)

The Spree River splits apart 100km southeast of Berlin and branches out over the countryside in an intricate maze of streams, canals, meadows, and primeval forests stretching over 1000km². Local traditions blossomed here when the tiny villages were first settled in the Middle Ages, and the folklore is still especially strong. The **Sorbs** (see **The Absorbing Sorbs,** p. 630), Germany's native Slavic minority, originally settled the region and continue to influence its cultural identity.

In this popular vacation spot for Berliners, locals use the ubiquitous canals for transportation, earning the region the title "Venice of the North." Farmers row to their fields and children paddle home from school. The fields and forests teem with owls, otter, deer and foxes, making the Spreewald strikingly idyllic. Because the forest is now recognized as a *Biosphärreservat* (a biosphere nature reserve) by the UN, some sections are off-limits to the public; other sections are closed during mating and breeding seasons but not tourist season. Guided tours are offered by reservation, camping spots abound, bicycles can be rented everywhere, and excellent hiking trails and footpaths weave through the peaceful forest. Each local tourist office has information on leisure activities and advice on how to be environmentally responsible in protected areas.

Lübben and **Lübbenau,** two tiny towns that open into labyrinths of canals, are popular destinations that lie within daytrip-range of Berlin. The park is divided into two sections: the **Unterspreewald,** north of Lübben, and the **Oberspreewald,** from Lübben down past Lübbenau. The Unterspreewald has more extensive bike paths; the Oberspreewald, a web of rivers and canals, is best explored by boat.

LÜBBEN ☎ 03546

With canals and trails fanning out from its northern and southern ends, little Lübben fills with German tourists milling around the colorful Altstadt and gliding by in kayaks, canoes, and gondolas. Lübben offers easy access to wooded bike paths and hiking trails, so pack your backpack, grab some juicy *Gurken* (pickles, the region's specialty) for the road, and get ready for an adventure.

▐▀▐▌ TRANSPORTATION AND PRACTICAL INFORMATION. Lübben is on the Cottbus-Berlin *Regional Express* line, making the city easily accessible by **train.** Trains go to: **Berlin Ostbahnhof** (50min., 1 per hr., €9); **Cottbus** (30min., 1 per hr., €5.50); **Lübbenau** (10min., 2 per hr., €1.70). For a **taxi** call ☎48 12 or ☎30 39. Rent **bikes** at the station (€5.50 per day, €3.50 with a train ticket; open M-F 6:30am-8:45pm, Sa-Su 9am-7:45pm) or at the tourist office (€5.50 per day, €4 each subsequent day). The **tourist office** is at Ernst-von-Houwald-Damm 15. From the station, head right on Bahnhofstr., make a left on Luckauer Str., veer left onto Lindenstr., cross the two bridges, and the office will be on the right, on the *Schloßinsel* across the bridge. The staff finds private rooms (€15-40) for a €3 fee. After hours, they post a list of private rooms outside the entrance. (☎30 90 or 24 33; fax 25 43. Open Apr.-Oct. daily 10am-6pm; Nov.-Mar. M-F 10am-4pm.) The **post office,** 15907 Lübben, is at Poststr. 4. (Open M-F 9am-6pm, Sa 9am-noon.)

CREATURES OF THE SPREEWALD

n addition to waterfowl and innumerable trees, royal snakes and ost souls roam the legendary Spreewald. This region of Brandenburg considers snakes to be good luck; the Sorbs used to keep hem as protectors of the house, and stories about a wealthy snake who bestows his riches upon the generous still dominate folktales. f you're lucky enough to spot this snake (he wears a crown), lay out a white tablecloth for him to set his headgear upon and then snatch it like the famed Graf ynar once did.

Not all beings in the Spreewald are benign. The *Irrlichter,* lights hat flicker on the moors and waterways at night, are said to be either evil fairies hungry for human flesh or the souls of those who've died on the moor, luring others to the same end. One such wanderer is a knight who married a beautiful woman from the forest on the condition that she be allowed to go alone to the river once a week. Of course, the knight followed her, only to discover that she was a mermaid replenishing her powers in the water. She lost her ability to transform into a woman and the knight killed himself, his soul cursed to wander the Spreewald.

Science now says the Irrlichter are bursts of spontaneously igniting methane gas, but as you sit in a boat gliding through the misty trees, you can decide for yourself what to believe.

ACCOMMODATIONS AND FOOD. The **Jugendherberge Lübben (HI) ❷,** Zum Wendenfürsten 8, is in a field at the edge of town. To get there, follow Bahnhofstr. to its end and turn left on Luckauer Str. Turn right on Burglehnstr. before the big crossing and right again on Puschkinstr., which becomes Cottbusser Str. After 1.5km, take a left on Zum Wendenfürst, and follow it for another 1.5km. Signs point the way. Though remote, the hostel is a dream, and offers easy access to wilderness paths. (☎30 46; www.jh-luebben.de. Sheets €3.30. Reception 9am-7pm. Dorms €12-13. Camping spots €8.) For convenience, **Pension am Markt ❸,** Hauptstr. 5, can't be beat. Each room has a kitchen and fold-out couches. (☎32 72. Breakfast included. €25-28; 1- to 4-person apartments €60-90.) **Spreewald-Camping Lübben ❶** is closer than the Jugendherberge. Follow directions to the Jugendherberge until Puschkinstr., and then turn left at the sign. (☎70 53; www.spreewald-camping-luebben.de. Boat rental €3.50 per hr., €20 per day; for campers €2.70/€16. Bike rental €6.50 per day. Reception 7am-1pm and 3-10pm. Open mid-Mar. to Oct. €5.50 per person, €3.50-4.50 per tent. 2- to 3-person cabins €18-24.)

While in Lübben, be sure to sample the Spreewald's pickled delicacies, famous throughout Germany. **Gurken Paule ❶,** at the entrance to the tourist office plaza on the Schloßinsel, is an outdoor stand offering the freshest of the Spreewald's unique pickle assortment: *Salzdillgurken* (dill), *Senfgurken* (mustard), and *Gewürzgurken* (spicy), and sundry other varieties. They're sold by weight, averaging about €0.40 per pickle or €2.50 for a jar. (Open daily 9am-6pm.) More varied local cuisine and evening music ranging from *Schlager* to country can be found at **Bubak ❸,** Ernst-von-Houwald-Damm 9, named after the Sorbian bogeyman who carries naughty children off into the forest. Sample the *Gurken-Kartoffelsuppe* (pickle-potato soup; €2.80) or an entree for €5.50-15. (☎18 61 44; www.bubak.de. Open M-F 11:30am-3pm and 5:30-10:30pm, Sa-Su 11:30am-11:30pm.)

SIGHTS AND OUTDOOR ACTIVITIES. The busy Altstadt's architectural pride is the newly restored **Paul-Gerhardt-Kirche,** named for the most famous German hymn writer since Martin Luther. (Open May-Aug. W 10am-noon and 3-5pm.) Gerhardt is buried inside (no one knows quite where) and immortalized outside in stone. The entrance to Lübben's lush forested park, **Der Hain,** is at the end of Breite Str., which begins where Hauptstr. ends. To the south, the **Schloßinsel,** an island whose park is more impressive than the modest palace also located there, houses the tourist office, several docks, and pricey cafes. The **Schloß** contains a small exhibit on Lübben's history and culture. (Open May-Sept. Tu-Su 10am-6pm; Oct.-Apr. W-F 10am-4pm, Sa-Su 1-5pm.) Most of Lübben's attractions are in the forests surrounding the town. The **Fährmannsverein "Lustige Gurken" Lübben/Spreewald**, Ernst-von-Houwald-Damm 15 on the Schloßinsel, offers boat trips exploring the Spreewald. (☎71 22; www.lustigegurken.de. Open daily 9am-4pm. 1½-10hr., €7-18.) The **Fährmannsverein "Flottes Rudel,"** at the end of the parking lot across Lindenstr. from Am Spreeufer, offers boat and barge trips with picnics starting daily at 10am. (☎82 69; www.flottesrudel.de. 1½-2hr., €7; 4hr., €12; all-day trips to Lehde or Schlepzig €15-20.) Or, rent a **kayak** or **canoe** at **Bootsverleih Gebauer**, Lindenstr. 18. From Luckauer Str., turn right on the street before the tourist office onto Lindenstr. (☎71 94; www.spreewald-bootsverleih.de. ID required. Open daily Apr.-Oct. 9am-7pm. One-person kayaks €2.50-4 per hr., €15-18 per day.)

LÜBBENAU ☎03542

Tiny Lübbenau is the most famous and perhaps the most idyllic of the Spreewald towns. For tourists, the village serves as a springboard for trips into the kingdom of the *Irrlichter* (see **Creatures of the Spreewald**, p. 158). The landscape here is dense with waterways, and has more gondolas than houses. Buried in the forest, the neighboring village **Lehde** has houses with straw roofs and a museum that recreates life as it once was among the Spreewald Sorbs.

█⁊ TRANSPORTATION AND PRACTICAL INFORMATION. Trains go to: **Berlin** (1hr., 1 per hr., €9.30); **Cottbus** (25min., 1 per hr., €4.50); **Lübben** (10min., every 30min., €1.70). For a **taxi** call ☎31 53 or 836 88. **Kowalsky's**, near the station at Poststr. 6, rents **bikes**. (☎28 35. €7 per day. Open M-F 9am-12:30pm and 2-6pm, Sa 9am-noon, Su call in advance.) Rent a **kayak** at the campsite (p. 159) or at **Franke,** Dammstr. 72. From the station, turn right down Bahnhofstr. and left at Dammstr. (☎27 22. Paddleboats €2-5 per hr. Open Apr.-Oct. daily 8am-7pm.) **Hannemann**, Am Wasser 1, rents **boats** at the other port. Follow Spreestr. to the end, cross the bridge, then continue to the next bridge. (☎36 47. One-seaters €3-4 per hr. Call ahead to reserve a boat. Open daily 8am-7pm.) The **tourist office**, Ehm-Welk-Str. 15, at the end of Poststr., has maps and finds rooms for a €4 fee. (☎36 68; fax 467 70. Open May-Oct. M-F 9am-6pm, Sa 9am-4pm; Nov.-Apr. M-F 9am-4pm.) The **post office**, 03222 Lübbenau, is at Kirchpl. 6. (Open M-F 9am-6pm, Sa 9am-noon.)

█▐ ACCOMMODATIONS AND FOOD. Though the closest hostel is in **Lübben**, 10min. away by train (p. 158), finding a room isn't a problem in friendly Lübbenau. Check for "Zimmer frei" signs or ask for the *Gastgeberverzeichnis* brochure at the tourist office. **Pension Erlenhof ❸**, Lindenstr. 5, is the cheapest pension around, but it's in Krimnitz—the next village over. From the train station, it's a 30min. walk. Turn left onto Bahnhofstr. and go straight until Wiesengrund appears on the right; take a right and then a quick right onto Lindenstr. (☎460 73. Free bike loan. Call ahead. Singles €23; doubles €40.) Directly on the road to Lehde and surrounded by water, **Campingplatz "Am Schloßpark" ❶** has 125 tent plots with cooking and bathing facilities on site, as well as a convenience store. (☎35 33. Bikes €6 per day; single boats €15 per day. Reception 7:30am-12:30pm and 2-9pm. €4.50 per person, €2 per child, €3-4 per tent. 2- to 8-person bungalows €19-44.)

For cheap food—and pickles, beets, and beans by the barrel—check out the snack bars and stands along the **Großer Hafen.** Cheerful yellow **Cafe Fontane ❸** dishes out delicious local cuisine near the church; try a salad with baguette (€7-9) or spring for the *Heringsfilet nach Hausfrauen Art* (herring à la housewife; €7.90). Homemade cakes make dessert a must. (Open daily from 11:30am.) The spacious, bright **Spreewald Idyll ❸**, Spreestr. 13, serves regional specialties like *Grützwurst* with potatoes (€6), fish dishes, and salads (€2-14) within spitting distance of the Kleiner Hafen. (☎14 22 51. Open M-Sa 10am-10pm, Su 10am-9pm.)

◙◪ SIGHTS AND HIKING. The Altstadt is a 10min. walk from the station. Go straight on Poststr. until you reach the marketplace and the Baroque **Nikolaikirche.** The stone pillar in front served as an 18th-century crossroads post marking the distance to nearby towns in hours of walking time. (Open May-Oct. M-F 2-4pm.) The requisite **Schloß** is now a handsome (and expensive) hotel and restaurant with lush grounds that are open to the public. Across the marketplace in the gatehouse (a prison until 1985) is the ◪**Spreewaldmuseum,** Topfmarkt 12, which gives a historical overview of the Spreewald and its customs. (☎24 72. Open Apr. to mid-Oct. Tu-Su 10am-6pm. €3, students €2.) The **Haus für Mensch und Natur,** Schulstr. 9, has a free exhibit on the local ecosystem. (Open Apr.-Oct. daily 10am-5pm.)

Gondola tours of the forest depart from the **Großer Hafen** and the **Kleiner Hafen.** The Großer Hafen, along Dammstr. a block behind the church, offers a wider variety of tours, including 2- and 3hr. trips to Lehde. The boats take on customers starting at 9 or 10am and depart when full (about 20 passengers) throughout the day. **Genossenschaft der Kahnfährleute,** Dammstr. 77a, is the biggest company. (☎22 25. Open Mar.-Oct. daily 9:30am-6pm. 2hr. round-trips to Lehde €7, children €3.50; 3hr. trips €9/€4.50; 5hr. tour of the forest €12.50/€6.25.) From the Kleiner Hafen, less-touristy but nearly identical wilderness trips are run by the **Kahnfährmannsverein der Spreewaldfreunde,** Spreestr. 10a. (☎40 37 10. Open Apr.-Oct. daily 9am-6pm or later. Tours 2-10hr.; 4-5hr. tours recommended. €7-20, children €3-10.)

It's only a hop and a paddle from Lübbenau to the haystacks and thatched-roof houses of **Lehde,** a UNESCO-protected landmark that is accessible by foot (15min.), bike, or boat. Follow the signs from the Altstadt or Großer Hafen, or take a boat from the harbor. Check out the **Freilandmuseum,** a recreated 19th-century village, portraying a time when entire Spreewalder families slept in the same room and newlyweds literally went for a "romp in the hay." (☎24 72. Open Apr. to mid-Sept. Tu-Su 10am-6pm. €3, students and seniors €2, children €1.) Just before the bridge to the museum lies the **Fröhlicher Hecht ❷** (Jolly Pike), Dorfstr. 1, a large cafe, restaurant, and *Biergarten* with a patio right on a river. Try *Kartoffeln mit Quark* (potatoes with curd cheese) in a special Spreewald sauce (€5.90) or pickles with a side order of *Schmalz* (lard; €1), another Spreewald "specialty." Say a prayer for your heart and dig in. (☎27 82. Open daily 11am-7pm.)

MECKLENBURG-VORPOMMERN (UPPER POMERANIA)

Nature takes center stage in sparsely-populated Mecklenburg-Vorpommern. Over 1700 lakes lie nestled between thick forests and peaceful towns, stretching northward to breathtaking cliffs and sandy beaches along the Baltic Sea coast. A popular tourist destination at the turn of the 20th century, Mecklenburg-Vorpommern (especially the islands of Rügen and Usedom) have been rediscovered by the west in the wake of reunification. Even now, dramatic Hanseatic architecture continues to emerge from rubble as restoration continues in Germany's poorest *Land*.

HIGHLIGHTS OF MECKLENBURG-VORPOMMERN

BATHE IN THE SEA or sun on the beautiful beaches of **Rügen Island** (p. 179).

HIKE the white chalk cliffs of **Jasmund National Park** (p. 180).

STEP BACK into the Middle Ages in **Stralsund** (p. 176), birthplace of the glazed brick Gothic architectural style.

SCHWERIN ☎ 0385

Founded in 1018, Schwerin is the grandfather of Mecklenburg-Vorpommern's cities, now capital of the province. Encircled by lakes and largely free of communist "architectural innovations," Schwerin brims with well-preserved townhouses and retains a regal flair with its magnificent **Schloß**. The undeniable cultural center of the *Land*, Schwerin houses numerous galleries and venues that bring dozens of art festivals and concerts to the city during the year. Schwerin is home to some of the region's finest traditional cuisine, and also boasts a number of classy bars.

◼ TRANSPORTATION AND PRACTICAL INFORMATION

Schwerin is on the Magdeburg-Rostock rail line and is accessible from all major cities on the Baltic coast. **Trains** run to: **Berlin** (2½hr., 1 per hr., €27-33); **Lübeck** (1¼hr., 1 per hr., €11.10); **Rostock** (1¼hr., 1 per hr., €13). An efficient system of **buses** and **trams** covers the city and outlying areas (single ride €1, day pass €3). The city's two **Räder Center** shops, at Schusterstr. 3 and at the "Service Point" booth in the train station, rent **bikes,** recommend trails, and lead personal tours. (☎ 500 76 30. M-F €6, Sa-Su €7. Rentals mid-Apr. to Oct. daily 9am-6pm.)

The **tourist office,** Am Markt 10, books hotel rooms for free and leads 1½hr. walking tours. (Daily 11am. €4.50.) From the train station, go right on Grundthalpl. and continue as it turns into Wismarsche Str.; take a left on Arsenal, a right on Mecklenburgstr., and another left on Schmiedestr. Pick up a free copy of *piste* for reviews and listings of clubs and parties. (☎ 592 52 12; www.schwerin.de. Open Apr.-Sept. M-F 9am-7pm, Sa-Su 10am-6pm; Oct.-Mar. M-F 9am-6pm, Sa-Su 10am-4pm.) Do **laundry** at **Schnell & Sauber,** on Pl. der Freiheit. (☎ 592 52 12. Wash 6kg €3, including soap. Dry €0.50 per 12min. Open daily 6am-11pm.) An **Apotheke,** Pushkinstr. 61/65, is just off the Markt. (☎ 59 37 90. Open M-F 8am-6pm, Sa 9am-12:30pm.) **Internet** is available at **Netz-Games,**

Ritterstr. 1, on the corner of Salzstr. (☎ 593 69 60. €0.50 per 10min., €2 per hr. Open M-F 2pm-midnight, Sa-Su 4pm-midnight.) The **Stadtsbibilothek,** Wismarsche Str. 144, also offers Internet. (☎ 590 19 21. €2 per hr. Open M-W and F 10am-6pm, Th 2-7pm, Sa 9am-1pm.) The main **post office** is at Mecklenburgstr. 4-6, 19053 Schwerin. From the Markt, go down Schmiedestr. and turn right. (Open M-F 8am-6pm, Sa 9am-noon.)

▐ ACCOMMODATIONS

Family-run ▐**Zimmervermietung Familie Kuhnert ❷,** Voßstr. 44, is in the blue house next to Café Bernstein (p. 163). Take bus #10 or 11 from the train station to "Alter Friedhof" and cross the street at the intersection. The rooms have TVs and would feel just like home—if your home had windows overlooking a castle. Scrapbooks testify to its popularity with artists, musicians, and backpackers. (☎ 79 79 79. Breakfast €5. Singles €20-30; doubles €30-40; €225-350 per month.) The always-booked **Jugendherberge (HI) ❷,** Waldschulweg 3, is 3km south of town in the woods by the lake. From the station, take a right on Wismarschestr. to Marienpl. Take bus #14 to the end of the line at "Jugendherberge" and take the road into the woods; the hostel is on the left. (☎ 326 00 06; fax 326 03 03. Breakfast and sheets included. Reception 4pm-midnight. Curfew midnight. Dorm beds €18, under 27 €15.)

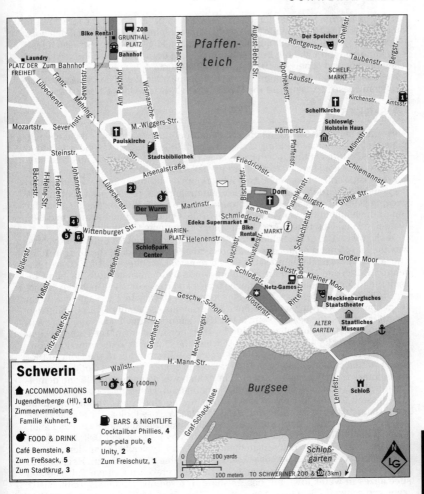

Schwerin

ACCOMMODATIONS
Jugendherberge (HI), **10**
Zimmervermietung
Familie Kuhnert, **9**

FOOD & DRINK
Café Bernstein, **8**
Zum Freßsack, **5**
Zum Stadtkrug, **3**

BARS & NIGHTLIFE
Cocktailbar Phillies, **4**
pup-pela pub, **6**
Unity, **2**
Zum Freischutz, **1**

FOOD

Schwerin's coziest micro-brewery, **⬛Zum Stadtkrug ❸**, Wismarschestr. 126, serves German specialties and award-winning beer. The local *Schweriner Altstadtbräu* (€1.40 for 0.2L) complements an intimidating *Brauhauspfanne* (pig roll, smoked turkey, lung sausage, sauerkraut, and vegetables) for €8. (☎593 66 93. Open daily 11am-1am.) Potato lovers can't afford to miss the gigantic stuffed potatoes (€5-6.50) at **Zum Freßsack ❸** (at the feedbag), Wittenburgerstr. 52, at the corner of Voßstr. The restaurant's more obscure Mecklenburger specialties, like *gepökeltes Eisbein* (pickled pig's knuckles on sauerkraut; €8.50), are for the adventurous. (☎760 71 72. M-Tu and Su 11:30am-10pm, F-Sa 11:30am-midnight.) While away an evening in the relaxed and friendly atmosphere of **Café Bernstein,** Voßstr. 44. Take bus #10 or 11 from the train station to "Alter Friedhof" and cross the street at the intersection. This "Amber Cafe" fills with people sipping iced drinks and delicious *Milchkaffee* (€2.40) served in giant bowls. (Open daily 9am-3am.) Strings of fast-food joints run through both **Der Wurm,** a mall on Marienpl. whose courtyard paths resemble a worm (open M-F 9:30am-7pm, Sa 9:30am-4pm) and the neighboring **Schloßpark Center,** a larger, more modern shopping complex. The **Edeka supermarket,** Schmiedestr. 10, is just off the Markt. (Open M-F 7am-8pm, Sa 8am-4pm.)

◎ SIGHTS

Schwerin's fairy-tale **Schloß,** on an island south of the city center, is a glitzy amalgamation of grandiose building styles. Begun in the 1500s, the castle was added onto into the 19th century, when it served as the seat of the dukes of Mecklenburg. The exterior's gold-capped towers are partially shrouded by ongoing restoration, but the inside still shines. Mahogany inlay floors lead through ornate chambers to the grand throne room, with its marble columns and wall-to-wall ornamentation. A sweeping view of the castle and its grounds can be had from atop the hill at the far end of the adjoining *Schloßgarten.* (☎56 57 38. Open Tu-Su mid-Apr. to mid-Oct. 10am-6pm; mid-Oct. to mid-Apr. 10am-5pm. €4, students €2.50, family €7.)

On the other side of the Schloß, the **Alter Garten,** now used for outdoor concerts, was the site of mass demonstrations preceding the downfall of the DDR in 1989. The adjacent **Staatliches Museum** houses a remarkable collection of 15th- to 19th-century Dutch and German art, including works by Rembrandt, Rubens, and Cranach the Elder. A room full of Barlach statues and the extensive Duchamp collection will please modernists. (☎595 80. Open Apr. 15-Oct. 14 Tu 10am-8pm, W-Su 10am-6pm; Oct. 15-Apr. 14 closes 5pm. €6, students €4, family €12.) Uphill from the Alter Garden, the nearest spire is the 13th-century Gothic **Dom.** Napoleon's soldiers once used the chapel as a stable for their horses. Many of the church's treasures, including its 42 altars, were lost when the Dom was redecorated in New-Gothic style at the beginning of the 19th century. Restoration of the Dom to (not New-) Gothic style took place in 1970-1988. The church's striking Gothic triumph cross comes from Wismar's Marienkirche, which was damaged in 1945 and demolished in 1961. (Open M-Sa 10am-5pm, Su noon-5pm. Donation requested. Tower €1; children €0.50.) In front of the Rathaus on the Markt, a towering **lion statue** pays tribute to Schwerin's founder, **Henry the Lion.** A close look at the statue's base will reveal amusingly irreverent scenes. The **Schleswig-Holstein-Haus** has small, rotating exhibitions that have included sketches by Picasso and Dalí. (Puschkinstr. 12. ☎55 55 27. Open daily 10am-6pm. Prices vary; typically €3, students €2.)

Animals cavort at the **Schweriner Zoo.** Take tram line #1, 2, or 3 (dir.: Hegelstr.) to "Zoo." From Bernhard-Schwentener-Str. turn left onto Am Grünen Tal. The zoo specializes in water fowl, but has its share of ferocious mammals. (☎39 55 10; www.zoo-schwerin.de. Open Apr.-Oct. M-F 9am-5pm, Sa-Su 9am-6pm; Nov.-Feb. daily 10am-3pm, Mar. 10am-4pm. €7, students and children €3.50.) In summer, **ferries** leave every hr. from the docks between the Schloß and the museum to tour the Schweringersee lake, including a loop around the **Kaninchenwerder** (rabbit haven) island. (Departures Tu-Sa 10am-5pm. €8-11.50, children €2.50.) North of the Markt, the **Pfaffenteich,** a much smaller lake, offers a walk spotted with statues.

♫ ◉ ENTERTAINMENT AND NIGHTLIFE

The cream-pillared building next door to the Staatliches Museum is the **Mecklenburgisches Staatstheater Schwerin,** which puts on the most elaborate and expensive plays, ballets, and symphonies in town. (☎530 01 23. Tickets €20-60; €10 student discount.) Buy tickets for most shows through **Ticketservice am Markt,** in the tourist office. (☎56 05 00. Open M-F 9am-7pm, Sa 10am-noon.) Schwerin's best sights often double as performance spaces; in the summer, the steps of the museum are converted into an opera stage, and in the nearby Schloß, the throne room is a regal venue for monthly concerts (around €26, students €18). **Der Speicher**, Röntgenstr. 20-22, airs cult films and hosts literary readings and folk music shows, mostly on weekends. (☎51 21 05. Entrance on Schelfstr.)

Most Schwerin bars are open daily, closing around midnight on Sundays. **Zum Freischutz**, Am Ziegenmarkt 11, a popular bar near the Speicher, covers the cracks on its dimly lit walls with an odd combination of Beethoven portraits, stuffed ravens, and butterflies. The crowd is young, the beer (€2) is good, and the drink menu is on a rotating wheel. (☎56 66 55. Open daily from 6pm.) The Altstadt empties at night, but trendy, dimly-lit **Unity**, Arsenalstr. 35, attracts a crowd of students to its wooden tables and overstuffed sofas. (☎55 50 98 30. Beer €1.50, *Glühwein* €2. Open daily from 6pm.) The cozy **pup-pela pub** is just down Wittenburgerstr. from Zum Freßsack. Enjoy a beer (€1.50-3) while pondering the crooked paintings and trinket-encrusted walls. (Open W-Sa from 8pm.) Across the street, join the Schwerin glitterari at **Cocktailbar Phillies**, Wittenburgerstr. 51, for fancy cocktails (€6.50-8) and Cuban cigars (€4.50) from an extensive list. (☎71 31 01. Open daily from 8pm. Free movies in the garden during the summer Su 10pm.)

MECKLENBURGISCHE SEENPLATTE (MECKLENBURG LAKE PLAIN)

When things got hectic in Berlin, Chancellor **Otto von Bismarck** often found refuge in the beauty of the **Mecklenburgische Seenplatte**, the lowland lake district of southern Mecklenburg-Vorpommern. The region's landscapes are a product of glacial activity during the Ice Age; hundreds of lakes are scattered about the Seenplatte, lined by wetlands and deciduous forests. A popular destination throughout the past century, the area fills with hikers, bikers, and paddlers during the summer.

MÜRITZ NATIONAL PARK

In the heart of the Seenplatte, Müritz National Park boasts thick forests, rolling grasslands, and over 100 lakes. The relatively compact park is easily accessible from small towns scattered around it, and the park's numerous bike trails, hiking paths, and canoeing opportunities make it well suited to nature enthusiasts of all levels of expertise. Müritz is also home to a number of rare birds. Although camping is perhaps the best way to enjoy the park, the lively town of Waren, on the shores of Lake Müritz, is a haven for weary bikers and backpackers.

■ ORIENTATION

The two separate regions of Müritz National Park are west and east of the town of **Neustrelitz**. The much larger western area is bordered on the west by **Lake Müritz**, Germany's largest freshwater lake. At the northwestern corner, the port town of **Waren** is a major jumping-off point for tourists. When calling from outside the cities, the appropriate **phone code** for Neustrelitz is **03981**; for Waren, **03991**. The park's southwestern quarter along the lake, mostly wetland, is home to much of its wildlife. The remainder of the western portion is forest interspersed with rolling fields and sparkling lakes. Müritz's eastern region has more hills and is thickly forested, but is also dotted with lakes and brooks. The **Hirschberg**, not exactly looming at a mere 143.5m, is the highest point in the park. Other major towns around

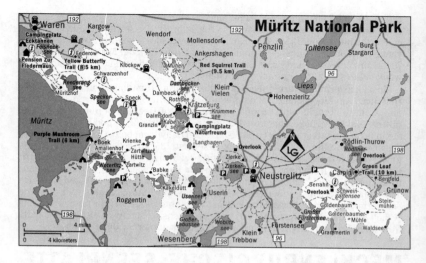

the park are **Kratzeburg**, in the center of the western region; **Speck**, west of Kratzeburg; **Federow**, on the north edge of the park southeast of Waren; and **Serrahn**, somewhat west of center in the eastern region. Maps of the park (€5.50) are highly recommended and available at all national park information offices.

⌐ TRANSPORTATION

Trains: Nearly everyone gets to the park through Neustrelitz or Waren, both of which are on the Berlin-Rostock rail line. Trains head to **Waren** from **Berlin** (2hr., 1 per hr., €20-21) and **Rostock** (1hr., 1 per 2hr., €12.90); to **Neustrelitz** from **Berlin** (1½hr., 1 per 2hr., €16.20) and **Rostock** (1½hr., 1 per 2hr., €17). Waren, directly on the park, is a better departure point, but Neustrelitz is only a 30min. bike ride from either section.

Public Transportation: Getting around the park is easy. The **Müritz-Nationalpark-Ticket** runs **buses** every hr. from 9am-4pm (July-Aug. until 5pm) from Waren to **Boek** through Federow and Speck. The line also includes a ship that connects Waren, Klink, and Roebel on the Müritz lake. Buy tickets on board buses or boats or at tourist information centers. Day ticket €6.50, students and children €3, family €13; with unlimited boat travel €13/€6/€26. 3- and 7-day passes also available. Check the schedule: many tours are free with purchase of these passes. **Trains** also shuttle between Waren and Neustrelitz every 2hr., stopping in **Kargow, Klockow,** and **Kratzeburg** (€5.70).

Taxis: In Waren, call ☎ 12 22 55.

Biking: Renting a bike is an efficient way to be mobile in Müritz. Rental stores are ubiquitous, even in the smaller towns like Boek, Schwarzenhof, and Carpin. In the more central areas, **Burau Mobil,** Loydstr. 2b, on the Track 1 side of the Waren train station, rents for €5 per day. (☎73 25 50. Open M-F 9am-6pm, Sa 9am-noon.) **Pedal Point,** Strelitzer Chausee 278, is near the Neustrelitz station. (☎44 16 38. €7 per day. Open M-F 9:30am-12:30pm and 1-6pm, Sa 9am-noon.)

⚡ PRACTICAL INFORMATION

Emergency: Police ☎ 110. **Ambulance** and **fire** ☎ 112.

Climate and Seasonality: The best time of year to visit the park is May-Oct. The much-touted cranes only live here Sept.-Oct.; June and July still bring other species. Müritz enjoys less rain than most other parts of Germany, and a mild range of temperatures.

National Park Information Centers: Hiking maps (€5.50), brochures, and advice are available at Müritz National Park's *Nationalparkinformation* offices:

Waren, Am Teufelsbruch (☎ 66 27 86). Follow the directions to Ecktannen (p. 167) but stay on Am Seeufer as it becomes Specker Str., then turn left on Am Teufelsbruch at the park sign. Or, take Waren's bus #1 to "Schabernack" at the end of the line. Open May-Sept. daily 9:30am-5pm.

Neustrelitz, Am Tiergarten (☎ 03981 20 32 84). Take Marienstr. from the train station past the *Opfern des Faschismus* monument on your right and veer left onto Friedrich-Wilhelm-Str. Continue straight past the traffic circle and follow the signs. Wheelchair accessible. Open May-Oct. daily 10am-5pm.

Nationalparkamt Müritz, Schloßpl. 3, 17237 Hohenzieritz (☎ 039824 25 20; info@nationalpark-mueritz.de), is the office to contact for information before you arrive.

Additional branches are located in Boek, Federow, Friedrichsfelde, Kratzeburg, Schwarzenhof, Serrahn, Speck, and numerous other locations throughout the park region. See the park webpage (www.nationalpark-mueritz.de) for more information.

Gear: In Waren, **Sport-Assmuß,** Friedensstr. 17, sells tents (€42-60) and other camping gear. (☎ 67 47 92. Open M-F 9am-6pm, Sa 9am-4pm.)

Tours: Free, themed walking and bike tours of parts of the park, including family tours, are available May-Oct. Tours last 1½-5hr., most around 3hr., and depart several times a day. For a list of dates, durations, and meeting points, visit the park website or any park center. **Boat tours** of the lake are offered by **Warener Schifffahrtsgesellschaft,** Am Stadthafen (☎ 12 56 24) and **Müritzwind Personenschifffahrt,** on Strandstr. (☎ 66 66 64), both in Waren. Tours run 1-7hr. (€5-20, children half-price).

Laundry: Waschsalon Wirbelwind, Strandstr. 1, in Waren (☎ 66 26 63). Wash and dry €8. Open M-F 9am-6pm, Sa 9am-2pm.

Pharmacy: Löwen-Apotheke, Neuer Markt 21, in Waren, next to the tourist office (☎ 78 11 11). Open M-F 8am-6pm, Sa 8am-12:30pm.

Internet Café, in Waren on Große Grüne Str. at the edge of the Alter Markt (☎ 66 45 48). €2.50 per hr. Open M-F 2-8pm, Sa-Su 2-7pm.

Post Office, Neuer Markt 19, Waren (☎ 67 39 30). Open M-F 9am-6pm, Sa 9am-noon.

ACCOMMODATIONS AND FOOD

Signs lead from the train station to **Campingplatz "Naturfreund" am Käbelicksee ❶**, at Dorfstr. 3 outside Kratzeburg, on a secluded lakeshore in the park. (☎ 039822 202 85. Boat rental €3-6 per hr. Reception 8:30am-8pm. Open year-round. €4.50 per person, €2-4 per tent.) **Campingplatz Ecktannen ❶**, in Waren, is on Fontanestr., near the lake. Take bus #3 (dir.: Ecktannen) to the last stop. (☎ 66 85 13. Reception 8am-1pm and 3-6pm, in summer until 9:30pm; if you get there later, camp outside the gate and check in the next day. Open April-Oct. €5.10 per person, €3-4 per tent.)

Though it may be the best way to spend the night in Müritz, **camping is legal only in designated campgrounds.** There are campgrounds near the park in Blankenforde, Boek, Klockow, Kratzeburg, Mirow, Waren, Wesenberg, Zietlitz, and Zwenzow; ask at information centers for exact locations. Most do not rent tents. Also, **the Waren youth hostel has closed,** though signs still point to it.

Waren's beautifully situated marina and cheerful atmosphere make it a hot spot for German vacationers. With hundreds of pensions, vacation apartments, and single rooms for rent, it's easy to find a place to stay: you can search the streets for signs and inquire within, or try the town's **tourist office**, Neuer Markt 21, which finds rooms (from €25) for a €3 fee. From the train station, turn right onto the footpath and follow it across the bridge over Schweriner Damm; go left on Friedenstr. and left again on Langestr. (☎66 61 83; www.mueritz-info.m-vp.de. Open May-Sept. daily 9am-8pm; Oct.-Apr. M-F 9am-6pm, Sa 10am-3pm.) The **Pension Zur Fledermaus ❸**, Am Teufelsbruch 1, has little rooms, a meadow view, and an unbeatable location in the northern part of the park, 3km from the harbor. Follow the directions to Waren's national park information center (p. 167), and continue another 1km along the dirt road. (☎66 32 93; www.pension-fledermaus.de. Breakfast included. Singles €27; doubles €48; triples €72. Bath €3 extra per person. 1-night stays €3 extra per person. Beds without breakfast €13 per person per night.)

The pedestrian zone along Langestr. and Neuer Markt in Waren's Altstadt is crammed with bakeries and *Imbiße*. Pricey cafes and restaurants line the bustling harbor, but budget-conscious diners can still enjoy a waterfront view at **Schnitzel-König ❷**, Strandstr. 3, tucked away in a quiet corner of the harbor. The log-hewn picnic tables afford an excellent view of the lake, and the tasty *Schnitzel* dishes (€5.50-6.50) make good meals. Predictably, vegetarian options are somewhat limited. (☎66 90 11. Open daily from 11am.) The **SPAR** supermarket, Neuer Markt 23, may be the cheapest way to eat. (Open M-F 8am-8pm, Sa 8am-2pm, Su 9am-2pm.)

🚶 ⛰ HIKING AND OUTDOOR ACTIVITIES

HIKING. Trails in Müritz are marked by colored images rather than names; many trails have the same symbol, differentiated only by the location of the trailhead. Grünow is the best starting point for trails in Müritz East, while the trails in Müritz West begin in many different towns. The extensive booklet *Wandern im Müritz-Nationalpark*, available at National Park Information Centers, describes all the trails and has color maps (€12). **Be aware that in high-protection areas in the core zone of the park you may not leave the marked trails.** Some of the good ones include:

🐿 Rotes Eichhörnchen (Red Squirrel; 9.5km). To reach the trailhead, leave Kratzeburg on the road leading to highway B-193 (dir.: Neustrelitz); the beginning of the trail will appear on your left, across from a small parking area. A local favorite that passes several of Müritz's lakes. The trail has a closed loop in the north: 2hr. takes you around the little lily-padded **Wienpletschsee** and then by the banks of the Müritz and Binnenmuritz, where the *Strandpromenade* is scalloped with tiny beach alcoves.

Violetter Pilz (Purple Mushroom; 6km). Follows the coastline of the Müritzsee from starting point Boek, providing good opportunities to spot wildlife. In fall, wild swans are everywhere, while in summer, fish-hawks hunt for lunch on the water.

Gelber Schmetterling (Yellow Butterfly; 8.5km). Follow Strandstr. past site of the former Waren Jugendherberge to reach the trailhead. In the north near Waren, this trail makes a circuit around the Feisnecksee, with grassy fields and views of the lake. The small *Burgwallinsel* in the middle of the lake is a remnant of a former Slavic settlement.

Grünes Blatt (Green Leaf; 10km). Beginning from Grünow in Müritz East, this path meanders through rolling country hills, forests, and along lakeside paths.

BIKING. Bike trails are nearly as common as hiking trails; some recommended ones are the **Gelber Vögel** (yellow bird) near Grünow, the **Violette Blüme** (purple flower) south of Waren, and the comprehensive 163km **Müritz-Nationalpark-Weg**. The road to Federow is good for biking, and Federow itself is a good place for setting off into the park. From Neustrelitz, there are several ways of getting into the west section. To get to the heart of Müritz West, bike on road B-193 in the direction of Penzlin (signs indicating this road begin at the town's main traffic circle on Strelitzer Str.) and then fork left to Kratzeburg, as indicated by road signs. The road to

Userin, on the southern border of the park (in the opposite direction of Penzlin), leads to a number of roads and trails that veer north into Müritz West. To get to Serrahn, in Müritz East, take B-198 from Neustrelitz east in the direction of Carpin and fork right at the sign. Following the signs on the road will get you to Grünow, another good springboard for trips into the eastern area of the park.

WATER SPORTS. The stretch of the Havel River between the Käbelicksee and the Granzinersee has the most scenic **canoeing** in Müritz. **Bootsvermietung Hecht,** Dalmsdorf 6, just outside of Kratzeburg, rents canoes, kayaks, and rowboats, and runs a tiny, but spectacularly cheap, campsite. (☎ 039822 202 41; www.kanu-hecht.de. Boats €6-17 per 4hr. Camping €3 per person, €2 with boat rental.) In Waren, the bar **Zur Kegelbahn,** Am Tiefwarensee, has a few boats you can take out on the lake. From Langestr., take Friedensallee to the end and go over the pedestrian bridge. (☎ 12 59 33. €3-5 per hr. Open daily 10-11:30am and 1-6pm.) **Sailing** and **windsurfing** are popular on the Müritzsee; rentals are readily available in Boek.

GÜSTROW ☎ 03843

Though graced with winding bike trails and a striking Renaissance *Schloß*, Güstrow is most famous for its collection of paintings and sculptures by prolific 20th-century artist **Ernst Barlach.** Barlach, a longtime resident of Güstrow, fiercely opposed German nationalism and filled the town with pacifist sculptures, causing the Nazis to condemn his work as *"Entarte Kunst"* (degenerate art). The rows of abandoned, crumbling buildings scattered throughout the inner city are signs of a continuing economic slump, but Güstrow's Altstadt is slowly regaining its sparkle as a result of the EXPO 2000 urban renewal project.

⛶ TRANSPORTATION AND PRACTICAL INFORMATION. Central Güstrow is south of the **train station.** Follow Eisenbahnstr. three blocks until it becomes Lindenstr., then turn left onto Pferdemarkt. Güstrow is connected to **Rostock** via the **S-Bahn** and **Regional Express** trains (both 30min., 1 per hr., €4.60), as well as to **Waren** (30min., 1 per 2hr., €8.40). Güstrow's **tourist office,** Domstr. 9, finds rooms for a €1 fee. (☎ 68 10 23; fax 68 20 79. Open May-Sept. M-F 9am-7pm, Sa 9:30am-4pm, Su 10am-4pm; Oct.-Apr. M-F 9am-6pm, Sa 9:30am-1pm.) **Walking tours,** hosted by the tourist office, leave Franz-Parr-Pl. daily at 11am. (May 15-Oct. 3. €2, students €1.) **Rats-Apotheke,** Am Markt 24, is the local **pharmacy.** (Open M-F 8am-6pm, Sa 8am-noon.) **Internet** access is available at **Lennys Computer,** Gleviner Str. 23. (€1 per 30min. Open M-F 10am-1pm and 2-6pm, Sa 9:30am-1pm.) The **post office,** 18271 Güstrow, is at Pferdemarkt 52-56. (Open M-F 9am-6pm, Sa 9am-noon.)

⛶ ACCOMMODATIONS AND FOOD. Güstrow's gorgeous **Jugendherberge (HI) ❷,** Heidberg 33, is 5km from town, serviced by buses #205, 224, and 252, which run only five times per day (€1.80; last bus around 5pm). It is 20min. from the Altstadt by bike. The picturesque hostel lies at the edge of the woods and is surprisingly luxurious, boasting modern 2- to 4-bed rooms, most with bath. (☎ 84 00 44. Breakfast included. Curfew 10pm. €19.50-21, under 27 €16.50-18.) At the heart of Güstrow, **Café Central ❷,** Neuer Markt 35, offers pizza (€5-8), pasta (€5-7), gyros (€7) and more to hungry crowds on the patio. (☎ 68 68 98.)

⛶ SIGHTS. Güstrow's 13th-century **Dom,** on the southwest side of town, houses Barlach's most famous sculpture, *Der Schwebende Engel* (the hovering angel), created as a tribute to the victims of WWI. The statue was first cast in 1926, but was publicly melted into bullets by the Nazis in 1941. After WWII, a plaster cast of the statue was unearthed in West Germany, the angel was restored and rededicated to the victims of both wars in 1952. (Open M-Sa 10am-5pm, Su 2-4pm. Free.)

The white Renaissance **Schloß** rises above you as you walk back toward Domstr. The palace's *Festsaal* has a forest mural with antlers sprouting out of the walls, and the upper floors house Renaissance art from Italy, Germany, and the Netherlands. The basement is filled with altars and suits of armor from the Middle Ages. Windows look out over a manicured **Schloßgarten** surrounded by shrub archways. (☎75 20. Open Tu-Su 9am-5pm. €3, students €2, family €6. German tours daily 11am and 2pm; €1.50, students €1.) On the west side of town, the **Gertruden-kapelle**, Gertrudenpl. 1, houses a collection of Barlachs in an octagonal white chapel. (☎68 30 01. Open Apr.-Aug. daily 10am-5pm; Sept.-Oct. Tu-Su 10am-5pm; Nov.-Mar. Tu-Su 11am-4pm. €3, students €2.) On the Neuer Markt, in the **Pfarrkirche St. Marien**, a folding golden altar crafted by Brussels artist **Jan Borman** in 1522 displays over 180 sculpted figures. (Open June-Oct. M-Sa 10am-5pm, Su 2-4pm; Nov.-May M-Sa 10am-noon and 2-4pm, Su 2-4pm. Tower €1, students €0.50.)

Barlach's **Atelierhaus** (studio), Heidberg 15, contains the world's largest collection of his works, including some 300 sculptures, in the house in which they were created. Next door, the elegant *Ausstellungsforum* hosts passing exhibits related to Barlach's life. It's a 1hr. walk from the Altstadt, so renting a bike is the best way to visit. Head down Gleviner Str. from the Marktpl. and continue as it turns into Plauer Str. until you see the "Barlachweg" signs. Take this path around the lake past the grassy beach; continue 100m through the woods and the museum will be on the left. (☎822 99. Open Tu-Su 10am-5pm. €4, students €3.)

WISMAR   ☎ 03841

After destruction wrought by WWII and years of neglect under socialist rule, massive restoration efforts in Wismar are finally underway. The Altstadt, centered around the largest marketplace in Northern Germany and ringed with magnificent churches, is rapidly regaining its former beauty. In 2002, UNESCO recognized Wismar as a World Heritage Site because of the town's architectural and historical significance as a founding member of the **Hanseatic League** in the 1300s. Later conquered by Sweden, it was expanded to become the largest fortress in Europe. The 1903 end of Swedish rule is commemorated by the annual **Schwedenfest**, a celebration of Swedish culture held during the third week of August.

■⚐ **ORIENTATION AND PRACTICAL INFORMATION.** Wismar's shipping industries are located to the north of the **Alter Hafen** (old harbor), at the **Wismarbucht** (bay) which connects to the Baltic. To the east of the Altstadt on Bahnhofstr. is the park **Lindengarten**. The **Bahnhof** lies at the northern edge of the Altstadt. Trains run every hr. until 10pm to **Rostock** (40min., €4) and **Schwerin** (40 min., €5.50). The **ZOB** is a block away (bus ticket €1, day pass €3). Bus #430 runs to the sandy beaches of the nearby island of Poel ("Timmendorf Strand;" 1-2 per hr. until 6pm; €3.90). The **tourist office**, Am Markt 11, in the southwest corner of the Markt, books rooms for free, provides maps, and offers guided tours in German. (☎251 30 25; www.wismar.de. Open daily 9am-6pm. 2hr. tours daily Apr.-Oct. 10am, Sa and Su also 2pm. €4, students €3.) A bulletin board outside the office lists rooms.

▐⚑ **ACCOMMODATIONS AND FOOD.** The new **Jugendherberge (HI) Wismar ❷** is accessible by bus lines B/D, C, or E to "Phillip-Müller-Str./Kinderkrankenhaus." Backtrack one block, and turn left on Juri-Gagarin-Ring. (Rents bikes. Sheets and breakfast included. Curfew 4am. Dorms €19.50, under 27 €16.50.) The Alter Hafen area, the center of Wismar's nightlife, has seafood restaurants aplenty. The popular Altstadt bar **Der Schlauch**, Lübsche Str. 18., bills itself as a place for "jazz, art, and companionship." (☎20 06 55. Open daily 10pm-2am.) **Kellerkassel**, Lübsche Str. 26, is a cozy cellar bar down the street. (Open Tu-Sa from 8pm.)

MECKLENBURG-VORPOMMERN

◆ SIGHTS. Of Wismar's many churches, **St.-Georgen-Kirche** is currently the most noticeable. Once a place of worship for craftsmen, it has been their place of work for over a decade now, and will remain so until 2010 when Germany's largest church restoration will finish. Although the exterior remains obscured by scaffolding, the interior of the church has been partially reopened, and contains an exhibition on Christian history and the church's Gothic architecture. (Open daily 10am-6pm. €3, student €2.) All that remains of the nearby **St.-Marien-Kirche,** severely damaged by bombing in 1945 and all but demolished by the DDR in 1960 for "political reasons," is the imposing (and inaccessible) 81m tower. The bells still toll every 15min., and during the summer months, concerts and exhibitions are held outside. The Gothic **St.-Nikolai-Kirche** survived WWII intact, and houses portions of the interiors of St.-Georgen-Kirche and St.-Marien-Kirche that were removed from the two churches shortly before the bombings. Construction on the St.-Nikolai-Kirche began in the 14th century, but after the tower collapsed in 1703, much of the church was rebuilt in the Baroque style. (Open daily May.-Sept. 8am-8pm; Oct. and Apr. 10am-6pm; Nov.-Mar 11am-4pm. Requested donation €1.) The **Heilige-Geist-Kirche,** the Altstadt's other major church, has medieval art, an ornately painted altar and organ, and a year-round nativity scene. The attached "Lange Haus" originally served as a hospital. From the Markt go three blocks west on Lübschestr. (Open M-Sa 10am-5pm. Requested donation €1.)

The **Marktplatz's** dizzying variety of architecture is a record of Wismar's history of destruction and reconstruction. The **Rathaus** was rebuilt in 19th-century Neoclassical style after the roof collapsed in 1807 and destroyed most of the original building. In 1992 the building's roof collapsed again, requiring another renovation. The basement of the new Rathaus contains an exhibition on the city's history. (Open daily 10am-6pm.) Across the Marktpl., the **Wasserkunst,** an ornate Dutch Renaissance style well-house completed in 1602, was the village spigot for almost 300 years. A plaque sums up the German's sense of priority with regard to the well-house: "most importantly, it delivered water to the breweries." Located near St. Nikolai, the **Schabbelhausmuseum,** Schweinsbrücke 8, the city's historical museum, houses a wide-ranging collection. On display are artifacts from medieval Wismar's past, rotating works by local artists, and an exhibition on medical history that includes a historically recreated dentist's office (complete with a set of canines), an *Apotheke* (pharmacy), and an X-ray room. (☎28 23 50. Open Tu-Su May-Oct. 10am-8pm; Nov.-Apr. 10am-5pm. €2, students €1, under 18 free. F free.)

ROSTOCK   ☎0381

A victim of socialist ambitions in the wake of WWII, the port city of Rostock, the largest in sparsely-populated Mecklenburg, was reconstructed but never fully restored. Fortunately, most of the concrete eyesores erected during the DDR-era are relegated to the city's suburbs. Hints of Rostock's thriving past as a member of the **Hanseatic League** hide between modern buildings downtown. Rostock's university, the oldest in the Baltic region, infuses the city with youthful energy, contributing to a thriving nightlife. Tourists flock to the charming resort town of **Warnemünde,** whose wide, sandy beaches are just minutes away.

▐ TRANSPORTATION

Trains: To: **Berlin** (2½hr., 1 per 2hr., €30); **Dresden** (5¼hr., 1 per 2hr., €57); **Hamburg** (2½hr., 1 per hr., €26); **Schwerin** (1hr., 1 per hr., €12.90); **Stralsund** (1hr., 1 per hr., €11.10); **Wismar** (1¼hr., 1 per hr., €8.40).

Public Transportation: Take trams #5 or 6 from the train station to reach the Altstadt. Single bus/tram ticket €1.50. The *Tageskarte* (€3.10) allows 1 day of travel on all public transportation in greater Rostock. To get to the **bus station** for lines to smaller towns,

Rostock

⌂ ACCOMMODATIONS
City-Pension, **6**
Jugendgästeschiff Rostock, **5**
Jugendherberge Warnemünde, **1**
Pension Am Doberaner Platz, **10**

🍴 FOOD & DRINK
Café Central, **9**
Kettenkasten, **2**
Mensa, **13**
Salsarico, **3**
Tre Kroner, **7**

🍸 NIGHTLIFE
Calamaris, **4**
diesseits, **11**
Sebastian, **8**
Studentenkeller, **12**

leave the train station through the Südstadt exit. Bus service thins out after 10pm; after midnight, the *Fledermaus* (bat) buses run to a few central stops, generally once per hr., until full service resumes the next morning.

Ferries: Boats for **Scandinavia** leave from the **Überseehafen** docks. **TT-Line** runs to **Trelleborg, Sweden.** (☎67 07 90. 5hr.; 2-3 per day; round-trip €51-65, children and students €25-40.) **Scandlines** sails to **Gedser, Denmark.** (☎673 12 17. 2hr.; 3 per day; one-way €9, children €4.) **Silja Linie** (☎0451 589 92 22; www.siljaline.de), operates ships to **Helsinki, Finland.** (28hr.; one-way from €70) and **St. Petersburg, Russia** (38hr., one-way from €90).

Bike Rental: Radstation, Am Bahnhof (☎252 39 90), to the right from the Hauptbahnhof's north exit. €7 per day. Open M-F 10am-6pm, Sa 10am-1pm.

🗺️ 🛈 ORIENTATION AND PRACTICAL INFORMATION

Rostock lies on the Warnow river, slightly more than 10km inland from the Baltic Sea. The city's main attractions are within the Altstadt, which is bordered to the north by the Warnow, and encircled on the other three sides by segments of the old city wall. Stretching across the Altstadt from **Kröpeliner Tor** in the west to the Rathaus in the east is Kröpeliner Str., the city's main pedestrian zone and shopping district, also home to the city's university. Many of the city's cafes and bars are to the west of the Altstadt in the lively student quarter near **Doberaner Platz.** The Hauptbahnhof is south of the Altstadt. The beaches of Warnemünde lie 11km to the northwest of Rostock, where the Warnow river meets the Baltic Sea.

Tourist Office: Neuer Markt 3 (☎194 33; fax 381 26 01), in the post office building. From the train station, take tram #5 or 6 to Neuer Markt. The staff books rooms for €3 and leads 1½hr. **tours** (in English for groups on request) of the town (May-Oct. M-Sa 2pm, Su 11am. €4.) Open June-Aug. M-F 10am-7pm, Sa-Su 10am-4pm; May and Sept. M-F 10am-6pm, Sa-Su 10am-4pm; Oct.-Apr. M-F 10am-5pm, Sa-Su 10am-4pm.

Currency Exchange: Deutsche Bank, Kröpeliner Str. 84 (☎456 50), changes traveler's checks, has **ATMs** downstairs. Open M-Tu and Th 9am-6pm, W 9am-1pm, F 9am-3pm.

Library: Kröpeliner Str. 82. Open M-Tu and Th-F 10am-6pm, W noon-6pm, Sa 9am-1pm.

Gay and Lesbian Resources: rat + tat, Leonhardtstr. 20 (☎45 31 56), above the bar **Sebastian** (p. 176). Open Tu and Th 9am-5pm.

Emergency: Police ☎110. **Ambulance** and **Fire** ☎112.

Pharmacy: Rost Apotheke, Neuer Markt 13 (☎493 47 47). Open M-F 8am-6pm, Sa 8am-1pm.

Internet: Treffpunkt, Am Vögenteich 23 (☎643 80 67), inside the Sparkasse building. 20min. **Free Internet** with purchase of coffee or drink (€1-2). **Kek Ui,** Am Bahnhof, to the right from Hauptbahnhof's north exit. €2.50 per hr.

Post Office: Neuer Markt 3-8, 18055 Rostock. Open M-F 9am-6pm, Sa 9am-noon.

ACCOMMODATIONS

If the hostels are full and you find Rostock's hotels too expensive, the tourist office's **room booking** service may be your best bet.

Jugendgästeschiff Rostock - MS Georg Buchner (HI), Am Stadthafen 72 (☎670 03 20). Tram #5 to "Kabutzenhof," turn right onto Am Kabutzenhof, walk 5min. until you reach the water. A converted cargo ship, now permanently docked in Rostock's harbor, serves as a small hotel and a 50-bed youth hostel. Beautiful waterfront views and a wood-paneled officers' mess hall make up for the tightness of the 2-, 4-, and 6-bed quarters. Breakfast included. Sheets €4. Dorms €20, under 27 €17. ❷

Jugendherberge Warnemünde (HI), Parkstr. 47 (☎54 81 70), 1km west of the Warnemünde harbor; take bus #36 or 37 to "Warnemünde Strand." Near the beach, housed in the bottom floors of a former weather tower. The 40 rooms with bath and 20 with hallway facilities fill up quickly. In-room **Internet** jacks for laptops (access fee applies). Breakfast and sheets included. Dorms €24, under 27 €20. ❷

Pension Am Doberaner Platz, Doberanerstr. 158 (☎49 28 30; fax 492 83 33). Take streetcar #3 or 6 to "Doberaner Pl." and follow the signs down the driveway. Large, quiet rooms come with shower and breakfast. Located near the student quarter, steps away from public transport. Singles €46; doubles €69. ❸

City-Pension, Krönkenhagen 3 (☎252 22 60; fax 252 26 24). Located directly in the Altstadt, this comfortable house has rooms with TV, radio and bath. Sauna and exercise facilities in the building. Breakfast included. Wheelchair accessible. Check-in after 2pm. Check-out 10am. Singles €49; doubles €85. ❹

FOOD

Dining options in Rostock are limited but pleasant; most meals come with a view of the marketplaces and churches. **Neuer Markt,** on Steinstr. across from the Rathaus, fills with vendors touting sundry produce. (Open M-F 8am-5pm, Sa

HOW DO YOU LIKE YOUR BUNS?

Every morning across Germany, millions of people are sitting in front of the same breakfast: baskets brimming with bread and a multitude of toppings to spread, stack, sprinkle, or shovel on top. As a rule, there are always plenty of *Brötchen* (stiff-crusted rolls) to go around, and slices of rye, wheat, or varieties of local bread. The first category of toppings is cold cuts and cheeses. These are presented on serving trays alongside dainty serving forks, with individually wrapped sausages and little round blocks of cheese in a bowl. Soft cheeses are packed in little wedges and are often flavored with garlic or herbs. The other category is everything spreadable. This of course includes butter and jam, but there are also some uniquely German items to be tried. In Germany it is never too early for chocolate, and most Germans smear Nutella on their bread, fruit and fingers. Another specialty is *Quark*, a smooth, creamy spread with a mildly sweet flavor and the tang of cream cheese, that is actually made from cottage cheese. Most Germans spread varieties flavored with onion, garlic, or bacon on their breakfast rolls, though it is also popular to eat sweet-flavored Quark from a cup, or slathered over berries. All of these toppings (reliable, sensible, and filling, in true German fashion), combine to make an ordinary morning into a feast.

8am-1pm.) For groceries, try **Spar,** at the corner of Paulstr. and Hermannstr. (Open M-Th 8am-7pm, F 8am-8pm, Sa 8am-2pm.) The bakeries on Kröpeliner Str. sell cheap sandwiches and pastries. In **Warnemünde,** dozens of more expensive restaurants lining the harbor serve the bounties of the sea.

🔯 **Salsarico,** Am Leuchturm 15 (☎319 35 65), just down the street from the lighthouse in Warnemünde. Tasty, though not particularly authentic, Mexican food including tostadas, burritos, and fajitas (€9-13) and a variety of tequilas (€2-3). Lounge in wicker chairs as rows of mechanized handheld fans send a welcome breeze. Knock-out specials include €8 steak on W, unlimited chicken on M (€8), and free wine for women (Th 8-11pm). Happy hour daily 5pm-6pm. Open M-F from 1pm, Sa-Su from noon. ❸

Café Central, Leonhardstr. 22 (☎490 46 48), fills with a 20-something crowd that spills out into the street. Take in the creative artwork on the walls over light pasta dishes (€4-8) or a drink (€2-4). Open M-Sa 9:30am-2am, Su 10am-2am. ❷

Tre Kronor, Lange Str. 11 (☎490 42 60). Traditional Swedish dishes in a glass-walled building on a small hill above the harbor. Entrees (€8-14) include an excellent steak with berries and pepper sauce (€13) and reindeer (€10). Open daily noon-10pm. ❸

Kettenkasten, Am Strom 71 (☎512 48), in Warnemünde. Tourists eat *Ostseeheringe* (herring; €12) and other fish, accompanied by maritime tunes on the accordion, W-Su 8-10pm (€2 cover). Open M-F noon-midnight, Sa-Su 11am-midnight. ❹

Mensa, 104-107 St.-Georg-Str., near the Leibnizpl. tram stop, in the basement of the cream stucco *Studentenwerk* building. Super-cheap cafeteria lunches (€1-4) feed a university crowd. Open M-F 11:15am-2pm, Sa noon-1:30pm. ❶

🔘 SIGHTS

KRÖPELINER STRAßE. Rostock's main pedestrian mall runs west from the Rathaus to 12th-century **Kröpeliner Tor,** the former town gate. Although much of the city was destroyed in WWII, many of the half-timbered and glazed-brick houses along this stretch have been restored. The main buildings of **Rostock University,** the oldest in Northern Europe, are located near the middle of Kröpeliner Str., surrounding the massive Rococo fountain at Universitätsplatz. Next to the university, along the remains of the city wall, is the **Kloster zum heiligen Kreuz,** a restored cloister founded by the Danish Queen Margaret in 1270. It now houses the **Kulturhistorisches Museum,** featuring medieval artifacts, an exhibit on life in the cloister, and a selection of local landscape paintings from the early 20th century. *(Open Tu-Su May-Sept. 10am-6pm; Oct.-Apr. 11am-5pm. €3, students €1.)*

ZOO. During WWII, Rostock housed some of its zoo's animals in public offices during WWII; the apes were guests of the police station. Since then, the zoo has grown to include over 2000 animals, especially arctic and aquatic species, and is justifiably proud of its polar bear breeding program. *(Streetcar #3 or 6 to "Zoo." ☎ 208 20. Open daily 9am-7pm; Nov.-Mar. closes at 5pm. €8, students €7, children €4.)*

SCHIFFFAHRTSMUSEUM. Paintings, photographs, and intricate models tell the story of ships from Vikings to modern day. Functional navigation devices dazzle the seafaring eye, while a hands-on maritime knot exhibit frustrates visitors. *(August-Bebel-Str. 1. ☎ 25 20 60. Open Tu-Su May-Sept. 10am-6pm; Oct.-Apr. 11am-5pm. €3, students €1.)*

MARIENKIRCHE. This 13th-century brick basilica is at the end of Kröpeliner Str. near the Neuer Markt. In the final days before the fall of the Berlin Wall, services here overflowed with political protesters who came to hear the sermons of **Pastor Joachim Gauck.** In one of his bolder gestures, Pastor Gauck began to publicly chastise the secret police by calling out the names of those *Stasi* members he could identify from the pulpit. After reunification, Gauck was entrusted with the difficult job of overseeing the fate of the *Stasi* archives. The highlight of the church's interior is the 12m-high **astronomical clock** contracted in 1472. The intricate mechanical workings display the date, time, and positions of the sun and moon. At noon, a set of miniature apostles pop out, traveling around a figure of Jesus in circular procession. *(Open May-Oct. M-Sa 10am-5pm; Nov.-Apr. M-Sa 10am-12:30pm and 2-4pm; July-Sept. also Su 11:15am-5pm; Oct.-June 11:15am-noon. Requested donation €1. Organ concerts July-Sept. W 8pm. Tours daily 11am and 2pm; €4, students €2.)*

ALTER MARKT. The Alter Markt is older than the Neuer Markt in name alone; since bombs leveled the whole area, all the buildings, including the church, have been built anew. Reconstruction of the magnificent **Petrikirche** began in the 1950s, but it was not until 1994 that the church's lofty spire was restored. Visitors can ascend the tower by stair or elevator for a view of all of Rostock. *(Open Apr.-Oct. daily 10am-5pm; Nov.-Mar. M-F 10am-4pm, Sa-Su 10am-5pm. Tower €1.50.)*

JEWISH ROSTOCK. Rostock was once home to a substantial Jewish population. Nazis razed the synagogue on Augustenstr., and the SS began deportations soon after. The small **Jewish cemetery** was damaged in the war; in the 1970s, the government decided to turn the remaining gravestones face-down to create the city's **Lindenpark.** Pressure from the international Jewish community convinced the city to right most of the stones and add a memorial in 1988, though a walk through the fringes of the park will reveal gravestones still scattered in the underbrush. *(Take streetcar #3 or 6 or bus #24 to "Saarpl.," then walk south through the park.)*

WARNEMÜNDE. To the north of Rostock, accessible by S-Bahn, is the beach town **Warnemünde.** *(S-Bahn or Fledermaus bus to "Warnemünde." 20min., 4 per hr. 4:45am-8:30pm. Less frequent service during the night. Rostock tram/bus day ticket is valid for the ferry across the Warnemünde harbor.)* Warnemünde's **Alter Strom** (old harbor) rings with the sounds of fishing boats and clicking cameras. Across the bridge from the Bahnhof, stands selling snacks and trinkets line the long waterfront promenade. **Tourist information** is at Am Strom 59. *(☎ 54 80 06; fax 548 00 30. Open M-F 10am-7pm, Sa-Su 10am-4pm.)* Climb the **lighthouse** by the Alter Strom for a view of shores stretching far into the distance. *(Open Apr. to early Oct. 10am-7pm. €2, students €1, family €4.)* Walk long enough, and you can disrobe at the **nude beaches** (look for *FKK* signs at beach entrances). Just off Kirchenpl., the **Heimatmuseum,** Alexandrinerstr. 31, gives an overview of life in the tiny, colorful *Pfister* houses here. *(Open W-F*

10am-6pm, Sa-Su 10am-8pm. €3, students and children €1.) Though summer brings beach parties nearly every weekend, the largest celebrations hit during **Warnemünde Woche** in July, when the town hosts a sailing regatta.

🎵 NIGHTLIFE

At night, Rostock's lively students come out to play, congregating along Kröpeliner Str., Wismarische Str., and Barnstorfer Weg. Check out *Rostock Szene*, which lists local clubs and performances, and *Nordost Eventguide*, a chic booklet that covers clubs in all of Mecklenburg-Vorpommern. Both are free at the tourist office.

Studentenkeller, Universitätspl. 5 (☎ 45 59 28; www.studentenkeller.de). Entrance on Schwaansche Str., across from the Marriott. The nexus of Rostock's university crowd, which fills the large brick cellar and attached garden. The *Keller* hosts DJs, parties, and movies most nights; check the website for a schedule. Open Tu-Sa from 10pm.

diesseits, Margaretenstr. 41 (☎ 203 68 95), serves pastas and steaks (€4-8) at outdoor tables that line the quiet Margaretenpl. The bar heats up at night, and has a long list of cocktails (€3-5). Open daily 9am-1am. Breakfast M-F 9am-1pm.

Sebastian, Leonhardstr. 20 (☎ 459 14 07). Mixed clientele relax by candlelight at sleek black tables. Drinks €2-3. Open M-Sa 10pm-2am, Su 10pm-midnight.

Calamaris, Am Leuchtturm 2, in Warnemünde, down the stairs from the lighthouse. Fish (€6-12), beer (€2-3), and dessert (€3). Open M-Th noon-10pm, F-Su from noon.

STRALSUND ☎ 03831

Stralsund is famous for the distinctive red brick *Backsteingotik* architecture pervading its lively Altstadt. Founded in 1234, the city became an instrumental member of the **Hanseatic League** and amassed great wealth as a trading and shipbuilding center. Stralsund came under Swedish rule after the Thirty Years' War before being annexed by Prussia in 1815. Although it was heavily damaged by air raids in WWII, reconstruction efforts have maintained the architectural integrity of the Altstadt. In 2002, the city, in conjunction with nearby Wismar, was recognized as a UNESCO World Heritage Site. Sadly, a slumping economy in the wake of reunification has left many of the city's historic buildings to decay, but tourism in this town of 60,000 is now blossoming and the atmosphere is upbeat. Stralsund's fantastic sights and an array of excellent new restaurants make it well worth a visit.

🚉 TRANSPORTATION AND PRACTICAL INFORMATION

Stralsund's historic **Altstadt** sits on a small island, bordered to the south and west by the **Frankenteich** and **Knieperteich,** two large natural ponds, and to the east by the **Stralsund,** a straight separating Rügen Island from the mainland. Two of 11 city gates remain, the **Kütertor** in the west and the **Kniepertor** to the north. A segment of the old city wall stretches between them. Stralsund's main pedestrian zone, **Ossenreyerstr.,** runs north-south through the center of the Altstadt from the **Alter Markt** towards the **Neuer Markt.** The distinctive spires of the town's three main churches are landmarks that simplify navigation within the Altstadt. Stralsund's train station lies near the Altstadt's southwest corner across the Tribseer Damm.

Trains: To: **Berlin** (3½hr., 2 per hr., €30.80); **Binz** and **Saßnitz** on Rügen (both 1hr., 1 per hr., €8.40); **Hamburg** (3-4hr., 1 per hr., €33-40); **Rostock** (45-75min., 1 per hr., €11.10-14.80).

Buses: Intercity buses depart from the ZOB at **Frankenwall,** in the south of the Altstadt. Take Tribseer Damm right from the train station and then another right at the split onto Frankenwall. Within Stralsund, bus #1 circles the Altstadt. Lines #2-6 serve the Altstadt and the outskirts of town. Single ride €1.30, day pass €3.

Ferries: Reederei Hiddensee (☎0180 321 21 50) runs 3 times per day to **Kloster, Vitte,** and **Neuendorf** on Hiddensee (round-trip €16-17, children €7-9, bikes €7.50).

Bike Rental: Fahrradverlieh, Tribseer Damm 75 (☎30 61 58). To your right as you exit the train station. From €4.50 per day. Open M-F 9am-5pm, Sa 9am-1pm.

Tourist Office: Alter Markt 9 (☎246 90; fax 24 69 49). From the station, turn right onto Tribseer Damm follow the signs to the tourist office just past the Rathaus (10min.). Or take bus #4 to "Kütertor." The office distributes free maps, finds rooms for €3, and rents **audio guide tours** (€5) of the Altstadt in several languages. Free walking tours depart daily at 11am and 2pm May-Sept. from the tourist office. Open May-Sept. M-F 9am-7pm, Sa 9am-2pm, Su 10am-2pm; Oct.-Apr. M-F 10am-5pm, Sa 10am-2pm.

Emergency: Police ☎110. **Fire** and **Ambulance** ☎112.

Pharmacy: Tribseer Damm 6 (☎29 23 28), across the street from the train station. Open M-F 8am-6pm, Sa 8am-noon.

Internet Access: Internet Cafe im Speicher, Katherinenberg 35. €3 per hr., students €1.50. Open M-F 10am-9pm. Access also available in the **tourist office,** €0.50 per 10min., €2.50 per hr.

Post Office: Neuer Markt 4, 18439 Stralsund. Open M-F 9am-6pm, Sa 9am-noon.

▚ ACCOMMODATIONS

Hotel Schweriner Hof, Neuer Markt 1 (☎28 84 80, reservations 739 37 32; www.schweriner-hof.de). On one of Stralsund's 2 main squares, a stone's throw from the Marienkirche, this straightforward hotel has large rooms with TV, bath, radio, and minifridge. Breakfast included. Singles €40-53; doubles €55-68; triples €66-84. ❹

Pension Cobi, Jacobiturmstr. 15 (☎27 82 88; www.pension-cobi.de), by St. Jakobi on Bottcherstr. Located in one of the Altstadt's quiet residential neighborhoods, this pension has brightly-lit, basic rooms with TV and bath. Breakfast included. Singles €37-42; doubles €46-62. No credit cards. ❸

Jugendherberge Stralsund-Devin (HI), Strandstr. 21 (☎49 02 89). From the station, take bus #3 to the end of the line at "Devin" (20min., €1.30). Take the path that veers right into the woods, continue on the trail on the left side of the *Kurhaus-Devin,* and turn left when you hit Strandstr. (5min.). Located in the seaside village of Devin, this tired-looking hostel sprawls in 20 buildings near the beach. Breakfast and sheets included. Reception 7:30am-10:30pm. Check-in 3-7pm. €18, under 27 €15. ❷

▐ FOOD

Stock up on **groceries** at **Edeka-Neukauf,** on the corner of Rudolf-Breitscheid-Str. and Mariakronstr. From the train station, follow Jungfernstieg to Rudolf-Breitscheid-Str. and turn left. (Open M-F 8am-7pm, Sa 9am-1pm.) The many restaurants near the harbor serve fresh seafood late into the night, while cheaper bakeries and sidewalk cafes line Ossenreyerstr. as well as both Neuer and Alter Markt.

Hansekeller, Mönchstr. 48 (☎70 38 40), occupies a Renaissance-era basement where customers relish regional specialties such as fish, duck, and *Sauerfleisch* (€9.50-14). Come hungry. Open daily 11am-11pm. ❸

Al Porto, Seestr. 14 (☎ 28 06 20). Devour pricey pizza, pasta, and fish (€6-14) at this waterfront Italian eatery. A walk to the end of the pier affords a stunning view of the town skyline. Open daily 11am-11pm. ❸

Fischermann's, An der Fährbrücke 3 (☎ 29 23 22). Massive, lively restaurant-bar sprawling onto the pier serves well-prepared fish dishes (€8-14). Open daily 10am-2am. ❸

🅖 SIGHTS

■ **DEUTSCHES MUSEUM FÜR MEERESKUNDE UND FISCHEREI.** Between the Alter and Neuer Markt, Stralsund's two major museums have replaced the monks of the **St. Katharinen** monastery. An international center for marine research, and Germany's largest oceanographic museum, the **Meeresmuseum** is home to four aquariums, including a lightless tank for deep-sea fish and a tide pool environment. *(On the corner of Mönchstr. and Böltcherstr. ☎ 265 00. Open daily June-Sept. 10am-6pm; Oct.-May 10am-5pm. Feedings Sa-Su 11am. €5.50, students €4, family €14.)*

■ **KULTURHISTORISCHES MUSEUM.** Sharing the rooms of St. Katharinen with the Meeresmuseum, this wide-ranging collection covers all aspects of Stralsund's history with a display that includes ice-age relics, medieval altarpieces, and a furnished living room from the 1960's. The highlight of the collection is the spectacular **Goldschatz von Hiddensee,** a set of intricate gold jewelry created by the Vikings of Schleswig in the 9th century. The treasure washed up on the shores of nearby Hiddensee between1873 and 1874, and contains 596 grams of pure gold. *(☎ 287 90. Open daily 10am-5pm. €3, students €1.50, family €8.)*

ALTER MARKT. As the name would suggest, the Alter Markt is surrounded by some of Stralsund's oldest buildings. The well-preserved 14th-century *Backsteingotik* facade of the **Rathaus** sports coats-of-arms from members of the Hanseatic League, including Stralsund's trademark green-and-gold 12-point stars. A pleasant inner courtyard opens to the street on all sides of the building. Next to the Rathaus, **St. Nikolaikirche** has watched over the town since the 13th century. The church's interior glows with fresh paint and recently restored altarpieces. Efforts are underway to replace the missing second spire, destroyed in WWII. *(Open Apr.-Sept. M-Sa 10am-5pm, Su 2-4pm; Oct.-Mar. M-Sa 10am-noon and 2-4pm, Su 2-4pm.)*

NEUER MARKT. After the wealthier half of Stralsund built St. Nikolai, merchants from the other part of town responded by erecting the **Marienkirche** on Neuer Markt. The city's most impressive church, this late-Gothic colossus is best known for its rare mid-17th-century Stellwagen organ. The largest and best-preserved of its kind in the world, its pipes range from 8mm to 10m. *(Concerts W 8pm, around €10.)* Climb 100m to the top of the church tower for a spectacular 360° view of Stralsund. *(Open M-F 9am-6pm, Sa-Su 10am-5pm. Tower €1.50, students and children €1.)*

JOHANNISKLOSTER. One block up Külpstr. from the Alter Markt is the Johanniskloster, a Franciscan monastery built in 1254, 45 years after St. Francis of Assisi founded the order. Inside the red-brick Gothic hallways are 14th-century mosaics, murals, and the town archives. On the upper floor, check out the unique *Raucherboden* (smoking attic), with a row of small chambers used as kitchens. The smoke from the stoves within these chambers vented directly into the chimneyless attic, which helped preserve the wooden beams of the rafters and imparted the distinctive smoky smell that is still noticeable today. *(Monastery open May-Oct. daily 10am-6pm. €2.10, students €1.70, family €4.)* Next to the monastery is the former **Johanniskirche;** destroyed in 1944, the ruins now host occasional open-air concerts and theater performances. The monestary courtyard contains a dramatic Ernst Barlach sculpture in which Mary holds the stiff body of her dead son Jesus, who wears a war helmet; their bodies form a cross. In the public courtyard outside is a **memorial** to Stralsund's lost Jewish community. Originally in the Apollonienmarkt, near the former site of the synagogue, it was placed in the cloister after it was vandalized by neo-Nazis in 1991. A permanent swastika remains. (*Outer courtyard free.*)

ST. JAKOBIKIRCHE. At the eastern end of Böttcherstr., St. Jakobi is the third of Stralsund's monumental churches. It was damaged in 1944 and later mutilated during DDR days; the organ pipes were removed and used as rain gutters. Financial constraints have hampered restoration efforts, nonetheless, the crumbling church currently hosts a number of theatrical performances and concerts. (*☎ 29 04 02. Open M-F 10am-5pm, Sa-Su 11am-3pm. Free.*)

RÜGEN ISLAND

Bathing in the Baltic Sea northeast of Stralsund, Germany's largest island is a natural paradise of impressive variety, boasting white beaches, rugged chalk cliffs, beech forests, meadows, heaths, and swamps. Ancient stone burial sites and monuments scattered about the island are remnants of Rügen's past dating back to the stone age. The island's modern history began when Teutonic tribes inhabiting the island were pushed out by the Slavs in the 5th century. The Danes came to the

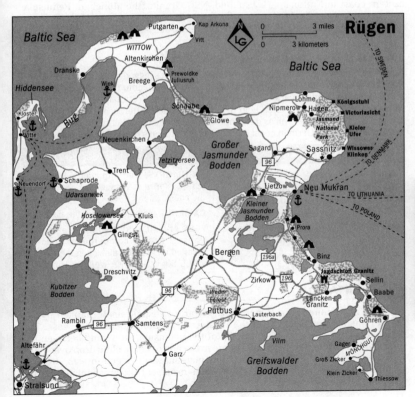

MECKLENBURG-
VORPOMMERN

island 500 years later, converting the Slavs to Christianity. Under Swedish control after the Thirty Years' War, Rügen later became part of Prussia. Wilhelm Malte I, the *Fürst*, or Prince, of Putbus, was the first to introduce bathing tourism to the island in the early 1800s, and by the beginning of the 20th century the island was a favorite destination for nobility. The fall of the Berlin Wall opened up Rügen to a flood of westerners, and the island is fast becoming one of Germany's favorite vacation destinations, attracting bikers, hikers, and throngs of eager beachgoers.

Trains leave Stralsund, the mainland gateway to Rügen for Binz and Sassnitz (1hr., 1 per hr., €8.40) via Bergen, an unattractive transportation hub in the center of the island. **Buses** connect Stralsund with Rügen's largest towns, and a **ferry** runs from Stralsund to Schaprode, near Hiddensee, on Rügen's west coast.

Most visitors drive onto the island and public transportation tends to be expensive. To get to Kap Arkona in the north or Göhren in the south you'll have to take an **RPNV** bus from Bergen. (☎ 03838 194 49. 1 per hr.; €3-6, day pass €8.20, bicycles €1.50 per ride.) The **Rasender Roland,** a narrow-gauge rail line with historic steam locomotives, runs every 2hr. from Putbus to Göhren (€8) with stops in many spa towns; however, with a top rate of 30km per hr., the railway is more of a tourist attraction than a means of speedy transportation. The best way to appreciate Rügen's stunning scenery and picturesque towns is by hiking and biking. Although the whole island is criss-crossed and circled by trails, the best are found along the eastern coast in Nationalpark Jasmund, NSG Granitz, the Mönchgut Peninsula, and on Hiddensee Island to the west. There are 21 campgrounds in Rügen, with the majority to the southeast on the Mönchgut Peninsula.

JASMUND NATIONAL PARK

Carved by massive glaciers 12,000 years ago, Jasmund's jagged, white *Kreideklippen* (chalk cliffs) drop into an emerald-green sea. Due to erosion, the sheer faces of the tooth-like cliffs hang precariously over the stormy coast. Fortunately, the roots of the red beech trees above the cliffs help the chalk to weather fierce Baltic winds. These 5000-year-old groves, as well as miles of canopied forest (the Baltic's largest), and the highest cliffs on the German coast make Jasmund Rügen's most attractive landscape.

THE PARK AT A GLANCE

AREA: 30km². Highest point 161m.

CLIMATE: Island weather, changing quickly between sun and rain. Warm, sunny summers; wet and windy winters.

FEATURES: Chalk cliffs, beech forests, wet grasslands, rolling meadows.

GATEWAY: Sassnitz.

HIGHLIGHTS: Cliff formations: Königsstuhl (118m) and Wissower Klinken along the coast.

CAMPING: Forbidden within the park.

FEES AND RESERVATIONS: Reservations at nearby campgrounds recommended in summer; parking in the Hagen lot €5.80; in Sassnitz "Wedding Lot" €4.

■ ORIENTATION

Jasmund is a peninsula of Rügen that is nearly an island itself, flanked by the Großer Jasmunder Bodden on the west and the Baltic Sea on the east. The national park is at the easternmost tip of the peninsula, stretching between the towns of Sassnitz in the south and Lohme in the north. Chalk cliffs drop over 100m into the sea along the coast and Stubnitz plateau, while beech forests, orchids, springs, lakes, moors, and ancient gravesites ornament the areas inland. Hiking and biking trails run throughout the park.

⌐ TRANSPORTATION

Rügen is small enough that no matter where you stay, getting to the park will not take long. Trains run from Stralsund to Sassnitz, the gateway to the park. (1 per hr., last return train 11pm, €8.40.) Once in Jasmund, bikes and feet are the best modes of transportation, as trails are plentiful and well-marked. Many of the more scenic coastline trails are off-limits to bikes because of numerous stairways. Bus #408 runs from the Sassnitz train station to "Stubbenkammer," 100m from the park's most famous site, the **Königsstuhl**. (3 per hr. in summer, until 5:40pm, €1.30.) Private cars are not permitted on the 3km stretch of road leading to the Königsstuhl. Drivers must park their cars in Hagen (€5.80 per hr.), and take the #419 "Pendelbus" shuttle to the Königsstuhl. (Every 10min. in summer, €2.40.)

⚡ PRACTICAL INFORMATION

Emergency: Police ☎ 110. **Fire** and **Ambulance** ☎ 112.

Climate: Summer is the best time to come, as temperatures are generally warm enough for hikers to wear shorts and t-shirts. Surprise rain-showers spring up year-round.

Ranger Stations: The brand-new **Nationalparkhaus am Königsstuhl** (☎ 038392 66 17 66; www.koenigsstuhl.com), by the entrance to the Königsstuhl lookout point has maps and information on hand, as well as multimedia exhibits about the park. Open daily Apr.-Oct. 9am-6pm; Nov.-Mar. 10am-6pm. The #6 ("Wedding") parking lot in Sassnitz is also staffed daily 9:30am-6pm.

Gear: Light hiking boots are adequate for the trails here. Bike trails are mostly bumpy cobblestone paths, so a mountain bike and an extra tire tube are recommended. Rain gear is a good idea at any time of year.

Tours: Free 2hr. tours of the Königsstuhl area leave from the Hagen parking lot daily at 11am. Adler Schiffe (☎ 038378 477 90) runs ferries past the Jasmund Park shoreline, departing daily from Göhren, Sellin, and Binz. (2½-4hr., €12.50-14.50.)

⛺ CAMPING

The closest campsite to the park is **Wald-Camping-Nipmerow ❶**, 4km west of Königsstuhl. Take bus #408 from the Sassnitz station (dir.: Stubbenkammer) to "Nipmerow." Most buses do not make the complete trip; be sure to ask before boarding. Otherwise, get off at "Stubbenkammer," take the #419 "Pendelbus" to Hagen, then hike the remaining 2km to reach the campground in Nipmerow. (☎ 038302 92 44. Bike/tent rental available. Reception 7am-6pm, but arrive anytime and check in the next morning. €3.50 per person, €2.50-3 per tent.)

🏔 HIKING

◼**KÖNIGSSTUHL HOCHUFERWEG.** The park's signature trail is an 8.1km, 3hr. hike that starts in the #6 ("Wedding") parking lot in Sassnitz at the end of Wedding-str. and runs the length of the park's coastline, with other trails branching off of it. The trail leads fairly easily from one scenic lookout to the next, often over enormous flights of stairs. When hiking, you can follow the white blazes with blue horizontal stripes painted on trees, but the signs at trail crossings or maps from the ranger station are more reliable. 600m into the trail, the **Piratenschlucht** offers a chance to make for the beach, but the trail continues on to the beautiful **Wissower Klinken** (2km) chalk cliffs. Three kilometers farther is the **Kieler Bach** lookout.

From here, you can walk the next stretch along the rocky water's edge or head back up the trail to the **Victoriasicht** lookout. This little balcony over the cliff offers a dramatic view with fewer tourists than the famous **Königsstuhl** a half kilometer farther. If you follow the mob there, you'll have to pay for the view (€1), which is only slightly better than what you can see from Victoriasicht for free. According to local legend, the first man to climb the crumbling cliff face to this chair-like formation became king of Rügen—hence *Königsstuhl* or "king's throne."

HERTHASEE. Running from the Hagen parking lot to the Königsstuhl beneath the shelter of red beech trees, this 3km trail offers an alternative to the shuttle bus. Two kilometers into the walk is the **Herthasee**, a lake named after the German harvest goddess. According to myth, Hertha drowned her mortal servants in this lake, and their spirits are said to gather on the banks each night. The **Herthaburg**, a U-shaped earth wall built by the Slavs in the 7th century, still stands near the shore.

BINZ
☎ 038393

Blindingly white seaside villas with frilly wooden gables and wide balconies exemplify the *Bäderarchitecktur* (spa architecture) of Rügen's largest, liveliest, and most elegant resort town. Tanned Germans get shade from *Strandkörbe* (covered wicker beach chairs) and tents. On warm days, the water teems with swimmers.

Pauli's Radshop, Hauptstr. 9a rents bikes from €5.50 per day. (☎ 669 24. Open daily 9am-6pm.) A **tourist office**, Hauptstr. 1, books rooms for free. From the station, take a right on Dollahner Str., which becomes Jasmunder Str., and turn left at Haupstr. (☎ 134 60; www.binz.de. Open M-Sa 9:30am-6pm.) A city-run office also books rooms; head right out of the station, and curve right at the next street onto Proraer Chausee. (☎ 337 89. Open M-F 10am-6pm, Sa 10am-5pm. Internet €1 per 10min.) For a **taxi**, call ☎ 03838 25 26 27. A **laundromat, SB Waschsalon**, is at Proraer Chaussee 3c. (Wash €4. Dry €1 for 13min. Open daily 6am-11pm.) The **post office**, 18609, is at Zeppelinstr. 7. (Open M-F 9am-1pm and 2-5pm, Sa 9:30am-12:30pm).

Accommodations in Binz fill up quickly and run €5-10 more than those on other parts of the island. *Ferienwohnungen* (vacation apartments) are the best options, but only for couples or groups staying for a minimum of three days. The most cost-effective (doubles €40-70 per night) line the narrow alley at the eastern edge of Binz that climbs the Klünderberg. The little homes are opposite a quiltwork slope of individual garden plots, and the view of the Schmachter lake to the south is truly stunning. The room squeeze doesn't spare Rügen's youth hostel, ◪ **Jugendherberge Binz (HI) ❷**, Strandpromenade 35. Judging by its location and gourmet breakfast, one could mistake the hostel for a luxurious beach hotel. (☎ 325 97; www.jugendherberge-binz.de. Breakfast included. Curfew 11pm but you can get the access code. Dorms €22; under 27 €19.) If the hostel in Binz is full, you can try the **Jugendherberge Sellin (HI) ❷**, Kiefernweg 4, a block away from the train station in the neighboring resort town of Sellin. (☎ 0381 77 66 70. Breakfast included. Dorms €24; under 27 €20.) Also in Sellin, **Haus Sellin ❸**, Wilhelmstr. 9, occupies a historic gabled home along the town's main promenade. (☎ 038303 153; www.haus-sellin.de. Singles without bath €31-36; doubles €46-59.)

Nudists enjoy Binz's *FKK* beaches, tastefully situated at the far ends of town. Jazz crooners and oompah bands make frequent appearances on the outdoor stage by the pier at the *Kurplatz*. At the end of Zepplinstr. **Edeka Neukauf**, Schillerstr. 5 sells groceries. (Open M-F 8am-8pm, Sa 8am-6pm, Su 2-6pm.) Binz also teems with restaurants, bars, and ice cream stands. The **Strandcafé Binz ❸**, Strandpromenade 29, sets in pizza, pasta, and herring to the tune of €6-9. (Open daily from 11am.)

GRANITZ AND GÖHREN ☎038308

The 🏰 **Jagdschloß Granitz,** in the heart of the dense Granitz forest, is an odd, castle-like hunting lodge designed in 1836 by Prussian architect **Friedrich Schinkel,** whose unmistakable creations can be seen all over the island. Built on top of the Tempelberg hill, its 38m tower offers a breathtaking panorama of the island. Faint of heart, beware: 164 animal heads are mounted in the **Jagdmuseum,** and antlers have been crafted into chairs and chandeliers. (Open May-Sept. daily 9am-6pm; Oct.-Apr. Tu-Su 10am-4pm. €3, students €2.50.) The *Roland* rail line stops at the Jagdschloß, as does the **Jagdschloßexpress,** which leaves from the *Kurhaus* in Binz (round-trip from Binz past the Jagdschloß to Göhren €7, children €3). From the *Roland* "Jagdschloß" stop, head uphill on the trail off to the right to reach the castle. To walk or bike the 5km from Binz, take the red-striped trail near the top of the Klünderberg hill in eastern Binz. Heading south from the "Jagdschloß" stop to the village of Lancken-Granitz, you'll pass huge prehistoric graves dating back to 2300 BC; even larger ones lie southwest of town. The *Roland*'s final stop is **Göhren,** on the easternmost tip of the forested **Mönchgut Peninsula,** which was settled by monks in the 13th century. The city sits on a hill, with a view of Greifswald across the sea from the church off Strandstr. Numerous **hiking** and **bike trails** lead through peaceful beaches, forests, and the rolling hills of the **Zickerschen Berge.**

An excellent bike trip (approximately 2hr.) follows the well-marked trail from Göhren through Theissow to Klein Zicker on the tip of the peninsula. Catch the bus back from Klein Zicker, or retrace the route to return to Göhren. Göhren's main attractions are the **Mönchguter Museen,** four tiny museums scattered about the town. The first of these, the **Heimatmuseum,** describes the geology of the Mönchgut peninsula, and traces the evolution of Göhren from a fishing village to a tourist resort. A block away, the **Museumshof** displays antique farming machinery. On Thiessower Str., off Strandstr., the **Rookhus** has a display of fishing equipment inside a historic building. Farther down the hill on Theissower Str., you can peer inside the cargo hold of the 20m-long **Museumsschiff Luise,** or learn knot-tying skills in the summer every Wednesday from 10am-noon. (☎21 75. Heimatmuseum and Museumshof: open daily mid-Apr. to May and Sept. to mid-Oct. 10am-5pm; mid-Oct. to mid-Apr. 10am-4pm. Rookhus: June-Aug. 10am-2pm; mid-Apr. to May and Sept. to mid-Oct. 11am-2pm; closed winter. Museumsschiff: June-Aug. 1-5:30pm; mid-Apr. to May and Sept. to mid-Oct. 1-5pm. Each museum €3, with *Kurkarte* and students €2.50; day card for all 4 museums €8/€6, family €15.)

Navigating in Göhren is simple, as almost everything is either on **Strandstraße** or just off it. To get to town center from the train station, turn left and take Bahnhofstr. until it turns into Strandstr., then follow it up the hill. Frequent **buses** connect Göhren to Binz, Bergen, and Sassnitz to the north and Klein Zicker to the south (€3-6). The **Fahrradverleih,** Kastanienalle 8, rents touring bikes for €5 and mountain bikes for €6. (☎254 06. Open daily 9am-noon and 4-6pm.) To get to the **tourist office,** Poststr. 9, follow Strandstr. from the train station up the hill as it turns into Poststr.; the office is on the right. (☎667 90; www.goehren.de. Open M-F 9am-6pm, Sa 9am-noon.) The **Fremdenverkehrsverein,** Berliner Str. 8, a block past the Kurverwaltung, books rooms. (☎259 40; info@zimmervermittlung-goehren-ostsee.de.) A **Pharmacy** is at Strandstr. 3. (☎911 94. Open M-F 8am-12:30pm and 2:30-6pm, Sa 9am-noon.) The **post office,** 18586 Göhren, is inside the **Edeka** grocery store at the corner of Strandstr. and Waldstr. (Open M-F 8am-7pm, Sa-Su 8am-1pm and 4-6pm.) Göhren's **campground, Regenbogen Camp Göhren ❶,** is one block to the right of the train station, near the beach. The site boasts a restaurant, cinema (€4.50), **laundromat,** and **Spar** grocery. (☎901

CONDOMS, ANYONE?

For the stereotypically straight-faced German, the country's rising incidence of sexually transmitted disease is embarrassing. In a bold effort to de-stigmatize condom usage, the government has unleashed a series of public service announcements aimed at youth. First came the surreal TV commercial in which a group of school-children in a streetcar toss around colorful wrappers; a close-up reveals these to be filled not with candy, but condoms.

Another campaign uses posters with eye-catching double entendres such as the famous "Gummi, Bärchen?" under a giant, multi-colored teddy bear. Innocent enough, until closer inspection shows the cuddly guy to be a mosaic of condoms, *Gummi* referring not to sweets of the small, chewy HARIBO variety, but, er, to that... other kind.

The state-backed PR campaign has drawn criticism from many groups. Meanwhile, the private sector has capitalized on the ads, packaging condoms in pink hearts filled with glitter and selling them next to stuffed animals. Despite the admonitions to "mach's mit," (join in), condom sales have actually dropped in recent years. To get the public involved, two competitions have been held for poster ideas, the winners being sent on a trip to the Olympics. The effectiveness of the initiative won't be seen for years, but in the meantime, Germans are getting a good laugh out of it.

20; www.regenbogen-camp.de. Reception Su-Th 8am-9pm, F-Sa 8am-10pm. €4.90 per person, €6.90 per tent, less in off-season. Reservations possible only for stays of 3 or more days.) For a hot meal try **Zum Leuchtfeuer ❷**, Max-Dreyer-Str. 6, an inexpensive restaurant close to the center of town. From Strandstr., turn onto Max-Dreyer-Str.; the restaurant is up the hill on the left. Fish and meat dishes range €6-9. (Open daily 11:30am-2pm and 5-11pm.)

KAP ARKONA AND VITT ☎038391

At Rügen's northernmost extreme, the dramatic **Kap Arkona**—Germany's only cape—lies on the charming half-island of Wittow (in the local *Plattdeutsch*, "land of the wind"). Quieter and less accessible than Rügen's southern regions, Wittow is carpeted with wildflowers. Near Kap Arkona is the tiny fishing village of Vitt, with its 13 reed homes. **Buses** run every hr. from Sassnitz (#419, 40min., €3) and Bergen (#110, 1hr., €3) to Altenkirchen, where you can transfer to bus #403 to Putgarten (15min., €1), 1.5km away from the cape and its three lighthouses. The 1km walk along the coast between Kap Arkona and Vitt is jaw-dropping: in spring and summer, flowering bushes and brilliant red poppies carpet the hills. The gorgeous 4.6km loop between Putgarten, Kap Arkona, and vitt is perfect for biking. (Rent bikes by the tourist office. Open daily 10am-6pm. €2.50 per hr., €7 per day.) You may pass the painfully slow *Arkonabahn*, a tourist train that connects these destinations for a modest fee. (30min. round-trip; 2 per hr.; €2 one-way to either Kap Arkona or vitt from Putgarten, or €4 round-trip to both, children 6-13 €0.50/€1.50.) **Horse-drawn carts** also make the loop at a leisurely pace (1½hr. tour; 2 per hr.; €8, children €4). The combination souvenir shop and **tourist office**, in Putgarten's parking lot, 300m down the road from the bus stop in the direction of Altenkirchen, books rooms. (☎41 90; www.kap-arkona.de. Open M-F 9am-5pm, Sa 10am-5pm, Su 11am-5pm.) The **Wittower Campground ❶**, is 2km east of Altenkirchen. (☎133 20; www.wittower-campingpark.de. Reception 9am-noon and 3-6pm. Open Apr.-Oct. €4.50, €2.50 per child, tents €4-5.)

Before reunification, the three lighthouses on Kap Arkona were part of a restricted area belonging to the DDR's National People's Army. The distinctive short, rectangular **Schinkelturm**, designed by architect Karl Friedrich Schinkel, was built from 1826 to 1827. It guarded the DDR's sea borders, but has been open to the public since 1993. Next door, the **Neuer Leuchtturm,** with its 148 numbered steps, towers above the other two lighthouses, offering the best views. (Schinkelturm open daily 10am-7pm. Neuer Leuchtturm open daily 11am-6pm. Both €3, students €2.50.) From the two lighthouses, you can make the 42m descent to the beach below on the wooden steps of the **Königstreppe**. The nearby **Marinepeilturm** was built in 1927 and rigged with a fancy electronic system to listen in on British radio communications. The wide tower now houses art and museum exhibits along the stairway spiraling up to the observation deck. (Open daily 10am-6pm, €2, students €1.50; combination ticket €6/€5.) Next to the Marinepeilturm is the **Slawischer Burgwall,** the remains of an old Slavic fortification. (Open daily 10am-5:45pm. €1.) Dining options in the area are limited, but there are a few pleasant outdoor cafes in Vitt, and fishermen usually smoke and sell their catch at the town's tiny harbor.

◪ DAYTRIP FROM RÜGEN: HIDDENSEE ☎038300

West of Rügen is Hiddensee, called by the *Plattdeutsch*, *"das söte Länneken"* (the sweet little island). The majority of it is now protected as part of the **Nationalpark Vorpommersche Boddenlandschaft** (Vorpommern Lagoon National Park), and Hiddensee remains the same sliver of unadulterated natural beauty that drew Sigmund Freud, Albert Einstein, and Thomas Mann to its shores. Automobiles are prohibited—even garbage trucks are horse-drawn—so bikes rule the island.

Hiddensee makes a great daytrip from Stralsund or anywhere on Rügen. You can easily see the entire island in a day with a **bike.** Bike rentals *(Fahrradverleih)* are hard to miss; the standard rate is €5 for a 5-speed. Since many of the island's roads are either muddy country trails or sandy beach paths, a mountain bike with fat tires and plenty of gears is best. **Reederei Hiddensee** (☎03831 26 81 38) operates ferries from Stralsund to Hiddensee's three towns: Neuendorf, Vitte, and Kloster. (90min.; round-trip €14-18 including Hiddensee Kurkarte, bike allowance €6.50/€7.50.) To get to Schaprode, take bus #410 from Bergen. (30min., €3.40.)

Vitte, with 650 residents, is Hiddensee's main town and home to the island's best beaches. As Hiddensee has neither a hostel nor a campground, visit the **tourist office,** Norderende 162, in Vitte, to book a room. (☎642 26; www.seebad-insel-hiddensee.de. Open May-Sept. M-F 8:30am-5pm, Sa-Su 10am-noon; Oct. M-F 8:30am-4pm; Nov.-Mar. M-F 9am-3pm) The **National Park Information Center,** Norderende 2, at the northern edge of Vitte on the way to Kloster, can provide further assistance, and hosts a display on the unique geological history of the island. (☎680 41. Open daily in summer 10am-4pm; winter 10am-3pm.) The **weather station** on Hiddensee, which also forecasts for all of Rügen, will keep you posted on approaching thunderstorms (☎680 70). In Vitte, you can catch lunch at **Godewind,** Süderende 53, before you start exploring. Try the fresh fish (€8-14), and a glass of *Sanddornsaft*, a rust-colored, honey-like local specialty drink (€3.50), also available in bottled form from many stores on the island (€3-6 per bottle, €8-13 for the alcoholic variant.) For groceries, there is an **Edka Markt** a block from the Vitte Harbor on Wallweg. (☎66 00. Open M-F 8am-7pm, Sa 8am-6pm, Su 1-5pm.)

GREIFSWALD ☎03834

Graced with one of Germany's oldest and smallest universities, Greifswald belongs to the students. Small gold plaques throughout the historic college town commemorate Greifswald's 545 years of professors, and the cobblestone streets swarm with students on bikes. Even in the summer, students populate the handful of bars tucked between the historic churches of the remarkably well-preserved Altstadt, which was never a target of Allied air raids.

⚡📠 ORIENTATION AND TRANSPORTATION. Greifswald is the easternmost city on Germany's Baltic coast, 60km west of the Polish frontier. Signs of life in Greifswald are confined to the Altstadt, home to all of the city's historic architecture and the majority of the restaurants and nightlife. **Trains** run to: **Berlin** (3½-4hr., 1 per hr., €28-34); **Rostock** (1¾hr., 1 per 2hr., €15); **Schwerin** (3hr., 1 per hr., €27); **Stralsund** (20min., 1 per 30min., €6). The **bus station (ZOB)** is across from the train station. (Single ride €1.50, daypass €3.50.) To get a **taxi**, call ☎50 22 22. Rent **bikes** at **Zweirad Kruger**, Gützkowerstr. 81-82, on the way to the hostel from the station. (☎50 22 68. Bikes from €5 per day. Open M-F 9am-6:30pm and Sa 9am-1pm.)

🗒 PRACTICAL INFORMATION. At the **tourist office** in the Rathaus am Markt, book a room for free or get a free map of the Altstadt. (☎52 13 80; www.greif-swald.de. Open May-Sept. M-F 9am-6pm, Sa 10am-2pm;, July-Aug. also Su 10am-2pm. Oct.-Apr. M-F 9am-5pm.) Do **laundry** at **Schnell und Sauber**, Gützkowerstr. 19. (Wash €3. Dry €0.50 per 15min. Open daily 6am-11pm.) A **pharmacy** is at Markt 1. (☎21 38 or 25 35. Open M-F 7:30am-6:30pm, Sa 9am-noon.) The **post office** is down the street at Markt 15-19, 17489 Greifswald. (Open M-F 9am-6pm, Sa 9am-noon.)

🏠🍴🎵 ACCOMMODATIONS, FOOD, AND NIGHTLIFE. Greifswald's friendly and modern **Jugendherberge Griefswald (HI) ❷**, Pestalozzistr. 11-12, is 15min. from the Altstadt. From the station, take a right on Bahnhofstr., a right on Gützkowerstr., then a left on Pestalozzistr. Students and parents sip beers in the small cafe upstairs. (☎516 90; fax 51 69 10. Breakfast, 7:30-9am, and sheets included. Reception 8am-10pm. Dorms €21, under 27 €18. Nonmembers add €3 per night.)

For **groceries**, go to **SPAR**, in the Dompassage mall near the entrance at Weissgerberstr. 11. (Open M-F 9am-8pm, Sa 9am-4pm. Also at Gützkowerstr. 37. Open M-F 8am-6:30pm, Sa 7am-noon.) Ritzy cafes line the cobblestone Market in front of the Rathaus. Nearby, **Das Sofa ❷**, Bruggstr. 29 has light pasta and pizza (€4), lots of comfy sofas, and a kitschy film motif. (Open daily from 11am.) **Café Malanders ❶**, Lange Str. 49, inside the *Soziokulturelles Zentrum*, offers small entrees, such as soup or bratwurst, for €2-3. (☎89 95 51. Open Tu-Th 11:30am-5pm, F 11:30am-4pm.) **Café Caspar ❷**, Fischstr. 11, serves tasty breakfasts (€3-5), baguettes (€4), and salads (€5-7) in a sophisticated environment, and doubles as a bar at night. (☎89 13 00. Open daily from 10am.) Greifswald's **Mensa ❶** is located at Am Schießwall, off Schulhagen. (☎86 17 11. Full meals €3-4. Open M-F 11am-2pm and 5-7:30pm.) Thursday and Saturday nights it reopens as **Mensaclub**, fueled by youthful spirit and rock music. The Mensa also shows movies twice a week. (Su German films, W English blockbusters. Movies 8pm, €1. Club: cover Th €3.50, students €1.50, Sa everyone €1.50. Open Th from 10pm, Sa from 11pm.) When they're not at the Mensa, the Uni students flock to **Mitt n' Drin**, Domstr. 53 (☎89 95 14. Open M-F 9am-3am, Sa-Su 2pm-3am.), or **Domburg**, Domstr. 21, with deep-red, high-backed sofa chairs. (☎77 63 51. Open M-F from 11am, Sa-Su from 5pm.) At **CoMiX**, Steinbeckerstr. 30, an able team of student bartenders mixes on both floors. (Open daily 11am-3am.) **Pariser**, Kapaunenstr. 20, was founded in 1991 in an abandoned building and runs, among other projects, a bar with a made-from-scratch feel, where bold guests can sign up to DJ. (☎85 55 89. Open W-Su from 8pm.)

🅖 SIGHTS. Stretching high above the Greifswald skyline is the **St. Nikolaikirche**, Domstr. 54. Around the tower of the 14th-century basilica, a small viewing platform is accessible by a narrow, 60m-high spiral staircase. Like the rest of the Altstadt, the church survived WWII partly because a German general risked death by surrendering the city to the Soviets in April of 1945. (☎89 79 66. Open May-Oct. M-Sa 10am-4pm, Su 11:30am-1pm; Nov.-Apr. M-F 11am-3pm, Su 11:30am-1pm. €1.50, students €1. Tours W 2pm, €2.) Cannonballs that struck the east wall of the 13th-century **St. Marienkirche**, Friedrich-Löfferstr. 68, during a war with Brandenburg in 1678, are still lodged there. The early Gothic interior is also worth a look. (☎22 63. Open June-Oct. M-F 10am-5pm, Sa 10am-noon, Su 10:45am-noon; Nov.-Apr. M-F noon-1pm, Su 10:45am-noon; May M-F 10am-noon, Su 10:45am-noon. Free.)

The harshness of the university professors has been memorialized in the **Karzer,** entrance at Rubinenstr. 1. These prison cells in the basement of the main university building were used to punish students for various archaic offenses, including chasing "strange women" and drinking too much. The rowdiest served sentences of up to 10 days, although by the early 20th century it was common practice to let student prisoners out for a couple of hours each day to eat and socialize. Some of the best parties were purportedly held in *Karzer* cells—students would climb walls to be let in the windows. (☎86 11 22. Open M 1-3pm. Turn left once inside the building, entrance next to the AStA office at the end of the hall.)

The **Gemäldegalerie,** Mühlenstr. 15, displays a large collection of paintings from the Romantic and Impressionist eras, including a Van Gogh. (☎89 43 57. Open Tu-Su 10am-6pm. €3, students €1.50.) Near the train station, the university's modest **botanical garden,** Münterstr. 11, features pleasant gardens and a greenhouse with lush hanging vines and spiky cacti. (☎86 11 30. Open M-F 9am-3:45pm; Apr.-Nov. also Sa-Su 1-4pm; May-Sept. also Sa-Su 1-6pm. Dec.-Feb. also Sa-Su 1-3pm.)

Just east of Greifswald, the coastal villages of **Wieck** and **Eldena** supply the city with fresh fish. Several festivals take place on the waterfront during the summer, but the area's main attractions are the crumbling arches and hollow sanctuary of the **Klosterruine** in Eldena, across from Wolgaster Str. Take bus #6 (dir.: Wieck Brücke) to the end of the line. Turn towards Greifswald and follow the signs 450m down Studentensteig, the pedestrian path. This 12th-century Cistercian monastery once housed Danish monks, but was destroyed by Swedish soldiers plundering for raw materials. **Caspar David Friedrich** immortalized the cloister ruins in his color-infused paintings, some of which are displayed in the Gemäldegalerie. In summer, the ruins become a venue for concerts and theater performances.

USEDOM ISLAND

During the 19th century, Usedom was a favorite vacation destination for Germany's elite, earning it the nickname "Berlin's bathtub." Depression and war scattered the tourists, but their beach toys—enormous, gaudy houses and long piers—remain. Today, the island is the playground of the *petit bourgeoisie;* a swarm of upper-middle-class families fills the beaches and rents rooms in the restored palaces. A hilly bike trail spans the island's tall, sun-dappled woods, offering access to secluded warm water beaches. Given the island's natural beauty, you may want to stick to the wilderness and use the tourist-packed towns only as refueling stops.

⌐ TRANSPORTATION

Usedom lies at the northeastern corner of Germany; the easternmost portion of the island belongs to Poland. Tourists fill the island in July and August, so it's a good idea to reserve rooms in advance. Usedom is connected to the national rail system at **Züssow,** via **Wolgast.** From the station at Züssow, take the **Usedomer Bäderbahn (UBB)** to get onto the island (€5 to Zinnowitz). The UBB line also runs the length of the island, connecting all of Usedom's towns (€1-5, daypass €10). **Adler-Schiffe** (☎038378 477 90) runs **ferries** from the Usedom resorts to Binz on the island of **Rügen** every Friday (2½hr., €19). The price of a *Kurkarte* is automatically added to your accommodation bill (€2 per day; under 18 May-Sept. €1, Oct.-Apr. €0.50), but the card is a good investment in any case, as it offers free access to all beaches as well as discounts at many of Usedom's tourist spots.

ZINNOWITZ

☎ **038377**

Commercially upscale, this resort town is packed with a diverse crowd of beachgoers. For a **taxi** call ☎ 405 67. At the corner of Neue Strandstr. and Dünenstr., the **Kurverwaltung** (spa administration), Neue Sandstr. 30, books rooms for free. (☎ 49 20; fax 422 29. Open M-F 9am-6pm, Sa-Su 10am-3pm.) They also offer **bike tours** that leave from the office. (M 9:30am, Tu and Th 10am. €3, with *Kurkarte* €1.50.) Rent **bikes** at **Fahrradverleih Meister Betrieb**, Dr.-Wachsmann-Str. 5. (☎ 428 69. May-Aug. €4, Sept.-Apr. €3. Open daily 8am-noon and 1-7pm.) There is a **pharmacy** at Neue Strandstr. 39. (☎ 421 66. Open July-Aug. M-F 8am-7pm, Sa 8:30am-1pm; Sept.-June M-F 8am-6pm, Sa 8:30am-noon.) The **library**, in the back of the Kurverwaltung building at Neue Sandstr. 30, offers **Internet** access. (€1.02 per 15min. Open M-F 9am-noon, and M 1-4pm, Tu 1-6pm, Th 1-6pm, F 1-4pm.) The **post office** is at Neue Strandstr. 38, 17454 Zinnowitz. (Open M-F 8am-6pm, Sa 8am-noon.)

The **Sportschule ❷**, Dr.-Wachsmann-Str. 30, caters to sports teams, but opens up its big, airy dorms to individuals as well. The track, soccer field, handball court, and ping-pong tables are free for guests. (☎ 422 68; fax 422 80. Breakfast €6. Book well in advance. Dorms €20.) Just down the street, the expansive **Campingplatz Pommernland**, Dr.-Wachsmann-Str. 40, rents **camping plots ❶** and has several new but expensive **bungalows ❹**. (☎ 403 48; fax 403 49. Reception daily 8am-noon and 2-9pm. Camping €5 per person, €4 per student, €4-6 per tent. Less for off-season and longer stays. Bungalows: doubles €80; quads €100; 6-person €110.) Restaurants line the Neue Strandstr. and the Strandpromenade, while the **Edeka Neukauf** supermarket, Neue Strandstr. 38, provides the ingredients for a beach picnic. (Open M-F 8am-8pm, Sa 8am-6pm, Su noon-6pm.)

KOSEROW

☎ **038375**

At Usedom's narrowest point, forests of moss-covered trees fall onto stunningly beautiful beaches in what is, refreshingly, the least touristed of Usedom's resort towns. Koserow's central location on the island makes it a good base for hiking and biking excursions. A short climb to **Streckelsburg**, the island's highest point (58m), affords a beautiful view. An observation tower on this peak was used for tests of Germany's revolutionary V2 rockets until its destruction in 1997. For a **taxi** call ☎ 202 07. **Fahrrad Ortmann**, at Bahnhofstr. 2, rents **bikes**. (☎ 213 60. €3-5 per day. Open M-F 9am-noon and 2-6pm, Sa 9am-noon.) The **tourist office**, Hauptstr. 34, has free maps and hiking tips. (☎ 204 15; www.seebad-koserow.de. Open July-Aug. M-F 9am-6pm, Sa-Su 9am-noon; May-June and Sept. M-F 9am-6pm; Jan.-Apr. and Oct.-Mar. M-F 10am-4pm, Sa 9am-noon.) The **Zimmervermittlung**, Hauptstr. 11, will find you a place to sleep. (☎ 210 62; fax 210 64. Open M-F 9am-6pm, Sa 9am-2pm.) Most services line the Hauptstr., which connects to the train station via Bahnhofstr.: a pharmacy, **Apotheke**, Schulstr. 1b (☎ 207 26; open M-F 8am-6:30pm, Sa 8am-noon); **Internet** access at **Hotel Nautic**, Hauptstr. 46e (open daily 8am-10pm; €2.80 per 30min.); and a small **post office**, Hauptstr. 49a, near the train station, 17459 Koserow (open M-F 8:30am-12:30pm and 2:30-5:30pm, Sa 9-11am).

While nearly every house in the small town advertises rooms for rent, they are usually booked well in advance. **Wald und Meer**, above the beach on the west end of town 1km from Hauptstr. at the end of Forster-Schrödter-Str., runs a large **pension ❹** with lots of fake wood, and bare dorm-style accommodations in the **Radlercamp ❷**. (☎ 26 20; www.koserow.de. Breakfast included. Sheets €5. Camp: beds €18.

Pension: singles €48; doubles €76-82.) **Campingplatz Am Sandfeld ❶** has the best view on the island. By the station end of Hauptstr., take a right onto Siemenstr. and follow the signs for 15min. (☎207 59; fax 214 05. Laundry €2.50 per hr. Reception 8am-1pm and 3-10pm. Open Apr.-Sept. €5 per person, €2-4 per tent, €2.25 per car.) The best places to eat in Koserow are the bakeries along Hauptstr. and the *Salzhütten* by the pier, where fishermen packed herring during the 19th century, and where **Udo's Fischräucherei ❷** now smokes delicious salmon and sells *Fischbrötchen* (€1.50-3) and fish plates for €3-5. (Open 10am-5:30pm.) A **Netto** supermarket, Hauptstr. 67, sells groceries. (Open M-Sa 8am-8pm, Su noon-6pm.)

HERINGSDORF ☎038378

Heringsdorf has long been the most elite of Usedom's resort towns, as illustrated by the rows of ornate villas that line the waterfront. It was a favorite vacation spot of **Kaiser Wilhelm I**, who paid his first visit in 1820. His house, Delbrückestr. 6, is privately owned, but you can see it from the street. Although Heringsdorf was a popular destination for dignitaries straight through the DDR years, interest has spurted in the wake of reunification. The town's thriving tourist trade is evidenced by the new pier, the busy shops lining the **Platz des Friedens**, and the crowds strolling down the long beachfront promenade. To get to the *Platz*, which lies at the heart of Heringsdorf, turn left on Bülowstr. from the station, right on Friedenstr., and follow it to the end. A kilometer down the beach at Maxim-Gorki-Str. 13, **Villa Irmgard**, the former home of Russian writer **Maxim Gorki**, is now a museum housing Gorki's personal possessions and interesting temporary exhibits upstairs. (☎223 61. Open Apr.-Oct. and during Christmas Tu-Su noon-6pm; Nov.-Mar. Tu-Su 10am-4pm. €3, with *Kurkarte* €2, students €1, children under 14 free.)

Most tourist services cluster around the *Platz*. For a **taxi**, call ☎229 92. Rent a **bike** at **Fahrradverleih Elegant**, Kulmstr. 26a. (☎223 14. €5 per day. Open daily 9am-6pm.) Heringsdorf's **tourist office** is at Kulmstr. 33, next to the Rathaus. (☎24 51; fax 24 54. Open M-F 9am-6pm, Sa-Su 10am-3pm.) The **police office** is right down the street at Seestr. 12. A **pharmacy, Apotheke Heringsdorf,** is at Seestr. 40. (☎25 90. Open M-F 8am-6:30pm, Sa 8am-12:30pm.) Get your **Internet** fix at **Kaiserbäder I-Café,** Seestr. 17. (☎330 86. €4 per hr. Open M 2-6:30pm, Tu-Sa 2-10pm, Su 2-6pm.) The **post office,** Heringsdorf 17424, is at Seestr. 17. (☎228 80. Open M-F 9am-noon and 2-6pm, Sa 9am-noon.) During the high season (July-Aug.), it is virtually impossible to find accommodations in Heringsdorf; most vacationers reserve early in the year. The stunning **Jugendherberge Heringsdorf (HI) ❷**, Puschkinstr. 7, has taken over a set of old beach houses between Heringsdorf and Ahlbeck. From the train station, turn right on Liehrstr. and follow the signs right onto Delbrückestr. (☎223 25; www.jh-heringsdorf.de. Breakfast and sheets included. Reception 7am-10pm. Curfew 10pm. Reservations required. €18, over 26 €22.) If the hostel is full, call or email the *Zimmervermittlung* for rooms (☎01805 58 37 83; zimmervermittlung@drei-kaiserbaeder.de). Food in Heringsdorf is generally expensive and aimed at an older crowd, though the terraces of many cafes provide stunning beach views. **Terrassen Kaffee ❸**, Kulmstr. 29, serves traditional German dishes (€8-14) on a patio a block from the beach. (☎225 40. Open daily 11:30am-11pm.)

MECKLENBURG-VORPOMMERN

SCHLESWIG-HOLSTEIN

 The only *Land* to border two seas, Schleswig-Holstein bases its past and present livelihood on the trade generated at its port towns. Between the western coast of the North Sea and the eastern coast of the Baltic, the velvety plains are populated primarily by sheep and bales of hay. Although Schleswig-Holstein became a Prussian province in 1867 following Bismarck's defeat of Denmark, the region retains close cultural and commercial ties with Scandinavia. Linguistically, Schleswig-Holstein is also isolated from its southern neighbors by its various dialects of *Plattdeutsch* (literally, "flat German"), and, to a lesser extent, the Dutchlike Frisian spoken throughout the *Land*. The most noticeable difference is the greeting *Moin* or *Moin moin*, a *Plattdeutsch* salutation used all day.

HIGHLIGHTS OF SCHLESWIG-HOLSTEIN

BARE ALL on the barren dunes of the island **Sylt** (p. 205), Germany's favorite beach.

LOSE YOURSELF in the many museums of **Schleswig's Schloß Gottorf** (**p. 210**), or the winding streets of the charming fishing village of **Holm**.

SAVOR legendary marzipan from **Lübeck's I.G. Niederegger Marzipan Café** (p. 193) while listening to the strains of the world's largest mechanical organ echo through the magnificent **Marienkirche** (p. 194).

LÜBECK   ☎ 0451

At night, a medieval aura seems to linger in the shadowy facades of Lübeck's old homes and around the lit steeples of its many churches. In its heyday, the city was capital of the **Hanseatic League,** controlling trade across Northern Europe. Later it was home to literary giants **Heinrich and Thomas Mann,** who had a tempestuous relationship with the local bourgeoisie. Though most of the city was destroyed in WWII, the expert reconstruction efforts have left few scars. It may no longer be a center of political and commercial influence, but tourists still flock to Lübeck because of its history, its famous marzipan, and its red-blonde *Duckstein* beer.

⌐ TRANSPORTATION

Trains: To: **Berlin** (3½hr., 1 per hr., €35); **Hamburg** (45min., 1 per hr., €9); **Kiel** (1¼hr., 1 per hr., €13); **Rostock** (2hr., 1 per hr., €18); **Schwerin** (1¼hr., 1 per hr., €11).

Mitfahrzentrale: Beim Retteich 10, next to ZOB Bussteig #20 (☎194 40). Open daily 10am-9pm. To: **Berlin** (€17); **Dresden** (€28); **Frankfurt** (€29); **Munich** (€43).

Public Transportation: The Altstadt is easily seen on foot, though Lübeck also has an excellent bus network. The **ZOB** (central bus station) is across from the train station. Single ride €1.50-2, children €1; day pass €5.60. To reach the Lübeck airport, take Bus #6 (dir.: Blankenese/Seekamp) to "Flughafen." Direct questions to the **Service Center am ZOB** (☎888 28 28). Open M-F 5:15am-8pm, Sa-Su 10:15am-6pm.

Schleswig-Holstein

Ferries: Many ferries run tours of the canals out of the waterfront on An der Obertrave and An der Untertrave. **Quandt-Linie,** An der Obertrave (☎ 777 99), cruises around the Altstadt, canal, and harbor from the bridge in front of the Holstentor. €7, students €5.50. Daily every 30min. 10am-6pm.

Car Rental: Hertz, Willy-Brandt-Allee 1 (☎ 70 22 50), next to the Mövenpick near the train station. From €49 per day. Open M-F 7am-6pm, Sa 7am-1pm, Su 9-10am.

Bike Rental: Jugendwerkstatt Leihcycle, Schwartauer Allee 39 (☎ 426 60), at the intersection with Marienstr., in a back courtyard, rents bikes for €5 per day and has maps and bike path info. Open M-F 9am-5pm, Sa 10am-noon.

◪ PRACTICAL INFORMATION

Tourist Office: At Holstentorplatz 1 (☎ 122 54 20; fax 122 54 19), next to the Hostentor. The informed and helpful staff books rooms for free and sends you off with a €0.30 map. Open M-F 9:30am-6pm, Sa-Su 10am-3pm. The Lübeck **Happy Day Card,** sold at the tourist office, provides unlimited access to public transportation and offers discounted admission to a number of museums. 1 day €5, 3 days €10.

Currency Exchange: Deutsche Bank, Kohlmarkt 7 (☎ 14 90), center of the Altstadt near the bus stops. Open M-Tu and Th 8:30am-6pm, W 8:30am-1pm, F 8:30am-4:30pm.

Groceries: Aldi, just north of Hundestr. on Kanalstr. Open M-F 9am-7pm, Sa 8am-3pm.

Laundromat: McWash (☎ 702 03 57), on the corner of An der Mauer and Hüxterdamm. Wash 7kg €4, soap included. Dry €0.80 per 15min. Open daily 6am-9pm.

Emergency: Police ☎ 110. **Fire** ☎ 112. **Ambulance** ☎ 192 22.

Rape Crisis Center: Musterbahn 3 (☎ 70 46 40). Center open daily 5-7pm. Phone consultations M and W-F 10am-noon, Tu 5-7pm.

Pharmacies: Adler-Apotheke, Breite Str. 71 (☎ 798 85 15), across from the Marienkirche. Open M-F 8:30am-7pm, Sa 8:30am-6pm. After hours call ☎ 710 81.

Internet Access: Netzwerk, Wahmstr. 58 (☎ 396 80 90). €0.60 per 10min. Open M-F 1-10pm, Su 10am-10pm.

Post Office: Königstr. 44-46, 23552 Lübeck. Across the street from the Katharinenkirche. Open M-F 8:30am-6:30pm, Sa 8:30am-1pm. Has a 24hr. international **ATM.**

ACCOMMODATIONS AND CAMPING

Rucksack Hotel, Kanalstr. 70 (☎ 70 68 92; fax 707 34 26), on the north side of the Altstadt by the canal. Bus #1, 11, 21, or 31 from the station to "Pfaffenstr.," then right at the church on Glockengießerstr. This popular hostel is a member of a collective of com-

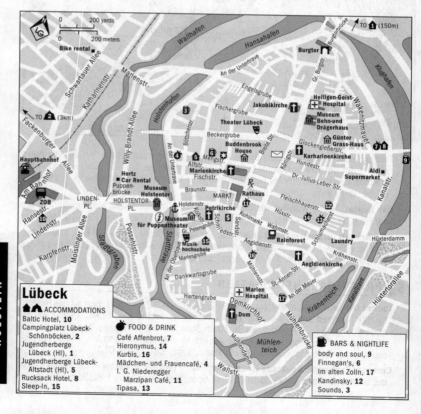

Lübeck

ACCOMMODATIONS
Baltic Hotel, **10**
Campingplatz Lübeck-
　Schönböcken, **2**
Jugendherberge
　Lübeck (HI), **1**
Jugendherberge Lübeck-
　Altstadt (HI), **5**
Rucksack Hotel, **8**
Sleep-In, **15**

FOOD & DRINK
Café Affenbrot, **7**
Hieronymus, **14**
Kurbis, **16**
Mädchen- und Frauencafé, **4**
I. G. Niederegger
　Marzipan Café, **11**
Tipasa, **13**

BARS & NIGHTLIFE
body and soul, **9**
Finnegan's, **6**
Im alten Zolln, **17**
Kandinsky, **12**
Sounds, **3**

munalist, eco-friendly shops in a former glass factory. Guests get access to lectures, parties, and juggling performances. Breakfast €3. Sheets €3. Reception 10am-1pm and 5-9pm. 6- to 10-bed dorms €13; doubles with bath €40; quads €60-68. ❷

Jugendherberge Lübeck-Altstadt (HI), Mengstr. 33 (☎ 702 03 99; fax 770 12). From the station, head for the Holstentor, cross the river, turn left on An der Untertrave and then right on Mengstr. Typical hostel, unbeatable location. Breakfast and sheets included. Reception 7:30am-noon, 1:15-6pm, and 7:15pm-midnight. Lockout midnight; guests 18+ can get a key. Reservations recommended. Dorms €20.10; singles and doubles from €25.60 per person, under 27 €23. Discounts for longer stays. ❸

Jugendherberge Lübeck "Vor dem Burgtor" (HI), Am Gertrudenkirchhof 4 (☎ 334 33; www.djh-ris.de). Just north of the Altstadt, off Travemünder Allee. This large, recently renovated hostel is brimming with activity. It fills up quickly with those who realize it's only 15min. from the town center. **Internet** €0.50 per 5min. Breakfast and sheets included. Laundry €2.60. Dorm beds €19.20, under 27 €16.50. ❷

Sleep-In (CVJM), Große Petersgrube 11 (☎ 719 20; www.cvjm-luebeck.de), near the Petrikirche in the Altstadt, 10min. from the station. Walk past the Holstentor, turn right on An der Obertrave, left on Große Petersgrube, and look to the right for the sign. This lodge, run by the CVJM Christian organization, offers beds in a cozy community atmosphere. The pub downstairs often echoes with jazz. No locked rooms or lockers. Sheets €4.50. Key with €10 deposit. Reception M-F 8am-10pm, Sa-Su 8am-noon. 4- to 8-bed dorms €10-12; doubles €20-40; apartments €16-20 per person. ❶

Baltic Hotel, Hansestr. 11 (☎ 855 75; www.baltic-hotel.de), across the street from the ZOB and 8min. from the Altstadt. Cheerfully bright and clean rooms with telephones and TVs. The owner is a veritable encyclopedia of Lübeck's history. Breakfast included. Reception 7am-10pm. Singles €35-45; doubles €58-65; triples from €80. ❹

Campingplatz Lübeck-Schönböcken, Steinrader Damm 12 (☎ 89 30 90; www.vcsh.de/ PLAETZE/schoenboecken.htm), 3km west of the city. From the ZOB, take bus #7 to "Schönböckener Hauptstr." Showers, washing machines, and cooking facilities. €4.50 per person, €2 per child, €5 per site. ❶

🔂 FOOD

While the rest of Germany swims in beer, Lübeck drowns in coffee, with no street corner more than a saucer's throw away from a caffeine fix. Of course, this is still Germany, so Lübeck's cafes stay open until the wee hours of the morning and become the nightlife venue of choice. The hippest, most popular cafes line **Mühlenstraße** in the eastern part of the city. A local specialty is *Lübecker Marzipan*, a sweet, colored almond paste molded into thousands of different shapes.

🔲 **Café Affenbrot**, Kanalstr. 70 (☎ 721 93), on the corner of Glockengießerstr. A vegetarian cafe and *Biergarten*, Café Affenbrot is part of the same *Werkhof* that brings you the **Rucksack Hostel**. Sit at tables crafted from antique sewing machines and indulge in a variety of light dinners created from organic ingredients (€4-8), or join the crowds there for breakfast (€3.50-9). Open daily 9am-midnight. Kitchen closes at 11pm. ❷

🔲 **I.G. Niederegger Marzipan Café**, Breitestr. 89 (☎ 530 11 26). This famous confectionery shop and cafe is *the* place to eat marzipan cake (€1.65) or buy candies shaped like pigs, jellyfish, or the town gate (cheaper at the counter than in the cafe). The **Marzipan Salon**, a free exhibit dedicated to the history and preparation of the sweet, is located upstairs. Cafe and Salon both open M-F 9am-7pm, Sa 9am-6pm, Su 10am-4pm. ❷

Kurbis, Mühlenstr. 9 (☎ 707 01 26). Though a *Kurbis* (pumpkin) theme pervades the decor right down to the orange salt and pepper shakers, no gourds of any kind are on the menu. Happy couples still fill the place, dining beneath the oak rafters of this laid-back restaurant-bar. Pasta dishes and *Pfanne,* pan-cooked meals topped with cheese, run €7-8. Open Su-Th 11am-1am, F-Sa 11am-2am. Kitchen closes 30min. earlier. ❸

SCHLESWIG-HOLSTEIN

PUPPETMAN

Fritz Fey, owner of Lübeck's Puppet Theater Museum (p. 195), talks about his inspirations.

I always liked traveling and meeting people from other countries—I was fascinated by the orient and by India from the time I was a young boy. I got a job at a television studio as a cameraman. I loved my job; it gave me the chance to travel all around the world—we made documentary films—to North America, to Africa. While traveling, I had the chance to meet old puppet players, and I found out that the tradition is a very old one, and that it exists in nearly every country. As I learned more, my interest increased.

I started my collection in 1971, and invested everything that I earned into it. After exhibiting my collection a few times, the idea came to me to create a museum. I eventually got the chance to rent a small house for the museum in Lübeck. I have expanded the collection every year since then... We still have about 20 times more figures than there is space to display...

My vision is to make this a haven for children and those fascinated by the history of theater. I want the museum to become an island in Lübeck's old city—a place for international friendship, where people see the figures from their culture displayed among figures from all over the world, as part of a larger tradition aimed at creating beautiful things and bringing happiness to people.

Tipasa, Schlumacherstr. 12-14 (☎ 706 04 51). Cave art on the walls adds neolithic charm to this student haunt. Pizza €4-7, meat dishes €8-10. The *Tipasa-Topf* (€6.60) is a zesty tomato, beef, mushroom, and pepper stew. *Biergarten* in back. Open M-Th and Su 1am, F-Sa noon-2am. Kitchen closes 30min. earlier. ❸

Hieronymus, Fleischhauerstr. 81 (☎ 706 30 17). Choices abound on a long menu of pan-European cuisine. The massive fireplace, dark lighting, and exposed wooden beams are very 15th-century. Lunch specials (€5-7) M-F before 5pm. Meat dishes €8-12, pizzas €4-7. Open Su-Th noon-1am, F-Sa noon-2am. ❸

Mädchen- und Frauencafé, An der Untertrave 97 (☎ 122 57 46), on the 2nd fl. Friendly women-only cafe serves more as a meeting than an eating ground, hosting frequent breakfast chats, girls' clubs, literature discussion groups, and discos. Check the door for postings about events and opening times.

👁 SIGHTS

To see Lübeck from on high, hop on the double-decker **LVG Open-Air-Stadtrundfahrt.** The red buses provide tours of the city, leaving from the "Kohlmarkt/Wahmstr." stop. (1 per hr. July-Aug. daily 11am-4pm, June and Sept. Sa-Su only. €5.50, children €3.80, families €14.50). If you have less money or more energy, it is easy enough to walk the Altstadt yourself. Pick up a guide of suggested routes in the tourist office. The streets of Lübeck are filled with little surprises. Be on the lookout for the hundreds of blue signs mounted on walls (all with English translations) that describe the fascinating history of many of Lübeck's buildings. In the northeastern section of the Altstadt, you can find dozens of narrow passages, or *Gänge,* which lead from the street into beautiful courtyard gardens.

HOLSTENTOR. Between the Altstadt and the station is Lübeck's city symbol, the imposing Holstentor, built in the 15th century. Inside, in the Museum Holstentor, you can read about the city's rise to prominence while exploring the tower's massive walls, gun bays, and limestone troughs for dumping hot tar on the enemy outside. Ironically, Napoleon, the only invader since its construction, entered the city from the north, bypassing the gate entirely. (☎ 122 41 29. Open Apr.-Sept. daily 10am-5pm; Oct.-Mar. Tu-Su 10am-5pm. €4, students and seniors €2, families €8.)

MARIENKIRCHE. The Marienkirche's two brick towers dominate the Lübeck skyline. Construction of the church began around 1200 in the

Romanesque style, but it was completed as a Gothic cathedral in 1350. The gigantic building, which houses the largest mechanical organ in the world, sustained heavy damage during WWII. Despite reconstruction efforts, the effects of the attacks are still visible. A giant bronze bell, warped and splintered, lies embedded in the shattered marble floor where it fell during the air raids of 1942. Pictures of the church's famous **Totentanzbild,** an intricate mural depicting the "dance of the dead," hang in the left apse, where the original, lost in the fires that followed the attacks, once stood. To the left of the pews is the church's newly restored astronomical clock. On your way out, take a peek at the little devil sitting just outside the main door. *(Open daily in summer 10am-6pm; in winter 10am-4pm. Suggested donation €1. Tours Apr.-Oct. Sa 3:15pm. June-Sept. also W 3:15pm, €3.50, students €2.50.)*

RATHAUS. Lübeck's beloved city hall, at the center of the Altstadt, is a somewhat schizophrenic conglomeration of three contrasting architectural styles. The original building, constructed in the 13th century, is the portion with the striking glazed black and red brick. New wings were added in the 14th and 15th centuries. *(Admission only with tour (in German). M-F at 11am, noon, and 3pm. €2.60, students €1.50.)*

BUDDENBROOKHAUS. Authors **Heinrich and Thomas Mann** lived here as children. Thomas, who won the 1929 Nobel Prize, used the house as the setting for his novel *Buddenbrooks.* The building is now a museum dedicated to the life and works of both brothers. The exhibit's lengthy text displays are all accompanied by English translations. Special events are held during the summer, including a "literary walk" through Lübeck on Sundays from June to August. *(Mengstr. 4, beside the Marienkirche.* ☎ *122 41 92. Open daily 10am-6pm. Admission €5, students €2.60; combo ticket with Günter Grass-Haus €7/€4. Walks last 2hr., €8.)*

DOM. Founded by Henry the Lion in 1173, Lübeck's oldest church shelters a majestic crucifix and is guarded by a distinctive lion statue. Approach the church from the north and you'll be able to tell people you walked through Purgatory (the street *Fegefeuer*) to reach the cathedral. *(Domkirchhof, at the southernmost end of the inner island.* ☎ *747 04. Open Apr.-Sept. 10am-6pm; Mar. and Oct. 10am-5pm; Nov. 10am-4pm; Dec.-Feb. 10am-3pm. Free. Organ concerts July-Aug. Su 5pm, €6, students €3)*

PETRIKIRCHE. An elevator climbs 50.5m to the viewing platform inside the 13th-century steeple for a sweeping, windy view of the Altstadt and Lübeck's many spires. The nave of the church exhibits modern art. *(East of the Rathaus on Schmiederstr. Church open daily 11am-5pm. Tower open daily Apr.-Oct. 9am-7pm, Mar. and Nov. 11am-5pm, Dec. 9am-7pm. Requested donation €1. Tower €2.50, students €1.50.)*

JAKOBIKIRCHE. Traditionally a place of worship for seafarers, the whitewashed, high-ceilinged church is lined with bronze chandeliers and contains an enormous wooden organ bordered by detailed pictures of the saints. *(North of the Rathaus on Breitestr., near Koberg. Open daily 10am-6pm. Requested donation €1. Organ concerts W 5pm and Sa 8pm. €6, students €3.)*

MUSEUM FÜR PUPPENTHEATER. Exquisitely detailed hand, string, shadow, and stick puppets from across the globe pack the museum's five floors, forming the largest such collection in the world. Check out the fully-preserved Chinese theaters, watch videos of puppet performances, or ask to hear the barrel organs, which the owner will happily play for you. Across the street, the puppet theater puts on daily performances at 3pm (€4), and Sa also at 6pm or 7:30pm (€8, students €6.50.) *(Kolk 14. Just below the Petrikirche.* ☎ *786 26. Open daily 10am-6pm Apr.-Sept., till 4pm in Oct., till 3pm Nov.-Mar. €3, students €2.50, children €1.50.)*

SCHLESWIG-HOLSTEIN

GÜNTER GRASS-HAUS. The cousin of the Buddenbrookhaus, this museum contains a visually enticing presentation of bronze sculpture, sketches, and watercolors created by acclaimed author and Nobel laureate **Günter Grass,** who lived in Lübeck for many years. Grass makes occasional appearances for readings and special events. *(Glockengießerstr. 21.* ☎ *122 41 92. Open daily Apr.-Oct. 10am-6pm, Nov.-Mar. 10am-5pm. Admission €4, students €2.20; combo ticket with Buddenbrookhaus €7/€4.)*

MUSEUM BEHN- UND DRÄGERHAUS. In this creaky 18th-century house is an exhibition of furnishings from the early 19th century, a collection of Impressionist and Realist art, and a unique display of historical musical instruments. Also on display are portraits by Edvard Munch, and the violin fitted with tubes to make it double as a trumpet. The artists' cooperative in the **sculpture garden** outside showcases local artists. *(Königstr. 9-11.* ☎ *122 41 48. Open Apr.-Sept. Tu-Su 10am-5pm; Oct.-Mar. 10am-4pm. €3, students €1.50, children 6-18 €0.50, family €6. First F of every month free.)*

🎵 ENTERTAINMENT

Lübeck is world-famous for its **organ concerts** at the Jakobikirche (at 5pm) and the Marienkirche (at 6:30pm) on Saturdays (€6, students €4); the full schedule is in the brochure *Musik in Lübecks Kirchen,* available at both churches. The city's music academy, the **Musikhochschule,** Gr. Petersgrube 17-29, plays frequent free concerts, often of professional caliber. (☎ 150 50; www.mh-luebeck.de.) For entertainment listings, pick up *Heute, Piste, Szene, Zentrum,* or (for women) *Zimtzicke* at the tourist office. Lübeck's two main theaters offer student discounts, but are closed from July to August. The huge **Theater Lübeck,** Beckergrube 16, puts up operas, symphonies, and plays. (☎ 745 52; www.theaterluebeck.de. Tickets €15-36; student tickets from €5. Box office open Tu-F 10am-6:30pm, Sa 10am-1pm, and 30min. before shows.) The smaller **Theater Combinale,** Hüxstr. 115, shows avant-garde works. (☎ 788 17. Tickets €8-14.)

🎟 NIGHTLIFE

Most of the better *Diskotheken* are scattered around the perimeter of the Altstadt or just outside it. Avoid the northwestern part of the island along the waterfront late at night, when dealers and addicts frequent the area.

Finnegan's, Mengstr. 42 (☎ 711 10). The 2-story Irish pub serves Guinness and other dark, yeasty beers (€3-4) to 30-something locals and Irish backpackers. Live music W, F, and Sa at 8:30pm. Open Tu-Sa 7pm until late.

body and soul, on a stationary boat in the water at the corner of Kanalstr. and Höhe Glockenstr. (☎ 706 06 00; www.bodyandsoul.de). Walk up the red carpet and dance with a student-aged crowd to a mix of hip-hop, pop, and rock in the two-level interior. Cover usually €4. Open Tu and Sa from 10pm, F from 10:30pm.

Sounds, An der Untertrave 81-83 (☎ 772 70; www.soundsclub.de). Club in the Altstadt pulses with hip-hop and techno/house. Mix of university students and older, alternative crowd hangs out on the metal-grate stairways. Cover around €5. Open Tu and Th-Sa.

Kandinsky, Fleischhauerstr. 89 (☎ 702 06 61). More than 30 tables in the street, a mile-long drink list of teas, coffees, and beer (€2-3), and live jazz every Tu night. Snug environment, gold walls, and a student-aged crowd. Open Su-Th 1pm-1am, F-Sa 1pm-2am.

Im alten Zolln, Mühlenstr 93 (☎ 723 95). Don't come here for a visa: the "old customs office" is currently decked out with classy wood paneling and a grand piano. Beer €2-4, cocktails €5-6. Open daily noon-1am.

HOLSTEINISCHE SCHWEIZ (HOLSTEIN SWITZERLAND)

PLÖN ☎ 04522

Nestled in the ancient glacial moraines of wooded *Holsteinische Schweiz*, Plön is situated in the middle of lake country. The town balances on a land bridge between the **Kleiner Plöner See** and the **Großer Plöner See**, where the sparkling waters and the opportunities to paddle, sail, and fish lure school groups and nature lovers alike. The red brick steeple of Plön's central church and the white facade of its elegant castle dominate the quiet, picturesque town.

🖪🖊 TRANSPORTATION AND PRACTICAL INFORMATION. Plön lies on the main rail line between Lübeck and Kiel. **Trains** travel every hr. to: **Eutin** (15min., €2.30); **Kiel** (30min., €4.55); **Lübeck** (40min., €6.60). For a **taxi,** look outside the station or call ☎26 00, 35 35, or 88 88. Rent **bikes** at **Wittich,** Lange Str. 39. (☎27 48. €6 per day. Open M-F 9am-6pm, Sa 9am-2pm.) Trails snake off in all directions and loop around the lakes. Rent **boats** at the **Kanucenter Plön,** Ascheberger Str. 76, on the campground (☎41 43. €5 per 2hr. Open daily 9am-dusk.); also try the **Segelschule Plön** next to the Jugendherberge, Aschebergstr. 70. (☎41 11. Kayaks €4 per 2hr., €7.50 per day; canoe €2.50/€5.) If you have time, head northeast through the Kleiner Plöner See and up the Schwentine River for extraordinary birdwatching. Otherwise, take a 30min. paddle east into the vast Großer Plöner See to get an unobstructed view of the Schloß. **Großer Plöner Seerundfahrt** chugs around the lake from the dock on Strandweg. (Daily 10am-5pm. Round-trip €7.50, students €4.50, children €4.) The **tourist office,** Am Lübschen Tor 1, is 200m from the train station; follow the signs. The staff distributes maps and books rooms (€15-50) for free. (☎509 50; www.ploen.de. Open in summer M-F 9am-6pm, Sa-Su 10am-1pm; less frequently in winter.) Check **email** downstairs at the library. (€1.50 per 30min. Open M-F 9:30am-1:30pm and 3-6pm.). Or, try **MB Computer,** next door to the tourist office. (€4 per hr. Open M-Th 9am-1pm and 2-6pm, F 3-6pm, Sa 9am-noon.) The **post office,** Lange Str. 18, 24306 Plön, is off the walkway near the square. (Open M-F 9am-1pm and 2-6pm, Sa 9am-12:30pm.)

🖪🖸 ACCOMMODATIONS AND FOOD. 2km outside of town, Plön's **Jugendherberge (HI) ❷,** Asheberger Str. 67, looks like a big elementary school. Follow the signs from the city center, or take bus #360 (1 per hr) to "Spitzenort." With a beach volleyball court, a soccer field, and ping-pong and picnic tables by the shores of the Großer Plöner See, this enormous hostel attracts noisy school groups. (☎25 76; fax 21 66. Breakfast and sheets included. Check-out 9am. Lock-out 10pm-7am, but you can get a key. Dorms €16.50, under 27 €14.) **Hotel Zum Hirschen ❸,** Bahnhofstr. 9, across from the station, has small, clean rooms with telephone and TV, in a convenient location. (☎24 23. Breakfast included. Singles €30-37; doubles €54-68.) On the road right before the hostel, **Naturcamping Spitzenort ❶,** Ascheburger Str. 76, has many grassy spots along the water and offers the latest amenities. (☎27 69; www.spitzenort.de. €4.50 per person, €2 per child 4-14, €4-6 per tent; €3-6 in off season.) If you're looking for a less-developed patch of grass, kayak to one of six other campgrounds farther south on the Großer Plöner See. Ask for a map at the kayak rental. For food, Plön's colorful pedestrian zone along Lange Str. and its main square are full of cafes with outdoor tables. **Eisenpfanne ❸,** Lange Str. 47, serves the massive *Plöner Teller* (€11), a specialty consisting of three kinds of local fried fish. The restaurant also serves Greek, Italian, and Mediterranean fare.

(☎ 22 90. Main dishes €8-12. Open daily 11am-11pm.) **Antalya-Grill ❷**, Lange Str. 36, offers grill platters (€7) and spicy Turkish pizzas (€4-7), as well as the *Döner* (€2.50-€4) expected of any good Turkish restaurant. (☎ 39 82. Open M-F 11am-1am, Sa-Su 11am-2am.) **Sky**, Markt 1, has the lowest prices and the longest hours of any grocery store in the area. (Open M-F 8am-8pm, Sa 8am-4pm, Su 11am-6pm.)

◪ SIGHTS. Though it now serves as a boarding school (you can't go inside), the late Renaissance **Schloß** is still the most noticeable building in town. On top of the Schloßberg, the path in front of the palace affords a spectacular view out over the surrounding lake and town. Wooded trails lead away from the castle to the stately brick **Prinzenhaus** (also closed to the public, except for special tours; inquire at the tourist office) amid the white-flowered fields of the **Schloßgarten**. To the southwest, the **Prinzeninsel** stretches out from the mainland into the Großer Plöner See. A tiny canal spanned by a footbridge divides it from the shore. Down the eastern slope of the Schloßberg is Plön's small 19th-century **Rathaus**. Though the **Nicolaikirche** in the square has an antique-looking Baroque exterior, the inside was remodeled during the 1960s in a jarringly angular style. (Open daily 10am-4pm.)

Housed in a former apothecary, the **Museum des Kreises**, Johannisstr. 1, at the intersection of Hamburger Str. and Lange Str., displays 17th-century glassware, porcelain, and other treasures swiped from the Schloß. (☎ 74 43 91. Open mid-May to Sept. Tu-Su 10am-noon and 2-5pm; Jan. to mid-May Tu-Sa 2-5pm. €1.50, students €1.) Resting atop a small hill across the street, the **Johanniskirche's** uneven brick, wood, and copper construction communicates the elegance and rustic flavor of a folk church. The subtly beautiful building was designed in 1685 for the ducal couple Johann Adolph and Dorothea Sophie. (Open daily 10am-4pm. Free.) Far east of the town center on the ridge that runs between the two lakes, the **Parnaßturm**, a former lookout tower, provides an amazing view well worth the 20min. climb up Rodomstorstr. (Open Easter-Oct. 9am-7pm. Free.)

KIEL   ☎ 0431

Site of the 1936 and 1972 Olympic sailing events, the waters around Kiel swim ceaselessly with brightly colored sails between giant ocean liners. The city's fascination with ships is most apparent during the **Kieler Woche**, which attracts some 3.5 million visitors, including 5500 sailors and 2500 boats, every year during the last full week in June. This famous regatta—the largest in the world—turns the harbor into a massive party and floods the town with music, food, and beer (☎ 90 19 05 for more information). During the rest of the year, this city of 250,000 residents quiets down considerably. Residents ignore the somewhat plain downtown and keep their eyes on the sea, working to push ships through the **Nord-Ostsee-Kanal** and maintain ferry connections to Scandinavia.

▛ TRANSPORTATION. Trains run every hr. to: **Flensburg** (70min., €13); **Hamburg** (70min., €15); **Lübeck** (70min., €12). The **Mitfahrzentrale**, Königsweg 25, is three blocks west of the train station. (☎ 67 50 01. Open M-F 9am-6pm, Sa 10am-3pm, Su noon-3pm.) At an average €2 per ride, Kiel's extensive **public transportation** system will quickly drain your wallet. Avoid fiscal bloodletting with the **Tageskarte** (1-day €5.30; all zones €8.70; 3-days €11.20). Most of Kiel's buses pass through the rows of stops outside the train station on Sophienblatt; those on the train station side of the street generally head north, while those on the Sophienhof side go south. Call ☎ 750 00 for a **taxi**. All **ferries** except those bound for Norway and the Baltics leave from the piers on the west side of the harbor (port information at www.port-of-kiel.de). **Stena Line**, on the west side near the station at **Schwedenkai**, will take you to Sweden. (☎ 90 99; www.stenaline.de.

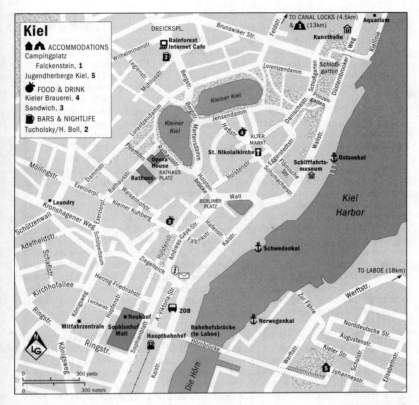

Kiel

ACCOMMODATIONS
Campingplatz
  Falckenstein, **1**
Jugendherberge Kiel, **5**

FOOD & DRINK
Kieler Brauerei, **4**
Sandwich, **3**

BARS & NIGHTLIFE
Tucholsky/H. Boll, **2**

Departures daily at 7:30pm arrive in Göteborg at 9am the next morning. €65, F and Sa €75, add €20 per person for a basic bed; cheaper in off-season) The posh **Color Line** at **Norwegenkai,** on the opposite side of the harbor, sails to Oslo,. (☎73 00 300; www.colorline.com. Daily at 1:30pm. Single cabin €90-98; doubles €110-240; cheaper on weekdays and off-peak months.) Boats bound for Kaliningrad and the Baltics leave from **Ostuferkai.**

◪ PRACTICAL INFORMATION. Kiel's **tourist office,** Andreas-Gayk-Str. 31, is in the post office building, two blocks north of the train station. The staff finds rooms for free and books them for a €3 fee. (☎01805 56 56 700; www.kiel-tourist.de. Open M-F 9am-6pm, Sa 9am-1pm.) **Laundry** can be done at **Waschcenter,** Exerzierpl. on Ziegelteich or Holtenauer Str. 154. (Wash €2.50 including detergent. Dry €0.50 per 12min. Both open Su-Th 6am-midnight, F-Sa 6am-11pm.) For **Internet,** cross the Kleiner Kiel lake to the **Rainforest Internet Café,** Bergstr. 17. (€0.75 per 15min. Open daily 9am-4am.) The **post office,** Stresemannpl. 1-3, 24103 Kiel, is just past the bus station from the train station. (Open M-F 8:30am-7pm, Sa 9am-2pm.)

◪◪ ACCOMMODATIONS AND FOOD. Perched on a hill, **Jugendherberge Kiel (HI) ❷,** Johannesstr. 1, has a panoramic view of the harbor, which means...it's a trek. From the train or bus station, head toward the water, over the Bahnhofsbrücke and continue straight. Take the stairs or elevator up and over the railroad tracks and highway (700m). Or take bus #11 from platform D and get off at "Kieler Str." Turn around and walk south on Schulstr., then turn right onto Johannisstr. about 100m down. A happy crowd relaxes in the pleasant indoor courtyard of this hostel, which offers spacious quads. (☎ 73 14 88; fax 73 57 23. Breakfast and sheets included. Reception 7am-1am. Check-out 9:30am. Curfew 1am. Dorms €19.20, at least 2 nights €18, under 27 €16.50/€15.20.) **Campingplatz Falckenstein ❶**, Palisadenweg 171, is a distant 13km from the center. Take bus #501 or #502 (dir.: Strande) to "Preis." Follow the signs, approx. 25min by foot. (☎ 39 20 78; www.campingkiel.de. Open Apr.-Oct. €4.35 per person, €5-7.50 per site.)

Neukauf, on the ground floor of the Sophienhof Mall, sells groceries (open M-F 9am-7pm), as do the open-air produce stands along Holstenbrücke, the country's oldest designated *Fußgängerzone* (pedestrian zones). Join the crowds enjoying traditional German fare at the ◪**Kieler Brauerei ❸**, Alter Markt 9, which has dark suds (€3-4), roast sausages, and potatoes. Watch the *Bräumeister* tending the copper tanks upstairs or examine the giant brew vats reducing *Kieler* in the basement. The Brauerei offers unlimited beer for €10 every other Sunday from 11:30pm-1:30am. (☎ 90 62 90. Entrees €7-10. Open Su-Th 10am-1am, F-Sa 10am-2am.) Near the markets, **Sandwich ❶**, Holstenstr. 92 (on Europaplatz), with zebra-patterned sofas and painfully yellow tables, sells diminutive versions of its namesake for €1.50-3. (Open M-Sa 8am-5pm, Su 9am-5pm.) In the evening, you can follow the throngs from nearby **Christian-Albrechts Universität** to the clubs and bars on Bergstr. Descend into the labyrinthine **Tucholsky/H. Boll,** Bergstr. 17, and lose yourself in dozens of rooms full of bars, billiards, foosball, darts, dance floors, and fluorescent pink air hockey tables. (Drinks €1-4. Open daily 8pm-4am.)

◪ SIGHTS. The harbor is the obvious focal point of the city. The highlight on the water is the largest series of **canal locks** *(Schleusen)* in the world, situated just north of Kiel, where the 99km-long **Nord-Ostsee-Kanal** enters the Baltic Sea. A tour of the facility (in German) will teach you more than you knew you didn't know about locks. (Bus #11 from the station to "Wik-Kanal," then take the free ferry that runs every 15min. Walk right 10min. along Kanalstr. from the ferry dock to the Schleuseninsel. Or, take bus #1 or 41 to "Schleuse." Tours 1½hr.; 9 and 11am, 1 and 3pm. €2.30, students €1.50.) Running from the Schloßgarten, the **Kiellinie** pedestrian walkway affords spectacular harbor views. Near the Kiellinie's southern end, the **Kunsthalle,** Düsternbrooker Weg 1, is worth a look. The antiquities gallery (free admission) exhibits hundreds of Roman and Greek statues. The museum's permanent and rotating exhibitions are housed upstairs and include works by Max Liebermann and other German impressionists, as well as a large collection of 20th-century artwork. (☎ 880 57 56. Open Tu-Su 10:30am-6pm, W until 8pm. Exhibits €6, students €4.) North of the Kunsthalle, along the Kiellinie, is a small **Aquarium** at the Institut für Meereskunde. (Open Apr.-Sept. 9am-7pm, Mar. and Oct. 9am-5pm, €1.60, children €1.) Along the waterfront a few blocks south, the **Schifffahrtsmuseum,** Wall 65, raises the ruins of submarines and other ships from the deep. Hundreds of model boats and old photographs recreate German trading vessels and Nazi ships of war. (☎ 34 28. Open mid-Apr. to mid-Oct. daily 10am-6pm; mid-Oct. to mid-Apr. Tu-Su 10am-5pm. Requested donation €1, children €0.50.) At the north end of the pedestrian zone, the **St. Nikolaikirche** towers over the center of the Alter Markt. While the building itself is a reconstruction, its venerable old roof, pulpit, and frescoes were brought to a nearby monastery for safekeeping during WWII and returned unharmed. (Open M-F 10am-6pm, Sa 11am-1pm. Free.)

SCHLESWIG-HOLSTEIN

WATTENMEER NATIONAL PARK (SCHLESWIG-HOLSTEIN)

Schleswig-Holstein's Wattenmeer National Park is one of three such parks in Germany, the other two located farther down the coast in Hamburg and Lower Saxony. The *Watt* refers to the mud—miles and miles of it—that sustains a wide variety of unique plant and animal life. The region is filled with small towns that label themselves health resorts, capitalizing on the invigorating salt-laden air that circulates through the region and the purported curative properties of the mud. The Wattenmeer National Park witnesses a seasonal migration of birds and tourists alike, with resort towns more than tripling in population during the summer.

THE PARK AT A GLANCE

AREA: 2850km².

CLIMATE: Mild summers, wet winters. Windy year-round.

FEATURES: Sandy beaches, *Wattenmeer* mud flats, grassy dunes, historic towns, spas.

HIGHLIGHTS: Guided hikes through the *Watt* extensive network of bicycle paths, Multimar National Park Center in Tönning, relaxing on Sylt and Amrum's wide beaches.

GATEWAYS: Tönning, St. Peter-Ording.

CAMPING: Not allowed within the park, but common on its fringes.

✸ ORIENTATION

Wattenmeer National Park stretches along Schleswig Holstein's western coast, situated on the North Sea. **Tönning,** (p. 203) in the central region of the park, is a good place to begin exploring. Twenty-five kilometers to the west, the resort town of **St. Peter-Ording** (p. 204) offers access to Wattenmeer wildlife and a spectacular beach that extends for miles. To the northwest lie the North Frisian Islands, including **Sylt** and **Amrum,** with beautiful white sand beaches on their western shores and wide stretches of Wattenmeer tidal flats on their sheltered eastern sides.

WHAT IS THIS WATT? Created by the radical fluctuation of tides, the Wattenmeer is an area of mudflats stretching along the North Sea from the Dutch to the Danish coasts. The Watt is classified into three unique bands: the *Sandwatt,* as its name suggests, includes the sandy part of the shore where sea worms burrow to hide from predatory birds. Farther inland, the *Mischwatt,* a bank of mixed sand and mud, teems with species from bacteria to mussels. Extending to the highest water line is the charcoal-black *Schlickwatt,* where only the most resilient organisms live in the oxygen-poor mud that is marketed to health-seekers as a nutrient-rich skin treatment. A relatively rare ecosystem, the Wattenmeer habitat supports some 3200 different types of animals. Among the most visible are the mussels that filter the ocean water, the fish that stock the plankton-rich waters with their eggs, the birds that feast at low tide on creatures trapped in shallow pools, and the seals that frolic on sandbanks just offshore.

▐ TRANSPORTATION

Trains provide easy access to nearly all National Park towns and sights along the coast. Most trains within the greater Wattenmeer Park area are NOB (Nord-Ostsee-Bahn) regional trains; tickets for these can be purchased from the on-board ticket machines. **Bus** connections are generally less frequent and less extensive than train connections. The region's bus terminals often lack information centers, so you'll have to plan ahead and inquire about bus routes in town, or decipher the posted schedules on your own.

⚡ PRACTICAL INFORMATION

Emergency: Police ☎110. **Fire** ☎112.

Wattenmeer Information Line: ☎04861 616 70; www.wattenmeer-nationalpark.de.

Information Centers: Schutzstationen (protection stations) are on each of the islands and in the major towns along the mainland coast. The staff gladly answer questions, and offer guided tours of the *Watt*. (See city listings for locations and contact info.) In addition to the network of *Schutzstationen,* information pavilions, part of the **Besucher-informationenssystem (BIS),** are at the beginning of many paths in the region.

Boat Tours: Adler-Schiffe (☎04842 90 00 30) offers 2½hr. excursions to the seal banks (p. 204), while **Reederei Rahder** (☎04832 36 12; www.rahder.de), conducts 2½ and 6hr. loops departing from Büsum through the Wattenmeer and seal habitat in Dithmarschen (€11-19).

🏠 ACCOMMODATIONS

Youth **hostels** dot the North Sea coast. In addition to the hostels described in the city listings, other HI hostels in the region are listed here (prices exclude *Kurkarte;* over age 26 add €2.70):

Büsum, Dr.-Martin-Bahr-Str. 1, Büsum (☎04834 933 71). €14.80.

Heide, Poststr. 4, Heide, on Holstein island (☎0481 715 75). €13.80.

Husum, Schobüller Str. 34, Husum (☎04841 27 14). €14.80.

Niebüll-Deezbüll, Deezbüll Deich 2, Niebüll (☎04661 93 78 90). €14.80.

Niebüll-Mühlenstraße, Mühlenstr. 65, Niebüll (☎04661 93 78 90). €14.80.

Wyk auf Föhr, Fehrstieg 41, Wyk, on Föhr Island (☎04681 23 55). €15.

⚠ OUTDOOR ACTIVITIES

WATTWANDERN. When the tides ebb, the mud flats of the Watt are exposed, making it possible to walk (barefoot or in rubber boots) across the terrain. To arrange a tour, call the National Park Service (☎04861 616 70) or a nearby *Schutzstation*. Private companies also offer tours. **Adler-Schiffe** leads walks across the Watt between the islands of Amrum and Föhr. The 2½hr. trip departs from Nordstrand, near Husum, and includes the cost of ferry rides to and from the islands. (☎04842 900 00. €24, children €13.50.) **Reederei H.G. Rahder** offers 2hr. guided hikes of the Watt in the vicinity of Büsum. (☎04834 36 12; www.rahder.de. €6, children €3, plus *Kurtaxe*. Reservations recommended.) If you insist on striking out independently, pick up a free "Ebbe und Flut" tide chart, and seek advice from one of the information centers.

BEACHES AND SWIMMING. Most costal towns levy fees called *Kurtaxe* for beach access. The cost varies, but is generally €1.50-3 per day for adults, €0.50 for children. Hotels and pensions in the area automatically add the cost of the *Kurkarte* to your bill. Guests not staying overnight can purchase a day card granting beach access for roughly the same cost. Swimming is allowed at all beaches in

> **BEACH SAFETY.** *Let's Go* does not recommend hiking the Watt without a guide. Tour guides are familiar with the tides, and can steer you away from dangers such as **quicksand.** Be sure to heed the markings on the Watt: **orange balls** forbid entrance, **yellow flags** warn that the sandbank island will be submerged, and **green flags** encourage caution around high tide.
>
> On any beach, watch out for special areas which are off-limits to protect roosting birds, and stay aware of the wickedly fast tides—crossing streams that are ankle-deep at low tide may mean you will end up swimming home.

the park, although the water can be uncomfortably cool year-round. Nude beaches are common and are marked with signs labeled *FKK Strand*, a reference to the *Freier Körper Kultur* ("free body culture") association.

HIKING AND BIKING. Biking is an incredibly popular and effective way to explore the park, both on the mainland and the islands. The park has a broad network of paved and gravel trails, and the powerful North Sea wind can send you flying along at exhilarating speeds—or slow progress to a painful crawl. Hiking trails criss-cross the park as well, visit the local information centers for maps. For information on renting bikes, see individual town listings below.

TÖNNING ☎ 04681

The charming little town of Tönning bills itself as a gateway to the Wattenmeer, offering a variety of accommodations options as well as close proximity to the national park headquarters and harbor. Easily accessible by rail, Tönning is a great place to start your trip.

☐☑ TRANSPORTATION AND PRACTICAL INFORMATION. NOB regional **trains** run every hr. to **St. Peter-Ording** (25min., €3.10), and **Husum** (30min., €3.50). Exiting the train station, the city center is a 5min. walk to the right. Across the square, near the church, is the **tourist office**, Am Markt 1. (☎614 20. Open May 15-Sept. 30 M-W 9am-noon, Th 2-5pm, F 9am-noon; June 22-Sept. 11 also Sa 10am-noon; Oct.-May 14 M-W 9am-noon, Th 2-4pm and F 9am-noon.) Pamphlets including accommodations listings (€0.50) are available from a machine outside the office door. The main **park center** is in Tönning at Schloßgarten 1 (☎04861 61 60; www.wattenmeer-nationalpark.de). It is primarily an administrative center, but the staff can help you plan your itinerary.

☐☑ ACCOMMODATIONS AND FOOD. To reach the **Jugendherberge Tönning ❷,** Badallee 28, turn left when exiting the train station and follow Badallee for 15min. until you see the *Jugendherberge* sign. The building doubles as an environmental study center, offering various programs on Watt biology. (☎04861 12 80. **Internet** €0.05 per min. Breakfast and sheets included. Check-in 4:30, 7:45, or 9:50pm. Check-out 9am. Curfew 10pm but keys are available. Excluding *Kurkarte* €18.20, under 27 €15.50.) Halfway to the hostel, **Camping Eiderblick ❶,** Strandweg 19, is small and right on the water. (☎04861 15 69. Laundry €2. Dry €2. €3 per adult, €2 per child, €5 per tent.) Past the Jugendherberge, in farmland 2.5km outside Tönning, **Campingplatz Lilienhof ❶,** Katinger Landstr. 5, is surrounded by birch trees. (☎04861 439. Gate closed 11pm-8am. €4.50 per adult, €2 per child, €7 per site. Toilets, showers, laundry, and electricity available.) There are some relatively inexpensive hotels in the city center; consult the tourist office. To stock up on food, visit the **SPAR** grocery, Am Markt 8, located in the main square. (Open M-F 7:30am-6pm, Sa 7:30am-12:30pm.) Steps away from the train station, **Peper's Fischerhütte ❹,** Westerstr. 17, serves fresh regional fish entrees (€8-14) accompanied by generous portions of potatoes, salad, and vegetables. The tasty fish sandwiches and plates (€2-9) make **Fischimbiß ❷**, am Hafen 33, an affordable choice amongst Tönning's expensive harbor-side cafes. (☎740. Open M-F 9am-6:30pm, Sa-Su 10am-7pm.) The restaurants near the market are generally less expensive and offer more variety than those along the harbor.

■ **SIGHTS.** From the town square, white fish painted on the sidewalk past the harbor lead to the **Multimar Wattforum,** Am Robbenberg, a combined museum, aquarium, and research station whose exhibits describe the unique Wattenmeer environment. (☎96 20 38; www.multimar-wattforum.de. Open daily Apr-Oct. 9am-7pm; Nov.-Mar. 10am-6pm. €8, children €5.50.) **Adler Schiffe** runs 2½hr. trips to the seal banks in the North Sea (☎04842 90 00 30; www.adler-schiffe.de; Tu, Th, Sa 10:30am and 1:30pm; €10.50, children €7) from Tönning's harbor. Tönning is also home to a pleasant **Schloßgarten,** which faces the market square.

ST PETER-ORDING   ☎04683

St. Peter-Ording is broken up into three parts: St. Peter-Bad to the northwest, St. Peter-Dorf in the middle, and St. Peter-Böhl to the south. Although all offer convenient access to the shore, the most beautiful beach is the seemingly endless swath of sand accessible from St. Peter-Bad.

■ ■ **TRANSPORTATION AND PRACTICAL INFORMATION** Trains run every hr. from St. Peter-Ording to: **Berlin** (5½hr., €66); **Hamburg** (3hr., €33); **Hannover** (5hr., €57); **Tönning** (25min., €3.10). To reach St. Peter-Bad from the train station, take the shuttle bus that meets the trains, or cross Eiderstedter Str. and follow the dirt path through the woods until it reaches Im Bad (5min.). In St. Peter-Bad, **rent bikes** at **Fahrrad Depot,** Im Bad 12. (☎22 98. €4.50-6 per day, €20-30 per wk. Open M-Sa 9am-12:30pm and 2:30-6pm, Su 10am-12:30pm and 3-6pm.) Directly off Im Bad, inside the "Dünen-Therme" building is the **tourist office,** which provides information and books rooms and tour packages. (☎99 90. Open M-F 9am-8pm, Sa-Su 10am-4pm.) Additional **branches** are located in Ording, Dorf, and Süd. The fee for a *Kurkarte* is €1.25 a night, but the card also provides free access to the town's bus service. The **Wattenmeer Park Info Station** (☎53 03), Schulstr. 1, in Dorf on the Markt, runs daily Watt tours. Two blocks from the tourist office, the **Internet Cafe,** along Im Bad, charges €4 per hr. For **groceries,** try **Spar,** Dorfstr. 39 in St. Peter Dorf. (Open M-F 7:30am-6:30pm, Sa 7:30am-6pm, Su 10am-12:30pm.) The **post office** is across the street from the bike shop.

■ ■ **ACCOMMODATIONS AND FOOD** Because it is a beach resort, hotel rooms are expensive and can be hard to come by during the summer months, and most private pensions only rent by the week. Offering a bit of luxury at moderate expense, the **Strand Hotel Garni ❹,** Im Bad 16, has very large rooms a block from the beach (☎969 60. Breakfast included. Reception until 10pm. Singles €62; doubles €70-90.) For more affordable accommodations, check with the tourist office about pensions accommodating short-term stays. Of the three neighboring campgrounds on the *Salzwiesen* in St. Peter Böhl, **Camping Rönkendorf ❶,** Böhler Landstr. 171, is the largest. (☎51 95. €3 per adult, €2 per child, €8 per tent.) The long strip along Im Bad in St. Peter-Ording is lined with restaurants. For a more personable atmosphere, head to the cluttered-living-room-bar **Benen Diken ❸,** Badallee 29, near Dorf. Traditional skillet-cooked *Pfanne* meals (€9-12) and *Spargel* (asparagus) are the specialties, but fish (€8-13) is just as popular. (☎15 50. Open daily 11:30am-2pm and from 5pm.)

■ **OUTDOOR ACTIVITIES** Free **bike tours** leave every Monday at 2pm from the **Ording-Hus,** Dreilanden 5, north of St. Peter-Bad. Those exploring on their own can follow the path that extends several miles to the north and south along the dike.

The main attraction, of course, is the sea, which is accessible via a long wooden walkway beginning at the music pavilion. For those looking to avoid the chilly waters and stiff ocean breeze, the **Dünen-Therme,** in St. Peter-Ording directly off Am Kurbad, offers aromatic saunas and therapeutic pools. At a Swedish sauna 50m outside the bath complex, guests relax as ice balls melt over live coals. (☎99 91 61; www.duenen-therme.de. Open Apr.-Oct. M-Sa 9:30am-10pm, Su 10am-7pm, €5.70 per 2hr., students €3.30, plus €3.10 for sauna access.)

SYLT ISLAND

☎04651

The windswept island of Sylt, with its miles of trails, white sand beaches stretching 39km along the mainland shore, and traditional thatched roof Frisian houses, has long been Germany's favorite vacation spot. Westerland, the island's largest city and its transportation hub, was founded as a resort town in the middle of the 19th century. Long regarded as a playground for the rich, the island is now the destination of choice for everyone from the biggest Teutonic celebrities to the nation's most typical vacationing families. Trains from the mainland cross the 10km-long **Hindenburgdamm** to deposit eager tourists at the beach. Others arrive by ferry to the town of Hörnum, at the extreme south end of the island, or to List, which is Germany's northernmost town. North of List, the dunes of the slender Ellenbogen peninsula separate the Wattenmeer from the open ocean. Bike paths connect the island's towns parallel to the highway or snaking through the dunes. The rich congregate in Kampen, just north of Westerland, while everyone else spreads out along the island's miles of beaches, where vacationers sit in wicker "beach baskets" to shield them from the stiff North Sea breeze, while they watch windsurfers battle the challenging surf.

█▟ TRANSPORTATION AND PRACTICAL INFORMATION. Trains run from Westerland to: **Flensburg** (2½hr., €18); **Hamburg** (3hr., €27); **Hannover** (5½hr., €56); **Tönning** (1½hr., €18). **Buses** with bike racks circuit the island, leaving the ZOB terminal to the left of the train station. (3 per hr. Single trips €1.35-€5.75. Day card €11.50, family day card €16.50.) **Ferries** run from List harbor to Havneby on the Danish island of Rømø. Call **Rømø-Sylt Linie** in List for reservations. (☎0180 310 30 30; www.sylt-faehre.de. 1hr.; 7-12 per day 5:30am-7:15pm; €6.50, children €4.50.) **Adler-Schiffe,** Boysenstr. 13, in Hörnum Hafen, runs daytrips to Amrum or Fohr. Buy tickets 30min. in advance at the ticket booth at the Hörnum harbor, and try to board early. (☎987 00. Open daily 9am-5:30pm, round-trip €17.50, children €12.) Sylt's bus company SVG offers **bus tours** of the island leaving daily from the Westerland ZOB. (☎83 61 00. 2hr. tour Apr.-Nov. 11am. 3hr. tour Apr.-Nov. 2pm; Dec.-Jan. 1pm.) For bike rentals, the most convenient is **Fahrrad am Bahnhof** at the station, across from track 1. (☎58 03. €5-7 per day, €22-42 per wk. Open daily 8:30am-6:30pm.) The **tourist office** in the train station books rooms for a €6 fee and requires an 11% deposit for stays longer than one night, and the big bulletin boards in front of the station also list available rooms. (☎99 88; fax 99 85 55. Open summer M-F 9am-4pm, Sa 9am-2pm.) Near the train station is **grocery** store **Sky,** Wilhelmstr. 6. (Open M-F 8:30am-8pm, Sa 8am-6pm, Su 11am-6pm.) In non-emergencies, the **police** in Westerland can be reached at ☎70 47. A **pharmacy, Friesen Apotheke,** is on Friedrich Str. next to the grocery store. (☎51 69. Open M-F 8:30am-6:30pm, Sa 8:30am-1pm.) Check **email** for free at **Stadtbücherei Westerland,** Alte Post, Stephanstr. 6b, across from the Rathaus. (☎227 10. Open M-Tu 10am-12:30pm and 2:30-6pm, Th 10am-12:30pm and 2:30-7pm, F 10am-12:30pm and 2:30-5pm, Sa 10am-12:30pm) You can also get online at **Syltfoto** (☎14 55), Kirchenweg 5, in front of the train station. (€2 per 30min., students €1. Open M-F 9am-1pm, Sa 10am-2pm.) To

THE LOCAL STORY

BADEKULTUR

Germans' fascination with the beach began years before most citizens could swim. Perhaps it's something magical in the crisp sea air, or maybe it's the views; but Germans have a *Badekultur* bathing culture) all their own.

In the 19th century, elaborate acation homes appeared on the North and Baltic seacoasts. These stately houses with white facades and ornamented balconies were built in such quantities that many are now affordable to rent.

Perhaps the best symbol of a German beach is the *Strandkorb*. Invented about 120 years ago, roughly 170,000 of these wicker huts shield beachgoers from the sun and wind of Germany's north- ern shores. Those who want even more shelter from the elements go to the massive indoor *Schwim- mbäder* to enjoy saunas, water slides, and therapeutic pools.

Germans also seem to love nude beaches, designated FKK or *Freikörperkultur* (literally "free body culture"). The movement had its roots in the 1920s, when nude bathing was still punishable by fines. One of the country's first nude beaches opened on Hidden- see before WWII, and the "free- dom" inherent in nude bathing was especially popular after the war. Today, nearly every German beach has FKK portions. Advo- cates claim that nudism is part of a larger philosophy promoting exercise, freedom, and enjoyment of the outdoors. Others are just glad not to see another Speedo.

reach the **post office,** Kjeirstr. 17, 25980 Sylt, and its **24hr. ATM,** follow Kjeirstr. out of the train station for 300m. (Open M-F 8am-6pm, Sa 8am-1pm.)

☎❏ ACCOMMODATIONS AND FOOD. For rooms in List, call ☎952 00; in Hörnum, ☎96 26 26; in Kampen, ☎46 98 33. Sylt has three youth hostels. **Jugendherberge Hörnum (HI) ❷,** Friesenpl. 2, is a standard hostel set among the gentle *Südspitz* dunes 10min. from the water. From the ZOB, take bus #2 (dir.: Hörnum Hafen) to "Hörnum-Nord" and continue 2min. along Rantumer Str., turning left at the *Jugendherberge* sign. (Reception 12:30-1:30pm and 5-9pm. Curfew 11:15pm, but you can get a key. Dorms €18, under 27 €15.30, plus €0.50 *Kurtaxe* €2.20, under 27 €1, under 18 €0.50.) Sylt's newest hostel, **Jugendherberge Wester- land - "Dikjen Deel" ❷,** Fischerweg 36-40, is primarily a tent site for youth groups, but the main building con- tains 50 beds. (☎835 78 25. Breakfast and sheets included. Reception 8-9:30am, 10am-noon, 4-7pm, and every hour at 8, 9, and 10pm. Dorms €18, under 27 €15.30, plus *Kurtaxe* of €2.90.) Three kilometers northwest of List, **Jugendherberge Mövenberg ❷** is a monolithic complex settled alone on the edge of Nördsylt, the island's largest nature preserve. Catch bus #1 (dir.: List Hafen) from the Westerland ZOB and take it to the end of the line (€3.60). From mid-April to October you can change to bus #5 to "Mövenberg" (every 2hr.); otherwise, return to the second intersec- tion before the bus stop, turn right and follow the *Jugendherberge* sign for 35min., past the sheep and dunes. School groups love the hostel's proximity to the youth beach. (☎87 03 97; fax 87 10 39. Breakfast and sheets included. Reception 8-9am and 2-8pm. Cur- few 11pm. Reservations strongly recommended. Open Feb.-Oct. Dorms €18, under 27 €15.30, plus *Kurtaxe*.) Camping is an affordable alternative to the expensive pensions and hotels. Near the beach and minutes away from ritzy Kampen, **Campingplatz Kampen ❶,** Mövenweg 4, is one of Sylt's most appealing sites. (☎420 86; www.campen-in-kampen.de. Reception 8am-1pm and 3-5pm.) Dining options on Sylt cater to the luxury automobile crowd that frequents the island. Those with money to burn can head to Stroenwai in Kampen, also known as "Whiskey Alley" because of the many bars and cafes that line the road. The cash- conscious go to **Toni's Restaurant ❸,** Norderstr. 3, (☎258 10) which, despite the tacky decor and poster- sized menus, serves cheap, but surprisingly decent, examples of German cuisine (€5.80-13).

☎🏊❏ BEACHES, OUTDOOR ACTIVITIES, AND SIGHTS. The best way to explore the 39km-long island from tip to tip is by bicycle. The main bike path hugs the highway, making it good for inter-town travel, while the smaller dirt and gravel paths meander through the dunes, with alternating views of the ocean, flowering hills, and dense heath below. The most spectacular view is from atop **Uwedüne,** the island's highest point, located near Kampen. Western Sylt offers sparsely populated beaches, including the famous nude beach **Bühne 16.** *Kurtaxe* (visitor's taxes) for most beaches are €2-3. Beginning windsurfers flop around on the eastern side of the island, while the more experienced and daring brace themselves against the cold, turbulent water of the unprotected western side at **Wenningstedt, Hörnum,** and **List.** List is also an excellent base for hikers and bikers wishing to explore the trails leading into the remote dunes of Ellenbogen, 8km north of town. The Wattenmeer Park's **Schutzstation Hörnum** (☎88 10 93), 100m south of bus stop "Steintal," offers information about the region and a leads a variety of Watt-related activities. Westerland's brand new **Aquarium,** Gaadt 33, focuses on fish of the North Sea but has its requisite share of sharks. Take bus line A from the ZOB to "Schützenpl.," or walk 15min. (☎836 25 22. Open daily 10am-7pm. students and children €9.) Next to the aquarium, the **Aussichtspunkt** provides a panoramic view of the windy beach to the west, and the sprawling city to the east.

AMRUM ISLAND
☎04682

Although it is the smallest of the North Frisian Islands, Amrum possesses all of Sylt's beauty and charm, in a quieter, more personal environment. The island's main attractions are, not surprisingly, nautical in nature: lighthouses and some of the wildest beaches in Europe.

▊▊ TRANSPORTATION AND PRACTICAL INFORMATION. Boats to the town of Wittdün, run by **Adler-Schiffe,** (☎04651 987 00) leave from Hörnum on Sylt and Nordstrand, near Husum. (Hörnum to Wittdün 50min. 11:55am and 5:10pm. Round-trip €17.50, children €12.) For more frequent service, the **Wyker Dampfschiffs-Reederei** goes to Wittdün from Dagebüll harbor, next door to Dagebüll's train station. (☎01805 08 01 40; www.faehre.de. 5 per day. €7.70, round-trip €14.70.) At the southern end of the island is the town of **Wittdün,** which is home to Amrum's ferry terminal. Following the main road north, you can reach the island's four other towns: Süddorf, Steenodde, Nebel, and Norddorf. Amrum's **bus lines** connect the towns (Apr.-Nov. €1.20-2 per ride, day ticket €6.80). **Bikes** are available for rent all over the island, but prices go up the closer you are to Wittdün and the ferry. (A good price is around €3 per half-day, €4.50 per day.) The **tourist office,** Am Fähranleger, on the road across from the ferry terminal, provides a free room-inquiry service but does not book rooms. (☎940 30; www.amrum.de. Open M-F 9am-5pm, Sa 9:30am-12:30pm.) The Wattenmeer National Park's **Schutzstation Wittdün** (☎27 18), Mittelstr. 34, is near the hostel and offers guided tours of the Watt (€3). Though the danger of **quicksand** pits makes it advisable to take a guided tour, at low tide some hikers cross the Wattenmeer to the neighboring island, **Föhr.** Do **laundry** at **Marlene's Münz Wasch,** Inselstr. 56, about 700m from the ferry landing. (Wash €3. Dry €2. Open daily 8am-8pm.) The **post office** is on Inselstr., but the address is Hauptstr. 30, 25940 Amrum. (Open M-Tu and Th-F 9am-12:30pm and 2-5pm, W and Sa 9am-noon.)

▊▊ ACCOMMODATIONS AND FOOD. Plan on booking far ahead to stay anywhere on the island in the summer. To get to ⬛**Haus Eckart ❷,** Mittelstr. 20., walk away from the ferry dock past Inselstr. on V-Quedens-Weg, then turn right onto Mittelstr. Family-run since 1902, the home offers easy beach access, a garden perfect for picnicking, and occasional in-house yoga seminars run by the cheery owner. (☎20 56; www.haus-eckart.de. Breakfast included. Linen charge €5 for stays less than 3 nights. Dorms €15; singles €25; doubles €40.) **Jugendherberge Wittdün ❷,** Mittelstr. 1, 100 yards before House Eckart, has large, clean rooms, some with beach views. (☎20 10.

Breakfast and sheets included. Reception 7-9am, noon-1pm, and 5-9:30pm. Open Apr.-Nov. Dorms €15.30; singles €20.05-25.15; doubles €45.20. Add €2.70 if over 26 and €2.50 for required *Kurtaxe*.) **Campingplatz Amrum ❶**, Inselstr. 125, Wittdün, is nestled in the dunes and has many amenities, including its own *Biergarten*. (☎22 54; www.amrum-camping.de. Tents €5-9, €6.50 per person, plus *Kurtaxe*.) Restaurants in Wittdün tend to be fairly expensive, but there are two **SPAR** supermarkets on Inselstr., close to the docks. (Open M-F 7:45am-12:30pm and 2:30-6pm, Sa 7:45am-noon and 2-5pm.) Those with a sweet-tooth should sample the dainty *Friesenwaffeln* (waffles with plum sauce and whipped cream; €2.60) or down an invigorating *Eiergrog* (egg, sugar, and hot rum; €4.90) in Nebel's time-tested **Friesen-café ❷**, Vasterstigh 7. (☎966 20. Open daily 11:30am-6pm.) Nestled in a basement a block away from Wittdün's ferry dock, **Restaurant Klabautermann ❹**, Inselstr. 13, serves big portions of reasonably priced (€8-14) fish and meat, next door to the restaurant's private bowling alley. (☎21 39. Open daily 11am-1:30pm and 5-9:30pm.) In the evening, crowds fill **Die Blaue Maus,** Inselstr. 107 in Wittdün. This cozy pub is Amrum's most beloved bar, and even has its own bus stop. (☎20 40. Open M-W and F-Su 8pm-3am.)

🇬🇧🏞 **SIGHTS AND OUTDOOR ACTIVITIES.** Wittdün has a pleasant main street, Hauptstr., as well as a souvenir- and *Imbiß*-free **Strandpromenade** (beach walkway). To the west lies the **Kniepsand,** a wild stretch of North Sea beach. Between the *Kniepsand* and the towns lies a strip of grassy dunes crisscrossed by hiking trails and crowned by the **Amrumer Leuchtturm,** the tallest lighthouse on Germany's North Sea coast. (Open Apr.-Oct. M-F 8:30am-12:30pm. €2, children €0.50.) A view of the island can also be earned at the tops of *Aussichtsdünen* (lookout dunes) along the island's trails. **Nebel,** a village of traditional thatch-roof Frisian houses, is unquestionably the cultural center of the island. The **Mühlenmuseum,** in an old thatched windmill, has exhibits on the history of Amrum and its lighthouse. (☎38 89. Open Apr.-Oct. M-Sa 10am-noon and 2:30-5pm, Su 2-5pm. €2, children €0.50.) Amrum's Frisian culture is exhibited inside the **Ömrang Hüüs,** Waaswai 1. The 18th-century captain's home captures the harshness of life in austere Nordfriesland—in the tiny closet bedroom, the whole family slept sitting up to keep from freezing during the night. (☎10 11. Open M-F 10am-noon and 3-5pm, Sa 3-5pm. €1 requested donation.) **St. Clemens,** Nebel's small church, is also worth a visit. Outside Nebel, two trails run to Norddorf: the **forest trail** (7.9km, marked by green triangles), through the western portion of the island and the more scenic **Wattenmeer trail** (7.4km, marked by yellow dots), cutting through the villages and open pasture along the east shore of the island. Cut left on the smaller paths that branch off of the green triangle path to reach the 2km-wide *Kniepsand* beaches.

SCHLESWIG   ☎ 04621

One of the oldest towns in Northern Europe, Schleswig has held the Schlei river in its horseshoe embrace since around 800 AD. Over the centuries Schleswig was strengthened by the Vikings and made grand by the **Gottorfer** dukes, small-time nobles who set themselves up in a showy island castle. Though the grandeur of the past is now confined to museums and the swords of the Vikings sheathed under meters of earth, Schleswig remains a noble steward of its cultural heritage. Every two years, the city hosts an elaborate **Viking Festival,** complete with longboats and reenactments, drawing crowds from afar. (Look for the next one in August 2006.)

▐ TRANSPORTATION

Trains every hr. to: **Flensburg** (30min., €5.50); **Hamburg** (2hr., €18); **Kiel** (50min., €8.10). **Buses** run from the train station to the **ZOB,** on the corner of Königstr. and Plessenstr. Single rides on Schleswig's bus network cost €1.15; day-pass €3.60.

Schleswig

🏠🏡 ACCOMMODATIONS
Hotel Schleiblick, 3
Jugendherberge (HI), 1
Wikinger Campingplatz, 5

🍖 FOOD & DRINK
Asgaard-Brauerei, 2
Fischrestaurant
  Schleimöwe, 4

Bus line 1 uses bus #1501 and 1502, line 2 is #1503, line 3 is #1504, etc. For **taxis**, call ☎ 333 33 or 50 60. Rent **bikes** at **Radsport Splettstößer**, Bismarckstr. 13. Take Plessentstr. away from the water up the hill until it turns into Bismarckstr. It's just past Lutherstr. on the left. (☎ 241 02. €4.50 per day. Open M-F 8:30am-12:30pm and 1:30-6pm, Sa 8:30am-12:30pm.)

🌞🛈 ORIENTATION AND PRACTICAL INFORMATION

Unlike most German towns, Schleswig centers on its **bus terminal** rather than its train station. The train station, a 20min. walk or 5min. ride on the #1, 2, 3, 6, or 7 buses from the Altstadt, is to the south of the Schlei River, across the inlet. On the other side of the Schlei, a few hundred meters north of the bus station, the pedestrian shopping street **Stadtweg** runs through the town center. South of Stadtweg, paved paths, parks, and cafe-restaurants line the waterfront. Halfway between the bus and train stations is the expansive **Schloß Gottorf**, while east of the yacht harbor the **Altstadt** and the fishing village of **Holm** remain in pristine condition.

The **tourist office**, Plessenstr. 7, is up the street from the harbor; from the ZOB, walk down Plessenstr. toward the water. (☎ 98 16 16, room reservations 98 16 17; fax 98 16 19. Open May-Sept. M-F 9:30am-5:30pm, Sa 9:30am-12:30pm; Oct.-Apr. M-Th 10am-4pm, F 10am-1pm.) Do **laundry** at **Waschcenter**, Stadtweg 70. (Wash €3.50. Dry €0.50 per 12min. Open M-Sa 6am-10pm.) Snackbar **Kochlöffel**, Stadtweg 36, has **Internet**. (€1 per 30min. Hamburgers €1-3. Open M-Sa 9:30am-10:30pm, Su 11am-10:30pm.) The **post office**, 24837 Schleswig, is just off Stadtweg at Poststr., and has a 24hr. **ATM**. (Open M-F 9am-6pm, Sa 9am-1pm.)

🏠🏢 ACCOMMODATIONS AND FOOD

The **Jugendherberge (HI) ❶**, Spielkoppel 1, is near the center of town. Take bus #2 (dir.: Hühnhauser Schwimmhalle) from the train or bus station to "Schwimmhalle;" and walk one block south. Or walk along Königstr. and turn right onto Poststr., keep going as it changes to Moltkestr., and take a left on Michaelisallee. About 400m later, take a right on Spielkoppel; the hostel is on the right across from the school. The facilities are standard issue, but just seconds from a park with a commanding view of Schleswig's jumbled rooftops and the Schlei's swirling waters. The Stadtweg is just downhill, either through the meadow or down the set of stairs. (☎238 93. Breakfast and sheets included. Reception 7am-1pm and 5-11pm. Curfew 11pm. Dorms €16.50, under 27 €14; singles €20.20/€17.50.) **Hotel Schleiblick ❸**, Hafengang 4, overlooks the glimmering harbor. Follow Plessenstr. toward the harbor. Continue as it turns into Am Hafen, take a right on Hafenstr., bear left, and take a quick left onto Hafengang. Tucked away on a sidestreet, this centrally-located hotel offers bright, airy rooms with baths. (☎/fax 234 68. Free bike loan. Breakfast included. Reception 8am-3pm and 6-9pm. Singles €36; doubles €63.) The **Wikinger Campingplatz ❶**, Am Haithabu, is a spacious, though windy, campsite on the water. The Vikings set up camp near here over 1200 years ago, when they established their settlement at Haithabu in AD 800. (☎324 50; www.camping-haithabu.de. Reception 8-11am and 4-6pm. €3.50 per person, €2 per child, €6 per tent.) Closer to the Altstadt, fresh and cheap seafood can be found at the *Imbiße* along Am Hafen. The Stadtweg is also lined with cheap eateries. Witness the production of beer at Schleswig's own **Asgaard-Brauerei ❸**, Königstr. 27, where descendants of Eric the Red nurture cloudy brews in big copper tubs and tubes. Look for the converted fire engine parked outside—it sprays *Bier!* (☎292 06. Meals €9-10; beer €2-3. Open M-Th 5pm-midnight, F 5pm-2am, Sa 11am-2am, Su 11am-midnight.) The **Fischrestaurant Schleimöwe**, Süderholmstr. 8, serves excellent fish straight from the Schlei, with a waterfront view of the quaint village of Holm. Small dishes are €6-7, full dinners run €8-14. (☎234 09. Open M-F 11:30am-2pm and 5-10pm.)

👁 🏛 SIGHTS AND MUSEUMS

A 20min. walk along the harbor from the Altstadt or a quick ride to "Oberlandesgericht" on buses 1, 2, 4, or 5 brings you to the 18th-century ◨**Schloß Gottorf**, home to the **Landesmuseen**. These six museums are Schleswig's primary attraction, and it is no wonder, given the incredible breadth of the collections. On the ground floor of the Schloß, the left wing contains altarpieces, religious statues, a Gutenberg Bible, and the gorgeous *Schloßkapelle*, the castle chapel. Renaissance art and works by the Dutch masters fill the hall to the right of the entrance, while a large collection of furnishings, porcelain, and silver are exhibited in the rear. In the Art Nouveau display on the second floor, even the carpets are part of the exhibit. Ascending further, you reach the **Archäologisches Landesmuseum**, which showcases prehistoric artifacts from Schleswig-Holstein and around the world. Across from the castle, the Kreuzstall and adjacent buildings house the **Museum des 20. Jahrhunderts**, an extensive collection devoted to the works of 20th-century artists. In particular, the **Gallerie der Klassische Moderne** exhibits the paintings, sketches, and sculpture of contemporary Germans. The **outdoor sculpture museum**, in the park surrounding the castle, showcases other modern works. (☎81 32 22; www.schloss-gottorf.de. Open Apr.-Oct. daily 10am-6pm; Nov.-Mar. Tu-F 10am-4pm, Sa-Su 10am-5pm. Admission to everything €6, students €3, families €13.)

A few minutes away from Schloß Gottorf, on the south side of the harbor, is the **Stadtmuseum Schleswig**, Friedrichstr. 9-11, which houses an exhibition on the history of Schleswig-Holstein, a series of special exhibits, and **Das Teddy Bär Haus**, a collection of teddy bears spanning 100 years. (☎93 68 20; www.stadtmuseum-schleswig.de. Open Tu-Su 10am-5pm. Admission €3; students, children, and seniors €1.50; families €5.50.)Elsewhere in the city, a typical assortment of shops and department stores lines **Stadtweg**, the main pedestrian zone. Schleswig's Altstadt, a few blocks above the harbor, is crisscrossed by cobblestone streets meandering through the town's hilly terrain. The **St. Petri Dom** dwarfs the Altstadt's townhouses. The bird's-eye view of Schleswig from its 12th-century tower will take your breath away, if you still have any after the 240-stair ascent. The highlight of the church is Brüggemann's incredibly intricate **Bordesholmer Altar.** Choral and organ concerts take place here in the summer. (Open May-Sept. M-Sa 9am-5pm, Su 1:30-5pm; Oct.-Apr. M-Sa 10am-4pm, Su 1:30-5pm. €1 suggested donation. Tower donation €1, children €0.50. Concerts W evenings at 8pm; usually free.) The **Holm,** an old fishing village where a ring of miniature houses and a tiny church are carefully tended, begins east of Knud-Laward-Str.

From the harbor, a 20min. journey across the Schlei will bring you to the **Wikinger Museum Haithabu.** (Ferries leave from Stadthafen am Dom, dock number 2, every hr. 12:30-4:30pm. One-way tickets €2, children under 12 and students €1.50; round-trip €3.50/€2.50.) Follow the signs along the winding path to the cluster of buildings housing the museum. Many of the artifacts displayed inside were found right next door at Haithabu, the site of Schleswig's first Viking settlement. Don't miss the hall containing the full-size frame of a partially reconstructed longboat. (Open Apr.-Oct. daily 9am-5pm; Nov.-Mar. Tu-Su 10am-4pm. €4, students and children €2.50, families €9.)

FLENSBURG   ☎ 0461

Minutes from the Danish border, Nordic Flensburg has some of the best sailing in Germany. Separated from the industrial harbor to the north, Flensburg's Altstadt savors the waterfront view from windswept cafes and restaurants, drinking in the mild scene of sea and sails. Spared from all but two bombs in WWII, Flensburg's medieval architecture and churches remain in near-perfect condition. In 1945, Flensburg played reluctant host to an SS army on the cusp of surrender, briefly making the city the Nazi provisional capital. On curving cobblestone and brick pedestrian streets, crowds of young Germans and Danes take advantage of the city's cosmopolitan flair over home-brewed *Flensburger Pilsener.* Visitors to Flensburg embark on boat rides around the harbor and to nearby towns in Denmark, which lies within sight across the inlet.

◨◪ TRANSPORTATION AND PRACTICAL INFORMATION. Trains travel to: **Copenhagen** (4hr., 5 per day, €41); **Hamburg** (2hr., 1 per hr., €22); **Kiel** (1¼hr., 1 per hr., €13); **Schleswig** (30min., 1 per hr., €5.50). To get to the **ZOB** from the train station, turn right at the end of the Bahnhofstr., and take the left fork that curves as Süderhofenden for two blocks. **Buses** leave for Denmark every 20min., leaving from gate B4 (20min., €1.35). Flensburg's **public transportation** system saves a lot of uphill walking: most buses circulate through the ZOB two blocks from Holm below the harbor (€1.35, day pass €4.20). A few blocks from the ZOB, Nordlicht Reisen's **Hansalinie** sails round-trip to **Glücksburg.** (☎ 04631 617 10; www.nordlicht-reisen.de. 1hr.; 1 per 2hr. 9:30am-5:30pm, return 1 per 2hr. 10:30am-6:30pm; round-trip €4, children €3.) To reach the **tourist office,** Rathausstr. 1, go to the corner of Norderhofen and Rathausstr. near the ZOB. The staff books rooms for free and in July and August arranges German tours of the *Flensburger* brewery and the Altstadt for €5. (☎ 909 09 20; www.flensburg.de. Open July-Sept. M-F 9am-6pm, Sa 10am-1pm; Oct.-June M-F 9am-1pm and 3-6pm.) Local services include: **Waschcenter,** Angelburgerstr. 45 (Wash €3.50, soap included. Dry €0.50 per 12min. Open daily 6am-10pm.); **police,** Norderhofenden 1 or Rathausstr. 2a from 8am-6pm (☎ 484 41 10; in **emergencies** police ☎ 110 or fire ☎ 112); **Internet** at **NetFun Center,** Hafermarkt 8 (☎ 182 42 00; €2 per 30min; open daily 2-10pm); **post office,** Bahnhofstr. 40, 24939 Flensburg (open M-F 7am-6pm, Sa 8am-1pm).

◨◧◪ ACCOMMODATIONS, FOOD, AND NIGHTLIFE. Nestled in the leafy Volkspark northeast of the Altstadt, Flensburg's **Jugendherberge (HI) ❷**, Fichtestr. 16, sits between two centers of learning: Heldenheim Universität and a Marines training ground. To reach the hostel from the ZOB, take bus #2, 3, 5, or 7 to "Stadion," then follow the signs past the stadium. Standard hostel fare in 2-, 4-, and 6-bed flavors. (☎377 42; fax 31 29 52. Sheets and breakfast included. Reception 8-8:45am, 5-6pm, and 9:30-10pm. Dorms €16.20, under 27 €13.50.) A bargain compared to the overpriced hotels on Süderhofenden, economy-chain **ETAP Hotel ❸**, Süderhofenden 14, offers rooms with TVs and baths right at the bus station. Get lower rates by checking in at their credit card automat, open 10am-6pm. (☎48 08 920; www.etaphotel.com. Reception M-Sa 6:30-11am and 5-10pm, Su 7-11am and 5-10pm. Singles €35; doubles €42. Cheaper in low season.) Cheap *Currywurst* joints, bakeries, and ice cream parlors coexist with the boutiques of the pedestrian zone. The popular **Nordermarkt** simmers with classy cafes and bars. Nearby, **Hansen's Brauerei ❸**, Schiffbrücke 16, serves a tourist crowd home-brewed beer by the meter (12 drinks lined up along a meter-long board for €15) and German food in equally absurd quantities, such as 1kg of ribs for €10.20 on Saturday and Sunday. (☎222 10. Open M-Th and Su 11am-midnight, F-Sa 11:30-2am.) As you head north on Schiffbrücke, the streets become seedier, but the best bars and clubs are on this street in the first few blocks along the waterfront north of Neuestr.

◪ SIGHTS. Flensburg surrounds the natural harbor formed by the inland banks of the Flensburger Förde; streets run up from the water's edge into the hills. In the Südermarkt, the 14th-century **Nikolaikirche** boasts an impressively large organ and a series of post-Reformation paintings of comparable magnitude. One painting shows Christ crucified when viewed from one angle, and from another angle depicts him rising from the dead. (Open Tu-F 9am-7pm, Sa 10am-5pm. Free.) Up Große Str., beyond the Nordermarkt, is the larger **Marienkirche**, with modern stained-glass windows and a spectacular two-story Baroque altar depicting the Last Supper. (Open M-Sa 10am-5pm; winter until 4pm. Free.) The **Marientreppe**, across from Norderstr. 50, gives a panoramic glimpse of Flensburg and Denmark from atop its 146 stairs. In the **Schiffahrtsmuseum**, Schiffbrücke 39, four packed floors document Flensburg's nautical history, its role in Denmark's once-thriving Caribbean trade, and its long-touted production of rum. Models of galleons, a pair of looming mastheads, and a basement full of rum-barrels and grog-delivery bicycles make the exhibit worthwhile. (Open Apr.-Oct. Tu-Su 10am-5pm; Nov.-Mar. Tu-Su 10am-4pm. €3.50, students €1.50, families €7.) Near Südermarkt, the **Deutsches Haus**, Friedrich-Ebert-Str. 7, (☎128 00) and the **Theater Flensburg**, Rathausstr. 22, put on plays, artsy films, and concerts. (☎150 50 00; www.sh-landestheater.de. Box office open M-F 10am-1pm and 3-6pm, Sa 10am-1pm.) Up the hill from the city theater is Museumsberg, upon which sit the two buildings containing the Städtische Museen. The bottom floor of the **Heinrich-Sauermann-Haus** contains Flensburg's **Naturwissenschaftliches Museum,** with hundreds of stuffed birds, mammals, and insects on display. The upper floors house a series of furnished rooms filled with artifacts of Schleswig-Holstein's cultural history. The adjacent building, the **Hans-Christiansen-Haus** Museumsberg 1, contains a unique collection of 19th-century paintings by regional artists and a collection of modern art. (☎85 29 56. Open Tu-Su 10am-5pm; Nov.-Mar. until 4pm.)

HAMBURG

Water shapes every aspect of life in the harbor city of Hamburg, Germany's second-largest city. Joggers and walkers flock to the Alster lakes to enjoy the area's beauty, while the bustling port on the Elbe floods the city with new people, ideas, and trade. The many canals that cross Hamburg reflect images of spectacular church steeples alongside modern facades. A walk through the city is a walk over water—with a grand total of 2478 bridges, Hamburg has more than Venice.

A hub for commerce since its early history, Hamburg was a founding member of the Hanseatic trade league in the 13th century. Overland trade from the Baltic Sea brought prosperity in the 16th century, leading to the establishment of the first German stock exchange here in 1558. By the 17th century, Hamburg's influence had spread, and it gained the title of "Free Imperial City" in 1618. Along with Berlin and Bremen, it is one of the three remaining city-states among Germany's 16 *Länder*. Hamburg still values its independent attitude, which, along with great sea-trade wealth, has brought the city through many hardships.

The Great Fire of 1842 levelled the entire downtown, but a massive rebuilding effort brought the city out of the ashes. The reborn Hamburg emerged in the industrial age as a powerhouse in naval construction and home of the Hamburg-America Line, then the world's largest shipping firm. In WWII, a series of air raids once again turned the downtown to rubble. Over 50,000 tenants of the crowded buildings on the waterfront were killed in a single strike in July of 1943. Thanks to a massive reconstruction effort begun in the 1960s, Hamburg has restored many of its most beloved buildings.

Today's Hamburg is progressive, cosmopolitan, and accepting. The city is Germany's most diverse, with large ethnic populations including many Turkish and Portuguese residents. The district of **St. Georg** is also home to a flourishing gay scene. As the cultural center of Germany, Hamburg houses world-renowned opera and theater companies and many of the country's finest museums. Modern art and music have a home here as well. Hamburg's venues hosted The Beatles before they were famous, and a thriving independent and experimental music scene exists today. The city boasts a spectacular array of nightlife. Tens of thousands of revelers flock every weekend to the infamous red-light district of the **Reeperbahn,** and bars and pubs throughout the city fill up nearly every night of the week.

HIGHLIGHTS OF HAMBURG

BARGAIN for the freshest fish in the *Land* while listening to local **rock bands** play on Sunday morning at the **Fischmarkt** (p. 225).

DANCE UNTIL DAWN in the midst of **Hamburg's** spectacular nightlife (p. 230).

MARVEL at the works of the old masters and contemporary artists in the museums along the **Kunstmeile** (see **Orientation,** p. 216).

✖ INTERCITY TRANSPORTATION

Flights: Air France (☎01805 83 08 30) and **Lufthansa** (☎01803 80 38 03) are the 2 heavy hitters flying into Hamburg's **Fuhlsbüttel Airport** (☎507 50). **Jasper Airport Express** buses (☎22 71 06 10) run from the Kirchenallee exit of the Hauptbahnhof to the airport (25min.; every 15min. 5am-7pm, then every 20min. 7-9:20pm; €4.60, under 13 €2). Or take U1 or S1/S11 to "Ohlsdorf," and then an **express bus** to the airport (every 10min. 4:30am-11pm, every 30min. to 1am. €2.20, children 4-12 €0.80).

HAMBURG

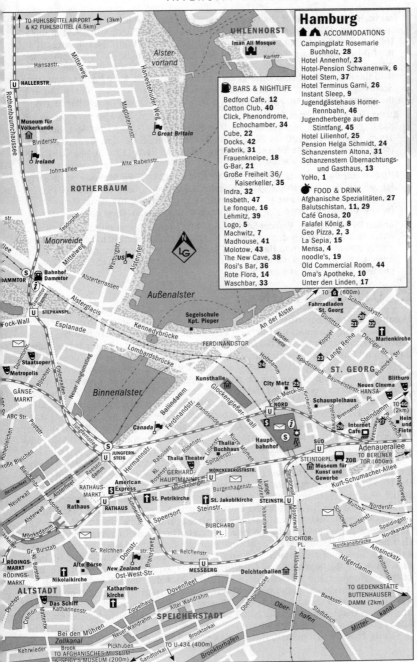

Hamburg

🏠 🏕 ACCOMMODATIONS

Campingplatz Rosemarie
  Buchholz, 28
Hotel Annenhof, 23
Hotel-Pension Schwanenwik, 6
Hotel Stern, 37
Hotel Terminus Garni, 26
Instant Sleep, 9
Jugendgästehaus Horner-
  Rennbahn, 46
Jugendherberge auf dem
  Stintfang, 45
Hotel Lilienhof, 25
Pension Helga Schmidt, 24
Schanzenstern Altona, 31
Schanzenstern Übernachtungs-
  und Gasthaus, 13
YoHo, 1

🍺 BARS & NIGHTLIFE

Bedford Cafe, 12
Cotton Club, 40
Click, Phenondrome,
  Echochamber, 34
Cube, 22
Docks, 42
Fabrik, 31
Frauenkneipe, 18
G-Bar, 21
Große Freiheit 36/
  Kaiserkeller, 35
Indra, 32
Insbeth, 47
Le fonque, 16
Lehmitz, 39
Logo, 5
Machwitz, 7
Madhouse, 41
Molotow, 43
The New Cave, 38
Rosi's Bar, 36
Rote Flora, 14
Waschbar, 33

🍎 FOOD & DRINK

Afghanische Spezialitäten, 27
Balutschistan, 11, 29
Café Gnosa, 20
Falafel König, 8
Geo Pizza, 2, 3
La Sepia, 15
Mensa, 4
noodle's, 19
Old Commercial Room, 44
Oma's Apotheke, 10
Unter den Linden, 17

HAMBURG

Trains: The **Hauptbahnhof** has connections every hr. to: **Berlin** (2½hr., €42); **Copenhagen** (5hr., €66); **Frankfurt** (3½hr., €86); **Hannover** (1½hr., €34); and **Munich** (6hr., €96); frequent trains to **Amsterdam** (5hr., 3 per day, €68). The efficient staff at the **DB Reisezentrum** sells tickets. Open M-F 5:30am-10pm, Sa-Su 7am-10pm. **Dammtor** station is near the university; **Harburg** station is south of the Elbe; **Altona** station is to the west of the city; and **Bergedorf** is to the southeast. Most trains to and from Schleswig-Holstein stop only at Altona. Frequent local trains and the S-Bahn connect the stations. **Lockers** are available 24hr. for €1-4 per day, follow the overhead signs.

Buses: The **ZOB** is across Steintorpl. from the Hauptbahnhof, just past the Museum für Kunst und Gewerbe. Terminal is open M-Th 5am-10pm, F-Sa 5am-midnight, Su 5am-10pm. **Autokraft** (☎280 86 60) goes to **Berlin** (3¼hr., 8 per day, €23). **Gulliver's** (☎24 71 06) to **Amsterdam** (5½hr., daily, €36) and **Paris** (12hr., daily, €55). Discount rates for students and children.

Mitfahrzentrale: Citynetz, Ernst-Merck-Str. 12-14 (☎24 85 95 25; www.citynetz-mitfahrzentrale.de). Open M-F 9:30am-6:30pm, Sa 9:30am-2:00pm. To: **Berlin** (€15.50); **Cologne** (€24); **Frankfurt** (€24); **Munich** (€37). **Mitfahr2000,** Ernst-Merck-Str. 8 (☎194 40; www.mitfahr.org) 2 doors down, has similar prices. Open daily 8am-8pm.

Ferries: DFDS Seaways, Van-der-Smissen-Str. 4 (☎38 90 30; www.dfdsseaways.co.uk), about 1km west of the Fischmarkt (S1 or 3 to "Königstr."). Overnight ferries run from the nearby port of Cuxhaven to **Harwich, UK** (18hr.; summer every other day, winter 3 per week; €113, winter €59, under 26 25% discount.) Open M-F 10am-4:30pm; reserve by phone M-F 9am-6pm, Sa 9am-2pm.

✚ ORIENTATION

Hamburg lies on the northern bank of the Elbe river, 100km inland from the North Sea. The ideally situated harbor, one of Europe's busiest, has shaped the city's growth. Hamburg's center is between the Elbe and the nearby Alster lakes, **Außenalster** and **Binnenalster,** which are formed by the confluence of the Alster, Bille and Elbe rivers. A ring of roads, once adorned with defensive fortifications, encircle the city. A chain of parks, including the beautiful **Planten un Blomen** (p. 224), skirt the western boundary of the downtown and arch northward from the **Landungsbrücken** (piers) of **St. Pauli** all the way to the western shore of the Alster lakes. The Hauptbahnhof lies at the eastern edge of the city center, along Steintorwall. Bisecting the downtown, the **Alsterfleet canal** separates the **Altstadt** on the eastern bank from the **Neustadt** on the west. The city's predominant museums, galleries, and theaters are located within these two districts.

Extending from the Kirchenallee exit of the Hauptbahnhof, the predominantly gay district of **St. Georg** follows the Außenalster's east bank. Here, the seediness of the Hansapl. area near the station falls away to a quiet cafe scene along the Lange Reihe. Outside the Hauptbahnhof's main exit on Steintorwall is the **Kunstmeile** (Art Mile), a row of museums extending from the Alster Lakes to the banks of the Elbe. Perpendicular to Steintorwall, **Mönckebergstraße,** Hamburg's most famous shopping street, runs westward to the **Rathausmarkt.** The Neustadt's **Hanseviertel,** nestled between Rathausmarkt and Gänsemarkt, is crammed with banks, shops, galleries, and auction houses. The area's glamour turns window-shopping into high art, while the nearby *Fleete* (canals) give the quarter a Venetian charm. North of the city center, the **university** dominates the **Dammtor** district and the western portion of **Rotherbaum,** sustaining a vibrant community of students and intellectuals. To the west of the university, the **Schanzenviertel** is a politically active community that is inhabited by artists, students, and a sizable Turkish population. The **Altona** district was once a Jewish community and, in the 17th century, an independent city ruled by Denmark, but as power shifted these groups were ousted.

Altona's bustling pedestrian zone, the Ottenser Hauptstr., runs west from the Altona station. Hamburg's wealthiest neighborhoods, such as **Winterhude** and **Harvesthude**, line the shores of the Außenalster. Toward the west, **Eppendorf** is home to the most beautiful outdoor markets in the city. At the southwest end of the city center, an entirely different atmosphere reigns along the Elbe in **St. Pauli**, where the raucous **Fischmarkt** (fish market) takes place blocks away from the equally wild **Reeperbahn**, home to Hamburg's infamous sex trade and most of its discos.

▆ LOCAL TRANSPORTATION

Public Transportation: HVV operates an efficient U-Bahn, S-Bahn, and bus network. Short rides within the downtown cost €1.50, one-way in greater Hamburg €2.40; 9hr. pass €4.65, 1-day €5.50; 3-day €13.30. The **Hamburg Card** provides unlimited access to public transportation, reduced admission to museums, and discounts on bus and boat tours for groups of 1 adult and up to 3 children under 12. (Available at tourist offices. €7.30 per day; €15 for 3 days) The **Group Card** provides the same benefits for up to 5 people of any age. (1-day €13; 3-day €23.)

Ferry: Alster-Kreuz-Fahrten (☎357 42 40) runs between 9 stops on the Binnen- and Außenalster daily 10am-6pm. €1.20 per stop; €6 for 5 stops or more; €8 for a full loop; children half-price.

Taxis: Taxiruf, ☎44 10 11. **Taxi Hamburg,** ☎666 666. Really.

Car Rental: Avis (☎32 87 38 00), in the Hauptbahnhof near track #12. Cars from €345 per wk., with insurance and 24hr. emergency assistance. International reservations ☎01805 55 77 55. Open M-F 7:30am-9pm, Sa 8am-6pm, Su 10am-6pm. **Hertz,** Kirchenallee 34-36 (☎280 12 01, international reservations 0180 533 35 35), is across the street and to the left. Cars from €305 per wk., including insurance. Open M-F 8am-6pm, Sa 8:30am-6pm.

Boat Rental: Segelschule Kpt. Pieper, An der Alster/Atlantikstieg (☎24 75 78, www.segelschule-pieper.de), directly across from the Hotel Atlantic at the foot of the Kennedybrücke on the Außenalster. Paddleboats and rowboats €12 per hr.; sailboats for up to 6 people €15-18 per hr. Open daily 10am-9pm.

Bike Rental: Fahrradladen St. Georg, Schmilinskystr. 6, (☎24 39 08), is off the Lange Reihe towards the Außenalster. €8 per day; €56 per wk. with a €50 deposit. Open M-F 10am-7pm, Sa 10am-1pm. **Fahrradstation Dammtor/Rothebaum,** Schlüterstr. 11 (☎41 46 82 77), is run by students but rents to all for the best price in Hamburg. €3 per day. Open M-F 9am-6pm.

▐ PRACTICAL INFORMATION

CITY CODE:	The city code for all of Hamburg is ☎**040**.

TOURIST AND FINANCIAL SERVICES

Tourist Hotline: The Hamburg Hotline (☎30 05 13 00) has English speaking operators who book rooms (€4), sell event tickets, and answer questions. Open daily 8am-8pm.

Tourist Offices: Hamburg's main tourist offices supply free English-language maps and pamphlets. All sell the **Hamburg Card,** a cheap way to explore the city (p. 217). The **Hauptbahnhof office,** in the *Wandelhalle* near the Kirchenallee exit (☎30 05 12 01; www.hamburg-tourism.de), books rooms for a €4 fee. Open daily 7am-10pm. The **St. Pauli Landungsbrücken office,** between piers 4 and 5 (☎30 05 12 03; fax 31 35 78), is less crowded than the Hauptbahnhof office. Open Oct.-Mar. daily 10am-5:30pm; Apr.-Sept. M, W, Su 8am-6pm, Tu and Th-Sa 8am-7pm.

Tours: Information booths for many tours are located at the St. Pauli Landungsbrücken and in the Hauptbahnhof.

Top-Tour Hamburg (☎641 37 31) operates sightseeing tours on double-decker buses, leaving from the Kirchenallee exit of the Hauptbahnhof and from the St. Pauli Landungsbrücken, every 30min. daily Apr.-Oct. 9:30am-5pm; fall and winter tours are less frequent. If a sight seems particularly intriguing you can hop off the bus and catch the next one after a more thorough inspection. For a tour in English, ask as you board. Adults €12, children €6, families €24.

Stattreisen Hamburg (☎430 34 81; www.stattreisen-hamburg.de). Offbeat 2hr. neighborhood- and themed walks, with titles such as "Reeperbahn by Night," "Merchants and Catastrophes Downtown," and "Neon lights, Seedy Bars and Catholics in St. Pauli." Most tours are given in German; however, English tours are offered on a less-frequent basis. Call (☎43 19 09 94) for times and locations, or ask at the tourist office. €6-10.

ADFC Allgemeiner Deutscher Fahrradclub (☎390 70 50; www.hamburg.adfc.de), offers guided bike tours through a variety of neighborhoods. Tours vary in length and difficulty. Mar.-Dec. Sa-Su. Call for exact times, or pick up a current schedule from the tourist office. €10.

Alster-Touristik, on Jungfernstieg by the Außenalster (☎357 42 40). Walk to the Außenalster or take the U1 or 2, or S1 or 3 to Jungfernstieg. 50min. boat rides around the lakes. Tours leave daily Apr.-Oct. every 30min. 10am-6pm, €9.50, children up to 16 €4.50, families €22.50.

Consulates: The majority of consulates flank the ritzy neighborhoods on the western shore of Außenalster, Harvestehuder Weg, and the smaller streets branching off of them. **Canada:** Ballindamm 35, S or U-Bahn to "Jungfernstieg", between Alestertor and Bergstr. (☎460 02 70). Open M-F 9:30am-12:30pm. **Ireland:** Feldbrunnenstr. 43 (☎44 18 61 13). U1 to "Hallerstr." Open M-F 9am-1pm. **New Zealand:** Domstr. 19, on the 3rd fl. of Zürich-Haus (☎442 55 50). U1 to "Messberg." Open M-Th 9am-1pm, 2-5:30pm, F 9am-1pm, 2-4:30pm. **UK:** Harvestehuder Weg 8a (☎448 03 20). U1 to "Hallerstr." Open M-Th 9am-4pm, F 9am-3pm. **US:** Alsterufer 26-28 S or U to Dammtor. (☎41 17 11 00). Open M-F 9am-noon.

Currency Exchange: ReiseBank, (☎32 34 83), on the 2nd floor of the Hauptbahnhof near the Kirchenallee exit, arranges money transfers for Western Union, cashes traveler's checks (1% commission with a €4 min. for American Express and 1% with a €6 min. for other types), and exchanges currency for a steep 4-5% fee, plus a fixed charge of €3 for exchanges of up to €25, and €5 for larger amounts. Open daily 7:30am-10pm. ReiseBank also has branches in the Altona and Dammtor train stations. For better rates, try one of the dozens of exchanges and banks (most of which are open M-F 9am-5pm) near the train station or downtown.

American Express: Rathausmarkt 10 (☎30 39 38 11). U3 to "Rathaus." Across from the bus stop, on the corner of Hermanstr. All banking services. Mail (letters only) held for members up to 5 wk. Open M-F 9:30am-6pm, Sa 10am-2pm.

LOCAL SERVICES

Bookstores: Thalia-Buchhaus, Spitalerstr. 8 (☎48 50 11 22), U2 to Mönkeburgstr., is one of the city's largest bookstores. **Heinrich-Heine Buch,** Grindelallee 24-28 (☎441 13 30), has an excellent travel section and a decent selection of English-language novels. Open M-F 9:30am-7pm, Sa 10am-4pm. **Buchladen,** Schulterblatt 55 (☎439 13 49), in the heart of the Sternschanze area, has about 100 English novels. Open M-F 9:30am-6:30pm, Sa 10am-4pm.

Library: Staats- und Universitätsbibliothek, Von-Melle-Park 3 (☎428 38 22 33). Hamburg's university library contains study areas and a good English-language collection. Open to the public M-F 9am-9pm, Sa 10am-1pm.

Gay and Lesbian Resources: St. Georg is the center of the gay community. Try picking up the useful, free **hinnerk** magazine and "Friends: The Gay Map" from **Café Gnosa,** Lange Reihe 93 (p. 223). Other organizations include: **Hein und Fiete,** Pulverteich 21

(☎24 03 33). Walk down Steindamm Str. away from the Hauptbahnhof, turn right on Pulverteich and look out for a rainbow-striped building. Open M-F 4-9pm, Sa 4-7pm. **Magnus-Hirschfeld-Centrum**, Borgweg 8 (☎27 87 78 00). U3 or bus #108 to "Borgweg." Daily films and counseling sessions, and an evening cafe, **Feelgood Cafe**, (☎27 87 78 01) open daily 5pm-midnight. The center operates hotlines for gays (☎279 00 69, M-F 2-6pm, Tu-W also 7-10pm) and lesbians (☎279 00 49, W 7-9pm).

Laundry: Schnell und Sauber, Grindelallee 158, in the university district. S21 or 31 to "Dammtor," then bus #4 or 5. Wash 6kg €3.50, soap included. Dry €1 per 15min. Open daily 7am-10:30pm. Other locations at Pferdemarkt 27 and Nobistor 24 have the same prices and hours. Sip a beer while waiting for your clothes at **Washbar**, Ottenser Hauptstr. 56 in Altona, a unique bar/cafe/laundromat (p. 232).

EMERGENCY AND COMMUNICATIONS

Emergency: Police, ☎110. From the Kirchenallee exit of the Hauptbahnhof, turn left and follow signs for "BGS/Bahnpolizei" (non-emergency ☎309 68 10). Also on the **Reeperbahn** at the corner of Davidstr. and Spielbudenpl. (non-emergency ☎428 65 15 10), and in the courtyard of the Rathaus. **Fire and Ambulance:** ☎112.

Rape Crisis Line: ☎25 55 66. Open M and Th 9:30am-1pm and 3-5pm, Tu 9:30am-1pm and 3-4pm, F 9:30am-1pm. English speaking staff available. The **Seelsorge Center** (☎31 65 43) near the Reeperbahn also takes calls Tu and Th-F 10:30am-5:30pm.

Pharmacy: Senator-Apotheke, Hachmannpl. 14 (☎32 75 27 or 33 92 92). Exit the Hauptbahnhof on Kirchenallee and turn right. English-speaking staff. Open M-F 7am-8pm, Sa 8am-4pm.

Internet Access: Internet Cafe, Adenaueralle 10 (☎28 00 38 98), directly across from the ZOB, offers one of the best deals in town, €0.70 for 30min. Open M-Sa 10am-midnight, Su 1pm-midnight. **Teletime**, Schulterblatt 39 (☎41 30 47 30), a callshop/Internet cafe in the heart of the Sternschanze district, charges €0.50 per 10min. Open M-Sa 10am-midnight. Near the U3 "Schlump" stop, **Spiele-Netzwerk**, Kleiner Schäferkamp 24, (☎45 03 82 10) costs €2 for 30min, €3 per hr., and is open later (daily 10am-2am). Second location with same hours and prices near U2 Mundsburg at Hamburger Str. 1 (☎22 92 71 36). By the Altona station is **Webdome**, Offenser Hauptstr. 17 (☎30 39 17 77). €0.98 per 30min., €1.95 per hr.

Post Office: At the Kirchenallee exit of the Hauptbahnhof, 20099 Hamburg. Open M-F 8am-8pm, Sa 9am-6pm. **Poste Restante** can be mailed to: Post Hamburg-Hauptbahnhof, 20099 Hamburg.

ACCOMMODATIONS

The vibrant **Schanzenviertel** area, filled with students, leftist dissidents, and a large ethnic community, houses two of the city's best backpacker hostels near many excellent, inexpensive cafes and shops. More expensive hotels are plentiful around the Binnenalster and eastern Außenalster. A slew of small, relatively cheap pensions (often renting by the hour) line **Steindamm, Steintorweg, Bremer Weg**, and **Bremer Reihe**, around the Hauptbahnhof. The area has its share of drug addicts, prostitutes, and wannabe mafiosi, but the hotels are, for the most part, safe. There are nicer, but still cheap, options north of the Bahnhof around and on **Ernst-Merck-Straße, Holzdamm**, and **Lange Reihe**. The tourist office's free *Hotelführer* can help direct you. For stays longer than two weeks, try the **Mitwohnzentrale Homecompany**, Schulterblatt 112. (S21 or 31 or U3 to "Sternschanze." ☎194 45; www.homecompany.de. Open M-F 9am-1pm and 2-6pm, Sa 9am-1pm.) A passport is required, as well as a deposit of one month's rent.

HOSTELS AND CAMPING

▨ **Schanzenstern Übernachtungs- und Gasthaus,** Bartelsstr. 12 (☎439 84 41; www.schanzenstern.de). S21 or 31, or U3 to "Sternschanze." Left onto Schanzenstr., right on Susannenstr., and left to Bartelsstr. In the middle of the electrifying Schanzenviertel, the Schanzenstern maintains bright, hotel-like rooms on the upper floors of a renovated pen factory. Wheelchair-accessible. Breakfast €4-6. Reception 6:30am-2am. Reservations needed in the summer. Dorms €18; singles €36; doubles €51; triples €61; quads €74; quints €92. ❷

▨ **Instant Sleep,** Max-Brauer-Allee 277 (☎43 18 23 10; www.instantsleep.de). S21 or 31 or U3 to "Sternschanze." From the station, take a right onto Schanzenstr., turn left on Altonear Str., and follow it until it becomes Max-Brauer-Allee. Helpful, bilingual staff contributes to a family feel at this backpacker hostel. Guests lounge together waiting for laundry, reading books from the improvised library, or cooking dinner in the communal kitchen. **Internet** €1 per 15min. Bike rental €4 per 6hr., €6 per day (midnight to midnight). Lockers €5 deposit. Sheets €2. Reception 8am-2am. Check-out 11am. Dorms €15-18; singles €28; doubles €44; triples €60. ❷

Schanzenstern Altona, Kleiner Rainstr. 24-26. (☎39 91 91 91; www.schanzenstern-altona.de). From Altona station, take the Offenser Hauptstr. exit. After 2 blocks, turn right on Bahrneldstr., then immediately left on Kleine Rainstr. Just as nice as its counterpart in the Schanzenviertel. Close to the Altona station with frequent S-Bahn service. Dorms €18; singles €40; doubles €55-65; triples €70; quads €80. ❷

Jugendherberge auf dem Stintfang (HI), Alfred-Wegener-Weg 5 (☎31 34 88). S1 or 3, or U3 to "Landungsbrücke," then just up the hill on the wooded path. Well-furnished rooms with large windows overlook the woods or the harbor. Signs warn to not wander St. Pauli alone at night and to be wary of swindlers nearby. Breakfast and sheets included. Dinner buffet €5. Laundry €3.50, including soap. Reception 12:30pm-12:30am. Lockout 2-6:30am. Dorms €21.50-24.50, under 27 €18.80-21.80. ❷

Jugendgästehaus und Gästehaus Horner-Rennbahn (HI), Rennbahnstr. 100 (☎651 16 71; www.jugendherberge.de/jh/hamburg-horn). U3 to "Horner-Rennbahn," then bus #213 to Tribünenweg, hostel is 150m farther. Adjacent to a horse-racing track, this hostel is far from Hamburg's city center, but extremely clean and secure. Breakfast (7-9am) and sheets included. Check-in noon-1am. Check-out 7-9:30am. Curfew 1am, stragglers admitted at 2am. Dorms €21.50; doubles €24.50-26; under 27 €2.60 discount; less for longer stays. Family rooms €17-20 per person. ❷

Campingplatz Rosemarie Buchholz, Kieler Str. 374 (☎540 45 32; www.camping-buchholz.de). From Altona train station, take bus #183 to "Basselweg" (20min., 2-3 per hr., 5am-midnight), then walk 100m farther. An enclosed plot of land with tightly packed campers, surrounded by houses and just off a busy road. Breakfast €4. Reception 8am-1pm and 2-10pm. Quiet hours 10pm-7am. Check-out noon. €4.30 per person, €8-11 per tent. Showers €1. ❶

HOTELS

Pension Helga Schmidt, Holzdamm 14, directly across from the Hotel Atlantic (☎280 83 90; www.home.t-online.de/home/Pension-Schmidt). Located in a decent neighborhood only 2 blocks from the Hauptbahnhof. Well-furnished rooms have telephone, TV, and a small collection of books; some have a view of the Alster. Cheaper rooms have hall shower. Breakfast €6. Singles €35-37; doubles €55-65; triples €82. ❸

Hotel-Pension Schwanenwik, Schwanenwik 29 (☎220 09 18; www.hotel-schwanenwik.de). From Hauptbahnhof, take bus #6 to Mundsburger Brücke, cross street, walk 200m down Hartwicusstr. and turn right onto Schwanenwik. The beautiful lakeside rooms are quiet and spacious, the more expensive ones with private showers. Breakfast included. Reception until 10pm. Singles €44-68; doubles €62-90. ❹

Hotel Terminus Garni, Steindamm 5 (☎280 31 44; www.hotel-terminus-hamburg.de). From the Hauptbahnhof Kirchenallee exit, turn right. Although located at the foot of the somewhat-seedy Steindamm, the hotel itself is clean and secure. Spacious rooms, standard all the way, with TV, telephone, and shower. Wheelchair-accessible. Breakfast included. Reception 24hr. Singles €35-50; doubles €62-76. ❸

Hotel Lilienhof, Ernst-Merck-Str. 4 (☎24 10 87; www.hotel-lilienhof.de). From the Hauptbahnhof Kirchenallee exit, turn left, hotel is at the intersection of Ernst-Merck-Str. and Kirchenallee. Basic rooms with TVs, telephones, and radios right in the center of town. Cheaper rooms have hall bathrooms. Breakfast included. Singles €31-41; doubles €61-71; triples and quads start at €87. ❸

Hotel Annenhof, Lange Reihe 23 (☎24 34 26; www.hotelannenhof.de). From the Hauptbahnhof's Kirchenallee exit, turn left. Pass the Schauspielhaus on your right, then turn right onto Lange Reihe. The brightly colored rooms are simply furnished and have soft beds. Singles €35; doubles €63; triples €80. ❸

Hotel Stern, Reeperbahn. 154 (☎31 76 99 90; www.stern-hamburg.de). Newly opened, with 308 rooms, located in a courtyard off the Reeperbahn, right next to the Große Freiheit. Singles and doubles €49. Website offers occasional dirt-cheap deals. ❹

YoHo - The Young Hotel, Moorkamp 5 (☎28 41 91; www.yoho-hamburg.de). U2 or 3 to "Schlump," walk 200m on Schäferkampsallee, turn right. A team of young architects from Hamburg used glass, steel, and mood lighting to transform this turn-of-the century villa into a destination for the style-conscious crowd. Breakfast €10. The hotel also houses "Maza," an upscale Syrian restaurant, on the main level. Reception M-F 6am-midnight, Sa-Su 6:30am-midnight. Singles €77, under 26 €57; doubles €87/€67. ❹

◪ FOOD

Seafood is everywhere in Hamburg, as you'd expect in a port city. Some of the most common varieties of fish include *Lachs* (salmon) and *Thunfisch* (tuna). Herring is the specialty, from the *Matjes* (white herring), pickled and served on sandwiches or in spreads, to the grilled *Brathering*. Sweet and salty tastes blend in the traditional *Aalsuppe* (eel soup), which combines dried fruit and chunks of eel. The **Daniel Wischer** and **Nordsee** fast-food chains offer cheap, greasy fish dishes throughout the city. Far more prolific and popular than the traditional regional food, however, are the hundreds of Turkish *Imbiße*, serving up cheap *Döner Kebap* and falafel wraps. The Portuguese community of Hamburg serves its own seafood dishes in the area between the Michaeliskirche (p. 223) and the river.

In early spring when asparagus is in season, it's hard to find a restaurant that doesn't serve *Spargelcremesuppe* (asparagus cream soup), and late summer sees a similar burst in *Blumenkohl* (cauliflower) dishes. For the sweet tooth, *Rote Grütze* is a beloved pudding made of red berries, usually served with vanilla sauce. Small markets selling cheap fresh fruit and Persian flatbread line Suzannestr. in the Schanzenviertel.

SCHANZENVIERTEL

In the Schanzenviertel, Turkish fruit stands, Asian *Imbiße*, and avant-garde cafes entice the hungry passersby. **Schulterblatt, Susannenstraße,** and **Schanzenstraße** host a slew of funky cafes and restaurants.

◪ **La Sepia,** Schulterblatt 36 (☎432 24 84). This Portuguese restaurant prepares some of the city's tastiest and most reasonably priced seafood. For your pocketbook's sake, come for lunch (11am-5pm), when €5 gets you a big plate of grilled tuna with sauteed and scallioned carrots and potatoes, a basket of fresh bread, and a bowl of soup. Lunch €4-6. Dinner €7-15. Open daily 11am-3am. ❸

ON THE MENU

HAMBURGER

While the residents of Frankfurt happily grill their *Frankfurter* sausages and the citizens of Berlin savor their *Berliner* donuts, the people of Hamburg carry the name of the world's most beloved sandwich: the hamburger.

The hamburger's history spans many years and thousands of miles. Although descriptions of ground beef date back to Roman times, the burger's development began in earnest in medieval Russia, where the nomadic Tartars ate raw, chopped beef mixed with spices. German sailors observed the preparation of this *Beef tartar* in Russian ports. After deciding (thankfully) that the meat should be cooked instead of eaten raw, they brought this creation back to the docks of Hamburg.

The "Hamburger steak" would have to leave Germany before it could gain a bun. German immigrants brought recipes for the steak (still bunless) with them to America in the 1870s, where it became popular in restaurants. In 1904, an enterprising vendor first served the hamburger on bread at the World's Fair in St. Louis. Its popularity exploded in America in the years before WWI.

The burger in its present form was slow to return to Germany, and many German restaurants still serve *Hamburger steak* without a bun. But globalization and fast-food empires have popularized the bunned version, and millions of Germans now chomp down on juicy hamburgers daily.

Unter den Linden, Juliusstr. 16 (☎43 81 40). Join happy couples and intellectuals reading complimentary papers with *Milchkaffe* (coffee with milk, €3.20), breakfast (€4.20-6.70), or monster salads (€3.50-6) in a relaxed atmosphere underneath, as the name suggests, the linden trees. Open M-F 11am-11pm, Sa-Su 10am-11pm. ❷

noodle's, Schanzenstr. 2-4 (☎439 28 40). The aptly-named establishment serves up a variety of excellent noodle dishes like gnocchi in cream sauce with chives and roasted pine nuts (€7), in addition to generously-portioned salads. By day, the restaurant maintains a coffee shop feel, while at night it becomes a trendy bar. Beer €3. Open Su-Th 10am-1am, F-Sa 10am-3am. ❷

Oma's Apotheke, Schanzenstr. 87 (☎43 66 20). Old-style ambience and portions large enough to make grandma proud. Most come for drinks, but the Apotheke also serves a curious mixture of German, Italian, and American cuisine. *Schnitzel* platter €7.50; hamburger with a pound of fries €6.60. Open daily 9am-1am, F-Sa until 2am or later. ❷

Falafel König, Schanzenstr. 115 (☎43 09 27 65). Right across from the S-Bahn station. Join the crowd of taxi drivers for fresh falafels (€3-5), made individually on order. With long hours and excellent vegetarian options, this tiny Lebanese *Imbiß* outshines its neighbors. Open Su-Th 9am-4am, F-Sa 24hr. ❶

UNIVERSITY

Slightly cheaper establishments can be found in the university area, especially along **Rentzelstraße, Grindelhof,** and **Grindelallee.**

Mensa, Von-Melle-Park 5. S21 or 31 to "Dammtor," then bus #4 or 5 to Staatsbiliothek (1 stop). Large student crowd, massive plates of cafeteria food, and a bulletin board of concerts and special events. Meals €1.50-3.50 with student ID. Non-students add up to €0.70. Open M-Th 10am-5:30pm, F 10am-4:30pm. ❶

Geo Pizza aus dem Holzbackofen, Beim Schlump 27 and 53 (☎45 79 29). U2 or U3 to "Schlump." Geo has vegetarian options, but carnivorous diners will melt for the Inferno Pizza's incendiary blend of jalapeños, red peppers, beef, onions, salsa, and corn. Pizzas €4-8. Open M-F 11am-1am, Sa 5pm-1am, Su 5pm-midnight. ❷

ELSEWHERE IN HAMBURG

In **Altona,** the pedestrian zone along Ottenserstr. next to the train station is packed with ethnic food stands and produce shops. A decidedly younger and more boisterous crowd eats and drinks at Altona's A.-Wartenberg-Pl. In a pinch, the shopping arcade at the

Hauptbahnhof has about a dozen fast-food joints (open daily 6am-11pm). **Lange Reihe,** in the heart of St. Georg, offers good but overpriced Portuguese, Italian, and Spanish restaurants. Gänsemarkt and Gerhard-Hauptmann-Pl. have decent options in the city center.

Balutschistan, Bahrenfelderstr. 169 (☎390 22 29) on A.-Wartenberg-Pl. in Altona, corner of Friedensalle. Serves beautifully prepared Pakistani food in a quiet, elaborately decorated environment. Enjoy the *Kofta curry lichi* (vegetable balls in curry with sweet lichee fruit and almonds, €9.50) and the pink, nutty *doodh* soda (€3). Entrees €8-13, lunch plates €5-6. Open daily noon-midnight. A second location at Schulterblatt 88, (☎43 36 61), has the same hours. ❸

Café Gnosa, Lange Reihe 93 (☎24 30 34). A social focal point for the gay community of St. Georg. Serves drinks (€2-5), desserts (€3-5), and tasty light entrees (€5-7) in a bright, comfortable atmosphere to 20-somethings of mixed orientation. Free gay publications like *hinnerk* and Hamburg's *Gay Map* available. Open Su-Th 10am-1am, F-Sa 10am-2am. ❶

Old Commercial Room, Englische Planke 10 (☎36 63 19), directly across from St. Michaeliskirche. The name is English but the atmosphere and food is authentic Hamburg at this century-old institution. Sample one of the many seafood specialties (€14-17) or other local fare, such as lightly salted pork and vegetables (€14.50). The restaurant has hosted a long list of celebrities including former German chancellor Helmut Schmidt, Berlin's ex-mayor Willy Brandt, Paul Hogan (of Crocodile Dundee fame), and rocker Jon Bon Jovi. The throne-like painted wooden toilet in the men's bathroom is truly a work of art. Open daily 10am-midnight. ❹

Afghanische Spezialitäten, on the corner of Steindamm and Pulverteich. This *Imbiß*-style Afghan grill serves a variety of creative kebabs and rice dishes. Wash down the huge *Kabeli Osbaki* (brown rice with raisins, lamb, and meat sauce, €6) with thick *dogh* (bitter buttermilk drink with mint and pickle bits, €1). Open daily 9am-9pm. ❷

◎ SIGHTS

ALTSTADT

GROßE MICHAELISKIRCHE. Affectionately called "Michel" by the Hamburgers, the tower of the gargantuan 18th-century Michaeliskirche is a symbol of the city. The church has had a tumultuous past, having been destroyed numerous times by lightning, accidents, and Allied bombs. Guarded by a dashing, Satan-crushing St. Michael, the newly renovated church's wide nave and scalloped walls resemble a concert hall. Indeed, the church hosts frequent evening concerts and performances. The tower affords the best view of Hamburg and an elevator can cut the 462-stair climb to only three flights. A small exhibition about the history of the church is housed in the crypt. *(☎37 67 81 00. Open May-Oct. M-Sa 9am-6pm, Su 11:30am-5:30pm; Nov.-Apr. M-Sa 10am-4:30pm, Su 11:30am-4:30pm. Organ music Apr.-Aug. daily at noon and 5pm. €1 requested donation. Screenings on the history of the church Th and Sa-Su every hr. 12:30-3:30pm. €2.50. Tower open until 9pm in summer. €2.50. Crypt open June-Oct. daily 11am-4:30pm; Nov.-May Sa-Su. 11am-4:30pm. €1.)*

RATHAUS. The great fire of 1842 destroyed Hamburg's old seat of government. Rebuilding efforts and economic troubles caused Hamburg to remain without a city hall for over 55 years. The new Rathaus, completed in 1897, was worth the wait, however, and its 647 lavishly furnished rooms contain intricate mahogany carvings, multiple-story murals, and spectacular chandeliers. The building still serves as the seat of both city and state government, and the Rathausmarkt out front holds constant festivities, ranging from political demonstrations to medieval

HAMBURG

fairs. (☎ 428 31 24 70. *Tours of the Rathaus in German every 30min. M-Th 10am-3pm, F-Su 10am-1pm. Tours in English every hr. M-Th 10:15am-3:15pm, F-Su 10:15am-1:15pm. €1.50, children under 14 €0.50.*)

MÖNKEBERGSTRAßE. Two majestic spires punctuate Mönkebergstr., Hamburg's glossiest shopping zone, which stretches from the Rathaus to the Hauptbahnhof. The first spire belongs to the **St. Petrikirche,** the oldest church in Hamburg, which survived WWII entirely intact but still suffers from damage done when Napoleon wintered his horses here in 1813. The 123m-high platform in the tower makes it the highest climbable tower in Hamburg, but the 544-step journey is only for the enthusiastic. (*Tower open M-Tu and Th-F 10am-6:30pm, W 10am-7pm, Sa 10am-5pm, Su 9am-9pm. €2, children under 15 €1.*) The second tower belongs to **St. Jakobikirche,** known for its 14th-century Arp-Schnittger organ. (☎ 303 73 70. *Open M-Sa 10am-5pm.*)

NIKOLAIKIRCHE. The blackened spire of this neo-Gothic ruin, destroyed during allied air raids in July of 1943, has been preserved as a memorial for the victims of war and persecution. An exhibition underneath the glass pyramid in the former apse of the church displays chilling photos of Hamburg in the aftermath of the attacks. (*Exhibition open M-F 11am-5pm, Sa-Su 11am-6pm. €2, children €1.*) Behind the church lies a zig-zagging maze of canals and bridges surrounding the **Alte Börse** (old stock market). The spires of buildings along nearby **Trost-Brücke** sport copper models of clipper ships—a testament to Hamburg's enduring sea wealth. (*Just south of the Rathaus, off Ost-West-Str.*)

SPEICHERSTADT. East of the docks, near the copper dome of the **St. Katherinenkirche,** is the historic warehouse district of Speicherstadt. These elegant, late 19th-century brick storehouses are still used today—look to see carpets, electronics, and other goods being hoisted up into the storerooms. The tiny **Afghanisches Kunst-und Kulturmuseum,** built in 2002, has already received a visit from German chancellor Gerhard Schröder. Enjoy the paintings and photographs of regional monuments while sipping on a cup of the complimentary Afghan tea. (*Am Sandtorkai 32. From St. Katherinenkirche, cross the street and continue over the Jungfernbrücke and the Neuerwegsbrücke, then turn right on Am Sandtorkai.* ☎ 37 82 36. *€3, students €2.50. Open daily 10am-5pm.*) Upstairs, **Spicy's Gewürzmuseum** appeals to epicures with its collection of 500 years' worth of seasonings. Sensual exhibits display the production of spices and show the progression of packaging techniques. (☎ 36 79 89. *Open Tu-Su 10am-5pm. €3, children under 13 €1.*)

ELSEWHERE IN CENTRAL HAMBURG

■ **PLANTEN UN BLOMEN.** This large expanse of gardens is one among a crescent of parks that extends from the TV tower to the Dammtor station and south to St. Pauli. The stunning flower displays and relative quiet lure families and romantics to the park, where they can wander on miles of scenic paths. (*S21 or 31 to Dammtor. Open 7am-11pm*) The park houses the largest Japanese garden in Europe and also contains a botanical garden exhibiting an array of exotic plants. (*Open Mar.-Oct. M-F 9am-4:45pm, Sa-Su 10am-5:45pm; Nov.-Feb. M-F 9am-3:45pm, Sa-Su 10am-3:45pm.*) Children can enjoy three playgrounds, a water slide, giant chess sets, and water-jet soccer, in addition to a newly opened mini-golf course and trampoline. Daily 3pm performances by groups ranging from Irish step dancers to Hamburg's police choir shake the outdoor *Musikpavillion* from May-Sept. The nightly *Wasserlicht-konzerte,* perhaps the most popular event at the park, draws large crowds to the lake, where they watch choreographed fountains and underwater lights. (*May-Aug. 10pm; Sept. 9pm*) By long-standing tradition, septuagenarians go to dance and find late love at the two park cafes on Wednesday and Saturday-Sunday.

FISCHMARKT. A Hamburg tradition since 1703, the Sunday morning Fishmarket is a swirl of veritable anarchy as charismatic vendors hawk fish, produce, flowers, and clothing. Early risers mix with Reeperbahn partyers who head straight to the marketplace after a long night of revelry. Things get frantic and great deals can be had near closing time. Bands of varying style entertain shoppers with loud rock music from the stage of the fish auction hall. *(U- or S-Bahn to "Landungsbrücken" or S-Bahn to "Königstr." or "Reeperbahn." Open Apr.-Oct. Su 5-10am; Nov.-Mar. 7-10am.)*

ST. PAULI LANDUNGSBRÜCKEN. Hamburg's harbor, the second largest port in Europe, lights up at night with ships from all over the world. Although crowded with tourists and lined with *Imbiße*, the piers provide an exceptional view of the Hamburg harbor, and are a starting point for most cruises and tours. **Kapitän Prüsse** departs every 30min. from Pier 3. *(☎31 31 30. 1 hr.; daily summer 9am-6pm, winter 9am-4pm; German only; €9, children €5.)* **HADAG** offers elaborate cruises of outlying areas from Pier 2. *(☎311 70 70. 1½hr.; departures M-Sa every hr. 10am-5pm, Su 11am-5pm; €9, children €5.)* Docked at Pier 1 is the tri-masted, 97m-long **Windjammer Rickmer Rickmers.** Constructed in 1896, the ship has been renamed five times and served as many different roles. It transported nitrates, was captured during WWI, and served as a Portuguese cadet training ship before finally coming to rest in the harbor as a museum. All quarters have been painstakingly restored to the original 1890s decor. The ship houses a large special exhibit space, an account of the vessel's unique history, and a cafe. *(☎319 59 59. Open daily 10am-5:30pm. €3, students €2.50, families €7.)* Behind pier 6, inside the building with the large copper cupola, is the entrance to the Old Elbtunnel. Although most vehicles now use the newer tunnel located farther to the west, this one, completed in 1911, is still active today. Cars and pedestrians descend 23.5m in an elevator, then travel through the two 426.5m-long tubes running under the Elbe. Benches on the other side offer an impressive view of the Hamburg skyline. *(Pedestrians: open daily, free. Cars: open M-F 5:30am-8pm, €2.)*

ALSTER LAKES. Just north of the city center, the Alster river, flowing from Schleswig-Holstein, expands into the two Alster lakes before converging with the Elbe. Elegant promenades surround the **Binnenalster,** while a series of parks, popular among joggers, encircle the larger **Außenalster.** Many windsurfers, sailboats, and paddle boats use the lake, in addition to the ferries that shuttle tourists between the banks. On the far northeastern shore of the Außenalster, the brilliant blue **Iman Ali Mosque** is home to the world's largest circular rug.

BEYOND THE CENTER

KZ NEUENGAMME. A concentration camp where 110,000 people were forced into labor between 1938 and 1945, Neuengamme was built in an idyllic agricultural village east of Hamburg. Close to 55,000 of its inhabitants died from overwork or execution. In 1948, some of the buildings were cleared to make way for a new German prison, which still stands today at the center of the site, although the government recently decided to close the facility. A mile-long path, constructed in 1989, begins at the **Haus des Gedenkens,** a memorial building containing banners and books inscribed with the names and death-dates of the victims. The path skirts the remains of the camp's brick-making factory, passes labor barracks, and finally leads to the former **Walther-Werke** factory, which contains an exhibit about the history of the camp, including recorded testimony from survivors. Exhibits in English. *(Jean-Doldier-Weg 39. S21 to "Bergedorf," then bus #227 to "Jean-Doldier-Weg." Bus runs from Bergedorf M-Sa every hr., Su every 2hr. ☎428 96 03. Museum and memorial open May-Oct. Tu-F 10am-5pm, Sa-Su 10am-6pm; Oct.-Mar. Tu-Su 10am-5pm. Path open 24hr. Tours Su noon and 2:30 pm.)*

JENISCH PARK. This park, and the museums within, sit upon a beautiful swath of green running up from the Elbe. **Ernst-Barlach-Haus,** the plain, white building, contains many of the Expressionist artist's most esteemed wood-carvings. (☎82 60 85. S-Bahn to "Klein-Plottbek," go left on Jürgensallee, then right on Baron-Vought-Str. Follow the signs. Open Tu-Su 11am-6pm. Free tour Su 11am. €4, students €3, families €6.) Fifty paces from the Barlach Haus is **Jenisch Haus,** former residence of Hamburg's famous senator, Martin Jenisch. The 19th-century house contains furnished rooms, an art collection, and a large special exhibition space. (☎82 87 90. Open Tu-Su 11am-6pm. Tours Su noon and 3pm €2. €4.50, students €3. Combination tickets €5 for both museums.) Directly across from the S-Bahn station, you can also visit the beautiful **Botanical Gardens,** whose expansive grounds center around a large pond. (Open daily 9am-8pm. Free.)

U-434. The world's largest non-nuclear sub now resides in Hamburg. After being decommissioned in 2002, the ship was purchased from the Russian navy and towed to the harbor where it now stands open to curious tourists. A visit affords a glimpse at a piece of Cold War history. The 90m-long ship and its 84-man crew were stationed off the American coast on reconnaissance missions from 1976-1978, after which the ship served on patrols of the North Sea. The maze of pipes and instruments will fascinate the mechanically-inclined. Tours offered in German only. (Vermannstr. 23c. Shuttles to the ship (€3 round-trip) leave from the St. Pauli Landungsbrücken, call ☎32 00 49 34 for details. Otherwise, it is a 25min. walk from U1 Messberg: heading towards Katherinenkirche, turn left over the 1st bridge and continue over 3 more until you reach Booktor, which becomes Versmannstr. Located on the right after 15min. www.u-434.de. Open Apr.-Oct. M-Th 10am-6pm, F-Su 9am-7pm; Oct.-Mar. daily 10am-6pm. Tour €3. €8, students €7, families €18.)

HAGENBECK'S TIERPARK. Founded in 1907 by the enthusiastic and slightly eccentric collector of exotic animals Carl Hagenbeck, Hamburg's zoo maintains its quirky character today. Animals wander about the park freely, while children clamber up the inside of the man-made mountain at the center of the park to gaze down on the many lions, tigers, and elephants. (U2 to "Hagenbeck's Tierpark." ☎540 00 10; www.hagenbeck.de. Open daily 9am-6pm. €14.50, children €8.50.)

GEDENKSTÄTTE BULLENHUSER DAMM UND ROSENGARTEN. In the midst of a warehouse district, the Janusz-Korczak School and its adjoining rose garden serve as a memorial to the 20 Jewish children who underwent "medical testing" at KZ Neuengamme and were brought to the school and murdered only hours before Allied troops arrived on April 20, 1945. Visitors are invited to plant a rose in memory of the victims, whose photographs line the fence of the flower garden. Inside the school, a small exhibition tells the story of the children and those who tried to save them. (Bullenhuser Damm 92. S21 to "Rothenburgsort." Follow the signs to Bullenhuser Damm along Ausschläger Bildeich, over the bridge. The garden is on the far left side of the intersection with Grossmannstr.; the school is through the garden, 200m farther. ☎428 13 10. Rose garden open 24hr. Exhibition open Su 10am-5pm and Th 2-8pm. Free.)

KZ FUHLSBÜTTEL. Within weeks of coming to power in 1933, the Nazis began imprisoning political opponents at this site. Over the next 12 years, the prison's ranks swelled with Hamburg's resistance fighters, Social Democrats, communists, gypsies, gays, beggars, and prostitutes. A small exhibit (German only) in the gatehouse profiles some of the victims who died here, and a reconstructed solitary cell provides a chilling glimpse into life at the prison. (Suhrenkamp 98 in Torhaus. S1 or 11, or U1 to "Ohlsdorf." From the "Im Garten Grund" exit, follow signs. ☎428 96 03. Open Su 10am-5pm. Talks by survivors and other witnesses every Su 11am and noon. Free.)

BLANKENESE STEPS. The wealthy suburb of Blankenese is tucked into the hillside above the outer Elbe, west of Hamburg. Dozens of narrow, cobbled staircases wind down to the shore around the terraced homes and their immaculate gardens, affording a beautiful view of the river. *(S1 or 11 to "Blankenese." From the station go right, take the 1st left on Blankenese Bahnhofstr., and head straight until the road hits a "T" and you see the river. Or take a HADAG boat from the St. Pauli Landungsbrücken.)*

ERNST-THÄLMANN-GEDENKSTÄTTE. In 1923, Communist leader Ernst Thälmann led a march on police headquarters, setting off a riot that left 61 protestors and 17 policemen dead. Thälmann was later murdered by the Nazis at Buchenwald, making him the first martyr of the DDR. His life and times are chronicled in a small museum. *(Tarpenbekstr. 66, at Ernst-Thälmann-Pl. U1 to "Hudtwalckerstr." Turn right on Hudtwalckerstr., go over the bridge, turn right on Ludolfstr. and walk 10min. until the intersection with Tarpenbekstr. ☎ 47 41 84. Open W-F 10am-5pm, Sa 10am-1pm. Donation requested.)*

🏛 MUSEUMS

Hamburg's many museums are filled with everything from African war masks to 18th-century pornography. The **Hamburg Card** provides discounted admission to most of these museums, though not the Deichtorhallen, Harry's Hamburger Hafen Basar, or the Erotic Art Museum. Hamburg also has a thriving contemporary art scene; pick up a list of current gallery exhibits at any of the tourist offices. The free newspaper *Museumswelt Hamburg* lists museum exhibitions and events and can be picked up at the tourist offices. Most museums are closed on Mondays and open 10am-6pm the rest of the week, and until 9pm on Thursdays.

HAMBURGER KUNSTHALLE. It would take days to fully appreciate this expansive art museum, regarded as one of the finest in Germany. The collection spans seven centuries, and is organized chronologically. Highlights include a set of medieval altars, works by Rembrandt and other 17th-century Dutch painters, and a large impressionist gallery. The lower level houses many popular temporary exhibitions. In the connected four-level building, **Galerie der Gegenwart,** contemporary art takes a rather noisy stand—it is hard not to notice the pneumatic dancing legs on the top floor. *(Glockengießerwall 1. Turn right from the "Spitalerstr./City" exit of the Hauptbahnhof and cross the street. ☎ 428 13 12 00. www.hamburger.kunsthalle.de. Open Tu-Su 10am-6pm, Th until 9pm. €8.50, students €5, families €11.)*

MUSEUM FÜR KUNST UND GEWERBE. The city's applied arts museum houses a large array of furniture, jewelry, musical instruments, and household objects spanning a broad range of times and countries. A huge exhibit containing over 430 historical keyboard instruments such as harpsichords, clavichords, and hammerklaviers illustrates the development of the modern piano. The museum also has an extensive photography collection, an impressive Art Nouveau display, and a treasure-trove of antique gold jewelry. *(Steintorpl. 1. 1 block south of the Hauptbahnhof. ☎ 428 54 27 32; www.mkg-hamburg.de. Open Tu-Su 10am-6pm, Th until 9pm. €8.20, students and seniors €4.10, under 16 €2.)*

DEICHTORHALLEN HAMBURG. Hamburg's contemporary art scene thrives inside these two former fruit markets, which house photography, paintings, and video. Each season brings new exhibits to the large, vaulted halls. The vaulted hall will be closed for renovations until April 2005. *(Deichtorstr. 1-2. U1 to "Steinstr." Follow signs from the subway station; look for 2 entwined iron circles. ☎ 32 10 30; www.deichtorhallen.de. Open Tu-Su 11am-6pm. Each building €6.50, students €4.50, families €9.50. Combination ticket €10.50/€7.50/€17.)*

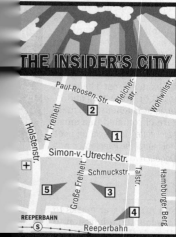

WITH THE BEATLES

The Beatles got their first break when a promoter landed them a gig in Hamburg. The experience they gained performing in clubs here played an integral part in shaping the group, and by the time they returned to England they were well on their way to stardom.

1 **64 Große Freiheit:** John, Paul, George, and Pete Best played their first Hamburg shows at the **Indra** (p. 233), beginning August 17, 1960. The 8hr. gigs were grueling and the pay was poor, but the group learned how to keep audiences satisfied. A plaque at the front of the building commemorates the group's performances.

2 **33 Paul-Roosen-Str.:** while playing at the Indra, the Beatles slept in tiny quarters upstairs at the **Bambi Kino,** the blue-gray house. Look for the small plaque on the door.

3 **36 Große Freiheit:** after the police shut down the rough-and-tumble Indra, the Beatles moved down the street to the

HAMBURGER MUSEUM FÜR VÖLKERKUNDE. This museum of world cultures is an anthropologist's paradise. Exhibits include an extensive collection of masks from Africa and the South Pacific, Egyptian mummies, and an archive on witchery. The exhibit on European cultures is particularly interesting. (Rothenbaumchaussee 64. U1 to "Hallerstr." ☎01805 30 88 88; www.voelkerkundemuseum.com. Open Tu-Su 10am-6pm, Th 10am-9pm. €6, with Hamburg Card €2, students €2, children €1. F adults half-price.)

MUSEUM FÜR HAMBURGISCHE GESCHICHTE. On the edge of the Große Wallanlagen gardens near St. Pauli, this four-story complex has a representative sampling of artifacts, costumes, statues, and coats-of-arms from throughout Hamburg's 800-year history. Numerous city models, the largest model train display in Western Europe, and the entire bridge of the steamer ship "Werner" capitalize on the building's spaciousness. The top floor houses an exhibition on the history of Hamburg's Jews. (Holstenwall 24. U3 to "St. Pauli." ☎4281 32 23 80. Open Tu-Su 10am-5pm. €7.50, with Hamburg Card €1.50, students €4, families €12. F everyone €1.)

HARRY'S HAMBURGER HAFEN BASAR. After spending a lifetime sailing the world and collecting its wares, Harry dropped anchor here in 1954. Ever since, his family has run this small, cluttered museum-shop—a veritable maze crammed with over 1000 gawking, screaming dance masks, and gazelle-hide drums. Collectors will be thrilled that everything here except for the shrunken heads and the stuffed leopard is for sale. (Balduinstr. 18. S1 or S3 to Reeperbahn, or U3 to St. Pauli. From Reeperbahn or St.-Pauli-Hafenstr., take Davidstr to Erichstr. At the corner of Balduinstr. and Erichstr. ☎31 24 82; www.hafenbasar.de. Open Tu-Su noon-6pm. €2.50, children €1.)

EROTIC ART MUSEUM. Recently moved off the Reeperbahn, the museum now occupies four floors, containing everything from the *Kama Sutra* to Victorian pornography and gigantic Russian dolls in varying degrees of undress. Drawings by Picasso add fame and propriety to an otherwise shocking display. The top floor contains an exhibit on the history of the Reeperbahn. (Bernhard-Nocht-Str. 69. S1 or 3 to Reeperbahn. ☎317 47 57; www.erotic-art-museum.de. Open Su-Th 10am-midnight, F-Sa 10am-2am. €8, students €5. Children under 16 not admitted.)

♫ ENTERTAINMENT

Hamburg's lively entertainment scene has something for all tastes and ages. In addition to the regular offerings of music, theater, and film, the Rathausmarkt and other locations often host lively street fairs, especially during the summer. Hamburg owes its prosperity to Friedrich Barbarossa, who granted the town the right to open a port on May 7, 1189. The city still celebrates its anniversary with the **Hafengeburtstag** (harbor birthday, May 5-8, 2005), which attracts about 1.5 million people to watch the ship parade and fireworks and party onshore. During April, August, and November the **Heiligengeistfeld** north of the Reeperbahn metamorphoses into the **"Dom,"** a titanic amusement park. The festival's beer and wild parties have eclipsed its historical connection to the church.

MUSIC

The **Staatsoper,** Große Theaterstr. 36, houses one of the best **opera** companies in Germany. The associated **ballet company** is considered the dance powerhouse of the nation. (☎ 35 68 68. U2 to "Gänsemarkt." Open M-Sa 10am-6:30pm and 90min. before performance. Tickets €4-77.) **Orchestras** abound: the Philharmonie, the Norddeutscher Rundfunk Symphony, and Hamburg Symphonia all perform at the **Musikhalle** on Johannes-Brahms-Pl. (U2 to "Gänsemarkt.") The Musikhalle (☎ 34 69 20; www.musikhalle-hamburg.de) also hosts **chamber music** concerts on a regular basis, and the occasional jazz performance. Hamburg's churches (see **Sights,** p. 223) offer a wide variety of classical concerts, often for free.

Live music of all genres prospers in Hamburg. Superb traditional jazz swings at the **Cotton Club** and **Indra** (see **Nightlife,** p. 230). On Sunday mornings, musicians talented and otherwise play at the **Fischmarkt.** Rock groups jam at **Große Freiheit** and **Docks** (p. 232). The renowned **Fabrik,** in Altona (p. 232), features everything from funk to punk. The magazine *Szene* (€3) has an exhaustive listing of events. During the summer, big name bands come to the **Stadtpark** (☎ 41 80 68; www.karsten-jahnke.de). The **West Port** jazz festival, Germany's largest, runs in mid-July. Call the Konzertkasse (☎ 32 87 38 54) for information. The most anticipated festival, **G-Move,** is known as the "Love Parade of the North" (May 28, 2005; www.gmove.de.) Tens of thousands of ecstatic ravers in orange hats storm the city for this techno-fest, following the slow procession of floats down the city streets.

THEATER AND FILM

Most theaters sell reduced-price tickets to students at the regular box office as well as at the evening box office, generally open 1hr. before performances. In July and August, many theaters close down, but only to make way for the summer arts festivals; pick up a schedule of programs at one of the tourist offices.

Kaiserkeller (p. 232), where they played shows from Oct. 4 to Nov. 30, 1960. It was here that the group first met drummer Ringo Starr, who joined them when Pete Best fell ill. A sign on a pillar outside the door marks this bit of history.

4 After spending time in Liverpool, the Beatles returned to Hamburg to play the **Top-Ten-Club** at 136 Reeperbahn. They lived upstairs while playing the gigs, which lasted from April 1 to July 1, 1961. The club has since changed its name to **Glam.**

5 The Beatles played their final Hamburg show on New Year's Eve 1962 at the **Star Club,** 39 Große Freiheit. The recordings were later released as the famous "Star Club Tapes." Directly across from the Kaiserkeller, go through the archway and look to the left, immediately inside the arch. A guitar-shaped marker denotes the site where the building housing the Star stood until a 1987 fire destroyed it.

CSD

Among the seemingly endless string of festivals occurring throughout Germany in the summer are the "Christopher Street Day" parades, gay-pride celebrations that take over the streets of most major German cities every year between June and August. The English name stems from the events of June 27, 1969, when patrons of the Stonewall Inn, a gay bar on Christopher Street in New York City, clashed with local authorities. The police, allegedly there to investigate a claim that the bar was selling alcohol without a license, made offensive comments and attempted to throw patrons out of the bar. The unhappy customers revolted, barricading the police inside in what has become a symbol for the gay-rights movement worldwide.

In Germany, gays and straights alike now commemorate "CSD" by crowding the streets to watch dancers and floats wind their way through the city to the blasting techno music. Street fairs spring up along the routes, and the day becomes a giant carnival that has transcended its activist roots.

Hamburg's parade attracted close to 500,000 people last year, and consisted of 10 days of parties leading up to the event. The city's 2005 parade will take place on June 12; Berlin and Cologne have similarly extravagant festivities, which will occur in 2005 on June 25 and July 1, respectively.

The acclaimed **Deutsches Schauspielhaus,** Kirchenallee 39, is directly across from the Hauptbahnhof. The theater presents primarily contemporary international works interspersed with the masterpieces of Shakespeare and Sophocles. (☎ 24 87 13; www.schauspielhaus.de. Box office open M-Sa 10am-7pm or showtime. Student tickets from €5.) The satellite **Polittburo,** Steindamm 45, puts on more experimental performances to a young, intellectual crowd. (☎ 28 05 54 67. Open 1hr. before showtime. Tickets also available at the Deutsches Schauspielhaus. €5-14.) The **English Theater,** Lerchenfeld 14, entertains both natives and tourists with its English-language productions. (U2 to "Mundsgurg." ☎ 227 70 89. Performances M-Sa at 7:30pm; matinees Tu and F at 11am. Box office open M-F 10am-2pm and 3:30-7:30pm, Sa 3:30-7:30pm, and 1½hr. before show. Tickets €23-28, students €11-12.) **Thalia,** Alstertor 1, sets up adventurous avant-garde musicals, plays, and staged readings. (S1 or 3, or U1 or 2 to "Jungfernstieg." ☎ 32 81 44 44.) Regular performances are also held in the **Hamburger Kunsthalle.** The German **cabaret** tradition lives on at several venues, including **Das Schiff,** at Holzbrückestr 2. (Head east 1 block on Ost-Weststr. then turn right—it's docked at the bridge. ☎ 69 65 05 60.)

The movie scene in Hamburg is invigoratingly diverse, ranging from the latest American hits to independent film projects by university students. **Metropolis,** Dammtorstr. 30a (☎ 34 23 53), a non-profit cinema, shows new independent films and revivals from all over the globe. **Kino 3001,** Schanzenstr. 75 (☎ 43 76 79), shows artsy alternative and international flicks. An intellectual crowd packs **Abaton-Kino,** Allendepl., off Grindelhof Str. (☎ 41 32 03 21; www.abaton.de), and its adjoining cafe for classics and new releases in English and German. In Altona, the **Zeise Kinos,** Friedensalle 7-9 (☎ 39 90 76 37), projects films in the open-air courtyard of Altona's Rathaus during the warmer months. The **Grindel Palast,** Grindelberg 7a, screens American blockbusters in their original English (☎ 44 93 33. €7.50, Tu €4).

■ NIGHTLIFE

The Sternschanze and St. Pauli areas host Hamburg's unrepressed nightlife scene. The infamous **Reeperbahn,** a long boulevard which makes Las Vegas look like the Vatican, is the backbone of St. Pauli. Sex shops, strip joints, peep shows, and other establishments seeking to satisfy every lust compete for space along the sidewalks next door to fast-food stands and regular theaters. Though the Reeperbahn itself is reasonably safe for both men and women, it is not recommended for women to venture onto some of the less populated side streets alone. **Herbertstraße,** Hamburg's "official" prostitution strip, runs parallel to the Reeperbahn; its bright red barrier opens only to men 18+, but prostitutes surround the area and nearby Davidstr. The industry is regulated: all the prostitutes on Herbertstr. are licensed and required to have health inspections. If you attract unwanted attention, simply ignore it or respond with a firm *"Nein."* Despite some seedy offerings, the area contains many of the city's best bars and clubs and young, energetic crowds.

Those who'd rather avoid the hypersexed Reeperbahn should head north to the trendy, ethnic streets of the **Schanzenviertel.** Unlike St. Pauli, this area is centered on cafes and weekend extravaganzas of an alternative flavor. Filled with spectacular graffiti that crosses the boundary into "public art" and posters that could be the products of high-end design schools, the neighborhood is steeped in creative energy. Much of Hamburg's **gay scene** is located in the **St. Georg** area, near Berliner Tor and along Lange Reihe. Gay and straight bars in this area are more welcoming and classier than those in the Reeperbahn. In general, clubs open late and close late, with some techno and trance clubs remaining open until noon the following day. *Szene,* available at newsstands (€2.50), lists events and parties, while the gay magazine *hinnerk* and the more condensed *Gay Map* list gay and lesbian events. Though bars are not as picky, you must be at least 18 to hit most clubs.

SCHANZENVIERTEL

Bedford Cafe, Schulterblatt 72, (☎43 18 83 32), on the corner of Schulterblatt and Susannesstr. College students and other 20-somethings pack the inside, outside, and whole street corner—one of the trendiest bars in the Schanzenviertel. Salads and sandwiches €4-7, beer €2-3.40, cocktails €5-6. Open daily from 10am.

Logo, Grindelallee 5 (☎410 56 58; www.logohamburg.de), keeps the college crowd cultured with its eclectic lineup of *plattdeutsch* folk rock, samba, and tribadelic techno. Cover €4-15. Doors open 8pm; music starts 9pm, check website or call for schedule.

Machwitz, Schanzenstr. 121 (☎43 81 77). Get in on a feisty game of foosball in the back room between beers (€2.30). Students mix with an older crowd. Open daily 10am-4am, on weekends until 5-6am. Kitchen closes at 11pm.

THE HIDDEN DEAL

ROTE FLORA

Curiously poised amongst trendy shops and bars in the Schanzenviertel, the decrepit, graffiti-covered Rote Flora Theater appears on the brink of collapse. It would have been long-gone if the government had their way. The story of the building's survival in an increasingly gentrified neighborhood is a testament to the district's fierce independence and spirit of counterculture protest.

Built in 1888, the *Concerthaus Flora* housed operettas, boxing matches, a movie theater, and a housewares retailer. When the government announced plans to demolish the building in 1989 to make way for a new theater for *Phantom of the Opera,* Sternschanze leftists protested in the traditional German fashion: by occupying the building.

Having fended off government threats, the Rote Flora is now a hotbed of community activism, venue for demonstrations, and birthplace of manifestos. On weekends, drum'n'bass and punk concerts shake the building, and on weekdays, small groups gather for art exhibitions, motorcycle maintenance clinics, and movie screenings. A dump behind the theater is now a park, but while the graffiti is sumptuous and the four-story climbing wall tempting, the area is questionable at night. *(Schulterblatt 71. ☎439 54 13. Beer €3-5. Weekend cover usually €3-5. Cafe open M-F 6-10pm. Music starts around 10pm, crowds show up after midnight.)*

Le fonque, Juliusstr. 33 (☎430 75 15; www.fonque.de), a block off of Schulterblatt on Juliusstr. The funk here is mellow but cool with live DJs most nights, no cover and cheap drinks (€2-3). Open daily from 9pm.

Frauenkneipe, Stresemannstr. 60 (☎43 63 77). S21 or 31 to "Holstenstr." Visitors disconcerted by the Reeperbahn and its objectification of women find relief at this bar and meeting place. For women only, gay or straight. Open Tu-Sa from 8pm, Su 3pm-12:30am.

ST. GEORG

Cube, Lange Reihe 88 (☎24 87 07 07). Mixed bar in the heart of St. Georg provides a relaxed alternative to the raucous pubs near the Reeperbahn. Many drinks (€2-6) on Cube's extensive list are served with the bar's perfectly formed ice cubes. W and Su "Groove Lounge" starts at 7pm. Open M-F from 5pm, Sa-Su from 2:30pm.

G-Bar, Lange Reihe 81 (☎28 00 46 90; www.g-bar.de). Soft red and violet neon lights illuminate the trendy, comfortable "Generation Bar." Under the subtle glow, men in skin-tight shirts serve beer (€2-3) and cocktails (€7-9) with a smile to a mixed, but primarily gay clientele. Open daily noon-2am.

ALTONA

■ **Fabrik,** Barnerstr. 36 (☎39 10 70; www.fabrik.de). From Altona station head toward Offenser Hauptstr., go right on Bahrenfelderstr., it is 4 blocks up on the right. 2 blocks from A.-Wartenburg-Pl. Look for the rusted-out crane on top or the corroded, crossed missiles out front. This former weapons factory now cranks out beats instead. For years, crowds have packed the 2-level club to hear big-name rock acts and an eclectic mix of other bands, with styles ranging from latin to punk. Music nearly every day, beginning at 9pm. Tickets €18-25. Live DJ most Sa nights at 10pm, cover €6-7.

Waschbar, Ottenser Hauptstr. 56. (☎0179 232 59 18). Enjoy hot chocolate (€2.80) and light fare (€4-7), while your clothes sit in one of the washers (€3.50 for 6kg, including soap) or dryers (€0.50 for 30min.). A clean, hip environment a far cry from your average laundromat. Residents crowd the popular long bar at night. Live DJ 4 nights a week. Open daily 9am-1am, F-Sa until 2am or later.

Insbeth, Bahrenfelder Str. 176 (☎390 19 24). S1, 3, or 31 to "Altona." From Offenser Hauptstr., make a right on Bahrenfelderstr.; it's located at A.-Wartenberg-Pl. The over-the-top decor defies categorization, but the 3-room-cafe is a comfy and crowded hangout spot, especially popular for its cheap, tasty breakfast (€2.65-5), served daily 10am-2:30pm. Open daily from 10am.

ST. PAULI

Große Freiheit 36/Kaiserkeller, Große Freiheit 36 (☎317 77 80; www.grossefreiheit36.de). The Beatles played on the small Kaiserkeller stage downstairs during their early years. Today, diverse young people and couples pour in to hear everyone from Radiohead to the Roots stomp about on the big stage and dance floor upstairs. Cover €5-6, live bands €10-30. Live music or DJs usually 10:30pm-5am. Frequent free entry until 11pm—if get your hand stamped you can return later.

Docks, Spielbudenpl. 19 (☎31 78 83 0; www.docks.de). Off the Reeperbahn, between Davidstr. and Taubenstr. A massive dance floor, multiple bars, oil drum tables, and an alter ego as a movie theater makes the Docks unique and popular. Drinks €4. Cover usually €4, sometimes €1 or free for students or women. Open Th-Sa 10 or from 11pm.

Madhouse, Hans-Albers-Pl. 15b. (www.madhouse-club.de). "The oldest disco in Europe" just relocated, but their funk and hip-hop repertoire still attracts a battalion of posh dancers to the smoky, underground floor. Cover €6-8. Beer €3, Cocktails €6.50-9. Open Th 11pm-4am, F 11pm-5am, Sa 11pm-6am.

Lehmitz, Reeperbahn 22 (☎31 46 41). A strange mix of students and tatooed biker punks gather round the clock for lots of €2 beers. Corrugated-metal bar and long tables spill out onto the Reeperbahn. Loud thrashing music W and weekends. Open 24hr.

Molotow, Spielbudenpl. 5 (☎31 08 45; www.molotowclub.com), parallel to the Reeperbahn. This basement lives at the fringes of Hamburg's club scene. Grunge decor, 70s music, great bands, and good dancers keep this small club rocking. Cover €3-4, live bands €5-10. Open M-Tu from 9pm, W-Th from 10pm, F-Su from 11pm.

The New Cave, Reeperbahn 48. This cave keeps things interesting with its multiple mirrored dance floors, and draws large crowds throughout the week. Cover €5-7. Open Th-Su from 10pm-5am. Th and Sa hip-hop and rap. F best new music, Su techno. Those unwilling to end their F and Sa partying don't have to leave—the club remains open from 5am-noon blasting techno.

Click, Nobistor. 24, 2nd floor (☎43 66 20; www.click808.com), 1 of 3 clubs housed inside a former department store, has become the mecca of Hamburg's techno scene. White couches line the long hallway, while video jockeys project their work in the large side rooms. The club hosts innovative events, such as the "silent disco," in which all 150 partyers wear headphones and groove to the music while bystanders look on, bemused. Opens at midnight, crowds show up after 1am. On top floor, **Echochamber** (☎43 66 20) blasts its own techno beat, and offers a spectacular view of the Reeperbahn from its windows. On the way out the door, **Phonodrome,** 1st floor (☎43 66 20; www.phonodrome.de) keeps the music flowing till the early hours of the morning.

Rosi's Bar, Hamburger Berg 7. Normalcy 1 block off the Reeperbahn? It's not an oxymoron, it's Rosi's. The crowd packs this *"richtige Kneipe"* (authentic bar) to enjoy comfortable retro furniture, cheap beer (€2-2.50), and free live DJ W-Sun. Open M-F 9pm-4am, Sa-Su 9pm-6am.

Cotton Club, Alter Steinweg 10 (☎34 38 78; www.cotton-club.de). U3 to "Rödingsmarkt." A Hamburg institution for over 45 years, the Cotton Club draws a crowd of regulars for New Orleans, dixie, swing, and big band in a warm setting. A mostly older crowd appreciates the boisterous jazz and intimate atmosphere. Cover €5 for Hamburg bands, more for guests. Open M-Th 8pm-midnight, F-Sa 8pm-1am. Shows start at 8:30pm.

Indra, Große Freiheit 64 (☎0174 49 74 61 23; www.indramusikclub.com) The newly-formed Beatles played a series of shows here in 1960, and nostalgia-inspiring photos continue to invoke their presence. The club has updated its image with a small stage and acts focusing on blues, hip-hop, and R&B, and has succeeded in drawing the younger crowd back to this somewhat-neglected block of the Große Freiheit. No cover most nights. Open W-Su from 6pm; music starts around 11pm.

NIEDERSACHSEN (LOWER SAXONY) AND BREMEN

Niedersachsen extends from the Ems River in the west to the Harz Mountains in the east, and from the North Sea down to the hills of central Germany. The deep forest around the Weser that inspired Grimm Brothers' fairy tales has retreated in the face of agriculture—a train ride through the region is a blur of corn and barley fields, windmills, and languid cows. In the remote East Frisian islands, fishermen still cling to their traditional language and culture, while the cities to the south constantly strive to outdo one another with new subway lines and skyscrapers. The sea-faring cities of Bremen and Bremerhaven have united to make up Germany's smallest *Land*, a popular summertime destination.

HIGHLIGHTS OF LOWER SAXONY AND BREMEN

EXPLORE the independent *Land* of **Bremen** (p. 264) and its **feisty** residents, **liberal** political climate, and uncontainable **nightlife** in the student-dominated **Viertel.**

PEDAL along beautifully barren island trails in the **East Frisian Islands** (p. 275) before hitting one of the North Sea's **superb beaches.**

PONDER the works of modern artists at the **Sprengel Museum,** Hannover (p. 234).

SMELL THE ROSES in the **Herrenhausen** gardens, the wild animals at the **Erlebnis-Zoo Hannover** (p. 239), or **Hannover's** sweaty nightlife scene (p. 245).

SPLAT your way across the healthy mud in **Wattenmeer National Park** (p. 277).

HANNOVER (HANOVER) ☎0511

Hannoverian **George I** ascended the British throne in the 18th century, making the past three centuries of "English" royals *Deutsch* by lineage. The German-British connection endowed Hannover with prominent status and numerous English gardens. Broad avenues, pedestrian zones, and parks make the city a model of effective urban planning. Add to that a famous opera house, expansive museums, endless summer outdoor festivals, and vibrant nightlife, and the result is a cosmopolitan dreamboat on the river Leine. Hannover is the railroad hub of northwestern Germany, and an efficient system of subways and buses connects the city to outlying areas. The 2000 World's Fair left a shining exhibition hall, new municipal facilities, and improved tourist services in its wake, and Hannover is already gearing up for another monumental event: five matches of the 2006 World Cup.

⌐ TRANSPORTATION

Available at the tourist office and hostel, the **Hannover Card** provides public transportation within the city and to the airport, as well as admission or discounts at several museums (1 day €8; 3 days €12; group ticket for up to 5 people €15/€25). The card is valid from 7pm the day before use and the entire 24hr. of the day of use, so plan ahead and buy your ticket one day early.

> **Flights:** Hannover's airport is 20-30min. from the Altstadt. *Schnellbuslinie* (express bus) #60 and the S-bahn run from the Hauptbahnhof to the airport. (M-F every 20min. 5am-7pm, every 30min. 7-10:30pm; Sa-Su every 30min. 5:30am-10:30pm. €5.) Call ☎977 12 23 for information. Flights depart to many European cities.

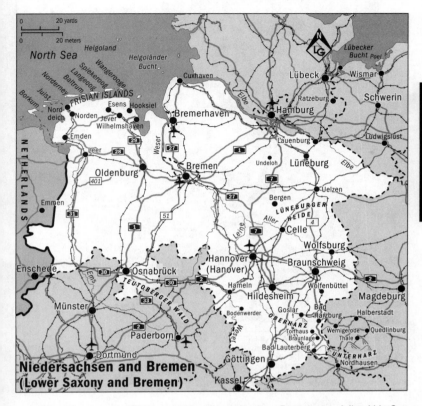

Niedersachsen and Bremen
(Lower Saxony and Bremen)

Trains: Hannover is well-connected to cities in Northern Europe, especially within Germany. Trains leave at least 1 per hr. to: **Amsterdam** (4½-5hr., €56); **Berlin** (2hr., €49); **Frankfurt** (2½hr., €65); **Hamburg** (1½hr., €29); **Munich** (9hr., €95).

Public Transportation: ÜSTRA, Hannover's mass-transit system, is extremely efficient. Pick up a free map of the U-Bahn and bus lines at the tourist office or the aluminum stand at the "Raschpl." bus stop behind the station. Stand open M-W and F 8am-6pm, Th 8am-7pm, Sa 9am-2pm. Buy tickets at machines or from drivers. Hannover has 3 zones with varying prices. *Kurzstrecke* (3 stops) €1; single ride €1.80-3, children 6-11 €1; day ticket €3.30-5.30; group ticket for up to 5 people €6.60-10.60. The Altstadt and Mitte are both in Zone 1. **If your ticket does not have the date printed on it, you must punch it in a blue machine or risk a €30 fine.** For more info and maps, call the ÜSTRA customer service office (☎ 16 68 22 38) in the Kröpcke station. Open M-W and F 8am-6pm, Th 8am-7pm, Sa 9am-2pm.

Taxis: Taxi Ruf (☎ 214 10), or **Funk Taxi Zentrale** (☎ 38 11).

ORIENTATION AND PRACTICAL INFORMATION

The Old Saxon *Hon overe* means "high bank," referring to the city's position on the river **Leine**. The Hauptbahnhof is in **Mitte**, the heart of Hannover. Bahnhofstr. leads to the landmark **Kröpcke Café** and eventually into the Altstadt. Below sprawls

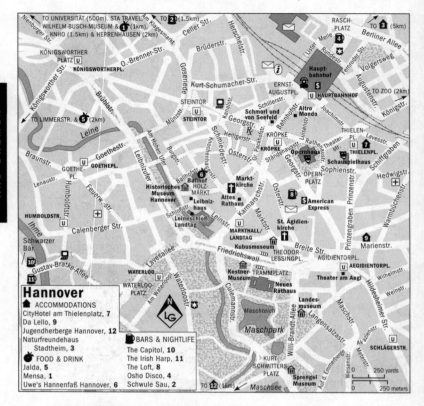

Hannover

♠ ACCOMMODATIONS
CityHotel am Thielenplatz, 7
Da Lello, 9
Jugendherberge Hannover, 12
Naturfreundehaus
  Stadtheim, 3

🍎 FOOD & DRINK
Jalda, 5
Mensa, 1
Uwe's Hannenfaß Hannover, 6

🍸 BARS & NIGHTLIFE
The Capitol, 10
The Irish Harp, 11
The Loft, 8
Osho Disco, 4
Schwule Sau, 2

the underground **Passerelle,** a mall-like cave of cheap diners and souvenir shops. Behind the station is **Raschplatz,** home to a disco and club scene. A pedestrian zone connects most of the center, including the shopping districts along **Georgstraße** and the Altstadt. The vibrant student quarter surrounding the university to the northwest of the city center is often overlooked. West of Mitte and just south of the university, **Limmerstraße** runs through **Linden,** historically a working-class area and now home to many artists and immigrants.

Tourist Office: Hannover Information, Ernst-August-Pl. 2 (☎ 16 84 97 00). Turn right from the train station. In the same building as the post office. Friendly staff find rooms for a €6.50 fee (free by phone, ☎ 12 34 55 55), provides maps and information on cultural events, sells tickets to concerts and exhibits, and runs a full travel agency. Free hotel list available. Open M-F 9am-6pm, Sa 9am-2pm; May-Sept. also Su 9am-2pm.

Tours: The **tourist office** offers 12 themed tours, including "Hannover's Cemeteries" and "Animal Magic." (☎ 16 84 97 34. €3-15.) To experience Hannover fully, follow the **Red Thread,** a 4km walking tour along a painted red line connecting all the sites. The *Red Thread Guide* (€2), available from the tourist office, details the tour in English.

Travel Agency: STA, Callinstr. 23 (☎ 131 85 31), in the same building as the Mensa. Open M-Th 9am-5pm, F 9am-4pm, Sa 10am-1pm.

Currency Exchange: ReiseBank, to the left just before the main exit of the train station. Reasonable commissions. Open M-Sa 8am-9pm, Su 9am-9pm.

American Express: Georgstr. 54 (☎368 10 03), near the opera house inside ReiseLand. Travel agency and full cardmember services. Mail held up to 4 wk. for card members and Traveler's Cheque clients. Open M-F 9am-noon and 1-6pm, Sa 10am-1pm.

Bookstore: Schmorl und von Seefeld, Bahnhofstr. 14 (☎367 50), has a tremendous selection of English-language novels. Open M-Sa 9:30am-8pm.

Gay and Lesbian Resources: ☎ 194 46; www.hannover.gay-web.de.

Women's Resources: Rape Crisis Line ☎33 21 12. **Shelter** ☎66 44 77.

Laundromat: Münz Waschcenter, at the corner of Hildesheimer Str. and Siemensstr. From the station take U1, 2 or 8 (dir.: Aegidientorpl.) to "Altenbekener Damm." Backtrack 1 block; it's on the left. Wash €3.50, including soap. Dry €0.60 per 15min. Open daily 6am-11pm, last wash 10pm.

Emergency: Police ☎110 or 10 90. **Fire** ☎112. **Ambulance** ☎192 22.

Pharmacy: Europa Apotheke, Georgstr. 16 (☎32 66 18; fax 363 24 63), walk down Bahnhofstr. and turn right on Georgstr.; it's 150m down on the left. Assistance available in several languages. Open M-Sa 8am-8pm.

Medical Assistance: EMS ☎31 40 44. **Medical Information** ☎31 40 44.

Internet Access: Weltcafe Telefon & Internet Cafe, on Kanalstr. (☎21 35 91 01) off the Georgstr. pedestrian zone near Steintor. Access the **Internet** (€1.25 per 30min.) or call home for cheap (€0.10 per min. to US/Canada/UK). Open M-Sa 9am-midnight. **Das Netz Internet-C@fe,** Humboldtstr. 1, at the corner of Gustav-Bratke-Allee, charges slightly more. €2.90 per hr. Open daily noon to midnight.

Post Office: 30159 Hannover. Right of the train station exit, just beyond the tourist office. Open M-F 9am-7pm, Sa 9:30am-2pm.

◤ ACCOMMODATIONS

Finding budget accommodations in Hannover means nabbing a spot in the youth hostel or *Naturfreundehaus*. Otherwise, try calling the **reservation hotline** (☎811 35 00; fax 811 35 41; or through the tourist office: 12 34 55 55; fax 123 45 55 67). If all else fails, staying in the hostels in nearby Braunschweig or Celle is cheaper than settling for one of Hannover's royally priced hotels.

▨ Jugendherberge Hannover (HI), Ferdinand-Wilhelm-Fricke-Weg 1 (☎131 76 74; jh-hannover@djh-hannover.de). Located near the Maschsee and 500m from the soccer stadium. U3 or 7 (dir.: Wettbergen) to "Fischerhof/Fachhochschule." From the stop, walk 10m back, turn right, cross the tracks, follow the path as it curves, and cross Stammestr. Go over the enormous red footbridge and turn right. Hostel is 50m down the dark road on the right. The Cadillac of youth hostels—spacious rooms with balconies, an airy dining room, and a fully-stocked bar. Rooms come in 6-, 4-, and 2-bed, and single varieties. **Internet** €0.10 per min. Sheets and breakfast included. Reception 7:30am-1am. After 1am, doors open every hr. on the hr. €19-30, under 27 €17-28. ❷

▨ CityHotel am Thielenplatz, Thielenpl. 2 (☎32 76 91; info@smartcityhotel.com). From the station, turn left onto Joachimstr. and go 1 block to Thielenpl. Prime location a few hundred yards behind the Opernhaus. Luxurious miniature lobby and 150 beds in well-maintained, furnished rooms, all with TV and bath, some with panoramic views of the city. Breakfast €5. Check-out 11:30am. Singles €40, with shower €57, weekends €37/€45; doubles with shower €75, weekends €65. ❹

Naturfreundehaus Stadtheim, Hermann-Bahlsen-Allee 8 (☎69 14 93; www.naturfreundehaeser-nds.de/hannover.html). U3 (dir.: Lahe) or 7 (dir.: Fasanenkrug) to "Spannhagengarten." Walk back to the intersection and follow Hermann-Bahlsen-Allee to the left for 5min.; follow the sign to your right and into the narrow path. An environmentally-friendly hostel with small rooms, on the outskirts of town. Breakfast included. Reception 8am-noon and 3-10pm. Singles €29, under 27 €25. ❸

Da Lello Ristorante-Hotel am Aegi, Marienstr. 5 (☎32 07 05; www.dalello.de), offers rooms above an Italian restaurant in a small shopping arcade half a block from the convenient U-bahn stop "Aegidientorpl." Breakfast included. All rooms have bathrooms with showers; call ahead for the cheaper rooms. Singles €38-62; doubles €56-90. ❹

🍴 FOOD

Hannover is about high culture, not cuisine. The pedestrian zone's expensive cafes cater to tourists—even the beloved **Kröpke** diner, a favorite local meeting place for the last 50 years, has been bought out by ice cream tsar Mövenpick. Find **groceries** at **Euro-Spar** by the Kröpke U-Bahn stop (open M-Sa 7am-8pm) or walk from the Hauptbahnhof to the **Markthalle,** a food court where varied snacks, meals, and booze await. (Open M-W 7am-8pm, Th-F 7am-9pm, Sa 8am-5pm.) Along Limmerstr., restaurants and *Imbiße* serve up cheap international flavors.

Uwe's Hannenfaß Hannover, Knochenhauerstr. 36 (☎32 16 16), in the timber-framed house that was once home to Hannover's master brewer. Decor as heavy and dark as the food and drink. The house-brewed *Hannen Alt* (€3.65 for 0.5L), accompanies steaming potato casserole *Niedersachsenschmaus* (€5), *Jägerschnitzel* (€6.50), or other German specialties. Open M-Th and Su 4pm-2am, F 4pm-4am, Sa noon-4am. ❷

Jalda, Limmerstr. 97 (☎212 32 61), serves popular Italian, Greek, and Arabic dishes, pizza, and salads (€5-10). Weekdays bring 3-course lunch specials (€7). Eat dinner by candlelight to funk beats. Take U10 (dir.: Ahlem) to "Ungerstr." Open M-Th and Su 11:30am-11pm, F-Sa 11:30am-1am. ❷

Mensa, Callinstr. 23 (☎768 80 35). U4 or 5 to "Schneiderberg/W.-Busch-Museum." Take a right up Schneiderbergstr., just past the pedestrian bridge in the green-trimmed building on the left. Meals €3-4 for guests. Open M-F 11:30am-2:30pm. ❶

👁 SIGHTS

HERRENHAUSEN GARDENS. In 1714, the crown of the United Kingdom was handed to **George I,** son of Hannover's Princess Sophie, in order to maintain Protestant rule in Britain. His descendants reigned over both Hannover and the UK until 1837, when the Hannoverians refused to accept the rule of Queen Victoria. The city owes much to Princess Sophie, who built the three Herrenhausen gardens. Here, Sophie would wait to inherit the crown from her niece, Queen Anne, only to die just weeks too soon. The centerpiece of the gardens is the Baroque **Großer Garten,** where striking geometry manifests itself in square trees and spiral bushes, all overseen by countless godly statues. The **Große Fontäne,** one of Europe's highest fountains, builds to an astounding 80m and sprays unwitting downwind bystanders with cool mist. At the end of August, a dazzling fireworks contest adds to the spray in the sky. *(Fountain spurts Apr.-Oct. M-F 11am-noon and 3-5pm, Sa-Su 11am-noon and 2-5pm. Garden open daily Apr. to mid-Oct. 9am-8pm; mid-Oct. to Mar. 8am-dusk. Entrance €4, including admission to Berggarten. Concerts and performances June-Aug.; ☎16 84 12 22 for schedule.)* The wide-open meadows and broad, tree-lined paths of the **Georgengarten** might convince you that you are hundreds of kilometers from anything resembling a city. *(Open 24hr. Free.)* The **Berggarten** has an indoor **rainforest** with a winding path ascending through the canopy amid tropical birds and butterflies. *(Berggarten open same hours as Großer Garten. €2. Rainforest open Apr.-May and Sept.-Oct. M-Th 10am-5pm, F-Su 10am-8pm; June-Aug. M-Th 10am-6pm, F 10am-10pm, Sa-Su 10am-8pm; Nov.-Mar. M-Th 10am-4pm, F-Su 10am-6pm. €8.50, students €5.50. Combination ticket for gardens, rainforest, and a museum €10, students €7.50, children €5.)*

ERLEBNIS-ZOO HANNOVER. More than 2500 animals live at this "experience zoo" specially designed to give visitors the sensation of observing wildlife out in nature. Themed areas include the **African Sambesi**, the **Indian Jungle Palace**, and **Gorilla Mountain**. The swift lory, a colorful tropical bird, might decide to perch on your head inside the **Tropical House**. Swarms of people, dogs, and strollers fill the zoo on sunny, summer afternoons. All shows free with admission. *(Adenaueralle 3.* ☎ *28 07 41 63; www.zoo-hannover.de. Take U11 to "Zoo." Open daily Mar.-Oct. 9am-6pm; Nov.-Feb. 10am-4pm. €16, children €11.50, under 4 free; dogs €6.)*

NEUES RATHAUS. On the outskirts of the Altstadt, built over swampland and filled in with piles of beech trees, is the spectacular Neues Rathaus. Don't be fooled by the palatial turn-of-the-century style: this beauty is indeed the *new* city hall, painstakingly recreated by Hannoverians after WWII. Inside, models depict the city in 1689, 1939, 1945, and today. Take the famous slanted elevator up the tower and scout out the **Maschsee**, a 2km long lake south of the Rathaus covered with sailboats and rowboats during the summer and ice skaters in winter. *(Open May-Sept. M-F 9am-11pm, Sa-Su 10am-11pm. Elevator runs M-F 9:30am-6:30pm, Sa-Su 10am-6:30pm, ticket sales until 6pm. €2, students €1.50.)*

ALTSTADT. Post-war reconstruction and the recent development boom for the World's Fair have given much of the city center a decidedly modern feel. However, many older sights still stand in Hannover's **Altstadt**, a 15min. walk from the train station. Walk down Bahnhofstr. and continue as it becomes Karmarschstr.; take a right on Knochenhauerstr. Immediately to the right is Hannover's **Altes Rathaus**. Used for official purposes until 1913, it has become, in a final burst of glory... a shopping area and cafe. Just past the Altes Rathaus, the 14th-century brick **Marktkirche** towers over Hans-Lilje-Pl. *(Open daily 10am-6pm; check for concerts.)*

LEIBNIZHAUS. A beautifully restored Baroque mansion, this house, which cost over €11 million to restore, was home to brilliant mathematician, philosopher, man of letters, and royal advisor Gottfried Wilhelm Leibniz until his death in 1716. *(Holzmarkt 5.* ☎ *62 44 50. Open Su 10am-1pm and 1:30-6pm. Free.)*

ST. ÄGIDIENKIRCHE. Across the street from Leibnizhaus is the magnificent **Leineschloß**, seat of the Diet of Niedersachsen. Farther down Leinstr., the road leads to the ivy-covered **St. Ägidienkirche,** a powerful monument kept in the state that WWII left it. Colored squares of glass suspended in empty window frames symbolize elaborate stained-glass designs that once filled them, and memorial plaques and rough-hewn timber crosses serve as reminders of the folly of war. *(Open 24hr. Free.)*

▥ MUSEUMS

SPRENGEL MUSEUM. A 20th-century art lover's dream, with works by James Turrell, Henry Moore, Dalí, Picasso, Magritte, and hometown hero Kurt Schwitters. Exhibits include Warhol self-portraits (through Jan. 16, 2005) and *The Mouse House* by Claus Oldenburg (May 29-Sept. 4, 2005). One modernist installation holds you in a pitch-dark space for 15min. so your mind can become attuned to the light that is actually there. *(Kurt-Schwitters-Pl. At the corner of the Maschsee and Maschpark, near the Neues Rathaus.* ☎ *16 84 38 75; www.sprengel-museum.de. Open Tu 10am-8pm, W-Su 10am-6pm. Permanent collection €3.50, students €2; with special exhibits €6/€3.50.)*

KESTNER-MUSEUM. August Kestner, Hannover's emissary to Rome, began this collection with Egyptian and Greco-Roman artifacts he picked up abroad: miniature Egyptian figurines, ancient Mediterranean blown glassware, and a sofa shaped like enormous lips. *(Trammpl. 3. Next to the Neues Rathaus.* ☎ *16 84 21 20; www.kestner-museum.de. Open Tu-Su 11am-6pm, W until 8pm. €2.60, students €1.50; F free.)*

HISTORISCHES MUSEUM HANNOVER. Catch a glimpse of everyday life in Niedersachsen over the centuries, chronicled by items such as a 10th-century fortress replica and Nazi regalia. Paintings, family trees, and a row of ornate horse-drawn carriages attempt to unravel the convoluted relationship between the British and Hannoverian monarchies. *(Pferdestr. 6, next to the Leibnizhaus.* ☎ *16 84 23 52. Open Tu and Th 10am-7pm, W and F-Su 10am-5pm. €3, students and children €2, under 12 free; F free.)*

WILHELM-BUSCH-MUSEUM. Busch was the 19th-century German cartoonist responsible for **Max und Moritz,** two troublemakers who have simultaneously amused and frightened German children into good behavior for several generations. This small museum contains many original sketches and paintings, and hosts rotating exhibits of children's book illustrations. *(Georgengarten 1. U4 (dir.: Garbsen) or #5 (dir.: Stöcken) to "Schneiderberg/W. Busch Museum."* ☎ *16 99 99 16; www.wilhelmbusch-museum.de. Open Tu-Sa 11am-5pm, Su 11am-6pm. €4.50, students and children €2.50.)*

LANDESMUSEUM. The playful displays inside this child-friendly cultural museum include exotic lizards and fish, a non-European "cultural" exhibit (jumbles of African masks and Inuit huts), Neanderthal skulls, and paintings by Lieberman, Rubens, and Monet. *(Willy-Brandt-Allee 5.* ☎ *980 75; www.nlmh.de. Open Tu-Su 10am-5pm, Th until 7pm. €4, students €3, children €1.50.)*

KUBUSMUSEUM. This Hannoverian artists' co-op shows contemporary art with origins ranging from local to international in a large one-room gallery on the second floor. *(Theodor-Lessing-Pl. 2, near the Ägidienkirche.* ☎ *16 84 57 90. Open Tu-F 11am-6pm, Sa-Su 11am-4pm. €3, students €2.)*

🎵 🎭 ENTERTAINMENT AND NIGHTLIFE

More than 20 theaters supply Hannover with ballet, opera, drama, and musicals. The four largest are the **Opernhaus,** Opernpl. 1; the **Ballhof,** Ballhofstr. 5; the **Schauspielhaus,** on Theaterpl.; and the **Theater am Ägi,** on Ägidientorpl. Tickets for most shows (from €10) are sold at the tourist office (ticket line ☎ 30 14 30). Advance tickets for the opera and the Schauspielhaus are available at the Opernhaus. (Open M-F 10am-7:30pm, Sa 10am-2pm. ☎ 99 99 11 11). Student tickets are generally sold at the box office 1hr. before shows at a 25% discount; student rush opera tickets are €8. The monthly *Hannover Vorschau* and *Hannover Live,* free at the tourist office, list theater shows and more. The Opernhaus provides its own free guide to opera and ballet. **KNHO,** Schaufelder Str. 30 (☎ 70 38 14; www.kino-imsprengel.de), near the university, shows art-house flicks. Take U6 or 11 to "Kopernikusstr.," exit left onto An der Lutherkirche and turn right on Schaufeldstr.

If you're within a 100km radius of Hannover the first week in July, detour to its **Schützenfest** (marksmanship festival), the largest such *fête* in the world. Every summer since 1539, Hannoverians have congregated—weapons in hand—to test their marksmanship before retreating to the beer gardens. The 10-day festival in early July comes complete with parade, fireworks, and amusement park rides, but its main attraction is the *Lüttje Lage,* a feisty traditional drink: you down the contents of two shot glasses simultaneously, holding them side by side in one hand and trying not to spill; one glass contains *Weißbier,* the other *Schnapps.* This party is a mere warm-up for the **Maschseefest** (late July to early Aug.) that provides another wild mix of concerts, masked balls, and street performances. Finally, Hannoverians let loose at the **Altstadtfest** the first or second weekend in August. The **Flohmarkt** (flea market) on the **Leibnizufer** hits town every Saturday 7am-2pm.

When the sun goes down, Hannover lights up with an array of packed cafes and pumping discos. The university crowds swarm **Linden-Nord,** the area beginning at Goethepl. and running along Limmerstr., filling the cafes and *Kneipen.* For parties, snoop around the Mensa for signs, or check *Prinz* (€1) or *Schädelspalter* (€2.50), both outstanding nightlife guides, available at the tourist office and newsstands. The free *MagaScene* lists clubs and concerts, and it's also online (www.magascene.de). For live music, check out **The Capitol** (p. 241) or **Altro Mondo**, Bahnhofstr. 8 (☎32 33 27), in the City-Passage. (Tickets available at ☎41 99 99 40.)

▨ The Loft, Georgstr. 50a (☎473 93 10), near Kröpcke. The mood-lighting at this hip joint draws packs of students on weekends. Go through the alleyway to enter this chic bar or its companion bistro **Masa**. Enjoy falafel (€3.50) and milkshakes (€3) by candlelight or next to the waterfall in the garden. Happy hour M-Th and Su 8-9pm, F-Sa 1-2am. Masa open daily noon-1am. Loft open daily 8pm-2am, F-Sa until 4am.

The Capitol, Schwarzer Bär 2 (☎929 88 18; tickets 44 40 66). U9 to "Schwarzer Bär," and walk back toward the river. Loosen up in a sea of bumping bodies. F nights "Dancing Queen" or Destiny's Child. Sa nights the disco moves to the main hall to make way for live indie rock bands. Cover €2-4. Open F 10pm-3am, Sa 10pm-6am.

The Irish Harp, Schwarzer Bär 1 (☎336 06 06). Across the street from The Capitol, take a break from disco fever in this laid-back pub, where you might share a pint of Guinness (€3.50) with some of Hannover's numerous Irish expatriates. Live Irish ensemble every Su beginning at 5pm. Battle the locals on pub quiz night, in German and English, M 9pm. Open daily Su-Th 5pm-1am, F-Sa 5pm-3am.

Osho Disco, Raschpl. 7L (☎34 22 17). At the round, banner-covered building just behind the Hauptbahnhof, DJs spin everything from house and pop to Latin beats and Frank Sinatra. Rest your feet upstairs with the dolphins. Every W is "Forever Young"—no cover for anyone over 30. 18+. Cover €3-5. Open W-Su from 10pm.

Schwule Sau, Schaufeldstr. 30 (☎700 05 25). U6 or 11 to "Kopernikusstr.," exit left onto An der Lutherkirche and turn right on Schaufeldstr. It's on the left, entrance on the far side of the building. Popular gay and lesbian bar in the university district. On good nights, the 3-person sofa can seat 15. Tu ladies only. W men only. Tea Su afternoons.

GÖTTINGEN   ☎0551

Home to Europe's first free university, Göttingen remains a college town to the core, boasting alumni **Otto von Bismarck** and **J.P. Morgan** and former teachers the **Brothers Grimm**, but its real fame comes from the hard sciences. Forty-two Nobel laureates have been students or faculty members here, including **Max Planck** (the father of quantum mechanics) and **Werner Heisenberg** (the head of the Nazi atomic bomb project, rumored to have secretly sabotaged the process). The university has historically taken extreme political positions—left in 1734 after its founding, reactionary right in the 1920s, and back again to the left in the 1950s, earning its reputation as a *rote Uni* (red university). Students carry on in the proud tradition with frequent protests when they aren't hanging out at Göttingen's pubs and cafes.

▐ TRANSPORTATION

Trains: Every hr. to **Berlin** (2½hr., €62). 2 per hr. to: **Frankfurt** (2hr., €34); **Hamburg** (2hr., €53); **Hannover** (1hr., €20); **Kassel** (1hr., €16).

Public Transportation: Most city buses stop at the central "Markt" in one direction and "Kornmarkt" in the other. Single ride with 1 transfer €1.60. Day tickets (€3.80) good for 24hr. from the time of purchase, available on any bus. Most buses run until 11pm.

Taxis: Taxi Night & Day ☎650 00.

Car Rental: Europcar, Groner Landstr. 17a (☎0180 580 00). Open M-F 7:30am-6pm, Sa 8am-noon, Su 9-11am.

NIEDERSACHSEN AND BREMEN

Göttingen

🏠 ACCOMMODATIONS
Hotel Garni Gräfin
   Holtzendorff, **4**
Hotel-Gaststätte
   Berliner Hof, **1**
Jugendherberge (HI), **2**

🍎 FOOD & DRINK
Claudio, **11**
Shucan, **7**

Villa Cuba, **10**
Zentral-Mensa, **3**

🍷 BARS & NIGHTLIFE
Blue Note, **9**
Cafe Kollektiv
   Kabale, **12**
Electro Osho, **6**
Irish Pub, **5**
Trou, **8**

Bike Rental: Fahrrad-Parkhaus (☎ 599 94), to the left facing the station's main exit. Bikes from €11 per day. Open M-Sa 5:30am-10pm, Su 8am-11pm.

✈ 🛈 ORIENTATION AND PRACTICAL INFORMATION

The Altstadt, still encircled by the old wall, is cut north to south by Weenderstr. At the center are the **Altes Rathaus** and **Wilhelmsplatz**, original site of the university.

Tourist Office: Markt 9 (☎ 49 98 00; www.goettingen-tourismus.de), in the Altes Rathaus. From the station, cross Berliner Str. to perpendicular Goetheallee, follow it several blocks as it becomes Prinzenstr., and turn right onto Weender Str. In the Markt., climb the stairs to find free maps, a free room-booking service, or **city tours**, (1½hr., F-Su at 11:30am, €5). Open Apr.-Oct. M-F 9:30am-6pm, Sa-Su 10am-4pm; Nov.-Mar. M-F 9:30am-1pm and 2-6pm, Sa 10am-1pm.

Currency Exchange: Commerzbank, Prinzenstr. 2 (☎ 40 80). Open M-W 9am-4pm, Th 9am-6pm, F 9am-3:30pm.

American Express: Goetheallee 4a (☎ 52 20 70). In case you left home without it. Open M-F 9am-6pm, Sa 9:30am-1pm.

Bookstore: Deuerlich, Weender Str. 33 (☎ 49 50 00), offers a good selection of English-language paperbacks. Open M-W 9:30am-7pm, Th-F 9:30am-8pm, Sa 9:30am-6pm.

Women's Resources: Frauenhaus (☎521 18 00). Some English spoken. Open 24hr.

Laundromat: Wasch-Salon, Ritterplan 4, opposite the Städtisches Museum. Wash 2.50, soap €0.50. Dry €0.50 per 12min. Open M-Sa 7am-10pm.

Emergency: ☎110. Non-emergency **police** ☎49 10. Groner Landstr. 51. **Fire** ☎112.

AIDS Hotline: AIDS-Beratung ☎400 48 31.

Pharmacy: Universitäts-Apotheke, Markt 6 (588 49). Helping students cure headaches, choler, and "other illnesses" since 1734. Open M-F 8:30am-7pm, Sa 9am-4pm.

Internet Access: Computerwerk, Düsterestr. 20 (☎48 80 50 90). €1 per 15min. Open M-Sa 10am-midnight, Su 4pm-midnight.

Post Office: Heinrich-von-Stephan-Str. 1, 37073 Göttingen, to the right facing the train station. Open M-F 8am-6pm, Sa 9am-1pm. There is a smaller **branch** near the city center at Groner Str. 15/17. Open M-F 9am-6pm, Sa 10am-1pm.

ACCOMMODATIONS

Jugendherberge (HI), Habichtsweg 2 (☎576 22; fax 438 87). Bus #6 (dir.: Klausberg) to "Jugendherberge," then cross the street to the path. Helpful staff, a pool table, and **Internet** (€0.10 per min.). Breakfast and sheets included. Key deposit €10. Reception 6:30am-midnight. Curfew midnight, or get a key with a €15 deposit. Check-out 9am. €18.60, under 27 €15.60; singles €21.60/€18.60. ❷

Hotel-Gaststätte Berliner Hof, Weender Landstr. 43 (☎38 33 20; www.berlinerhof.de). From the station, take bus #15 (dir.: Steffensweg) to "Kreuzbergring." Or walk left from the station up Berliner Str. and turn left on Weender Str. Bordering the university, Berliner Hof offers cheery rooms with TVs, phones, and a friendly staff. Large 3-bedroom suites (€77) are ideal for families or groups. Breakfast included. Reception 8am-11pm. Singles €32, with shower €36-44; doubles with the works €64. ❸

Hotel Garni Gräfin Holtzendorff, Ernst-Ruhstrat-Str. 4 (☎639 87; fax 63 29 85). From the station, take bus #13 (dir.: Esebeck) to "Florenz-Sautorius-Str." Continue in the direction of the bus and take the 1st left. In a somewhat distant industrial area, but a courtyard garden offers relief from the drab neighboring buildings. Many rooms have TVs. Breakfast included. Singles €27-37, with bath €45; doubles €45-50/€65. ❸

FOOD

Göttingen's most appetizing produce comes from its **fruit markets**—adjacent to the Deutsches Junges Theater (Tu, Th, and Sa 7am-1pm), and in the square in front of the Rathaus during the summer (Th 2-8pm). **Goetheallee,** running from the station to the city center, and parallel **Groner Straße,** have Greek, Italian, and Turkish restaurants that stay open late. Bakeries and other snack stops line **Weender Straße** and **Jüdenstraße.** The streets surrounding **Wilhelmsplatz** have a variety of pizza joints and other restaurants that cater to the student population.

Villa Cuba, Zindelstr. 2 (☎488 66 78). Behind Kirche St. Johannis. The stucco interior, huge picture of Che Guevara, and imported Cuban beer will bring back those Havana nights. The food is plentiful and surprisingly authentic. Tapas €4-5, delicious Creole specialties €4.80-8.80. Open Su-Th 10am-2am, F-Sa 10am-3am. ❸

Shucan, Weender Str. 11 (☎48 62 44). Join the people-watchers in this lively, tropical-themed cafe and bar. Baguettes (€5) are exceptional, and the creative, fruit-garnished ice cream dishes (€2-5) are a treat. Open daily 9am-2am. ❷

Zentral-Mensa, Pl. der Götthinger Sieben 4 (☎39 51 51). Follow Weender Landstr. onto Pl. der Göttinger Sieben, turn right into the university complex, and walk until you reach the mammoth *Studentenwerk* on the left. Meals €1-3 for students, others €4. Buy meal tickets downstairs. Open M-F 9am-3:30pm, Sa 10am-2:30pm. The **Café Central** sells baguettes and pastries. Open M-Th 9am-8pm, F 9am-7pm. ❶

Claudio, Lange Geismarstr. 39, near Kornmarkt, is probably the source of the ice-cream cones in the hands of happy Göttingeners walking around the Marktpl. The generous *Kugeln* (€0.60) come in more than 15 flavors. ❶

🔍 SIGHTS

ALTES RATHAUS. Built in the 13th century, the Altes Rathaus and its courtyard formed the focal point of the city. Now, 700 years later, the courtyard is the Marktpl., hemmed in by outdoor cafes producing a continuous stream of idle chatter. The flow of students, tourists, and street musicians wandering through or gathering around the *Gänseliesel* fountain will enthrall people-watchers.

BISMARCK SIGHTS. The **Bismarckhäuschen,** built into the city wall in 1459, is a tiny stone cottage. Here, the 17-year-old law student Otto von Bismarck took up residence after authorities expelled him from the inner city for overzealous partying. On display is young Otto's 1832-1833 class schedule, as well as a wooden student ID. *(From the Markt, walk down Zindelstr. and follow it as it becomes Nikolaistr.; just before Bürgerstr. turn right by the bus stop onto the footpath on top of the wall; the house is on your left.* ☎ *48 62 47. Open Tu 10am-1pm, Th and Sa 3-5pm. Free.)* The **Bismarckturm,** in the Hainberg forest east of town, commemorates the larger-scale trouble-making of his later career. From the top of the old stone tower, there's a Göttingen-wide view. *(Im Hainberg. Bus #9 to "Hainbundstr.," then continue up the hill, following Bismarckstr. as it winds into the woods—also a great place for a walk. After about 1km, watch for signs pointing to the tower, on your left.* ☎ *561 28. Open Sa-Su 11am-6pm. Free.)*

MEDIEVAL CHURCHES. Göttingen is home to several notable churches. The **Jacobikirche's** 72m tower rises up next to the stone lambda structure called *Der Tanz.* Inside the modern and the ecclesiastical collide: geometric stained-glass windows (1997) on the left side face more traditional ones (1900) on the right, surrounding candy-striped columns (built in 1480) straight out of a book of optical illusions. *(☎ 575 96. Corner of Prinzenstr. and Weender Str. Open daily 11am-4pm. Free. Tower open Sa from 11am. €2.)* Behind the Altes Rathaus stands the fortress-like **Kirche St. Johannis,** whose tower has housed students since 1921. The church is undergoing renovations until 2005. *(☎ 48 62 41. Open M-F 11am-noon, Sa 10am-noon. Tower open Sa 2-4pm.)*

GEORG-AUGUST-UNIVERSITÄT. The university, established in 1737, fills an area bounded by Weender Landstr., Humboldtallee, and Nikolausberger Weg, just northeast of town. The best and brightest rush around, many by bicycle.

STÄDTISCHES MUSEUM. The municipal museum, a cut above average, gives a detailed examination of the city over the last several millennia. Jewelry from the Bronze Age, medieval altarpieces and robes, and 1950s furniture fill out a benign history, while the model of a child dressed in Hitler youth regalia, and a postcard showing a swastika rising over the city are considerably more chilling. *(Ritterplan 7. 1 block north of the Jakobikirche on Jüdenstr. ☎ 400 28 43. Open Tu-F 10am-5pm, Sa-Su 11am-5pm. Permanent exhibit €1.50, children €0.50; temporary exhibits €1.50/€1.)*

SYNAGOGUE MEMORIAL SCULPTURE. On Untere Maschstr., the steel sculpture stands over the site where a Göttingen synagogue was razed in 1938. The silver structure has plaques listing the names of Jews from the synagogue who died during WWII. Viewed from above, the memorial forms a Star of David.

MEDIEVAL HOUSES. Göttingen's Altstadt is scattered with colorful *Fachwerkhäuser* (half-timbered houses) dating back to 1337. The flamboyant **Junkernschänke,** on the corner of Barfüßerstr. and Jüdenstr., is adorned with bright carvings of Biblical scenes, and was built in 1431. Others can be found on Rote-Str.

♫ ENTERTAINMENT

Most of Göttingen's renowned theaters close mid-July until September.

Deutsches Theater, Theaterpl. 11 (☎ 49 69 11; www.dt-goettingen.de), puts on classics and contemporary productions. Check out the slick *DT* catalogue. So classy that even the students dress up to come here. Open M-F 10am-1:30pm and 5-8pm, Sa 11am-2pm, and 1hr. before shows. Tickets at the box office, from €6.

Junges Theater, Hospitalstr. 6 (☎ 49 50 15), an edgier, but top-notch, alternative theater presents a new outlook on both classic and the innovative works. Box office open M-F 11am-4pm, Sa 11am-2pm, and 1hr. before shows. Tickets €10, students €7.

Cinema: Ruthlessly dubbed blockbusters and German-language flicks play at **Cinema Filmkunstkino,** Weender Str. 58 (☎ 588 88) or at the gigantic **Cinemaxx** (☎ 521 22 00) complex behind the train station. The artsy **Lumière,** Geismarer Landstr. 19 (☎ 48 45 23), housed in Cafe Kabale (p. 245), is more cosmopolitan (€5, students €4).

◉ NIGHTLIFE

Trou, Burgstr. 20 (☎ 439 71). This 500-year-old, candle-lit cellar has been Göttingen's most intimate watering hole for 40 years. People cluster amidst light jazz and good conversation around barrels that serve as tables. A specialty is *Altbierbowle mit Erdbeeren* (strawberries in a 0.3L-bowl of *Diebels* beer, €2). Konrad, the owner, is known to give lectures on the history of brewing in Germany. Open M-Th 7:30pm-2am, F-Su until 3am.

Irish Pub, Mühlenstr. 4 (☎ 456 64), one of the most popular student watering holes, with a ton of Gaelic *Gemütlichkeit*, lots of Guinness, and live Irish music every night at 10pm (summer 3 times per wk.). Open daily 3pm-2am.

Blue Note, Wilhelmspl. 3 (☎ 469 07), under the Aula. The most diverse venue for music and fun in the Altstadt. A different theme every day (Jazz, reggae, and African pop are favorites). W Latin music, Sa Salsa dancing, both no cover. Other nights €1.50-2.50, concerts (at least once a week) €4-16. Open M-Th 10pm-3am, F-Sa 10pm-4:30am.

Electro Osho, Weender Str. 38 (☎ 517 79 76). Students dance until the sun comes up in this relatively new underground club. Its central location is unbeatable—it's almost like there's a rave in the Rathaus. W night hip-hop, F night techno, Sa night disco. Cover usually €3, more for live music. Open W 11pm-3am, F-Sa 11pm-6am.

Cafe Kollektiv Kabale, Geismarlandstr. 19 (☎ 48 58 30; www.cafe-kabale.de). Far outside the old city past the Neues Rathaus (15min.); watch for the sign on your left. Hidden behind a stone wall and tall trees, this crazy house is brimming with art, film, food, and drink. Theme parties twice a month, art exhibitions, and poetry readings. Call for the schedule. Lesbian bar Tu 8:30pm. Open M-F 4pm-1am, Sa 2pm-1am, Su 10-1am.

GOSLAR   ☎ 05321

Tiny Goslar is one of Niedersachsen's most historically and culturally prominent cities. Its 11th-century palace, once home to German emperors, towers over the perfectly-preserved Altstadt (the product of fortunes unearthed in nearby silver mines), full of sculptures, fountains, and miniature witches. In WWII, Goslar's citizens proclaimed it neutral and painted red crosses atop their homes, banning soldiers. Under the Geneva Convention, this act made the town safe from bombing. Goslar's beauty and proximity to the Harz Mountains draw intimidating crowds of tourists, but the town retains the charm that once lured Goethe and Henry Moore.

NIEDERSACHSEN AND BREMEN

🖂 🔋 TRANSPORTATION AND PRACTICAL INFORMATION

Trains roll to: **Braunschweig** (45min., 1 per hr., €5.60); **Göttingen** (1¼hr., 1 per hr., €12); **Hannover** (1½hr., 2 per hr., €12). The hub of an extensive bus network, Goslar serves as a convenient gateway to any part of the region (ticket €1.70, *Tageskarte* €4). **Hotel Der Achtermann**, Rosentorstr. 20 (☎ 700 09 99), rents bikes even to non-guests; as you walk out of the station, turn left. The **tourist office**, Markt 7, across from the Rathaus, books rooms (from €20) for free and sells maps of the Harz. From the station, turn left onto Rosentorstr. Follow it as it winds to the right and turns into Hokenstr., which leads to the Marktpl. The office is on your left. (☎ 780 60; www.goslar.de. Open May-Oct. M-F 9:15am-6pm, Sa 9:30am-4pm, Su 9:30am-2pm; Nov.-Apr. M-F 9:15am-5pm, Sa 9:30am-2pm.) **Tours** (€3-5) depart regularly from the Marktpl. The **post office** is just to the right of the train station at Klubgartenstr. 10, 38640 Goslar. (Open M-F 8:30am-6pm, Sa 9am-12:30pm.)

🖂 🍴 ACCOMMODATIONS AND FOOD

The half-timbered Goslar **Jugendherberge (HI) ❷**, Rammelsberger Str. 25, is a bit of a hike; it's best to take bus #808 from the train station (dir.: Bergbaumuseum) to "Theresienhof." (1 per hr. until 6pm). Continue along in the same direction, and take a sharp left up the hill at the big white "Jugendherberge" sign (5min.). Once the luggage is off your back, the walk from Marktpl. becomes pleasant. Take the twisty Bergstr. from the church southwest until it ends at Clausthaler Str. Cross the intersection and follow the signs for the hostel down Rammelsberger Str. (25min.). The path is not lit at night. Rooms are small but provide a good view of the mountains or surrounding farmland; for an additional €2.50, you can claim a double as a private single. (☎ 222 40; fax 413 76. Breakfast and sheets included. Reception 7am-2:30pm and 3-10pm. Curfew 10pm. Dorms €16.70, under 26 €14.) **Gästehaus Elisabeth Möller ❷**, Schiefer Weg 6, offers a dollhouse-like ambience with lacy, pastel decor, poofy beds, and delightful garden. From the station, take a right on Klubgartenstr., which becomes Am Heiligen Grabe; cross Von-Garssen-Str., and turn right on Schiefer Weg. (☎230 98. Singles €22, with shower €27, with full bath €35; doubles €45-60.) **Campingplatz Sennhütte ❶**, Clausthaler Str. 28, is 3km from town along the B241 highway; bus #830 (dir.: Hahnenklee or Clausthal-Zellerfeld) to "Sennhütte" (6min., 1-2 per hr.) This site is a short hike from the lake, with a kiosk, WC, and laundry room. (☎224 98. €3 per person, €2 per tent, €1.50 per car.) The town has a mountain **market** (Tu-F 8am-1pm) and the beautiful surrounding square is ringed with pricey restaurants. **Markt Treff ❷**, Fleischscharren 6 (☎30 67 61), serves German favorites, like *Currywurst* with french fries (€4-6), at prices that put the other outdoor cafes to shame. Cheaper places can be found along Hokenstr., where *Imbiße* provide meals for €2-4. Music, beer, and the local 20-something crowd converge at **Brauhaus Wolpertinger,** a giant *Biergarten* complex set in a 16th-century courtyard just off Marstallstr. (open M-Sa from noon, Su from 10am), or the nearby **Kö Musik-Kneipe,** Marktstr. 30, which offers **free Internet** access to customers. (☎268 10. Open Su-Th 4pm-2am, F-Sa 4pm-3am.)

🔲 SIGHTS

Guarded by a pair of bronze Braunschweig lions, the austere 🏰**Kaiserpfalz,** Kaiser-bleek 6, is a massive Romanesque palace that served as the ruling seat for 11th- and 12th-century emperors. Glory was short-lived, and the palace was abandoned, becoming a den of undesirables and eventually a prison. By the 19th century it had fallen into disrepair, but romantic infatuation with the Middle Ages and the loving care of Prussian aristocrats restored the palace to its present majesty. The interior of the **Reichssaal** is plastered with gargantuan murals displaying carefully selected incidents from German history in a uniquely mythic, pompous manner. In the palace's **Ulrichskapelle**, Kaiserpfalz, Heinrich III's heart lies inside a massive sarcophagus, while the entrance still bears evidence of its stint as town prison. (☎311 96 93. Open daily Apr.-Oct. 10am-5pm; Nov.-Mar. 10am-4pm. Last entry 30min. before closing. €4.50, children €2.50.) Below the palace is the **Domvorhalle**, Kaiserbleek 10, a restoration of a 12th-century cathedral destroyed 170 years ago.

Each day in the market square, figures of court nobles and miners dance to the chiming bells on the treasury roof in the **Glocken-und-Figurenspiel** (9am, noon, and 6pm). Behind the Rathaus loom the twin towers of the reconstructed 12th-century **Marktkirche**. The church contains the stained-glass saga of St. Cosmas and St. Damian, 3rd-century twin doctors and martyrs. In classic Roman excess, the saints were punished by drowning, burning at the stake, stoning, and crucifixion. (☎229 22. Tours M 12:30 and 3:50pm. Open daily 10am-5pm. Free.) On the way back from the Kaiserpfalz the fantastic **⬛Musikinstrumente- und Puppenmuseum**, Hoher Weg 5, feels like the inside of a children's book. The owner, once a musical clown with a traveling circus, has spent over 50 years assembling Germany's largest private instrument collection, that now includes mandolins, musical saws, violins, deformed fiddles, and Thomas Jefferson's glass harmonica. (☎269 45. Open daily 11am-5pm. €3, children €1.50.) The **Mönchehaus**, Mönchestr. 1, has modern art and cutting-edge exhibitions in a traditional *Fachwerk* home. The museum awards the prestigious annual *Kaiserring* to a modern artist based on a vote by the townspeople; the first went in 1975 to Henry Moore, and other recipients include Anselm Kiefer, Willem de Kooning, and Cindy Sherman. (☎295 70; www.moenchehausmuseum.de. Open Tu-Sa 10am-5pm, Su 10am-1pm. €3, students €1.50.)

HAMELN (HAMELIN) ☎05151

In the 700 years since the Pied Piper last strolled out of town, his talents have kept this once-obscure German village in the limelight. On June 26, 1284, after Hameln failed to pay the piper his rat-removal fee, he walked off with 130 children in thrall. Today, this legend of the *Rattenfänger* draws tourists as steadily as his flute drew rodents. Rats are back in town, but nobody's complaining—this time, they are made of bread and marzipan. Outside the souvenir zone, the Weser beckons to hikers. Hameln is a gateway to the region; buses connect through picturesque rolling hills to nearby countryside castles and fairy-tale villages.

▐▌ TRANSPORTATION AND PRACTICAL INFORMATION

Hameln bridges the Weser River and is 45min. from Hannover by **train** (2 per hr., €8.40). **Flotteweser,** Deisterallee 1 (in the same building at the tourist office), runs **ferries** up and down the Weser to Bodenwerder, Holzminden, and Hannoversch Münden. (☎93 99 99. Operates Mar.-Oct. Call for schedule. 1hr. trip €6, children €3; 2hr. €9.50/€3.) For a **taxi**, call ☎74 77, 33 38, or 122 00. Rent **bikes** from **Troche Fahrrad-Shop**, Kreuzstr. 7. (☎136 70. €10 per day. Open M-F 9:30am-12:45pm and 2:30-6pm, Sa 9:30am-12:30pm.) The **tourist office**, Deisterallee 1, on the Bürgergarten, tracks down rooms (from €15) for free and lists hotels and pensions. From the station, cross Bahnhofpl., make a right onto Bahnhofstr., and turn left onto Deisterstr., which becomes Deisterallee. (☎95 78 23; www.hameln.de. Open May-Sept. M-F 9am-6:30pm, Sa 9:30am-4pm, Su 9:30am-1pm; Oct.-Apr. M-F 9am-6pm, Sa 9:30am-1pm.) **Tours** (with or without Pied Piper) leave from the tourist office. (M-Sa 2:30pm, Su 10:15am. €4, children €2.) To reach the pedestrian Altstadt, cross the road just beyond the tourist office. **Matthias Buchhandlung**, Bäckerstr. 56, has

English paperbacks. (☎947 00. Open M-F 9am-7pm, Sa 9am-6pm.) Access the **Internet** at **Witte,** Kopmanshof 69. (☎994 40. €2 per 30min.) The **post office** is on Stubenstr., 31785 Hameln, a block past the Markt. (Open M-F 8am-6pm, Sa 8am-1pm.)

ACCOMMODATIONS AND FOOD

Hameln's tourist boom has spawned a large number of pensions. The best deal is probably **Gästehaus Alte Post ❸,** Hummenstr. 23, in the Altstadt, offering colorful rooms complete with Picasso prints. TVs, phones, and clock radios. (☎434 44; ottokater@aol.com. Breakfast included, in the pub downstairs. Reception 11:30am-2:30pm and 5pm-midnight. Check-out 11am. Singles €25-35; doubles €50-65.) The beautifully located **Jugendherberge (HI) ❶,** Fischbeckerstr. 33, sits on a gentle bend in the Weser, a short walk north of the Altstadt. From the station, take bus #5 or 20 to "Langer Kreis/Jugendherberge," then backtrack 100m and look for the sign on your right. (☎34 25; fax 423 16. Breakfast included. Reception 12:30-1:30pm only if you call ahead and 5-9pm. Curfew 10pm, but key available with €15 deposit. €17.10, under 27 €14.40.) Southeast of the city center on the shores of Tönebon Lake, **Campground Jugendzeltplatz ❶,** Tönebonweg 8, has warm showers and a sauna. Take bus #44 or 51 (only runs a few times per day) to "Südbad." (☎262 23. Reception 8am-10pm. Open May-Sept. €3 per person.)

Hamelners flock to the open-air **market** on the *Bürgergarten* for fruit, vegetables, and other treats. (W and Sa 8am-1pm.) The streets of the Altstadt around Osterstr. and Pferdemarkt are lined with restaurants and cafes, but the chances of finding a bargain are slim. Some good deals wait along Bäckerstr. near the *Münster* or in the alleys branching off from the touristy cafe area. **Mexcal ❸,** Osterstr. 15, serves excellent German-Mexican meals, and the lunch specials (noon-3pm) are a good deal (burritos €5). Dinners run €6-10. Happy hour (3-6pm and 11pm-close) lowers cocktails to €4. (☎428 06. Open daily noon-midnight.) Little crusty souvenir bread-rats are €1.70 at the excellent bakery in the **Schmelz Reformhaus,** Osterstr. 18, in the Altstadt. It carries all-natural foodstuffs in a town otherwise filled with cellophane-wrapped candy. (Open M-F 8:30am-6pm, Sa 8:30am-3pm.)

SIGHTS

If you want to make your own escape from rats, you may have to venture out of the Altstadt: the Piper motif is ubiquitous. A small exception is the **Bürgergarten,** near the tourist office, where the locals relax and play life-sized chess. (Open daily 7am-10pm.) At Rathauspl. is the **Theater Hameln,** featuring a musical about the Piper and other theater, opera, and dance. (Information and tickets ☎91 62 22 or 91 62 20. Box office open Tu-F 10am-7pm, Sa 10am-3pm.) Trek 100m into the *Fußgängerzone* to the **Leisthaus,** Osterstr. 8-9, where the **Museum Hameln** exhibits an eclectic collection of pieces from Hameln's history, among them some fossils, 1960s rock albums with the Piper theme, and a cane with a hidden *erotisches* skeleton—use your imagination. (☎20 22 15. Open Tu-Su 10am-4:30pm. €3, students and children €1.50.) The *Rattenfänger* tale is enacted zealously by the community theater every Sunday at noon in a **Freilichtspiel** outside the 17th-century Hochzeithaus on Osterstr., as well as in ■ **RATS: Das Musical,** every Wednesday, 4:30pm, in the same place. (May-Sept., weather permitting. Free.) At 9:35am, the **Glockenspiel** on the **Hochzeithaus** plays the haunting *Rattenfängerlied* (Pied Piper song); at 11:45am the *Weserlied;* and at 1:05, 3:35, and 5:35pm, a tiny stage emerges from the Hochzeithaus and "rats" circle around a wooden flautist.

For something completely different, head to the **Glashütten Hameln,** Pulverturm 1, a glassware shop with a glass-blower's workshop upstairs. (☎272 39. Open M-F 9:30am-1pm and 2-6pm, Sa 9:30am-2pm, Su 10am-5pm. Workstation entrance €1, children €0.80.) Removed from Piperville, the **Schloß Hämelschenburg** comes with horses, babbling brooks, a waterwheel, and a pond full of huge goldfish. To get there, take bus #40 from "Münster" on the south edge of the Altstadt toward Emmerthal (30min., 1 per hr., €2). This Weser Renaissance style castle shelters gargoyles next to a trail with views of the surrounding countryside. Wonder over the mysteriously empty pyramid near the trailhead. (☎05155 95 16 90. Open Apr.-Oct. Tours every hr. Tu-Su 10am-noon and 2-5pm. €5, students €2.50. Admission only with tour.) For **hiking,** try one of the trails that lace the woods, meadows, and hills of the area surrounding the castle. For routes ranging from 5-14km, check out the big map next to the bus stop or pick up a hiking map at the tourist office (€7).

HANNOVERSCH MÜNDEN ☎ 05541

Declared "one of the seven most beautifully located cities in the world" by Alexander von Humboldt, Hannoversch Münden lies between forested hills where the Fulda and Werra Rivers combine to form the Weser. With more than 700 preserved *Fachwerkhäuser*, this is one of the most attractive of Germany's six zillion half-timbered towns. A miniature world of architectural charm, it is best appreciated with aimless strolls through the alluring Altstadt and over its many bridges.

🛈 PRACTICAL INFORMATION. Hann. Münden is reachable by **train** once per hr. from **Göttingen** (40min., €5.60) and **Kassel** (20min., €4.70). **Ferries** navigate the Fulda and Weser rivers and run **water tours** of the town (1¼ hr., €6.50, children €3). Information is available at the tourist office or the ferry landing. Tours around Hann. Münden leave from Kasseler Schlagd, two blocks from the Rathaus. Fulda trips begin left of the Pionierbrücke and Weser rides go from the tip of the island *Unterer Tanzwerder*, across the Mühlenbrücke. Rent **bikes** and **canoes** at **Busch Freizeit,** at Campingpl. Münden. (p. 249. ☎66 07 77; Open 8am-6pm. Bikes €9.50 per day, discounts for multiple days; boats €15 per day.) The **tourist office** in the Rathaus books rooms for free, gives out simple maps and sells hiking maps (€3.25-7.50). Tours of the town (€3, children €1) depart from the office daily May-Oct. at 2pm; call for English tours. (☎753 13; www.hann.muenden.de. Open May-Sept. M-F 8am-5:30pm, Sa 10:30am-3pm, Su 11am-3pm; Oct.-Apr. M-Sa 8am-4pm. Always closed noon-1pm.) When the office is closed, try the information counter in the same building. (☎750. Open daily May-Sept. until 9pm; Oct.-Apr. until 8pm.)

🛏🍴 ACCOMMODATIONS AND FOOD. The **Jugendherberge (HI) ❶,** Prof.-Ölkers-Str. 10, is just outside the town on the banks of the Weser. From the station, walk down Beethovenstr., turn left at Wallstr., cross the Pionierbrücke, and turn right along Veckerhäger Str. Follow the road left across the bridge, and look for signs (40min.). Or, take bus #135 (about 1 per hr.) from the train station (dir.: Veckerhäger-/Kasseler Str.) to "Jugendherberge." This riverside hostel has spacious 2- to 6-bed rooms. (☎88 53; jh-hann-muenden@djh-hannover.de. Breakfast and sheets included. Reception 7am-noon and 5-7pm. Curfew 10pm, but keys available. Closed weekends Nov.-Feb. €16.90, over 27 €14.20.) **Hotel-Garni zur Fulda ❸,** Ziegelstr. 62, is a peachy sandstone and stucco building in a narrow street in the Altstadt. Spacious rooms have new furniture and lots of natural light. (☎954 30; fax 95 43 27. Breakfast included. Singles €30; doubles €55.) Pitch your tent in view of the city walls at **Campingplatz Münden ❶,** Oberer Tanzwerder, 10min. from the train station on an island in the Fulda. From Blasiuskirche, take Tanzwerderstr. and cross the bridge. The site boasts a great location and ultra-modern facilities. (☎122 57; fax 66 07 78. Reception 8am-1pm and 3-8pm. €4.50 per person, €3 per child, from €4 per tent.) Search out the cheap eats at the bakeries along **Lange Straße** or at the **market** in front of the Rathaus (W and Sa 7am-1pm). **Plus,** Ziegelstr.

20, alongside the Blasiuskirche, stocks **groceries.** (Open M-F 8am-7pm, Sa 8am-2pm.) Restaurants throughout the Altmarkt are pricey, but cheap pizza parlors and *Imbiße* are scattered through town. **Il Piccolo Abruzzo ❷,** Lange Str. 14, serves pizza and pasta (€4-8) with background music and a touch of class, one block from the Werra. (☎728 46. Open daily noon-3pm and 6-11pm; Nov.-Mar. closed M.)

◪ SIGHTS. The town centers around the ornate **Rathaus,** a prime example of the Weser Renaissance style that originated in the area around 1550. From the station, cross the street and walk down Beethovenstr.; make a right onto Burgstr. and a left on Marktstr. Centuries-old Weser flood heights are recorded on the Rathaus's corners and colorful carvings adorn the front of the building. Figurines appear in the upper windows of the Rathaus for the ringing of the bells daily at noon, 3, and 5pm. The featured figure is Hann. Münden's favorite tourist gimmick, **Doctor Eisenbart,** an 18th-century traveling physician with a flare for the dramatic; in the days before anesthesia, he would have harlequins and tumblers put on a loud show outside his office to mask the shrieks of pain from patients inside. Watch his story on the stage in front of the Rathaus. (June-Aug. most Su 11:15am; check at the tourist office for dates. €2.50, children €1.50.) The **Blasiuskirche,** opposite the Rathaus, is decked out in periwinkle and emerald hues. (Open May-Oct. daily 11am-4pm. Free.) Around the church and the Rathaus are a number of interactive sculptures called Traces of Water, created for the World's Fair in 2000. Weave through the angled side streets to admire the 14th-century *Fachwerkhäuser* (half-timbered houses); some of the best are down **Ziegelstraße** and **Hinter der Stadtmauer.** On the edges of the city, seven of the original defense towers still stand, as well as the **Alte Werrabrücke** bridge, built in 1329, and the 12th-century **Ägidienkirche.**

Hann. Münden's three islands—**Doktorwerder, Unterer Tanzwerder,** and **Oberer Tanzwerder**—are accessible by small bridges on the outskirts of the Altstadt. The islands are all tiny and give a view of the city from the outside. Tanzwerder has several small parks, a *Biergarten,* and a parking lot for all the visitors. The camp grounds are on Oberer Tanzwerder. To escape crowds, hike one of the many trails in the thick beech forests on the other side of the Fulda. Cross the Pionierbrücke and take the path across the road up to the **Tillyschanze** tower, built in 1882 to memorialize the failed defense of the town during the Thirty Years' War, when **General Tilly** stormed through Münden, killing more than 2000 citizens. (Open daily Apr.-Oct. 9am-8pm; Nov.-Mar. 11am-8pm, M until 1pm. €1.10, children €0.60.)

HILDESHEIM   ☎05121

According to legend, Emperor Ludwig der Fromme (the Pious) lost his way while hunting and fastened a relic of the Virgin Mary to the branch of a conspicuous rose bush. He found his way home, and the next day returned to find it frozen to the branch. Since it was summertime, he saw this as a divine sign and erected a chapel on the site, around which grew the majestic Dom and the town of Hildesheim. Superstition holds that as long as the bush flourishes, so will Hildesheim. On March 22, 1945, Allied bombers flattened the town, yet remarkably, the bush survived. The collapsed ruins of the Dom sheltered the roots from the flames, and eight weeks later, 25 buds of the *tausendjähriger Rosenstock* (thousand-year-old rose bush) were growing strong. So did Hildesheim, and it is now a busy suburb.

◪◪ TRANSPORTATION AND PRACTICAL INFORMATION. Hildesheim is 45km southeast of Hannover, with **trains** to: **Braunschweig** (45min., 2 per hr., €7); **Göttingen** (30min., 1 per hr., €22); **Hannover** (30min., 1 per hr., €6). **Bus** tickets within the city cost €1.50 and are valid for 1hr.; a *Tagesticket* (€4) is valid all day. Rent **bikes** at **Räder-Emmel,** Dingworthstr. 20-22. From the "Dammtor" busstop, walk away from the Altstadt 3 blocks and turn right (☎ 438 22. Open M-F 9am-6pm, Sa 9am-1pm. €5 per day.) Located in the Marktpl.,the **tourist office**, Rathausstr. 18-20 (inside Gerstenberg bookstore), on the Markt offers brochures, hotel lists, maps, and city guides. They also book hotel and private rooms for free. From the Hauptbahnhof, take Bernwardstr. (straight ahead and slightly right), which becomes Almsstr. and then Hoher Weg; turn left on Rathausstr. Or from the "Schuhstr." busstop, walk down Hoher Weg and take your first right (☎ 179 80; www.hildesheim.de. Open M-F 9:30am-7pm, Sa 9:30am-4pm.25) The tourist office also offers 2hr. city **tours** in German, which leave from the Rathaus; English tours if you call ahead. (☎ 10 66. M-F 2pm, Sa 9:30am; €4). Open M-F 9am-7pm, Sa 9am-4pm.) **Internet** access and pastries await in **@Il Giornale**, Judenstr. 3. (Open M-Sa 9am-9:30pm. €2 per 30min) **Münz Waschcenter**, Bahnhofsallee 10, is 3 blocks from the train station. (Open daily 6am-11pm, last wash 10pm. Wash €3.50, including soap. Dry €0.50 per 10min.) The **post office**, Bahnhofpl. 3-4, 31134 Hildesheim, is diagonally across from the train station. (Open M-F 8am-6pm, Sa 8am-1pm.)

▐▌▐▐ ACCOMMODATIONS AND FOOD. Hildesheim's **Jugendherberge (HI) ❷**, Schirrmanweg 4, is literally the king of the hill, with a sweeping view across a sea of gently-swaying grass to the town below and hills beyond. Take bus #1 (dir.: Himmelsthür) to "Schuhstr." and then bus #4 (dir.: Bockfeld) to "Triftstr." Cross the street and climb 15min. uphill to the hostel. (☎ 427 17; jh-hildesheim. Breakfast included. Reception 9am-10pm. Check-out 10am. Curfew 10pm, but key available with an ID. €18.10, under 26 €15.40.) For privacy, cable TV, and a little bit of luxury, **Pension Kurth ❸**, Küsthardstr. 4, has rooms not far from the Markt. Walk down Schustr. with the Markt on your left, to the intersection with Wollenweberstr. (Hindenburgpl.); cut through the platz into Küsthardstr., the passage between the cafes. (☎ 36 272. Breakfast included. Singles €30, doubles €56.)

Hildesheim's culinary scene has plenty of variety and reasonable prices. **Plus Supermarkt,** Hannoversche Str. 28 is one block to the left, past the right side of Bahnhofspl. (Open M-F 8am-7pm, Sa 8am-2pm.) Culture shoppers will prefer the open-air **market** in both the Marktpl. and the Neustädter Markt, one block beyond Pension Kurth. (Open W and Su 8am-1pm.) The **Amsthausstuben ❹**, Markt 7, serves German dishes from €7 inside the Knochenhaueramtshaus (see **Sights**, p. 251) across from the Rathaus. (☎ 288 99 09. Open daily 9am-midnight, kitchen 11:30am-2:30pm and 5:30-10pm.) For fresh vegetarian and vegan fare, check out **Scheidemann's Salad & Toast Bar ❷**, Osterstr. 18, a stand-up cafe with 20 salads, sandwiches, and pizzas to choose from (€3-8). Meat dishes are available, too, as are a few chairs and stools for the weary. (☎ 390 04. Open M-Th 9am-7pm, F 9am-6pm.)

◪ SIGHTS. Hildesheim is a city of many churches, and the best way to see all of them is to follow the *Rosenroute* (rose path), a do-it-yourself tour following spray-painted white blossoms. Ludwig's favorite chapel, the Annenkapelle, and the famous 1000-year old *Tausendjähriger Rosenstock* are featured in the **Dom**'s courtyard. (Open M-Sa 9:30am-5pm, Su noon-5pm. Courtyard €0.50, children and students €0.30.) The **Dom-Museum**, through the door on the right near the altar, showcases countless chalices, a jewelled monstrance, and other ecclesiastical goodies. (☎ 17 91 63. Open Tu-Sa 10am-5pm, Su noon-5pm. €3.50, students €2.50.) Walk one block down Pfaffenstieg to reach the **◪ Römer- und Pelizaeus-Museum,** Am Steine 1-2, one of the largest collections of Egyptian artifacts in Europe. In addition to countless statues and ceramic bowls, the exhibits show how Egyptian burial rituals increased in complexity over the centuries. The top floor has a few mummified pets. Also an excellent display on Peruvian culture. (☎ 936 90; www.rpmuseum.de. Open daily 10am-6pm. €6, students €5.) The **Marktplatz** is a plaza of reconstructed half-timbered buildings and archways featuring the majestic **Knochenhaueramtshaus** (butcher's guild house). The lavish facade is painted with German proverbs like, *Arm oder reich, der Tod macht alles gleich*—"poor or rich, death makes everyone equal." Next to the restaurant is a museum displaying religious relics, pharmacy jars, animal-shaped doorknockers, and a recreated 19th-century hospital operating room. (☎30 11 63. Open Tu-Su 10am-6pm. €2.50, students €1.50.) South of the center at the corner of Gelber Stern (Yellow Star) and Lappenberg, the **Mahnmal am Lappenberg** stands in memorial amid the remains of Hildesheim's **synagogue,** which was torched on *Kristallnacht* in 1938.

⬛⬛ ENTERTAINMENT AND NIGHTLIFE. The **Theaterhaus Hildesheim,** Langer Garten 1 (☎642 76), hosts visiting theater and dance companies, plays artsy flicks, and stages concerts. It's between railtracks to left of the station. The **Stadttheater,** Theaterstr. 6, hosts operas, ballets, and plays. (☎16 93 53; www.stadttheater-hildesheim.de. Box office open M-F 10am-4pm, Sa 10am-6:30pm, Su 11am-2pm.) **Vier Linden,** Alfelder Str. 55b, exhibits art and shows a range of concerts from rock to techno to jazz. (☎272 44; www.vierlinden-hildesheim.de.) **KulturFabrik Löseke,** Langer Garten 1, in the same building as the Theaterhaus, hosts grittier alternative concerts, films, and theater productions. (☎553 76; www.kufa.info.) The Irish pub **Limerick,** Kläperhagen 6, has pizzas, omelettes (€4-8), and Irish draughts. (☎13 38 76. Open M-Th 11am-1am, F-Sa 11am-2am, Su 11am-midnight.)

BODENWERDER
☎05533

Deep forests of hundred-year-old trees engulf small clusters of wood-frame houses along the banks of the Weser river in this haven for backpackers and cyclists. It was in this small village that the legendary soldier, wanderer, and liar **Baron von Münchhausen** finally settled down. His tall tales of riding on cannon balls and flying with a team of ducks are now immortalized in statues all over the town.

⬛⬛ TRANSPORTATION AND PRACTICAL INFORMATION. Bodenwerder is best reached from **Hameln** and, unless you plan to hike or bike, demands only an afternoon of attention. Take bus #520 (dir.: Stadtoldendorf) to "Weserbrücke, Bodenwerder," leaving from the train station or from "Münster," on the south edge of Hameln's Altstadt (40min.; 1 per hr., weekends 1 per 2 hr.; €5). A great way to see the countryside is to rent a **bike** from **Karl-Heinz Greef,** Danziger Str. 20. From the end of Große Str. go left on Mühlentor, take the 5th right and then the first left.(☎33 34. €8 per day. Open Mar.-Oct. daily 8:30am-6pm.) The **tourist office,** Weserstr. 3, sells maps (€3) of the trails in the area and a biking map of northwest Germany (€10). (☎405 41; fax 61 52; www.bodenwerder.de. Open M-F 9am-12:30pm and 2:30-6pm, Sa 9am 12:30 pm). **Tours** meet in front of the office. (May-Sept. W at 3pm. €1.50.) Surf the **internet** at **Net L@den,** Mühlentor 3. (☎407 97 90. €2 per hr. Open 9am-noon, 3-6pm.) The **post office** is across from the Rathaus, 37619 Bodenwerder. (Open M-F 8:30am-noon and 3-5:30 pm, Sa 8:30-11:30am.)

⬛⬛ ACCOMMODATIONS AND FOOD. The tourist office prints a list of hotels and private rooms. You can see the pastel-green building of Bodenwerder's **Jugendherberge (HI) ❷,** Richard-Schirmann-Weg (☎26 85; fax 62 03), from the bridge—it's halfway up the steep little mountain. Walk across the Weser and turn left, then turn right on Siemensstr., and follow the signs up Unter dem Berge. Clean rooms and nice views await. (Breakfast included. Reception 4:30-7pm and 9:30-10pm. Curfew 10pm, but you can get a key. 6-bed dorms €17.10, under 26 €14.40.) Bodenwerder's culinary offerings are short of crazy: pizza, baked goods, ice cream. **Akropolis ❷,** Große Str. 44, grills up budget-friendly Greek food, with pitas starting at €3 and heaping grill plates €6-9. (☎931 20. Open 10am-10pm.)

⊙ ♫ SIGHTS AND ENTERTAINMENT. Near the tourist office, Münchhauspl. has Bodenwerder's one sight: the **Münchhausen-Museum Bodenwerder.** On display are a few of the Baron's personal effects, including the legendary pistol he used to shoot his horse down from a steeple. Colorful illustrations of his exaggerated adventures line the walls. (☎405 41. Open daily Apr.-Oct. 10am-noon and 2-5pm. €2, children €1.50). Once a month, a **play** in the gardens reenacts Münchhausen's exploits. (May-Oct. first Su of each month at 3pm. Free.) On the second Saturday of August, Bodenwerder sets the Weser ablaze with its pyrotechnic **festival of lights.** Head to the ▓**Rodelbahn,** Grüne Schleite 1, for the chance to **toboggan** down the mountain on a railed track. Follow the signs in town, or from the tourist office, head away from the river. (☎93 48 00; www.rodelpark.de. 1 ride €2, 3 rides €5.60. Children under 16 €1.50/€4. Open Apr.-Oct. 10am-6pm. Beer garden May-Aug. 10am-7pm.) To enjoy the countryside, bike along the river and through the hills or hike through the forest to various hilltops. Though there are many **bike trails** right along the Weser, the best route is to follow the road left or right from the Weserbrücke bus stop. **Trails** leave from behind the Jugendherberge (on the left as you climb the hill), or from across the river: from the Weserbrücke bus stop, cross the bridge and follow the road as it curves left. Maps are available at the tourist office.

BRAUNSCHWEIG   ☎0531

Now that Braunschweig's duties as a Cold War border town are over, this middleweight city is a thriving cultural center. In 1166, Braunschweig (known in English as Brunswick) was settled by **Henry the Lion.** He erected the famous Braunschweig lion statue (now the city's emblem), built **Burg Dankwarderode,** and inaugurated Braunschweig's growth into a thriving religious and commercial center. Today, in addition to its stunning cathedrals and museums, Braunschweig draws national attention for its 130-year-old soccer tradition and new American football team (the "Lions," of course), thriving shopping centers, and cosmopolitan nightlife.

▐ TRANSPORTATION

Trains: Braunschweig is on the Hannover-Berlin line. To: **Berlin** (1½hr., 1 per hr., €43); **Hannover** (45min., 2 per hr., €9); **Magdeburg** (1¼hr., 2 per hr., €12).

Mitfahrzentrale: Wollmarkt 3 (☎194 40). Walk to the northern tip of the pedestrian zone and up Alte Waage, which turns into Wollmarkt. Open M-F 10am-noon and 2-6pm, Sa 10am-1pm.

Public Transportation: A thorough system of **streetcars** and **buses** covers Braunschweig and its environs (including **Wolfenbüttel;** p. 258). Pick up a **free map** at the tourist office. For more info call ☎383 20 50 or stop by the information center in front of the Hauptbahnhof. Single-ride ticket, valid for 1½hr. and any number of transfers is €1.70. Daypass €4; family day ticket (valid for up to 2 adults and 3 kids) €6.80. Most buses make their final run around 11:30pm.

Taxis: ☎555 55 or 666 66 or 59 91. **Women's Taxi** (Frauennacht-Taxi) ☎444 44.

Car Rental: Europcar, Berliner Pl. 3 (☎24 49 80), across from the train station. Open M-F 7:30am-6pm, Sa 8am-noon, Su 9-11am. €50-110 per day.

Bike Rental: Glockmann + Sohn, Ölschlägern 30 (☎469 23). €10 per day. Open M-F 9:30am-6:30pm, Sa 10am-2pm.

◤◢ ORIENTATION

Braunschweig oversees the farmland between the Lüneburger Heide and the Harz Mountains. The city center is an island ringed by the **Oker** river. The renovated **Hauptbahnhof** is a short way from the city, connected to the south-east-corner of

NIEDERSACHSEN AND BREMEN

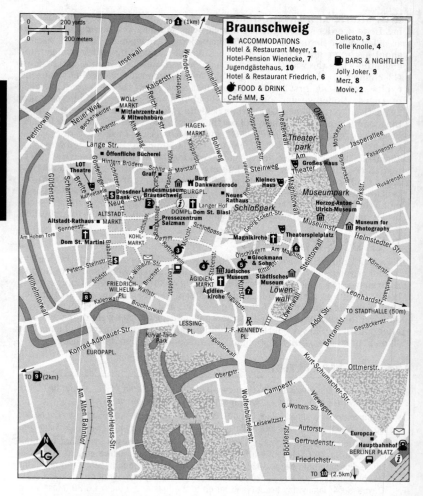

Braunschweig

ACCOMMODATIONS
Hotel & Restaurant Meyer, **1**
Hotel-Pension Wienecke, **7**
Jugendgästehaus, **10**
Hotel & Restaurant Friedrich, **6**

FOOD & DRINK
Café MM, **5**

Delicato, **3**
Tolle Knolle, **4**

BARS & NIGHTLIFE
Jolly Joker, **9**
Merz, **8**
Movie, **2**

the city (called **John-F.-Kennedy-Platz**) by the busy **Kurt-Schumacher-Straße.** North on Auguststr. are **Ägidienmarkt** and **Bohlweg,** the wide eastern boundary of the pedestrian zone. Turn left at Langer Hof to get to the Rathaus. Most streetcars and buses pass through "Rathaus/Bohlweg" stops (downtown) or "JFK-Pl./K.-Schumacher-Str." (15min. from the station). Streetcars #1 and 2 go to all these stops.

⚡ PRACTICAL INFORMATION

Tourist Office: Next to Dom St. Blasi at the corner of Vor der Burg and the Dompl. (☎27 35 50; www.braunschweig.de). Open M-F 9:30am-6pm, Sa 10am-2pm, Su 10am-12:30pm. Staff finds rooms (from €25) and hands out maps for free.

Housing Office (Mitwohnbüro): Wollmarkt 3 (☎130 00; fax 152 52), finds apartments and sublets. Open M-Th 10am-6pm, F 10am-4pm, Sa 10am-1pm.

Currency Exchange: Dresdner Bank, Neuestr. 20, near the Altstadtmarkt. **24hr. ATM.** Open M-Tu and Th 9:30am-6pm, W 9:30am-4pm, F 9:30am-1pm.

Bookstores: Pressezentrum Salzman, in the Burgpassage near the stairs, sells English-language paperbacks and periodicals. Open M-F 9:30am-7:30pm, Sa 9:30am-6pm. **Graff,** a block from the Burgpassage on the corner of Sack and Schild, also has English-language books. Open M-F 9:30am-7pm, Sa 9:30am-6pm.

Library: Öffentliche Bücherei, Hintern Brüdern 23 (☎470 68 38), off Lange Str. Main building open M-F 10am-7pm, Sa 10am-2pm. **Foreign language library** only open Tu noon-6pm, F 11am-4pm. €1 locker for bags. **Internet** €2 per hr.

Emergency: Police ☎110. **Ambulance** ☎192 22. **Fire** ☎112.

Pharmacy: Apotheke am Kennedy-Pl., Auguststr. 19, corner of Kurt-Schumacherstr. (☎439 55). Open M-F 8:30am-6:30pm, Sa 9am-1pm.

Internet Access: Telecafe (on Friedrich-Wilhelm-Str. next to the *Döner Kebap* shop). €1.50 per hr. Open daily 9am-11pm.

Post Office: Berlinerpl. 12-16, 38106, the 16-story building to the right of the train station. Open M-F 8:30am-7pm, Sa 9am-1pm. Smaller **branch,** Friedrich-Wilhelm-Str. 3, is in the Altstadt. Open M-F 9am-7pm, Sa 9am-1pm.

ACCOMMODATIONS

Pick up *Hotels und Gaststätten* (free) at the tourist office for a listing of accommodations and cafes with prices, phone numbers, and city maps.

Jugendgästehaus (HI), Salzdahlumerstr. 170 (☎26 43 20; fax 264 32 70), is right at the bus stop "Klinikum Salzdahlumerstr." on lines #431 or 439 (dir.: Stöckheim). Or, walk left from the station on Berliner Pl. and follow the cab turn-around until you hit Salzdahlumerstr. Turn left, go under the overpasses (be careful after dark), and walk straight (30min.). Large, clean rooms. Breakfast and sheets included. Key deposit €15 or ID. Reception 7-10am and 4-10pm in the building through the gate on the left. €17, under 27 €13.50; triples and doubles also available. ❷

Hotel & Restaurant Meyer, Wenderring 18 (☎34 03 61; fax 33 68 67). Take bus #429 (dir.: Hamburger Str.) or #439 (dir.: Weststadt Donaustr.) to "Maschpl." It's the 2nd building on your right. This family-run hotel offers comfortable rooms with cable TV. Breakfast included. Singles €23-25.50, with bath €46; doubles €41-46/€62. ❷

Hotel & Restaurant Friedrich, Am Magnitor 5 (☎417 28). In the Magniviertel, by the Städtisches Museum. Friendly chatter from cafes below drifts through the windows into spacious, airy rooms right out of *Home & Country;* dreamy top fl. doubles with sofas and large bathrooms. TVs and stereos in all rooms. Restaurant (entrees €4-15) open daily 5pm-midnight. Singles €35; doubles €52. ❹

Hotel-Pension Wienecke, Kuhstr. 14 (☎464 76; www.koehler-wienecke.de). From the station, walk up Kurt-Schumacher-Str. to JFK-Pl. Bear right onto Auguststr. and then Kuhstr. (15min.). Rooms have private bathrooms, fridges, TVs, and big windows that overlook a pedestrian street near the city center. Breakfast buffet included. Singles €35-40, with bath €47-75; doubles with bath €65-99. ❹

FOOD

Bars and *Imbiße* along **Bohlweg** serve pizzas, salads, soups, and small sandwiches at reasonable prices. The Altstadt hosts an open produce market each week (W and Sa 8am-1:30pm). The open **Kohlmarkt** area, southeast of the Altstadtmarkt in the city center, bustles with many pleasant (not cheap) cafes and restaurants. The **Magniviertel's** winding streets, boutiques, and half-timbered houses provide a great setting for a meal or drink. Late-night cavorters head to the Turkish delis and fast food on **Friedrich-Wilhelm-Straße,** near the clubs and bars of the pedestrian zone.

ON THE MENU

OF APES AND OWLS

On a fountain across from the Bäckerlint house in Braunschweig, a curious, smirking little man sits among the animals. Frozen in his amusement for centuries, this Medieval tramp is Till Eulenspiegel, the notorious prankster whose tricks are the subject of many German folk tales. The nationally beloved Till was born in 1350 in Kneitlingen, a little village just east of Braunschweig. Baptized thrice and clever to a fault, Till traveled extensively and made a living on the gullibility of the supposedly educated kings, doctors, artists, and scholars who crossed his path.

Legend has it that Till was working at a bakery in Braunschweig during a rest from his travels. On his first day, he asked the head baker, "What shall I bake?" The baker, thinking this a silly question, replied "Uulen und Aapen" (owls and apes). The next morning, the baker arrived to find hundreds of little cake owls and apes for sale, but no bread.

Although this little trick cost Till his job, the citizens of Braunschweig found it amusing enough to keep the tradition alive. Throughout the city, bakeries sell little bread animals next to their standard wares. Once ridiculed by the baker, Till's owls and apes now occupy a place of honor, promising to make any ordinary sandwich into an entertaining treat.

Café MM, Kuhstr. 6 (☎ 422 44; www.cafe-mm.de), near Hotel-Pension Wienecke. Stylish bistro sells omelettes (€3.50-5) and pasta (€5-7). Weekday lunch specials €3-5. Open M-Th 9am-midnight, F-Sa 9am-1am, Su 10pm-midnight; winter Su-Th until 11pm. ❷

Tolle Knolle, Stobenstr. 15-16 (☎437 33), near the "Bohlweg/Damm" stop. Potato soups, potato omelettes, potato salads, baked potatoes, even "Potatoes of the World," (€3-14). Mr. Potato Head gives his blessing from the bar. Open M-Sa 11:30am-3pm and 5:30-11:30pm, Su 11:30am-3pm and 5:30-10pm. ❷

Delicato, Münzstr. 9 (☎40 07 16), on the corner of Münzstr. and Kattreppeln. A Turkish potluck of gourmet salads and meats. Food sold by weight; a plateful costs around €5. Open M-F 9am-10pm, Sa 9am-4pm. ❷

◎ SIGHTS

All of Braunschweig was once crowded on a small island between offshoots of the Oker; those streams now form a moat around the Altstadt. The city's medieval sights ring the cobbled **Burgplatz,** guarded by the 1166 **bronze lion** of Henry the Lion.

DOM ST. BLASI. From its perch in the southwest corner, the Dom looms over the city center. In 1173, Henry oversaw the destruction of a tiny wooden church on this spot and began the Dom's construction, a project that would take 22 years. The finished basilica contains only one sign of its inheritance: a hauntingly beautiful wooden crucifix above the nave. Fading frescoes cover the ceilings, illustrating the lives of Christ, Mary, John the Baptist, and Thomas of Canterbury. The original stone grave plate portraying Henry and his consort Mathilde stands in front of the altar, but their sarcophagi (and many others) rest in the gloomy **crypt;** pick up a guide at the crypt entrance. *(Open daily 10am-5pm. Crypt €1.)*

DOM ST. MARTINI. Built concurrently with the Dom St. Blasi, the cathedral's magnificent interior includes a Baroque communion altar and a pulpit decorated with sculptures of the "Wise and Foolish Virgins." Wise were the virgins who held their lamps upright as they waited for their grooms, foolish were those who let their lamps tip and got left in the dark. *(An der Marktkirche 10, next door to the Altstadt-Rathaus. Open Tu-F 10am-1pm and 3-5pm, Sa 10am-5pm, Su 10am-noon and 3-5pm. Free.)*

LÖWENWALL. The relaxing Löwenwall is a circular park behind the Städtisches Museum. The obelisk in the center, flanked by lions and two splashing fountains, is a monument to city nobles who died in the Napoleonic Wars. *(Walk up Kurt-Schumacher-Str. from the train station; the Löwenwall will be on your right just before you reach JFK-Pl.)*

MUSEUMS

If you're planning to do a run of Braunschweig's museums in one day, you may want to purchase a *Braunschweiger Museumsverbund Tageskarte* (€5), a day pass valid at all museums and available at all museum desks and tourist offices.

HERZOG-ANTON-ULRICH MUSEUM. One of the first on the continent to welcome the public, this museum houses a small but eye-popping collection of great Western art (mostly Dutch Masters), as well as rotating shows of art and handiwork from all over the world. *(Museumstr. 1. From the pedestrian zone, walk across Bohlweg and down Georg-Eckert-Str., which turns into Museumstr. Or, ride streetcar #5 to "Museumstr." ☎ 122 50. Open Tu and Th-Su 10am-5pm, W 1-8pm. €2.50, students €1.30.)*

BURG DANKWARDERODE. This 19th-century reconstruction of Henry's castle exhibits his medieval collections of tapestries and religious and secular art, including a mantel owned by emperor Otto IV in 1200. The **Rittersaal** (knights' hall) has golden frescoes of Henry and his favorite knight, guarded by the original Braunschweig lion. *(Burgpl. ☎ 12 15 26 18. Museum open Tu and Th-Su 11am-5pm, W 1-2:30pm and 4-8pm. Rittersaal open Tu and Th-Su 10-11am, W 2:30-4pm. €2.50, students €1.30.)*

MUSEUM FOR PHOTOGRAPHY. This constantly evolving museum hosts the work of a different (usually German) contemporary artist every few months. The small building is full of light, and avant-garde flair makes it a nice break from the heavy-duty history of the town. *(Helmstedter Str. 1. Just down Museumstr. from the Ulrich museum. Or, take bus #413 or 443 to "Steintor." ☎ 750 00. Open Tu-Su noon-6pm. €3, students €1.50.)*

LANDESMUSEUM- JÜDISCHES MUSEUM. A branch of the Landesmuseum, the Jewish museum's reconstruction of the old synagogue's main room is, ironically, located in a Gothic monastery. The synagogue's furniture and altar were rescued from the deteriorating building in Hornburg; relics of German Jewish culture complete the collection, with a small exhibit on the British freeing of Bergen-Belsen. The museum is in the monastery of the looming, gothic **St. Aegidienkirche;** the exceptionally peaceful courtyard, dotted with sculptures, is worth a short walk. *(Hinter Ägidien. ☎ 12 15 26 61. Open Tu-Su 10am-5pm. Free.)*

LANDESMUSEUM BRAUNSCHWEIG. The main part of the Landesmuseum has three branches in town and one in Wolfenbüttel. The primary collection is in the **Vierweg-Haus** and ranges from equine armor to dainty Victorian dollhouses; the museum also has a collection of dolls' books with Hitler on the cover and other WWII-era playthings. *(Burgpl. 1. Across from the tourist office. ☎ 121 50. Open Tu-W and F-Su 10am-5pm, Th 10am-8pm. €1.50; combination ticket to all 4 branches €2.50.)*

ENTERTAINMENT AND NIGHTLIFE

Braunschweig's theatrical scene became prominent in 1772 with the first performance of Lessing's *Emilia Galotti* and in 1829 with the premiere of Goethe's *Faust*. The monumental **Staatstheater** (☎ 123 40), built in the Florentine Renaissance style, replaced the old hall in 1861. The **Großes Haus,** Am Theater (☎ 484 28 00), is one of three stages run by the state theater; the other two are the **Kleines Haus,** Magnitorwall 18 (☎ 484 28 00) and the **Theaterspielplatz,** Hinter der Magnikirche 6a (☎ 484 27 97). The Großes Haus presents big-name operas, ballets, musicals, and orchestral concerts (€4-25); the Kleines Haus has everything from Goethe to Mamet to modern dance; Theaterspielpl. also hosts children's theater. (☎500 01 41 for information. Tickets for all three theaters available at the Großes Haus box office M-F 10am-6:30pm, Sa 10am-1pm.) The **LOT Theater,** Kaffeetwete 4a (☎173 53), is the home of a local avant-garde company that puts up comedies, satires, and farces. (Up Gördelingerstr. from the Altstadtmarkt. Box office open M-F 11am-2pm. Tickets €7-10.) The **Stadthalle,** Leonhardpl. (☎707 07), hosts the **Braunschweiger Staatsorchester,** the city orchestra. Several free monthly magazines offer details on local events: *Subway, Da Capo, Cocktail,* and *Braunschweig Bietet.* It's telling that these magazines sometimes direct readers to cities as far away as Hamburg. Still, the Braunschweig scene reaches a simmer on weekends. The most lively area is the intersection of Sack, Vor der Burg, and Schuhstr., and also nearby Neue Str. The **Magniviertel** brims with cafes, bars, and Braunschweig charm.

Movie, Neue Str. 2 (☎437 26), is a bar with a pop music theme. The beer (€2.60 for 0.3L) flows as fast as the conversation, and droves of locals quickly fill the small space. Rock and blues constitute the "feature presentation." Open daily 9am-2am.

Merz, on the corner of Gieseler and Kalenwall near Europapl., is a huge bar in the evening and a club after midnight. The patio swims in beer and night air, while its interior mixes it up with disco-funk, heavy metal, classic rock, and an occasional live band. Cover €3. Su brunch 10am-2pm. Open M-W and Su 3:30pm-2am, Th-Sa 3:30pm-4am.

The Jolly Joker, Broitzemerstr. 220 (☎281 46 60). Streetcar #5 or 6 to "Jodebrunnen," then follow the crowd. This titanic joint has it all: 3 dance floors, a *Biergarten,* fast food, movies, and more bars than you can count. Young regulars show off nasty dance moves. Cover €1.50, movies included. Open F-Sa 9pm-4am.

▶ DAYTRIP FROM BRAUNSCHWEIG: WOLFENBÜTTEL

Catch bus #420 or 421 (€2.35, day pass €5.50) or the train (10min., 2 per hr., €2.40) from Braunschweig's Hauptbahnhof. Phone code ☎05331.

Only a few kilometers away from Braunschweig, Wolfenbüttel maintains a small-town peace. It's hard to believe that until a few centuries ago Wolfenbüttel was the more prominent cultural center, developed with care by the literature-loving dukes of Braunschweig-Lüneburg from 1432 to 1754. However, with the world's largest collection of medieval manuscripts, a brightly painted castle and Altstadt, and a scenic "Little Venice" system of canals, this town can stand alone.

To get to the **tourist office,** Stadtmarkt 7, exit the station and turn right on Bahnhofstr., continuing as it becomes Kommissstr. Just before it bends right, continue straight onto the pedestrian path Wasserwege and follow it to the Markt, where the office is on the far left. The office lists hotels, pensions, and private rooms, and gives city information, including maps, in English. (☎862 80; www.wolfenbuettel-tourismus.de Open M-F 9am-5pm, May-Sept. also Sa-Su 11am-2pm.)

The phrase "paint the town red" may well have been referring to Wolfenbüttel, where many of the historic sights have been slathered in bright candy-colored hues. The pink, towerless **Trinitatskirche** in the Holzmarkt looks more like a palace than a church; only a viewing of the elaborate interior, with three levels of balconies and a glorious altar, reveals its true purpose. (Open Tu 11am-1pm, W 11am-1pm and 2-4pm, Th 3-5pm, Sa 11am-4pm.) In recent years, even the Schloß has jumped in on the radical red action with a new paint job. The castle has the foundation of a 13th-century fortress of the Welfs, but its current appearance is pure Baroque, with a beautifully proportioned 17th-century clock tower. A tour through the painstakingly recreated front rooms of the **Schloßmuseum,** Schloßpl. 13, is like walking through a life-size royal dollhouse. (☎924 60. Open Tu-Su 10am-5pm. €3, students €2.) The Schloß's courtyard hosts open-air performances nearly every day from mid-June to mid-July. Get tickets at the *Braunschweiger Zeitung* office in Wolfenbüttel, Löwenstr. 6 (☎ 800 10).

Priceless, beautiful medieval and Renaissance books line the walls of the ▨ **Herzog-August-Bibliothek.** Founded by Duke Julius in the 16th century, the library later became the largest in Europe under the loving attention of bookworm **Duke August;** his equally bookish relatives donated their collections, including the 1100 Bibles given by quirky Duchess Elizabeth Sophie Marie, some of which are on display. The reading room is to your right as you enter. The library puts on rotating, theme-oriented exhibits which display the priceless collection, including a facsimile of the intricate and stunning **Evangeliar Heinrichs des Löwen,** a gospel drawn up in the late 12th century at the request of Henry the Lion for which the state of Lower Saxony shelled out over €2.5 million in 1983 (the most expensive book in history), which is kept safely locked away. (☎ 80 82 13; www.hab.de. Open Tu-Su 10am-5pm.) Intellectual greats Leibnitz and Lessing were head-librarians here; Lessing, a contemporary of Goethe and celebrated playwright, critic, and journalist, loved the library so much that he lived next door. The **Lessing House** displays early editions of his *Nathan der Weise* and countless personal letters. (Open Tu-Su 10am-5pm.) Across from the castle is the 17th-century **Zeughaus,** whose magenta, high-gabled facade belies its former role as an armory. It now serves as a library annex holding the other half of the Herzog-August collection. (Open M-F 8am-8pm, Sa 9am-1pm. Combination ticket with Lessing House and Zeughaus €3, students €2, under 19 €1, family €6.) The city's other major sight, the **Hauptkirche St. Marien,** stretches its hulking, stony spires across town. A jutting four-faced clock tower and life-sized statues of saints grace the church's exterior. The interior is gift-wrapped in gold and green. (Open Tu-Sa 10am-noon and 2-4pm.)

LÜNEBURGER HEIDE (LÜNEBURG HEATH)

Germany's literary greats have often written about the heather-carpeted **Lüneburger Heide,** which stretches between the Elbe and Aller rivers: the delicate *Heidenröslein* (heath rose) found a role in one of Goethe's *Lieder,* while Heine once compared one lady's bosom to the "flat and bleakly desolate" landscape of the *Heide* (heath). Careful preservation efforts, including a ban on cars, have allowed the Heide to remain the largest moor in Europe, and you'll frequently see horse-drawn carriages and roving gangs of cyclists criss-crossing its 200km width. The undulating countryside oscillates from farm to forest; green gives way to purple from July to September, when the heather flowers. If you want to see the grassy *Heide* during the flowering season, but would prefer not to sleep on it, make reservations now—it seems like all of Germany comes here to bike, hike, motor, and otherwise frolic in the late summer. The most important regional towns are **Lüneburg** and **Celle.** In Lüneburg, the **housing office,** Barckhausenstr. 35 (☎ 04131 737 30; fax 426 06), finds rooms and vacation homes in remote hamlets barely on the map. This office is a wellspring of information, much of it in English, about the Heide, including maps and various tour packages. The staff at the **AG Urlaub und Freizeit auf dem Lande,** Lindrooperstr. 63, 27283 Verden (☎ 04231 966 50; www.bauernhof-ferien.de), provides information on the Heide's *Heu-Hotels* (hay hotels), functioning barns with rooms that farmers rent out to travelers for around €10. They take their name from the hay on which travelers lie (bring a sleeping bag), but all have showers and toilets, and many are surprisingly luxurious.

To see the greater Heide, a **bike** is your best bet. The tourist offices in both Lüneburg and Celle have information on self-guided and group tours. Extensive and detailed maps outline the Heide's major bike tours. The most popular is an 80km route from Lüneburg that follows main roads through the endless woods and pastures of the countryside near Lüneburg and neighboring Harburg. The tour is marked only with tiny white and green bicycle signs, so bring a map. The comprehensive 350km Heide-Rundtour also passes through Lüneburg. Tourist and housing offices will help you plan your trip, including suggesting accommodations in each town along your route, and also help plan **horseback** tours at a number of local farms. Your best bet for **hiking** information is not the tourist office, but the bookstore, which sells a number of hiking and biking guides for the area.

LÜNEBURG ☎ 04131

Legend has it that Lüneburg's salt deposits were discovered when a wild boar fell into a pit and shook salt loose from his bristles as he crawled out. Boar or no boar, Lüneburg made its money during the Middle Ages by supplying nearby trading centers like Lübeck and Hamburg with the salt needed for shipping, storing, and seasoning fish. Although "salt shocks" no longer pose a threat to the world economy and Lüneburg's broader influence has faded, neither the industry nor the town are obsolete. Salt is channeled into the city's famed rejuvenating baths, and the town, with its brick Altstadt and elegant half-timbered houses, retains an ancient grace. Streets are marked by a certain upscale sophistication, brimming with boutiques and chic cafes. It was in this environment that Lüneburg native Heinrich Heine penned one of Germany's greatest Romantic poems, *Die Lorelei*.

▐▐ ▐▌ TRANSPORTATION AND PRACTICAL INFORMATION

Lüneburg serves as the transportation center of the *Heide*. **Trains** run to: **Hamburg** (30min., 2 per hr., €6.90); **Hannover** (1-2hr., 1 per hr., €18.20-22); **Lübeck** (1hr., 1 per hr., €11.10). The city's **bus terminal** is directly outside the train station. (Single ride €1.50, 6-ride card €7.40). Summon a **taxi** by dialing ☎ 520 25 or 520 77, or find one at the main square on Am Sande. The only place to rent **bikes** is **Radspeicher am Bahnhof**, Bahnhofstr. 4, next to the train station. (☎ 26 63 58. €5 per 3hr., €10 per day. €100 deposit and ID required. Reservations recommended. Open M-F 6am-8pm, Sa-Su 9am-8pm.) The **tourist office**, Am Markt, is next to the Rathaus, and books rooms for free. From the station, turn right and then make a left on the first street, Bleckeder Landstr., which becomes Lünertorstr. At the end, turn left onto Bardowickerstr. (☎ 207 66 20; www.lueneburg.de. Open M-F 9am-6pm; also May-Oct. Sa-Su 9am-4pm; Nov.-Apr. Sa-Su 9am-2pm.) **Tours** of the Altstadt leave from the office. (1½hr., May-Oct. daily 11am, Sa also 2pm; Nov.-Apr. Sa 11am only. €5, students €4.) Tickets to shows and concerts can be bought at **LZ Kartenverkauf**, Am Sande 17. (Open M-F 9am-5pm, Sa 9am-1pm). **Deutsche Bank**, Bardowickerstr. 6, is a block from the Rathaus. (Open M-Tu and Th 9am-1pm and 2-3pm, W 9am-1pm, F 9am-2:30pm.) Do **Laundry** at **Wasch Fuxx**, Altenbrückertorstr. 6, a block away from the Johanniskirche. (Wash €3-4, soap included. Dry €1.30 per 15min. Open daily 8am-8pm.) There is a **pharmacy** at Grapengießerstr. 48, just off Am Sande. (Open M-F 8:30-7pm, Sa 8:30-4pm.) **Internet** is available at **The Internet Cafe**, Am Sande 10. (☎ 22 13 17. €1.50 per 30min. Open daily 10am-8pm.) The **post office**, 21335 Lüneburg, is at Sülztorstr. 21. (Open M-F 8:30am-6pm, Sa 9am-1pm.)

⌐⌐ ACCOMMODATIONS AND FOOD

Hotels fill up when the Heide blooms from July to September. The **Jugendherberge Lüneburg (HI)** ❷, Soltauer Str. 133, was somewhat optimistically scheduled to open in August 2004 after remodeling; call before you visit to make sure they're ready for you. Take bus #11 (dir.: Rettmer/Häcklingen) to "Scharnhorststr./DJH" (M-Sa 6am-7:30pm and Su after 1pm; €1.45.) from the train station. (☎418 64; fax 457 47.) **Das Stadthaus** ❹, Am Sande 25, may lighten your wallet, but its location is unbeatable, with a spectacular view of Am Sande square and the Johanniskirche. (☎444 38; www.das-stadthaus.de. Breakfast included. Singles €44-68; doubles €76-92; triples €108.) There are a number of official **campgrounds** along the Elbe and in the wooded suburbs; contact the tourist office for further information.

The overabundance of salt must make Lüneburgers thirsty—at one time the tiny city hosted 80 breweries. Schroederstr. and the city squares are lined with many restaurants and cafes filled with crowds sipping *Lüneburger Pilsner*. **Spar**, Am Sande 8, sells groceries. (Open M-F 8:30am-6:30pm, Sa 8:30am-2:30pm.) **Central** ❸, Schroederstr. 1, offers a broad menu in a dark-wooded, big-windowed tavern a block from the Markt. Try local favorite fish and chips (€6.50), pasta (€5-8) or the big morning breakfast buffets while you get a dose of local chatter on the courtyard patio. (☎40 50 99. Open M-Th 8am-2am, F-Sa 8am-3am, Su 10am-1am.)

◐ ♫ SIGHTS AND ENTERTAINMENT

The fruits of the salt trade are evident in the **Rathaus**, Am Markt, where impressive gold statues stand outside. You'll have to take a tour (German only) to see the interior, which includes fancifully painted walls, elaborate woodcarvings, and a glass jar supposedly containing a bone from Lüneburg's mythic wild boar. (☎30 92 30. Tours daily at 10, 11:30am, 1, 2:30, and 3:30pm. €4.50, students €3.50) The **Deutsches Salzmuseum**, Sülfmeisterstr. 1, is a sleek, dimly-lit shrine to the city's 1000-years of salt production. From the Rathaus, follow Neue Sülze to Salzstr.; follow the signs past the Neukauf supermarket. The wide-ranging exhibit, housed in the town's last remaining salt factory, covers the history, science, and production of the once-precious substance. Evidence of the mines' importance can be seen in a document on display, written by Pope Paulus II in 1465, which granted the Lüneburg mines permission to operate on Sundays and religious holidays. (☎450 65. Open May-Sept. M-F 9am-5pm, Sa-Su 10am-5pm; Oct.-Apr. daily 10am-5pm. €4, students €2.70, family €11. German tours M-F at 11am, 12:30 and 3pm; Sa-Su 11:30am and 3pm. €1.80, children €1.10, family €3.) On the way back to town is the **Brauereimusuem**, Heiligengeiststr. 39, a former brewery that operated for over 500 years. The museum contains an exhibits on every aspect of the brewing process, from the complex purifying machine at the top to the gigantic **wort kettle** at the bottom. Across the courtyard, check out the collection of elaborately decorated historic beer steins. (☎448 04. Open Tu-Su 1pm-4:30pm. Free.)

Lüneburg's giant churches make navigation easy. At Bardowicker Str. and Lünerstr. on the edge of the Rathauspl., **St. Nicolai** and its brick flying buttresses threaten to eclipse the sun. (☎73 15 42. Open daily 9am-5pm. €1 suggested donation. Organ concerts Su 4pm. €6, students €4 during the summer.) Cobbled side streets with ivy-covered houses and boutiques lead to the Gothic **Michaeliskirche**, on Johann-Sebastian-Bach-Pl. in the Altstadt. The imposing brick, wood, and ceramic church was built in 1418 on a foundation of salt; the massive pillars have warped considerably since then, so the interior of the church may induce vertigo. Bach was a student here between 1700 and 1702. (☎314 00. Open M-Sa 10am-5pm,

Su 1:30pm-6pm; Oct.-Apr. until 4pm only.) The majestic **Johanniskirche,** Am Sande, soars over late 13th-century walls sheltering a Gothic altar and Baroque organ. (☎445 42. Open M-W and Su 10am-5pm, Th-Sa 10am-6pm; winter shortened hours and closed M. Free 30min. organ concerts in summer M-F at 12:30pm. Tours of the tower W 1:10pm in summer, June-Sept. also Sa-Su 1 and 3pm.) The town's old **water tower** offers a good view of the city. Tourists take the elevator up to the top, then meander down the stairs through the interior of the water tank, past exhibits on water and the environment. (Open daily Apr.-Oct. 10am-6pm; Nov.-Mar. Tu-Su 10am-5pm. Evening cultural events every full moon. €3.30, students €2.30.)

A trip to the old **Kloster Lüne** makes for a nice jog or a 20min. walk. Take Bardowicker Str. out of the town center, then turn right on Stadtring and make a left on Bockelmannstr. On the far side of the street, walk through the forest to the cloister. The site is also home to Lüneburg's **Teppich Museum,** with a collection of historic rugs and tapestries. (☎52 38. Grounds open summer daily until 6pm. Museum open Tu-Sa 10:30am-noon and 2:30-5pm, Su 11:30am-noon and 2:30-5pm. Closed Oct. 16-Mar. 31. Tours €4, students €3. Museum €3/€2. Combo €6/€4.) Swans chill on the river as locals fill the cafes and bars along picturesque Am Stintmarkt. At night, the sound of rushing water is drowned out by the sound of gushing beer. Groove junkies park in the **Garage,** Auf der Hude 74-80, a 20min. walk from the Altstadt, a large club with DJs playing a variety of modern music. (☎358 79; www.discothek-garage.de. Drinks €2-4. Cover W €1; F €1 before 11pm, €3 thereafter; Sa €1 before 11pm, €4 thereafter. Open F-Sa from 10pm, also June-Aug. W.)

CELLE   ☎05141

The powerful prince electors of Lüneburg moved to Celle (pronounced "TSEL-luh") in 1398 after the **Lüneburg War of Succession** and stayed here until 1705 when the last duke died. During those 307 years, the royalty lavished funds on their home, building a massive castle and promoting the city's growth. The well-maintained half-timbered houses that line Altstadt used to be taxed based on the number of diagonal beams on their facades, which quickly became status symbols.

⬛🏻 TRANSPORTATION AND PRACTICAL INFORMATION. Trains run twice per hr. to **Braunschweig** (1½hr., €11) and **Hannover** (45min., €7). Rent **bikes** at **Fahrradverleih Am Bahnhof,** Bahnhofstr. 27. (€7.50 per day. Open M-F 8:30am-1pm and 3-6pm, Sa 9am-1pm.) The **tourist office,** Markt 14-16 in the Altes Rathaus, reserves rooms for free and sells tickets for the theater at the Schloß (see **Sights,** p. 263). From the train station, walk up Bahnhofstr., which becomes Westcellertorstr., then turn left onto Poststr., which becomes Markt. Or, take bus #3 or 4 to "Schloßpl." and follow the signs. (☎12 12; www.region-celle.de. Open mid-May to mid-Oct. M-F 9am-7pm, Sa 10am-4pm, Su 11am-2pm; mid-Oct. to mid-May M-F 9am-5pm, Sa 10am-1pm.) **Tours** in German start from the bridge in front of the Schloß. (1½hr. May-Oct. and Dec. M-Sa 2:30pm, Su 11am. Apr. and Nov. Sa 2:30pm and Su 11am; €4.) **Decius,** at the corner of Markt and Neue Str. next to the Rathaus, carries English-language paperbacks. (Open M-F 9am-7pm, Sa 9am-4pm.) **Internet** access is available at **Spiel-Treff,** Am Heiligen Kreuz 7. (18+. €0.50 per 7½min., €4 per hr. Open M-Sa 8am-11pm, Su 11am-11pm.) The **post office,** 29221, Runde Str. 8, near Schloßpl., has a 24hr. **ATM.** (Open M-F 8:30am-6pm, Sa 8:30am-1pm.)

🏠🏡 ACCOMMODATIONS AND FOOD. Budget travelers in Celle compete with school groups for limited space. The **Jugendherberge (HI) ❶,** Weghausstr. 2, covered with sky-blue siding and conveniently located near an aromatic cow pasture, reaches new levels in barn-chic. From the train station, take bus #3 (dir.: Boye) to "Jugendherberge." Or walk along the pedestrian path to the left, which becomes Biermannstr., turn left on Bremer Weg, and take the first right onto Petersburgstr.;

it's on the left after 20-30min. (☎532 08; jh-celle@djh-hannover.de. Breakfast included. Lunch €4.50. Reception until 10pm. Curfew 10pm, but a €10 deposit gets you a key. Dorms €17, under 26 €14.20.) **Hotel zur Herberge ❸,** Hohe Wende 14, still feels new and offers stylishly simple, well-outfitted rooms with TVs and showers, albeit at some distance from town. From the tourist office, go left and immediately turn left, walk through the Markt, which becomes Hehlentorstr., and walk straight for 30min., then turn right onto Hohe Wende and continue until the sign. Or, take bus #5 from Schloßpl. (dir.: Vorwerk) and get off at "Harburger Heer Str.," continuing in the direction of the bus to the intersection where Hohe Wende begins. (☎20 81 41; www.nacelle.de. Breakfast included. Singles €42; doubles €58; triples €85.) **Campingplatz Silbersee ❶** is 7km northeast of the town. Take bus #6 (dir.: Vorwerk) to "Silbersee." (☎312 23. €3 per person.) Cafes have cropped up along most every street in the Altstadt. **Alex's Antikcafé ❷,** Schuhstr. 6, in a secluded patio combines simple food (€4-6) with myriad old doodads. (☎236 36. Open M-Sa 8:30am-6pm, Su 9am-6pm.) On the other side of the Altstadt, **Millennium,** Bergstr. 16-17, is a cheap restaurant by day, Irish pub by night. Have a salad (€4.50) or stick with the slightly greasy fish and chips (€2.50) as you scan British tabloids on the ceiling. (☎21 70 16. Open daily 10am-11pm, F-Sa until midnight.)

◪ SIGHTS. Some of the city's finest houses are tucked down alleys; wander any of the smaller streets radiating from Schloßpl. or Großer Pl. in the Altstadt. The **oldest house** in the area, at Am Heiligen Kreuz 26, was built in 1526. The **Stadtkirche** hosts concerts and art exhibits, as well as regular services. A trumpeter plays a church hymn every day at 9am and 5pm from the tower, which provides a view of red- and brown-shingled roofs fading into the countryside. (☎77 35. Church open Tu-Su 10am-6pm. Tower open Apr.-Oct. Tu-Su 10-11:45am and 12:15-4:45pm. €1, children €0.50.) In the Altstadt, the **Rathaus** is richly wrought in the Weser Renaissance style. Right across the road, figures from Celle's colorful history mark the hour on the **Glockenspiel** (daily every hr. 10am-5pm). The ◪**Bomann-Museum Celle,** Schloßpl. 7, has rooms modeled after early Cellean houses, a history of the town and the *Heide* (including an exhibit on Celle's famed *Zweiback* and a room of live heather), and modern art. Special exhibits are on the top and bottom floors. (☎123 72. Open Tu-Su 10am-5pm. €3, students €2.) Celle's landmark **Herzogschloß,** Schloßpl. 13, which stretches out just west of the Altstadt directly across from the Bomann-Museum, has foundations dating to 1292 and grounds with a willow-draped pond and picnickers. Inside is a macabre exhibit of artifacts pertaining to executions and a section devoted to the history of the kingdom of Hannover. (☎55 07 14. Open Tu-Su 10am-5pm. Mandatory 50min. tours for castle rooms Apr.-Oct. Tu-Su 11am-3pm on the hour; Nov.-Mar. 11am and 3pm. €3.50, students €2.50.) The 1740 Baroque **Synagogue,** Im Kriese 24, is one of the nation's oldest standing places of Jewish worship and a memorial to Celle's once-thriving Jewish community. (☎55 07 14. Open Tu-Th 3-5pm, F 9-11am, Su 11am-1pm. Free.)

▶ DAYTRIP FROM CELLE: BERGEN-BELSEN

Take bus #11 from the Celle train station to "Belsen-Gedenkstätte." (1hr., M-F 12:05 and 1:36pm, return 4:54 and 5:34pm.) €4.70. ☎05051 60 11. Open daily 9am-6pm.

The Bergen-Belsen **concentration camp** was founded in 1940 as a "labor camp" for prisoners of war. For five years, 20,000 Soviet prisoners were held here, performing futile, torturous tasks like rolling heavy stones up and down hills, or refilling ditches they had just dug. In January 1945, the POW camp was dissolved and the SS took over, bringing in thousands of Jews, homosexuals, and political dissidents from Auschwitz and other concentration camps. For four unimaginable months, tens of thousands of people lived in cramped conditions and suffered the mindless torture of the Nazis. Over 35,000 died of hunger and typhoid fever, including **Anne Frank,** whose symbolic gravestone is near the Jewish memorial. In total, Bergen-Belsen claimed more than 100,000 lives. In the documents building near the entrance, a permanent exhibit displays the history of the camp and shows a film made by British liberation forces. At the camp boundary, a gap in the trees shows where the fence once stood. Though the grounds of the camp contain no original buildings (they were burned after liberation to prevent the spread of disease), recent excavations have begun to reveal the foundations of buildings that have been covered over by earth and plants. Grass-covered mounds of mass graves can be found throughout the site. A path through the woods leads to the memorial cemetery for Russian POWs (20min.). A stone obelisk commemorates the 30,000 Jewish victims, and a wall is inscribed with memorial phrases in the languages of the victims. Self-guided tours for the camp are available in several languages.

BREMEN ☎ 0421

In the Grimm Brothers' fairy tale, a donkey, dog, cat, and rooster—the Bremen Town Musicians—were on their way to Bremen when their singing terrified a band of robbers. Today, thousands of tourists make a similar pilgrimage, arriving for a photo at the statue of the famed animals. Less photographed but just as meaningful for the town's residents is the statue of semi-mythical **Knight Roland,** a representative of freedom and justice. Bremen is proud of its fiercely-protected independence; this city of a half-million makes up its own autonomous *Land* along with nearby Bremerhaven. Like Hamburg, its Hanseatic sister city to the north, Bremen's medieval ambience has given way to a thriving cosmopolitanism in which cathedrals compete with video art for tourists' attention. The city, though small, is surprisingly lively—its renowned cultural institutions and busy bar scene rival cities several times as large. Even so, Bremen remains proud of its traditions. Every day, horse drawn carriages can be seen delivering the city's supply of **Beck's beer** from the brewery, located just across the banks of the Weser River.

▐ TRANSPORTATION

Flights: Airport Bremen (☎ 559 50) is 3.5km from the city center; take S6 (15min.). Frequent flights to major German cities, the East Frisian Islands, and international destinations (including London, Amsterdam, and Mallorca).

Trains: 2 per hr. to: **Bremerhaven** (1hr., €8.80); **Hamburg** (1-1½hr., €16.80-€21); **Hannover** (1-1½hr., €17.20-22); **Osnabrück** (45min.-1¼hr., €17-24).

Public Transportation: An integrated system of streetcars and buses covers the city and suburbs. 1 ride €1.95, day pass €4.65. In the round building opposite the station, a **VBN** information center has tickets and transportation maps. Open daily 7am-7pm.

Ferries: Hal Över, Schlachte 2, (☎ 33 89 89) shuttles to suburbs and towns on the Weser, ending in Bremerhaven. (3½hr., May-Sept. Sa 8:30am; June-Aug. also W and Th 8:30am, Su 9:30am. €13, round-trip €21). Also offers 1½hr. harbor tours Apr.-Oct. 5 times daily (€8, students €6, children €4). **Reederei Warrings** "speedy" ferries make round-trips to Bremerhaven (€27). Take S2, 3, 4, 6, or 8 to "Domsheide," walk straight to the end of the street, turn right and follow the river to the ships. Both depart from the *Martinianleger,* directly behind Martinikirche.

Taxi: Pick up a taxi at the front or back exits of the Hauptbahnhof or call ☎ 140 14. **Frauen Nachtaxi** (☎ 133 34) operates a women's taxi service daily 6pm-6am.

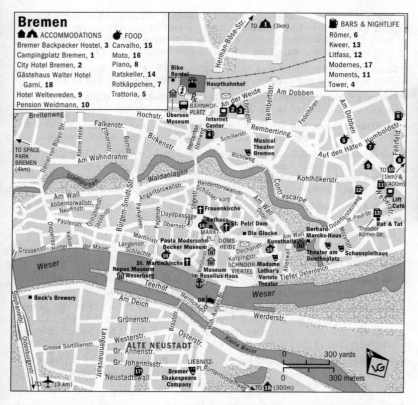

Bremen

▲▲ ACCOMMODATIONS

Bremer Backpacker Hostel, 3
Campingplatz Bremen, 1
City Hotel Bremen, 2
Gästehaus Walter Hotel
    Garni, 18
Hotel Weltevreden, 9
Pension Weidmann, 10

🍴 FOOD

Carvalho, 15
Moto, 16
Piano, 8
Ratskeller, 14
Rotkäppchen, 7
Trattoria, 5

🍸 BARS & NIGHTLIFE

Römer, 6
Kweer, 13
Litfass, 12
Modernes, 17
Moments, 11
Tower, 4

Car Rental: Avis, Bahnhofpl. 15 (☎ 163 36 99, 24hr. reservations 0180 555 77), in the train station. Open M-F 7am-8pm, Sa-Su 8am-8pm.

Bike Rental: Radstation (☎ 30 21 14), between the Hauptbahnhof and the Überseemuseum. €9 per day; weekend €20; week €35. Open M-F 6am-10pm, Sa-Su 9am-8pm.

🔧 🛈 ORIENTATION AND PRACTICAL INFORMATION

Where the Weser River meets the North Sea, Bremen's four neighborhoods await: the tourist-filled **Altstadt,** containing most sights and the oldest architecture; the **Alte Neustadt,** a residential neighborhood south of the Weser; the **Schnoor,** an old neighborhood-turned-shopping-village; and the **Viertel,** a student quarter filled with college kids, clubs, and cheap food. The city is perfect for a stroll, though perhaps not around Ostertorsteinweg or Am Dobben late at night. An **EntdeckerCARD Nordwest,** available at the tourist office, offers free entrance to several attractions in Bremen and the rest of the region, as well as free public transportation within Bremen, and on certain regional train segments. (Valid for 72hr.; €39, children €29.)

Tourist Office: The central office (tourist hotline ☎ 01805 10 10 30, €0.12 per min.; www.bremen-tourismus.de) in the Altstadt on Obernstr. at the Liebfraukirchenhof (S2 or 3 to "Obernstr."), has free maps of the city center, makes room reservations for free, and sells tickets for concerts and festivals. Open M-W 9:30am-6:30pm, Th-F 9:30am-8pm, Sa-Su 9:30am-4pm. A **second office** inside the Hauptbahnhof performs the same tasks. Open M-F 8am-8pm, Sa-Su 9:30am-6pm. **Walking tours** of the Altstadt leave daily from the central office. (2hr., daily at 2pm, Apr.-Sept. also Sa 11am. €6.50.)

Consulate: UK, Herrlichkeit 6 (☎59 07 01). Open M-F 9am-noon and 2:30-3:30pm. They don't handle visa problems; for those, call Düsseldorf (☎0211 944 81 60).

Currency Exchange: Reisebank, inside the Hauptbahnhof. Exchanges currency and wires money via Western Union. Open daily 8am-8pm.

Bookstores: Thalia, Sögerstr 36-38 (☎30 29 20) in the pedestrian zone; helpful staff will lead you to the English paperbacks. Open M-F 9:30am-8pm, Sa 9:30am-6pm.

Gay Resources: Rat- & Tat-Zentrum, Theodor Körnerstr. 1 (☎70 00 07). Take S2 or 3 to "Theater am Goethepl.," and continue on, veering right onto St.-Pauli-Str. Provides information about gay events and services. Open M-F 11am-1pm. Also in the building is the **AIDS Beratungsstelle** (☎70 41 70). Open M, W, F 11am-1pm, Tu 3-6pm.

Women's Resources: Info pertinent to women travelers is available on the web at www.gesche.bremen.de. The tourist office sells women's city maps for €1.

Laundromat: Schnell and Sauber, Vor dem Steintor 105. Take S2, 3, or 10 to Brunnenstr. Wash €3.50. Dry €0.50 per 12min. Open daily 6am-11pm.

Emergency: Police ☎ 110. **Fire** and **Ambulance** ☎ 112.

Pharmacy: Päs Apotheke, Bahnhofspl. 5-7 (☎144 15). Straight from the station's main exit, on the right side of the Platz. M-F 8am-6:30pm, Sa 8am-2pm.

Internet Access: Internet Center Bremen, Bahnhofspl. 22-28 (☎277 66 00), in the DGB building to the left of the main entrance. €1 per 20min. Open M-Sa 10am-10pm, Su noon-8pm. Also at **Lift Internetcafe,** Weberstr. 18 (☎774 50), just off Ostertorsteinweg. Take S2 or 3 to "Wulwesstr." €1.60 per hr. Open M and W-Su 3pm-midnight.

Post Office: Main office at Domsheide 15, 28195 Bremen (☎367 33 66), near the Markt. Open M-F 7am-7pm, Sa 9am-1pm. **Additional office** on Bahnhofspl. 21, left of the train station. Open M-F 9am-8pm, Sa 9am-1pm.

▚ ACCOMMODATIONS AND CAMPING

▨ **Bremer Backpacker Hostel**, Emil-Waldmann-Str. 5-6 (☎223 80 57; www.bremer-backpacker-hostel.de). A 5min walk from the station's main exit: turn left, walk down An der Weide, turn right onto Löningstr., and make another right onto Emil-Waldmann-Str. Fully-stocked kitchen, washing machines, and a room with TV and **Internet** (€1 per 30min.). 5- to 7-bed rooms €16; singles €27; doubles €44; triples €60; quads €18. ❷

Pension Weidmann, Am Schwarzen Meer 35 (☎498 44 55). Take S2, 3, or 10 to "St. Jürgen-Str." and follow the left fork for 2 blocks; pension is on the right. Decor is dated, but plush comforters and well-kept rooms complete with coffee-makers and TVs are fit for royalty. Breakfast included. Call ahead. Singles from €21; doubles from €42. ❷

Gästehaus Walter Hotel Garni, Buntentorsteinweg 86 (☎55 80 27; fax 525 95 10). Take S4, 5, or 6, or N6 or 11 to "Theater am Leibnizpl." Left onto Buntentorsteinweg. Large rooms with hardwood floors in a quiet neighborhood. Breakfast included. Singles €25-40; doubles €40-60. ❸

Hotel Weltevreden, Am Dobben 62 (☎780 15), off Ostertorsteinweg. S10 (dir.: Sebaldsbrücke) to "Humboldtstr." On your right after 1 block. Comfortable rooms just steps from Bremen's boisterous nightlife. Breakfast included. Reception daily 8am-8pm. Singles €32, with shower €42, with shower and toilet €50; doubles €52/€56/€65. ❸

City Hotel Bremen, An der Weide 18-19 (☎364 80 52; www.city-hotel-bremen.de). From the station, head left on An der Weide; it's the peach facade on the right. This new hotel makes up for lack of personality with sparkling rooms and a great location. Breakfast €6.50. Reception 24hr. Singles €40, with shower €50; doubles €55/€75. ❸

Camping: Campingplatz Bremen, Am Stadtwaldsee 1 (☎21 20 02; fax 21 98 57). Shaded campground near the university. Take S8 to "Kulenkampfallee," then bus #28 to "Campingpl." Wash and dry €2.50 each. Reception daily 8am-1pm and 3pm-10pm. €4-6 per site, €4.50 per adult, €2.65 per child. Showers and electricity free. ❶

🍴 FOOD

For cheap eats try the open-air **market** (daily 8am-2pm) or follow the bronze pig statues to the take-out cafes on **Sögerstraße** in the Marktpl. To escape the tourist mob, head to **Auf den Häfen,** where even locals get lost in the tiny cobblestone alleys crammed with gourmet restaurants and trendy *Kneipen.* Student pubs proliferate farther east in the **Viertel** and around **Ostertorsteinweg** (see **Nightlife,** p. 270). The immensely popular **Schlachte,** on the banks of the Weser, is home to a long stretch of bars and restaurants with huge outdoor seating areas. For **groceries,** there is a **EuroSpar** at the back of the train station. (Open M-Sa 8am-8pm.)

🎹 Piano, Fehrfeldstr. 64 (☎785 46). S2, 3, or 10 to "Sielwall," walk a block towards the Altstadt; it is on your right. Students and locals flock to this neighborhood institution for coffee, conversation, the huge breakfast spreads (€5-8), and big pizzas (€5-8). Open daily from 9am. Breakfast M-F until 4pm, Sa-Su until 5pm. ❷

Trattoria, Auf den Häfen 12-15 (☎70 03 35). S10 to "Humboldtstr.," turn right on Auf den Häfen and then right again down the corridor beneath the neon sign. Ideal for a warm summer evening. Italian bistro with excellent pasta dishes (€5-8) and tasty, if somewhat more expensive, meat dishes (€12-19). ❸

Rotkäppchen, Am Dobben 97 (☎754 46). S10 to "Humboldtstr." Has heaping lunch specials (€6-7), weekend breakfast buffets (€5-8.50), and light salads, crepes, and veggie meals (€4-9) under skylights in a mellow atmosphere. Open daily 10am-2am. ❷

Carvalho, Kolpingstr. 14 (☎336 50 80). S2, 3, 4, 6, or 8 to "Domsheide," 2 blocks behind the post office. Carvalho combines colorful tapas (€7-10) and specialty dishes (€9-14) with good tequila and an electric atmosphere. Open daily from 6:30pm. ❸

Moto, Schlachte 22 (☎30 21 13). S1, 2, 3, or 8 or bus #25, 26, or 27 to "Am Brill" and turn left along the river. A great deal on the wildly popular Schlachte, this understated pan-Asian restaurant serves tasty soup (€3-5) and noodle dishes (€7-10) with tons of veggie options. The best deals are the €7 lunch specials. Open daily noon-midnight. ❸

Ratskeller, Am Markt 1, (☎32 16 76) in the basement of the Rathaus. S2 or 3 to "Obernstr." German wine has been served in these vaulted chambers since 1405. Try one of the 650 wines (€4-6 per glass), or treat yourself to a meal (€10-18 for meaty entrees such as *Rinderrouladen*; €6.70 lunch special). Open daily 11am-midnight. ❹

👁 SIGHTS

ST. PETRI-DOM. A survivor of WWII, the 1200-year-old St. Petri Dom was excavated from 1973 to 1976, revealing many treasures that were used to restore the church to its medieval glory. The interior now explodes with color, its canopied vaults embellished by wall paintings. The Gothic architecture of the present-day Dom dates back to the first half of the 13th century. If you look closely, you can see the "Bremen Church Mouse," a tiny rodent carved into a pillar near the south entrance to the choir. A climb up 265 steps offers a meshed-over glimpse of the hubbub in the market square below. *(Sandstr. 10-12. ☎ 36 50 40. Cathedral open M-F 10am-5pm, Sa 10am-2pm, Su 2-5pm. Free. Tower open Easter-Oct. €1, children €0.70.)* In a corner of the cathedral is the **Dom Museum,** whose dim corridors preserve original 15th-century frescoes and the remains of 900-year-old silk attire, recovered from the bodies of entombed archbishops unearthed during the archaeological dig. *(☎ 365 04 41. Open Apr.-Oct. M-F 10am-5pm, Sa 10am-1:30pm, Su 2-5pm; Nov.-Mar. M-F 11am-4pm, Sa 10am-noon, Su 2-5pm. Call in advance for English tours. €2, students and children €1.)* Walk around and behind the church into the **Bibelgarten,** which provides the only access to the macabre **Bleikeller,** in the basement of the Dom. Here, an assortment of mummified corpses have been on display for three centuries, including the unfortunate loser of a student duel, a soldier from the Thirty Years' War, and a 100-year-old mummified monkey and cat; not for the squeamish. *(Open M-Sa 10am-5pm, Su noon-5pm. €1.40, children €0.70.)* Just past the *Domshof,* turn left on Domsheide to reach the **Schnoorviertel,** Bremen's district of historic, tiny red-roofed houses, which now house a variety of small shops and restaurants.

RATHAUS. Bremen's Altstadt surrounds the Rathaus and its stunning Renaissance facade. Impressively, the hall and surrounding market square are largely preserved in their original states, since the English WWII bomber assigned to obliterate the area deliberately missed his target. On the west side of the Rathaus is Gerhard Marcks's famous 1951 sculpture *Die Musikanten*—the town's symbol—which portrays the Grimms' donkey, dog, cat, and rooster in their robber-foiling stance. *(Take S3 or 4 to "Obernstr." Entrance only with tours, lasting 45min., offered M-Sa 11am, noon, 3 and 4pm. €4, children and students €2.)*

BECK'S BREWERY. Guides usher wide-eyed beer aficionados through this giant brewery, explaining the drink's Sumerian origins and inspiring awe with mind-boggling statistics (e.g., Beck's annual export of 320 million liters). The highlight arrives at the end of the 2hr. tour with a tasting challenge and two free rounds of beer for the winners. The free beer itself is worth more than the cost of admission; don't miss the bitter regional specialty, Haake Beck, or the family's newest member, Beck's Gold. Reservations required, but a few afternoon spots are held for drop-ins. *(Am Deich 18-19. Take S1, 2, 3, or 8, or bus #25, 26, or 27 to "Am Brill." Cross the Bürgermeister-Smidt Bridge, then turn right on Am Deich. Walk towards the Stephan Bridge to get to the Visitors Center. ☎ 50 94 55 55; www.becks.de. Open Tu-Sa 11am-5pm, Su 10am-3pm. German tours every hr. on the hr. English tours daily 1:30pm. €3; children under 13 free.)*

BÖTTCHERSTRAßE. A project of Ludwig Roselius, millionaire inventor of decaffeinated coffee, this street was transformed from a cramped artisans' quarter to a graceful unity of Art Nouveau and Expressionist architectural elements. The **Museum im Roselius-Haus,** a melange of ornate tapestries and medieval tableware, displays Roselius' living quarters. *(Böttcherstr. 6-10. Take S2, 3, 4, 6, or 8 to "Domsheide." ☎ 336 50 77. Open Tu-Su 11am-6pm. €5, students and children €3, includes admission to Paula Modersohn-Becker Museum.)* Tourists huddle every day at noon, 3, and 6pm awaiting the magic of the **Böttcherstraße Glockenspiel.** Bells ring and part of the tower rotates to reveal 10 images that depict the exploits of famous explorers.

🏛 MUSEUMS

The strong civic spirit in Bremen has created a long and proud tradition of citizens rallying around the arts, leading to a rich collection of museums. Indeed, Bremen has high hopes of being named "cultural capital" of Europe in 2010.

KUNSTHALLE. Bremen's excellent art collection includes paintings and sculptures dating from the 15th century to the present. Modern works offering new interpretations of old classics are interspersed throughout the galleries. The museum's best holdings are those of the German Expressionists and French Impressionists. *(Am Wall 207. Take S2 or 3 to Theater am Goethepl. ☎32 90 80. Open Tu 10am-9pm, W-Su 10am-5pm. €5, students €2.50.)*

NEUES MUSEUM WESERBURG BREMEN. Almost all of this museum's collection is privately owned, which allows it to display an evolving array of works by contemporary artists from across the globe. Captions in both English and German. *(Teerhof 20. Off the Bürgermeister-Smidt Brücke on an island in the Weser River. Take S1, 2, 3, or 8, or bus 25, 26, or 27 to "Am Brill." ☎59 83 90. Open Tu-F 10am-6pm, Sa-Su 11am-6pm. €5, students and children €3. Tours daily in German; €7, students and children €4.)*

ÜBERSEE MUSEUM. This museum delivers a *"Weltreise im Minutentakt"* (a trip around the world in minutes), with displays ranging from a Shinto garden to a South Sea fishing village. When you're finished with the life-size wildlife dioramas and artifacts, head upstairs for an exhibit on the history of Bremen, Bremerhaven, and the container shipping business. *(Bahnhofspl. 13, next to the train station on the right. ☎16 03 81 01. Open Tu-F 9am-6pm, Sa-Su 10am-6pm. €6, students €4, children €2.50.)*

PAULA MODERSOHN-BECKER HAUS. In honor of Modersohn-Becker's work, Ludwig Roselius established this museum, the first ever dedicated to the work of a female artist. Her pre-Expressionist paintings, rooted in an omnipresent maternal theme, are accompanied by works of other German artists such as **Bernard Hötger,** an artist and the architect responsible for many of the Böttcherstr.'s buildings. *(Böttcherstr. 6-10. Take S2-6 or 8 to "Domsheide." ☎336 50 77. Open Tu-Su 11am-6pm. Tours Su 11:30am and W 6pm. €5, students €3, including admission to Roselius Haus.)*

GERHARD-MARCKS-HAUS. Devoted to contemporary sculpture, this elegant indoor and outdoor sculpture garden features works by Marcks (1889-1981), creator of Bremen's famous *Die Musikanten*, along with changing exhibitions of avant-garde sculpture. *(Am Wall 208. Next to the Kunsthalle. ☎32 72 00. Open Tu-Su 10am-6pm. Tours Th at 5pm. €3.50, students and children €2.50.)*

🎭 ENTERTAINMENT

Known for operas, musicals, and dance, the 900-seat **Theater am Goetheplatz**, Am Goethepl. 1-3, is the largest of Bremen's theaters. Take S2 or 3 to "Theater am Goethepl." Its sister theaters are the **Schauspielhaus,** Ostertorsteinweg 57a, directly behind the Theater am Goethepl., which performs new drama, and the **Musical Theater Bremen,** Richtweg 7-13, which favors musicals. Take S4, 6, or 8 to "Herdentor." Tickets for all three theaters range from €12-50 and must be purchased at the Theater am Goethepl. box office. (☎365 33 33. Open M-F 11am-6pm, Sa 11am-2pm.) The **Bremer Shakespeare Company,** in the Theater am Leibnizplatz, enjoys an unrivaled national reputation for its productions of some obscure English playwright. Take S4, 5, or 6 to "Theater am Leibnitzpl." (☎50 03 33. Box office open Tu-Sa 3-6pm. Tickets €7.50-16.) For the more bizarre, check out the two-part show at **Madame Lothar's Variete Theater,** Kolpingstr. 9, a cabaret *Travestie* comedy performed W-Sa. Shows start at 9:30pm; doors open at 8pm. Take S2-6 or 8 to "Domsheide" and turn right onto Komturstr. (☎337 91 91 Tickets W-Th €15, F-Sa €22) The **Bremer Philharmoniker** and the more experimental **Deutsche Kammerphilharmonie Bremen** both perform inside Bremen's new concert hall, **Die Glocke,** Domsheide 4-5, renowned for its excellent acoustics. (Tickets ☎33 66 99.)

The last two weeks of October find Bremen residents drinking beer and eating tubs of lard cakes in honor of the city's market rights during the colorful **Freimarkt** fair—an annual event since 1035. Bremen also hosts big concerts often held in the **Stadthalle** (☎35 36 37; box office open M-F 8am-6pm, Sa 9:30am-1pm), located behind the train station, and the **Weserstadion**. (☎491 31 10.) Summertime brings performances to parks around the city; a children's production of Bremen's famous fairy tale takes place on the main Platz every Sunday at noon and 1:30pm. Check the tourist office, the theaters, or the free publication *Bremer Umschau* for schedules and prices. *Foyer*, free at many museums, lists theater, music, film, and art events. *Belladonna* lists cultural events of special interest to women. The indispensable *Prinz* provides monthly party listings and the lowdown on the Bremen scene (€1 at the tourist office and newsstands). *Partysan*, a Hamburg magazine, also lists big parties in Bremen (free at many cafes).

🎧 NIGHTLIFE

To experience Bremen's raucous pub culture, head for the **Viertel;** for slightly more touristed, multi-floor clubs, hit the **Rebertiring**, across from the main station.

Modernes, Neustadtswall 28 (☎50 55 53; www.modernes.de). S1 or 8, or bus #26 or 27 to "Hochschule Bremen," backtrack 1 block, and turn right on Neustadtswall. In a gutted movie theater, this popular disco hosts weekly specials ranging from flamenco concerts to Depeche Mode parties. On warm nights, the retractable roof makes way for a starry canopy. Cover €3.50-4.50. Special events €9. Disco open F-Sa 11pm-4am.

Litfass, Ostertorsteinweg 22 (☎70 32 92). S2 or 3, or N12 to "Wulwesstr." An all-day, all-night bastion of alternative chic in bar form. A big outdoor terrace and open facade make it the place to see and be seen. Open Su-Th 10am-2am, F-Sa 10am-4am.

Moments, Vor dem Steintor 65 (☎792 66 33; www.club-moments.de). S2 or 3, or N12 to "Sielwall," and another 1½ blocks farther. A mixture of live music and dance hall fun. Hosts events such as the Turkish music nights. Open Th-Sa 10pm-6am.

Römer, Fehrfeldstr. 31 (☎70 09 64), 2 blocks off Oststeintorweg. Tram 10 to "Humboldtstr.," follow Humboldtstr., turn right on Fehrfeldstr. Long bar and big dance floor with a young crowd. Weekends €2-4. Open Tu-Th 10pm-2am, F-Sa 10pm-4am.

Tower, Herdentorsteinweg 7 (☎32 33 34). From the train station cross Bahnhofpl. and continue onto Herdentorsteinweg. Behind an electric blue facade, Bremen's goth and grunge types groove to heavy alternative beats. Weekend cover €3.50. Open Tu and F-Sa from 9:30pm until the party's over.

Kweer, Theodor Körnerstr. 1 (☎70 00 08). S2 or 3 to "Theater am Goethepl.," and veer right onto St.-Pauli-Str. Though Bremen isn't known for gay nightlife, the relaxed atmosphere of this intimate cafe and *Kneipe* attracts a crowd of regulars. All proceeds go to AIDS education. Open 1st and 3rd Tu of the month. Open 8pm-midnight, every W 8pm-midnight, F 8pm-1am, Su 3-6pm.

BREMERHAVEN ☎0471

Flooded with maritime culture, the port city of Bremerhaven was established in the 18th century to handle an ever-increasing number of ships that couldn't clear the shallow passage to Bremen, farther south along the Weser River. Bremerhaven has long been Germany's main point of immigration, a fact reflected today in the diversity of its inhabitants. Many of the city's residents are employed at the harbor —Bremerhaven boasts one of the world's largest container ports. The city celebrates its maritime tradition at the end of every July with a massive **Hafenfest** (harbor festival). Bremerhaven's main commercial avenue, **Bürgermeister-Smidt Straße,** surrounds the **Columbus Center Mall,** across from which towers the elaborate single spire of the **Große Kirche.** From the train station, take bus #502, 505, 506, 508, or 509 to "Große Kirche." Nearby, the carnivalesque **Alter Hafen** (Old Harbor) overflows with beer and snack stands. Most of Bremerhaven's attractions are located along the **Seemeile,** a "sea mile" of shore by the harbor. The harbor is one block behind the Columbus Center; take bus #526 from the Hauptbahnhof to "Alter Hafen."

Bremerhaven is easily reached from Bremen by **train** (45min., 1-2 per hr., €8.80) and a daily **ferry** (p. 264). Local **bus** tickets cost €1.85; a day pass is €4.65. Rent **bikes** from **Der Rad Geber,** Bürgermeister-Smidt-Str. 138 (☎941 38 30. €7 per day, €19 for 3 days, €33 per week. Open M-F 9:30am-1pm and 2-6:30pm.) The **tourist office,** on the second floor of the Columbus Center, provides free maps and accommodations listings. (☎430 00; www.bremerhaven-tourism.de. Open M-W 9:30am-6pm, Th-F 9:30am-7pm, Sa 9:30am-4pm.) A branch at the harbor, **TouristCenter Hafeninsel,** H.-H.-Meier-Str. 6, has the same services (☎94 64 61 20. Open daily 9am-6pm.) Find **Internet** at the **call shop** on the corner of Friedrich-Ebert-Str. and Bismarckstr. across from the train station. (€2 per hr. Open M-Sa 9am-midnight, Su 11am-midnight.) The **post office,** Friedrich-Ebert-Str. 77, 27570 Bremerhaven, is to the left as you leave the train station. (Open M-F 8:30am-6pm, Sa 8:30am-12:30pm.)

The ▣**Deutsches Schifffahrtsmuseum** is along the harbor at Hans-Scharoun Pl. 1. Take bus #501 or 511 to "Deutsches Schifffahrtsmuseum." Models, relics, and full-size boats fill the expansive interior, documenting the evolution of shipbuilding and sea travel. The museum's prized possessions are its original Viking boats and the *Hansekogge,* a Hanseatic merchant ship built in 1380 and painstakingly reconstructed with remnants salvaged from the deep. Drive remote-control boats in the basement "Miniport," or climb aboard museum ships docked in the harbor outside. (Open Apr.-Oct. daily 10am-6pm; Nov.-Mar. Tu-Su 10am-6pm. Museum ships open Apr.-Oct. only. €5; students, seniors, and children €3.50, family €12.) Across the docks, clamber through the hatches of the 1945 **Technikmuseum U-Boot Wilhelm Bauer,** one of the few German WWII submarines that was neither sunk nor scrapped. The control room is off-limits, but visitors can man a periscope, examine torpedo tubes, and feel the claustrophobia of the living quarters. (Open Apr.-Oct. daily 10am-6pm. €2.50, under 18 €2.) Farther up the harbor, sea lions, mountain lions, chimpanzees, and penguins cavort in the **Zoo am Meer,** but the polar bears are the stars of the show. (☎420 71. €6, students 4.50. Open Apr.-Sept. 9am-7pm, Mar. and Oct. 9am-6pm, Nov.-Feb. 9am-4:30pm. Polar bear feeding 4pm.)

Though Bremerhaven's attractions are easily experienced as a daytrip from Bremen, those opting to spend the night can find relatively cheap, spartan rooms far from the pedestrian center; anything near the harbor is probably overpriced. The **Jugendgästehaus-Jugendherberge (HI) ❷,** Gaußstr. 54-56, offers a dazzling array of amenities, including a mini-gym and sauna. Take bus #502, 509, or 511 to "Gesundheitsamt." All the rooms in the *Gästehaus* are private. (☎856 52 or 98 20 80; fax 874 26. Breakfast included. Reception 7am-6pm. Reservations strongly recommended. €18.10; under 27, €15.40. Bedding €1.10 extra.) In the Lehe district, **Hotel Columbus ❸,** Lange Str. 145, provides functional rooms with TVs and bath at fair prices. Take bus #502 or 508 to "Lange Str." (☎454 40. Singles from €34; doubles from €59.) Bremerhaven's nightlife center, littered with international eateries and late-night *Kneipen,* can be reached on bus #505, 506, or 511 to "Schleusenstr." or by taking Bürgermeister-Smidt-Str. northwest from the pedestrian zone. Closer to the downtown, **Mendocino,** Grazerstr. 55, a cozy cocktail bar and dance club one block off Bürgermeister-Smidt-Str., attracts a crowd of 20- and 30-somethings. After a bar-hopping Saturday night, stop by for a free Sunday breakfast beginning at 3:30am. (☎300 22 22. Open F-Sa from 10pm.)

OSNABRÜCK ☎ 0541

Around the year 1300, the inhabitants of two century-old villages built a wall that surrounded both and called the unified town Osnabrück. It quickly became an important commercial center, and when warring parties sat down to end the Thirty Years' War, they divided their negotiations between Osnabrück and Münster. After five years of tedious summits, peace was announced to Osnabrück's citizens from the steps of the Rathaus. The townspeople gaped incredulously, then began singing. Their song is over, but 350 years later, Osnabrück remains at peace.

E7 TRANSPORTATION AND PRACTICAL INFORMATION. Trains to: **Düsseldorf** (2hr., 1 per hr., €28); **Hannover** (1½hr., 1 per hr., €19); **Münster** (30min., 1-2 per hr., €11). **Buses** travel around the city center (€0.80) and to the outer zones (€1.50-3.70). A *Tageskarte* (€2.70-7.20) is good for a day of unlimited travel from 9am-midnight. For a **taxi**, call ☎320 11. Rent **bikes** at **Radstation Osnabrück**, to the right as you exit the train station. (☎25 91 31. ID required. €6 per day, €25 per week. Open M-F 6am-10pm, Sa-Su 8am-8pm.) The **tourist office**, Bierstr. 22-23, is across the street from the Rathaus. Take bus #31 to "Heger Tor" and follow Hegerstr., or from the station, walk up Möserstr. as it turns into Herrenteich Str., follow the curve around, and turn onto Krahnstr., which becomes Bierstr. The staff books rooms and provides city maps for free. (☎323 22 02; www.osnabrueck.de. Open M-F 9:30am-6pm, Sa 10am-4pm.) Wash clothes at **Münz Waschcenter**, on the corner of Kommenderiestr. and Johannistorwall. (Wash €3.50, soap included. Dry €0.50 per 15min. Open daily 6am-11pm.) **Internet** is available at the Stadtbibliothek across from the tourist office. (€0.50 per 12min. Open Tu-F 10am-6pm, Sa 10am-1pm.)

▐▐ ACCOMMODATIONS AND FOOD. South of the town center is the standard and clean **Jugendgästehaus Osnabrück ❷**, Iburger Str. 183a. From the station, take bus #62 (dir: Zoo) to "Kinderhospital." (☎542 84; fax 542 94. Wheelchair accessible. Breakfast and sheets included. Reception 7am-midnight. Dorms €19, under 27 €15.60.) The sparkling independent hostel **Penthouse Backpackers ❶**, Möserstr. 19, lures travelers with luxurious facilities and a rooftop terrace. Walk down Möserstr. from the station; it's on the right. (☎600 96 06. Reception 8-11am and 5-8pm. Dorms €13; doubles €30.) **Hotel Jägerheim ❸**, Johannistorwall 19a, has basic singles and large doubles. From the station, turn left on Konrad-Adenauer-Ring, which becomes Petersburgerwall and then Johannistorwall. (☎216 35. Reception until 9pm. Reservations recommended. Singles €22-24, with bath €34; doubles €44/€52.) **Camp** at **Freizeitpark Attersee ❶**, Zum Attersee 50. From the station, take bus #13 to "Attersee." (☎12 41 47. €2.80 per person, €3 per tent.)

A number of discount **supermarkets** line Johannisstr. For sit-down fare, **Crêperie ❷**, Markt 24, matches filling salads and crepes (€3-8) with an endless complimentary bread basket. (☎227 15. Open 10:30am-midnight.) **Paradieschen ❸**, Osterberger Reihe 10, serves up vegetarian specials (small portions €3.80-5, large portions €7.20-9) and fresh juices. (☎243 40. Open M-F 11am-7pm, Sa 11am-4pm.) Occupying a 19th-century warehouse, **Lagerhalle**, Rolandsmauer 26, is the town's nightlife nucleus, with a popular *Kneipe*, a restaurant with international and vegetarian specials (all from €3), an art-house movie theater, and frequent rock concerts, cabarets, and dance parties. Take bus #11 or 12 to Heger Tor. (☎33 87 40, www.lagerhalle-osnabrueck.de. Open M 7pm-1am, Tu-Th 6pm-1am, F-Sa 6pm-2am, Su 6:30-11pm. Summer closed Su.) Retreat to the trendy bar **Pferde haben keine Flügel** (horses have no wings), Am Kamp 81-83, to enjoy tapas (€1.50-5) and beer (€2.20) under a soothing panoramic projection of ocean waves or next to the horse mural. (☎202 79 10. Open daily 2pm-midnight.)

◙ SIGHTS. Osnabrück's perfectly preserved late-Gothic style **Rathaus** has much of the original furnishing and decor, thanks to town officials with the foresight to hide valuable items in the countryside during WWII. A stately series of portraits depicting 17th-century leaders hangs in the **Peace Hall,** where they participated in the endless debates. (Open M-F 8am-8pm, Sa 9am-4pm, Su 10am-4pm. German tours Sa-Su 11am. Free.) Next to the Rathaus, the **Marienkirche** was almost completely destroyed during the war and then rebuilt in the Baroque style. Tread lightly; the choir floor is a sea of stones marking clergymen buried below. (Open Apr.-Sept. M-Sa 10am-noon and 3-5pm; Oct.-Mar. M-Sa 10:30am-noon and 2:30-4pm. Climb the tower Su from 11:30am-1pm; €1.50, students €1, children under 12 €0.50.) Osnabrück's massive **Dom,** Kleine Domsfreiheit 24, has been accumulating religious relics for centuries, including the remains of the cathedral's patron saints, acquired by Charlemagne himself. (☎31 84 81. Open Tu-F 10am-6pm, Sa-Su 11am-2pm. Free. Treasury open Tu-Su 11am-6pm. €2, students €1.)

The ◙**Felix Nussbaum Haus** exhibits the largest collection of the artist's work, paintings that capture the anxiety and horror the Holocaust. As a promising Jewish avant-garde artist in the 1930s, Nussbaum was increasingly persecuted as the Nazis gained power. After fleeing to Belgium, he and his wife were eventually transported to Auschwitz, where they were executed in 1944. The collection of over 160 works are displayed in a deconstructionist building, designed by American architect **Daniel Libeskind** to evoke an external realization of the artist's tangled emotions and make visitors feel as disoriented as the subjects of the paintings. Insightful English audio commentary clarifies the significance of each room. The attached **Kulturgeschichtliche Museum** thoroughly chronicles the city's history. The German victory over Roman troops near Osnabrück in AD 9 is still a source of local pride; a legionnaire's facemask is on display. (Both museums open Tu-F 11am-6pm, Sa-Su 10am-6pm. €4, students €2. Audio tours in German, English and Dutch, €3.50.) Osnabrück's most famous son is **Erich Maria Remarque,** the author of *Im Westen nichts neues (All Quiet on the Western Front).* Though Allied bombing completely destroyed his house on Hafenstr., literary travelers can tour the **Erich Maria Remarque Friedenszentrum,** Am Markt 6, which documents his life and work in German. The author's archives are also stored here. (☎323 21 09. Open Tu-F 10am-1pm and 3-5pm, Sa and first Su of the month 11am-5pm. Free.) **Theater Osnabrück,** next door to the Dom, fills seats for operas, musicals, and other theater. (☎760 00 76; www.theater.osnabrueck.de. Box office open Tu-F 10:30am-6:30pm, Sa 10:30am-2pm, and 1hr. before shows. Tickets €12-35.)

OLDENBURG ☎0441

First settled as early as 1108, the city of Oldenburg was spared destruction in the Thirty Years' War due largely to **Count Anton Günther,** who raised the most beautiful horses in Germany. Oldenburg today has more to offer—Frisian culture runs deep, and is actively preserved by its people. Though the city's varied museums and bustling shopping center fill daily with tourists, most outsiders miss the beautiful neighborhood west of Alexanderstr., the cemetery, and the lush *Schloßgarten.*

▐▌ TRANSPORTATION AND PRACTICAL INFORMATION

Trains to: **Bremen** (30-50min., 3 per hr., €6); **Jever** via **Sande** (1hr., 1 per hr., €9); **Osnabrück** (1½hr., 1-2 per hr., €16). The old, moated city lies along an offshoot of the Weser River and serves as a take-off point for excursions to East Frisia. For a **taxi** call ☎22 55. **Rent bikes** at the **Fahrradstation,** adjoining the back of the train station. (☎218 82 40. €7 per day. Open M-Sa 6am-11pm, Su 8am-11pm.)

HIGHWAY BOWLING

Road safety tip for East Frisia: during winter months, watch out for half-drunk Germans bowling on country lanes. The game is **Boßeln** and it developed here in the mid-19th century. Essentially, two teams compete to see who can roll their 3-inch diameter wooden ball (filled with lead) farther down the road. A team scores when it takes the other team more turns to roll the ball the same distance. *Boßeln* began in towns, but had to be moved to the countryside because the church disapproved of the drinking that always went along with it.

The association of *Boßeln* with winter derives not from a need for snow, but because that is the time of year when **Grünkohl und Pinkel** (kale and sausages) is abundant. After a hard day of drinking beer and playing *Boßeln*, the whole group shares this hearty meal. *Grünkohl* is a kind of cabbage that develops a sweet flavor after the first frost of the year; *Pinkel* is the local term for the ox intestines originally used to make it (modern Pinkel uses pork and oatmeal).

These Frisian delights can be enjoyed on a *Boßeln* tour arranged by the Oldenburg tourist office (p. 273). A local expert on the game takes the group out on country roads, where they learn how to play and down a wagon full of beer, followed by a *Grünkohl und Pinkel* dinner back in town.

The **tourist office,** Wallstr. 14, hands out free maps, finds rooms for free and sells North Sea brochures for €1.50. From the train station, go right on Moslestr., continue as it becomes Heiligengeistwall, and turn left on Wallstr. (☎361 61 30; www.oldenburg-tourist.de. Open M-F 10am-6pm, Sa 10am-2pm.) **Internet** access is at **Telecafe,** Ritterstr. 15, at the corner of Mühlenstr. (☎95 50 40. 1st hr. €2, then €1 per hr. Open M-Sa 9am-8pm, Su 11am-8pm.) Two blocks away, **Teleking,** Staustr. 18, near the corner of Poststr., lets you stay connected later. (☎217 62 39. €2 per hr. Open daily 10am-10pm, Sa until 11pm.) The **post office,** 26123 Oldenburg, is to the right as you exit the train station. (Open M-F 8am-6:30pm, Sa 9am-1pm.)

■■ ACCOMMODATIONS AND FOOD

The **Hotel Hegeler ❸,** Donnerschweer Str. 27, is a convenient bet. Exit from the rear of the station and turn left onto Donnerschweer Str. (☎875 61; fax 885 03 59. Breakfast included. Singles €25-31, with bath €47; doubles €55, with shower €80.) The city's **Jugendherberge (HI) ❷,** Alexanderstr. 65, is 1.5km from the station. Take bus #302 or 303 to Von-Finckh-Str. or take a right out of the train station, pass the post office on your right and continue straight until you reach Staulinie. Cross the street, take a right, and go straight until Pferdemarkt. Go left at the fork in the road onto Alexanderstr.; it's on the left. This concrete complex offers cheap rooms. (☎871 35; www.djh.de/unterweser. Breakfast included. Reception 5-11pm. Curfew 10pm; key available. Dorms €15.20; singles €19.50; doubles €37.)

Oldenburg's market overwhelms the **Rathaus** square with fresh produce (Tu, Th, Sa 8am-2pm). To get to the rose-covered facade of ◪**Marvin's ❷,** Rosenstr. 8, head up Bahnhofstr. from the train station, and go left on Rosenstr. You'll arrive at a priceless local hangout with an entertaining menu. Purists stick to "Moon Trip" or "First Aid," from the drinks menu (from €1.30); those who want a snack choose from a selection of salads, soups, and sandwiches for €2.50-6. (Open M-Th and Su 7pm-2am, F-Sa 8pm-3am.) **Tandour ❷,** Staustr. 18, lets you scribble your order of savory gyros, pastas, or lunch specials (€2.50-7) on scraps of paper and bring them to the counter to be cooked. (☎170 75. Open daily 11am-midnight.) **Picknick ❷,** Markt 6, cooks regional specialties, like potato pancakes with applesauce (€4.50), across from the church and Rathaus. (☎273 76. Open M-Sa from 10am.) Check out Wallstr. for a selection of cheap late-night pizza and pasta places.

◨▯▣ SIGHTS, ENTERTAINMENT, AND NIGHTLIFE. The **Landesmuseum für Kunst und Kulturgeschichte** combines three museums, all near the Schloßgarten: the Schloß, Augusteum, and Prinzenpalais. The yellow **Schloß**, Schloßpl. 26, presents the city's history using early reliefs depicting executions in the Middle Ages, 17th-century armor, Nazi propaganda and 1950s cocktail dresses. Don't miss the paper theater display on the top floor. Begin heading down Damm to find the **Augusteum**, Elisabethstr. 1, which houses paintings by the "old masters" of Germany, France, Italy, and the Netherlands from the 12th century onward. Across the street, the **Prinzenpalais**, Damm 1, contains a modern collection, including numerous works by German Expressionists and a room devoted entirely to eerie **Franz Radziwill** canvases. (All 3 museums: ☎220 73 00; www.landesmuseum-oldenburg.de. Open Tu-F 9am-5pm, Th until 8pm, Sa-Su 10am-5pm. Combined ticket €3; students, seniors, and children €1.50.) Walk another 300m to get to the **Landesmuseum für Natur und Mensch**, Damm 38-44, a pink building containing spearheads, mastodons, and other ghosts of Oldenburg's primeval past. (☎924 43 00; www.naturundmensch.de. Open Tu-Th 9am-5pm, F 9am-3pm, Sa-Su 10am-5pm. €3, students and children €1.50.) At the other end of the pedestrian zone, just off Moslestr., the **Stadtmuseum**, Am Stadtmuseum 4-8, preserves old, color-coordinated, stately rooms. The attached **Horst-Janssen-Museum** hosts rotating exhibits on the prolific 20th-century printmaker. (☎235 29 81; www.oldenburg.de/stadtmuseum; www.horst-janssen-museum.de. Both museums open Tu-Su 10am-6pm. Stadtmuseum €1.50, students €0.75. Horst-Janssen-Museum €3.50/€1.50. Combined ticket €4/€2.25.)

Nightlife in Oldenburg is centered around **Wallstraße's** thumping beats and late-night *Kneipen*. **Der Schwan**, Stau 34, across from Kaiserstr., is a beer garden with occasional live music. Boats streak across the harbor while patrons down cheap beer under strings of white lights. (☎261 89. Breakfast buffet served until noon; M-F €5.30, Sa €7, Su €9. Open daily 9am-2am, F-Sa until 3am.) Farther down the street, **Cinemaxx**, Stau 79-85, is a modern cinema that features a different current English release each week. (☎217 70; www.cinemaxx.de. Shows M around 8pm and W around 5pm, call for exact times. €4.50-7.)

OSTFRIESLAND (EAST FRISIA)

Germany's North Sea shoreline and the seven sandy islands that hug its coast appear to belong to the Netherlands. The flat landscape, dotted with windmills, impenetrable clouds and foreboding seascapes, contrasts sharply with Germany's bustling river valleys and modern skylines. The seafaring Frisians, whose dialect is a close linguistic relative to English, treasure their strong **tea**, which is customarily served in elaborate porcelain sets over sugar candies called *Kluntje*. A traditional tea ceremony may be filling (it's impolite to drink fewer than three cups), but there's always room for the region's culinary delicacies. Try some *Ostfriesische Rosinenstütten*, a sweet raisin loaf, on display in every bakery. Though buses and trains in the area are often inconvenient, miles of breathtaking beaches, green fields, and rolling dunes compensate for the planning required. German tourists certainly seem to think so; in the summer the shores fill with vacationing families.

JEVER ☎04461

Jever received city rights 450 years ago from its patroness, Lady Mary, who commissioned art, building fortifications, and a school. The town's modern patron is the nationally famous local brewery. A regional **rail line** runs to Jever from **Oldenburg** and **Osnabrück** via **Sande** (2½hr., 1 per hr., €15.20). For a **taxi** call ☎30 30. The **tourist office**, Alter Markt 18, across from the Schloß, books rooms for free. From the train station, follow Anton-Günther-Str. to the right, turn left at Mühlenstr. and

Ostfriesische Inseln (East Frisian Islands)

North Sea

Norderney   **Nordstrand**

Norderney
Kalfamer

Juist

Im Loog   Juist

Memmert

Nationalpark Niedersächsisches Wattenmeer

Norddeich

Borkum

Ostland

Borkum

Lütje Hörn

Westland   Reede Borkum

Norden

Norden

TO EEMSHAVEN,
NETHERLANDS

TO EMDEN

TO EMDEN
(26km)

72

0   5 miles
0   5 kilometers

N
LG

it will be near the Schloßpl. on the left. (☎ 710 10; www.stadt-jever.de. Open Mar.-
Oct. M-F 9am-6pm, Sa 9am-1pm; Nov.-Feb. M-F 9am-5pm.) The tourist office is
located at the edge of the pedestrian zone, and from there signs indicate the way to
major sights. Near the Alter Markt, the **post office** is one block off Neue Str. on Kattrepel, 26441 Jever. (Open M-F 9am-5:30pm, Sa 9am-12:30pm.)

⬛Im Schmidz Pension ❹, Alter Markt 2, offers friendly service in the center of
town. (☎ 75 90 36. Breakfast included. Singles €38; doubles €70; discounts for
multiple nights.) The **Jugendherberge Jever (HI) ❶** is at Mooshütterweg 12. From the
train station, take a right onto Anton-Günther-Str. and turn left on Mooshütterweg.
(☎ 35 90; jugendherberge-jever@t-online.de. Breakfast and sheets included. Check-
in M-F and Su 5-5:30pm, Sa 5:30-6pm; late check-in 9:45pm or call from the front
desk. Curfew 10pm, key available. Open Apr.-Oct. €15.50, under 27 €12.70.)

Balu ❸, Kattrepel 1a, across from the post office in a quiet courtyard off the Altstadt, cooks African specialty dishes like yam wings and plantains, as well as a
range of other finger foods (€10-13). *Salat a la Rosemarie* (€9.90), with chicken,
avocado, orange slices, and warm pita bread, is life-affirmingly good. (☎ 70 07
09. Open daily 10am-10pm.) A late night option in Jever is **La Casetta Pizzeria ❷**,
Bahnhofstr. 44. Don't let the 34 pizzas on the menu distract you from the delicious
tortellini. (☎ 725 89. Entrees €3-8. Open daily noon-3pm and 5pm-midnight.)

North of the Altstadt, the **Freisisches Brauhaus**, Elisabethufer, is a futuristic
glass brewing complex that puts Jever on the map—and on tap—all over northern Germany. To reserve **tour** tickets or purchase the essential Jever survival
gear (sweatshirt, sun visor, watch, and beer mug), head for **Der Jever-Shop**, Elisabethufer 18. (☎ 137 11; www.jever.de. Open M-F 9am-7pm, Sa 9am-2pm. 45min.
German tours begin at half past every hr. €6.50, including a souvenir mug and 2
glasses of beer. Sa tours go to museum only.) Most Jeverians dismiss pilsner as
their claim to fame by insisting that their finest offering is the castle across
from the tourist office. Each room in the salmon-colored, 15th-century **Schloß**
details a facet of East Frisian heritage, from exquisite, hand-painted chests to
18th-century clothing. The castle's centerpiece is the remarkable wooden ceiling in the audience hall where Lady Mary received emissaries from far off lands.

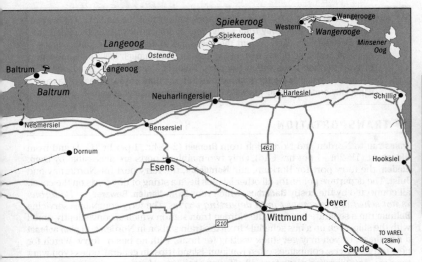

(☎ 96 93 50; www.schlossmuseum.de. Open Tu-Su 10am-6pm; July-Aug. also M 10am-6pm. €1, students €0.80, children €0.50. Tower €0.50.) Outside, the **Lady Mary Statue** is the city's greatest monument to its beloved patroness. Just outside the castle entrance at the Hof von Oldenburg is a **Glockenspiel,** which goes off every hr. from 11am-noon and 3-6pm, releasing figurines from Jever's history through its trap doors. The cheerful characters, among them Lady Mary and a Russian Empress, extend their hands in greeting. On Kirchpl., the **Stadtkirche** is a product of the citizens' dedication; after it burned down, they reconstructed and modernized it. The ornate brick facade of the Renaissance **Rathaus** is a few blocks away from the main square.

WATTENMEER NATIONAL PARK (NIEDERSACHSEN)

Twice daily, tides rush out of the Wattenmeer National Park, laying bare kilometers of the ocean floor. The slowly sloping continental shelf along the coast that creates this dramatic ebb and flow sustains a unique ecology at this, the westernmost of Germany's three Wattenmeer parks (p. 201). Dunes formed here millions of years ago, protecting the islands from erosion and the flora and fauna from salt water. Hundreds of local plant and insect species interact in the protected island interiors, while various fish, birds, and invertebrates have evolved to thrive on the surrounding ocean floor mudflats (see **What is this Watt?,** p. 201). Familiar with the intricacies of the Watt terrain and timing of the tides, local experts lead popular *Wattwanderung* (Watt walk) groups out onto the flats during low tides, describing this specialized ecosystem as everyone enjoys a romp in the mud.

◼ ORIENTATION

The Niedersachsen Wattenmeer National Park stretches along the coast from the mouth of the **Ems River** to the mouth of the **Weser River.** It includes the coastline as well as the seven **East Frisian Islands.**

WATT NOT TO DO. A few rules apply throughout the park. First, **always keep at least 500m away from seals.** Your approach will frighten them and as they flee they are likely to hurt their sensitive underbellies. Second, nesting areas are restricted during bird mating season, April through July, so **do not venture off marked trails within the park.** Third, in areas labeled "Schutzzone I: Ruhezone," **never leave the marked trails at any time of year.** These areas are especially protected, and you will be **fined** if a ranger catches you.

⌐ TRANSPORTATION

Trains run to Norden and Norddeich from **Bremen** (2-2½hr., 1 per hr., €24) and from **Oldenburg** (1½-2hr., 1 per hr., €16). Only two mainland ports are accessible by train: **Emden,** the ferry port for Borkum, and **Norddeich,** the ferry port for Norderney and Juist. The departure points for all other islands lie in a string of tiny ports on the coast, all connected by the costly **Bäderbus,** which runs from **Norden. Beware:** *the Bäderbus is not scheduled to connect with departing ferries.* The ferry companies servicing **Baltrum** run a separate bus from the Norden train station which is conveniently timed with the ship. Pick up a bus schedule from the train station in Norden and **plan at least a day ahead,** or you may get stuck waiting for hours with no bus or ferry. Watch for new ferry services; companies often run inter-island trips. In general, unless you want to take a tiny, vibrating plane for €40-150, you can't travel between islands—you must return to the mainland. To learn all the ins and outs of your chosen island, buy its brochure (in German only) at a tourist office in the region. These pamphlets contain extensive accommodations listings and full explanations of local attractions.

ⓘ PRACTICAL INFORMATION

Climate and Seasonality: The best time to visit is summer, when the weather is typically mild and the migrating birds have arrived. Keep in mind, however, that North Sea weather is a tad temperamental; windy and rainy days are not uncommon even during peak tourist season (July-Sept.). The salt marsh flora bloom late July to early Aug.

Information Centers: A series of **National Park Häuser** offer information and tours; locations include **Baltrum** and **Norderney** (see town listings). Town information centers also have transportation and hiking information, as well as accommodations listings.

Tours: The National Park Häuser offer themed nature tours (see above). Private guided tours of the Watt are also available; see individual town listings.

⚠ HIKING AND BIKING

ON BALTRUM. As you leave the harbor in Baltrum, the **National Park Haus** is the first building on the right. To get to the trailhead from the house, take a right and continue for 600m. Take the fourth left (past the pond on your right) and then the first right (in front of the grassy dune studded with thick brush). Follow this path as it curves to the right before a big house. From there take an immediate left and then the following left; take the stairs over the large sand dune with its peak enclosed by green fences and continue east on the middle path for 400m. Stay left when the path merges as you enter the *Ruhezone* after another 300m.

From here, there are two options. For a **short hike** (1¾hr.), continue straight for 500m and make a right onto the riding and hiking path marked alternately with red and green markers. The trail eventually brings you back to the road from which you began. For a **long hike** (3hr.), go left toward the beach; from there you can walk through the sand dunes or on the beach. For the dunes, take the first right. For the beach, walk until you hit the sand, then turn right. Both paths head east to the end of the island. Once there, you can either double back the way you came, or, at very specific times of the day, take the **Watt Trail;** check in first at the National Park Haus, as **it is only accessible from 1hr. before until 1hr. after low tide.** Taking this trail adds 1hr. to the long hike. If you hike the Watt trail in the other direction, be careful not to miss the trailhead coming back into town. To enter the Watt trail, go to the *Jugendstätte* campground, then fork right, curving around to the south. When you hit the Watt, lose your shoes and enjoy the 1hr. walk east through the mud.

ON NORDERNEY. A bike is almost a necessity on Norderny. There are two rental shops across the street from the harbor (p. 282). There are three good ways to see the island: a bike trail, a medium hike, or a long hike. All three begin by leaving the bike shop and traveling down Deichstr. past the large industrial cylinders on your right. As you round the long curve in the road, cross the street and take the path above the dike. The trail curves sharply to the left 300m later; follow it and then go right along the street for another 500m past the golf course.

If you want to do the ☒**bike trail,** look for a sign for Trail 4 on your right (if you get to the forest, you've gone too far). Cross onto Trail 4, which will take you along the coast. After 5km, you'll ride into **Parkplatz Ostheller.** Look for the bike path on your left as you go down the ramp from the dike trail. Take this path to the lighthouse. If you keep going straight, you can return to town (12km, about 2hr.), or to continue, make a right onto Trail 2. After about 1km it stops abruptly, but continues 50m to your right. Once you reach the town of Norderney, take Emsstr. past rows of houses, straight through the pedestrian zone and Fannenstr. Make a left onto Poststr., which will eventually bring you to the harbor (17km, 3½hr.).

To **hike,** follow the bike trail to Parkplatz Ostheller, park your bike, and walk up the ramp over the dike. Trail 5 begins to the right. Continue on Trail 5 until you reach the **Möwendune,** a huge wooden lookout tower. Loop around the tower to head back to the parking place (1km biking, 6km hiking, 2½-3hr. total). For a **longer hike,** continue on Trail 5 to the end of the island. Here, a large colony of seals calls Norderney's tip home. Continue down

ily Chronicle

IN RECENT NEWS

TURBINE TUMULT

Graceful white windmills fill the Frisian countryside, capturing sea breezes on lowland plains. One of the most environmentally conscious nations on the planet, Germany is taking a lead role in using renewable energy resources.

More than 15,000 modern windmills currently call Germany home, generating a whopping 40% of the world's wind energy and meeting 6% of Germany's energy demands. An overwhelming majority of Germans support the proliferation of windmills, and this wind is being used to pick up the slack created by a government decision to discontinue the use of nuclear power by the year 2020. Germany hopes to triple the percentage of power from wind within the next 10 years.

Not all Germans welcome the burgeoning windmill population, arguing that wind energy is inefficient and expensive for taxpayers. However, many are fighting more just to preserve the pristine appearance of the countryside— they call windmill construction *"Verspargelung der Landschaft"* (asparagus-ing the countryside)— and are sick of what they call the "disco effect" of humming turbines and flashing lights.

Recent legislation suggests that new windmills be built offshore, where swift air currents help generate more output per machine. It is possible that wind energy in Germany has a promising future that may be pleasing to everyone after all.

the beach to the left, keeping the trail markers in sight. With the Möwendune on your left, walk toward it from the beach. Turn right on the trail and head back to the parking lot (14km, 4½-5hr.).

ON BORKUM. The bike loop on Borkum is 25km, with numerous trails along the way allowing for shorter hikes over the sand dunes. Begin the bike trail at the beachfront in town and follow the Strandweg path to the right, keeping to the shoreline until you reach the sand dunes. This path will wind up to the northern shore and follow the beach all the way to the easternmost tip of the island. From here the *Deich- und Salzwiesenweg* path continues to your right, bringing you back out of the dunes, through grassy plains, across the main highway, and to the far southern shore. The path follows the coast to the right and meets up with Strandweg, leading back to town. Though overnight accommodations are usually available only with reservations at least a month in advance, the ferry schedule allows travelers enough time to enjoy the island's splendid beaches.

NORDEN   ☎ 04931

Norden is the transportation hub excursions around East Frisia. **Trains** go to **Emden** (1 per hr., €5) and **Norddeich** (2 per hr., €1.70), and the **Bäderbus** provides easy access to most other port towns. The **train station** is 2km from the city center; from the station follow Bahnhofstr. to the right and veer right at the fork onto Neuer Weg. At the pedestrian zone, turn left on Osterstr. to the main market square. Visit the **tourist office,** Am Markt 36, inside the Teemuseum, for specific transportation information or to book rooms (from €18) for free. (☎98 62 01; fax 98 62 90. Open M-F 9am-12:30pm and 2-5pm, Sa 9am-4pm.) Turn right at the market to find the **post office,** 26506 Norden. (Open M-Sa 8:30am-12:30pm, M-F also 2:30-5:30pm.) **Hotel Smutje ❹,** Neuer Weg 89, has impeccably clean and comfortable large rooms near the marketplace. (☎942 50; www.hotelsmutje.de. Breakfast included. Singles €39; doubles €58. Discounts after 2 nights.) **Das Kleine Pizzastübchen ❷,** Neuer Weg 121 (☎53 34), near the corner of Osterstr., dishes out an affordable (€3-7) array of pizza, gyros, pasta and salad. (Open M-Sa 11am-10pm.) Across the street, **Mittelhaus ❶,** Neuer Weg 11 (☎97 18 81), has apple strudel and baguettes (€2.70-3), beer (€1.65), and coffee liquor cocktails for €3.50. (Open daily 10am-1am.)

A couple blocks off Neuer Weg, the **Rathaus,** Am Markt 15, looks across the market green at the imposing tower of the 15th-century **Ludgerikirche.** The intricate woodwork and pleasant blue pews inside are lovingly tended by Norden's townspeople. (Open Apr.-Sept. M 10am-12:30pm, Tu-Su 10am-12:30pm and 3-5pm. Organ concerts every W 8pm. €5, students €3.50.) Experience the church's **Glockenspiel** at 9am, noon, 3, or 6pm. The great East Frisian fascination with tea is explained at the **East Frisian Teemuseum,** Am Markt 36, in the old Rathaus on the southwest side of the market. The museum houses myriad teacups, pots, and silverware associated with northern German tea culture. For €0.50, participate in an East Frisian **tea ceremony** (July-Sept. W 2pm.) The **Heimatmuseum** in the same building covers the other elements of East Frisian culture, including dike construction and shoemaking. (☎121 00; www.teemuseum.de. Both museums open Mar.-Oct. Tu-Su 10am-4pm; July-Aug. also M 2-5pm. Joint admission €2.50, students and children €1.) For some treasures of the sea, try the **Muschel-&-Schnecken-Museum,** In der Gnurre 40, a collection of shells inside an old windmill just off Bahnhofstr. (☎126 15. Open Apr.-Oct. Tu-F 2:30-6pm. €1.50, children €0.50.)

NORDDEICH   ☎ 04931

The busy port of Norddeich, 3km from its sister city of Norden, is a more logical base camp for budget travelers, offering more affordable accommodations, easy access to the ferry network, and spectacular seascapes along a string of beaches.

The most convenient train station is **Norddeich-Mole,** which is the end of the line. To reach town, follow the crowds up and over the dike to the right. Badestr. runs parallel to the dike and intersects Dörper Weg after 800m. **Ferries** leave Norddeich daily for Norderney and Juist. Pick up schedules in the ferry ticket offices right outside of the train station. **Bike** rental shops line Dörper Weg; many also rent go-carts (single or family-size) from €3 per hr. (Bikes about €5 per day, €21 per week. ID required.) The patient staff at the Norddeich **tourist office,** Dörper Weg 22, finds rooms for free, hands out ferry schedules, gives information about **Watt tours,** and offers the only **Internet** access (€4 per hr.; €10 deposit) for miles. (☎98 62 00; www.norddeich.de. Open M-F 9am-5pm, Sa 10am-5pm, Su 10am-1pm.) For a **taxi,** call ☎80 00. The **post office,** 26506 Norddeich, is in the Fernseh Hemken building on Frisiastr., which intersects Badestr. near the train station.

The town's **Jugendherberge (HI) ❷,** Strandstr. 1, is excellent for exploring the region: it's cheap, clean, and right in the center of town. From Badestr., turn left just past the Hotel Regina Maris; the hostel will be on the next corner on the left. The main hostel compound is generally filled with school groups, but the adjacent pine cabins *(Blockhütten)* provide some escape. (☎80 64; fax 818 28. Breakfast included. Reception 5-8pm. Book far, far in advance. €17, under 27 €14. €5.80 to pitch your own tent in the backyard.) **Hotel Seeblick ❸,** Badestr. 11, provides snug rooms near the beach at unbeatable prices. (☎80 86; fax 16 84 84. Breakfast included. Reception 8am-10pm in the restaurant below. June-Sept. singles €23; doubles €42. Oct.-Apr. €22/€40.) **Gästehaus Merlan ❸,** Kakteenweg 7, just off of Deichstr., has roomy doubles and red-bricked apartments, each with cable TV, radio, and private bath. (☎816 30; fax 816 15. Reservations strongly recommended. Doubles €48, including breakfast; 2- to 6-person apartments €23 per person.) **Nordsee-Camp ❶,** Deichstr. 21, is 20min. farther down Badestr., which becomes Deichstr. It has impressive views (though dike-side camping gets chilly), and a convenient bar and grocery store on the grounds. (☎80 73; fax 80 74. Reception until 10pm. Open mid-Mar. to Oct. €2.60 per person, €6.80 per day. *Kurtaxe* €1.50.) **⛱Diekster Köken ❸,** Deichstr. 6 (☎822 42) is a local hotspot with tourist charm. Specialties include delicious potato pancakes (€3-15), served with almost anything, and fresh seafood. (Open daily 9am-10pm.)

At the **Seehundstation,** Dörper Weg 22, in the park behind the tourist office, injured North Sea seals are rehabilitated before their return to the wild. Get up close and personal with the playful sea critters, who entertain with their underwater acrobatics on the other side of a glass wall. (☎89 19; www.seehundstation-norddeich.de. Open daily 10am-5pm. €3, children €1.50, family €7.)

BALTRUM ISLAND ☎04939

The smallest of the Frisian Islands with only 500 permanent residents, Baltrum is run by its bold wildlife—rabbits and pheasants regularly emerge from the brush to size you up. A ban on motor vehicles creates a much-treasured silence, broken only by the occasional animal call or clopping of horse hooves. Houses are numbered in the order they were built, which seems quaint until you have to find one.

To reach Baltrum, take the ferry company bus from the Norden train station to **Neßmersiel.** Ferry times *vary greatly,* as the boats can only travel this route close to low tide. The first ferry leaves for Baltrum anywhere between 6am and 2:30pm, the last ferry returns between 2 and 9:30pm. (June-Nov. 2-3 per day. Open-ended return €21, children €10. Daytrip €16/€7.50.) Buses leave Norden about 1hr. before the ferry (€6 round-trip). Check the schedule in any tourist office or at the information signs at the market square in Norden. For a daytrip, your best bet is to hit the first ferry, or you'll only have a couple hours before the last boat leaves for home. For more information, call the ferry company, **Reederei Baltrum Linie** (☎913

00), or visit the **tourist office,** in the Rathaus, Nr. 130. Turn right at the harbor exit and then take the third left, it's near the end of the road on the left. They book private rooms for free. (☎800; www.baltrum.de. Open M-F 9am-noon, Sa-Su 10am-noon.) For hiking tips and bird-call lessons, head to the **National Park Haus,** Nr. 177, to your right as you leave the harbor. (☎469. Open Tu-F 10am-noon and 3-7pm, Sa-Su 3-7pm.) The **post office** is across the street, Nr. 43, 26579 Baltrum. (Open M-F 9am-noon and 3-5pm, Sa 9am-noon.) **Watt tours** between the island and the mainland during low tide are quite popular. For tour times, call a local *Wattführer* or look for signs at the tourist office. Family Ortelt runs tours between Baltrum and Neßmersiel. (☎04933 17 06; www.wattfuehrer.com. 2½hr. €20, children €13, including ferry.) Hansjürgen Barow also leads a tour to the mainland. (☎918 20. 2½hr. €21, children €13, including ferry.)

It may be easier to spend the night on the island than to work out the intricacies of the ferry schedule. To get to **Haus Störtebeker ❷,** Nr. 167, from the National Park Haus, turn right and take the third left, between two brick walls. Take the next right and walk down this street; it will be on your right, overlooking the water. (☎295; www.stoertebeker-baltrum.de. Kitchen available. All rooms €16-19.) **Jugendbildungsstätte ❶** lets you camp within the National Park. Turn right immediately after the harbor and continue for 1.5km along the bike path. (☎04941 99 11 64. Cot and tent included. Open June-Sept. €6.50 per person, €4.50 per child. *Kurkarte* €2.30/€0.50.) For cheap eats, **Strandcafe ❷,** Nr. 70, contains a cafeteria-style restaurant (all items under €10) apparently staffed by every teenager on the island. Go past Haus Störtebeker until the road splits, turn left, and continue until you reach the sand dunes at the end of the road; it will be on your left. (☎200. Open daily 10am-midnight. Closed M in off season.) Where the road splits after Haus Störtebeker, **Kiek Musikkniepe,** Nr. 123, lights up with late entertainment and occasional live music. (☎89 60. Open Su-Th 9pm-2am, F-Sa 9pm-3am.)

NORDERNEY ISLAND   ☎04932

The holiday destination of **Otto Van Bismarck** and **Heinrich Heine,** Norderney celebrates tourist success with postcard and beach-bucket shops and some of the best-maintained trails in the national park. Though only 6500 people call the island home, tides of sunburned Germans swell the population to 60,000 on warm days.

Ferry Company Frisia runs from Norddeich to Norderney. (☎04931 98 70 in Norden; ☎91 30 in Norderney; www.reederei-frisia.de. 1hr. 9-13 per day. 1st departure July-Aug. daily 6:35am; Sept.-June Sa-Su 7:30am. Last return between 6 and 7:15pm. Check schedules for exact times. Round-trip €14.50.) A bike is essential for getting around on Norderney; be sure to walk it through pedestrian zones designated by blue and white signs. ID is often required. For a **taxi,** call ☎23 45 or 33 33. Two **bike rental** shops are located just beyond the harbor. **Dicki Verleih** is on Gorch-Fock-Weg and also at Jann-Berghaus-Str. 62 in the town center. (☎33 78. €1.50-2 per hr., €6.50-8 per day. Open daily 9am-6pm.) **Reinke's Fahrradverleih am Hafen,** Hafenstr. 1, is 300m down Hafenstr. as you step off the ferry. (☎13 26. Open daily 9am-6pm. €1.50-2 per hr., €5.50-6.50 per day.) To spend the night, check in at the busy **tourist office,** Bülowallee 5, at the end of Hafenstr. The staff, who speak only German, find rooms (typically €50-60) for a €4 fee. (☎918 50; fax 824 94. Open M-F 9am-12:30pm and 2-6pm, Sa 10am-3pm, Su 11am-2pm.) There is also a **National Park Haus,** directly on your left as you leave the ferry, that sells hiking maps (€1.95), teaches (in German) about the local wildlife, and displays stuffed birds. (☎20 01. Open May-Oct. Tu-Su 10am-6pm, Nov.-Apr. Tu-F 10am-5pm, Sa-Su 2-5pm.)

Norderney has two youth hostels, both of which are relatively expensive. To get to **Jugendherberge Südstraße ❷,** Südstr. 1, turn right on Deichstr. just outside the harbor, then turn onto Südstr.; it's on the right. This small house is one of

Germany's oldest hostels, offering 8- to 14-bed dorms. (☎24 51; fax 836 00. Full board and sheets included. Reception 5-5:30pm. Reserve in advance. HI members only. Open Mar.-Oct. Dorms €24.90, after 3 nights €23.10; under 27 €22.20/€20.40; all prices include *Kurtaxe*.) The **Jugendherberge Dünensender ❸**, Am Dünensender 3, is a full 7km inland. If you miss the hourly #2 bus to "Leuchtturm," you'll have to rent a bike in town or walk 1½-2hr. Follow Deichstr. to its end, and head right on Karl-Rieger-Weg, where signs point your way. (☎25 74; fax 832 66. Breakfast included. Reception 5-6pm. Open Apr.-Oct. €24.90, under 27 €22.20.) In the summer you can also **camp ❷** at the hostel and use its facilities. (☎16 14. Breakfast included. HI members only. €17 per person, with tent.) **Haus Westend ❸**, Friedrichstr. 40, has elegant rooms with ocean views. (☎26 85; www.haus-westend.de. Breakfast included. Singles €36-43; doubles €66-72. 10-20% less Nov.-Apr.) **Hotel Aquamarin ❹**, Friedrichstr. 5, has sparkling rooms and a sunny veranda. (☎928 50; www.hotel-aquamarin-norderney.de. Breakfast included. All rooms €45 per person.) The main campsite on the island is **Camping Booken ❶**, Waldweg 2. (☎448; fax 478. Wash €3, dry €3. €6.40 per person, €4.50 per tent. Showers free.)

Norderney's restaurants are pricey (entrees typically €10-20), and adorned with fake lobsters and fish netting. Perhaps the best seafood in town is at **Bootshaus ❸**, Am Hansendamm 1. From the ferry dock walk around the harbor; it's on the other end. The fresh crab soup (€5.20) is creamy and delicious. (☎28 50. Entrees from €7.20. Open daily from 11am. Kitchen closes 10pm.) For groceries, try **Plus**, Hafenstr. 6, 200m from the harbor exit. (Open M-Sa 8am-8pm, Su 10am-3pm.)

The town's tiny 16th-century **▓Evangelische Inselkirche** sits in the center of town near the end of Bülowallee. Model ships hang from the bright orange ceiling, and contrasting white trim adds elegance among the straight-backed pews. (Open M-Th 8am-5pm, Su after the service until 5pm. Free.) Away from town, the dunes and beaches of the eastern two-thirds of the island are part of the national park. Areas designated **FKK** are nude beaches. To go for a Watt tour, call local expert seaman Kurt Knittel (☎04931 30 96; www.mit-kurt-ins-watt.de); his **tour** is 3hr., complete with a bus from Norddeich to Neßmersiel, an explanation of sea creatures along the walk to Norderney (in German), and a ferry ticket back to Norddeich. (€21; pick up a schedule at the ferry office or call for departure times.)

BORKUM ISLAND   ☎04922

Lodged in an inlet halfway between Germany and the Netherlands, Borkum is where industrious Germans go to do nothing. The island is festive and laid-back—tiny painted trains cart vacationers through a serene, flower-filled landscape to the bustling town at the far end of the island. Every year, Borkum's beaches transform thousands of pale German legs into vicious sunburn, but still they return.

AG-EMS (☎01805 18 01 82; office in the Emden train station open M-F 8:30am-5pm) runs a **ferry** from Emden's *Außenhaven* (outer harbor) to the island (2hr.; June-Sept. 2-3 per day; morning ferry departs for Borkum at 8am; last return ferry leaves Borkum Apr.-Dec. 4:30pm; Jan.-Mar. 1:30pm. Open-ended return €26.50; one-way €14. Ticket window opens 1hr. before departure.) For more money, you can get to the island in half the time on the **catamaran**. (1hr.; first departing ferry Apr.-Dec. 9:15am; Jan.-Mar. 12:30pm. Last return ferry 5:30pm, earlier Jan.-Mar. Round-trip €32.) On Borkum, unless you are staying at the hostel, take the train to town (fare included in ferry ticket). In town, rent **bikes** at the **Fahrradverleih** in the train station. (☎30 90. €2.10 per hr., €6.40 per day. Open M-Sa 7am-6pm, Su 8:30am-6pm.) Borkum's **tourist office**, Am Georg-Schütte-Pl. 5, across from the train station in town, books rooms for free. (☎93 30; www.borkum.de. Open M-F 9am-12:30pm and 2-5:30pm, Sa 10am-noon and 2-5pm; Su 11am-noon and 2-5pm.)

It is difficult to find a bed in Borkum without reservations. The **Jugendherberge (HI) ❷**, Reedestr. 231, a 5min. walk from the dock, prefers guests to write at least one month in advance. (☎579; jh-borkum@djh-unterweser-ems.de. Full board included. Curfew 10:30pm, key provided. Closed Dec. Dorms €21, under 27 €18.80; singles €32.50; doubles €65; *Kurtaxe* €2.50.) **Pension Stella-Maris ❸**, Alte Schulstr. 9, is just around the corner from the station; follow Strandstr. and take the first right. (☎26 14 or 510. Breakfast included. Singles €20-24; doubles €48-66.) **Insel-Camping ❶**, Hindenburgstr. 114, is 15min. from the train station. Even pitching a tent may require reservations. (☎10 88; fax 42 34. €12.50 per person, tent included. *Kurtaxe* €2.50.) Restaurants line Bismarckstr. A trendy crowd snacks on baguettes, wraps, and desserts among the leopard-skin bar stools of **Cafe Coffee? Bar ❷**, Bismarckstr. 16 (☎92 42 86. Main dishes €2-7. Open daily 9am-2am.)

If you've had too much sun for one day or if the North Sea weather turns foul, Borkum also offers some indoor attractions good for a few hours of fun. Though the 19th-century **Alter Leuchtturm** (old lighthouse) no longer operates, tourists can still ascend the attractive brick tower to savor the panoramic views. From the station, follow Strandstr. until it ends and turn right on Wilhelm-Bakker-Str. (Open M, W, Sa 10am-noon; July-Sept. also F 10am-noon. €1.50, students €1.) One block past the lighthouse, the **Heitmatmuseum** displays interesting articles of island culture, including a full whale skeleton and a knot collection that would make any sailor proud. (☎48 60. Open Apr.-Oct. Tu-Su 10am-noon and 3-5pm; Nov.-Mar. Tu and Su 3pm-5pm. Tours Apr.-Oct. W 5pm; €4. Museum €3, children €1.50.) On the grassy knoll just behind the train station, the **Neuer Leuchtturm,** successor to the old lighthouse, is also open for your stair-climbing enjoyment. (Open daily 10-11:30am and 3-4:30pm; Apr.-Oct. also M, W, F-Sa 7-9pm. €1.50, students €1.)

NORDRHEIN-WESTFALEN (NORTH RHEIN-WESTPHALIA)

In 1946, the victorious Allies attempted to expedite Germany's recovery by merging the traditionally distinct regions of Westphalia, Lippe, and the Rheinland to unify the economic and industrial nucleus of post-war Germany. The resulting *Land*, Nordrhein-Westfalen, defies all German stereotypes. A dense concentration of highways and rail lines forms the infrastructure of the most heavily populated (17 million inhabitants) and economically powerful region in Germany, where an industrial boom during the late 19th century sparked social democracy, trade unionism, and revolutionary communism. Despite downturns in heavy industry and persistently high unemployment, the enormous wealth of the region continues to support a multitude of cultural offerings for the citizens and visitors of its lively urban centers. While industrial squalor may have inspired the philosophy of Karl Marx and Friedrich Engels, the natural beauty of the Teutoburg and Eifel mountains, coupled with the intellectual energy of Cologne and Düsseldorf, have spurred the muses of writers from Goethe to Heine to Böll.

HIGHLIGHTS OF NORDRHEIN-WESTFALEN

GULP DOWN CHOCOLATE from an endless fountain (or *Kölsch*) in **Cologne** (Köln, p. 285), internationally admired for its immense **Dom.**

PAY YOUR RESPECTS at **Beethoven's birthplace** (in Bonn, p. 296) and **Aachen's** (p. 303) collection of **Charlemagne's body parts,** or visit **Münster's** (p. 318) **Leprosy Museum,** but don't worry, these hip university towns are alive and well.

STRUT WITH STYLE down the "**Kö**"—a glitzy strip of designer boutiques in **Düsseldorf** (p. 307), the nation's undisputed fashion cop. By night, its citizens retire to the procession of over 500 *Kneipen* (the "longest bar in the world") lining the city's Altstadt.

KÖLN (COLOGNE)   ☎ 0221

Founded as a Roman colony (*colonia*, hence Köln) in 32 BC by Agrippina, wife of Roman Emperor Claudius, Cologne was Petrarch's "city of dreams" when the rest of Germany was just wilderness. The city's location at the crossroads of several trade routes ushered in a golden age during the Middle Ages, foreshadowing its present status as a German commercial and communications center. Cologne's modern prosperity camouflages the staggering damage it sustained in WWII, when relentless air raids crumbled 90% of the city center. Looming over the city skyline, the legendary Dom serves as a constant reminder of a turbulent past; though it eclipses all other churches in Gothic splendor, discolored stones mark old war wounds. The cathedral miraculously remained intact despite the 14 bombs that struck its north end, and currently sees 22,000 visitors daily. Today, the city is the largest city in North Rhein-Westphalia and its most important cultural center, with a wide range of world-class museums and theatrical offerings. The city's long history includes a variety of traditionally extravagant festivals and celebrations. Each year *Karneval*

NORDRHEIN-
WESTFALEN

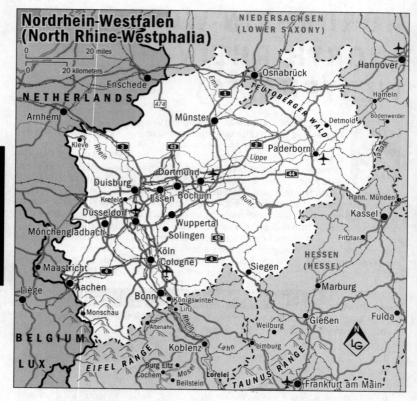

Nordrhein-Westfalen
(North Rhine-Westphalia)

plunges Cologne into a frenzy of parades, costume balls, and intoxication for the week before Lent. Meanwhile, locally brewed *Kölsch* beer helps to instill a festive mentality all year, and the city's expanding nightlife scene indulges eclectic tastes of the university crowd.

⌐ TRANSPORTATION

Flights: Flights depart from **Köln-Bonn Flughafen.** Flight information ☎01803 80 38 03. S13 leaves the train station every 20min. during the week, every 30min. weekends. Shuttle to **Berlin** 24 times per day 6:30am-8:30pm.

Trains: to: **Berlin** (4½hr., 1 per hr., €85); **Düsseldorf** (30min.-1hr., 5-7 per hr., €7); **Frankfurt** (1¼-2hr., 2 per hr., €51); **Hamburg** (4hr., 2-3 per hr., €63); **Munich** (4½-5hr., 1-2 per hr., €105); 1 per 2hr. to: **Amsterdam** (2½-3½hr., €46); **Paris** (4hr., €78).

Ferries: Köln-Düsseldorfer (☎208 83 18; www.k-d.com) begins its popular Rhein cruises here, where Salzg. meets the Rhein. Sail upstream to **Koblenz** (€34 one-way/€37 round-trip) or see the castles along the Rhein to **Mainz** (€46/€53). Ships to **Bonn** (€10.80/€12.80) offer a scenic alternative to trains. Children ages 4-13 travel for €3.20 on all scheduled cruises, seniors half-price on M and F. Many trips are covered by Eurail and German railpasses.

Public Transportation: VRS (Verkehrsverbund Rhein-Sieg) offices have free maps of the S- and U-Bahn, bus, and streetcar lines; 1 office is downstairs in the Hauptbahnhof, at the U-Bahn station. Major terminals include the **Hauptbahnhof, Neumarkt, Appellhofplatz,** and **Barbarossaplatz.** Single ride tickets €1.20-8, depending on distance traveled. Day pass €5.50. The Minigruppen-Ticket (from €7.50) allows up to 5 people to ride M-F from 9am to midnight and all day Sa-Su. Week tickets €12-20.

Gondolas: Kölner Seilbahn, Rhiehlerstr. 180 (☎547 41 84), U17-19 (dir.: Ebertpl./ Mülheim) to "Zoo/Flora." Float over the Rhein from the Zoo to the Rheinpark, enjoying the spectacular cityscape. €3.80, children (4-12) €2.20; round-trip €5.50/€3. Open Apr.-Oct. daily 10am-6pm, last ride 5:45pm.

Taxis: Funkzentrale, ☎28 82.

Car Rental: Hertz, Bismarckstr. 19-21 (☎515 08 47). Open M-F 7:30am-6pm, Sa 8am-noon.

Bike Rental: Kölner Fahrradverleih, Markmannsg. (☎0171 629 87 96), in the Altstadt on the Rhein. €2 per hr., €10 per day, €40 per week. Open daily 10am-6pm.

Mitfahrzentrale: Citynetz Mitfahrzentrale, Maximilianstr. 2 (☎194 40). Turn left from the back of the train station. Open daily 9am-7pm.

Hitchhiking: Let's Go does not recommend hitchhiking. Opportunities in Cologne are not numerous; hitchers have been known to look for rides at the train station or the airport.

■◢ 🛈 ORIENTATION AND PRACTICAL INFORMATION

Eight bridges unite Cologne across the Rhein, though nearly all the sights are on the western side. The **Altstadt** (also called the **Innenstadt**) is split into two districts: **Altstadt-Nord** is near the main train station; **Altstadt-Süd** is just south of the Severinsbrücke. The convenient **Köln WelcomeCard,** sold at the tourist office, gives generous discounts on city museums, Rhein cruises, and bike rentals as well as free use of public transportation (1-day card €9; 2-day card €14; 3-day card €19).

Tourist Office: KölnTourismus, Unter Fettenhennen 19 (☎22 13 04 10; www.koelntourismus.de), across from the main entrance to the Dom, provides free city maps and books rooms for a €3 fee. The €1 booklet called Köln im (current month) gives city information and event schedules, and a brochure offers maps and overviews of all the sights (€2). Open M-Sa 9am-9pm, July-Sept. until 10pm; Su 10am-6pm.

Budget Travel: STA Travel, Zülpicher Str. 178 (☎44 20 11). U8 or 9 to "Universität." Open M-F 10am-6pm, Sa 11am-2pm.

Currency Exchange: At the Reisebank in the train station. Open daily 7am-10pm.

American Express: Burgmauerstr. 14 (☎925 90 10), near the Dom. Open M-F 9am-6pm, Sa 10am-1pm.

Bookstore: Gonski, Neumarkt 18a (☎20 90 90). Great selection of English bestsellers and classics on the 5th fl. Open M-Sa 9:30am-8pm.

Women's Resources: Frauenamt, Markmansg. 7 (☎22 12 64 82), has a friendly staff ready to field questions. Open M-Th 8am-4pm, F 8am-noon, appointments preferred.

Laundry: Eco-Express Waschsalon, at the corner of Richard-Wagner-Str. and Händelstr. Wash €1.50-2. Soap €0.50. Dry €0.50 per 10min. Open M-Sa 6am-11pm. **Waschsalon,** Severinstr. 74. Wash €3. Dry €0.50 per 10min. Open M-Sa 6am-11pm.

Emergency: Police ☎110. **Fire and Ambulance** ☎112. A police station is located at Maximinenstr. 6 (☎299 61 30), behind the train station.

Pharmacy: Apotheke im Hauptbahnhof, at the back of the train station, near platform 11 (☎139 11 12). Open M-F 6am-8pm, Sa 9am-8pm.

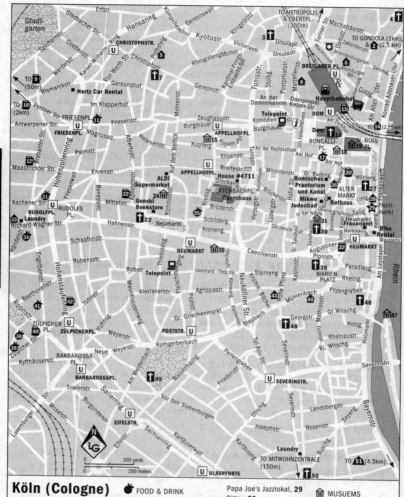

Köln (Cologne)

🏠🏚 **ACCOMMODATIONS**

Campingplatz Poll, 51
Das Kleine Stapelhäus'chen, 28
Hotel Am Rathaus, 26
Hotel Berg, 6
Hotel Heinzelmännchen, 43
Hotel Hubertus Hof, 44
Hotel Im Kupferkessel, 5
Jugendgästehaus Köln-Riehl, 2
Jugendherberge Köln-Deutz, 14
Pension Jansen, 33
Station Hostel for
    Backpackers, 8

🍎 **FOOD & DRINK**

Brauhaus Früh am Dom, 17
Café Magnus, 39
Eis Café Firenze, 25
Engel Bät, 41
Feynsinn, 38
Ganesha, 34
Joe Champs, 21
Päffgen-Brauerei, 11

📖⭐ **BARS & NIGHTLIFE**

Alter Wartesaal, 13
Das Ding, 42
Gloria, 22
Hotel Timp, 32
M20, 12
MTC, 40

Papa Joe's Jazzlokal, 29
Pitter, 20
Stadtgarten, 9
Underground, 10

🕆 **CHURCHES**

Alt St. Alban, 30
Dom, 16
Groß St. Martin, 27
St. Aposteln, 23
St. Georg, 48
St. Gereon, 7
St. Kunibert, 4
St. Maria im Kapitol, 36
St. Maria Lyskirchen, 46
St. Pantaleon, 49
St. Severin, 50
St. Ursula, 3

🏛 **MUSUEMS**

Käthe-Kollwitz-
    Museum, 24
Museum Ludwig, 19
NS-Dokumentations-
    Zentrum, 15
Römisch-Germanisches
    Museum, 18
Schokoladen-
    museum, 19
Museum Schnütgen, 35
Wallraf-Richartz
    Museum, 31

Internet: Telepoint Callshop & Internet C@fe, Komödenstr. 19 (☎250 99 30), by the Dom, or Fleischmengerg. 33 (☎397 52 05), near Neumarkt. €1 per 30min., €1.50 per hr. Both open M-F 8am-midnight, Sa-Su 9am-midnight.

Post Office: Hauptpostamt, 50667 Köln, at the corner of Breite Str. and Tunisstr. in the WDR-Arkaden shopping gallery. Open M-F 9am-7pm, Sa 9am-2pm.

⚐⚑ ACCOMMODATIONS AND CAMPING

Cologne's hotels fill up in the spring and fall, when trade winds blow conventioneers into town and inflate the prices of rooms; hostels see high traffic in summer. The main hotel haven is **Brandenburger Straße,** on the less exciting side of the train station. Trying to find last minute rooms during *Karneval* is an exercise in futility—a year in advance is not too early to book. The **Mitwohnzentrale,** Im Ferkulum 4, finds apartments for longer stays. (☎ 194 45. Open M-F 9am-1pm and 2-4pm.)

▩ **Hotel Heinzelmännchen,** Hohe Pforte 5-7 (☎21 12 17; hotel.koeln@netcologne.de). Bus #132 (dir.: Frankenstr.) to "Waidmarkt," or walk down the Hohe Str. shopping zone until it becomes Hohe Pforte. Fairy-tale pictures decorate the clean, quiet rooms of this family-run hotel. Breakfast included. Reception 6am-10pm; call if you'll arrive later. Singles €35-40; doubles €60-65; triples from €75-85. Discounts for stays over 2 nights. ❸

Pension Jansen, Richard-Wagner-Str. 18 (☎25 18 75), on the 3rd fl. U1, 6, 7, 12, or 15 to "Rudolfpl." and follow Richard-Wagner-Str. for 2 blocks. Family-operated pension with social atmosphere, sky-high ceilings, and shared bathrooms. Breakfast included. Singles €31-42; doubles €62. Discount for longer stays. Cash only. ❸

Jugendherberge Köln-Deutz (HI), Siegesstr. 5 (☎81 47 11; jh-koeln-deutz@djh-rheinland.de), just over the Hohenzollernbrücke. U1 or 7-9 to "Deutzer Freiheit." Exit the station toward Siegesstr.; the hostel is 100m down. This newly-built, 7-story 520-bed hostel with minishop boasts superbly clean rooms, all with shower and toilet. **Internet** access €4 per hr. Breakfast and sheets included. Laundry €1. Reception 24hr. Curfew 1am. Dorms €22.50; singles €39; doubles €59; quads €92. ❷

Hotel Im Kupferkessel, Probsteig. 6 (☎270 79 60; info@im-kupferkessel.de). From the Dom, follow Dompropst-Ketzer-Str. as it becomes An der Dominikan, Unter Sachenhausen, Gereonstr., and then Christophstr.; Probsteig. is on the right. Spacious, simple rooms with TV and telephone. Breakfast included. Singles €30-49; doubles €66. ❸

Das Kleine Stapelhäus'chen, Fischmarkt 1-3 (☎272 77 77; stapelhaeuschen@compuserve.com). Cross the Altenmarkt from the back of the Rathaus and take Lintg. to the Fischmarkt. An old-fashioned *Rheinisch* inn with a green-and-pink front, featuring rooms with carved oak bed frames. Reception in the restaurant below. Breakfast included. Singles €39-51, with shower or full bath €52-81; doubles €64-85/€90-141. ❹

Station Hostel for Backpackers, Rheing. 44-48 (☎912 53 01; www.hostel-cologne.de). From the station, walk 1 block along Dompropst-Ketzer-Str. and take the 1st right on Marzellenstr. Abuzz with chill backpackers and a dorm atmosphere. **Free Internet** access. Breakfast €3. Sheets included. Towels €1, €5 deposit. Laundry €2. Reception 24hr. Check-in 2pm. Check-out noon. 4- to 6-bed dorms €16-18; singles €27-35; doubles €40-50; triples €63. Cash only. ❷

Jugendgästehaus Köln-Riehl (HI), An der Schanz 14 (☎76 70 81; jh-koeln-riehl@djh-rheinland.de). U17-19 (dir.: Ebertpl./Mülheim) to "Boltensternstr." Or, walk along the Rhein on Konrad-Adenauer-Ufer as it becomes Niederländer Ufer and finally An der Schanz (40min.). Big common areas and spacious lockers. Breakfast included. Reception 24hr. 4- to 6-bed rooms €22; singles €34; doubles €54. HI members only. ❸

Hotel Am Rathaus, Bürgerstr. 6 (☎257 76 24; fax 258 28 29). On your right as you stand on the front porch of the Rathaus, demonstrating the true value of location. Reception in the bar below. Breakfast included. Singles €35-40; doubles €55-60. ❸

Hotel Berg, Brandenburger Str. 6 (☎12 11 24; hotel@hotel-berg.com). Bear left on Johannisstr. from the train station's back exit and take the 3rd left onto Brandenburger Str. Tidy rooms away from the crowds and near the station. Breakfast included. Reception 24hr. Singles €44-62; doubles €49-72. ❹

Camping: Campingplatz Poll, Weidenweg (☎83 19 66), southeast of the Altstadt on the Rhein. U16 to "Heinrich-Lübke-Ufer," cross the bridge (15min.). Reception 8am-noon and 5-8pm. Open mid-Apr. to Oct. €4.50 per person, €2.50 per tent or car. ❶

◖ FOOD

Cologne's local cuisine centers on sausage, but also offers hungry visitors delicious *Rievkooche*—slabs of fried potato to dunk in *Apfelmus* (apple sauce). Don't pass through without sampling the city's smooth *Kölsch* beer. Local brews include *Sion, Küppers, Früh,* and the devout *Dom.* Cheap restaurants and small cafes packed with students line **Zülpicher Straße.** Take U8 or 9 to "Zülpicher Pl." Mid-priced restaurants with a fine selection of ethnic cuisine are concentrated around the perimeter of the Altstadt, particularly from Hohenzollernring to Hohenstaufenring. The city's best inexpensive food is found in the Turkish district on Weideng. North of Ebertpl., an open-air **market** on **Wilhelmsplatz** takes over the northern **Nippes** neighborhood. (Open M-Sa 8am-1pm.) **ALDI,** Richmodstr. 31, is a cheap, no-frills supermarket. (Open M-F 9am-7pm, Sa 8am-4pm.)

▣ **Brauhaus Früh am Dom,** Am Hof 12-16 (☎261 32 11). A trip to Cologne isn't complete without a visit to Früh am Dom or Päffgen (below). The combination of hearty, well-priced *Kölsch* (€1.35) and pleasantly persistent waiters is sure to take effect in no time. Drink your beer with one of their filling regional specialties (€4-18). Open daily 8am-midnight, menu until 11:45pm. ❸

Päffgen-Brauerei, Friesenstr. 64-66 (☎13 54 61). Take U3-6, 12, or 15 to "Friesenplatz." A local favorite since 1883. Legendary *Kölsch* (€1.25) is brewed on the premises and enjoyed in cavernous halls or in the *Biergarten;* bring your friends—the room seats 600. Meals €2-16. Open daily 10am-midnight. Kitchen open 11:30am-11pm. ❸

Café Magnus, Zülpicherstr. 48 (☎24 16 14 69). Take U8 or 9 to "Zülpicher Pl." Though students dominate the night scene, locals of all ages come here for funky tunes, artfully prepared meals (from €4), and vegetarian options (€5-7). Open daily 8am-3am. ❷

Ganesha, Händelstr. 26 (☎21 31 65), at the corner of Richard-Wagner-Str. Take U1, 6, 7, 12, or 15 to "Rudolfpl." This elaborately-draped restaurant offers a broad range of Indian specialties, from samosas (€3) to spicy chicken vindaloo (€9). Most entrees €7-12. Open daily 6pm-midnight, Tu-Su also 12:30-3pm. ❸

Engel Bät, Engelbertstr. 7 (☎24 69 14). U8 or 9 to "Zülpicher Pl." Scrumptious crepes (€2-8) and myriad vegetarian and dessert options. Open daily 11am-midnight. ❷

Joe Champs, Hohenzollernring 1-3 (☎257 28 54). Take U6, 15, 17, or 19 to "Rudolfplatz." A 2-story sports bar and grill serves huge burgers (€6-10) both veggie and meat, and motley cocktails (€6.50-8). Shows major US sporting events on TVs scattered around the 1st fl. and on 2 big screens upstairs. Happy hour 5-7pm and after 11pm. Open Su-Th noon-midnight, F-Sa noon-2am. ❸

Feynsinn, Rathenaupl. 7 (☎24 09 210). U8 or 9 to "Zülpicher Pl." Swank university crowds chatter under a star-spangled ceiling and over an endless menu of drinks. Breakfast served M-F until 4pm, Sa-Su until 5pm. Open daily 9am-1am, Sa-Su from 10am. ❸

Eis Café Firenze, Krebsg. 1 (☎257 53 22). Elaborate ice cream dishes (€3-8) and Italian landscape murals make this a great pit stop near the flurry of Neumarkt.

SIGHTS

🏛 DOM

Directly across from the train station. ☎ 52 19 77. Open daily 6am-7:30pm. **Tours in German** *M-Sa 11am, 12:30, 2, and 3:30pm; Su 2 and 3:30pm. €4.* **Tours in English** *M-Sa 10:30am and 2:30pm, Su 2:30pm. €4, children €2. Dom free.* **Organ concerts** *June-Sept. Tu 8pm. Free.* **Tower** *open daily May-Sept. 9am-6pm; Mar.-Apr., and Oct. 9am-5pm; Nov.-Feb. 9am-4pm. €2, students €1.* **Domschatzkammer** *open daily 10am-6pm; €4, students €2.* **Diözesanmuseum** *open M-W and F-Su 11am-6pm. Free.*

It's impossible not to stare in wonder and amazement at the Dom that has dominated Cologne since its erection. With its colossal spires, a canopied ceiling towering 44m above the floor, and 1350m² of exquisite stained glass casting a harlequin display of colored light, the cathedral is the perfect realization of High Gothic style. At 157m, the Dom was the tallest building in the world for four years after its completion, until the U.S.'s Washington Monument eclipsed it in 1884. Today, construction continues to repair the damage wrought by WWII as well as by centuries of pollution, pigeons, and acid rain. Beneath the scaffolding permanently affixed to its spires, the body of the cathedral is being meticulously replaced with new stone. As you cross the threshold, a section of original stone is on display to the right side of the nave, its once-intricate detail blunted by weather and war.

A chapel to the right of the choir houses a 15th-century **triptych** painted by Stephen Lochner to represent the city's five patron saints. St. Ursula and her bevy of female attendants dominate the left wing, St. Gereon the right, and in the center, the Three Kings pay tribute to a newborn Christ. Gilded silver, gold, and thousands of encrusted jewels ornament the **Shrine of the Magi,** which reportedly holds the remains of the Three Kings. Transplanted to Cologne by an archbishop in 1164, the reliquary demanded an appropriately opulent building to house this treasure, which led to the start of the grand cathedral's construction in 1248. The shrine's golden front depicts the Three Kings bringing their gifts, and careful observation shows that a fourth king has snuck into the back of the scene. This is Germany's own **Holy Roman Emperor Otto IV,** who donated the gold and thereby earned patron saint status. To see a model of the Dom's predecessor, move to the opposite side of the choir, where a floor mosaic depicts the former cathedral. The **Chapel of the Cross** holds the 10th-century **Gero crucifix,** the oldest intact sculpture of **Christus patiens** (a crucified Christ with eyes shut). Nearby, a doorway leads into the **Domschatzkammer** (treasury), which holds the requisite clerical artwork and reliquaries: thorn, cross, and nail bits, as well as pieces of 18 saints.

Back at the entrance, 15min. and 509 steps are all it takes to scale the **Südturm** (south tower) and peer down at the river below. Catch your breath at the **Glockenstube** (about three-quarters of the way up), a chamber for the tower's nine bells. Four of the bells date from the Middle Ages, but the 19th-century upstart known affectionately as **Der große Peter** (at 24 tons, the world's heaviest swinging bell) is loudest. Those who prefer the view from below can attain a sense of the tower's immenseness at the plant-like statue located directly opposite the front door is a scale replica of the cathedral's crowning pinnacles. Find more ecclesiastic treasures in the **Diözesanmuseum,** just outside the south portal in the red building. The allure of the cathedral illuminated from dusk to midnight is irresistible, drawing natives and tourists to the expansive **Domvorplatz** to admire it.

INNENSTADT

In the shadow of the cathedral, the **Hohenzollernbrücke** crosses the Rhein. The majestic bridge empties out onto a promenade flanked by equestrian statues of the imperial family. A monumental flight of stairs leads from the Rhein to **Heinrich-Böll-**

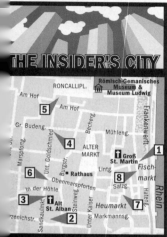

THE INSIDER'S CITY

KUNST, KULTUR, AND *KÖLSCH* IN THE KÖLN ALTSTADT

1 Reconstructed after the war, most of the Fischmarkt's colorful Rheinisch facades aren't original, but the mellow riverside atmosphere and inescapable accordion melodies are timeless.

2 Statues of the Roman generals Marcus Agrippa and Marsilius keep watch from their perches on the facade of the impressive 14th-century Gothic **Gürzenich.** Inside, a restored 15th-century celebration hall is still used for parties and conventions. (Martinstr. 29, at the corner of Gürzenichstr. ☎92 58 99 90.)

3 The eerie skeleton of the Romanesque **Alt St. Alban** today frames a replica of Käthe Kollwitz's statue "The Mourning Parents," dedicated to the memory of the citizens who died in WWII. The artist herself could relate to such pain, having lost her son in WWI. (Martinstr., next to the Gürzenich.)

Platz and its cultural center (see **Museums,** p. 294), a complex of modern architecture that complements the Dom. Farther on, the squares and crooked streets of the **Altstadt** and old **Fischmarkt** district open onto paths along the Rhein; the cafe patios give way to an expanse of grass along the river, perfect for a picnic serenaded by musicians.

HOUSE #4711. In the 18th century, Goethe noted "How grateful the women are for the fragrance of *Eau de Cologne.*" The recipe for this revolutionary water was presented to Wilhelm Mühlens on his wedding day in 1792. Though it was once prescribed as a potable curative containing 80% alcohol, today it is treasured merely for its scent, which is supposed to enhance one's senses. Genuine bottles say *Echt kölnisch Wasser* (real Cologne water) and have a "4711" label. The name comes from Mühlens's residence, called House #4711 under a Napoleonic system that abolished house names because it confused soldiers. The home now functions as a boutique, where a corner fountain bubbles with the scented water and elegantly-attired attendants dole out small samples. The free upstairs museum has a full history of the famous fragrance. *(Glockeng., at the intersection with Tunisstr. From Hohe Str., turn right on Brückenstr., which becomes Glockeng. Open M-F 9am-7pm, Sa 9-6pm.)*

RATHAUS. Bombed in WWII, Cologne's city hall has been reconstructed in its original mongrel style. A Gothic tower stands guard over Baroque cherubs encircling an ornate 1570 Renaissance arcade, the only part that survived the war. The tower is a diverse array of historical and cultural figures; Marx and Rubens loom above rows of popes and emperors. The *Glockenspiel* plays daily every hour from noon-6pm. *(Open M-Th 7:30am-4:15pm, F 7:30am-12:15pm. Free.)*

RÖMISCHES PRAETORIUM UND KANAL. Classical historians and *Ben Hur* fans will be impressed by the excavated ruins of the former Roman military headquarters. In addition to offering access to the nearby baths, this underground museum displays remnants of Roman idols and an array of rocks left by early inhabitants. It is set to reopen in late summer of 2004 after extensive renovations. *(From the Rathaus, turn right toward the swarm of hotels, then left onto Kleine Budeng. Open Tu-F 10am-4pm, Sa-Su 11am-4pm, €1.50, students €0.75.)*

MIKWE JUDENBAD. Look through the mini Louvre glass pyramid to the left as you exit the Rathaus. Underneath it is a 12th-century Jewish ritual bath that burrows 15m to groundwater. Once part of the center of one of the oldest Jewish communities in Germany, it was destroyed in 1349 when the Jews were driven out of the city. To enter, trade your passport for a key at the *Praetorium* on Kleine Budeng. *(Open M-Th 8am-4pm, F 8am-noon, Sa-Su 11am-3pm. Free.)*

CHURCHES

The Romanesque period saw the construction of 12 churches in a rough semi-circle around the Altstadt, each containing the holy bones of saints to protect the city. Though dwarfed by the splendor of the Dom, these churches attest to the glory and immense wealth of what was the most important city north of the Alps. In addition to those below, other Romanesque churches include **Alt St. Alban** (Martinstr.), **St. Maria in Lyskirchen** (An Lyskirchen 10), **St. Georg** (Georgspl. 17), **St. Pantaleon** (An Pantaleonsberg 2), **St. Severin** (Im Ferkulum 29), **St. Kunibert** (Kunibertskloster. 2), and **St. Aposteln** (Neumarkt 30).

ST. GEREON. This magnificent rose-colored medieval church was constructed in the 11th century over the remains of its patron **St. Gereon,** a Roman soldier who refused to kill fellow Christians. Its decagon structure contains a gilt mosaic of a sword-wielding David tackling oafish Goliath. *(Gereonsdriesch 2-4. ☎13 49 22. Open M-Sa 9am-6pm, Su 1:30-6pm; decagon open M-Sa 10am-noon and 3-5pm, Su 3-5pm. Free.)*

GROß ST. MARTIN. Along with the Dom, **Groß St. Martin** defines Cologne's skyline. Near the Rathaus in the Altstadt, the church was reopened in 1985 after near destruction in WWII. The interior is tiled with mosaics from the Middle Ages, and crypts downstairs house an esoteric collection of stones and diagrams. *(An Groß St. Martin 9. ☎257 79 24. Open M-Sa 10am-6pm, Su 2-4pm. Free. Crypt €0.50.)*

ST. CÄCILIEN. This church dates back to the 9th century, but after many centuries and post-WWII restorations it is no longer used for services, and instead holds the **Museum Schnütgen,** a collection of religious artifacts and artwork. *(Cäcilienstr. 29. ☎22 12 23 10. Accessible only through Museum Schnütgen, p. 295.)*

ST. MARIA IM KAPITOL. Possessing Germany's second largest crypt, this church, built in 1030 above a Roman capitol temple, also features 11th-century door panels whose reliefs detail the life of Christ. *(Marienpl. 19. Entrance around the corner on Kasinostr. ☎21 46 15. Open M-Sa 9am-6pm, Su 11:30am-5pm.)*

ST. URSULA. North of the Dom, this church commemorates Ursula's attempts to maintain celibacy despite her betrothal. This was easier after she was struck by an arrow in 383 when an untimely arrival in Cologne put her and 11,000 of her chaste compan-

4 Appreciate the fine art of Roman plumbing at this **elevated sewer ruin.** Nearby, the **Praetorium** exhibits even more ancient artifacts. (At the intersection of Unter Goldschmied and Kleine Budeng.)

5 Experience modern culture at the brewery **Brauhaus Früh am Dom,** where the best *Kölsch* in town has been served since the 19th century. (Am Hof 12-164. ☎261 32 11. See p. 487.)

6 Though your vision may be blurry from all that beer, don't worry; so are these canvases. Check out the upstairs Impressionist collection inside the **Wallraf-Richartz Museum.** (Martinstr. 39. ☎22 12 11 19. See p. 294.)

7 If the *Kölsch* brew doesn't faze you, the dialect still might. Even so, the puppet shows at the **Hänneschen-Theater** are good for loads of laughs. Call ahead for tickets; these are among the most popular seats in town. (Eisenmarkt 2-3. ☎258 12 01. Box office open M-Sa 3-6:30pm, Su 1:30-6pm.)

8 Slip back a few generations with tinted lighting and traditional jazz at the priceless **Papa Joe's Jazzlokal.** (Buttermarkt 37. ☎257 79 31. See p. 296.)

ions in the midst of a Hunnish siege. Relics and more than 700 skulls line the walls of the **Goldene Kammer.** *(Ursulapl. 24.* ☎ *13 34 00. Open M 9am-noon and 1-5pm, W-F 10am-6pm, Sa-Su 11am-6pm. Church free. Kammer €1, children €0.50.)*

🏛 MUSEUMS

Major museums are free with the **Köln WelcomeCard** (p. 287).

NEAR THE DOM

▧ MUSEUM LUDWIG. In Heinrich-Böll-Pl., this museum features works by virtually every big-name artist of the 20th century, including a collection of pop art and one of the world's largest Picasso collections. *(Bischofsgartenstr. 1, behind the Römisch-Germanisches Museum.* ☎ *22 12 61 65. Open Tu-Th and Sa-Su 10am-6pm, F 11am-6pm. €7.50, students €5.50.)*

WALLRAF-RICHARTZ MUSEUM. Recently relocated to accommodate its bountiful collection, the pastel galleries of this museum are lined with masterpieces spanning the Middle Ages through Post-Impressionism. *(Martinstr. 39. From the Heumarkt, take Gürzenichtstr. 1 block to Martinstr.* ☎ *22 12 11 19. Open Tu 10am-8pm, W-F 10am-6pm, Sa-Su 11am-6pm. German tours W 4:30pm, Th 6pm, Sa 11:30am, and Su 11:30am and 3pm. Call ahead for English tours, min. 10 people. €5.80, students and children €3.30, children under 7 free.)*

RÖMISCH-GERMANISCHES MUSEUM. Discovered in 1941 during the excavation of an air raid shelter, a 3rd-century **Dionysus Mosaic** is the foundation for this extensive collection. Three floors of artifacts overflow with ancient toys, gambling dice, and fields of Roman statues. *(Roncallipl. 4., next to the Dom.* ☎ *22 12 44 38. Open Tu-Su 10am-5pm. German tours Su 11:30am. €4.50, students and children €2.70.)*

ELSEWHERE IN COLOGNE

▧ IMHOFF-STOLLWERCK-MUSEUM (SCHOKOLADENMUSEUM). This museum not only demonstrates how to make candy and hollow chocolate soccer balls, but also displays artifacts from the first cultures who cultivated (and revered) the cocoa bean in Central and South America. Salivate at every step of chocolate production, from rainforests of cocoa trees to the gold fountain that spurts a stream of free chocolate samples. *(Rheinauhafen 1a. Near the Severinsbrücke. From the train station, head for the river, and walk along the Rhein heading right. Proceed under the Deutzer Brücke and take the 1st footbridge across to the small bit of land jutting into the Rhein.* ☎ *931 88 80. Open Tu-F 10am-6pm, Sa-Su 11am-7pm. Last entry 1hr. before closing. Museum €6, students, seniors, and children €3.50.)*

NS-DOKUMENTATIONS-ZENTRUM. Once Cologne's Gestapo headquarters, this museum now portrays the city as it was during the Nazi regime. The *Mutterkreuz* an award given to mothers of three or more children for doing their part to help build a strong Nazi state, is on display. Explore prison cells in the basement, where political prisoners memorialized themselves in over 1200 wall inscriptions, including poems of protest, simple calendars, love letters, and self-portraits. English translations available. *(Am Appellhofpl. 23-25. At the corner of Elisenstr., on the far side from the Dom.* ☎ *22 12 63 32. Open Tu-F 10am-4pm, Sa-Su 11am-4pm. €3.60, students €1.50.)*

KÄTHE-KOLLWITZ-MUSEUM. The world's largest collection of sketches, sculptures, and prints by the brilliant artist and activist (p. 67). Dark and deeply moving images chronicle the struggle of common life and pains of personal loss against the stark black-and-white landscape of early 20th-century Berlin. *(Neumarkt 18-24. On the top fl. in the Neumarkt-Passage. Take U1, 3, 7-9, 16, or 18 to "Neumarkt."* ☎ *227 23 63. Open Tu-F 10am-6pm, Sa-Su 11am-6pm. German tours Su at 3pm. €5, students €1.50.)*

MUSEUM SCHNÜTGEN. Showcasing one of the largest collections of medieval art with over 5000 Romanesque and Gothic stone sculptures and 2000 works in silver, gold, ivory, and bronze, this museum is a bastion of ecclesiastical art from its very beginnings. Also included are an extensive collection of stained glass windows, tapestries, and priestly fashions. *(Cäcilienstr. 29. In St. Cäcilien, p. 293. ☎22 12 23 10. Open Tu-F 10am-5pm, Sa-Su 11am-5pm. €4.20, students €2.90.)*

ENTERTAINMENT

Cologne explodes in festivity during ◧**Karneval,** a week-long pre-Lenten festival. Celebrated in the hedonistic spirit of the city's Roman past, *Karneval* is made up of 50 neighborhood processions in the weeks before Ash Wednesday. **Weiber-fastnacht** (Feb. 3, 2005), is the first major to-do: the mayor mounts the platform at Alter Markt and abdicates leadership of the city to the city's *Weiber* (a regional, untranslatable, and unabashedly politically incorrect term for women). In a demonstration of power, the women then traditionally find their husbands at work and chop their ties off. In the afternoon, the first of the big parades begins at Severinstor. The weekend builds up to the out-of-control parade on **Rosenmontag,** the last Monday before Lent (Feb. 8, 2005). Everyone's in costume and gets and gives a couple dozen *Bützchen* (Kölsch dialect for a kiss on the cheek). Arrive early, get a map of the route, and don't stand anywhere near the station or cathedral or you'll be pulverized by the crowds. While most revelers nurse their hangovers on Shrove Tuesday, pubs and restaurants set fire to the straw scarecrows hanging out their windows. For more information on the festival and tickets to events, inquire at the **Festkomitee des Kölner Karnevals,** Antwerpener Str. 55 (☎57 40 00), or pick up the *Karneval* booklet at the tourist office (available in Nov. or Dec. of 2004).

Cologne has more than 30 theaters, including the **Oper der Stadt Köln** and **Kölner Schauspielhaus** near Schilderg. on Offenbachpl. The **box office** for the opera sells tickets for both. (☎22 12 84 00. Open M-F 10am-7:30pm, Sa 11am-7:30pm. Tickets €8-55.) **KölnTicket,** in the same building as the Römisch-Germanisches Museum (p. 294), also sells tickets for the opera as well as other venues, from Cologne's world-class **Philharmonie** to open-air rock concerts. (☎28 01; www.koelnticket.de. Open M-F 10am-7pm, Sa 10am-4pm. Tickets €30-150.) For more on Cologne's theaters, check the *Köln im (current month),* available at the tourist office. For information on special summertime productions, check out the KölnTicket's website. **Metropolis,** Ebertpl. 19, plays new releases in their original language, and children's movies dubbed into German. (☎739 12 45. Shows daily from 2pm, on weekends from 1:45pm. Last screenings start around 10pm. €4-7, all shows €4 on Th.)

NIGHTLIFE

Roman mosaics dating back to the 3rd century record the wild excesses of the city's early residents, but Cologne has come a long way: instead of grape-feeding and fig-wearing, modern life here focuses on a more sophisticated bump-and-grind. Many bars and clubs change their music nightly; the best way to know what you'll get is to pick up the monthly magazine *Kölner* (€1). The closer to the Rhein or Dom you venture, the more quickly your wallet will get emptied. After dark, in **Hohenzollernring** crowds of people move from theaters to clubs and finally to cafes in the early hours of the morning. Students congregate in the **Bermuda-Dreieck** (Bermuda Triangle), bounded by Zülpicherpl., Roonstr., and Luxemburgstr. The center of gay nightlife runs up Matthiasstr. to Mühlenbach, Hohe Pforte, Marienpl., and up to the Heumarkt area by *Deutzer Brücke.* Radiating westward from Friesenpl., the **Belgisches Viertel** is spiced with slightly more expensive bars and cafes.

At the various *Brauhäuser*, where original *Kölsch* is brewed, servers will greet you with a friendly "Kölsch?" and then bring glass after glass until you fall under the table or cover your glass with a coaster. Unless your waiter keeps a tally, make sure that the lines on your coaster correspond to the number of beers you actually drank—it's said they might count on the fact that you won't be able to count.

■ **Papa Joe's Jazzlokal,** Buttermarkt 37 (☎257 79 31; www.papajoes.de). Papa Joe's has a legendary reputation for great music and good times. Local groups play fantastic traditional jazz 7 days a week. Drinks are pricey, but a 0.4L *Kölsch* (€3.60) goes a long way. Grab some peanuts when the sack comes around. Open daily 7pm-1am, weekend until 3am. Music starts at 9pm.

■ **Stadtgarten,** Venloerstr. 40 (☎952 99 40). From Friesenpl. follow Venloerstr. for several blocks. 2 clubs in one location: downstairs techno and house; upstairs, a concert hall renowned for live jazz recordings. Cover €7. Open M-Th 9pm-1am, F-Sa 9pm-3am.

Das Ding, Hohenstaufenring 30-32 (☎24 63 48). Smoky and very *noir,* this popular and eclectic student bar and disco has dirt-cheap drink specials (€1 and under). W 70s and 80s night. Open Tu, Th, Su 9pm-3am; W 9pm-2am; F-Sa 9pm-4am. Cover around €4.

Alter Wartesaal, Johannisstr. 11 (☎912 88 50; www.wartesaal.de). In the basement of the train station, this enormous dance floor fills with trendily clad 20-somethings. Cover €8. Check their website to find out the night's theme and hours.

M20, Maastrichter Str. 20 (☎51 96 66). From Rudolfpl. follow Hohenzollernring and turn left at Maastrichter Str. Distinguished DJs deliver some of the city's best drum'n'bass, rock, and punk to intimate crowds of locals. Open daily 10pm-2am, F-Sa until 4am.

MTC, Zülpicherstr. 10 (☎240 41 88). Near Zülpicher Pl. Take U8 or 9 to "Zülpicher Pl." Frequent live bands, generally of the rock persuasion. Cover €5, includes 1 drink; on concert night €5-15. Open daily from 10pm, earlier on concert nights.

Underground, Vogelsangerstr. 200 (☎54 23 26). Take U3 or 4 to "Venloer Str./Gürtel." Catering to an alternative student crowd, this chill beer garden transforms into a typical club when it's not hosting live experimental music. Open daily from 10pm.

GAY- AND LESBIAN-FRIENDLY VENUES

■ **Hotel Timp,** Heumarkt 25 (☎258 14 09; www.timp.de), right across from the U-bahn stop. This outrageous gay-friendly club and hotel has become an institution for travesty theater. Nightly crowds come here for the gaudy and glitter-filled cabarets. No cover, but your 1st drink is €8, weekends €13. Open daily from 11am. Shows daily from 1-4am.

Gloria, Apostelnstr. 11 (☎25 44 33; www.gloria-theater.com). A former movie theater, this popular gay-friendly cafe and theater and occasional club is at the nexus of Cologne's trendy gay and lesbian scene. Call for schedule of themed parties. Cover €7-8. Open Tu-Sa noon-9pm, until 5am on party nights.

Pitter, Alter Markt 58-60 (☎258 31 22). Warm evenings bring a primarily male crowd to the outside patio of this easygoing gay pub. Open daily noon-1am.

BONN ☎0228

Known derisively for the past 50 years as the *Hauptdorf* (capital village), Bonn was basically a non-entity before falling into the limelight by chance. **Konrad Adenauer,** the Federal Republic's first chancellor, resided in the suburbs, and the occupying Allied powers made Bonn the "provisional capital" of the Western Occupation Zone before they baptized it the capital of the fledgling Republic. The summer of 1991 brought headlines of "Chaos in Bonn" as Berlin fought to reclaim the seat of government in a political melee that divided every party in the German political spectrum. By the narrowest of margins, Berlin won, and in 1999, the

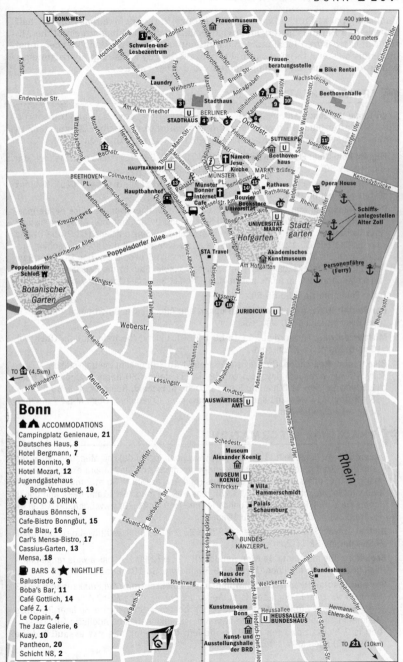

Bonn

🏠🏚 ACCOMMODATIONS
Campingplatz Genienaue, 21
Dautsches Haus, 8
Hotel Bergmann, 7
Hotel Bonnito, 9
Hotel Mozart, 12
Jugendgästehaus
   Bonn-Venusberg, 19
🍎 FOOD & DRINK
Brauhaus Bönnsch, 5
Cafe-Bistro Bonngôut, 15
Cafe Blau, 16
Carl's Mensa-Bistro, 17
Cassius-Garten, 13
Mensa, 18
🍷 BARS & ★ NIGHTLIFE
Balustrade, 3
Boba's Bar, 11
Café Gottlich, 14
Café Z, 1
Le Copain, 4
The Jazz Galerie, 6
Kuay, 10
Pantheon, 20
Schicht N8, 2

Bundestag packed up and moved east. Though Berliners joke that Bonn is "half the size of a Berlin cemetery and twice as dead," the sparkling streets of the Altstadt hide treasured local pubs in an intimate atmosphere. Bonn's exceptional museums bolster a thriving cultural scene and the city is also rapidly becoming a center for Germany's technology industry and cyber-culture.

▐ TRANSPORTATION

Bonn Regio WelcomeCard, available at the tourist office, covers public transportation (M-F after 9am; all day Sa-Su) and admission to more than 20 museums in Bonn and the surrounding area (one-day €9; two-day €14; three-day €19).

Flights: Köln-Bonn Flughafen (☎ 02203 40 40 01 02). Bus #670 runs from the train station (every 30min. 5am-10pm; €3, children €1.50).

Trains: To: **Cologne** (20min., 5 per hr., €5); **Frankfurt** (2hr., 3 per hr., €25); **Koblenz** (45min., 3 per hr., €8).

Public Transportation: Bonn is linked to Cologne and other riverside cities by the massive **VRS** *(Verkehrsverbund Rhein-Sieg)* S-Bahn and U-Bahn network. Areas are divided into **Tarifzonen;** the farther you go, the more you pay. Single tickets (€1.20-5.60) and day tickets (€5.50-12.10) are available at *Automaten* and designated vending stations. With the *Minigruppenkarte* (€8.30-23 per day) 5 people can ride M-F after 9am and all day on weekends. Week passes also available. Stop by the **Reisezentrum** in the train station to pick up a free transit map. Open M-Sa 6am-10pm, Su 7am-10pm.

Taxis: Funkzentrale ☎ 55 55 55.

Car Rental: Hertz, Avis, InterRent Europcar, and **Alamo** have airport offices. **Kurscheid** (see Bike Rental, below) also rents cars.

Mitfahrzentrale: Herwarthstr. 11 (☎ 69 30 30), behind the train station. Open M-F 10am-6:30pm, Sa 10am-2pm.

Bike Rental: Radstation, Quantiusstr. 26 (☎ 981 46 36), behind the train station. €7 per day, €6 per day for 2 days, €5 per day for 5+ days, €30 deposit. Open M-F 6am-11:30pm, Sa 7am-11:30pm, Su 8am-11:30pm. **Kurscheid,** Römerstr. 4 (☎ 63 14 33). €8 per day; €11 weekend special. Also rents cars. ID required. Open M-Sa 7am-7pm, Su 9am-1pm and 3-7pm.

▐ PRACTICAL INFORMATION

Tourist Office: Windeckstr. 1 (☎ 194 33; www.bonn-region.de), off Münsterpl. near the cathedral. Staff doles out free black-and-white maps or slightly more exciting colored maps for €1, offers sightseeing bus tours (mid-Apr. to Oct. W-Su at 2pm; Nov. to mid-Dec. and Jan. to mid-Apr. Sa only; €13), runs walking tours (Sa 11am; free), and books rooms via phone for a €2 fee or online for free (☎ 910 41 70; www.bonn.de). Open M-F 9am-6:30pm, Sa 9am-4pm, Su 10am-2pm.

Budget Travel: STA Travel, Kaiserstr. 22 (☎ 22 14 71; bonn@statravel.de). Open M-F 9:30am-6pm, Sa 11-2pm.

Bookstore: The mammoth **Bouvier,** Am Hof 28-32 (☎ 72 90 10), has a wide range of foreign books on the top floor. Open M-F 9:30am-8pm, Sa 10am-8pm.

Gay and Lesbian Resources: Schwulen- und Lesbenzentrum, Am Frankenbad 5 (☎ 63 00 39; www.zentrumbonn.de), is at the far left corner of the *Mobil Autoöl* parking lot. From Münsterpl., follow Windeckstr., which becomes Sternstr., to Berliner Pl. Cross Berliner Pl. to Bornheimer Str. and after 3 blocks take a right on Adolfstr.; Am Frankenbad is 2 blocks down the street on the left. **Counseling** and **gay assault hotline** (☎ 194 46) open M-W 7-9pm.

Women's Resources: Frauenberatungsstelle, Kölnstr. 69 (☎65 95 00). Open M and Th 5-7:30pm, W and F 10am-noon.

Laundromat: Eco-Express Waschsalon, Bornheimer Str. 56 (☎560 26 03). Wash 6-10am €1.50, 10am-11pm €2. Dry €0.50 per 10min. Open M-Sa 6am-11pm. Last wash at 10:15pm.

Emergency: Police (☎110), inside the train station. **Fire** and **Ambulance** ☎112.

Pharmacy: Bahnhof-Apotheke, Poststr. 19 (☎65 30 66). Open M-W and F 8am-7pm, Th 8am-8pm, Sa 9am-6pm.

Internet: Cheap access can be found at **Bonner Internet Cafe & Tele-Service,** Maximilianstr. 26, 1 block from the train station. €2 per hr., €5 for 3hr. Open M-Th 8pm-1am, F-Sa 8pm-2am, Su 9pm-1am.

Post Office: Münsterpl. 17, 53111 Bonn. Open M-F 9am-8pm, Sa 9am-4pm.

▐ ACCOMMODATIONS AND CAMPING

Jugendgästehaus Bonn-Venusberg (HI), Haager Weg 42 (☎28 99 70; jgh-bonn@t-online.de). Take bus #621 (dir.: Ippendorf Altenheim) to "Jugendgästehaus," or bus #620 (dir.: Venusberg) to "Sertürnerstr." Turn left on Haager Weg and walk 10min. A modern hostel in the suburbs: automatic glass doors, bar, and clean rooms with bath. Wheelchair-accessible. Breakfast and sheets included. Laundry €4. Curfew 1am. Dorms €21.50; singles €35.70; doubles €51.20. ❷

Hotel Bergmann, Kasernenstr. 13 (☎63 38 91; ajbergmann@web.de). From the station follow Poststr., turn left at Münsterpl. on Vivatsg., then right on Kasernenstr.; the hotel is on the left after 10min. Small family-run hotel with elegant rooms and a homey feeling. Shared bath. Breakfast included. Singles €35; doubles €50. Cash only. ❸

Deutsches Haus, Kasernenstr. 19-21 (☎63 37 77; info@hotel-deutscheshaus.net). Simple rooms with TVs, pets welcome. Breakfast included in a cheerful room with tulip decor. Singles €34-38.50, with bath €52-55.50; doubles €60-77, triples €75-95. ❸

Hotel Bonnito, Kölnstr. 45 (☎63 80 89; info@bonnito.de). Right around the corner from the Hotel Bergmann. Functional rooms with phones, TVs, and colorful sheets. Entrance in the Spanish restaurant below. Breakfast €8. Reception 7am-10pm. Singles €40; doubles €70; triples €90. ❹

Hotel Mozart, Mozartstr. 1 (☎65 90 71 74; www.hotel-mozart-bonn.de). From the south exit of the station turn right onto Herwarthstr., left on Bachstr., then right on Mozartstr. From the piano in the front foyer to the large, trim rooms, this hotel delivers just the kind of Viennese elegance you'd expect in such a classy neighborhood. Breakfast included. Singles €41-80; doubles €60-95. ❹

Campingplatz Genienaue, Im Frankenkeller 49 (☎34 49 49). U16 to "Bad Godesberg," then bus #613 (dir.: Giselherstr.) to "Guntherstr." Turn left on Guntherstr. and right on Frankenkeller. Rhein-side camping in suburban Mehlem, 30min. from the city. Reception 9am-noon and 3-10pm. €5.10 per person, €3-5 per tent. ❶

▐ FOOD

The **market** on **Münsterplatz** teems with haggling vendors and determined customers. At the end of the day, voices rise and prices plummet. (Open M-Sa 8am-6pm.) There is also a **supermarket** in the basement of the Kaufhof department store on Münsterpl. (Open M-F 9:30am-8pm, Sa 9am-4pm.)

▩ **Cafe-Bistro Bonngôut,** Remigiusstr. 2-4 (☎65 89 88). Revel in sleek furniture and floor-to-ceiling windows and indulge in filling meat entrees (€10-15) or delicious dessert crepes (€3.50-4.50) at this popular cafe. Huge breakfasts (€5-10) served M-F until noon, Sa until 1pm, Su until 3pm. Open M-Sa 9am-1am, Su 10am-midnight; kitchen open until 11:30pm. ❸

Cassius-Garten, Maximilianstr. 28d (☎ 65 24 29), at the edge of the Altstadt facing the station. Take a break from meaty German specialties at this fresh, sunny veggie bar. 50 kinds of salads, noodles, and whole-grain baked goods. €1.50 per 100g. Restaurant open M-F 11am-10pm, Sa 11am-6pm; bistro open M-Sa from 9am for breakfast. ❷

Cafe Blau, Franziskaner Str. 5. Crowds of students flock to this pastel cafe across from the university. If you can get the attention of the waitstaff, delicious pasta and heaps of salad (€3-6) await you. Breakfast from €1.20. Open daily 9am-1am. ❷

Carl's Mensa-Bistro, Nassestr. 15, has filling restaurant-quality meals (i.e., huge portions of pasta) served cafeteria-style at a price only slightly higher than the Mensa's. Chili and burritos (€3-4), bratwurst and fries (€2.60), and salad (€0.65 per 100g). Open M-Th 10:30am-10pm, F 10:30am-3pm. ❷

Brauhaus Bönnsch, Sterntorbrücke 4 (☎ 65 06 10), pours its own *Bönnsch* (€2.10 for 0.2L), the smooth-as-butter illegitimate son of Cologne's *Kölsch*. At this busy restaurant, *Bönnsche Flammkuchen*, made from an old Alsatian recipe, come in many delicious varieties, including vegetarian (€8-10). Open M-Th 11am-1am, F-Sa 11am-3am, Su noon-midnight. ❸

Mensa, Nassestr. 11, a 15min. walk from the station along Kaiserstr. Filling meals don't get cheaper than at this student center. The 2nd fl. serves the day's meat specialty while the 3rd fl. cooks pasta. All meals €1.65-3. €1 extra for non-students. Lunch M-Th 11:30am-2:15pm, F 11:30am-2pm, Sa noon-1:45pm. Dinner M-F 5:30-7:30pm. ❶

◉ SIGHTS

While most of Bonn's bureaucracy has been packed up and shipped out, the hulls remain; most government buildings are now ministries. These erstwhile seats of power have a historical novelty factor, but Bonn's more interesting sights include its many museums and castles just outside the city center.

▓ BEETHOVENHAUS. Attracting music aficionados of all sorts, Beethoven's birthplace hosts a fantastic collection of the composer's personal effects, including over 1000 manuscripts, his primitive hearing aids, and his first violin. The symphonic ghost haunts Bonn annually during the **Beethoven Festival.** The first fête, in 1845, was a riot, with Franz Liszt brawling with French nationalist Berlioz while King Ludwig's mistress Lola Montez table-danced. This historic 18th-century residential house is one of the few from its era that has been preserved. *(Bonng. 20. ☎ 981 75 25. Open Apr.-Oct. M-Sa 10am-6pm, Su 11am-4pm; Nov.-Mar. M-Sa 10am-5pm, Su 11am-4pm. Last entry 30min. before closing. €4, students €3.)*

RATHAUS. This voluptuous birthday cake of a Baroque building is frosted with pastel pink, blue, and gold trim, providing a backdrop for countless celebrity photo-ops: from these steps Charles de Gaulle, John F. Kennedy, and Elizabeth II have all charmed the crowds. In the absence of foreign dignitaries, the scenic Rathaus now provides a performance space for concerts and town presentations.

MÜNSTER. Three stories of arches within arches finally yield to a gorgeous gold-leaf mosaic inside the impressive Münsterbasilika, home to the remains of martyrs Cassius and Florentius. A 12th-century cloister laced with crossways and passages branches off under the doorway labeled "Kreuzgang." Keep an eye out for the incongruous blue-red windows, designed by expressionist Heinrich Campendonk. *(Münsterpl., or Gerhard-von-Are-Str. 5. ☎ 63 33 44. Open daily 9am-6pm. Cloister open M-Sa 9am-5:30pm, Su 1:30-6pm. Free.)*

BUNDESHAUS. In its heyday, this Bauhaus-inspired structure earned the title of "least prepossessing parliament building" in the world. Its transparent walls were meant to mark a new German democracy where the governors truly felt their responsibility to the people. *(Take U16, 63, or 66 to "Heussallee" or bus #610 to "Bundeshaus." Inside open by tour only, Sa-Su at 2 and 3pm; request free tickets in the tourist office.)*

PALAIS SCHAUMBURG. The imposingly gated and guarded structure was home to Konrad Adenauer, Germany's first chancellor and Bonn's guiding light. The less majestic **Denkmal,** in the Bundeskanzlerpl. outside the *Palais,* was also erected in Adenauer's honor, though arguably by people with strange ideas of honor: the 2m hollow-cheeked bust looks like it was lifted from a pirate flag. Engraved into his cranium are allegorical figures: various animals, a pair of bound hands, and two French cathedrals. *(Adenauerallee 135-141. Take U16, 63, or 66 to "Museum Koenig.")*

OTHER SIGHTS. Forty-thousand students study in the **Kurfürstliches Schloß,** the huge 18th-century palace now serving as the center of **Friedrich-Wilhelms-Universität** (also called **Universität Bonn**). The Schloß is the gateway to the open grassy spaces and tree-lined walkways of the **Hofgarten** and **Stadtgarten,** gathering places for students, picnickers, dog-walkers, and punks. To uncover Bonn's "other" palace, stroll down Poppelsdorfer Allee to the 18th-century **Poppelsdorfer Schloß.** The palace boasts a French facade and an Italian courtyard, and is surrounded by the beautifully manicured **botanical gardens.** Poppelsdorfer Schloß also houses the university **mineralogy museum** *(Museum open W 3-5pm, Su 10am-5pm. €2.50, students €1.50, 16 and under free. Gardens open Apr.-Sept. M-F 9am-6pm, Su 9am-1pm; Oct.-Mar. M-F 9am-4pm. Greenhouses open year-round M-F 10:30am-noon and 2-4pm; Apr.-Sept. also Su 9am-1pm. Free.)*

🏛 MUSEUMS

Bonn enjoyed nearly 50 years of generous federal funding, and much of this wealth has been channeled into over 20 museums. The **"Museum Mile"** begins at the **Museum Alexander Koenig.** Take U16, 63, or 66 to "Heussallee" or "Museum Koenig." The **WelcomeCard** (p. 298) gives free admission to most museums.

▧ HAUS DER GESCHICHTE. This museum examines the history of a nation grappling with its past acts and future potential, beginning in the broken landscape of post-WWII Germany, and culminating in a thoughtful chronicle of modern issues. Along the way, enjoy the artful arrangement of exhibits, including Konrad Adenauer's first Mercedes, surviving rubble of the Berlin Wall, and a genuine moon rock. *(Willy-Brandt-Allee 14. ☎ 916 50. Open Tu-Su 9am-7pm. Free.)*

KUNSTMUSEUM BONN. Unveiled in 1992, this immense contemporary building designed by Berlin architect Axel Schultes houses an even more impressive collection of 20th-century German art. Highlights include the genre-defying canvases of Gerhard Richter, cameo works by Warhol and Duchamp, and an extensive selection of oils and sketches by local expressionist August Macke. *(Friedrich-Ebert-Allee 2. ☎ 77 62 60. Open Tu and Th-Su 10am-6pm, W 10am-9pm. €5, students €2.50. Joint entrance to Kunstmuseum Bonn and Ausstellungshalle €10, students €5.)*

KUNST- UND AUSSTELLUNGSHALLE DER BRD. This modern hall has no permanent art collection; scheduled shows vary widely, and include *Genghis Khan and His Heirs* (June 17-Sept. 25, 2005). The 16 columns flanking the *Ausstellungshalle* represent Germany's federal states. *(Friedrich-Ebert-Allee 4. ☎ 917 12 00. Open Tu-W 10am-9pm, Th-Su 10am-7pm. €7, students €3.50.)*

MUSEUM ALEXANDER KOENIG. If taxidermy had a *Louvre,* this would be it. This recently renovated zoology museum displays superb specimens in natural poses amid detailed dioramas. Vivarium with live lizards in the basement. *(Adenauerallee 160. ☎ 912 20. Open Tu-Su 10am-6pm, W until 9pm. €3, students €1.50.)*

FRAUENMUSEUM. These vast galleries shine with the talent of over 700 works that span centuries of female artists, including Yoko Ono. *(Im Krausfeld 10. ☎ 69 13 44. U61 to "Rosental/Herrstr." Open Tu-Sa 2-6pm, Su 11am-6pm. €4.50, students €3.)*

AKADEMISCHES KUNSTMUSEUM. A world's worth of masterpieces resides under one roof in Germany's largest collection of plaster casts. Exhibits include Venus de Milo, the Colossus of Samos, and Laocöon. *(On the far side of the Hofgarten, facing the Kufürstliches Schloß. ☎ 73 77 38. Originals collection open Tu and Su 10am-1pm, Th 4-6pm. Casts collection open Su-W and F 10am-1pm, Th 10am-1pm and 4-6pm. Closed in Aug. Guided tours Su 11am. €1, students free.)*

NIGHTLIFE

Of Bonn's monthly nightlife glossies, *Schnüss* (€1) is unbeatable and more complete than the free *Szene Bonn*. The tourist office sells tickets to most of Bonn's extensive theater offerings through **BonnTicket.**

The Jazz Galerie, Oxfordstr. 24 (☎ 65 06 62). There's no jazz to be found at this jumping bar and disco, popular with swank youths. Party for ages 30 and over Th 9pm-2am. Cover Th €5, F-Sa €7.50; includes one drink. Open Tu, Th 9pm-3am; F-Sa 10pm-5am.

Balustrade, Heerstr. 52 (☎ 63 95 96). Enjoy a beer (€2-2.50) or *caipirinha* (Brazilian cocktail; €4.50) in front of the huge TV screen at this hip bar. Monthly theme nights include beach, snowball, and jungle parties. Open M-Th 7pm-1am, F-Sa from 7pm.

Pantheon, Bundeskanzlerpl. 2-10 (☎ 21 25 21; www.pantheon.de.), in the shadow of an enormous Mercedes logo. Follow Adenauer-Allee out of the city until you reach Bundeskanzlerpl. The popular disco also hosts concerts, stand-up comedy, and art exhibits. German-only website lists shows and events. Cover €6.50-8. Disco open 11pm-4am.

Café Gottlich, (☎ 65 99 69), Fürstenstr. 4, near the university. Modern decor and mellow jazz rule this popular student scene. Serves drinks (€2-5) into the wee hours. Open M-Th 9am-2am, F-Sa 9am-4am, Su 10am-2am.

Schicht N8, Bornheimer Str. 20-22 (☎ 963 83 08). The quirkiest club in Bonn rocks with a different kind of party every night. Su gothic, Tu theme nights (such as karaoke), Th ladies night (free entry and half-price drinks for women), F pop, Sa rock. Cover Th-Sa €3. Open Tu-Th, Su 10pm-3am, F-Sa 10pm-5am.

Kuay, Theaterstr. 2 (☎ 96 96 39 00). This new, trendy bar caters mostly to men but welcomes everyone. An open and friendly staff, luminescent decor, and theme nights suggest that Kuay will succeed. Open daily 9pm-3am, F-Sa open end, after-hours party Su 6am.

GAY AND LESBIAN

Café Z, in the **Schwulen- und Lesbenzentrum** (p. 298). This upstairs bar with colorful wall art is the center of gay and lesbian life in Bonn. Gay night M, lesbian party Tu, youth-group (ages 16-27) W, and mixed gay-lesbian Th. Open M-Th 8pm-midnight.

Boba's Bar, Josephstr. 17 (☎ 65 06 85). A chill bar drawing a lively and varied crowd of lesbians and gay men. Open Tu-Su 8pm-3am.

Le Copain, Thomas-Mann-Str. 3a (☎ 63 99 35). Comfortable bar serving cheap drinks (beer €1.25) to mostly local men. Open M-Sa 4pm-1am, Su until 11pm.

DAYTRIP: KÖNIGSWINTER AND DRACHENFELS

*The ruins can be reached from Bonn and Königswinter, the town in the valley below. From Bonn, take U66 (dir.: Königswinter/Bad Honnef) to "Königswinter Fähre" (30min., every 10min., €3.60). Or take the **Bonner Personen Schifffahrt** ferry (☎ 0228 63 63 63. 4-8 per day; €5.50, round-trip €7.50). From Königswinter, follow Drachenfelsstr. (about 45min. uphill), or take the **Drachenfelsbahn** up Germany's oldest rack railway. (Drachenfelsstr. 53; ☎ 02223 920 90. €8.50, round-trip €10.)*

"The castled crag of Drachenfels frowns o'er the wide and winding Rhein," wrote Lord Byron in *Childe Harold's Pilgrimage*. According to the *Nibelungenlied* and local lore, epic hero **Siegfried** slew a dragon who once haunted the crag. Siegfried then bathed in the dragon's blood and would have been invincible if not for the bare spot left by a leaf on his back. The **Nibelungenhalle,** where the dragon once devoured its prey, is now home to scale-covered creatures big and small—A newly opened **reptile zoo** is located halfway between the museum and the ruins. (Open daily mid-Mar. to mid-Nov. 10am-6pm, mid-Nov. to mid-Mar. Sa-Su 11am-4pm.) The Drachenfels' little brother **Schloß Drachenburg** (☎ 02223 90 19 70), an impressive 19th-century castle, flaunts its ornate turrets just uphill from Nibelungenhalle. The castle's neo-Gothic style features interlacing patterns, intricate panelling, and rich oil murals. Marvel at a commissioned Nibelung wall painting featuring Siegfried in famous scenes from the epic, or other eccentricities left behind by more recent owners, such as antlered furniture and a dummy organ. The castle is undergoing renovations, so call ahead to find out when tours will be given. (Grounds open Apr.-Oct. Tu-Su 11am-6pm. Castle and grounds €2.50, children €1.)

AACHEN   ☎ 0241

Aachen bustles day and night in four different languages, exuding a youthful internationalism in spite of its age. Bordering Belgium and the Netherlands, with the Dutch town of Maastricht just a few minutes away, Aachen has been tossed between empires for centuries, retaining a few historical treasures from each. The Romans took advantage of the city's hot springs and turned the town into a recreational center, building luxurious thermal baths. The ruins of the baths have been long since built over, but visitors can still relax as the Romans did at Aachen's modern spa. The capital of Charlemagne's Frankish empire in the 8th century, Aachen has preserved his palace and cathedral—not to mention fragments of his body. Renowned as a thriving forum for up-and-coming European artists, Aachen is a beautiful daytrip from Cologne or a relaxing and fulfilling longer stay.

▐ TRANSPORTATION

Trains: To **Brussels** (2hr., 1 per 2hr., €20) and **Cologne** (1hr., 2-3 per hr., €11). The **Airport Aixpress shuttle** stops at Elisenbrunnen en route to the Düsseldorf and Köln/Bonn Airports, daily every 60-90min. 3:30am-7pm.

Public Transportation: The main **bus station** is on the corner of Peterskirchhof and Peterstr. Tickets are priced by distance; one-way trips run €1-6. *24-Stunden* tickets provide a full day of unlimited travel within Aachen from €5.

▟ PRACTICAL INFORMATION

Tourist Office: (☎ 180 29 60; fax 180 29 30). From the train station, cross the street and head up Bahnhofstr., turn left onto Theaterstr., which becomes Theaterpl., then right onto Kapuzinergraben, which becomes Friedrich-Wilhelm-Pl. The office is in the Atrium Elisenbrunnen on your left. Also a stop for most of the city's buses. The helpful staff dispenses literature, runs tours in English if you call ahead, and finds rooms for free. Open M-F 9am-6pm, Sa 9am-2pm; Apr.-Dec. also Su 10am-2pm.

Currency Exchange: At the Citibank, Großkölnstr. 64-66 (☎ 470 34 80), near the Rathaus. Up to €500 exchanged per day for a €3 fee. Open M-F 9am-1pm and 2-6pm.

Gay and Lesbian Resources: Schwulenreferat, Kasinostr. 37 (☎ 346 32). Office open Th noon-2pm. Cafe open Tu, F, and Su 7:30am-midnight.

NORDRHEIN-
WESTFALEN

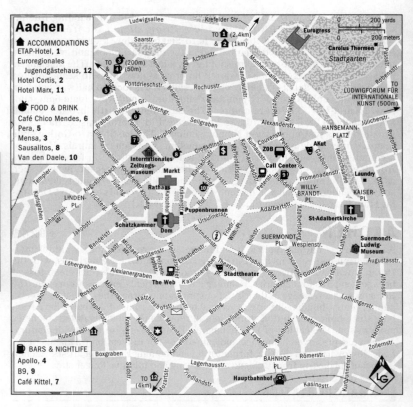

Aachen

🏠 **ACCOMMODATIONS**
ETAP-Hotel, **1**
Euroregionales
  Jugendgästehaus, **12**
Hotel Cortis, **2**
Hotel Marx, **11**

🍎 **FOOD & DRINK**
Café Chico Mendes, **6**
Pera, **5**
Mensa, **3**
Sausalitos, **8**
Van den Daele, **10**

🍸 **BARS & NIGHTLIFE**
Apollo, **4**
B9, **9**
Café Kittel, **7**

Laundromat: Münz Washcenter, Heinrichsallee 30. Wash €1. Dry €0.50 per 15min. Open M-Sa 6am-11pm, last wash at 10pm.

Emergency: Police ☎110. Police station: Kasernenstr. 23 (☎95 77 12 02). **Fire and Ambulance** ☎112.

Internet Access: Call Center & Internet Cafe, Peterstr. 11 near the main bus station. LAN connections for laptops. €2.60 per hr. Open M-Sa 10am-11pm, Su 1-11pm. **The Web,** Kleinmarschierstr. 74-76. Computers on the 2nd fl. €4 per hr., F-Sa after 11pm €2.40 per hr., Su €3 per hr. Open M-W 11am-11pm, Th 11am-midnight, F-Sa 11am-3am, Su noon-10pm.

Post Office: An den Frauenbrüdern 1, 52062. Open M-F 9am-6pm, Sa 9am-2pm.

🏠 ACCOMMODATIONS

Many hotels are closed in early January. The **Mitwohnzentrale,** Stefanstr. 56, finds lodging for longer stays. (☎194 45. Open M-Th 9am-1pm and 2-5pm, F 2-5pm.)

Euroregionales Jugendgästehaus (HI), Maria-Theresia-Allee 260 (☎71 10 10; jh-aachen@djh-rheinland.de). From the "Finanzamt" stop on Lagerhausstr. Bus #2 (€1.90, dir.: Preusswald) to "Ronheide." Pristine rooms in a hilltop hostel next to a cattle pasture. Reservations strongly recommended. Breakfast and sheets included. Wash, including soap, €2. Dry €1.50. Curfew 1am. Dorms €21; singles €35; doubles €52. ❸

Hotel Marx, Hubertusstr. 33-35 (☎375 41; www.hotel-marx.de). From the station, take a left on Lagerhausstr. which becomes Boxgraben. Turn right on Stephanstr., then left on Hubertusstr. Well-kept rooms near the Altstadt, and a real duck pond in back. Breakfast included. Singles €34-49; doubles €62, with bath €77. ❹

Hotel Cortis, Krefelderstr. 52 (☎997 41 10; fax 99 74 14). Bus #51 to Rolandstr. Walk to the end of street and turn left. Hotel is next to the gas station. A comfortable bed and breakfast combo not far from the city center. Reception until midnight. Singles €28; doubles €50-55, with shower and bath €61. ❸

ETAP-Hotel, Strangenhäuschen 15 (☎91 19 29; fax 15 53 04). From the bus station, take bus #51 to "Strangenhäuschen," then walk back to the end of the street, turn left and it is on the left side. A clean chain hotel far from the city center. Breakfast €4.90. Reception M-Sa 6:30-11am and 5-10pm, Su 7-11am and 5-10pm. Automated check-in by credit card in the afternoon. Check-out noon. Singles €35; doubles €42. ❸

FOOD

Food in Aachen has a distinctly international character; here, quiche and crepes meet *Wurst* and *Kartoffeln*. Aachen's specialties include popular desserts *Reisfladden*, a rice pudding cake often served with strawberries or cherries, and *Printen*, spicy gingerbread biscuits from an old Belgian recipe.

Sausalitos, Markt 45-47 (☎40 19 37). This Mexican cocktail bar and restaurant is one of Aachen's most popular places to eat. The gigantic bar serves jumbo drinks like "Killer Cool Aid" (€8.40) and "Mega Mojito" (€11) and the best enchiladas, tacos, and burritos for miles (€7-13). Open daily noon-1am, F-Sa until 2am. ❸

Pera, Pontstr. 95 (☎409 37 80). Minimalism reaches new heights here, but not on the drinks list. Sample one of their Mediterranean dishes (from €3.50) or splurge on an ornate Su brunch (€10.80). Lunch buffets €6. Open M-Th 11am-1am, F-Sa 11am-2am, Su 10am-1am. Su brunch 10am-3pm. ❸

Café Chico Mendes, Pontstr. 74-76 (☎470 01 41), located inside the Katakomben Studentenzentrum, is the Catholic College's lively cafe (food €4-6). Over 80 board games provide hours of simple pleasure. Cheap beer F-Su 6-8pm and all night M. Open M-Th 4:30pm-1am, F-Su 6pm-1am. Kitchen open 6-10pm. ❷

Van den Daele, Büchel 18 (☎357 24), just off the Markt. This cafe and bakery occupies the oldest house in Aachen, built in 1655. Enjoy a homemade selection of Aachen's famed local delicacies, like *Printen* or *Reisfladden* (€2.50). Filling English, French, and Dutch breakfasts from €5-11. Open M-Sa 9am-6:30pm, Su 11am-6:30pm. ❷

Mensa, Turmstr. 3 (☎80 37 92), in the teal-trimmed building on Pontwall, near the Ponttor. Look for the sign "Studentenwerk Aachen." Cafeteria style meals €1.50-7. Open M-F 11:30am-2pm. ❷

SIGHTS

In 765, the Frankish King Pepin the Short liked to unwind at the hot springs north of Aachen's present city center. After assuming power, his son **Charlemagne** (**Karl der Große,** p. 52) made the family's former vacation spot the capital of a rapidly expanding kingdom, casting a wide shadow of Carolingian influence.

DOM. With its three-tiered dome, intricate marble inlays, and dazzling blue-gold mosaics, the city cathedral rings with echoes of Charlemagne's "second Rome." Inaugurated in 805 as his palace chapel, the magnificent Dom is said to fall under the emperor's protection to this day—in WWII, a bomb aimed at the cathedral was apparently deflected by a statue of Charlemagne. For 700 years after his death, new Holy Roman Emperors traveled to this cathedral to be crowned and to sit in the simple throne still displayed upstairs, linking themselves to the greatest king Europe had ever known. The ornate gold filigree and Gothic stained glass are the modest attempts of these rulers to join in his glory. Though Charlemagne was originally buried in the marble "Proserpina Sarcophagus" (located in the Schatzkammer), today his remains reside in the jewelled reliquary behind the altar. *(☎ 470 91 27. Visiting hours M-Sa 7am-7pm, Su 12:30-7pm, except during services. Tours M 11am and noon; Tu-F 11am, noon, 2:30, and 3:30pm, plus 1, 4:30, and 5:30pm on demand; Sa-Su 1, 2, 3, and 4pm, extra tours at 5pm on demand. Access above the 1st fl. by guided tour only.)*

SCHATZKAMMER. One of the largest collections of late antique and early medieval devotional art (i.e., gold stuff to put bones into), the Schatzkammer's reliquaries contain everything from John the Baptist's hair and ribs to nails and splinters from the true cross and Christ's scourging rope. Charlemagne is also well-divided among numerous containers. The most famous likeness of him, a gold-plated silver bust, was made in Aachen in 1349 and donated by Emperor Charles IV. The bust, which contains Charlemagne's skull, was carried to the city gates for coronations so that the ancient ruler could "welcome" his spiritual successors. *(Klosterpl. 2. Around the corner to the right from the Dom, tucked into the Klosterg. ☎ 47 70 91 27. Open M 10am-1pm, Tu-W and F-Su 10am-6pm, Th 10am-9pm. Last entrance 30min. before closing. Tours must be arranged by phone, min. 10 people, German and English available. €4, students, seniors, and children €3. Tours €3.50/€3.)*

MARKTPLATZ. The 14th-century stone **Rathaus,** which looms over the wide Marktpl., was built on the ruins of Charlemagne's palace. The upstairs **Empire Hall** contains his sabre, and is garnished with magnificent 19th-century frescoes of military scenes. The hall also contains a 17th-century statue of Charlemagne, a replica of which guards the outside fountain. On the facade stand 50 statues of former German sovereigns, 31 of whom were crowned in Aachen. *(☎ 432 17 10. Open daily 10am-1pm and 2-5pm, last entrance 15min. before closing. €2, students and children €1.)* The **Puppenbrunnen,** a fountain whose interactive bronze figures portray Aachen's townspeople, gurgles happily at the intersection of Krämerstr. and Hofstr.

🏛 MUSEUMS

LUDWIGFORUM FÜR INTERNATIONALE KUNST. Aachen has focused its cultural energies on acquiring cutting-edge visual arts, with the Ludwigforum at the center of this endeavor. In addition to hosting impressive international exhibits, the museum explores artistic expression in all media. Exhibits from the permanent collection rotate monthly. The **Space,** underneath the museum, is a forum for modern dance, music, and theater. *(Jülicher Str. 97-109. Bus # 1, 16, or 52 to "Lombardenstr." ☎ 180 70. Open Tu-Su noon-6pm. Free German tours Su noon. Last entry 30min. before closing. €3, students €1.50. Events at Space €7-18.)*

INTERNATIONALES ZEITUNGSMUSEUM. Housed in a 15th-century building, this museum stores more than 165,000 different international newspapers from the 17th century to the present, covering the revolutions of 1848, the World Wars, the day Hitler died, and the fall of the Berlin Wall in 1989. The museum also has a reading room of current papers, including the *International Herald Tribune. (Pontstr. 13. Up the street from the Markt. ☎ 432 45 08. Open Tu-F 9:30am-1pm. Free.)*

SUERMONDT-LUDWIG-MUSEUM. This museum's rotating exhibits showcase everything from Etruscan vases to photography, and its permanent collection specializes in religious works from the Middle Ages through the Baroque era. *(Wilhelmstr. 18. ☎ 47 98 00. Open Tu-Su noon-6pm, W until 9pm. Last entry 30min. before closing. Free tours Su 11am and W 7:30pm. Museum €3, students and children €1.50.)*

🎵 🎭 ENTERTAINMENT AND NIGHTLIFE

Most nightlife in Aachen centers on Pontstr. and Pontwall. People flow between bars to enjoy the night air, creating a huge outdoor crowd. Aachen has a lively theater scene, led by the **Stadttheater,** on Theaterpl. in the central city. (☎478 42 44; www.theater-aachen.de. Box office open M-Sa 11am-2pm, 5-7pm, and 30min. before performances. Tickets €8-20; up to 40% discount for students.) A small strip of newer, edgier theaters lines Gasborn, spearheaded by the **Aachener Kultur- und Theaterinitiative (AKuT),** Gasborn 9-11 (☎274 58). The free *Klenkes Magazin,* available at newsstands, has movies and music listings. The thorough *Stonewall TAC,* available in university cafes and at newsstands, lists gay and lesbian events.

Apollo, Pontstr. 141-149 (☎900 84 84). A multi-screen cinema, mellow terrace cafe, space-age underground *Kneipe,* and a grab-and-go bar outside for pre-movie beer runs. Cafe open Tu-F noon-8pm, Sa 9am-2pm. *Kneipe* open M-Th and Su noon-midnight, F-Sa noon-1am. Movie times vary—check their weekly schedule for times.

Café Kittel, Pontstr. 39 (☎365 60), maintains a hip student following with a beer garden and trendy waitstaff. Posters smother the door with announcements for live music and parties. Drinks from €1.30, pizza €4. Open Su-Th 10am-2am, F-Sa 10am-3am.

B9, Blondelstr. 9 (www.b9-aachen.de). A central disco that fills nightly with students getting down to chart toppers. Posters all over town give their weekly program of events, including Freaky Friday and Student Night. Crowds line up 1hr. early for Free Beer Tu—€4.50 cover for all you can drink 10pm-midnight. Drinks €2-3.50. Cover weekdays €2, weekends €4 (includes 1 drink). Open M-Th 10pm-4am, F-Sa 10pm-5am.

DÜSSELDORF ☎0211

As Germany's fashion and corporate hub, the capital of densely populated North Rhein-Westphalia crawls with German businessmen and stylish socialites. Founded in the 13th century, Düsseldorf has thrice rebounded after pummelings in the Thirty Years' War, the War of Spanish Succession, and WWII. Today, it is Germany's "Hautstadt," a pun on *Hauptstadt* (capital) and the French *haute*, as in *haute couture.* The stately, modern metropolis, has an Altstadt that features beautiful promenades and a boisterous nightlife along the Rhein. Just beyond the riverbank is the **Königsallee ("the Kö"),** a kilometer-long catwalk that sweeps down both sides of the old town moat. By day, the social scene revolves around sipping espresso in Kö boutiques. By night, cast-away remnants of propriety (and sobriety) litter the streets as thousands of Düsseldorfers flock to the 500 pubs lining the Altstadt for glasses of local *Alt* beer and a good time.

Summer is low season for Düsseldorf's tourist industry; from Aug. to Apr. the city swarms with trade fairs. Hotels in often double prices for conventions. Call at least a month ahead and confirm the price of your room upon arrival.

▐ TRANSPORTATION

Flights: S7 and a Lufthansa shuttle travel from the main train station to **Flughafen Düsseldorf.** Call ☎421 22 23 for flight information. Open 5am-12:30am.

Trains to: **Amsterdam** (3hr., 1-2 per hr., €39); **Berlin** (4½hr., 1 per hr., €82); **Frankfurt** (2½hr., 3 per hr., €56); **Hamburg** (4hr., 2 per hr., €57); **Munich** (5hr., 1-2 per hr., €109). It's cheaper to take the S-Bahn to **Aachen, Dortmund,** and **Cologne.**

NORDRHEIN-WESTFALEN

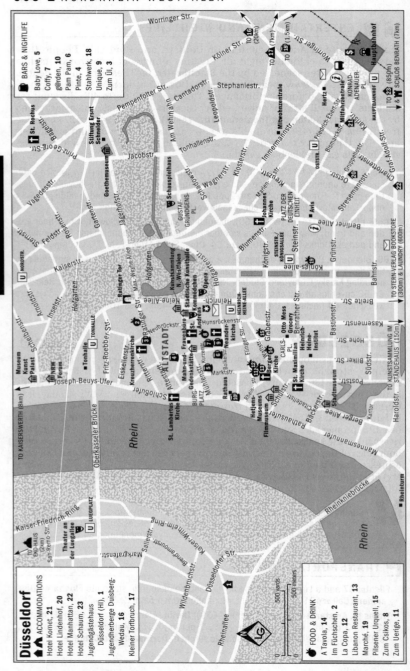

Düsseldorf

▲ ACCOMMODATIONS
Hotel Komet, 21
Hotel Lindenhof, 20
Hotel Manhattan, 22
Hotel Schaum, 23
Jugendgästehaus
  Düsseldorf (HI), 1
Jugendherberge Duisberg-
  Wedau, 16
Kleiner Torfbruch, 17

🍴 FOOD & DRINK
A Tavola, 14
Im Füchschen, 2
La Copa, 12
Libanon Restaurant, 13
Marché, 19
Pilsener Urquell, 15
Zum Csikos, 8
Zum Uerige, 11

🍸 BARS & NIGHTLIFE
Baby Love, 5
Coffy, 7
g@rden, 10
Pam Pam, 6
Pinte, 4
Stahlwerk, 18
Unique, 9
Zum Ül, 3

Public Transportation: The **Rheinbahn** includes subways, streetcars, buses, and the S-Bahn. Single tickets €1-7.10 depending on distance. A *Tagesticket* (€6.70-17.50) is the best value—up to 5 people can travel for 24hr. on any line. Düsseldorf's S-Bahn is integrated into the regional **VRR** *(Verkehrsverbund Rhein-Ruhr)* system, which connects most surrounding cities. Schedule information ☎582 28.

Taxi: ☎333 33, 999 99 or 21 21 21.

Car Rental: Hertz, Immermannstr. 65 (☎35 70 25). Open M-F 7am-6pm, Sa 8am-noon. **AVIS,** Berliner Allee 26 (☎865 62 20). Open M-F 7:30am-6pm, Sa 8am-noon.

Mitfahrzentrale: Bismarckstr. 88 (☎194 40). Open daily 9am-7pm.

Mitwohnzentrale: Immermannstr. 24 (☎194 45).

Bike Rental: Zweirad Egert, Ackerstr. 143 (☎66 21 34). S6 (dir.: Essen) to "Wehrbahn," turn right from the exit on Birkenstr., then right onto Ackerstr. and walk 10min. Call ahead to check availability. Bikes €7.50 per day, €12 per weekend. €30 deposit and ID required. Open M-F 10am-6:30pm, Sa 10am-2pm.

🔢 PRACTICAL INFORMATION

Tourist Office: Immermannstr. 65 (☎172 02 28; www.duesseldorf-tourismus.de). Walk up and to the right from the train station and look for the Immermannhof building. A haven of information. Free German monthly *In Düsseldorfer* details local goings-on. Open for event ticket sales (their 12% fee is better than a 20% surcharge at the door) and general advice M-F 8:30am-6pm, Sa 9am-12:30pm, or call the Düsseldorf ticket hotline ☎01805 64 43 22. Books rooms for free (€5 during fairs) M-F 9:30am-6:30pm, Sa 9:30am-2pm. The **branch office,** Berliner Allee 33 (☎300 48 97), is open M-F 10am-6pm.

Consulates: Canada and **UK,** Yorckstr. 19 (☎944 80). Open M-F 8:30am-12:30pm, F also 1:30-4:30pm.

Currency Exchange: ReiseBank, in the station. Open M-Sa 7am-10pm, Su 8am-9pm.

American Express: An office is located inside the main tourist office. Open M-F 9:30am-1pm and 1:30-5:30pm, Sa 10am-1pm.

Bookstore: Stern-Verlag, Friedrichstr. 24-28 (☎388 10). Paperbacks in many languages plus Internet (€3 per hr.). Open M-F 9:30am-8pm, Sa 9:30am-6pm.

Women's Resources: Frauenbüro, Mühlenstr. 29 (☎899 36 03), 3rd fl., entrance next door to Mahn-und-Gedenkstätte. Open M-Th 8am-4pm, F 8am-1pm; call to make an appointment.

Gay and Lesbian Resources: Cafe Rosa Mund, Lierenfelderstr. 39 (☎99 23 77; www.rosamund.de). Events for gays and lesbians. **Aids-Hilfe Zentrum,** Oberbilker Allee 310 (☎77 09 50; www.duesseldorf.aidshilfe.de). S6 to "Oberbilk" or U74 or 77 to "S-Bhf. Oberbilk." Open M-Th 10am-1pm and 2-6pm, F 10am-1pm and 2-4pm.

Laundromat: Wasch Center, Friedrichstr. 92, down the street from the "Kirchpl." streetcar stop. Wash €3. Dry €0.50 per 15min. Open M-Sa 6am-11pm, last load at 10pm.

Emergency: Police ☎110. **Ambulance and Fire** ☎112. Emergency doctor ☎192 92. Police station: Heinrich-Heine-Allee 17 (☎870 91 13).

Pharmacy: Apotheke im Hauptbahnhof. Open M-F 7am-8pm, Sa 8am-4pm. Emergency pharmacy ☎01 15 00.

Internet Access: Internet shops line Graf-Adolf-Str., and **g@rden** (p. 315) offers access.

Post Office: Konrad-Adenauer-Pl., 40210 Düsseldorf, to the right of the tourist office. Open M-F 8am-6pm, Sa 9am-2pm. Limited service M-F 6-8pm. **Branch office** in Hauptbahnhof open M-F 7am-6:30pm.

▐ ACCOMMODATIONS AND CAMPING

Jugendgästehaus Düsseldorf (HI), Düsseldorfer Str. 1 (☎55 73 10; jh-duesseldorf@djh-rheinland.de), just over the Rheinkniebrücke from the Altstadt. Take U70 or 74-77 (dir.: Heinrich-Heine-Allee) to "Lügpl.," then walk 500m down Kaiser-Wilhelm-Ring, or to "Belsenpl." and take bus #835 or 836 (dir.: Graf-Adolf-Pl.) to "Jugendherberge." Full of large student groups. Reception 7am-1am. Curfew 1am; doors open every hr. on the hr. 2-6am. Dorms €20.90; singles €26; doubles €48. ❸

Jugendherberge Duisburg-Wedau (HI), Kalkweg 148e (☎0203 72 41 64; www.jh-duisburg@dmx.net). S1 or 21 to "Duisburg Hauptbahnhof," then bus #934 to "Jugendherberge." These dorm beds are too far from the city to accommodate wild nights since streetcars to Duisburg (40min.), stop by 1am and taxis are expensive. Breakfast included. Sheets €3.60. Wash and dry €1.25 each. Reception 8am-10pm. Closed mid-Dec. to mid-Jan. €18.30, under 27 €15.60. Discounts for stays over 2 nights. ❷

Hotel Lindenhof, Oststr. 124 (☎36 09 63; fax 16 27 67). Spacious rooms in the center of town with friendly reception, TV, telephone, and private bath. Breakfast included. Singles €45; doubles €65. ❹

Hotel Schaum, Gustav-Poengsen Str. 63 (☎311 65 10; fax 31 32 28). From the train station, exit left onto Graf-Adolf-Str., follow the first left along the tracks to Gustav-Poengsen-Str. Or, take the S-Bahn 1 stop to "Düsseldorf-Friedrichstadt," exit onto Hüttenstr., and take the first left onto Gustav-Poengsen-Str. Smoking rooms with TV, phone, and bathrooms provide a comfortable retreat from the bustle of downtown. Breakfast included. Singles from €30; doubles from €50. ❸

Hotel Manhattan, Graf-Adolf-Str. 39 (☎602 22 50; www.hotel-manhattan.de), 4 blocks from the station. The mirror-plated reception hallway reflects neon signs and Coca-Cola posters into infinity. Clean and basic rooms with TV and phone. Breakfast included. Reception 24hr. Singles from €34; doubles from €54. ❸

Hotel Komet, Bismarckstr. 93 (☎17 87 90; www.hotelkomet.de). Straight down Bismarckstr. from the train station. Bright, snug rooms 10min. from the Altstadt. Singles €30-85; doubles €45-120; higher prices during conventions. ❹

Camping: Kleiner Torfbruch (☎899 20 38). S-Bahn to "Düsseldorf Geresheim," then bus #735 (dir.: Stamesberg) to "Seeweg." Pitch your palace and live like a king. Open Apr.-Oct. €4 per person, €2.50 per child, €5 per tent. ❶

◖ FOOD

For a cheap meal, there are rows of pizzerias, *Döner kebap* stands, and Chinese diners reaching from Heinrich-Heine-Allee to the banks of the Rhein. The **Markt** on Carlspl. has plenty of foreign fruits and a local favorite, *Sauerbraten* (pickled beef). (Open M-F 9am-6pm, Sa 9am-4pm.) **Otto Mess** is a popular **grocery** chain; the most convenient location is at the eastern corner of Carlspl. in the Altstadt. (Open M-F 8am-8pm, Sa 8am-4pm.)

▨ Libanon Restaurant, Bergerstr. 19-21 (☎13 49 17). A touch of the exotic. Splurge on the *Masa* (€29) or join the early birds and eat anything on the menu for half-price during the day. Meals €7-14. Belly dancing W-Sa from 9pm. Open daily noon-midnight. ❹

Zum Uerige, Bergerstr. 1 (☎86 69 90). This heavy-wood, heavy-food restaurant competes with Im Füchschen for the best beer in town. Breezy *Rheinisch* nights can be savored over a *Schlösser Alt* or one of their own *Uerige* beers. Meals from €2. Open daily 10am-midnight. Kitchen open M-F 6-9pm, Sa 11am-4pm. ❷

Im Füchschen, Ratinger Str. 28 (☎13 74 70). A popular local favorite. *Blutwurst* (blood sausage) and Mainz hand cheese (€3.50) go well with Im Füchschen's own delicious beer, *Füchsenbier* (€1.35 for 0.25L). Open daily 9am-midnight, F-Sa until 1am. ❷

A Tavola, Wallstr. 11 (☎ 13 29 23). Score a seat on the outdoor patio and delight in bottomless bread baskets, meticulously prepared pastas (most €7.50-9), and an Italian-speaking waitstaff. The tomato-smothered bruschetta (€4.90) is only a hint of the culinary wonders to come. Open daily noon-3pm and 6-11pm. ❸

Pilsener Urquell, Grabenstr. 6 (☎ 13 13 67). The local outlet of a Czech brewery specializes in meaty eastern European specialties (from €4). Open M-Sa 10am-1am, Su 4pm-midnight. Kitchen open M-F 10am-3pm and 5-11pm, Sa noon-11pm, Su 4-10pm. ❷

Zum Csikos, Andreasstr. 9 (☎ 32 97 71; www.csikos.de). This colorful little *Kneipe* is bursting with character and Hungarian cuisine. Though some brave the bear meat, less experimental taste buds will revel in the tasty *Gulyassuppe* (Hungarian stew; €5). Frequent live Hungarian music. Open Tu-Su 6pm-midnight, F-Sa until 1am. Closed Aug. ❷

Marché, Königsallee 60 (☎ 32 06 81), downstairs in the Kö-Galerie mall. Well stocked with salad, pasta, and meat options, this cafeteria-style restaurant provides a rarity: cheap food on the Kö. Entrees from €3.50. Buffet daily 6pm to close (€11.80). Open M-F 8am-9pm, Sa-Su 8am-8pm. ❷

La Copa, Bergerstr. 4 (☎ 323 88 58). Traditional Spanish restaurant serving 50 tasty types of *tapas* (€2-9). Rinse with sangria. Open daily 11am-midnight. ❷

👁 SIGHTS

KÖNIGSALLEE. The glitzy Kö, just outside the Altstadt, embodies the vitality and glamour of wealthy Düsseldorf. While it doesn't have the fashion-center status of Milan or New York, it packs in enough boutiques and pretension to fill Fifth Avenue. Its title (which means King's Avenue) actually originated as an attempt to placate an angry King Wilhelm IV after he was hit with a piece of manure. Stone bridges span the little river that runs down the middle, which trickles to a halt at the toes of an ornate **statue** of the sea god Triton. Midway up is the highbrow **Kö-Galerie**, a marble-and-copper shopping mall showcasing one haughty store after another. (*Head 10min. down Graf-Adolf-Str. from the train station.*)

SCHLOß BENRATH. Originally built as a retreat for Elector Karl Theodor, this 18th-century palace is one of the latest examples of Baroque architecture in western Europe. Though the architect used strategically placed mirrors and false exterior windows to make the pink castle appear larger than it is, the vast French gardens and central fountain put the building in perspective. Walk along the reflecting pool behind the castle or

THE LOCAL STORY

TURNING TRICKS

Düsseldorf may be a modern city focused on efficient business and the latest fashions, but one of its historical legacies has less sophisticated, more dizzy roots. In 1583, the first cartwheel in recorded history took place on its streets. During a royal wedding celebration, local boys impressed the guests with their ability to spin down the street head over heels, and the town's children have been spinning head over heels ever since.

Cartwheels came into prominence in the late 19th century as some young boys discovered that adults were willing to part with a penny if their trick was good enough. Spinning down the street became a profitable endeavor and soon every kid in town was competing against their friends to see who could earn the most money.

Today, cartwheelers are scattered about the city—mostly just as statues, keychains, and pictures on tour buses. But every year during the last week in June, the local youth once again take their sport to the streets. An annual tradition since 1937, *Radschlägen Turnier* is a competition to seek out both the fastest and the most stylish cartwheels in town. Around 500 boys and girls descend on Königsallee to show off in front of the crowds and compete in 20m cartwheel races.

explore the tree-lined paths in the park. *(Benrather Schloßallee 100-106. S6 (dir.: Köln) to "Schloß Benrath." ☎ 899 38 32. Castle open Tu-Su mid-Apr. to Oct. 10am-6pm; Nov. to mid-Apr. 11am-5pm. Tours on the hr., in English if requested. €4, students and children €2.)*

HEINRICH-HEINE-INSTITUT. Beloved poet **Heinrich Heine** is Düsseldorf's melancholic son. His birthplace and homestead are marked by plaques, and every third restaurant and fast-food stand bears his name. This institute is the official shrine, with a collection of manuscripts, Lorelei paraphernalia, and an unsettling death mask. *(Bilker Str. 12-14. ☎ 899 55 71; www.duesseldorf.de/kultur/heineinstitut. Open Tu-F and Su 11am-5pm, Sa 1-5pm. €2, students €1.)*

HOFGARTEN. At the upper end of the Kö, the Hofgarten park (the oldest public park in Germany) is an oasis of lush green. Stroll to the eastern end of the garden, where the 18th-century **Schloß Jägerhof** houses the **Goethe-Museum** (see **Museums**, p. 313) behind a peach facade and white iron gates. The Neoclassical **Ratinger Tor** gatehouse leads into the garden from Heinrich-Heine-Allee.

KAISERSWERTH. North on the Rhein in tiny Kaiserwerth are the **ruins** of Emperor Friedrich's palace. Built in 1184, it was destroyed by the French in 1702 in the War of Spanish Succession, but the gloomy frame remains. Some fearless travelers climb the ruins at night (with the aid of flashlights) and check out the blinking lights of the **Rheinturm,** a huge clock tower over 8km away. From bottom to top, the dots represent one second, 10 seconds, 1min., 10min., 1hr., and 10hr. *(Take U79 to "Klemenspl.," then follow Kaiserswerther Markt left to the Rhein, turn left and walk another 150m.)*

EKO-HAUS. Across the Rhein from the Altstadt, the EKO-Haus celebrates Düsseldorf's Japanese population (one of the largest in Europe) with a beautiful garden, temple, and cultural center that hosts frequent tea ceremonies and readings from Buddhist texts. *(Brüggener Weg 6. Take U70 or 74-77 to "Barbarossapl." Follow Arnulfstr., turn right on Kirchweg and then left on Brüggener Weg. Take the path to the left that leads to a small gate. ☎ 577 91 80; www.eko-haus.de. Open Tu-Su 1-5pm. €2.50, students €1.50.)*

▥ MUSEUMS

Düsseldorf takes pride in its many museums, especially the collections of contemporary art from the last century. Museums cluster around **Ehrenhof** above the Altstadt and **Grabbeplatz** near the center. The **Düsseldorf WelcomeCard** (available at the tourist office) includes entrance to major museums, as well as free public transportation and other discounts. (One-day card €9; 2-day card €14; 3-day card €19.)

▨ K21: KUNSTSAMMLUNG IM STÄNDEHAUS. Once home to the *Land*'s parliament, this enormous building reopened in April 2002 as the companion museum to the *Kunstsammlung Nordrhein-Westfalen*, focusing on experimental art from the late 20th century onward. A box fan swinging like an erratic pendulum greets you as you prepare to delve into the most progressive styles the art world has to offer. Featuring prolific modern artists such as Sigmar Polke and Katharina Fritsch, each exhibit has German and English captions. *(Ständehausstr. 1. Take streetcar #704, 709, or 719 to "Graf-Adolf-Pl." Walk 1 block down Elisabethstr. and turn right on Ständehausstr. ☎ 838 16 00; www.kunstsammlung.de. Open Tu-F 10am-6pm, Sa-Su 11am-6pm, 1st W of month until 10pm. €6.50, students €4, German and English audio guides €1.)*

▨ FILMMUSEUM. Generations of movie madness are chronicled through demonstrations of early animation, dubbed clips from notable directors, and lots of Greta Garbo. Learn how to impress your friends with excellent shadow puppets or transport yourself using blue screen technology. The **Black Box** theater (p. 314), in the same complex, specializes in recent cult flicks. *(Schulstr. 4. between Carlspl. and the Rhein. ☎ 899 22 32. Open Tu-Su 11am-5pm, W until 9pm. €3, students €1.50.)*

HETJENS-MUSEUM. Connected to the Filmmuseum, the Hetjens-Museum fills four floors with 8000 years of pottery and ceramics, including intricate Islamic tilework, 19th-century porcelain pets, and Precolumbian American relics. (*Schulstr. 4.* ☎899 42 10. *Open Tu-Su 11am-5pm, W until 9pm. €3, students €1.50; exhibitions €1 extra.*)

K20: THE KUNSTSAMMLUNG NORDRHEIN-WESTFALEN. Within this black glass edifice, skylights lavish sunshine on Matisse, Picasso, Surrealists, and Expressionists. The collection of works by hometown boy Paul Klee is one of the most extensive in the world. The museum also hosts rotating exhibits of modern art and film. (*Grabbepl. 5. U70, 74-79 or streetcar #706, 713, or 715 to "Heinrich-Heine-Allee" and walk north 2 blocks.* ☎838 11 30; *www.kunstsammlung.de. Open Tu-F 10am-6pm, Sa-Su 11am-6pm, 1st W of month until 10pm. Tours W 3:30pm, Su 11:30am. €3, students €1.50.*)

STÄDTISCHE KUNSTHALLE. Across the square from K20 is this forum for rotating modern art exhibits of every shape and size. The stove-pipe on the museum is a piece by Joseph Beuys meant to symbolize the link between art and the real world. (*Grabbepl. 4.* ☎899 62 43; *www.kunsthalle-duesseldorf.de. Open Tu-Sa noon-7pm, Su 11am-6pm. Admission depends on exhibit; usually €5, students and children €4.*)

MUSEUM KUNST PALAST. A dizzying display that mingles masterworks of antiquity with modern creations. On the ground floor, glassware, tapestries, dishes, and some astonishingly intricate locks memorialize 11 centuries of aristocratic decor. The museum's rotating contemporary exhibits lie beyond some impressive stained-glass windows. (*Ehrenhof 4-5.* ☎899 24 60; *www.museum-kunst-palast.de. Open Tu-Su 11am-6pm. Tours Th and Su 3pm. €6, students and children €3.50.*)

NRW FORUM. Dedicated to works that combine art and industry, the Forum's past exhibits have included Herb Ritts's portraits, Verner Panton's retro furnishings and Frank Miller's comic book art. (*Ehrenhof 2, across from the Kunstmuseum.* ☎892 66 90. *Open Tu-Su 11am-8pm, F until midnight. €5.50, students €3.50.*)

STADTMUSEUM. This museum recounts the history of Düsseldorf from the prehistoric to the Industrial Revolution and the aftermath of WWII. Also featured are works by the Young Rheinland artists group and a Napoleon room. (*Berger Allee 2.* ☎899 61 70. *Take streetcar #704, 709, or 719 to "Poststr." or U-bahn to "Heinrich-Heine-Allee," the museum is 1 block from the Rhein. Open Tu-Su 11am-5pm, W until 9pm. €2.60, students and children €1.30.*)

MAHN- UND GEDENKSTÄTTE. Through photographs, videotapes, and audiotaped interviews, the Gedenkstätte documents the persecution of individuals during the Nazi era. Established as a memorial in 1987, this museum addresses the Christian Churches' and workers' movements as well as racial persecution. (*Mühlenstr. 29.* ☎899 62 05. *Open Tu-F and Su 11am-5pm, Sa 1-5pm*).

GOETHE-MUSEUM. Goethe only visited Düsseldorf for 4 weeks in 1792, but this museum houses the world's largest collection of artifacts related to his life. Upcoming exhibits include "Goethe as a geologist" (Mar.-Apr. 2005), which explores his views on nature. (*Jakobistr. 2. In Schloß Jägerhof, at the east end of the garden. Streetcar #707 or bus #752 to "Schloß Jägerhof."* ☎899 62 62. *Open Tu-F and Su 11am-5pm, Sa 1-5pm. Library open Tu-F 10am-noon and 2-4pm. €2, students and children €1.*)

🔳 🔳 ENTERTAINMENT AND NIGHTLIFE

Folklore holds that Düsseldorf's 500 pubs make up *die längste Theke der Welt* (the longest bar in the world). Every night, pubs in the Altstadt are standing-room-only by 6pm, and foot traffic is shoulder-to-shoulder by nightfall, when it is nearly impossible to see where one pub ends and the next begins. The tourist-friendly **Bolkerstraße**

RIVER RIVALRY

Drinking etiquette in Düsseldorf is fairly straightforward, but always recall one simple rule of thumb: never, under any circumstances, order a *Kölsch*. The rationale behind this dictate is twofold. First, according to the 1985 Kölsch Convention, this special beer can only be served within a 20mi. radius of Cologne. More important, though, is the long-standing (and unexplained) rivalry between Düsseldorf and its upstream neighbor Cologne.

Historians date the rift back to 1288 when Count Adolf vom Berg (of what was then Duseldorp) led 6000 troops into battle against the Archbishop of Cologne in one of the bloodiest spectacles of the Middle Ages. Some locals say that mere jealousy fuels the hatred: Cologne resents the fact that its protégé has become an international corporate and fashion headquarters, and Düsseldorf remains envious of the art, history, and Dom it will never have.

Others argue that the fierce competition is founded on more serious grounds: beer. Nothing elicits town pride more than the local brew: Cologne boasts a gold fountain of *Kölsch* (known by its yellow-gold color and subtle, fruity flavor), while Düsseldorf prides itself on its coppery reservoirs of *Altbier* (copper-colored, bitter, and thick). Fortunately, travelers can experience (and taste) the charms of both cities, which are under an hour apart. Just keep your preferences to yourself.

is jam-packed with street performers of the musical and beer-olympic varieties, while locals head to **Ratingerstraße.** Though the Altstadt makes a casual and friendly setting for all ages, the city's young debutantes flaunt their most recent designer purchases in various up-scale bars and clubs; don't expect to mingle if you don't dress the part. Clubbers should watch their valuables while hanging out around Charlottenstr. after nightfall. *Prinz* (€3) is Düsseldorf's fashion bible; it's often free at the youth hostel. *Facolte* (€2), a gay and lesbian nightlife magazine, is available at most newsstands. Free cultural guides *Coolibri* and *Biograph* are useful, though less complete.

Kommödchen is a tiny, extraordinarily popular theater behind the Kunsthalle on Kay-und-Lore-Lorentz-Pl. (☎32 94 43. Box office open M-Sa 11:30am-8pm, Su 5-8pm.) To avoid a service charge, purchase ballet and opera tickets at the **Opernhaus,** Heinrich-Heine-Allee 16a. (☎890 82 11. Box office open M-F 10am-8pm, Sa 10am-6pm, and 1hr. before each performance. Tickets €8-59.) **Black Box,** Schulstr. 4 (☎899 24 90), off Rathausufer along the Rhein, serves the art-film aficionado with foreign flicks in their original format (€5, students €4). Tickets for all events are available by phone, at the box office, or from the tourist office.

▓ **Unique,** Bolkerstr. 30 (☎323 09 90). Instead of joining in the endless beerfest with neighboring bars, this aptly-named, red-walled club focuses on the music and draws a younger, trendier crowd. Cover €5. Open W-Sa from 10pm.

Pam-Pam, Bolkerstr 32 (☎854 93 94). This minimally lit basement disco is filled to overflowing by midnight, yet the crowds keep coming. Dance the night away to house, rock, pop, and plenty of American music. No cover. Open daily 9pm-5am.

Zum Ül, Ratinger Str. 16 (☎32 53 69). The quintessential German *Kneipe.* The crowd congregating out front renders the street impassable; inside people of all ages down glasses of *Füchschenbier* (€1.40 for 0.2L). Open daily 10am-1am, Sa-Su until 3am.

Baby Love, Kurzerstr. 2 (☎828 43 45). This favorite that throbs with lively tunes. W is reggae and soul, Th punk, F-Sa techno. No cover. Open Tu-Th 9pm-3am, F-Sa 9pm-5am.

Stahlwerk, Ronsdorfer Str. 134 (☎73 03 50; www.stahlwerk.de). U75 to "Ronsdorfer Str." This classic 2-floor factory-turned-disco packs in 1500 or more of the city's most divine for events like their famous 80s nights and Diebels beer parties. Be prepared to dance the night away. Cover €4-6. Open F-Sa and the last Su of the month from 10pm.

Coffy, Mertensg. 8 (☎868 16 50). Hipsters materialize at this popular bar and disco, draping themselves across cubical cushions or assembling in the cavernous downstairs disco. In nice summer weather, the whole bar moves to the square outside Tonhalle from 3-11pm. Cover F-Sa €3. Cafe open daily from noon. Disco open F-Sa 11pm-4am.

g@rden, Rathausufer 8 (☎86 61 60). A futuristic cafe with **Internet** access (€1.60 per 30min., €2.60 per hr.), a view of the Rhein, and DJs who spin everything from R&B to techno. Checking email never felt so cool. Open Mar.-Sept. Cafe open 10am-1am. Club open from 9pm on 1st and 3rd Sa of the month.

Pinte, Volkardeyer Weg 12 (☎41 03 89). One of the older pubs in the Alstadt, good music and lots of beer (€1.45 for 0.2L) attract a mellow gathering by day. After dark the younger crowd shows up to shake their groove thing, sometimes overflowing onto the sidewalk. Open daily 1pm-1am, weekends until 5am.

RUHRGEBIET (RUHR REGION)

On the banks of the Ruhr River, this region of Germany leapt from near obscurity to industrial powerhouse when factories began to crop up all over the countryside in the mid-19th century. As the Industrial Revolution swept across Europe, the pace at which train tracks, rail cars, and guns streamed from these factory floors increased, catapulting the region into industrial preeminence in just 25 years. During this time, mounting economic pressures, coupled with labor strikes and Marxist rhetoric, kindled fears of Communist revolt; the popular moniker "Red Ruhr" had little to do with the color of the water. Nevertheless, residents remained loyal to the government; the region was felled not by Marxist revolution but by Allied bombing in WWII. Thanks to the reconstruction program in later years, the cities of the Ruhr emerged from the rubble healthier and more welcoming to tourist sojourns, as public parks and museums replaced factories and smokestacks.

ESSEN ☎0201

For a millennium after the Bishop of Hildesheim founded a nunnery on the premises in AD 852, Essen remained just another German cathedral town. By the eve of WWI, however, it had become the industrial capital of Germany, thanks to seemingly limitless deposits of coal and iron. Essen capitalized on the utter annihilation inflicted by Allied air raids, reinventing itself as a city free of soot and full of culture. Though today visitors benefit from revamped historical sights and an outstanding museum, the city maintains its reputation as the industrial cornerstone of the Ruhr with shiny skyscrapers and rows of chain stores.

⊟⊠ TRANSPORTATION AND PRACTICAL INFORMATION. Trains go to **Düsseldorf** (30min., 5 per hr., €10) and **Dortmund** (20-30min., 3 per hr., €9). U-Bahn and streetcar rides cost €1-1.85, depending on distance; day tickets €6.70. The **tourist office,** Am Hauptbahnhof 2, opposite the station, books rooms for free and offers information. (☎194 33; www.essen.de. Open M-F 10am-7pm, Sa 10am-6pm.) **Internet** is at **Web & Call,** Hachestr. 5, one block to the left of the train station's main exit (€2 per hr. Open daily 9am-11pm.) The **post office,** 45127 Essen, is on Willy-Brandt-Pl. across from the station. (Open M-F 8am-7pm, Sa 8:30am-3:30pm.)

⌐⌐⊡ ACCOMMODATIONS AND FOOD. The **Jugendherberge (HI) ❷,** Am Pastoratsberg 2, is in the middle of a quiet forest in Werden, a suburb noted for its 8th-century *Abteikirche* and *Luciuskirche*, the oldest parishes north of the Alps. Take S6 to "Werden" (25min.) and bus #190 to "Jugendherberge." Rooms are standard but far from the city. (☎49 11 63; jh-essen@djh-rheinland.de. Breakfast and sheets included. Reception 7am-10pm. Curfew midnight. Dorms €19; singles €30; doubles €50.) The basic, comfortable **Hotel Kessing ❸**, Hachestr. 30, is close to the train station; go left as you exit the station onto Hachestr. (☎23 99 88; fax 23 02 89. Breakfast included. Singles €30, with shower €40, with bath €45; doubles with bath €70.) Camp at **Stadt-Camping Essen-Werden ❶**, Im Löwental 67, on the west bank of the Ruhr. Take the S-Bahn to "Werden," then walk under the bridge and continue straight. The campground is on the left. (☎49 29 78. Reception 7am-1pm and 3-9pm. €4 per person, €8 per tent.)

The **Porscheplatz**, near the Rathaus, mixes outdoor cafes with cheap mall food. Take the U-Bahn to "Porschepl." The **Mensa**, Segerothstr. 80, is in the yellow-trimmed cafeteria building at the university. Take the U11 or 17 to "Universität," exit to "Segerothstr.," head toward the rail overpass, and the Mensa is on the left. (☎18 31. Open M-F 11:15am-2pm.) Next door, the university-sponsored bar/restaurant **KKC ❷**, Universitätsstr. 2, hosts occasional parties and serves up cheap food (€2-8) and drinks. (☎205 02. Open M 9am-8pm, Tu-F 9am-midnight.) Across the street, **Beaulongerie ❷**, Segerothstr. 81, offers delicious foot-long sandwiches (€3-4) on fresh-baked bread. (☎32 62 12. Open M-Sa 10am-10pm.) The **Ihr Platz** in the train station sells basic **groceries.** (Open M-Sa 6:30am-9:30pm, Su 9am-9:30pm.)

◪ **SIGHTS.** The **Museumszentrum,** Goethestr. 41, houses two museums. Take streetcar #101, 107, or U11 to "Rüttenscheider Stern," follow signs to the Museumzentrum, and continue north on Rüttenscheiderstr., then turn left on Kuhrstr. and right onto Goethestr. Or, walk down Hachstr. from the train station, turn left on Bismarckstr. and the museum is 500m on the right. Unrivaled among Essen's modern attractions is its internationally renowned ◪**Museum Folkwang** (☎884 53 00; www.museum-folkwang.de), a stunning collection featuring defining works from the repertoire of every important artist of the 19th and 20th centuries. The Folkwang's **Fotographische Sammlung** takes on camera work from the early days, with photographs capturing the grit of urban life. Also worth a look is the attached **Ruhrlandmuseum** (☎884 50 10), which has an artistic display of fossils, gemstones, and Egyptian artifacts, in addition to an exhibit on the Ruhr in its industrial heyday. Visitors can live a day in the life of a miner without dirtying their hands through sundry paraphernalia, tools, and medical evaluations surrounding an old mining elevator. (Both museums open Tu-Su 10am-6pm, F until midnight. Single admission €5, students and children €3.50. Combined admission €8/€5.50.)

Nineteenth-century arms and railroad mogul **Alfred Krupp** perfected steel-casting in industrial Essen. **Villa Hügel,** Hügel 15, the longtime Krupp family home (or rather, palace), was given to the city in the 1950s to brighten the company's image, once tarnished by its Nazi affiliation. Inside, the museum details the history of this illustrious man, his family, and his business. Even the gargantuan mahogany staircases and intricate carvings pale in comparison to the rotating exhibits that fill the mansion's main hall with exotic artifacts from afar. The next exhibition is scheduled for 2006. (S6 to "Essen-Hügel." ☎61 62 90. Museum open Tu-Su 10am-6pm, grounds open 8am-6pm. €1, children under 14 and seniors free.)

Built as a nunnery in the 9th century, Essen's **Münsterkirche,** near the city center on Burgpl., served as the focus of life for centuries. Today, its towers are dwarfed by Essen's industrial edifices, but the cloistered string of flowering courtyards and hexagonal crypts are still impressive. Next to the choir, a candlelit shrine surrounds the 1000-year-old, doll-like *Goldene Madonna*—the church's most cherished item and the oldest three-dimensional sculpture of the Virgin Mary in the world. (☎220 44 19. Open daily 7:30am-6:30pm. Free. Treasury open Tu-Sa 10am-5pm, Su 12:30-5pm. €2.50, students €1.) Though Nazis gutted Essen's **Alte Synagogue,** Steeler Str. 29, in 1938, the largest synagogue north of the Alps now serves as a memorial to Jews oppressed and murdered by the regime. Take the U-Bahn to

"Porschepl." and follow the signs to the Schützenbahn; as you head south on the Schützenbahn, the synagogue, with the aqua-colored roof, is on your left. The ground floor presents German Jewish history from the Middle Ages through the "Final Solution," while temporary exhibits on the second floor portray life during the Nazi regime. Exhibits are in German and English. (☎ 884 52 18 or 884 52 23. Open Tu-Su 10am-6pm. Free.) Across the street, the **Theaterplatz,** site of the Grillo theater, along with the Rathaus theater at Porschepl., hosts a range of productions. (☎ 812 22 00. Box office in the Rathaus open M-F 10am-5pm, Sa 10am-1pm.)

DORTMUND ☎ 0231

Dortmund's fame for steel and coal production made it a prime target for bombing raids during WWII. The city has since rebuilt in modern fashion, with a mix of small family-owned shops and large department stores blending the charms of an earlier time with the fast-paced society of today. Spacious parks found just outside of the city center complete its suburban appearance. Budget flights from the nearby airport make Dortmund a requisite stopover for many travelers.

▊▐ TRANSPORTATION AND PRACTICAL INFORMATION. Trains to: **Düsseldorf** (1hr., 3 per hr., €12); **Cologne** (1¼-1½hr., 2-3 per hr., €15); **Münster** (20min., 3 per hr., €9); **Hannover** (2hr., 2 per hr., €33). The airport shuttle departs from the train station once per hr. 4:30am-10:30pm. U-Bahn and streetcar rides cost €1-1.80; day tickets €6.70. The **tourist office,** Königswall 18a, across from the station, books hotel rooms for free and hands out info on city sights and free maps of the Altstadt. Detailed tourist maps of the area are also available for €0.50. (☎ 18 99 91 12; www.dortmund-tourismus.de. Open M-F 9am-6pm, Sa 9am-1pm.) Rent bikes next door at **Fahrradvermietung.** (€8 per day, €30 deposit. Open M-F 6am-9pm.) Find English **books** on the second floor of **Mayersche Bücher,** on the corner of Hansastr. and Westenhellweg. (Open M-F 9:30am-8pm, Sa 9am-8pm.) Do laundry at **Eco-Express Waschsalon,** Burgwall 17; follow Königswall left from the train station until it becomes Burgwall. (Wash €1.50, soap €0.50. Dry €1 per 15min. Open daily 6am-11pm, last wash 10pm.) The **post office,** 44137 Dortmund, is at Kurfürstenstr. 2, behind the train station. (Open M-F 7:30am-8pm, Sa 8am-3:30pm.)

▐▐ ACCOMMODATIONS AND FOOD. The Jugendgästehaus Adolph Kolping (HI) ❷, Silberstr. 24-26, is centrally-located in the Altstadt. Follow Königswall left from the train station, turn right on Hansastr., and right on Silberstr. The entrance, in a small alley to the left, leads to modern rooms. (☎ 14 00 74; www.djh.de/jh/dortmund. Breakfast and sheets included. Reception 24hr. Dorms €19.90; singles €30; doubles €50.) A few blocks from the train station, **Hotel Carlton ❸,** Lütge-Brückstr. 5-7, provides basic rooms with TV in the Altstadt. From Hansastr. turn left on Lütge-Brückstr.; it's on the left. (☎ 52 80 30; fax 55 38 42. Breakfast included. Singles €30-45; doubles €60-90.) **Pension Göhler ❸,** Sudermannstr. 40, has bright rooms with private bath outside the city center. Take the U-bahn to "Kampstr.," and then streetcar #403 or 404 (dir.: Dorstfeld) to "Heinrichstr." and backtrack to Sudermannstr. Or, follow Königswall right from the train station, turn right on Rheinische Str. and left on Sudermannstr. (☎ 16 44 49; pensiongoehler@aol.com. Singles €29; doubles €45; multiple nights discounted.)

Many pricey restaurants line the spacious streets and squares in central Dortmund, where the locally brewed *Hövels* is the beer of choice. One that shouldn't be passed up is ▨**Boomerang ❸,** Kuckelke 20, an Australian restaurant and pub with superb food. Write home with stories of how you tackled the emu burger (€8) or wrangled an entire crocodile steak (€18.50). Pizza and pasta (€5.50-6.50) are available for more timid taste buds. From Hansastr., turn left on Friedhof and left again at Kuckelke. (☎586 29 11. Open daily 11am-midnight, F-Sa until 1am.) **ALEX ❷**, Ostenhellenweg 18-21, maintains a hip atmosphere under brightly-colored chandeliers. Located in the C&A building, this cafe/bar has salads, baguettes, and warm entrees, all €3-8. (☎589 78 50. Open daily 8am-1am.)

🅂 **SIGHTS.** Dortmund has numerous parks in the vicinity of the Altstadt. 🄺 **West-falenpark**, 2km southeast, is known for the magnificent rose gardens that cover its gentle hills. Several playgrounds on the east end of the park keep children occupied for hours. Ascend **Florianturm**, the 212m radio tower, for a view of the city or a bite to eat at the rotating restaurant. Take U45 or 49 to "Westfalenpark," or U41 or 47 to "Märkische Str." (☎502 61 00. Open daily 10am-11pm. €1.80, children €1. Florianturm €1.50. Combination ticket €3.10, children €2.50.

MÜNSTER
☎ 0251

NORDRHEIN-WESTFALEN

Long ago, the citizens of Münster chose the crowing cock as an appropriate city symbol; they have a little more swagger and a lot more fun than most towns their size. Locals meet nightly for dinner and a drink to celebrate almost anything—Wednesdays, for instance. The green *Promenade* and surrounding parks teem with joggers, dog-walkers, and people taking the scenic route to work. As capital of the Kingdom of Westphalia, Münster witnessed the treaty that ended the Thirty Years' War and defined the borders of German mini-states for centuries. Residents never tire of retelling the story of the 1648 Peace of Westphalia over a cold beer.

▐ TRANSPORTATION

Flights: Flughafen Münster-Osnabrück, to the northeast of the city, has flights to major European cities. Bus #S50 shuttles between the train station and the airport. **Flight information:** ☎02571 940.

Trains To: Cologne (2hr., 2-3 per hr., €23); **Düsseldorf** (1½hr., 2-3 per hr., €18); **Emden** (2hr., 1-2 per hr., €24).

Car Rental: Hertz, Weseler Str. 316 (☎773 78). Weekly rates start at €270, including insurance. Open M-F 7:30am-6pm, Sa 7:30am-1pm.

Bike Rental: Radstation, in front of the station (☎484 01 70), look for the big glass triangle. €6 per day, €25 per week. Open M-F 5:30am-11pm, Sa-Su 7am-11pm.

Mitfahrzentrale: AStA, Schloßpl. 1 (☎405 05). Open M-F 9am-4pm, F until 2pm.

▟✱▛ ORIENTATION AND PRACTICAL INFORMATION

Münster is at the confluence of the lower channels of the Ems River, in the midst of the Münsterland plain. The magnificent Promenade surrounds the Altstadt, which is west of the train station.

Tourist Office: Heinrich-Brüning-Str. 9 (☎492 27 10; www.tourismus.muenster.de). Just off the Marktpl. From the station, cross Bahnhofstr. and head into the Windhorstr. pedestrian zone. Veer right as the street becomes Stubeng.; the office is on your left as Stubeng. crosses Klemenstr. Staff books rooms for free and offers tours and theater tickets. German tours daily 11am. English tours Sa 11am. €5, children, students, and seniors €4. Open M-F 9:30am-6pm, Sa 9:30am-1pm.

Budget Travel: STA Travel, Frauenstr. 25 (☎41 43 90; fax 414 39 20). Open M-F 10am-6pm, Sa 10am-2pm.

Bookstore: Thalia Bücher, Prinzipalmarkt 24 (☎41 86 00). A decent selection of English paperbacks and classics. Open M-F 9:30am-8pm, Sa 9:30am-4pm.

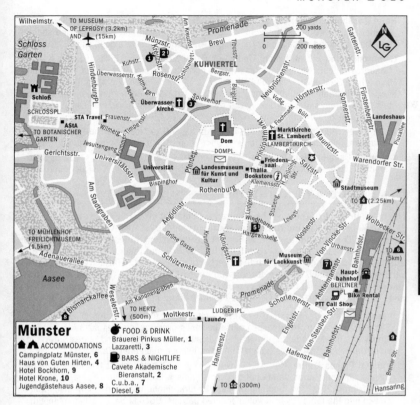

Münster

🏠🏕 **ACCOMMODATIONS**
Campingplatz Münster, 6
Haus von Guten Hirten, 4
Hotel Bockhorn, 9
Hotel Krone, 10
Jugendgästehaus Aasee, 8

🍎 **FOOD & DRINK**
Brauerei Pinkus Müller, 1
Lazzaretti, 3

🍺 **BARS & NIGHTLIFE**
Cavete Akademische
  Bieranstalt, 2
C.u.b.a., 7
Diesel, 5

Laundromat: Münz Waschcenter, Moltkestr. 5-7. Wash €3.50, soap included. Dry €0.50 per 15min. Open M-F 6am-11pm. Last wash 10pm.

Emergency: Police ☎ 110. **Fire** and **Ambulance** ☎ 112.

Internet Access: **PTT Call Shop & Internet Café,** Bahnhofstr. 8-10, directly across from the train station. €3 per hr. Open daily 9am-10pm.

Post Office: Berliner Pl. 35-37, 48143 Münster. To the left as you exit the train station. Open M-F 8am-7pm, Sa 8am-1pm. Another **branch,** Dompl. 6-7, is across from the Dom. Open M-F 9am-7pm, Sa 8:30am-2pm.

🏠 ACCOMMODATIONS

The cheapest accommodations are outside of the city center, near the station.

🛏 **Jugendgästehaus Aasee,** Bismarckallee 31 (☎ 53 02 80; jgh-muenster@djh-wl.de). Bus #34 (dir.: Roxel) to "Hoppendamm." Overlooking the scenic Aasee, this friendly hostel provides guests with every possible convenience, including in-room bath, sheets, an **Internet** kiosk, late-night bistro, and pool table. Bike rental €5 per day; €10 deposit. Breakfast included; other meals €6.90. Reception 7am-1am. Lockout 1am, doors open for 5min. on the hr. 2-6am. Dorms €21.70; singles €37; doubles €59; quads €87. ❸

Hotel Bockhorn, Bremer Str. 24 (☎655 10). From the station's rear exit, walk right on Bremer Str. for 400m. Rooms with TV, close to the station and the city's club scene. Breakfast included. Reception 24hr. Singles €35, with bath €50; doubles €60/€90. ❹

Haus vom Guten Hirten, Mauritz Lindenweg 61 (☎378 70; fax 37 45 49). Bus #14 to "Mauritz Friedhof." Or, take a 40min. walk: from the rear entrance of the train station, turn left on Bremer Str., right on Wolbecker Str., left on Hohenzollernring, right on Manfred-von-Richthofen-Str., and finally left on Mauritz Lindenweg. Managed by the church, this hotel offers suites big enough to debunk ideas of church asceticism. Breakfast included. Reception 6am-9pm. Singles €32; doubles €54; triples €77. ❸

Hotel Krone, Hammerstr. 67 (☎738 68). Bus #1 or 9 to "Josephkirche," Above a chic restaurant, this small hotel has large, if worn, rooms. Singles €33; doubles €57. ❸

Camping: Campingplatz Münster, Wolbecker Str. 7 (☎31 19 82). Bus R22 or 32 to "Freibad," near the pool. Reception 8am-midnight. €4 per person, €4-7 per tent. ❶

🏠🍴 FOOD AND NIGHTLIFE

The plaza in front of the Dom hosts a **farmer's market** (W and Sa 7am-1:30pm). Fridays 12:30-6pm you'll find the **Biomarkt,** the organically grown version of the regular market. The student district, **Kuhviertel** (cow quarter), hides cheap eateries and cafes. Bars line the streets across from the *Schloß* and discos reign between the train station and the harbor, while large party venues litter Hafenweg. Upcoming parties are advertised outside student hangouts. Münster also has frequent performances; tickets for all concerts can be bought at the tourist office or box office. (☎41 46 71 00; fax 59 09 205. Open Tu-F 9am-1:30pm and 3:30-7pm, Sa 9am-1pm.)

Diesel, Windthorstr. 65 (☎579 67), in the Altstadt, at the intersection of Windthorstr., Stubeng. and Lörstr. Trendy types nurse cocktails over phenomenal pizzas (€4-7) in a smoky pub filled with Keith Haring art. A gas pump stands guard and James Brown provides the soundtrack. Open daily 10am-1am. Kitchen open until 10pm.

Brauerei Pinkus Müller, Kreuzstr. 7-10 (☎451 51). Directly across the street from the Cavete, this enormous traditional beer hall brims with locals and *Original Pinkus Alt* (€1.80 for 0.25L). The meaning of life may lurk among the overlapping inscriptions carved into the tables by less well-mannered patrons. Open M-Sa 11:30am-midnight.

Cavete Akademische Bieranstalt, Kreuzstr. 38 (☎457 00). Founded in 1959, this first student pub in Westphalia serves homemade spinach noodles in thick sauces (€6-8) in a dark, carnivalesque atmosphere. Open daily 7pm-1am. Kitchen closes M-Th and Su 11:30pm, F-Sa 12:30am.

C.u.b.a., Achtermannstr. 10-12 (☎548 92; www.cuba-muenster.de). A late-night hotspot for Münster's alternative crowd, this 2-floor cultural center, disco, and *Kneipe* throws specialty parties W and Sa. Open daily 6pm-1am. Kitchen open until 11pm.

Lazzaretti, Spiekerhof 26 (☎48 42 333). This stylish bistro and outdoor patio is a popular student haunt by day. Pasta €6-12. Giant sundaes €4-7. Open daily 10am-11pm.

🎯 SIGHTS

🏛**DOM.** The heart of Münster's religious community is the huge **St. Paulus-Dom** in the center of the Altstadt. Though the church was founded under the direction of Charlemagne in 792, the cathedral standing today dates from the 13th century, now beautifully restored after WWII bombings. A stone from the similarly bombed Cathedral of Coventry stands in the entryway, carrying a wish for mutual forgiveness between Britain and Germany. Inside is the pulpit where Bishop Clemens von Galen delivered three courageous sermons against the

Nazi program of euthanasia for so-called "incurables." Fearing revolt if he arrested the popular bishop, Hitler took out his frustration by sending 37 priests and clergy to concentration camps in von Galen's place; 10 of them died there. Transcripts of his sermons can be purchased in English or German at the treasury. An exceptional feat of both artistry and intellectual precision, a 16th-century **astronomical clock** dominates the choir ambulatory. Adorned with hand-painted zodiac symbols, the clock will operate until the year 2071, when its calendar will end and restart at the year 1540. Meanwhile, it continues to keep accurate time, trace the movement of the planets, and play a merry Glockenspiel tune. *(M-Sa noon and Su 12:30pm.)* A wide selection of diocesan vestments in the basement display church fashion from the late Middle Ages. *(Dom open M-Sa 6:30am-6pm, Su 6:30am-7:30pm. Free. Courtyard open Tu-Sa 9am-6pm, Su 2-6pm. Free. Treasury open Tu-Su 11am-4pm. €1, students €0.50.)*

MARKTKIRCHE ST LAMBERTI. Münster's piety shows its macabre side at the Marktkirche St. Lamberti, where three cages hang above the clock face. In 1535 one cage held the corpse of anabaptist zealot Jan van Leiden, who ordered the town's citizens to relinquish all property and be rebaptized as polygamists. The menacing cages still hang as a "reminder." Suspended inside the church is Germany's only free-hanging organ. Following a tradition dating to 1481, the watchman plays a copper horn every 30min. from 9am-noon, daily except Tuesday. *(Kirchhermg. 3, off the Prinzipalmarkt. ☎448 93. Free concerts 1st Sa of the month at noon.)*

PROMENADE. When Goethe's carriage turned onto the linden-tree-lined Promenade encircling Münster's Altstadt, he would slow it and smell the flowers. Today the Promenade remains an idyllic setting for the many cyclists, families and couples that enjoy its shady sidewalks. In the west, the Promenade meets the Schloßgarten, where centuries-old trees continue to grow, moss-covered and majestic. The Baroque **Schloß,** designed by local architect Johann Conrad Schlaun, is now part of Wilhelmsuniversität. *(Open daily Apr.-Sept. 7am-7pm; Oct.-Mar. 7am-8pm.)* The **botanical gardens,** behind the Schloß, are the perfect spot for a walk. *(☎832 38 27. Open daily mid-Mar. to mid-Oct. 8am-5pm; mid-Oct. to mid-Mar. 8am-4pm.)*

FRIEDENSSAAL. Beside the elegant gabled houses of Prinzipalmarkt, the Friedenssaal (Hall of Peace) commemorates the end of the Thirty Years' War. Within these hallowed halls, which kept a band of woodcarvers busy for a very long time, the Peace of Westphalia was signed in 1648. Fortunately, all important artifacts were stored away in the coutryside during WWII, so after thorough renovations it was possible to bring the hall to its original splendor. Inside, guarded by a golden cockerel, a centuries-old human hand is on display—no one seems to know why. *(Open Tu-F 10am-5pm, Sa-Su 10am-4pm. €1.50, children and students €1.)*

▥ MUSEUMS

Münster treasures its historical and cultural artifacts in a well-maintained **Landesmuseum,** but its real gems are the small collections. Ask the tourist office for information about these offerings, including the **Railway Museum, Carnival Museum,** and **Museum of Organs,** all in nearby suburbs.

LANDESMUSEUM FÜR KUNST UND KULTUR. Spiraling around a central atrium, a series of modern galleries include visions of Franz Marc's paradise and a procession of Kirchner canvases (one of which is positioned sideways at the artist's request). A separate wing explores religious art from the Middle Ages to the Baroque period and hosts traveling exhibitions. *(Dompl. 10. ☎59 07 01. Open Tu-Su 10am-6pm. €3.50, students €2.10, children €2.)*

LEPRAMUSEUM (LEPROSY MUSEUM). It's a little far away, but the novelty factor never wears thin and the exhibits (all strictly hands-off) possess unique appeal. Highlights include playful little leper-puppets. *(Kinderhauser Str. 15. Northwest of the Altstadt; take bus #6, 9, or 17 to "Kristiansandstr." ☎285 10. Open Su 3-5pm. Call for an appointment on other days. Free.)*

MÜHLENHOF-FREILICHTMUSEUM. This open-air museum allows visitors to sample daily life in an 18th-century farm town. Inhale the pungent odor of strung sausages in an old miller's cottage or improvise a picnic lunch on a millstone from 1868. Loaves of indestructible *Schwarzbrot* (€2) and authentic wooden clogs (€12) for purchase. *(Theo-Breider-Weg 1, near the Aasee and Torminbrücke. ☎98 12 00. Open mid-Mar. to Oct. daily 10am-6pm, last entry 5pm; Nov. to mid-Mar. M-Sa 1-4:30pm, Su 11am-4:30pm, last entry 4pm. €3, students and seniors €2, children €1.50.)*

MUSEUM FÜR LACKKUNST. This museum presents a selection of the highly refined lacquer crafts of East Asian and Islamic art from India and Persia. Statues and vases fill perfectly polished cases, and ornate furnishings seem to glow with abalone and mother-of-pearl inlays. Visiting exhibits glisten in the basement, including Burmese art exhibition January-March 2005. *(Windthorststr. 26, just off the Promenade. ☎41 85 10. Open Tu noon-8pm, W-Su noon-6pm. €3, students €2. Free on Tu.)*

STADTMUSEUM. Abounding with ancient vases, courtly frocks, and models of the evolving history, this museum follows Münster from its inauspicious beginning early in the 8th century. *(Salzstr. 28. Open Tu-F 10am-6pm, Sa-Su 11am-6pm. Free.)*

DETMOLD ☎05231

Although Detmold's attractions may not seem outstanding, the town is an ideal base for exploring the *Teutoburger Wald*. Here, Germany's picture-perfect forested hills melt into pastures full of horses grazing serenely as eagles soar overhead. More fancy fowl can be seen at the local aviary, and other living museums include a scenic bird and flower park and a historical open-air village.

⊡⊿ TRANSPORTATION AND PRACTICAL INFORMATION. Trains to: **Bielefeld** (45min., 1-2 per hr., €9); **Münster** (2hr., every 2hr., €16); **Osnabrück** (1¼hr., 1 per hr., €13). The **tourist office,** Rathaus, am Markt, will help you prepare for pastoral adventures. From the station, head left on Bahnhofstr., turn right on Paulinenstr., then left on Bruchstr. into the pedestrian zone, and walk another 5min. to the peach Rathaus. The tourist office is on the right side of the building. The city brochure is excellent and has a detailed map of the area (€1.50). For wider-ranging hikes, ask for the green *Hermannsland* map (€8), a detailed trail map with elevations, or *Wanderschuh* (free), a handy guide that gives hike distances and durations. The staff books rooms for free and posts an accommodations list outside the building. (☎97 73 28; www.detmold.de. Open M-F 10am-6pm, Sa 10am-2pm.) Altstadt **tours** (in German) leave from the main entrance of the Residenzschloß. (Apr.-Oct. Sa 10am, Su 11am. €2, students €1.) The tourist office also gives out a free self-guided tour in English. Save money with an *extraTour* ticket (€14.50, children €5.90), valid at the Hermannsdenkmal, Adlerwarte, Vogel- und Blumenpark, Residenzschloß, and Landesmuseum. Hop on the **Internet** at **Internet-Bistro,** Lange Str. 84. Turn left out of the tourist office and walk straight; it's on the left. (☎98 11 12. €2.50 per 30min., €3.60 per hr. Open M-F 1-10pm, Sa noon-8pm, Su 2-10pm.) The **post office** is between the station and the pedestrian zone, on the corner of Paulinenstr. and Bismarckstr. (M-F 8am-6pm, Sa 8am-12:30pm.)

NORDRHEIN-WESTFALEN

▐▐ ACCOMMODATIONS AND FOOD. In addition to the regular pack of wild school children, the **Jugendherberge Detmold ❷**, Schirrmannstr. 49, houses Socke the mule, who meanders quietly around the isolated but charming stucco house and its orchard setting. From Bussteig 3 at the train station, take bus #704 (dir.: Hiddesen; 1-2 per hr.) to "Auf den Klippen," and walk 10min. down the picture-perfect country road across the street from the stop. Or, it's a 45min. walk from the station: turn right on Paulinenstr., right on Freiligrathstr. (which becomes Bandelstr.), left on Bülowstr., right onto Schützenberg, and right onto Schirmannstr. (☎247 39; www.jh-detmold.de. Breakfast and sheets included. Lunch €4.50, dinner €4. Reception until 10pm. Curfew 10pm, but guests get keys. Dorms €17, under 26 €14.) A few blocks from the Rathaus, find luxurious accommodations at **Hotel Nadler ❹**, Grabbestr. 4. Rooms are bright and spacious, with TV and telephones. (☎924 60; www.hotel-nadler.de. Breakfast included. Singles €29-44; doubles €65-76; triples €92.) A variety of delicious crepes, potatoes, and salads await at **Knollchen ❶**, Lange Str. 21. (☎283 99. €2-4. Open M-F 10am-7pm, Sa 10am-4pm.) Down the street at **Fuchsbau ❷**, Lange Str. 13, get baguette sandwiches (€2-5), *Schnitzel*, pasta, and drinks from the straw-hut bar (€4-7). All pizzas are €4 from 5-8pm. (☎280 22. Open M-F 5-11pm, Sa noon-3pm and 5-11pm, Su 5-11pm.) Though there is no grocery store in the Altstadt, fresh produce can be picked up at the **market** in front of the Rathaus. (Open Tu, Th, Sa 7am-2pm.)

◐ SIGHTS. Most of Detmold's activities lie beyond the city limits, but cannons still arm the courtyard of the **Fürstliches Residenzschloß,** a Renaissance castle in the town's central park. (☎700 20. Obligatory 40min. tours daily on the hr. 10am-4pm, except 1pm; Apr.-Oct. also 5pm. €3.50, children €2.) Other sights unfold across the countryside. It's not hard to walk from sight to sight, though bus #792 (dir.: Scheider) shuffles weekend sight-seers between locations, leaving from *Bussteig* 6 at the train station once per hr. on weekends, and weekdays at 8:10am, 9:10am, and 3:10pm. (Day ticket for all sights below €7.10, 5 people €11.10; excluding Externsteine €3.70, 5 people €6.60). Other bus routes are listed below with individual sights; timing during the week is tricky, but the tourist office has bus schedules and advice on how to get from place to place. There are also many trails that criss-cross the Teutoburger Wald, making for lovely hikes between sights. A trail map from the tourist office may save you from hours of aimless wandering.

A good place to start is the **Adlerwarte,** a nature trail featuring more than 80 birds of prey. Time your arrival to catch a free flight exhibition, where falcons pass inches above startled faces, eliciting shrieks from children and adults alike. The view of the hill and valleys from the exhibition platform can't be beat. Take bus #792 or 701 (€1.65) from Detmold (dir.: Weidmüller/Berlebeck) to "Adlerwarte." (☎471 71. Open mid-Mar. to mid-Nov. daily 9:30am-5:30pm. Displays 11am and 3pm. May-Sept. also 4:30pm. €4, children €2.) To exchange eagles for emus, follow signs on the trail (about 20min.) behind the Adlerwarte to the relaxing **Vogel- und Blumenpark** (bird and flower park), home to ostriches and peacocks. If you aren't up for the hike, take bus #792 or 782 (€1.65) from Detmold to "Vogelpark." (☎474 39. Open mid-Mar. to Oct. daily 9am-6pm. €4.50, students €3.50, children €2.50.) After soaking in the birds and blossoms, take the main road in front of the park left toward the **Hermannsdenkmal** (about 30min.), which commemorates the victory of the Germanic chief Hermann over the Romans, proclaiming him liberator of the German people. Overeager nationalists erected Hermann's likeness on an old encampment in 1875, and **Kaiser Wilhelm I** even came to cut the ribbon. Complete with winged helmet, the statue wields a 7m sword with the disconcerting inscription, "German unity is my power; my power is Germany's might." Research continually relocates the battle site; the only consensus is that the colossus does *not* mark it. Climb 75 steps inside the base of the statue for a great view; you'll still only be at his feet. (Bus #792. Open daily Mar.-Oct. 9am-6:30pm; Nov.-Feb. 9:30am-4pm. €1.50, children €0.50.) At the Hermannsdenkmal, a number of marked **hiking** trails head out in various directions. Heading from Hermann's front left leads into thickly wooded hills. The path on his right side leads back into Detmold.

Also among the hills south of town, massive pillars of rock at **Externsteine** emerge incongruously from the surrounding forest. Cleaved out of the mountains during an ice age, the exposed rock faces were carved and etched by people long ago to mark celestial events. By climbing the stairs and crossing the bridge to the central pillar, you will arrive at the upper chapel and see in the wall a hole that lets light fall on the pedestal only at sunrise on the summer solstice. Atop one of the towering cliffs, a large rock nicknamed "grave rock" appears to teeter precariously close to the edge, prepared to tumble and earn its name. Actually quite stable, the rock won't be going anywhere for a while. Take bus #792 or 782 (€3.30) to "Abzweig Externsteine." (Stairways open Apr.-Oct. daily 9am-6pm. €1.50, students €1.) Detmold's **Westfälisches Freilichtmuseum** is miraculously untouristed: spread over 80 hectares, this outdoor museum consists of more than 100 restored and rebuilt 17th- to 19th-century German farm buildings. A horse-drawn carriage takes you from the entrance to the museum's far end. (€1.50, children €1.) Take 792 or bus #701 (dir.: Weidmüller/Berlebeck) to "Freilichtmuseum." (☎70 61 05. Open Apr.-Oct. Tu-Su 9am-6pm. Last entrance 5pm. €5, students €3.50, children €2.)

NORDRHEIN-WESTFALEN

HESSEN

Prior to the 20th century, Hessen was known for exporting mercenary soldiers to rulers such as **King George III,** who enlisted them to put down an unruly gang of colonials on the other side of the Atlantic in 1776. Today, Hessen's ivy-covered castles and soaring steeples are reflected in the region's ultramodern skyscrapers. Hessen is the busiest economic center in the country, led by the financial center of Frankfurt. Overshadowed by this giant, the rest of Hessen attracts little attention from tourists, leaving the medieval delights of Marburg's *Uni*-culture and the more modern offerings of Kassel blessedly off the beaten path.

HIGHLIGHTS OF HESSEN

LAND at **Frankfurt's** busy airport (p. 325), and stay for the **Römerberg,** fast-paced nightlife, and superb museums.

PARTY ALL NIGHT LONG in the hip university town of **Marburg** (p. 341), which influenced the writings of the **Brothers Grimm** and has spawned a hip youth culture.

WALK THROUGH A FAIRY-TALE in **Wilhelmshöhe Park,** where waterfalls and castles complement the curious cosmopolitanism of **Kassel** (p. 346).

FRANKFURT AM MAIN   ☎069

Though Frankfurt may lack the traditional architecture of many German cities, its glass and steel buildings give it modern glamour. Looking at the sleek skyline, it is hard to believe that this city dates back to 794. It is said that while fleeing the Saxons, **Charlemagne** and his Franks saw a deer crossing the Main River in a shallow *Furt* (ford) and followed the animal to the safety of the opposite bank, where Charlemagne proceeded to found a city. In 1356, Frankfurt rose to prominence when the **Golden Bull** of imperial law made it the site of emperors' elections and coronations until the Holy Roman Empire dissolved. Since then, hordes of Frankfurters have influenced Western culture. **Goethe** and **Anne Frank** lived here, and the **Oppenheim** and **Rothschild** families built up Frankfurt's economic power.

Ten years after Allied bombers destroyed nearly all of the city in March 1944, Frankfurt received a complete concrete makeover, paid for by the countries that had ruined it. Today, skyscrapers loom over crowded streets and dark-suited stock traders scurry about. It's easy to see how cell-phone-infested Frankfurt acquired the nicknames "Bankfurt" and "Mainhattan"—the EU's central bank is even based here. Frankfurt has a reputation for being the most Americanized city in Europe, but the government works hard to preserve the city's rich history; Frankfurt spends more on cultural attractions than any other German city.

▛ TRANSPORTATION

Flights: The ultra-modern **Flughafen Rhein-Main** (☎01805 372 46 36) welcomes hundreds of airplanes and thousands of travelers from all over the world daily. From the airport, Schnellbahn trains S8 and 9 travel to the Hauptbahnhof every 15min. Buy tickets (€3) from green ticket machines marked *Fahrkarten* before boarding. Most public transportation as well as trains to major cities depart from Terminal 1; a free streetcar runs between the terminals every 15min.

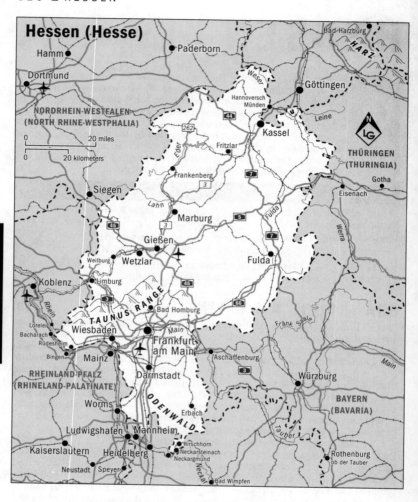

Hessen (Hesse)

HESSEN

Trains: ☎ 0180 599 66 33 for reservations and information. Trains from Frankfurt's **Hauptbahnhof** to: **Amsterdam** (4hr., 2 per hr., €67-91); **Berlin** (5-6hr., 2 per hr., €74-92); **Cologne** (2½hr., 3 per hr., €34-52); **Hamburg** (3½-5hr., 2 per hr., €67-86); **Munich** (3½-4½hr., 3 per hr., €56-69); **Paris** (6-8hr., 2 per hr., €74-90).

Mitfahrzentrale: Baseler Str. 7 (☎ 23 64 44). Take a right on Baseler Str. at the side exit of the Hauptbahnhof (track 1) and walk 2 blocks. Arranges rides to **Athens** (€105), **Berlin** (€29) and elsewhere. Open M-F 8am-6:30pm, Sa 8am-4pm, Su 10am-4pm.

Public Transportation: Single-ride tickets are valid for 1hr. in 1 direction, transfers permitted (€1.70. 6-9am and after 4pm €2). Eurail passes valid only on S-Bahn trains. For unlimited access to the S- and U-Bahn, streetcars, and buses, the *Tageskarte* is valid until midnight the day of purchase. (€4.70, children €2.80). Some machines take credit cards. **Passengers without tickets face a €40 fine.** At the Hauptbahnhof, the S-

Bahn departs from the level below the long-distance trains. Escalators to the U-Bahn platforms are in the shopping passage. Streetcars #10, 11, 16, 19, and 21 pass by the island platform directly outside the main (northeast) entrance, while buses #35, 37, and 46 leave from the right of the main entrance. The Hauptbahnhof has an **information desk** on the main level. Public transportation runs until 1am.

Taxis: ☎23 00 01, 23 00 33, or 25 00 01. €1.38-1.53 per km.

Boat Rides: Several companies offer Main tours, departing near the Römerberg (1¾hr.; 2 per hr.; €7.80, children 2.80). ▨**Primus Linie** also cruises to beautiful wine towns along the Main. (☎122 83 70; www.primus-linie.de. Rudesheim €23, Loreley €31.)

Bike Rental: Die Bahn (DB) runs the citywide bike rental service, **Call a Bike.** These bikes (marked with the red DB logo) are found in squares and street corners throughout the city. To rent one, call the service hotline (☎0700 05 22 55 22), dial 0 during the recording, and ask for an English-speaking operator for further instructions. www.callabike.de. Credit cards only. €0.06 per min. or €15 per day.

Hitchhiking: *Let's Go* does not recommend hitchhiking as a safe mode of transport. Hitching on the highway itself is strictly forbidden. However, hitchers report that those heading south to Munich take buses #36 or 960 from Konstablerwache to the *Autobahn* interchange. Those heading to Cologne or Düsseldorf take S1 or 8 to "Wiesbaden Hauptbahnhof," then S21 (dir.: Niedernhausen) to "Auringen-Medenbach," and turn right, walk 800m, and take the access road to the Autobahn rest stop.

◢◣ ORIENTATION

A sprawling collage of steel, concrete, glass, and scaffolding, Germany's fifth-largest city bridges the **Main** (pronounced "mine") 35km east of its confluence with the Rhein. The train station is at the end of Frankfurt's red-light district, among airline offices, sex shops, and banks. From the station, the city center is a 20min. walk down Kaiserstr. or Münchener Str., which both lead to the Altstadt. Just north of the river, the Altstadt contains the well-touristed **Römerberg** square. Take U4 (dir.: Seckbacher Landstr.) to "Römer" or walk down Liebfrauenstr. from **Hauptwache** (S1-6, 8, or 9, or U1-3, 6, or 7). The commercial heart of Frankfurt, north of Römer, is an expanse of department stores and ice cream vendors stretching along Zeil from Hauptwache to **Konstablerwache** in the west (one S-bahn stop farther) and to **Opernplatz** in the east (U6 or 7 to "Alte Oper"). Students, cafes, and services cluster farther northwest around the university in **Bockenheim**. Take U6 or 7 to "Bockenheimer Warte." On the southern bank of Main, **Sachsenhausen** draws *Äpfelwein*-lovers, pub-crawlers, and museum-goers. (U1, 2, or 3 to "Schweizer Pl.")

The **Frankfurt Card**, available at tourist offices and most travel agencies, allows unlimited travel on all trains and buses including the airport line. It also gives discounts on 21 museums, the *Palmengarten*, the zoo, guided city tours, river cruises, and ▨**free beer.** (1-day €7.80, 2-day €11.50.) The **Museumsufer Ticket** gets you in to 26 museums for two days, but doesn't include travel or beer (€12, students €6, family €15). See **Museums,** p. 332 for more information.

◢ PRACTICAL INFORMATION

TOURIST AND FINANCIAL SERVICES

Tourist Office: (☎21 23 88 00; www.frankfurt-tourismus.de). In the Hauptbahnhof reception hall, next to the main exit. Maps (€0.50-1), brochures, tours, and more. Books rooms for a €3 fee; free if you call or email ahead. Open M-F 8am-9pm, Sa-Su and holidays 9am-6pm. Another **branch,** at Römerberg 27, doesn't book rooms. Open M-F 9:30am-5:30pm, Sa-Su 10am-4pm.

HESSEN

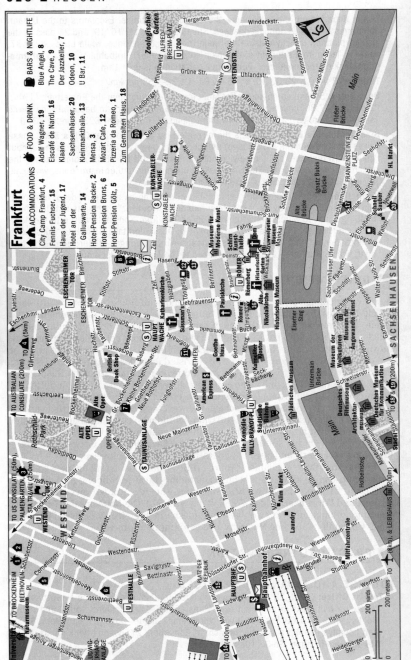

Frankfurt

▲▲ ACCOMMODATIONS
City Camp Frankfurt, **4**
Fennis Fuchser, **15**
Haus der Jugend, **17**
Hotel an der
  Galluswarte, **14**
Hotel-Pension Backer, **2**
Hotel-Pension Bruns, **6**
Hotel-Pension Gölz, **5**

♦ FOOD & DRINK
Adolf Wagner, **19**
Eiscafé de Nardi, **16**
Klaane
  Sachsenhäuser, **20**
Kleinmarkthalle, **13**
Mensa, **3**
Mozart Cafe, **12**
Pizzeria da Romeo, **1**
Zum Gemalten Haus, **18**

■ BARS & NIGHTLIFE
Blue Angel, **8**
The Cave, **9**
Der Jazzkeller, **7**
Odeon, **10**
U Bar, **11**

Tours: Depart daily 10am and 2pm (in winter only 2pm) from the Römerberg tourist office, and 15min. later from the Hauptbahnhof tourist office. Tours last 2¼hr. 8 languages offered. €25, students €20, children under 12 €10.

Budget travel: STA Travel, Bockenheimer Landstr. 133 (☎70 30 35; frankfurt.uni@statravel.de), near the university. U to "Bockenheimer Warte." Books flights and sells ISICs. Open M-F 10am-6pm, Sa 11am-2pm.

Consulates: Australia, Grüner Burgweg 58-62 (☎90 55 80). Open M-Th 9am-4:30pm, F 9am-4pm; phone hours M-F 9am-5pm. **UK:** Bockenheimer Landstr. 42 (☎170 00 20; fax 72 95 53). Open M-Th 9am-noon and 2-4pm, F 9am-noon; phone hours M-Th 8:30am-1pm and 2-5pm, F 8:30am-1pm and 1:30-3:30pm. **US:** Siesmayerstr. 21 (☎753 50; fax 74 89 38). Open M-F 8-11am; phone hours M-F 8am-4pm.

Currency Exchange: At any bank. Banks in the airport and station have poor rates.

American Express: Kaiserstr. 10 (☎21 93 88 60; 24hr. hotline 979 70), in Reiseland Shop. Exchanges currency, handles Traveler's Cheques, and arranges hotel reservations and car rentals. Open M-F 9:30am-6pm, Sa 10am-2pm.

LOCAL SERVICES

Bookstores: Süssman's Presse und Buch, Zeil 127 (☎131 07 51), behind the Katharinenkirche. Many current English titles. Open M-W 9am-7pm, Th-F 9am-8pm, Sa 9am-6pm. **British Book Shop,** Börsenstr. 17 (☎28 04 92). Classics, Shakespeare, popular novels, and non-fiction in English. Open M-F 9:30am-7pm, Sa 9:30am-6pm.

Gay and lesbian hotline: Rosa Hilfe Frankfurt (☎194 46). Open Su 6-9pm. In an emergency call ☎0171 174 57 21.

Laundromat: Waschsalon, Wallstr. 8, near the hostel in Sachsenhausen. Wash €3 (soap included). Dry €0.50 per 15min. Open daily 6am-11pm. **Miele Washworld,** Moselstr. 17, is a 10min. walk from the Hauptbahnhof. Small wash €3.5; large €7 (soap included). Dry €1 per 15min. Change machine. Open M-Sa 6am-11pm.

EMERGENCY AND COMMUNICATIONS

Emergency: ☎110. **Fire** and **Ambulance:** ☎112.

Women's Helpline: ☎70 94 94.

AIDS hotline: ☎405 86 80.

Disabled travelers: Transportation access info at www.vgf.ffm.de. **Frankfurt Forum,** Römerberg 32 (☎21 24 00 00), publishes a guide to accessible locations in Frankfurt. Open M and W 10am-4:30pm, Tu and Th 10am-6pm, F 10am-2pm.

Pharmacy: In the train station's **Einkaufspassage** (☎23 30 47). Open M-F 6:30am-9pm, Sa 8am-9pm, Su 9am-4pm. After hours, call ☎192 92 for medical emergencies.

Internet Access: Alpha, in the Hauptbahnhof's gambling salon, past track 24 on the north side. €3.50 per hr. Open Su-Th 9am-11pm, F-Sa 9am-midnight. The cheapest is **Telewave,** Elisabethenstr. 45-47 (☎66 76 99 38), but it charges in 1hr. units (€1.50 per hr.). Open M-F 10am-8pm, Sa 10am-4pm.

Post Office: Filiale Frankfurt 2, Zeil 90/Schäferg., 60313 Frankfurt (☎13 81 26 21), inside the Karstadt department store. U- or S-Bahn to "Hauptwache." Take a right on Zeil with your back to the church until you see the Karstadt building. Open M-Sa 9:30am-8pm. **Branch office,** 60329 Frankfurt, on the upper level of the Hauptbahnhof. Open M-F 7am-7:30pm, Sa 8am-4pm.

■ ACCOMMODATIONS AND CAMPING

In the financial center of Europe, deals are rare, and trade fairs make rooms scarce. The **Westend/University** area has a few budget options. There are also hostels under 45min. away: **Darmstadt** (p. 337), **Mainz** (p. 362), and **Wiesbaden** (p. 335).

▧ **Haus der Jugend (HI),** Deutschherrnufer 12 (☎610 01 50; www.jugendherberge-frank-furt.de). Bus #46 from the station to "Frankensteiner Pl." Turn left along the river; the hostel is at the end of the block. Its location bordering the pubs and museums of the Sachsenhausen district makes it popular with student groups and youngsters. Breakfast and sheets included. Check-in after 1pm. Check-out 9:30am. Curfew 2am. Locks available for €5 deposit. Dorms from €20, under 27 from €15. ❷

▧ **Hotel-Pension Bruns,** Mendelssohnstr. 42 (☎74 88 96; www.brunsgallus-hotel.de). U4 to "Festhalle." Exit onto Beethoven Str. and turn left. At the traffic circle, continue on Mendelssohnstr. (the 3rd street to the right). The hotel is immediately to the right. In the wealthy Westend area near the *Uni*, Bruns has 9 Victorian rooms with high ceilings, hardwood floors, cable TV, and free breakfast in bed. Ring the bell; it's on the 2nd fl. Showers €1.50. Singles €40-45; doubles €50-55; triples €65-70; quads €75-80. ❸

Hotel-Pension Gölz, Beethovenstr. 44 (☎74 67 35; www.hotel-goelz.de). U6 or 7 to "Westend." One street north of Pensions Backer and Bruns. Quiet, beautiful rooms with TVs, phones, and couches, some with balconies. Big breakfast included. Singles €36-64; doubles €70-105; triples €85-120. Non-smoking rooms available. ❹

Fennis Fuchser, Mainzer Landstr. 95 (☎25 38 55). Near the Hauptbahnhof, this hotel is a convenient place to crash. From the station, take a left on Düsseldorfer Str., walk 2 blocks, and take a left onto Mainzer Landstr.; the hotel is 1 block down on the left. Enter through the popular bar downstairs (meals €5.40-29.70). Special rates for stays longer than 1 night. Singles €20; doubles €60. ❷

Hotel an der Galluswarte, Hufnagelstr. 4 (☎73 03 000; www.brunsgallus-hotel.de). S3, 4, 5 to "Galluswarte." From the "Mainzer Landstr." exit, turn right, walk 1 block, then turn right again onto Hufnagelstr. Large rooms with TVs, baths, and phones. Breakfast included. Singles €45; doubles €65-95. Prices rise during conventions. ❹

City Camp Frankfurt, An der Sandelmühle 35 (☎57 03 32; www.city-camp-frank-furt.de). U1, 2, 3 to "Heddernheim," leave through the unmarked exit (not labeled "Sub-ahnhof"), take a left at the *Kleingartnerverein* sign and continue down the road until you reach the *Sandelmühle* sign. Then cross the stream and turn left, following the signs until you reach the campground. Reception open daily 9am-1pm and 4-8pm. €5.20 per person, €2.30 per child, €3.50 per tent. Showers €1 per 4min. Cash only. ❷

◖ FOOD

Frankfurters love sausages and beer, but they have their own regional specialties as well: Goethe's favorite, *Handkäse mit Musik* (cheese curd with raw onions); *grüne Sosse* (a green sauce with various herbs, usually served over boiled eggs or potatoes); and *Ebbelwei*. Large mugs (0.3L) of this apple wine (*Äpfelwein* up north) should never top €2. The old district of Frankfurt, **Sachsenhauser,** is famous for its *Ebbelwei* bars. Non-German foods abound, including crepes, T-bone steaks, samosas, lo mein, and those ubiquitous meat-filled *Döner Kebap*.

For those on a budget, **supermarkets** are plentiful. Just a few blocks from the youth hostel is a well-stocked **HL Markt,** Dreieichstr. 56 (open M-F 8am-8pm, Sa 8am-4pm), while **Alim Markt,** Münchener Str. 37, is near the Hauptbahnhof (open M-F 8:30am-7:30pm, Su 8am-2pm). The most reasonably priced meals are around the university in **Bockenheim** and nearby **Westend** (U6 or 7 to "Bockenheimer Warte"), and many pubs in **Sachsenhausen** serve food at a decent price. Take U1, 2, or 3 to "Schweizer Pl." Bockenheim and the **Zeil** attract carts and stands.

▧ **Kleinmarkthalle,** on Haseng. between Berliner Str. and Töngesg. Make your own lunch in this 3-story warehouse of bakeries, butchers, and fruit and vegetable stands. Cutthroat competition among the many vendors pushes prices way down. Enough meat and sausage to feed a small nation, possibly Monaco. Open M-F 8am-6pm, Sa 8am-4pm. ❶

Pizzeria da Romeo, Mendelssohnstr. 83 (☎ 74 95 01). Across the street from the Pension Backer. Owner Romeo Marzocchi and company prepare excellent Italian dishes (from €3.50) and fresh pizzas with humor, charm, and fantastic service. Lots of vegetarian options as well. Open M-F 10:30am-3pm and 4-9:30pm. ❷

Adolf Wagner, Schweizer Str. 71 (☎ 61 25 65). Saucy German dishes (€5-17) and mugs of *Äpfelwein* (€1.40 per 0.3L) keep the patrons of this famous corner of old Frankfurt jolly. Locals sit elbow-to-elbow with travelers. Tasty vegetarian options on the menu, like salad with grilled mushrooms and apples (€7.90). Open daily 11am-midnight. ❸

Mozart Cafe, Töngesg. 23-25 (☎ 29 19 54). Lauded by locals, this cafe serves huge breakfasts and a variety of local foods like the delicately prepared *Spargel* (white asparagus), only available in May and June, and a wide selection of pastas, salads, and huge desserts. Meals €4.90-6.80. Open M-Th and Sa 8am-11pm, F and Su 9am-9pm. ❷

Klaane Sachsenhäuser, Neuer Wall 11 (☎ 61 59 83). Here, the Wagner family has served customers homemade *Ebbelwei* (€1.40) and Frankfurt specialties (€6.20-15) since 1886. The restaurant is named after the 1st of the Wagners who, while hunting, hit 2 rabbits at the same time with just 1 bullet. Open M-Sa 4pm-midnight. ❸

Zum Gemalten Haus, Schweizer Str. 67 (☎ 61 45 59). The long tables of this Sachsenhausen institution have seen generations of locals savor *Wurst, Kraut,* and homemade wine (€7). Relaxed, jovial atmosphere. Open W-Su 10am-midnight. ❸

Eiscafé de Nardi, Römerberg 13 (☎ 29 42 97), in the corner of Römer next to the Alte Nikolaikirche, serves eye-catching fruit sundaes and milkshakes (€4-9) to rejuvenate tourists between museum visits. Open M-Sa 10am-9pm, Su 11am-10pm. ❷

Mensa, U6 (dir.: Heerstr.) or 7 (dir.: Hausen) to "Bockenheimer Warte." Follow signs for "Palmengarten Universität." Exit to "Mensa" and take the first left before STA travel. The *Mensa* is inside the courtyard to your right. A state-owned, 2-fl. cafeteria dedicated to feeding poor students. Guest meals €2.80-4.30. Open M-F 11am-6:30pm. ❶

◙ SIGHTS

Much of Frankfurt's historic splendor lives on only in memories and reconstructed monuments. After the Allied bombing of 1944 destroyed everything but the cathedral, the industrious Frankfurters, knowing they couldn't build the same city again, engineered the resurrection as a testament to both pre- and postmodern times. A walk around town quickly reveals the resulting architectural variety.

RÖMERBERG. A voyage through Frankfurt should begin in this central area of the Altstadt, among the half-timbered architecture and medieval-looking fountains that appear on most postcards of the city. To celebrate the 13 coronations of German emperors that were held in the city, the **statue of Justice** in the center of the square once spouted wine. Unfortunately for all, she has since sobered up.

RÖMER. At the west end of the Römerberg, the gables of Römer have marked the site of Frankfurt's city hall since 1405. It was also the original stop on the Main for the merchants who began the city's long trade tradition. The building's upper floors are open to the public, including the **Kaisersaal,** a former imperial banquet hall adorned with portraits of 52 German emperors, from Charlemagne to Franz II. *(Entrance from Limpurgerg. German Tours every hr. Open daily 10am-1pm and 2-5pm. €2.)*

HISTORISCHER GARTEN. Between the Dom and the rest of the Römerberg are the **Schirn Kunsthalle** and a plantless "garden" of building foundations dating back to the 2000-year-old Roman settlement. Two simple plaques provide explanation.

DOM. East of the reconstructed Römerberg stands the only major historical building in the city center that escaped the bombings. The red sandstone Gothic cathedral contains several splendidly elaborate altarpieces. The seven electors of the

Holy Roman Empire chose emperors here, and the Dom served as the site of coronation ceremonies between 1562 and 1792. Reconstruction of the viewing tower atop the Dom should be finished by 2008. The **Dom Museum** inside the main entrance has architectural studies of the Dom, intricate chalices, and the venerated robes of imperial electors. *(☎ 13 37 61 86. Open Tu-F 10am-5pm, Sa-Su 11am-5pm. German tours Tu-Su 3pm; €3, students €2. Admission €2/€1.)*

PAULSKIRCHE. St. Paul's Church stands directly across Braubachstr. from the Römerberg. The church was the site of the 19th century's last chance for constitutional government over a united Germany (p. 54). Here, the liberal bourgeoisie sided with order in the face of peasant revolts in 1848 and watched the slaughter of their one-time political allies. Non-history-buffs will find a conference center and a political memorial to German democracy. *(Open daily 10am-5pm. Free.)*

ALTE NIKOLAIKIRCHE. This church raises its modest spires south of the Römerberg. With foundations dating back to the 11th and 12th centuries, this church was named for **St. Nicholas of Myra** (AD 350), patron saint of dangers associated with water, in order to protect the church from bad weather and flooding from the nearby Main. The sparse interior hosts occasional organ concerts. *(Open daily Apr.-Sept. 10am-8pm; Oct.-Mar. 10am-6pm. Free.)*

■ **PALMENGARTEN.** Couples, tourists, families, and a variety of native and exotic birds take refuge in the sprawling grounds of this garden in the northwest part of town. Boat rentals are available by the lake. *(€2.50 per 30min., each additional person €0.50.)* The garden's greenhouses contain seven different "worlds," from the tropics to frozen wastes, and is a relaxing place to see performances in the summer. *(Palmengartenstr. 1. U6 or 7 to "Bockenheimer Warte." ☎ 21 23 39 39. Open daily Feb.-Oct. 9am-6pm; Nov.-Jan. 9am-4pm. €5, students €2, family €9.50; with special exhibits €7/€3/€15.)*

GOETHEHAUS. The master was born in Frankfurt in 1749, found his first love (a girl named Gretchen, said to be the inspiration for the Gretchen/Margarete character in *Faust*), and penned some of his best-known works here, including *The Sorrows of Young Werther*. Unless you're a huge Goethe fan, the house is little more than a typical 18th-century showroom for a well-to-do family. It was one of the first buildings to be reconstructed after the war and refurnished with the family's original belongings, many of which the renowned author hated. *(Großer Hirschgraben 23-25, northwest of the Römer. ☎ 13 88 00. Open M-F and Su 10am-5:30pm and Sa 10am-6pm; last Sa of month 10am-8pm. Tours in German daily 10:30am and 2pm. Audio tours, in German or English, €4.50, 2 people €6.50. €5, students €2.50, family €8.)*

ZOO. Over 650 species, ranging from commonplace to exotic, live here. Daily feedings are around 11am. *(Alfred-Brehm-Pl. 16. U6 or 7 to "Zoo." ☎ 21 23 37 30. Open daily summer 9am-7pm; winter 9am-5pm; last entry 30min. before closing. €8, students €4.)*

▥ MUSEUMS

Pick up a **Frankfurt Card** or a Museumsufer Ticket (p. 327) for museum savings, or go on the last Saturday of the month, when most museums are free.

MUSEUMSUFER

The **Schaumainkai,** also known as **Museumsufer,** hosts an eclectic range of museums housed in opulent 19th-century mansions and more contemporary buildings on the south bank of the Main between the Eiserner Steg and the Holbeinsteg. The Museumsufer is also home to Frankfurt's weekly **flea market** (open Sa 9am-2pm during the warm months) and the **Museumsuferfest,** a huge cultural jamboree that draws more than a million visitors over three days in late August. Frankfurt also has nearly 50 commercial **art galleries** clustered around Braubachstr. and Saalg.

■ **STÄDEL.** The Städel has the remarkable distinction of being one of the few museums to have equally vital paintings from nearly every period in Western tradition. It hosts extensive collections of Impressionist and Expressionist art, as well as many works by the Old Masters. Some notable names include Kirchner, Monet, Renoir, Picasso, and Beckmann. *(Schaumainkai 63, between Dürerstr. and Holbeinstr. ☎ 605 09 80. Open Tu and F-Su 10am-5pm, W-Th 10am-8pm. Audioguides available in English and German, €2. €6, students €5, family €10, under 12 free. Last Sa of the month free.)*

■ **DEUTSCHES FILMMUSEUM.** Trace the progression of film from a 19th-century obsession with optical illusions and see the Lumiere brothers' founding work in cinema. On the second floor, a Nickelodeon plays silent comedy classics. In 2005 the special "Angels in Film," in partnership with the Stadel and Liebieghaus museums, will run through April. All captions are in German. *(Schaumainkai 41. ☎ 21 23 33 69; www.deutsches-filmmuseum.de. Open Tu, Th-F, Su 10am-5pm; W 10am-8pm; Sa 2-8pm. Tours Su 3pm. €5, students €3.30. Last Sa of the month free. Films €5.50/€4.50.)*

MUSEUM FÜR KOMMUNIKATION. Reopening in 2005 and guarded by a sheep fashioned from telephone cords, this museum is dedicated to the importance of communication technology. Go behind the scenes at the post office, learn how telephones work, and trace the rise of the Internet. Interactive video displays are in German; English audio tours available. *(Schaumainkai 53. ☎ 606 00. Open Tu-F 10am-5pm, Sa-Su 11am-7pm. €2, children €1.)*

MUSEUM DER WELTKULTUREN. This museum of ethnology holds rare collections from Indonesia, Africa, the Pacific, and the Americas. Call ahead for current exhibitions. *(Schaumainkai 29. ☎ 21 23 59 13; www.mdw.frankfurt.de. Open Tu, Th-F, and Su 10am-5pm; W 10am-8pm; Sa 2-8pm. €3.60, students €2. Last Sa of the month free.)* **Galerie 37,** a small gallery of rotating, ethnically-themed exhibitions, is connected to the museum. *(☎ 21 23 57 55. Same opening times. Prices vary with exhibition.)*

ARCHITEKTURMUSEUM. Highlights of German architecture over the past decade, plus classical and modern city models. *(Schaumainkai 43. ☎ 21 23 88 44. Open Tu and Th-Su 10am-5pm, W 10am-8pm. Tours Sa-Su 3pm. €5, students €2.50. W half-price.)*

LIEBIEGHAUS. The castle-like building and gardens contain antique, medieval, Renaissance, Baroque, Rococo, and Classical busts, statues, friezes, and other sculpted material. *(Schaumainkai 71. ☎ 21 21 86 17. Open Tu and Th-Su 10am-5pm, W 10am-8pm. Tours W 6:30pm and Su 11am. €4, students €2.50. Last Sa of the month free.)*

MUSEUM FÜR ANGEWANDTE KUNST. The museum of applied arts displays arts and crafts from around the world. The permanent collection includes handiwork from the Chinese Ming dynasty to Baroque Frankfurt. *(Schaumainkai 17. ☎ 21 23 40 37. Open Tu-Su 10am-8pm. €5, students €2.50. Last Sa of the month free.)*

ELSEWHERE IN FRANKFURT

■ **MUSEUM FÜR MODERNE KUNST.** Just a few blocks from the Dom, this triangular building (a "slice of cake") is an ideal setting for the modern art within. Though the museum has works by luminaries Roy Lichtenstein and Jasper Johns, it prides itself on exhibiting new and unknown artists and forms—hence the hall of suspended clay heads. The basement shows films and slides. *(Domstr. 10. ☎ 21 23 04 47; www.mmk-frankfurt.de. Open Tu and Th-Su 10am-5pm, W 10am-8pm. €6, students €3.)*

SCHIRN KUNSTHALLE. The Schirn has no permanent exhibits, but morphs eight to 10 times a year—it might currently be a sedate Baroque gallery or a cutting-edge video installation. *(Next to the Dom; through the alley. ☎ 299 88 20; www.schirn.de. Open Tu and F-Su 10am-7pm, W-Th 10am-10pm. Admission €4-10, varies by exhibit.)*

HESSEN

TAP THAT

Although droves of tourists visit Germany to sample its renowned beer, few understand the intricacies of German *Bierkultur*. German beer is typically served by the quart *(Maß)*, ask for *"Ein Maß, bitte,"* or sometimes by the pint *(halb-Maß)*. If you feel short-changed (most glasses have measurement lines on them), say *"Bitte nachschenken"* for a top up. There are countless brews to savor in Germany. A **Helles** is a typical light, often Bavarian, beer. Those looking for a more bitter, less malty beer with more alcohol order the foam-crowned **Pils**, and often search long and wide for the perfect head.

Similar to an English shandy, **Radlermaß** (bikers brew) is a 50-50 blend of *Helles* and sparkling lemonade, named because Germans seem to think that it's ok to cycle while only half drunk. **Weißbier** is a cloudy, strong beer made with wheat *(Weizen)*. Some fans like it with lemon, some abhor this fruity mix.

A toasted malty lager, **Dunkeles**, however, is not the strongest beer. If you're in the mood for severe inebriation, try a **Bock** (strong beer) or a **Doppelbock** (even stronger). Both of these potent beers are often brewed by monks, presumably because they have the restraint to keep from drinking it all themselves.

You have picked the perfect nation to visit to appreciate beer, but be warned, watery domestics may never please you again...

STRUWWELPETER-MUSEUM. On the side of the Schirn Kunsthalle, this small museum is dedicated to the German storybook character. Be sure to comb your hair and clip your fingernails before entering, or else "Pfui!" You too might be declared a "modern satyr" like Struwwelpeter! *(Benderg. 1. Entrance next to Historischer Garten. ☎ 28 13 33. Open Tu-Su 11am-5pm. Free.)*

HISTORISCHES MUSEUM. This museum houses exhibitions on the history of Frankfurt, including a permanent *Äpfelweinmuseum*, an display of Frankfurt art, and a comparative display of the city before and after the WWII bombings. It also has good children's exhibits. *(Saalg. 19. ☎ 21 23 55 99. Open Tu, Th, and Su 10am-5pm; W 10am-3pm; F 10am-5pm; Sa 1-5pm. €4, students €2, family €9. Last Sa of the month free.)*

NATURMUSEUM. The largest natural history museum in Germany attracts the largest school groups in Frankfurt to its impressive works of taxidermy and giant whales. Children will love all of the interactive dinosaur exhibits and fully mounted skeletons. *(Senckenberganlage 25. U6 or 7 to "Bockenheimer Warte." ☎ 754 20. Open M-Tu and Th-F 9am-5pm, W 9am-8pm, Sa-Su 9am-6pm. €5, students €2, under 18 €1.50.)*

JÜDISCHES MUSEUM. Chronicling Jewish life in Frankfurt from the Middle Ages to the modern world, this museum houses a model of the 15th-century Jewish ghetto, the "Judengasse," as well as a number of cultural artifacts from Jewish life in Frankfurt. It also explores the November pograms and *Kristallnacht*, when the synagogues were set on fire and over 10,000 Jews from Frankfurt were either deported or committed suicide out of desperation. *(Kurt-Schumacher-str. 10. ☎ 297 74 19. Open Tu and Th-Su 10am-5pm, W 10am-8pm. €2.60, students €1.30.)*

♫ 🎭 ENTERTAINMENT AND NIGHTLIFE

When it comes to entertainment, Frankfurt leaps to the head of the class. Its first-rate ballet, theater, and opera receive massive endowments from the city. There are two major theaters. The **Alte Oper**, Opernpl. (U6 or 7 to "Alte Oper;" ☎ 134 04 00), a magnificent classical building rebuilt in the 1980s, offers a full range of classical music, while the **Städtische Bühne**, Untermainanlage 11 (U1-4 to "Willy-Brandt-Pl;" ☎ 21 23 71 33), stages ballets, operas, and experimental renditions of traditional German plays. For productions in English, the **English Theater**, Kaiserstr. 52 (☎ 24 23 16 20; www.english-theatre.org) near the Hauptbahnhof, puts on comedies and musicals. **Die**

IT'S AS EASY AS

one, two, three

uno, dos, tres

un, deux, trois

один, два, три

일 , 이 , 삼

Immerse yourself in a language.

Rosetta Stone® software is hands-down the fastest, easiest way to learn a new language — and that goes for any of the 27 we offer. The reason is our award-winning Dynamic Immersion™ method. Thousands of real-life images and the voices of native speakers teach you faster than you ever thought possible. And you'll amaze yourself at how effortlessly you learn.

Don't force-feed yourself endless grammar exercises and agonizing memory drills. Learn your next language the way you learned your first — the natural way. Order the language of your choice and get free overnight shipping in the United States!

Available for learning:
Arabic • Chinese • Danish • Dutch • English
French • German • Hebrew • Hindi • Indonesian
Italian • Japanese • Korean • Latin • Pashto
Polish • Portuguese • Russian • Swahili • Swedish
Spanish • Thai • Turkish • Vietnamese • Welsh

Personal Edition. Solutions for Organizations also available.

The guaranteed way to learn.

Rosetta Stone will teach you a language faster and easier than other language-learning methods. We guarantee it. If you are not satisfied for any reason, simply return the program within six months for a full refund!

Learn what NASA, the Peace Corps, thousands of schools, and millions around the world already know: Rosetta Stone is the most effective way to learn a new language!

FREE OVERNIGHT SHIPPING
In the United States
(Use promotion code lge005s)
1-800-788-0822
www.RosettaStone.com/lge005s

Komoedie, Neuer Mainzerstr. 14 (U1-4 to "Willy-Brandt-Pl;" ☎28 45 80), produces lighter theatrical fare. Shows and schedules of the city's stages are detailed in several publications, including *Fritz* and *Strandgut* (free at the tourist office), and the *Journal Frankfurt* (€2), available at any newsstand. Students can often buy tickets at reduced prices 1hr. before a show. Regular prices range from €5 for a youth orchestra performance to €108 for a prime opera seat. For ticket information for most venues, call **Frankfurt Ticket** (☎134 04 00).

For drinks, head to the **Sachsenhausen** district between Brückenstr. and Dreieichstr. to find a huge number of rowdy pubs and taverns specializing in *Äpfelwein*. The complex of cobblestone streets centering on **Grosse** and **Kleine Rittergasse** teems with cafes, bars, restaurants, and gregarious Irish pubs. Frankfurt has many thriving clubs and prominent techno DJs, mostly in the commercial district between Zeil and Bleichstr. In general, things don't really heat up until after midnight. Wear something dressier than jeans—unless they're *really* hip jeans—if you plan to get past the picky bouncers. Most clubs are 18+; cover runs €5-16. For more on Frankfurt's club scene, visit www.nachtleben.de.

■ **U Bar,** Roßmarkt (www.u60311.net), on the corner of Goethepl. Frankfurt's best DJs, and some international stars, spin in this old subway station. When the whole station is open for the weekend, it spans the entire breadth of subterranean Goethepl. Lines start at 9pm F nights. Cover €6-15. Open from 10pm. Techno/house club opens F-Su 11pm.

■ **Der Jazzkeller,** Kleine Bockenheimer Str. 18a (☎28 85 37; www.jazzkeller.com). Founded in September 1952, this is the oldest jazz club in Germany and has hosted many masters, including Dizzy Gillespie. Popular events include jazz jam sessions W and dance mix F. Cover €4-15. Open W-Sa from 9pm, Su from 8pm.

Odeon, Seilerstr. 34 (☎21 99 58 77). Look for the converted medieval villa with cut-out octopi on the door. This 2 fl. club vibrates with house, soul, and hip-hop. Theme nights: Th student night (special drinks half-price and free buffet from 11:30pm). M and Th-F drinks half-price until midnight. Cover €5, students €3. Open Tu-Sa from 10pm.

Blue Angel, Brönnerstr. 17 (☎28 27 72; www.blueangel-online.de). Techno music and flashing lights dominate the interior of the liveliest gay club around, a Frankfurt institution for 27 years. Ring the bell to be let in. Crowd doesn't begin to arrive until after 1am. Cover €5. Open daily 11pm until at least 4am.

The Cave, Brönnerstr. 11. Features goth and metal every night in a catacomb-like locale. Concerts Sa. Cover €3. Open Tu-Sa 10pm-6am, Su 10pm-4am.

WIESBADEN ☎0611

While most German cities rotate around their castles and cathedrals, Wiesbaden's center of gravity is its ritzy casino. The city's boutiques and hip citizens still pay homage to the heady 19th century, when European aristocrats came to frolic away their time and money. A bit of the old Wiesbaden is still here for the taking; you can shop on the cobblestone streets of the Marktpl., take the hydraulic funicular to the top of the Neroberg, and gamble away your savings at the 200-year-old casino.

⊟? TRANSPORTATION AND PRACTICAL INFORMATION. Frequent trains to: **Frankfurt** (45min., €5.90); **Heidelberg** (2hr., €14.40); **Koblenz** (1¾hr., €14.20); **Mainz** (15min., €6). Wiesbaden is a convenient daytrip from Mainz (p. 362), as the two cities share a **public transportation** system. Wiesbaden's **tourist office,** Marktstr. 6, down Bahnhofstr. from the train station, books rooms for free. (☎172 97 80; www.tourist.wiesbaden.de. Open M-F 9am-6pm, Sa 9am-3pm.) **Internet** can be found at **Telefoninternet,** Helenerstr. 2, near Bleichstr. (☎732 26 65. €2.50 per hr. Open daily 9am-11pm.) The **post office,** Kaiser-Friedrich-Ring 98, is across the street and left from the station. (Open M-F 8am-6pm, Sa 8am-12:30pm.)

▐▐▐ **ACCOMMODATIONS, FOOD, AND NIGHTLIFE.** The **☒Jugendherberge (HI) ❷**, Blücherstr. 66, has cheap beds, good facilities, and a friendly staff. Take bus #14 (dir.: Klarental) to "Gneisenaustr." Turn left as you step off the bus and walk 200m up the street. (☎486 57; wiesbaden@djh-hessen.de. Breakfast included. Lockers €10 deposit. Reception until midnight. Check-in after 2pm. Quiet time 10pm, curfew midnight, but you can get a key for a €20 deposit. 6-bed dorms €19; singles €25; doubles €44.) The **Ring-Hotel ❹**, Bleichstr. 29, is a few minutes from the pedestrian zone. From the Hauptbahnhof take bus #1 (dir.: Dürenpl.) to "Bleichstr." This family-owned hotel once housed renowned musicians like Jimi Hendrix and Tom Jones. (☎949 02 77; fax 949 02 77. Breakfast included. Singles €39, with shower or bath and TV €46-62; doubles with shower and TV €62.)

The pedestrian zone is brimming with pubs, restaurants, fruit stands, bakeries, and cafes right on the Marktpl. To the north of it, Goldg. is packed with Italian restaurants (pizza/pasta €5-10). Mauerg., home to many economical seafood and German restaurants, is your best bet for lunch. The jolly staff at **Setzkasten ❸**, Wagemannstr. 33, serves up Bavarian specialties like *Leberkäse* or *Weißwurst* for under €6. The lunch special (€3.90) is different every day. (☎30 64 75. Open daily noon-4am; kitchen closes at 3am.) **The Irish Pub**, Michelsberg 15, rocks with live music every night from 9pm, offers enormous Irish breakfasts on Sundays (11am-3pm), and serves drinks until the wee hours. Sunday through Thursday shot specials (4 shots for €5) and cocktail specials (all €4) Monday, Tuesday, and Thursday. (☎30 08 49. Open M-Th 5pm-1am, F 5pm-2am, Sa 3pm-2am, Su 4pm-1am.)

▐▐ **SIGHTS AND ENTERTAINMENT.** In early June, the **Kurpark** and Wilhelmstr. fill with a cultural extravaganza known as the **Theatrium** street festival, and in mid-August the pedestrian zone turns into the "longest wine bar in the world" during the **Rheingauer Weinwoche** festival dedicated to local wines. If you've always wanted to try your luck at a game of chance, then put on your best clothes (or rent a jacket and tie there for €2.50) and head for the **Kurhaus Casino** in the Kurpark. The main hall, illuminated by two giant crystal chandeliers and filled with roulette tables and tuxedo-clad waiters, is reminiscent of the high Wilhelminian era. Game explanations on Friday and Saturday are a perfect chance to try your luck risk-free (☎53 61 00; www.spielbank-wiesbaden.de. 18+. Open daily 2:45pm-4am. Entry €2.50.) Or, flout dress codes and get down and dirty with the slots next door at **Kleines Spiel.** (18+. Open daily 1pm-4am. Entry €1.) The Kurhaus Casino complex, situated off Wilhelmstr., is bordered on two sides by the expansive **Kurpark**, where locals unwind under century-old willows. (Take bus #1 or 8 to "Kurhaus/Theater.")

On the other side of the *Kurhaus* is the stately **Staatstheater,** inscribed with the rather demanding instruction *Der Menscheit Würde ist in Eure Hand gegeben, bewahret Sie.* ("The dignity of mankind is in your hands, preserve it.") Honoring this code, the *Staatstheater* and neighboring **Kleines Haus** present ballets, operas, and plays for as little as €5.50. (☎13 23 25. Box office for both open Tu-F 11am-6pm, Sa-Su 11am-1pm, and 1hr. before performances.) On the corner of Quelleng. and Burgstr., west of the *Staatstheater*, the **world's biggest cuckoo clock** is topped by a giant moose head. The birds strut every 30min. from 8am-8pm. Toward the train station on Friedrich-Ebert-Allee, the **Museum Wiesbaden** houses temporary exhibits of modern German art. (☎335 22 50; www.museum-wiesbaden.de. Open Tu 10am-8pm, W-Su 10am-5pm. €2.50, students and seniors €1.25, children €0.50.) The **Marktkirche** is on the Markt near the tourist office. Organ concerts (Sa 11:30am) are followed at noon by a 30min. carillon concert on the church's 21-ton, 49-bell glockenspiel. (Open Tu-W and F-Sa 10am-12:30pm, Th 3:30-5:30pm.)

The **Neroberg,** a low hill at the north end of town, provides an alternative to Wiesbaden's bustle. Take bus #1 to "Nerotal" and walk or take the **Nerobergbahn** hydraulic funicular to the summit of the 254m hill crowned by the **Nerobergturm** tower. (☎780 23 98. Funicular open May-Aug. daily 9:30am-8pm; Apr. and Sept. W noon-7pm, Sa-Su 10am-7pm; Oct. W and Sa-Su noon-6pm. €1.40, round-trip €2.80; family €5.60.) Head down the hill to take a dip in the **Opelbad** or enjoy the scenery and tan with the locals. (☎172 98 85. Open 7am-8pm. €6, after 5pm €4; students €4.) Still farther down the mountain is the **Russische Kirche,** a richly decorated Russian Orthodox church modeled after the Cathedral of Christ the Redeemer in Moscow. The 1885 church is also the tomb of Princess Elizabeth of Nassau, the niece of a Russian tsar, who was married to a local duke. (Open Apr.-Oct. daily 10am-5pm; Nov.-Mar. Sa 11am-4pm, Su 10am-4pm. €1, children €0.50.)

DARMSTADT ☎06151

Nestled among winding streets and quiet residential quarters, the **Technical University** and the **German Academy of Language and Literature** distinguish Darmstadt from a dozen other sleepy towns. While the university grants Darmstadt a youthful vigor year-round, the German Academy commands the whole nation's attention once a year with the awarding of the **Georg-Büchner Prize,** Germany's highest literary honor. The colony of artists that congregates around the Academy adds to Darmstadt's cultural pretensions. The city has some superb *Jugendstil* (Art Nouveau) architecture, and is a surprisingly diverse, yet untouristed, city close to Frankfurt.

⌷ TRANSPORTATION

Frequent **trains** and S3 run from Frankfurt to Darmstadt (30min., 1 per hr., €5.90). Local **S-Bahn** and **bus** tickets cost €1.30, children €0.80; day pass €2.80/€1.70; week pass €8.40. For a **taxi,** call **Funk** (☎194 10). Rent **bikes** at **Minigolf,** next to the pond; take S1 to "Prinz-Emil-Garten." (☎66 40 90. Bikes €4 per day. Mini-golf €1.50, students €1. Open M-F 8am-8pm, Sa-Su 2-8pm.)

◪ PRACTICAL INFORMATION

The **ProRegio tourist office** on the Luisenpl., in the pavilion adjacent to the fountain, books rooms for a €4 fee (free by phone or email), sells area maps (€0.60), and provides free city maps and hotel guides. (☎95 15 013; www.proregio.darmstadt.de. Open M-F 9:30am-7pm, Sa 10am-3pm; summer and Christmas also Sa 9:30am-6pm) Another branch is on the Am Carre 4a, off Luisenstr. (☎95 15 00; fax 95 15 050). The **Darmstadt Card** allows free travel on public transportation and access to museums (1-day €5, 2-day €8). **STA Travel,** Alexanderstr. 37-39, handles all student travel needs. (☎225 22. Open M-F 9:30am-1pm and 2-6pm, Sa 9:30am-1pm.) For English books, visit **The British Shop,** Alexanderstr. 26, on the corner of Mauerstr. (☎753 80. Open M-F 11am-1pm and 2-7pm, Sa 10am-2pm.) Check email at **Netzwerk game café** on the corner of Rheinstr. and Saalbaustr. (☎96 32 90; www.netzwerk-darmstadt.de. €3 per hr.) The **post office,** 64283 Darmstadt, to your left as you exit the station, sends faxes. (Open M-F 7am-6:30pm, Sa 8am-12:30pm.)

▙▐ ACCOMMODATIONS AND FOOD

The **Jugendherberge (HI) ❷,** Landgraf-Georg-Str. 119, has spotless rooms and friendly service. Take Bus L (dir.: Ostbahnhof) to "Woog." (☎452 93; fax 42 25 35. Breakfast included. Lockers €5 deposit. Reception until 1am. Check-in 9:30am-10pm, later with reservation. Curfew 1am. €21.10, over 26 €23.80; singles €32/

€35, doubles €28.10/€31.) The hostel overlooks local swimming hole **Großer Woog,** an artificial lake. (☎13 23 93 or 13 38 66. Open daily mid-May to mid-Sept. 9am-8pm. Last entry 7pm. €2, students €1. Boats €3 per hr. Showers €0.50.) **Zentral Hotel ❹,** Schuchardstr. 6, is pricier, but well worth it. From Luisenpl., walk along Luisenstr. with the Luisencenter mall on your right and turn left onto Schuchardstr. Just off the popular Luisenstr., this hotel has lavish rooms with bath, telephones, and TVs; some doubles have ovens and fridges. The cheapest singles are not on the list of offered rooms; ask for them specifically. (☎264 11 12; fax 268 58. Breakfast included. Singles €50-62; doubles €72-82.)

Eating in Darmstadt can be pricey, but **Markthalle Caree,** across the street from the Zentral Hotel, is an exception with its wonderland of bakeries, fruit stands, Chinese groceries, and *Imbiße.* (Open M-F 11am-10pm, Sa 11am-8:30pm.) Every morning except Sunday, Marktpl. is crowded with fruit and sausage vendors. A few inexpensive restaurants can be found at the beginning of Landgraf-Georg-Str., west of the Schloß. The university **Mensa ❶** also dishes out cheap meals. With your back to the northern side of the Schloß, cross Alexanderstr., then take a right and walk past the yellow *Staatsarchiv* and the first university building on your left. Turn left down the stairs, then right into the University's Otto-Bernd-Halle. The *Mensa* is on the second floor. A decent selection of snacks are available for €0.85-4. (Open M-Th 8:30am-6pm and F 8:30am-3:45pm.) Right in front of the Schloß, loungers at the outdoor tables of **Cafehaus Bormuth ❷** enjoy quirky sundaes (€2.90-4.70) and fresh snacks and salads (€4-8) while taking in the bustle of the Marktpl. (Open M-Sa 8am-7pm, Su 6am-10pm.) For a grander atmosphere, try **La Java ❸,** in a restored Renaissance school building. From the southwestern corner of the Schloß, take Holzstr., then continue on Kirchstr. and turn left on Pädagogstr. (☎391 97 77; www.lavajava.de. Entrees €7-15. Open M-Sa 6pm-1am.)

◉ SIGHTS

▨MATHILDENHÖHE. The mecca of Darmstadt's *Jugendstil* architecture (p. 67), this artists' colony on a hill west of the city center was founded by Grand Duke Ernst Ludwig in 1899. The Duke fell in love with *Jugendstil* and invited seven artists to build a "living and working world" of art, funding the transformation of the urban landscape into the nature-friendly predecessor to Art Deco. The result is this architectural complex, heavy on flowered trellises and somber fountains. *(Walk east from the Luisenpl. along Erich-Ollenhauer-Promenade, or take bus F to "Lucasweg/Mathild." and take a right on Lucasweg.)* Like a monstrous jukebox against the sky, the **Hochzeitsturm** (wedding tower) on top of the Mathildenhöhe was the city's wedding present to Ernst Ludwig in 1908. The 48m tower offers a scenic view of Darmstadt. *(Open Mar.-Oct. Tu-Su 10am-6pm. €1.50, students €0.50.)* The **Museum Künstlerkolonie** to the southeast of the tower houses Art Nouveau furniture and modern art exhibits. *(Alexandra Weg 26. ☎13 33 85. Open Tu-Su 10am-5pm. Tours 1st Su of each month 11:30am, call ☎13 27 78. €3, students €2, family €6.)* The **Russische Kapelle,** a gilded, triple onion-domed Russian Orthodox Church, lies to the south of the tower. The chapel was imported stone by stone from Russia at the behest of the last Tsar Nicholas II when he married Darmstadt's Princess Alexandra. Its foundations are built upon earth from every state in the Russian empire so that it would stand on Russian soil. Today, because of its association with the martyred Royal Family, it is a pilgrimage site for Russian Orthodox Christians living in the diaspora. *(Nikolaiweg 18. ☎42 42 35. Open daily 10am-4pm. €0.80, students €0.60.)*

ROSENHÖHE. This brooding park houses a rose garden and a mausoleum of the city's deceased dukes. Planted in 1810 at the request of Grand Duchess Wilhelmine, the garden is supposed to breathe "the free, noble Spirit of Nature." With its overgrown lawns, hulking evergreens, and cemetery-like serenity, it seems to fulfill Wilhelmine's wish. *(Corner of Seitersweg and Wolfskehlstr.)*

BRAUN MUSEUM. The home of the Braun design collection showcases the evolution of the company's appliances since 1955—everything from Aunt Ulrike's blender to Uncle Franz's cutting-edge electric razor. *(Eugen-Bracht-Weg 6. Right off of Alexandraweg near Mathildenhöhe.* ☎ *42 48 81. Open Tu-Sa 10am-6pm, Su 10am-1pm. Free.)*

SCHLOß. The gigantic coral-and-white palace is smack-dab in the middle of the city. Built between 1716 and 1727, it was modeled after Versailles by a wistful Frenchman. Since WWII, the Schloß has served as a public university library and police station. A small museum tucked in the eastern wing holds 17th- to 19th-century ducal clothing and furniture. *(*☎ *24 03 53. Open M-Th 10am-1pm and 2-5pm, Sa-Su 10am-1pm. Obligatory 45min. tour leaves every hr. on the hr. €2.50, students €1.50.)* The **Herrngarten,** a lush expanse of greenery north of the Schloß, provides space for loafing students, frolicking dogs, and flapping ducks. In its northwestern corner is the even more exquisite **Prinz-Georg-Garten,** arranged in Rococo style. *(Open daily Mar.-Oct. 7am-7pm; Nov.-Feb. 8am-5pm.)* Next to it, the **Porzellanschlößchen** (little porcelain castle) displays an extensive china collection. *(Schloßgartenstr. 10.* ☎ *71 32 33. Open M-Th 10am-1pm and 2-5pm, Sa-Su 10am-1pm. €2.50, students €1.50.)*

⬛ NIGHTLIFE

Jazz, rock, poetry, and boxing: **Central Station,** Im Caree, has it all. From the tourist office on Marktpl., follow Luisenstr. and take the first left. This three-story cultural center showcases a dizzying variety of talents and in winter (peak season) hosts acts almost every night. The website lists the latest attractions. *(*☎ *94 23; www.centralticket.de. Hours vary. Closed Aug.)* In the center, locals recommend **Nachrichten-Treff,** Elisabethenstr. 20, for cheap beer (€2.10) and chill atmosphere. From Luisenpl. take Luisenstr. and the first right onto Elisabethenstr. *(*☎ *238 23. Open 9am-1am.)* **Kuckucksnest** is a happening after-hours establishment two blocks from the Schloß. The music is loud, the pool tables are always busy, and beer flows for €1.50-4. *(*☎ *208 25. Cover M, W, F €5. Open daily 8pm-5am.)* For late-night *Kneipe*-hopping, take buses K, U, or H to "Kopernikus Pl.," then walk down the Lauteschlägerstr. Darmstadt parties annually the first weekend in July during **Heinerfest** with beer, music, fireworks, and rides in the city's center.

LAHNTAL (LAHN VALLEY)

The peaceful Lahn River flows through this verdant valley, and the hills on either side of it are dappled with vineyards and quiet hamlets, as well as with German families in search of outdoor fun. Every spring and summer, campgrounds and hostels fill with people who have come to take advantage of the hiking, biking, and kayaking available along the Lahn. Rail service runs regularly between Koblenz in the west and Gießen at the eastern end of the valley, as well as between Frankfurt and Limburg. Visit local bookstores to pick up hiking maps, and inquire at town tourist offices for locations of bike and boat rentals.

LIMBURG AN DER LAHN   ☎ 06431

Limburg an der Lahn serves much the same function today as it did during the Middle Ages: a stop for merchants traveling from Cologne to Frankfurt. With the most important train station between Koblenz and Gießen, Limburg is an excellent base for exploring the Upper Lahn Valley. **Trains** run every hour to **Koblenz, Gießen,** and **Frankfurt,** making Limburg a popular weekend getaway for these city-dwellers. Largely unscathed by WWII, the Altstadt is a maze of narrow, brick streets that provide a charming backdrop for an afternoon stroll. The little town's pride is the **St. Georg-Dom,** a majestic cathedral that looms above the rest of the Altstadt. The landmark red-and-white structure is one of a kind, its combination of Romanesque and Gothic styles is filtered through the traditional German architectural sensibility, and the result might be the biggest, holiest *Fachwerkhaus* you'll ever see. Inside are a number of well-preserved frescoes and devotional artworks. From the train station, follow Bahnhofstr. until it ends in the Altstadt and take a left on Salzg. Take a sharp right onto the Fischmarkt and from there follow Domstr. for 25min. all the way up to the Dom. (☎ 29 53 32. Open daily Apr.-Oct. 9am-6pm; Nov.-Mar. 9am-5pm. Tours M-F at 11am and 3pm, Sa at 11am, Su at 11:30am. Free.) Next to the cathedral, the **Diözesanmuseum und Domschatz,** Domstr. 12, display a small, impressive collection of medieval religious artifacts dating from the 12th century, including jewel-encrusted crucifixes and elaborate robes. (☎ 29 53 27. Open mid-Mar. to mid-Nov. Tu-Sa 10am-1pm and 2-5pm, Su 11am-5pm. €2, students €1.)

The **tourist office,** Hospitalstr. 2, offers a guide to the town and provides a list for finding rooms. Exit the station, turn left and make a quick right on Hospitalstr. The office is at the intersection with Grabenstr., in the big *Verkehrsamt* building. The office itself is poorly marked; walk in from Hospitalstr., and it's the first door on the right. (☎ 61 66; fax 32 93. Open Apr.-Oct. M-F 9am-5pm, Sa 10am-noon; Nov.-Mar. M-Th 9am-5pm, F 9am-1pm.) The **post office,** 65549 Limburg, is at the corner of Grabenstr. and Eschhöfer Weg. (Open M-F 8:30am-5:30pm, Sa 9am-12:30pm.)

The **Jugendherberge (HI) ❷,** Auf dem Guckucksberg, in Eduard-Horn-Park, provides spacious rooms, pristine facilities, and a friendly staff at its hilltop location. From the station, turn right and take the stairs down to an underpass, then take the left exit toward Frankfurter Str. Follow Im Schlenkert right until it empties onto a larger road, and take this until Frankfurter Str. forks off on the left; stay right and keep on up the hill to the hostel (40min.). Or take bus #603 from Hospitalstr. (dir.: Am Hammerberg; 1 per hr. 8am-6pm) to "Jugendherberge." (☎ 414 93; fax 438 73. Breakfast included. Sheets €3. Reception 5-10pm. €17, under 27 €14.) For a better location in the middle of the Altstadt, **Gasthaus Schwarzer Adler ❸,** Barfüßerstr. 14, has rooms above its Franconian restaurant in a restored stucco building dripping with historical charm (☎ 63 87; www.schwarzeradler.de. Reception from 5:30pm. Doubles €48). To avoid the pricey hotels in town, call charming local couple Herr and Frau Hantl, who offer comfortable **Privatzimmer ❸,** Walderdorffstr. 25. From the station, take a left on Weiersteinstr., and after two blocks bear left onto Parkg. Walderdorffstr. will be on your right. The rooms are large and well outfitted with private bathrooms, but they fill fast. (☎ 38 05. Breakfast included. Singles €28; doubles €52.) **Lahncampingplatz ❶** is on the far bank of the Lahn, just outside the Altstadt. Follow directions to the Dom until the Fischmarkt, then bear left (instead of right on Domstr.) along Fahrg. downhill to Brückeng. and the Lahnbrücke. On the other side of the Lahn, turn right onto Schleusenweg and walk 10min. along the Lahn to the campground. (☎ 226 10. Reception M-F 8am-1pm and 3-10pm, Sa 8am-1pm and 3-5pm, Su 8am-1pm. Open May-Oct. €4 per person. Tents €3.) The tangle of narrow streets below the Dom are filled with cheap (but still overpriced) bakeries offering sweets and sandwiches. Just off the Fischmarkt, you will feel like you have stepped into Spain at ◼️**Bodega Dali Loco** ❸, Rütsche 11, which serves delicious *tapas* (€2-6), amazing homemade bread and a wide range of dinner options (€8.50-20) ❸. Another good deal is **Sockenschoss** ❷, Barfüßerstr. 5, a German pub with a sign that reads (in German): "Normal is boring...we're not." You'll find *Schnitzel* and other culinary standards for €4-7. Theme nights (such as soccer night) are held at least twice per month, and games are available at the bar (☎28 81 46. Open daily 11am until late.) **Da Sandro** ❷, Schiede 26, offers pizza and pasta dishes in an upscale restaurant for low prices (€4-7). From the Bahnhof, turn left and walk along Weiersteinstr. and take the right side of the fork onto Schiede. (Open Tu-Su noon-2:30pm and 6pm-midnight.)

MARBURG   ☎06421

In 1527, Landgrave Philip founded the world's first Protestant university in **Marburg,** then an isolated town on the banks of the Lahn River. Since then, the university has produced an illustrious list of alumni, including **Martin Heidegger, T.S. Eliot, Richard Bunsen** (of burner fame), and the **Brothers Grimm.** It seems that nothing in this college town is at a right angle—teetering rows of *Fachwerkhäuser* look as though they will topple into the Lahn at any moment. The city's cramped perch between the mountains and the river provides a dramatic setting where tourists and students alike enjoy varied watersports, cafes, monuments, and nightclubs.

◼️◼️ TRANSPORTATION AND PRACTICAL INFORMATION

Trains: To **Cologne** (3hr., 2 per hr., €32); **Frankfurt** (1hr., 1 per hr., €12); **Hamburg** (3½hr., 6 per day, €60); **Kassel** (1½hr., 1 per hr., €15).

Public Transportation: Buses run throughout the city. Single tickets €1.25.

Taxi: Funkzentrale (☎477 77).

Tourist Office: Pilgrimstein 26 (☎991 20; www.marburg.de), 150m from Rudolphspl. Bus #1, 2, 3, 5 or 6 to "Rudolphspl.," and exit to the north along Pilgrimstein; the office is on the left. By foot, walk across the bridge straight out of the train station, turn left on Elisabethstr. as you pass the post office, and continue straight. Provides free maps, books rooms for free and offers a variety of city tours (€3). Inquire at the office about specific themes and schedules. Open M-F 9am-6pm, Sa 10am-2pm.

ATM: 24hr. ATM at **Deutschebank,** at the corner of Pilgrimstein and Biegenstr.

Bookstore: N.G. Elwert, Pilgrimstein 30 (☎17 09 34), 1 block from Rudolphspl., has a sophisticated selection of English books. Open M-F 9:30am-7pm, Sa 9:30am-5pm.

Women's Resources: Autonomes Frauenhaus, Alter Kirchainer Weg 5 (☎16 15 16). Open M and W 10am-1pm, Th 4-7pm.

Laundromat: Waschcenter, at the corner of Gutenbergstr. and Jägerstr. From the youth hostel, cross the wooden bridge, then another bridge, turn left onto Frankfürterstr. and quickly hang a right onto Gutenbergstr. Sip a beer in the adjacent **Bistro Waschbrett** during rinse cycle. **Internet** kiosk takes coins (€3.90 per hr.). Wash €3. Dry €0.50 per 15min. Open daily 8am-midnight, closed Su during school holidays.

Emergency: Police ☎110. **Fire** ☎112.

Internet Access: Internet Treff, Pilgrimstein 27 (☎92 47 05), right across from the tourist office. Choose from a variety of hot and cold drinks (€1.50-3) while surfing the web (€1.50 per 30min.). Open M-Sa 10am-2am, Su noon-1am.

Post Office: Bahnhofstr. 6, 35037 Marburg. A 5min. walk straight out from the train station. Open M-F 9am-6pm, Sa 9am-12:30pm.

HESSEN

ON THE MENU

THE BEST WURST

So you're finally in Germany and tching to get your teeth into your irst authentic German *Wurst*. With over 1500 varieties, you'll have plenty of choices. All have one thing in common: German aw mandates that sausages can only be made of meat and spices—if it has cereal filling, it's not Wurst.

Bockwurst: This tasty sausage is common roasted or grilled at street stands, and is usually served dripping with ketchup and mustard in a soft Brötchen. Although Bock means billy-goat, his Wurst is made of finely ground veal with parsley and chives. Complement your Bockwurst with some Bock beer.

Thüringer Bratwurst: Similar o the Bockwurst both in content and presentation, the Bratwurst has a little pork too, plus ginger and nutmeg.

Frankfurter: Unlike the American variety (whose origin is believed to be the Wienerwurst), he German Frankfurter can only have this name if made in Frankfurt. It's made of lean pork ground nto a paste and then cold smoked, which gives it that orange-yellow coloring.

Knockwurst: Shorter and plumper, this sausage is served with sauerkraut. It's made of lean pork and beef, and a healthy dose of garlic. Pucker up!

Weißwurst: Cream and eggs give this "white sausage" its pale coloring. Weißwurst goes with rye bread and mustard.

ACCOMMODATIONS AND CAMPING

Marburg boasts more than 30 hotels and pensions, but competition hasn't done much to keep prices down. Plan ahead if you intend to spend less than €30.

Jugendherberge (HI), Jahnstr. 1 (☎234 61; marburg@djh-hessen.de). Bus line C (dir.: Marburg Stadtwerke P+R) to "Auf der Weide," backtrack and turn right into a small street that becomes a bridge. Cross the metal bridge, then the wooden one. Or, from the tourist office, go to Rudolphspl.; cross the bridge and turn right onto the river path; the hostel is on the left (40min.). Scenic riverbank location, close to the town center. Large rooms, some with bath. Breakfast and sheets included. Reception 7:30am-11:30pm. House keys available with ID or €25 deposit. €21, under 26 €18. ❷

Tusculum-Art-Hotel, Gutenbergstr. 25 (☎227 78; www.tusculum.de). Follow Universitätsstr. from Rudolphspl. and take the first left on Gutenbergstr. Many tourists visit modern art museums, but here you can feel like you're staying in one. Each room is decorated with a different theme—bathroom fixtures can get pretty ridiculous. Singles have TV. Reception 4-9pm. Singles €37; doubles €66, with shower €74. ❹

Hotel und Gasthaus Zur Sonne, Market 14 (☎171 90; fax 17 19 40), on the Markt square in a 1569 *fachwerk* building. Location, history, delicately painted furniture, and kind owners make this a good base from which to explore Marburg, if you can get a room. Office closed M. Singles €41-51; doubles €77-87. ❹

Camping: Lahnaue, Trojedamm 47 (☎213 31; www.lahnaue.de), on the Lahn River. Follow directions to the hostel and continue downriver another 5min. €5 deposit for use of electricity and toilets. Laundry €2.50. The **Terrassencafe** has moderately priced food and drink near the mini-golf course. Open Apr.-Oct. €4 per person, €3 per tent. ❶

FOOD

Marburg's cuisine caters to its students, with *Wurst*, pizza, and the omnipresent *Marburger* beer. The streets surrounding the Markt are full of cafes serving sandwiches for around €3. **ALDI** supermarket has **groceries;** from Rudolphpl. take Universitätstr. and turn left on Gutenbergstr. (Open M-F 9am-7pm, Sa 8am-4pm.)

Bistro-Café Phönix, Am Grün 1 (☎16 49 69). Tucked in a short alley between Rudolphspl. and Universitätsstr., this bistro/bar serves pizzas, salads, and baguettes for €3-6. Ice-cold piña coladas €5. Open M-Th 6pm-1am, F-Sa 6pm-3am. ❷

Café Barfuß, Barfüßerstr. 33 (☎253 49), is packed with locals and students. Big breakfast menu (€3-8) served until 3pm, and a one of a kind *Fladenbrot*-meets-pizza 'Fetizza.' The comfortable booths and picnic tables, as well as the laid-back staff and regulars, make this the kind of place to sit at all afternoon. Open daily 10am-1am. ❷

Havana, Am Grün 58 (☎16 49 60), tucked a short way off the street next to a canal. A student hot spot. Dozens of cocktails (€4-8). Serves tapas, baked roll-ups, lasagna, and salads (€5-10). Open daily 6pm-1am, F-Sa until 2am, Su until midnight. ❸

Café Vetter, Reitg. 4 (☎258 88) A 90-year-old cakeshop proud of its city-view terrace on the edge of the Oberstadt. Extensive photo-history of the cafe is included in the menu. Live piano music Sa-Su afternoons in good weather (Sa 5pm, Su 3pm). Cake and coffee €5. Open M and W-Sa 8:30am-6:30pm, Tu 11am-6:30pm, Su 9:30am-6:30pm. ❷

🔵 SIGHTS

UNIVERSITÄTSMUSEUM FÜR BILDENDE KUNST. The university's impressive little collection of 19th- and 20th-century German painting and sculpture is housed in a modest building that belies the quality of the works. Pieces by Paul Klee and Otto Dix compete with temporary exhibits of provocative modern work and a section on Expressive Realism and the lost generation of artists who matured during the Nazi period. *(Biegenstr. 11. ☎282 23 55. Open Tu-Su 11am-1pm and 2-5pm. Free.)*

LANDGRAFENSCHLOß. The exterior of this castle looks almost as it did in 1500 when it was a haunt of the infamous Teutonic knights. In 1529, Count Philip brought rival Protestant reformers **Martin Luther** and **Ulrich Zwingli** to his court to convince them to reconcile. Inside, the Schloß has been completely re-made into the **Museum für Kulturgeschichte,** which exhibits Hessian history and art, including wooden shields and ornate crosses. The basement holds a 7th-century skeleton and recently unearthed 9th-century wall remnants now protected by glass. The **Landesherrschaft** floor is a war buff's dream come true. Behind the Schloß is a quiet green garden that provides a good place to rest your feet after the climb, and great views in all directions. *(From Rudolphspl. or Markt take bus #16 (dir.: Schloß) to the end, or hike the 250 steps from the Markt. ☎282 23 55. Open Tu-Su Apr.-Oct. 10am-6pm; Nov.-Mar. 11am-5pm. Last entry 30min. before closing. €2.60, students €1.)*

ELISABETHKIRCHE. Save some ecclesiastic awe for the oldest Gothic church in Germany, modeled on the French cathedral at Rheims. The name of the church honors the town patroness, a widowed child-bride (engaged at 4, married at 14, dead by her 20s) who took refuge in Marburg, founded a hospital, and snagged sainthood four years after death. The reliquary for her bones is the centerpiece for the elaborate choir, which is like a church-within-a-church, so overdone it's glorious. The somber brown interior is illuminated by glowing stained-glass windows. *(Elisabethstr. 3. With your back to the train station, walk down Bahnhofstr. 10min. and turn left on Elisabethstr. ☎655 73. Open Apr.-Sept. M-Sa 9am-6pm, Su 11:15-5pm; Oct.-Mar. daily 10am-4pm. Church free; reliquary €2, students €1.50.)*

RUDOLPHSPLATZ. The modern university building was erected in 1871, but the original Alte Universität on Rudolphspl. was built on the rubble of a monastery conveniently empty after Reformation-minded Marburgers ejected the resident monks. The enormous stone building stands at the foot of the big hill, anchoring the Altstadt that spreads up and out behind it. The **Aula,** or main hall, bears frescoes illuminating Marburg's history, but you can see it only by reservation (call ☎991 20). The nearby houses are former fraternities, and the topsy-turvy state of their frames attest to a proud, *Bier*-soaked tradition.

OTHER SIGHTS. In front of the 16th-century Gothic **Rathaus** is the **Markt,** a plaza surrounded by open-air cafes and shops. To get there, take the **Altstadt Aufzug** elevator between the tourist office and the bookstore, or wind up the steep hill from the Alte Universität. Even farther up the hill, the 13th-century **Lutherische Pfarrkirche St. Marien** features amber-colored stained glass and an elaborate organ. The view overlooking the old city rivals the one from the Schloß perched near the top of the hill. *(Lutherische Kirchhof 1.* ☎*252 43. Open daily 9am-5pm. Free organ concerts Oct.-July Sa 6:30pm.)* Down Kugelg., the 15th-century Catholic **Kugelkirche St. Johannis** (sphere church) owes its peculiar name not to its shape but to the *cuculla* (hats) worn by the religious order that founded it. Back down by the river, visit the newly relocated **Kunstverein,** a cavernous gallery that hosts temporary exhibitions of contemporary art and an annual show of local artists. *(Biegenstr. 1.* ☎*258 82; www.marburger-kunstverein.de. Open Tu and Th-Su 11am-5pm, W 11am-8pm. Free.)*

🎵 🎭 ENTERTAINMENT AND NIGHTLIFE

Marburg's upper village alone has over 60 bars and clubs. Live music, concert, theater, and movie options appear in the weekly *Marburger Express,* available at bars and pubs. Posters plaster the main streets to announce larger events. The **Hessisches Landestheater** hosts an array of theatrical and dance productions. Ask for a program of upcoming performances at the tourist office, and buy tickets at the Stadthalle, Biegenstr. 15. (☎256 08; www.hlth.de. Open M-F 9am-12:30pm and 4:30-6pm.) There are a number of movie theaters; **Marburger Filmkunsttheater,** Steinweg 4, shows old American hits and more unusual recent releases; one movie per week is undubbed; check out the website or posters by the door. (☎672 69 or 626 77; www.marburgerfilmkunst.de.) Things get hopping the first Sunday in July, when costumed citizens parade onto the Markt for the rowdy **Frühschoppenfest.** Drinking officially kicks off at 11am when the brass rooster on top of the Rathaus flaps its wings. Unofficially, the barrels of *Alt Marburger Pils* are tapped at 10am when the ribald old *Marburger Trinklieder* (drinking ballads) commence.

🏛 **Hinkelstein,** Markt 18 (☎242 10). This medieval cellar now features tunes from the Kinks and the Stones, and "No Techno!" as the barstaff likes to attest. A blue jeans-friendly pub with a sturdy cast of regulars at the bar sipping beer (€3 for 0.5L). Walking uphill from the Markt, it's on the left. Opens daily at 7pm; closes Su-Th 3am, F-Sa 5am.

Discothek Kult, Temmlerstr. 7 (☎941 83). Bus #A1 (dir.: Pommernweg) or A2 (dir.: Cappeler Gleiche) to "Stadtbüro." This warehouse-like building is the place to dance the night away with Marburg's teens on one of 3 dance floors, to bass-throbbing techno, hip-hop, or oldies, or join the 20-somethings at any of the 4 bars. Lots of different theme nights; call for the schedule. Cover €2-4. Open Tu-W 9pm-3am, F-Sa 9pm-4am.

Bolschoi Café, Ketzerbach (☎622 24). From Rudolfspl. walk up Pilgrimstein to the Elizabethkirche and turn left on Ketzerbach; it's at the end of the block. The decor is communist kitsch: red candles, walls, and ceiling, and 20 kinds of vodka (€1.50-3), though the atmosphere is that of a down-to-earth pub. Open M-Sa 8pm-2am.

FULDA ☎0661

Only 30km from the former East-West border, Fulda gained notoriety during the Cold War as the most likely target for a Warsaw Pact invasion, earning it the undesirable nickname the "Fulda Gap." The city's central location changed from burden to asset as reunification turned Fulda into a transportation hub. Its treasures do not draw an overwhelming number of visitors, and the beautiful Baroque quarter and gardens are lively and refreshingly free of tourist cliches.

■▐ TRANSPORTATION AND PRACTICAL INFORMATION. Fulda offers good rail connections from its strategic location. **Trains** to: **Frankfurt** (1hr., 2-3 per hr., €25); **Hamburg** (3hr., 2 per hr., €69); **Kassel** (1½hr., 2 per hr., €16); **Nürnberg** (1½hr., 1 per hr., €33); **Weimar** (2hr., 1 per hr., €40). Public transit consists of two **bus** fleets, with the hub located up the stairs to your left as you step outside the train station. The **tourist office** (☎102 18 14; www.tourismus-fulda.de) is across the intersection from the Schloß. It distributes maps and self-guided tour booklets and books rooms for free. (Open M-F 8:30am-6pm, Sa 9:30am-4pm, Su 10am-2pm. Tours Apr.-Oct. daily 11:30am; Nov.-Mar. Sa-Su 11:30am; call ahead for English. €2.50, children €1.50.) Find a **24hr. ATM** at the **Sparkasse** on Rabanusstr. Do **laundry** at **Wash n' Dry,** Floreng. 18. From behind Stadpfarrkirche, take Steinweg, which becomes Floreng. (Wash €3.60. Dry €0.80. Open daily 7am-10pm.) The **post office,** 36037 Fulda, is on Heinrich-von-Bebra Pl. (Open M-F 8am-6pm, Sa 8am-1pm.)

▐▐ ACCOMMODATIONS AND FOOD. Fulda's **Jugendherberge (HI) ❷,** Schirmannstr. 31, can be reached from the train station by bus #5052 or #1B to "Stadion." Proceed 5min. up the hill and it will be on your left. Its small size, purple halls, and friendly family staff make for a pleasant experience. (☎733 89; fulda@djh-hessen.de. Breakfast and sheets included. Curfew 11:30pm. Dorms €18.70, under 27 €16; singles €22.50/€20; doubles €45/€39.) The ebullient Frau Kremer maintains technicolor accommodations at the **Gasthaus Kronhof ❸,** Am Dronhof 2, behind the Dom just outside the old city walls. Take bus #7, AS 5, or AS 12 to "Hinterburg/Am Kronhof" and continue down Kronhofstr. Or from the Schloß, walk downhill on Johannes-Dyba-Allee. After it becomes Wilhelmstr., take a right along the city wall on Kronhofstr. and look for a pink building three blocks down on the left. If you're lucky, you might get one of the top floor singles that open onto the roof deck, complete with flowers and lawn furniture. (☎741 47. Breakfast included. Singles from €23; doubles from €55.) For something a bit more upscale, try the family-run **Hotel Garni Peterchens Mondfahrt ❹,** Rabnusstr. 7. Posh rooms include cable TV, telephones, modem connections, and cosmically decorated bed linens. (☎90 23 50; Harnier@t-online.de. Breakfast included. Singles €58-68, F-Sa €48-58; doubles €78-98/€58-78; family suites €88-108.)

Mercado ❷, Gemüsemarkt 15, offers a different vegetarian meal every day, as well as staples like veggie burgers, all for €3-5. To get there, from the Stadtschloß, follow Friedrichstr. past the Stadtpfarrkirche and down Mittelstr. and take a right into Gemüsemarkt. (☎229 88. Open M-F 9am-6pm, Sa 9am-4pm.) Taking a left past the church down Marktstr. brings you to the **Buttermarkt,** where cheap dinner options abound. **Vini & Panini ❸,** Steinweg 2-4, is a cozy Italian delicatessen between Karstadt and Pfarrkirche. Enjoy gourmet pasta or risotto (€6-12) or sip fine wine (from €4) while you sit at a candlelit table among bottles of olive oil. (☎774 93. Open M-Sa 9:30am-2am, kitchen until 11pm.)

◪ SIGHTS. Prince-abbots reigned in Fulda for 700 years, leaving behind a glorious, if small, *Residenz* palace. Built in 1706 as the centerpiece of the town, the historical **Stadtschloß** now contains offices and a one-room exhibit on Fulda's Nobel Prize-winning **Carl Braun,** inventor of the television tube. Particularly striking are the **Spiegelsäule** (mirror rooms) and the **Fürstensaal,** ringed with paintings from Greek mythology. One corner room has 420 mirrors and 46 tiny paintings. Every Friday morning the castle closes for Fulda's wedding ceremonies, held here because the *Schloß* serves as the de facto city hall. Entrance to the castle also includes access to the **Schloßturm** (tower), where you can look out over the town. To reach this yellow behemoth from the train station, head down Bahnhofstr. and turn right onto Rabnusstr. Enter across from the tourist office. (Castle open M-Th and Sa-Su 10am-6pm, F 2-6pm; last tower entrance 5:30pm. Castle and tower €2, students €1.50. Tower only €1/€0.50.) Behind the palace is the luxurious **Schloßpark** lined with terraces; just beyond the fountain sits the 18th-century **Orangerie,** a striking structure topped with golden pineapples, originally built to house the royal garden of imported lemon trees, now a ritzy cafe and convention center. The Baroque **Floravase** sculpture graces the steps of the Orangerie.

Across the street from the Schloß is the stunning 18th-century **Dom,** which houses the tomb of St. Boniface. An 8th-century English monk and missionary known as "the apostle of Germany," Boniface founded the Fulda abbey in 744, around which the town was eventually built. Dozens of alabaster saints and cherubs are scattered among marble pillars and various gilded alcoves, including a well-crafted plaster skeleton posing near the pulpit. (Open daily 7:30am-7:30pm. Free.) To the left of the cathedral is the **Dommuseum,** where you'll find an array of Baroque relics and other sacred items. (Open Apr.-Oct. Tu-Sa 10am-5:30pm, Su 12:30-5:30pm; Nov.-Mar. Tu-Sa 10am-12:30pm and 1:30-4pm, Su 12:30-4pm. €2.10, students €1.30.) To the right of the Dom is one of Germany's oldest and most unusual churches, the medieval **St. Michaelskirche,** built in 820. Take the stairs to the right of the circular sanctuary for a taste of adventure in the eerie, twisting crypt. (Open daily Apr.-Oct. 10am-6pm; Nov.-Mar. 2-4pm. Free.)

KASSEL

☎ 0561

After Napoleon III and his soldiers were captured in the Battle of Sedan in 1870, the Aacheners jeered *"Ab nach Kassel"* (off to Kassel) at the crestfallen monarch as he was marched into Kassel's **Schloß Wilhelmshöhe.** Far from being an icon of defeat, Kassel has developed into a city of modern architecture, unique museums, and artsy citizens. From bizarre castles and monuments to sweeping vistas, as well as **documenta,** an international explosion of contemporary art (next in 2007), Kassel offers plenty to draw the curious and brave in search of a truly unique locale.

⌐ TRANSPORTATION

Trains: From Bahnhof Wilhelmshöhe-Kassel to: **Düsseldorf** (3½hr., 1 per hr., €38); **Frankfurt** (2hr., 2 per hr., €41); **Hamburg** (2½hr., 2 per hr., €57); **Munich** (4hr., 1 per hr., €78).

Ferries: Personenschifffahrt Söllner, Die Schlagd/Rondell (☎77 46 70; www.personenschiffahrt.com), offers daily 3hr. Fulda Valley tours May to mid-Sept. 2pm and W, Su, and holidays 9:30am (leaves Hannoversch Münden 3pm). One-way to Hann. Münden €11, round-trip €17; children €6/€8.

Public Transportation: Kassel's sophisticated system of buses and streetcars is integrated into the **NVV** *(Nordhessischer Verkehrsverbund).* Tickets are priced by distance; single rides range from €1.25 (up to 4 stops) to €2.50 (anywhere in Kassel). The **Multiticket** (€5) is valid for 2 adults and 3 children throughout Kassel.

Taxis: ☎881 11.

Car Rental: City-Rent Autovermietung, Kurt-Schumacher-Str. 25 (☎77 08 21). Open M-F 7:30am-6pm, Sa 9am-noon.

Bike Rental: FahrradHof, Wilhelmshöhe station (☎31 30 83). €10 per day, €40 per wk. Open M-F 9am-1pm and 2-6:30pm; Apr.-Oct. Sa 9am-3pm; Nov.-Mar Sa 9am-1pm.

▣▢ ORIENTATION AND PRACTICAL INFORMATION

When Deutsche Bahn chose Kassel to be an InterCity Express connection, they rebuilt **Bahnhof Wilhelmshöhe-Kassel** to its streamlined contemporary specs. While the new station elevated Kassel's status as a connected urban hub, it also had the

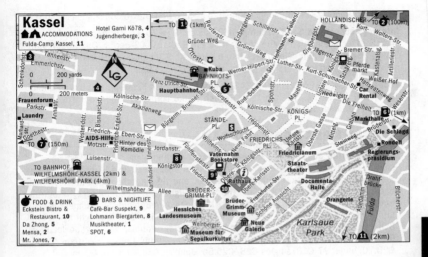

Kassel

▲▲ ACCOMMODATIONS

Fulda-Camp Kassel, **11**

Hotel Garni Kö78, **4**

Jugendherberge, **3**

🍴 FOOD & DRINK

Eckstein Bistro & Restaurant, **10**

Da Zhong, **5**

Mensa, **2**

Mr. Jones, **7**

🍺 BARS & NIGHTLIFE

Café-Bar Suspekt, **9**

Lohmann Biergarten, **8**

Musiktheater, **1**

SPOT, **6**

HESSEN

effect of taking a lot of the "action" away from the old city center, since it is at the far western end of Wilhelmshöhe Allee at the edge of an enormous park (see **Sights**, p. 349). The old Hauptbahnhof overlooks the economically depressed downtown area. Now marketed as more of a cultural center than a train station, the old Hauptbahnhof has been outfitted with postmodern adornments, including the popular Gleis 1 nightclub and one of the documenta exhibitions, the **Caricatura** (p. 350). IC, ICE, and some IR trains stop only at Wilhelmshöhe, but frequent trains and streetcar #7 shuttle between the stations. Streetcars #1-4 run between the Altstadt and the Wilhelmshöhe areas. Be careful walking along the underground walkway in the streetcar station alone after dark. **Treppenstraße,** Kassel's original pedestrian zone (the first in all of Germany), takes you down the hill from the front of the station and brings you to **Obere Königsstraße,** the main pedestrian zone and site of the majority of shops and eateries.

Tourist Office: The main office is in the Rathaus, Obere Königstr. 8 (☎70 77 07; www.kassel.de). They book rooms for a €2.50 fee and offer free maps. A smaller **branch** at the far left exit of the Kassel-Wilhelmshöhe Allee station provides the same services (☎340 54; fax 31 52 16). Ask about the **Kassel Card,** which gives free public transportation and tours, and museum discounts. 1-day card €7, 3-day card €10; 2 persons €10/€13; 4 persons €15/€19. Both offices open M-F 9am-6pm, Sa 9am-2pm.

Currency Exchange: Commerzbank, Königspl. 32-24 (☎789 90). Open M and F 9am-4pm, Tu and Th 9am-6pm, W 9am-1pm. 24hr. **ATM.**

Bookstore: Buchhandlung Vaternahm, Obere Königsstr. 7 (☎78 98 40). Broad selection of English paperbacks. Open Su-F 9:30am-8pm, Sa 9:30am-6pm.

Women's Resources: Frauenforum, Annastr. 9 (☎77 05 87). **Mädchenhaus,** Annastr. 9 (☎717 83).

Laundromat: Wasch-Treff, Friedrich-Ebert-Str. 83, near the hostel. Wash €3.50, including soap. Dry €0.50 per 12min. Open M-Sa 5am-midnight.

Emergency: Police ☎110. **Fire** and **Ambulance** ☎112.

AIDS-Hilfe: Motzstr. 4 (☎10 85 15; www.kassel.aidshilfe.de), in a small complex of medical facilities. Open M-W and F 10am-1pm, Th 1-4pm.

Hospital: Klinikum Kassel, Mönchebergstr. 41-43 (☎98 00; www.klinikum-kassel.de).

Internet Access: Red Sea Telecafé, Fünffensterstr. 9 (☎70 33 40), has computers and comfy office chairs around the corner from the Rathaus. €2 per hr. Open daily 9am-9pm, F-Sa until 10pm. **@Internet,** Untere Königsstr. 72, halfway between Königpl. and the Universität on the 2nd fl. €2 per hr. Open daily noon-8pm.

Post Office: Untere Königsstr. 95, 34117 Kassel, between Königspl. and the university. Open M-F 8am-6pm, Sa 8am-1pm. **Branch** at the corner of Friedrich-Ebert-Str. and Bürgerm.-Brunner-Str., has the same hours.

ACCOMMODATIONS AND CAMPING

Jugendherberge am Tannenwäldchen (HI), Schenkendorfstr. 18 (☎77 64 55; kassel@djh-hessen.de). From Bahnhof Wilhelmshöhe take streetcar #4 (dir.: Lindenberg) to "Annastr." Backtrack on Friedrich-Ebert-Str. and take a right on Querallee, which becomes Schenkendorfstr. Or, take the bus straight to "Jugendherberge." From the Hauptbahnhof, take the *Südausgang,* go up the stairs onto Bürgmeister-Brunner-Str., and turn right on Kölnische Str., walk straight for about 15min., then turn right again onto Schenkendorfstr. (30min.). Spacious cafeteria, clean rooms, and a good location. Breakfast included. Sheets €4. Reception 9am-11:30pm. Curfew 12:30am. Dorms €20.70, under 27 €18; singles €28/€25.50; doubles €50.40/€45. ❷

Hotel Garni Kö78, Kölnische Str. 78 (☎716 14; www.koe78.de). From the Hauptbahnhof, exit through the *Südausgang,* walk up the stairs, and turn right on Kölnische Str. From Bahnhof Wilhelmshöhe, follow the directions to the Jugendherberge, and from the streetcar stop walk up Annastr. Turn right onto Kölnische Str. Handsome brick townhouse with luxurious rooms, many with balconies, and a pretty garden hidden behind the building. Most rooms have cable TV and telephone. Breakfast included. Reception 7am-10pm. Singles €32, with bathroom and shower €41-51; doubles €51/€61-75. ❸

Camping: Fulda-Camp Kassel, Giesenallee 7 (☎224 33). Bus #16 (dir.: Aüstadion) from Königspl. or bus #25 (dir.: Lindenberg) from Kirchweg on Wilhelmshöher Allee to "Damaschkebrücke." Located on the Fulda, it's a short walk south of Karlsaue. Reception 7am-10pm. Open Mar.-Oct. €4 per person, €2.50 per child, €6 per tent. ❶

FOOD

Friedrich-Ebert-Straße, the upper part of **Wilhelmshöher Allee,** and the area around **Königsplatz** all have supermarkets, bakeries, *Imbiße,* and cafes sprinkled among department stores and fashion boutiques. The **Markthalle,** a block from the Fulda off Brüderstr. hosts an indoor and outdoor **market** (Th-F 7am-6pm, Sa 7am-1pm).

Eckstein Bistro & Restaurant, Obere Königstr. 4 (☎71 33 00), at the corner of Fünffensterstr. Filling pizzas and veggie meals (€5-9), as well as standard *Schnitzel* delights (€7). Lunch M-Sa 11:30am-5pm (€5.10). Open daily 11am-midnight. ❷

Da Zhong, Kurfürstenstr. 8 (☎739 88 53), just downhill from the Hauptbahnhof. Lavish, crimson decor sets the mood for exquisite Chinese specialties, served near a fountain and goldfish pond. Though main courses cost €7-12, the *Schnellmenü* offers entrees for €4-6 with soup or spring roll. Open daily 11:30am-3:30pm and 5:30-11pm. ❸

Mr. Jones, Goethestr. 31 (☎71 08 18), at the corner of Querallee. Good, plentiful food of the American sort (burgers €6, salads €5) and several Indian dishes (€3-6). Extensive drink menu including the "Mr. Jones" (ingredients unspecified—try it if you dare). Open Su 10am-midnight, M-Th 11am-midnight, F-Sa 11am-1am. ❷

Mensa, on Arnold-Bode-Str. (☎804 31 32) Walk down Unter-Königsstr. from the pedestrian zone or take streetcar #1 to "Holländischer Pl." Cross through the underground passage and veer right on Diagonale, which cuts through campus. €2.50-4, students €1 off. Lunch M-F 11:30am-2:15pm. The **Moritz-Restaurant** (☎804 33 90), in the same building, serves a more elaborate lunch with much shorter lines. €4, students €3. open M-F 11am-2:30pm. Cafe-like **Studentwerke-Pavillon** is a cheap cafe just around the corner on Diagonale. Open M-Th 8am-5pm, F 8am-3pm. ❶

🅖 SIGHTS

Kassel's sights center around two main areas: the Rathaus and the far end of Wilhelmshöhe Allee. The Rathaus area is home to various museums, many of which are devoted to Kassel's pride and joy: **documenta** (every five years, next in summer 2007). The area around the Schloß Wilhelmshöhe offers an adventurous jaunt into German history. The museums belonging to the **Staatliche Museen Kassel—Schloß Wilhelmshöhe, Ballhaus, Hessisches Landesmuseum, Neue Galerie,** and **Orangerie**—are covered by the *Tageskarte*, for sale at any of the museums (€7, students €5).

DOCUMENTA AND RATHAUS AREA

For the past 50 years documenta has showcased cutting-edge art in a week-long festival that virtually takes over the town. Exhibitions question the role of contemporary art within global culture, usually with emphasis on politics and social conscience. Though it only happens every five years, the international event leaves indelible and provocative marks on Kassel. Several works from past documentas have become permanent exhibitions: visit Claus Oldenburg's *Pick-axe* on the banks of the Fulda near the Orangerie and Joseph Beuys's *7,000 oak trees*, both from Documenta VII in 1982.

MUSEUM FÜR SEPULKRALKULTUR. An ultramodern structure houses death-ritual-related paraphernalia. The museum strives to "arrest the taboo process which surrounds the subject of 'death and dying' in today's world, and open it to public discussion." Painted skulls, black mourning garb, elaborate crucifixes, and stone monuments are sure to satisfy morbid fascinations. Artistic depictions of death include a photography series cataloging the last day of a man's life, and a dozen TVs displaying movie stills of death throes. *(Weinbergstr. 25-27. From the Rathaus, cross Fünffenster to Wilhelmshöhe, and go left on Weinberg. ☎91 89 30. Open Tu-Su 10am-5pm, W until -8pm. €4, students €2.50.)*

MUSEUM FRIEDRICIANUM. The large yellow Friedricianum is the oldest public museum on the continent. During documenta years, it functions as the central exhibition hall; in off years it houses work from past festivals, as well as other exhibitions of modern art. *(Friedrichspl. 18. ☎707 27 20. Open W-Su 10am-6pm, Th until 8pm. Single exhibition €4, students €3; entire museum €6/€4. W Free.)*

NEUE GALERIE. Whatever the documenta leaves in its wake, the Neue Galerie picks up and puts on display. Their well-rounded collection also includes paintings dating back to the 1700s and important works from the "Neue Sachlichkeit" movement. *(Schöne Aussicht 1. From Königspl., walk down Obere Königsstr. and turn left on Friedrichstr. ☎70 96 30. Open Tu-Su 10am-5pm, W until 8pm. €3.50, students €2.50. F free.)*

BRÜDER GRIMM-MUSEUM. Rooms are filled with drawings and life-sized cutouts of characters from the Grimm Brothers's tales, as well as large busts and a few personal effects that bring to life the men who wrote down so many joyful and often frightening German folktales. Exhibition of *1001 Nights*, including lots of Aladdin artwork, until March 2005. *(Schöne Aussicht 2, across from the Neue Galerie. ☎787 20 33; www.grimms.de. Open daily 10am-5pm. €1.50, students €1.)*

KUBA. Short for KulturBahnhof, it houses **Caricatura**, the self-proclaimed "gallery for bizarre art." Nothing is off-limits—missing limbs and scatological humor are the main currency at this off-color museum. *(Bahnhofspl. 1. ☎77 64 99. During exhibitions, Caricatura open Tu-F 2-8pm, Sa-Su noon-8pm. €3, students €2.)*

KARLSAUE. This English garden has picnic-perfect lawns along the Fulda. At its southern tip is the **Insel Siebenbergen,** Karlsaue's unique "Island of Flowers." *(From Königspl., hop on bus #16 (dir.: Auestadion) to "Siebenbergen.")* The **Orangerie,** in a yellow manor house at the north end of the park, contains the mechanical and optical marvels and a planetarium of the **Astronomy and Technology Museum.** *(Karlsaue 20c. ☎70 13 20. Open Tu-Sa 10am-5pm. €3.50, students €2.50. F free. Planetarium shows in German Tu and Sa 2pm; W, F, Su 3pm; Th 2, 3, and 8pm. €3-5, students €3-4.)*

HESSISCHES LANDESMUSEUM. This museum appears to be the work of an interior decorator run amok with huge sums of money. Surprises include 16th-century embossed leather-and-gold Spanish hangings, a rare depiction of the battle of Austerlitz, a six-color wallpaper printer, and a letter from Goethe to Schiller mentioning wallpaper order. The museum also houses several other collections, including a floor of prehistoric artifacts. *(Brüder-Grimm-Pl. 5. In the yellow Landesmuseum near the Rathaus. ☎31 68 03 00. Open Tu-Su 10am-5pm. €3.50, students €2.50. F free.)*

■ WILHELMSHÖHE

The Wilhelmshöhe area is a hillside park that must be seen to be believed. Impeccably manicured gardens and emerald lawns surround one enormous castle, while another sits crumbling on a wooded hill above. Towering over both castles by a few hundred meters is a Greek titan, visible from miles away. To fully experience this dream world, allow yourself a full afternoon, good walking shoes, and good old-fashioned wonderment. From Bahnhof Wilhelmshöhe, take streetcar #1 to Wilhelmshöhe, at the eastern end of the park.

SCHLOß WILHELMSHÖHE. The rulers of Kassel used to call this mammoth building home. Napoleon III was imprisoned here after the Battle of Sedan. Although the main wing was rebuilt in the aftermath of WWII, the museums inside are truly impressive. The **Antikensammlung und Gemäldegalerie Alte Meister** collection includes works by Rembrandt and Rubens, and the pride of the town—Dürer's 'Elsbeth Tucher', featured on the former 20-*Deutschmark* bill. A tour through the **Museumsschloß** reveals the palace's extravagant private rooms. *(From the streetcar stop, walk under the overpass, and take the path straight or right. ☎937 77. Gemäldegalerie open Tu-Su 10am-5pm. Museumsschloß open Tu-Su Mar.-Oct. 10am-5pm; Nov.-Feb. 10am-4pm. Obligatory tours every hr., last tour 1hr. before closing. Each museum €3.50, students €2.50.)*

SCHLOß LÖWENBURG. Landgrave Wilhelm IX of Kassel, a Teutonic Don Quixote obsessed with the year 1495 and fancying himself a time-displaced knight, built this architectural fantasy, complete with a moat and functioning drawbridge, for his concubine in the 18th century. To make it look crumbling and medieval, Wilhelm demanded rapidly deteriorating basalt as the construction material and dictated that some stones should be left missing. This plan was too successful; the castle has passed the "weathered" stage and is starting to fall apart. The ever-eccentric Wilhelm also sent the architect to Britain to study castles for two years and requested the inclusion of a Catholic chapel in the Schloß to date it to before the Reformation, though he himself was a Protestant. *(Facing up the hill at Schloß Wil-*

helmshöhe, take the path to the left of the pond; follow it as it bends left, and then go left when it ends at the paved road. ☎935 72 00. Open Tu-Su Mar.-Oct. 10am-5pm; Nov.-Feb. 10am-4pm. Obligatory tours on the hour 10am-3pm. €3.50, children €2.50.)

CASCADES. The **fountain displays** are timed so that a walk down the clearly designated path lands you at the next one just as the show begins. *(Spurts mid-May to Sept. W, Su 2:30pm.)* The finale comes an hour later with a grand 52m gush (except when there isn't enough water to properly "cascade"). Stake out a spot early. *(Follow the road uphill from Schloß Löwenburg toward Herkules to the base of the fountain.)*

HERKULES. Kassel's mighty emblem stands atop a massive pedestal, jeering at conquered giant Encelades, whose head pokes out of the rocks at the top of the cascades. All told, the structure is 108m tall—even from the base, you can see for miles. If you're not exhausted by the climb up the hill and hundreds of steps, you can climb onto Herkules's pedestal and up into his club. *(Access to the base of the statue free. Pedestal and club open mid-Mar. to mid-Nov. daily 10am-5pm. €2, students €1.25.)*

🎵 🎭 ENTERTAINMENT AND NIGHTLIFE

The stretch along Friedrich-Ebert-Str. and Obere Königsstr., between Bebelpl. and Königspl., is home to numerous bars and clubs; the free monthly magazines *Fritz* and *Xcentric* list schedules of parties at most of the city's clubs. Kassel fosters a lively **film** culture. Theaters cluster around the Altstadt; **Bali** (☎71 05 50; www.balikinos.de) in the Hauptbahnhof shows movies in their original language. Kassel hosts an **outdoor film festival** every summer behind the Museum Fridericianum at the theater **Dock 4** (www.filmladen.de; info and ticket sales at the Bali). Shows (€6.50, students €6; all tickets €4.50 on M) range from the likes of *Fahrenheit 9/11* to *Star Wars*. The **Staatstheater** (☎109 43 33) on Friedrichspl. hosts plays, concerts, operas, and ballet from mid-Sept. to early July.

🎵 Musiktheater, Angersbachstr. 10 (☎840 44). Bus #14 or 18 to "Drei Brücken," or #27 to "Naumburgerstr.," or follow Schenkendorfstr. as it curves left and over the tracks behind the hostel. A disco-party mecca where eternal 20-somethings congregate. 3 massive dance floors fill 2 city blocks with techno, house, and pop. Theme areas include "Hell's Kitchen" (heavy metal) and the Gothic "Dark Place." The area is dimly lit and sparsely traveled; use caution or take public transportation. Cover W €1.50, F-Sa €3. Open W 8:30pm-3am and F-Sa 10:30pm-5am.

Lohmann Biergarten, Königstor 8 (☎701 68 75). From the Rathaus, walk up Fünffensterstr. and make a left on Königstor. One of Kassel's oldest beer gardens, and the only one open late. Serves beer (€3 for 0.5L) and sparkling *Äpfelwein* (€1.70), and tasty dishes like 12 kinds of *Schnitzel* (€5-6.50). Open daily 11am-1am, kitchen until 11pm.

SPOT, Ölmühlenweg 10-14 (☎562 09; www.spot-kassel.de). Take streetcar #4 or 8 (dir.: Kaufungen Papierfabrik) to "Hallenbad Ost," backtrack 10m toward the city, and turn right on the path through the parking lot. Move to techno, drum'n'bass, and hip-hop on 3 dance floors, or hit the quieter front bar. Cover €3-6. Most nights start at 9pm.

Café-Bar Suspekt, Fünffensterstr. 14 (☎10 45 22). A popular hangout, probably because of the laid-back and friendly ambience. By day a pleasant cafe (Tu-Su 1-8pm), at night a bar (Tu-Su 8pm-1am, F-Sa until 2am).

NEAR KASSEL: FRITZLAR   ☎05622

Fritzlar was (ironically) named *Frideslar* (Place of Peace) in 723, when St. Boniface chopped down the huge **Donar's Oak,** the pagan religious symbol of the Thor-worshipping Chatti tribe. The "Apostle of Germany" used the timber to build his own wooden church, which today is the beautiful **Petersdom.** Heinrich (Henry) I was proclaimed king here in 915, inaugurating the medieval Holy Roman Empire. Since then, this diminutive medieval town has become happily isolated from the main routes of commerce. Having survived both WWII and zealous post-war building projects, Fritzlar is content with its role as a postcard-perfect town of half-timbered houses on the **Märchenstraße**, the German Fairy Tale Road.

The gem of Fritzlar is the 12th-century Petersdom, with its splendid golden altar, stained-glass windows, and sizable treasury, which includes the 11th-century diamond and pearl-covered **Heinrichkreuz** (Cross of Heinrich) and numerous precious robes and relics. A statue of the axe-toting Boniface stands in the square just outside the Dom. (Dom open M-F 8am-1pm and 2-6pm, Sa-Su 9am-noon and 1-5pm. Free. Treasury and crypt open May-Oct. M 2-5pm, Tu-F 10am-noon and 2-5pm, Sa 10am-noon and 2-4:30pm, Su 2-4:30pm; Nov.-Apr. Su-M 2-4pm, Tu-Sa 10am-noon and 2-4pm. €2, students €1.) On the western end of the still-standing medieval city wall, the austere 39m **Grauer Turm** is the tallest defense tower in Germany. It no longer serves its original purpose, but does offer a view from the top. (Open Apr.-Oct. daily 9am-noon and 2-5pm.) On the way to the tower from the Markt you'll pass the **Hochzeitshaus**, which has hosted weddings and festivals since the 16th century. It also houses the **Regionalmuseum,** a fairly small collection of earthenware, tools, and other artifacts from throughout Fritzlar's history. (☎98 86 28. Open Mar.-Dec. Tu-F and Su 10am-noon and 3-5pm, Sa 10am-noon. €1.50, children €0.50.) For a nice walk through the Altstadt, follow Mainzer Ring, the road that runs parallel to the Mühlengraben stream. Little German towns like Fritzlar spawn big festivals; the **Pferdemarkt** happens annually during the second weekend of July (July 9-10, 2005), and the **Altstadtfest** takes place every other August (Aug. 20-21, 2005). Both inspire a mad array of *Lederhosen*, traditional music, and beer steins.

Fritzlar is an ideal afternoon jaunt from Kassel, reachable from either of its main stations by **train** (40min., 3-4 per day, €6) or **bus** #50 (45min.-1hr.; M-F 1 per hr., Sa-Su 3 per day; €5). The **tourist office,** Zwischen den Krämen 5, next to Fritzlar's Rathaus, built in 1109, is the oldest official building in Germany. Make a left out of the train station and a quick right onto Gießener Str., following it up the hill until it reaches Marktpl., then go left onto Zwischen den Krämen. (☎98 86 43; www.fritzlar.de. Open M 10am-6pm, Tu-Th 10am-5pm, F 10am-4pm, Sa-Su 10am-noon.) The staff doesn't make reservations, but has a free list of hotels. Town tours (five people min.) leave from the Rathaus. (1½hr. Mid-Apr. to mid-Oct. Tu-Sa 10:30am, Su 11am. €2.50.) The **post office,** 34560 Fritzlar, is at the corner of Nikolausstr. and Gießener Str., near the Markt. (Open M-F 9am-noon and 2:30-6pm, Sa 9am-noon.)

RHEINLAND-PFALZ (RHEINLAND-PALATINATE) AND SAARLAND

With a legacy of sharply carved hillsides, scattered hamlets, and weathered castle ruins, Rheinland-Pfalz is a virtual time-warp to medieval ages. The fatal call of Lorelei sirens and the fireside folklore of Nibelung treasure echo across the dramatic landscape. The region is not without actual nourishment—the vineyards of the Rhein and Mosel valleys produce delicious wines. The Rheinland has had power since its electors chose the kings of the Holy Roman Empire, and the Saarland's minerals have been the envy of Germany and France for centuries.

HIGHLIGHTS OF RHEINLAND-PFALZ

BIKE OR HIKE the **Mosel Valley** (p. 365), which keeps up the German tradition of gorgeous, ubiquitous castles and are surrounded by endless vineyards.

REFLECT ON ROMAN RUINS in 2000-year-old **Trier** (p. 368), which make the typical German *Schloß* seem like a sandcastle.

SAVOR WINE among the poetic cliffs of the lush **Rhein Valley** (p. 358).

KOBLENZ ☎ 0261

Koblenz sits at the strategic point where the Rhein and Mosel rivers meet, which led the Romans to name the city *confluentes* (confluence), and also explains why the city has hosted every empire seeking to conquer Europe in the last two millenia. Before reunification, Koblenz was West Germany's largest munitions dump, but the blasts that light up the city now are decorative, not destructive—Koblenz turns into a flaming spectacle during **Rhein in Flammen** (May 7, 2005).

▶ TRANSPORTATION

Trains: Koblenz is on the line connecting Frankfurt to Cologne. To: **Bonn** (30min., 3 per hr., €4.20-8.40); **Cologne** (1½hr., 4 per hr. €10.50); **Frankfurt** (1½-2hr., 2-3 per hr., €12.50); **Mainz** (1hr., 3 per hr., €9); **Trier** (1½-2hr., 2-3 per hr., €16).

Public Transportation: 10 main bus lines cruise around the city and into the suburbs for €1.25-3 per ride. **Zentralplatz,** serviced by all bus lines, offers the most convenient access to the Altstadt. Purchase tickets from the driver.

Taxis: Taxi Koblenz ☎ 330 55 or **Funk Taxi** ☎ 121 51

Bike Rental: Biking the Rhein and Mosel valleys can be invigorating. See the pamphlet *Rund und Rad,* sold in bookstores. **Fahrradhaus Zangmeister,** Am Löhrrondell (☎ 323 63), rents bikes for €8 per day. ID required. Open M-F 10am-8pm, Sa 8am-2pm.

◢ ▯ ORIENTATION AND PRACTICAL INFORMATION

Koblenz's sights are clustered in the strip of Altstadt between the **Deutsches Eck** (a spit of land jutting into the Mosel and Rhein) and the **Markt.** The train station lies farther inland, but busy **Löhrstraße,** lined with shops, runs from there to the Markt.

**Rheinland-Pfalz and Saarland
(Rhineland-Palatinate and Saarland)**

Tourist Offices: The main office, Bahnhofpl. 17 (☎ 100 43 99; www.koblenz.de), across from the train station, hands out boat schedules and maps and books rooms for free. Open May-Oct. M-F 9am-7pm, Sa-Su 10am-7pm; Nov.-Apr. daily until 6pm. A **branch** in the Rathaus (at the entrance to Jesuitenpl.) has the same services and hours.

Bookstore: Reuffel, Löhrstr. 62, fills 3 stories on Koblenz's main shopping street. Current mainstream English books on the top floor.

Laundromat: Eco-Express Waschsalon, on the corner of Rizzastr. and Löhrstr. Wash €3. Dry €0.50 per 10min. Soap included. Open daily 6am-11pm, last wash 10pm.

Emergency: Police, ☎ 110. **Fire** and **Ambulance,** ☎ 112. Police station at Moselring 10-12 (☎ 10 31).

Pharmacy: Medico Apotheke, Bahnhofpl. 6 (☎ 91 46 60; fax 91 46 622), directly in front of the train station past the buses. Open M-F 8am-6:30pm, Sa 9am-1pm.

Internet: ▧ **Chatpoint,** Am Plan 10. Internet access among palm trees, funky booths, and plastic dolphins, with drink specials, baguettes (€2-4), and pizza (€4). Bring your own laptop for discounted **wireless access.** €3 per hr., after 7pm €3.50, happy hour 10am-noon. Open M-Th 10am-midnight, F-Sa until 2am, Su noon-midnight.

Post Office: The Hauptpostamt, 65068 Koblenz, is to the right of the train station exit. Open M-F 7am-7pm, Sa 8:30am-1:30pm.

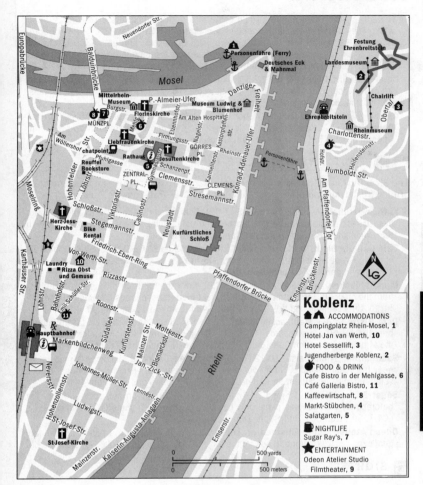

Koblenz

⌂▲ ACCOMMODATIONS
Campingplatz Rhein-Mosel, 1
Hotel Jan van Werth, 10
Hotel Sessellift, 3
Jugendherberge Koblenz, 2

🍴 FOOD & DRINK
Cafe Bistro in der Mehlgasse, 6
Café Galleria Bistro, 11
Kaffeewirtschaft, 8
Markt-Stübchen, 4
Salatgarten, 5

🍸 NIGHTLIFE
Sugar Ray's, 7

★ ENTERTAINMENT
Odeon Atelier Studio
Filmtheater, 9

🏠 ACCOMMODATIONS AND CAMPING

Rooms in Koblenz are expensive, so it may be worthwhile to make the really long, really uphill trek across the river to the hostel. Make reservations early.

Hotel Jan van Werth, Von-Werth-Str. 9 (☎365 00; fax 365 06). From the station, walk up Bahnhofstr. and take a right on Van-Werth-Str. This classy family-run establishment is inexpensive living with a touch of elegance—and by far one of the best values in Koblenz. Large breakfast buffet included. Reception 6:30am-10pm. Singles from €23, with shower and toilet €41; doubles from €53/€62; triples €60-70. ❸

Jugendherberge Koblenz (HI), in **Festung Ehrenbreitstein** (p. 356), (☎97 28 70; fax 972 87 30). Take bus #9 or 10 from the bus station to "Charlottenstr." If you intend to hike uphill, continue along the Rhein side of the mountain on the main road, following the DJH signs. Within minutes you'll come to a path leading to the Festung (20min. walk). The chairlift *(Sessellift)* is a block further. (runs Easter-May, Oct. 10am-4:50pm; June-Sept. 9am-5:50pm; €4.20 one-way, €5.80 return; students €2.50/€3.50). Within the fortress, this hostel has a great view of the city and its rivers. Breakfast included. Reception 7:15am-10pm. Curfew 11:30pm. Dorms €16.50; doubles €44. ❷

Hotel Sessellift, Obertal 22 (☎752 56; fax 768 72), next to the "Obertal" bus stop; take bus #9 or 10. Though a bit far from town, this hotel offers basic, functional rooms with showers. Breakfast included. Singles €25; doubles €42; triples €60. ❷

Campingplatz Rhein-Mosel, Am Neuendorfer Eck (☎827 19), across the Mosel from the Deutsches Eck. Cross the river by ferry (€0.80). Reception 8am-1pm and 3-10pm. Open Apr.-Oct. 15. €4.50 per person, €2.50 per site. ❶

🌃 🎷 FOOD AND NIGHTLIFE

The **Rizza Obst und Gemüse** grocery store, Rizza Str. 49, provides an assortment of drinks, fresh fruit and other necessities. (Open M-F 7am-7pm, Sa 7am-2pm.)

📸 **Kaffeewirtschaft,** Münzpl. 14 (☎914 47 02). Crimson and navy walls, candlelight, and fresh roses set the scene at this hip bar and cafe. Filling meals (€8-10). Open M-Th 9am-midnight, F-Sa 9am-2am, Su 10am-midnight. ❸

Café Galleria Bistro & Pizzeria, Emil-Schüllerstr. 45 (☎337 58), to the left of the train station. Great pizzas and pastas from €5 in this bright, classy cafe. Open daily 10:30am-midnight, F-Sa until 3am. ❷

Markt-Stübchen, Am Markt 220 (☎755 65), down the hill from the hostel, one block from the chair lift. Local atmosphere with great food (most entrees €7 or less). Open M-Tu, Th, Su 11am-midnight; W 11am-2pm; F 4pm-1am; Sa 11am-1am. ❷

Cafe Bistro in der Mehlgasse, Mehlg. 12 (☎144 57). Sandwiches on tasty ciabatta bread (€4.4.50), fresh salads (€3.50-7), and a chill ambience on the street opposite the Mittelrheinmuseum. Open daily 9:30am-11pm, F-Sa until midnight. ❷

Salatgarten, Gymnasialstr. 10-12 (☎364 55), where Casinostr. becomes Gymnasialstr. near the Jesuitenkirche. Stuff your plate with a wealth of vegetarian wonders at this salad-bar style restaurant for under €6. Open M-F 10am-7pm, Sa 10am-4pm. ❷

Sugar Ray's, Münzpl. 15 (☎42 19), specializes in blue neon and rock and roll. Eat beforehand, because this place only has drinks: beer (€2), shots (€2), and cocktails (€4-7, Su-Th €3.50). Su-Th 8pm-1am, F-Sa 8pm-2am. ❷

Odeon Atelier Studio Filmtheater, Löhrstr. 88 (☎311 88), plays recent English-language movies 1 W per mo. (Look for the huge "Kino" sign outside.) €6.50, students €5.

👁 SIGHTS

FESTUNG EHRENBREITSTEIN. Towering 118m over the town, this 11th-century fortress offers a bird's-eye view of the clear Mosel as it blends into the muddy Rhein. Stay at the **Jugendherberge Koblenz** (p. 355), or marvel at the defensive pits and portcullises on the grounds. *(Hourly tours start at tourist office, weekend before Easter until mid-Nov. 10am-5pm, €1.10. Fortress €1, students €0.60, free for hostel guests.)*

DEUTSCHES ECK. The Rhein, the Mosel, and German nationalism converge at the Deutsches Eck (German Corner). This are allegedly witnessed the first stirrings of the German nation in 1216 when the Teutonic Knights settled here. Erected in 1897, the large monument at the top of the steps stands in tribute to Kaiser Wilhelm I for his forced reconciliation of the internal conflicts of the German Empire. The 14m equestrian statue of the Kaiser that once topped the monument was toppled in 1945 and replaced by a duplicate in 1993. Beginning in 1953, the corner also became know as **Mahnmal der Deutschen Einheit** (Monument of German Unity) as a reminder of the bonds still shared by a divided East and West Germany.

CHURCHES. Koblenz's Altstadt is dotted with churches, many of which received post-WWII facelifts. The 12th-century **Florinskirche** was used as a slaughterhouse during the Thirty Years' War. *(Open daily 11am-5pm. Free.)* Nearby, oval Baroque towers rise above intricate ceiling latticework of the **Liebfrauenkirche,** whose choir windows depict women's roles in the Passion of Christ. *(Open M-Sa 8am-7pm, Su 9am-8pm. Free.)* More stained-glass windows hide behind a masterful *Rheinish* facade in the modern interior of the **Jesuitenkirche** on the Marktpl. *(Open daily 7am-6pm. Free.)* The 19th-century new Roman style **Herz-Jesu-Kirche** dominates the city center and looks down upon the **Schängelbrunnen.** At the top of the fountain, a statue of a young boy spits water on passersby every two minutes. *(Church open daily 7:30am-7pm. Free.)* On the other side of the train station, the inside of **St.-Josef-Kirche** is bathed in light from yet more stained glass. *(Open daily 9am-6pm. Free.)*

BLUMENHOF. In the understated gardens next to Museum Ludwig, there is more national braggadocio to be had, though this time not on the part of the Germans. Here, an overconfident Napoleon erected the fountain to commemorate the "certain impending victory" in his Russian campaign. The Russians, after routing the French army, added the mocking inscription "seen and approved."

🏛 MUSEUMS

Koblenz's Museums are outstanding and diverse, and a 4-day pass (€5.10), available at tourist offices and museums, gets you into all those listed below, as well as the **Festung Ehrenbreitstein, Schloß Stolzenfels,** and the **Wehrtechnische Studiensammlung** (military technology museum).

MUSEUM LUDWIG IM DEUTSCHHERRENHAUS. Just behind the Deutsches Eck, this art museum showcases modern French artists and presents high-caliber exhibitions every six to eight weeks. Regular tours offer a penetrating glance into the works. The permanent collection is on the 2nd floor. *(Danziger Freiheit 1. Behind the Mahnmal.* ☎ *30 40 40. Open Tu-Sa 10:30am-5pm, Su 11am-6pm. €2.50, students €1.50.)*

MITTELRHEINMUSEUM. This museum's three floors of art are largely devoted to religious sculpture and a number of romantic landscapes depicting the Rhein Valley. The 2nd floor holds changing exhibits. *(Florinsmarkt 15-17 next door to the Florinskirche.* ☎ *129 25 20. Open Tu-Sa 10:30am-5pm, Su 11am-6pm. €2.50, students €1.50.)*

LANDESMUSEUM KOBLENZ. A permanent collection of shiny antique automobiles and regional artifacts, including huge wooden wine-presses. *(Hohe Ostfront, in Festung Ehrenbreitstein.* ☎ *970 30. Open daily mid-Mar. to mid-Nov. 9am-12:30pm and 1-5pm. Last entrance 30min. before closing. €2, students €1.50.)*

RHEINMUSEUM. A private museum devoted to all things *Rheinisch.* Four floors of maritime history and more model boats than you ever wanted to see. *(Charlottenstr. 53a. Bus #9 or 10 to "Charlottenstr."* ☎ *97 42 44. Open Tu-Su 10am-5pm. €3, children €2.)*

🔁 DAYTRIPS FROM KOBLENZ

SCHLOß STOLZENFELZ

Take bus #650 (dir.: Boppard) from the train station to "Stolzenfels Mitte" (10min., 2 per hr., €2), then walk 10min. up the winding Schloßweg. ☎ *0261 516 56 for information, or call the Koblenz tourist office (*☎ *0261 100 43 99). Obligatory 45min. tours in German (English descriptions available). Open daily Jan.-Mar. and Oct.-Nov. 9am-5pm; Apr.-Sept. 9am-6pm. Last entrance 1hr. before closing. €2.60, students €1.30, children €1.*

5km outside of Koblenz, the orange structure that is Schloß Stolzenfels sprawls with the typical decadence one might expect of a 13th-century stronghold turned 19th-century court (after its destruction during a French siege). Since King Wil-

FROM THE ROAD

ROYAL TREATMENT

I took the bus to Sayn because of a 3-line description in a tourist brochure, expecting that I would snap a few photos of the colorful butterflies and head back to Koblenz for an early dinner. I was not expecting that a prince would tell me about 800 years of family history inside his ancestral estate.

The owner of the butterfly garden, Gabriela, guided me around the indoor butterfly house, describing everything we saw, then suggested we go across the street to *Schloß Sayn*, where her husband Alexander was working.

Inside the castle, Alexander explained its history beginning in the 12th century, showing me sketches and photographs in the entryway. The beautiful woman in one of the magnificent paintings was not just some artist's model, but Princess Leonilla (Alexander's great-grandmother), who returned with her husband Ludwig from Russia to reestablish the family line in Germany. In another room, paintings and scrapbooks tell the family's history through the perspective of its women.

Eschewing the pastel shades that frost many German castles, Prince Alexander and Princess Gloria had painted many rooms in bold reds, blues, and greens. In a stained sweatshirt and jeans, I felt slightly underdressed for my surroundings. But, encouraged by the genuine friendliness of my hosts, I forgot about fashion and enjoyed my personal castle tour.

— *Melissa Much, 2004*

helm IV died in 1863, the only people to stay in the castle have been refugees from Koblenz during WWII. Glossy imported fabrics, paneled ceilings, intricate antiques, and countless mirrors tastefully adorn every room. See the ideal merging of medieval and Romantic styles inside the chapel, enhanced by the apse mural and meticulous cast-iron staircase. The **pergola garden,** garnished with dangling flowerpots, rose-shaded trellises and languishing statues, feels like an Italian villa.

SCHLOß SAYN AND BUTTERFLY GARDEN

Take bus #8 (dir.: Bendorf/Sayn) from the train station or Zentralpl to Sayn Schloß (last stop), 30min., 1-2 per hr., €3.15). The castle is next to the bus stop and the butterfly garden is inside the park at the left. Castle museum (☎ 02622 902 40; www.sayn.de) and butterfly house (☎ 02622 154 78) both open Mar.-Sept. 10am-6pm, Oct. 10am-5pm, Nov. 10am-4pm. Admission to both €6, students €5; castle museum only €3/€2. Falconry show (☎ 02622 907 98 40) Mar.-Nov. Tu-Su at 5pm. €3.50, students €2.50.

A variety of activities await in Sayn, 15km north of Koblenz. Walk through clouds of colorful wings in the tropical paradise of the **Garten der Schmetterlinge** (Butterfly Garden). Located inside the **Schloßpark,** this glass house has more than just butterflies; turtles, fish, and birds fill the streams and dart across paths. Visitors who arrive early may see butterflies breaking from their cocoons in the butterfly house.

Across the street is the dignified **Schloß Sayn** (see **Royal Treatment,** p. 358). The Sayn family originally lived in the 12th-century castle at the top of the hill, but left after it was ruined in the Thirty Years' War. After returning in the mid-19th century, they bought the medieval palace at the bottom of the hill and had it redone in the popular neo-Gothic style by François Girard, who would later become chief architect of the Louvre. Inside, the Sayn-Wittgenstein family history is told through the unique perspective of its female members. The castle is also home to the **Rheinische Eisenkunstguss Museum** (Rhein Cast Iron Museum), commemorating an local iron foundry. Further up the hill, the **Falconry** opens up in the afternoon for a show. At the crest of the hill, the ruins of **Burg Sayn** look over the Rhein Valley.

RHEINTAL (RHEIN VALLEY)

Though the Rhein River runs from Switzerland to the North Sea, the Rhein of the poetic imagination exists in the 80km gorge stretching from Bonn to just north of Mainz. Here the river rolls by whirlpools and craggy shores, with castle silhouettes crowning the coarse terrain. From the Lorelei cliffs, a golden-haired siren lured passing sailors to their deaths on the rocks below. Heinrich Heine immortalized the spot with his 1823 poem "Die Lorelei," but he can hardly claim sole credit for the river's resonance. Inspired by the Germanic *Nibelungenlied* saga, Wagner recalled the Rhein's mythic legacy in his *Der Ring des Nibelungen*, while British Romantics like Turner captured its elusive sublimity with violent brushstrokes.

Two different train lines (one on each bank) traverse this fabled stretch; the line on the west bank runs between Koblenz and Mainz and sticks closer to the water, providing superior views. Many, undeterred by tourist crowds, opt instead to experience the landscape by boat, affording even better vistas. The **Köln-Düsseldorfer (KD) Line** covers the Mainz-Koblenz stretch four times per day during the summer, with more frequent excursions along shorter stretches of the river.

LORELEI CLIFFS AND CASTLES

Though sailors were once lured to these cliffs by the infamous Lorelei (sometimes spelled "Loreley") maidens, their hypnotic song is now unnecessary; today hordes of travelers are seduced by scenery alone. Hillsides jut from the churning Rhein, cloaked in slanting vineyards, romantic villages, and medieval ruins. In peak season, the river brims with passenger ships, while tour buses trickle in from the towns of **St. Goarshausen** and **St. Goar. Trains** run to St. Goarshausen from Cologne (1hr., €18) and Mainz (1½hr., €9.40) and to St. Goar from Cologne (1½hr., €22) and Mainz (1hr., €8.40). These two towns host the spectacular **Rhein in Flammen** (see **Rhein in Flammen**, p. 362) fireworks celebration in mid-September. St. Goarshausen, on the east bank, provides access to the Lorelei statue and the infamous cliffs. Facing the Rhein, follow Rheinstr. left to the statue's peninsula. To reach the cliffs, take the stairs across the street from the base of the peninsula (45min.).

St. Goarshausen's **tourist office**, Bahnhofstr. 8, hands out free maps and local listings. (Phone code: 06771. ☎91 00; loreley-tourist-info@t-online.de. M and Sa-Su 9:30am-noon, M also 2-4:30pm; Th 2-4:30pm; F 2-5:350pm.) The **police station**, Bahnhofstr. 12 (☎932 70; emergency ☎110), is a few doors down. Twenty minutes up the Lorelei Cliffs, the hostel **Jugendheim Loreley ❶** lures travelers with its spectacular location, only to drown them in crashing waves of schoolchildren. From the cliffs, walk past the red and white parking gate down the road and take a left. (☎26 19; tuhe@loreley-herberge.de. Breakfast included. Sheets €3.50. Curfew 10pm. €8.50 per person. Call in advance for doubles.) Still in St. Goarshausen, **Nassauer Hof ❸**, Bahnhofstr. 22, offers bright, modern rooms near the river. (☎80 28 40. Breakfast included. Singles €33; doubles €48.) To reach **Campingplatz Loreleystadt ❶** from the station, face the Rhein and go right on Rheinstr. to Rheinpromenade (8min. ☎25 92. €4.80 per person, €2.60-4.50 per tent.) To be closer to the famed cliffs, try **Campingplatz Auf der Loreley ❶**. Follow signs from the Lorelei statue area. (☎430. €3 per person, €5 per tent.) Directly above St. Goarshausen, the fierce **Burg Katz** (Cat Castle) eternally stalks its prey, the smaller **Burg Maus** (Mouse Castle). Fortunately, the mouse escapes by hiding a few kilometers upstream in the Wellmich district of Goarshausen. Though all of Burg Katz is a privately-owned bed and breakfast (rooms from €250) closed to sightseers, Burg Maus, at the end of a very strenuous 1¼hr. hike up cliffs, offers falconry demonstrations daily at 11am and 2:30pm. If you're lucky, you can watch falcons snatch rats off the heads of small children. (☎76 69. €6.50, children €5.50.)

The "Loreley V" **ferry** crosses the river to and from St. Goar, another base for Lorelei explorations. (Phone code: 06741. Ferries M-F 6am-11pm, Sa-Su from 7am. €1.70, round-trip €2.) St. Goar's **tourist office**, Heerstr. 86 in the pedestrian zone, books rooms for free. (☎383; www.talderloreley.de. Open M-F 8am-12:30pm and 2-5pm, Sa 10am-noon.) The **Jugendherberge (HI) ❶**, Bismarckweg

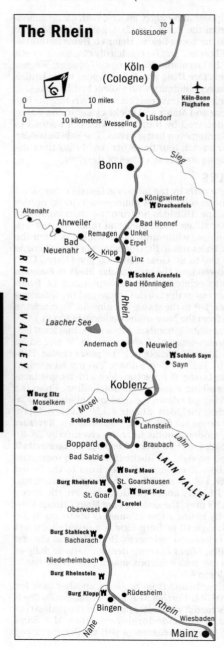

The Rhein

TO
DÜSSELDORF

Köln
(Cologne)

Köln-Bonn
Flughafen

0 ——— 10 miles

0 ——— 10 kilometers

Wesseling

Lülsdorf

Sieg

Bonn

Königswinter
Ħ Drachenfels

Altenahr

Ahrweiler

Bad Honnef

Remagen   Unkel

Bad   Erpel

Neuenahr   Kripp

Ahr   Linz

Ħ Schloß Arenfels
Bad Hönningen

Rhein

Laacher See

Andernach   Neuwied

Ħ Schloß Sayn
Sayn

Koblenz

Ħ Burg Eltz
Moselkern

Mosel

Schloß Stolzenfels Ħ   Lahnstein

Boppard   Braubach

Bad Salzig   Lahn

LAHN VALLEY

Ħ Burg Maus

Burg Rheinfels Ħ   St. Goarshausen

St. Goar   Ħ Burg Katz

Oberwesel   ■ Lorelei

Burg Stahleck Ħ
Bacharach

Niederheimbach

Burg Rheinstein Ħ

Burg Klopp Ħ   Rüdesheim

Bingen
                Wiesbaden
Rhein

Nahe   Mainz

RHEINLAND-PFALZ
RHEIN VALLEY

17, is 10min. from the station. With your back to the tracks, follow Oberstr. left. At the end of Oberstr., make a left under the bridge. Bismarckweg is the next right. Close to the castle, this cheap hostel packs in beds with admirable efficiency. (☎388; fax 28 69. Breakfast and sheets included. Reception 8-9am, 5-6pm, and 7-8pm. Curfew 10pm, but you can get a key. Dorms €12.70.) ◪**Hotel Hauser ❸,** Heerstr. 77, has central, spotless rooms with balconies. (☎333; fax 14 64. Breakfast included, plus discounts on meals at the restaurant downstairs. Singles €26-38; doubles €55-60.) The view from the cliffs on this, the eastern side of the Rhein, is spectacular. The beautiful, age-worn **Burg Rheinfels** (☎77 53) is a sprawling, half-ruined castle with underground passages—it doesn't get more *romantisch* than this. Beware of slippery slopes. (Open daily Mar.-Sept. 9am-6pm; Oct. 9am-5pm. €4, students €3, children €2, families €10. Bring a flashlight, or buy a candle in the museum for €0.50.)

BACHARACH   ☎06743

Bounded by a lush river promenade, a resilient town wall, and dramatic sloping vineyards, Bacharach retains an irrepressible sense of identity in the face of increasing tourist traffic. The **tourist office,** Oberstr. 45, and the Rathaus share an old building at one end of the town center. It offers **Internet** access (€0.50 per 5min.) and books rooms for free. (☎91 93 03; fax 91 93 04. Open Apr.-Oct. M-F 9am-5pm, Sa-Su 10am-2pm; Nov.-Mar. M-F 9am-noon.) To start the steep 15min. trek, take a right out of the station pathway, turn left at the Peterskirche, and take any of the marked paths leading up the hill to the ◪**Jugendherberge Stahleck (HI) ❷.** This hostel is about as close to a fairy tale as most of its 40,000 yearly visitors will get. A converted 12th-century castle, it provides dazzling panoramas of the Rhein Valley. Painstaking details include individually named rooms and cheerful plaid sheets. (☎ 12 66; fax 26 84. Breakfast included. Reception 24hrs. Curfew 10pm, bar open until midnight. €15.10; doubles €73.60.) For those weary of uphill treks, a dynamic mother-son duo runs two centrally-located pensions. Frau Dettmar owns clean and flowery **Haus Dettmar ❷**, Oberstr. 8. (☎/fax 26 61. Rooms €17-25, all with shower and toilet.) Jürgen's **Hotel Am Markt ❸**, Oberstr. 64, is in an even better location. (☎ 17 15; fax 29 79. Doubles €42-56.) More luxury awaits at the **Gästehaus Schloß Furstenberg ❸**, Mainzer Str. 22. From the station turn left; the hotel is a 2min. walk from the town center. The rooms are large and clean, with baths, the staff is friendly, and full apartments start at just €37 a night. (☎ 91 90 00; fax 91 90 10. Singles from €26; doubles from €33-44. Lower prices for stays over 4 days.) Turn right from the station (downhill towards the river), then walk south for 10min. to reach **Campingplatz Bacharach ❶**, directly on the Rhein. (☎ 17 52. €4.20 per person, €3 per tent, €6 per site.)

Once home to a stone altar to Bacchus (hence the town name), today Bacharach fills with pilgrims journeying to worship at the town's numerous *Weinkeller* and *Weinstuben* (wine cellars and pubs), tucked between half-timbered houses. Try some of the Rhein's best wines and cheeses at **Die Weinstube ❸**, Oberstr. 63. (Open M-F from 11pm and Sa-Su from noon.) Behind the historical **Altes Haus,** whose half-timbered perfection has acquired minor fame, this family-owned business makes its own wine on the premises. Entrees are €8-15, and wine with cheese €3-8. (☎ 12 08. Open M-W and F 1-11pm, Sa-Su from noon. Closed Th.) The price is right at the 🄬**Café Restaurant Rusticana ❸**, Oberstr. 40, where a bubbly German couple serves three-course meals of regional dishes for €6-11. The apple strudel (€2) is baked daily from a Romanian recipe that locals have been trying to replicate for years. (Open May-Oct. M-W and F-Su. 11:30am-9:30pm.) On Oberstr., just up the steps next to the late-Romanesque **Peter-skirche,** is the 14th-century **Wernerkapelle,** the ghost-like Gothic skeleton of a chapel that took 140 years to build but only a few hours to destroy in the Palatinate War of Succession in 1689.

RÜDESHEIM   ☎ 06722

From opposite the Rhein, Rüdesheim looks like a Romantic's dream come true—terraced vineyards stretch steeply up from a colorful village framed by two stone castles. The town's photographic skyline, coupled with its convenient location in the center of the **Rheingau** wine-producing region, has spawned a tourism industry that specializes in dishing out nostalgia to elderly visitors.

The **tourist office,** Geisenheimerstr. 22, is a 10min. walk from the station. Facing the Rhein, take a left, walk down Rheinstr. and continue onto Bleichstr; the office will be on your left in the bus park. The staff offers brochures and books rooms for free. (☎ 296 21 94 33; www.ruedesheim.de. Open Apr. to mid-Sept. M-F 8:30am-6:30pm, Sa-Su 11am-5pm.) The **post office,** Rheinstr. 4, towards Brömserburg, has an **ATM.** (Open M-F 8:30am-noon and 2:30-5pm, Sa 9am-noon.) Email to your heart's content at **Internetcafe Rüdesheim,** located on Marktstr. (☎ 46 96. €3 per 30min. Open daily from 11am-8pm.) The **Jugendherberge (HI) ❷,** Jugendherberge 1, has simple, clean rooms a steep 25min. walk above town. From the station, walk down Rheinstr. and take a left on any street you please. At Oberstr., turn right. Bear left at the fork onto Germaniastr. and follow it to Kuhweg and the Jugendherberge signs. (☎ 27 11; fax 482 84. Breakfast and sheets included. Curfew 9pm. Dorms €15; singles €17.50, with bath €21.50; doubles €32/€37.) In town, **Zur Lindenau ❸,** Löhrstr. 9, has airy rooms and a secluded courtyard. (Breakfast included. Singles from €34; doubles €56.) **Campingplatz am Rhein ❶** has riverside plots and a swimming pool next door. From the station, walk past town along the river. (☎ 25 28. Reception 8am-10pm. Open May-Sept. €4.40 per person, €4.60 per tent.)

RHEIN IN FLAMMEN

Every summer in the lower Rhein river valley, age-old castles are showered in bursts of flaming color for the annual fireworks display known as *Rhein in Flammen*. During this dazzling event, illuminated boats loaded with spectators float along the Rhein to form a "light boat parade."

On July 2, 2005, starting promptly at 6pm, the flotilla will pass the towns of Rüdesheim, Bingen, and Assmannshausen. At 10pm the first fireworks explode from beneath the castle *Reichenstein* and continue at castle *Rheinstein*. Farther along the Rhein, the ruins of the ancient castles Ehrenfels and Klopp produce a "Bengel fire" of sparks, igniting in front of an awestruck audience. The finale is in Rüdesheim at 11:30pm, when countless falling firecrackers turn the river into a ribbon of flame. High the town, the enormous *Niederwaldenkmal* monument provides a stellar view of the final festivities.

To reach the monument, take the *Sesselift*, which runs later due to the celebration. Check with the local tourist office in Rüdesheim for operating times and prices. Visitors who plan far enough in advance can also participate in the boat parade. Many cruise ships offer live music and dancing with a magnificent view of all of the festivities from the water. Tickets can be ordered in advance with departures from a number of local cities. (€41; www.rhine-river-lights.com.)

Bordered on both sides by a small vineyard, the picturesque 12th-century **Brömserburg** castle, Reinstr. 2, is a **wine museum,** where you can see wine technology from the Stone Age onward. From the station or ferry docks, walk 5min. toward town along Rheinstr. Ask for details about their wine tasting tours. (☎23 48. Open mid-Mar. to Nov. 9am-6pm. Last admission 5:15pm. €3, students and children €2.) Servings of kitsch abound on the nearby **Drosselgasse,** a tiny alley where merchants peddle fake cuckoo clocks and lots of wine. Up Drosselg. to the left are signs for ■**Siegfried's Mechanisches Musikkabinett,** Oberstr. 27-29. The myriad self-playing musical instruments from the 18th to 20th centuries make the generic ballerina-in-a-box look disgracefully primitive. Delightful women in 19th-century dress lead visitors through the collection, and allow visitors to play one of the instruments themselves. (☎492 17. Open Mar.-Dec. daily 10am-10pm. 45min. mandatory tours every 15min. €5.50, students €3.) The **Mittelalterliches Foltermuseum,** Oberstr. 49, displays medieval torture devices intended to inspire repentance. After seeing these 80 antiquated instruments, several with blood-ied mannequins, beheading seems charitable. (☎475 10. Open daily 10am-6pm. €5, students €4.)

The **Niederwalddenkmal,** a 38m monument crowned by the unnervingly figure of Germania wielding a 1400kg sword, looms above town. Erected on the establishment of the Second Reich in 1871 after victory over France, the frieze features legions of aristocrats pledging loyalty to the Kaiser, while winged emblems of war and peace stand guard. A ■**chairlift** *(Seilbahn),* Oberstr. 37, runs to the statue from the top of Christoffelstr.; take a left directly before the tourist office. (10min. each way. Open Apr. daily 9:30am-4:30pm; May-Aug. M-Th 9:30am-6pm, F-Su 9:30am-7pm; Aug.-March daily 9:30am-5pm. €4, round-trip €6, children half-price.) To reach the monument by foot (35min.), go towards the station on Oberstr. and turn onto Feldtor, which winds through vineyards toward the monument.

MAINZ   ☎06131

Johannes Gutenberg, Mainz's favorite son, invented the movable-type printing press in 1455, and the city houses a printing museum and holds an annual fair in his honor. Mainz used to be the greatest Catholic diocese north of the Alps, and the archbishop-dukes who ruled the city played a central role in German politics until the Napoleonic wars. The monumental Dom at the heart of the maze of cobblestone streets is a living symbol of the long-thriving town.

TRANSPORTATION

Trains run to: **Frankfurt** (30min., €6); **Heidelberg** (1hr., €17); **Koblenz** (1hr., €17). Mainz shares a **public transportation** system with Wiesbaden; to get there, take bus #6. The Köln-Düsseldorf **ferry** (☎23 28 00) docks in Mainz and departs from the wharfs on the other side of the Rathaus. To: **Köln** (11hr., €66, students €33).

ORIENTATION AND PRACTICAL INFORMATION

Streets running parallel to the Rhein are marked with blue nameplates, while streets perpendicular to the river have red ones. The **tourist office** in Brückenturm has free maps, conducts **tours**, (2hr. Sa 2pm, May-Oct. also W and F 2pm; in German and English. €5.) and reserves rooms for a €2.50 fee. (☎28 62 10; www.info-mainz.de/tourist. Open M-F 9am-6pm, Sa 10am-3pm.) The **Mainz Card** grants access to all museums and is also a one-day travel pass (€6, families €10). The **AIDS-Hilfe hotline** (☎22 22 75) has the scoop on GLBT life in the city. For **Internet**, visit **Spiel-in.** (In Rebstorkpl. From Markpl. follow Schusterstr. and then go right onto Korbg. 18+. €3 per hr. Open M-Sa 8am-11pm.) The **post office,** 55001 Mainz, is a block down Bahnhofstr. from the station. (Open M-F 8am-6pm, Sa 8:30am-12:30pm.)

ACCOMMODATIONS

Jugendgästehaus (HI), Otto-Brunfels-Schneise 4 (☎853 32; jh-mainz@t-online.de), is in Weisenau in a corner of the Volkspark. Take bus #62 (dir.: Weisenau), 63 (dir.: Laubenheim), or 92 (dir.: Ginsheim) to "Viktorstift/Jugendherberge" (10min.) and follow the signs. Bright, clean rooms with private baths make the trek worth it. Breakfast included. Reception 6:30am-10pm. 4- to 6-bed rooms €16.90; doubles €43.80. ❷

Altstadt Hotel Rebstock, Heiliggrabg. 6 (☎23 03 17; fax 23 03 18), has 8 clean, basic rooms over a small winehouse. Friendly staff and great location in the Altstadt. Breakfast included. Reservations recommended. Singles €37-59; doubles €60-85. ❹

Hotel Stadt Coblenz, Rheinstr. 49 (☎629 04 44; www.stadtcoblenz.de. Bus #61, 60, 71, or 90 to "Rheingoldhalle/Rathaus" and turn down Rheinstr. away from Rheingoldhalle. Go through the Havana Restaurant on your right to get to reception. Inexpensive rooms across the street from the Rathaus on the outskirts of the Altstadt. Breakfast included. Singles €40; doubles €60, with bath €70; triples €80. ❹

FOOD

In warm months, local butchers and farmers peddle their goods in an outdoor **market** in the shadow of Mainz's cathedral on the Dompl. (Tu and F-Sa open 7am-2pm.) Wonderful smells wafts through Augustinerstr. in the evening, where you can get meals for under €6. If you're in a hurry, stop on almost any street-corner to pick up a fresh pretzel or mini-pizza from one of the **Ditsch** stands (€0.50-1.25).

Der Eisgrub-Bräu, Weißlilieng. 1a (☎22 11 04). On the edge of the Altstadt, with the motto "Bier Erleben" (experience beer). Beer is brewed in-house and served from vats, without refiltering (€2.70 for 0.4L). Entrees €5-13. Breakfast buffet daily 9am-noon €2.90; lunch buffet M-F 12:30-4pm €5.10. Open Su-Th 9am-1pm, F-Sa 9am-2pm. ❸

News Cafe, Göttelmannstr. 40 (☎98 98 37), in the Volkspark adjacent to Mainz's Jugendgästehaus. An ideal backyard to the hostel with playgrounds, roller rinks, wading pools, ice cream stands, and a small train for kids to ride. Sandwiches €5.50-7, entrees under €10. Open M-Th 8am-2pm, Sa 9am-2pm, Su 9am-1pm. ❷

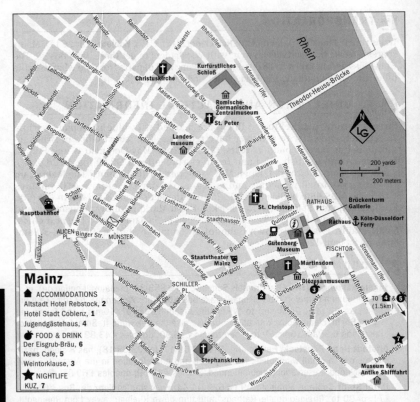

Mainz

🏠 ACCOMMODATIONS
Altstadt Hotel Rebstock, **2**
Hotel Stadt Coblenz, **1**
Jugendgästehaus, **4**
🍴 FOOD & DRINK
Der Eisgrub-Bräu, **6**
News Cafe, **5**
Weintorklause, **3**
⭐ NIGHTLIFE
KUZ, **7**

Weintorklause, Weintorstr. 11 (☎ 22 21 67). The walls of this small restaurant are decorated by banknotes of foreign guests' currencies. Traditional German meals €5-8. Open daily 11am-2pm and 6-9pm; closed W. ❸

👁 SIGHTS

MARTINSDOM. In the heart of the city is the resting place of the archbishops of Mainz. This colossal sandstone cathedral is a memorial to ecclesiastic power. The archbishops' extravagant tombstones line the walls, under a stained-glass timeline from AD 975. (☎ 25 34 12. Open Mar.-Oct. Tu-F 9am-6pm, Sa 9am-2pm, Su 1-2:45pm and 4-6:30pm; Nov.-Feb. M-F 9am-5pm, Sa 9am-4pm, Su 12:45-3pm and 4-5pm. Free.)

STEPHANSKIRCHE. The Gothic Stephanskirche, on a hill south of the Dom, was almost completely destroyed by the bombings of WWII and later reconstructed using the original stones. In the 1970s and early 1980s, the church comissioned Russian artist-in-exile **Marc Chagall** to create the magnificent stained-glass windows. Working until he was 98 years old, the Jewish artist finished only four months before his death. The Biblical themes symbolize the Abrahamic bond between Jews and Christians and a pledge of international peace between France and Germany. (On Stefansberg. ☎ 23 16 40. Open daily 10am-noon and 2-5pm. Free.)

KIRCHE ST. CHRISTOPH. The reputed site of Gutenberg's baptism was devastated in WWII. Its walls stand as haunting reminders of war. *(On Christofsstr.)*

🏛 MUSEUMS

GUTENBERG-MUSEUM. Johannes Gutenberg, father of movable type, is immortalized at the **Gutenberg-Museum,** which contains several Gutenberg Bibles, historic presses, an impressive collection of text art, early Asian calligraphy, and other relics of the early printing industry. Every hour, the staff prints a page from the Bible using an exact replica of the original printing press. *(Liebfrauenpl. 5, across from the Dom. ☎ 12 26 44. Open Tu-Sa 9am-5pm, Su 11am-3pm. €3, students €2.)*

DIÖZESANMUSEUM. Adjacent to the Martinsdom, the **Diözesanmuseum** looks out on a beautiful courtyard and houses changing exhibitions on religious themes and a permanent exhibition of religious sculptures in the cellar. *(Enter at the back of the Dom or from Domstr. ☎ 25 33 44. Open Tu-Su 10am-7pm. €7; students €5. Cellar free.)*

OTHER MUSEUMS. The **Römisch-Germanisches Zentralmuseum,** housed in the Kurfürstliches Schloß on the bank of the Rhein, traces human existence from prehistory to the Middle Ages with period artifacts. *(☎ 912 40. Open Tu-Su, 10am-6pm. Free.)* The **Museum für Antike Schifffahrt** displays remnants of Roman ships recovered near Mainz and other ship-related objects. *(Neutorstr. 2b. ☎ 28 66 30. Open Tu-Su, 10am-6pm. Free.)* Witness archeological discovery in action at the nearby excavation of a former **Roman Theater.** *(From the Schifffahrt museum, cross the street and take the uphill road past the yellow house. Continue underneath a bridge and up the stairs; the dig will be on your right.)* A comprehensive collection of art and archaeology, including a Judaica division and Roman arches, awaits in the **Landesmuseum.** *(Große Bleiche 49-51. ☎ 28 57 25. Open Tu 10am-8pm, W-Su 10am-5pm. €2, students €1.50. With special exhibits €5/€3.)*

🎭 NIGHTLIFE

On the third weekend in June, Mainz celebrates **Johannisnacht,** three days of revelry, Gutenberg style, when the Altstadt fills with wine, sausage, and sweet stands. **KUZ (Kulturzentrum),** Dagobertstr. 20b, packs two dance floors with local youth. Take bus #90 to "Holzturm," face the shopping center across the street, and turn right; walk one block and turn left on Dagobertstr. (☎ 28 68 60; www.kuz.de.)

MOSELTAL (MOSEL VALLEY)

Before its inevitable surrender to the Rhein at Koblenz, the Mosel River meanders slowly past the sun-drenched hills, scenic towns, and the ancient castles of its softly cut valley. The slopes can't compete with the Rhein's narrow gorge, but the less-touristed vineyards on the Moseltal's gentle hillsides have been pressing quality wines since the Romans first cultivated them 2000 years ago. The only local complaints are that summers are too dry and the winters too wet. The valley's scenery is best viewed by boat, bus, or bicycle—the train line between Koblenz and Trier cuts through the unremarkable countryside rather than following the river. Passenger boats no longer make the complete Koblenz-Trier run, but several companies do run daily trips along shorter stretches in summer.

COCHEM
☎ 02671

Like many German wine-making villages, the hamlet of Cochem is often overrun by busloads of elderly Germans looking for the quaint, idyllic village of yesteryear. Cochem's vineyard-covered hills and majestic **Reichsburg**, however, simply can't be cheapened. Atop a hill adjacent to the village, the castle's turrets lend the town a fairy-tale quality, deepened by the gnarled streets lined with clapboard houses.

⌐◪ TRANSPORTATION AND PRACTICAL INFORMATION. Unlike much of the Mosel Valley, Cochem is easily accessible by **train** from Koblenz (1hr., 2-3 per hr., €8) and Trier (1hr., 2 per hr., €9). Although Cochem is equidistant from the two cities, the route from Koblenz is more scenic, hugging the Mosel River and affording spectacular views. The **tourist office,** Endertpl. 1, next to the bus station, books rooms for free. From the train station, go to the river and turn right. (☎ 600 40; www.cochem.de. Open Apr.-Oct. M-Th 9am-5pm and F 9am-6pm; May to mid-July also Sa 9am-3pm; mid-July to Oct. also Sa 9am-5pm and Su 10am-noon. Nov.-Mar. M-F 9am-1pm and 2-5pm only.) The **police station** is located at Moselstr. 31. (☎ 98 40; **emergency** ☎ 110. Open 24hr.) **Internet** access is at **Murphy's @ Internet Cafe,** on Endertstr. (€1.60 per 30min. Open daily Mar.-Oct. 1pm-midnight; Nov.-Feb. M-F 7pm-midnight, Sa-Su 1pm-midnight.) The **post office,** 56812, is at the corner of Ravenestr. and Josefstr. (Open M-F 9am-5pm, Sa 9am-noon.)

⌐◨ ACCOMMODATIONS AND FOOD. Spacious rooms await at ▨**Gästehaus Zum Onkel Willi ❹**, Endertstr. 39, a welcoming family-operated guesthouse and restaurant. Phenomenal service sets this hotel apart from the rest. Located a few blocks away from the bustle of the city center. (☎ 73 05; www.zum-onkel-willi.de. Breakfast included. Singles €40; doubles with bath €60.) Cochem's **Jugendherberge (HI) ❷**, Klottener Str. 9, is 15min. from the train station on the opposite shore. Cross the Nordbrücke to the left as you exit the station; the family-owned youth hostel is next to the bridge on the right. (☎ 86 33; fax 85 86. All rooms have shower and toilet. Breakfast included. Dorm beds €16.90; singles €31; doubles €44.) Down the street from Gästehaus Zum Onkel Willi, **Hotel Holl ❹**, Endertstr. 54, combines large, bright, and comfortable rooms with a good restaurant serving steaks and *Schnitzel*. (☎ 43 23; www.hotel-holl.de. Breakfast included. Singles €36; doubles €52.) **Gästehaus Bambeg ❷**, Schloßstr. 5, supplies comfortable rooms uphill on your way to the Reichsburg. (☎ 70 56; fax 98 01 28. Breakfast included. Singles €22; doubles €34-38.) If you've got your own tent, walk down the path below the hostel to the **Campingplatz am Freizeitzentrum ❶** on Stadionstr. (☎ 44 09; fax 91 07 19. Laundry €0.80. Bike rental €7.50 per day. Reception 8am-9pm. Open Easter-Oct. €4 per person, €4 per campsite.) The cheesy yet good-hearted **Weinhexenkeller ❸**, on Hafenstr. across the Moselbrücke and immediately to the right, serves traditional food (€5-9) and savory Mosel wine. Local legend says that guests who imbibe too much fall under a witch's spell—modern science says they become drunk. Either way, the live music and dancing is entrancing. (☎ 977 60. Music begins at 7pm June-Aug. daily, Sept. F-Su. Open M-F 11am-1am, Sa-Su 10am-2am. Kitchen closes at 10pm.) On the Marktpl. next to the bridge, the **Café-Restaurant Mosella ❸** provides good coffee and filling meals. (Meals €8-13. Open daily Apr.-Oct. 9am-10pm.) **La Baia Ristorante Pizzeria ❷**, Liniusstr. 4, near the Moselbrücke, serves excellent pizza and pasta (€5-7) on a second-floor terrace. (☎ 80 40. Open Su-Th 11:30am-2:30pm and 5-11:30pm, F-Sa until midnight.) At **Filou ❸**, down Bernstr., sample homemade potato cakes smothered in cheese and veggies (€9), or splurge on one of the rich desserts. Comfortable indoor/outdoor seating. (Open daily 9am-6pm.)

◉ ⚐ SIGHTS AND ENTERTAINMENT. The neo-Gothic **Reichsburg** dominates the valley from 100m above the Mosel. The view more than warrants the 15min. climb along Schloßstr. from the Marktpl. to this 19th-century refurbishment of a nearly destroyed 11th-century original. The only way to see the castle interior is with one of the lively tour guides. Inside, a falconer teaches visitors the proper way to call an owl. (☎ 255. Open daily Mar.-Nov. 9am-6pm. 40min. tour; written English translations available; last tour at 5pm. €4, students €3.50, children €2. Falconry show €3, children €2.) Another popular hillside attraction is the **Sesselbahn** chairlift on Endertstr. The lift brings visitors to the level of the family-friendly **Wildpark** (30min. walk from the top), which has thrill rides and wildlife, as well as the **Pinnerkreuz**, a lone cross on a high peak illuminated by 10,000-watt bulbs at night. (☎ 98 90 63. Lift runs Apr.-June 10am-6pm, July-Aug. 9:30am-7pm, Sept.-Oct. 10am-6pm, until mid-Nov. 10am-5pm. €4, round-trip €5.50; children €1.90/2.50.) For **hiking** *sans* crowds, a relaxing journey awaits across the street from the Sesselbahn. Follow the stone steps to a trail that ends at the hill's summit, then head down the opposite side, turn left on the highway, and follow the trail branching off with the sign for "Maria Hell," (*hell* is German for "light"). The 2hr. hike leads through vineyards with marvelous views of Cochem's castle. For theme-park-style thrills, head across the river and follow the *Freizeitzentrum* signs to reach the gigantic **Schwimmbad**, a complex of pools, saunas, jacuzzis, and waterslides 5min. north of the *Nordbrücke*, the bridge near the train station. (☎ 979 90. Indoor pool open daily 10am-10pm. Outdoor pool open daily June-Aug. 10am-6:30pm. Day ticket €10.70, students €6.70, ages 6-11 €4.60, under 6 free. Outdoor pool only €3, students €2.) The **Weinwoche** (wine week; May 25-29, 2005) runs 1½ weeks after *Pfingsten* (Pentecost) and showcases some of the Mosel's best vintages. On the last weekend of August (Aug. 25-29, 2005) the **Heimat-und-Weinfest** peaks in a dramatic fireworks display.

⧉ DAYTRIP FROM COCHEM: BURG ELTZ. Originally constructed in the 11th and 12th centuries, **Burg Eltz** was one of the few castles in the Rheinland to escape destruction by Louis XIV's troops in the 17th century. Though the castle's secluded valley location didn't hurt, the Eltz family claims it was their ancestors' diplomacy that kept the castle intact. This political savvy was stretched thin in the 1330s when Baldwin, Elector of Trier, decided to tighten the law within his land. Two years of rock-slinging later, the Eltz family surrendered to Baldwin's terms: they retained the castle, but served him as vassals. Today the Eltz family still has rooms in the castle but lives elsewhere, leaving more of the Burg open to tourists. The shadowed forest path snakes along a quiet stream, culminating in the sudden appearance of the Gothic monument atop a spire of rock in the valley floor. The castle's interior can only be seen on a tour; guides identify medieval armory, Chinese porcelain, decaying tapestry, and spiral staircases. The recreations of castle life are done exceptionally well, especially explanations of medieval bedding and plumbing. Dazzling gold and silver pieces can be found in the **Schatzkammer** (treasury), which is separate from the tour. (☎ 02672 95 05 00; www.burg-eltz.de. Open daily Apr.-Oct. 9:30am-5:30pm. Tours every 15min. English tours given if you call ahead or with sufficient demand (about 15 people), typically 1 per hr. €6, students €4.50. Schatzkammer €2.50/1.50.) The nearest town connected to Burg Eltz by **train** is Moselkern. (20min., 1 per hr., €3.15.) With your back to the train station, head right on Oberstr. through town until it passes under a bridge and becomes a slightly winding road along the Eltz brook. The road ends at **Ringelsteiner Mühle**—from here the path through the woods is well marked. The mildly strenuous hike to the Burg is 1¼hr. each way, and the castle is only accessible by foot or car.

BEILSTEIN ☎ 02673

A tiny hamlet of half-timbered houses, crooked cobblestone streets, and about 300 residents, Beilstein takes pride in being the smallest official town in Germany. Spared in WWII, Beilstein's untarnished beauty has made it the idyllic backdrop of several movies and political summits, including the creation of the European Economic Community (now the European Union). By day, Beilstein's natural charm draws a tourist crowd that gives the town the illusion of size, but after 6pm, the spell breaks, and the peaceful town is yours. **Burg Metternich** (of the same family as the 19th-century Austrian statesman) is the local castle; though little survived a French sacking in 1689, the tower's view is spectacular. (☎ 936 39. Open daily Apr.-Oct. 9am-6pm. €2, students €1, children €0.50.) The Baroque **Karmelitenkirche,** also on the hill, has an intricately carved wooden altar and the famous **Schwarze Madonna von Beilstein,** a 16th-century Montserrat sculpture left behind by Spanish troops reintroducing Catholicism to the region. (Open daily 9am-7pm.)

The town can be reached by **bus** #716, which departs from the bus station at Endertpl. in Cochem (15min.; M-F 14 per day, Sa 5 per day, Su 3 per day; €3). The boats of **Personenschifffahrt Kolb** also float to Beilstein. (☎ 15 15; fax 15 10. 1hr.; May-Oct. 5 per day; €8, round-trip €11.) Hotels fill up quickly for October's grape harvest, so call well in advance. At **Hotel Gute Quelle ❸,** Marktpl. 34, the cordial staff will show you to a quaint room with private bath. (☎ 14 37; fax 13 99. Breakfast included. Doubles €60-70.) **Klapperburg ❸,** Bachstr. 33, offers spacious rooms with private baths and serves breakfast (included) and heavenly desserts in the cafe below. (☎ 14 17. Reception open Tu-Su 8am-6pm. Singles €35; doubles €48-56; triples €78.) Or try **Winzerschenke ❸,** An der Klostertreppe 29, which has comfortable doubles not far from the Karmelitenkirche. (☎ 13 54; fax 96 23 71. All rooms with bath. Breakfast included. Singles €28; doubles €38.) The ▨**Klostercafé ❷** outside the church offers traditional food (€5-12), fantastic Mosel wine, and a view that tops both. (☎ 16 74 or 16 53. Open daily 9am-7pm.) **San Donato ❷,** Fürst-Metternich-Str. 28, sells pizza and pasta dishes (€4-7) along with tasty fish and vegetarian specials (€6.50-15. ☎ 90 00 69. Open daily 11am-midnight.)

TRIER ☎ 0651

The oldest town in Germany, Trier has weathered more than two millennia in the western end of the Mosel Valley. Founded by Romans during the reign of Augustus, Trier reached its zenith in the early 4th century as the capital of the Western Roman Empire and a major center for Christianity in Europe. This rich historical legacy, coupled with the tiered vineyards of the surrounding valley, inspires awe in the tourists who crowd the streets day and night. Alongside these ruins, Trier has also become a fresh, young city with a large and highly visible student population.

▊ TRANSPORTATION

Trains: To: **Cologne** (2½hr., 2-3 per hr., €24); **Koblenz** (1½hr., 2 per hr., €16); **Luxembourg** (45min., 1 per hr., €11); **Saarbrücken** (1½hr., 2 per hr., €13).

Buses: Although most sights are within walking distance of the town center, buses run everywhere for €1.40. A Trier Card may save you money (see below).

Taxis: Taxi-Funk ☎ 120 12.

Bike Rental: Fahrradservicestation (☎ 14 88 56), in the main train station building on track 11. From €7.50 per day with €30 deposit. Open daily May-Oct. 9am-7pm, Nov.-Apr. 9am-5pm. Reservations recommended for groups.

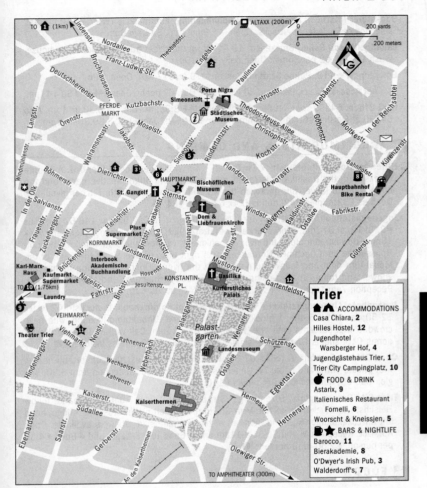

TO ↑ (1km)
TO 🖥 ALTAXX (200m)

200 yards
200 meters

Nordallee
Franz-Ludwig-Str.
Theobaldstr.
Engelstr. ❷
Paulinstr.
Deutschherrenstr.
Bruchhausenstr.
Lindenstr.

Porta Nigra
Simeonstift
Petrusstr.
Theodor-Heuss-Allee
Christophstr.
Göbenstr.
Thebäerstr.
Molkestr.
In der Reichsabtei

PFERDE-MARKT
Kutzbachstr.
Städtisches Museum
ⓘ

Orenstr.
Langstr.
Windmühlenstr.
Böhmerstr.
Deutschherrenstr.

Moselstr.
Jakobstr.
Walramsneustr.
Dietrichstr.
Simeonstr.
Rindertanzstr.
Kochstr.
Flanderstr.
Dewerastr.
Bahnhofstr.

Hauptbahnhof Bike Rental ❽
Kürenzerstr.

HAUPTMARKT ❻
St. Gangolf
Sternstr.
Bischöfliches Museum
Fleischstr.
Grabenstr.
Liebfrauenstr.

Dom & Liebfrauenkirche

Windstr.
Predigerstr.
Baldunstr.
Ostallee
Fabrikstr.
Güterstr.

Plus Supermarket
KORNMARKT
Brotstr.
Palaststr.
Konstantinstr.
Interbook Akademische Buchhandlung
Hosenstr.
Jesuitenstr.

KONSTANTIN-PL.

Karl-Marx-Haus
Kaufmarkt Supermarket
Nagelstr.
Fahrstr.
Brotstr.

Mustorstr.
Basilika ⛪
Kurfürstliches Palais

Gartenfeldstr. ⓬

TO ❿ (1.75km)
Laundry
❾

VEIHMARKT-PL.
Theater Trier
Viehmarkt-str.
Neustr.

Rahnenstr.
Weberbach
Am Palastgarten

Palast-garten
Landesmuseum
Ostallee
Weimarer Allee
Schützenstr.
Egbertstr.

Hindenburgstr.
Wechselstr.
Kahrenstr.
Kaiserstr.
Südallee

Kaiserthermen
Hermesstr.
Hettnerstr.

Eberhardstr.
Saarstr.
Gerberstr.
An den Kaiserthermen
Oleweiger Str.

TO AMPHITHEATER (300m)

Trier

🏠🏕 ACCOMMODATIONS
Casa Chiara, 2
Hilles Hostel, 12
Jugendhotel
 Warsberger Hof, 4
Jugendgästehaus Trier, 1
Trier City Campingplatz, 10

🍴 FOOD & DRINK
Astarix, 9
Italienisches Restaurant
 Fornelli, 6
Woorscht & Kneissjen, 5

🍺★ BARS & NIGHTLIFE
Barocco, 11
Bierakademie, 8
O'Dwyer's Irish Pub, 3
Walderdorff's, 7

RHEINLAND-PFALZ

🔲❓ ORIENTATION AND PRACTICAL INFORMATION

Trier lies on the Mosel River fewer than 50km from the Luxembourg border. The entrance to the Altstadt, the **Porta Nigra** (Black Gate), is a 10min. walk from the train station down Theodor-Heuss-Allee or Christophstr. A **Trier Card,** available at the tourist office, offers free inner-city bus fare and discounts on museums and Roman sites over a three-day period (€9, family card €15).

Tourist Office: (☎ 97 80 80; www.trier.de), in the shadow of the Porta Nigra, runs English tours every Sa at 1:30pm (€6, students €5). Open Apr.-Oct. M-Sa 9am-6pm, Su 10am-3pm; Nov.-Dec. and Mar. M-Sa 9am-6pm, Su 10am-1pm, Jan.-Feb. M-F 10am-5pm, Sa 10am-1pm.

Bookstore: Interbook Akademische Buchhandlung, Kornmarkt 3 (☎97 99 01). Small selection of English paperbacks. Open M-F 9am-7pm, Sa 9am-6pm.

Laundry: Wasch Salon, Brückenstr. 19-21, down the street from Karl Marx's old house. Wash €5. Dry €2 per 30min. Open daily 8am-10pm.

Emergency: ☎110. **Police Station,** Salvianstr. 9 (☎977 90). Open 24hr.

Internet Access: Altaxx, Paulinstr. 80 (☎991 93 03). €2 per hr. Open M-F and Su 4-11pm.

Post Office: 54292 Trier, on Bahnhofpl. Open M-F 8:30am-7pm, Sa 8:30am-1pm. Also 54290 at Fleishstr. 60 in the Kornmarkt. Open M-F 9:30am-6pm, Sa 9:30am-1pm.

ACCOMMODATIONS AND CAMPING

Hilles Hostel, Gartenfeldstr. 7 (☎710 27 85; www.hilles-hostel-trier.de). A couple blocks from the Basilika, this family-run hostel offers bright, festive decor and the opportunity to leave your photo on the wall. All rooms have bath. Kitchen available. Doubles €32; triples €42; quads €56; 6-person €84. ❷

Jugendgästehaus Trier (HI), An der Jugendherberge 4 (☎292 92; fax 146 62 30). Bus #2, 8, 12, or 87 (dir.: Trierweilerweg or Pfalzel/Quint) to "Zur Laubener Ufer," and walk 10min. downstream along the river embankment. Or, from the station follow Theodor-Heuss-Allee as it becomes Nordallee, forks right onto Lindenstr., at the bank of the Mosel turn right and follow the path along the river (30min.). Riverside rooms with shower and toilet, and a talking bird in the lobby. Breakfast and sheets included. Reception 7am-10pm. Singles €32; doubles €46; quads €70. ❸

Jugendhotel/Jugendgästehaus Warsberger Hof im Kolpinghaus, Dietrichstr. 42 (☎97 52 50; fax 975 25 40), 1 block off the Hauptmarkt. Unbeatable location, with halls crowded with students until late. Reception 8am-11pm. Call well in advance. Hostel dorms €15, sheets €2.50; hotel singles €25; doubles €42, sheets included. ❷

Casa Chiara, Engelstr. 8 (☎27 07 30; www.casa-chiara.de), has comfortable rooms with private baths and cable TV. Generous brunch included. Reception from 6:30. Singles €50-60; doubles €80-95; triples €110. ❹

Trier City Campingplatz, Luxemburger Str. 81 (☎869 21). From Hauptmarkt, follow Fleischstr. to Bruckenstr. to Karl-Marx-Str. to the Römerbrücke. Cross the bridge, head left on Luxemburger Str., and then left at the camping sign. Showers available. Open Apr.-Oct. Reception M and Sa-Su 8-11am and 4-6pm; Tu-F 8-11am and 4-8pm. €4.50 per person, €2.50-4.50 per tent. ❶

FOOD

For **groceries,** head to **Kaufmarkt,** at the corner of Brückenstr. and Stresemannstr. (open M-F 8am-8pm, Sa 8am-4pm), or check out **Plus** near the Hauptmarkt, Brotstr. 54 (open M-F 8:30am-8pm, Sa 8:30am-6pm).

Astarix, Karl-Marx-Str. 11 (☎722 39). Squeezed in a passageway, Astarix can be reached from the Trier Theater area or by walking down Brückenstr. toward the river. Excellent, cheap food combined with a mellow atmosphere and good music. Hip waitstaff. Tortellini and pizzas from €4. Open daily 11am-11:30pm. ❷

Italienisches Restaurant Fornelli, Jakobstr. 34 (☎433 85), serves up large scrumptious pizza (€5-7) and filling pasta dishes (€6-9) for the lunch and dinner crowds. Open daily 11:30am-11pm. ❸

Woorscht & Kneissjen, Simeonstr. 27. Combined bakery and butcher shop sells large, tasty sandwiches made with traditional *Wurst* (from €1). Open M-Sa 8:30am-7pm. ❶

ⓒ SIGHTS

Budding archaeologists will want to pick up a one-day combination ticket valid at all Roman monuments (€6.20, students €3.10).

PORTA NIGRA. Trier is full of Roman history, the most impressive remnant of which is the Porta Nigra (Black Gate). This massive sandstone construction was originally light yellow, but now stands tarnished by years of weathering and pollution. Built in the 2nd century AD, the gate was simply an entrance to the city until a local archbishop named it a church and pilgrimage site in the 11th century. It has survived relatively unscathed over time, though Napoleon's troops did melt the metal roof into bullets. Climb to the top for a great view. *(Open daily Apr.-Sept. 9am-6pm; Oct.-Mar. 9am-5pm. Last entry 30min. before closing. €2.10, students €1.60.)*

DOM. This convoluted 11th-century cathedral shelters the tombs of archbishops. The *Tunica Christi* (Holy Robe of Christ) is reputedly enshrined at the eastern end of the cathedral. Tradition holds that this relic was brought from Jerusalem to Trier around AD 300 by St. Helena, mother of Emperor Constantine. The *Tunica* is shown to the public only on rare occasions, usually once every 30 years. Near the south end of the cathedral, outside the doorway, stands a fractured granite pillar supposedly cracked by the devil himself. Also within the Dom, the **Schatzkammer** holds a treasury of holy relics. Behind the cathedral is the **Bischöfliches Dom- und Diözesanmuseum,** a surprisingly modern building showcasing large archaeological collections and restored frescoes. *(Dom open daily Apr.-Oct. 6:30am-6pm; Nov.-Mar. 6:30am-5:30pm. Free. Schatzkammer open Apr.-Oct. M-Sa 10am-5pm, Su 2-5pm; Nov.-Mar. M-Sa 11am-4pm, Su 2-4pm. €1.50, children €0.50. Diözesanmuseum, Windstr. 6-8. ☎ 710 52 55. Open M-Sa 9am-5pm, Su 1-5pm; Nov.-Mar. closed M. €2, students €1.)*

AMPHITHEATER. A short walk from the city center, the Trier Amphitheater stands in memorial to the brutal sort of fun and revelry appreciated by ancient Roman society. Shows in this 20,000-seat venue would begin in a light tone, with tumblers and jesters, followed by displays of exotic animals captured from distant lands. Then the gladiator games would commence, pitting men against wild animals or against other men. The amphitheater is now a stage for city productions; check with **Theater Trier** performance listings. *(The signs will lead you to a 10min. walk uphill from the Kaiserthermen along Olewiger Str. Admission and hours same as the Porta Nigra.)*

KAISERTHERMEN. Though vivid when viewed from the top, these ruins of 4th-century Roman baths are most memorable for gloomy, underground passages remaining from the ancient sewer network. Paths intersect everywhere, making it easy to get lost below. *(Entrance on the north through the Palastgarten. Open daily Apr.-Sept. 9am-6pm, Oct.-Mar. 9am-5pm; last admission 30min. before closing. €2.10, students €1.60.)*

LIEBFRAUENKIRCHE (CHURCH OF OUR LADY). Adjacent to the Dom is the magnificent Gothic Liebfrauenkirche. Angular red- and blue-patterned stained-glass windows dominate the insides of this plainly decorated church. *(Liebfrauenstr. 2. ☎ 425 54; fax 403 13. Open daily Apr.-Oct. 7:30am-6pm; Nov.-Mar. 7:30am-5:30pm.)*

KARL-MARX-HAUS. The walls of Karl's humble birthplace are plastered with articles, photographs, and other memorabilia interesting to die-hard Marxists and social scientists. Copies of the Communist Manifesto abound. *(Brückenstr. 10. ☎ 430 11. Open Apr.-Oct. M 1-6pm, Tu-Su 10am-6pm; Nov.-Mar. M 2-5pm, Tu-Su 10am-1pm and 2-5pm. Audio guides available in English €2, students €1.)*

AROUND THE BASILIKA. Built as a throne room for Emperor Constantine, the Basilika is the only remaining Roman brick structure in Trier. This towering building served as a palace and church over the years before it was heavily damaged by bombing during WWII. Unadorned walls and simple wood benches reveal little of its former splendor. *(Open Apr.-Oct. M-Sa 10am-6pm, Su noon-6pm; Nov.-Mar. Tu-Sa 11am-noon and 3-4pm, Su noon-1pm. Free.)* Next door is the bubble-gum pink **Kurfürstliches Palais,** a former residence of the archbishops and electors of Trier that today houses municipal government offices. The lavish landscaping of the **Palastgarten** completes the Rococo motif. On the eastern edge of the garden lies the **Landesmuseum,** a terrific collection of Roman stonework, sculpture, and mosaics. Check out the meticulous model of 4th-century Trier. *(Weimarer Allee 1. Open M-F 9:30am-5pm, Sa-Su 10:30am-5pm; Nov.-Apr. closed M. Audio guides available in English. €5.50, students €3.)*

SIMEONSTIFT. An 11th-century monastery inside the Porta Nigra's courtyard, the Simeonstift holds the **Städtisches Museum,** which has special modern art exhibits and a permanent collection of oils, sculptures, and porcelains. *(☎718 14 59. Open Mar.-Oct. daily 9am-5pm; Nov.-Feb. Tu-F 9am-5pm, Sa-Su 9am-3pm. €2.60, students €1.50.)*

🎵 🍷 ENTERTAINMENT AND NIGHTLIFE

Several annual festivals spice up Trier's atmosphere. The **Altstadtfest** (June 24-26, 2005) brings live music, wine, and beer to the streets during the fourth weekend in June. The second weekend in July brings the **Moselfest** (July 8-11, 2005), with Saturday night fireworks over the water, and the first weekend in August welcomes the **Weinfest** (Aug. 5-8, 2005) in the nearby town of Olewig. The **Weihnachtsmarkt** (Nov. 21-Dec. 22, 2005) of the Christmas season is also known as "Glühweinmarkt" to the local college students because of the featured spiced wine version of the local vintage. The **Theater Trier,** Am Augustinerhof, has three stages and a wide variety of shows. (☎718 18 18; www.theater-trier.de. Tickets range from €8 to 28. Box office open Tu-F 9:30am-2pm and 3:30-8pm, Sa 10am-12:30pm.) Pubs, clubs, and *Kneipen* of all flavors fan out from the Hauptmarkt, with dense collections on **Judengasse** and the **Pferdemarkt.** Check posters and the free weekly *Der kleine Dicke* for parties and concerts.

Walderdorff's (☎994 44 12; www.walderdorffs.de), across from the Dom. By day a mellow cafe, by night a trendy multi-room bar and disco. Beer €2, cocktails €5.50-9. Cover €4-5. Cafe/bar open M-Th 9:30am-1am, F 9:30am-2am, Sa 10am-2am, Su 10am-1am. Disco open W and F-Sa 10pm-4am, dancing starts around 12:30am. Refer to website for a list of additional events.

Barocco, Viehmarktpl. 10 (www.barocco.de). Magnified works of art, Romanesque pillars, and decadent velvet couches contribute to the ambience of this chill bar and club combo. Half-price cocktails 6-9pm. Salsa night F 10pm-2am. R&B/Hip-Hop on Sa nights. Open daily 10:30am-1am, F-Sa until 4am.

O'Dwyer's Irish Pub, Jakobstr. 10 (☎495 39; www.irish-pub.de), fills up with local crowds on regular theme nights, including "U2 Tuesdays," featuring free Guinness or Bailey's every time a U2 song is played. Karaoke M at 9pm (€2, students €1.50). Cheaper drinks for students on Su and Th. Open Su-Th 11am-1am, F-Sa until 2am.

Bierakademie, Bahnhofstr. 28 (☎994 31 95), ½block from the station. With 100 beers and numerous local wines, Bierakademie is all about the drinks. Foosball, billiards, and a dart board in back (€2-3). Open M-Sa noon-1am, Su 3pm-midnight.

SAARBRÜCKEN ☎0681

For centuries, Saarbrücken's proximity to the French border and rich natural resources have involved it in countless wars, leaving virtually none of its Altstadt intact and clearing the way for rampant industrial development. Today, postmodern architecture and a dynamic downtown point to Saarbrücken's cosmopolitan future, while road signs, ethnic cuisine, and a few surviving monuments preserve its diverse cultural past. From its expanding cityscape to its progressive punk population, the capital of Germany's smallest *Land* features all the flavor of an urban center, minus the throngs of tourists.

TRANSPORTATION AND PRACTICAL INFORMATION

Saarbrücken is connected by **train** to **Trier** (1½hr., 2 per hr., €13) and **Mannheim** (1½hr., 2 per hr., €19). The **tourist office**, Reichstr. 1, located across from the station to the right of the McDonalds, books rooms for free. (☎938 09 39; www.saarbruecken.de. Open M-F 9am-6pm, Sa 10am-4pm.) Do **laundry** at **Waschhaus**, Nauwieserstr. 22, two blocks from the Rathaus (Wash €3. Dry €0.50 per 10min. Open daily 8am-10pm) or **Münz-Waschsalon**, Eisenbahnstr. 8, across the street from the Ludwigsplatz. (Wash €3, Dry €0.50 per 10min. Open daily 7am-10pm) The **police station** is located at Karcherstr. 5. (☎96 20; **emergency** 110. Open 24hr.) **Internet** is at **Phone Center**, Bahnhofstr. 104 (876 46 84; €2 per hr. Open daily 10am-11pm.), and the **post office**, 66111 Saarbrücken, is to the right of the station. (Open M-F 9am-6pm, Sa 9am-1pm.)

ACCOMMODATIONS AND FOOD

The **Jugendgästehaus Europa (HI) ❸**, Meerwiesertalweg 31, is a 25min. walk from the station. Head downhill and to the left; at the intersection veer left on Ursulinenstr., turn right onto Mozartstr., left onto Dudweilerstr., and right onto Meerwiesertalweg. Or take bus #69 (€1.50; dir.: Uni-Campus) to "Prinzenweiher" and backtrack 70m to the hostel. On a scenic back street, this modern hostel has private bathrooms and a lively cafe/bar. (☎330 40; jh-saarbruecken@djh-info.de. Breakfast and sheets included. Reception 7:30am-1am. Curfew 1am. Dorm beds €17.50; singles €32; doubles €46; quads €70.) Nearby, **Gästehaus Weller ❸**, Neugrabenweg 8, offers larger rooms with showers, phones, fridges, and TVs. A 20min. walk from the station. go down Ursulinenstr., right on Mozartstr., continue on to Schumannstr., left on Fichtestr., and cross the bridge to Neugrabenweg. (☎37 19 03; fax 876 47 60. Reception in corner restaurant M-F 6am-11pm, Sa 6am-10pm, Su 6am-9pm. Singles €29-42; doubles €47-60.) **Hotel Schloßkrug ❸**, Schmollerstr. 14, at the corner of Bruchwiesenstr., has simple and spacious rooms with showers and TVs 15min. from the station. Go left onto Ursulinenstr., right on Richard-Wagner-Str., and right on Schmollerstr. Or take tram #1 to Landespl. (☎367 35; fax 37 50 22. Singles €28, with shower and bath €36; doubles €51, with shower €59, with bath €64; triples with bath €87.) **Campingplatz Saarbrücken ❶**, Am Spicherer Berg, is far from the station. Take bus #42 to "Spicherer Weg," then cross Untertürkheimstr. and head uphill on Spicherer Weg. (☎517 80. Reception 7am-1pm and 3-10pm. Open Mar.-Oct. €4 per person, €6 per campsite.)

Pick up some fresh bread, fruits, or meat at one of the market stalls in the **Diskonto Passage**, under Bahnhofstr. near Dudweilerstr. The streets around **St. Johanner Markt** brim with beer gardens and ethnic restaurants. A handful of Chinese restaurants can be found in the **Chinesenviertel** between Rotenbergstr., Richard-Wagner-Str., Dudweilerstr., and Großherzog-Friedrich-Str., a nighttime hotspot for college students. While you're there, stop by the funky ▓ **Fleur de Biere**, Cecilieustr. 3. Don't worry if after a few French specialty drinks you see miniature boats, volcanoes, and a plastic frog suspended from the ceiling. The upside-down scenery is part of the decor. (☎355 33. Open daily 8pm-1am.) **Baldes Braustübel ❸**, on the corner of Uferg. and Bahnhofstr., allows a respite from pedestrian traffic. Fill up on fish or spaghetti entrees (€7-14) amid a friendly crowd. (☎37 16 96. Open 11am-

10pm, Sa until 5pm.) The laid-back **Schnokeloch ❷**, Kappenstr. 6, serves *Flammekuchen* (a delicious Alsatian twist on pizza) and filling salads for €5-7. (☎333 97. Open M-F noon-2:30pm and 6pm-1am, Sa noon-1am, Su 6pm-1am.)

👁 🎵 SIGHTS AND ENTERTAINMENT

Saarbrücken is mainly remarkable for its super-modern commercial district, **St. Johanner Markt,** but also boasts some pretty pieces of old Europe. The details on the bronze doors of the **Basilika St. Johann** have faded since its 1754 construction, and now it's difficult to tell whether the engraved figures are writhing in hell-fire or ecstatic with heavenly bliss. Take Kappenstr. from the market and turn right onto Katherinen-Kirche-Str.; the church is on the left. (Open M, W, F 8:30am-6:30pm; Tu, Th, Sa-Su 9:30am-6:30pm. In winter closes W at 5pm. Free.) A walk along Am Stadtgraben leads to the **Moderne Galerie,** Bismarckstr. 11-19, which features a fantastic selection of Impressionists from Rodin, Matisse, and Franz Marc to lesser-known German artists. Admission also grants entry to the **Alte Sammlung,** Karlstr. 1, across the street, with a collection of medieval Madonnas, French porcelain, and silver beer steins; attached is the **Landesgalerie,** introducing promising regional artists. (☎996 40. All museums open Tu-Su 10am-6pm; W until 10pm. €1.50, students and children €1. Special exhibits €6, students €2.) Children and adults alike can take a reprieve at **Tifliser Platz** on Saarstr., next to the river. Captain the playground boat, relax on a swing, or bring your own paddles for a game of table tennis on the large, stone tables. The **Saarbrücker Schloß,** on the other side of the Saar river, has been transformed many times since its Renaissance construction and now sports a towering glass facade. It currently houses offices of local officials. (☎50 63 13. Open M-F 8:30am-noon and 2-6pm, Sa-Su 10am-6pm. German tours Sa-Su at 3pm. Free.) The Schloßpl. is officially the **Platz des unsichtbaren Mahnmals** (Place of the Invisible Reminder), one of the most interesting memorials you'll never see. From 1990 to 1992, students at a nearby art school dug up stones in the plaza, carved the names of former Jewish cemeteries on their undersides, and replaced them carved side down. The 2146 commemorative stones make up the center of the path leading straight out from the Schloß.

Three museums surround the town plaza. To the south, adjacent to the Schloß, the **Historisches Museum** includes a disturbing collection of war propaganda and a prison cell once used by WWI secret police, with graffiti in Russian and German. (☎506 45 01. Open Tu-W, F, and Su 10am-6pm; Th 10am-8pm; Sa noon-6pm. €3, students €1.50.) To the north, the **Museum für Vor- und Frühgeschichte,** Schloßpl. 16, holds a Celtic countess's grave and jewelry from the 4th century BC. (☎95 40 50. Open Tu and Sa 9am-5pm, Su 10am-6pm. Free.) The 1498 **Altes Rathaus** west of the Schloß hosts the wacky **Abenteuermuseum** (Adventure Museum), overflowing with anthropological loot collected by globe-trotter Heinz Rox Schulz on his tropical expeditions. Photographs and exhibits illustrate his daring escapades, which included tales of cross-country horse races and shrunken heads. (☎506 43 43. Open Tu-W 9am-1pm, Th-F 9am-1pm and 3-7pm. €2, children €1.50.)

WORMS
☎06241

Worms was forever immortalized as the city whose imperial council, the **Diet of Worms,** sent Martin Luther into exile for refusing to renounce his heretical doctrine that religious truth existed only in scripture. There are numerous Jewish memorials, cemeteries, and synagogues scattered throughout the city, which was a cultural center for Jews before the Holocaust. A historical town that bustles by day, Worms quiets down at night in the shadow of its tall, dark monuments.

📧📱 TRANSPORTATION AND PRACTICAL INFORMATION. Get to Worms from Mainz by **train** (45min., 2 per hr., €6.90). The **tourist office**, Neumarkt 14, is in a complex across the street from the Dom St. Peter. (☎250 45; www.worms.de. Open M-F 9am-6pm, Sa 9:30am-1:30pm. Nov.-Mar. closed Sa.) Walking **tours** (in German) meet at the south entrance to the Dom. (2hr. Apr.-Oct. Sa 10:30am and Su 2pm. €3.) **Exchange money** at the **Deutsche Bank** down Wilhelm-Leuschner-Str. from the station. (Open M-Tu 8:30am-12:30pm, W 8:30am-2pm, Th 8:30am-12:30pm and 2-6pm, F until 3:30pm.) The **police station**, Hagenstr. 5, is located behind the city council building. (☎85 20; **emergency** ☎110. Open 24hr.) Log on to the **Internet** at **Aduni Call Shop** across from the station at Siegfried Str. 25. (€2.50 per hr., students €2. Open M-Sa 9am-11pm, Su 10am-11pm.) The **post office**, 67547 Worms, is in the Kaiser Passage shopping center in Markt Pl. (Open M-F 9am-8pm, Sa 9am-4pm.)

📷📱 ACCOMMODATIONS AND FOOD. To get to centrally located ▧**Jugendgästehaus (HI) ❷**, Dechaneig. 1, follow Bahnhofstr. right from the station to Andreasstr., turn left, and walk until the Dom is on your left; the hostel is on your right. Bright 2- to 6-bed rooms, each with bath, await you. (☎257 80; fax 273 94. Breakfast and sheets included. Reception 7am-11pm. Doors lock at 11pm. €16.90; singles €31; doubles €43.80.) **Weinhaus Weis ❸**, Färberg. 19, is another convenient option, adjoining a wine bar. (☎235 00. Breakfast included. Singles €25, with private bath €33; doubles €42/€60.) Though many believe the famous Nibelungen treasure to be lost forever under the Rhein, the family that owns **Hotel Boos ❸**, Mainzerstr. 5, claims to have found it. From the train station, walk down Siegfriedstr. and turn left. The hotel boasts superb rooms for the right price with TVs and bath. Over the delightful breakfast buffet, keep your eyes peeled for the precious stained-glass windows chronicling the "Nibelungenlied" which the owner and his son pieced together by hand over two years. (☎94 76 39; fax 94 76 38. Singles €35; doubles €51.) The university **Mensa ❶** serves predictable cafeteria grub. Turn right as you exit the station, go right across the first bridge, walk down Friedrich-Ebert-Str., and turn left after eight blocks on Erenburger Str. It's 1½ blocks up on your right, past the US Army barracks. (Open M-F 9am-7pm. Student ID required.) Otherwise, **Cafe Schmitz ❸**, on Weckerling Pl. provides patio seating and tasty meals. (☎41 35 35. €5-9. Open 10am-1am, kitchen open until 11pm. Concerts and theater from Sept.-May.)

🎭📱 SIGHTS AND ENTERTAINMENT. The site of Luther's confrontation with the Diet is memorialized at the **Lutherdenkmal.** The 1868 statue, inscribed with the words, "Hier stehe ich. Ich kann nicht anders" (Here I stand. I cannot do otherwise), is three blocks southeast of the station along Wilhelm-Leuschner-Str. Luther never actually said these words; after leaving the trial, he said, "I am finished!" Then he headed home with a letter of safe conduct, but was "kidnapped" by friends who knew that the council had proclaimed him a heretic, and therefore an open target for murder. Across the walkway toward the Dom, the rose-colored **Kunsthaus Heylshof** showcases a small collection of late Gothic and Renaissance artifacts including Rubens' *Madonna with Child* and a huge number of beer steins. (Open May-Sept. Tu-Su 11am-5pm; Oct.-Apr. Tu-Sa 2-5pm. €2.50, students €1.) The inviting lawns and paths of the **Heylshofgarten** surround the museum.

Crowning Worms with its distinctive Romanesque spirals, the **Dom St. Peter** rises from ancient Celtic foundations. Balthasar Neumann designed the spectacular altar in the 18th century. (Open daily Apr.-Oct. 9am-6pm; Nov.-Mar. until 5pm. Donation requested.) The recently constructed **Nibelungen Museum** offers an interactive glimpse into the legendary *Nibelungenlied* by bringing the anonymous writer of the 13th-century epic back from the dead to navigate guests through tales of blood-drinking soldiers, *Übermensch* queens, and dwarves with mythical treasure. Follow Petersstr. until you reach the town wall and turn right. (☎20 21 20. Open Tu-Su 10am-5pm, last entrance 3:15pm; F until 10pm. €5.50, students €4.50; price includes mandatory headset available in multiple languages.)

The 900-year-old **Heiliger Sand**, the oldest Jewish cemetery in Europe, is the quiet resting place of rabbis, martyrs, and a few celebrities. Enter through the gate on Willi-Brandt-Ring, just south of Andreasstr. On the opposite end of the Altstadt, the cobblestoned streets around **Judengasse** stand witness to the 1000-year legacy of Worms's Jewish community (once known as "Little Jerusalem"), which prospered during the Middle Ages but disappeared completely during the Holocaust. The **Synagoge,** just off Judeng., was the center of Jewish learning north of the Alps until *Kristallnacht* (Nov. 10, 1938), when the it was torched by the Nazis. In 1961 it was rebuilt; stones and foundations from many eras now testify to the long Jewish presence in Worms. (Open daily Apr.-Oct. 10am-12:30pm and 1:30-5pm; Nov.-Mar. 10am-noon and 2-4pm. Required yarmulkes available at the door.) Behind the synagogue is the **Jüdisches Museum** in the **Raschi-Haus,** which presents a chronology of Worms's Jewish population and original commentary by the 11th-century Talmudic scholar Rabbi Shlomo Ben-Yitzhak, better known as Raschi. (☎853 47 01. Open Tu-Su 10am-12:30pm and 1:30-5pm. €1.50, students €0.80.)

A happy student crowd and cheap drinks (under €3) liven up the **Taberna,** a groovy *Studentenkneipe* in the basement of the building opposite the Mensa. (Weekly disco Th from 9pm. Often closed July-Sept. Open M-Th 7pm-1am.) Late nights transform the electric blue bar of **Ohne Gleichen,** Kriemhildenstr. 11, into an aquarium of tropical drinks. Go down Bahnhofstr. to the right of the station. (☎41 11 77. Open daily 9am-1am.) The Worms open-air **jazz festival** takes place each summer (in early July) in the center, while the **Backfischfest** brings a wine-soaked party of 70,000 people to Worms for nine days starting the last weekend in August.

SPEYER   ☎06232

Speyer's political star rose when the Salian dynasty came to the German throne in the 11th century. The charming Rhein town, which boasts the largest Romanesque cathedral in Germany, hosted 50 meetings of the Imperial Diet, including the 1529 meeting at which the name "Protestant" was coined for the followers of Martin Luther. Speyer's importance fell after it was burned to the ground by the French in 1689, but the town was rebuilt, and escaped destruction in both World Wars.

⌨️ TRANSPORTATION AND PRACTICAL INFORMATION. Trains go to: **Ludwigshafen** (25min., 2 per hr., €4) and **Mannheim** (30min., 1 per hr., €4). **Bus** #7007 from **Heidelberg** (1½hr.) leaves passengers at the steps of the Kaiserdom. A **shuttle bus** (line 565) runs the length of the city every 10min. (shuttle day ticket €1, other buses €2 per ride). The **tourist office,** Maximilianstr. 13, two blocks before the Dom, has free maps and an accommodations list. From the station, take bus #565 to "Maximilianstr." (☎14 23 92; www.speyer.de. Open M-F 9am-5pm; also Apr.-Oct. Sa 10am-3pm and Sun 10am-2pm, Nov.-Mar. Sa 10am-2pm.) The police office is beside the Dom, Maximilian Str., 6. **Internet** access is available at **Silver Surfer Internet Cafe** on Schulerg. (☎60 51 62; €3 per hour). The **post office,** 67346 Speyer, is on Wormser Str. 2-4. (Open M-F 8:30am-6pm, Sa 8:30am-12:30pm.)

⌨️ ACCOMMODATIONS AND FOOD. Speyer is blessed with the incredible new **Jugendgästehaus Speyer (HI) ❷,** Geibstr. 5, which has a sunbathers' park, a backyard *Fußball* field, and pool nearby. Take the city shuttle (line 565) to "Freibad/Jugendherberge." (☎753 80 or 615 97; www.djh-info.de. Breakfast and sheets included. Reception daily 7:30am-7pm. Curfew M-F 11pm, Sa-Su midnight. Dorms with bath €17.50; singles €30.90; doubles €46.) **Pension Grüne Au ❸,** Grüner

Winkel 28, has sunny, comfortable rooms with flowers. Take Bus #562 from the train station to "Eselsdamm," turn right as you step off, cross Eselsdamm and continue on Grüner Winkel. (☎721 96; fax 29 28 99. Reception closed 2-5pm and Sa. Singles €29, with bath €37; doubles €45/€55; triples €60/€70.) North of Maximilianstr., excellent restaurants line **Korngasse** and **Große Himmelsgasse**. The wine cellar **Zur Alten Münz ❸**, Korng. 1a, just off Maximilianstr. and three blocks from the Dom, serves *Pfälzen* dishes (€6.90-9.10) in a quaint 18th-century residence. (☎797 03. Open daily Apr.-Oct. 11am-midnight; Nov.-Mar. 11am-3pm and 5pm-midnight.)

◑ SIGHTS. Since the 12th century, the immense Kaiserdom has been the symbol of Speyer. The crypt under the east end cradles the remains of four German kings, four Holy Roman Emperors and their wives. The cathedral is undergoing renovations until 2008. (☎771 70. Open Apr.-Oct. M-Sa 9am-7pm, Su noon-6pm; Nov.-Mar. M-Sa 9am-5pm, Su 1:30-5pm. Call ☎100 92 18 for morning tours in German.) South of the Dom, the Historisches Museum der Pfalz, Dompl., gives an overview of Palatinate history, including museums on wine and the Romans, and hosts highly-touted special exhibits on subjects from pop art to Napoleon. Among the exhibits are the exquisite Domschatzkammer (treasury) and the oldest bottle of wine in the world—a slimy leftover from a Roman blowout in the 2nd century. (☎132 50. Open Tu-Su 10am-6pm. €7, ages 3-5 6-18 €3, €2.50, families €15.) From the Dom, take Große Pfaffeng. one block and turn right on Judeng. to reach the Judenbad, a Jewish **mikwe** (ritual bathhouse) from the 12th century. (☎14 23 92. Open Apr.-Oct. daily 10am-5pm. €1, children €0.50.) Maximilianstr., Speyer's main thoroughfare, spreads westward from the Dom, culminating in the medieval Altpörtel, an exquisitely preserved five-story village gate. Climb it. (Tower open Apr.-Oct. M-F 10am-noon and 2-4pm, Sa-Su 10am-5pm. €1, students €0.50.) From the Altpörtel, a southward jaunt on Gilgenstr. leads to the Josefskirche (open Apr.-Oct. M-Sa 9am-7pm, Su noon-6pm; Nov.-Mar. M-Sa 9am-5pm, Su 1:30-5pm) and, across the street, the Gothic arches and beautiful stained glass of the Gedächtniskirche. (Open M-Sa 10am-noon and 2-6pm, Su 2-6pm.) The Technikmuseum, Geibstr. 2, fills a gigantic warehouse with different types of transportation, many of which visitors can climb into and explore. The museum also has an IMAX theater (☎67 08 50) and an "adventure-simulator." Take bus #565 to "Technikmuseum," or walk through the Dom Garten until you see the IMAX sign. (☎670 80. Open daily 9am-6pm. €11, children €9; IMAX €7.50/€5.50; combination ticket €15.50/€11.)

THE LOCAL STORY

SUNKEN TREASURE

If the *Nibelungenlied* can be trusted, budget-strained backpackers in Worms need look no farther than the nearby Rhein to replenish their supply of cash: the medieval epic claims that the greatest treasure ever known is still buried beneath the river.

According to the legend, Worms was home to the Burgundian princess Kriemhild and her elder brother Gunther. Tales of her unsurpassed beauty attracted dragon-slaying hero Siegfried to court her, and Gunther consented to this romance so long as Siegfried helped him woo Brunhild, a stunningly beautiful Bergundian princess with extremely high standards. After both couples wed, a spat ensued between Kriemhild and Brunhild regarding the respective prowess of their men. Brunhild was shamed after learning that Gunther had needed Siegfried's aid to impress her. Hagen, Gunther's vassal, in turn murdered Siegfried and threw Siegfried's famous Nibelung treasure (endless mounds of gold) into the Rhein. To learn more about the history of the Nibelung story, which was later made famous in Wagner's "Ring" cycle, and also influenced Tolkien's *The Lord of the Rings*, visit the Nibelungen Museum in Worms.

(Nibelungen Museum. Fisherpförtchen 10. ☎20 21 20. Open Tu-Su 10am-5pm, F until 10pm. €5.50, students €4.50.)

THE GERMAN WINE ROAD

Stretching 85km through Germany's most productive grape-growing region and crowned by the mighty Riesling, the Wine Road (or *Weinstraße*) runs through countless vineyards and small villages. The Palatinate vineyards produce more wine than any other region in Germany. Every town and village hosts festivals in tribute to *Wein;* there is one almost every weekend during the summer. Check tourist offices for details. If the booze doesn't relax you, the Haardt Mountains, castle ruins, the Palatinate forest, and half-timbered houses will.

NEUSTADT AN DER WEINSTRAßE   ☎ 06321

Bordering the Palatinate forest and the Haardt mountains, Neustadt and its surrounding villages are the midpoint of the German wine road and the easiest to reach; **trains** run to **Mannheim** (3-4 per hr., €8.20) and **Saarbrücken** (1-2 per hr., €14). Neustadt's tourist industry centers on all the family-owned *Weingüter* in the area, where you can taste and buy wines. The surrounding villages, particularly Haardt and Deidelsheim, regularly produce internationally lauded wines and are 10min. away by bus. Customers who intend to buy wines may taste them at will; an official tasting, including 7-9 wines and food, will last 1-3hr. and cost from €6.

In Haardt, at **Weingut Probsthof,** Probstg. 7, the family Zimmermann takes guests on a tour of traditional German viticulture with samples of red and white wines from their own vineyards. Generous wine tasting session from €6, with *Sekt* (German sparkling wine) from €7. Take bus #512 to "Haardt, Winzer" and walk up the street, then turn right. (☎63 15; fax 602 15. Open M-Sa 8am-6pm.) In Diedesfeld, **Schönhof,** Weinstr. 600, has similar tastings in its in-house restaurant. Ride bus #501 to "Diedesfeld" and walk up the street. (☎861 98; fax 868 23. €6.50 for 7 wines. Open daily 9am-6pm; call ahead on Su.) In town, the antique **Haus des Weines,** Rathausstr. 6, sells tastes and bottles of hundreds of regional specialties. (☎35 58 71. Open Tu-F 10am-1pm and 2:30-6:30pm, Sa 9:30am-3pm.)

Though the site dates back to Roman times, the **Hambacher Schloß** was built in the 11th century and later flourished as a retreat for Speyer Bishops. At the 1832 "Hambach Festival," held by local vintners, 20,000 citizens demanded freedom and national unity. The 30min. trail starts from the end of Waldstr.; follow the red dashes. Otherwise, the hourly #502 bus will deliver you there. (☎96 13 28. Open Mar.-Nov. daily 10am-6pm. Castle grounds free. Castle €4.50, students €1.50.)

The **tourist office,** Hetzelpl. 1, is across from the train station, selling hiking maps of the Palatinate forest (€6) and running wine tastings on Fridays. (☎92 68 92; www.neustadt.pfalz.com. Open May-Oct. M-F 9:30am-6pm, Sa 10am-noon; Nov.-Apr. M-F 9:30am-5pm. 8 wines for €6.) Neustadt's youth hostel, the **Jugendgästehaus Neustadt ❷,** Hans-Geiger-Str. 27, has sparkling 2- and 4-bed rooms and a cafe/bar and cafeteria. From the train station, walk left, angling back past the post office and across the footbridge. Follow signs uphill on Alter Viehberg, turn left on Kiesstr., then head right on Hans-Geiger-Str. (☎22 89; www.djh-info.de. Sheets and breakfast included. Reception 8am-11pm. Dorms €16.90; singles €30.20; doubles €43.80.) **Bistro am Markt ❸,** left off Hauptstr. coming from the train station, across from the fountain, serves big salads (€6-8) and large soups for €4. (Open M-Th 9am-1am, F-Sa 9am-2am, Su 10am-1am.) The **police station** is at Karl-Helferich-Str. 11 (☎85 40; **emergency** ☎110. Open 24hr.). Nearby is **Net-Cafe,** which has **Internet** at Konrad-Adenauer-Str. 5. (€2 per 30min. Open M-F 11am-midnight, Sa 3pm-midnight, Su 3-11pm.) The **post office,** Bahnhofstr. 2, 67434 Neustadt an der Weinstraße, is next to the train station. (Open M-F 8:30am-6pm and Sa 9am-12:30pm.)

BAD DÜRKHEIM   ☎ 06322

Thanks to the vibrant wine community and the natural baths, Dürkheim's (only outsiders use the *Bad*) dense system of parks and amusements create a resort atmosphere. **Römerplatz** and **Stadtplatz**, in front of the train station, form the center of the old city. From Römerpl., Kurgartenstr. empties into the **Kurpark**—several acres of green grass, flowers, and gurgling fountains. The **Salinarium**, outside the Kurpark, has a pool and sauna. (☎93 58 65. Open M-Tu and Th 9am-10pm, W 6:45am-10pm, F 9am-11pm, Sa 9am-8pm, Su 9am-8pm. €5, children €2.50.) Located a block away from the Kurzentrum exit of the Kurpark is the **Große Faß**, the largest wine barrel in the world. With a capacity of 1,700,000L, it eclipses even the *Faß* in Heidelberg (p. 388), though it has never been used. Head across the street for tasting **Weingut Fitz-Ritter**, Weinstr. Nord 51. (☎53 89. Open M-F 8am-noon and 1-6pm, Sa 9am-1pm. Wine tasting free.) Dürkheim hosts the **Wurstmarkt**, the world's largest wine festival (2nd and 3rd weekends in Sept.), which began as a pilgrims' march to the nearby **Michaelskapelle** on St. Michael's Day.

The **⬛Gradierbau Salina** lies near the salinarium. Here, brine springs to the surface and is pumped up and across a 330m long, three-story high wall before trickling down what looks like giant fish gills. The thick surrounding air tastes like the ocean and allegedly does wonders for your respiratory system. (Open mid-Apr. to Oct. M 1-6pm, Tu-Su 10am-6pm. €1, or sit for free at one of the public benches nearby.) One kilometer from the city center is the **Pfalzmuseum für Naturkunde**, devoted to indigenous life. (☎941 30. Open Tu and Th-Su 10am-5pm, W 10am-8pm. €2, students €1.30.) **Schloß Limburg**, 2km west of Römerpl. (follow the blue stripes from the cemetery), now lies in ruins, but at various times housed Celtic princes, Salian dukes, and Benedictine monks.

The friendly **tourist office** is at Kurbrunnenstr. 14. Cross the plaza in front of the train station and continue onto Kurgartenstr. Go through the park, turn right, and watch for "Kurzentrum." They book rooms for free and sell hiking maps for €6-8. (☎956 62 50; www.bad-duerkheim.de. Open M-F 9am-7pm, Sa-Su 11am-3pm.) The **police station** is on Weinstr. Süd. (☎96 30; **emergency** ☎110. Open 24hr.) The **Internet C@fe Click**, Kurbrunnenstr. 21, is in the Jugendhaus across the street. (☎98 06 79. €1 per hr. Open Tu and Th 3-8pm, F 4-9pm.) The **post office** is across from the station at Mannheimerstr. 11a, 67098. (Open M-F 8am-6:30pm, Sa 8am-1pm.)

The **Jugendgästehaus St. Christopherus-Haus ❷**, Schillerstr. 151, is a 20min. walk uphill, but worth it. From the train station, turn left and follow Leningerstr. and continue along Schillerstr. The *Haus* is on your left. The multi-bed rooms fill quickly with school groups. (☎631 51; fax 624 42. Sheets and breakfast included. Lockout 10pm, ask for a key at front. Singles €16, with shower €21.) **Pension Dürkheimer Weineck ❸**, Weinstr. Süd 14., provides quiet and convenient lodging. From the train station, turn left on Mannheimerstr. until Weinstr. (☎/fax 83 61. Singles €35; doubles €55.) **Campingpark Bad Dürkheim ❶**, In den Almen 3, is next to a lake. Take bus 487 from the Hauptbahnhof (1 per hr. ☎613 56; fax 81 61. Reception open daily 8am-1pm and 3-10pm. €5 per person, €9 per site. Electricity €2.)

BADEN-WÜRTTEMBERG

Once upon a time, the states of Baden, Württemberg-Hohenzollern, and Württemberg-Baden were all separate. When the Federal Republic was founded in 1951, the Allies combined the states into Baden-Württemberg. However, the Badeners and the Swabians (*never* "Württembergers") still proudly proclaim their distinct regional identities. Today, two powerful German stereotypes—the brooding romantic of the Brothers Grimm and the modern *homo economicus* exemplified by Mercedes-Benz—battle it out in Baden-Württemberg. Pretzels, cuckoo clocks, and cars were all pioneered here, and the region is as diverse as its exports. Rural customs live on in the bucolic hinterlands of the **Schwarzwald** (Black Forest) and the **Schwäbische Alb**, while the modern capital city of Stuttgart celebrates the ascendancy of the German industrial machine. The province also plays home to the ritzy resort of Baden-Baden, the **Bodensee** (Lake Constance—Germany's Riviera), and the historic university towns of Freiburg, Tübingen, and Heidelberg.

HIGHLIGHTS OF BADEN-WÜRTTEMBERG

GAZE AT THE ALPS or roam among the manicured gardens of **Mainau**, on the **Bodensee** (p. 427), tropical for Germany, with beautiful beaches and turquoise waters.

HIKE through stretches of pine forest in the **Schwarzwald** (p. 418); its towering mountains and serene lakes extend from **Freiburg** (p. 411) to **Baden-Baden** (p. 409).

RELAX YOURSELF in the indulgent mineral baths and lush **Schloßgarten** of **Stuttgart** (p. 380), sleek corporate home of Mercedes and Porsche.

RIDE A CABLECAR to **Heidelberg's** (p. 388) crumbling **Schloß** or enjoy stunning views while strolling on the **Philosophenweg**.

SIP JAVA in the cozy Altstadt of **Tübingen** (p. 396), a gorgeous university town.

STUTTGART   ☎ 0711

Life is always faster in the city, but Stuttgart has the help of Porsche, Daimler-Benz, and a host of other corporate thoroughbreds to keep it racing along. After almost complete destruction in WWII, Stuttgart was rebuilt in an uninspiring style. Luckily, its lush setting of forested hills, parks, and vineyards lends some tranquility to the busy capital of Baden-Württemberg. The mineral baths draw visitors looking to unwind after a day of museums or a trip to the castles of Ludwigsburg.

◪ TRANSPORTATION

Flights: Flughafen Stuttgart (☎ 94 80). Take streetcars S2 or S3 (30min., €2.65).

Trains: Stuttgart is the transportation hub of southwestern Germany. To: **Basel** (3½hr., 2-4 per hr., €37-49); **Berlin** (6hr., 2 per hr., €109); **Frankfurt** (1-2hr., 2 per hr., €39-46); **Munich** (2½-3½hr., 2 per hr., €32-44); **Paris** (6½hr., 4 per day, €80).

Ferries: Neckar-Personen-Schifffahrt (☎54 99 70 60; www.neckar-kaeptn.de). Boats leave the Bad Cannstatt dock by Wilhelma Zoo. Take U14 (dir.: Remseck) to "Wilhelma." Ships cruise the Neckar daily Easter-Oct. Round-trip 1-7hr., €7-20.

Public Transportation: Single ride €1.60-5.50. A 4-ride *Mehrfahrkarte* is €6.10-20.40; a *Tageskarte*, valid 24hr. on all trains and buses, is €4.90; €10 including suburbs. A **3-day tourist pass** (€8.40/€11.50) is available at the tourist office and most hotels.

Car Rental: Offices in the station at track 16 for: **Avis** (☎223 72 58; fax 229 15 26); **Europcar** (☎224 46 30; fax 22 44 63 66); **Hertz** (☎226 29 21; fax 226 27 10); **Sixt/ Budget** (☎223 78 22; fax 223 78 24). At least 1 office open M-F 7am-9pm, Sa 7:30am-9pm, Su 8:30am-9pm.

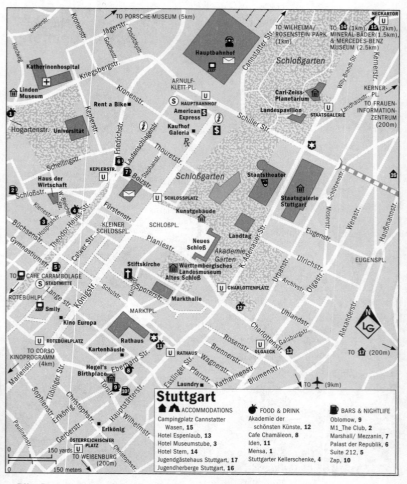

Stuttgart

🏠 🏕 ACCOMMODATIONS
Campingplatz Cannstatter
  Wasen, 15
Hotel Espenlaub, 13
Hotel Museumstube, 3
Hotel Stern, 14
Jugendgästehaus Stuttgart, 17
Jugendherberge Stuttgart, 16

🍴 FOOD & DRINK
Akademie der
  schönsten Künste, 12
Cafe Chamäleon, 8
Iden, 11
Mensa, 1
Stuttgarter Kellerschenke, 4

🍺 BARS & NIGHTLIFE
Oblomow, 9
M1_The Club, 2
Marshall/ Mezzanin, 7
Palast der Republik, 6
Suite 212, 5
Zap, 10

Bike Rental: Rent a Bike, Kronenstr. 17 (☎ 209 90), in Hotel Unger. €9.50 for 6hr., €13 per day; students €6/€8. Bikes can go on the U- and S-Bahn for the price of a children's ticket except M-F 6-8:30am and 4-6:30pm; never on buses.

Mitfahrzentrale: Stuttgart West, Lerchenstr. 65 (☎ 636 80 36 and 194 48). Bus #42 (dir.: Schreiberstr.) to "Rosenberg/Johannesstr." Open M-F 9am-6pm, Sa 10am-1pm, Su 11am-1pm. **Hauptstätter Str. 154** (☎ 194 40). U14 (dir.: Heslach/Vogelrain) to "Marienpl." Open M-F 9am-6pm, Sa 10am-1pm, Su 11am-1pm.

✽ 🛈 ORIENTATION AND PRACTICAL INFORMATION

The heart of Stuttgart is an enormous pedestrian zone cluttered with shops and restaurants. **Königstraße** and the smaller **Calwerstraße** are the main pedestrian thoroughfares; from the train station, both are accessible by the underground **Arnulf-**

Klett-Passage. To the left sprawls the tranquil **Schloßgarten**, to the right the thriving business sector, including **Rotebühlplatz**, two blocks right from the end of Königstr. The **Stuttcard** (€17, without transportation €11.50) offers three days of inner city transportation, admission to most museums, and discounts for guided tours, theaters, mineral baths, the zoo, and other sights.

Tourist Offices: I-Punkt, Königstr. 1A (☎222 80; www.stuttgart-tourist.de), in front of the escalator down into the Klett-Passage. I-Punkt offers daily tours of the city in German or English (11am-12:30pm; €6). Open Apr.-Oct. M-F 9am-8pm, Sa 9am-6pm, Su 11am-6pm; Nov.-Mar. daily 1-6pm. **tips 'n' trips,** Lautenschlagerstr. 22 (☎222 27 30; www.jugendinformation-stuttgart.de), hands out youth-oriented pamphlets on the Stuttgart scene. Open M-F noon-7pm, Sa 10am-2pm.

American Express: Arnulf-Klett-Pl. 1 (☎226 92 67; fax 223 95 44), cashes cheques. Open M-F 9:30am-noon and 1-6pm, Sa 10am-1pm.

ATM: Königstr. 1A, at the tourist office entrance.

Gay and Lesbian Resources: Weißenburg, Weißenburgstr. 28a (☎640 44 94; www.zentrum-weissenburg.de), is Stuttgart's gay and lesbian center. Cafe open M-F 7-10pm, Su 3-10pm. **Erlkönig,** named for the famous Goethe poem, Nesenbachstr. 52 (☎63 91 39), is a popular bookstore. Open M-F 10am-8pm, Sa 10am-4pm.

Women's Resources: Fraueninformationzentrum, Landhausstr. 62 (☎26 18 91).

Laundromat: Fl Lavomagic, Katherinenstr. 21d (☎259 98 48). U-Bahn to "Rathaus." Wash €3.50. Dry €0.50 per 10min. Open M-Sa 8am-11pm.

Emergency: ☎110. **Police,** Hauptstätterstr. 34 (☎89 90 31 00). **Fire** ☎112.

Pharmacy: Königstr. 4 (☎29 02 14). Open M-F 8am-8pm, Sa 9am-6pm.

Hospital: Katharinehospital, Kriegsbergerstr. 60, near the train station (☎27 80).

Internet access: Surf the web in air-conditioned comfort at **Smily Call-Internet Shop,** Calwerstr. 58 near Rotbühlpl. (☎253 67 93). €2 per hr. Open M-Sa 8am-12.30am, Su 10am-12:30am. For late night email try **Cafe Carambolage,** Rotebühlstr. 81 (☎615 09 27). €3 per hr. Open M-F 10am-2am, Sa-Su 4pm-2am.

Post Office: Inside the train station, Arnulf-Klett-Pl. 2, 70173 Stuttgart. Open M-F 8:30am-6pm, Sa 8:30am-12:30pm. The **branch** at Bolzstr. 3 does not hold mail. Open M-F 8am-7pm, Sa 9am-2pm.

◤ ACCOMMODATIONS AND CAMPING

Hotels around the pedestrian zone and train station cater to customers paying top euro—call ahead for better deals. Most of Stuttgart's budget beds are on the two ridges surrounding the downtown area and are easily accessible by streetcar. **tips 'n' trips** (see **Tourist Offices,** p. 383) can often help you find cheap accommodations.

◤ **Jugendgästehaus Stuttgart (IB),** Richard-Wagner-Str. 2 (☎24 11 32; jgh-stuttgart@internationaler-bund.de). Streetcar #15 (dir.: Ruhbank) or night bus N8 to "Bubenbad." Take the next right; the hostel is on the right in a quiet residential neighborhood. Comfortable rooms with views. Breakfast and sheets included. Dinner offered M-Th (€7). Laundry facilities available. Key deposit €10. Reception 24hr. Dorms €16; singles €21; doubles €37. With bath, add €5. 1-night stays, add €2.50. ❷

Jugendherberge Stuttgart (HI), Haußmannstr. 27 (☎24 15 83; www.jugendherberge-stuttgart.de). Follow the signs along the path beside the police station (near Staatsgalerie). Or take streetcar #15 (dir.: Heumaden) to "Eugenspl." Walk uphill and take a left at the sign.; the entrance is about 5min. down Kernerstr., up the stairs with the red handrail. A lively mix of nationalities shack up in 4- or 6-bed rooms, most with city views. Reserve ahead by email. **Internet** €0.50 per 5min. Breakfast and sheets included. Locks for the lockers €5. Reception 24hr. Use night bell at back door 1-5am. 1st night dorms €20.10, under 27 €17.40; additional nights €17/€14.30. ❷

Hotel Espenlaub, Charlottenstr. 27 (☎21 09 10; www.hotel-espenlaub.com). U5, 6, or 7 or streetcar #15 to "Olgäck." Pricey, but only 5min. from Schloßpl. Breakfast, TV, and phone included. Singles €44, with bath €62; doubles €51/€87; triples €72/€98. ❹

Hotel Stern, Neckarstr. 215a (☎269 69 41; sternhotel@gmx.de), is 5min. from the station and city center. U1 or 14, or streetcar #2 to "Metzstr." Close to the mineral baths, with impeccable little rooms. Breakfast and TV included. Reserve in writing. Singles €46-64; doubles €52-82; triples €77-97. ❸

Hotel Museumstube, Hospitalstr. 9 (☎29 68 10; fax 120 43 59). Take U9 or 14 to "Keplerstr." Small family-run hotel close to the station and the city center. €30, with breakfast €35; doubles €45/€55, with bath €65/€75; triples €60. ❸

Campingplatz Cannstatter Wasen, Mercedesstr. 40 (☎55 66 96; www.campingplatz-stuttgart.de), in Bad Cannstatt. S1 (dir.: Daimler-Stadion). Turn back and follow Mercedesstr. to the tree oasis across from the parking lot. Reception daily Apr.-Oct. 7am-noon and 2-10pm; Nov.-Mar. 8-10am and 5-7pm. Wash €4.50. Dry €2.80. Shower €1.55. €5 per person, €2.20 per child, €2.20 per car, €3.10-€6.50 per campsite. ❶

🍴 FOOD

Stuttgart's Swabian cuisine is some of the best in Germany: *Spätzle* (thick egg noodles) and *Maultaschen* (pasta pockets filled with meat and spinach). Reasonably priced restaurants lie along the pedestrian zone between Pfarrstr. and Charlottenstr., while Rotebühlpl. has more *Imbiße*. The basement of the **Kaufhof Galeria** at Königstr. 6, has a **supermarket** (open M-F 9:30am-8pm, Sa 9am-4pm).

Stuttgarter Kellerschenke, Theodor-Heuss-Str. 2a (☎29 44 45; fax 223 72 49), under the uninspiring Gewerkschaftshaus. The high ceiling and backlit windows lend a pleasant feel. Meals are among the cheapest in town (€3-14), with Swabian specialties from €5.60. Daily specials are a good deal at €5.20, €7.20, and €10, with soup of the day and salad. Open M-F 10am-11pm. ❸

Mensa, Holzgartenstr. 11. From the train station, take Kriegsbergstr. to Holzgartenstr. Cafeteria is on the right. Or take bus #40, 42, or 43 to "Hegelpl." Small cafeteria offering bakery items and drinks, and a more spacious eatery upstairs. Meals €3.85-4.10. Open during the semester M-F 11:15am-2pm, cafeteria M-F 11am-3pm. ❷

Akademie der schönsten Künste, Charlottenstr. 5 (☎24 24 36). U-Bahn to "Charlottenpl." High ceilings, art-covered walls, and a shaded garden draw visitors of all ages to this restaurant-bar. Considered the perfect date setting among trendy Stuttgarters. Entrees €1.50-7.50. Open M-Th 6am-midnight, F 6am-1am, Sa 9am-1am, Su 9am-6pm. Kitchen closes 10pm. ❸

Iden, Eberhardstr. 1 (☎23 59 89). U-Bahn to "Rathaus." Good organic vegetarian fare served cafeteria-style. 50 kinds of salads (€1.53 per 100g) and several noodle and potato dishes, all served in a bright atmosphere with lots of Nordic furniture. Head back to the buffet for some of the desserts. Open M-F 11am-8:30pm, Sa 10:30am-5pm. ❸

Cafe Chamäleon, Eberhardstr. 35 (☎96 01 20). Popular cafe sells baked goods, mugs of coffee and a small selection of appetizing dishes (€3.20-7.50). Lunch menu €4.81, vegetarian €2.81. Open M-F 6:15am-8pm, Sa 6:15am-6pm, Su 10am-6pm. ❷

🔆 SIGHTS

MINERALBÄDER. Stuttgart boasts amazing mineral baths, formed from Western Europe's most active mineral springs. The 22 million liters of spring water pumped out every day are said to have curative powers. All the baths offer a spectacular array of pools, saunas, and showers. Loll in the **Mineralbad Leuze,** an official health-care facility. *(Am Leuzebad 2-6. U1 or streetcar #2 to "Mineralbäder." Past the volcano-like fountains. ☎216 42 10. Open daily 6am-9pm. Day card €13, students €8.30; 2hr. soak €6.40/ €4.80. 6-8am 1½hr. soak €5, ages 3-18 €3.20.)* **Mineralbad Berg** is less expensive and less luxurious. *(Am Schwanenpl. 9. U1 or 14 or streetcar #2 to "Mineralbäder," just behind the U-Bahn station. ☎923 65 16. Open M-F 6am-8pm, Sa 6am-7pm, Su 6am-1pm. Day card €6, under 16 €5. Last entry in both baths 1hr. before closing.)*

SCHLOßGARTEN. Almost 20% of Stuttgart is under a land preservation order, resulting in something known as "the green U," crowned by the **Schloßgarten,** Stuttgart's principal municipal park. Running from the station south to the Neues Schloß and northeast to the Neckar, the Schloßgarten is crammed with fountains and manicured flowers. The huge **Rosensteinpark,** at the north end of the Schloßgarten, holds the **Wilhelma,** a zoological and botanical garden containing 9000 species of animals and plants. *(Take U14 (dir.: Remseck) to "Wilhelma" or bus #52, 55, or 56 to "Rosensteinbrücke." ☎540 20. Open daily Mar. and Oct. 8:15am-6:30pm; Nov.-Feb. 8:15am-6pm; May-Aug. 8:15am-6:45pm; Apr. and Sept. 8:15am-7pm. Free 1½hr. tours Sa 2pm, Su 10am. German guidebooks €3.30. €10.20, after 4pm or Nov.-Feb. €7; ages 6-17 €5.10/€3.50.)*

SCHLOßPLATZ. The Schloßgarten runs to **Schloßplatz,** off Königstr., to the elegant Baroque **Neues Schloß,** where the mythological figures perched on top guard the stodgy bureaucrats working inside. The 16th-century **Altes Schloß,** across the street on Schillerpl., offers a graceful, colonnaded Renaissance courtyard, and the **Württembergisches Landesmuseum** (p. 386).

CARL ZEISS PLANETARIUM. Stuttgarters stargaze at the Carl Zeiss-Planetarium, named after one of the most famous telescope manufacturers in the galaxy. Enjoy the shows with informative German voiceovers, cool visual effects, and spacey background music. *(Willy-Brandt-Str. 25. U1, 4, 9, or 14 or streetcar #2 to "Staatsgalerie," or walk from the train station into the Schloßgarten. ☎162 92 15; www.planetarium.stuttgart.de. Open 1hr. before shows. Be punctual; stragglers not admitted. Shows Tu and Th 10am and 3pm; W and F 10am, 3, and 8pm; Sa-Su 2, 4, and 6pm. €5, students €3.)*

HEGEL'S BIRTHPLACE. Learn more about the philosopher's labyrinthine phenomenology firsthand by exploring this large collection of his letters, manuscripts, and academic regalia. *(Eberhardstr. 53, a couple blocks east from the end of Königstr. Take S1-6, U14, or streetcar #2 or 4 to "Rotebühlpl. (Stadtmitte)." ☎216 67 33. Exhibit in German, brochures in English. Open M-W and F 10am-5:30pm, Th 10am-6:30pm, Sa 10am-4pm. Free.)*

🏛 MUSEUMS

▧ STAATSGALERIE STUTTGART. A superb collection in two wings: the stately paintings in the **old wing** date from the Middle Ages to the 19th century, while the **new wing** contains a first-rate collection of moderns including Picasso, Kandinsky, Beckmann, and Dalí. *(Konrad-Adenauer-Str. 30-32. ☎47 04 00; www.staatsgalerie.de. Open Tu-W and F-Su 10am-6pm, Th 10am-9pm; 1st Sa of the mo. 10am-midnight. Tours €3, students €1.50. Museum €4.50/€3, children under 14 free; permanent exhibits free W.)*

▧ MERCEDES-BENZ MUSEUM. In the words of one young fan, *"Oh, das ist mega-geil!"* (This is mega-cool!). The original workshop where Herr Daimler first built a Benz now has a modern exhibit. Ogle a century's worth of gleaming models and hold high-tech "soundsticks" to your ear. Tight security weeds out BMW spies. *(Mercedesstr. 137, in Stuttgart-Untertürkheim. S1 (dir.: Plochingen) to "Daimlerstadion." Continue on Mercedesstr. and look for signs. ☎172 25 78. Open Tu-Su 9am-5pm. Free.)*

BADEN-WÜRTTEMBERG

LINDENMUSEUM STUTTGART. This museum features collections from America, the South Seas, Africa, and Asia, and friendly personnel with intimate knowledge of every exhibit. (*Hegelpl. 1. 10min. west of the train station on Kriegsbergstr. Bus #40, 42, or 43 to "Hegelpl." ☎202 23; www.lindenmuseum.de. Open Tu and Th-Su 10am-5pm, W 10am-8pm. €3, students €2. W after 5pm free, except special exhibits.*)

WÜRTTEMBERGISCHES LANDESMUSEUM. Located in the Altes Schloß, this museum details the culture of the Swabian region and people, with an emphasis on local archaeology. Excellent exhibits on Bronze Age Celtic metalwork, along with fascinating skulls, crown jewels, and a rich coin collection. The ticket also allows entry to a collection of musical instruments located at Schillerpl. 1. (*Schillerpl. 6. ☎27 90. Open Tu-Su 10am-5pm. €3, students €2, under 14 free.*)

KUNSTGEBÄUDE. Houses the **Württembergischer Kunstverein's** temporary exhibits (☎22 33 70). The gallery features contemporary art in a variety of media. (*Schloßpl. 2, directly across from the Altes Schloß. Both museums open Tu and Th-Su 11am-6pm, W 11am-8pm. Special exhibits usually €3-5, students €2-4. Obligatory cloak room €0.50.*)

PORSCHEMUSEUM. A glorified showroom, but Porsche fans will enjoy gawking at this conglomeration of sexy curves. For a factory tour, call well in advance. (*Porschestr. 42, in Stuttgart-Zuffauhausen. S6 (dir.: Weil der Stadt/Leonberg) to "Neuwirtshaus"; exit the station to the right; cross the intersection and take a left on Moritz-Horkheimer-Str. ☎911 56 85. Open M-F 9am-4pm, Sa-Su 9am-5pm. Free.*)

🎵 🎭 ENTERTAINMENT AND NIGHTLIFE

The **Staatstheater,** across the plaza from the Neues Schloß, is Stuttgart's most famous theater, with operas, ballets, plays, and concerts. (Reservations ☎20 20 90. Box office open M-F 10am-6pm, Sa 10am-2pm, and 1hr. before performances. Tickets €8-155; student tickets €7-12 with student ID.) Stuttgart's 25 other local theaters are usually much cheaper. The tourist office provides schedules and sells tickets, as does **Kartenhäusle,** Geißstr. 4 at Hans-im-Glück-Brunnen. (☎210 40 12; fax 210 40 39. Open M-F 9am-6pm, Sa 9am-4pm.) **Kino Europa,** Königstr. 58 (☎299 19 74) and **Corso Kinoprogramm,** Hauptstr. 6 in Vaihingen (☎73 49 16; U1 to "Schillerpl."), show undubbed films.

The **Stuttgarter Weindorf** (wine village) is the largest wine festival in Germany. From August 31 to September 11, 2005, wine lovers will descend upon Schillerpl., Marktpl., and Kirchstr. to sample Swabian specialties and 350 kinds of wine. Beer gets two weeks in the spotlight during the 160-year-old **Cannstatter Volksfest,** a fair on the Cannstatter Wasen (Sept. 24-Oct. 9, 2005). The **Christopher Street Day** (☎0179 464 46 94) gay and lesbian festival occurs July 22-31, 2005 (see **CSD,** p. 230).

From pleasant chats over fine Italian coffee to techno-fueled hysteria, Stuttgart offers a full spectrum of nightlife. The cafes along Königstr. and Calwerstr. get going in the early evenings; later on, the nightlife clusters around Eberhardstr., Rotebühlpl., and Calwer Str. *tips 'n' trips* (see **Tourist Offices,** p. 383) publishes up-to-date guides to the evening scene in German and English. For more on current events, see the monthly *Lift* magazine (www.lift-online.de). For gay and lesbian nightlife, check the monthly magazine *Schwulst* (www.schwulst.de).

Suite 212, Theodor-Heuss-Str. 15 (www.suite212.org). Stand around and chat with the crowd on the sidewalk, or come inside, sit on the soft chairs, and let the videos above the bar soothe your mind. DJ and video-mixing on weekends. Beer €2.50, cocktails €6.50-8. Open M-W 11am-2am, Th 11am-3am, F-Sa 11am-5am, Su 2pm-2am.

Oblomow, Torstr. 20 (☎236 79 24). This jungle-deco cafe throws open its doors late at night so its upbeat music can flood the street. The chillest bar in town. Snacks €3-6 (served 3pm-4am), drinks €3-8. Open M-Th 4pm-5am, Sa 11pm-6am, Su 4pm-5am.

Zap, Hauptstätter Str. 40 (☎ 23 52 27), entrance from the back in Josef-Hirn-Pl. Marble-heavy club is a glitzy social mecca. Dance to live music on Th. Cover Th €11, students €8; W 20+ €3. Free entry before 10pm W-Th. Open W-Th 10pm-3am, F 11pm-5am, Sa 10pm-6am, Su 9pm-2am.

M1_The Club, Seidenstr. 20 (☎ 284 79 40; www.m1-theclub.com), downstairs across from the HL Markt, in the Bosch Areal complex. Take U9 or 14 to "Berliner Pl.," continue to the intersection, then turn right. Large nightclub with 2 dance floors specializing in house, techno, and hip-hop. Beer €3.50. Cover €10. Open Th-Sa from 9pm.

Palast der Republik, Friedrichstr. 27 (☎ 226 48 87). This round wooden pavilion blasts music for the after-hours aficionados who congregate on the sidewalk to down reasonably priced drinks. Open M-Tu 11am-2am, Th-Sa 11am-3am, Su 2pm-1am.

Mezzanin, Bolzstr. 8 (☎ 284 68 78). This artsy bar sells 45 different types of cigars (€1-65) and plays chill music to a slightly older crowd. The adjoining **Marshall** fills with fun-loving 20-somethings and popular music. Beer €1.80-3. Cocktails €5.70-8.70. Open M-Th 8:30am-1am, F-Sa 11am-3am.

⬛ DAYTRIP FROM STUTTGART: LUDWIGSBURG

From Stuttgart, take S4 (dir.: Marbach) or S5 (dir.: Bietigheim; 20min., 4 per hr., €2.65).

Ludwigsburg's **tourist office,** Marktpl. 6, has free maps and guides. (☎ 07141 91 75 55; info@lust.ludwigsburg.de. Open M-F 9am-6pm, Sa 9am-2pm.) **Panda Imbiß ❷,** Marstallcenter 28, beside the train station, serves Chinese and Thai meals (€4-8), sit down or take away. (☎ 07141 91 60 88. Open daily 10:30am-11pm.)

This town sprang up in the early 18th century, when Duke Eberhard Ludwig of Württemberg decided what he needed more than anything else was a residential castle in the duchy's new capital. Though Eberhard died before its completion, Ludwigsburg was brought to life in the middle of nowhere—a lively Baroque city with a trio of luxurious palaces. A 1½hr. guided journey is the only way to see the curiosities inside the opulent Baroque **Residenzschloß**—Ludwig's 3m long bed (he was almost 7 ft. tall) and the rest of the lavish gold, marble, and velvet interior. From the train station, walk down the street to the right of the bank, then go right at the intersection. At the end, take a left on Schloßstr., and look for signs. (☎ 07141 18 64 40. Open mid-Mar.-Oct. daily 10am-6:30pm (No entry after 5pm); Nov. to mid-Mar. 10am-noon and 1-4pm. Tours in German: summer every 30min.; winter M-F 4 per day; Sa-Su 8 per day; in English: summer M-Sa 1:30pm, Su 11am, 1:30 and 3:15pm. €5, students €2.50; combined ticket with gardens and Schloß Favorite €13/€6.50.) The castle, often called "the Swabian Versailles," is situated in an expansive 30-hectare garden that earned the title **Blühendes Barock,** or "blooming Baroque." There are gardens of every kind, from rose-bushes to greenhouse to forest paths. (☎ 07141 97 56 50. Open Mar.-Oct. daily 7:30am-8:30pm. €7, students €3.30.) Inside, a perennial **Märchengarten** recreates scenes from major fairy tales in a large park of wild vegetation. (Open daily 9am-6pm.) The **Schloß Favorite,** behind the *Residenzschloß* garden, is an excellent destination for a stroll or picnic. The interior of Duke Carl Engler's Baroque hunting lodge and party venue has been elaborately restored. (☎ 07141 18 64 40. Open mid-Mar. to Oct. daily 10am-12:30pm and 1:30-5pm; Nov. to mid-Mar. 10am-12:30pm and 1:30-4pm. Guided tours in German every 30min. €2.50, students €1.20.) If you're not Schloßed out, stop to pet the wild deer (at your own risk) as you continue through the **Favoritenpark.** (Open daily Apr.-Aug. 8am-7pm; Sept.-Oct. 9am-6pm; Nov.-Jan. 9am-4pm; Feb.-Mar. 9am-5pm. Free.) Marvel at the third Ludwig palace—the Rococo **Monrepos.** (1½hr. from entrance.) The castle is private, but you can rent a **boat** on the peaceful lake nearby. (☎ 07141 327 96. Open Apr. to mid-Oct. daily 10am-7pm in good weather; boats €5-6 per

30min.) All three palaces host the annual **Ludwigsburger Schloßfestspiele**, a series of open-air performances that runs from mid-June to mid-Sept. For information on tickets, call the Forum am Schloßpark. (☎07141 93 96 36; www.schloss-festspiele.de. Open M-F 8:30am-6:30pm, Sa 9am-1pm.)

HEIDELBERG ☎06221

Over the years, this sun-drenched town on the Neckar and its crumbling Schloß have lured scores of writers and artists: Mark Twain, Wolfgang von Goethe, Friedrich Hölderlin, Victor Hugo, and Robert Schumann, to name a few. During the summer, roughly 32,000 tourists answer the call every day. Even in the off season, legions of camera-toting fannypackers fill the length of Hauptstr., where postcards and t-shirts sell like hotcakes and every sign is posted in four languages. The incessant buzz of mass tourism is worth enduring, however, for Heidelberg's beautiful hillside setting, Germany's oldest university, and a lively nightlife.

▐ TRANSPORTATION

Trains: To: **Frankfurt** (50min., 2 per hr., €12.90-23); **Mannheim** (20min., every 30min., €8.40); **Stuttgart** (40min., 1 per hr., €20-26).

Ferries: Rhein-Neckar-Fahrgastschifffahrt (☎201 81), on the southern bank in front of the *Kongresshaus*, runs up the Neckar to Neckarsteinach and back (3hr., every 1½hr. Easter-Oct. 19 9:30am-4:50pm; €9.50, children €5.50), and all over Germany.

Public Transportation: Single **bus** ride prices vary with destination, around €2. Day passes (€5) valid on all streetcars and buses for 24hr. from the time stamped. On weekends and after 9am on weekdays, up to 5 persons can travel on a single day pass.

Taxis: ☎30 20 30.

Bike Rental: Per Bike, Bergheimer Str. 144 (☎16 11 48). €10, weekend €20, week €40. Open M-F 9am-6pm, call for Sa reservations.

Boat Rental: Bootsverleih Simon, (☎41 19 25) north shore of the Neckar by Theodor-Heuss-Brücke. 3-person boat €6 per 30min. Open daily 11am-dusk.

Hitchhiking: *Let's Go* does not recommend hitchhiking as a safe mode of transportation; those who do hitch wait at the western end of Bergheimer Str.

▐ ORIENTATION AND PRACTICAL INFORMATION

About 20km east of the Neckar's confluence with the Rhein, Heidelberg stretches along the river for several kilometers, with almost all of the city's attractions in the eastern quarter. To get to the Altstadt from the station, take any bus or streetcar to "Bismarckpl.," where **Hauptstraße** leads into the city's heart. Heidelberg has a huge population of bicyclists who like to ride fast—stay out of the red bike lanes. A **Heidelberg Card,** which includes use of public transit and admission to most sights, is available at the tourist office (2-day card €12, family €24; 4-day card €20).

Tourist Office: (☎13 881 21; www.cvb-heidelberg.de), in front of the station. Books rooms for €3 plus a small deposit. If you speak German, pick up a copy of the magazines *Meier* (€1) or *Heidelberg Aktuell* (€0.60) to see what's up. Open Apr.-Oct. M-Sa 9am-7pm, Su 10am-6pm; Nov.-Mar. M-Sa 9am-6pm. Additional offices at the **Schloß** (☎211 44; open daily June-Sept. 9am-5pm; Oct.-May 10am-4pm) and at **Neckarmünzplatz** (☎137 40; open daily June-Sept. 9am-6pm; Oct.-May 10am-4pm).

Currency Exchange: Sparkassen on Universitätspl. and Bismarckpl., or try the exchange office in the train station. Open M-F 7:30am-8pm, Sa 9am-5pm, Su 9am-1pm.

Heidelberg

▲▲ ACCOMMODATIONS
Camping Haide, **20**
Camping Heidelberg-
 Schlierbach, **19**
Jugendherberge (HI), **1**
Hotel-Pension Elite, **7**
Hotel-Pension Schmitt, **6**
Pension Jeske, **16**
Schnookeloch, **15**

🍴 FOOD & DRINK
Hemingway's, **9**
Goldener Anker, **12**
Großer Wok, **8**
Mensa, **13**
Merlin, **4**
Thanner, **5**

🍸 BARS & NIGHTLIFE
Destille, **14**
Mata Hari, **17**
Nachtschicht, **3**
O'Reilly's, **10**
Schwimmbad Musikclub, **2**
VaterRhein, **11**
Zum Sepp'l, **18**

BADEN-
WÜRTTEMBERG

English books: Piccadilly English Shop, Kurfürstenlage 62 (☎16 77 72), B6 Chemie Haus behind the Hauptbahnhof bus station. Small selection including bestsellers, children's books and books on tape. Open M-F 10am-8pm, Sa 10am-6pm.

Women's Resources: Emergency hotline ☎582 54.

Laundry: Rohrbacherstr. 10 (☎48 57 75), on Adenauerpl. 6kg wash €3.70. Dry €2.10. **Internet** €1 per 30min. Open M-F 8:30am-9:30pm, Sa 8:30am-4pm.

Emergency: ☎110. **Fire** and **Ambulance** ☎112.

Police: Römerstr. 2-4 (☎99 17 00).

AIDS Hotline: ☎194 11.

Internet Access: 30min. free with student ID at **Info Café International,** Grabeng. 18. Open M-Th 10am-4pm, F 10am-3pm. **Call Shop Internet Cafe,** Hauptstr. 144 (☎893 63 61); €2 per hr., students €1.50 per hr.

Post Office: Sofienstr. 8-10, 69115 Heidelberg. Open M-F 9am-6pm, Sa 9:30am-1pm.

▚ ACCOMMODATIONS AND CAMPING

In summer, save yourself a major headache by arriving early in the day or calling ahead. There are **youth hostels ❷** in **Neckargemünd.** (1hr. away. ☎06223 21 33. Breakfast included. Dorms €16.80, age 3-5 €9.90; singles €21.30; doubles €37.60.) Also, try **Zwingenberg,** 45min. away. (☎06251 759 38. Breakfast included. €17.70, under 27 €15.) These Neckar Valley towns lie along the Heidelberg-Heilbrunn railroad; train service is reliable and regular between them.

▨ **Pension Jeske,** Mittelbadg. 2 (☎237 33; www.pension-jenke-heidelberg.de). From the station, bus #33 (dir.: Ziegelhausen) or 11 (dir.: Karlstor) to "Rathaus/Kornmarkt." Perfect Altstadt location complements delightfully unique rooms. Reserve well in advance. Doubles €50, with bath €60; triples €60/€75; quints with bath €100. Cash only. ❸

Schnookeloch, Haspelg. 8 (☎13 80 80; fax 138 08 13), has luxurious rooms in a beautifully restored early modern building with huge baths, TVs, and telephones. Breakfast included. Singles €60-97; doubles €85-120. ❺

Jugendherberge (HI), Tiergartenstr. 5 (☎65 11 90; www.jugendherberge-heidelberg.de). From Bismarckpl. or the station, bus #33 (dir.: Zoo-Sportzentrum) to "Jugendherberge." This neighbor to the Heidelberg Zoo also teems with wildlife in the form of schoolchildren. Small pub serves beer 7-11:30pm. Partial wheelchair access. Breakfast and sheets included. Lockers €2 deposit. Reception until 11:30pm. Check-out 7-9am. Lockout 9am-1pm. Curfew 11:30pm; sign the "late-entry list" to get in until 2am. Reserve at least 1wk. ahead. Dorms €23, under 27 €20; singles or doubles add €5 each. ❷

Hotel-Pension Elite, Bunsenstr. 15 (☎257 34; www.hotel-elite-heidelberg.de), 4 blocks south of Bismarckpl. Elegant rooms with high ceilings, baths, and TVs. Breakfast included. Parking €3. Singles €56; doubles €66; triples €77; quads €87; €20 per additional person. Show your *Let's Go* for reduced rates. €3 credit card charge. ❹

Hotel-Pension Schmitt, Blumenstr. 54 (☎272 96). Near the station. Rooms boast sparkling baths and TVs. Breakfast included. Singles €65; doubles €77; triples €100. ❸

Camping: Haide (☎06223 21 11; http://camping-haide.de), on the banks of the Neckar. Bus #35 to "Orthopädischen Klinik," then cross the river and turn right; campground is on the right 20min. away. Bike rental €8 per day. Wash €2.60. dry €1.60. Reception 8-11:30am and 4-8pm. Open Apr. 11-Oct. 31. €4.70 per person, €3 per tent/RV, €1 per car. Cabins €12. Showers €0.50 per 5min. ❶

Camping: Heidelberg-Schlierbach, (☎80 25 06; www.camping-heidelberg.de), between Ziegelhausen and Neckargemünd. Bus #35 (dir.: Neckargemünd) to "Im Grund." Cafe open 7am-10pm. Wash and dry €5. Bike rental €5 per day. Check-in 6am-10pm. €5.50 per person, €2.35 per child, €2.50-6 per tent, €2 per car. Caravan rental €12.50. ❶

◘ FOOD

Most of the restaurants around Hauptstr. are pricey, but the *Imbiße* are cheaper. Just outside the central area, good values can be found in historic student pubs.

Hemingway's Bar-Café-Meeting Point, Fahrtg. 1 (☎ 16 50 33). This crowded patio restaurant along the Neckar is well-shaded by an enormous central tree. Lunch menu M-F 11:30am-2:30pm (€4.10). Open Su-Th 9am-1am, F-Sa 9am-3am. ❷

Mensa "Zeughaus," in the stone fortress on Marstallstr. Bus #35 to "Marstallstr." €0.80 per 100g. Open M-Sa 11:30am-10pm. A popular **cafe** next door serves snacks and beer (€1.70). Open M-Sa 11:30am-1am. **Branch** on Grabeng. 18, across from Alte Universität. A CampusCard, needed to pay at most Mensas, can be obtained at **Info Café International,** Grabeng. 18, for €5 deposit. Open M-Th 10am-4pm, F 10am-3pm. ❷

Goldener Anker, Untere Neckar 52 (☎ 18 42 25), near the river and the Alte Brücke. This quaint *fachwerk* house offers a traditional German lunch menu 11:30am-3:30pm (€5.90-6.50). Dinner (€7-17) served 5:30-10:30pm. ❷

Großer Wok, Bergheimer Str. 1a (☎ 60 25 28), near Bismarckpl. Filled with appetizing aromas of Chinese specialties (€3-7). Eat in or take out. Open M-Th and Su 11am-11pm, F-Sa 11am-noon. The **Großer Wok Upstairs,** Bergheimer Str. 7, has a larger selection and more seats. Open M-Sa 11am-10pm, Su 1-10pm. ❷

Merlin, Bergheimer Str. 85 (☎ 65 78 56). Large, friendly sidewalk cafe away from the rush of Hauptstr. Lunch menu M-F 11:30am-4pm (€6). Open Su-Th 10am-1am, F-Sa 9am-3:30am. Kitchen open daily until 1hr. before closing. ❷

Thanner, Bergheimer Str. 71 (☎ 252 34), the only *Biergarten* in Heidelberg allowed to play music, serves up impressive dishes from an eclectic international menu. Entrees €5.50-15.50. Open daily 8:30am-2am. Garden open daily until 11pm. ❸

◉ SIGHTS

▨ **HEIDELBERGER SCHLOß.** The crown jewel of a striking city, the Schloß stands careful watch over the armies of tourists below. Its construction began early in the 14th century, and after 1329 it housed the Prince Electors, whose statues remain in front of the entrance. Over a period of almost four centuries, the castle's dwellers commissioned additions ranging in style from Gothic to High Renaissance. Thrice destroyed, twice by war (1622 and 1693) and once by nature (lightning in 1764), the castle became a popular subject for Romantic artists, who depicted tension between the ruins and the thriving forest. The cool, musty wine cellar. houses the **Großes Faß,** the largest wine barrel ever used, holding 221,726L and topped by a dance floor; the **Kleines Faß** holds a mere 125,000L. The Schloß is accessible by a steep path or the **Bergbahn,** one of Germany's oldest cable cars, which runs from the "Bergbahn/Rathaus" bus stop to the castle. *(Trams depart from Kornmarkt parking lot next to the bus stop every 10min. Mar.-Oct. daily 9am-8pm; every 20min. Nov.-Feb. daily 9am-6pm. Take bus #11 (dir.: Karlstor) or 33 (dir.: Ziegelhausen). Cable car round-trip €3.50. Castle ☎ 53 84 14. Grounds open daily 8am-5:30pm. English audio tours €3.50. Guided tours daily 10am-4pm, in English every 15min.; €3.50. Schloß €2.50, students or group members €1.20.)*

UNIVERSITÄT. Heidelberg is home to Germany's oldest (est. 1386) and perhaps most prestigious (more than 20 Nobel laureates) university. It was here that **Max Weber** made sociology a legitimate subject. The oldest remaining buildings border the stone lion fountain of the Universitätspl. Other university buildings dot the western Altstadt. The **Museum der Universität Heidelberg** traces the university's long history; in the same building is the **Alte Aula,** Heidelberg's oldest auditorium. *(Grabeng. 1. ☎ 54 21 52. Open Apr.-Oct. M-Sa 10am-4pm; Nov.-Mar. Tu-F 10am-2pm. €2.50, stu-*

dents €2; also includes Studentenkarzer. Call ahead to make sure the Aula is not being used by the university.) Before 1914, students were exempt from prosecution by civil authorities; instead, naughty youths were tried and punished by the university faculty. Guilty students were jailed in the **Studentenkarzer.** It wasn't much of a prison in its final years—students were allowed to bring their own beds to ease their stay, and even to attend classes and return to the jail at their leisure. The walls are covered with poetic graffiti painted with soot from the students' stoves. (Augustinerg. 2. ☎ 54 35 54.) The **Bibliothek** has a collection of medieval manuscripts. (Plöck 107-109. ☎ 54 23 80. Open M-W 9am-5pm, Th 9am-6pm, Sa 9am-1pm. Free.)

PHILOSOPHENWEG. Named the "philosopher's path," this favorite stroll of famed thinkers Goethe, Lugwig Feuerbach and Ernst Jünger stretches along the Neckar, high on the side of the **Heiligenberg,** and offers fantastic views of the city. On top of the Berg are the ruins of the 9th-century **St. Michael Basilika,** the 13th-century **Stefanskloster,** and an **amphitheater** built under Hitler in 1934 on the site of an ancient Celtic gathering place. (To the west of the Karl-Theodor-Brücke, in the direction of the Theodor-Hüss-Brücke. Take streetcar #1 or 3 to "Tiefburg," for the longer route. Or use the steep footpath 10m west of the Karl-Theodor-Brücke, across from the #34 or 734 bus stop "Alte Brücke Nord.")

KURPFÄLZISCHES MUSEUM. The museum is crammed with artifacts like the jawbone of an unfortunate homo Heidelbergensis, a.k.a. "Heidelberg man," one of the oldest humans ever discovered. Elsewhere in the museum you'll find well-preserved works of art by Dürer and a great archaeology exhibit. (Hauptstr. 97, near Universitätspl. ☎ 58 34 00. Open Tu-Su 10am-6pm. €3, students €1.80; Su €1.80/€1.20.)

KARL-THEODOR-BRÜCKE (ALTE BRÜCKE). No trip to Heidelberg would be complete without a walk along the northern bank of the Neckar. On both sides of the Karl-Theodor-Brücke, plump statues of the bridge's namesake, the prince elector who commissioned the bridge as a symbol of his modesty, stand guard.

MARKTPLATZ. The Altstadt centers on the Marktpl., a cobbled square where a contemplative Hercules directs water at **Hercules' Fountain.** In the 15th century, "witches" and heretics were burned at the stake here; now legions of tourists savor steak in outdoor cafes. Two of the oldest structures in Heidelberg border the square. During Louis XIV's invasion of the town, terrified inhabitants fled to the 14th-century **Heiliggeistkirche,** now used for Protestant worship. For a great view of the town and the surrounding mountains, climb the tower's 204 steps. (Open M-Sa 11am-5pm, Su 1-5pm. Church free; tower €0.50, children €0.30.) Opposite the church's southern face is the ornate 16th-century facade of the **Haus zum Ritter,** a local hotel and restaurant since 1705. The stately **Rathaus** stands at the far end of the square.

🎵 🎭 ENTERTAINMENT AND NIGHTLIFE

The first Saturdays in June and September and the second Saturday in July draw giant crowds to fireworks in front of the Schloß. The **Faschingsparade** (carnival) cavorts through the city on Shrove Tuesday. The **Handschuhsheim Fest** lures revelers the third weekend in June, while the **Schloßfestspiele Heidelberg** features a series of concerts and plays at the castle in July and August (☎ 58 20 00 for tickets). For the last weekend in September, the **Heidelberger Herbst** brings a medieval market to the Altstadt, which later hosts the **Weihnachtsmarkt** for four weeks before Christmas. The **Marktplatz** is the hub of the city's action; most popular nightspots fan out from here. **Untere Straße,** on the Neckar side of the Heiliggeistkirche, boasts the densest conglomeration of bars in the city. During fair weather, drunken revelers fill the narrow way until 1 or 2am. **Hauptstraße** also harbors a fair number of venues, and a few dot the north side of the river as well.

Nachtschicht (☎43 85 50, infoline 438 55 22; www.nachtschicht.com), in Landfried-Komplex. From the Hauptbahnhof, take Mittermaierstr.; take the first left onto Alte Eppenheimerstr. and enter the 2nd parking lot on the right. University students jam to a variety of music in a basement resembling an old factory. €3.50; M and F students €1.50. Open M and Th-Sa 10pm-4am, W 10pm-3am.

Schwimmbad Musikclub, Tiergartenstr. 13 (☎47 02 01; www.schwimmbad-musik-club.de), on the opposite side of the river as the Altstadt. Only close to the youth hostel. 4 levels of live music, dancing, and movies. Open W-Th 8pm-3am, F-Sa 8pm-4am.

VaterRhein, Untere Neckarstr. 20-22 (☎213 71). Students enjoy plentiful, cheap food (spaghetti €1.70) here until late under poster-plastered walls. Open daily 8pm-3am.

O'Reilly's (☎41 01 40), on the corner of Brückenkopfstr. and Uferstr. Cross Theodor-Heuss-Brücke, turn right, and follow the noise to Guinness's "1999 Highly Recommended" pub, where a young crowd drinks the black stuff (€4.20 for 0.5L). Karaoke Sa 9:30pm. Open M-Th 5pm-1am, F 5pm-3am, Sa noon-3am, Su noon-1am.

Destille, Unterstr. 16 (☎228 08). In the evenings locals and tourists of all ages come for pinball and *Pils* (€1.50-3). Open Su-Th noon-2am, F-Sa noon-3am.

Mata Hari (☎18 18 08), on Zwingerstr. near Oberbadg. A small nightclub for gays and lesbians where "everyone who loves gays is welcome." Tu men only. Beer €2.80. Open daily 10pm-3am.

Zum Sepp'l, Hauptstr. 213 (☎230 85). This student lair accented by stained glass windows hosts a piano player and a loud crowd M-Tu and F-Sa. Open daily noon-10:30pm.

NECKARTAL (NECKAR VALLEY)

The Neckar Valley—a swath of the dense Oden Forest sliced by the Neckar River—reaches from Heilbronn to Heidelberg. Centuries ago, a series of enterprising royals decided to build castles to "protect merchants from pirates," and reaped hefty tolls for their services. Today, their medieval castles, largely unspoiled by tourism, dot the hilltops of the Neckartal, forming part of the **Burgenstraße** (Castle Road) that stretches from Mannheim to Prague.

Two train lines connect Heidelberg and Heilbronn, with stops in the small towns along both sides of the valley. Local buses also traverse the Neckar Valley; these are often faster than the infrequent trains. Schedules are posted at bus stops. More expensive 1- and 3-day passes (€8/€22) from Heidelberg are valid for connections in the valley; check at the train station in Heidelberg for details. One of the best ways to explore the valley is by biking along the many well-maintained routes. In Hirschhorn, **Josef Riedel,** Hainbrunner Str. 6 (☎20 18), rents bikes for €6 per day. The **Rhein-Neckar Fahrgastschifffahrt** runs **boat tours** from Easter to Oct. 19 between Heidelberg, Neckargemünd, Neckarsteinach, Hirschhorn, and Eberbach. (☎06221 201 81 or 06229 526. Round-trips cost €2.50-16.)

NECKARSTEINACH ☎06229

Fourteen kilometers upstream from Heidelberg, Neckarsteinach is a fishing village made famous by its four picture-perfect castles. To stay, visit the **tourist office** (inside Schreibwaren), Hauptstr. 15, which lists private rooms. (☎920 00; www.neckarsteinach.com. Open M-Tu and Th-F 8:30am-12:30pm and 2:30-6pm, W 8:30am-12:30pm, Sa 8:30am-1pm.) The **post office** is at Hauptstr. 9, 69239. (Open M-Tu and Th-F 8:30am-12:30pm and 2:30-6:30pm, W 8:30am-12:30pm, Sa 8:30am-1pm). **Vierburgeneck ❹,** Unterhalb der Ruine, has large rooms with balconies overlooking the Neckar. From the train station, walk 1.5km west along the river. TVs, private baths, and telephones are in every room. (☎542; www.neckarstein-ach.com/hotel. Singles €59; doubles €84; triples €100. Extra bed €14.) For **camp-**

ing, head across the river to **Unterm Dilsberg ❶.** On foot, walk south on Bahnhofstr., cross the footbridge and turn right; by car, head to Neckargemünd and follow the signs from there. (☎06223 725 85; www.camping-dilsberg.de. Open Apr.-Sept. €6 per person, €4 per child, €7.50 per site. Showers €1.)

The famous castles were built during the 12th and 13th centuries by the Stein-achs, feudal tenants of the Bishop of Worms. The two westernmost castles stand romantically in ruins, while the two to the east have been rebuilt in the traditional style of the nobility—commoners are not allowed inside. All lie along 3km of the north bank of the Neckar, and can be reached by foot via the **Burgenweg.** From the train station, turn right on Bahnhofstr. and follow it until you reach Hauptstr. Along the right side of Hauptstr. watch for a brick path labeled *Schloßsteige* veering up the mountain. At the end of the path, turn right to admire the view of the two private castles. Continue on the path behind the castles to the left to reach the **Hinterburg.** Enter the ruins and climb the unlit tower staircase at your own peril; the view is worth it. To reach the fourth castle, head uphill from the Hinterburg and follow the handrailed path along the river valley. Fireworks burst above the town on the second Saturday after Pentecost in June and on the last Saturday in July for the **Vierburgenbeleuchtung** (four-castle lighting).

HIRSCHHORN AM NECKAR   ☎06272

Just south of Neckarsteinach is Hirschhorn am Neckar, whose reconstructed medieval Altstadt sits squeezed between the Neckar river and the Stöckberg mountain. Maps of local hiking trails are available at the **tourist office,** Alleeweg 2, which also helps find rooms. From the station, turn left on Bahnhofstr., continue on Neckarsteinacher Str. and follow it to the intersection as it curves to the right. Turn right and walk downhill toward the river. The office is in the rear of the yellow museum on the right. (☎17 42; www.hirschhorn.de. Open Apr.-Sept. Tu-F 8am-noon and 2-5pm, Sa 9am-1pm and 2-5pm; Oct.-Mar. M-F 8am-noon and 2-5pm.) The **post office,** Hauptstr. 27, 69434 Hirschhorn, is on the main pedestrian road. (Open M and W-F 8:30am-12:30pm and 2:30-6pm, Tu 8:30am-12:30pm, Sa 8:30am-1pm.)

This small settlement thrived for centuries under the protection of the Knights of Hirschhorn. Though a curse laid on the House of Hirschhorn ended the dynasty in 1632, the beautiful architecture remains a tribute to their influence. For overnight accommodations, check the hotels and pensions along Hauptstr. and the board outside the tourist office. **Haus La Belle ❸,** Hauptstr. 38, has cushy rooms with TV. (☎14 00. Breakfast included. Reserve in advance. Singles €21.) Camp at **Odenwald Camping ❶,** Langenthaler Str., 1km outside of town; follow the signs from the tourist office. (☎809; www.odenwald-camping-park.de. Open Apr.-Oct. 15. Showers and heated swimming pool included. €4.50 per person; €3.10 per child 5-14, €1.80 per child 1-4, €6.20 per site. Dogs €1.60. Caravan rental €25-30. 10% rebates for extended stays and spring/fall camping.) **Schloß Hirschhorn ❺** now houses a posh hotel/restaurant complex. (☎920 90; www.castle-hotel.de. Annex single €63-75; annex doubles €98; at the castle €110.) The castle is still worth a look, and the surrounding countryside is excellent for hiking. By foot, follow the gray brick of Schloßstr. diagonally across from the *Bürgerhaus* intersection (10min.); do not follow the road signs unless you are in a car. The castle's terraces offer a fine panorama; an even better one can be seen from the tower. (Open 7am-7pm. €0.30.) Stone stairs curl from the castle down to the Altstadt, passing the 15th-century **Karmeliterklosterkirche,** with its graceful Gothic interior. The tourist office building also houses the **Langbeinmuseum,** the eclectic collection of Hirschhorn innkeeper Carl Langbein (1816-1881), which includes 17th- and 18th-century wooden statues, weaponry, and a diorama that crams 180 types of native fauna into a space of a king-size bed. (Open W and Su 3-5pm. €1, children €0.50.)

🄳 DAYTRIP FROM HIRSCHHORN: BURG GUTTENBERG

*To reach Burg Guttenberg, take the train from Neckargemünd (see **Neckar Valley**, p. 393). Get off at "Gundelsheim Neckar," head southeast on the tracks, take the 1st right, cross the bridge past the campsite, and follow the signs for 2km along the road (30min.).*

Thirty kilometers south of Hirschhorn, the well preserved **Burg Guttenberg** towers above the museum detailing its 800-year history. (☎06266 388; www.burg-guttenberg.de. Open Apr.-Oct. daily 9am-6pm. Museum and castle €4.) Also within the castle walls is an **aviary** for eagles and vultures, maintained by prominent ornithologist Claus Fentzloff. Each day, Fentzloff or a well-trained assistant sends eagles and vultures flying inches above the heads of the crowds, plucking chicks out of the sky, while he launches into lengthy scientific diatribes in German. Get a seat by the railing to see the birds soar over the valley. (Apr.-Oct. 11am and 3pm; Mar. and Nov. 3pm only. €8; with castle €11.)

BAD WIMPFEN   ☎07063

Downstream from Heilbronn is the village of Bad Wimpfen, whose fairy-tale sensibility was once one of southwest Germany's best-kept secrets. The friendly **tourist office** in the train station finds reasonable private rooms. (☎972 00; fax 97 20 20. Open Nov.-Easter M-F 9am-1pm and 2-5pm; Easter -Oct. M-F 9am-6pm, Sa-Su 10am-12:30pm and 1-2:30pm.) 🄷**Hotel Garni Neckarblick ❹**, Erich-Salier-Str. 48, will pick you up from the train station if you call; or, take a right from the Hauptbahnhof, follow Hauptstr. to Erich-Salier-Str., and hang a right. Walk for 15min. along the street as it curves around the hillside; the hotel is on the right. Offers affordable luxury, hospitality, and a stunning view of the valley. All rooms have TV, telephone, and bath. They rent **bikes** for €12 per day (guests 25% off), and will pick you up at the end of the bike tour. (☎96 16 20; www.neckarblick.de. Breakfast included. Call ahead. Singles €46; doubles €71-85; triples €98; special prices for stays longer then 3 days.) Contradicting Benedictine stoicism, **Gästehaus der Benediktinerabtei Grüssau ❸**, Lindenpl. 5. has large, comfortable rooms, a few with baths. From the station, turn away from town and follow the main road to Wimpfen im Tal for 15min. The monastery is on the left. Call or email at least one day ahead. (☎970 40; www.abtei-gruessau.de. Singles €35; doubles €58.) **Dobel's Maultaschen ❸**, Hauptstr. 61, draws locals with *Maultaschen* for €3.80-9. (☎82 12. Open daily 10am-11pm.) **Gasthaus Hirsch ❸**, Hauptstr. 88, serves filling entrees with a salad for €7. (☎86 88. Open M and W-Su 11am-2:30pm and 5-10pm.)

The twisty-turny **Altstadt** is a 10min. walk from the ornate train station. Follow Karl-Ulrich-Str. or take the steep hiking trail to the right of the station, go up the stairs at the top and follow the old wall until you find an entrance. Laid out along the northern side of town, easily accessible points on the ancient battlements offer incredible views of the valley and the surrounding countryside. Next to the **Roter Turm** (Red Tower; open Sa-Su 10am-1pm and 2-5pm; free), the **Pfalzkapelle** hosts the **Kirchenhistorisches Museum,** which exhibits ecclesiastical artifacts from the town's monastery and churches, including two Luther Bibles. (Open Apr.-Oct. Tu-Su 10am-noon and 2-4:30pm. €1, students €0.70.) The **Blauer Turm** (blue tower), Burgviertel 9, offers a striking view. (☎89 68. Open Tu-Su 10am-noon and 2pm-4:30pm. €1, children €0.50; pay at the top.) The **Galerie der Stadt,** Hauptstr. 45, features a small exhibit on contemporary artwork, while the **Reichstädtisches Museum** recounts the history of Bad Wimpfen. (☎95 03 13. Both open Tu-Su summer 10am-5pm; after Oct. 10am-noon and 2-5pm. Galerie free. Museum €1.50, students €1.) The world's only **Schweine Museum,** Kronengäßchen 2, on the turn beside Hauptstr. 67, details the role of swine (a good luck symbol in Germany) with collectors' items and charms. In the summer, a real pig named Timmy often joins the exhibits. (☎66 89. Open daily 10am-5pm. €2.60, students €1.30.) A **museum pass** is available to the Museum in Stienhaus, Museum in Alten Spital, Ödenburger Heimatmuseum, and Museum in der Pfalzkapelle (€3, students €2).

TÜBINGEN   ☎07071

Thirty kilometers south of Stuttgart, Tübingen straddles the Neckar River on the edge of the Schwarzwald, in the geographic heart of Baden-Württemburg. People here feel good—the city was awarded the title of "highest quality of life in Germany." Nearly half of Tübingen's residents are affiliated with the 500-year-old university, keeping the Altstadt a lively center of discussion and discovery.

⌐ TRANSPORTATION

Trains and buses: Tübingen is well connected to **Stuttgart** (by bus or train, 1hr., 2 per hr., €9) and many small towns in the Schwäbische Alb.

Taxis: ☎92 05 55.

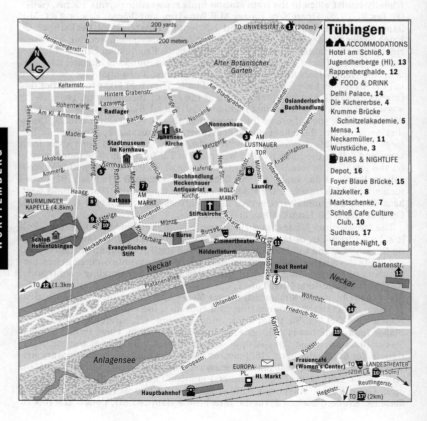

Tübingen

♠♠ ACCOMMODATIONS
Hotel am Schloß, **9**
Jugendherberge (HI), **13**
Rappenberghalde, **12**

🍴 FOOD & DRINK
Delhi Palace, **14**
Die Kichererbse, **4**
Krumme Brücke
    Schnitzelakademie, **5**
Mensa, **1**
Neckarmüller, **11**
Wurstküche, **3**

🍺 BARS & NIGHTLIFE
Depot, **16**
Foyer Blaue Brücke, **15**
Jazzkeller, **8**
Marktschenke, **7**
Schloß Cafe Culture
    Club, **10**
Sudhaus, **17**
Tangente-Night, **6**

BADEN-WÜRTTEMBERG

Bike Rental: Radlager, Lazarettg. 19-21 (☎55 16 51). €7-10 per day. Open M, W, F 9:30am-6:30pm; Tu and Th 2-6:30pm; Sa 9:30am-2:30pm; winter Sa until 1pm.

Boat Rental: Bootsverleih Märkle, on the river under the tourist office. (☎315 29. €7-9 per hr. Open Apr.-Sept. daily 11am-8pm.)

◪ PRACTICAL INFORMATION

Tourist Office: (☎913 60; www.tuebingen-info.de), on the Neckarbrücke. From the front of the station, turn right, walk to Karlstr., turn left, and walk to the river. City maps available. **Tours** (in German) €3.50, children €1.50. Ask for a schedule. Call ahead for English tours. Open M-F 9am-7pm, Sa 9am-5pm.

Bookstores: The 400-year-old **Osianderische Buchhandlung,** Wilhelmstr. 12 (☎920 11 29; www.osiander.de), carries a selection of English-language literature and occasionally hosts English authors. Open M-W 9am-7pm, Th-F 9am-8pm, Sa 9am-6pm.

Women's Resources: Frauencafé, Karlstr. 13 (☎328 62), in the magenta house 1 block from the station, has a popular, women-only night spot/safe zone on the 2nd fl. Open M-F 8pm-12:30am. Enter over the fire escape.

Laundromat: Waschsalon, Mühlstr. 8 (☎36 08 41). Wash 6kg €3.50; 10kg €5.90. Dry €0.90 per 10min. Cappuccino €0.90. Open M-Sa 7am-10pm.

Emergency: Police ☎ 110. **Fire** and **Ambulance** ☎ 112.

Internet Access: Handy Shop, Europapl. 5 (☎25 24 60). €0.50 per 15min. Open M-F 10am-8pm, Sa 10am-4pm.

Post Office: Europapl. 2, 72072 Tübingen. The modern building 100m to the right of the station. Open M-F 8am-6:30pm, Sa 8:30am-1pm.

◪ ACCOMMODATIONS AND CAMPING

Jugendherberge (HI), Gartenstr. 22/2 (☎230 02; www.jugendherberge-tuebingen.de). Cross the bridge past the tourist office and turn right, or take bus #22 (dir.: Neuhaldenstr.) to "Jugendherberge." Enter on Herman-Kurz-Str. Newly renovated, with a terrace overlooking the river. Wheelchair-accessible. Breakfast included. Lockers €2 deposit. Reception 1pm-midnight. Curfew midnight. Dorms €22.20, under 27 €19.60; extra nights €19.10/€16.40. Singles and doubles, some with shower, add at least €5. ❷

Hotel Meteora, Weizsäckerstr. 1 (☎227 35; www.hotel-meteora.de). Follow Wilhelmstr. past the university and turn right on Weizsäckerstr. Or take bus #1 or 7 to "Pauline-Krone-Heim" and walk back 1 block. Friendly management, clean facilities, and a Greek/Swabian restaurant. All rooms with phones and TVs. Breakfast included. Singles €31, with shower €36; doubles with shower €59; triples with bath €72. ❸

Hotel am Schloß, Burgsteige 18 (☎929 40; www.hotelamschloss.de), on the hill leading to the Schloß. 3-star lodgings in a picturesque location. All rooms with showers, phones, and TVs. Breakfast included. Singles €51-67; doubles €76-92; deluxe €105-118. Cheaper rooms in the Gästehaus next door. ❹

Camping: Rappenberghalde (☎/fax 431 45; www.neckarcamping.de). Follow Neckarhalde away from town until Hirschauerstr. and finally Rappenberghalde (25min.). Or take bus #9 to "Rappenberg" and follow the river to your left. Bike rental €4.50 per day. Wash €2.10. Dry €2.10. Reception daily 8am-12:30pm and 2:30-10pm. Open Mar. to mid-Oct. €5.30 per person, €3.50 per child, €1.70 per site, €3.80 per tent, €4.50 per caravan, €2.50 per car. Showers free. ❶

THE BIG SPLURGE

DAYS OF PINTS AND PUNTS

On any bright summer day in Tübingen, the quiet Neckar is flooded with long boats full of singing, laughing students. In accordance with local law, only fraternities and student clubs are allowed to own these "punts," or floating party-boats, but visitors have a way to take part in this age-old tradition. For €52, you can rent a 12-seat boat and the services of a sturdy student punter for an hour. Let your guide glide you along the picturesque riverfront through the Altstadt, or instruct you in the art of punting. For the most authentic experience, don't forget to pack a picnic (the Friday morning Tübingen market is the best place to stock up) and a few cases of Pils.

The students reclaim the Neckar every year on the second Thursday of June, when they come together for the informal competition known as "The Punting Race." It is a wild and chaotic spectacle of jamming, collisions, screaming and laughing—nothing like the precisely organized crew races of Oxford or Cambridge. The winners receive a keg of beer, while the losers are doomed to down half-liters of cod-liver oil for the crowd. So seek a beer-bellied punter as your instructor and enjoy this unique Swabian Gemütlichkeit.

To rent a punt, visit the Tübingen tourist office on the Neckar., p. 397.)

🄲 FOOD

Tübingen's superb restaurants seduce students and tourists alike. Most inexpensive eating establishments cluster around **Metzgergasse** and **Am Lustnauer Tor**. Modern *Imbiße* crowd Kornhausg. Buy **groceries** at **HL Markt**, Europapl. 8, across from the post office and down by the underpass. (Open M-F 7am-8pm, Sa 8am-8pm.) There is a **market** on Am Markt (M, W, F 7am-1pm).

🄴 **Krumme Brücke Schnitzelakademie,** Kornhausstr. 17B (☎224 66). This pleasant, 300-year-old restaurant near the Rathaus serves up Swabian specialties, especially sizable *Schnitzel* (€3-8.30). Open daily 11am-3pm and 5-11pm. ❸

Neckarmüller, Gartenstr. 4 (☎278 48), is close to the youth hostel and next to the bridge. Young and old alike eat, drink, and schmooze under trees beside the Neckar, or indoors among brewing apparati. Try the house brew (€2.70 for 0.5L). Swabian food starts at €5.70, daily specials €5.60. Open daily 10am-1am. ❸

Wurstküche, Am Lustnauer Tor 8 (☎927 50). The staff teaches you Swabian dialect while you enjoy traditional German food (€4-15). Open daily 11am-midnight. ❸

Delhi Palace, Wohrdstr. 25 (☎355 22), on the corner of Friedrich-Str. and Poststr. Great Indian food in a *Biergarten* on the Neckar. Ping-pong and a fire at night. Tu-Su lunch buffet (€8). Lunch €4.50-5.50. Dinner from €9.50. Open daily 11am-midnight. ❸

Die Kichererbse, Metzgerg. 2 (☎521 71). Simple eatery prepares fresh Middle Eastern vegetarian meals for €3-6. Open M 11am-6:30pm, Tu-F 11am-7pm, Sa 11am-4pm. ❷

Mensa, the turquoise-and-glass building on Wilhelmstr. between Gmelinstr. and Keplerstr., 5min. from Lustnauer Tor. Buy meal tickets upstairs (€5.25 for guests). Open during the semester M-Th 11:30am-2pm and 6-8:15pm, F 11:30-2pm and 6-7:45pm. The **cafeteria** downstairs has cold food and desserts (€0.60-1.40). Open Sept.-June M-Th 8am-8pm, F 8am-6:30pm; July-Aug. M-Th 8am-7pm, F 8am-5:30pm. ❶

👁 SIGHTS

🄼 **SCHLOß HOHENTÜBINGEN.** This 11th-century castle stands atop the hill in the center of town. A dark tunnel and staircase on the far side of the courtyard lead through the castle wall to breathtaking views of the surrounding valleys. *(Accessible from Am*

Markt. Castle grounds open daily 7am-8pm. Free.) Occupied by various university institutes, the Schloß is also home to the excellent **Museum Schloß Hohentübingen,** the largest university museum in Germany, featuring a rich collection of ethnographic and archaeological artifacts. Greek coins, cuneiform tablets, an Egyptian burial chamber and the **oldest surviving hand carving,** an ivory horse sculpture from 35,000 BC. *(Enter at Burgsteig inside courtyard. ☎ 297 73 84. Open May-Sept. W-Su 10am-6pm; Oct.-Apr. W-Su 10am-5pm. €3, students €2.)*

STIFTSKIRCHE. The 15th-century church serves as the focal point of the Altstadt's winding alleys. In the **chancel** are the tombs of 14 members of the House of Württemberg. Life-size stone sculptures of the deceased top the memorials. The church **tower** offers a rewarding view after the 172-step climb. *(☎ 431 51. Open daily 9am-5pm. Chancel and tower open Aug.-Sept. Tu-Su 11am-5pm; Oct.-July F-Su 11am-5pm. Organ concerts July-Aug. Th at 8pm. €1, students €0.50.)*

HÖLDERLINTURM. The great 18th- and 19th-century poet Friedrich Hölderlin spent the final 36 years of his life writing quatrains on the four seasons in this tower, while certifiably insane. The tower now contains a small museum dedicated to his life. *(Below Bursag. on the river. ☎ 220 40. Tours Sa and Su 5pm. Open Tu-F 10am-noon and 3-5pm, Sa-Su 2-5pm. €1.50, students €1.)*

PLATANENALLEE. The buildings of the **Neckarfront** are best viewed from this quiet tree-lined avenue that runs the length of the man-made island on the Neckar. Punting trips down the Neckar are available from university students; inquire at the tourist office. *(Boats seat 12. M-F and Su €52 per hr., Sa €55)*

WURMLINGER KAPELLE. The simple but beautiful chapel (built in 1685) and cemetery atop an idyllic pastoral hill (475m) has a rare panoramic view. Follow Kapellenweg to the hill from the Schloß, then continue up the hill through the vineyards; at the first fork take a left, then a right at the second fork (6km). Or, take bus #18 (dir.: Rottenburg) to "Hirschau Kirchpl." *(10min., 2 per hr., €1.50. Chapel open Mar.-Oct. Su 9am-5pm; Nov.-Mar. Su 9am-4pm; or call ☎ 221 22.)*

OTHER SIGHTS. Across from the **Stiftskirche** is **Buchhandlung Heckenhauer Antiquariat,** Holzmarkt 5, where **Hermann Hesse** worked from 1895 until 1899. The old-fashioned store sells rare books. *(☎ 230 18; www.heckenhauer.de. Open M-F 2-6:30pm, Sa 11am-3pm.)* Stop to admire the facade and gilded rostrum of the ornate **Rathaus,** Am Markt, towards the castle from the church. Nearby, the **Kornhaus** contains the **Stadtmuseum,** Kornhausstr. 10, with exhibits on the city's history. *(☎ 204 17 11. Open Tu-F 3-6pm, Sa and Su 11am-6pm. €2.50, students and children €1.50.)* Above the river is the **Evangelisches Stift,** Klosterberg 2. This theology dorm was once a monastery that housed such luminaries as Kepler, Hölderlin, and Hegel.

🎵 🎭 ENTERTAINMENT AND NIGHTLIFE

Tübingen's nightlife is laid-back, mostly revolving around cafes in the Altstadt that begin brewing quiet cups of coffee at 10am, and serve beer to students late into the night. In warm weather, students come to sip drinks and sit on Am Markt's pavement, stairs, or fountain. For after-hours transportation, wait for the **Nachtbus,** which leaves Lustnauer Tor (Th-Sa night 12:45-2:45am), or call **Nacht-SAM** to pick you up (☎ 340 00). Tübingen also has two major theaters: the progressive **Zimmertheater,** Bursag. 16., (☎ 927 30; open M-F 10am-1pm and 3-6pm, Sa 2-7pm and 1hr. before shows; tickets also available at the tourist office and Mensa, M-Th 11:30am-3pm, F 11:30am-2:15pm) and the **Landestheater,** Eberhardstr. 8. (☎ 931 31 49; fax 15 92 70. Open Tu-F 2-7pm, Sa 10am-1pm.)

■ **Schloß Cafe Culture Club,** Burgsteige 7 (☎96 51 53), near the Schloß. This brand-new student lair is decorated with an eclectic mix of couches, old church pews, and other slapdash furnishings. Live music and DJs on weekends, poetry readings, jam sessions, open mics and more. Board games and student-priced drinks abound. Beer €2.50. Cocktails €5. Open M-Sa 11am-2am, Sun until midnight.

Sudhaus, Hechinger Str. 203 (☎46 96; www.cityinfonetz.de/sudhaus). Bus #3 or 5 or night bus N95 to "Fuchsstr.," then go under the busy road. This "socio-cultural center," in a former brewery, hosts wacky art films, dance parties, and live acts. Schedules are plastered all over town. Cover €5-16. In winter, **Takco Bistro** serves up food, cocktails, and fluctuating music M-F 11:30am-2pm and 6pm-midnight, Sa 6pm-3am. In the summer, head to Takco *Biergarten* instead, May-Aug. 11:30am-11pm. **Takco Bar** (☎76 07 67) opens its small dance floor and cocktail bar (€7-9) on weekends, F-Su 10pm-3am.

Depot, on Eisenbahnstr. (www.depot-tuebingen.de), is across the river and close to the rail tracks. Take bus #35 to "Hügelstr." or night bus N84 or 85 to "Landestheater," turn back and cross the highway by the tunnel. Large dance fl. and alternating DJs for beat freaks. Drinks €5-6. Cover varies. Open F-Su 10pm-4am.

Tangente-Night, Pfleghofstr. 10 (☎230 07), at the corner of Lustnauer Tor. A student hangout for evening beers or morning reading over coffee. Beer €1.90-€2.90. Cocktails €6.50. Techno DJ W 9pm. Karaoke M. Open daily 10am-3am; summer 4pm-3am.

Foyer Blaue Brücke, Friedrichstr. 12 (☎53 82 44). Take bus #3 or night bus N87 to "Blaue Brücke." This 2-fl. disco, which once housed French officers, now attracts an even more party-oriented crowd. Rock upstairs; top 40 downstairs. Beer €2.10-3.30. Cocktails €4.50-5. Cover €5. Open F-Sa 10pm-3am.

Jazzkeller, Haagg. 15½ (☎55 09 06). From jazz to funk to salsa and back again, in style. There's also a disco downstairs, with occasional live gigs (€3-4). Happy hour M-Tu and Th 11:30pm. Open daily from 7pm; mid-June to Aug closed Su.

Marktschenke, Am Markt 11 (☎220 35). Trendies gather at this modern bar to sip their *Hefeweizen* (€2.90 for 0.5L), indoors or out. Open M-Th 9am-1am, F-Sa 9am-2am, Su 10am-1am.

MANNHEIM ☎0621

Though the alphanumeric street names are straight out of a game of Battleship and several sights and museums are undergoing restoration, city-loving travelers in search of the real modern Germany will enjoy Mannheim. This commercial power-house is a good base for visiting Heidelberg while avoiding the crowds of tourists.

▐▟ TRANSPORTATION AND PRACTICAL INFORMATION

Trains run to **Frankfurt** (1hr., 2 per hr., €17.20) and **Stuttgart** (40min., 1 per hr., €23). **Streetcars** cost €1.90. The **tourist office,** Willy-Brandt-Pl. 3, a block from the station, distributes maps and accommodations info. (☎10 10 11; www.tour-ist-mannheim.de. Open M-F 9am-7pm, Sa 10am-1pm.) A **laundromat, Waschinsel,** is on Seckenheimer Str. 8, two blocks northeast of the station. (Wash €3.70. Dry €2.20. Open M-F, Su 8am-8pm, Sa 9am-4pm.) A **pharmacy, Bahnhof-Apotheke,** is at block L15, across from the station and to the left. (☎12 01 80. Open M-F 7am-8pm, Sa 8am-8pm.) Check email at **Chat Corner,** #16-17 L14, 2 blocks from the train station. (€1 per 20min. Open daily 9am-3am.) The **post office,** Willy-Brandt-Pl. 13, 68161 Mannheim, is one block east of the station. (Open M-F 9am-6pm, Sa 9am-noon.)

ORIENTATION

Mannheim is on the peninsula created by the junction of the Rhein and Neckar rivers. The **Innenstadt** is bounded by a horseshoe road, known as **Parkring** to the west, **Luisenring** to the northwest, **Friedrichsring** to the northeast, and **Kaiserring** to the east. Bismarckstr. connects the southern ends. The train station is just outside the southeast corner. **Kurpfalzstraße** and **Breite Straße** bisect the horseshoe, which is divided into a grid of 144 blocks: each block is named by a letter and a number; blocks along Kurpfalzstr. have increasing numbers the farther away you get from the central axis. Blocks to the west of Kurpfalzstr. are designated south to north by the letters **A** through **K**, while streets to the east are similarly lettered **L** through **U**. East of Kaiserring, streets assume regular names.

ACCOMMODATIONS AND FOOD

Mannheim's **Jugendherberge (HI) ❶**, Rheinpromenade 21, has small rooms and aging facilities, but compensates with a super-convenient location 10min. from the station. Walk through the underground passage for the tracks at the east end of the station and take a right up the stairs at the very end. Take the path to the left of the big glass building, cross the tracks, and, with the park on your right, continue down Rennershofstr. for about a block. At the intersection with Gontardstr., take the stairs on the right side into the shrubbery. Or take streetcar #7 (dir.: Neckarau) to "Lindenhofpl." (☎82 27 18; www.jugendherberge-mannheim.de. Breakfast 7:30-8:30am and sheets included. Key deposit €10. Reception 7-9:30am and 4-10pm. Dorms €19, under 27 €16.30; additional nights €15.90/€13.20. Singles or doubles add €5.) **Goldene Gans ❸**, Tattersallstr. 19, two blocks northeast of the train station, opens onto Bismarckpl. during the day, but after midnight the entrance is around the corner. This inn offers clean, sunny rooms, many with large baths. (☎10 52 77; fax 422 02 60. Breakfast included. Reception M-Sa 6am-midnight, Su 7am-6pm. Singles €30, with bath €64; doubles €78; family apartments €100. Cheaper rates for weekends.) Bakers and grocers gather at the **market** in the square at the intersection of Kurpfalzstr. and Kirchstr. in the center of the city grid. (Open Tu, Th, Sa 7am-1:30pm.) The cheapest meals in town (€4.70-5) are at the **Studentenwerk Mannheim Mensa ❶**, behind the Residenzschloß in the southwest corner (open M-F 11:30am-2pm), and the adjacent **cafeteria**. (Sandwiches, €1-1.80. Open M-Th 8:30am-4pm, F 8:30am-3:45pm.) For local specialities (€6-9), head to the **Kurfürst ❸**, #15 R1, one block east of the Marktpl. (☎262 75. Open daily 9am-11pm.) **Stonehenge Irish Pub ❸**, #8-9 M4, has regular theme nights with drink discounts. (☎122 39 49; www.pub.de. Open Su-Th 5pm-2am, F-Sa until 3am.) **Flic Flac**, #12 B2, is a local student favorite. Decorated as a 1920s zeppelin, this bar has a daily happy hour after 9pm, €5.90 pasta buffet (M), and live bands on Thursday. (☎225 53. Open Su-Th 9am-1am, F-Sa until 2am.) Blocks **G2** through **J6** have a dense array of *Imbiße* and ethnic restaurants, where food is generally €3-7.

SIGHTS

The bustling **Paradeplatz**, with its intriguing Baroque fountain, is the heart of Mannheim. Restaurants, department stores, cafes, and movie theaters surround the square and extend along the pedestrian zones on Breite Str. and Planken. At the end of Planken is the city's emblematic masterpiece, the elegant sandstone **Wasserturm**, said to be "the most beautiful water tower in the world," and the surrounding gardens on **Friedrichsplatz**. South of the manicured foliage of Friedrichspl. is the

Kunsthalle, Friedrichspl. 4, a museum surveying art from the mid-19th century to today, including works by Manet and Van Gogh. (☎ 293 64 13 30. Open Tu-Su 11am-6pm. Hours extended for special exhibitions. €2.10, students €1.)

The giant **Kurgürtliches Residenzschloß,** the largest Baroque palace in Germany, now houses the **Universität Mannheim** and a small museum, which will return bigger and better when it reopens in 2007. The pink-striped **Schloßkirche** entombs Karl Phillip's third wife, Violante von Thurn und Taxis. (☎ 213 63. Open Apr.-Oct. Tu-Su 10am-5pm; Nov.-Mar. Sa-Su 10am-5pm. Free.) The huge **Reiss-Engelhorn-Museen,** around block C5, northwest of the Schloß, has buildings dedicated to archaeology, ethnology, and natural science. The archaeology wing is under construction until 2007. (☎ 293 31 55. Open Tu-Su 11am-6pm. Tours Sa 3pm, Su 11:30am and 3pm; €3, under 18 €1. €6, under 18 €2.50, family €12.) The recently restored **Jesuitenkirche,** between the museum and the Schloß at block A4, was built for the Pfalz court's return to Catholicism. (Open daily 8am-noon and 2-5pm.)

On the other side of the Innenstadt, several blocks northeast of the Wasserturm, is the 100-acre **Luisenpark.** (☎ 410 05 20. Open daily May-Aug. 9am-9pm; Sept.-Apr. 9am-sunset. Day card in summer €7, winter €2.50; students €3/€1.80.) The greenhouses, flower gardens, aviary, zoo, water sports, mini-golf, frequent afternoon concerts, and boat rides offer something for everyone. South of Luisenpark, seven blocks due east of Friedrichspl. on the **Augustanlage,** lies the terrific **Landesmuseum der Technik und Arbeit,** Museumstr. 1, which displays the inner workings of big, creaky, rusty things through fun hands-on exhibits and demonstrations. Through six stories connected by tunnels and ramps, the museum follows the impact of technology on German society since the introduction of textile factories 250 years ago. Take streetcar #6 to "Landesmuseum." (☎ 429 87 22. Open Tu and Th-F 9am-5pm, W 9am-8pm, Sa 10am-5pm, Su 10am-6pm. €3, students €2, family €6. W afternoon free.) The **Museumsschiff "Mannheim"** floats in the Neckar, just by the Kurpfalzbrücke. Once the steamer *Mainz,* which sank in 1956, it was dredged from the murky Rhein's and now houses a history of navigation. (☎ 156 57 56. Open Tu-Sa 10am-4pm, Su 10am-6pm. €1, children under 6 free. W afternoons free.)

SCHWÄBISCHE ALB (SWABIAN JURA)

The limestone plateaus, sharp ridges, and pine-forested valleys stretching from Tübingen in the north to the Bodensee in the south are collectively known as the Schwäbische Alb. This roughly-hewn landscape is scenic yet stubborn, and the climate is harsh. Lofty ruins crowning the peaks are all that remain of for-tifications erected by the once powerful dynasties that held the region. The **Schwäbische Albstraße** (Swabian Jura Road) bisects the plateau, crossing the Romantic Road at Nördlingen (p. 534). A web of trails serves hikers; maps are available at regional tourist offices in most towns. Train service to many points is roundabout and spotty; plan to make use of the local bus routes and keep track of schedules.

SCHWÄBISCH HALL ☎ 0791

An urban oasis in the Swabian countryside, Schwäbisch Hall is a colorful gather-ing of red roofs, church towers, and crumbling stone walls. Its steeply-sloping and many-staired Altstadt is one of the most expansive and well-preserved in Ger-many. Tourism is still in its infancy in Schwäbisch Hall, leaving the town almost entirely to its residents and the few travelers wandering its ancient streets.

🄵 🄽 TRANSPORTATION AND PRACTICAL INFORMATION

Schwäbisch Hall has two **train** stations. The **Hauptbahnhof** is close to town, but the more important station is in **Schwäbisch Hall-Hessental**, on the main rail line to **Stuttgart** (1¼hr., 1 per hr., €11.10). Bus #4B connects the two stations (15min., 2-3 per hr., €1.50). All **bus** lines stop at "Am Spitalbach Ost" or "West," a few blocks northwest of the tourist office. *Stadtbus KundenCenter*, Am Spitalbach 4, sells *Tageskarten* (€4.50), valid all day or all weekend on buses (☎97 19 00. Open M-F 9:30am-6:15pm, Sa 9am-1:30pm.) For a **taxi** call ☎61 17. Rent bikes at **Radsport Fiedler**, Kirchstr. 4. (☎93 02 40. From €7.50 per day. Open Su-F 9am-7pm, Sa 9am-2pm.) **Kocherflotte**, on the river by the Haalpl. parking lot, rents boats. (☎430 64. €5 per hr. Open May to mid-Oct. daily 12-6pm.) Schwäbisch Hall's **tourist office**, Am Markt 9, has free maps, room lists, and a ▉**town guide.** (☎75 12 16; www.schwaebischhall.de. Open May-Sept. M-F 9am-6pm, Sa-Su 10am-3pm; until 8:30pm during *Freilichtspiele* (p. 403); Oct.-Apr. M-F 9am-5pm.) The **Baden-Württembergische Bank**, on Neue Str. by the river, has an **ATM**. The **Hirsch-Apotheke pharmacy** is on Gelbingerg. 18. (Open M-F 8am-12:30pm and 2-6pm, Sa 8:30am-12:30pm.) Check the **Internet** at **Populaire**, Heimbacherg. 8. (☎63 08. €0.50 per 10min. Open daily 10am-1am.) The **post office** is on Hafenmarkt 2, 74523 Schwäbisch Hall. (Open M-F 9am-12:30pm and 2-5:30pm, Sa 8:30am-noon.)

🄰 🄲 ACCOMMODATIONS AND FOOD

Schwäbisch Hall's **Jugendherberge (HI)** ❷, Langenfelder Weg 5, is beyond the Michaelskirche on the Galgenberg., accesible by bus #1, 5 or 4C at the "Schwäbisch Hall Hölzmarkt." Follow Crailsheimer Str. up 200m from the church and take a left onto Ziegeleiweg, then Langenfelder Weg, or head through the stone arch at the corner of Ziegeleiweg. The hostel, in the orange building on the left, offers modern accommodations behind an overgrown stone terrace. (☎410 50; fax 479 98. Excellent breakfast buffet included. Reception 4:30-7:30pm. Dorms €19.70, under 27 €17.40; singles €25/€22.60; doubles €30/€27.50. Reduced prices for stays over 1 night.) **Gasthof Krone** ❸, Klosterstr. 1, offers basic, clean rooms. Follow the street to the right of Michaelskirche all the way up and around the corner on the right or take bus #1, 5 or 4C to "Schwäbisch Hall Hölzmarkt." (☎60 22. Breakfast included. Singles €20-25; spacious doubles with bath €50-60; triples €60-80. Cash only.) There is a **Campingplatz** ❶ at Steinbacher See. Take bus #4B to "Steinbach/Mitte" (5min., 2-3 per hr., €1.40), then turn back and follow the signs. (☎/fax 29 84; www.camping.hohenlohe2000.de. Reception 7am-1pm and 3-10pm. Laundry €0.50. €4.60 per person, €3.60 per child, €5.10 per site. Showers €0.50.) An **HL Markt** is three blocks down the hill from the Marktpl. on Neue Str. (☎978 10 74. Open M-F 8:30am-8pm, Sa 8am-4pm.) **Warsteiner Ilge's** ❷ terrace above the Kocher River, Im Weiler 2, provides delicious fruit shakes, cocktails, or beer (€1.60-9.90) as well as soup, salads, and baguettes (€3.80-5.40), hot or cold. (☎716 84. Open daily 11am-1am.) Restaurants along **Gelbinger Gasse** offer a variety of cuisines, including typical Swabian specialties at **Sonne** ❸, Gelbinger G. 2. (☎97 08 40. Entrees €7-12.50. Open Tu-Su 11:30am-2pm and from 5:30pm.) *Imbiß*-style **Burger-House** ❷, Hallstr. 8, serves hamburgers and *Döner Kebap* near the river for €2-6.50. (☎97 30 53. Open M-F 10am-noon,; Sa-Su 11am-1am.)

🄾 🄽 SIGHTS AND ENTERTAINMENT

On summer evenings from mid-May to mid-August, the **Freilichtspiele**, a series of plays running the gamut from Shakespeare to Brecht, are performed at several locations in Hall, including the steps of the Michaelskirche and the Haller Globe theater on the river island. Contact the tourist office for tickets. (☎ 75 16 00. €4-27.50, student discount €5.50.) On the weekend of Pentecost, in late May or early June (May 15-16, 2005), Schwäbisch Hall celebrates the **Kuchen- und Brunnenfest,** during which locals don 16th-century salt refiner costumes and dance jigs around a 100 lb. cake. During the **Sommernachtsfest** (the last Sa in Aug.), 30,000 candles are set alight in patterns along the Ackeranlage and around town.

■**HOHENLOHER FREILANDMUSEUM.** In nearby Wackershofen, this museum reenacts life in a German agricultural village with 51 authentic low-ceilinged houses amidst scenic countryside. Admire the haystacks, pigs, sheep, and the Schnapps-making process. Most weekends from Apr.-Nov. have special events, ranging from a southern German cheese market to the "Schwäbisch-Hällischen pig day." A free guide in English is available in the village office. *(Take bus #7 from Spitalbach West to "Freiland Museum" (15min.; M-F 3 per hr., Sa-Su less frequent; €1.55). Or, hike the 1½hr. trail #3 from central Hall to the museum. ☎ 97 10 10. Open June-Aug. daily 9am-6pm; May and Sept.-Oct. Tu-Su 9am-6pm; Mar. 22-Apr. and Oct.-Nov. 9 Tu-Su 10am-5pm. Tours €4; call 2 wk. early to arrange English tours, €28. €5, students €3.)*

ALTSTADT. Thrice charred by fires, Hall's half-timbered center was built in the 18th century. The Romanesque tower and Gothic nave of the **Michaelskirche** perches atop a steep set of stone stairs. The church is Lutheran thanks to local **Johannes Brenz,** the reformer who converted Hall to Protestantism in the 1520s. Organ music often echoes in the church (check board for concert information), rattling the pile of human bones and skulls in the medieval ossuary—pass to the right of the altar to gaze into the underground mass grave. The **Turmzimmer** atop the church's tower provides a great view of the town. *(Open Mar. to mid-Nov. M 2-5pm, Tu-Sa 9am-5pm, Su 11am–5pm. Tower €1, students €0.50.)*

Narrow half-timbered alleys wind outwards from Marktpl. To the south, Untere Herrng. leads to the eight-story Romanesque **Keckenturm,** on Keckenhof, which houses the **Hällisch-Fränkisches Museum.** The museum has a lovely Baroque room and exhibits on the town's history. *(☎ 75 13 60. Open Tu-Su 10am-5pm, W 10am-8pm. €2, students €1.)* Feed the ducks in the shady gardens of the **Ackeranlage,** along the Kocher. Headless copper statues guard the modern **Würth** gallery, Lange Str. 35, across the river. *(☎ 94 67 214. Open daily 10am-6pm. English audioguide €4. Free.)*

KLOSTER GROßCOMBURG. Steinbach, the only suburb of Hall that remained Catholic during the Reformation, holds Kloster Großcomburg, a former castle and 11th-century Benedictine monastery. Today the cloister houses the **Staatliche Akademie Comburg,** a museum, and a small cafe. From inside, the 460m wall has peep holes for views of the valley, but you must take a **tour** (call in advance, especially for English tours, 6 people minimum) to see the museum and gilded interior of the reconstructed Baroque church. *(Take bus #4B (5min., 2-3 per hr., €1.50) to "Steinbach/Mitte." Cross the street, head back toward the town and take an immediate sharp right onto the Bildersteige path. ☎ 93 81 85. Cafe open Tu-F 10am-noon and 2-5pm, Sa-Su 2-5pm. Tours Apr.-Oct. Tu-F 11am, 2, 3, and 4pm, Sa-Su 2, 3, and 4pm; Nov.-Mar. by appointment. €2.30, students €1.20, family pass €5.80.)*

SCHWÄBISCH GMÜND ☎07171

The oldest town in the Staufenland, Schwäbisch Gmünd has been a smithing center since the 14th century. Locally wrought jewelry can be found in many shops in the center, which bristles with Baroque plaster facades and *fachwerk* buildings. The town is a also good base for excursions into the northern Swabian Jura.

Trains run to **Stuttgart** (30-50min., 1-2 per hr., €8.40-11.80). Regional **buses** leave from the bus terminal next to the train station. The lively staff at the **tourist office,** Marktpl. 37/1 (close to Lederg.), has free town maps and area hiking guides. (☎ 603

42 50; www.schwaebisch-gmuend.de. Open M-F 9am-5:30pm, Sa 9am-1pm.) There's an **ATM** at Deutsche Bank on Lederg. 12, and a **pharmacy, Pfauen Apotheke,** at Kornhausstr. 3. (☎23 29. Open M-Tu and Th 8:15am-6:30pm, W and F 8:15am-6pm, Sa 8:30am-1pm.) The **post office** is in **City Center,** a large shopping complex on Kalter Markt. (Open M-F 9am-7pm, Sa 9am-1pm.) Reach the clean rooms at **Gasthof Weißer Ochsen ❷,** Parlerstr. 47, by bus #2 or 4 to "Weißer Ochsen." (☎28 12; Weisserochsen@T-online.de. Singles €20; doubles €38; extra bed €12.) An open-air **market** fills Münsterpl. W and Sa (7am-1pm). **Grillmeister ❷,** Lederg. 57, has standard *Imbiß* food (€1.35-5.50) and a large seating area. (☎665 03. Open M-Th and Su 10am-11pm, F-Sa 10am-midnight.) **Gasthaus Zum Lamm ❸,** Rinderbacher G. 19, has a daily Swabian menu for €6.50-14. (☎26 61. Open M from 6pm, Tu-F 10:30am-2pm and 6pm-midnight, Sa and Su 11am-2pm.)

To reach the cafe-filled **Marktplatz** from the train station, pass the post office and use the pedestrian underpass to cross the first street. Take the first left, then the first right onto Lederg. and follow it to the end. At the far end of the square is the pink Baroque Rathaus; turn right in front of it to get to Münsterpl., with its 14th-century **Heiligkreuzmünster,** the oldest hall church in southern Germany (☎24 64). Terrible gargoyles depicting screaming, tortured human figures and fanged beasts protrude from the church exterior horizontally in every direction. The original church towers collapsed in the late 1400s. The replacement is a boxy compromise, though safe to enter—view the elaborate Gothic architecture daily 8am-6pm. The **◪St. Salvator Chapel** was carved directly into the caves above town in the early 17th century. The **Way of the Cross,** with detailed, life-like statues from 1737, leads to the chapel from behind the train station. Walking toward the post office inter-section, take a sharp left to the tunnel under the tracks, then briefly follow Taubentalstr. to the sign for St. Salvator. Where the path forks, take the cobble-stone stairs on the right (15min. from train station). The **Silberwaren- und Bijouterie-museum,** Milchgäßle 10, behind the Rathaus to the right, features silversmiths tooling silver in the traditional style each Sunday afternoon. The museum exhibits the cluttered detritus of silver-, gold-, and leather-smiths. (☎389 10. Open Sa-Su 11-5; 1hr. tour Su at 2pm in German. €3, students €1.) The edge of the Altstadt is flanked by seven medieval towers; only the **Königsturm** is open for visitors (Su 1:30-4pm; €0.50). For hiking, head to the nearby Kaiserberge.

ULM ☎0731

When Napoleon designated the Danube as the border between Württemberg and Bavaria, Ulm was split into two distinct cities, Ulm and Neu-Ulm. Brochures claim that they are Siamese twins, but it's pretty clear from a tourist's perspective that the younger sibling got the shaft. The looming peak of the Münster, the tallest church steeple in the world, provides a fantastic backdrop to a lively pedestrian district crowded with shopping bags and beer mugs. Ulm is also known for sci-ence, having raised both **Albert Einstein** and **Albrecht Berblinger,** the "tailor of Ulm," best known for his 1811 attempt at human flight that landed him in the Danube.

▊⌖ TRANSPORTATION AND PRACTICAL INFORMATION. Ulm is connected by **train** to all of southern Germany, with trains to **Munich** (1½-2hr., 2-3 per hr., €20-29) and **Stuttgart** (1hr., 2-3 per hr., €14-22). **Public transport** costs €1.50 per ride, children €0.75. A day ticket, valid for four people (children count as half a person) on the day of purchase, is €6. Rent **bikes** from **Ralf Reich,** Frauenstr. 34. (☎211 79. €8 per day. Open M-F 9am-12:30pm and 2-6:30pm, Sa 9am-2pm.) The **tourist office,** Münsterpl. 50 in the Stadthaus, books rooms for free, sells city guides (€0.50), and offers tours of Ulm in German (€5, students/disabled €2.50, family €8); arrange in advance for English. (☎161 28 30; www.tourismus.ulm.de. Open M-F 9am-6pm, Sa 9am-1pm. May-Dec. also

Sa 9am-4pm, Su 10:30am-2:30pm.) An **ATM** is at Citibank, behind the Stadthaus. **Free Internet** can be found at **Alberts Cafe**, Kornhauspl. 5 (☎ 15 30 23; open M-Sa 10am-10pm), or on the 2nd and 3rd floors of the **Stadtbibliothek**, Weinhof 12. (☎ 161 41 00. Open M-W and F 10am-6pm, Th 1-6pm, Sa 10am-12:30pm.) The **post office**, Bahnhofpl. 2, 89073 Ulm, is to the left of the station. (Open M-F 8:30am-6:30pm, Sa 9am-1pm.)

⌐⌐ ACCOMMODATIONS AND FOOD. Ulm's **Jugendherberge Geschwister Scholl (HI) ❷**, Grimmelfinger Weg 45, was named in memory of Ulm's **Hans and Sophie Scholl**, members of the **Weiße Rose** resistance movement who were executed by the Nazis in 1943 (p. 56). Take bus #1, 3, 7, 8, or 10 from the train station to "Ehinger Tor," and change to bus #4 or 8 (dir.: Kuhberg) to "Kuhberg Schulzentrum." Walk through the underpass just up the road and follow the "Jugendherberge" signs for 5min. (☎ 38 44 55; info@jugendherberge-ulm.de. **Internet** €5 per hr. Breakfast and sheets included. Lunch €4.50, lunch and dinner €7.80. Lockers €10 deposit. Reception 7-10:30am and 4-10:30pm. Curfew 10:30pm; key available with €10 deposit. €20.10, under 27 €17.40. Additional nights €16.90/€14.20.) The newly renovated **Münster-Hotel ❸**, Münsterpl. 14, is to the left of the Münster. Enjoy small rooms in a great location, but beware the early bells. (☎/fax 641 62. Breakfast included. Singles with bath €40; doubles €55, with bath €60; triples with shower €75.) **Pension Rösch ❸**, Schwörhausg. 18, has compact, bright rooms and baths. (☎ 657 18; fax 602 25 84. Breakfast included. Singles €24, from 2nd night €21, with bath €42; doubles with bath €53-58; triples €72.)

A **farmer's market** springs up on Münsterpl. (W and Sa mornings 7am-1pm). Ulm's restaurants reflect both Bavarian and Swabian culinary influences, including *Schupfnudel*, a half-potato, half-wheat noodle dish served with cabbage and bacon. Sandwich-serving bakeries and *Imbiße* dominate the Ladenpassage in front of the train station and line the way to the Münster along **Bahnhofstraße** and **Hirschstraße**. For the most variety, try the territory between **Neue Straße** and the river. For **groceries** head to **Plus**, Münsterpl. 15. (Open M-F 8:30am-7pm, Sa 8:30am-4pm.) **Ulmer Münz Cafe ❸**, across from the Schiefes Haus, serves a small selection of dishes (€3-11.90) or mid-afternoon drinks in Ulm's former mint. (☎ 151 78 87. Open Tu-Su 11am-10pm. Closed Jan.) Near the Münster, **Spanische Weinstube ❷**, on the corner of Münsterpl. and Rabeng., serves Spanish, Bavarian, and Swabian specialities and many salads; daily specials start at €5.90. (☎ 632 97. Open Tu-Su noon-midnight.) A **Mensa ❶** is on the left of the "Eingang Süd," the southern entrance to the university area. Take bus #3 (dir.: Wissenschaftsstadt) to "Universität Süd." (Meals €5.80. Buffet open M-F 11:30am-1:30pm.)

◪ SIGHTS. At 161m, the steeple topping the ▪**Münster** is the tallest in the world. During the Middle Ages, wealthy guild members decided to fund the building of the cathedral, and in 1377 the foundation stone was laid. Many generations passed away before the enormous steeple was completed, 513 years later. Ulm became Protestant in the early 1500s, and many altars and ornate decorations were destroyed. Among those saved was *The Man of Sorrows*, a stone sculpture of Christ by 15th-century sculptor Hans Multscher, next to the front portal of the cathedral. Inside the Gothic walls are some stunning wooden choir stalls carved by Jörg Syrlin the Elder. On a clear day, climb the tower's 768 corkscrewing steps to see all the way to the Alps. (☎ 967 50 23. Church open daily July-Aug. 8am-7:45pm; May-June and Sept. 8am-6:45pm; Apr. 9am-6:45pm; Mar. and Oct. 9am-5:45pm; Nov.-Feb. 9am-4:45pm. Tower closes 1hr. earlier. €3, children €2.)

The nearby white building that houses the tourist office is also home to the **Stadthaus**. Designed by New Yorker Richard Meier, its postmodern style, in conspicuous contrast to the Gothic Münster, raised great controversy among Ulm's residents. The basement holds interesting archaeological and historical exhibits on the Münsterpl. and the painstakingly slow construction of the Münster. (Open M-W and F-Sa 9am-6pm, Th 9am-8pm, Su 11am-6pm. Free.) Toward the river on Neue Str., the **Rathaus,** built in 1370, is decorated with brilliant murals and an elaborate astronomical clock, both dating from 1540. The old **Fischerviertel** (fishermen's quarter), down Kroneng. from the Rathaus, is full of half-timbered houses, cobblestone streets, and primitive footbridges. One of the oldest houses in Ulm, the **Schiefes Haus** (crooked house), at Schwörhausg. 6, is now a hotel.

Across from the Rathaus to the East is the **Ulmer Museum,** Marktpl. 9, which features outstanding exhibits on contemporary art and the archaeological past of the area. (☎ 161 43 30. Open Tu-Su 11am-5pm, special exhibits also Th 11am-8pm. €3, students €2, family €4. F Free. Tours Th 6pm.) The **Deutsches Brotmuseum,** Salzstadelg. 10, documents 6000 years of bread-making and waxes philosophical about "the *Leitmotif* of Man and Bread." Temporary exhibits with surprisingly diverse artwork fill the first and fourth floors. (☎ 699 55. Open daily 10am-5pm, W 10am-8:30pm. Last entrance 1hr. before closing. €3, students €2, family €8.) Max Bill's red-marble monument on Bahnhofstr., marks **Albert Einstein's birthplace;** the house itself gave way long ago to a modern cube of a bank.

On even years, during the **International Danube Festival,** the riverbanks fill with handcraft and food stalls, artists, and musicians from the countries that lie on the river's way to the Black Sea. (Next in 2006. ☎96 99 69 02; www.donaufest.de.) The mayor's annual oath to uphold the town constitution is an excuse for another round of festivities on the Danube during **Schwörmontag** (3rd M in July).

KARLSRUHE   ☎0721

By German standards, Karlsruhe (Karl's rest) was born yesterday. In 1715, Markgrave Karl Wilhelm built a castle retreat for himself and his mistresses. Inspired by the abundant sunshine, he designed a city with streets radiating out from the castle. This lively city is home to Germany's two highest courts, the **Bundesgerichtshof** (Federal Supreme Court) and the **Bundesverfassungsgericht** (Federal Constitutional Court), as well as Germany's oldest technical university.

▐▐ TRANSPORTATION AND PRACTICAL INFORMATION

From the station, the town center is a 25min. walk along Ettlinger Str. and Karl-Friedrich-Str., or a streetcar ride to "Marktpl." or "Europapl." (€1.90 per ride, 24hr. ticket €4, press "city" on the machine). For a **taxi,** call ☎914 94. The **tourist office,** Bahnhofpl. 6, across the street from the station, books rooms and distributes *Karlsruhe Extra,* a free, annually updated guide in English with great maps. (☎37 20 53 83; www.karlsruhe.de/tourismus. Open M-F 9am-6pm, Sa 9am-1pm.) A **branch office,** Karl-Friedrich-Str. 22, provides the same services, but is closer to town center. (☎37 20 53 76; tickets 250 00. Open M-F 9:30am-6:30pm, Sa 10am-3pm.) The Karlsruhe **WelcomeCard,** available at the tourist office, covers regional transportation for 2 days during the week or 3 on weekends, and admission to all museums for two days (€9.50). **Laundromat Waschhaus** is at the corner of Scheffelstr. and Sophienstr. (☎243 81 67. Wash €3.50. Soap €0.50. Dry €0.50 per 10min. Open M-Sa 6am-11pm.) A central **pharmacy** is **Stadt Apotheke,** Karlstr. 19. (☎235 77. Open M-F 8am-7:30pm, Sa 9am-6pm.) **Internet** is at **Ch@t,** Kaiserstr. 136-138. (☎249 58 57. €1.65 per 30min. Open M-Sa 11am-midnight, Su noon-midnight.) The **post office,** 76133 Karlsruhe, is inside the Post Galerie on Europapl. (Open M-F 9:30am-8pm, Sa 9:30am-4pm.)

■ 🏠 ACCOMMODATIONS AND FOOD

Karlsruhe's **Jugendherberge (HI) ❷**, Moltkestr. 24, is close to the Schloß, but far from the train station. Take streetcar 1 or 6 to "Europapl.," then walk to the end of Karlstr. and follow the signs (10min.). The sunny, spacious hostel is on the right, set back from the street. (☎282 48; www.jugendherberge-karlsruhe.de. Breakfast and sheets included. Reception 7:30-9am, 9:30am-noon, 4-8pm and 8:30-10:30pm. Curfew midnight; house key available with €5 deposit. 2-, 4-, or 6-bed dorms €20, under 27 €17.40.) **Pensions Zebra** and **Am Zoo ❸**, Ettlingerstr. 33, share an entrance and offer spacious, comfortable rooms close to the station and the Marktpl. (Zebra ☎352 47 01, Am Zoo 336 78; pension.zebra@freenet.de. Singles €26-40; doubles €42-55.) **Hotel Handelshof ❹**, Reinhold-Frank-Str. 46a, is on the boundary of the city center, next to Mülburger Tor. (☎91 20 90; HotelHandelshof@aol.com. All rooms with bath, phones, and TVs. Breakfast included. Singles €40-53; doubles €60-73.) Camp at **Turmbergblick ❶**, Tiengererstr. 40, in Durlach. Take streetcar 1 to "Durlach Turmberg," then turn back, take a right, and follow the signs. (15min. ☎49 72 36; www.azur-camping.de. Reception 9am-1pm and 3-10pm. Laundry €3. Dry €3. Open mid-Mar. to mid-Nov. €6 per person, €4.50 per child, €2.10 per tent, €4.60 per tent with car or RV. Free showers.)

Imbiße and ice-cream shops line Kaiserstr. and Marktpl. (burgers and *Wurst* €2-3). Buy produce at the **market** on Marktpl. (Open mid-Jan. to mid-Nov. M-F 9am-6pm, Sa 9am-2pm.) Many cafes on Ludwigspl. stay open until 1am. **Harmonie ❷**, Kaiserstr. 57, is a pub and *Biergarten*, featuring an amusing collection of vintage posters and good, cheap food. (☎384 31 12. Regional specialties €4.20-8.50. Beer €2-3.90. Open M-Th 11am-1am, F-Sa 11am-3am, Su 5pm-1am. Kitchen open 11am-3pm and 5-11pm.) **Pasta-Pasta ❷**, on the corner of Amalienstr. and Karlstr., serves up Italian specialities. During the week, 11am-3pm all pasta and 18" pizzas are €4.50. (☎247 62. Open Tu-Su 11am-4am.)

🅖 SIGHTS

In Karlsruhe, all roads lead to the classical yellow **Schloß** north of Marktpl. The impeccable **Schloßgarten** stretches out behind the castle for nearly half a kilometer. (Open daily until 10pm. Free.) The Schloß houses the **Badisches Landesmuseum,** with elaborate special exhibits and an extensive permanent collection of antiques, including the flashy **Türkenbeute,** a legacy of Turkish invaders. Beginning in Oct. 2005 it will host an exhibit on the Roman Empire. (☎926 65 14. Open Tu-Th 10am-5pm, F-Su 10am-6pm. €4, students €3, free F after 2pm.) Around the corner, the **Kunsthalle,** Hans-Thomas-Str. 2, and the **Kunsthalle Orangerie,** Hans-Thomas-Str. 6, are two smashing art museums. European masterpieces from the 15th to the 19th centuries adorn the Kunsthalle while the Orangerie contains a smaller collection of modern art. (☎926 33 59. Both open Tu-F 10am-5pm, Sa-Su 10am-6pm. €4, students €2.50. Orangerie only €2.50/€1.50.) The **Museum beim Markt,** Karl-Friedrich-Str. 6, dedicated to design and illustration after 1900, has a particularly fascinating Art Deco collection. (☎926 65 78. Open Tu-Th 11am-5pm, F-Su 10am-6pm. €2, students €1, family €4. Free F after 2pm, if there are no special exhibits. Combo ticket with Badisches Landesmuseum €4/€3/€8.) On the upper floors of a former mansion, the recently renovated **Prinz-Max-Palais,** Karlstr. 10, has a local history display with the first bicycle in the world. (☎133 42 34. Open Tu-W, F, Su 10am-6pm; Th 10am-8pm; Sa 2-6pm. Free.) Poets like von Scheffel and Hebel inhabit the adjoining **Museum für Literature.** (Same hours as Prinz-Max-Palais museum. Free.)

In late May, the appetizing **Brigande-Feschd** brings a huge display of dishes from local restaurants to Marktpl. Two weeks later, students clutch their steins at **Unifest,** the largest free open-air concert in Germany.

BADEN-BADEN   ☎07221

In its 19th-century heyday, the Baden-Baden's guest list read like a *Who's Who* of European nobility. Although its status has since declined, Baden-Baden remains primarily a playground for the well-to-do; minor royalty, nouveaux riches, and the like gather here all year to bathe in the mineral spas and drop fat sums of money in the elegant casino. The surprisingly affordable luxury baths and up-and-coming restaurants are good chances to indulge without spending huge sums of money.

▐ ▌ TRANSPORTATION AND PRACTICAL INFORMATION

The **train station** is 5km from town. Walk 1½hr. along a path, or take **bus** #201, 214, 216, 244, or 245 (dir.: Stadtmitte) from the station to "Leopoldspl." (€1.90; day pass €4). **Trains** to: **Frankfurt am Main** (1½hr., 1 per hr., €23.40); **Munich** (4hr., 1 every 2hr., €50-63); **Stuttgart** (1½hr., 1 per hr., €17). For a **taxi** call ☎53 888 or 621 12. The **tourist office** is inside the Trinkhalle on Kaiserallee. Take bus #201 to "Hindenburgpl." (☎27 52 00; www.baden-baden.de. Open M-Sa 10am-5pm, Su 2-5pm.) The **laundromat** is at Scheibenstr. 14. (☎248 19. Wash €4. Dry €3 per 5min. Open M-Sa 7:30am-9pm.) Get cash at the **ATM** at the "Leopoldspl." bus stop. Check **email** at the **Stadtbibliothek,** on Lange Str. near Hindenburgpl. (€2 per hr. Open Tu-W and F 10am-6pm, Th 11am-7pm, Sa 10am-1pm.) The **post office,** 76530 Baden-Baden, is in the Wagener store next to Hindenburgpl. (Open M-F 9:15am-7pm, Sa 9:15am-6pm.)

▌ ▐ ACCOMMODATIONS AND FOOD

Rooms in the center of town are expensive with few exceptions, and all hotels charge the *Kurtaxe* of €2.50 per day per person. The modern **Werner-Dietz-Jugendherberge (HI) ❷,** Hardenbergstr. 34, is between the station and the town center. Take bus #201, 205, or 216 to "Große-Dollen-Str." (€2) and follow the signs uphill for 10min. (☎522 23; jh-baden-baden@t-online.de. Sheets and breakfast included. Reception every hr. on the hr. 5-11pm. Curfew 11:30pm; house key available for €25 or ID deposit. Dorms €20.90, under 27 €17.90. Additional nights €17.70/€14.70.) **Hotel am Markt ❸,** Marktpl. 18, has comfy rooms in an ideal location between the Friedrichsbad and the Stiftskirche, close to the spas. (☎270 40; www.hotel-am-markt-baden.de. Breakfast included. Reception 7am-10pm. Singles €30-32, with shower €41-47; doubles with bath €58-62, with shower or bath €72-80; triples from €88.) **Hotel Laterne ❹,** Gernsbacher Str. 10-12, has luxurious rooms in a 300-year-old half-timbered house a few meters below the Rathaus. (☎299 99; fax 383 08. Breakfast included. Deposit or credit card number required with reservations. Singles €40-70; doubles €65-85.) **Altes Schloß ❸,** Alter Schloßweg 10, gives you a chance to live where nobles did: in a reconstructed wing of the **Hohenbaden** castle. The rooms are comfortable, and the atmosphere priceless. It's a 1hr. uphill trek on gravel roads, so a taxi (about €18 from the station, €12 from the town center) is recommended. (☎269 48; fax 39 17 75. Breakfast included. Singles €35, additional nights €28; doubles €70/€56; 1- to 4-person apartments €40 per person.) Most restaurants in Baden-Baden are far from cheap. For **groceries** head to **Pennymarkt,** at the "Grosse-Dollen-Str." bus stop near the hostel. (Open M-F 8am-8pm, Sa 8am-4pm.) **Pizzeria Roma ❸,** Gernsbacher Str. 14, offers affordable pasta (€6.50-8.50) right below the Rathaus. (☎251 51. Open M and W-F 11:30am-4pm and 5:30pm-midnight, Sa-Su 11:30am-midnight.) **Sindbad's Kebap-Haus ❷,** Seilerstr. 5, off Augustapl., sells Turkish meals for €2-8. Get the food to go, or sit on the terrace. (☎335 84. Open daily 10am-2am.) If you decide to climb to the **Altes Schloß ❹**, treat yourself to roast wild boar. (€13-15.50. Open daily 10am-9pm.)

☑ SPAS

Baden-Baden's history as a resort goes back nearly two millennia to the time when the Romans started soaking themselves in the area's **thermal baths**. The ☑**Friedrichsbad**, Römerpl. 1, is a beautiful 19th-century bathing palace where visitors are parched, steamed, soaked, scrubbed, doused, and pummeled by trained professionals for 3hr. Fifteen tubs of varying temperatures, as well as saunas, showers, and hot rooms, await nude bathers, and at the end everyone wraps up in pink blankets for a 30min. nap. Mark Twain put it best: "Here at Friedrichsbad you lose track of time within ten minutes and track of the world within twenty." (☎27 59 20; www.roemisch-irisches-bad.de. Open M-Sa 9am-10pm, Su noon-8pm. Last entry 2hr. before closing. Baths are co-ed; M and Th men and women bathe separately. Standard Roman-Irish bath €21, with soap and brush massage €29.) The invigorating **Caracalla-Thermen**, Römerpl. 1, next door, is cheaper, attracts a local crowd, and allows bathing suits, except in the saunas upstairs. (☎27 59 40; www.carasana.de. Open daily 8am-10pm. Last entry 9pm. Thermal bath €12 for 2hr., €14 for 3hr.) The **Hardberg** public **swimming pool** next to the hostel has a giant slide and five pools. (Open May-Sept. daily 10am-8pm in good weather. Last entry 7pm. €2.60, with *Kurkarte* €1.70; students €1.70.)

◎ ☑ SIGHTS AND HIKING

When they're not busy preening themselves at the baths, Baden-Baden's affluent guests head to the oldest **casino** in Germany, which movie star Marlene Dietrich called the "most beautiful casino in the world." You must be 21 in order to gamble here, men must wear a coat (rentals €8) and tie (€3), and women must avoid jeans or tennis shoes. (☎210 60. Open M-Th and Su 2pm-2am, F-Sa 2pm-3am. Entrance fee €3, min. bet €2.) There is no dress code for the **slot machine wing** downstairs (same hours as casino), or for the casino tour. (Tours 9:30-11:45am; €4, children €2.) Next to the casino, the massive Neoclassical **Trinkhalle** contains a marble fountain, souvenir shop, and a gallery of murals immortalizing local folktales. The free *Heilwasser* (healing water) is allegedly good for your health and tastes it: very warm and saline. (Open daily 10am-6:30pm. Free.) A few blocks in the opposite direction, down the paths of the verdant Lichtentaler Allee, the **Kunsthalle** showcases six to 10 modern art exhibits per year. (☎31 83 60. Open Tu-Su 11am-6pm, W until 8pm. Admission €5, students €3, children 6-16 €2.) For a pretty view of the surrounding valleys, head up the steep **Schloßstafeln** stairwell from Marktpl. to the **Neues Schloß**. Once the home of the Margraves of Baden, the castle now hosts the **Römische Sammlung**, which displays some of the area's Roman ruins. (☎93 22 72. Open daily 11am-5pm. €2, children €1.) For an exquisite view extending all the way to the French frontier, head to the 12th-century **Altes Schloß**. Its majestic ruins, the **Ruine Hohenbaden**, are accessible by the **trail** starting from behind the Neues Schloß. From the trailhead, glance at the visible Altes Schloß on your left for orientation. Head towards the wooden gazebo at the edge of the forest, then follow the trail that leads up and to the right; keep an eye out for *Altes Schloß* signs. For even more breathtaking views of the surrounding landscape, and to check out daring climbers, proceed to the **cliffs** ("Felsen" trails) above the Altes Schloß. Several trails connect the castle and the end of bus line #214 at **Eberstenburg** (about 15min. to Leopoldspl., 1-2 per hr., last bus down around 8pm).

Longer **hiking** trails traverse the 668m **Merkur** peak east of town. Take bus #204 or 205 from Leopoldpl. to "Merkurwald," then hike to the top, where a slew of trails plunge into the Schwarzwald. At the bottom, the 37km, more-or-less level **Panoramaweg** (marked by white signs with a green circle) connects the best lookout points. For a general idea of the trails pick up the "Outline map" at the tourist office (€1.50); for more serious hiking buy one of the tourist maps (€5).

FREIBURG IM BREISGAU ☎0761

It's not difficult to see why German *Luftwaffe* pilots mistakenly bombed their own city of Freiburg in May 1940. It is tucked in the far southwest corner of Germany, and looks rather French. Despite its status as the "metropolis" of the Schwarzwald, Freiburg and its students have yet to succumb to hectic rhythms. Paths link the medieval **Schwabentor** to the German trail network, and all traces of urbanity dissolve into serene countryside a few kilometers from the city.

TRANSPORTATION

Trains: To: **Basel** (1hr., 3 per hr., €11.60-15.40); **Karlsruhe** (1¾hr., 1 per hr., €19-28).

Public Transportation: Single fare on Freiburg's bus and streetcar lines €1.90. *Regio24* day pass €4.60; 2 people €6.50. Most transportation stops at 12:30am, but a system of **night buses** covers major stops through the night (€4 per ride; €2 with day pass; F-Su every hr. 1:30-4:30am). The streetcar stop at the train station is on the overpass.

Taxis: ☎55 55 55.

Bike Rental: Mobile, Wentzingerstr. 15 (☎292 79 98), the round wooden structure under the overpass. €7.50 per 6hr., €10 per day. Open daily 5:30am-1:30am.

Hitchhiking: *Let's Go* does not recommend hitchhiking as a safe mode of transportation. Hitchers have been known to take public transit to departure points: for points north, streetcar #5 (dir.: Zähringen) to "Reutebachg." and walk back 50m; for points east: streetcar #1 (dir.: Littenweiler) to "Maria-Hilf-Kirche."

ORIENTATION AND PRACTICAL INFORMATION

The city's sights and restaurants are concentrated in the Altstadt, a 10min. walk from the main train station down tree-lined Eisenbahnstr. to Rathauspl.

Tourist Office: Rotteckring 14 (☎388 18 80; www.freiburg.de). Take the underpass from the station, then walk 2 blocks down Eisenbahnstr. Office books rooms for a €2.55 fee and has free city maps. 24hr. automated displays in front of the office and the train station can help you find lodging as well. Open June-Sept. M-F 9:30am-8pm, Sa 9:30am-5pm, Su 10am-noon; Oct.-May M-F 9:30am-6pm, Sa 9:30am-2pm, Su 10am-noon.

Currency Exchange: The closest to the train station is the **Volksbank** across from the main entrance. Open M-W and F 8am-4:30pm, Th 8am-6pm. **24hr. ATM.** The **Volksbank** at the Martinstor has an **exchange** machine and **ATMs.** Open daily 6am-1am.

Gay Resources: Rosa Hilfe, Eschholzstr. 19 (☎251 61).

Laundromat: Wasch&Fun, Egonstr. 25 (☎28 72 94), behind the train station. Wash €3. Soap €0.50. Dry €2. For €5.50 they will wash, dry, and fold your laundry for you; pick it up the next day. Open M-Sa 9am-10pm; laundry service until 5pm.

Public Restrooms: At Augustinerpl., under the stone terrace.

Emergency: Police: ☎110. **Fire and Ambulance:** ☎112.

Rape Crisis Hotline: ☎285 85 85.

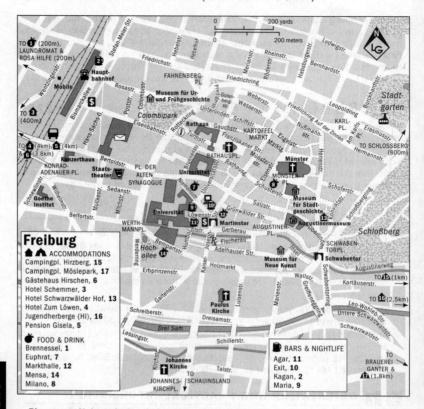

Freiburg

▲ A ACCOMMODATIONS
Campingpl. Hirzberg, **15**
Campingpl. Möslepark, **17**
Gästehaus Hirschen, **6**
Hotel Schemmer, **3**
Hotel Schwarzwälder Hof, **13**
Hotel Zum Löwen, **4**
Jugendherberge (HI), **16**
Pension Gisela, **5**

🍴 FOOD & DRINK
Brennessel, **1**
Euphrat, **7**
Markthalle, **12**
Mensa, **14**
Milano, **8**

▶ BARS & NIGHTLIFE
Agar, **11**
Exit, **10**
Kagan, **2**
Maria, **9**

Pharmacy: Holzmarkt-Apotheke, Kaiser-Joseph-Str. 255 (☎313 21), is by the Martinstor, on Holzmarkt. Open M-Tu and Th 9am-7pm, W and F 9am-6:30pm, Sa 9am-2pm.

Internet Access: Ping-Wing, Niemensstr. 3, (☎409 87 32), near Martinstor. €1.20 per 15min.; M-Sa after 6pm €1.50 per 30min. Open M-F 11am-9pm, Sa 10am-8pm.

Post Office: Eisenbahnstr. 56-58, 79098 Freiburg. 1 block straight ahead from the train station. Open M-F 8am-6:30pm, Sa 8am-2pm.

🏠 ACCOMMODATIONS AND CAMPING

🏨 **Pension Gisela,** Am Vogelbach 27 (☎89 78 980; www.hausgisela.com). From the station, take streetcar 1 to Padua-Allee, then bus #10 (dir.: Au) to "Hofackerstr." Continue to "Im Wolfswinkel" and follow the signs. Luxurious studios or 2-room apartments, stocked with the owner's homemade jams. Phone and TV, kitchen, bath, and plenty of insider Freiburg tips. Within 10min. of a small lake and park. Laundry service €3. Singles €38; doubles €48; 2-room apartments €62, for 3 people €68, 4 people €72. ❹

Jugendherberge (HI), Kartäuserstr. 151 (☎676 56; www.jugendherberge-freiburg.de). Bus #1 to "Lassbergstr." Take a left and then a right onto Fritz-Geiges-Str. The signs will take you from there (800m). Rampant schoolchildren sleep in packed, brightly colored rooms. In-house disco or movie nights. Breakfast and sheets included. Reception every hr. on the hr. Check-in after 1pm. Curfew 2am. Dorms €22.50, under 27 €19; doubles €24.50; additional nights €19.10/€16.40/€21.40. ❷

Hotel Zum Löwen, Breisgauer Str. 62 (☎809 72 20 or 846 61; fax 840 23). Take streetcar #1 to "Padua-Allee," then bus #19, 31 or 32 to "Kirchbergstr." Or, backtrack 20m along the tracks and walk down Breisgauer Str. for 5min. Marble floors defy the budget prices. Enter through the parking lot; the front door leads to a more expensive guesthouse. Breakfast included, most rooms with TVs. Singles €35; doubles €55-85. ❸

Hotel Schemmer, Eschholzstr. 63 (☎20 74 90; fax 207 49 50). Behind the station: over the overpass, past the church and to the left. Beautiful rooms, some with balconies. Breakfast included. Reception M-F 7am-7pm, Sa-Su 7-11am and 4-7pm. Singles €35-37, with shower €39-45; doubles €49-62; triples €66-€78; quads €85. ❸

Gästehaus Hirschen, Breisgauer Str. 47 (☎821 18; fax 879 94). Down the street from Hotel Zum Löwen. An old farmhouse in a quiet neighborhood featuring cozy rooms with TVs. Singles €28, with bath €42; doubles €45/€57. ❸

Hotel Schwarzwälder Hof, Herrenstr. 43 (☎380 30; www.hotel-schwarzwaelderhof.de). Comfortable and well-stocked rooms 2 blocks north of the Schwabentor. Breakfast included. Singles €36-59; doubles €65-89; triples €100; family suite €120-160. ❹

Camping: Möslepark, Waldseestr. 77 (☎729 38; fax 775 78). S1 to "Stadthalle." Head south on Möslestr., cross the tracks, and keep going straight on Waldseestr. past the park (about 15min.). Ideally situated for either roughing it on the beautiful hiking trails or pampering yourself at the neighboring *Waldkurbad* (M-Sa 9:30am-11pm, Su 9:30am-10pm). Wash and dry €6.65. Reception 8am-noon and 3:30-10pm. Open Mar.-Oct. €5 per person, €1.60-2.60 per child. €2.10-2.60 per tent, €5 with car. ❶

Camping: Hirzberg, Kartäuserstr. 99 (☎350 54; www.freiburg-camping.de), is a 20min. walk from the Altstadt. S1 to "Stadthalle," then take the underpass to the left and walk through the park. (If you reach the train tracks, you are going in the wrong direction). Cross the river and go straight. After the 2nd bridge, turn left; it will be on the right side. Multilingual staff. Kitchen €0.50 per 30min. Summer tent rental €5-10. Bikes €8 per day. **Internet** €1 per 10min. Wash €2.50. Dry €2.50. Reception 8am-1pm and 3-9:30pm; July-Aug. until 10pm. €5 per person, €2 per child, €3-4 per tent. ❶

🄵 FOOD

With more than 23,000 university students to feed, Freiburg's budget eateries dominate the city. During the daytime, the **Freiburger Markthalle**, next to the Martinstor, is home to foodstands serving ethnic specialties for €3-7. The main entrance is one block up on Grünwälderstr. (☎38 11 11. Open M-F 7am-7pm, Sa 7am-4pm.)

Brennessel, Eschholzstr. 17 (☎28 11 87), behind the station, serves specialties from ostrich to pancakes (€1.80-9.20). Funk and jazz abound. Open M-Sa 6pm-1am, Su 5pm-1am. Kitchen open until 12:30am, but only 4 meals available after 11:30pm. ❷

Euphrat, Niemensstr. 13, prepares tasty Middle-Eastern plates and wraps in fresh tortillas (€2.50-6.50). Open M-F 11am-midnight, Sa 11am-1am, Su noon-midnight. ❷

Milano, Schusterstr. 7 (☎337 35), 1 block from Münsterpl. With its leather and brass interior, this *ristorante* feels more upscale than it costs. Delicious pizza and pasta (€4-10) served with Italian flair. Open daily 11am-midnight. ❷

Mensa: Hochallee, Rempartstr. 18. 3 kinds of meal tickets buy everything from soup to full meals (€3.10-4.40, students €2.05-2.55). No cash; a card must be obtained from the Mensa Service Point on Hochallee for a €7 deposit. Open M-F 11:30am-2pm and 5:30-7:30pm, Sa 11:30am-1:30pm. ❶

GOBLIN BREAD?

Though not a utopia for vegetarians, Baden Württemburg is the *Musterländle* (model region) of German cuisine. Its Swabian cuisine is best known for *Maultaschen*, ravioli-like pockets of meat and spinach, often served in broth. Swabians combine simple, fresh ingredients into hearty meat and potato dishes. Swabian baking (sweet, flour-based *Mehlspeisen*) is also delectable.

Rarely absent from a Swabian meal is the steaming, buttery dish known as *Spätzle*. These traditional flour and egg noodles are made by hand and scraped from the cutting board into boiling water, where they form into noodles. A particularly delightful version is *Käsespätzle*, in which the noodles are baked with layers with cheese. In Baden Württemburg, *Spätzle* are often served with *Linsen* (lentils) flavored with spices and ham. Another trademark dish of Baden Württemburg, especially in Stuttgart, is *Gaisburger Marsch*, a stew of *Spätzle* with diced beef, potatoes, vegetables, and fried onions.

A goblin in Stuttgart invented another famous local food, *Hutzelbrot*, according to 19th-century poet Eduard Möricke. This "wrinkled" bread, served at Christmas, is made from an assortment of dried fruits. During the rest of the season, visitors and locals alike may indulge in *Apfelküchle mit Eis*: apple and yeast dough baked into little round cakes and topped with ice cream.

🜲 SIGHTS

In only one night in 1944, the Allies finished the bombing job the *Luftwaffe* had mistakenly started, obliterating most of the old city. Since then, the citizens of Freiburg have painstakingly recreated the city's architecture and public spaces.

MÜNSTER. Freiburg's pride and joy is its majestic cathedral, which towers 116m over the Platz. With sections constructed between the 13th and 16th centuries, this architectural melange immortalizes in stained glass the different medieval guilds that financed its construction. Trudge up 209 steps to the ticket counter (the windows on the way up afford a free view), then climb 126 more to ascend the tower. (☎ 298 59 63. *Open M-Sa 9:30am-5pm, Su 1-5pm. Tours M-F 2-3pm, Sa-Su 2:30-3:30pm. Tower open M-Sa 9:30am-5pm, Su 1-5pm. €1.50, students €1, under 12 €0.50.*)

SCHLOßBERG. From the Schwabentor, take the overpass across the busy Schloßbergring and climb the **Schloßberg** for a superb view of the city. Or, reach the **Oberer Schloßberg** on the cable car from the Stadtgarten at Leopoldring. (*Open Apr.-Oct. daily 11am-7pm; Nov.-Mar. W-Su 11am-5pm. Round-trip €3.60, ages 4-14 €2.60.*) To get to the top on foot, start at Schloßbergring across from Hermannstr. (20min.).

AUGUSTINERMUSEUM. A good bet for old art enthusiasts, the Augustiner impresses with medieval sculpture and art and heart-warming depictions of Schwarzwald life, set in a 13th-century monastery. (*Augustiner at Augustinerpl. in an old monastery 2 blocks south of the Münster. ☎ 201 25 31. Open Tu-Su 10am-5pm. €2, students €1, family €4.*)

MUSEUM FÜR UR- UND FRÜHGESCHICHTE. The immaculate, early Victorian *Colombischlößle* sits atop a hill of vineyards and flowers. Inside, myriad odds and ends track the fascinating history of the South Baden region from the stone age to early medieval times. (*Rotteckring 5. In Colombipark across from the tourist office. ☎ 201 25 71. Open Tu-Su 10am-5pm. €2, student €1. English guide €1.50.*)

OTHER SIGHTS. On the south side of Münsterpl. is the red **Kaufhaus,** a merchants' hall dating from the 1500s. Two medieval gates stand within blocks of each other in the southeast corner of the Altstadt. The **Schwabentor,** at the bottom of the Schloßberg, houses a museum of tin figurines illustrating the numerous battles in the area. (☎ 243 21. *Open mid-May to Sept. Tu-F 2:30-5pm, Sa-Su noon-2pm. €1.20, students €0.50, children €0.30.*) The **Martinstor,** which served as a revolutionary barricade in the politically tumultuous year of 1848, is now a McDonald's.

🎵 🎭 ENTERTAINMENT AND NIGHTLIFE

Freiburg is a city of wine and music, awash in *Weinstuben* and *Kneipen*, though clubs are less abundant. For current events listings, pick up a free copy of *Freiburg Aktuell* from the tourist office, or drop by the *Badische Zeitung* office, Bertoldstr. 7, off Universitätstr., where you can buy tickets for upcoming fêtes. (☎555 66 56. Open M-F 9am-7pm, Sa 9am-2pm.) The **Freiburger Theater**, Bertholdstr. 46, holds plays, ballets, musicals and concerts. (☎201 23 50; www.freiburgertheater.de. Ticket office open Tu-F 10am-6pm, Sa 10am-1pm.) The **Freiburger Weinfest** is held on Münsterpl. the first weekend in July. Sample some 400 different vintages (€1.50-3 per glass) to live swing music. The two-week international **Zelt-Musik-Festival** (tent music festival; early July) brings big-name classical, rock, and jazz acts to two circus tents at the city's edge. Tickets (€8-20) sell fast and can be bought over the phone (☎50 40 30; www.zmf.de), or through the *Badische Zeitung* office. Take streetcar #5 to "Bissierstr." and catch the free shuttle to the site.

Freiburg's nightlife keeps pace with its students—afternoon cafes become pubs and discos by night. The scene centers around the streets near the university: **Niemensstraße, Löwenstraße, Humboldtstraße**, and the nearby alleyways.

Agar, Löwenstr. 8 (☎38 06 50; www.agar-disco.de), next to Martinstor. Beer €3, drinks €5.50. Th 80s night; other nights range from house to hip-hop. 18+. Cover €3, weekends €4. Tu free with student ID, Su over 30 free. Open Tu and Th 10pm-3am, F-Sa 11pm-4am, Su 10pm-2am. Last entry 1hr. before closing.

Maria, Löwenstr. 3-5 (☎217 22 04). A stylish bar usually packed full with students. Through the back door is the smaller, quieter **R&B.** Beer €1.80-3, drinks €4-6, cocktails from €5.90, half-price 6-9pm. Both open M-Sa 9am-1am, Su 11am-1am. Bar open summer Su at 4pm.

Exit, Kaiser-Joseph-Str. 248 (☎365 36; www.exit-freiburg.de). A thick layer of sand is the perfect foundation for each summer's month-long beach party. Summer special: beer €0.50 on tap. Cover around €3. Open M, W, F-Sa 10pm-5am.

Kagan, Bismarckallee 9 (☎767 27 66; www.kagan-lounge.de). The top 2 floors of the Sonnenturm next to the Bahnhof host a fashionable bar and lounge at night. Beer €2.60-4.50. Cocktails €6.50-8.50. Su Salsa night. W and F-Sa 20+ only. Cover €8, Th €5, Su €2-3. Open W 9pm-3am, Th-F 10pm-4am, Sa 10pm-3am.

🥾 HIKING

Freiburg's plentiful accommodations and easy access by train make it a superior base for hikes in the Schwarzwald. **Mountain biking** trails also traverse the hills; look for symbols with bicycles (maps €3.50-6 at tourist office). The **Schwarzwaldverein** office, Schloßbergring 15, provides trail information. (☎38 05 30; www.schwarzwaldverein.de. Open M-Th 8am-noon and 2-4pm, F 8am-noon.)

A good starting spot in Freiburg is **Schauinsland**. Take streetcar #4 (dir.: Günterstal) to "Dorfstr." (15min. from Hauptbahnhof; 1 per 10min.), then bus #21 to "Talstation" (7min., 2 per hr.). From the station, the red circle trail takes you to the top (3hr.), or ride the spectacular 3.6km **Bergbahn**. On top is the **Bergwelt Schauinsland**, with a wildlife park and 🪨 **mining museum**. Guides here fit visitors with helmets, head lanterns, and gloves before taking them down slippery metal ladders into the mountain. The tour explores 800 years of mining history with demonstrations and detailed descriptions of the muddy, narrow passages and huge caverns. Wear closed-toe, waterproof shoes that can get dirty. (☎264 68; 1½ and 2½hr. tours W and Sa-Su 11am and 2pm. €17.50/€23.) It also offers a 7km downhill roller ride and varied hiking and biking trails. (☎29 29 30. Bergbahn runs May-Sept. 9am-6pm; Oct.-Apr. 9:30am-5pm. Round-trip €10.20, students €8.60, ages 6-14. €5.60. Roller ride €20.) Take the red-dot trail down (2hr.). Simple maps are free at the bottom.

Slightly longer, the yellow circle trail from the top of the mountain connects "Schauinsland Gipfel," "Rappeneck," and "Kappel," after which you can take the bus #17 back to Freiburg (4hr.). A **Rundweg** also takes you from the top station in a panoramic circle around the top (1hr.). Trails around Schauinsland are loaded with forested vistas of Freiburg and the Schwarzwald.

For a **day hike**, part of the red-diamond **Westweg Pforzheim-Basel** to Feldberg runs just a couple of hours from Schauinsland. The hike requires about 7hr. from **Schauinsland** to **Feldberg-Bärental** and shows a cross-section of the Schwarzwald—cow pastures, barns, and soaring trees. Particularly noteworthy are the scenic meadows and thick forest between Feldberg and Notschrei. To reach the trail from Schauinsland top station, take a right and head down the driveway to the parking lot. Follow the blue diamond trail to Halden and keep going; it meets the red-diamond Westweg between Halden and Notschrei (3-4hr.).

 GRABBING THE WEED BY ITS THORNS. There is a reason German hikers wear those untrendy wool socks hiked up to their knees: a little weed known as **Brennessel** (stinging nettles). These waist-high weeds grow in clusters across the German landscape, and are recognizable by long, saw-toothed leaves and furry yellow bunches. The leaves and stems are covered with needle-like thorns that snag an unsuspecting hiker's flesh and inject formic acid, the same poison in bee and ant stings. A few minutes later, the spot will burn unmercifully and develop a **tingling red rash with white circular bumps.** The pain will stop in around 20min. and the rash, which doesn't spread, will disappear in a day or so on its own, but both can be averted using the nettle itself. The juicy pulp of the plant's leaves, if rubbed on a sting immediately, is said to prevent a rash from forming. Needless to say, it's advisable to put a layer of cloth or paper between your skin and the leaves you are mushing.

Those who don't harbor grudges against the plant find nettles to be quite useful. The leaves cook like spinach to make a tasty dish, and when dried and steeped in hot water they brew a tea rich in vitamin C. During WWI, the German army used fibers from the plant to make uniforms, and more recently, Italian designers have been using nettles to make fashionable (non-stinging) blue jeans.

BREISACH AND THE KAISERSTUHL ☎07667

Twenty-five kilometers west of Freiburg, Breisach is separated from French Alsace by the Rhein. The beautiful Altstadt is in an exquisite location, surrounded by unending vineyards. Near Breisach is the **Kaiserstuhl**, a clump of lush hills that used to be volcanoes. Now they attract hikers who come to see the unique flora and fauna usually found in warmer climes.

◰ **TRANSPORTATION. Trains** arrive from **Freiburg** (30min., every 30min., €4.60). The Freiburg-Breisach train also stops at the towns of Ihringen and Wasenweiler, both on the Kaiserstuhl's southern fringes. **Buses** handle the route straight into the hills; check the schedule at the Breisach Hauptbahnhof (☎361 72; www.suedbadenbus.de). Rent **bikes** at **Firma Schweizer**, Richard-Müller-Str. 22, behind the main pedestrian drag. (☎76 01. €10 per day. Open M-F 9am-12:30pm and 2-6:30pm, Sa 9am-1pm.) Jaunts along the Rhein in big white **boats** are available through **Breisacher Fahrgastschifffahrt**, Rheinuferstr., on the Rhein. Occasional trips to: **Basel** (€45, children €23); **Colmart** (€26/€13); **Strassburg**

(Strasbourg) (€45/€23.) Buy tickets at the dock or tourist office. (☎94 20 10; www.bfs-info.de. M-F 9am-5:30pm. 1 or 2hr. rides €6.50-8, children €3-4; check the webpage for schedule.)

◪ PRACTICAL INFORMATION. For hiking, biking, and town maps, visit the Breisach **tourist office**, Marktpl. 16. From the train station, turn left onto Bahnhofstr., follow Neutorpl. right from the rotary intersection, keep the fountain on your right, and go down Rheinstr. into the Marktpl. (☎94 01 55; www.breisach.de. M-F 9am-12:30pm and 1:30-6pm, Sa 10am-1pm; Nov.-Mar. M-F 9am-12:30pm and 1:30-5pm.) The **Volksbank**, across from the station, has an international **ATM**. (Bank open M and F 8am-noon and 2-4:30pm, Tu and Th 8am-noon and 2-6pm, W 8am-noon; ATM open daily 5am-midnight.) The Stadt-Apotheke **pharmacy**, Neutorstr. 2, is down the street from Marktpl. (☎218. Open M-F 8am-6:30pm, Sa 8am-1pm.) Follow the "Postamt" signs for the **post office**, Richard-Müller-Str. 3a, 79206 Breisach. (Open M-F 9am-12:30pm and 2:30-6pm, Sa 9am-12:30pm.)

◪◪ ACCOMMODATIONS AND FOOD. Breisach's modern **Jugendherberge ❷**, Rheinuferstr. 12, boasts a stunning riverside location and charming stone rooms, most with baths, and many with a wonderful view of the Rhein. From the train station, take a left and then go left again at the rotary intersection. Take the path leading under the main road and cross the bridge, then turn right and walk along the river. Turn left at the hostel sign; it's the third house down the road. (15min. ☎76 65; www.jugendherberge-breisach.de. Sheets included. **Internet** €1 per 12 min. Wash €3 (hang dry). Reception 7am-11pm. Curfew 11:30pm, but housekey available for €10 deposit. Call ahead to reserve. Dorms €21.40, under 27 €18.70; singles €26.10/€23.40; Some doubles available for no extra charge.) A farmer's **market** sets up on Marktpl. (Sa 9am-1pm). The **Bahnhofsgaststätte ❸**, in the train station, has good prices entrees (€5-10) and a large collection of military medals. (☎15 76. Open M-F 10am-midnight, full menu 11:30am-2:30pm and 5:30-10pm.) For some *Flammkuchen* and appetizers (€3.30-6) try **Humpen ❷**, Neutorstr. 20. (☎91 26 25. Open Su-Th 11am-midnight, F-Sa 11-2am; winter closed Su.)

◪◪◪ SIGHTS, ENTERTAINMENT AND HIKING. Breisach's **St. Stephansmünster** towers dramatically over a steep riverfront promontory crowded with clapboard houses. Constructed between the 12th and 15th centuries, the church's interior is plain compared to nearby cathedrals, but the remnants of the church's frescoes are beautiful, and the wooden altar, the work of the 16th-century Master Hans Loy, is stunningly intricate. Take a look at the unusual open crypt supporting the base of the choir area; since the hilltop was too small for the cathedral, it was extended with this graceful space. The stone wreath of thorns around the central pillar is a war memorial. (Church open daily summer 9am-6pm; winter 9am-5pm.)

The **Radbrunnenallee** runs from the Münster to the **Schloßberg** garden, which has panoramic views of the countryside. The entrance to the garden is on Tullag., next to Kapuziner Hotel. Down the hill in the 17th-century **Rheintor**, the **Museum für Stadtgeschichte**, Rheintorpl. 1, contains a large collection of artifacts, including 3000-year-old ceramics and chain-link skivvies from 15th-century northern Italy. (☎70 89. Open Tu-F 2-5pm, Sa 11:30am-5pm, Su 11:30am-6pm. Free.) In summer, the **Schloßberg** garden becomes a theater for the annual **Festspiele**, hosting plays most weekends between mid-June and mid-September. (Call the tourist office for tickets, ☎90 77 60. €8-12, students €7-11.) Breisach also hosts the **Weinfest Kaiserstuhl und Tuniberg,** during the last weekend in August, when local wines are sipped on the banks of the Rhein. Wine connoisseurs can register for a tour of **Badischer**

Winzerkeller, Zum Kaiserstuhl 16 (☎90 02 70), one of the largest wine cellars in Europe. The cellar is a 1km walk east of town. From the train station, go right on Bahnhofstr. and head to the very end of Im Gelbstein (3-7 samples €3-5).

The most famous of the Kaiserstuhl's lush trails (maps €5-7) is the **Kaiserstuhl Nord-Südweg,** which braves the overgrown hills and valleys, forging from Ihringen 16km northward to Endingen. From the Ihringen train station, turn left and walk past Hotel Luise; the first trailpost is on your right. The Nord-Südweg is marked by a blue diamond on a yellow field. The last leg of the 108km long **Querweg Donaueschingem-Breisach** also winds through the hills; the trail is marked by a red diamond on yellow. For information on other trails, visit the Breisach tourist office.

SCHWARZWALD (BLACK FOREST)

It might be an overstatement to say that Germans are obsessed with the macabre, but from the earliest fairy tales, a sense of the sinister has lurked in the German consciousness. This collective mystique finds a home in the Schwarzwald, a tangled expanse of evergreen covering the southwest corner of Baden-Württemberg. The forest owes its name to the eerie darkness that prevails under its canopy of vegetation, and was the source of inspiration for many German fairy tales, including *Hänsel and Gretel*, and a slew of poetry and folk traditions. Many of these regional quirks, from cuckoo clocks to *Lederhosen*, are now exploited at ubiquitous kiosks, which conspire to erode the region's authenticity.

Myriad trails wind through the hills, leading willing hikers into secluded parts of the forest. Skiing is also available in the area; the longest slope is at Feldberg, near Titisee. The main entry points to the Schwarzwald are Freiburg, in the center; Baden-Baden to the northwest; Stuttgart to the east; and Basel, Switzerland, to the southwest. Most visitors use a bike, as public transportation is sparse. Rail lines encircle the perimeter, with only two train lines cutting through the region. Bus service is more thorough, but is slow and less frequent.

HOCHSCHWARZWALD (HIGH BLACK FOREST) ☎07655

Enthralling and still, the Hochschwarzwald is named for its high, pine-carpeted mountains, towering above lonely lakes and remote villages. The best source of information for the area is the **Schwarzwaldverein** office in Freiburg (☎0761 38 05 30. Open M-Th 8am-noon and 2-4pm, F 8am-noon.).

At 1493m, the **Feldberg** is the Schwarzwald's tallest mountain. The tourist office, Kirchg. 1, offers information about the Feldberg and 16 other ski slopes in the area. (☎80 19; www.feldberg-schwarzwald.de. Open Tu-F 10am-6pm, Sa-Su 10am-noon.) The Westweg Pforzheim-Basel runs over the Feldberg as well. From the Feldberg-Bärental train station follow the blue circle trail to the glacial Feldsee (2hr.), then pick up the red diamond Westweg to the Feldberg (2hr.). The **Feldbergbahn** ski lift will carry you part of the way (€6, children €4.50; lift open daily 9am-5pm). On a clear day, the Swiss Alps are visible, along with an alarming, unfenced drop into the Feldsee. Several paths extend from the top, including trails to Titisee. The gentle 30min. hike back down to the ski lift station is magnificent in the early summer, when it winds through the meadows of fragrant white *Edelweiß* and red, yellow, and purple wildflowers. Sporadic bus service also runs from Titisee via the train station to **Feldbergerhof,** right next to the ski lift. (Bus #7300; 15min., about 6 per day, €1.80. Dec.-Apr. also a **Skibus,** €13 per day.). The tourist office is in the ground floor of the Feld-

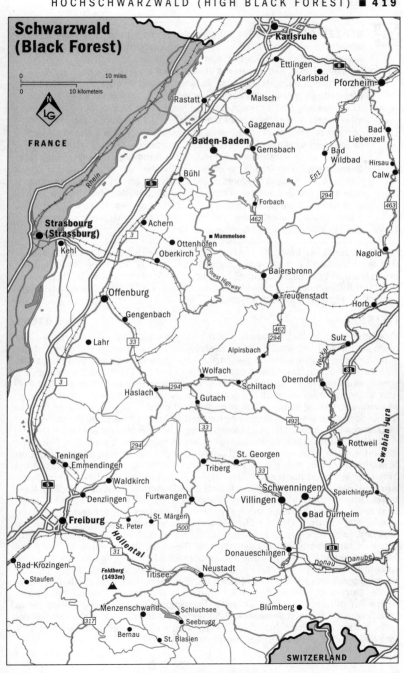

Schwarzwald
(Black Forest)

0 _____ 10 miles
0 _____ 10 kilometers

N
LG

FRANCE

Karlsruhe

Ettlingen

Karlsbad

Pforzheim

8

Malsch

Rastatt

Gaggenau

Bad
Liebenzell

Baden-Baden

Gernsbach

Bad
Wildbad

Hirsau

Calw

Bühl

Forbach

Enz

294

Achern

462

Mummelsee

463

Strasbourg
(Strassburg)

3

Kehl

Ottenhöfen

Oberkirch

Nagold

Black Forest Highway

Baiersbronn

Offenburg

Freudenstadt

Horb

Gengenbach

Sulz

Lahr

33

Alpirsbach

462
294

Oberndorf

81

Wolfach

Schiltach

Haslach

294

Gutach

Neckar

33

492

Rottweil

Teningen

St. Georgen

Swabian Jura

Emmendingen

Triberg

33

Waldkirch

Schwenningen

Spaichingen

Denzlingen

Furtwangen

Villingen

Freiburg

St. Peter

St. Märgen

Bad Dürrheim

500

Höllental

31

Donaueschingen

81

Bad-Krozingen

Feldberg
(1493m)

Titisee

Neustadt

Donau

(Danube)

Staufen

Menzenschwand

Schluchsee

Blumberg

317

Seebrugg

Bernau

St. Blasien

SWITZERLAND

Rhein

5

BADEN-
WÜRTTEMBERG

BLAZES OF GLORY. The Schwarzwald may be a hiker's paradise, but its labyrinth of twisting trails can quickly become a tangled hell. The *Schwarzwaldverein* (Black Forest Association) has set up a system of markers for the major trails in the area. **Red or part-red diamonds on a white field** mark the north-south summit trails, including the 285km Westweg Pforzheim-Basel odyssey. **Diamonds on yellow fields** denote east-west trails, the longest of which is the 178k, Querweg Freiburg-Bodensee. Together with the **blue diamond** trails that mark access routes, these trails often involve a lot of climbing and rewarding panoramas. The Schwarzwaldverein is also introducing **yellow diamond** markers for the major local trails to complement or replace local marking systems. Local trails are often eccentrically named, but a **Rundweg** is always a loop; a **Seerundweg,** which follows the shoreline of a lake, will be less taxing. Paths with stunning views of the surrounding landscape are called **Panoramaweg.** After trail junctions and intersections, look for a trail marker 50m down the path to confirm you are on the right track. If there is no sign at the intersection, always continue straight. New trail maps are forthcoming; for now, Atasco or Kompas hiking maps are often the best bet.

bergerhof hotel. At 1234m above sea level, Feldberg's **Jugendherberge Hebelhof (HI) ❷**, Passhöhe 14, may be the highest in Germany. Take the Freiburg-Seebrugg train to Feldberg-Bärental (1 per hr., €4.35), then the bus to "Hebelhof." (☎221; info@jugendherberge-feldberg.de. Sheets €3.10. Reception 8am-10pm. Curfew 10:45pm. Dorms €20.10, under 27 €17.40.)

TITISEE   ☎07651

The Titisee and Schluchsee are two of the most beautiful lakes in the region. The more scenic and touristed Titisee (TEE-tee-zay) is mobbed by Germans on hot summer days, and its lakeside pedestrian zone throngs with souvenir shops and *Imbiße*. The 30min. train ride from Freiburg (2 per hr., €4.60) glides through the scenic **Höllental** (Hell's Valley). Between the **Hintergarten** and **Himmelreich** (heavenly kingdom) train stops, in a gap of sky in the midst of tunnels, watch for the **Hirschsprung,** a regal statue of a stag crowning the cliff in a narrow part of the valley. According to legend, a deer once escaped its hunter by making the impossible leap across the chasm. The placid **Seerundweg** (1½hr.) is nice for a relaxing stroll.

Titisee's **tourist office,** Strandbadstr. 4, books rooms for a small fee. From the station, hang a right onto Parkstr., left across the square and another right on Strandbadstr. The office is in the *Kurhaus* (☎980 40; www.titisee.de. Open May-Oct. M-F 8am-noon and 1:30-5:30pm, Sa 11am-1pm, Su 10am-noon; Nov.-Apr. M-F 8am-noon and 1:30-5pm.) Hiking trails start in front of the office. Rent **boats** from vendors along Seestr. (Paddleboats from €4 per 30min.) Guided **boat tours** depart from the same area, run by **Bootsverleih Schweizer.** (☎82 14. 25min. €4, children €1.50.) There's a **pharmacy** on the corner of Seestr. and Jägerstr. (☎82 02. Open M-F 8:30am-12:30pm and 1:30-6pm, Sa 8:30am-2:30pm.) Titisee's **Jugendherberge (HI) Veltishof am Titisee ❷**, Bruderhalde 27, is on the lake 2km outside of town. Continue on Strandbadstr. past the tourist office or take bus #7300 (1 per 1-2hr. until 6pm) to "Jugendherberge." (☎238; www.jugendherberge-titisee-veltishof.de. For reception, ring the bell 8:30am-10pm. Dorms €20.10, under 27 €17; plus €1 *Kurtaxe*.) Contact the tourist office for details regarding Titisee's 4 **campgrounds** and many **private rooms** (starting at €13). **Hotel Someneck ❹**, Parkstr. 2, a 2min. walk to the right of the train station, has clean, luxurious rooms with well-stocked minibars and TVs. (☎82 46. €32-57 per person depending on season.)

SCHLUCHSEE   ☎ 07656

If the tourist density in Titisee is too intense, head south to the Schluchsee, home to a snarl of first-rate hiking trails. The simple **Seerundweg** circumvents the lake (18km, about 4hr.; red dot markers). More difficult and rewarding trails depart from the **Sportplatz** parking lot, a 15min. walk up Dresselbacherstr. past the huge resort hotel. For a 15km, 3-4hr. trek, follow Kreuzwaldweg to the **Vogelhaus,** home to a traditional workshop. (☎13 47. Open Tu-Su 1-6pm. Free.) Then follow the yellow diamond signs for **Hingerhäuser, Fischbach, Bildstein,** and **Aha** before returning to Schluchsee. For a great view of the lake, climb to the **Riesenbühlturm** tower: from Dresselbacherstr. take either the red diamond marked Mittelweg (steep climb) or the Kreuzwaldweg (longer) until you come across signs for the tower. Cruise around the lake on the **Seerundfahrten T. Toth,** which runs **boat trips** between Schluchsee, Seebrugg, and Aha. (☎92 30; www.seerundfahrten.de. May-Oct. daily every hr. 10am-5pm; less frequent trips 11am-5pm off-season. 1hr. ride €5.50, children €1.50-3.) **Boat rentals** are available at the Seerundfahrten dock. From the train station, cross the tracks, turn left facing the lake and follow the path (☎0171 72 37. Open mid-May to mid-Oct. daily 8:30am-6pm. Paddleboats and rowboats from €6 per hr., additional person €0.50.) The **Aqua Fun Spaßbad,** with a heated pool, big waterslide, a playground, and a beach, is next to the docks (☎571. Open May-Sept. daily 9am-7pm. €3.80, students €2).

Hourly double-decker **trains** chug from Titisee to Schluchsee and Seebrugg (20min., €1.90). Rent **bikes** in town at **Hotel Schiff** by the church. (☎975 70; fax 97 57 57. €7.70 per day, children €3.60. Open daily 8am-10pm.) Schluchsee's **tourist office** is a block into the pedestrian zone in the *Kurhaus.* There's a reservations phone and a hotel map at the train station and outside the tourist office. From the train station, turn right on Bahnhofstr., walk through the underpass, and turn left up Kirchsteige. The office is at the corner of Fischbacherstr. and Lindenstr., next to the Rathaus. (☎77 32; www.schluchsee.de. Open year-round M-Th 8am-6pm, F 9am-6pm; May-Sept. Sa 10am-noon, July-Aug. Su 10am-noon, Aug. also Sa 4-6pm.) The **post office,** 79859 Schluchsee, is down Fischbacherstr. from the tourist office. (Open M-Tu and Th-F 8:30am-noon and 2:30-5pm, W and Sa 8:30am-noon.)

The **Jugendherberge Schluchsee-Wolfsgrund (HI) ❷,** Im Wolfsgrund 28, is ideally situated for a stunning lake view. From the station, cross the tracks and follow the path right, over the bridge parallel to the tracks, and go straight. (☎329; fax 92 37. Laundry €3. Reception 7am-11pm. Check-in 4:30-5:30pm. Curfew 11pm, key available for €10 deposit. Dorms €20, under 27 €17.30. Additional nights €16.90/€14.20.) **Schiff ❹,** Kirchpl. 7, has large rooms with baths, TVs, and phones, some with balconies facing the lake. (☎975 70; www.hotel-schiff-schluchsee.de. Breakfast included. Singles €33-36; doubles €52-98; extra bed €17.50-20.50; children €13-16.) Pitch a tent at **Campingplatz Wolfsgrund ❶.** Walk left up Bahnhofstr. and continue onto Freiburger Str., take a left on Sägackerweg, follow it past Am Waldrain, and take a left. (☎573. Laundry €2.50. Dry €2.50. Kitchen €0.50 per 25min. €4 per person, €2.40 per child, €6.50 per site. Free showers.) Add a *Kurtaxe* of €1-1.50 to all room prices. **Schluchseestüble ❸,** Dresselbacherstr. 11, provides good, filling meals for €4-14.30, while the adjacent *Biergarten* has food for under €5. (☎98 85 99. Open daily from 11am.)

ST. BLASIEN   ☎ 07672

Were it not for its towering cathedral, St. Blasien would be an average town tucked into the green-velvet folds of the Black Forest's southern mountains. Third in size only to St. Peter's in Rome and Les Invalides in Paris, the **Dom** is constructed in a monumental classical style, rising above a charming Altstadt and a white-and-salmon **Rathaus.** The cathedral's history stretches back to the 9th century, when the relics of St. Blasius were brought from Rome to Rheinau. On the way, the Benedictine monks settled in the well-protected Alb Valley. Since then, the monastery has weathered a peasants' revolt and four fires, and was Neoclassically resurrected in the late 18th-century. (Open daily May-Sept. 8am-6:30pm; Oct.-Apr. 8:30am-5pm. Donation requested.) In the same building as the tourist office is the **Museum St. Blasien,** with exhibits on the Dom's past and the town's history, and natural and artistic surroundings. (☎414 37. Open Tu-Su 2:30-5pm; closed Nov.-Dec. €1.60, students €0.50. June-Aug. concert series every Tu and Sa 8:15pm.) The first week of September, St. Blasien hosts an **wood-carving contest.** Contestants from around the globe gather on Hauptstr. to spend a week carving themed wood.

Trails dart through the virgin wilderness of St. Blasien's surrounding mountains. **Philosophenweg** offers an excellent view of the Dom. From the Rathaus, follow Hauptstr. to Friedrichstr., then take a left on Bötzbergstr. and another left onto Philosophenweg (45min. round-trip). The other leg of the fork at the end of Bötzbergstr., **Blasiwälder Weg** (marked by a blue diamond), leads to the "Kletteranlage" climbing rocks and the Windberg creek (1½hr. round-trip). On the other side of town, more trails scale the idyllic **Holzberg.** From the **Kurgarten** next to the Dom, take **Tuskulumweg** and head through the tunnel, following the blue diamond markers. Numerous marked trailheads await on the highway's other side.

A 20min. **bus** ride (#7319, 1 per hr., €2.75) connects St. Blasien with Seebrugg and the train system. The **tourist office,** Am Kurgarten 1-3, has hiking maps (€5), a free town map, and a room catalog. From the main bus station, cross Umgehungsstr., turn down and right and head for the "Haus des Gastes." The tourist office is inside. (☎414 30; www.st-blasien-menzenschwand.de. Open M-F 10am-noon and 3-5pm; May-Sept. also Sa 10am-noon.) A **pharmacy** is on Hauptstr., across from the Rathaus. (☎515. Open M-F 8:30am-1pm and 2:30-6:30pm, Sa 8:30am-12:30pm). The **Sparkasse** across the street has a **24hr. ATM.** The **post office,** 798 37 St. Blasien, is in the Quelle shop on Hauptstr. 45. (Open M-F 8:30am-5:30pm, Sa 8:30-12:30pm.)

The cheapest night's stay in St. Blasien is **Hotel Garni Kurgarten ❷,** Fürstabt-Gerbert-Str. 12, across from the tourist office. Most rooms have balconies facing the Dom and Rathaus, some have TVs. (☎527. Singles €22; doubles €43-55. All rooms with showers. €1.35 *Kurtaxe* per person.) The nearest hostel, along with many private rooms, is in **Menzenschwand.** (10km away. Bus #7321, 15min., runs almost every hr. until M-F 6:45pm, Sa 6:15pm, Su 5pm; €2.25.) There, the **Jugendherberge Menzenschwand (HI) ❷,** Vorderdorfstr. 10, offers cheap lodgings in an authentic wood chalet. Ask about the illuminated waterfalls. (☎07675 326; info@jugendherberge-menzenschwand.de. Breakfast and sheets included. Reception 5-9pm. Dorms €20, under 27 €17.30. Additional nights €16.90/€14.20. *Kurtaxe* €0.50.) Rooms in Menzenschwand and St. Blasien run from €13 per night. Contact the Menzenschwand **tourist office,** Hinterdorfstr. 15, near the "Hirschen/Hintertor" bus stop. (☎07675 930 90. Same hours and website as the St. Blasien office.)

ST. PETER AND ST. MÄRGEN

Deep in a valley of cow-speckled hills 17km from Freiburg are St. Peter and St. Märgen. **Bus** #7216 runs from Freiburg to St. Märgen via St. Peter, but the more common route requires a **train** ride along the Freiburg-Titisee line to "Kirchzarten" (3rd stop), where bus #7216 heads to St. Peter (25min., 1-2 per hr.). A 24hr. *RegioKarte* (€6), valid for both buses and trains, is the best deal for round-trips from Freiburg. Only half the buses continue on to St. Märgen (15min., last bus 7:40pm, €1.80); always check with the driver.

St. Peter, closer to Freiburg and surrounded by cherry orchards, breaks through a crown of dark pine. Its **Klosterkirche** rises above the timid skyline and sports a Baroque interior of gold and mauve marble. Take the tour to see the inside of the abbey and its striking library. (☎07660 910 10. Open during the day. Tours Su 11:30am, Tu 11am, Th 2:30pm. €3.) The **tourist office** is in the Klosterhof.

Get off the bus at Zähringereck; the office is up the hill in front of the church under the *Kurverwaltung* sign. (☎07660 91 02 24; www.st-peter-schwarzwald.de. Open May-Oct. M, W, F 9am-6pm; Th 9:30am-6pm; Sa-Su 10am-1pm. Nov.-Apr. closed Sa-Su.) For latecomers, a **reservations** phone is out front. **Zähringer Apotheke,** Zähringer Str. 12, is by the bus stop. (Open M-F 8:30am-12:30pm and 2:30-7pm, Sa 8:30am-12:30pm.) **Public restrooms** are under the Rathaus next to the tourist office. Many well-marked hiking paths begin at the tourist office and abbey. A relatively easy and scenic 8.5km path leads to St. Märgen; follow the blue diamonds of the **Panoramaweg** past *Vogesenkapelle* and *Kapfenkapelle*. From the abbey, make a sharp right alongside the Klosterkirche, heading for the *Jägerhaus*, before crossing the highway. The trail meanders through the dark evergreen-scented forest into vast wildflower meadows with stunning views of surrounding peaks. A tiny chapel dedicated to travelers and decorated with chalk paintings of cows inside is a great rest stop about halfway through (2-2½hr.).

A little village with links to all major Schwarzwald trails and a number of gorgeous day hikes, **St. Märgen** rightfully calls itself a *Wanderparadies*. Most of the trails are marked from Hotel Hirschen, uphill from the bus stop. A challenging local trail leads to the **Zweibach waterfall;** follow signs with a black dot on a yellow field (15km, 4-5hr.). To reach the start of the trail from the town center, walk along Feldbergstr., turn left onto Landfeldweg, and follow signs for the Rankmühle. **Bike** rentals are available at **Stihldienst Saier,** on Rankhofstr. 28, uphill past the gas station. (☎07669 279. Bikes €5-13 per day. Open M-F 8am-12:30pm and 2-6pm, Sa 8am-noon.) The **tourist office** is in the Rathaus 100m from the "Post" bus stop, downhill to the right of the Volksbank. A **reservations** phone and a hiking trail map await at the bus stop. (☎07669 91 18 17; www.st-maergen.de. Same hours as the office in St. Peter.) A **24hr. ATM** is at **Sparkasse,** on Feldbergstr. 2 near the bus stop. There are **public restrooms** in the Rathaus. **Greber,** by the bus station, has **groceries** and a **post office** counter. (Open M-Tu and Th-F 7:30am-12:30pm and 2:30-6pm, W and Sa 7:30am-12:30pm.)

CENTRAL BLACK FOREST

TRIBERG ☎07722

Tucked in a lofty valley 670m above sea level, the tiny village of Triberg is well-known for its waterfalls, the highest in Germany. Its misty spruce forests filled with friendly brown squirrels are a mecca for hikers. On the hour, the village echoes with the sounds of cuckoo clocks, for which the town is known.

▐▊ TRANSPORTATION AND PRACTICAL INFORMATION. Trains puff from Triberg to **Freiburg** (1½-2hr., 1-2 per hr., €26-24) and **Donaueschingen** (40min., 1 per hr., €5-10.40). Call ☎42 90 for a **taxi.** Triberg's **tourist office,** Luisenstr. 10, hides on the ground floor of the local *Kurhaus.* From the station, turn right on Bahnhofstr. and follow the signs: cross the bridge, go under it, and head up steep Fréjusstr., which turns into Hauptstr. Or, take any **bus** to Marktpl. (€1.35). Pass the Marktpl. and take a left on Ludwigstr. before the **Wasserfall** park entrance; the office is in the building behind the flags. (☎95 32 30; www.triberg.de. Open M-F 9am-12:30pm and 2-5:30pm, Sa 10am-noon.) **Sparkasse** at Marktpl. has an **ATM.** The friendly **Stadt-Apotheke pharmacy,** Am Marktpl., is in the town center right next to the Rathaus. (☎45 37. Open M-F 8:30am-12:30pm and 2:30-6:30pm, Sa 8:30am-12:30pm.)

▐▐ ACCOMMODATIONS AND FOOD. Many private rooms and holiday apartments are available at good prices; ask for a list at the tourist office. The town's modern **Jugendherberge (HI) ❷,** Rohrbacher Str. 35, sits (far) up a (steep) mountain and offers plunging views of two valleys, though getting there requires a masochistic 30min. climb straight up Friedrichstr. (which turns into Rohrbacher Str.) from the tourist office. A taxi from the station costs about €7. (☎41 10; www.jugendherberge-triberg.de. **Internet** €0.15 per min. Sheets and breakfast included. Reception 5-7pm and 9:45pm. Curfew 10pm, but housekey available. €20.10, under 27 €17.40; additional nights €17/ €14.30. Mostly 4- or 6-bed dorms, but some doubles available at no extra charge.) Closer to the center, the friendly family who owns **Hotel Zum Bären ❷**, Hauptstr. 10 (on the way into town from the station), go out of their way to make guests feel comfortable and provide lots of advice about the area. Rooms are clean, comfortable, and most have showers. (☎44 93; fax 47 43. Breakfast included. Singles €24; doubles €46; triples €60; quads €69, all with bath.) *Imbiße* around the entrance to the **Wasserfall** park or down Hauptstr. toward the train station offer cheap food. **Zur Lilie ❹**, Wallfahrtstr. 3, near the water-falls, serves an array of homemade Schwarzwald specialties (€8.50-13.50) and cakes (€2.30-2.70), including a particularly delicious Black Forest cake. (☎44 19. Open daily from 11:30am to around midnight.)

◨ SIGHTS. The locals brag in superlatives about the **Gutacher Wasserfall**—the highest waterfall in Germany—a series of bright cascades tumbling over moss-covered rocks for 163 vertical meters. Swarming with more than 400,000 visi-tors every year, these falls are tame by Niagara standards, but the idyllic hike through the lush, towering pine trees makes up for it. The steep climb dissuades the cardiovascularly underprivileged from ascending **Kaskadenweg** to the top of the waterfall (1hr. round-trip; marked with a squirrel symbol). Taking the **Kultur-weg** and **Naturweg** to the same place is less strenuous but takes longer; pick up a trail map at the park entrance. (Park always open and lighted until midnight. Admission 9am-7pm. €1.50, students €1.20, under 18 €0.50, family €3.50.) The signs for the **Wallfahrtskirche** point along Kulturweg to the small **Pilgrimage church**, *Maria in der Tanne*, where, according to legend, the pious have been miraculously healed since the 17th century. (☎45 66. Closes around 6 or 7pm.) At the tiny *Bergsee* uphill from the church, rent rowboats (€1.50 per 30min., under 14 €1.20) or paddleboats (€4.20 per 30min.) from the kiosk. (Open M-W and F-Su 8:30am-7pm.) Cross the main road onto Kroneckweg and follow the **"Panoramaweg"** signs for hiking with an excellent view of the valley. The **Schwarzwald Museum**, Wallfahrtsstr. 4, back in town, is just across the street and left from the waterfalls. This fun museum is packed with Schwarzwald para-phernalia of every variety, including Europe's largest collection of barrel organs, luminscent rocks from local mines, magnificent wood carvings and fes-tival costumes. (☎44 34. Open daily 10am-5pm. €4, students and children 14-18 €2.50, children 5-13 €2.) This little town also manages the completely impossi-ble feat of possessing *two* "world's biggest cuckoo clocks." One of these mar-vels, the first and the oldest, is a bit out of town toward Schonach on L109. (☎46 89. Open daily 9am-noon and 1-6pm.) The other is 15min. away from the train station; turn left on Bahnhofstr. and follow it to the end, then continue on Franz-Göttler-Weg. After the road below enters a tunnel, take the next right, down to the clock park. (☎962 20. Open Easter-Oct. M-Sa 9am-6pm, Su 10am-6pm; Nov.-Easter M-Sa 9am-6pm. €1.50. Audio guide €1.)

The region's splendid surroundings ensure magnificent hikes. Numerous trail signs on the outskirts of town point the way to a portion of the Pforzheim-Basel **Westweg** (red diamond trail markers; access via blue diamond markers). The tour-ist office sells maps for hiking (€6), biking (€4), and mountain biking (€4).

DONAUESCHINGEN ☎0771

Ever since a 10-year-old Mozart visited Donaueschingen on his way from Vienna to Paris and played three concerts in the castle, musical luminaries and average travelers alike have stopped here (and the local *Fürstenberg* beer). Located on the Baar Plateau between the Schwarzwald and the Schwäbische Alb, it is an ideal starting place for forays into the **Black Forest**, the **Bodensee** region, and the **Wutach Schlucht** 15km to the south.

🖳🛈 TRANSPORTATION AND PRACTICAL INFORMATION. Trains connect Donaueschingen to **Triberg** (40min., 1 per hr., €5-10.40), and **Rottweil** (40min., 1 per hr., €6.60-8.10). Rent **bikes** at **Zweiradhaus Rothweiler,** Max-Egon-Str. 11, for €10 per day. (☎131 48. Open M-Tu and Th-F 9:30am-12:30pm and 2:30-6pm, W 9:30am-12:30pm, Sa 9:30am-1pm.) The **tourist office,** Karlstr. 58, helps find rooms (from €15); for latecomers there's a reservation phone up the street. Follow Josefstr. and its continuation from the station (10min.) and turn left at Karlstr. (☎85 72 21; www.donaueschigen.de. Open May-Oct. M-F 9am-6pm, Sa 10am-noon; Nov.-Apr. M-F 9am-5pm.) The office gives info on the city's annual **Musiktage** in mid-October (Oct. 14-16, 2005), a modern music festival. Get cash at the **ATM** at the **Baden-Württembergische Bank's,** across the street on Schulstr. Nurse blisters at the **Hofapotheke,** Karlstr. 40. (Open M-Tu and Th-F 8:30am-12:30pm and 2:30-6:30pm, Sa 8:30am-12:30pm.) **Internet** is available at the **Stadtbibliothek,** at Max-Rieple-Pl. behind the tourist office. (☎85 72 45. €2 per hr. Open M and W-Th 2-6pm, Tu 9am-noon, F 9am-2pm, Sa 9:30-11:30am.) The **post office,** Donaueschingen 78166, is on the corner on Schulstr. 5-7. (Open M-F 9am-noon and 2-6pm, Sa 9am-noon).

🖍🏠 ACCOMMODATIONS AND FOOD. Rest weary feet at **Hotel Bären ❸,** Josefstr. 7-9, on the way from the train station to town. (☎25 18. Check-in after 4:30pm. Breakfast included. Large singles €25; doubles €50, with bath €65.) Try **Fürstenberg Bräustübe ❹,** Postpl. 1-4, across from the church in the corner of the pink house, for carefully prepared traditional fare (€8-17). Beer from the brewery next door is €1.90-2.40. (☎36 69. Open M-Tu and Th-Su 11am-midnight, kitchen 11am-2pm and 6-10pm.) **Pizzeria da Alfredo ❷,** Villinger Str. 4, across from the Rathaus, serves Italian cuisine (€3-18. ☎29 95. Open M and W-F 11am-2pm and 5:30pm-midnight, Sa 11am-2pm and 6pm-1am, Su 10am-2pm and 5:30pm-midnight.) Head to **City Markt,** Karlstr. 44a, for groceries. (Open M-F 7:30am-7pm, Sa 7am-4pm.)

◪ SIGHTS. Donaueschingen's somewhat dubious claim to fame is its status as the "source" of the 2860km Danube, the second-longest river in Europe. The river officially begins east of the city center where the Brigach and Breg Rivers converge, but the Fürstenberg princes decided to overlook this minor detail and glorify a spring in the garden of their **Schloß Fürstenberg** instead. The **Donauquelle** (source of the Danube) is a round sandy basin encased in overpowering 19th-century stonework, located (conveniently) right next to the Fürstenberg souvenir booth. The Schloß contains an art gallery, spectacular tapestries, and a cavernous shining marble bathroom with a massage-shower; no, you don't get to try it. (Open May-July. Garden open 24hr. Obligatory tours leave daily at 11am, 2:30pm. €10.) Across the street from the Schloß, the **Fürstlich-Fürstenbergische Sammlungen,** Am Karlspl. 7, is a museum cluttered with former possessions of the Fürstenberg princes. (☎865 63. Open Mar.-Nov. Tu-Th 10am-1pm and 2-5pm, Su 10am-5pm. Last entry 30min. before closing or lunch break. €5, students €4, family €10.) The museum, Schloß, and spring are all within a 10min. walk of the train station; follow the signs.

If the Fürstenberg decor leaves you envious, you can at least get royally smashed on free samples of the family beer at the **Fürstliche Fürstenberger Brauerei,** Postpl. 1-4, behind Haldenstr. (☎862 06. M-F 1½hr. brewery tours followed by 1hr. of beer tasting and appropriate snacks. €4, students €2. Call at least 2 weeks in advance for reservations.) Bike fiends can rejoice: Donaueschingen is a stop on the **Danube bicycle trail,** which hugs the river all the way to Vienna. The tourist office sells a map (€11.20, Donaueschingen-Passau). For shorter trails, head to the **Fürstenberg Park.** Hikers can also take heart: part of the Schwarzwald rings the western edge of town and the 108km **Schwarzwald-Kaiserstuhl-Rhein Querweg** to Breisach begins at the train station.

ROTTWEIL   ☎0741

High on a plateau with a view of the Swabian Alps, Rottweil is the oldest settlement in Baden-Württemberg. A free city under the Holy Roman Empire, Rottweil's contributions to civilization have included both flameless gunpowder and pernicious canines. The town's main attraction is the **Fasnet celebration,** which draws gawkers from all over Germany to watch 4000 *Narren* (fools) storm through the well-preserved Altstadt in wooden masks and extravagant costumes in an attempt to expel winter; the next outbreak is February 7-8, 2005.

🖪🖪 TRANSPORTATION AND PRACTICAL INFORMATION. The **train** station lies in the valley 20min. below the town center. Turn right after exiting the station, head uphill, and cross the bridge; Hauptstr., the second block on your left, is the town center (10min.). Or take **bus #11** from the train station to "Friedrichspl." (€1). Trains go to **Stuttgart** (1½hr., 1 per hr., €15.60-21). Rent **bikes** at Alfred Kaiser, Balingerstr. 9, at the end of the bridge leading out of town from Hauptstr. (☎89 19. From €15 per day, weekend €30-50. Open M-W 9am-12:30pm and 2-6:30pm, Th-F 9am-12:30pm and 2-7pm, Sa 9am-3pm.) The **tourist office,** Hauptstr. 21-23, reserves rooms and offers maps, an English city guide, and *Freizeit Spiegel,* a publication detailing artistic offerings in the area (all free). Free city tours start here May-Oct. Sa 2:30pm; call one week ahead to reserve. (☎49 42 80; www.rottweil.de. Open Apr.-Sept. M-F 9:30am-5:30pm, Sa 9:30am-12:30pm; Oct.-Mar. M-F 9:30am-12:30pm and 2-5pm.) Head to the mint-colored building at Hauptstr. 26 to get cash at the **ATM. Untere Apotheke,** Hochbrücktorstr. 2, is the central **pharmacy.** (☎77 75. Open daily 8:30am-12:30pm and 2-6:30pm.) Surf the **Internet** at **CyNet,** Bruderschaftg. 2-4, in the Neues Rathaus. (☎49 43 53. €2 per hr. Open M, W, F 4-9pm.) The **post office,** 78628 Rottweil, is at Königstr. 12. (Open M-F 8:30am-12:30pm and 2-6pm, Sa 9am-noon.)

🖪🖪 ACCOMMODATIONS AND FOOD. Pension Goldenes Rad ❷, Hauptstr. 38, above a friendly restaurant, offers nice rooms in a central location. (☎74 12. Breakfast included. Reception M-Tu and Th-Su 11:30am-2pm and 6pm. Singles €25; doubles €45.) Save money on food by heading across the bridge to the Königstr./Stadionstr. intersection, or buy **groceries** from **Edeka Neukauf Maier,** Kriegsdamm 7-9. (Open M-F 8:30am-8pm, Sa 8m-4pm.) At **Rotuvilla ❸,** Hauptstr. 63, feast on wood-oven pizzas (€3.50-10.20) and other Italian dishes in a folksy half-timbered dining room. (☎416 95. Open Su-M and W-Sa 11:30am-2pm and 5pm-midnight.)

🖪 SIGHTS. Rottweil's fanatic adherence to tradition is not limited to festivals. The town is a living architecture museum, its buildings graced with historic murals and meticulously crafted window boxes. The **Schwarzes Tor,** built in 1230 and enlarged in 1571 and 1650, guards the Altstadt. At the summit of the hill, the 54m **Hochturm** watchtower offers a stunning view all the way to the Swabian Alps. To scale it, pick up the key to the tower from the tourist office (or at Cafe Schädle down the street on weekends) in exchange for €1 and an ID. Across Hauptstr. from the tourist office and the Gothic **Altes Rathaus** is the **Stadtmuseum,** Hauptstr. 20, which houses a still-valid 15th-century defense treaty between Rottweil and 13 Swiss towns and a collection of wooden masks from the *Fasnet* celebrations. Don't miss the 16th-century *Pürschgerichtskarte*, a panoramic map of the view from the Hochturm. (☎ 942 96 34. Open Tu-Su 10am-noon. €1.) Behind the Altes Rathaus, the Gothic **Heilig-Kreuz-Münster** (Cathedral of the Holy Cross) houses an array of gilded lanterns that are carried through town in the annual **Corpus Christi** procession. Subject to the winds of architectural fancy, this cathedral was tossed from 12th-century Romanesque to 15th-century Gothic to 17th-century Baroque and back to 19th-century Gothic revivalist. Behind the pastel pink Rococo **Predigerkirche**, the refreshingly modern **Dominikanermuseum** is on Kriegsdamm. The museum houses a beautiful collection of medieval representations of saints and an excellent exhibit on Rottweil's Roman past, highlighted by a 2nd-century 570,000-tile mosaic. (☎ 78 62. Open Tu-Su 2-5pm. €2.) To find the stone decorations of the medieval **Kapellenturm** off Hochbrücktorstr., drop by the tiny **Lorenzkapelle**, Lorenzg. 17, constructed in the 1330s. (☎ 942 96 33. Open Tu-Su 2-5pm. €1.) While there, enjoy a view of the bucolic **Neckar valley** from the terrace beyond, and marvel at the crooked houses of **Lorenzgasse**. The 92km **Lahr-Rottweil Querweg** and other **hiking** trails are marked on a tree at the corner of Hochbrücktorstr. and Bahnhofstr.

BODENSEE (LAKE CONSTANCE)

Mostly landlocked, Germany has no white sand beaches like the French Riviera, no sparkling waters like the Greek islands, no sun-bleached stucco like Italy— except for a strip of land on the **Bodensee**. In this stretch of southern Baden-Württemberg, potted palms line the streets, public beaches are filled with sunbathers tanning to a melanomic crisp, and business is conducted with profoundly un-German casualness. With the snow-capped Alps soaring in the background, the turquoise Bodensee is one of Germany's most breathtaking destinations.

Getting to the region by **train** is easy; **Konstanz** and **Friedrichshafen** have direct connections to many cities in southern Germany. Rail transport within the region requires long rides and tricky connections because no single route encircles the lake. The bright white boats of the **BSB** (*Bodensee-Schiffs-Betriebe;* Konstanz office ☎ 28 13 98.) and other ferries, known collectively as the **Weiße Flotte,** provide a calmer and quicker alternative. Ships leave every hr. from Konstanz and Friedrichshafen for ports around the lake. The **BodenseeErlebniskarte** gives discounts on most transportation, sights, and tours. (www.bodensee-tourismus.com. €49 for 3 days, €63 per week; ages 6-15 €29/€39.)

KONSTANZ (CONSTANCE)   ☎ 07531

Spanning the Rhein's exit from the Bodensee, Konstanz rubs elbows with Switzerland and Austria. Its location saved the elegant university town from bombardment in WWII, as the Allies were leery of accidentally striking its neighbors. The unique location has been a constant blessing for the city, giving it an open, international flair. Its narrow streets wind around beautifully painted Baroque and Renaissance facades in the central part of town, while gabled and turreted 19th-century houses glow with gentility along the river promenades. The green waters of the Bodensee lap the beaches and harbors.

⌐ TRANSPORTATION

Tickets for the **BSB** ship line to **Meersburg** (€4), **Mainau** (€5.20), and beyond are on sale on board or in the building behind the train station, Hafenstr. 6. (☎ 28 13 89; www.bsb-online.com. Open Apr.-Oct. daily 7:45am-6:35pm.) **Giess Personenschiff-**

Bodensee (Lake Constance)

fahrt (☎07533 21 77) runs boats every 40min. from Dock 2 to **Freizeitbad Jakob** and **Freibad Horn** (p. 431; both €2). **Buses** in Konstanz cost €1.70 per ride, €3 for a *Tageskarte*, and €4.50 for a 1-day ticket that covers two adults, children, and a dog. For a **taxi**, call ☎222 22. A stay of two or more nights in the city requires a €1 *Kurtaxe* per adult per night. This gets you **Gästekarte** coupons, providing free transit within Konstanz and discounts on sights. Rent **paddleboats** (€4 per 30min.; €7 per hr.), **rowboats** (€3.50/€6) or **motorboats** (€14/€24) at Am Gondelhafen, by the Stadtgarten. (☎218 81. Open Apr.-Oct. daily 10am-dusk.) Rent **bikes** from **Kultur-Rädle**, Bahnhofpl. 29. (☎273 10. Open M-F 9am-12:30pm and 2:30-6pm, Sa 10am-12:30pm; Easter-Sept. also Su 10am-12:30pm. €10 per day, €18 for 2 days.)

🛈 PRACTICAL INFORMATION

The tiny but friendly **tourist office**, Bahnhofspl. 13, to the right of the train station, provides a helpful walking map (€1) or a city map with index (€2). The staff finds rooms in private homes (€21-30) for a €2.50 fee (3-night min. stay), and hotels. (☎13 30 30; www.konstanz.de. Open Apr.-Oct. M-F 9am-6:30pm, Sa 9am-4pm, Su 10am-1pm; Nov.-Mar. M-F 9:30am-12:30pm and 2-6pm.) The **Deutsche Bank** across from the station changes currency and has a 24hr. **ATM**. (Open M-W 9am-4:30pm, Th 9am-6pm, F 9:30am-6:30pm.) Get beach reading at the **English Bookshop**, Münzg. 10. (☎150 63. Open M-Th 1-6:30pm, F-Sa 10am-4pm.) Do **laundry** at **Waschsalon & Mehr**, Hofhalde 3. (☎160 27. Wash €4.50, soap €0.60. Dry €3.50. Open M-F 10am-7pm, Sa 10am-4pm.) **Internet** is at **clixworx.net**, Bodanstr. 21. (☎99 12 11. €0.50 per 5min. Open M-Sa 10am-8pm.) The **post office**, 78462 Konstanz, Marktstätte 4, is near the train station. (Open M-F 8:30am-6pm, Sa 9am-noon.)

🛈🛏 ACCOMMODATIONS AND FOOD

Trying to find last-minute lodging in Konstanz can cause massive migraines. **Jugendherberge Otto-Möricke-Turm (HI) ❷**, Zur Allmannshöhe 18, isn't within walking distance, but this former water tower has a terrific view. Take bus #4 from the train station to "Jugendherberge;" turn back and head uphill on Zur Allmannshöhe. (☎322 60; www.jugendherberge-konstanz.de. Breakfast included; dinner €4.50, compulsory for stays over 1 night. Sheets €3.10. Reception Apr.-Oct. 8am-noon and 3-10pm; Nov.-Mar. 8am-noon and 5-10pm. Lockout 9:30am-noon. Curfew 10pm, housekey for €20 deposit. Call at least 2 months ahead. €22.20, under 27 €19.50; additional nights €19.10/€16.40.) If you don't need a visa for Switzerland, call ahead to secure a place at **Jugendherberge Kreuzlingen (HI) ❷**, Promenadenstr. 7. South of the Swiss border in Kreuzlingen, but closer to downtown than the Konstanz hostel, it commands the tip of a small lakefront hill and features cushy furniture and a friendly, multilingual staff. The best way there is by foot (20min.). From the train station, turn left, then left again to cross the tracks, turn right, and go through the parking lot to the border checkpoint "Klein Venedig." Walk along Seestr. until the sharp right curve. Instead of following the street, continue on the gravel path between the children's park and the bushes through the field and vineyard up to the gray building with a flag on top. The hostel rents bikes for €10 per day, kayaks for €8 per hr. (From Germany and ☎00 41 71 688 26 63; from Switzerland 071 688 26 63; kreuzlingen@youthhostel.ch. Breakfast and sheets included. Reception 8-10am and 5-9pm. Closed Dec.-Feb. €28.) **Jugendwohnheim Don Bosco ❷**, Salesianerweg 5, offers rustic lodgings. From the station, take bus #1 or 4 to "Tannenhof." Turn back along Mainaustr. and follow the signs (off the left side). Take in some cable TV in the lively dayroom. (☎622 52; www.donbosco-kn.de. Breakfast included. Sheets €3.25. Call at least 5 days ahead. €16.50.) In the center of town, **Pension Gretel ❸**, Zollernstr. 6-8, offers bright, inexpensive rooms. (☎45 58

25; www.hotel-gretel.de. Breakfast included. Call at least a month ahead in summer. Singles €29; doubles €48, with bath €58; triples €75; quads €87; extra bed €18. Apr.-Oct. €6-7 cheaper per person.) **Hotel Barbarossa ❹**, Obermarkt 8-12, has rooms with medieval beds and trimmings, baths, and telephones. (☎12 89 90; www.barbarossa-hotel.com. Breakfast included. Singles €38-62; doubles €85-105, extra bed €18.) Fall asleep to lapping waves at **DKV-Campingplatz Brudehofer ❶**, Fohrenbühlweg 50. Take bus #1 to "Staad," and walk for 10min. with the lake to your left. The campground is on the waterfront. (☎313 88; www.campingkonstanz.de. Reception closed noon-2:30pm. €3.50 per person, €2 per child, €3.10-4.50 per tent, €7.50 per RV, €0.50 per bike, €2.60 per car. Warm showers €1.) Three other campsites are near Konstanz; contact the tourist office.

Find **groceries** in the basement of the Karstadt department store, on Augustinerpl. (Open M-F 9:30am-8pm, Sa 9:30am-7pm.) Stroll through the small streets surrounding the Münster's northern side; it is the oldest part of Konstanz and the center of its alternative scene, with health-food stores, left-wing graffiti, and student cafes. The **Fachhochschule Mensa ❶** stands in a modern building on Webersteig, overlooking the Rhein. An ISIC is required for a meal card; ask in the cafeteria downstairs. The hassle is worth it—meals cost only €4.70-5.30. (Open M-F 11am-1:45pm. Cafeteria open M-Th 7:30am-4pm, F 7:30am-2pm.) **Café Zeitlos ❷**, St.-Stephans-Pl. 25, cooks all meals (€5.10-7.70) strictly from local ingredients. (☎18 93 84. All-you-can-eat brunch Su 10am, €12.50. Weekly beer and wine specials. Snacks €2.50-3.60 until 10pm. Open daily 10am-1am, kitchen 10am-3pm and 6-10pm.) Near the train station, the **Creperie Salat ❶**, Bodanstr., has a fresh salad buffet (€3.50) and tasty, inexpensive crepes (€2-2.90). With your back to the train station, take a left and walk down the street until you see the big "Lago!" mall. The creperie is across the street. (Open daily 9am-10pm.)

👁 📷 SIGHTS AND BEACHES

Konstanz's **Münster,** built over the course of 600 years, has a 76m soaring Gothic spire (under construction until 2006) and a display of ancient religious objects. Don't miss the *Kreuzgang* frescoes, downstairs to the left of the crypt. (Church open M-F 10am-6pm, Sa and Su noon-5pm.) The **Rathaus,** Kanzleistr. 15, off Wessenbergstr., tells the tale of Konstanz's history in elaborate late-16th-century frescoes; in the courtyard, enter the first tower to the left with the "Historische Bilder" sign. Farther south, off Bodanstr., the 13th-century **Schnetztor** shows off its proud layers of battlements, guarding a network of busy shopping streets behind. Choose from two picturesque promenades to enjoy the view across Lake Konstanz: **Rheinsteig,** along the Rhein, or **Seestraße** on the lake across the bridge. The tree-filled **Stadtgarten,** next to Konstanz's main harbor, gives an unbroken view of the Bodensee and of the voluptuous *Imperia* statue guarding the harbor. She is based on a 16th-century Italian courtesan described by French novelist Honoré de Balzac in his "Contes Drolatiques." In her arms high above the sea she balances two figures—one wearing a crown representing world power, and another a papal tiara symbolizing the church. Across the Rhein from the Altstadt, near the "Sternenpl." bus stop, is the **Archäologisches Landesmuseum,** Benediktinerpl. 5, an assemblage of ancient things from Baden-Württemberg—old town walls, re-assembled skeletons, and spearheads. (☎980 40. Open Tu-Su 10am-6pm. €3, students €2, family €6.) Visit the aquatic critters of the Rhein at the **Sea-Life Museum,** Hafenstr. 9, on the way to the Swiss border. Beginning with an ice cave, the museum traces the history of sea life, with a special focus on the Bodensee region. Exhibits include a large trout tank and a walk-though shark tunnel promoting Greenpeace. (☎12 82 70. Open July-Sept. daily 10am-7pm; May-June and Oct. daily 10am-6pm; Nov.-Apr. M-F 10am-5pm, Sa-Su 10am-6pm. Last entry 1hr. before close. €10.50, students €8.50.)

Konstanz boasts a number of **public beaches;** all are free and open May to September. **Freibad Horn** (take bus #5) is the largest and most crowded; it has a nude section enclosed by hedges. In inclement weather, immerse yourself in **Bodensee Therme Konstanz,** Wilhelm-von-Scholz-Weg 2, near Strandbad Horn, a modern pool complex with thermal baths, saunas, and sun lamps. Take bus #5 to "Bodensee Therme Konstanz." (☎611 63. Open daily 9am-9pm. €4.60, evening €3; students €3.) Closer to town, go for a dip at the **Kur- und Hallenbad,** Spanierstr. 7, on the north bank of the Rhein, between the bridges. (☎662 68. Outdoors open May-Sept. daily 9am-9pm; indoors open mid.-Sept. to mid.-May Tu 2-6pm, W 6:45-7:45am and 3-7pm, Th 2-9pm, F 6:45-7:45am and 2-7pm, Sa 1-6pm, Su 9am-noon. €2, students €1.50.)

▶ DAYTRIP FROM KONSTANZ: MAINAU

To get to Mainau, take bus #4 (dir.: Bettingen) to "Mainau" (20min., 1-2 per hr., €1.70), or a boat from behind the train station (1hr., every 1-2 hr., €5). Apr.-Oct. 7am-8pm; Nov.-Mar. 9am-6pm. Apr.-Oct. €11, students €5, under 16 €3, family €21; half-price after 4pm, free after 7pm; Nov.-Mar. €5.50, students €4, children free.

The island of **Mainau** is all one rich and magnificently manicured garden, the result of the horticultural prowess of generations of Baden princes and the Swedish royal family. A lush arboretum, exotic birds, and huge animals made of flowers surround the pink Baroque palace and church built by the Teutonic Knights in the 13th century. Now thousands of happy tourists scamper across the footbridge from Konstanz to pose with the blooming peacocks and take in an unparalleled view of the Bodensee amid 30 varieties of butterflies.

▶ DAYTRIP FROM KONSTANZ: MEERSBURG

*Reach Meersburg by boat (30min.; 1-2 per hr., last boat around 6:30pm; €3.80). To reserve rooms, consult the welcoming **Reiseverkehrsbüro,** Daedorstr. 34, 1 block in and ½ a block toward the castle from the dock. Free maps. ☎804 40; www.mittlerer-bod-ensee.de. Open M-F 9am-noon and 2-6pm, Sa 9am-noon. €1 reservation fee, €4 for advance arrangements.*

Glowering over the Bodensee, the massive medieval fortress **Burg Meersburg** is the centerpiece of this gorgeous town and was formerly displayed on the 20-*Deutschmark* bill. The first watchman moved into **oldest inhabited castle** in 628 and the fortress now shelters deer antlers, rusting armor, and a deep dungeon. Also on display are the living quarters of **Annette von Droste-Hülshoff,** generally recognized as Germany's greatest female poet. (☎800 00. Open daily Mar.-Oct. 9am-6:30pm; Nov.-Feb. 10am-6pm; last entry 30min. before closing. €5.50, students €3.50, children €3. With a tour of the tower, Apr.-Oct. only, €8/€5.50/€4.75.)

In the 18th century, a prince bishop rejected King Dagobert's **Altes Schloß** and commissioned the sherbert-pink Baroque **Neues Schloß** up the hill on Schloßpl. The house now houses the town's art collection in the **Schloßmuseum.** The **Dorniermuseum** has models of Dornier airplanes. (☎41 40 71. Open Apr.-Oct. daily 10am-1pm and 2-6pm. €4, with Guest Card €3; family €8/€6; children €1. Combo card with entrance to the Weinbaum Museum and the Stadtmuseum €5/€4.) Meersburg's **Zeppelinmuseum,** Schloßpl. 8, crams the world's largest collection of Zeppelin memorabilia (everything from the *Hindenburg's* original silverware to Zeppelin's own models) into a tiny building. (☎79 09. Open Mar.-Nov. daily 10am-6pm. €3, children €2.) For a view of the Bodensee against an

AIRSHIPS REBORN

Almost every city in Southwest Germany has a street named after the Graf Zeppelin, the rigid airship that beloved engineer Hugo Eckener (so popular that Hitler considered him a threat and banned all mention of his name in the press) piloted around the globe in 1928-1938. It was named after Count Ferdinand Graf von Zeppelin, who flew the world's first untethered airship, the LZ-1, for 17min. on July 2, 1900, before landing in Lake Constance.

In 1910, Zeppelin designed Germany's first commercial airship, the *Deutschland*. The German government commissioned 67 ships during WWI; only 16 survived the war. The horrendous inaccuracy of their city bombing runs led the British to believe that the Germans were targeting English cows. After post-war restrictions were lifted, Germany built the greatest Zeppelins in history, including the Graf Zeppelin and the Hindenberg, which exploded while landing on May 6, 1937, killing 35 passengers. After this catastrophe (caused in part by the U.S. government's refusal to sell safe helium gas to the Nazis) and with the start of WWII, the zeppelins were scrapped.

In Friedrichshafen, visitors to the **Zeppelin museum** can walk through a model of the Hindenberg (p. 432), or take a ride on the **Deutsche Zeppelin-Reederei GmbH** (€190-370; www.zeppelin-flug.de), which now soars over Lake Constance again.

alpine backdrop, trek up past the Altstadt, through the Obertor gate up the hill from the Marktpl., left on Stettenerstr., and follow signs for Friedrichshöhe. Or, just stroll along the **Uferpromenade**, east of the harbor.

FRIEDRICHSHAFEN   ☎07541

A former Zeppelin construction base, Friedrichshafen had trouble getting back off the ground after Allied bombings in 1944. The town was finally rebuilt with sweeping, wide promenades—a bit overwhelming for the little city. The tree-lined boulevards open onto breathtaking panoramas of the Alps across the water. The city's flagship attraction is the superb ☒**Zeppelinmuseum**, Seestr. 22, which details the history of the flying dirigibles (see **Airships Reborn**, p. 432). The fleet of 16 scale models is overshadowed by a 33m reconstruction of a section of the *Hindenburg*, which went down in flames in 1937. Climb aboard for a peek at the recreated passenger cabins. Upstairs, the museum also displays art, including some medieval and early modern pieces and an impressive gallery of Otto Dix's early 20th-century work, like his *Temptation of St. Anthony*. (☎380 10. Open May-Oct. Tu-Su 10am-6pm; Nov.-Apr. 10am-5pm. Last admission 30min. before closing. English audioguide €3. €7.50, students €3, family €13.) Afterwards, climb the metal **tower** by the dock, off Seestr. and across from Salzstr., to improve your view. The spires in the east belong to the exquisite **Schloßkirche** on Klosterstr. Take Friedrichstr. away from town and turn left on Olgastr. and then immediately right on Klosterstr. (☎213 08. Open mid-Apr. to Oct. M-Th and Sa 9am-6pm, F and Su 11am-6pm.) The beach is at the **Strandbad**, Königsweg 11, replete with a pool and volleyball nets. Follow the hedged path from Schloßkirche entrance away from town for 10min. (☎280 78. Open daily mid-May to mid-Sept. in good weather 9am-8pm. €1.40, children €0.70.) Popular among cyclists, Friedrichshafen provides access to a number of **biking paths**, including the beloved **Bodensee-Radweg**, a 260km trail around the Bodensee. The path is marked by signs of a cyclist with a blue back tire.

There are two train stations in Friedrichshafen: the main **Stadtbahnhof** and the **Hafenbahnhof** at the docks behind the Zeppelinmuseum. **Trains** connect the two stations (2-4 per hr., €1.50). Trains run to **Munich** (3-4hr., 1-2 per hr., €30.20-41) and **Lindau** (20-40min., 2 per hr., €4). Frequent **buses** and **boats** also run to Lindau and **Meersburg**. For the boat to Konstanz (1½hr., 1 per 2hr., €7.80), buy tickets on board or at the **ticket counter** next to the Zeppelinmuseum. (☎923 83 89.

Open Apr.-Oct. daily 8:30am-5:40pm; Nov.-Mar. M-F 8:30am-12:30pm and 1:30-4:40pm, Sa 8:20am-1pm.) Rent a boat at the **Gondelhafen** by Seestr., but don't shoot for Konstanz in it, and watch the fickle skies. (☎07 54 12. Rowboats and paddleboats €7.50 per hr., motorboats €20-25 per hr. Open May-Sept. daily in good weather 9am-dusk.) Rent **bikes** from Zweirad Schmid, Ernst-Lehmann-Str. 12. (☎218 70. €10.50 per day, additional days €7.50; mountain bikes from €15 per day. Open M-F 8am-noon and 2-6pm, Sa 9am-12:30pm.) The **tourist office**, Bahnhofpl. 2, in the striped building to the left of the Stadtbahnhof, gives out maps, suggests biking routes, and books rooms for a €3 fee. (☎300 10; tourist-info@friedrichshafen.de. Open Nov.-Mar. M-Th 9am-noon and 2-4pm, F 9am-noon, Apr. and Oct. M-Th 9am-noon and 2-5pm, Sa 10am-2pm; May-Sept. M-F 9am-6pm, Sa 9am-1pm.) The **post office**, Friedrichshafen 88045, is across from the tourist office. (Open M-F 8:30am-12:30pm and 2-6pm, Sa 9am-12:30pm.)

Friedrichshafen's enthusiastic **Jugendherberge Graf Zeppelin (HI) ❷**, Lindauer Str. 3, named after the first Zeppelin to circumnavigate the world, is clean, recently renovated, and 50m from the water. From the Hafenbahnhof, walk 10min. down Eckenerstr. away from Buchhornpl. From the Stadtbahnhof, walk left down Friedrichstr., and continue onto Eckenerstr. (20min.). Or take bus #7 to "Eberhardstr." (☎724 04; www.jugendherberge-friedrichshafen.de. Breakfast and sheets included. Wash (hang dry) €3.10. Lockers €2 deposit. Reception 7-9am, 2-7:30pm and 8:30-10pm. Lockout 9am-noon. Curfew 10pm, key available for guests over 18. €22.20, under 27 €19.10. Additional nights €19.50/€16.40.) More luxurious lodging awaits in **Gasthof Rebstock ❸**, Werastr. 35. From train station, take bus #1, 2 or 5 to "St. Elisabeth, Werastr." (☎216 94; gasthof-rebstock@victorvox.de. Breakfast included. Singles €35, with bath €48; doubles €50/€68; triples €68/€83.) Rebstock's **restaurant ❸** serves huge local dishes for €4-12. (Open daily 11:30am-2pm and 5:30-9pm.) For **groceries**, head to **Lebensmittel Fehl** on the corner of Seestr. and Salzg. (Open Sa-Th 7am-midnight.) **Naturkost am Buchhornplatz ❶**, Buchhornpl. 1 (☎243 35), serves vegetarian food to take out or eat in. (☎243 35. Salads €1.70-3.45. Lunch specials €2.90. Baked goods €0.85-3.10. Open M-Sa 9am-6pm.)

LINDAU IM BODENSEE   ☎08382

Connected to the mainland only by a narrow causeway and lapped by aquamarine waves, the island of Lindau is a perfect tourist lure.

🖪🎵 TRANSPORTATION AND PRACTICAL INFORMATION. Ferries link Lindau with **Konstanz**, usually stopping at **Friedrichshafen, Mainau** and **Meersburg** along the way (3½hr., 3-6 per day, €11.60). Or take the **train** to Konstanz (1-2hr., 1 per hr., €14.40). **Public transport** in Lindau costs €1.50 per ride or €3.50 for a 24hr. ticket (family €2.60/€6). Rent **bikes** at the train station. (☎212 61. €5-10 per day. Open M-F 9am-1pm and 2-6pm, Sa 9:30am-1pm; May-Sept. in good weather also Su 9am-noon.) **Boats** await next to both bridges at the Kleiner See between the island and the mainland (☎55 14. Motorboats €25 per hr.; row- and paddleboats €6-8 per hr. Open late Mar.-Oct. 9am-9pm.). The **tourist office**, Ludwigstr. 68, across from the station, finds rooms for €3. (☎26 00 30; www.lindau-tourismus.de. Open mid-June to mid-Sept. M-F 9am-6pm, Sa-Su 10am-2pm; Apr. to mid-June and early Sept.-Oct. M-F 9am-1pm and 2-6pm, Sa 10am-2pm; Nov.-Mar. M-F 9am-noon and 2-5pm.) **Tours** leave from the office at 10am. (Tu and F in German, M in English. €5, students and overnight guests €4. Audioguide €7.50.) The **Bodenseebank**, across the street at Maximilianstr. 27, offers **currency exchange** and an **ATM.** (Open M-W and F 9am-noon and 2-4pm, Th 9am-noon and 2-5:30pm.) Do laundry at **Lindauer Wäschecenter**, Holdereggenstr. 21A. (☎66 98. Wash €6.15. Dry €5.15. Open M-F 9am-12:30pm and 2:30-6:30pm.) The **post office**, 88131 Lindau 1, is 50m to the left of the station. (Open M-F 8am-noon and 2-5:30pm, Sa 8:30am-noon.)

ACCOMMODATIONS AND FOOD. All accommodations in Lindau charge a *Kurtaxe* of €1.40 per person per night. The modern **Jugendherberge (HI) ❷**, Herbergsweg 11, lies across the Seebrücke. Cross the bridge, turn right onto Bregenzer Str., right again on Kolpingstr., and left onto Herbergsweg after the Limare indoor swimming pool (20min.). Or, take bus #1 or 2 from the train station to "Anheggerstr./ZUP," then bus #3 (dir.: Zech) to "Jugendherberge." (☎967 10; fax 96 71 50. Under 27 and families with children only. Breakfast and sheets included. Wash €1.50. Dry €1.50. Reception 7am-10pm. Curfew midnight, door code available. €19-20, less for additional nights.) **Hotel Pension Norris ❸**, Brettermarkt 13, has comfortable rooms right off the promenade. (☎36 45; fax 10 42. Large, delicious breakfast included. All rooms with bath. Singles €30-35; doubles €70-72.) **Park-Camping Lindau Am See ❶**, Frauenhofer Str. 20, is 3km to the east on the mainland, within spitting distance of the Austrian border. *Let's Go* does not recommend spitting at Austria. Take bus #1 or 2 to "Anheggerstr./ZUP," then bus #3 (dir.: Zech) to the next-to-last stop, "Laiblachstr."; exit the bus and turn right, then left onto the large Bregenzer Str., where the campground is marked. (☎722 36; www.park-camping.de. Reception 8am-noon and 2-8pm. €4.50-5.50, €1.50-2.50 per child, €1.50-5.50 per site. Free showers. Grocery store and restaurant open daily 7am-9pm.) Get French grub at **Insel Bar Cafe-Bistro ❸**, Maximilianstr. 42, which serves crepes (€4.20-6.90), ice cream dishes (€2.80-5.20) and other dishes. (☎15 46. Open M-Sa 10am-7pm, Su 11am-7pm.) For seafood (lakefood, really) head to **Neptun Fishhandlung ❷**, In der Grub 6. Daily specials (€5.50-6.80) include remoulade and potato salad. (☎56 39. Open M-F 9:30am-6pm, Sa 8:30am-1pm.)

SIGHTS AND BEACHES. The 14th-century gabled houses on **Maximilianstraße** form the central part of town. Halfway along Maximilianstr., the **Altes Rathaus** is a blend of frescoes, completed in 1436. The muraled **Cavazzen-Haus** in the Marktpl. houses the **Stadtmuseum,** whose endless rooms display a collection of furniture and art, ranging from fine French porcelain to portraits of pompous-looking nobles. Tours of a small mechanical instruments exhibit take place in the afternoon. (☎94 40 73. Open Apr.-Oct. Tu-F and Su 11am-5pm, Sa 2-5pm. €2.50, students €1, family €5. Tours 3 and 4:15pm. €2.50, students €1.50. Combined ticket €4/€2, family €6.) Cross Marktpl. and compare the ornate interior of the Catholic **Stiftskirche,** on the right, with the more sober Evangelical **Kirche St. Stephan.** A walk down **In der Grub** leads to the Rapunzel-esque **Diebsturm** (thieves' tower). The medieval **Peterskirche** next door, now a memorial to all victims of the World Wars, contains the only surviving murals by Hans Holbein the Elder. At the harbor, the yellow-topped **Mangturm,** a 12th-century lighthouse, keeps watch over the waves of tourists but does not let any inside. Climb the new lighthouse at the harbor entrance for a great view of the lake and the Alps. (Open late Mar. to early Nov. daily 10am-sunset. €1.60, children €0.50.) Lindau has four major beaches, the biggest and busiest of which is **Eichwald,** with three heated pools and a slide. Walk to the east along Uferweg for 30min. or take bus #1 or 2 to "Anheggerstr./ZUP," then bus #3 to "Kamelbuckel." (☎55 39. Open daily May-Sept. 9:30am-8pm. Last entry 1hr. before closing. €3, ages 6-18 €2.) **Römerbad,** on the island left of the harbor, is the smallest and most casual. (☎68 30. €2.50, ages 6-18 €2. Warm showers €0.50.) To reach the quieter **Lindenhofbad,** take bus #1 or 2 to "Anheggerstr./ZUP" and then bus #4 to the end, "Alwind."; then take the hedged road uphill. (☎66 37. Römerbad and Lindenhofbad both open June to mid-Aug. daily 10am-8pm; May-Sept. M-F 10:30am-7:30pm, Sa-Su 10am-8pm. Last entry 1hr. before closing. €2.50, ages 6-18 €2. Warm showers €0.50.) The luxurious heated pool of **Strandbad Bad Schachen** is also in the Lindenhofpark; it's in the shadow of a posh hotel. (Open May-Aug. daily 9am-7pm. Daypass weekends €9.50, weekdays €7.)

BAYERN (BAVARIA)

Bavaria is the Germany of Wagnerian opera, fairy tales, and Teutonic myth. From tiny forest villages to stately Baroque cities along the Danube and castles perched high in the Alps, the region attracts more visitors than any other part of the country. When foreigners conjure up images of Germany, they are thinking of Bavaria: land of beer gardens, sausage, and *Lederhosen*. But tourists soon discover that there is much more to Germany's largest federal state than the cliches it indulges. From international powerhouses like BMW and Audi to thriving university towns; from the burgeoning Turkish population to scattered Jewish immigrant communities, Bavaria is much too dynamic to be regarded as an open-air museum.

It's true that the region's residents have always been Bavarians first and Germans second. Through wars with France and Austria, Otto von Bismarck pulled Bavaria into his orbit, but it remained its own kingdom until 1918. Local authorities still insist upon using the *Land*'s proper name: *Freistaat Bayern* (Free State of Bavaria). On a local level, Franconians, upper Bavarians and Swabians take great pains to assert their unique cultures. Despite such long-standing cultural identities, modern cosmopolitanism is combining with historical preservation to animate the truly individual character of Germany's southernmost state.

HIGHLIGHTS OF BAVARIA

ABSORB the culture, and the *Bier*, of **Munich** (p. 435), which offers not only the notorious **Oktoberfest** (Sept. 19-Oct. 4, 2004; p. 463), but also an opera festival, sleek bars, lively museums and a park three times the size of New York's Central Park.

BEAR WITNESS to Germany's Nazi past at the **Dachau** memorial, **Nürnberg's** Nazi ruins (p. 540) and **Berchtesgaden's Eagle's Nest** (p. 484).

BIKE for a week in stunning natural surroundings from the gorgeous pastel stucco town of **Eichstätt,** or check out fossils in the **Altmühltal Nature Preserve** (p. 508).

CHUG extra-strength monks' brew at **Andechs,** a hilltop monastery still serving the 12% alcohol beer it has produced since the 16th century (p. 465).

DISCOVER the medieval splendor of the **Romantic Road** (p. 526). For more feudal fun, try the castles in **Burghausen** (p. 497) and **Landshut** (p. 499).

DRINK MILK practically straight from the cow in the spectacular **Berchtesgaden National Park** (p. 478), a stunning setting for hikes and other outdoor activities.

SURVEY eccentric King Ludwig II's extravagant **Königsschlößer** (royal castles; p. 472), in the Alps and on the **Chiemsee,** or sleep in his bed in **Passau** (p. 512).

MÜNCHEN (MUNICH)　☎089

Tourists who step past the stereotypes of *Lederhosen* and pot-bellied conservatives will be pleasantly surprised to discover that Munich is both the sleek southern capital of German affluence and the leafy home of true German merriment. The city's unique cosmopolitan attractions and its long-standing tradition of enjoy-

ing beer, life, and nature (in that order) make it a place both relaxing and stimulating. World-class museums, handsome parks and architecture, and a rambunctious art scene conspire to create a city of astonishing vitality.

Even in the depths of winter, citizens meet in outdoor beer gardens to discuss art, politics, and (of course) *Fußball*. A bubbling mixture of sophistication and earthy Bavarian *Gemütlichkeit* keeps the city awake at (almost) all hours. Müncheners party zealously during *Fasching*, Germany's Mardi Gras (Jan. 7-Mar. 8, 2005), shop with abandon during the *Weinachtsmarkt* (Christmas Market; Nov. 28-Dec. 24, 2004), and imbibe unfathomable quantities of beer during the legendary **Oktoberfest** (Sept. 17-Oct. 2, 2005; see p. 463 for more information).

HISTORY

Although Munich stands today as the eternal *Hauptstadt* of Southern Germany, the city was actually founded by a Northerner. In 1158 Henry the Lion built Munich to control the only bridge over the Isar River and, with it, the profitable salt trade. Soon Munich came under the rule of one of Europe's most stalwart dynasties, the **Wittelsbachs,** who elbowed their way to the top of the Bavarian aristocracy by the end of the Middle Ages and controlled the city with strict Catholic piety until the 18th century. Following Napoleon's defeat, Bavaria became a kingdom and leapt into a Golden Age with an efficient state administration that promoted commerce and the arts. **Ludwig I** and Maximilian I contributed hugely to the evolution of the city, building many museums, while Bavaria's eccentric king **Ludwig II** began the construction of "fairy-tale" castles (p. 472). In 1871, after Bismarck's wars solidified Prussian dominance over Germany, Bavaria was absorbed into the greater *Reich*, a process facilitated by Bismarck's funding of Ludwig's grandiose architectural projects. Munich became a cultural powerhouse, rivaling Berlin (to *Müncheners*, a glorified garrison town), as artists flocked to its blossoming scene.

Germany's defeat in WWI ended 700 years of Wittelsbach rule in Bavaria. Postwar depression and the reparations required by the treaty of Versailles sent the economy into hyperinflation. The instability of Weimar Munich gave rise to reactionary, anti-Semitic movements. **Adolf Hitler** found the city such a fertile recruiting ground for the new National Socialist German Workers' Party (Nazis) that he later called it "the capital of our movement." In 1923, Hitler and hundreds of Nazis unsuccessfully attempted to capture several municipal government officials in the **Beer Hall Putsch,** leading to a year in jail for the future Führer. Echoes of the Nazi era still haunt Munich—the Nazis' first concentration camp was constructed just outside the city at **Dachau** (p. 464). Despite Munich's location deep inside German air defenses, Allied bombs obliterated over 70% of the city center; much of it has since been rebuilt. The **1972 Olympics** (although marred by terrorism) brought modernization to Munich. Large portions of the city center were pedestrianized and the subway system was extended, bringing a new era of glory to the city.

◼ INTERCITY TRANSPORTATION

Flights: Flughafen München (☎97 52 13 13). S1 makes the 40min. trip into Munich (sit in the rear of the train), as does S8. Trains between the airport and the train station depart every 10min, costing €8 or 8 stripes on the *Streifenkarte* per person; 2-5 adults can pay a group rate of €15 (see Public Transportation, p. 440). A **Lufthansa shuttle bus** runs between the Hauptbahnhof and the airport (45min.), with a stop at the "Nordfriedhof" U-Bahn station in Schwabing. It leaves from Arnulfstr., on the northern side of the train station, every 20min. 5:10am-8:10pm. Buses return from Terminal A *(Zentralbereich)* and Terminal D every 20min. 6:20am-9:50pm. €9.50, round-trip €15.

Trains: Munich's **Hauptbahnhof** (☎22 33 12 56) is the transportation hub of southern Germany, with connections to: **Amsterdam** (7-9hr., 1 per hr.); **Berlin** (6½hr., 2 per hr.); **Cologne** (6hr., 2 per hr.); **Frankfurt** (4hr., 2 per hr.); **Füssen** (2hr., every 2hr.); **Hamburg** (6hr., 1 per hr.); **Innsbruck** (2hr., every 2hr.); **Paris** (8-10hr., 6 per day); **Prague** (6-7hr., 4 per day); **Salzburg** (1¾hr., 2 per hr.); **Vienna** (5hr., 1 per hr.); **Zürich** (4½-5½hr., 4-5 per day). For 24hr. schedules, fare information, and reservations (in German), call ☎01805 99 66 33. The improved **Bayern-Ticket** (single €15, 2-5 people €22) is now valid for all train transit from 9am (midnight on weekends) to 3am the next day, and can take you all the way to Salzburg. **EurAide,** located next to track 11 in the station, provides free train information in English and books train tickets. **Reisezentrum** information counters are open daily 7am-9:30pm.

Mitfahrzentrale: McShare Treffpunkt Zentrale, Lämmerstr. 6 (☎194 40). Open daily 8am-8pm. **Frauenmitfahrzentrale,** Klenzestr. 57b, arranges ride shares for women only. Open M-F 8am-8pm.

Hitchhiking: *Let's Go* does not recommend hitchhiking as a safe mode of transportation. Those looking to share rides scan the bulletin boards in the **Mensa,** Leopoldstr. 13. Otherwise, hitchers try *Autobahn* on-ramps; those who stand behind (on the autobahn side of) the blue sign with the white auto may be fined. Hitchers going to Salzburg take U1 or 2 to "Karl-Preis-pl." Hitchhikers to Stuttgart take streetcar #17 to "Amalienburgstr." or S2 to "Obermenzing," then bus #73 or 75 to "Blutenburg." Those heading to Nürn-

TO **1** (750m)

THERESIENSTR. U

TO **2** (500m)

3

Dachauerstr.

TO OLYMPISCHE PARK (3km)
& BMW MUSEUM (3km)

Heßstr.

TO SCHLOSS
NYMPHENBURG,
BOTANISHER
GARTEN (4.5km),
16 (3km), **17** (2km),
& **18** (4.5km)

Gabelsbergerstr.

Theresienstr.

Steinheilstr.

Enhuberstr.

Luisenstr.

13

Arcisstr.

Neue
Pinakothek

Batty Baristas

Theresienstr.

Barer Str.

Schleißheimer Str.

Rottmanstr.

Augustenstr.

R.-Wagner-str.

Gabelsbergerstr.

Alte
Pinakothek

14

Volkstheater

Cinema

**Second
Hand Sports
Cinema München**

19

Nyphenburgerstr.

U STIGLMAIERPLATZ

Briennerstr.

Hauptschule für
Musik und Theater

20

Pinakothek
der Moderne

Lenbachhaus

KÖNIGSPL. U

KÖNIGSPL.

Glyptothek

Markuskirche

Prinz-Ludwig-Str.

Türkenstr.

Oskar-von-Miller-Ring

Jägerstr.

Finkenstr.

TO **21** (6.5km) & **22** (1.5km)

23

Karlstr.

Luisenstr.

Meiserstr.

Antikensammlung

Obelisk

KAROLINENPLATZ

Universitäts
Hospital

Seidlstr.

Dachauer Str.

Amerika Haus

Barer Str.

Max-Joseph-Str.

Briennerstr.

Marsstr.

Sophienstr.

Ottostr.

26

27

MAXIMILIANS-
PLATZ

SALVATORPLATZ

33

24

25

Hirtenstr.

TO **29** (250m), **30** (500m)
& **31** (4.5km)

Arnulfstr.

32

Elisenstr.

Alter
Botanischer
Garten

U LENBACHPLATZ

KARLSPL.

Pranner-str.

Kard.-Faulhaber-Str.

Bike rental

S HAUPTBHF.

Justizpalast

Prielmayerstr.

Pacellistr.

Maxburgstr.

PROMENADEPLATZ

Maffeistr.

Hauptbahnhof

BAHNHOF-
PLATZ

DB Mobil

Schützenstr.

KARLSPLATZ

S KARLSPL.

American
Express

Löwen-grühe

U HAUPTBHF.

Bayerstr.

Neuhauser Str.

Michaelskirche

Frauenkirche

72

TO **36** (250m), **37** (500m)
& **38** (2km)

Senefelderstr.

39

**International
Phone World**

Schlosserstr.

Adolf-Kolping Str.

Herzogspitalstr.

Herzog-
Wilhelm-
Str.

Eisenmannstr.

Altheimer Eck

Kaufingerstr.

FRAUEN-
PLATZ

Neues
Rathaus

Wehrstr.

40

46

47

Schwanthalerstr.

**Deutsches
Theater**

Sonnenstr.

Damen-
stiftstr.

Brunn-str.

Hackenstr.

Hotterstr.

Rosenstr.

Rosental

MARIENPL. S

Peterskirche

41

Jospehspitalstr.

Landwehrstr.

Schillerstr.

50

Sonnenstr.

Wilhelm-
Str.

Kreuzstr.

Sendlinger Str.

Schmider
Hackenstr.

Duftstr.

Rindermarkt

Münchener
Stadtmuseum

ST. JAKOBS
PLATZ

TO **59** (2km),
60 (100m), &
THERESIENWIESE (250M)

61

Pettenkoferstr.

Asamkirche

51

Oberanger

Klosterhofstr.

Unterer Anger

Blumenstr.

Goethestr.

Nußbaumstr.

Lindwurmstr.

**Matthäus-
kirche**

Sendlinger
Tor

SENDLINGER
TOR U

Blumenstr.

Kreuzstr.

Unterer Anger

Corneliusstr.

Müllerstr.

Blumenstr.

0   250 yards

0   250 meters

65

66

Müllerstr.

Staatstheater am
Gärtnerplatz

Laundry ■

Klenzestr.

N

Thalkirchner str.

Pestalozzistr.

Hans-Sachs-Str.

Fraunhoferstr.

Müllerstr.

Jahnstr.

TO **68** (3km), **69** (2km), **70** (5km),
71 (3km) & TIERPARK HELLABRUNN ZOO

TO **73** (50m)

72

BAYERN

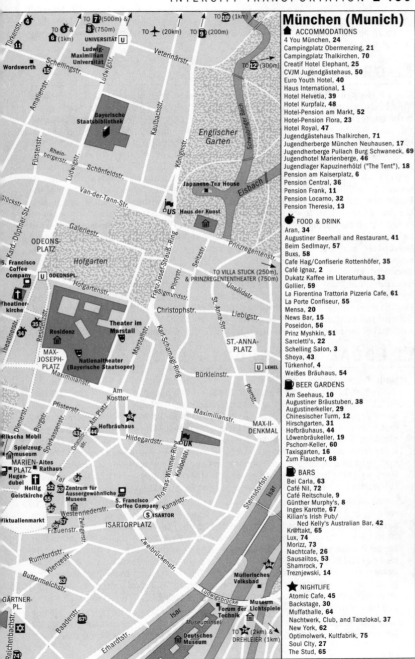

München (Munich)

ACCOMMODATIONS
4 You München, 24
Campingplatz Obermenzing, 21
Campingplatz Thalkirchen, 70
Creatif Hotel Elephant, 25
CVJM Jugendgästehaus, 50
Euro Youth Hotel, 40
Haus International, 1
Hotel Helvetia, 39
Hotel Kurpfalz, 48
Hotel-Pension am Markt, 52
Hotel-Pension Flora, 23
Hotel Royal, 47
Jugendgästehaus Thalkirchen, 71
Jugendherberge München Neuhausen, 17
Jugendherberge Pullach Burg Schwaneck, 69
Jugendhotel Marienberge, 46
Jugendlager Kapuzinerhölzl ("The Tent"), 18
Pension am Kaiserplatz, 6
Pension Central, 36
Pension Frank, 11
Pension Locarno, 32
Pension Theresia, 13

FOOD & DRINK
Aran, 34
Augustiner Beerhall and Restaurant, 41
Beim Sedlmayr, 57
Buxs, 58
Cafe Hag/Confiserie Rottenhöfer, 35
Café Ignaz, 2
Dukatz Kaffee im Literaturhaus, 33
Gollier, 59
La Fiorentina Trattoria Pizzeria Cafe, 61
La Porte Confiseur, 55
Mensa, 20
News Bar, 15
Poseidon, 56
Prinz Myshkin, 51
Sarcletti's, 22
Schelling Salon, 3
Shoya, 43
Türkenhof, 4
Weißes Bräuhaus, 54

BEER GARDENS
Am Seehaus, 10
Augustiner Bräustuben, 38
Augustinerkeller, 29
Chinesischer Turm, 12
Hirschgarten, 31
Hofbräuhaus, 44
Löwenbräukeller, 19
Pschorr-Keller, 60
Taxisgarten, 16
Zum Flaucher, 68

BARS
Bei Carla, 63
Café Nil, 72
Café Reitschule, 9
Günther Murphy's, 8
Inges Karotte, 67
Kilian's Irish Pub/
  Ned Kelly's Australian Bar, 42
Kreftakt, 65
Lux, 74
Morizz, 73
Nachtcafe, 26
Sausalitos, 53
Shamrock, 7
Treznjewski, 14

NIGHTLIFE
Atomic Cafe, 45
Backstage, 30
Muffathalle, 64
Nachtwerk, Club, and Tanzlokal, 37
New York, 62
Optimolwerk, Kultfabrik, 75
Soul City, 27
The Stud, 65

BAYERN

berg and Berlin take U6 to "Studentenstadt" and walk 500m to the Frankfurter Ring. Those heading to the Bodensee and Switzerland take U4 or 5 to "Heimeranpl.," then bus #33 to "Siegenburger Str."

■**:** ORIENTATION

Munich rests on the banks of the Isar in the middle of south-central Bavaria, with King Ludwig's castles and the Alps only a short trip past its outskirts. **Marienplatz**, is the center of Munich's sight-strewn Altstadt. To get there from the **Hauptbahnhof**, take any S-Bahn to "Marienplatz," or head out the main entrance and across Bahnhofpl. Continue east on Prielmayerstr. past the fountain at **Karlsplatz** (called **Stachus** by locals) and through the **Karlstor**; Marienpl. is straight ahead down the pedestrian mall. The huge **Deutsches Museum** lies on the well-named **Museumsinsel** in the middle of the Isar river. North of the Altstadt is the **Residenz**, the former home of the Wittelsbach rulers; the **Hofgarten** beyond stretches to the corner of the **Englischer Garten**, which in turn sprawls toward the northeast reaches of the city. On the other side of town, the grand **Schloß Nymphenburg** rests beside the manicured **Botanical Gardens**. Sports fans head north of town to the **Olympiapark**, built for the 1972 Olympic Games. The University of Munich (a.k.a. **Ludwig-Maximilians Universität**) is north, next to **Schwabing's** student-friendly restaurants and bookstores. The Technical University is also north of the city, near the museums of the Königspl. area. South of town is the **Glockenbachviertel**—filled with nightspots, including many gay bars. The area around the **Hauptbahnhof**, formerly dominated by sex shops, is improving, and now houses many hotels. The large, open **Theresienwiese**, southeast of the train station on the U4 and 5 lines hosts **Oktoberfest**. Several publications help visitors navigate Munich; the most comprehensive (in English) is the monthly *Munich Found* (€3 at newsstands and bookshops).

■ LOCAL TRANSPORTATION

Public Transportation: MVV, Munich's public transport system (☎41 42 43 44), runs Su-Th 5am-12:30am, F-Sa 5am-2am. S-Bahn to the airport starts running at 3:30am. Eurail, InterRail, and German railpasses are valid on the S-Bahn (S) but *not* on the U-Bahn (U), streetcars, or buses. Buy tickets at the blue *MVV-Fahrausweise* vending machines and **validate them** in the blue boxes marked with an "E" **before entering the platform.** Payment is on an honor system, but disguised agents often check for tickets; if you sneak on or don't validate correctly, you risk a €40 fine. Always descend from the right-hand side of the S-Bahn. **Transit maps** and **maps of wheelchair accessible stations** are at the tourist office or EurAide and at MVV counters near the subway entrance in the train station. *Fahrpläne* (schedules) cost €1 at newsstands.

Prices: Single ride tickets €2.10 (valid for 3hr.). **Kurzstrecke** (short trip) tickets €1.10 (one hr. or 2 stops on the U- or S-Bahn, or 4 stops on a streetcar or bus). A **Streifenkarte** (10-strip ticket) costs €9.50 and can be used by more than 1 person. Cancel 2 strips per person for a normal ride, or 1 strip for a *Kurzstrecke*. Beyond the city center, cancel 2 strips per zone. A **Single-Tageskarte** (single-day ticket) is valid until 6am the next day (€4.50). At €11, the **3-Day Pass** is a great deal. Alternatively, a **Partner-Tageskarte** (€8) can be used by up to 5 adults. The much-touted **Munich Welcome Card** gives public transportation discounts. The **München XXL Ticket**, offers day-long transit on all transport in Munich and surroundings (€6 single; €10.50 for up to 5 individuals), and can be used to reach Dachau.

Taxis: Taxi-München-Zentrale (☎216 10 or 194 10) has stands in front of the train station and every 5-10 blocks in the city center. Women can request a female driver.

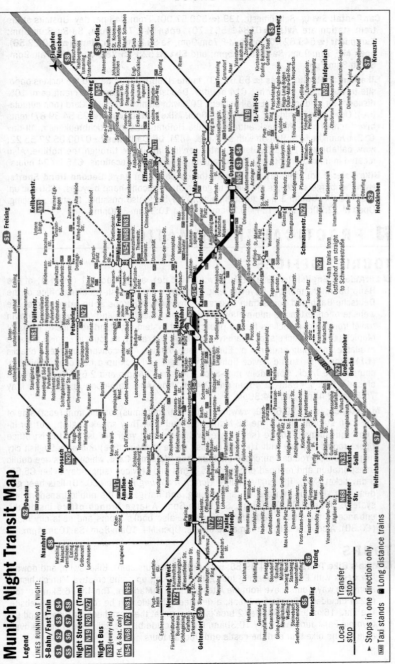

Munich Night Transit Map

Legend

LINES RUNNING AT NIGHT:

S-Bahn/Fast Train
S1 S2 S3 S4
S5 S6 S7 S8

Night Streetcar (Tram)
N17 N19 N20 N27

Night Bus
N33 (every night)

(Fri. & Sat. only)
N54 N68 N72 N81 N95

Local stop

Transfer stop

▲ Stops in one direction only
🚕 Taxi stands
■ Long distance trains

After 4am trains from
Ostfriedhof run straight
to Schwanseestraße

BAYERN

Car Rental: Swing, Schellingstr. 139 (☎520 57 00). From €43 per day. Upstairs at the train station are **Avis** (☎01841 501 70), open M-F 7am-9pm, Sa-Su 8am-5pm; **Europecar** (☎549 02 40), open M-F 7am-9pm, Sa-Su 8am-7pm; **Hertz** (☎550 22 56), open M-F 7am-9pm, Sa-Su 9am-5pm; and **Sixt** (☎525 25 25), open M-F 7am-9pm, Sa-Su 8am-7pm.

Bike Rental: Radius Bikes (☎59 61 13), in the Hauptbahnhof behind the lockers opposite tracks 30-36. €3 per hr., €14 per day. Deposit €50, passport or credit card. 10% discount for students and Eurail-holders, 20% with Munich Welcome Card (non-cumulative). Open May to mid-Oct. daily 10am-6pm. **Mike's Bike Tours** (☎25 54 39 87) rents bikes across from the back entrance of the Hofbräuhaus, on Hochbreukenstr. All day €12, overnight €18. Half-off with a tour (p. 442). **DB CallBikes** (☎0700 05 22 55 22, www.callabike.de) is a Deutsche Bahn service, available through the hotline. Also located in front of the Hauptbahnhof and in select central locations. €15 for 24 hours.

Bike Sale: If you are staying for more than a couple of days, **Second Hand Sports,** Nymphenburgerstr. 29, is the place to go for cheap second-hand bicycles. (€50 and up; ☎59 70 74. UBahn 1 or 7 to Stiglmaierpl.) Buyback also possible. In-store servicing. Open M 12:30pm-7pm, Tu-F 10:30am-7pm, Sa 10:30am-3:30pm.

⁊ PRACTICAL INFORMATION

TOURIST OFFICES

▓ **EurAide in English** (☎59 38 89; www.euraide.de), along track 11 (room 3) of the Hauptbahnhof, near the Bayerstr. exit. EurAide is the English-speaking office of the Deutsche Bahn and books train tickets for anywhere in Europe at no extra charge. The website offers extensive information not available elsewhere, and can be used to plan travel from abroad. Tickets for the public transit system (at standard prices), maps of Munich (€1), and tickets for a variety of walking, bus, and bike tours in English are also available, including ones run by EurAide (see below). Also converts traveler's checks (€1). Drop in for sound advice from the manager and pick up a free copy of his brochure *Inside Track.* Open daily June-Sept. 7:45am-12:45pm and 2-6pm (Su afternoon closed); Oct. 7:45am-12:45pm and 2-4pm; Nov.-Apr. 8am-noon and 1-4pm; May 7:45am-12:45pm and 2-4:30pm.

Main Office: (☎23 39 65 00; www.muenchen.de/Tourismus), on the front (east) side of the train station, next to the SB-Markt on Bahnhofpl. They speak English, but for in-depth questions, EurAide (see above) will better suit your needs. The tourist office books rooms (for free with 10-15% deposit made to their office) and sells English city maps (€0.30). You can purchase the **München Welcome Card,** which offers free public transportation and reduced prices for 35 sights and services (single-day ticket €6.50, 3-day ticket €16). The English guide *Munich for Young People* (€0.50) lists beer gardens and gives tips on cycling, sightseeing, and navigating the public transportation system. Open M-Sa 9am-8pm, Su 10am-6pm. A large **branch office** inside the entrance to the Neues Rathaus on Marienpl. also books rooms and sells city maps (€0.30). A counter sells performance tickets. Open M-F 10am-8pm, Sa 10am-4pm.

TOURS

▓ **Mike's Bike Tours** (☎25 54 39 88; www.mikesbiketours.com). Bike, swim, and down a few beers with English-speaking tour guides, picking up some creative Munich history along the way. Tours leave from the Altes Rathaus in Marienpl. The 4hr., 6.5km city tour (€22) includes a *Biergarten* break; a detailed schedule can be found on the website. The 7hr., 16km tour (€33) has 2 breaks and stops at the Nymphenburg Palace and the Olympic Park. June-July daily 10:30am. Prices include bike rental. Combo tickets available for the bike tour and the castle and Dachau tours.

Spurwechsel Bike Tours (☎ 692 46 99; www.spurwechsel.info). Entertaining tour guides focus on the secrets of Munich's landmarks. Tours in German. 2hr. tours meet F-Su and holidays 11:15am at the Marienpl. fountain. €13; bike rental included. Theme tours (such as the "political tour" or "nature tour") available on request to groups of 8 or more, as are tours in English; call for reservation details. Bike rentals €12.50 per day.

The Original Munich Walks (☎ 55 02 93 74; www.munichwalks.com). Native English speakers give historical walking tours of the city with 2 different slants: the 10am introductory tour of the Altstadt (May-Oct. daily; Nov.-Mar. M, W, Sa) and the Third Reich tour (May-Oct. 9:30am and 3pm). Each 2½hr. tour is €10, students €9, under 14 €5. Combo tickets available for both the walking tours and the Munich Walks guided tour of Dachau. Walking tours meet at the **EurAide** office next to track 11, 10 min. early, or beneath the Neues Rathaus at Marienpl. 10 min. after the listed time.

Munich Walk Tours (☎ 017 12 74 02 04; www.munichwalktours.de) leads 2 hr. walks around Munich for €10, students €9. Beer- and Nazi-themed tours also available. Discounts apply when multiple tours are taken. Tours offered daily mid-Oct. to Apr. at 10:45am (in Dec., Christmas market tours start at 2:45pm), and May to mid-Oct. twice daily at 10:45am and 2:45pm. Meeting point is the Neues Rathaus.

Rikscha-Mobil (☎ 0700 80 90 10 20; www.rikscha-mobil.de) offers 1 hr. tours for two people for €27 each (€21 on weekdays) in a bicycle rickshaw. 30 or 45min. tours also available; briefer tours of the center range €4-15.

Panorama Tours, Arnulfstr. 8 (☎ 55 02 89 95; www.muenchenerstadtrundfahrten.de). 1hr. bilingual double-decker **bus tours** leave from the train station's main entrance on Bahnhofspl., Apr.-Oct. daily 1 per hr. 10am-4pm, with additional bus at 2:30pm. €11, children €6. 2½hr. tours leave daily at 10am and 2:30pm. Tours include admission and a guide at the sites; ask for each day's destinations. €19-23, children €10-12. A 4½hr. Munich By Night tour runs Apr.-Nov. F-Sa 7:30pm. €60. Hotel pick-up available. Office open M-F 7:30am-6pm, Sa 7:30am-noon, Su 7:30-10am. Also offers daytrips.

City Sightseeing Tours (www.city-sightseeing.com), available in nearly 70 cities worldwide, offers a 1hr. tour in a double-decker bus for €11. Tours leave from the Hauptbahnhof square 10am-5pm on the hour, and Fr-Su on the half-hour as well. €11, children under 12 €6. Recorded information in 8 languages covers the city's highlights and includes stops to allow a walk through the pedestrian historical center.

Castle Tours: There are many ways to be guided into the magical realm of mad King Ludwig II (see p. 472 for more castle info). **EurAide** (p. 442) leads a day-long, half-bus, half-train *Schloß*-schlep in English including **Neuschwanstein, Linderhof,** and the Rococo **Wieskirche**. Meet June-July W 8:15am by track 11 in front of EurAide. €41; with Eurailpass, InterRail, or Flexipass €35. Castle admission not included. Book ahead. **Panorama Tours** (see above) offers a 10½hr. bus excursion (in English) to **Neuschwanstein** and **Linderhof** leaving Apr.-Oct. daily 8:30am; Nov.-Mar. Tu-Su 8:30am. €41, children €21; Castle admission not included. Book ahead. **Mike's Bike Tours** (www.busbavaria.com), offers guided day trips (in English) aimed at a younger audience, by bus (or train) and bike that include a visit to **Neuschwanstein,** a bike through the area, swimming, a stop at the alpine slide (€1.30) and spectacular views. Tours leave most days during the high season, check website for meeting times and places. Bus tours €49, train tours €39 (castle admission not included).

Dachau Tours: Before taking a tour, make sure your guide is qualified by The Dachau Memorial. **Radius Touristik** (☎ 550 29 374) gives a 4½hr. English tour of Dachau. Meet at the Radius office opposite tracks 30-36 in the station 20min. before daily tours begin at 9:20, 11:20am and 12:40pm. In Apr. and Oct. only the first and last tours take place. From Nov. to Mar. one tour takes place at noon. Tickets also available at EurAide. No reservations necessary. €19, children under 14 €9.50. **Mike's Bike Tours** (p. 442) provides transportation and a self-guided audio tour. Meet outside the main tourist office in the station Apr. 15-Oct. 31 Tu-Su 9:50am. €14, or €29 for both the Dachau and bike tour, same day only. **Panorama Tours** goes to Dachau on Saturdays from mid-May to mid-October for 4½hr., €22 (children €12).

CONSULATES

Canada: Tal 29 (☎219 95 70). S1-8 to "Isartor." Open M-Th 9am-noon and 2-5pm, F 9am-noon.

Ireland: Dennigerstr. 15. (☎20 80 59 90). Open M-F 9-11am.

UK: Bürkleinstr. 10 (☎21 10 90; www.britishembassy.de), 4th fl. U4 or 5 to "Lehel." Phone hours M-F 8:30am-noon and 1-5pm (F to 3:30pm), consul open M-F 8:45-11:30am and 1-3:15pm.

US: Königinstr. 5 (☎288 80; www.usembassy.de/consular/munchen/index.htm). Open M-F 8-11am. For visa info, call ☎0190 850 0550; €1.86 per min (M-F 7am-8pm).

FINANCIAL SERVICES

Currency Exchange: ReiseBank (☎551 08 37; www.reisebank.de), at the front of the train station on Bahnhofpl. Slightly lower processing fee than other banks. Open daily 7am-10pm. Or, around the corner from EurAide at track 11. Open M-Sa 9:15am-12:30pm, 1-4:15pm.

American Express: Promenadepl. 6 (☎228 014 65; 24hr. hotline ☎08001 85 31 00), to the left of the Hotel Bayerischer Hof. Cashes Traveler's Cheques. Open M-F 9am-1pm and 2-6pm, Sa 9:30am-12:30pm. **Branch** office at Neuhauser Str. 47 (☎22 80 13 87). Open M-F 9:30am-6pm, Sa 10am-1pm.

LOCAL SERVICES

DER Reisebüro (☎55 14 02 00; www.der.de) is in the main hall of the train station and sells train tickets and railpasses. Open M-F 9:30am-6pm, Sa 10am-1pm.

Luggage Storage: 24h. at the **airport** (☎97 52 13 75). Staffed storage room *(Gepäck-aufbewahrung)* in the main hall of the **train station** (☎13 08 50 36). €0.50-3 per day, for a maximum storage time of 3 days. Lockers in main hall and opposite tracks #16, 24, and 28-36. €1-2 per day. Open daily 4am-12:30am.

Lost and Found: Fundbüro, Ötztaler Str. 17 (☎233 00). U6 to "Partnachpl." Open M-F 8am-noon, Tu also 2-6:30pm. **Hauptbahnhof** (13 08 66 64), Bayerstr. 10a, across from track 26. Open M-F 6:30am-11:30pm, Sa 7:30am-10:45pm, Su 7:30am-11pm.

Mitwohnzentrale: An der Uni, Adalbertstr. 6 (☎286 60 60; www.mwz-munich.de). U6 to "Universität." Apartments available for 1mo. or more. Open M-F 10am-6pm. **City Mitwohnzentrale,** Lämmerstr. 4 (☎194 20; www.mitwohnzentrale.de), lists apartments and houses throughout Germany. Open M-F 10am-1pm and 2-6pm. **Studentenwerk,** Leopoldstr. 15 (☎38 19 60; www.studentenwerk.mhn.de), offers inexpensive housing for students. Open M-Th 8am-5pm, F 8am-4pm.

Bookstores: Words Worth, Schellingstr. 19 (☎280 91 41), has an orderly array of English titles in a quiet alcove off the main street. Open M-Tu and F 9am-6:30pm, W-Th 9am-8pm, Sa 10am-3pm. **Hugendubel,** Marienpl. 22, (☎48 44 84; www.hugendubel.de) is a 5-story bookstore and cafe offering hundreds of English titles in print, audio and video. Enjoy books before purchase (rare in Germany) in the unforgettable cabbage-shaped reading corners. Open M-F 9:30am-8pm, Sa 9:30am-2pm.

Libraries: Bayerische Staatsbibliothek, Ludwigstr. 16 (☎28 63 80; www.bsb-muenchen.de), U6 to Universität. The largest university library in any German-speaking country with over 6.5 million books, magazines and newspapers. Open M-F 9am-9pm, Sa-Su 10am-5pm; Aug.-Sept. closes earlier. **Bookshelf,** Blumenstr. 36 (☎61 62 27), is an English library. U1 or 2 to "Sendlinger Tor." Open M, W, F 3-6pm, Sa 11am-1pm.

Visitor Publications: New In the City (www.new-in-the-city.com) a yearly publication in both German and English (€6.50). Available at newsstands. Also investigate **SZ Woche**, the Süddeutsche Zeitung's Thursday supplement with cultural listings.

Gay and Lesbian Resources: Gay services information (☎260 30 56), open 7-10pm. Another point of reference is the 24hr. reception of **Hotel Deutsche Eiche**, Reichenbachstr. 13 (☎331 166-0). **Lesbian information** at the **LeTra Lesbentraum**, Angertorstr. 3 (☎725 42 72). Phone times M and W 2:30-5pm; Tu 10:30am-1pm; open Th 7-9pm. See also **Gay and Lesbian Munich**, p. 462.

Women's Resources: Kofra Kommunikationszentrum für Frauen, Baaderstr. 30 (☎201 04 50). Job advice, magazines, lesbian politics, and books. Open M-Th 4-10pm, F noon-6pm. **Frauentreffpunkt Neuperlach**, Oskar-Maria-Graf-Ring 20-22 (☎670 64 63 or 679 209 71; www.frauenzentrum-neuperlach.de). Services and venues for women. Cafe open M 3-5pm to women and young children; Tu 10am-1pm to women without children; and Th 4-6pm for "international coffeehouse." Open Tu and Th-F 10am-1pm, W 10am-1pm and 3-6pm. **Lillemor's Frauenbuchladen**, Barer Str. 70 (☎272 12 05), is a women's center. Open M-F 10am-6:30pm, Sa 10am-2pm.

Disabled Resources: Info Center für Behinderte, Schellingstr. 31 (☎211 70; www.vdk.de/bayern), lists Munich's resources for disabled persons. Open M-Th 9am-noon and 12:30-6pm, F 9am-5pm.

Ticket Agencies: To order almost all event tickets by phone call **München Ticket** (☎54 81 81 81; www.muenchenticket.de). Advance tickets are available at the **Ticket Service** desks in the Kaufhof department store on **Marienpl.**, 3rd fl. (☎260 32 49) or at **Karlspl.**, ground fl. (☎512 53 36). Marienpl. location open M-F 10am-8pm, Karlspl. M-F 11am-8pm. Both open Sa 10am-7pm.

Laundromats: SB-Waschcenter, Lindwurmstr. 124. U1 to "Sendlinger Tor." Wash €3.50 (soap €0.30), dry €0.60 per 10min. Open daily 7am-11pm. Also at Untersbergstrasse 8. U2, 7 and 8 to "Untersbergstrasse." **Free wireless Internet**. Same prices and hours.

Swimming Pools: 15 local pools. Outdoor pools open May to mid-Sept., but most places have indoor pools too. Pick up *Münchener Bäder* at the tourist office for full listings. Realize your dreams for gold at the **Olympic Pool** (☎306 72290) in Olympiapark. U3 (or bus 36, 136, 41, 43, 81, or 184) to Olympiazentrum. Open daily 7am-11pm.

EMERGENCY AND COMMUNICATIONS

Emergency: Police ☎110. **Ambulance** and **Fire** ☎112. **Emergency medical service** ☎192 22, home service 551 771. **Emergency road service** ☎0180 222 22 22.

Bahnhofsmission: The experienced staff at this walk-in center can help in case of emergencies ensuing at or near the train station. Near track 11, just past EurAide.

Rape Crisis Line: Frauennotruf München, Güllstr. 3 (☎76 37 37).

AIDS Hotline: ☎194 11 or 23 32 33 33. M-F 7-9:30pm.

Pharmacy: Bahnhofpl. 2 (☎59 41 19 or 59 81 19), on the corner outside the train station. Open M-F 8am-6:30pm, Sa 8am-2pm.

Medical Assistance: Klinikum Rechts der Isar, across the river on Ismaninger Str. U4 or 5 to "Max-Weber-Pl." Free and anonymous STD/AIDS tests at **Münchener AIDS-Hilfe**, Lindwurmstr. 71 (☎544 64 70). Open M-Th 9:30am-6pm. F 9:30am-2pm. UK and US consulates carry lists of English-speaking doctors.

Internet Access: Easy Everything, on Bahnhofspl. next to the post office. Over 500 computers, also offers printing and other services. €2.40 per hr. Unlimited passes for periods of 24hr. (€4); 7 days (€10); or 30 days (€25). Open 24hr. **Internet Cafe**, Marienpl. 20 (☎20 70 27 37; www.icafe.spacenet.de.) serves cocktails and food all night. €1 per 30min. Open 24hr. **International Phone World**, Schillerstr. 8. From the Hauptbahnhof, walk half a block down Schillerstr. Internet €1 per 20min. A variety of international phone cards and phones available (€2.20 per min. to Australia, Canada, and the US). **Wireless access** for your laptop can be found in many places (p. 37), including some locations of the trendy **San Francisco Coffee Company** (☎ 995 29 73), near the Isartor at Tal 15, or in Theatinerstr. 23/Odeonsplatz. Access vouchers on sale at the counter, €2.50 per hr., €3.90 per day, €24.90 per mo. Open M-F 7:30am-11pm; Sa 8am-11pm, Su 9am-10pm. Another wireless hotspot at **Times Square Bistro,** (☎ 51 26 26 00) in the train station on Bayerstr. 6. €3 per hr., payable only by credit card. Open Su-W 7:30am-1am, Th-Sa 7:30am-3am. **Batty Baristas,** Barer Str. 42 (☎ 28 77 91 62), just opposite the Neue Pinakothek, offers customers **free** wireless access. Surf to your heart's content for the price of coffee (espresso €1.50).

Post Office: Bahnhofpl., 80335 Munich (☎ 59 90 87 16). The yellow building opposite the train station exit. Open M-F 7:30am-8pm, Sa 9am-4pm.

▐ ACCOMMODATIONS AND CAMPING

Munich's accommodations seem to fall into one of three categories: seedy, expensive, or booked solid. During Oktoberfest, only the last category exists—if you're hoping to imbibe the brew, begin your search for accommodations up to a year in advance. Be forewarned that the **rates rise by 10-15% during the Oktoberfest** for *all* types of accommodations. In summer, it's best to call before noon, or book a few weeks in advance. For extended stays in Munich, call the *Mitwohnzentrale* or try bargaining with a pension owner. At most of Munich's hostels you can check in all day, but start your search before 5pm. Don't even think of sleeping in a public area, including the Hauptbahnhof; police patrol all night long.

HOSTELS

Munich has a vibrant hostel scene, with options to suit all tastes (and budgets). Most hostels only admit guests under 26, or families with children.

NEAR THE HAUPTBAHNHOF

▨ **Euro Youth Hotel,** Senefelderstr. 5 (☎ 59 90 88 11; www.euro-youth-hotel.de). From the Bayerstr. exit of the Hauptbahnhof, turn left on Bayerstr., then right on Senefelderstr.; the hotel is on the left. Friendly, well-informed English-speaking staff offers loads of information and spotless, recently repainted rooms. Bar serving *Augustinerbräu* (€2.80) open daily from 7pm. Breakfast buffet €4.90. Wash €2.80. Dry €1.30. Reception 24hr. Dorm beds €19.50; 3-5 person rooms €23.50. Singles without bathroom €45; doubles €27.50, with private shower, telephone and breakfast €36; triples €28; quads €21, all per person. Cash only. ❷

CVJM Jugendgästehaus (YMCA), Landwehrstr. 13 (☎ 552 14 10; www.cvjm-muenchen.org). Take the Bayerstr. exit from the train station, head straight down Goethestr., and take the 2nd left onto Landwehrstr.; it's 1½ long blocks on the right. Central location, pretty rooms, and hall showers. Restaurant open W-F 6:30-10:30pm; meals €7.50. Co-ed rooms for married couples only. Breakfast and sheets included. Reception 8am-12:30am. Lockout 12:30am-7am. Hostel closed on Easter and Dec. 20-Jan. 7. Singles €32-40; doubles €27-29; triples €25-27. Reduced rates Dec.-Feb. ❸

4 You München, Hirtenstr. 18 (☎ 552 16 60; www.the4you.de), 200m from the Hauptbahnhof. Exit at Arnulfstr., go left, quickly turn right onto Pfefferstr., then left onto Hirtenstr. Hostel is 1½ blocks ahead on the right. Has a restaurant and bar, hang-out areas, a playroom, and wheelchair-accessible everything. Breakfast buffet €5. Sheets included. Reception 24hr. Reserve in advance. 4-, 6- or 8-bed dorms €20-23; 12-bed dorms €18; singles €35; doubles €50. Prices slightly higher for customers over 26. Add €3 during Oktoberfest. Hotel rooms also available with private bathrooms and telephones. Breakfast included. Singles €44; doubles €70; triples €95. ❷

Jugendhotel "In Via" Marienherberge, Goethestr. 9 (☎ 55 58 05; invia.muenchen.marienherberge@t-online.de), less than 1 block from the train station. Take the "Bayerstr." exit and walk down Goethestr. An unmarked yellow building with a big black door. **Open only to women.** The rooms are spacious, cheery, and spotless. Kitchen, laundry, and TV facilities. Breakfast included. Wash €1.50, dry €1.50. Reception 8am-midnight. Check-out 9am. Lockout midnight-6am. 6-bed dorms €22, ages 26 and up €27; singles €30/€35; doubles €40/€50; triples €60/€75. ❷

ELSEWHERE IN MUNICH

🏕 **Jugendlager Kapuzinerhölzl ("The Tent"),** In den Kirschen 30 (☎ 141 43 00; www.the-tent.de). Streetcar #17 from the Hauptbahnhof (dir.: Amalienburgstr.) to "Botanischer Garten" (15min.). Follow the signs straight on Franz-Schrank-Str. and turn left onto In den Kirschen; The Tent is on the right. Night streetcars run at least once an hour all night. Join 250 fellow international "campers" under a big tent on a wooden floor. Evening campfires. **Internet** €0.50 per 15min. Bike rental €6 per day. Free city tours in German and English. Free lockers. Kitchen and laundry facilities available. Wash €2, dry €1.50. Passport required as key deposit. Reception 24hr. Open June-Aug. €8.50 gets you a foam pad, wool blankets, bathrooms, showering facilities, and breakfast. Actual beds €11. Camping available for €5.50 per campsite plus €5.50 per person. ❶

🏕 **Jugendherberge Pullach Burg Schwaneck (HI),** Burgweg 4-6 (☎ 74 48 66 70; www.jugendherberge-burgschwaneck.de), in a castle 12km outside the city center. S7 (dir.: Wolfratshausen) to "Pullach" (20min.). Exit the station from the Munich side and follow signs down Margaretenstr. toward the huge soccer field (10min.). Caters largely to the under-18 crowd. Bowling €6.50 per hr. Breakfast and sheets included. Meals €4.80. Reception 11am-11pm. Curfew 11:30pm. 6- to 8-bed dorms €15.50; singles €23.50; doubles €42; quads €66. ❷

Jugendherberge München Neuhausen (HI), Wendl-Dietrich-Str. 20. (☎ 13 11 56; jhmuenchen@djh-bayern.de). U1 (dir.: Westfriedhof) to "Rotkreuzpl." Go down Wendl-Dietrich-Str past the Galeria Kaufhof; the entrance is about 2 blocks ahead on the right. The most "central" of the HI hostels (3km from the city center). Free safes in the reception area. Bike rental €10. Breakfast and sheets included. Sit-down dinner €4.40. Key deposit €15. Reception 24hr. Check-in starts at 11:30am. Big co-ed dorm (37 beds) €17.80; 4- to 6-bed dorms €22.55; doubles €46. ❸

Jugendgästehaus Thalkirchen (HI), Miesingstr. 4 (☎ 723 65 50 or 723 65 60; YGH-muenchen@djh-bayern.de). Take U1 or 2 to "Sendlinger Tor," then U3 (dir.: Fürstenried West) to "Thalkirchen" (15min.). From the Thalkirchnerpl. exit, follow Schäftlarnstr. toward Innsbruck and bear right around the curve, then follow Frauenbergstr. and head left on Miesingstr.; the hostel will be in front of you. TV room, billiards, and a washer/dryer (€3 each). **Internet** available, payable with Euro coins (€3 per hour). Sheets and breakfast included. Reception 24h. Check-in from 2pm (call first if after 6pm). 2- to 15-bed dorms €19.20; singles €22. Discounts for groups apply. Only accepts under-26 year-olds, but families with children welcome. ❸

Haus International, Elisabethstr. 87 (☎ 12 00 60; www.haus-international.de). U2 (dir.: Feldmoching) to "Hohenzollernpl.," then streetcar #12 (dir.: Romanpl.) or bus #33 (dir.: Aidenbachstr.) to "Barbarastr." It's the 5-story beige building behind the BP gas station. Pleasantly clean rooms with no age limit. Billiards, ping pong, small *Biergarten*, TV room, cafeteria and groovy disco with bar. Reception 24hr. Singles €30, with bath €46; doubles €52, with shower €72; triples €78, quads €98, quints €115. ❸

CAMPING

Munich's campgrounds are open from mid-March to late October.

Campingplatz Thalkirchen, Zentralländstr. 49 (☎ 723 17 07; fax 724 31 77). U1 or 2 to "Sendlinger Tor," then U3 to "Thalkirchen," change to bus #135 and get off at the "Campingplatz" bus stop (20min.). 550 sites on the lush banks of the Isar. Jogging and bike paths nearby. TV lounge and restaurant. Wash €4. Dry €0.50. Reception open 7am-11pm. €4.50 per person; €1.30 per child under 14. €3-4 per tent; tent rental €8 per night. €4.30 per car. Showers €1. Caravans also available at €11 per person. ❶

Campingplatz Obermenzing, Lochhausener Str. 59 (☎ 811 22 35; fax 814 48 07). S3, 4, 5, 6, or 8 to "Pasing" then exit toward track 9 and take bus #76 to "Lochhausener Str." Head up Lochhausener Str. from the bus stop; it's on the left after 10min. Friendly and well-kept, but right next to the *Autobahn*. Reception 7:30am-noon and 3-7pm; 7:30am-7pm July-Aug. Wash €4. Dry €1 per 7min. €4.50 per person; €2 per child under 14; €3.85 per tent; €6 per car (car and tent together €6.85). Showers €1. ❶

HOTELS AND PENSIONS

Munich—reputedly a city of 80,000 guest beds—has many affordable options for those who prefer the amenities of a hotel to sharing rooms in hostels. Rooms fill quickly, so call ahead. Expect 10-20% rate increases during Oktoberfest.

NEAR THE HAUPTBAHNHOF

☒ **Hotel Helvetia,** Schillerstr. 6 (☎ 590 68 50; www.Hotel-Helvetia.de), at the corner of Bahnhofspl., just beyond the Vereinsbank, to the right as you exit the station. Possibly the friendliest hotel in Munich. Many recently renovated rooms are outfitted with wood floors and oriental rugs. **Free Internet.** Breakfast included. Reception 24hr. Singles €30-35; doubles €40-55, with shower €50-65; triples €55-69; quads €75-88; 5-bed room separable into 2 rooms €95-110. ❸

☒ **Creatif Hotel Elephant,** Lämmerstr. 6 (☎ 55 57 85; www.munich-hotel.net). 300m from the train station. From the Arnulfstr. exit, take a quick right on Pfefferstr., turn left on Hirtenstr., and right on Lämmerstr. All newly renovated rooms with fabulously colorful decor, private baths, telephones, and TVs. **Free Internet.** Reception 24hr. Singles €30-40; doubles €40-65; extra bed €10. ❸

Hotel Kurpfalz, Schwanthaler Str. 121 (☎ 540 98 60; www.kurpfalz-hotel.de). From the Bayerstr. station exit, walk 1 block down Schillerstr., then turn right onto Schwanthaler Str., continue for 5-6 blocks until after the Holzapfelstr. intersection (15min.). Or take streetcar #18 or 19 to "Holzapfelstr." and walk from there. Private baths, satellite TVs and phones in all rooms of this hip hotel. Breakfast included. Laundry service available. Reception 24hr. Singles €30-40; doubles €45-65; doubles with cots €84. Book early, prices increase steeply as availability decreases. ❹

Pension Locarno, Bahnhofspl. 5 (☎ 55 51 64 or 55 51 65; www.pensionlocarno.de). From the Bahnhofspl. exit of the station walk left across Bahnhofspl. Look for the building with the large "Pension" sign. Comfortable, carpeted rooms, all with cable TV and phone. Reception 7:30am-5pm. Singles €43; doubles €56; triples €72. ❹

Hotel-Pension Flora, Karlstr. 49 (☎ 59 41 35; www.hotel-flora.de). Take the Bayerstr. exit from the train station and go left on Dachauerstr. Located 2 blocks down on the left (5min.). Close to the station, this hotel offers reasonable prices that include sheets and breakfast. **Internet** is €1 for 10 minutes. Singles €40, with shower €55; doubles €50/€75; triples €75-130/€90-130. ❷

Hotel Royal, Schillerstr. 11a, (☎ 59 10 21). To the right as you exit the station, two blocks down Schillerstr. on the left. This new pension has spacious rooms with large windows, bathrooms and TVs. **Free Internet.** Breakfast included in the sunny and spacious dining hall. The 24hr. reception will help you book tours and plan your stay in Munich. Singles €35-45, doubles €55-65, triples €65-79, quads €80-100. ❹

Pension Central, Bayerstr. 55 (☎543 98 46; pension.central@t-online.de). Go right out of the station's Bayerstr. exit and walk 5min. up Bayerstr.; it's on the left. Large pension with modern decor. Breakfast included. Reception 24hr. Singles €34, with shower €40; doubles €52/€67; triples €69/€78; quads €92/€104; quints €115/€130. ❸

ELSEWHERE IN MUNICH

▨ **Pension Theresia,** Luisenstr. 51 (☎52 12 50; fax 542 06 33). U2 to "Theresienstr." Take the Augustenstr. S.O. exit, follow Theresienstr.; take 2nd right onto Luisenstr. Red curtains complement spacious rooms. TV available upon request. Breakfast included. Reception (3rd fl.) 7am-9pm. Singles €30-33, with shower €46-50; doubles €46-52/€68-72; triples €66-69/€87-93; quads €80-88/€96-100, quints €100-110. ❸

▨ **Pension Frank,** Schellingstr. 24 (☎28 14 51; www.pension-frank.de). U3 or 6 to "Universität." Take the Schellingstr. exit, then the 1st right onto Schellingstr.; Pension is 2 blocks down on the right. Schwabing location is fabulous for cafe and bookstore aficionados. **Internet** €2 per hour. Breakfast included. Reception 7:30am-10pm. Check-out 11am. 3- to 6-bed dorms €25-28; singles €45-49; doubles €57-60; triples €75-81; quads €100-108; quints €125-135. ❹

Pension am Kaiserplatz, Kaiserpl. 12 (☎34 91 90). U3 or 6 to "Münchener Freiheit," take the escalator to Herzogstr., then turn left; take a left three blocks later onto Viktoriastr.; it's at the end of the street on the right (10min. from the U-Bahn stop). A few blocks from nightlife central. Motherly owner offers elegant rooms, each one in its own style, from Victorian to Modern. Breakfast included and served directly to the room. Reception 8am-8pm. Singles €31, with shower €47; doubles €48-53/€55-57; triples €63/€66; quads €84; quints €105; 6-bed rooms €126. ❸

Hotel-Pension am Markt, Heiliggeiststr. 6 (☎22 50 14; hotel-am-markt.muenchen@t-online.de). Smack dab in the city center, just off the Viktualienmarkt. S1-8 to "Marienpl.," then walk past the Altes Rathaus and turn right down the little alley behind the Heiliggeist church. Small but spotless rooms are wheelchair accessible. Breakfast included. Singles €38, with shower €66; doubles €68/€92; triples €100/€123. ❹

◨ FOOD

The vibrant **Viktualienmarkt,** 2min. south of Marienpl., offers both basic and exotic foods and ingredients, but prices can be steep. (Open M-F 10am-8pm, Sa 8am-4pm.) On every corner, ubiquitous **Biergärten** (beer gardens) serve savory snacks and booze. For

THE LOCAL STORY

BREZN AND BAKLAVA

Bavaria, with its sausages and beer, seems an unlikely home for Muslims, yet the Turkish community of Munich is vibrant. Mehmet Kargöz, owner of a restaurant in a Turkish neighborhood, has lived in Bavaria for nearly thirty years.

On life in Germany: The Turkish community of Munich used to be very closed, but it is not anymore, there is much more openness. The way of thinking of young Turks is mostly German. Even marriage is much more flexible nowadays. If you live here, it affects you a lot, even the way you think. The people who have been here for a while now are getting a lot back from their new home.

On German: Older Turkish people only speak broken German, but the third generations speak German perfectly, and usually some English as well.

On Bavarian cuisine: Turkish families eat a lot more green vegetables than Germans do. That's why we have our own markets. And I don't sell alcoholic drinks. Bavarians are all about their culture, but this does not pose any sort of problem. My customers for example are mainly German; the rest are Italian, Turkish, etc.

On returning to Turkey: For the third generation of German-born Turks, Turkey is just a holiday destination. Of the first generation, 60-70% stay in Germany even after retiring. It does not depend on the working situation; they are simply used to living here.

an authentic Bavarian lunch, spread some *Brez'n* (pretzels) with *Leberwurst* (Liverwurst) or cheese. *Weißwürste* (white veal sausages) are another native bargain, served with sweet mustard and a soft pretzel on the side, but real Müncheners only eat them before 11am. Slice the skin open and devour the tender meat. *Leberkäse*, a local lunch, is a pinkish mix of ground beef and bacon which contains neither liver nor cheese. *Leberknödel* are liver dumplings served in soup or with *Kraut; Kartoffelknödel* (potato dumplings) and *Semmelknödel* (bread and egg dumplings) should be eaten with a hearty chunk of German meat. Herbivorous travelers can enjoy a plate of *Spargel* (asparagus), with a *Germknödel* (a sweet, jelly-filled dumpling topped with vanilla sauce) for dessert.

SCHWABING

The lively university district off **Ludwigstraße** clusters cafes and restaurants on **Schellingstraße, Amalienstraße,** and **Türkenstraße** (U3 or 6 to "Universität").

■ **Schelling Salon,** Schellingstr. 54 (☎272 07 88). Bavarian *Knödel* and billiards since 1872. Rack up at tables where Lenin, Rilke, and Hitler once played (€7 per hr.). Breakfast €3-5.10, German entrees €4-11. Open M and Th-Su 6:30am-1am, kitchen open until midnight. A free **billiard museum** displays a 200-year-old Polish table and the history of pool dating back to the Pharaohs. Museum open Su night or upon request. ❸

News Bar, Amalienstr. 55 (☎28 17 87), at the corner of Schellingstr. Trendy cafe teeming with students. Large portions at reasonable prices. Breakfast menu €3-9. A wide assortment of salads, sandwiches, or pasta (€4-12). Open daily 7:30am-2am. ❸

Türkenhof, Türkenstr. 78 (☎280 02 35), offers a wide selection of global cuisine, from Middle Eastern to Mexican to Thai. Popular with the low-key student population. Smoky and buzzing from noon until late. Variable daily menu with numerous veggie options. Entrees €5-8. Open M-Th and Su 11am-1am, F-Sa 11am-2am. ❸

Mensa, Arcisstr. 17, to the left of the Pinakothek just below Gabelsbergstr. on Arcisstr. U2 or 8 to "Königspl." Students from the Technical University hit the cafeteria on the ground floor for light meals (€0.70-2). The actual Mensa upstairs serves large portions of cheap food (€2-4), with at least 1 vegetarian dish. To eat there, get a "Legic-Karte" in the library (€5 deposit plus €5 toward purchases). Student ID required. Lunch 11am-2pm. Open M-Th 7:45am-5:30pm, F 7:45am-4pm; during vacations M-F 8am-4pm. ❶

ELSEWHERE IN MUNICH

■ **Dukatz Kaffee im Literaturhaus,** Salvatorpl. 1 (☎291 96 00). The center of literary events in Munich since 1997, this cafe is the place to see and be seen. This home for struggling artists serves gourmet food (€6-8) to complement creative drink options (€2-4). Sip a cup of coffee and people-watch—you will unwittingly be observing the city's writers at rest. Open M-Sa 10am-1am (Sa 3pm) and 6:30pm-10:30pm. ❹

■ **Sarcletti's,** Nymphenburgerstr. 155 (☎15 53 14; www.sarcletti.de), has the best ice cream in town. Take U1 to "Rotkreuzpl." Cones €0.70 per scoop. Mouth-watering specialities €5-12. Open Apr.-Sept. M-F 9am-11:30pm; Oct.-Mar. M-F 9am-11pm. ❸

Poseidon, Westenriederstr. 13 (☎29 92 96), off the Viktualienmarkt. Bowls of *bouillabaisse* (soup) with bread for €10 in a bustling fish-market atmosphere. Other fish and seafood dishes €4-13. Join Müncheners in the know for the special sushi menu on Th (€20). Open M-W 8am-6:30pm, Th-F 8am-7pm, Sa 8am-4pm. ❸

Augustiner Beerhall and Restaurant, Neuhauser Str. 27 (☎23 18 32 57). This restaurant, between Marienpl. and the train station, offers Bavarian specialties and Augustiner brew (*Maß* €6). English menu. Entrees €4-13.50. Open daily 10am-midnight. ❸

La Porte Confiseur, Heiliggeiststr. 1, (☎29 16 21 12). The La Portes have made delicious truffles and chocolates in the back of this boutique for over ten years. Most items sell at €5 for 100g. The French couple also makes crêpes and hot chocolate. ❸

Shoya, Orlandostr. 5 (☎29 27 72), across from the Hofbräuhaus. The most reasonably priced Japanese restaurant in town. Fill up on rice dishes, teriyaki and sushi (€4-10). Open daily 10:30am-midnight. Also at Frauenstr. 18 (☎24 20 89 89), open Tu-Su, 11am-midnight. Shoya also has a market location at the Viktualienmarkt. ❸

Weißes Bräuhaus, Tal 7 (☎29 98 75), across from the McDonald's at the end of Marienpl. Traditional restaurant founded in 1490, in present incarnation since 1872. Brims with dishes like the €7.90 "Münchener Voressen" made of calf and pig lungs. Choose from 40-50 options on the daily menu (€3-17) served by waitresses in classic Bavarian garb. Smaller portions on request (€4.50-10). Open daily 8am-midnight. ❸

Cafe Hag/Confiserie Rottenhöfer, Residenzstr. 25-26 (☎22 29 15), across from the Residenz. Munich's oldest *Konditerei* specializes in an array of sweets (€2-4), which dominate the menu and the elegant interior. Open M-F 8:45am-7pm, Sa 8am-6pm. ❷

Beim Sedlmayr, Westenriederstr. 14 (☎22 62 19), off the Viktualienmarkt. This renowned *Weißwurst* joint serves only Bavarian meat. Specials €4-14. Open M-F 9am-11pm, Sa 8am-4pm. Kitchen open M-F 9am-9:30pm, Sa 8am-3:30pm. ❸

La Fiorentina Trattoria Pizzeria Cafe, Goethestr. 41 (☎53 41 85), a few blocks from the train station. Italian-speaking waitstaff serves up large pasta dishes at reasonable prices (€6-8). Daily menu, ask about the regional dishes; main courses €5-17, pizzas €4-8. Open M-F 11:30am-11:30pm, Sa 11:30am-3pm and 6pm-10:20pm. ❸

VEGETARIAN RESTAURANTS

SCHWABING

▨ Café Ignaz, Georgenstr. 67 (☎271 60 93). U2 to "Josephspl.," take Adelheidstr. 1 block north and turn right on Georgenstr. Earth-friendly bakery and cafe serves delicious food to a low-key clientele. Dinners, ranging from crepes to stir-fry dishes, €5-9. Breakfast buffet M and W-Fr 8-9am (€5), 9-11am (€7). Lunch buffet M-F 12-2pm (€5.50); brunch buffet Sa-Su 9am-1:30pm (€8). Open M-F 8am-10pm, Sa-Su 9am-10pm. ❷

Aran, Theatinerstr. 12 (☎255 469), is the most creative bakery in Munich, with inexpensive panini (pick a loaf and have it toasted with basil and mozzarella for €3.50). Also serves strong coffee. Open M-Sa 10am-8pm. ❷

ELSEWHERE IN MUNICH

Buxs, Frauenstr. 9 (☎291 95 50), on the southern edge of the Viktualienmarkt on the corner of Frauenstr. Artful pastas, salads, soups, and bread in an indoor/outdoor setting. Self-serve, with a weight-based charge (€2 for 100g). Take-away available in glass (€3) or recyclable (€0.25) containers. Open M-F 11am-6:45pm, Sa 11am-3pm. ❸

Gollier, Gollierstr. 83 (☎50 16 73). U4 or 5, or S7 or 27 to "Heimeranpl." Take a left onto Ridlerstr. and walk 2 blocks west; turn right onto Astallerstr. and then left on Gollierstr. Serves delicious pizzas, casseroles, and crepes (€7-10). Buffet is especially convenient: M-F 11:30am-2:30pm (€6), also Mondays at 5pm. Open M-F 11:30am-2:30pm and 5pm-midnight, Sa 5-midnight, Su 10am-midnight. ❸

Prinz Myshkin, Hackenstr. 2 (☎26 55 96). S1-8 to "Marienplatz," then head 3 blocks down Rosenstr. and turn right. This internationally recognized restaurant is pricey but unique, with Asian-influenced cuisine featuring luscious paneers. Main courses are €9.50-15. Open daily 11am-12:30am; kitchen closes at 11pm. ❺

◉ SIGHTS

▨ RESIDENZ. Down the pedestrian zone from Odeonspl., the richly decorated Residenz is the most visible presence of the Wittelsbach dynasty, whose apartments and State Rooms now comprise the **Residenzmuseum.** The luxurious apartments range from Renaissance to 17th-century Baroque, 18th-century Rococo and 19th-century

RESURRECTING THE FRAUENKIRCHE

For 200 years the bell-shaped cupola of Dresden's Frauenkirche Church of Our Lady) was the crowning glory of a stunning sky-ine. The Baroque church, completed in 1743, was built by master architect George Bähr as a symbol of strength, community and durability. But the Allied fire-bombing of February 1945 reduced the church to rubble, along with over three-fourths of he surrounding city.

The church lay in ruins for 45 years, until the reunification of Germany brought about the rebuilding of many of Dresden's historical buildings. Reconstruction plans were made in 1990, and the internationally supported work began three years later.

In June 2004, the famous dome once more topped the church. The same golden cross that crowned it 250 years ago was salvaged from the rubble and refurbished—by a British craftsman whose father flew in the 1945 air raid—and presented to Dresden by Great Britain as a gesture of change and reconciliation.

One sixth of the new exterior is composed of stones from the original church that have been meticulously placed in their original positions. Although work on the church will continue through 2005, the completed silhouette of the Frauenkirche is a symbol of healing for many Dresdeners and a sign that the rebirth of a city, and a nation, is almost complete.

Neoclassical styles. Also on display are also collections of European porcelain, gold and silverware, and a 17th-century court chapel. Highlights include the Rococo **Ahnengalerie,** hung with over 100 "family portraits" tracing the royal lineage, and the spectacular Renaissance **Antiquarium,** the oldest room in the Residenz. Behind the Residenz, the beautifully landscaped **Hofgarten** shelters a small temple. *(Max-Joseph-pl. 3. Take U3-6 to "Odeonspl." ☎ 29 06 71. Open daily from Apr. to mid-Oct. 9am-6pm, Th 9am-8pm; in winter daily 10am-4pm. Last admission 30min. before closing time. German language tours meet just outside the museum entrance Su 11am. Entrance €6, students €5, children €3.)* The **Schatzkammer** (treasury) contains the most precious religious and secular symbols of Wittelsbach power: crowns, swords, crosses and reliquaries collected during the Counterreformation to increase the dynasty's Catholic prestige. *(Open same hours as Residenzmuseum. €6; students, seniors, and group members €5; children under 18 free with adult. Combination ticket to Schatzkammer and Residenzmuseum €9; students and seniors €8.)* A collection of **Egyptian art** is also housed on the premises *(☎ 28 92 76 30; open Tu-Fr 9am-5pm, Sa-Su 10am-5pm. Entrance €4, students and seniors €3.)* Across Max-Joseph Platz lies the golden-yellow Baroque **Theatinerkirche,** constructed by Ferdinand Maria from 1663 to 1675 in honor of his son's birth. The crypt houses the bronze coffins of the Wittelsbach clan. *(Church tours June-Sept., Th at 2pm, €3.50. Crypt open M-Fr 10am-1pm and 1:30-4:30pm, Sat 10am-3pm. €2)*

MARIENPLATZ. Sacred stone spires tower above the Marienpl., a major S-Bahn and U-Bahn junction and the social nexus of the city. The plaza, formerly known as *Marktplatz,* takes its name from the ornate 17th-century monument to the Virgin Mary at its center, the **Mariensäule,** built in 1638 to celebrate the fact that, during the Thirty Years' War, the city survived both the Swedish army and the plague. At the neo-Gothic **Neues Rathaus** (built in medieval style at the dawn of the 20th century), the **Glockenspiel** chimes with a display of a victorious Bavarian jouster. The dancing coopers below are a reminder of how the barrel-makers coaxed townspeople out of their homes, singing and dancing, at the end of the plague of 1517. *(Daily 11am, noon, 3pm, also 5pm in summer.)* At 9pm a mechanical watchman marches out and the Guardian Angel escorts the *Münchner Kindl* ("Munich Child," a symbol of the city) to bed. On the face of the **Altes Rathaus** tower, to the right of the Neues Rathaus, are all of Munich's coats of arms—with the notable exception of the Nazi swastika-bearing shield. Hitler commemorated his failed 1923 putsch in the ballroom, which is still used for official functions. *(Tower open M-F 9am-7pm; Sa-Su 10am-7pm. €1.50, under 19 €0.75, under 6 free.)*

FRAUENKIRCHE. One block west from Marienplatz, towards the Hauptbahnhof (see **Resurrecting the Frauenkirche**, p. 452).

ASAMKIRCHE. This small Rococo masterpiece of a church commemorates Prague's patron **St. John of Nepomuk,** who was allegedly thrown in the Moldau on the orders of the Emperor for refusing to violate the confidentiality of confession (in reality it was a political move). The frescoes on the ceiling narrate the story in detail. To either side of the church stand the residences of the two Asam brothers, Cosmas Damian and Egid Quirin, who financed its construction and decorated its interior. Doors still connect their houses (donated to the priests after the brothers' deaths) to the elevated church balcony. The church looks more expensive than it is; while the red marble is real, the blue-gray surface is just stucco. *(Sendlinger Str. 32; 4 blocks down Sendlinger Str. from the Marienpl. Tours June-Sept. at noon. €3.50.)*

PETERSKIRCHE. The 12th-century Peterskirche represents Munich's ecclesiastical past; its golden interior, which contains the skeleton of **Holy Munditia,** patron saint of single women, was "Baroquified" in the 18th century. Atop the tower, christened **Alter Peter** by locals, a spectacular view of Munich and (on clear days) the Alps awaits those with the *Irxenschmalz* (Bavarian for muscle power) needed to scale the 300 steps. *(Rindermarkt and Peterspl., across Marienpl. from the Neues Rathaus. Open M-Sa 9am-7pm, Su 10am-7pm. Tower €1.50, students €1, children €0.30.)*

MICHAELSKIRCHE. Ludwig II of Bavaria (of castle fame) rests peacefully with 40-odd other Wittelsbachs in the crypt of the 16th-century Jesuit Michaelskirche. Together with the later **Dreifaltigkeitskirche** and Asamskirche, it represents the pinnacle of the Bavarian Counterreformation, dubbed "Barockboom," by art historians. The construction of the church, intended by Wilhelm V "the Pious" to flaunt the city's Catholicism, almost bankrupted the state, and was marred by the immediate fall of the tower. Thinking that St. Michael had destroyed it for being too small, Wilhelm expanded construction, but the tower was never rebuilt for fear that St. Michael might see a new one as a challenge. Father Rupert Mayer, one of the few German clerics who spoke out against Hitler, preached here. *(Kaufingerstr. and Ettstr., four blocks from Marienplatz on Kaufingerstr. in direction of the Hauptbahnhof. ☎ 231 70 60. Church open M-W and F-Sa 8:30am-7pm, Th 8:30am-9pm, Su 6:45am-10pm. Concerts Su at 9am. Crypt open M-F 9:30am-4:30pm, Sa 9:30am-2:30pm. €1.50, children under 15 €1.)*

ENGLISCHER GARTEN. Three times bigger than New York's Central Park, the Englischer Garten is the largest metropolitan public park in Europe. On sunny days, all of Munich turns out to fly kites, ride horses, or sunbathe. A couple of beer gardens are on the grounds, as is a Japanese tea house, Chinese pagoda, and Greek temple. Nude sunbathing areas are designated **FKK** on signs and park maps: consider yourself warned. Daring Müncheners daring surf the white-water rapids of the Eisbach, the artificial river that flows through the park. The bridge on Prinzregentenstr., close to the Haus der Kunst, is a great vantage point for these stunts.

SCHLOß NYMPHENBURG. Constructed to celebrate the birth of Max Emanuel in 1662 (after 10 years of failed attempts), the breathtaking Schloß Nymphenburg is an ode to the overambitious hopes of the Wittelsbach dynasty. The gorgeous park was added in 1715 and remodeled in the English style at the beginning of the 19th century. Modeled after Versailles, the palace was built and extended in the two centuries when France dominated Europe, culturally and politically. The Rococo decorations and the neoclassical themes in the grandiose two-story marble hall are reminiscent of the Sun King's (Louis XIV) France, while the empire-style furniture in the electors' apartments is Napoleonic. The **Gallery of Beauties** is a fascinating collection of portraits of both noblewomen and commoners whom the king fancied or bedded. Particularly famous are **Helene Sedlmayer,** a market girl protected by the king, and **Lola Montez,** an English theatrical dancer with whom Ludwig had an affair well into his 70s, and who later led the 1848 revolution that caused his deposition. In the landscaped gardens the Amalienburg, the Badenburg and the oriental Pagodenburg, richly decorated, intimate manors, were once the locations of exclusive parties. The faux-ancient **Magdalen hermitage** was meant, with its fashionable grotto-style walls, to provoke penance in the courtiers. See how royalty rode and ate in style at the **Marstallmuseum** (carriage museum) and the porcelain collection. *(Streetcar #17 (dir.: Amalienburgstr.) to "Schloß Nymphenburg." ☎ 17 90 80. Complex open Apr. to mid-Oct. daily 9am-6pm, Th 9am-8pm; late Oct. to Mar. daily 10am-4pm. Museum and Schloß open Tu-Su 9am-noon and 1-5pm. Badenburg, Pagodenburg, and Magdalen hermitage closed in winter. Schloß €5, students €4. Manors €2/€1. Marstallmuseum €4/€3. Entire complex €10/€8; children under 18 free with adult.)*

BOTANISCHER GARTEN. Next door to Schloß Nymphenburg, the greenhouses of the immense Botanischer Garten shelter rare and wonderful flora from around the world. Ask at the entrance what is flowering (rhododendrons in June, roses in July), but be sure not to miss the greenhouses with turtles scuttling about beneath the orchids, the alpine hill over the lake, and other exotic landscapes. *(Streetcar #17 (dir.: Amalienburgstr.) to "Botanischer Garten." ☎ 17 86 13 10. Open daily May-Aug. 9am-7pm; Apr. and Sept. 9am-6pm; Feb.-Mar. and Oct. 9am-5pm; Nov.-Jan. 9am-4:30pm. €2, students €1.)*

NAZI-RELATED SIGHTS. Mixed with Munich's Baroque elegance are visible traces of Germany's Nazi past. Buildings erected by Hitler's regime that survived the 1945 bombings stand as grim reminders of Munich's role as the ideological *Hauptstadt der Bewegung* (capital of the movement). The ceiling of the **Hofbräuhaus,** where the Nazi party held its first political rallies, still bears faint swastikas. The **Haus der Kunst,** built to enshrine Nazi principles of art, serves as a modern art museum; swastika patterns have been left on its porch as reminders of its origins (see **Museums,** p. 455). The gloomy limestone building now housing the **Hauptschule für Musik und Theater** was built under Hitler's auspices and functioned as the **Führerbau,** his Munich headquarters. From its balcony he viewed the city's military parades; it was also here that Chamberlain signed away the Sudetenland in 1938. At the **Königsplatz,** one block away from the Führerbau between the Antikensammlung and the Glyptothek Museums, thousands of books were burned on the night of May 10, 1933. Memorials dedicated to the **White Rose student movement,** whose leaders were executed in Munich in 1943 for speaking out against the Third Reich, stand at the Ludwigs-Maximillians Universität and in the Hofgarten past the Staatskanzlei.

OLYMPIAPARK. Built for the 1972 Olympic Games in Munich, the lush and green Olympiapark contains the architecturally bold, tent-like **Olympia-Zentrum** and the 290m **Olympiaturm,** the tallest building in Munich. Three **tours** in English are available: the "Adventure Tour" of the entire park leaves Apr.-Oct. daily at 2pm from the Info-Pavilion, while a tour of just the soccer stadium meets Mar.-Oct. daily at 11am. The **Roof Climb,** daily 2:30pm, is a 2hr. exploration of the **Olympiastadion** with a rope and hook. *(Meet at the north box office of the Olympic Stadium. Architectural tour available upon request for groups of 10 or more. Adventure tours €7, students and ages 6-15 €5. Soccer Stadium tour €5/€3.50. Roof climb €25/20, weekends €30/25.)* Tourists can marvel at the view from the top of the Turm or attend various outdoor events all summer, from flea markets to bungee jumping, in the park itself. *(Take U3 to "Olympiazentrum." Info Pavilion ("Besucherservice") at skating rink ☎ 30 67 24 14. Open M-F 10am-6pm, Sa 10am-3pm. Tower open daily 9am-midnight. €3, ages 6-15 and students €2, children under 6 free.)*

TIERPARK HELLABRUN. Animals are allowed to roam (relatively) freely and interact with each other in Munich's zoo, built in 1911. There are no large fences to obstruct the view; the creatures are kept in by a series of meandering streams. In the hall of bats, night dwellers fly around your head. The sign outside the entrance lists the feeding times of many animals, including penguins and tigers. *(Tierparkstr. 30. U3* to *"Thalkirchen,"* then follow signs over the Isar to the Tierpark. ☎ *62 50 80; www.zoo-munich.de. Open Apr.-Sept. daily 8am-6pm; Oct.-Mar. daily 9am-5pm. Wheelchairs can be borrowed from the front desk. €9; students €6.50; children 4-14 €4.50; children under 4 free.)*

🏛 MUSEUMS

Munich has been a superb museum city ever since Ludwig I decided to make it into an "Athens on the Isar" in the 19th century. The *Münchner Volkshochschule* (☎ 48 00 62 29) offers many museum tours for €6. The tourist office sells day passes for all of Munich's state-owned museums (€15), which are free on Sunday.

MUSEUMSINSEL

DEUTSCHES MUSEUM. One of the world's largest and best science and technology museums. Exhibits include an early telephone, the work bench upon which Otto Hahn first split an atom, and a recreated subterranean labyrinth of mining tunnels. An impressive aerial electrical demonstration takes place daily (11am, 2pm, 4pm). A walk through the museum's 50+ departments covers over 17km; grab an English guidebook (€4). There is also an impressive **flight museum** in a WWI hangar in Schleißheim. *(☎ 315 71 40; Effnerstr. 18. S-Bahn to Oberschleißheim, then follow signs. Open daily 9am-5pm. Admission €3.50, students and seniors €2.50.)* The **planetarium** shows educational films during the day and music and laser shows at night. *(€7, students €6; combination tickets for planetarium and museum €11.50/€9)* The **IMAX screen** shows a variety of 45-min. films, both 2D and 3D every hour on the hour, while the **Forum cinema** screens contemporary European comedies and children's movies *(€7, students €6, M-Tu €5; IMAX 2D €7, students €6, 3D €8.50/7.50. All attractions located at Museuminsel 1. S1-8 to "Isartor" or streetcar #18 to "Deutsches Museum." ☎ 217 91; www.deutsches-museum.de. Open daily 9am-5pm. €7.50, students €3, children under 6 free.)*

KÖNIGSPLATZ

PINAKOTHEK DER MODERNE. A uniquely rich collection of 20th century art is on display at this Pinakothek, which opened in 2000. The sleek space designed by *Münchener* Stephan Braunfels is particularly strong on "classical" modernism: great works of expressionism, surrealism, futurism and cubism, but also Jasper Johns, Gerhard Richter, Lucio Fontana, all the way to exciting contemporary sculptural and video installations. The **design section** has something for everyone, from cars to jewelry. The museum's two other departments feature graphic art and architecture. *(Barerstr. 40. U2 to "Königspl." Take a right at Königspl., and a left after 1 block onto Meiserstr. Walk 1½ blocks to the museum. ☎ 23 80 53 60. Open W, F-Su 10am-5pm, Tu-Th 10am-8pm. €9, students €5. Day pass for all 3 Pinakotheken €12/7.)*

ALTE PINAKOTHEK. This world-famous hall contains Munich's finest art from the 14th to 18th centuries, from religious triptychs to portraits and landscapes. Northern European artists are particularly well-represented, including Dürer, Cranach, Brueghel, Rembrandt and Rubens, but Italian, French and Spanish masterpieces are also on display. *(Barer Str. 27. ☎ 23 80 52 16. Hours and prices same as Pinakothek der Moderne. Combination ticket for the Alte and Neue Pinakotheken €8/€5.)*

NEUE PINAKOTHEK. The 19th century in art, from Jacques-Louis David to Klimt. Special attention given to German art and overlooked movements such as that of the Nazarenes. The Impressionist rooms are particularly impressive. Look for the iconic portrait of Goethe, by Stiegler of Schönheitsgalerie fame. *(Barerstr. 29, next to the Alte Pinakothek. ☎ 23 80 51 95. Open M, W-Su 10am-5pm and Th until 10pm. Tour M noon. Same prices as the Alte Pinakothek.)*

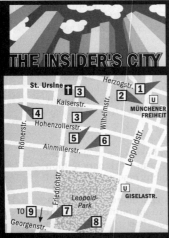

YOUNG SCHWABING: THE MUNICH BOHEME

In 1900, the Schwabing quarter of Munich was home to the blossoming community of artists and writers who developed *Jugendstil* (Art Nouveau), the first 20th-century art movement to completely break with tradition. Named after Munich's bohemian magazine *Die Jugend,* the style celebrated curvy floral motifs and bright colors, and can still be spotted on Schwabing facades.

1 **Erlöserkirche,** Ungererstr 13. The first Jugendstil church, built 1899-1901, has green ceiling decor, a baptismal font, Jugendstil column-tops, a clock, and a cock on the roof. *(U3 or 6 to "Münchener Freiheit." Open M-Th and Sa 8am-5pm.)*

2 Check out the floral facade of **Leopoldstr. 77.**

3 **Bayrischer Revisionsverein,** Kaiserstr. 14 and 29, display fruit and children, two typical elements of the style.

GLYPTOTHEK. Together with the Antikensammlung, the Glyptothek is a testament to the enduring German love for all things Greek, as well as Etruscan and Roman sculptures. The brightly painted plaster casts of Grecian sculpture will challenge your notions of classical art. *(Königspl. 3. U2 to "Königspl." Across Luisenstr. from the Lenbachhaus. ☎28 61 00. Open W and F-Su 10am-5pm, Th 10am-8pm. Free tour Th at 6pm. €3, students €2. €5/€3 together with Antikensammlung)*

ANTIKENSAMMLUNG. A collection of Greek and Etruscan vases and ceramic works of a stunning quality; the artwork brings mythological and everyday subjects to life, with pieces such as Dionysus's drinking bowl and the female bather. *(Königspl. 1. U2 to "Königspl." Across Königspl. from Glyptothek. ☎59 83 59. Open Tu-Su 10am-5pm, W until 8pm. Free tour W at 6pm. €3, students €2.)*

LENBACHHAUS. A rich assemblage of works chronicling Kandinsky's move to abstraction and the founding of the *Blaue Reiter* movement is housed in the opulent mansion of 19th-century painter **Franz von Lenbach.** His personal collection of masterpieces is on the upper levels. The museum also offers a collection of local landscapes and portraits. Together with the adjoining **Kunstbau,** the gallery shows modern exhibits of artists like Picasso and Klee. *(Luisenstr. 33. U2 to "Königspl." ☎23 33 20 02; www.lenbachhaus.de. Open Tu-Su 10am-6pm. Free tour Su 11am. €7, students €3.)*

ELSEWHERE IN MUNICH

MÜNCHENER STADTMUSEUM. Exhibitions present aspects of Munich's city life and history: film, fashion, weapons, puppetry, posters, and more. **Classic films** (€4) every evening at 6 and 9pm, plus 11am and 3pm on Sundays. Foreign films in the original language with German subtitles; call ☎23 32 41 50 for a program. *(St.-Jakobs-pl. 1. U3 or 6 or S1-8 to "Marienpl." Walk down Rindermarkt Str. for 3 blocks; turn left on St.-Jakobs-pl. ☎23 32 23 70; www.stadtmuseum-online.de. Open Tu-Su 10am-6pm. €2.50; students, seniors, and children €1.50; family pass €4; free admission Su.)*

ZAM: ZENTRUM FÜR AUSSERGEWÖHNLICHE MUSEEN. Munich's Center for Unusual Museums corrals such treasures as the Pedal-Car Museum, the Museum of Easter Rabbits, and the Chamberpot Museum. Buy a chamber pot of your own at the gift shop in the lobby. *(Westenriederstr. 41. S1-8 or streetcar #17 or 18 to "Isartor," or walk from Marienplatz. ☎290 41 21. Open daily 10am-6pm. €4, students and children €3.)*

BMW-MUSEUM. Bavaria's second-favorite export is on display at this sleek museum. Headphone stations (in English, German, French, and Spanish) and the brochure *Horizons in Time* (available in 10 languages) guide you through the spiral path to the top of the museum. A great trip for the car enthusiast. *(Petuelring 130. U3 to "Olympiazentrum," take the "Olympiaturm" exit and walk a block up Lerchenauer Str.; the museum will be on your left. ☎38 22 33 07. Open daily 9am-5pm. €3, students €2.)*

VILLA STUCK. This villa, designed by Munich artist **Franz von Stuck,** is the backdrop for paintings, design and graphic art of the early 20th century German *Jugendstil*, a movement which rejected tradition, celebrating nature, spring, the body and youth. *(Prinzregentenstr. 60. U4 to "Prinzregentenplatz," then head down Prinzregentenstr. ☎455 55 10; www.villastuck.de. Open W-Su 11am-8pm. €6, students €3.)*

HAUS DER KUNST. This Nazi construction at the edge of the English Gardens somehow survived the Allied bombing. It now houses art exhibits of all sorts, including the yearly "Große Kunstausstellung," a display of contemporary German art, from late April to late June. Also includes a permanent exhibit detailing the history of the building and its uses. *(Prinzregentenstr. 1. U4 or 5 to "Lehel," then streetcar #17 one stop in the direction of "Effnerpl." ☎211 27 12; www.hausderkunst.de. Open daily 10am-10pm. €5-9; students €3.50-7, depending on the exhibit; kids under 12 €2.50.)*

SPIELZEUGMUSEUM. Housed in the tower of the Altes Rathaus, this tiny toy-themed museum plays host to rotating exhibits on subjects such as "100 Years of Teddy Bears" and 'The History of Barbie." *(Marienpl. 15. In the Altes Rathaus. ☎29 40 01. Open daily 10am-5:30pm. €3.50, children under 15 €1, families €6. No wheelchair access.)*

🔌 ENTERTAINMENT

THEATER AND OPERA

Munich's cultural cachet rivals the world's best. Its natives are fun lovers and hedonists, yet they reserve a place for folksy kitsch. Sixty theaters of various sizes are scattered throughout the city. Styles range from dramatic classics at the **Residenztheater** and **Volkstheater** to comic opera at the **Staatstheater am Gärtnerplatz** to experimental works at the **Theater im Marstall** in Nymphenburg. Standing room tickets run around €8. The **Hochschule für Music** on Arcisstr. also offers an unconventional assortment of free performances by the future masters of German music. Munich's **opera festival** (July 1-July 31 2005) is held in the **Bayerische Staatsoper** (see below) and is accompanied by a concert series in the Nymphenburg and Schließheim palaces. *Monatsprogramm* (€1.50) and *Munich Found* (€3) list schedules for Munich's

4 **Römerstr 26** and **28** display cherubs and water, other common themes of Jugendstil.

5 Check out the pink **Hohenzollernstr. 10.**

6 Adam and Eve lie under a tree at **Ainmillerstraße 22,** the best-preserved *Jugendstil* building. Bourgeois contemporaries condemned the bright colors and threatening medusas when it appeared in 1899.

7 The floral motifs on **Friedrichstr. 3** imitate the Leopoldpark opposite.

8 **Georgenstr. 10,** brightly decorated with medallions of artists, sits on a street named after Schwabing poet Stefan George, next door to the neo-Baroque **Pacelli-Palais** (Georgenstr. 8).

9 The **Villa Stuck,** a former Jugendstil mansion, is now a museum (p. 457). Founded in 1903, the pub **Alter Simpl,** Türkenstr. 57 (☎272 30 83), is named after *Simplizissimus,* a Munich satirical review, which (together with *Die Jugend*) was the newspaper of choice of the Schwabing crowd. Weißbier €3.10. Open Su-Th 11am-3am, F-Sa 11am-4am.

stages, museums, and festivals. In **Schwabing,** Munich shows its more bohemian face with scores of small fringe theaters, cabaret stages, art cinemas, and bars. **Leopoldstraße,** the main avenue from the university, is magical on a summer night; milling crowds, artists hawking their work, and terrace-cafes create an exciting swarm. At the turn of the century this area was a center of European cultural and intellectual life, housing luminaries such as Brecht, Mann, Klee, Georgi, Kandinsky, Spengler, and Trotsky (see **Young Schwabing,** p. 456).

Bayerische Staatsoper, Max-Joseph-pl. 2 (tickets ☎21 85 01, recorded information 21 85 19 20; www.bayerische.staatsoper.de). U3-6 to "Odeonspl." or streetcar #19 to "Nationaltheater." Built by Max Joseph to bring opera to the people. Standing-room and student tickets (€4-10) sold 1hr. before shows at the entrance on Maximilianstr. Bring student ID and another form of ID—they do not accept ISIC. Box office open M-F 10am-6pm, Sa 10am-1pm. Tickets can also be bought online. No performances Aug. to mid-Sept. Summer concerts in Nymphenburg and Dachau.

Gasteig Kulturzentrum, Rosenheimer Str. 5 (☎48 09 80). S1-8 to "Rosenheimerpl." or streetcar #18 to "Am Gasteig." The hall rests on the former site of the Bürgerbräukeller, where Adolf Hitler launched his abortive Beer Hall Putsch, and houses a conservatory, music school and the **Munich Philharmonic.** Box office in the Glashalle open M-F 10am-8pm, Sa 9am-4pm, and 1hr. before performances.

Staatstheater am Gärtnerplatz, Gärtnerpl. 3 (☎20 24 11, box office 21 85 19 60). U1 or 2 to "Fraunhoferstr.," then follow Reichenbachstr. to Gärtnerpl.; or bus #52 or 56 to "Gärtnerpl." Stages comic opera and musicals. Standing room tickets €10, students €3. €7 student tickets for seats must be bought 2 weeks before the performance. Open M-F 10am-6pm, Sa 10am-1pm, and 1hr. before performance.

Drehleier, Rosenheimer Str. 123 (☎48 27 42). S1-8 or bus #51 to "Rosenheimerpl." One of the Munich's best cabaret scenes. Reservations required. All seats at tables, for food (€3-9) and drink. Tickets €18, student price €15. Open W-Su 6:30pm-1am, shows at 8:30pm, Sunday at 8pm. Opening times vary; call for precise info.

FILM

English films are usually dubbed; look for "OF" (original language) or "OmU" (subtitled) on the poster or in the listings. Munich's **Internationales Dokumentarfilmfestival** (www.dokfest-muenchen.de) will run from May 6-14, 2005. The broader **Filmfest München** (☎381 90 40; www.filmfest-muenchen.de) will take place from June 25 to July 2, 2005. *In München* and other publications list movie screenings.

Museum Lichtspiele, Lilienstr. 2, (☎48 24 03 to reserve tickets or 489 12 96 for program; www.museum-lichtspiele.de) shows only English-language films, both the latest Hollywood fare and arthouse productions. Admission €6.50, students €5.50.

Cinema München, Nymphenburgerstr. 31 (☎55 52 55; www.cinema-muenchen.com). U1 to "Stiglmaierpl.," then walk 2 blocks west on Nymphenburgerstr. This theater plays English-language films almost exclusively; most are current and American. So as not to forget you are in Munich, sip a *Maß* while the movie shows. Reserve tickets early online as movies do sell out. €8-9, students €7.

MUSIC

Tollwood Festival, (0700 38 38 50 24; www.tollwood.de) June 16-July 14, 2005, Munich's alternative culture festival, attracts a large, mainly German, youth audience. Featuring beer tents like *Oktoberfest,* Tollwood offers all forms of performing art, from mime, theater and dance to music, with international acts such as Air, Alice Cooper, and James Brown (in 2004). The *Tollwood* magazine, available from the tourist office, lists all performances, which can be booked through the hotline. Student discounts available. Take U3 to Olympiazentrum, then follow signs. Special buses depart from Westfriedhof (U1) and Scheidplatz (U2 or 3). Open M-F 2pm-1am, Sa-Su 11am-1am.

🎭 NIGHTLIFE

Munich's nightlife is a curious collision of Bavarian *Gemütlichkeit* and trendy cliquishness. Those of the latter persuasion are often called *Schicki-Mickis*— expensively dressed, coiffed, beautiful specimens of both sexes. With a healthy dose of students, the streets bustle with raucous beer halls, loud discos, and exclusive cafes every night of the week. Most locals begin their odyssey at a *Biergarten* or beer hall, which generally close before midnight and are most crowded in the early evening. Alcohol keeps flowing at cafes and bars, which, except for Friday and Saturday nights, close their taps at 1am. Then it's off to the bump and grind of the clubs and discos until 4am. The bars, cafes, cabarets, and discos along **Leopoldstraße** in **Schwabing** attract tourists from all over Europe. High-end venues dot the **Maximilianstraße** and the old center, and more "alternative" vibes can be found in the **Glockenbachviertel.** Many of these venues require you to at least try the hipster look (leave the shorts and T-shirts at home). Otherwise, more laid-back fun is to be had at large, less central venues such as **Kultfabrik, Muffathalle** and **Backstage.**

Munich's alternative concert scene centers on **Feierwerk,** Hansastr. 39-41 (☎769 36 00), which has seven stages and huge tents. Take U4 or 5 or S7 to "Heimeranpl." and walk left down Hansastr. (10min.) In summer, there's lots of independent rock, reggae, hip-hop, and electronica. Beer gardens open at 6pm, doors usually open at 8:30pm and concerts begin at 9pm. **Münchener Freiheit** (on the U3/6 line) is the most famous (and touristy) bar and cafe district. The southwestern section of Schwabing, directly behind the university on Amalienstr. and Türkenstr., is more low-key. Pick up *Munich Found, In München,* or *Prinz* at newsstands to help you sort out the scene. Big-name pop artists often perform at the **Olympiahalle,** while **Olympia-Stadion** on the north side of town hosts other mega-concerts.

BEER GARDENS

When Bavaria agreed to become a part of a larger Germany, it made one main and important stipulation: that it would be allowed to maintain its beer purity laws. Since then, Munich has remained loyal to six great labels: *Augustiner, Hacker-Pschorr, Hofbräu, Löwenbräu, Paulaner,* and *Spaten-Franziskaner.* Four main types of beer are served in Munich: *Helles* and *Dunkles* (standard light and dark beers); *Weißbier* (cloudy blond beer made from wheat instead of barley); and *Radler* (cyclist's brew: half beer and half lemon soda). Munich's beer typically has an alcohol content of 3.5%, though in *Starkbierzeit* (the first two

THE HIDDEN DEAL

PRICELESS ENTERTAINMENT

All the thrills of a concert without the uncomfortable seats and outrageous prices. That's what you'll enjoy when you join half the city to sit outside the stadium during one of Munich's many summer concerts. Every summer, famous artists (like AC/DC, Bruce Springsteen and Simon & Garfunkel) come and play to the lively Bavarian crowds at the former Olympic Stadium. Many *Müncheners,* however, know how to hear all of these accomplished musicians while relaxing in a beer garden or picnicing next to the swan-filled lake on the park grounds.

Thousands of locals crowd the banks of the lake and the sides of the hills where they can clearly hear the sounds of the concert. Entrance to this kind of concert is free, but the experience is priceless. The setting is beautiful and the beer and bratwurst plentiful as you lie in the grass listening to your favorite artist. Simply call the information office or check the website to see who's playing and then show up right before concert time to revel in a truly unique concert experience.

(Take U3 to "Olympiazentrum" and follow the crowds towards the stadium. For listings and schedules call ☎306 724 14 or check www.olympia-park-muenchen.de. Concerts usually start around 8pm.)

weeks of Lent), Müncheners traditionally drink *Salvator*, a dark beer that is 5.5% alcohol. To find the beer gardens, look for leaf symbols on the tourist map. *"Ein Bier, bitte"* will get you a liter, known as a *Maß* (€5-6). Specify if you want a half-*Maß* (€3-4), though many places serve only *Weißbier* in 0.5L sizes. While some beer gardens offer veggie dishes, vegetarians may wish to eat elsewhere before a post-meal swig. In general it's fine to bring food along; drinks, however, must be bought at the *Biergarten*. Bare tables usually mean self-service *(Selbstbedienung)*.

WITHIN MUNICH

▓ **Augustinerkeller,** Arnulfstr. 52 (☎ 59 43 93), at Zirkus-Krone-Str. S1-8 to "Hacker-brücke." Walk left out of the station on the bridge and take a left on Arnulfstr. Founded in 1824, Augustiner is viewed by many as the finest *Biergarten* in town, with dim light-ing beneath 100-year-old chestnut trees, and tasty, enormous *Brez'n*. The real attrac-tion is the delicious, sharp *Augustiner* beer (*Maß* €6). Food €2-14. Open daily 10am-1am; hot food until 10:30pm. *Biergarten* open daily 10:30am-midnight.

▓ **Hirschgarten,** Hirschgarten 1 (☎ 17 25 91). Streetcar 17 (dir.: Amalienburgstr.) to "Romanpl." Walk south to the end of Guntherstr. and enter the Hirschgarten. The largest *Biergarten* in Europe (seating 9000) is boisterous and always crowded. Families come for the grassy park and carousel, and to see the deer that are still kept on the premises. Entrees €5-15. *Maß* €5.50. Open daily 9am-midnight, kitchen open until 10pm.

▓ **Zum Flaucher,** Isarauen 8 (☎ 723 26 77) U3 to "Brudermühlstraße." Gorgeous 2000-seat Biergarten under the trees on the banks of the Isar. Lift a *Maß* with locals relaxing near the water, or take a swim yourself. The perfect destination for a cycling excursion along the Isar, easy to reach from one of the many bike trails along the river.

Hofbräuhaus, Platzl 9 (☎ 29 01 36), 2 blocks from Marienpl. Walk past the Altes Rathaus and take a left onto Sparkassenstr. Turn right onto Ledererstr., and take your first left on Orlandostr.; the Hofbräuhaus is straight ahead, opposite the Hard Rock Café. In 1589, Bavarian Duke Wilhelm the Pious earned his name by founding the Münchener Hofbräuhaus for the worship of Germany's most revered beverage. 15,000-30,000L of beer are sold per day. Many tables are reserved, and hundreds of locals keep personal steins in the beer hall's safe. Go in the early afternoon to avoid tourists, or in the evening to see the true bustle of the beer hall. *Maß* €6.40. *Weißwürste* €3.50. Open daily 9am-midnight with live Bavarian music in the large hall below.

Am Seehaus, Kleinhesselohe 3 (☎ 381 61 30). U6 to "Dietlindenstr.," then bus #44 (dir.: Giesing) to "Osterwaldstr." Directly on the Kleinhesseloher See in the Englischer Garten. In the evening, watch the sun set over the water as you enjoy a *Maß* (€6) and a pretzel (€3.10), or another delicacy from the cafeteria-style eatery. Open daily 10am-midnight, kitchen closes at 10:30pm.

Taxisgarten, Taxisstr. 12 (☎ 15 68 27). U1 to "Gern," then 1 block east on Tizianstr. This small (1500 chairs) *Biergarten* is a local gem. Serves a scrumptious green variety of the normally orange Bavarian specialty *Obazda* (a mix of cheeses; €2.10). *Maß* €5.90, *Weißbier* €3.20. Open daily 11am-11pm, last call for drinks at 10:30pm.

Chinesischer Turm (☎ 38 38 73 19), in the Englischer Garten next to the pagoda. U3 or 6 to "Giselastr." or bus #54 from Südbahnhof to "Chinesischer Turm." A fair-weather tourist favorite. Live, cheesy *Blasmusik* drifts from the pagoda while you enjoy a *Maß* (€6). Open daily in balmy weather 10am-midnight.

Löwenbräukeller, Nymphenburgerstr. 2 (52 60 21) U1 or 7 to "Stiglmaierpl." Castle-like entrance to a festive, enormous indoor beer hall and a shady garden tucked next to the massive Löwenbräu brewery. Come here to taste the real *Löwenbräu*, a bitter, some-what dilute brew with a core of loyal middle-aged followers. *Maß* €5.40, €2 deposit for your glass. Open daily 10am-midnight, kitchen closes at 11pm.

Augustiner Bräustuben, Landsberger Str. 19 (☎ 50 70 47). S1-8 to "Hackerbrücke." Walk down the bridge following Theresienwiese signs to Landsberger Str. and take a right. Rel-atively new beer hall in the Augustiner brewery's former horse stalls. Any devoted carnivore should try the *Bräustüberl* (duck, two types of pork, Kraut, and two types of dumplings; €9.60). Heaps of Bavarian food come at excellent prices (€5-7), although true to Bavarian tradition, you will get no *Weißwurst* after midday. Ask for the *Backerbsensuppe* (€1.60), an herby meat broth with baked balls of dough floating in it. Especially popular in winter. Open daily 10am-midnight. Kitchen open 11am-11pm.

Pschorr-Keller, Theresienhohe 7 (☎50 036 80). U4 or 5 to "Theresienwiese." At the original Oktoberfest, Prince Ludwig had a *Weißwurst* breakfast here. The rest is history. Raise a glass of the interesting, fruity brew in the company of locals at this outpost of the Hacker-Pschorr brewery (along with the Hackerkeller down the street), right next to the Oktoberfest grounds. *Maß* €6.20, entrees €6-12. Open daily 10am-11pm.

BARS
Many of the city's cafes double as night spots, often serving drinks after dark.

☒ Café Reitschule, Königinstr. 34 (☎38 88 76). U3 or 6 to "Giselastr." Above a club, overlooking a horseback-riding school. In the summer, a backyard *Biergarten* teems with students crowding under straw huts and around rose-filled fountains. *Weißbier* €3.20. Breakfast served all day (€7-10). Entrees €7-15. Open daily 9am-1am.

Günther Murphy's, Nikolaistr. 9a (☎39 89 11). U3 or 6 to "Giselastr." Irish cheer accompanies each plateful of Irish and American food (€6-15). Mostly English-speaking crowd. Guinness €4.40. Karaoke Su, happy hour M night and daily until 7pm. Open M-Th 6pm-1am, F 6pm-3am, Sa noon-3am, Su noon-1am.

Sausalitos, Im Tal 16 (☎24 29 54 94). U3 or S1-8 to "Marienpl.," walk past the Heiliggeist Kirche, and the bar is on your right. Mexican bar and restaurant jumping with crowds of local 20-somethings. Hearty entrees (including vegetarian options) €9-13. Drinks €6-9. All cocktails half-price during happy hour, daily 5-8pm. Margaritas half-price after 11pm. Open daily from 11am.

Kilian's Irish Pub and **Ned Kelly's Australian Bar**, Frauenpl. 11 (☎24 21 98 99 and 24 21 99 110). U3 or S1-8 to "Marienpl.," behind the Frauenkirche. Two venues in one, with live music, Irish and Australian beer and food, and live sports coverage. Kilian's also features an outdoor *Biergarten*. Kilian's open M-Th 4pm-1am, Fr midday-1am, Sa-Su 11am-1am. Ned Kelly's daily 5pm-1am.

Lux Bar and Restaurant, Reichenbachstr. 37 (☎20 23 83 93). U1, 2, 7, or 8 to "Frauenhofer." Enjoy French cuisine, including a variety of fish dishes, at one of the black lacquer tables, or sit at the bar among elegant 30-somethings. Specials €3-15. Restaurant until about 10pm, later a socializing hot spot. Beer €2.60 for 0.4L. Open M-W 6pm-1am, Th-Sa 6pm-3am. Kitchen open until 2:30am

Tresznjewski, Theresienstr. 72 (☎28 23 49). U2 to "Theresienstr." Handsome bar with dark wood and stylish frescoes. Good cocktails and chatty crowds until late. Entrees €7-11. Beer €3. Open Su-Th 8am-3am, F-Sa 8am-4am.

Nachtcafe, Maximilianspl. 5 (☎59 59 00). U4 or 5 or S1-8 to "Karlspl." Chic, slightly older crowds rub shoulders or dance to live jazz, funk, soul, and blues until the wee hours in this dark red bar. Easy-going weekdays; very picky on weekends when you'll have to look the part. Main courses €5-14. No cover, but outrageous prices (beer €5 per 0.3L) so do your drinking beforehand. Open M-Th 9pm-6am; Fr-Sa 9pm-9am. Live music 11pm-4am; things really get rolling at midnight.

Shamrock, Trautenwolfstr. 6 (☎33 10 81). U3 or 6 to "Giselastr." Nightly live music runs the gamut from blues to fiddling to rock in this Irish pub. Live soccer. Guinness €4 (0.5L). Open M-F 7pm-3am, Sa-Su 2pm-3am.

CLUBS
In adjacent lots lie **☒Kultfabrik** (☎49 00 90 70; www.kultfabrik.info), at Grafinger Str. 6, and **☒Optimolwerk** (☎450 69 20; www.optimolwerke.de), Friedenstr. 10, two massive complexes which together provide dozens of nocturnal venues

playing all kinds of music. To get there take U5 or S1-8 to "Ostbahnhof," then follow the constant stream of people onto Friedenstr. and then Grafingerstr. Optimolwerk, with 13 clubs, is smaller and caters to a slightly older crowd (mid-twenties to early thirties) than Kultfabrik (23 clubs; late teens to mid-twenties). At the Optimolwerk, **K41** (☎ 638 92 90) is one of the most established and hippest venues, with 70s disco music and house, and a Th 80s night. Open M-Sa. The unconventional **Salon Erna,** (☎ 63 89 29 11) is open all week, and on Su night becomes Germany's rock 'n' roll capital, with lessons for dancers of all ages. If it's your birthday, enjoy free entry on Th and a complimentary bottle of champagne. Over at the Kultfabrik, party the Russian way at **Kalinka** (☎ 40 90 72 60), recognizable by its seven-foot Lenin bust. Choose from 100 types of vodka and dance to techno under the hammer and sickle. The massive **Freudenhaus,** (☎ 40 28 77 28) with two dance floors and eight bars, plays hip-hop and top 40. Hours, covers, and themes vary—call or check the website. All clubs have relaxed door policies, particularly in the summer.

Muffathalle, Zellstr. 4 (☎ 45 87 59 90; www.muffathalle.de), in Haidhausen. Take S1-8 to "Rosenheimerpl." and walk toward the river on Rosenheimer Str. for 2 blocks, or take streetcar #18 to "Deutsches Museum." This former power plant generates techno, hip-hop, spoken word, jazz, and dance performances. Features a *Biergarten*. Open M-Sa 7pm-4am, Su 4pm-1am. Cover from €5. Buy tickets online or through München Ticket.

Backstage, Wilhelm-Hale Str. 16, (☎ 126 61 00; www.backstage-online.com). Streetcar #16 or 17 to "Steubenpl." or #18 or 19 to "Elsenheimerstr." Underground scene, playing hardcore, indie rock and electronica. Primarily local crowd is usually a reflection of the artist. *Maß* €2 from 7pm-11pm; *Biergarten* also shows movies and soccer games. Check online or call for live concert listings. Open Su-Th 7pm-3am, F-Sa 7pm-5am.

Nachtleben, Maximilanstr. 34, (☎ 22 80 17 00) formerly known as *Reich und Schön* (rich and beautiful), this is the fun and chic place to be for the 18-25 crowd. Enjoy the glossy decor and the music, which veers between house and top-40. Cover €5-8 depending on the night. Drinks are €3-7. Open Wed 10pm-4am, F-Sa 10pm-6am.

Nachtwerk, Club, and Tanzlokal, Landsberger Str. 185 (☎ 578 38 00). Streetcar #18 or 19 or bus #83 to "Lautensackstr." After 15 years, Nachtwerk (open W, F, Sa 10pm-4am) may be past its prime, but younger crowds still enjoy it. **Club,** the little sister next door, plays soul and R&B (open Th-Sa). M night brings German oldies. Th 70s night. **Tanzlokal** (open F-Sa) has hip hop on F. Beer €2.50 at all venues; cover €5.50.

Atomic Cafe, Neuturmstr. 5 (☎ 228 30 52), around the corner from the Hofbräuhaus, is the Bavarian take on late-60s mod glory. Has a feel of its own, and sticks to its 60s and 70s beats, avoiding a mainstream 70s disco sound. Young audiences come also for the live britpop, R&B, ska, reggae. Cover €3. Beer €3.20 for 0.5L. Happy hour (10-11pm) cocktails €5.50, beer €2.20. Open Tu-Th 10pm-3am, F-Sa 10pm-4am, Su 10pm-3am.

◼ GAY AND LESBIAN MUNICH

Although Bavaria has the reputation of being more conservative than the rest of Germany, gay nightlife is a alive in Munich, centering around Müllerstr. in the **Glockenbachviertel,** and stretching from south of the Sendlinger Tor through the Viktualienmarkt/Gärtnerpl. area to the Isartor. Friday and Saturday are the busy nights; the crowd is mostly late 20s to 40s. Pick up *Sergej,* Munich's "scene magazine" at **Max&Milian Bookstore,** Ickstattstr. 2 (☎ 260 33 20; open M-F 10:30am-2pm and 3:30-8pm, Sa 11am-4pm), or any other gay locale, for listings of gay hotspots and services (also try *Our Munich,* available at the tourist office). **Sub: Schwules Kommunikations- und Kulturzentrum,** Müllerstr. 43, (www.subonline.org) offers an array of services and a cafe for gay men. (information ☎260 30 56, staffed daily 7-10pm; violence hotline ☎192 28, daily 10am-7pm. Some English spoken. Center open Su-Th 7-11pm, F-Sa 7pm-midnight.) For lesbian information, call **Lesbentelefon.** (☎725 42 72. Open M and W 2:30-5pm, Tu 10:30am-1pm, Th 7-9pm.)

GLOCKENBACHVIERTEL

▨ Bei Carla, Buttermelcherstr. 9 (☎22 79 01). S1-8 to "Isartor," then walk 1 block south on Zweibrückenstr., take a right on Rumfordstr., turn left on Klenzestr., then another left onto Buttermelcherstr. This friendly lesbian cafe and bar is one of Munich's best-kept secrets. Women in their 20s and 30s flock here for pleasant conversation, a few cocktails, and a round or two of darts. Open M-Sa 4pm-1am, Su 6pm-1am.

Morizz, Klenzestr. 43 (☎201 67 76). U1 or 2 to "Frauenhofer Str." Settle into low chairs for a cocktail (€5-8.50) at this mixed cafe and bar. European and Thai dishes available Su-Th until 12:30am, F-Sa until 2:30am. Open Su-Th 7pm-3am, F-Sa 7pm-4am.

Inges Karotte, Baaderstr. 13 (☎201 06 69). U1 or 2 to Frauenhoferstr or S1-8 to "Isartor." This friendly lesbian pub has a unique atmosphere, with bizarre decor and lively music. Serves diverse drinks to its mixed clientele. Open M-Sa 6pm-1am, Su 4pm-1am.

The Stud, Thalkirchenstr. 2, (☎260 84 03), Bavaria's biggest leather disco is an underground bar featuring house and techno on F and Sa nights, which transforms into a "cruising labyrinth" on Th and Su. Open Th-Su 11pm-5am.

Kr@ftakt, Thalkirchenstr. 4 (☎21 58 88 81), Munich's only gay Internet cafe, features a bar and a street cafe, popular for breakfast (€3.90) and brunch. The clientele is here more to socialize than for the **Internet connection.** Wed 9pm-11pm happy hour with €1 beers. Open Su-Th 10am-1am, F-Sa 10am-3am.

New York, Sonnenstr. 25 (☎59 10 56). U1-3 or 6 to "Sendlinger Tor." Fashionable gay men dance the night away. Laser show. Cover F-Su €5 (includes drinks). Happy hour 10pm-midnight, drinks €5. Open Su-Th from 10pm-6am, F-Sa from 10pm.

Cafe Nil, Hans-Sachs-Str. 2 (☎26 55 45). U1 or 2 to "Fraunhofer Str." Take a right out of the U-Bahn down Klenzestr., a right on Ickstattstr., and a right on Hans-Sachs-Str. Sleek cafe and meeting place for gay men in their 20s and 30s. Mobbed on weekends. Beer €3 for 0.4L. Open daily 3pm-4am.

ELSEWHERE

Soul City, Maximilianspl. 5 (☎59 52 72), at the intersection with Max-Joseph-Str. The biggest gay disco in Bavaria, with music from 70s to Latin to techno. Straight clubbers always welcome. Beer €4 for 0.3L. Cover €5-13. Call for info about live concerts. In the early evening Soul City becomes the theater **KleinKunst Fabrik,** with cabaret, poetry readings and erotic comedy (closed during summer). Club open W from 9pm, Th and Sa from 10pm, F from 11pm, Su 7pm-midnight.

OKTOBERFEST

Every fall, hordes of tourists make an unholy pilgrimage to Munich to drink and be merry in true Bavarian style. From noon on the penultimate Saturday of September through early October, it's all about consuming beer, and the numbers for this festival have become truly mindboggling: participants chug five million liters of beer, but only on a full stomach of 200,000 *Würste*. Oktoberfest is the world's largest folk festival—in fact, the festival has gotten so large (and sometimes out of hand) that the city of Munich has stopped advertising it.

BAYERN

Oktoberfest began on October 12, 1810 to celebrate the wedding of the future king Ludwig I of Bavaria. Representatives from all over Bavaria met outside the city gates, celebrating with a week of horse racing on fields they named **Theresienwiese** in honor of the bride (U4 or 5 to "Theresienwiese"). The bash was such fun that *Müncheners* have repeated the revelry (minus the horses) ever since. An agricultural show, inaugurated in 1811, is still held every three years, and fair fare, from carousels to touristy kitsch, remains to amuse beer-guzzling participants.

The festivities begin with the "Grand Entry of the Oktoberfest Landlords and Breweries," a parade that ends around noon with the drinking of the ceremonial first keg, to the cry of *O'zapft is!*, or "it's tapped," by the Lord Mayor of Munich. Other special events include international folklore presentations, a costume and rifleman's parade, and an open-air Oktoberfest concert. Each of Munich's breweries set up tents in the Theresienwiese. The touristy *Hofbräu* tent is the rowdiest. Arrive early (by 4:30pm) to get a table; you must have a seat to be served alcohol. Drinking hours are relatively short, about 9am to 10:30pm, depending on the day; fairground attractions and sideshows are open slightly later. For those who share a love of alcohol with their kin, family days have reduced prices.

◢ DAYTRIPS FROM MUNICH

DACHAU

From Munich, take S2 (dir.: Petershausen) to "Dachau" (20min., €4 or 4 stripes on the Streifenkarte, or use Munich XXL ticket), then bus #724 (dir.: Krautgarten) or 726 (dir.: Kopernikusstr.) from in front of the station to "KZ-Gedenkstätte" (10min., €1 or 1 stripe on the Streifenkarte). Camp open Tu-Su 9am-5pm. Informative 2½-hr. tours of the camp in English leave from the museum June-Aug. daily 1:30pm; Sept.-May Sa-Su at 1:30pm. A 30min. introduction takes place at 12:30pm daily and on weekends also at 11am. Tours are free; all donations go directly to the Holocaust Survivors' Association. Audio headsets in English and German are available inside the entrance to the camp for self-guided tours (€2.50; students and seniors €1.50). Museum guides available in German, English, Dutch, Hebrew, French, Spanish, Hungarian, Polish, and Russian €0.20; call ☎08131 17 41 for more information. Commercial tours also available.

The first thing prisoners saw as they entered Dachau was the inscription "Arbeit Macht Frei" (work will set you free) on the iron gate of the **Jourhaus,** the only entry to the camp. Dachau was the Third Reich's first concentration camp, opened in 1933 to house political prisoners on the former grounds of a WWI munitions factory. After Hitler visited the camp in 1937, it became a model for the construction of the 3000 other camps throughout Nazi-occupied Europe, and a training-ground for the SS officers who would work at them. Dachau was primarily a work camp, as opposed to extermination camps like Auschwitz; during the war, prisoners made armaments and were hired out to work sites in the area. Many prisoners were worked to death. Those who volunteered for medical experiments in hopes of release were frozen to death or infected with malaria in the name of science. Although Dachau had a gas chamber, for unknown reasons it was tested but never put into full use. The tightly-packed **barracks,** designed for 6000 prisoners, once held 30,000 men; two have been reconstructed for purposes of remembrance, but the rest were destroyed. Walls, gates, and a crematorium have also been restored since 1962 in a chillingly sparse memorial to the victims. On the site of the memorial are Jewish, Catholic, Lutheran and Russian orthodox prayer spaces.

The museum, in the former administrative buildings, examines pre-1930s anti-Semitism, the rise of Nazism, the establishment of the concentration camp system, and the lives of prisoners through photographs, documents, and artifacts. Also examined is the question of how much was known to the German population at large. Exhibits have captions in English. A short **film** (22min.) shows in English at

11:30am, 2pm, and 3:30pm. An additional display in the **bunker** chronicles the lives and experiences of the camp's prominent prisoners, including Georg Elser, the SS officer who attempted to assassinate Hitler in 1938.

ANDECHS MONASTERY AND BREWERY

From Munich, take S5 (dir.: Herrsching) to "Herrsching" (45 min., use a €9 Tageskarte). Once in Herrsching, you have a number of options: take a bus to Andechs (10min.), either the MVV which leaves only a few times a day, or a private bus which leaves every 30min. (€2.10); if you brought your bicycle, you can bike the 7km to Andechs; or walk there, following the brown signs through the town along the stream. Keep following the stream along Kienbachstr., then Andechstr., at the end of which, opposite a golden Madonna on a column, you can turn left onto the Kientalstr., a path which follows the river Kien through a wooded valley, or turn right and follow the (harder to find) scenic route. Each walk about 1hr.

Andechs, atop the Heiligenberg hill on the Ammersee, has been the destination of pilgrimages since the Middle Ages due to its location and its valuable collection of reliquaries. Its first cloister dates to 1392, but it gained notoriety in 1455, when Albrecht III founded a Benedictine monastery here. This started a century-long affiliation of the monastery with the Bavarian rulers. Albrecht and his family are buried at Andechs, along with a number of 20th-century Wittelsbachs. Shut down during the 1803 secularization of all church property, Andechs was bought back in 1843 by Ludwig I for an outrageous sum and reopened. 23 monks are current members of the monastery; eight of them live on the hill. The **Andechs monastery** can be visited M-F at 3pm on a German tour (€3; students and seniors €1.50).

If you don't visit the pink-and-white **Andechs Church,** with its sundial and typically Bavarian onion dome, *before* you hit up the brewery, you probably never will. The church was built after a fire in the 17th century destroyed its predecessor, and refurbished in full-blown Rococo for the 1755 tercentenary. Above the altar is a noteworthy fresco by **Johann Baptist Zimmermann.** (Admission free. Tower with panoramic view open M-Sa 9am-5pm, Su 12:15pm- 5pm. €1).

Modern-day pilgrims are motivated by the monks' famous Andechs brew, whose sale has financed the Benedictines' good works since 1455. Tours of the brewery, which produces 100,000 hectoliters of beer a year, take place Tu-W at 1:30pm. Andechs beer is delicious but uniquely strong: the *Helles* has an alcoholic content of 11.5%, and *Doppelbock Dunkles* reaches a dizzy 18.5%. Join the imbibing crowds of locals at the panoramic **Bräustüberl** (☎ 08152 37 62 61. Open 10am-8pm), featuring both a terrace and a lower-placed Biergarten. The beer is cheaper than Munich beer (*Maß* €4.80), and the fresh-baked pretzels with butter from the monks' own dairy are delicious (€2.60, butter €0.70). If you prefer seated service, the **Klostergasthof** (☎ 08152 930 90. Open 10am-11pm; kitchen open until 10pm) offers entrees for €7.50-18.50 or a *Maß* for €6. The monks also make their own spirits, in four varieties (herbs, apples and pears, berries, honey; available at the **Klosterladen,** open May-Sept. 8am-7pm; Oct.-Apr. 8am-6pm). Be careful on your way back down; many a drunken walker has come to an unhappy end in the Kien river. If you are still on your feet, the attractive Ammersee is worth viewing from one of the ferries departing from Herrsching, or take the bus to the Starnberger See, home to the highest income per capita of the whole Federal Republic.

ALLGÄU

Stretching from the shores of the Bodensee (Lake Constance) to the snow-capped peaks on the Austrian border, the Allgäu region boasts charming villages in an alpine landscape. Largely ignored by international tourists, the area is known among Germans as a haven for hiking and skiing.

BAYERN

ACROSS THE WAVES. For coverage of Lindau and the Bodensee, see **Baden-Württemberg,** p. 427.

IMMENSTADT AND BÜHL AM ALPSEE   ☎ 08323

Despite its 1360 name change from Immendorf, Immenstadt is still no city, but a largely untouristed village joined by the tiny hamlet of Bühl am Alpsee and huddled deep in the gorgeous mountains of the Allgäu south of Kempten, a world away from the lakeside resorts to the south. Streams flowing down from the Alps feed two lakes, the **Großer Alpsee** and the **Kleiner Alpsee,** whose clear waters are refreshing after hiking the surrounding hills.

Immenstadt can be reached by **train** from **Memmingen** (45min., 1 per hr., €8.40) and **Füssen** (2hr., 1 per hr., €14.20). The friendly **tourist office,** Marienpl. 12, finds rooms, gives out free area maps, and sells hiking maps (€5-6.60). They also offer seven-day transportation passes (€10) with a *Kurkarte,* which are given to hotel guests. (☎91 41 76; www.immenstadt.de. Open July to mid-Sept. M-F 9am-1pm and 2-5:30pm, Sa 10am-noon; mid-Sept. to June M-F 9am-noon and 2-5:30pm.) From the station, turn right onto Bahnhofstr. and follow it through to Marienpl. Bühl's **tourist office,** Seestr. 5, at Großer Alpsee, has many of the same maps and brochures as its Immenstadt cousin. Walk or take bus #(97)39, (dir.: Oberstaufen) to "Gästeamt" (5min., 1 per hr., €1.45); the office is right next to the bus stop. (☎91 41 78; fax 89 96. Open mid-June to mid-Sept. M-F 9am-noon and 2-5:30pm; mid-Sept. to mid-June M-F 9am-noon and 2-5pm, Sa 10am-noon.) Do your **Internet** business at **Riefler,** Bräuhauspl. 2. (☎85 69. Open M-F 9:30am-12:30pm and 1:30-6pm, Sa 9:30am-12:30pm. €0.08 per min.) The **post office,** Bahnhofstr. 38, 87509 Immenstadt, is across from the station. (Open M-F 9am-noon and 1:30-5:30pm, Sa 9am-noon.) For overnight stays, **Goldener Adler ❸,** Marienpl. 14, has spacious rooms with baths and cable TV. (☎85 49; fax 89 79. Breakfast included. €30 per person.) Camp on the Großer Alpsee at **Bucher's Camping ❶,** Seestr. 25, 5min. from the bus stop. (☎77 26; www.camping-allgaeu.de. No reservations. Reception 7am-noon and 1:30-10pm. €4-4.70 per person, €3.10-3.80 per child, €3.30-4.90 per tent, €1.25 per car, €4.35-6.20 per RV. Sept. to mid-Dec. and mid-Jan. slightly less. Free showers.) All accommodations charge a €1 per day *Kurtaxe,* children €0.50. A plentiful **market** of fruits, meats, and more pops up Saturday (8am-noon) on **Marienplatz;** a few fruit stalls may be there as well. For a sit-down meal, **Bistro Relax ❸,** on Bräuhausstr., serves Italian and German dishes at a reasonable €3.20-13.10. (☎77 87. Lunch menu €4.50, 11am-2pm. Open Su-Th 10am-2am, F-Sa 10am-3am.)

The **Kleiner Alpsee,** a 20min. walk from the center of Immenstadt, offers an extensive park where families play volleyball, take dips, and sunbathe. Check out swimming action at **Freibad Kleiner Alpsee,** Am Kleinen Alpsee on the other side of the lake, which has a heated pool. From the train station, walk left on Bahnhofstr. past the rotary, then take a right onto Badeweg and go straight for about 15min. (☎87 20. Open daily late May to early Sept. 9am-7pm. €2.60, ages 6-18 €1.40.) Proceed along the Badeweg to reach the Großer Alpsee and a free public beach. **Boat** rents paddleboats, rowboats, and sailboats. (☎21 03. €4.50-7.50 per hr.) Windsurfboards are also available. (☎522 00. €13 per hr.; €35 per day.) Two **skiing** areas are also close: **Alpsee Skizirkus** is in Ratholz, a 10min. ride on bus #(97)39 (dir.: Oberstaufen). (☎8325 252. Open June-Nov. weekends, July to mid-Sept. daily 9am-4:30pm.) **Mittag Ski-Rodel Center** is on the south edge of Immenstadt. (☎61 49. Open daily 8am-5pm. Day pass €17, under 16 €11, family €40.) The ski season runs roughly December to March. Ice skaters twirl in winter at **Viehmarktplatz** off Badeweg near the train station (☎521 90. Open 9am-5pm). Dozens of **hiking trails** dot the countryside. The exquisite **Hornweg** trail, which begins at the cemetery trailhead (follow signs for "Friedhof" from the town center), leads along the steep mountainside to the south (1½hr.). Or, take the left fork (Untere Steig) from the trail head and follow along picturesque **waterfalls;** a wooden chapel awaits at the top (20min.). For a rambling route, follow signs for **Ruine Rothenfels und Hugofels** from the northern bank of the Ach river (1-2hr.). The **Naturlehrpfad,** near Knottenried, a 2hr. walk north of town, is a family favorite. Several trails link Immenstadt and Bühl, of which the pleasant **Badeweg** is the quickest (30min.).

OBERSTDORF ☎ 08322

Oberstdorf is heaven for amateurs and hardcore hikers alike. Surrounded by the snow-layered Allgäu Alps, this mecca for lovers of the outdoors has accessible forest paths. The town is packed with guesthouses, restaurants, and stores, but beyond the streets, narrow dirt trails taper toward alpine lakes and solitary hillsides. Foreign tourists are few and far between, and Oberstdorf remains a health resort populated by Germans enjoying their native landscape.

Three **Bergbahnen** (cable cars) whisk hikers to the heady alpine heights. The closest one, in town, delivers acrophiliacs to the top of **Nebelhorn,** the highest accessible mountain in the Allgäu Alps at 2224m. (☎960 00; www.nebelhorn.de. **Weather info** ☎55 53 36 66. Operates May-Oct. daily 8:30am-4:30pm. Round-trip €23, children €17.50; round-trip to lowest station €13.50/€10.50.) The **Fellhornbahn** climbs 2037m for an equally thrilling view. (☎960 00; www.fellhorn.de. Mid-May to Oct. daily 8:20am-4:50pm. Round-trip €21, children €16.) The less ambitious **Söllereckbahn** carries hikers up 1358m to mountainous hiking paths. (☎57 57; www.soellereckbahn.de. Round-trip €12, children €10; families pay only for the 1st child.) On the mountain, gravel trails wind among flowery meadows and patches of snow. In winter, the Bergbahnen transport skiers and snowboarders (winter day pass €29, children €22.50). To reach the Nebelhornbahn station, walk down Nebelhornstr. from Hauptstr. To reach the Fellhornbahn, ride the "Fellhorn" bus from the train station. **Söllereck** is accessible by the bus marked "Baad."

For swimming fun against a mountain backdrop, splash around in the **Moorbad.** From the Marktpl., turn onto Oststr. and walk to the end. Follow the sign to the trail that leads to the Moorbad (15min. ☎48 63. Open in warm weather July-Aug. 9am-8pm; May-June and Sept. 10am-6pm. €2.80, students €2, children €1.50; after 5pm €1.70/€1.35/€1.) Three inconspicuous chapels in St. Loretto, south of town in an idyllic valley, conceal delicate altars and frescoes. Follow signs for Loretto from the Moorbad (15min.) or take Prinzenstr. and then Lorettostr. from the Marktpl. (20min.). One prime hiking route leads to the **Breitachklamm,** a chasm carved into the rock face by a frothy river; in winter, it's covered in fantastic ice formations. (☎08322 48 87. Trail open summer 8am-5pm; winter 9am-4pm.) The chasm is most easily approachable from Kornau, a sub-village of Oberstdorf. From the train station, take the bus (dir.: Baad) to "Kornau" (5min., every 15min., €1.80). Walk up the hill and hang a right after house #22. The road becomes a hiking trail over the Breitach river (1hr. to the Klamm). Or, from the train station, take the bus (dir.: Obermaiselstein/Bolsterlang) to "Breitachklamm."

Trains link Oberstdorf to Immenstadt (30min., 1-2 per hr., €4.20). Rent a **bike** at **Zweirad Center Hasselberger,** Hauptstr. 7, for €6-16 per day. (☎44 67. Open M-F 9am-noon and 2:30-6pm, Sa 9am-noon.) The bustling Oberstdorf **tourist office** at Marktpl. 7, hands out brochures; walk straight down Hauptstr. from the station. (☎70 00; www.oberstdorf.de. Open 8:30am-noon and 2-6pm, Sa 9:30am-noon; mid-July to mid-Oct. and Dec.-Jan. M-F 8:30am-6pm, Sa 9:30am-noon.) The **branch** office at Bahnhofpl. 3, across from the station, is more convenient to book rooms. For latecomers, there is a reservations phone outside. (☎70 02 17; fax 70 02 36. Open July-Sept. and Dec.-Jan. M-F 8:30am-8pm, Sa 9am-8pm, Su 9am-6pm; Oct.-

Nov. and Feb.-June M 8:30am-6pm, Tu-F 8:30am-1pm and 2-6pm, Sa-Su 9:30am-noon and 2-6pm.) The **post office**, 87561 Oberstdorf, is across from the station. (Open M-F 8:30am-12:30pm and 1:30-6pm, Sa 8am-12:30pm.)

Close to Oberstdorf, **Kornau** is home to the excellent **Jugendherberge Oberstdorf (HI) ❶**, Kornau Haus 8, in a gorgeous setting overlooking the Alps. Its spacious facilities include laundry (€0.50) and a rudimentary bar. Take the bus from Oberstdorf (dir.: Baad) to "Reute" (5min., 2-4 per hr., €1.50), continue in the direction of the bus, and take the first right. Be warned: the last bus leaves town by 9pm, weekends and winter 8pm. (☎22 25; jhoberstdorf@djh-bayern.de. Cross-country ski rental €4 for first day, then €3 per day. Breakfast and sheets included. Reception 7am-noon and 2-11pm. Closed 1st half of Dec. Under 27 only. Dorms €15.70-16.10, less for longer stays.) For a homey, carved-wood chalet in the center of the village near the station, try **Gästehaus Alois Zobel ❷**, Obere Bahnhofstr. 2. The house was rebuilt in 1866 after a fire destroyed most of Oberstdorf. (☎963 20. Singles €18; doubles €36. Off-season €16/€32). The tourist office will help you pick from their list of 1000 potential rooms in the area, starting at €10. Restaurants are expensive and close early; try the self-serve **Cafe Felixar ❸**, Nebelhornstr. 48, decorated with stuffed squirrels and ferrets, by the Nebelhornbahn. (Entrees €3-8. Open daily 8am-6pm, July-Sept. until 8pm) There are **grocery stores** on Bahnhofpl. and Obere Bahnhofstr. 2. **Vinzenz Murr ❶**, on Hauptstr. at Bahnhofpl., has meaty *Imbiß* dishes (€2-5) and a salad bar. (Open M-F 8:30am-6pm, Sa 8am-1pm.) For Chinese and Thai food with lots of veggies (€2-6.50), visit **Asia Schnellimbiss Samson ❷**, Weststr. 7. (☎80 01 70. Open daily 11:30am-10pm.)

MEMMINGEN   ☎08331

At the foothills of the Allgäu Alps, Memmingen is not a town of blinding glory, but the 13th-century fortifications and colorful Rococo buildings of this former free imperial city lend it a noble charm. The smells of Swabian and Bavarian specialties fill the air, and locals sip large mugs of beer along crowded pedestrian streets.

Trains arrive from: **Munich** (1½hr., 1 per hr., €16); **Oberstdorf** (1½hr., 1 per hr., €11.10); **Ulm** (30-60min., 2 per hr., €8.40). To get to the Altstadt, cross Bahnhofstr. and follow Maximilianstr. away from the station, then take a right on pedestrian Kramerstr. to **Marktplatz** (5min.). Rent **bikes** from **Matthäus Fickler**, Lindauerstr. 14. (☎22 58. €5 per day. Open M and F 9am-6pm; Tu-Th 9am-12:30pm and 2-6pm, Sa 9am-1pm.) The **tourist office**, Marktpl. 3, by the Rathaus, finds rooms and sells maps of nearby bike trails for €6-11. (☎85 01 72; www.memmingen.de. Open M-F 9am-5pm; Sa 9:30am-12:30pm.) An **ATM** is on Maximilianstr. 24, in **HypoVereinsbank**. **Internet** cafe **Treff**, Kuttelg. 22, has eight coin terminals. (☎45 39. €2 per 36min. Open daily 11am-1am.) The **post office**, Lindentorstr. 22, 87700 Memmingen, is near the Siebendächerhaus. (Open M-F 8:30am-5:30pm, Sa 9am-noon.)

Gasthaus Lindenbad ❷, Lindenbadstr. 18, offers plain but comfortable rooms. Turn right down Bahnhofstr., walk by an underpass, then turn right through the next one to Lindenbadstr. (☎32 78; fax 92 74 54. Breakfast and TV included. Singles €26, with bath €28; doubles €56.) Those hunting for food in the Altstadt needn't look far—Maximilianstr. is covered with *Imbiße* and *Bäckerei*.

The white **Rathaus** in the Marktpl. hides behind a 16th-century facade, spruced up in 1765 with some Rococo additions. Off the Marktpl. on Zangmeisterstr., the 15th-century Gothic **St. Martinskirche** has well-preserved frescoes depicting the Passion of Christ. Take a tour of the tower for a great view of the city. (☎85 69 20. Church open daily May-Sept. 10am-5pm; Oct. 10am-4pm; Apr. 11am-2pm, Free. Tower tours May-Oct. daily 3pm; €2, under 14 €0.50. Early July-Aug. 30min. organ concert and 30min. tour free Sa 11am.) Walking down Kramerstr. through the pedestrian zone and left onto Lindentorstr., you'll find Gerberpl. and the **Siebendächerhaus**, a half-timbered house with seven roofs. The house was designed in

1601 by tanners looking to maximize airflow over drying skins; it now houses a **pharmacy.** (☎31 48. Open M-F 8:30am-noon and 2-6pm, Sa 8:30am-12:30pm.) For a refreshing stroll, head north along Ulmer Str. to the green promenade along the **River Ach;** the **Stadtpark** north of Schumacherring contains a popular modern playground and plenty of crumb-hungry ducks.

In early June, Memmingeners drink tourists under the table during the annual *Bier, Wurst,* and *Musik* **Stadtfest.** The **Fischertag Heimatfest** takes place at the end of every school year in late July. At 8am men empty the stream of fish in a race to earn the title of "Fishermen's King." The children's celebration is on Thursday, but the real festivities take place on Saturday at 6pm, when hundreds of residents parade in period dress, with lots of beer, marching bands, and local dialect.

🔁 DAYTRIP FROM MEMMINGEN: OTTOBEUREN   ☎ 08332

From Memmingen, take bus #955 to "Ottobeuren," bus platform #2. (20min., €2.40), schedule available in the Memmingen tourist office or station ticket counter.

Ottobeuren is renowned for its towering basilica and 🖼**Benedictine Abbey,** representing the architectural height of the German Baroque. Since its founding in 764, Ottobeuren's abbey has morphed several times, finally to the 18th-century style. An easily missed 13th-century statue of Christ on the first altar is the abbey's most venerated piece of art. (Church open daily 7am-sunset. Free.) The most open and accessible monastery north of the Alps is still inhabited by 23 monks. Visitors are allowed to see the grandiose **library,** the impressive **Emperor's Hall,** adorned with statues of the Kaisers, and a **museum** of old church artifacts. (☎79 80. Open mid-Mar. to Dec. daily 10am-noon and 2-5pm; Jan. M-F 10am-noon and 2-4pm; Feb. to mid-Mar. Sa-Su 10am-noon and 2-4pm, last entry 20min. before closing. €2.50, students €1.50, family €4.50, under 10 free.) Stop and watch the rusty mobile **fountain** on Marktpl. churn water, fed by the tiny stream that divides the street. Behind the abbey and next to its former brewery, **Klosterbräustüble ❸,** Luitpoldstr. 42, serves traditional German meals (€3.10-11.70) in a 750-year-old tavern and in the *Biergarten* outside. (☎92 51 80. Open daily 10am-1am.)

BAYERISCHE ALPEN (BAVARIAN ALPS)

On a clear Munich day you can see a series of snow-covered peaks and forested slopes, a rugged and magical terrain spanning from southeast Germany across Austria and into Italy. Ludwig II of Bavaria, the mysterious "Fairy-tale King," built his idyllic palaces among mountain villages, glacial lakes, icy waterfalls, and world-class ski slopes. Castles, cows, and Christianity are some of the major players in the region—you'll see crucifixes high on mountaintops and hear the rattling of cowbells from across the valley. People still wear *Lederhosen,* and everyone, young or old, seems to be on the way to a hike. Rail lines are sparse; buses cover the gaps. For travel information, contact **Fremdenverkehrsverband Oberbayern,** Bodenseestr. 113, in Munich. (☎089 829 21 80. Open M-Th 9am-4pm, F 9am-12:30pm.)

FÜSSEN   ☎ 08362

The word *Füssen* means "feet," an apt name for this little town at the base of the Romantic Road, nestled in the foothills of the towering Bavarian Alps. Tourists are drawn year-round by the town's hiking routes and proximity to Ludwig's famed **Königsschlößer** (p. 472). Füssen's own castle, the **Hohes Schloß,** sits atop a hill overlooking a sea of red-tiled roofs and the calm River Lech. Cobblestone streets, once trod by monks, now lead tourists from old churches to Romanesque archways.

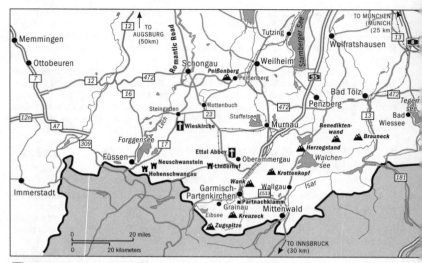

TRANSPORTATION. Trains to: **Augsburg** (2hr., every 2hr., €14.40) and **Munich** (2hr., every 2hr., €18.20). Füssen can be reached by **bus** #1084 or 9606 from Oberammergau (1½hr.; M-F €5-8 per day, Sa-Su €3-6, €7.20 with *Tagesticket*) and Garmisch-Partenkirchen (2¼hr., €7.20 with *Tagesticket*). Along the Füssen-Schwangau county line, there are 80km of cycling paths. For a **taxi** call ☎ 77 00 or 62 22. Rent **bikes** at **Preisschranke**, to the left of the station as you exit. (☎ 0178 374 02 19. Open Apr.-Oct. daily 9am-7pm. First day €8, 2nd day €7, €6 thereafter.)

PRACTICAL INFORMATION. The **tourist office** is at Kaiser-Maximilian-Pl. 1. From the station, turn left and walk the length of Bahnhofstr., then head straight across the roundabout to the big yellow building on your left. The staff finds rooms for free (but does not make reservations), sells hiking maps (€3-7), and organizes **guided hikes** of the area. (☎ 938 50 for information, 93 85 19 to reserve rooms in English during the office's off-hours; www.fuessen.de. Tours and hikes free with *Kurkarte*, €1.60 per person *Kurtaxe* with an overnight stay. Open July-Aug. M-F 8:30am-6:30pm; Sept.-Oct. and Apr.-June M-F 8:30am-6pm; Apr.-Sept. also Sa 10am-1pm; Oct.-Mar. M-F 9am-5pm, Sa 10am-noon.) The **police** station is at Herkomerstr. 17 (☎ 110), around the corner from the youth hostel. The **Bahnhof-Apotheke**, Bahnhofstr. 8, has a bell for night **pharmacy** service. (☎ 918 10. Open M-F 8:30am-1pm and 2-6:30pm, Sa 8:30am-12:30pm.) Access the **Internet** at **Videoland@Internet**, Luitpoldstr. 11. (€2 per 30min., €3 per hr. Open M-Sa 4-10pm, Su 4-8pm.) The **post office**, 87629 Füssen, is at the corner of Bahnhofstr. and Rupprechtstr. (Open M-F 8:30am-5:15pm, Sa 8:30am-noon.)

ACCOMMODATIONS AND FOOD. Füssen's **Jugendherberge (HI) ❷**, Mariahilfer Str. 5, shares a neighborhood with local homes, vacation condos, and some intrepid sheep unaffected by the passing trains. Turn right from the station and follow the railroad tracks for 15min. (☎ 77 54; fax 27 70. Laundry €3.60. Reception daily Mar.-Sept. 7am-noon and 5-11pm; Oct.-Apr. 5-10pm. Curfew 11pm, but you can get the access code. Closed Nov. €16.15, additional nights €15.55.) **Pension Haslach ❸**, Mariahilfer Str. 1b, is only a few doors down from

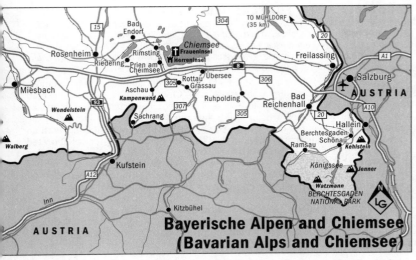

Bayerische Alpen and Chiemsee (Bavarian Alps and Chiemsee)

the youth hostel. Give the bell a ring and Grandma Haslach will tell you from the second-floor chalet window whether her rooms are *frei* or *belegt*. (☎24 26. Singles €25; doubles €45.)

Many fairly cheap bakeries, butcher shops, and *Imbiße* stand among the pricier cafes on **Reichenstraße,** particularly off the **Luitpold Passage. Pizza Pasta Americano,** 23 Ritterstr., serves slices from €1.50 and 32cm pies from €5. (☎50 53 28. Open daily 11am-10pm.) If you're trail-bound, head to the **Plus** supermarket, on the right towards to the rotary from the station. (Open M-F 8:30am-7pm, Sa 8am-3pm.)

🅖 **SIGHTS.** Reminders of the prince-bishop's medieval glory linger in Füssen's architecture. The inner walls of the **Hohes Schloß** courtyard display surreal *trompe l'oeil*—relics of a time when optical illusions of gold and marble were almost as valuable as the real thing. The late-medieval chambers and cloisters of the **Staatsgalerie,** inside the castle walls, feature regional art from the late Gothic period to the present. (☎90 31 64. Open Tu-Su Apr.-Oct. 11am-4pm; Nov.-Mar. 2-4pm. €2.50, students and seniors €2, children under 14 free.) Just below the castle is the Baroque **Mangkirche** and its abbey, dating from the 9th century. An ancient fresco discovered during renovations in 1950 lights up the church's 10th century subterranean crypt. The abbey hosts an 18th-century Baroque library. (☎48 44. Tours year-round after Su services, Jan.-Oct. also Sat 10:30am; May-June and Oct. also Tu 4pm; July-Sept. also Tu and Th 4pm.) Inside the **Annakapelle,** commemorating victims of the bubonic plague, 20 macabre skeleton-decked panels depict everyone from the Pope and Emperor to the smallest child engaged in the *Totentanz* (dance of death) with the following inscription: *Sagt ja, Sagt nein, Getanzt Müß Seyn* (say yes or say no, all must dance). The **Stadtmuseum** in the monastery details Füssen's history as a manufacturing center struck by flood, plague, and war. Attention is given to Füssen's lutemakers guild, Europe's oldest (est. 1562). Recreated workshops and displays showcase the Renaissance lute and its many-stringed cousins, from double-gutted violins to the miniscule Pochette favored by Mozart's father. (☎90 31 46. Open Tu-Su Apr.-Oct. 10am-4pm; Nov.-Mar. 2-4pm. €2.50, students and children €2.) The **Kombikarte,** admission to the Stadtmuseum and the Staatsgalerie (€3), can be purchased at either museum.

BAYERN

▶ DAYTRIP FROM FÜSSEN: WIESKIRCHE

Bus #73 leaves for the church from the station daily at 11:05am (M-Sa only), 12:35, 1:05, 2:05 (M-F only), 3:25, and 4:35pm and returns at 11:21am, 2:50, and 3:50pm. (check the schedule for less frequent weekend buses. Last return bus 3:50pm.) 1hr. One-way €2.80, round-trip €5.60. The 2hr. bike ride from Füssen is pleasant. Follow the signs for Munich until you see Wieskirche signs. ☎ 08862 93 29 30; www.wieskirche.de. Open daily 8am-7pm.

Count yourself lucky if your bus ride from Füssen or Oberammergau to the Ammergau Alps includes a brief stop at the **Wieskirche** (Church in the Meadows), a small gem set in the midst of yellow wildflowers. The Rococo pilgrimage church houses a relic from the Miracle of Wies in 1738, when the wood-and-cloth likeness of the Scourged Savior began to cry. The interior of the church is breathtaking, with an optical-illusion ceiling that is actually flat. The painter and sculptor collaborated to blend the gold-gilded ornaments into the frescoed walls and ceiling, eliminating the boundary between the two- and three-dimensional worlds—see if you can spot the mischievous cherub poking his foot through the ceiling. **Dominikus Zimmermann,** the architect who built the church from 1746 to 1754, was so devoted to the building that he lived in the adjacent house until he died. In the small **Abbot's Loge** on the east side of the church, the balustrade's monogram records the words of the church's founder, Abbot Marianus II Mayer, who supposedly scratched them into a window pane in the **Prelate Hall** with his diamond ring: *Hoc loco habit fortuna, hic quiescit cor* (Here in this place abides happiness; here the heart rests).

KÖNIGSSCHLÖßER (ROYAL CASTLES)

Perhaps it was to his credit that Maximilian II neglected to educate his sons in the mundane affairs of government, allowing them to cultivate a taste for literature and the arts instead. With Max's untimely death, the royal line was left in the hands of his naïve 18-year-old son Ludwig II. A frenzied visionary and fervent Wagner fan, Ludwig made his dreams into reality, creating fantastic castles soaring into the alpine skies, a veritable fantasia inspired by scenes from the opera *Lohengrin.* Whether the king was actually crazy has never been determined—some claim that his detractors fabricated medical evidence—but in 1886 a band of upstart nobles and bureaucrats deposed Ludwig in a coup d'état, had him declared insane, and imprisoned him in Schloß Berg on the Starnberger See. Three days later, the king and his psychiatrist were discovered dead in the lake under mysterious circumstances—murder, suicide or a failed escape attempt, no one knows. Today, thousands of tourists flock to his castles daily to explore the captivating enigma of Ludwig's life, death, and self-fashioned dream-world.

◼ HOHENSCHWANGAU AND NEUSCHWANSTEIN CASTLES

*From the Füssen train station, **bus** #73 or 78 marked "Königsschlößer," (10min.; 2 per hr.; €1.40, round-trip €2.80) puts you at the base of the castle hills in front of the **information booth.** (☎81 97 65. Open daily 9am-6pm.) The Ticket-Service Center is a short walk uphill on Alpseestr.; farther up the road, separate paths lead up to both castles. A less-touristed path to **Hohenschwangau** starts from the left side of the information booth and meanders through the moss-covered forest (10min.). Or, clip-clop to the top in a horse-drawn carriage (uphill €3.50, downhill €1.50) from Car Park D or Hotel Müller. To **Neuschwanstein,** walk up from Car Park D; it's the shortest but steepest trail to the top (20-40min.). There is also a carriage to Neuschwanstein (uphill €5, downhill €2.50). After exiting Neuschwanstein, continue past the castle for Pöllat gorge and the **Marienbrücke.** Consider trekking the trail on the other side of the bridge, through the dramatic gorge and back to the base of the hill (20min.; open only in summer). Private buses run from Hotel Lisl to Bleckenau, a beautiful vantage point 650m (steep) uphill from Neuschwanstein (round-trip €2.60). A Tagesticket (€5.60) entitles castle-hoppers to unlimited regional bus use (not including the bus to Bleckenau); buy it on the bus. (☎ 08362 93 08 30; www.ticket-center-hohenschwangau.de.) Both castles open daily Apr.-Sept. 9am-6pm;*

*Oct.-Mar. 10am-4pm. Required tours, available in 10 languages, included in entrance fee. Apr.-Sept. German and English tours of each castle every 20min.; Oct.-Mar. tours every 30min. Ticket sales for Neuschwanstein Apr.-Sept. 8am-5pm; Oct.-Mar. 9am-3pm. Hohenschwangau ticket sales close 30min. later. Tickets for both castles may be purchased at the Ticket-Service Center, Alpseestr. 12, about 100m uphill from the Hohenschwangau bus stop. **Arrive early in the morning to avoid long lines** at the Ticket-Service Center and to be placed in a tour group that departs as soon as possible, otherwise you may end up waiting many hours for your tour. Tickets may be reserved in advance with a credit card for a €1.60 fee per ticket. Each castle €9, children under 18 free with an adult; students/ seniors €8. Combination ticket for both castles €17/€15.*

Ludwig II spent childhood summers at **Schloß Hohenschwangau,** the bright yellow neo-Gothic castle rebuilt by his father on the sight of a crumbling medieval fortress. It was no doubt within these frescoed walls that he acquired a taste for romantic German mythology of the Middle Ages. After Maximilian II died, nocturnal Ludwig ordered servants to paint a night sky upon the royal bedroom ceiling. The vast constellations were inlaid with crystals so that the "stars" would twinkle when lit from above with oil lamps. The castle also houses the piano and bed that Richard Wagner used during his visits.

Ludwig's desperate building spree across Bavaria peaked with the construction of glitzy **Schloß Neuschwanstein,** begun in 1869 to create jobs in a period of rising unemployment. Germany's most clichéd tourist attraction and the inspiration for Disney's Cinderella's Castle is as mysterious and paradoxical as Ludwig himself. The first sketches of the Schloß were reportedly drawn by a set designer, not an architect, and young Ludwig II lived to spend a mere 173 days in the extravagant edifice before he was betrayed by a servant and imprisoned. The palace mirrors Ludwig's untimely death; 63 rooms are unfinished, and the platform in the lavish throne room is eerily lacking a throne. Completed chambers include a neo-Gothic Tristan-and-Isolde bedroom, a small artificial grotto, and an immense **Sängersaal** (singers' hall), an acoustic masterpiece built expressly for Wagnerian opera performances. Though the hall was never used during Ludwig's lifetime, concerts have taken place here since 1969, always in September (for more information, contact the Schwangau **tourist office, ☎** 08362 819 80; www.schwangau.de). Almost all the castle walls are painted with scenes from Wagnerian operas; the king and composer were united in affection for Teutonic myth and tragic heroes, and Wagner acted as a confidante during the king's spells of uncertainty and abdication.

For the fairy godmother of all views, hike up to the **Marienbrücke,** spanning the **Pöllat gorge** behind Neuschwanstein (10min.). Though some may flinch at crossing the circa-1860 bridge over a 149 ft. waterfall, those with stout hearts and legs can continue uphill from here for a view of the castle and nearby lake (1hr.). In the opposite direction, descend the mountain from Schloß Hohenschwangau to the lillypad-topped **Schwansee.** Follow the Schwansee-Bundweg path through fields of flowers to a beach and secluded swimming hole. Sane people and hang-gliders alike ride the **Tegelbergbahn** cable car to the top of the Tegelberg for similar panoramas. The valley station is to the left of the castles as you face the mountain. (☎ 983 60. *Open daily summer 9am-5:30pm; winter 9am-4:30pm. €9, students €8.50, children €4.50; round-trip €15/€14/€7.50.*)

SCHLOß LINDERHOF

Bus #9622 runs between Oberammergau (p. 474) and the park (9:50am-4:55pm). The last bus leaves Linderhof at 6:40pm (20min., 1 per hr., round-trip €5). Hikers and cyclists can follow the well-kept gravel path along the Ammer river to Linderhof (10km). From the Oberammergau tourist office head left on Eugen-Papst-Str.; when the road forks at the bridge, select the gravel bike path and follow signs to Linderhof. ☎ 08822 920 30. Open daily Apr.-Oct. 9am-5:30pm; Oct.-Mar. 10am-4pm. Apr.-Sept. obligatory castle tours €7, students and seniors €6; Oct.-Mar. €4/€3; accompanied children under 18 free. Park open all day to the public Apr.-Sept. Free. Lockers available to the left of the ticket office (€1).

Halfway between Füssen and Oberammergau is the exquisite **Schloß Linderhof,** Ludwig II's compact hunting palace, surrounded by a meticulously manicured park. In the design of the *Schloß*, Ludwig paid homage to the French Bourbon kings, in particular Louis XIV, just as he did with his *Herrenchiemsee* palace (p. 495). Though it lacks Neuschwanstein's pristine exterior, the decadent interior is a filled with royal goodies like Meissen porcelain (see **The Search For White Gold,** p. 621) and Gobelin chairs. The entire castle is slathered in 5kg of 24-carat gold leaf, except for the servants' room— they had to settle for silver. Across the ceiling in the entrance stretches the French Bourbon affirmation *Nec pluribus impar,* which loosely translates to "I'm too sexy for democracy." Living up to this motto, the royal bedchamber is unbelievably lush, with gold leaf and a crystal chandelier that weighs half a ton. Dark blue (the king's favorite color) velvet encases the bed, specially made to fit the 191cm (about 6'4") tall king. The "Dream King" was almost entirely nocturnal, waking at dusk and returning to bed after his breakfast, because he strongly disliked sunlight. He also disliked seeing people, so he had his dining table magically raised and lowered on a lift from the servants' quarters. The two malachite tables were gifts from Russian Tsarina Marie Alexandrovna, who tried to match Ludwig (a "confirmed bachelor" to his death) with one of her daughters. Ludwig kept the tables and rejected the girls. The final room of the tour is the irregularly shaped *Spiegelsaal.* Mirrors cover the walls, making the elaborate ivory-chandeliered room appear to stretch into infinity.

More impressive than the palace itself is the magnificent **park** surrounding it. The sheer force of water cascading down steps behind the palace powers the fountain in front. Once an hour, the dam is opened, and water shoots higher than the top of the palace. To the right of the palace and up the hill is an artificial **grotto;** red and blue floodlights illuminate a dream world of trellises and stalagmites. A subterranean lake and floating lettuce-leaf boat complete Ludwig's personal 19th-century Disney ride. Farther along, there are brilliant red-and-blue stained-glass windows on the **Maurischer Kiosk,** an elaborate, mosque-inspired building and the only sight on the grounds not built expressly for Ludwig. He saw it at the 1867 World Exposition in Paris and liked it so much that he had it brought home. Within these walls, Ludwig would sit on the peacock throne, smoke his water pipe, and order his servants to dress up in costumes and read him tales from *1,001 Nights.* Under the right moon, Ludwig the Sultan would even throw midnight Turkish orgies. Following the path down the hill to the left (20min.) is the reconstructed **Hunding-Hütte,** modeled after a scene in Wagner's *Die Walküre* from *Der Ring des Nibelungen.* In another of Ludwig's flights of fancy, bearskin-covered log benches surround a tree that is—surprise—artificial.

OBERAMMERGAU ☎ 08822

In a wide valley surrounded by mountains, meadows, and forests, the tiny alpine town of Oberammergau is home to the world-famous **Passion Play.** After the town was spared from the plague that swept through Europe in 1633, the inhabitants promised to re-enact the Crucifixion and Resurrection of Christ every 10 years— the next performance is scheduled for the summer of 2010. The cast is composed of 1000 locals who begin rehearsing (and growing their beards) far in advance. The plays last all day, with a short break for pretzels, *Wurst,* and beer around noon. The cheapest seats in the house go for around €55. Though the town is quieter in non-performance years, hiking trails, the handiwork of the town's myriad wood-carvers, and the nearby Schloß Linderhof and Ettal Abbey provide plenty to see.

◼◪ TRANSPORTATION AND PRACTICAL INFORMATION. Oberammergau can be reached by **train** from **Munich** (1¾hr., 1 per hr., €14.20) and **Augsburg** (2½hr., €16.20-20.40). It's also connected by **bus** to Garmisch-Partenkirchen (#1084 or

9606; 40min., 1 per hr., €3), and Füssen (#1084; 1¾hr., 8 per day, €7.20). The **tourist office** is at Eugen-Papst-Str. 9a. The staff has info on accommodations and hiking, and cycling maps for the area. Turn left from the station and right at the town center onto Eugen-Papst-Str. (☎923 10; www.oberammergau.de. Open M-F 8:30am-6pm, Sa 9am-noon; June-Sept. also Sa-Su 1-5pm.) The **police** are at Feldingg. 17 (☎110). The **post office**, 82487 Oberammergau, is across from the station. (☎920 70. Open M-F 8:30am-noon and 2-5pm, Sa 9am-noon.)

ⓘⓒ ACCOMMODATIONS AND FOOD. In a central location, ◪**Gästehaus Familie Richter ❸**, Welfeng. 2, offers large rooms with balconies, full bathrooms, showers, and huge fluffy beds with chocolates on the pillows. With your back to the train station, take a left on Bahnhofstr., then a sharp right before the bridge (5min.). (☎942 94; www.w-richter.com/dgaestehaus.htm. Breakfast included. Doubles €44.) Oberammergau's **Jugendherberge (HI) ❶**, Malensteinweg 10, hunches over the gently flowing Ammer River 7min. upstream from the train station. Go left from the station up Bahnhofstr. and take a right on the gravel path just before the bridge; follow the path, keeping the river on your left; the hostel is on the right. The 4- to 6-bed rooms are simple and spotless. (☎41 14; fax 16 95. Reception 8-11am and 4-10pm. Curfew 10pm. Closed mid-Nov. to Dec. Under 26 and families only. €14.90 plus €1.30 *Kurtaxe*.) Although most of the restaurants in town aren't well-suited for budget travelers, **Gasthof Bayerische Löwe ❸**, Dedelerstr. 2, serves hearty portions of Bavarian and vegetarian entrees for reasonable prices. Soups and salads run €2-4, while entrees are €6-12. Everything comes with a side of Bavarian folk tunes. To save money or prepare for a hike, pick up groceries at **A&P Tengelmann**, Bahnhofstr. 9. (Open M-F 8am-8pm, Sa 7:30am-4pm.)

◧ SIGHTS. The richly-painted ceiling frescoes of the 18th-century Rococo **St. Peter and Paul Church**, Herkulan-Schweigerg. 5, depict the martyrdoms of its two namesakes. The church's unique marble columns and its intricate stucco work add to the beautiful interior. From the tourist office, walk north on Eugen-Papst-Str., turn right on Verlegerg., and make another right onto Dorfstr. (Open dawn to dusk.) On your way, stop to admire the famous *Lüftlmalerei* (house fresco) on **Pilatushaus** (on Verlegerg.); painted in 1784 by Franz Zwinck, it illustrates Christ's condemnation by Pilate. A short walk around the town will take you past a number of other decorated houses, usually bearing religious or folk-themed images; a long walk will take you around the town twice.

In 1330, Ludwig I of Bavaria—not the Ludwig of Neuschwanstein fame—founded the enormous **abbey** in the tiny village of **Ettal**, 4km south of Oberammergau. Since then, the abbey has conducted a brisk business in house-fermented beer and spirits. The **Klosterladen,** to the right as you face the church, sells divine bottles of *Kloster*-brewed beer (€1.50). Stuccoed and ornamented with gold and precious stones, the double-domed **sanctuary,** built in the 14th century, assumed its Baroque form after 18th-century renovations. (www.kloster-ettal.de. Open daily Apr.-Sept. 7:45am-7:45pm; Oct.-Mar. 7:45am-noon. English tour €2.)

Buses #1084 and 9606 to Ettal from Oberammergau leave every hr. from the train station (€1.80). To **hike** to the abbey from the Oberammergau tourist office, turn left on Eugen-Papst-Str. When the road forks at the bridge, take the gravel path straight ahead to Ettal (1½hr.). The Ettal **tourist office**, Ammergauer Str. 9, lists rooms and has a map of hiking trails. (☎35 34; fax 63 99. Open M-F 8am-noon.) On the way to Ettal, be sure to climb up to the grotto on the hill after crossing the highway; it contains a beautiful devotional figure of Christ looking out at the river.

GARMISCH-PARTENKIRCHEN ☎ 08821

Once upon a time, the 1100-year-old hamlets of Garmisch and Partenkirchen were beautiful, unassuming Bavarian villages whose location at the foot of the **Zugspitze**—Germany's tallest peak—ensured their tranquil isolation. Once the 19th-century nature movement discovered the mountains, however, the two towns quickly became known for their magnificent ski slopes, trails and climbing routes. Hitler persuaded the mayors of Garmisch and Partenkirchen to combine the two villages in 1935 in anticipation of the 1936 Winter Olympic Games. The towns are still united and casually known as Garmisch, much to the dismay of Partenkirchen-ers. Though the fresco-filled town centers may look identical, Garmisch, in the west, is slightly more modern, while Partenkirchen, in the east, is more traditional.

⟐⟐ TRANSPORTATION AND PRACTICAL INFORMATION. Trains to Munich (1½hr., 1 per hr., €14.20) and **Innsbruck** (1½hr., 1 per hr., €10.40). **Buses** #1084 and 9606 arrive from **Füssen** (2hr., 6-7 per day, €7 with *Tagesticket*) and **Oberammergau** (40min., €3.50). **Public transportation** within the city costs €1, but it's free with a *Kurkarte* (issued at lodgings when you pay the mandatory *Kurtaxe*, €2). For a **taxi**, call ☎ 16 16 or 194 10. Rent **bikes** at **Sport Total**, Marienpl. 18 (☎ 14 25. Open M-F 9am-10pm, or call for an appointment; €15 per day. They can also arrange base jumps, hot air balloon rides, rafting, and other outdoor activities). The **tourist office,** Richard-Strauss-Pl. 2, distributes English hiking brochures and finds rooms for free. From the station, turn left on Bahnhofstr. and left again onto Von-Brug-Str. about 200m up the road (10min.), then enter the pink building on the square. (☎ 18 07 00; fax 18 07 55. Open M-Sa 8am-6pm, Su and holidays 10am-noon.) For **weather reports** for the Zugspitze or Alpspitze, call ☎ 79 79 79 or the tourist office. Do **laundry** at **Waschsalon**, Zugspitzstr. 17. (Wash €4.90, soap included. Dry €1.80 for 15min. Open June to mid-Sept. M-F 9:30am-6pm, Sa 9am-noon; mid-Sept. to May M-F 10am-6pm.) The **police** station is at Münchenerstr. 80 (☎ 110). A neon "A" marks the **pharmacy Bahnhof-Apotheke,** Bahnhofstr. 36, to the right as you face the station. (☎ 24 50. Open M-F 8:30am-12:30pm and 2-6pm, Sa 8:30am-noon.) **Internet Cafe,** Ludwigstr. 69, provides **Internet** access. (€1 per 10min. Open M-F 10:45am-6pm, Sa 10:45am-noon.) The **post office,** 82467 Garmisch-Partenkirchen, is across the street from the station. (Open M-F 8:30am-5:30pm, Sa 9am-noon.)

⟐⟐ ACCOMMODATIONS AND FOOD. Many *Gästehäuser* in town offer rooms with WC, shower, and breakfast for under €40, but they fill up fast. The Naturfre-undehaus ❶, Schalmeiweg 21, is a hostel on the edge of the forest by a small brook at the east end of Partenkirchen. From the station, walk straight on Bahnhofstr. as it becomes Ludwigstr., follow Ludwigstr. as it bends right, and turn left on Sonnen-bergstr. Continue straight as it becomes Prof.-Michael-Sachs-Str. and then Schalmeiweg (25min.). Sleep in lofts with up to 16 fellow backpackers and meet new friends in the communal bathrooms and kitchens. (☎ 43 22. Breakfast €4. Use of kitchen €0.50. Reception 6-8pm. 10- to 17-bed dorms €8; 3- to 5-bed dorms €10.) For a positively Bavarian experience, spend a night at Gasthof Werdenfelser Hof ❸, Ludwigstr. 58, in the heart of Partenkirchen's historic district. Cozy wood-paneled singles and doubles ooze subtle ambience. Amenities include a sink in every room. (☎ 36 21; fax 796 14. Breakfast included. €26.) Friendly atmosphere abounds in the restaurant-and-bar downstairs, with a broad menu for Bavaria (including vegetarian dishes). Enjoy dinner (€6-12) with a side of live traditional Bavarian music. (Open Tu-Su 11am-10pm.) Campingplatz Zugspitze ❶, Griesener Str. 4, is on highway B24 at the base of the Zugspitze; take the Eibsee bus from the station to "Schmölzabzweigung." (☎ 31 80; fax 94 75 94. Office open 8am-noon and 3-6pm. €5 per person plus €1.50 **Kurtaxe**, €3 per child. €3-5 per tent.)

Garmisch's restaurants are typically meat-centric and overpriced, but there are establishments that cater to a wider range of tastes and budgets. Get a big meal at **Saigon City Express ❸**, Am Kurpark 17a. Pad thai makes for a tasty break from *Wurst;* most dishes are €3-10. (☎96 93 15. Open Tu-Su 11am-2:30pm and 5-10:30pm. Delivery 5-10pm.) The fast-food joints on Von-Brug-Str. also offer cheap choices. Cheerful owners at **Taverne Thessaloniki,** Ludwigstr, 26, serve huge platters of perfectly seasoned souvlaki (€6.50) to the strains of soulful Greek ballads. (☎90 97 40. Greek specialities €3-6.50. Open Tu-Su 11am-2pm and 4-10pm.)

◙ ◙ SIGHTS AND HIKING. The story goes that Garmisch-Partenkirchen survived both the bubonic plague and the Thirty Years' War due to its piety, and today Christianity still plays a central role in the life of the town. The gilded interior of **Pfarrkirche Garmisch St. Martin,** between Marienpl. and Mühlbach, provides a glimpse into the local religious establishment and its powerful past. Equally charming is the **St. Sebastian Kapelle** on the corner of Hindenburgstr. and Ludwigstr.—ask at the tourist office for the story of the Kapelle

The mountains are the main attraction in town, offering marvelous glacial views in the summer and snowy alpine antics in the winter. There are three ways to conquer the **Zugspitze,** the highest peak in Germany, though they should be attempted only in fair weather for a decent view from the top. **Option 1:** Take the cog train *Zugspitzbahn* from the Zugspitzbahnhof (50m behind the Garmisch main station) to "Eibsee." (☎79 70; www.zugspitze.de. Departs every hr. 8:15am-3:15pm. 1¼hr.) Continue with the **Gletscherbahn** cable car to the top at the 2950m high *Zugspitzgipfel.* (Round-trip, including train and cable car, €43; ages 16-17 €30; children €25.) **Option 2:** Get off the cog train at Eibsee as in Option 1, but take the dramatically steep **Eibsee Seilbahn** to the top. (☎86 27. 80min. Departs every hr. from 8am; July-Aug. last return at 5:45pm, May-June and Sept.-Oct. 4:45pm. Closed for maintenance 2 6-week periods per year. Same prices as Option 1.) **Option 3:** Climb for about 10hr., usually as part of a 2-day trip. **Do not attempt this ascent unless you are an experienced climber.** Get a map and check weather at either ☎79 79 79 or www.zugspitze.de before leaving.

For other alpine views, take the new **Kreuzeckbahn** to Kreuzeck peak and sample the mild hikes. (1651m. Departures begin 8:30am; July-Oct. last return at 5:45pm, May-June 5:15pm. Round-trip €17, students €12, children €10.) Or try the **Alpspitzbahn** cable car from the station southwest of town to Osterfelderkopf peak. (2050m. 9min.; July-Oct. departures begin at 8am, May-June 8:30am, last return at 5pm. Round-trip €19, ages 16-17 €14, children €12.) The 3-day **Holiday Erlebnispass** is good for all cable cars, buses, and trains (except to the Zugspitze), and includes admission to the **Olympic Eissport Zentrum.** (€35, youth 16-17 €24, children 5-15 €20.) Biking to the **Eibsee,** 10km from Garmisch, can be a great daytrip. The soaring, snow-capped weight of the Zugspitze is reflected in the calm, crystal waters of a mountain lake. To avoid pedaling up the fairly steep uphill grade of the last 300m, take the Eibsee bus from Garmisch (one-way €4). On the other side of town, one of the most popular trails leads to the dramatic, 100m deep **Partnachklamm** gorge. Hikers walk up to the gorge from behind the Olympic ski stadium (35min.) and then meander for another 30min. in the narrow tunnels dug in the rocks, extremely close to the foaming water. (Entrance to the gorge from dawn to dusk, €2.) **WN Alpin,** Zugspitzstr. 51, specializes in mountaineering gear and rents **hiking and climbing equipment** (☎503 40; www.wn-alpin.de. Open M-F 9am-12:30pm and 2-6pm, Sa 9am-12:30pm). For information about hiking trails and rock climbing, contact the **German Alpine Association** in Munich (☎089 29 49 40).

BERCHTESGADEN NATIONAL PARK

The paintings of Romantic **Caspar David Friedrich** have impressed the iconic Watzmann peak in every German's mind, yet the sparkling blue lakes and majestic forests surrounding it, now known as **Berchtesgaden National Park,** are just as enchanting. For centuries, the region was controlled by a prior-prince who levied taxes from local herdsmen and shepherds. In the 19th century, Berchtesgaden became prized hunting grounds for the Bavarian kings. Soon artists, then tourists, flocked to these mountains, and the herdsmen became pension owners and guides. By 1978 they realized that the plant protection area they had set up was not enough to protect the ecosystem from the invading hordes of visitors, and the national park was established. Since the park's creation, much previously farmed land has been replanted as spruce forest, but about 4% remains alpine pasture.

Today, hiking takes precedence, primarily because of its minimal disturbance of the wildlife. There are many other activities here: biking, bobsledding, paragliding, rafting, rowing and skiing; most of these, however, are strictly regulated.

THE PARK AT A GLANCE

AREA: 210 km^2. Lowest point 603m at the Königssee, highest point 2713m at the summit of Mt. Watzmann.

CLIMATE: Snowy winters, rainy springs, mild (16°C/60°F) summers. Alpine at higher elevations, temperate at lower.

FEATURES: Extensive forest, steep rock faces, sparkling glacial lakes.

GATEWAYS: Berchtesgaden, Schönau, and Ramsau.

CAMPING: Strictly forbidden. A system of alpine huts accommodates outdoor enthusiasts within the park.

FEES AND RESERVATIONS: There are no entrance or trail fees. Parking runs from €1.50 per day. Reservations not usually needed for huts.

HIGHLIGHTS: Hiking through the Magic Forest, breathtaking views of the Königssee, the summit of the Watzmann.

✳ ORIENTATION

Berchtesgaden National Park is a German peninsula jutting into a sea of Austrian Alps. To the north, it encompasses the towns of **Berchtesgaden, Ramsau,** and **Schönau.** The park extends along three valleys; the fjord-like **Königsee** valley holds the ski-friendly **Jenner** and the notorious **Kehlstein** to the east, and the mighty **Watzmann,** highest peak in the park and second-highest in the country (2713m) to the west. According to legend, the cruel King Watzmann was turned into stone, and now looks down on Berchtesgaden with his wife and seven children—the **Kleiner Watzmann** and **Watzmann Kinder** peaks—by his side. On the far side of the Watzmann is the **Wimbach** valley, overlooked by the **Hochkalter** on the west. The third valley contains the picture-perfect **Hintersee,** starting at Ramsau and continuing as the **Klausbach** valley, where the only public bus in the park circulates. At the convergence of the three valleys in the south lie the **Steinernes Meer** massif and a number of Austrian peaks, with the Austrian town of **Maria Alm** in the valley on the far side. The park's major rivers, perfect for rafting, are the **Königsseer Ache** and the **Ramsauer Ache,** which combine downstream to form the **Berchtesgadener Ache.**

▐ TRANSPORTATION

Cars are not allowed into the park at all, with the exception of those bringing supplies to the many **Alpine Hütte** (huts) scattered throughout, although on the outskirts of the park several major roads lead to trailheads and nearby villages. The boat across the Königssee or the bus along the Klausbachtal are your best bet to quickly penetrate the depths of the park. Good bases outside the park include **Ber-**

Berchtesgaden National Park

○ TRAILS

Malerwinkelweg, **1**
Watzmann, **2**
Zauberwald, **3**
Jenner/Königssbachweg, **4**
St. Bartholomä, **5**
Wimbach Valley, **6**
Oberseeweg, **7**

BAYERN

chtesgaden, **Ramsau,** and **Schönau.** Berchtesgaden can be reached by bus and train, and offers bus connections to both Ramsau and Schönau. Once within the park, there are hundreds of well-marked **hiking trails,** six of which are navigable by **mountain bike** in the summer, and others by **skis** in the winter. You can start a hike from just about anywhere—trails run from every town, criss-crossing each other. If arriving by car, park in the parking lot at the end of Königsseerstr. in Schönau (€3 per day, €2 with *Kurkarte;* p. 484) or at one of the many smaller trailhead parking lots (€1-2 per day) and head into the park on foot.

🛈 PRACTICAL INFORMATION

Emergency: Fire or **ambulance** ☎ 112; **police** ☎ 110. For a hiking accident, you can also call ☎ 08652 192 22. If you have hiked into Austria, call ☎ 144 or 140. To send a distress signal, repeat a loud noise or visual signal 6 times in 1min., followed by a 1min.

pause, then repeat. The response is a signal given 3 times per min. Official visual signals include flashing a red scarf or raising both arms above your head. Standing with 1 arm raised and the other at your side signifies that you do not need assistance.

Climate and Seasonality: During winter, the park sleeps under many feet of snow. In spring and early summer it rains almost every day. Summer brings the warmest weather: average July temperature is around 16°C (60°F), about 4°C warmer in valleys. Autumn is also beautiful, with forests ablaze with color. For current **weather information,** call the **Nationalpark-Haus** (see below).

■ **Nationalpark-Haus,** Franziskanerpl. 7, Berchtesgaden (☎ 08652 643 43; www.nationalpark-berchtesgaden.de). From the main train station, follow the "Zum Markt" signs and bear right on Maximillianstr., which runs through Franziskanerpl. The info center is attached to the church on the right. A must for anyone interested in outdoor activities—the staff are hiking geniuses. Check out the extensive rotating and permanent exhibits, including a 3D map of the national park and its hiking routes, a kid's playroom, and an exhibit on peasant life. Open daily 9am-5pm.

National Park Information Centers: In addition to the main Nationalpark-Haus, there are 6 centers in the park located near most trail bases. Each houses an exhibit based around a certain theme and showers travelers with free brochures, posters, maps, and advice. Hikers will appreciate the green **Berchtesgadener Alpen für Wanderer und Bergsteiger map** (€6.50), which labels all hiking routes with numbers corresponding to signposts throughout the park, and shows the location of all of the Alpenhütte and *Gaststätte*. The **Nationalpark-Wanderbus-Hirschbichl map** is a good, though less detailed, option (free at the Nationalpark-Haus, €0.50 at the tourist information office), which also highlights Austrian trails. The free brochure "A National Park for Everyone," available in English, French and Italian, includes a map and scenic hike information.

Königssee, Seestr. 17 (☎/fax 08652 622 22), in the former Königssee train station by the parking lot. Houses exhibits about the lake ecosystem. Open mid-May to mid-Oct. M-Sa 10:30am-5pm.

Wimbachbrücke, Wimbachweg 2, in the Wimbachbrücke lot below Ramsau. Houses an exhibit on the formation and geological past and present of the Wimbach gorge. Open M-Sa 8am-5pm.

Hintersee, Hirschbichlstr. 26, at the foot of the Klausbach valley (☎ 08657 14 31). Houses an exhibit on woodpeckers and eagles in the park, and another on rustic gardening and natural experiences. Open Christmas-Oct. M-Sa 9am-5pm.

St. Bartholomä, at the St. Bartholomä ferry stop. Houses an exhibit on change and continuity in the wilderness. Open when the boats are running.

Engert-Holzstube, Hirschbichlstr., halfway up the Klausbachtal. Accessible from the Klausbachtal trail. Houses an exhibit on the transition from economic activity to environmental preservation on the park lands. Open in summer M-Sa 9am-5pm.

Fees and Reservations: Entrance to the park and all hikes are free. **Camping** within the park is strictly forbidden, along with all forms of fire, including campfires and camp stoves. **Parking** is available in the lot at the end of Königsseerstr. in Schönau (€3 per day) and at trailheads throughout the park (€1.50 per day; check map for locations).

Gear: Sport M+R Brandner in Berchtesgaden or Ramsau. Both rent **bikes** and stock **hiking boots** and other **equipment.** Rent **Skis** at the **M+R Brandner** in Berchtesgaden; at the **Ski School Berchtesgaden-Jenner** (☎ 08652 667 10); at the **Jenner base lodge** in Schönau; or the **Ski School Schwarzeck** in Ramsau (☎ 08657 674). A listing of 15+ additional rental locations servicing all of the major ski areas is also available at the Berchtesgaden tourist office (ask for the "Winter" brochure).

Tours: The park service leads **free guided nature hikes,** or *Wanderführungen,* throughout the year (depending on weather). Check the "Wandern" brochure at the Nationalpark-Haus for days, times, and meeting points. Tours in English on themes of your choice available for groups of 7 or more for a small fee with advance notice. The **tourist office** in Berchtesgaden (p. 484) also offers guided hikes.

ACCOMMODATIONS

The National Park is an easy day trip from the bordering towns. If you want to try longer routes or stay up in the high country, 26 **Alpine Hütte**—simple huts offering food and a bed for €15-20—are scattered throughout and just outside of the park. These are the only authorized accommodations and are usually only open from the end of May to October. Bring your own bedding or rent it at the huts, and don't expect many comforts; you'll be squished in next to others on mattresses on the floor, or in a bed for more money. The food is standard *Gaststätte* fare, usually quite good with plenty of choices. Reservations are (usually) not necessary, although weekends in June and July do get busy, and members of the German Alpine Society have priority over humble tourists. Camping is strictly *verboten*.

Alpeltalhütte, 1100m (☎08652 630 77). Obersalzburg ski region. 1½hr. hike from Vorderbrandstr. 39 beds, 22 mattresses. Open Dec. 25-Oct.

Blaueishütte, 1685m (☎08657 271 or 546). On Mt. Hochkalter. 2½-3hr. from Ramsau/ Hintersee. 20 beds, 63 mattresses. Open mid-May to mid-Oct.

Gotzenalm, 1685m (☎08652 69 09 00). On Gotzenberg. 15 beds, 65 mattresses. Open June-Sept.

Bergheim Hirschbichl, 1153m (☎00 43 6582 83 47). In Austria, 2hr. from Ramsau/ Hintersee. 40 beds. Open May to mid-Oct.

Ingolstädterhaus, 2119m (☎00 43 6582 72 72). In Austria, on Diesbachscharte, 6-7hr. from Wimbachbrücke. 14 beds, 83 mattresses. Open mid-June to Sept.

Kärlingerhaus am Funtensee, 1633m (☎08652 29 95). Steinernes Meer ski tour region, 4½hr. from St. Bartholomä. 48 beds, 182 mattresses. Open June to mid-Oct.

Carl-von-Stahl-Haus, 1736m (☎08652 27 52). Just below the Jenner on the border; ski tour region. 2hr. from Hintersee parking lot. 24 beds, 72 mattresses. Open year-round.

Kühroint-Hütte, 1420m (☎08652 73 39). On Watzmannkar. 2hr. from Königssee. 25 mattresses. Open June-Sept.

Purtschellerhaus, 1692m (☎08652 24 20). On Hoher Göll, 1hr. from Ofneralm bus stop. 10 beds, 50 mattresses. Open mid-May to Oct.

Riemannhaus, 2177m (☎00 43 582 733 00). In Austria, on Ramseiderscharte; ski tour region. 6hr. from St. Bartholomä. 20 beds, 120 mattresses. Open mid-June-Sept.

Schneibsteinhaus, 1700m (☎08652 25 96). On Torrenerjoch, just below the Jenner. 2hr. from Hinterband parking lot. 90 mattresses. Open May-Oct.

Störhaus, 1894m (☎08652 72 33). On Untersberg. 3½hr. from Bischofswiesen. 15 beds, 54 mattresses. Open June-Sept., with shelter available in winter.

Toni-Lenz-Hütte, 1551m (☎00 43 6641 34 16 90). On the Austrian border above Untersberg. 3hr. from Marktschellenberg. 58 mattresses. Open June to mid-Oct.

Traunsteiner-Hütte, 1570m (☎0171 437 89 19). On Reiteralm, 6hr. from Hintersee/ Böselsteig. 40 beds, 100 mattresses. Open April to mid-Oct.

Watzmannhaus, 1928m (☎08652 96 42 22). Way up the Watzmann, 3-4hr. from Wimbachbrücke. 50 beds, 140 mattresses. Open June to mid-Oct., shelter available in winter.

Wimbachgrieshütte, 1327m (☎08657 344). 2½hr. from Wimbachbrücke. 16 beds, 58 mattresses. Open May to mid-Oct.

Overnight accommodations are symbolized by a red hut on the *Berchtesgadener Alpen Wanderer* map. There are also houses which offer food but no accommodation; on the map these are represented by white huts outlined in red. On the

Nationalpark-Wanderbus-Hirschbichl map look for white huts; on the free "National Park for Everyone" map red numbered huts show both where food is available and where you are able to spend the night.

⬛ HIKING

Literally thousands of hikes can be put together from the network of marked trails that snake through the park. Most trail signs give the length and an estimated time for each section. The dotted lines are routes for experienced hikers only. A few of the more popular and scenic hikes include:

Obersee (3½hr. round-trip). Take the ferry to Salet. (☎96 36 18; www.bayerische-seen-schifffahrt.de. 2 per hr. 8am-6:30pm. Round-trip €14, under 14 €7. 10% discount before 9am.). Follow signs for the 15min. walk to the Obersee. From here, a counter-clockwise route leads, in under an hour, along the shimmering lake to the **Fischunkelalm,** which in summer dispenses milk and butter. Another 30min. of hiking leads to a stunning waterfall, with water clean enough to drink. On the return trip, overheated hikers splash in the refreshing Obersee. If you don't check the time of the last ferry on your way out, you might spend the night at the wrong end of the lake.

Watzmann (12km, full day). The Watzmann was first conquered in 1799, and the hike remains strenuous. Only start it if you know what you are doing; the National Park helicopter has to fly out daily to this route to rescue hikers who overestimated their ability. From Berchtesgaden, take bus #46 to "Wimbachbrücke" (15min., 1 per hr. 6:30am-7:45pm), where there is an Information Center. Then follow signs through the parking lot and onto **trail 441.** Most hikers take 3-3½hr. to reach Watzmannhaus—when you pass the cow pasture, you're halfway there. The steep 785m vertical to the top (only worth it on clear days) is **for experienced hikers only.** Pack a jacket and food.

Wimbachtal (18km; 6-8hr.). Long but rewarding. Take bus #46 to Wimbachbrücke (see Watzmann), and follow the signs to **Wimbachklamm** (gorge) to see the rock formations. Stroll along the Wimbach stream's striking valley to **Wimbachschloß,** buit in 1784, which serves refreshments in the summer. You can turn around at this point, or continue to the **Wimbachgrieshütte,** which boasts phenomenal views of the Hochkalter opposite.

St. Bartholomä and Eiskapelle (6km; 1½hr. round-trip). This popular Königssee hike starts from the beautiful St. Bartholomä church (get there by ferry). After a visit to the National Park Information Center, follow signs to the **Eiskapelle** (ice chapel), a dome formed at the front edge of the glacier by the river of melted snow running underneath.

Klausbachtaler Blaueis (2½hr.). Starting out on the same path as the Zauberwald hike (see **Ramsau,** p. 488), turn left 20min. into the hike. This strenuous hike heads up the side of Mt. Hochkalter to the Blaueishütte, 1680m over Ramsau. The incline steepens but the view of the valley is rewarding. The same valley also offers a great hike to the **Bindalm** (12km; 6-8 hr.). Head past the Engert-Holzstube information point up to the **Bindalm,** at which point you could hike into Austria or take the bus back from Weißbach to Hintersee, and from there to Ramsau, Schönau or Berchtesgaden.

Jenner/Königsbachweg (6.5km, 2hr. from the summit to the midstation). The hulking Jenner, a skiing paradise, can be hiked beginning with **trail 494** (trailhead at the Kessel stop on the Königssee) or **trail 493** (trailhead reachable by following Jennerbahnstr.). The less ambitious can take the **Jennerbahn** lift ("Berg-und-Talfahrt" ascent and descent €18; ascent only €13.50) to the top, then hike part of the way back down. Take bus #41 (dir.: Königssee) from the train station to the Königssee parking lot. (€2.30. Open summer 8am-5:30pm; winter 9am-4:30pm.) From the top, follow the signs to the Stahlhaus and then down over Königsbachalm to the Jennerbahn midstation, where you can ride the lift back down. Check out the Salzburg and Bayern signs outside the Stahlhaus, on the Austrian border.

Malerwinkelweg (1hr. round-trip). A short loop to "Painter's Outlook," one of the best scenic points on the Königssee, then back through a wooded area. From the Königssee National Park Center, follow Jennerbahnstr. to the lift station, and bear right onto the gravel path after the gondola statue, coming out by the Königssee Schifffahrt docks.

🚲 BIKING

Mountain bikes are only permitted (by law) on a limited number of routes around the edges of the national park, although in the rest of the Berchtesgaden area there is plenty to keep cyclists busy. Thoroughfares such as the **Mozart Route** are always buzzing with bikers. Official national park maps show bike routes with green dotted lines. If you're in shape and up for some steep climbs, your options include:

Klausbachtal. The whole Hirschbichl road from the Hintersee to the border with Austria is open only to the local bus, cyclists and hikers. From Ramsau you can also ride up to Seeklausköpfel for a panoramic view of the Ramsauer Tal.

Wimbachtal. One track goes across the lower northern face of the Hochkalter, while another leads along a valley to Eckau (hiking route #486). Another heads from the Wimbachbrücke up in an easterly direction, then south along the Watzmann massif past the Kühroint-Alm to the panoramic Archenkanze.

Jenner can be circled on a route which starts in Berchtesgaden and winds a semi-circle around the peak, then heads straight into the park along a valley above and parallel to the Königsee all the way to the Gotzenalm. Or continue around the Jenner all the way past the Carl-v.-Stahl hut into Austria. Routes run on the Kehlstein all the way to the Eagle's Nest, as well as into a small section of the park.

🏃 OUTDOOR ACTIVITIES

Treff Aktiv, Jennerbahnstr. 19 (☎ 08652 667 10; www.treffaktiv.de), on the way to the Jennerbahn base station, offers various outdoor adventure trips, including **rafting** (€26 per adult, €19 per child), **paragliding** (from €109), mountain bike tours (from €31), and **canyoning** (€45, beginners' route €29). They also offer **ski weekends, climbing, bobsledding, rapelling,** and **guided hikes.** To try out everything from ice climbing to paragliding to hot air ballooning, contact the **Berchtesgaden Outdoor Club** (☎ 08652 977 60; www.outdoor-club.de), with 13 locations in the area.

RESPECT THE ANIMALS. Although the park is first of all a wildlife sanctuary and only incidentally a vacation spot for humans, outdoor sports companies all too often will break rules in pursuit of money, and wildlife pays the price. Paragliding near eagles' nests, for example, should be avoided at all costs.

The Jenner is the largest **ski** slope around, serviced by the Jennerbahn. (☎ 08652 958 10. Day pass €21.50, children 6-15 €13.) The Berchtesgaden tourist office and most ticket counters also sell a five-day pass good for all 20 ski areas in the region (with *Kurkarte* €99, children 6-14 €55; a pass for 5 of 7 days on just Jenner, Hochschwarzeck and Götschen sells for €97/€60). For weather news, call ☎ 08652 96 72 97 or check http://schneebericht.berchtesgaden.de. For the **Ski School Berchtesgaden-Jenner,** call ☎ 08652 66 710. Ask at the tourist office in Berchtesgaden for a list of ski and snowboard schools in the area, most of which also rent equipment. You can also get a trip down the Kunsteisbahn **bobsledding** track with **Rennbob-Taxi** from mid-Oct. to February for €80, including all insurance and a "Bobsled Diploma." (☎ 08652 96 72 15; www.rennbob-taxi.de.)

BERCHTESGADEN ☎ 08652

Nestled in the southeast Bavarian Alps, Berchtesgaden wins the affection of many world travelers for the natural beauty of its surroundings. Once part of the Archbishopric of Salzburg, the region was annexed by Bavaria in 1809 for its salt deposits. Encircling this town are the alpine peaks of **Hoher Göll, Watzmann** (the highest, at 2713m) and **Hochkalter;** the **Königsee** and **Hintersee's** shimmering waters; and the **Zauberwald's** pristine forests. Berchtesgaden is also well-known for a more notorious attraction: Hitler's **Kehlsteinhaus**—the mountaintop retreat christened the "Eagle's Nest" by American troops who occupied it after WWII.

▗ TRANSPORTATION

Trains: Tickets and info in the station on Bahnhofstr. Open M-F and Su 8am-12:45pm and 2:15-5:40pm, Sa 8am-12:45pm. 1 train per hr. to: **Bad Reichenhall** (30min., €3.20); **Mühldorf** (2hr., €14.20); **Munich** (3hr., €15); and **Salzburg** (1hr., €6.90).

Buses: The main terminal is just outside the train station. Tickets can be purchased on the bus or at the ticket window (☎94 48 20). The *Urlaubsticket,* available at the bus station and all tourist offices, provides unlimited bus travel for your choice of 6 days out of the next 7 for €18, children under 13 €9 (with a *Kurkarte*). Buses run within Berchtesgaden until 7pm (€1). They also head to: **Bad Reichenhall** (€3.90); **Königssee** (€2.20); **Ramsau** (€2.50); **Salzburg** (€3.90).

Taxis: ☎40 41.

Bike Rental: Sport M+R Brandner, Bergwerkstr. 52 (☎14 34). From the tourist office, cross the bridge and turn right onto Bahnhofstr., which turns into Bergwerkstr., or take bus #48 (dir.: Oberau) to "Watzmann Therme." Bikes €18 per day. Also has **hiking and Nordic walking equipment.** Sticks €3. Runs guided tours on request. Open M-F 8:30am-noon and 2-6pm, Sa 8:30am-1pm.

✈🛈 ORIENTATION AND PRACTICAL INFORMATION

Berchtesgaden is a lone German outpost among Austrian mountains. The train station lies along the clear and swiftly-flowing **Berchtesgadener Ache;** the main **Marktplatz** is on the hill above. From the train station, turn right immediately and look for the alcove labeled "Zum Markt" on the right before the post office. Go up the stairs, over the footbridge, and follow the "Zum Markt" and "Ortsmitte" signs through the woods to the pedestrian zone. At night, travelers may prefer to take a better-lit route, turning left from the train station and following Bahnhofstr. as it branches off up the hill to the left. The manicured **Kurgarten** is on the right just before the Marktpl. Turn right at the Marktpl. and you will be in the relative quiet of the **Schloßplatz** (castle courtyard) beneath the matronly spires of the church.

Tourist Office: Königsseer Str. 2 (☎96 71 50, 96 70 for recorded hotel information; www.berchtesgadener-land.com), opposite the train station in an off-white building with blue shutters. The **Wanderpass** brochure includes tips (in German) on trails and hikes in the Berchtesgaden National Park. They also offer a list of daily guided tours, most of which are free. Visitors need a €1.80 *Kurkarte.* Open mid-June to Oct. M-F 8:30am-6pm, Sa 9am-5pm, Su 9am-3pm; Nov. to mid-June M-F 8:30am-5pm, Sa 9am-noon.

Kur und Kongresshaus, Maximilianstr. 9 (☎944 53 00; www.berchtesgaden.de/kongresshaus) is another visitor's haven, with a cafe-restaurant, garden, movie theater, and reading room. From the station, follow the "Zum Markt" signs and bear right along Maximilianstr.; it is on the right before the parking garage. The staff helps find rooms. Info and ticket offices open M-F 9am-6pm, Sa 9am-2pm, Su 10am-1pm and 2-6pm.

Tours: Short, English-language tours of the **Kehlsteinhaus** depart daily at 10:35 and 11:45am. (Meet at the tunnel entrance to the elevator. To catch the 1st tour, take the 9:45am bus from Berchtesgaden to Kehlstein; for the 2nd tour, the 10:45am bus. 35min. €4, children free.) A 4hr. tour (English) of the Kehlsteinhaus and the documentation center with the Nazi bunker system in Obersalzberg can be reserved 1 day in advance from **Berchtesgaden Mini Bus Tours** in the tourist office. (☎ 649 71, evenings 621 72; www.eagles-nest-tours.com. Meet at the tourist office mid-May to Oct. daily at 8:30am and 1:30pm. €38, under 13 €28, under 6 free.) The Bavarian hills are alive with the sound of minibuses—the same company also operates **Sound of Music Tours** around Salzburg. (4hr. tours leave from the Berchtesgaden tourist office M-Sa 8:30am. Reservations required. €28, children under 13 €18, children under 6 free.)

ATM: Exchange money at **Raiffeisen Bank,** Metzgerstr. 3, in the Marktpl. Open M-F 8:30am-12:30pm and 2-4:30pm.

Laundromat: Waschsalon im Wittelsbach, Maximilianstr. 16. Nice and centrally located. Wash €3. Dry €2. Open daily 7:30am-9pm.

Police Station: Bayerstr. 7 (☎ 946 70, emergencies 110). Follow "Zum Markt" signs from the station; bear left at the street. Follow Hanielstr. to Bayerstr. and take a right.

Pharmacy: Bahnhof Apotheke, in the front of the train station, to the left of the main exit. Open M-F 8am-7pm, Sa 8am-2pm.

Internet: Radio, Maximilianstr. 13. €2.50 per hr. Open M-F 9am-6pm. Access also available at the tourist information office. €4 per hr.

Post Office: Franziskanerpl. 2½, 83471 Berchtesgaden. Open M-F 9am-12:30pm and 2-5:30pm, Sa 9am-12:30pm.

ACCOMMODATIONS

Although most private rooms and pensions in Berchtesgaden run €38-77 per night, there are a few more budget options. If everything cheap is booked, as is often the case from mid-July to the end of August, try the neighboring town of **Ramsau** (p. 488). Take bus #46 from Berchtesgaden (30min., 2 per hr., €2.50).

Jugendherberge (HI), Gebirgsjägerstr. 52 (☎ 943 70; jhberchtesgaden@djh-bayern.de), is 25min. uphill from the station. Turn right from the station and follow Ramsauer Str. on the left for 15min., then take the first right on Gmundbrücke and follow the signs up the steep gravel path on the left. Or, take bus #39 (dir.: Strub Kaserne) to "Jugendherberge" (1 per hr., €2). Modern facility overlooking the mountains. Breakfast and sheets included. Reception 6:30-9am and 5-7pm. Check-in until 10pm. Curfew midnight. Closed Nov. 1-Dec. 26. 10-bed dorm €15.40, including *Kurtaxe.* ❷

Haus Gürtler, Weinfeldweg 7 (☎ 39 11). Head down Maximilanstr. to the Schloßpl., turn left when you can see the pink belltower, and head up the steps as the sidewalk rises high above the street. Take the path leading up to join Weinfeldweg; the pension is the 3rd house up on the left. Balconies overlook a flower-filled garden. The climb is steep, but where else can you watch goats baa-ing their way back to the stable in the evenings? Breakfast included. Singles €20, less for longer stays. ❷

Hotel Watzmann, Franziskanerpl. 4 (☎ 20 55; fax 51 74). From the station, take a right and follow the "Zum Markt" signs. Bear right onto Maximilianstr.; the hotel is on the left. Hallways filled with Bavarian artifacts in a great location. Singles €30-40 (including TV, showers, *Kurtaxe* and breakfast). Higher prices in summer and Nov.-Dec. ❸

Haus Achental, Ramsauer Str. 4 (☎ 45 49; fax 632 70). From the train station, take a right and walk 5min. down Ramsauer Str. Tidy rooms with private bathrooms right on the main road and train line near the center of town. Breakfast included. Singles €28 for 1st night, less for subsequent nights. ❸

Campingplatz Allweglehen (☎23 96; www.alpen-camping-allweg.de), at Untersalzberg, more than an hour's walk upstream from the station. Take a right on Ramsauer Str. and keep on trucking. €4.50 per person, €3.70 per child, €6 per tent and car. ❶

FOOD

Berchtesgaden is rife with expensive restaurants. Pick up a *Wurst* from a vendor, or score some groceries at the **Edeka Markt,** Königsseer Str. 22 (open M-F 7:30am-6pm, Sa 7:30am-noon) and fresh bread and pastries at the **Bäckerei-Konditorei Ernst,** Königseer Str. 10. (Open M-F 6:30am-6pm, Sa 6:30am-noon.)

Il Buon Gelato, Maximilanstr. 16. The family that runs this Italian *gelateria* knows its stuff: gigantic chocolate chips in generous scoops (€0.70). Open daily 9am-10pm. ❶

Bauern Schmankerl, Rathauspl. 2. From the *Königsschloß,* head through the courtyard and the arch to the left; Bauern Schmankerl is the 2nd door on the right. Anja, the owner, loves to practice her English while suggesting traditional dishes. Entrees €4-7. Open M and Su 7am-2pm, Tu and F 7am-6pm, Sa 8am-noon. ❷

Express-Grill Hendl, Maximilianstr. 8. Hamburgers with fries juxtapose traditional Bavarian dishes like bratwurst with sauerkraut (€4), or *bayerische Schweinhax'n* (pork steak with crunchy skin; €1.20 per 100g). Open daily 11am-9:30pm. ❶

Gasthof Goldener Bär, Weinachtsschützenpl. 4, has Bavarian entrees along with every kind of sausage you could ever want, including the beloved *Weißwurst* (€1.90 each). Other entrees (including vegetarian options) €6-13. Open daily 9am-10pm. ❸

SIGHTS

KEHLSTEINHAUS. The Kehlsteinhaus, called the Eagle's Nest by invading American soldiers, was built for the *Führer*'s 50th birthday as a place to entertain ambassadors. Though Hitler only visited the mountaintop "teahouse" 14 times (he was, ironically, afraid of heights and extremely claustrophobic, particularly in elevators), today it is a tourist must-see. A restaurant now fills the granite resort house, which survived the war intact, unlike the Nazi residences below. But the best reason for visiting—apart from the spectacular view from the 1834m mountain peak—is the trip up. The 6.3km road is an engineering marvel hewn from solid rock in less than two years by an army of 3000 men excused from conscription for health reasons. If you're making a day out of it, it's possible to hike all the way to the top from the "Kehlstein" bus stop. Reserve your spot on a return bus at the booth when you get off. Or, from the parking lot, go through the tunnel and marvel at the elevator that ascends up through the mountain to the summit. An hour should give you enough time to explore the mountaintop. A 5min. climb brings you to a cross memorializing the 10 men who died during the rapid construction of the Kehlsteinhaus. Beyond the cross, there's a beautiful 45min. hike to the summit which is only really worth it (and safe) in clear weather. Legend says the house's original brass mirrored walls were installed to quell Hitler's claustrophobia. (*Bus #38 (dir.: Hinterband) to "Kehlstein Busabfahrt;" every 30min. 6:45am-6:25pm. Buses return to Hintereck and Berchtesgaden every 30min., last one at 5:15pm. Buy an elevator ticket to the top of the mountain from the cashier's desk at the bus stop. Open May-Oct. daily except on days of heavy snow. €15, children €7; round-trip €16.10/€8.)*

DOKUMENTATION OBERSALZBERG. This permanent exhibition is located where Hitler and his inner circle once made their homes (bombed in 1945), which, along with SS barracks, rounded off the Nazi **Obersalzberg** village. If you walk around, you will still find the former **"Türken" Gasthof,** where the regime leaders met for beer, as well as the canteen of the **Platterhof,** the hotel which functioned as a vacation resort for the American army stationed in Germany until 1996. The museum offers an in-depth look into the history of Obersalzberg and the Nazi dictatorship. Audio guides in English and German to lead you through the hundreds of photographs and down to the cold bunkers that were reserved for party members in the case of an attack. *(Bus #38 (dir.: Hinterland) to "Kehlstein Busabfahrt." €3.50 round-trip. Open Apr.-Oct. daily 9am-5pm; Nov.-Mar. Tu-Su 10am-3pm. Audioguides €2. €2.50; military, teachers, students, and children free with ID.)*

KÖNIGLICHES SCHLOß. This castle belonged to an Augustinian prior who was also secular ruler of the area until 1803. A branch of the Wittelsbachs lived here in the 1930s. On display is fabulous furniture, an antique weapons collection, a strong gallery of Gothic art (including two early Riemenschneider pieces) and the largest hunting trophy in Germany, a pair of 18.3kg antlers. The 50min. obligatory tour is in German, but English translations are available. *(From Maximilianstr., veer right at the parking garage. Turn left by Gasthof Triembacher and follow the signs to the Schloß.* ☎ *20 85. Open Easter to mid-Oct. Su-F 10am-1pm and 2-4pm; mid-Oct. to Easter M-F 11am-2pm. €7, with Kurkarte €6, students €3.50, under 16 €3.)*

KÖNIGSSEE. Wedged between extraordinary alpine cliffs, the blue-green Königssee is generally considered clean enough to drink. The *Fußgängerweg* (footpath) from Berchtesgaden winds through fields and over brooks, and is also bike-accessible. *(From the train station, cross the street, turn right, and take a quick left over the bridge. Walk to the right of the green-roofed building, but not up the hill, and take a left onto the gravel path near the stone wall. Follow the "Königssee" signs for 5.5km footpath walk. Or, take bus #41 (dir.: Königssee) from the bus station (1 per hr., round-trip €3.70). Or, ride the touristy* Alpenexpress *tractor "train." Departs from Alpenexpress sign across the street and over the bridge from the train station (1 per hr. 10:20am-4:20pm; round-trip €4.40, under 16 €3.20). By foot, bus, or train, you'll end up in the Königssee parking lot.)* At the end of Seestr. is the Königssee dock and the **Bayerische Seen Schifffahrt** counter, which offers cruises to other points on the lake, including the famous **Echo Wall** and **St. Bartholomä** church. **Salet** is beautiful, and the 45min. walk around the Obersee is well worth it. *(☎ 96 36 18. Boats operate every 30min. 8am-5:30pm. Round-trip from €10.50, under 14 €5.30. 10% discount before 9am.)* Schifffahrt's *Ruderboote* house to the left of the docks rents **rowboats.** *(Open June-Sept. 11am-6pm; May and Oct. 11am-5pm. €5 per hr. for a 2-person boat, more for a 4-seater. €50 deposit or ID required.)* The gorgeous *Malerwinkel* (painter's outlook) lies to the left of the lake; start the 1hr. loop to the left of the base of the Jennerbahn cable car. The best aerial view is from the 1170m peak serviced by the **Jennerbahn** gondola (p. 482). If you're planning to do both the Königssee ferry and Jenner gondola, you can buy a **See-Gipfel-Ticket** at either ticket booth for just €26 (available May-Oct.).

SALZBERGWERK. In the *Salzbergwerk* (salt mines) near town, visitors dress in old miner's outfits, toboggan down snaking passages in the dark, and raft on a saltwater lake in mines that have been operating since 1517. Allow 2hr. for purchasing tickets, waiting, dressing up, and the tour itself. *(From the station, take bus #9548 to "Salzbergwerk" (1-2 per hr. 7:20am-7:20pm, €1). Or, trek 30min. left out of the train station down Begwerkstr., following the "Salzbergwerk" signs.* ☎ *600 20. Open May to mid-Oct. daily 9am-5pm; mid-Oct. to Apr. M-Sa 12:30-3:30pm. €12.50, children under 16 €6.80.)*

OBERSALZBERGBAHN. This cable car takes you 1000m up the face of the Kehlstein. From there, choose one of the many hiking trails leading around the mountain. *(Take a left out of the train station and walk along Bahnstr. for 5min. The station will be on your right, across from the tourist information office. Open 9am-5:50pm. Round-trip €7.50.)* For an adrenaline rush, slide down the 600m **Sommerrodelbahn,** a metal slide built into the side of the mountain, where riders reach speeds of up to 40km per hr. *(Open daily 10am-8pm, closed on rainy days. €2, children €1.50.)*

◼ NIGHTLIFE

If you're not too exhausted after conquering mountains, Berchtesgaden has a nightlife worth cleaning up for, especially the small, bustling bars in the center.

Kaserbar, Seestr. 2 (☎37 55). This bar draws a younger crowd 7 nights a week to (mostly) American music on a crowded floor, hang out at the sidelines enjoying the scene, or take advantage of the pool and foosball tables. Drinks €2.50-4. Open daily 10pm-3am. Night buses run the 6km back to the Bahnhof through the wee hours, but make sure to check the timetable.

Bobby's Inn, Bahnhofsweg 1 (☎48 31). From the train station, follow the *Zum Markt* signs up the gravel path. *Bobby's* is across the bridge along the gravel path leading up to town. Climbers, hikers, and bikers find their 2nd wind between the dart board and baby grand at this bar with a country-western flair. Enjoy a beer (€2.50) or cocktail (€3-6) with a snack (€3-5). Open W-Sa 7pm-1am.

Kuckuksnest, Bahnhofsweg, is where the cool cats hang out. Make new friends among a welcoming crowd of real climbers and hikers. Cover charge only for live events.

Heidi's Abendcafe. After Bobby's closes down, head here for a nightcap on the rooftop terrace. Snuggle up to the fire under the stars that always seem to shine in this alpine wonderland. Beer €2.50, cocktails €5-7, food €3-5. Open daily 8pm-3am.

Stehplatz, Maximilanstr. 16½ (☎629 67). Join a mixed crowd for a drink in the extremely friendly and laid-back atmosphere of this popular *Pils* pub. Beer €2.60, shots €1.80-2.30. Open Tu-W 6pm-1am, Th-Sa 6pm-3am.

NEAR BERCHTESGADEN: RAMSAU   ☎08657

Nestled among the Alps 10km southwest of Berchtesgaden, Ramsau is nirvana for hikers, cyclists, and skiers. Dominated by the magnificent, snow-capped Waltzmann and Hochkalter mountains, Ramsau is an ideal starting point for walks and mountain hikes in **Berchtesgaden National Park** (p. 478).

Ramsau can be reached from Berchtesgaden by bus, bike, or foot. Bus #46 runs every hr. from the Berchtesgaden bus station, to your right as you leave the train station (15min., 6:10am-7:30pm, €2.50). Get off at "Neuhausenbrücke" to reach the center of town. Rent **mountain bikes** (€15-20 per day) or buy hiking boots at **Sport M+R Brandner,** Im Tal 64. (☎790. Open M-F 9am-noon and 2-6pm, Sa 9am-noon.) The neat Ramsau **tourist office,** Im Tal 2, books rooms for free. (☎98 89 20; www.ramsau.de. Open Oct.-June M-F 8am-noon and 1:15-5pm; July-Sept. M-Sa 8am-noon and 1:15-5pm, Su 9am-noon and 2-5pm.) **Exchange money** and traveler's checks at **Volks-Raiffeisenbank,** Im Tal 89. (☎390. **24hr. ATM.** Open M-Tu and Th-F 8:30am-12:30pm and 2-4:30pm, W 8:30am-12:30pm.)

Ramsau sports a wide selection of fairly inexpensive pensions and *Gästehäuser.* **Gästehaus Marxen ❶,** Hinterseer Str. 22, is a quiet, friendly cottage just up the road from the bus #46 "Marxenbrücke" stop and very close to the Zauberwald trail head. (☎213. Breakfast included. €11-14.) **Haus Freiblick ❷,** Riesenbichl 38, is slightly more expensive but centrally located by the "Neuhausenbrücke" bus stop. Cross the street and bear right on Riesenbichl, following it up the hill. (☎436. Breakfast included. €15-20. Longer stays preferred.) **Campingplatz Taubensee ❷,** Am Taubensee 19, basks on the Lattenbach river 5min. from the "Taubensee" bus stop. (☎284. €4.60 per person, €2.30 per child, plus *Kurtaxe* €1.80/€0.80. Camper site €5.20. Tent site €4.60. Showers €0.60. Electricity €0.50 per kwh.) Among the trees, the **Gletscherquellenhütte ❸** is the most accessible restaurant via the hiking trails radiating from Ramsau. A wooden footbridge crosses the stream before the church. On the other side, follow the white gravel path to the right, then signs will guide you into the woods for a 15min. stroll to the Hütte. Here, beer (from €2) and

BAYERN

fresh milk and buttermilk (€2 per 0.25L) quench hikers' *Durst*, accompanied by tasty Bavarian *Brotzeiten*. (☎14 14. Open Apr.-Oct. and Dec. 26-Jan. 6 M and W-Su 10am-10pm.) The colorful **Café Waldquelle ❸**, Riesenbichl 25, offers seating on an outdoor patio with a view of the water-powered *Zwergspiele* (model dwarfs) in the garden, or indoors among the fauna of Bavaria. (☎291. Most meals €5-10. Open M-W and F-Su 11am-9pm.) At **Gasthof Oberwirt ❷**, Im Tal 86, enjoy hot strudel and other specialties as you gaze at the Hochkalter. (☎225. Open daily 11am-8pm.) Buy wine and cheese at the small **Edeka grocery store,** Im Tal 60 (open M-F 7:30am-12:30pm and 2:30-6pm, Sa 7:30am-noon) to go with bread and pastries from the **Bäckerei-Konditorei,** Im Tal 1. Some baked goods are half-price after 5pm. (☎12 51. Open M-F 6am-noon and 2-6pm, Sa 6am-noon.)

In winter, knicker-clad tourists take advantage of cross-country ski trails, sled runs, and ice skating on the Hintersee. The 16th-century **Pfarrkirche** (parish church), Im Tal 82 (☎988 60), rises magnificently from the Ramsauer Ache stream a few sheep pastures down the road from the tourist office. To clear your sinuses, follow the white gravel path across the stream from the church to the left, and turn right at Cafe Waldquelle to the **Kleingradierwerk Ramsau,** a small "outdoor brine inhalatorium." Saltwater drips down a wall of hundreds of mountain briar bush branches and the wind blows the healing fumes to those sitting on the surrounding benches. Past the inhalatorium, the pebbly path leads to the **Kneipp-Gesundheitsanlage,** a mountain stream wading pool built by a local doctor to improve his patients' circulation. The ice-cold water prepares feet for a day in the sun and cools them after a day's hike. A rewarding yet low-impact hike, the **Zauberwald** (enchanted forest) trail follows the Ache upstream through a forest to the sparkling Hintersee. Follow Im Tal from the Ramsau tourist office past the Pfarrkirche, taking a left on Fendtenweg by Cafe Brotzeitstation. Cross the bridge and, keeping the river on your right, follow the white gravel trail. From then on, follow the arrows labeled "Zauberwald-Hintersee." Bus #46 returns to Ramsau from Hintersee's bus station (10min., 1-2 per hr., €1.60). For more information on the network of well-marked hiking trails radiating from Ramsau, see p. 482.

NEAR BERCHTESGADEN: SCHÖNAU ☎08652

Though not as serene as Ramsau, Schönau is a perfect starting point for hiking in the Königssee area of the park. The village lies on a plateau above Berchtesgaden, extending to the bustling outdoor shopping street of Seestr. in the adjoining *Dorf* of Königssee. Schönau is a 30min. walk from Berchtesgaden. Follow the footpath to the Königssee and bear right when you cross Graf-Arco-Str.; it bridges the **Königsseer Ache,** leading to UnterSteinerstr. Bus #43 runs from the Berchtesgaden train station to "Unterstein" (every 45min. 5:55am-6:15pm, €1.80), which puts you 300m uphill from the **tourist office,** Rathauspl. 1. (☎17 60; www.koenigssee.com. Open M-F 9am-6pm, Sa-Su 9am-4pm.) If the office is closed, machines in the Königssee parking lot sell helpful pamphlets in several languages (€1).

For **accommodations,** check with the tourist office—everyone with a free room is registered (prices vary). One nice option is **Gästehaus Germania ❷,** Im Maltermoos 7. From the tourist office, head up UnterSteinerstr. and turn right at Waldhauserstr. Head up the incline and take a left onto Im Maltermoos, which curves to the right again; the building is on the left. (☎42 09; www.pension-germania.de. Singles €19-25; doubles €38-50.) The closest camping to the Königssee is **Campingplatz Grafenlehen ❶,** Königsseer Fußweg 71, about a 5min. walk to the lake. From Berchtesgaden, take bus #41 (dir.: Königssee) to "Königssee Tankstelle" by the gas station. Take a right on Schornstr. and another right onto Königsser Fußweg, following blue signs to the campground. (☎41 40. Shower included, warm water 6am-10pm. Reception 8am-8pm. €4.50 per person, €3 per child, €6 per car and tent.

Kurtaxe €1.80/€0.90.) **Spar Markt,** Untersteinerstr. 1, has groceries. (Open M-F 7:30am-noon and 2-6pm, Sa 7:30am-1pm.) Grab some *Wurst,* or a *Germknödel mit Vanillesoße* (dumpling with vanilla sauce) at **Brotzeitstüberl ❷,** Seestr. 29. (☎44 06. Many entrees €3.50-4.50. Open daily 10am-6pm.)

BAD REICHENHALL   ☎08651

For centuries the fortunes of this alpine town have depended on a mysterious elixir: "white gold," the natural salt water that flows from underground. The salt, once an important trading commodity, now draws pilgrims attracted by its purported healing powers. A large crowd of mostly older Germans flocks to Bad Reichenhall's baths and springs to breathe, drink, wade, and bathe in the city's briny symbol. Apart from salt, a wide array of adventure sports beckon, and the Bad Reichenhall—Salzburg bike trail connects Austria and Germany.

⌨🎵 TRANSPORTATION AND PRACTICAL INFORMATION. Trains run every hour to **Munich** (2hr., €15) and **Salzburg** (30min., €4). Both trains and **buses** connect to **Berchtesgaden** (35min., 1 per hr., €3.10). Most trains stop in Freilassing. Rent a **bike** at **Sport Müller,** Spitalg. 3. (☎37 76. €8 per day, children 20% off. Open M-F 9am-6pm, Sa 9am-1pm.) The **⬛tourist office,** Wittelsbacherstr. 15, is on the same road as the station, across from the Sparkasse. The staff provides maps and free guides for hiking, climbing, canoeing and nordic walking. (☎60 63 03; www.bad-reichenhall.de. Open M-F 8am-5pm, Sa 9am-noon.) **Club Aktiv,** Frühlingstr. 61, offers **rafting, canyoning, mountain biking** and **paragliding** packages. (☎672 38; www.rafting-fun.com. Half-day trips from €35.) Do laundry at **Abel Wäscherei,** Schacht-Str. 1 (open M-Tu and Th-F 8am-12:30pm and 2-6pm, W morning only, Sa 9am-noon), or at **Moni,** Getriedeg. 3. (Wash €3, soap €0.50. Dry €4 per 30min. Open M-Sa 8am-10pm.) The **police station** is at Poststr. 19 (☎97 00, emergency ☎110). For **Internet,** go to the **Kurgarten** (p. 492) or the popular **Cafe Amadeo,** Poststr., where surfing sets you back €3.75 per hr. (Open M-F 8am-1am, Sa-Su 9:30am-1am.) The **post office,** Bahnhofstr. 35, 83435 Bad Reichenhall, is to the right as you exit the station. (Open M-F 8am-6pm, Sa 8am-12:30pm.)

🏠🍴 ACCOMMODATIONS AND FOOD. Bad Reichenhall has no hostel, but private rooms abound in the area—the Bad Reichenhall tourist office keeps an extensive list. After one night at any accommodation you will have to pay the mandatory *Kurtaxe* (€2.50 or €1.90 depending on your location). In return you receive a *Kurkarte,* which gets you **discounts** and **free admission** at many area sites. **Gästehaus Villa Fischer ❷,** Adolf-Schmidt-Str. 4, is a small, pleasant hotel a short walk from the Kurgarten. Take a right out of the train station on Bahnhofstr., a left on Rinckstr., a right on Salzburger Str., and a left on Adolph-Schmidt. (☎57 64. Breakfast included. Giant singles €21.) While **Landhaus Kirchholz ❷,** Salzburger Str. 44c, is a 20min. walk from the train station, it offers comfortable rooms with balconies overlooking the Alps. Take a left on Bahnhofstr., a right on Zenostr., and a left on Salzburger Str. (☎55 82. Singles €19.) For camping, head to **Campingplatz Staufeneck ❶,** 2km past Bad Reichenhall, in Piding. (☎21 34 or 08654 503 15. Reception April-Oct. 8-11am and 5-10pm. €5.50 per person, €2.50 per tent. Showers €0.50. Electricity and washing machines available. Dogs allowed.) Campers park for 36hr. for free at the **Kirchholz** parking lot, just off the Salzburger Str. past the St. Zeno church and cemetery (water €2).

Endless cafes and shops alternate with flowers and fountains along the pedestrian zones of Salzburgerstr. and Ludwigstr.; follow Bahnhofstr. to the right out of the station, take a left on Kurstr., and a right on Salzburgerstr. Just past the *Alte Saline,* the **Harlekin Cafe/Bistro ❷,** Anton-Winkler-Str. 3a, in the yellow building, offers a simple daily menu beneath a hat-covered ceiling (soup of the day €2.30, pasta €3.50). The cafe is also a non-profit social project, employing workers who are reentering the work force or need a protective environment. (☎98 43 04. Open M-F 10:30am-5:30pm.) Try the world-famous, delectable *Mozartkugeln* (marzipan and chocolate balls) at the fabulously gaudy **Cafe Reber** ❸, 10 Ludwigstr. (€0.50 each. Open M-Sa 9am-6pm.) A quartet of bewigged Mozart impersonators perform free concerts Sa 11am-1pm. At **Gasthof Bürgerbräu** ❸, Am Rathauspl., throw back local beer direct from the in-house brewery (from €2.10 for 0.5L). The menu, punctuated jokes verging on the inappropriate, has Bavarian dishes (€6-10), vegetarian options and soup (€4-8), but the specialty are the plentiful grilled meats (€8.40-10), with names like "Macho Man." (☎71 52 98. Open M-Th and Su 9am-midnight, F-Sa 9am-1am.) At local favorite **Murat's** ❷, Poststr. 24, the friendly owner will enhance your *Döner Kebap* with delicious fried eggplant, zucchini and peppers (€4). The veggie variety is €3, and the "Big Döner," served on a plate, is €7. (☎76 72 76. Open daily 8am-8pm.) A **grocery** store, **Aldi**, is directly to the left of the train station in the parking lot. (Open M-F 8am-7pm, Sa 8am-2pm).

🢒 **SIGHTS.** The **Salzmuseum,** Alte Saline, is peppered with exhibits on the history and process of salt-making in the area. Obligatory 1hr. tours in German pass through briny underground passageways, past massive 15-ton wheels that have been turning uninterruptedly for 150 years. English tours by request; call a week in advance. (☎700 21 46. Tours May-Oct. daily at 10, 11:15am, 2, and 4pm; Nov.-Apr. Tu, Th, and 1st Su of the month 2 and 4pm. €5, with *Kurkarte* €4.50; children 6-16 €3. Combo ticket with the Berchtesgaden Salzwerk, p. 487, €14.50/€7.90.) The **Städtisches Heimatmuseum,** Getreidg. 4, offers a gigantic, haphazard collection of everything from prehistoric jewelry to troubling paraphernalia from the Nazi period celebrating local military "heroes." Also on view are strange *Naturplastiken*, unworked wooden pieces with strange resemblances to animals and people. (☎668 21. Open May-Oct. Tu-F 2-6pm and Su 2-6pm. €1.50, children €0.75.) At the museum or the tourist office, pick up a €3 guide to the **Reichenhaller Burgenweg,** an extensive, worthwhile circuit (hike, bike, or drive) of the castles and palaces of the Reichenhall valley. The route covers ancient watchtowers and ruins, but its culmination is **Schloß Marzoll,** the beautifully-preserved mansion of the wealthiest Reichenhall inhabitants during the Renaissance. Its interiors can be visited only on a guided tour (ask at the tourist office). The city's oldest church, **Münsterkirche St. Zeno,** was founded in the early 9th century. Thanks to a monetary gift from Barbarossa, it was rebuilt in stunning Romanesque style in

ON THE MENU

THE PROPER *PROST!*

In Germany, drinking beer is a time-honored tradition, so next time you head into a Biergarten, follow these tips to look the part:

Bavarian custom requires each drinker to wait until everyone has received his or her beverage before even thinking of touching a stein. Once the whole party is seated with beer in front of them, everyone greets everyone else with a hearty *"Prost!"* This is the German word for cheers and it is downright rude (and some say, catastrophic) not to perform the ritual properly—failure to make eye contact with the person whose glass you're clinking is supposed to result in seven years of bad sex. After glasses have been tapped all the way around the group, everyone hits their stein to the table before taking their first sip.

This final tap is said to date back to King Ludwig I, who was great in more ways than one—while doing wonders for Munich and Bavaria, he still had time to amass a large physical presence. When he would *Prost* his companions at the dinner table, he would be so exhausted from holding up his Maß that he had to set down his beer again before he could muster up the energy to drink.

So channel the spirit of Ludwig, get ready for some eye-contact, and *Prost* with heartfelt Bavarian pride.

the 11th century, although by the 16th century a fire destroyed nearly all of the original building. The church and much of its artwork, therefore, date to the Renaissance, but the impressive portal and the bas-reliefs in the adjoining cloister (one of which portrays Barbarossa himself) are striking reminders of the beauty of the more archaic building style. (Church open daily, cloister open Sa-Su.)

The center of the town's "water cure" circuit is the palatial **Kurgarten.** From the train station, turn right down Bahnhofstr., then left onto Kurstr. and walk until you see the garden on the left. (Open Apr.-Oct. daily 7am-10pm; Nov.-Mar. 7am-6pm. Free. Summer concerts €5, children €2.50, free with *Kurkarte*.) The **Altes Kurhaus** hosts events, and across the park the **Wandelhalle** has a music pavilion, a giant chess set, and a *Gurgelnraum*—a room devoted to gargling. The *Trinksole* (salt spring fountain) sells drinks from hot and cold springs. (Open M-Sa 8am-12:30pm and 3-5pm, Su 10am-12:30pm. Small cup €0.10, glass €1.50.) At the back of the hallway, beyond the fountain, is **free Internet** access for those with a *Kurkarte* (€2.50 per hr. without the card). The 170m **Gradierwerk** out front is a bizarre wall known as an "open air inhalatorium." Built in 1912, it's covered with 250,000 *Dornbündel* (bundles of branches, briars, and thorns) through which salt-water mist trickles. For intense results, stroll around the downwind side and inhale for 30min. daily (open Apr.-Oct.). The **Predigtstuhlbahn,** Südtirolerpl. 1, the oldest twin-cable car in the world (1928), ascends 1614m of skiers' paradise to a lookout point and restaurant across the river. From the top, you can hike to Berchtesgaden and other valleys. (☎21 27. 1 trip every 30min., 9am-5pm. Last uphill trip at 4pm. One way €9.50, children €5. Round-trip €15, with *Kurkarte* €14.50, under 18 €7.)

CHIEMSEE

Artists, architects, and musicians have chosen the Chiemsee region, situated between Munich and Salzburg, as the setting for their masterpieces for hundreds of years. The original inhabitants of these picturesque islands, meadows, forests, and marshlands surrounded by dramatic crescents of mountains were the 9th-century builders of the island monasteries later, aristocratic dynasties and their serfs. Much later, 11-year-old **Mozart** composed a mass in Seeon while on holiday, and **King Ludwig II** chose the Herreninsel island in the Chiemsee for his last and most extravagant fairy-tale chateau. Modern visitors to the "Bavarian Ocean" are artists of leisure; the area has been overrun by resorts and rising prices. Much of the lake itself is now a *Naturschutzgebiet* (Nature Preserve) and its waters remain pristine and potable despite droves of visitors. Even though it is prime real estate for the German elite, the Chiemsee area attracts a younger, more active audience as well, thanks to the variety of sports on tap, from wind-surfing and sailing to hiking and mountain biking. For information on white water rafting, contact **Sport Lukas,** Schleching (☎08649 243). **Prien,** the largest lake town, functions as a hub for the other towns around the lake, as well as Aschau, resort paradise Bad Endorf, Sachrang, the ski areas of **Kampenwand,** and the surrounding alpine range.

PRIEN AM CHIEMSEE ☎08051

Tranquil Prien's best qualities may be its Chiemsee proximity and its hub train station, but the Altstadt and the **Chiemgau Bahn** ride through the mountains are worth tearing yourself away from the waves.

◪ TRANSPORTATION. On the southwestern corner of the Chiemsee, Prien has **train** connections to Munich (1hr., 1 per hr., €12.90) and Salzburg (50min., 1 per hr., €9). **Buses** to nearby towns leave from the parking lot to the left as you exit the train station (€1.50-3). Rent **bikes** at **Radsport Reischenböck,** Bahnhofpl. 6 (☎46 31), 100m to your left after you exit the train station. (€8 per day. Open M-F 8am-noon and 2-6pm, Sa 8am-noon.)

7 PRACTICAL INFORMATION. The **train station** is a few blocks from the city center and a 20min. walk north of the lake. To reach the Altstadt, turn right on Hochriesstr. from the station and then turn left on Seestr., which becomes Alte Rathausstr. The modern **tourist office**, 5min. away on the left at Alte Rathausstr. 11, full of free maps and brochures, keeps a list of *Privatzimmer* and offers **free Internet.** (☎ 690 50; www.prien.chiemsee.de. Open M-F 8:30am-6pm, Sa 9am-4pm, Su 8:30am-noon.) There is an **ATM** at **Sparkasse**, 200m left of the Hauptbahnhof. (☎ 98 19 81. Open M-F 8:30am-6pm, Sa 8:30am-noon.) The Prien **police station** is two doors down on the left at Altes Rathausstr. 13 (☎ 905 70, emergencies 110). **Internet** is available at **Oscom Computer**, Seestr. 56. (€5 per hr. Open M-F 9am-noon and 1-5pm.) The **post office** is 400m to the left of the train station at Hochriesstr. 21. (Open M-F 8am-6pm, Sa 8am-12:30pm.)

7 ☐ ACCOMMODATIONS AND FOOD. Visitors with cars get the best deals in Prien, because outlying rooms, which offer better prices, are not well-serviced by public transport. The cheapest bed in town is at the **Jugendherberge (HI) ❷**, Carl-Braun-Str. 66, 20min. from the station and 10min. from the lake. From the station, turn right, then right on Seestr., and continue under the train overpass. After two blocks, go left on Staudenstr., which curves right and turns into Carl-Braun-Str. (☎ 687 70; fax 68 77 15. Breakfast included. Locker €2 deposit. Reception 8-9am, 5-7pm, and 9:30-10pm. Curfew 10pm, but door code available. Open early Feb. to Nov. 4- to 6-bed dorms €15.90, less for longer stays.) In town, **Haus Händlmayer ❸**, Rafenauerweg 7, offers pleasant rooms with bath. Exit the Bahnhof right and turn right onto Seestr., take the first left onto Hallwanger after the rail underpass, then the first right onto Rafenauerweg. (☎ 28 23. Singles €25; doubles with balcony €60; less for longer stays). Although remote, **Schmiedhof ❸**, Ludwigstr. 119, often has room when everything else is full. Take bus #9494 from the first platform at the bus stop (1 every 2-4hr., €1.50) to "Bachham;" Schmiedhof is two houses down on the right. Many rooms have balconies and alpine views. (☎ 18 41. Breakfast and afternoon coffee and cake included. Singles €25, less for longer stays; doubles €40.) **Campingplatz Hofbauer ❶**, Bernauer Str. 110, is a 25min. stroll from the center of town. From the station, turn left at Seestr., left again at the next intersection, and follow Bernauer Str. out of town past three gas stations and a McDonalds. (☎ 41 36; fax 626 57. Reception 7:30-11am and 2-8pm. Open Apr.-Oct. €5.30 per adult, €2.70 per child, €5.10 per site. Free showers.)

Descend into the bustling beer cellar of **Wieninger Bräu ❸**, Bernauer Str. 13b, for *Bayerische Käsespätzle* (Bavarian cheese noodles; €9) and *Lederhosen*-clad waitstaff. (☎ 610 90. Entrees from €10. Open M and W-F 10am-midnight, Su 9am-midnight.) For a delicious Italian meal, enter the faux-Italian ambience of **La Piazza ❸**, Seestr. 7. The lively waitstaff serves savory pasta dishes (€12-18) and large, thin-crust pizzas for €6-8. (☎ 56 52. Open Tu-Su 11am-2:30pm and 5-11:30pm.) For a cheap meal, try indoor/outdoor cafe **Bäckerei/Cafe Müller ❷**, Marktpl. 8 in the pedestrian zone behind the church. (☎ 40 31. Sandwiches from €3. Open M-F 6:30am-6pm, hot food until 3pm; Sa 6:30am-12:30pm, Su 7:30-10:30am.) Do as the locals do and buy veggies at the **farmer's market** behind the church. (Open F 9am-1pm.)

☐ ☐ SIGHTS AND ENTERTAINMENT. Prien's most exciting cultural feature, the ☒**Kirche St. Jakobus**, is in Urschalling, a pleasant 30min. walk from the center of town. From the tourist information office, head left along Alte Rathausstr., then left onto Beilhackstr., which soon becomes Trautersdorfer Str. Contine through Trautersdorf on what is now Bauernbergstr., then follow signs to Kirche St. Jakobus. Or, take the *Chiemgau Bahn* train for a 5min. ride to Urschalling (the stop is on request; speak to the conductor before departure). The church has a complete fresco cycle from the end of the 14th century:

B A Y E R N

it was considered crude by followers and covered over, but restoration has revealed the striking, archaic figures (Church open daily 8:30am-6pm.) **Mesnerstub'n,** Urschalling 4, next to the church, is a pleasant *Gaststätte* with delicious beer and upper Bavarian dishes (☎39 71.) Prien's *Kneipp* water cure at the **Kleiner Kursaal** gardens behind the tourist office soothes sore feet. Nearby, the red-and-blue marble interior of the **Himmelfahrt Church** boasts beautiful 18th-century chandeliers, paintings, statues, and ceiling frescoes by **Johann Baptist Zimmermann,** of Wieskirche fame. On the square behind the church the recently renovated **Heimatmuseum** tells the story of distinctive local Bavarian culture through exhibits of clocks, fishing rods, coins, ceramics, and stuffed local fowl. (☎927 10. Open Apr.-Oct. M-Sa 10am-noon and 2-5pm; Nov.-Mar. Tu and F 10am-noon and 3-5pm. €1.50, students and seniors €1.) **Galerie im Alten Rathaus,** Alte Rathausstr. 22, shows international art and photography. (☎08051 929 28. Open summer months M-F 2-5pm, Sa-Su 11am-1pm and 2-5pm.)

Bootsverleih Stöffl rents the cheapest **boats** in town. From the train station, turn left and walk to the end of Seestr. Turn left before the ferry dock. (☎16 16. Open Apr.-Oct. daily 9am-dusk. Pedal boats €4.50-6 per hr.; rowing boats €5 per hr.; electric €9-19.) Every week in summer the cinema **Mike's Kino,** Bernauer Str. 13a, shows the colorful historical drama "Ludwig." (☎96 66 76; www.mikes-kino.de. In German. Th 7:45pm.) **Prienavera Erlebnisbad,** Seestr. 120, just along the lakefront from the ferry wharf, has a sauna, fun pool, 25m pool, 70m slide, and an outdoor heated pool with view of the Chiemsee. (☎08051 60 95 70; www.prienavera.de. Open M-F 10am-9pm, Sa-Su 9am-9pm. Beach pool open summer 9am-8pm. Full-day admission €10.50, children under 15 €5. Sauna €3.) The 3hr. **Chiemsee Tanzschiff** (dance ship) lake cruises leave select Fridays in summer from the Prien dock. (☎60 90 for dates, or ask at the tourist office. Departs Prien at 6:30pm. €13.) For those bursting with energy, the Prien tourist office offers **guided mountain bike tours** in the area. (Meeting point at tourist office; sign up one day in advance. Tu and F evening tours from 6:30-9pm, €20 per person. Sa half-day 9am-1pm, €30. Price does not include bike rental.) Ask about the **Naturerlebnistouren,** guided nature tours, at the tourist office. Experts lead visitors to the delta of the **Tiroler Achen,** around remote areas of the lake, and along the Alz river for dawn and sunset trips on a wooden raft. (All tours take place regularly in summer; €8-20.)

ISLANDS ON THE CHIEMSEE

Chiemsee Schifffahrt ferries float across the waters of the Chiemsee from Prien to **Herreninsel** (Gentlemen's Island), **Fraueninsel** (Ladies' Island), and towns on the other side of the lake. Both islands are extremely popular with German tourists and school groups, so take a ferry before 10am to avoid crowds. (Departs from the Prien dock roughly every 30min. in summer and every hr. in winter, 7:15am-7:30pm. Last ferry from the islands to Prien leaves Fraueninsel 7:00pm, Herreninsel 7:10pm. Round-trip to Herreninsel €5.70, under 15 €2.80; to Fraueninsel or both islands €6.80/€3.40.) An Augustinian monastery on Herreninsel once complemented the still-extant Benedictine nunnery on Fraueninsel in religious isolation. Supposedly, mischievous members of the cloth met up on **Krautinsel** (Herb Island) and engaged in a scandalous practice: gardening. Today, the island is uninhabited and unferried. For more information on getting to the islands, call **Chiemsee-Schifffahrt** (☎60 90). To get to the dock, hang a right from the Prien train station's main entrance and follow Seestr. for about 15min. Or, a slow, green 19th-century steam train, the **Chiemseebahn,** takes visitors from the train station to the dock; follow the signs. (1 per hr., 10:10am-5:54pm. €2, round-trip €3; children under 15 €1/€1.50. Tickets can be purchased at the booth next to the tracks, or on the train. Or, buy the combination train/ferry ticket at the train station.)

◪**HERRENINSEL.** Frustrated by his powerlessness and already descending into the depression and delusion of his final days, King Ludwig II made one last stab at earthly perfection with the construction of the **Schloß Herrenchiemsee.** A monument to the "Sun King," Louis XIV of France, the ornate folly is a temple to Ludwig's admiration for his omnipotent 17th-century namesake (Ludwig is the German equivalent of Louis). Unfortunately, Ludwig's death in 1886 left the dream incomplete and the family coffers empty; the combination of overdone chambers and barren, uncompleted rooms in the palace betrays the sudden halt in construction. To get to the palace from the ferry landing, walk along the paved footpath (20min.) or ride in true kingly fashion in a horse-drawn carriage (every 15min.; €3, children 4-15 €1). The entire palace is an unparalleled extravagance, shamelessly copying Versailles, with a **Hall of Mirrors,** replicas of furnishings and artwork, and a lavish golden bed chamber dedicated to Louis's tradition of receiving his first and last appointments of the day while in bed. Ludwig II's private chambers include the most expensive chandelier ever produced by the famed Meissen porcelain factory (Ludwig had the blueprint destroyed to ensure the piece's uniqueness) and a dining room table that rose up through the floor, so that the king would never have to encounter another human being. Despite the lavish accommodations, Ludwig spent only 10 days total in the palace. A museum documenting his life through original garments and portraits is just inside the castle entrance and is included in the price of admission. (☎688 70. Open daily Apr.-Sept. 9am-6pm; Oct. 9:40am-5pm; Nov.-Mar. 9:40am-4pm. German tours every 10min.; English tours every hr. 10:45am-4:45pm. Admission and obligatory tour €5.50; seniors, students, and disabled persons €4.50; under 18 free with adult.) Halfway down the path back to the dock is the former monastery, known as **Altes Schloß** since the days when Ludwig stayed there during the construction of his new palace. Herreninsel came to the fore in the 1940s, when the Federal Republic's constitution was drafted here; an exhibit explains the event. Also on view are remnants of the original building and artwork, as well as a large collection of works by Chiemsee landscapist **Julius Exter.** In summer, the Hall of Mirrors hosts concerts; call the Prien tourist office for more information. (Open daily Apr.-Sept. 9am-6pm; Oct. 10am-5:45pm; Nov.-Mar. 10am-4:45pm. €3, students €2; free with admission to the castle.) On select Sundays (May-Sept.), two local storytelling grandmothers lead an evocative **fairy-tale walk** around the Herreninsel. (☎08667 71 99; www.maerchenwanderung.de. May-Sept. €8, children €6.)

FRAUENINSEL. Despite daily swarms of tourists, the Fraueninsel manages to maintain its rural island charm. Only footpaths wind through this restrained village realm of hard-working nuns and fishermen. From the dock, a path curls toward the **Klosterkirche** (cloister church), passing its medicinal herb garden. The nuns make their own marzipan, beeswax candles, and five kinds of *Klosterlikör* (€5 for 0.2L), for sale in the **Klosterladen** convent shop. (Open M-Sa 10am-5:45pm; Su 1-5pm.) The abbey, which dates back to at least AD 866, memorializes **St. Irmengard,** the great-granddaughter of Charlemagne and earliest known abbess of the cloister. Her corpse was exhumed in the 17th century and encased in the glass in 1928, though she's not much to look at after 1000 years. Facing the altar are countless messages written to Irmengard in thanks for deliverance after prayer. (Open M-Sa 7:30am-6pm.) The **Torhalle** (gatehouse) is the oldest surviving part of the cloister as well as the oldest completely preserved structure in southern Germany; its **Michaelskapelle** displays some archaic 11th-century frescoes and a few local artifacts with careful copies of prestigious medieval artwork, whose originals are everywhere from Italy to the Germanic Museum in Nürnberg. (Open May-Oct. daily 11am-5pm. €1.50.) The gatehouse also exhibits paintings of the lake by the 19th-century painters' colony that flourished on the island. If you're in the mood for a stroll, the entire Fraueninsel can be circumnavigated on foot in 45min. However, remember that restaurant prices

BAYERN

are somewhat higher than usual since owners know they have tourists trapped. On select weekends in November and December, the Fraueninsel hosts a charming *Christkindlmarkt* (Christmas market; ask at Prien tourist office for dates).

ELSEWHERE NEAR THE CHIEMSEE

While Prien is considered the "metropolis of the Bavarian sea," untold other towns melt into the landscape, offering idyllic resorts, nature hikes, and historical attractions. **Übersee,** which boasts the best and longest beachfront of the region, lies just past Prien on the Munich-Salzburg train line (€2.60 from Prien). In summer, it is also serviced by the ferry line. Contact their **tourist office,** Feldwieserstr. 24. (☎08642 295; www.uebersee.com. Open M-F 8am-noon and 2-6pm, Sa 9am-noon.) A great accommodation in Übersee is the beach-side **Chiemsee Camping Rödlgries** ❶, Rödlgries 1. (☎08642 470; www.chiemsee-camping.de. June-Aug. €7 per adult, €4.50 per child 8-17, €2.50 per child under 8. Sept.-May €6/€3.50/€2. Includes *Kurtaxe*. €5.50-8 per car and tent. Free beach access and showers.) Übersee also boasts the **Julius Exter Haus,** which is now a museum dedicated to the local artist, and still features a lush garden. The tourist office offers weekly guided hikes, but everyone can hike from town up the Westerbuchberg hill to the medieval **St. Peter-und Pauls-Kirchlein.** Übersee also features a **Natur-Pavillon,** Hochfellnweg 1, which educates visitors and school groups about the Chiemsee ecosystem. (In German. Open May-Oct. W-Su 2-5:30pm.) Just northwest of the Chiemsee is **Bad Endorf,** famed for its thermal baths; call the **tourist office,** Bahnhofstr. 6., for more information. (☎08053 30 08 22; www.bad-endorf.de. Open M-F 8am-5pm.) Little villages curl up at the foothills of the mountains. **Grassau** is on the other side of the Kampenwand mountain from Aschau; contact its **tourist office,** Kirchpl. 3. (☎08641 23 40; www.grassau.info. Open M-F 8am-noon and 1:30-6pm.) **Rimsting** is a 30min. walk north of Prien, and a great location for exploring the **Eggstätter Seeplatte** moors. Its **tourist office,** Schellstr. 4, will help you plan your visit. (☎08051 68 76 21; www.rimsting.de. Open summer daily 1-5pm; winter M-Th 8:30am-noon and 1-4:30pm, F 8:30-noon.) **Riedering** is a hamlet located near the small Simsee; to get there, take the train to Rosenheim or Stephanskirchen and then a bus. Its **tourist office,** Holzrotweg 9 (☎08036 615; open M-F 9:30am-11am) will supply more information. **Rottau,** just south of the Chiemsee, nestles in a mountain ridge; contact its **tourist office,** Grassauerstr. 7. (☎08641 27 73; www.rottau.de. Open summer M-F 8am-6pm, Sa 9am-noon; winter M-F 8am-noon and 1:30-5pm.)

Aschau, a beautiful mountain town southwest of the Chiemsee and positioned on the 410km Bodensee-to-Chiemsee bike route, offers everything from horseback riding to mountain gondola rides, as well as solaria, tobogganing, skiing, and sailing. From the Munich-Salzburg train line, get off at Prien and take the special **Chiemgau Bahn** (1 per hr.; €1.70) from platform 1a. Buses also run daily from the main street to Grassau and Rosenheim. Head first to the **tourist office,** Kampenwandstr. 38. From the train station, take a left on Bahnhofstr., which turns into Kampenwandstr. (☎08052 90 49 37; www.aschau.de. Open mid-May to mid-Oct. M-F 8am-6pm, Sa 9am-noon, Su 10am-noon; mid-Oct. to mid-May M-F 8am-noon and 1:30-5pm.) The **post office** is at Kampenwandstr. 37. (Open M-Sa 9am-noon, M-Tu and Th-F 1:30-4:30pm.) The office is in the middle of a small pond in front of the **Kurpark,** where weekly summer concerts are held. Walk 20min. farther down Kampenwandstr. and take a right onto Schloßbergstr. to reach the base of **Schloß Hohenaschau,** built by the Lords Konrad and Arnold von Hirnsberg as an outlook and protection point for the Prien valley in the 12th century. The Renaissance courtyard now hosts summer concerts, and the Holy Trinity Chapel features side altars by **Johann Baptist Zimmermann,** prime artist of Bavarian Rococo. (Obligatory tours May-Sept. Tu-F at 9:30, 10:30, and 11:30am; Apr. and Oct. Th only. Call ahead for tours in English. €3, children €2.) A museum devoted to the history of the valley is also on the premises; entrance is included in the price of the tour. (Open Apr.-Oct. Su 1:30-5pm.) The **Kampenwand**

Bahn gondola takes visitors on a picturesque ride up and down the mountain. You can also ski or make the 2hr. hike down. (☎08052 44 11. Runs daily July-Aug. 8:30am-5:30pm, €14.50, children 5-15 €8; ascent only €10/€5. May-June and Sept.-Nov. 8:30am-5pm, €12/€7; €8.50/€4.50. Dec.-Apr. 9am-4pm. Discounts before 9:30am or with *Kurkarte*.) For rooms, your best bet is to get in touch with the helpful tourist office, or try the central **Gästehaus Kirchlechner ❷**, Kampenwandstr. 30. (☎761. Open Christmas day-Oct. Singles €18; doubles €35, with bath €43. Discounts for longer stays.) Most restaurants in Aschau are expensive, but the **Penny Markt,** Kampenwandstr. 22, sells basics. (Open M-Sa 8am-8pm.) Just outside Aschau, the **Hochseilgarten,** Am Beerweiher 4, is a complex wooden climbing park. (☎54 60; www.chiemgauer-hochseilgarten.de; www.rafting-canyoning.de. 3-4 hr. with a trainer €48 per person.) The same company offers rafting and canyoning packages. For paragliding, contact **Flugschule Chiemsee,** Drelindenweg 7, whose intro session goes for €75. (☎94 94; www.flugschule-chiemsee.de.)

To reach the tiny town of **Sachrang,** an exquisite alpine village on the Austrian border, take bus #9502 from the stop in front of Aschau's train station (free with *Kurkarte*). For more information on excellent skiing, mountain climbing, and walking tours, stop by the **tourist office,** Dorfstr. 20. (☎08057 378; www.sachrang.de. Open May-Oct. M-F 8am-noon and 2-5pm, Sa 10am-noon; Nov.-Apr. M-Tu and Th-F 8am-noon and 2-5pm, W 8am-noon.)

BURGHAUSEN
☎08677

A proverbial castle on a hill overlooks tiny Burghausen, just over the Salzach River from Austria. Set in a lush alpine landscape, Burghausen was a residence of the Landshut line of Wittelsbachs from 1255 to 1503. On the 30min. walk between the ultra-modern train station and the fortress in the Altstadt, you'll become convinced not a day has passed since the Middle Ages. Locals sweeten the deal with a perfect combination of Bavarian beer and Austrian *Torte*.

▐▜ TRANSPORTATION AND PRACTICAL INFORMATION. Burghausen is most easily reached by **train** from: **Mühldorf** (30min., 2 per hr., €5.50); **Munich** (2hr., 1 per hr., €15); **Passau** (3hr., 2 per hr., €15). From Mühldorf, you can also take bus #33. From the front of the train station, follow Marktlerstr. to the right; it's a 30min. trek to the Altstadt. Or take bus #1 from the bus station to "Stadtpl." (Every 30min. 6:35am-7:50pm; fewer Sa-Su. €1.) For a **taxi,** call ☎914 20. The staff of the **tourist office,** Stadtpl. 112, in the peppermint-green Rathaus at the far end of the Stadtpl., books rooms for free. (☎88 71 40; www.burghausen.de. Open M-F 9am-6pm, Sa 10am-4pm.) To explore the Burghausen area by **boat,** join **Plättenfahrten** on a 1½hr. tour down the Salzach River on a reconstruction of the medieval wooden boats that brought salt from Bad Reichenhall. Tours leave from the dock at Tittmoning, 18km south of Burghausen, and land at the Salzach dock in Burghausen. A **shuttle bus** (€2.50) runs to Tittmoning from the Stadtpl. stop at 1:05pm, or from the Bahnhof 5min. later. (☎88 71 40. Mid-May to mid-Sept. every Su; Aug. and Sept. occasional weekdays at 2pm. Check the tourist office for scheduled dates. €10, children and disabled persons €4.) Another popular excursion from Burghausen is the **Helmbrecht Pfad,** a 30km bike or walking loop that hits up all the medieval sights of the area and also features informational signs in both modern and medieval German. Ask at the tourist office for maps of this and other gorgeous bike and walking routes in the Inn-Salzach area. Exchange your traveler's checks at the **Sparkasse,** Marktlerstr. 15. (Open M and Th 9am-noon and 2-5:30pm; Tu-W and F 9am-noon and 2-4:30pm.) Find **Internet** at the swinging **Cafe Liquid,** just off Marktlerstr. 47. (☎ 91 34 80. €3.80 per hr. Open daily 11am-2am.) The **post office,** Marktlerstr. 17, 84489 Burghausen, is in the Neustadt, between Stadtpl. and the train station. (☎917 20. Open M-F 9am-5pm, Sa 9am-noon.)

BAYERN

⌐⌐ ACCOMMODATIONS AND FOOD. The **Jugendherberge Burghausen (HI)**
❷, Kapuzinerg. 235, is close to cafe-heavy **In den Grüben.** Take city bus #1 from
the train station to "Heilige-Geist-Spital." Walk straight and turn left onto
Kapuzinerg. (15min.). Or from Stadtpl., continue through the arch at the far
side of the square onto In den Grüben. At the end, cross the intersection to the
left of the church onto Spitalg. and turn right onto Kapuzinerg. (45min.).
Immaculate rooms have impressive views of the castle. The staff speaks fluent
English. (☎41 87; fax 91 13 18. **Internet** €4.80 per hr. Sheets and breakfast
included. Reception 7-10am and 5-7pm. Reserve well in advance. €16.95.) **Pension Maria Hofbauer** ❷ has a great location between the Grüben and the main
square (☎25 17. Singles €25; doubles €43-47, some with view of the Salzach).
Private rooms (€12-22, some including breakfast) can be found through the
tourist office. For Bavarian dishes, **Hotel Post** ❸, Stadtpl. 39., knows its
Würstchen after 450 years. (☎96 50. Most meals €7-10, beer €2.50. Open daily
11:30am-11pm.) Buy **groceries** at Altstadt Markt, In den Grüben 170-2. (☎87 65
51. Open M-F 8:30am-6pm, Sa 7:30am-noon.)

◪ SIGHTS. The 900-year-old **Burg** extends over 1043m, making it the longest
medieval fortress in Europe. Primarily expanded between 1255-1503, when the
Wittelsbachs were divided into two competing clans, the Burg, together with **Burg
Trausnitz** in Landshut, housed the rulers of eastern Bavaria. Its imposing size would
have defended Bavaria from a Turkish attack, but the Turks only ever made it as
far as the gates of Vienna. Considered impregnable, the fort was breached once—
in 1742, lacking proper arms or reinforcements, Burghausen opened its gates without a fight to the Habsburg Empire. Days later, the brash 26-year-old *Hofka-
minkehrermeister* (Master Chimney Sweep) **Karl Franz Cura** recruited 40
grenadiers, and freed the castle and the city in one fell swoop.

These days, everyone can explore the **castle ramparts** after a 10min. scramble
up the steep **Hofberg** footpath. The Hofweg starts to the right of **St. Jakobskirche,**
a 12th-century church across from the Rathaus (look for the stairs). The grassy
park area up top, perfect for a picnic, offers a ravishing view of the town's red-
tiled roofs and colorful gables. A long series of courts will finally lead you to the
central, residential fortification. Here, the **Stadtmuseum** squats in the upper halls
of the Burg, offering glimpses of peasant and noble life in these parts. (☎651 98.
Open daily May-Sept. 9am-6pm; mid-Mar. to Apr. and Oct.-Nov. 10am-4pm. €2,
children €1.) Across the courtyard, the **Staatliche Sammlung** combines medieval
art with the furniture of the medieval inhabitants of the Burg. The **St. Elisabeth**
chapel has preserved its Gothic elegance. (☎46 59. Open daily Apr.-Sept. 9am-
6pm; Oct.-Mar. 10am-4pm. €3, students €2, children free.) Atop the tower in the
Sammlung, gain a splendid view of the grassy banks of the **Wöhrsee** far below,
popular in the summer months for refreshing swims. The eerie **Folterturm** (torture chamber), several courtyards away from the museums, was in use until
1918. (Open daily June-Sept. 9am-6pm; Apr.-May and in winter with good
weather 10am-5pm. €2, children €0.80.) The **Hexenturm** across the way held
accused witches until 1751. The excellent **Burg Cafe** serves home-made ice-
cream for €0.60 per scoop. Below the castle, the rows of pastel facades lining
the **Stadtplatz** shimmer with soft medieval splendor. At the far end of the Stadtpl.
looms the magnificent Baroque **Studienkirche St. Joseph,** a 1630 Jesuit convent.
Every summer on the second weekend in July, the Burg hosts **Burgfest
Burghausen,** a merry medieval romp involving everything from men in leggings
brandishing spears to circle dancing, madrigal choirs and wild boars on spits.
Away from the Altstadt in the direction of the train station is the **Stadtpark,**
recently renovated to host beautiful and varied flora.

Just upstream of the Stadtpl. is Burghausen's nightspot, **In den Grüben.** Most cafes, restaurants, and dance clubs open around 7 or 8pm and buzz until midnight. Every spring, In den Grüben hosts **B'Jazz Burghausen,** a jazz festival. Bronze plaques embedded in In den Grüben pay tribute to the groove masters who have played here. (☎14 11 or www.b-jazz.com for more information.)

LANDSHUT   ☎0871

The House of Wittelsbach did not always call the Munich *Residenz* home—Landshut, less than an hour from Munich by train, was the main seat of government until 1255. In the 15th century the Wittelsbach line split for three generations; half of Bavaria was ruled by the Landshut line, and this city on the Isar saw its golden age. The line died out in 1503, but the city is still the capital of Lower Bavaria. Its medieval hill castle overlooks red-roofed homes, flower gardens, and pedestrian walkways that run along the river and around the many pastel stucco facades. The setting is ideal for the **Landshuter Hochzeit** (starts June 25, 2005), a three-week medieval revel with authentic feasting, jousting, dancing, and period plays. First celebrated in 1903, the festival only comes around every four years, and re-enacts the magnificent *Hochzeit* (wedding) that Duke Ludwig arranged for his son Georg and his Polish bride Hedwig in 1475.

▛ TRANSPORTATION

Landshut is easily reached by **train** from: **Munich** (1hr., 1-3 per hr., €11.10); **Passau** (1½hr., 1 per 2hr., €16.50); **Regensburg** (45min., 1 per hr., €9.40). To get into town from the station, walk down Luitpoldstr. (the main street on the right) following the curve left and across the bridge. Go through the town gates, then continue straight ahead on Theaterstr.; turn left on Altstadtstr., and the Rathaus will be ahead on the right (25min.). Even better, use public transportation; all local **buses** that leave from the station, to the left as you exit, run to the town center (€1.50, students €1; day pass €1.90). Tickets can be bought on the bus. **Bicycle rental** is at **Fahrrad Geißler,** Länd 126, one block from the Altstadtstr., nearly behind the Residenz. Bikes (☎846 28; €10 a day).

▛ PRACTICAL INFORMATION

The **tourist office,** Altstadtstr. 315, in the Rathaus, has free maps of the Altstadt and better ones of the entire city for €1. The staff helps find hotel and private rooms. (☎92 20 50; www.landshut.de. Open M-F 9am-noon and 1:30-5pm, Sa 9am-noon.) Pick up the free *Monatsprogramm,* a monthly pamphlet listing all concerts, art shows, dances, and films in town in any given month. **St. Rosen Apotheke,** Altstadtstr. 339, lists 24hr. **pharmacies.** (☎891 49. Open M-F 8:30am-6pm, Sa 8:30am-2pm.) Check email at the **Internet Cafe** on Altstadtstr. 362, about two blocks to the right of the Rathaus. (€3 per hr. Open daily 9am-1am.) The **post office,** 84028 Landshut, is left of the station as you exit. (Open M-F 8:30am-6pm, Sa 8:30am-noon.)

▛ ▟ ACCOMMODATIONS AND FOOD

The **Jugendherberge (HI) ❷** is at Richard-Schirrmann-Weg 6. From the tourist office, walk to the left up Altstadtstr. and turn left onto Alte Bergstr. at the "Burg Trausnitz" sign. Take a right on Richard-Schirrmann-Weg. The elegant modern villa sits on quiet grounds overlooking the town and has comfortable but simple 4-to 8-bed dorms with private showers. In June and July, it fills with German schoolchildren. (☎234 49. Sheets and breakfast included. Reception M-F 9am-noon and 5-8pm, Sa-Su 5-8pm. Closed Dec. 23-Jan. 7. €19.35, multiple nights €13.70.) **Hotel Garni Bergterrasse ❸,**

Gerhart-Hauptmann-Str. 1, in the proximity of the Hofgarten (10min. from Altstadt), offers quiet rooms with TVs and phones. (☎891 90; www.hotel-bergterrasse.de. Singles €36-40; doubles €62-65.) Halfway between the train station and the Altstadt is **Hotel Park Cafe ❹**, Papiererstr. 36. From the station, walk straight on Luitpoldstr., turn left on Rennweg, and right onto Nikolastr. which becomes Papiererstr. (15min.). The hotel has clean, modern rooms with private baths, phones, and cable TV. (☎97 40 00; fax 974 00 40. Breakfast included. Singles €44; doubles €67. For a better deal, ask for the €26 single without bath.) **Campingplatz Landshut-Mitterwöhr ❶**, Breslauer Str. 122, is outside of town, but has mini golf along the banks of the Isar. From the Rathaus, walk right down Altstadtstr., straight ahead over Heiliger-Geist-Brücke, then follow the sidewalk and gravel path directly to the right of the bridge along the river for 20min. At the second bridge, Adenauerbrücke, take stairs up to the street and walk left down Adenauerstr.; turn right onto Breslauer Str. at the camping sign. Handicapped-accessible. (☎533 66. Reception 8am-12:30pm and 3-8pm. Open Apr.-Sept. €4.50 per person, €2.50 per child, €1 per dog, €3 per tent, €5.50 per site. Laundry €4.40. Hot showers and electricity included.)

Farmers sell produce in the **market** in front of the Rathaus (M-Th and Sa 7am-noon), and Friday on Am Alten Viehmarkt. For an excellent Greek meal, turn left out of the tourist office and head to ☑**Restaurant Pallas ❸**, Altstadtstr. 191. Their lunch buffet (M-F €6, Su €10) is luxurious. Try the special: gyros with onions, pilaf, and fries for €8.60. (☎233 33. English menu available. Open daily 11:30am-2pm and 5pm-1am.) **Café Cappuccino ❷**, Altstadtstr. 337, down the street from the Rathaus, has tasty pasta and pizzas (€4.70), salads and breakfast. (☎270 92. Open M-Th 9am-midnight, F-Sa 9am-1am, Su 2-6pm.) **Weißes Bräuhaus Krenkl ❸**, Altstadtstr. 107, across from the Rathaus, has been serving Bavarian food since 1457. (☎248 01. Entrees €7-12. Beer €2.25. Open M-Sa 9am-midnight, Su 9am-4pm.)

🟢 🎵 SIGHTS AND ENTERTAINMENT

On a lush hill above the **Altstadt,** which features rows of gabled Gothic and Baroque houses filled with glitzy shops and restaurants, sits **Burg Trausnitz.** The hefty brick and red-tiled fortress was built in 1204, and can be reached by scrambling over 350-odd steps. The seemingly impenetrable exterior conceals a pleasant courtyard with tiers of yellow arches. The castle was the luxurious abode of the Wittelsbach princes of Bavaria-Landshut until 1503, and its highlight is a tapestry series illustrating how Otto, founder of the Wittelsbach dynasty, gained his title of duke from Barbarossa by flashing his sword all over Italy. His fictional founding of Landshut is included for good measure. The amusing *Narrentreppe* (fool's staircase), which traverses the whole building, displays frescoed scenes from the famous Italian folk theater tradition, *Commedia dell'Arte.* The castle interior can only be seen on a German-language tour, but written translations are available in English. (☎92 41 10. Open daily Apr.-Sept. 9am-6pm, Th until 8pm; Oct.-Mar. 10am-4pm. Tours given every 30-45min., last tour 1hr. before closing. €4, students and seniors €3, children free with a parent.) The city **Hofgarten** next to the Burg offers lovely walking trails and beautiful views of the city. (Open dawn to dusk. Free.)

Down in the Altstadt, the world's highest brick church tower reaches a lofty 130m at the **St. Martinkirche.** Unfortunately, the last Landshut Wittelsbach died childless just as it was being completed. The 8m long crucifix crafted by Michael Erhart in 1495 hovers in front of a 1424 hewn stone altar. The 11th-century spiral stairs lead down to the original street level and first portal of the church. Outside the church, look for the bust of architect **Hans Burghausen** under the sculpture of Christ—it's one of the first cases of portraying the artist, since in the Middle Ages, they remained anonymous and faceless. (☎922 17 80. Open daily Apr.-Sept. 7:30am-6:30pm; Oct.-Mar. 7:30am-5pm.)

Across the street from the greenish-beige **Rathaus,** the unassuming facade of the **Stadtresidenz** conceals the only Italian Renaissance-style palace north of the Alps. Two sets of rooms overlook the spacious courtyard: flaking classical frescoes adorn the Renaissance rooms of the 16th-century duke Ludwig X, who had the Residenz built after a trip to Italy. The 18th-century apartments housed Ludwig I while he frequented the Ludwig-Maximilian university during its Landshut period (1800-1826), before his accession to the Munich throne. In the **museum** upstairs a collection of regional arts and crafts spans the Bronze Age to the present. (☎92 41 10. Brisk 35min. German tours of the apartments every hr. Apr.-Sept. Tu-Su 9am-5pm; Oct.-Mar. Tu-Su 10am-3pm. €4, students €3, under 18 free.)

At the edge of the Hofgarten park lies the **Skulpturenmuseum im Hofberg,** Am Prantlgarten 1, a collection of sculptures by German contemporary artist **Fritz Koenig.** His partially abstracted human figures are interspersed with an impressive international sculpture collection including Etruscan and Nigerian pieces. Also take a look at the remnants of the city wall on the premises. To get there, slide past St. Martin's church down Kirchg., then continue on Binderg., turning right at the end. Brown signs lead the way. (Open Tu-Su 10:30am-1pm and 2-5pm.) A stroll along the **Isarpromenade** is always pleasant; the river is dotted with attractive beer gardens alongside green banks.

BAYERISCHER WALD (BAVARIAN FOREST)

A national treasure, the Bayerischer Wald is the largest range of wooded mountains in central Europe. The peaks (60 of which are over 1km high) cover 6000km², and countless creeks and rivers stretch from the Danube to the Austrian and Czech borders. In recent years, an insect known as the *Buchdrucker* has attacked thousands of trees (be careful of falling branches), especially spruces, but new growth is now sprouting. The remoteness of the towns discourages most non-German visitors from visiting this year-round paradise of hiking, camping, and cross-country skiing. Twelve **HI youth hostels** dot the forest; Regensburg's tourist office (p. 520) has a helpful brochure with addresses for all of them.

The Bayerischer Wald is much more than just a blossoming paradise; palaces, churches, and castle ruins are tucked away in tiny villages. The region is famous for its crafts, particularly **glass-blowing.** The glass produced here is prized throughout the world, especially the dark green *Waldglas* (forest glass). Every forest town seems to have its own *Glashütte*, and Bavarian tourist officials have designated a 250km long route from Passau through the park as the *Glasstraße* (Glass Road).

BAYERISCHER WALD NATIONAL PARK

Founded in 1970, the **Bayerischer Wald Nationalpark,** the first national park in Germany, is a hiking mecca—clearly-marked trails lace 59,900 acres of forest. The park strictly prohibits any activities that might alter the ecosystem, including camping and building fires, but there are many campsites at the park's edge. The newspaper *Informationsblatt Nationalpark Bayerischer Wald* gives the latest forest news, *Grenzenlose Waldwildnis* is a free park map, *Ihre Gastgeber* lists accommodations in towns within the park and on its borders, and *Grüner Faden für den Gast* (available in a slightly out-of-date English version) lists information on the park. All brochures are available in park centers and area tourist offices.

█▞█ TRANSPORTATION AND ORIENTATION A series of open roadways run through the park, and many of the trailheads can be reached by car. Public transportation within the park is also very good. The environmentally-friendly *Igel-*

busse ("hedgehog buses") of **RBO** *(Regionalbus Ostbayern)* run from Grafenau, Neuschönau, and Spiegelau to places in the National Park. The **Bayerwald Ticket** (€5) allows unlimited travel on **buses** and **trains** within the park for one day. Your best bet is to pick the trails you want to cover and have one of the tourist offices tell you the precise connections to take.

The Bavarian Forest is located in east-central Bavaria. The park borders the Czech Republic's Bohemian Forest National Park on the east and stretches from Mauth in the south to Bayerisch Eisenstein in the north. Zwiesel is outside the western border of the park in the north, while Grafenau lies to the southwest. 98% of the park is forested, and the three most important (and hike-able) peaks within its borders are the **Lusen** (1373m), on the Czech border directly north of Neuschönau; the **Großer Rachel** (1453m), in the middle of the park; and the **Großer Falkenstein** (1315m), in the northern-most section of the park. Biking is more common in the northern regions, but the entire area is etched with extensive hiking trails.

🛈 PRACTICAL INFORMATION

Emergency: Police ☎ 110. **Ambulance** ☎ 192 22.

Climate and Seasonality: The park is open and accessible year-round. Precipitation is heavy, and winter is very snowy, with only select trails cleared by the park service for cross-country skiing. Summer is relatively cool and moist, with frequent thunder storms. Spring, which starts in May (snow remains until Apr.), and autumn (with its brilliant leaves) are warm and sunny. Sept. and Oct. are ideal times to visit. Vegetation is primarily coniferous forest at higher elevations, mixed forest at lower elevations.

Information Offices: There are 4 within the park, in addition to the administrative offices located in Grafenau.

🏛 **Informationszentrum Hans-Eisenmann-Haus,** Böhmstr. 35, 94556 Neuschönau (☎ 08558 961 50; www.nationalpark-bayerischer-wald.de). From Grafenau (p. 505), take Igelbus #7594 from stop 4 in front of the station to "Nationalpark Infozentrum" (approx. every hr. 7:30am-5pm). The Hans-Eisenmann-Haus is across the street. Exhibits, free pamphlets, a 20min. film (in English upon request), and *Wanderkarten* (**hiking maps;** €5.30). The *Südl Teil* (South Part) is for hiking in the area of the Haus, the *Nördl Teil* (North Part) for hikes to the north. Open Jan.-Oct. daily 9am-5pm.

Info-Stelle Luwigsthal, Eisensteiner Str. 8, 94227 Lindberg (☎ 09922 86 92 37). Open Jan.-Oct. M-Sa 9am-5pm.

Infostelle Spiegelau, Konrad-Wilsdorf-Str. 1, 94518 Spiegelau (☎ 08553 960 07). Open Jan.-Oct. M-Sa 9am-5pm.

Infostelle Mauth, Mühlweg 2, 94151 Mauth (☎ 08557 97 38 38). Open Jan.-Oct. M-Sa 9am-5pm.

Nationalparkverwaltung Bayerischer Wald, Freyunger Str. 2, 94481 Grafenau. (☎ 08552 960 00; fax 46 90.) The park's administrative offices. Open M-Th 7:45am-noon and 1-4pm, F 7:45am-2pm.

Gear: Rent bikes at **Radsport Leitl,** Theresienthalerstr. 25, Zwiesel (☎ 80 21 57), or **Radsportshop de Graaf,** Rosenauerstr. 20 (☎ 36 04), Grafenau, 15min. from Stadtpl. Open M-F 9am-12:30pm and 2-6pm, Sa 9am-1pm. **Intersport Fuchs** (☎ 14 36), Hauptstr. 16, Grafenau, rents **skis** and **snowshoes.** Open M-F 9am-6pm, Sa 9am-1pm.

Tours: Free guided hikes leave daily from the Hans-Eisenmann Haus (see above); contact them a day in advance to book a tour. The free seasonal "Führungen und Veranstaltungen" brochure, available at park info centers, lists tour times and themes.

🛏 ACCOMMODATIONS

Camping is forbidden on park lands, but several designated camping areas cluster just beyond its borders. *Ihre Gastgeber*, available at any National Park information office, lists information for campsites, hotels, and pensions in the tiny towns along the park border. There is one **youth hostel** in the park, located at Waldhäuser (☎ 08583 12 08). Two mountain huts, with limited amenities, are available to over-

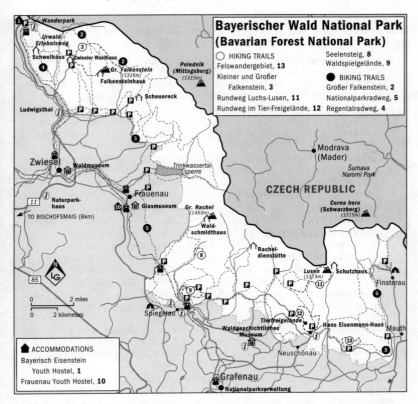

**Bayerischer Wald National Park
(Bavarian Forest National Park)**

○ HIKING TRAILS

Felswandergebiet, **13**

Kleiner und Großer
 Falkenstein, **3**

Rundweg Luchs-Lusen, **11**

Rundweg im Tier-Freigelände, **12**

Seelensteig, **8**

Waldspielgelände, **9**

● BIKING TRAILS

Großer Falkenstein, **2**

Nationalparkradweg, **5**

Regentalradweg, **4**

ACCOMMODATIONS

Bayerisch Eisenstein
 Youth Hostel, **1**
Frauenau Youth Hostel, **10**

night hikers all summer and on weekends in the winter (call ahead for reservations): **Lusenschutzhaus** (☎08553 12 12) is at the 1373m peak of Mt. Lusen in the southern section of the park; **Falkensteinhaus** (☎0992 590 33 66) is 1315m up the Großer Falkenstein in the northern reaches of the park. On free park maps, these huts are marked by a white house with a window and door. This is the same symbol that denotes other huts where only food is available, so check beforehand. Most of the trails through the park pass a restaurant or *Gaststätte* every hr. or so. Other hostels at the fringes of the park that are great to set out from include:

Bayerisch Eisenstein, Brennesstr. 23 (☎0992 510 20). Germany's highest youth hostel at 1330m is conveniently located for hikes around the big and small Arber mountains.

Bischofsmais, Oberbreitenau 1 (☎0992 02 55). From this hostel, discover the busy (touristy) streets of Bischofsmais, or take on a 2hr. hike to *Teufelstisch* (devil's table).

Frauenau, Haus St. Hermann, Hauptstr. 29 (☎0992 67 35). From Frauenau, hike around the beautiful *Trinkwassertalsperre,* a water reservoir in the middle of the park.

HIKING AND BIKING

The hiking trails around the park are marked with care that borders on obsession. All intersections are signposted and popular trails have inlaid wooden maps every 500m and color-and-picture coded signs on a tree every 100m. Trails with yellow signs are loops, and those with white markers lead from one trailhead to another. Guided hikes leave daily from the **Hans-Eisenmann-Haus** (p. 502). To explore the park on foot, pick up a *Wanderkarte* (hiking map).

Kleiner und Grosser Falkenstein (10km, 4-5hr. round-trip). In the northern section; take the bus from Zwiesel or Ludwigsthal to "Zwieslerwaldhaus." From the Falkenstein parking lot, follow the white signs of 2 bell-adorned pine branches for a 2½hr. climb over *Kleiner Falkenstein* and on to the top of its larger brother. Steep in places.

Seelensteig (1.3km, 1½hr.). From Grafenau, take the bus past Hans-Eisenmann-Haus to "Groupsäge," then the Rachel Bus to "Seelensteig." Or, from Spiegelau take the Rachel Bus (dir.: Gfäll) to "Seelensteig." This steep trail shows the life of the forest around cycles of life, death, decay, and regrowth. We warned you about the steep part.

Racheltour (4hr.). From Spiegelau, take the Rachel Bus to "Gfäll." Follow the bird symbols past the Liesl-fountain and the *Waldschmidthaus* (which serves beer). After a view of the *Rachelsee* you'll hit the highest peak in the park. Descent passes the *Rachelkapelle* and ends at the *Racheldiesthütte*, which offers food and the bus back down.

Waldspielgelände (1hr., plus playtime on the ziplines and see-saws). An outdoor adventure trail with playgrounds and physical challenges every 100m, starting in Spiegelau.

Rundweg im Tier-Freigelände (3hr. round-trip). A fun hike from the Hans-Eisenmann-Haus. Yellow signs mark this flat loop leading through a unique zoo: along the trail, animals such as brown bears, lynx, and wolves roam enclosures resembling their natural habitat. Carved wooden signs clarify strange German animal names. In the wild swine quarters, mama and baby pigs overrun the trail alongside the tourists.

Felswandergebiet (2hr.). From the Hans-Eisenmann-Haus, take the Finsterau Bus to "Jugendwaldheim." Cross the street and follow the yellow signs depicting a bird with a spotted chest. Hike curves up through the rocky hilltops to outlook points on top of the Kanzel mountains from which, on a clear day, you may see the Alps, or be able to peer west over the former Iron Curtain into the Czech Republic. Can also be reached via a pleasant hike by following the white signs with 3 trees on them and arrows to "Felswandergebiet" from the Hans-Eisenmann-Haus parking lot.

Rundweg Luchs-Lusen (2½hr.). Lace up your boots and climb one of the highest peaks in the Park. From Grafenau, take the bus past the Hans-Eisenmann-Haus to end of the line at the Lusen parking lot. From there, follow the yellow signs with the lynx (wildcat) picture. Past the granite outcroppings, the top affords a gorgeous view, and about 300m farther down, food awaits at the Lusenschutzhaus.

Many trails are also accesible by **bike**; signs at the start indicate whether or not wheels are allowed. Pick up a free **Radwander- und Mountainbikekarte** at the Hans-Eisenmann-Haus to check out bike trails in the park. Routes marked in purple are recommended only for fit folks with mountain bikes.

The Nationalparkradweg (100km) is the main trail through the forest, running southeast from Zwiesel and curving up to cross the Czech border. Accessible from Waldbahn-linked towns Eisenstein, Zwiesel, and Spiegelau, as well as towns on the Finsterau Igel bus line between Spiegelau and Finsterau.

The Regentalradweg, accessible from Bayerische Eisenstein, good for leisurely biking, follows the course from the Regen to Regensburg.

The Großer Falkstein is circled by a 50km trail for fit bikers. Good beginning and/or endpoints are the train stations in Zwieselau, Zwiesel, or Ludwigsthal.

The main activity in winter is **cross-country skiing**, which can be done on many of the hiking trails, making for a total of about 80km of skiing trails. The **Nationalparkgemeinde Neuschönau, Winter** map (free at the Hans-Eisenmann Haus) and the **Grafenau Winterland** maps shows winter trails for both hiking and skiing. Ask at the Hans-Eisenmann-Haus for info on guided skiing tours.

GRAFENAU   ☎ 08552

Just west of the Bavarian Forest National Park, easily-accessible Grafenau is an ideal place to begin excursions on the web of hiking trails that laces the park's southern half. The village is the last stop on the special **Waldbahn** (forest train) line from Zwiesel (50min., every 2-3hr., €5 with the *Bayerwald* ticket) and can also be reached from Munich (€15 with the Bayern ticket) or Passau (3hr., €15). Alternatively, you can catch the twice-daily **bus #8652** from Zwiesel, or the direct bus line from Passau (1hr., 10 per day 7:45am-6pm). Within Grafenau, the **city bus** runs from the Bahnhof to locations in town (€1, children 5-15 €0.50).

Once in Grafenau, walk left out of the train station until you reach the **Stadtplatz** (200m). Walk across the square and take a left, then follow the signs to the right to reach the friendly **tourist office** in the back of the Rathaus, which books rooms for free and conducts free guided hikes every Tuesday at 11am. (☎96 23 43; www.grafenau.de. Open summer M-F 8:30am-4:30pm, Sa 10-11:30am, Su 10-11am.) A computer outside lists available rooms and contacts prospective hosts for late arrivals. Other services include: **VR-Bank,** 100m to the left as you exit the train station, **24hr. ATM.,** the **Marien-Apotheke pharmacy,** Stadtpl. 10 (☎35 38; open M-F 8am-6pm, Sa 8am-noon) and the **post office,** 94481 Grafenau, on Spitalstr. (☎20 42. Open M-F 8:30am-noon and 2-5pm, Sa 9-11:30am.) To find the spotless, friendly rooms of **Pension Tauscher ❷,** at Stifterstr. 22., take a right out of the tourist office, make another right onto Freyungerstr., and a left when it forks onto Stifterstr. (☎626; www.pension-tauscher.de. Breakfast included. Singles €15; doubles €32.) **Bäckerei Konditerei Cafe Manzenberger,** Am Stadtpl. 17, on the left side of the Stadtpl., is a typical bakery (open M-F 6:30am-6pm, Sa 6:30am-noon), and the **Edeka Activ Markt,** Spitalstr. 32, is a grocery store. Follow the Stadtpl. down the hill to Kröllstr. and take a left when it intersects with Spitalstr. Walk past the post office and through the underpass; it will be on your right. (Open M-F 8am-6:30pm, Sa 8am-2pm.) After a long day in the woods, feast on salads, pizzas, meat and fish (€7-9) at **Cafe-Restaurant Fox ❸,** Stadtpl. 3. (☎92 03 77. Open daily 8am-midnight.) The gorgeous **Kurgarten** is just behind the Rathaus and the post office.

ZWIESEL   ☎ 09922

The abundance of train connections and its proximity to the park makes Zwiesel an excellent hub for scouting the Bavarian Forest. A skier's paradise in the winter, in summer the town highlights its 600-year history of glass-making. Summer nights heat up with the **Grenzlandfest,** a festival held in the city center in mid-July.

⌨ TRANSPORTATION AND PRACTICAL INFORMATION. Trains run every hour to **Munich** (3hr., €15) and **Plattling** (1hr., €8.30). There are four city **buses** (1 per hr. M-F 8:14am-6:14pm, Sa 8:14-11:14am). Tickets are €0.80 or free with a €1.30 *Kurkarte*, which should be given to you after a one-night stay. The Stadtlinie bus runs to the Stadtpl. from just outside the station. The **tourist office,** Stadtpl. 27, in the Rathaus, provides maps and information on hiking and biking tours and finds private rooms for free. Cross the bridge, turn left after the Greek restaurant and head up through the Stadtpl.; the **Rathaus** is on the left. (☎84 05 23; www.zwiesel.de. Open M-F 8:30am-5:30pm, Sa 10am-noon.) From the station, turn right and walk downhill on Dr.-Schott-Str. The **post office** is a block down on your right. (Open M-F 8:30am-noon and 2-8pm, Sa 8:30-11am.) Turn right when you come to a T-junction, then keep following the curve of the road. You will stumble past **Cafe Flair,** Dr.-Schott-Str. 18, a gaming salon with **Internet** access. (☎50 07 98. 18+. €2 per hr. Open M, W-Th, Su 11am-1am; F-Sa 11am-3am.)

⌨ ACCOMMODATIONS AND FOOD. Zwiesel no longer has a youth hostel, but groups can opt for **Arbeiterwohlfahrt ❶,** Karl-Herold-Str. 9, which offers small detached houses 15min. from the town center. (☎9175; www.awo-zwiesel.de. 6-7 person apartments €29-54 per night.) For a small, inexpensive pension, try **Haus Elfriede ❷**, Anton-Pech-Str. 4. From the tourist office continue up the Stadtpl. past Frauenauer Str. and the supermarket on your right. Bear right onto Oberwieselauer Str., walk up the hill, take a right on Böhmerwaldstr., and take the third left onto Anton-Pech-Str. The friendly owners love to suggest activities in the area and will pick you up from the train station. (☎30 17. Breakfast included. Singles €16; doubles €24-32.) A similar option is **Gästehaus Mühl ❷**, Badstr. 5. From the train station, walk left down Bahnhofstr. to the first intersection, take a left down Rabensteiner Str. and walk through the tunnel. Turn left onto Badstr.; the house is on the left (10min.). A common room with TV and a flower-filled balcony complement sunny rooms and a warm owner. (☎18 21. Breakfast included. Singles €15-17; doubles €26-30.) **Campingplatz Tröpplkeller ❶**, Tröpplkeller 48, is on a small hill above the Schwarzer Regen river, 2km from the center of town. From the train station, turn right and walk down Dr.-Schott-Str. Follow it to the right, then turn right onto Schlachthofstr. before the river. Walk 10min., then cut behind the supermarket and come out on Landdorferstr. Tröpplkeller is up the hill on the left. (☎17 09 or 603 91. €4 per person plus €1.30 *Kurtaxe*, €3 per child plus €0.50 *Kurtaxe*, €2 per tent, €2 per car, €3-4 per RV. Showers €0.80.)

The Stadtpl. brims with enticing restaurants. The **Eiscafe-Pizzeria Rialto ❸**, Stadtpl. 28, has outdoor seating for Italian meals (€5-12) and ice cream. (☎605 36, takeout 47 03. Open Tu-Su.) For Bavarian meals, try **Gasthaus zum Kirchenwirt**, Bergstr. 1, which offers dishes like *Schweinbraten* (pig roast with sauerkraut) for €6-11, and free *Volksmusik* nightly at 8pm. (☎25 70. Open daily 11am-1am.)

◪ SIGHTS. Just north of town is the **Glas Park Theresienthal**, a village of glass-blowing houses with a museum on how glass items are created. (Open M-F 9:30am-6pm, Sa 9:30am-4pm; June-Oct. also Su 11am-4pm.) Buses shuttle to the Glas Park from the Stadtpl. (M-F 11 per day from 8:30am; last return 6:30pm. €0.80.) The **Waldmuseum**, Stadtpl. 29, behind the Rathaus, tells the tinkly tale of glass-making and teaches about everyday life in the forest. (☎608 88. Open mid-May to mid-Oct. M-F 9am-5pm, Sa-Su 10am-noon and 2-4pm; mid-Oct. to mid-May M-F 10am-noon and 2-5pm, Sa-Su 10am-noon; closed Nov. €2, students €0.50.)

EICHSTÄTT   ☎ 08421

A collection of pastel-colored 17th-century facades, imposing churches and a castle on a hill are the remnants of the once-mighty bishopric of Eichstätt, a gorgeous Baroque town that lies at the center of the massive **Altmühltal Nature Preserve** (p. 508), on the margins of Franconia, Swabia, and Bavaria. The pilgrims who once flocked here have been replaced by droves of outdoorsy Germans, who use Eichstätt as a home base for exploring the park on walks, hikes, and bike trails. The 160km **Altmühltal Radweg** is one of the most scenic bike routes in Germany. Home to the only Catholic university in the country, the old city runs at a surprising pace.

◪⁊ TRANSPORTATION AND PRACTICAL INFORMATION. Eichstätt has two train stations. **Trains** run to Eichstätt-Bahnhof from **Ingolstadt** (20min., 1 per hr., €4.10) and **Nürnberg** (1¼hr., 1 per hr., €14.20). From Eichstätt-Bahnhof, another train takes you the last 5km to the Eichstätt-Stadt station closer to town (9min., 2 per hr., €1.20). The friendly **tourist office**, Dompl. 8, gives free **tours** of the old city (Sa 1:30pm), sells maps (€0.50) and event tickets, and helps find rooms for a €1.50 fee. Get off the train, walk through the station, turn right, and bear left across the Spitalbrücke; you'll see signs for the tourist office, which will be on the left. Ask about hiking opportunities. (☎988 00; www.eichstaett.de. Open Apr.-Oct. M-Sa 9am-6pm, Su 10am-1pm; Nov.-Mar. M-Th 10am-noon and 2-4pm, F 10am-noon.) Get money at **Hypo-Vereinsbank**, Marktpl. 18. (☎30 11. Open M and F 9am-3pm, Tu-Th 9am-12:30pm.) A convenient **pharmacy** is **Dom-Apotheke**, Dompl. 16. (☎15 20.

Open M-F 8am-6pm, Sa 8am-noon.) The only **Internet** access in town is on Westenstr. 7 off Marktpl. in the **Journal** cafe. (€6 per hr. Open daily 10am-1am.) The **post office,** 85072 Eichstätt, is at Dompl. 7. (Open M-F 8:30am-6pm, Sa 9am-noon.)

█ ⌂ ACCOMMODATIONS AND FOOD. Eichstätt's **Jugendherberge (HI) ❷,** Reichenaustr. 15, is modern and comfortable. Follow directions to Willibaldsburg (see **Sights,** p. 507), but turn right halfway up Burgstr. onto Reichenaustr. The hostel is 200m down the street on your left. (☎98 04 10; fax 98 04 15. Breakfast and sheets included. Wash €1.50. Dry €1.50. Reception 8-9am and 5-7pm. Curfew 10pm, but they'll give you an access code if you're over 18. Closed Dec.-Jan. 4- to 10-bed dorms €17.45, longer stays €15.05.) **Haus Kirschner ❷,** Elias-Holl-Str. 27. is a small pension 10min. farther down the street. Follow Reichenaustr. past the hostel; it becomes Elias-Holl-Str. Quiet, bright doubles come with hall bathrooms, access to TV, and **free Internet** connections. (☎54 42; fax 90 22 07. Singles €17; doubles €30.) The **Gasthof Ratskeller ❸,** Kardinal-Preysing-Pl. 8, a 5min. walk from the station, is slightly more expensive. Follow directions to the tourist office, but turn right after crossing the Spitalbrücke. Walk through the Residenzpl. and take the first right onto Leonrodpl. Take your first left onto Kardinal-Preysing-Pl.; the hotel is about 20m up on your right in a white building with pink trim. (☎901 258; fax 24 17. Singles €32-36; doubles €50-58.) Campers head to the **Wohnmobil und Zeltplatz der Stadt Eichstätt ❶,** 20min. out of town on the city's Volksfestpl. by the river. To get there, follow Ostenstr. until it becomes Römerstr. Keep walking for about 15min. Take a right the second time you see a street called "Schottenau." At the end of the street, take a left and then a quick right onto the street with circular signs of a car pulling a trailer, then follow the street until it ends. (☎90 81 47. Staffed from Apr.-Oct., but open year-round. RV area closed the last week of Aug. and the 1st week of Sept. for the *Eichstätter Volksfest.* €6 per night for either a tent or RV site. Electricity €2 for 24hr. Free showers.)

Walburgis Restaurant ❸, on Westenstr. 29 off the Marktpl., serves Croatian cuisine from the grill for €8-12. Their lunch menu (M-F) has eight choices for around €7. (☎14 81. Open daily 11am-2:30pm and 5pm-midnight.) **La Grotta ❷,** in back of Marktpl. 13, offers pizzas and pasta (€4-7) on a nice terrace. (☎72 80. Open daily 11am-2:30pm and 5-11pm.) **Desperado ❷,** Marktg. 9 has Tex-Mex food in a tiny street off the Marktpl. Dig into a plate of nachos or a pizza (€4-5) at one of the large wooden tables. (Happy hour daily 7-8pm and 11:30pm-12:30am. Cocktails €3.50. Open Su-Th 7pm-1am, F-Sa 7pm-2am.) **Netto Marken-Discount,** Buchtal 30, has cheap groceries. (Open M-F 8am-7pm, Sa 8am-2pm.) **Schneller's Backstub'n,** Marktpl. 20a, has fresh bread and pastries. (Open M-F 7am-6pm, Sa 6:30am-1pm.)

◘ SIGHTS. Perched conspicuously over town, the **Willibaldsburg,** Burgstr. 19, the former residence of the local bishops, now hosts two museums. To reach the castle, walk out the back of the train station and over the tracks to Weißenburgerstr. Cross the street, bear right, and then take a quick left on Burgstr. The 14th-century Burg, designed to control the city, was given its present look by the same architect who later built the famous Rathaus in Augsburg. Inside, the **Juramuseum** is filled with large tanks of rare tropical fish and coral, as well as Jurassic Period fossils from the Altmühltal Valley, which was once covered by a vast prehistoric sea. More importantly, Altmühltal was the site where **Archaeopteryx** fossils were found. One of these primitive birds is on display. The **Museum für Ur- und Frühgeschichte,** also in the Willibaldsburg, goes from *Homo sapiens* to the Roman era, and has a near-complete mammoth skeleton. (Juramuseum ☎29 56. Free tours Su at 2pm. Museum für Ur- und Frühgeschichte ☎894 50. Box office for both museums ☎47 30. Both open Tu-Su Apr.-Sept. 9am-6pm; Oct.-Mar. 10am-4pm. Both museums €4, students €3, free for art history students.) At the entrance to the museum, climb up 98 winding steps to the top of the tower to see the city from above, (closes daily at 5:45pm) or peek down the 76m well to see some water.

Across the river, Eichstätt proper centers on the extravagant **Residenzplatz,** where the bishops moved in the 17th century. German-language tours of the **Residenz** begin here for groups of at least five people. (☎702 20. Tours Easter-Oct. M-Th 11am and 3pm, F 11am, Sa-Su every 45min. 10:15-11:45am and 2-3:30pm. €1.) In a corner of Residenzpl., in the middle of a fountain, stands the **Mariensäule,** a sculpture of the Virgin Mary perched atop a slender column. Behind the Residenz is the 14th-century **Hoher Dom,** originally Gothic, although most of the interior is 19th-century neo-Gothic. (☎16 32. Open M and W-F 9:45am-4pm, Tu 9:45am-3:30pm, Sa 9:45am-3pm, Su 12:30-5pm.) The east apse features lush stained glass and the striking late-Gothic figures of the **Hochaltar,** while the north aisle shelters the intricate 1492 stone **Pappenheim Altar,** an once-resplendent depiction of the crucifixion. To the right of the main altar is the **Mortuarium** cloister, the resting place of Eichstätt's bishops. At the far end, follow the stairs up to the **Domschatz und Diözesanmuseum,** which house 8th-century religious pieces interspersed with modern, abstract art. (☎507 42. Open Apr.-Oct. W-F 10:30am-5pm, Sa-Su 10am-5pm. €2, students €1. Su and holidays free.) Two blocks farther on Leonrodpl. is the Baroque **Schutzengelkirche** ("guardian angel church"), built during the Thirty Years' War. Its richly carved wooden pews, striking golden sunburst above the high altar, and sculpted soaring angels (567 in all) are the most visible signs of the Jesuits who used Eichstätt as a base to reconvert Bavaria to Catholicism.

NEAR EICHSTÄTT: ALTMÜHLTAL NATURE PRESERVE

Spread over 3000km² in the center of Bavaria, the Altmühltal Nature Preserve follows the curve of the Altmühl river from its source at the Altmühlsee above Gunzenhausen through the river's merger with the Main-Donau-Kanal and to the end of the canal at Kelheim. Impressive cliffs are littered with fossils and the bike trails here are renowned, but hikers, kayakers, and climbers also love this lush valley.

🖬 PRACTICAL INFORMATION. Home to many adventure-friendly establishments, Eichstätt is the perfect jumping-off point for trips into the preserve. A car is not necessary, since a railway cuts across the park from Gunzenhausen to Ingolstadt, and the other part is covered by the **FreizeitBus** system, which connects Eichstätt and Riedenburg on weekdays, and also Riedenburg and Regensburg on weekends (day pass €5.50, €8.50 with bike, €5.50 without). The **Informationszentrum Naturpark Altmühltal,** Notre Dame 1, is cloistered in a former monastery downtown. To get there, walk through the Residenzpl. and take a right on Ostenstr. and then your first left; it's 200m up on the right. The center has exhibits on the natural and cultural history of the area, and weekly **nature tours** (€2, children €0.50) in the summer months; ask for dates and times. (☎987 60; www.naturpark-altmuehltal.de. Open Easter-Oct. M-Sa 9am-5pm, Su 10am-5pm; mid-May to mid-Sept. daily until 6pm; Nov.-Easter M-Th 8am-noon and 2-4pm, F 8am-noon.) For information on everything from movie theaters to beach volleyball in the preserve, grab an English copy of *Freizeit Infos von A bis Z. Experiencing.* The free *Holiday and Excursion Tips* booklet is slightly out of date but more detailed. Most brochures cost around €0.50, but the center will mail copies to your house for free.

🖪🖸 ACCOMMODATIONS AND FOOD. The Altmühltal Nature Preserve is strewn with little towns offering a wide range of establishments. Be sure to pick up the *Gastgeberverzeichnis* and the yellow camping brochure at the info center for a list of accommodations in the preserve. Most **camping** is available right along the river for the convenience of boaters and bikers on the Altmühltal Radweg; prices range €3-10 per person including tent. Boaters can also set up camp at various boat docks along the way for €3-5 per night per tent; look for signs along the river or pick up the yellow *Bootwandern* brochure for a list of locations.

⚠ 🜂 OUTDOOR ACTIVITIES. Within the preserve, the primary activities of choice are biking and canoeing. Of the 800km of paved and well-maintained bike paths, the 160km **Altmühltal Radweg**, which snakes along the river and runs straight through the middle of Eichstätt, is the most popular. **Bikes** can be rented all over the park. In Eichstätt, try **Fahrradgarage,** Herzogg. 3, in the alley between Marktpl. and the footbridge. (☎21 10; www.fahrradgarage.de. €8 per day. Open daily 9am-7pm.) The *Bayernnetz für Radler* map and the yellow *Radwandern* brochure will help you navigate. Another good resource is the *Freizeit* map (€3), which gives trail information. Wide brown signs with a picture of a bike mark trails.

Fahrradgarage can also outfit you with **canoes** for a trip down the river (€26 per boat per day), and **Glas Booteverleih,** Industriestr. 18, rents canoes and **kayaks.** (☎30 55. M-F €10 per day, Sa-Su €13; under 16 20% off. Transport to the river €24-50. Open daily 9am-7pm.) The tranquil Altmühl is generally very safe, especially if you stay to the right at the small rapids along the way. Inexperienced boaters should avoid Töging, where the river merges with the Main-Donau-Kanal and becomes more dangerous. Two major tour companies offer canoe and kayak excursions in the preserve, with guides, baggage transfer, bike rental and pick-up, and boat transport for longer trips. **San-aktiv-TOURS** is in Gunzenhausen, Bühringer Str. 8 (☎09831 49 36; www.san-aktiv-tours.de), while **NATOUR** has its offices in Weißenburg at Gänswirtshaus 34 (☎09141 92 29 29; www.natour.de).

Altmühl also offers extensive **hiking** and **rock-climbing** options. Pick up a *Mittleres Altmühltal* hiking map (€6.60) to help you navigate the trails around Eichstätt; paths are marked with yellow signs. Most good climbing is to the east of Eichstätt near the town of Dollnstein; see the yellow *Klettern* brochure for more info. For **horseback riding,** contact the Geyer family (☎52 42). The preserve is also a great place to try amateur **paleontology.** The Altmühl river valley was covered by a Jurassic tropical sea 150 million years ago and is now littered with limestone deposits rich in fossils. A prime location for digging is the open **Steinbruch Quarry** right outside of Eichstätt. To get there, take the bus from the Dompl. (in from of the Raiffeisenbank) to "Kinderdorf" (€3 round-trip). Beware—bus schedules vary greatly; you might want to bring a map along to navigate the 20min. walk back to town. Once there, you can visit a museum with some striking fossils and minerals, or rent some tools and start looking yourself. (Open year-round. Equipment €2, under 18 €1. Tool rental open mid-Apr. to mid-Oct. daily 9:30am-3pm.) The new 9km **mineralogy trail, which** departs from Eichstätt's Altstadt, provides an overview of fossils and minerals in the area. Inquire at either information office.

INGOLSTADT ☎0841

The old Danube town of Ingolstadt was the site of the first Bavarian university in 1472 and later a powerful Catholic center of the Counterreformation. Today, this city of 120,000 is shaped by the presence of luxury car manufacturer Audi, based here since WWII, which currently employs 25% of Ingolstadt's population. Modern stores and services came in the company's wake, but the old town's charm has been carefully preserved. Neoclassical fortifications, old town walls and beautiful churches are surrounded by greenery and the flow of the Danube. A lively place thanks to the university it shares with nearby Eichstätt, Ingolstadt kicks off its celebrations each summer with the **Festa del Vino** (Italian wine festival), which culminates 1½ weeks later with the **Bürgerfest** (city festival) the first weekend in July.

BAYERN

⌐ TRANSPORTATION

Trains to: **Augsburg** (1hr., 1 per hr., €9.40); **Munich** (1hr., 2 per hr., €12.90); **Regensburg** (1hr., 1 per hr., €11.10). **Bus** routes center on the Omnibusbahnhof in the middle of the city (single ride €1.60). Call a **taxi** at ☎194 10. **Rad Haus,** Münchener Str. 45 (☎730 27) and Kreuzstr. 2 (☎322 11), rents **bikes**.

🔃 PRACTICAL INFORMATION

Ingolstadt's **tourist office,** Rathauspl. 2, in the Altes Rathaus, hands out maps and helps find rooms. To reach the tourist office and the Altstadt from the distant train station, take bus #10, 11, 15, or 16 to "Rathauspl." Or, for the 2.5km walk, follow Bahnhofstr. to Münchener Str. and head straight over the bridge down Donaustr. to Rathauspl. (☎305 10 98; www.ingolstadt.de. Open M-F 8am-5pm, Sa 9am-noon. Extended and Su hours in summer.) Free tours of the old city (in German) depart from the office (May-Oct. Sa 2pm). Part of Mary Shelley's famous novel was set in Ingolstadt, as **Dr. Frankenstein's Murder & Mystery Tour** will eagerly remind you. The entertaining 70min. tour leaves the courtyard of Hohe Schule, June-October on select Fridays at 9:15pm. (☎95 19 99 61; www.frankenstein.at. Call ahead for exact dates. €7. Children under 14 not permitted.) **Exchange money** at **Volksbank,** Theresienstr. 32. (Open M-W 8am-12:30pm and 1:30-4:30pm, Th 8am-12:30pm and 1:30-5:30pm, F 8am-2pm.) **Franziskus-Apotheke,** Rathauspl. 13, posts 24hr. **pharmacy** information. (☎330 53. Open M-F 8am-6pm, Sa 8am-1pm.) Find **Internet** in the train station at **Internet Express,** off Gleis 1. (€3 per hr., €3.50 after 6pm; with your laptop €2.40 per hr. Open Su-Th noon-midnight, F-Sa noon-1am.) The **Stadtbücherei Ingolstadt** in Carrarapl. near the Neues Schloß. (€1 per hr. Open M-F 10am-6pm, Sa. 10am-1pm.) The **post office,** 85024 Ingolstadt, is right in front of the train station. (Open M-F 8:30am-6pm, Sa 9am-12:30pm.)

🏠🍴🎵 ACCOMMODATIONS, FOOD, AND NIGHTLIFE

Ingolstadt's **Jugendherberge (HI)** ❶, Friedhofstr. 4½, is in a renovated section of the town's old fortifications. From the tourist office, take Moritzstr. north and turn left on Theresienstr. to the Kreuztor. Walk through the gate and cross Auf der Schanz; the hostel is on the right (10min.). Large rooms have private sinks and cavernous hallways. (☎341 77; fax 91 01 78. Sheets and breakfast included. Reception 8am-11:30pm. Curfew 11:30pm. Dorms €14.85; subsequent nights €13.70-14.25.) **Gästehof Huber** ❷, Dorfstr. 12, offers simple rooms 15min. from the train station. Take bus #15 or 16 to "Unserherr Schule." (☎723 35; www.gasthof-huber.de. Breakfast included. Singles €21-30; doubles €36-52.) Campers can go to **Campingplatz am Auwaldsee** ❶, known as the "Blue Lagoon," off the E45/Autobahn A9. To get there without a car, take a right from the station and follow Bahnhofstr. to Münchener Str. Before the bridge, look for the "Brückenkopf" bus stop on the right side of the street; catch bus #60 (dir.: Kälberschüttstr. 1-6 per hr. M-Sa 5:35am-1:12am; 1 per hr. Su and holidays 8:19am-1:12am) to "Am Auwaldsee." (☎961 16 16; ingolstadt@azur-camping.de. €4.50-6.50 per person. €5.50-7.50 per tent and car.)

Edeka, Ludwigstr. 29 in the basement of Galeria Kaufhof, sells groceries. (Open M-Sa 9am-8pm.) The **Kreuztor** is the symbol of the Altstadt, but also the center of groove. Local nightlife clusters on **Kreuzstraße,** which turns into **Theresienstraße** toward the center of town. **Sigi's** ❷, Kreuzstr. 6, a few doors down from the Tor, is a small and chic cafe with nice outdoor seating. *Wurst*, sandwiches, and salads are all under €6. (☎329 52. Beer €2.50. Open M-Th 9am-2am, F-Sa 9am-3am, Su 2pm-2am.) **Restaurant Mykonos** ❸, Ludwigstr. 9, dishes up Greek delights in a mini-Athens. Omelettes (€4.50) and Mediterranean specialities (€6-17) come with a free shot of *ouzo*. (Open daily 11am-3pm and 5pm-1am.) **Neue Welt** ❷, Griesbadg. 7, off Kreuzstr., with its own stage, is home to the local art and music crowd. Try the chili (€4) or a homemade *Tsatsiki* for €3. (☎324 70. Beer €2.60. Cabarets, alternative and R&B concerts M-Tu and F. Open M-Sa 7pm-1am.) The university **Mensa ❶**, Konviktstr.1, near the Maria-de-Victoria church, charges students €3-4 for main courses. (Open M-F 11am-2:30pm.) Local students hang out at the outdoor tables of **Mohrenkopf Cafe ❷**, Donaustr. 8, one block from the river, as well as the adjacent Bar Centrale. (Breakfast until 2pm. Beer €2.70. Open M-F 7:30am-1am, Sa 8am-1am, Su 9:30am-1am.) For the latest entertainment, check out the publications *Megazin* and *Espresso*, available at the tourist office.

🅖 SIGHTS

The old city wall is magnificently represented by the turreted **Kreuztor** (built in 1385), topped by dainty stone ornaments. Just beyond the gate outside the city wall, the **Stadtmuseum**, Auf der Schanz 45, explains Ingolstadt's prehistoric origins, its years as a Roman town, and its flourishing as a Counterreformation center under **Johann Eck**, perhaps the most vehemently anti-Lutheran preacher ever. Also displayed is the embalmed horse of Protestant Swedish king **Gustavus Adolphus,** captured when he unsuccessfully attempted to lay siege to the town. (☎305 18 85. Open Tu-F 9am-5pm, Sa-Su 10am-5pm. €3, students and seniors €1.50.) Two blocks east of the Kreuztor is the late Gothic **Liebfrauenmünster**, full of ornate altars and immense columns. Eck preached here, in front of a depiction of the early martyr **St. Catherine** discussing theology with professors. A few blocks south on the aptly named Anatomiestr., the ▨**Deutsches Medizinhistorisches Museum** (medical history museum), Anatomiestr. 18-20, occupies the former medical laboratory that inspired Mary Shelley to use Ingolstadt as the setting for *Frankenstein.* The museum houses a collection of medical oddities, from a "do-it-yourself" enema stool to gruesome amputation saws and a "skeleton room." (☎305 18 60; www.ingolstadt.de/deutschesmedizinhistorischesmuseum. Open Tu-Su 10am-noon and 2-5pm. English guidebooks available. €3, students and seniors €1.50.) At the corner of Jesuitenstr. and Neubaustr. is the **Maria-de-Victoria-Kirche.** This once sparse chapel for students of the nearby Catholic school was "Rococoed" with a vengeance in 1732, with an awe-inspiring fresco by **Cosmas Asam,** of Munich fame. The African man to your left as you enter points his spear in your direction, no matter where you are. (Open Mar.-Oct. Tu-Su 9am-noon and 1-5pm; Nov.-Feb. Tu-Su 10am-noon and 1-4pm. €2, students and children €1.50, children free. Free organ concerts Apr.-Oct. Su noon.) Famous Catholic general Tilly died in 1632 in the building opposite the church (Neubaustr. 2) during the Thirty Years' War.

At the **Audi Forum** on Ettingerstr. the moving *Museum mobile* displays a selection of fabulous past Audis as well as imaginative prototypes. The name of this luxury car company was originally *Horch*, the last name of auto innovator and entrepreneur **August Horch,** and German for "hark." The Latin *Audi* (listen) was chosen in 1910 to help exports in an international market resistant to German-sounding products. Screens throughout display the names of Audi owners as they are called to pick cars up; the constant stream of new vehicles shooting out of the garage is also visible from the souvenir shop, the restaurant and the movie theater. (☎0800 283 44 44. Open daily 9am-6pm. Museum tours €1. Factory and workshop tours M-F 10:30am, 12:30, and 2:30pm; €4, students €3, under 18 €2. Admission €2/€1.50/€1. Films daily 5:30 and 8pm, Su 11am. Children's films Sa 3pm, Su 1 and 3pm. €6, children €4; Tu €3.) More of streamlined Ingolstadt is on show at the **Museum für Konkrete Kunst**, Tränktorstr. 6-8, off Donaustr. near Konrad-Adenauer-Brücke. The wild colors of the pieces, by international contemporary artists, are overwhelming. (☎305 18 71. Open Tu-Su 10am-6pm. €3, students €1.50, under 14 free.) Across town is the 15th-century white **Neues Schloß**, Paradepl. 4, a red-tiled castle now housing the **Bayerisches Armeemuseum**, a detailed exhibit of weapons and armor. (☎937 70. Open Tu-Su 8:45am-4:30pm. €3, students €2.50.)

PASSAU
☎ **0851**

Baroque arches cast long shadows across the cobblestone alleys of Passau, a 2000-year-old city situated at the confluence of the Danube, the Inn, and the Ilz rivers. The peninsular Altstadt has maintained much of its Baroque splendor from the era when Passau controlled lands in Austria, Bavaria and Bohemia (today the Czech Republic). The heavily-fortified castle, glorious cathedral, and a row of patricians' palaces stand alongside modern shops, cafes, and museums. This *Dreiflüssestadt* (three-river city), inspiration of the 12th-century epic *Nibelungenlied*, celebrates its culture with the **European Festival,** a summer-long art, music, theater, and film festival held every year since 1952 in support of a peaceful and unified Europe.

▐ TRANSPORTATION

Trains: 1 per 2hr. to: **Frankfurt** (4½hr., €49.60); **Munich** (2hr., €15); **Nürnberg** (2hr., €15); 1 per hr. to **Regensburg** (1-2hr., €15) and **Vienna** (3½hr., €32). The **Hauptbahnhof** is west of the center on Bahnhofstr. **Ticket counter** open M-F 5:50am-7:25pm, Sa 6am-5:25pm, Su 8:50am-7:25pm. **Lockers** €1-2.

Buses: Regionalbus Ostbayern (☎75 63 70) provides service from the train station to cities throughout eastern Bavaria. **SWP Passau** buses make a number of stops within the city and in neighboring towns. Single ticket €1.

Ferries: Donau Schifffahrt (☎92 92 92) sails to **Linz,** Austria (5hr.; May-Sept. Tu-Su 9am and 1pm, returns 8am and 2:20pm; €21, round-trip €24). The 45min. **"Three Rivers" tour** of the city leaves daily from docks 7 and 8, Mar.-Oct. every 30min. 10am-5pm and Nov.-Dec. at 11am, noon, 1 and 2pm (€6.50, under 15 €3.75).

Taxis: Call ☎570 73 or catch a cab at Ludwigspl.

Bike Rental: The stunning **Donau Radweg** bike path begins in Donaueschingen and continues through Passau into Austria—ask for a map at the tourist office. In the Bahnhof, **Rent a Bike** (☎490 58 72; www.fahrradverleih-passau.de) at the window farthest to the left in the Reisezentrum, charges €12 per day, €9.50 with a DB rail ticket. Open Sa-Su 9-11:30am and 3-5:30pm, weekdays by phone appointment.

▐▌ ☑ ORIENTATION AND PRACTICAL INFORMATION

To reach the city center from the train station, follow Bahnhofstr. to the right until you reach **Ludwigsplatz.** Bear left across Ludwigspl. to Ludwigstr., the beginning of the pedestrian zone, which becomes Rindermarkt, Steinweg, and finally Große Messerg. Continue straight onto Schusterg. when the street ends, and you'll soon be in the **Altstadt;** hang a left on Schrottg., and you'll stumble upon the **Rathausplatz** (30min.). Uphill lies the **Veste Oberhaus** fortress. Farther east, the three rivers converge at the tip of the peninsula. The **Inn** is on the right; to the left is the (not-so-blue) **Danube,** and the third and smallest river, the **Ilz.** East of the Altstadt, Innstr. runs along the Inn to the university. Bridges span the Danube towards **Innstadt,** a German enclave on the Austrian side of the rivers, home to nightlife hotspots.

Tourist Office: Tourist Information, Rathauspl. 3 (☎95 59 80; www.passau.de), on the banks of the Danube next to the Rathaus (p. 515). Free brochures, schedules, tour information, cycling maps and guides. The staff books rooms for a €3 deposit and provides information on cheaper hotels and pensions (€18-35) in the surrounding area. *WasWannWo,* a free monthly pamphlet, chronicles everything going on in Passau. Office open Easter to mid-Oct. M-F 8:30am-6pm, Sa-Su 9am-4pm; rest of the year M-Th 8:30am-5pm, F 8:30am-4pm. A smaller **branch** at Bahnhofstr. 36, across from the train station and to the left (☎95 59 80; fax 572 98), has free maps and brochures outside after hours. Open Easter to mid-Oct. M-F 9am-noon and 12:30-5pm.

Tours: German-language walking tours (1hr.) meet at the **Königsdenkmal** (king's monument) in front of the church at Dompl. Apr.-Oct. M-F 10:30am and 2:30pm, Sa-Su 2:30pm. €3, children €1.50.

Budget Travel: ITO Reisebüro, Bahnhofstr. 28 (☎540 48), across the street from the train station in the Donau Passage. Open M-F 8am-6pm, Sa 9am-1pm.

Currency Exchange: Go right out of the train station down Bahnhofstr. to reach **Volksbank-Raiffeisenbank,** Ludwigspl. 1 (☎33 50). €1.02 fee per traveler's check cashed. Open M-W and F 8:30am-12:30pm and 1:15-4:15pm, Th 1:15-5pm.

Laundromat: Rent-Wash, Neuburger Str. 19. From Ludwigspl., walk up Dr.-Hans-Kapfinger-Str., follow it to the end as it curves right and becomes Neuburger Str., then bear left. Wash €2.50. Soap €0.50. Dry €1.50. Open daily 7am-11pm.

Emergency: Police, Nibelungenstr. 17 (☎50 30). **Emergency** ☎110. **Fire** and **Ambulance** ☎112.

Pharmacy: Bahnhofstr. 17 (☎513 01). Open M-F 8am-6pm.

Hospital: Klinikum Passau, Bischof-Pilgrim-Str. 1 (☎530 00). **Emergency medical care** ☎19 92 22. Ahh, even the hospital has a view!

Internet: Comp Pass, Neuburger Str. 19, next to the laundromat (above). €3 per hr. Open daily 2-10:30pm, last admission 9:30pm. Or, get a drink at **Cafe Unterhaus,** Höllg. 12, a trendy art gallery, bookshop, and cafe, a few blocks from the Rathaus, and connect for **free.** Open Su-M and W-Sa 10am-1am (☎989 04 64).

Post Office: Bahnhofstr. 27 (☎959 50), 94032 Passau, to the right as you exit the station. Open M-F 8am-6pm, Sa 8:30am-12:30pm.

ACCOMMODATIONS AND CAMPING

Most pensions in downtown Passau start at €30, while those in the surrounding area run €11-35. The only hostel in town is usually swarming with German school-children, especially June and July.

Jugendherberge (HI), Veste Oberhaus 125 (☎49 37 80; fax 493 78 20). Perched high above the Danube, in the former quarters of the Veste Oberhaus sentinels. Cross the suspension bridge downstream from the Rathaus, look for the signs pointing up the steps, then follow the signs pointing to the right at the branch towards the museum (30-45min. uphill). Or, hop on the **shuttle** *(Pendelbus)* from Rathauspl. bound for the museum adjacent to the hostel (Easter to mid.-Oct. every 30min. M-F 10:30am-5pm, Sa-Su 11:30am-6pm; €2, same-day round-trip €2.50). Feels like sleeping in a museum (in a good way). Breakfast included. Reception 7am-9am, 9:30am-1pm, 1:30-7pm and 7:30-10pm. Curfew 10pm, but you can get an access code. Dorms €17.30. ❷

Pension Rößner, Bräug. 19 (☎93 13 50; www.pension-roessner.de). From the Rathaus, walk downstream along the Danube. Directly on the river, these pleasant rooms are cheap for the Altstadt. Call upstairs if no one is at the reception. All rooms with bath and radio, some with TV. Breakfast included. Singles €35; doubles €50-60. ❸

Rotel Inn, Hauptbahnhof/Donauufer (☎951 60; fax 951 61 00). From the train station, walk straight ahead down the steps, down Haisseng., and through the tunnel to this outlandish hotel right on the river. Built in 1993 in the shape of a sleeping man to protest Europe's decade-long economic slumber, this self-proclaimed "Hotel of the Future" packs travelers into small rooms bedecked with primary-color plastics. Radios in every room. Breakfast €5. Reception 24hr. Open May-Sept. Singles €25; doubles €30. ❸

Hotel Garni Herdegen, Bahnhofstr. 5 (☎95 51 60 or 541 78; www.hotel-herdegen.de). Located in the center of the Neustadt, this hotel offers large rooms with private bath and TVs. Breakfast included. Singles €41; doubles €66-72. ❹

Camping: Zeltplatz Ilzstadt, Halser Str. 34 (☎414 57). Downhill from the youth hostel at a beautiful location on the Ilz. Follow directions to the hostel but turn right before the steps and walk along Angerstr. until Halser Str.; follow it all the way to the riverbank, keeping right

THE BIG SPLURGE

A ROYAL TIME

Many towns offer guided tours through royal bedchambers, but only in Passau can you actually sleep in one. **Hotel Wilder Mann** has been at the center of town for long enough to have sheltered its share of both nobility and history. Originally a patrician home, this building with a great view of the Danube became, in the 19th century, a luxury hotel for the European beau monde traveling through Passau. Thanks to careful preservation, the furniture that surrounded these larger-than-life personalities remains as it was when they slept here. Besides a bed from Princess Sissi of Bavaria's stay in Corfu, the hotel also has a bed used by the Austrian empress's notorious nephew, mad King Ludwig II. You too, can savor the fancy setting that hosted the eccentric king.

The restaurant on the roof owns the largest collection of German cookbooks (16,200 volumes), and prepares a stunning array of dishes under candlelight and chandeliers. Keep an eye on your fellow diners: more recent notable guests have included Neil Armstrong, Reinhold Messner, and Otto of Habsburg. Where else will you be able to say you (nearly) slept with royalty?

The Princess Sissi room and the Ludwig II room €109 per person per night. Breakfast and bath included. Book ahead at ☎0851 350 71; info@wilder-mann.com. Restaurant ☎0851 350 75.)

when Halser Str. becomes Grafenleite. Or take bus #1-4 from "Exerzierpl." to "Ilzbrücke" at the start of Halser Str. Open May-Oct. Breakfast €3-4 (order the night before). Reception 8-10am and 5-9pm, but you can pitch your tent any time. €5.50, under 18 €4.50, under 6 free. No RVs. Phone and hot showers included. ❶

▣ FOOD

The student district centers on **Inn Straße** near the university. From Ludwigspl., head down Nikolastr. and turn right on Inn Str., which runs parallel to the Inn River; the street is dotted with good, cheap places to eat. **Norma** is a supermarket at Bahnhofstr. 16b. (Open M-F 8:30am-7pm, Sa 8am-2pm.) Get fresh food at **Schmankerl Passage**, Ludwigstr. 6. (Open M-F 7:30am-6pm, Sa 7:30am-4pm.)

▣ **Innsteg Café Kneipe**, Innstr. 15 (☎512 57), 1 block from Nikolastr. This hopping restaurant offers students and locals balcony seating and loud American music outside, and a sleek sports bar inside. Daily menu (€5.20) available until 2pm. Beer €2.40. Open M-Sa 10am-1am, Su 10am-midnight. ❷

Altes Bräuhaus, Bräug. 5 (☎490 52 52). Classic Bavarian and Austrian specialties in the Altstadt, on the Platz opposite the suspension bridge over the Donau. Main courses, such as *Jägerschnitzel mit Spätzle*, €6-10. Open daily 11am-1am. ❸

Cafe Kowalski, Oberer Sand 1 (☎24 87). From Ludwigspl., walk down Nikolastr. toward the Inn river; take a left on Gottfried-Schäffer-Str. and walk almost 2 blocks until you see the terrace on the left. Home to the largest *Schnitzel* in Passau. Hordes of college students chill with ice cream specialties (€3-5), mixed drinks (€2-5), fresh salads and pasta (€3-8). M is students' night: *Studentenbier* or tequila €1. Open M, W-Th, Su 10am-midnight, Tu and F-Sa 10am-1am. ❷

Cafe Kairo, Neuburger Str. 1 (☎756 07 55). Palm trees and wicker chairs are the backdrop to an all-you-can-eat brunch Sa-Su 10am-4pm (€8.80). Outdoor BBQ every Th from 6pm with live DJs. Daily menu, not at all Egyptian, offers meat (€5.50) and vegetarian (€4.80) options M-F 11am-6pm. Open Su-Th 9am-3am, F-Sa 10am-3am. ❷

◉ SIGHTS

STEPHANSDOM. When fire devastated Passau, Italian artists were brought in to rebuild the city. The cathedral, the largest Baroque structure north of the Alps, is their centerpiece, which remains cohesive despite the few Gothic remnants among white stucco and frescoes. The **world's largest church organ** stands above the choir loft. Its 17,774 pipes and multiple keyboards can hold five organists at once. *(Open daily summer 6:30am-7pm; winter 6:30am-6pm. Organ concerts May-Oct. and Christmas week M-F at noon, €3, students and children €1; Th 7:30pm, €5, students, seniors, and children €3. Daily tours May-Oct. and Christmas week M-F 12:30pm, meet in front of the side aisle; Nov.-Apr. M-F noon, meet underneath the main organ. €1.50, children €0.75.)*

VESTE OBERHAUS. Over the Luitpoldbrücke, up the footpath is the former palace of the bishop. Once a prison for the bishops' enemies and a fortress with control over the city and the rivers below, the complex now houses the **Cultural History Museum.** Hands-on displays for children, rotating special exhibits, and 54 rooms of art and artifacts chronicle 2000 years of Passau's history. The **tower** affords a great view of the city below. *(Shuttle bus from the Rathaus stops here every 30min. Last bus back leaves Oberhaus at 5:15pm. ☎49 33 50. Open early Apr. to Oct. M-F 9am-5pm, Sa-Su 10am-6pm; Nov.-Mar. Tu-Su 9am-5pm. €5, students €3. Tower €1, children under 16 €0.50.)*

GLASMUSEUM. This huge collection of fancy glass work celebrates Bohemian production from the Baroque era to the present, and includes an elaborate glass birdcage, a copy of da Vinci's *Last Supper* engraved on a chalice, and various psychedelic *Jugendstil* experiments. Two of the rooms in which Princess Sissi (Austrian Empress Elisabeth) once stayed have been preserved and can be viewed within the museum, complete with her gloves, socks, and toiletries. *(Am Rathauspl. ☎350 71. Open daily 1-5pm. €5, students €3, children free with parents. Get a 20% discount by showing your Passau boat tour ticket.)*

ALTSTADT. Behind the cathedral is the **Residenzplatz,** lined with former patrician dwellings, and the **Residenz,** the erstwhile home of Passau's bishops. The **Domschatz** (cathedral treasury) within the Residenz has an extravagant collection of the bishops' most precious items in its old library. Contemporary art exhibits are interspersed throughout the permanent collection. *(Enter through the back of the Stephansdom, to the right of the altar. Open Easter-Oct. M-Sa 10am-4pm. €1.50, students and children €0.50.)* The less opulent 13th-century Gothic **Rathaus** was appropriated from a wealthy merchant in 1298 to house the city government. The impressive high water marks from past floods (the last in 2002) are marked on the outside wall underneath the clock. Inside, the **Prunksaal** (Great Hall) is a masterpiece of rich wooden paneling and dark marble. *(Open Apr.-Oct. daily 10am-4pm. Free.)* In the heart of the Altstadt, bright lights shelter the **Museum Moderner Kunst,** a charming museum of paintings, sculpture, photography and video installations. *(Braug. 17. ☎383 87 90; www.mmk-passau.de. Open Tu-Su 10am-7pm. €5, students and children €3.)*

🔼 🔽 ENTERTAINMENT AND NIGHTLIFE

After a long day of study or work, Passau's students and young professionals party at the city's many bars and clubs on **Innstraße** by the university, or across the footbridge in **Innstadt.** The best way to keep abreast of the nightlife scene is to get hold of *Pasta,* a free monthly magazine with information on films, concerts, and more, available at most bars, clubs, and coffee houses. *Innside* is a similar publication, focusing on events in the Innstadt, available at the tourist office.

🔳 **Bluenotes,** Ledererg. 50 (☎343 77). Cross the Fünfersteg footbridge, make a left on Am Severinstor, and hang another left onto Ledererg. to find one of Passau's sultry bars. Enjoy your beer or cocktail outside in the *Biergarten,* next to the live events of the *Scheune* (inquire for details). Happy hour every night 8-9pm and midnight-1am and all night W (cocktails €4.50). Open daily 6pm-1am.

Colors, Mariahilfstr. 8 (☎322 20). Right across the Innbrücke in Innstadt, past the Kirchenpl. Gulp down a *Helles* (€2.20) as you throw darts, shoot pool, or relax in the *Biergarten.* Tu night happy hour: cocktails €3-5. DJs spin everything from reggae to easy listening. Open daily 7pm-1:30am.

Camera, Fraueng. (☎343 20), around the corner from the McDonald's on Ludwigspl. The city center's grooviest dance lair, its stark black exterior foreshadows an underground cavern of student angst and inebriation. Live music every Tu in spring, early summer, and fall; otherwise, get down to everything from house to hip-hop—check ahead for details. Open daily 10pm-3am, weekends and holidays until 4am.

The Frizz, Dr.-Hans-Kapfinger-Str. 3, directly below the Wirtshaus Bayerischer Löwe. The fast cats at The Frizz have received special dispensation to stay open later than all the other bars in town. Gulp down a "Desperado," long drink, or cocktail as you absorb the yellow marble interior and techno beats. Open W-Th 9pm-3am, F-Sa 9pm-4am.

Theater-Opernhaus Passau, Gottfried Schäfferstr. 2-4 (☎929 19 13; www.sudoest-bayerisches-staedtetheater.de). From Ludwigspl. walk down Nikolastr. to the river and take a left; the theater is just before the bridge. Classic operas and more modern plays. Closed early July to mid-Sept. Box office open Tu-F 10am-12:30pm and 4-5:30pm. Tickets from €7.50, reduced rates available 1hr. before showtime (usually7:30pm).

STRAUBING ☎09421

"They govern in Landshut, they pray in Passau, but you can really live in Straubing," said painter Carl Spitzweg of this historic Danube town, perched on the fringe of the forest—and live they do. Each summer, Straubing lets down its hair for the 10-day **Gäubodenvolksfest** (Aug. 12-22, 2005). The festival, called the "Fifth Season" by locals, started as an agricultural fair in 1812 under King Maximillian. It has since evolved into a tribute to inebriation second in size only to Oktoberfest. Accompanying the *Volksfest* is the **Ostbayernschau** (East Bavaria Show), a regional trade and industry exhibition (i.e., more beer; Aug. 13-21, 2005). Both are held in the Fest area "Am Hagen," 5min. north of the Markt. When they aren't reveling, Straubing's residents and visitors enjoy the city's beautiful churches, striking architecture, colorful houses, and cobbled pedestrian zone.

▐ TRANSPORTATION

The **train station** has an information counter. (☎01805 99 66 33. Open M-F 6am-5:30pm, Sa 7:30am-12:15pm, Su 1:10pm-6:20pm.) Trains run to: **Landshut** (1hr., 1 per hr., €8.40); **Munich** (1 per hr., €15); **Passau** (1hr., 1 per hr., €11.10); **Regensburg** (30min., 1 per hr., €6.90). **Stadt-BUS-Verkehr Straubing** runs buses (€1.25, day pass €2.80); the tourist office has maps and schedules. For **taxis** call ☎98 98 60.

◼▟ ORIENTATION AND PRACTICAL INFORMATION

The Altstadt is northwest of the train station, 5min. away on foot. Cross the street in front of the station and look left for the "Fußweg-Zentrum" sign that points you across a crosswalk and through a small park, then head down Bahnhofstr., through the pedestrian zone and the clock tower passage. The wide main pedestrian mall on Theresienpl. and Ludwigspl. is lined with shops and eateries. Most sights lie between the mall and the Danube.

The **tourist office,** Theresienpl. 20, is to the left after you walk through the clock tower passage. The office has free maps and brochures on Straubing and neighboring towns, and will help find private rooms (€15-18) for free. (☎94 43 07; www.straubing.de. Open M-W and F 9am-noon and 1:30-5pm, Th 9am-noon and 1:30-6pm, Sa 9am-1pm.) German 1½hr. tours of the Altstadt are offered mid-May to mid-October. (W and Sa 2pm. €3, students and seniors €2, family ticket €6.) Pick up cash at **SchmidtBank,** Bahnhofstr. 9, across from the train station (Open M and W 8:30am-1pm and 2-4pm, Tu and Th 8:30am-1pm and 2-5:30pm, F 8:30am-2pm.) The **Löwen-Apotheke** pharmacy is at Ludwigspl. 11. (☎106 65. Open M-F 8am-6pm,

Sa 8am-1pm.) **Terminal,** Bahnhofstr. 5 (under the red and white awning), has **Internet.** (18+. €4 per hr. Open daily 9am-11pm.) The **post office,** 94315 Straubing, is at Landshuter Str. 21. (Open M-F 8:30am-6pm, Sa 8:30am-noon.)

▗▖ ACCOMMODATIONS AND FOOD

Your best bet for a cheap stay in Straubing is to book a private room at the tourist office. Otherwise, the **Jugendherberge (HI) ❶,** Friedhofstr. 12, is 15min. from the train station. Turn right from the front entrance and follow the curve of Bahnhofspl. left. Turn immediately right onto Schildhauerstr. and take a second right after a block onto Äußere-Passauer-Str. Take a quick left onto Friedhofstr.; the Jugendherberge is on your right. This hostel, by a small park, features creaking hardwood floors, comfortable leather sofas, table-tennis, billiards, and a quiet location. (☎804 36; fax 120 94. Breakfast included. Sheets €0.80. Reception 7-9am and 5-10pm. New arrivals after 5pm only. Curfew 10pm, keys available with €5 deposit. Open Apr.-Oct. 4-, 6-, or 8-bed dorms €8.71, over 27 €11.71.) Most hotels and pensions in Straubing begin at €31; one small and tidy exception is **Weißes Rößland ❷,** Landshuter Str. 65. Walk left out of the station and left again down Landshuter Str.; the building is on your left after 10min. (☎325 81. Breakfast included. Singles €20; doubles €35; triples €50.) **Hotel Schedlbauer ❸,** Landshuter Str. 78, is right across the street from the Weißes Rößland and has very clean rooms, all with TVs. (☎338 38; fax 46 40. Breakfast included. Singles €21-36; doubles €40-52; triples €60.) A **Campingplatz ❶** is at Wundermühlweg 9. From the tourist office, head left down Ludwigspl., turn left on Stadtgrabenstr., and go over the bridge. Walk for about 10min. then veer left onto Chamer Str. by the "Ruderclub" sign; the site is on the left. Reception rents tents (2 for €10) and recommends local sights. (☎897 94. Open daily May to mid-Oct. Reception 7am-1pm and 3-10pm. €8 for 1 person with tent. €15 for 2 people with car and tent. €3 per additional person, €2 per additional child. Showers, water and electricity free.)

There is a **supermarket** on Ludwigpl. 29 (open M-F 8am-7pm, Sa 8am-4pm), but the Platz also offers a **market** (open M-F 8am-noon.) A **farmer's market** is held Saturdays on Theresienpl. (open 8am-2pm.) You can also find food, clothing, and more for next to nothing at the **flea market** *(Flohmarkt)* on Am Hagen (1st Sa of the month from 6am.) For food, head to **Unterm Rain ❸,** Unterm Rain 15, to sit under bright lights and large chestnut trees. Hearty Bavarian meat dishes go for €5.50-12. Falling chestnuts, while seldom deadly, have been known to distress diners. (☎227 72. Open daily 5pm-2am, beer garden open from 4pm.) Down the street in the direction of St. Peter's is **Cantina La Cueva ❸,** Rot-Kreuz-Pl. 3, a fun Mexican option, also with a small beer garden. Steer past the Caribbean-themed bar and head down the stairs for filling starters and entrees (€4-11. M night is wings and ribs buffet, €5.90). Happy hour (all drinks €3.60) at 6pm and 11:30pm. (☎853 34. Open M-Sa 5pm-1am, Su 11am-2pm.) Just opposite is the friendly **La Conchiglia ❷,** Rot-Kreuz-Pl. 5, where pizzas and pastas are €5-8.50. (☎815 05. Beer €2.30. Open M-Tu and Th-Su 11:30am-2:30pm and 5:30pm-midnight.) **Pallas ❷,** Ludwigspl. 27, offers a happy mixture of Italian and Greek specialties (€5-8), right on the main square. (☎28 55. Open Tu-Su 11am-11pm.) Across the street, cure your craving for cheap Sino-Japanese dishes (€5-8) at **Asia Bistro KM ❷,** Ludwigspl. 16. (☎108 14. Open M 11am-3pm, Tu-Su 11am-3pm and 5-10:30pm.)

◉ ▐▌ SIGHTS AND ENTERTAINMENT

Teal-green symbol of the city, the five-turreted Gothic **Stadtturm** (watchtower) with an inset gold figure of Mary, splits the Marktpl. (Tours mid-Mar. to mid-Oct. Th 2pm, Sa-Su 10:30am. €3, students and children €2, under 6 free. Meet at the tourist office.) Just north of Theresienpl., a patchwork of well-preserved stained glass gives the late-Gothic

BAYERN

Basilika St. Jakob, Pfarrpl. 1a, a dim and divine elegance. Look into the side chapel to the right of the main altar for some Asam brothers work in stucco and paintings. The second side chapel to the right of the north portal entrance contains a Madonna by Holbein. The **Gäubodenmuseum,** Frauenhoferstr. 9, traces the history of the city as far back as the Neolithic. Also on view is a unique collection of decorative Roman armor, the most complete in the world, retrieved during construction work in Straubing. (☎974 10. Open Tu-Su 10am-4pm. €2.50, students €1.50, children €1. Combination ticket with state museum €3.50, students and seniors 2.50.) From the Gäubodenmuseum, walk one block on Zollerg. to the late-Gothic **Karmelitenkirche,** Albrechtsg. 21 (☎843 70), built in the Middle Ages by the *Herzog* (duke) to support the **Carmelites** and shockingly jazzed up during the Baroque period, in a style that jars with the supposed modesty of this monastic order. The reason for the decor is the enduring popularity of the church with pilgrims, who came to pray to the Mary of the Nettles figure.

One block down on Burgg., the small but beautiful **Ursulinenkirche** rests behind a simple white facade. This was the last feat of the renowned Asam brothers, whose masterpiece is the church of St. John Nepomuk near the Sendlinger Tor in Munich. The overflowing opulence of Rococo screams "look at me," from the excessive gold stucco and the pink marble columns that twirl up to the ceiling frescoes. Down Fürstenstr. on the banks of the Danube, the irregular complex of the **Herzogsschloß** once housed the Wittelsbach branch that ruled Straubing. Some parts of the Schloß date to 1356, but most of the interior is now office space. The **state museum** in the palace displays an extensive collection of Christian *objets d'art* from the 17th to the 20th century, from all over Europe. (☎211 14. Open Th-Su 10am-4pm. €2.50, students €1.50.) The Jews were expelled from Straubing in 1442 by Duke Albrecht III, but the only **synagogue,** Wittelsbacherstr., in lower Bavaria dates to 1907 and is neo-Romanic in style. (☎13 87. Visits on request.)

The **Basilika St. Peter,** built in the 1180s, is the oldest church in town, standing on the remains of Roman fortifications. From the Stadtturm, walk east on Ludwigspl., turn left onto Stadtgraben Str., and turn right just before the bridge onto Donaug. Bear right when the road splits; St. Peter's is a 10min. walk. Inquire at the tourist office about tours of the complex. The Romanesque basilica is surrounded by a medieval graveyard with wrought-iron crosses, gravestones from as far back as the 14th century, and three Gothic chapels, which, because of vandalism, can only be viewed through the gates. Particularly noteworthy is the 18th-century **All Souls Chapel,** with a fresco cycle of the *Totentanz* (Dance of Death), in which the Grim Reaper pays everyone a visit, from the pope and the *Kaiser* to grave-diggers and nuns. The **Agnes Bernauer Chapel** is dedicated to the famous Augsburg commoner who secretly married a Wittelsbach duke, but was drowned in the Danube by his father, who only approved of aristocratic girls. (Open daily dawn to dusk.)

Straubing's large swimming pool complex, **AQUA-therm,** Wittelsbacherhöhe 50-52, has an 80m waterslide, several massage parlors, an indoor pool, a steam sauna, and a warm salt-water pool. Follow the tunnel to the left of the Bahnhof down Landshuter Str. and turn right onto Dr.-Otto-Höchtl-Str., which becomes Wittelsbacherhöhe; it's on the right. Or take bus #2 from Ludwigspl. to "Aquatherm." (☎86 44 55; www.stadtwerke-straubing.de/baeder/images/inhaltb.htm. Outdoor pool open daily mid-May to mid-Aug. 9am-8:30pm; Sept. 9am-8pm. Indoor pool open mid-Sept. to mid-May; call for hours. €3; students, seniors, children and adults after 5:30pm €1.80. Sauna entrance €8, after 5:30pm €6.) Straubing is also home to the only **zoo** in eastern Bavaria, with more than 1000 closely-quartered animals, a large aquarium, as well as reconstructed Danube habitats in which local otters and fish frolic. From the tourist office, walk right down Theresienpl. and follow the road as it becomes Regensburger Str.; continue for 20min. Walk through the parking lot and follow the "Fußweg zum Tiergarten" sign. (☎212 77. Open daily Apr.-Sept. 8:30am-7pm; Oct.-Mar. 9am-5pm. Last admission 1hr. prior to closing. €4.50, students and children 6-18 €2.50, under 6 free.)

NIGHTLIFE

The hippest spot in Straubing for nocturnal prowling is the ▦**Roxy**, Aprilg. 3, replete with ample bar, plentiful seating, a dance floor packed with a mix of teens to 30-somethings, and foosball. The DJ spins the best collection of classic rock this side of the Atlantic. From the tourist office, take a right down Theresienpl. and your first left onto Aprilg. (☎ 121 57. Cover €3. Open W and F 10pm-3am, Sa 10pm-4am.) **Freiraum**, Flurlg. 8, is a delectable bar on a tiny street off Luwigspl. Come here for the ice-cream and nightly specials (M desserts, Tu vegetarian dishes, F Asian, Sa all salads €6) or drinks. (☎ 96 09 62. Cocktails €4-6. Open M-Th 7:30am-1am, F 7:30am-2am, Sa 9am-2am, Su 10am-1am.) **Peaches**, Steinerg. 14, just south of the *Stadtturm*, is a mellow cocktail bar that offers half-price drinks on Tuesday nights. (☎ 105 92; www.peaches-straubing.de. Cover Tu €2. Open Tu-Su 7pm-1am.)

REGENSBURG   ☎ 0941

When Goethe visited Regensburg for the first time, he wrote: "Regensburg is beautifully situated; the area couldn't help but attract a city." Indeed, nearly two millennia ago in AD 179, Roman emperor and philosopher **Marcus Aurelius** laid the city's foundations by building the fortress **Castra Regina** where the Naab and Regen flow into the Danube. It was later the first capital of Bavaria, then the seat of the **Perpetual Imperial Diet,** and the site of the first German parliament. These days the city is alive with students, visitors and everything needed to satisfy them—Regensburg is said to have more cafes and bars by area than any other European city.

TRANSPORTATION

Trains: Ticket office open M-F 6am-7:30pm, Sa 6am-6:30pm, Su 7:30am-7:30pm. To: **Munich** (1½hr., 1 per hr., €15); **Nürnberg** (1-1½hr., 1-2 per hr., €14.20); **Passau** (1-1½hr., 1 per hr., €15).

Ferries: Regensburger Personenschifffahrt (☎ 553 59; www.schifffahrtklinger.de), on Thunerdorfstr. next to the Steinerne Brücke. Ferries tourists to **Walhalla** (p. 523), (45min.; Apr.-Oct. daily 10:30am and 2pm; round-trip €9.50, students €6.50, children €4.50, families €22). Also offers a city tour in German (50min.; Apr.-Oct. daily every hr. 10am-4pm; €6.50/€4.50/€3/€15).

Public Transportation: Routes, schedules, and fares for Regensburg's **bus** system are available at the *Presse & Buch* store in the train station, or at the tourist office (€1). The transport hub is "Bustreff Albertstr.," one block straight and then to the right from the train station. Single ride within zone 1 €1.60; day ticket for zones 1 and 2 €3.40. Buy tickets at the *Automaten* in bus shelters or from the driver and validate your ticket on the bus. Buses run until midnight.

Taxis: Taxi Funk Vermittlung Regensburg ☎ 194 10, 570 00, or 520 52.

Bike Rental: Bike Haus, Bahnhofstr. 18 (☎ 0800 460 24 60; www.bikeproject.de), across the street and to the left of the train station. Rents bikes and provides maps and route suggestions. Open M-Sa 10am-1pm and 2-7pm; Oct.-Mar. also open Su 10am-2pm and 3-7pm. €9.50 per day, children €6.

ORIENTATION AND PRACTICAL INFORMATION

The Altstadt sprawls on the southern bank of the Danube, opposite the islands formed by its confluence with the Regen. To the south of the Altstadt are the train station and Bahnhofstr. The modern Maximilianstr. leads from the station into the city. The university is behind the station, opposite the Danube.

Tourist Office: Rathauspl. (☎507 44 10; www.regensburg.de), in the Altes Rathaus. From the station, cross the street and follow the red signs *"Altes Rathaus"* down Maximilianstr. to Grasg. and take a left. Follow the street as it turns into Obermünsterstr., turn right at the end onto Obere Bachg. and follow it 5 blocks onto Rathauspl. The office, to the left across the square, provides free maps, sells English-language guide books (€2-7), and books rooms for free. Open M-F 9:15am-6pm, Sa 9:15am-4pm, Su 9:30am-2:30pm. Apr.-Oct. also open Su until 4pm.

Tours: 1½hr. English-language walking tours of the city leave from the tourist office May-Oct. and Dec. on W and Sa 1:30pm. €6, students €3. The "City Tour" bus leaves from the Dom Apr.-Oct. on the hour 10am-4pm; June-Oct. also 5pm, no 1pm tour. 1hr. recorded information in English, French and Italian. €6, reduced €4.50, families €15.

Bank: Volksbank, Pfaueng. 3 (☎584 70), 1 block from the Dompl. Open M-W 8:30am-4pm, Th 8:30am-5:30pm, F 8:30am-3:30pm.

Lost and Found: In the Neues Rathaus (☎507 21 05; fundamt@regensburg.de). Open M-W 8am-noon and 12:30-4pm, Th 8am-1pm and 1:30-5:30pm, F 8am-noon.

Bookstore: Book in a Box, Goldene-Bären-Str. 12 (☎56 70 14), near the Steinerne Brücke; entrance on Brückstr. This cluttered store has tons of discount books and a 2nd-fl. shelf of cheap English paperbacks. Open M-F 9am-6pm, Sa 9am-4pm.

Laundry: Wasch-Salon, Osteng. 4a. Open daily 6am-10pm. Wash €3. Dry €1.50.

Emergency: Police ☎110. **Ambulance** ☎192 22. **Fire** ☎112.

Crisis Hotline: In case of rape or other trauma, contact **Caritas** (☎502 10).

Pharmacy: Engel-Apotheke, Neupfarrpl. Open M-Th 8:30am-6:30pm, F 8:30am-6pm, Sa 9am-2pm.

Hospital: Evangelisches Krankenhaus, Emmeramspl. 10 (☎504 00), near the Thurn und Taxis Schloß, is the most centrally located.

Internet: The **tourist office** offers access for €3 per hr.; buy a PIN at their desk.

Post Office: Bahnhofstr., 93047 Regensburg, next door to the train station. Open M-F 9am-6pm, Sa 9am-12:30pm. The Dompl. branch has the same hours.

⌂ ACCOMMODATIONS AND CAMPING

What cheap lodgings Regensburg has need to be reserved, preferably at least a month ago. If the hotels and pensions are full, the tourist office has a list of private rooms (a few are in the €22-30 range; most are €35-65). Otherwise, the hotels in outlying parts of town are cheaper, and linked to the center by reliable bus service.

Jugendherberge (HI), Wöhrdstr. 60 (☎574 02; fax 524 11), is a 25min. walk away on an island in the Danube. From the station, walk down Maximilianstr. to the end. Turn right at the *Apotheke* onto Pflugg. and immediately left at the Optik sign onto tiny Erhardig. At the end, take the steps down and walk left over the Eiserne Brücke, then veer right onto Wöhrdstr. The hostel is on the right. Or take bus #3, 8, or 9 from the station to "Wöhrdstr." (€1.60). The hostel is just past the bus stop on the right. Standard, clean HI rooms overrun by school groups. **Internet** €2.40 per 30min. Breakfast and sheets included. Key deposit €10. Reception 7-10am and 3pm-midnight. Doors lock at midnight, but an access code is available. Dorms €18.50. ❷

Spitalgarten, St.-Katharinen-Pl. 1 (☎847 74; www.spitalgarten.de.), inside a 13th-century hospital with a river view. Cross the Steinerne Brücke and make a left into St.-Katharinen-Pl. at the sign. Pass through a gate and go past the church. Or take bus #17 from the station to "Stadtamhof." Enter by the pink *Biergarten*. Breakfast included. Reception until midnight. Call or write well ahead. Singles €22; doubles €44. ❷

Gaststätte Schildbräu, Stadtamhof 24 (☎857 24), is over the Steinerne Brücke; follow the street for 5min., and it's on the right. Or take bus #12 from the station to "Stadtamhof." Clean and orderly rooms with geraniums spilling from every window. Breakfast included. Reception 8am-9pm. Singles €35; doubles €60. ❸

Regensburg

🛏 ACCOMMODATIONS
Alte Mälzerei, 23
Azur-Camping, 1
Gaststätte Schildbräu, 3
Hotel Am Peterstor, 19
Jugendherberge, 6
Spitalgarten, 2

🍴 FOOD & DRINK
BaanThai Restaurant, 16
Cafe Galeria, 10
Cafe Felix, 18
Hinterhaus, 12
Kaufhof Cafe, 14
Mensa, 20

🍺 BEER GARDENS
Alte Linde, 5
Goldene Ente, 4
Historische
Wurstküche, 8

**★ ENTERTAINMENT &
NIGHTLIFE**
Alte Filmbühne, 11
Alte Mälzerei/
Cartoon, 22
Apo. Theke, 13
Cinemaxx, 21
Jazzclub, 15
Neue Filmbühne, 17
Peaches, 9
Wunderbar, 7

BAYERN

Alte Mälzerei, Galgenbergstr. 20 (☎ 78 88 115; www.alte-maelzerei.de). This converted malt processing plant hosts night-time fun (see Nightlife) and cheap accommodation. 4- to 6-bed dorms €12.50, students €10.50. Check-in M-F 10am-4pm. ❶
Hotel Am Peterstor, Fröhliche-Türken-Str. 12 (☎ 545 45; fax 545 42), 5min. from the station. Go down Maximilianstr. and take the 2nd left onto St.-Peters-Weg, which becomes Fröhliche-Türken-Str. Rooms are neat and simple, with bath and TV. Breakfast €5. Reception 7-11am and 4-10:30pm. Singles €35; doubles €40. ❸
Camping: Azur-Camping, Am Weinweg 40 (☎ 27 00 25; www.azur-camping.de). Bus #6 (dir.: Wernerwerkstr.) to "Westheim." Reception 8am-1pm and 3-10pm. €4.50-6 per person, €3.50-4.50 per child, €5.50-7.50 per site. Small tent site without car €3.50-4.50. Prices higher in summer, lower Sept. to mid-Dec. and mid-Jan. to Mar. ❶

◖ FOOD

The 17th-century English dramatist and diplomat Sir George Etherege commented that Regensburg's "noble, serene air makes us hungry as hawks." You can't walk two blocks without seeing a **supermarket;** the **Edeka** in the basement of **Galeria Kaufhof,** on the Neupfarrpl., is near the center. (Open M-Sa 9am-8pm.) The Viktualienmarkt, on Neupfarrpl., has fresh veggies and other basics. (Open daily 9am-4pm.)

▨ Hinterhaus, Rote-Hahnen-G. 2 (☎ 546 61), off Haidpl. down from Rathauspl. Crooked tables under dimly lit archways, black-and-white photographs, and white stucco walls create the perfect setting for chillin' out, maxin', or relaxin' all cool. A relatively young crowd mellows out to blues and jazz. Excellent vegetarian fare like baked camembert with salad or cheese tortillas (€4-8). Meat dishes €5-9. Open daily 6pm-1am. ❸
Cafe Felix, Fröhliche-Türken-Str. 6 (☎ 590 59; www.cafefelix.de). This crowded and lively cafe specializes in delicious, gigantic salads, with all possible ingredients from pineapple to prawns (€7-9). Beer €2.50 for 0.5L. Each night has happy hours (drinks €3.50) or special offers. Open M-Sa 9am-1am, Su 10am-1pm. ❸
BaanThai Restaurant, Dechbettenerstr. 6 (☎ 218 77), near the Dönberg park. Large, artistic meals served by the family owners outdoors among fish tanks and elephant statues. Top off classics such as pad thai (€9) or vegetarian meals like sauteed tofu with salad and rice (€7.50) with flambéed desserts of homemade sorbet (€4-5). Seafood specialties €10-14. Open Tu-Sa 5pm-midnight, Su noon-2:30pm and 5pm-midnight. ❸
Mensa, on Albertus-Magnus-Str., in the park on the university campus. Bus #6 (dir.: Klinikum) or 11 (dir.: Burgweinting) to "Universität Mensa." The cheapest meal in Regensburg, with a lively crowd. Student ID required to get a Mensa card. Meals €2-4. Open M-Th 11:15am-1:45pm and 5-7pm, F 11:15am-1:45pm and 5-6:30pm; Nov.-Feb. and May-July also open Sa 11:30am-1:30pm. No evening meals mid-Aug. to mid-Sept. ❶
Kaufhof Cafe, Neupfarrpl., on the 4th fl. of the Galeria Kaufhof. Fabulous view from the terrace, where you can enjoy a huge breakfast for only €3.85. Buffet offers pizzas, salads, sandwiches, cakes, cuisines from Indian to Bavarian (€3-7), and, of course, beer. Many veggie options. Food is freshest early in the day. Open daily 9am-8pm. ❸
Cafe Galeria, Kohlenmarkt 6 (☎ 56 14 08), near the Rathaus. *The* place to go for breakfast. The "small" breakfast of *Müsli* with yogurt, fresh fruit and a huge basket of rolls and croissants is just €4.50. A crowded and popular eatery (€3-9), and packed with beautiful youth at night nursing drinks on all 3 levels. Open daily 9am-8pm. ❸

BEER GARDENS
▨ Historische Wurstküche, Thundorfer Str. (☎ 590 98), next to the Steinerne Brücke with a view of the river. Relax, sip a beer, and watch the boats drift by. Having recently celebrated its 850th birthday, the Wurstküche is the oldest operating fast-food joint in Europe—12th-century workers who built the nearby bridge broke for lunch here. 6 small, delicious *Würste* from the kitchen come with sauerkraut and bread (€5.40). Beer €2.60 for 0.5L. Open Apr.-Oct. daily 8am-7pm; Nov.-Mar. Su 8am-3pm.

Alte Linde, (☎880 80) just over the Steinerne Brücke from the Wurstküche. Serves students and professors alike delicious food (entrees €4-7), but the beer is better (€5.20 for 1L). Offers some well-thought-out veggie options. Open daily 11am-midnight.

Goldene Ente, Badstr. 32 (☎854 55). Under magnificent chestnut trees on the banks of the Danube, just across the Eiserner Steg footbridge and upstream from the Steinerne Brücke. During summer this *Biergarten*, part of the oldest inn in Regensburg, serves steaks, *Würstchen*, and *Schnitzel* are grilled at friendly prices (€3-7). *Maß Helles* €4.70. Open daily 11am-1am.

🅖 SIGHTS

DOM ST. PETER. The Dompl. is a stable foundation for the soaring high-Gothic Dom St. Peter and the **Diözesanmuseum St. Ulrich** adjacent to the church. Begun in 1276, the cathedral was completed in 1486, but the delicately carved 105m twin spires were finished under King Ludwig I in the 19th century. *(☎516 88. Open Apr.-Nov. Tu-Su 10am-4:45pm. €1.50, students €0.75, families €4.)* The rich stained glass windows date from the 13th and 14th centuries. Inside the cathedral is the **Domschatz,** a collection of gold and jewels purchased by the Regensburg bishops in the days of indulgences. Check out the shriveled hand of Bishop Chrysostomus (who died in AD 407). Underneath the Dom is the resting place for many of Regensburg's bishops and recently-unearthed Roman ruins. *(Dom ☎586 55 00. Open daily Apr.-Oct. 6:30am-6pm; Nov.-Mar. 6:30am-5pm. 1¼hr. German-language tours May-Oct. M-Sa 10, 11am and 2pm, Su 12:30 and 2pm; Nov.-Apr. M-Sa 11am, Su 12:30pm. €2.50, students and children €1.50. English tours for groups only, call ahead. Dom entry free. Domschatz ☎576 45. Open Apr.-Oct. Tu-Sa 10am-5pm; Su noon-5pm; Nov.-Mar. F-Sa 10am-4pm, Su noon-4pm. €1.50, students €0.80, families €4. Combination ticket for the Domschatz and Diözesanmuseum €2.50. Wheelchair access via the Eselturm.)*

WALHALLA. Down the river from Regensburg, Walhalla, a faux Greek temple, is poised dramatically on the steep northern bank of the Danube. Ludwig I built the monument of ancient Germanic *Nibelungen* lore between 1830 and 1842 above the river, to honor Germans past and present. Modeled after the Parthenon in Athens and named after the legendary resting place of Norse heroes, Walhalla stares imposingly down 248 steep steps to the river below. This afterworld counts among its sculpted residents everyone from kings and generals to poets and scientists. Do not be fooled by the presence of Catherine the Great, as everyone here is German (she started off life as a Prussian princess). The plaques above the busts honor those whose faces are unknown, such as the author of the *Nibelungenlied*. Albert Einstein's visage proves that new members have been added since Ludwig's time: the Bavarian ministry for culture adds a bust every five or six years. Most recently, they chose **Sophie Scholl,** the young Munich student who was executed for leading the **Weiße Rose** resistance against Hitler in 1942 (p. 56). Even with the addition of Scholl, the number of females remains a paltry 11 of 191 total busts. In summer, the hallowed steps provide a lively evening hangout for students who come here for picnics and guitar-playing. *(Take the ferry from Regensburg (p. 519) or bus #5 from the Albertspl. bus station to "Donaustauf Walhallastr." for €2.20, then continue walking on Wörtherstr. to the gravel path leading up the hill. ☎96 16 80. Open Apr.-Sept. daily 9am-5:45pm; Oct. 9am-4:45pm; Nov.-Mar. 10-11:45am and 1-3:45pm. €2.50, students €2.)*

ALTES RATHAUS. A few blocks away from the cathedral is the yellow Gothic town hall, which served as the capitol building of the Holy Roman Empire in its final period, from 1663-1803. The town council had to move to the adjacent "Neues Rathaus." The permanent meeting of the **Imperial Diet** made Regensburg home to a German parliament of sorts. This brought little wealth to the city, for the Imperial delegation did not pay taxes on their imports, and did not even have to employ local artisans. The four long iron rods fastened to the side of the building date from its stint as town hall; they

BUSINESS FÜRST

Gloria, the *Fürstin* of Schloß Thurn und Taxis, blurs the line between history and celebrity gossip. She grew up in Africa and spent her teenage years as a rebel, joining the Young Socialists (because they threw the best parties). Between protests and partying, Gloria caught the eye of the playboy who was the last *Fürst* of Thurn und Taxis. In 1980 their wedding enthralled every housewife in Germany. She was 20, he was 54. Within three years, Gloria had given birth to three children, including the much-hoped-for male heir, and found her place as the doting matriarch of Regensburg's enormous *Schloß*.

When the *Fürst* died in 1990, the 30-year-old widow buried him according to family tradition—by having his organs removed and then embalming him. To save the decaying family property, Gloria paid the hefty inheritance tax by selling the family's jewelry to the government, and opened up the *Schloß* the public. The most elaborate rooms are now available for business functions (the ballroom costs €17,500, the palm garden €12,000). Gloria then bared all in a 2004 autobiography.

If you see the family banner flying above the *Schloß*, keep your eyes peeled: you just might spot the last representative of the great Thurn und Taxis dynasty (at one point related to the Hohenzollerns and the Hapsburgs) puttering about under dark hair and oversized sunglasses.

were the official measurement standards by which the merchants traded in the Middle Ages. The town hall also houses a **Reichstagsmuseum.** Chair heights reflect the legislators' political ranks: four steps high for the emperor, two for the electors (among them the Wittelsbachs), one for the 100 *Fürsten* (princes). The 50-odd free city representatives sat on ground level. *(German tours Apr.-Oct. every 30min. M-Sa 9:30am-noon and 2-4pm, Su 10am-noon and 2-4pm; Nov.-Mar. every hr. English tours May-Sept. M-Sa 3:15pm. €2.50, students €1.25.)*

KEPLERGEDÄCHTNISHAUS. The iconoclastic astronomer and physicist Johannes Kepler died here of meningitis in 1630. Period furniture, portraits, and facsimiles of his work are on display. Up the street at Keplerstr. 2 is **Keplers Wohnhaus,** a colorful house where Kepler spent time away from his gold-nosed patron and taskmaster, Tycho Brahe. It now houses a tanning salon. *(Keplerstr. 5. ☎507 34 42. Open Sa-Su 10am-4pm. 45min. tours at 10 and 11am, 2 and 3pm. €2, students €1, families €4.)*

DOKUMENT NEUPFARRPLATZ. Archaeological excavations from 1995 to 1998 revealed that under Regensburg's first Lutheran church (founded 1542) lie buried the remains of a Gothic synagogue destroyed in 1519, and other parts of a large Jewish quarter. Regenburg's Jews were expelled in the 16th century from the last surviving Jewish community in a German city. Until then, it had been a fertile and integral part of the city. The 624 gold coins from the 14th century that were found at the Neupfarrpl. dig bear witness to its wealth. Beneath the Jewish quarter are vestiges of ancient Roman constructions. A circular Nazi-era bunker is also on display. *(☎941 507. Accessible only with guided tour Th-Sa 2:30pm; Aug. also Su-M. Includes presentation. Buy tickets at the Tabak Götz, Neupfarrpl. 3. €5, students and seniors €2.50.)*

PORTA PRAETORIA. A Roman gateway, the Porta Praetoria is the only standing Roman ruin in Germany besides the Porta Nigra in Trier. Together with the ruins of its accompanying wall, it gives a hazy idea of the city's original fortifications, which have been incorporated into a house on Unter den Schwibbögen, between the Dom and the Danube. One of the earliest documents of Regensburg's past can be seen on the front wall of the house—a flat foundation stone from the Roman fort of Castra Regina, inscribed with the date AD 179. *(Open 24hr. Free.)*

FÜRST THURN UND TAXIS SCHLOß. Across from the station, this 11th-century Benedictine cloister became the 500-room residence of the Prince of Thurn and Taxis in 1812. The originally Italian family—Thurn und Taxis is the Germanized version of "Torriani e Tassi," (translates as "towers and badgers," symbols which feature prominently on their coat of arms)—earned its title in 1695, in recognition of the booming business it ran, the first efficient, Europe-wide postal service of the modern era. The Thurn clan ran the mail until it was taken over by Prussia in 1867. In 1991, when the latest Fürst died, controversial Fürstin Gloria (see **Business Fürst**, p. 524) opened 25 rooms of the palace to public tours. *(Emeramspl. 5. ☎504 81 33. Open Apr.-Oct. M-F 11am-5pm, Sa-Su 10am-5pm; Nov.-Mar. Sa and Su only. Tours Apr.-Oct. daily at 11am, 2, 3, and 4pm, Sa-Su additional tour at 10am; Nov.-Mar. Sa-Su at 11:30am and 2pm. €8, students €7. Kreuzgang only €4, students €3.50.)*

HISTORISCHES MUSEUM. Set within a former Franciscan monastery are a wealth of archaeological finds from Regensburg's Roman times, displayed to illustrate life in a fortress town of the Empire. Castra Regina was gradually taken over by Germanic tribes, also represented in the collection. St. Salvator, the massive Franciscan church, is also open to the public. *(Dachaupl. 2-4. Open Tu-Su 10am-4pm.)*

🎵 📷 ENTERTAINMENT AND NIGHTLIFE

Many of the cafes and beer gardens listed in **Food** double as local nighttime haunts. Ask at the tourist office for a free copy of *Logo, Was los?*, or *Stadtzeitung*—three monthly publications listing the liveliest events and the addresses of the hippest bars and cafes in Regensburg; you can also browse the streets of the Altstadt after hours and duck in at whichever of the city's offerings strikes your fancy. Beyond the bar and club scene, Regensburg is a fabulous city for movie- and theatergoers. Stop in at the central box office in the **Theater am Bismarckplatz**, Bismarckpl. 7 (☎507 24 24; fax 507 38 77), to inquire about theater, ballet, and opera performances in the city's three main theaters, or kick back to live jazz performances at the **Jazzclub** in Leeren Beutel, Bertoldstr. 9. (☎56 33 75; www.jazzclub-regensburg.de. Most performances at 8:30pm. Call or check online for upcoming events.) On the other side of the train tracks from the Hauptbahnhof, Regensburg's massive movie megaplex, **Cinemaxx**, Friedenstr. 25, plays new movies and offers some films in their original English version. (☎780 21 21; www.cinemaxx.de. Tickets €5-8, M-Th students €4.50, Th before 5pm, €3.50.)

Alte Mälzerei, Galgenbergstr. 20 (☎730 33, tickets ☎757 49). Regensburg's lively "Art and Culture Factory," an old malt processing plant, now hosts a beer garden (€1.90 for 0.5L) and a bar, **Cartoon,** (the "kleine Mälze"; ☎757 38. Beer €2.50 for 0.5L and simple entrees €4-6.50) with pop, jazz, funk, reggae, and blues. Garden open M-F 11am-1am, Sa-Su 2pm-1am. Bar open daily 2pm-1am. Events and times vary, check their calendar (available at the tourist office).

Peaches, Baumlackerg. 2 (☎53 481), near the Steinerne Brücke, is one of the classics of the Regensburg cocktail scene. 2 reasons to visit: 1st, the M night, 50cm pizza for €5.10 (get there at 6pm or fight the ravenous crowds); 2nd, if you have the guts to order it, the XXL Zombie, which is served in a unique 3.5L glass (€30). Open M-Th and Su 6pm-1am, F-Sa 6pm-3am.

Alte Filmbühne, Hinter der Grieb 8 (☎579 26). Look for the staircase leading down to a green gate. Regensburg's funkiest scene attracts a diverse and bizarre crowd. Film posters, strange art, and disco balls scattered everywhere. 18+. Open June-Sept. daily 9pm-1am; Oct.-May 8pm-1am.

Neue Filmbühne, Bismarckpl. 9 (☎570 37). This colorful hangout near the theater provides breakfast until 6pm, but most people are here for the typical Franconian *Flammkuchen* (€6-7), small pizza-like loaves with melted cheese and ham. Cocktails €5-6. **Free wireless Internet** access. Open daily 9am-1am.

Apo.Theke, Rote Hahneng. 8 (☎58 43 999). Candles on bare wood tables are the setting for a bohemian crowd sipping wine after 10pm (glass €3-4). Open M-Th 10am-1am, F 10am-2am, Sa 10am-3am, Su 6pm-1am.

Wunderbar, Keplerstr. 11 (☎ 531 30). Just a few staggers from the Steinerne Brücke, young late-nighters pack into the catacombs here. Elaborately crafted champagne cocktails €7-10. Cocktails €1.50 off during happy hour Su-Th 10pm-midnight. *Maß* €5.70. Open Su-Th 10pm-3am, F-Sa 9pm-3am.

ROMANTISCHE STRAßE AND BURGEN STRAßE (ROMANTIC ROAD AND CASTLE ROAD)

Vineyards, groomed fields of sunflowers and wheat, rolling hills, and dense forests checker the landscape between Würzburg and Füssen. Officially dubbed the **Romantic Road** in 1950, the area has become the most heavily touristed part of Germany. In 1954, Bavaria christened the **Castle Road,** which runs east-west through the same region. Both routes have breathed new life into the region, though some towns have preserved their authentic appeal more than others.

⌐ TRANSPORTATION. Every day, Deutsche Bahn's **Europabus** shuttles throngs of tourists from Frankfurt to Füssen and back on the **Romantic Road.** The **Castle Road,** which runs from Mannheim to Prague through Rothenburg, Nürnberg, and Bayreuth, is currently only covered by Europabus through Rothenburg ob der Tauber. Travelers then head on the Romantic Road bus in the direction of Füssen.

Europabus is the most popular way to travel the two routes, though it is also one of the least flexible—there is only one bus in each direction per day. However, the schedule is currently undergoing major change. A final stop in Munich is possible for the Romantic Road itinerary, and the Castle Road tour may be extended to Prague. Check out www.touring.de or http://uk.romantischestrasse.de/ for information, or to make reservations online. As of 2004, the 12hr. southbound journey begins in **Frankfurt** daily at 8am. Northbound buses depart from **Füssen** daily at 7:45am. Stops include Würzburg, Rothenburg ob der Tauber, Dinkelsbühl, Nördlingen, Ausburg, Wieskirche, Hohenschwangau and Neuschwanstein; the final arrivals are in Füssen at 7:55pm and in Frankfurt at 7:50pm. For the Castle Road (the Mannheim-Munich route) southeastbound buses currently leave Mannheim daily at 7:30am, while northwest-bound buses depart from Munich daily at 9am. Stops include Heidelberg, Schwäbisch Hall, Rothenburg ob der Tauber, Dinkelsbühl, Nördlingen, and Augsburg; the final arrivals are in Munich at 7:20pm, and in Mannheim at 8:55pm. The Europabus is the most expensive connection

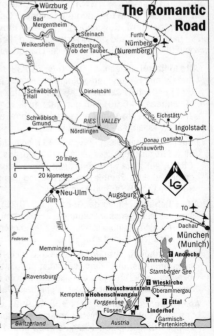

The Romantic Road

between destinations. (Frankfurt to: Rothenburg €37; Dinkelsbühl €43; Munich €70. Dinkelsbühl to: Hohenschwangau €38; Füssen €39. Students, under 26 and over 60 10% off, under 12 50% off, under 4 free. Railpass holders 60% discount.) For those without the railpass discount—or those who prefer to travel on their own schedule without a disembodied voice describing the view from the bus window—a more economical way to see both routes is (paradoxically) to use the faster and more frequent **trains,** which run to every town except Dinkelsbühl. If you plan to travel by train or local bus, take into account that both run less frequently (or sometimes not at all) on weekends. Those traveling by **car** may have to park in lots outside the old city walls of some towns, but will have easy access to many suburban budget hotels, private rooms, and campgrounds that lie outside the reach of bus or train. The Romantic Road is an excellent opportunity for a leisurely **bike** journey, with campgrounds 10-20km apart. Hardcore cyclists could finish the 350km route in a few days, but at a more modest pace you'll be on the road a week or two. Tourist offices offer excellent cycling maps and information on campgrounds along the road. For information or reservations, call **Deutsche Touring,** Am Römerhof 17, 60486 Frankfurt (☎069 79 03 50; www.touring.de). For more information on the Romantic Road, contact the **Romantische Straße Arbeitsgemeinschaft,** Marktpl., 91550 Dinkelsbühl (☎09851 902 71; www.romantischestrasse.de). For more information on the Castle Road, contact the **Burgen Straße Arbeitsgemeinschaft,** Rathaus, 74072 Heilbronn (☎07131 56 22 71). Even better, contact a **Euraide** office (for Munich location, see p. 442); they specialize in information and travel bookings (either route) for English-speaking tourists; all Euraide services are free.

AUGSBURG
☎0821

Unlike the many eternally medieval and Baroque cities in the Bavaria, Augsburg's zenith occurred during the Renaissance. Owing its name and 15 BC founding to the Roman emperor Augustus, it's no wonder that this town of 275,000 likes to consider itself the northernmost city of Italy. The second-oldest city in Germany, Augsburg was the financial center of the Holy Roman Empire and a major commercial city by the end of the 15th century; through the Via Claudia, it connected to Munich, Venice and, by extension, the Silk Road. The town owes its flourishing in great part to the **Fuggers,** an Augsburg family that virtually monopolized the banking industry; **Jakob Fugger "the Rich"** was personal financier to the **Hapsburg** Emperors. After the Thirty Years' war, however, Munich eclipsed Augsburg as Bavaria's most important city. WWII destroyed most of the town, and while major historical buildings were reconstructed, much of the city was simply built anew, but locals are increasingly attempting to protect their heritage.

▐ TRANSPORTATION

Augsburg is connected by **train** to: Berlin (8hr., 1 per 2hr., €80); Frankfurt (3hr., 1 per hr., €60); Füssen (2hr., 1 per hr., €15); Munich (45min., 3-5 per hr., €9-18); Nürnberg (1¾hr., 1 per hr., €20-29). Augsburg's **public transportation** hub is at Königspl., two blocks down Bahnhofstr. For transit information, head to the **VGA Info Center** there. (☎32 45 88 80. Open M-F 7am-6pm, Sa 9am-1pm.) A single ride is €0.95; a *Tageskarte* is €5.20. For a **taxi,** call ☎350 25 or 194 10.

▐ PRACTICAL INFORMATION

The **tourist office,** Rathauspl., (☎502 07 24 or 50 20 72 00 for reservations; www.regio-augsburg.de) offers free city maps and books rooms for a €2 fee. From the station, walk to the end of Bahnhofstr. and take a left at Königspl. onto

Annastr. Take the third right and Rathauspl. will be on the left; the tourist office is on the right. (Open Apr.-Oct. M-F 9am-6pm, Sa 10am-4pm, Su 10am-2pm; Nov.-Mar. M-F 9am-5pm, Sa 10am-2pm.) **Walking tours** of the city leave from the Rathaus (Apr.-Oct. daily at 2pm, Nov.-Dec. Sa at 2pm; €7, students €5), and cover both the Goldener Saal and the Fuggerei. From April to October, bus tours of the city in German and English leave from the same place (Th-Su at 10am; €9, students €7). Other services include: **Sparkasse**, Halderstr. 3, two blocks east of the station, (€1.50 per check cashed, open M and Th 8:30am-6pm; Tu-W 8:30am-4pm; F 8:30am-3pm.); **Bücher Pustet**, Karolinenstr. 12. (☎50 22 40; open M-F 9am-7pm, Sa 9am-6pm.); **laundromat** at Heilig-Kreuz-Str. 32; enter on Klinkertorstr. (€6-7 wash and dry. Open M-Sa 7:30am-5pm.) The **police station** is on the ground floor of the Rathaus (☎110). For a **pharmacy**, head to **Stern-Apotheke**, Maximilianstr. 27 on Moritzpl., behind the fountain. (☎308 38. Open M-Th and F 8:30am-6:30pm, W 8:30am-6pm, Sa 8am-1pm.) **Internet** access can be found at **TeleCafe**, Jakoberstr. 1 (☎50 85 80). €2.50 per hr. Augsburg's **post office**, Halderstr. 29, 86150 Augsburg, is on the right as you exit the station. (Open M-F 8am-6:30pm, Sa 9am-1pm.)

🏠🍴 ACCOMMODATIONS AND FOOD

Augsburg's tranquil **Jugendherberge (HI) ❶**, Beim Pfaffenkeller 3, has rooms that feel like converted second-grade classrooms. From the station, walk up Bahnhofstr. to Königspl., then cross the rotary onto Bürgmeister-Fischer-Str. and left onto Maximilianstr. to the Rathauspl. Continue straight as the street name changes to Karolinenstr., and then to Hoher Weg. Just after the Dom, turn right onto Inneres Pfaffergässchen, and bear left as it becomes Beim Pfaffenkeller (20min.). Or, take streetcar #2 from Königspl. to "Stadtwerke," and then follow the directions above from Karolinenstr. (☎339 09; fax 15 11 49. **Internet** €2.50 per 40min. Breakfast included. Key deposit €10 plus an ID. Reception 7-9am and 5-10pm. Curfew 1am. Closed Jan. Dorm beds €14.50, adults over 27 accompanying youth €16.60, children ages 3-6 €10.20, under 3 free.) The downtown area is not known for inexpensive accommodations. The cheapest privacy you'll find in a central location is at **Jakober Hof ❸**, Jakoberstr. 39-41, 20min. from the station, across from the Fuggerei. Follow the directions to Rathauspl., then head downhill on Perlachberg, which becomes Barfüsserstr., and Jakoberstr. The rooms are spacious and modern with cable TV, and the staff is friendly. (☎51 00 30; www.jakoberhof.de. Breakfast and parking included. Singles €26, with bath and TV €39; doubles €39, with shower €54, with bath €64.) If you're willing to throw down a heftier sum, you can find luxurious accommodations overlooking Königspl. at **Hotel Ost am Kö ❺**, Fuggerstr. 4-6, just 300m from the station down Bahnhofstr. It features vibrantly colored rooms equipped with bathrooms, TV, radios, and phones. (☎50 20 40; www.ostamkoe.de. Singles €65-75, weekends €55; doubles €85-100/€70.) Pitch your tent at **Campingplatz Augusta ❶**, ABA Augsburg-Ost, Am Autobahnsee. Take bus #23 (dir.: Firnhaberau) to "Hammerschmiede" and follow the signs 500m. (☎70 75 75; www.campingplatz-augusta.de. €4.10 per person. €3.10 per tent or car.)

Bahnhofstr., Annastr., Karolinenstr., and Maximilianstr. are lined with food stands in the summer, but some of the *Imbiß* fare can be surprisingly pricey. Try the **König von Flandern ❸**, Karolinenstr. 12 (under the bookstore), Augsburg's first Gasthof-brewery, where the warm smells of yeast and fermenting barley waft. Large portions of soup, salad, and meat entrees (€3-11) satisfy the most ravenous Bavarians. (☎15 80 50. Open M-Sa 11am-1am, Su 5pm-1am.) In the Italianate courtyard of the *Zeughaus*, the Renaissance armory that was later a fire department, **Zur Alten Feuerwache ❷**, Zeugpl. 4, is a traditional restaurant with an affordable beer garden. (Maß €4.40, food €2-6. ☎343 37 84. Open daily 10am-10pm.) A **Plus** supermarket is at the corner of Halderstr. and Hermannstr., at the southeast corner of the Konigspl. park. (Open M-F 8:30am-8pm, Sa 8:30am-4pm.)

📷 SIGHTS

Jakob Fugger "the Rich," once the wealthiest man on earth, founded the **Fuggerei** quarter in 1521 as the first welfare housing project in the world. His motivation was not entirely selfless: in exchange for free housing, the poor had to pray for the Fugger family. To this day, the narrow streets and 67 gabled houses are a haven for 150 low-income families, who even now must be Catholic and approved by the Fugger descendants. (€1, children under 15 €0.50. Includes entry to the museum.) The **Fuggereimuseum**, Mittlerg. 13, within the Fuggerei, is arranged to portray an early modern home, and is one of the only apartment buildings that survived WWII. To reach the Fuggerei from the Rathaus, walk behind the **Perlachturm** tower on Perlachberg, which becomes Barfüsserstr., then Jakoberstr., and turn right under the archway. (Open Mar.-Dec. daily 9am-6pm.) Fugger lived and tended to his business in the **Fugger Haus**, Maximilianstr. 36-38, where a dispute between Martin Luther and Cardinal Cajetan in October of 1518 precipitated the Reformation. Mostly destroyed by the 1944 bombing, this palace's former beauty can be glimpsed from the *Damenhof* courtyard, accessible through the bookstore. The Lutheran **St. Anna Kirche**, on Annastr. near the Königspl., is a strange mixture of Catholic and Protestant styles. Luther stayed here, and pioneered the Reformation in Augsburg from this church. St. Anna is also the Fuggers' final resting place. (Open Tu-Sa 10am-12:30pm and 3-6pm, Su noon-6pm.)

Overlooking the broad Rathauspl. in the city center is the huge **Rathaus,** which encloses the **Goldener Saal** on its third floor. The reconstructed frescoes surrounded by gold, centerpieces of the Augsburg Renaissance, still impress today. (☎32 40. Open May-Oct. daily 10am-6pm. €2, children under 15 €0.50.) Those willing to climb 258 narrow steps can catch a great view over Augsburg from the **Perlach Turm**, next to the Rathaus. (Open May-Oct. daily 10am-6pm. €1, children €0.50.) Behind the Rathaus is the former **artisans' quarter,** a maze of small lanes laced with canals, filled with pleasant open-air cafes to enhance summer evenings. Up Hoher Weg to the left is the **Hoher Dom,** the regional bishop's seat. Built in the 9th century, the cathedral was renovated in the 14th century in Gothic style, and later restored after WWII damage. The beautiful stained glass windows, depicting the prophets in Jewish costume reportedly date from 1140, making them the oldest in the world. (Open M-Sa 6am-5pm. German-language tours available M-Sa 10:15am-4pm.) The large, beautiful **Synagogue** is a testament to the 2000 Jews who lived in Augsburg until the 1930s. Turn right from the station on Halderstr.; the synagogue is on the left. Inside, the **Jewish Cultural Museum** displays valuable ritual objects. (☎51 36 58. Open Tu-F 9am-4pm and Su 10am-5pm. €2, students and children €1.50. Guided visits can be arranged.) **Bertolt Brecht's birthplace** by a stream in a serene old neighborhood was renovated in 1998, on the 100th anniversary of his birth. The museum chronicles the life of the influential 20th-century playwright and poet through photographs, letters, and poetry. From Rathauspl., head downhill on Perlachberg, and take the third left onto Auf dem Rain. (Open Tu-Su 10am-5pm. €1, students and children €0.75.) The new **Maximilanmuseum,** Philippine-Welser-Str. 24, displays Renaissance sculptures and historical exhibits, for now only on its ground floor. (Open Tu-Su 10am-5pm. €1.50, students and children €1.) Beyond the Fuggerhaus, walk through the garden of the Baroque **Schaezler Palace,** under renovation until 2006, to reach the **Staatsgalerie,** Maximilianstr. 46, a small but beautiful collection of religious art by artists including Cranach and Holbein. Also on view is a Dürer portrait of Jakob Fugger. The **Augsburg Puppenkiste** (Puppet Theater) Spitalg. 15, has a museum of the marionettes that still bring fame to the city. (Open Tu-Su 9am-7pm, ticket sales until 6pm. €3.20, children €2.20.)

ROTHENBURG OB DER TAUBER ☎ 09861

As the crossroads of the Romantic and Castle Roads, Rothenburg ob der Tauber caters to tourists seeking a one-day authentic medieval experience. But don't let the perpetual hordes of camera-wielding Americans and Japanese scare you away; this town, which originally blossomed around 1500, has been carefully preserved and is well worth a visit. A gorgeous reminder of Bavaria's architectural past, pastel-colored Rothenburg has great museums, quality handcrafts shopping, historical reenactments galore and horse-drawn carriages trotting over the cobblestones. It sometimes feels like Rothenburg is trying to be more medieval than the Middle Ages themselves—but it's all in the name of fun.

■? TRANSPORTATION AND PRACTICAL INFORMATION

Trains run to: Steinach (15min., 1 per hr., €1.80), where you can transfer to trains for Munich and Würzburg. **Buses** also serve the route, sometimes in place of the train in the evening. The **Europabus** (p. 526) leaves from the Busbahnhof, right next to the train station. For a **taxi,** call ☎20 00 or 72 27. Rent **bikes** at **Hiko Zweirad,** Mühlacker, next to the youth hostel. (☎34 95. €5 per day. Open M 1:30-6pm, Tu-F 9am-noon and 1:30-6pm, Sa 9am-1pm.) The cheap bikes, although not new, are nonetheless in prime condition, since Hiko also does repairs. Another option is **Rad und Tat,** Bensenstr. 17 (☎879 84. Open M-F 9am-6pm, Sa 9am-1pm. €2.50 per hr., €10 per day.) **Lidl,** Ehrlbacherstr. 48, is a conveniently cheap supermarket (open M-Sa 8am-8pm), located just opposite Rad und Tat.

Rothenburg's **tourist office,** Marktpl. 2, books rooms and supplies free maps. You can also access the **Internet** for 15min. free of charge. Walk left from the station, bear right on Ansbacherstr., and follow it straight to the Marktpl. (15min.); the office is on your right, across the square in the pink building. (☎404 92; www.rothenburg.de. Open May-Oct. M-F 9am-noon and 1-6pm, Sa-Su 10am-3pm; Nov.-Apr. M-F 9am-noon and 1-5pm, Sa 10am-1pm.) **Tours** in German depart daily from the steps of the Rathaus (90min., Apr.-Oct. and Dec. 11am and 2pm, €3), while English tours meet there daily at 2pm (€4). The night watchman leads a ◪**special tour** with his lantern and iron spear; meet at the Rathaus. (Daily Easter-Christmas, in English 8pm, €4; in German 9:30pm, €3.)

Other services include: **Laundromat,** Johanniterg. 9. (☎27 75. €5.50 for detergent, wash, and dry; open M-F 8am-6pm, Sa 8am-2pm.); **Police,** Ansbacherstr. 72 (☎110); **Löwen-Apotheke,** Marktpl. 3. (☎944 30; Open M-F 8am-6pm, Sa 8:30am-12:30pm). **Internet** is at **Der Computershop,** Ansbacherstr. 21a, a few blocks from the Rödertor. (Open M-F 11am-7pm, Sa 10am-4pm. €2 for the 1st 30min., €1 for each 30min. thereafter.). The **post office** is at Bahnhofstr. 15, 91541 Rothenburg, across from the station in the Zentro mall. (Open M-F 9am-5pm, Sa 9am-noon.)

⌂ ACCOMMODATIONS

An incredible number of private rooms (singles €15-30; doubles €28-45) not registered with the tourist office are available; look for "Zimmer frei" signs in the areas outside the city walls. Despite their abundance, don't expect same-day availability in the summer or around Christmas. There are also many pensions in town, some cheaper than others. The most charming budget one, ◪**Pension Raidel ❷,** Wengg. 3, in the Altstadt, is a half-timbered house with bright rooms and feather beds, each one built and decorated by the owner. From Marktpl., head down Obere Schmiedg. and make a left on Wengg. (☎31 15; www.romanticroad.com/raidel. Breakfast included. Singles €19, with bath €39; doubles €39/€49.) The smaller **Pension Pöschel ❷,** Weng. 2, across the street, has similar rooms. (☎34 30; pension.poeschel@t-online.de. Singles €20; doubles €35-45.) **Gasthof Goldene Rose ❸,** Spitalg. 28, on the main street of the town, has cheery, spacious rooms run by sisters with an eye for detail. Ask for a double in the detached blue house (€47) at the end of the garden. (☎46 38; fax 86 417. Singles €21-23; doubles €36, with bath €41-62.) In the Altstadt, the English-friendly **Pension Becker ❸**, Roseng. 23, offers conveniently-located rooms with private showers (☎35 60; fax 35 40; singles €29-31; doubles €40-47), as does **Gasthof Zum Ochsen ❸**, Galgeng. 26, (☎67 60; fax 87 657. Singles €18, with bath €26; doubles €48-53). **Pension Then ❸**, Johanniterg. 8a, is only 10min. outside the city walls. From the station, turn left, then right on Ansbacherstr. and right on Johanniterg. (☎51 77; fax 860 14. Breakfast included. Singles €25; doubles €40, with bath €45.) **Jugendherberge Rossmühle (HI) ❷**, Mühlacker 1, a horse-powered mill in the 16th century, now sports ping-pong and pool tables, a TV room with movies, **Internet** access (€2 per 30min.), and laundry machines. From the tourist office, take a left down Obere Schmiedg., and go straight for about 10min. until you see the small, white *Jugendherberge* sign to the right. From the train station, the *Stadtbuslinie* leaves every few hours; take it to "Spitalg." (€1), and backtrack a block before turning left onto Mühlacker. (☎941 60; jhrothenburg@djh-bayern.de. Sheets and breakfast included. Reception 7am-midnight. Curfew midnight, but they'll give you an access code. €18.)

⬛ FOOD

Rothenburg's festive *Schneeballen* (snowballs)—thin layers of fried dough rolled into a large ball—are available in any season. Their traditional powdered sugar coating now often gives way to elaborate and messy guises involving chocolate, coconut, cointreau, marzipan and amaretto. **Diller's ❶**, Untere Schmiedg. 24, Hofbronneng. 16, and Hafeng. 16, offers these doughy concoctions for €1-3. (Open daily 11am-6pm; Schmiedg. opens at 10am.) Special deals abound at **Cafehaus ❸**, Untere Schmiedg. 18, from the "Happy Meal" (try to dispel those fast-food associations)— soup, main course, dessert and a drink for €10—to the free glass of prosecco with breakfast, 9-10am. Pick from 111 different types of coffee (€4 for a jumbo cup), or try the Franconian specialties such as fried camembert (€7-9). The terrace in the back offers a dramatic view of the Tauber. (☎939 85. Open M-Sa 8am-7pm, Su 9:30am-6pm.) The international tourist traffic supports scores of overpriced restaurants near the Marktpl., but good deals abound. **Roter Hahn ❸**, Obere Schmiedg. 21, is the former home of the renowned **Mayor Georg Nusch**, whose tolerance for large doses of alcohol saved the town from destruction. *Let's Go* does not recommend attempting to "save the town." This restaurant caters to meat-lovers,

SOCIALIZE AND SAVE

Two strangers meet in front of a train station. With determination, the two stride towards one another. A tense, previously arranged greeting is exchanged. This scene is not the beginning of a noir film, but a commonplace occurrence in Germany. Since the Deutsche Bahn introduced its group ticket (€22, offering unlimited one-day travel within a single *Land* for groups of 2-5 people) Germans have been breaking social boundaries, approaching strangers without introduction in attempts to form a group of five.

The travelers who eye each other furtively around the ticket vending machines are simply trying to figure out who will be going their way. This impulse to share, is, of course, frowned upon by the Deutsche Bahn. It is becoming more common, however, and it's fun and often enriching to commune with Germans who are sharing the price of their ride with you. For €4.20 each, less than the price of last night's margaritas, five travelers can head from the opera at Bayreuth, in the northernmost part of Bavaria, all the way down to a festival in Austria (the Bayern ticket considers Salzburg a border station). The Internet-savvy can even run an online search for the many message boards where travelers advertise their travel plans and agree on meeting points. A rendezvous at the train station has suddenly gained totally new significance. When choosing a travel partner, always use common sense and trust your instincts.

though vegetarians will eat well, too. Meals on the lunch menu cost €5-9, while large dinners run €8-15. (☎97 40. Open daily 8am-10:30pm.) **Pizzeria Roma ❷**, Galgeng. 19, serves large portions of pasta, pizzas, and fresh salads (€4-7) at affordable prices. (☎45 40. Open Th-Tu 11:30am-midnight.) Dine in the oldest house in town at **Zur Höll** ("To Hell") ❸, Burgg. 8. Franconian food (€3-13) served on scarred wooden tables in dim candlelight, all on a foundation built in AD 980. (☎42 29. Open daily 5pm-1am.) If you lust for a *Biergarten*, look no further than **Gasthof Rödertor ❸**, Ansbacherstr., just by the Rödertor. It's no *Hirschgarten*, but the garden is pleasant and the beer (€2.50 for 0.4L) washes down the *Kartoffel*-centric entrees (€4-11) nicely. (Open daily 11:30am-2pm and 5:30pm-11pm.)

⑥ SIGHTS

The Renaissance **Rathaus** stands on the Marktpl., its 60m tower affording a nice view of town. (Open Apr.-Oct. daily 9:30am-12:30pm and 1:30-5pm; Nov. and Jan.-Mar. Sa-Su noon-3pm; Dec. daily noon-3pm. €1, children €0.50.) According to local lore, during the Thirty Years' War, the conquering Catholic general Johann Tilly offered to spare the town from destruction if any local could chug a keg containing 3.25L (almost a gallon) of wine. Mayor Nusch successfully met the challenge, passed out for several days, then lived to a ripe old age. His saving *Meistertrunk* (Master Draught) is reenacted with great fanfare each year (May 13-16, Sept. 4, Oct. 1 and 8, 2005). Hang around with all the other tourists for an anti-climactic version of the episode acted out by the clock over the Marktpl. in the pink building, every hour 11am-3pm and 8-10pm. Inside the courtyard behind the Rathaus are the **Historical Vaults**, once a medieval bakery, now a depiction of Rothenburg during the Thirty Years' War, the conflict that destroyed the wealth and prestige of both the city and the Holy Roman Empire. The first floor presents military and social history, while torture instruments lurk in the gloomy stone cells that form the dungeon. (☎867 51. Open Apr.-Oct. daily 9:30am-5:30pm; during Christmas market, 1-4pm. €2, students €1.50, children 3-6 €0.50.)

The macabre exhibits in the ■**Medieval Crime Museum**, Burgg. 3-5, present the creative ways in which Europeans punished one another. A strictly regulated social and legal order emerged through to such grim instruments as chastity belts, iron maidens, gag bonnets, the stocks, and the pillory. Downstairs, exhibits teach about torture; upstairs focuses on death and shaming devices. All displays explained in English. (☎53 59. Open daily Apr.-Oct. 9:30am-6pm; Dec. and Mar. 10am-4pm; Nov. and Jan.-Feb. 2-4pm. Last entry 45min. before closing. €3.50, students €2.40, children €1.70.) The **Jakobskirche**, Klosterg. 15, is famed for its **Altar of the Holy Blood,** a beautifully-carved wooden *Last Supper* by Würzburg master Tilman Riemenschneider, who idiosyncratically placed Judas at the center. The altar contains a famous reliquiary: three drops of Christ's blood in a crystal, once a pilgrims' prayer site. The **Altar of the Twelve Apostles** is also a masterpiece, with gleaming paintings by Nördlingen artist Friedrich Herlin. (☎70 06 20. Open Apr.-Oct. M-Sa 9am-5:30pm, Su 10:30am-5:30pm; Dec. daily 10am-5pm; Nov. and Jan.-Mar. daily 10am-noon and 2-4pm. €1.50, students €0.50. Free German language tours Apr.-Oct. 11am and 2pm. Free organ concerts July-Aug. W 6pm.) A 13th-century Dominican convent now holds the **Reichsstadtmuseum**, Klosterhof 5, with displays on local history and art. Highlights include the oldest kitchen in Germany, a collection documenting the history of Jews in the city, and Marie Antoinette's hunting rifle. (☎93 90 43. Open daily Apr.-Oct. 10am-5pm; Nov.-Mar. 1-4pm. €3, students €2.) The **Christmas Museum**, Herrng. 1, shows the holiday's evolution. (Open Apr.-Dec. daily 10am-6pm; Jan.-Mar. Sa-Su 10am-5pm. €4, students €2.50, children €2.)

DINKELSBÜHL ☎ 09851

Due to the Swedes' adoption of this small town as a garrison, as well as the residents payments of hefty ransoms, Dinkelsbühl escaped the widespread destruction caused by the Thirty Years' War. Two ensuing centuries of economic depression ensured that the town, once as prominent as Leipzig, remained quaint. Locals were too distracted by the violent civil strife between Catholics and Lutherans to attempt economic recovery. By the time they were ready to welcome modernity in, Ludwig I and his preservationist instinct got in the way, dictating in the early 19th century that no stone in Dinkelsbühl be touched. The presence of a large Catholic church at the center of a predominantly Lutheran town signals the continuing relevance of centuries of religious difference.

⌐ TRANSPORTATION. Getting to Dinkelsbühl is not easy. Trains only run from nearby **Nördlingen** (p. 534), with bus service continuing to Dinkelsbühl (7 per day, 2-4 per day on weekends, €4.10). Otherwise, buses go to and from **Rothenburg ob der Tauber** (M-F 9 per day, Sa-Su 1-3 per day; transfer at Dombühl or Feuchtwangen; €5.60.) For a **taxi**, call ☎ 76 27.

◢ PRACTICAL INFORMATION. The **tourist office**, on the Marktpl. across from the church, finds rooms for free. The office also rents **bikes** (€3.60 per day). From the "Bahnhof" bus stop, turn right on Luitpoldstr. and then left through the **Wörnitz Tor,** the oldest gate in the city, into the Altstadt. Veer right with the street to the Marktpl.; the tourist office is in the red building. (☎ 902 40; www.dinkelsbuehl.de. Open Apr.-Oct. M-F 9am-6pm, Sa 10am-noon and 1-6pm, Su 10am-noon; Nov.-Mar. M-F 10am-1pm and 2-5pm, Sa 10am-noon.) **Tours** of the town (in German) leave from St. Georgskirche. (Apr.-Oct. daily 2:30 and 8:30pm. At 9pm the night watchman gives a torchlight tour. €2, students €1.50.) The **police** are next door (☎ 110). The **pharmacy** is at Nördlinger Str. 11. (☎ 34 35. Open M-F 8am-12:30pm and 2-6pm, Sa 8am-noon.) Get on the **Internet** at **Fair Play**, Nördlingerstr. 9. (18+. €1 per 15min. Open Su-Th 9am-midnight, F-Sa 9am-1pm.) The **post office**, 91550 Dinkelsbühl, is at the "Bahnhof" bus stop on Luitpoldstr. (Open M-F 9am-5pm, Sa 9am-noon.)

⌐◖ ACCOMMODATIONS AND FOOD. Built in 1378 as a grain store, the **◪Jugendherberge (HI) ❶**, Koppeng. 10, is one of the most beautiful buildings in the HI network. Leaving the tourist office, turn right down Segringer Str., and take a right on Bauhofstr. after passing the new Rathaus. At the first bus stop, swing left onto Koppeng. and up the uneven cobblestoned street; it's the large building at the top on the right. The huge, ivy-covered fortress has a lush patio enclosed by tall stone walls; several forests worth of beams and paneling enclose the rooms. (☎ 95 09; fax 48 74. Breakfast included. Reception 5-7pm. Curfew 11pm. Open Mar.-Oct. 2- to 8-bed rooms €14.25.) **Frankischer Hof ❸**, Nördlingerstr. 10 offers simple rooms above a restaurant near the center of town. (☎ 579 00; www.fr-hof.de. Breakfast included. Singles €29-36, with bath €41-51; doubles €47-75). If you are traveling in a group of four, ask for Room 31 at the luxurious **Weisses Roß ❸**, Steing. 12. to get an antique, country-style 4-bed duplex on the top floor. (☎ 57 98 90; Hotel-Weisses-Ross@t-online.de. Breakfast included. €100 per duplex.) Camp at **DCC Campingpark Romantische Straße ❶**, north on Dürrwanger Str. (☎ 78 17; www.campingpark-dinkelsbuehl.de. €4 per person, €2.50 per child. €8.50 per tent and car.)

The Italo-Turkish **Istanbul Imbiß ❷**, Nördlinger Str. 8, serves quality *Döner*, pizza, and salads (€3-7), to go or to eat among guitars and *bouzoukis* mounted on colorful walls. (Open Su-Th 11am-11pm, F-Sa 11am-midnight.) **Gasthof Goldener Hirsch ❹**, Weinmarkt 6, has delicious Dinkelsbühl carp (fresh from Sept.-May; €7-14), classic Bavarian and vegetarian cuisine. (☎ 23 47. Open daily 8am-midnight.)

◨ ⬓ SIGHTS AND ENTERTAINMENT. The Romanesque tower of the **Münster St. Georg,** which dominates the Weinmarkt at the center of town, dates to the 13th century, though the late Gothic church was not begun until 1448. Once construction was underway, however, the locals realized they could not afford a new tower, so they extended their church to incorporate the old tower. Inside the sandstone walls, an altar contains the fragmentary skeletal glory of early martyr St. Aurelius, acquired in the 18th century. (Open daily 9am-noon and 2-7 pm. Free.) The lush **Parkring** promenade around the Altstadt separates the old and new parts of town and offers pleasant walks past a system of moats and dikes, punctuated by armies of ducks and willow trees. The **Museum of the Third Dimension,** just outside the Nördlinger Tor, lets visitors look through 3D glasses at optical wonders ranging from pin-up girls to the pope—both are divine. (☎ 63 36. Open Apr.-Oct. daily 10am-6pm; Nov.-Mar. Sa-Su 11am-4pm. €8, children under 6 free.) The **Historisches Museum,** Dr.-Martin-Luther-Str. 6b, chronicles the history of Dinkelsbühl and its fittingly passive role in the Thirty Years' War. (☎ 32 93. Open Tu-Su 10am-4pm. €3, children under 15 €1.) The town's miraculous survival of the Swedish occupation was later explained by the story that the tearful pleas of the town's children, led by the beautiful Lore Hirte, daughter of a watchman, moved the Swedes to compassion. The event is reenacted every year in the **Kinderzeche Festival** (Children's Feast, July 15-24, 2005), with parades, fireworks, dances, and, of course, Lore and her flock of crying kids, many of whom are frequent guests at local hostels.

NÖRDLINGEN IM RIES ☎ 09081

The pleasant town of Nördlingen, formerly a free city of the German *Reich*, sits proudly in a crater created by a meteor impact some 14.7 million years ago. The crater (known as the **Ries,** from *Raetia,* the name of the province under Roman rule), about 25km in diameter, was first an enormous lake. After the water drained naturally, the sediments it deposited gave the new town unusually fertile soil. As a result, Nördlingen grew into a trading center in the Middle Ages, with an important fair, the **Pfingstmesse,** which still takes place (May 28-June 6, 2005). Its almost perfectly circular wall, the only fully intact example in Germany, is built entirely from "Rieser Moonstones"—stones which formed here as a result of the collision.

◨ ⬓ TRANSPORTATION AND PRACTICAL INFORMATION. Trains to: **Augsburg** (1¼hr., 1 per hr., €11); **Munich** (2hr., 2-3 per day, €19); **Nürnberg** (2hr., 1 per hr., €18); **Ulm** (2hr., 1 per 2hr., €16). Bus #501 also runs from **Dinkelsbühl** (45min.; 7 per day, 2-4 per day on weekends; €4). The **tourist office,** Marktpl. 2, distributes maps and finds rooms for free. (☎ 43 80 or 841 16; www.noerdlingen.de. Open Easter-Oct. M-Th 9am-6pm, F 9am-4:30pm, Sa 9:30am-1pm; Nov.-Easter M-Th 9am-5pm, F 9am-3:30pm.) It also offers 1hr. tours (Apr.-Oct. 2pm) from the Rathaus, or by torchlight at 8:30pm (€3). The **police** can be found at Reimlingerstr. 7 (☎ 110). **Einhorn-Apotheke,** Polizeig. 7., is the oldest pharmacy in town, dating to 1387. (☎ 296 20. Open M-F 8am-6pm, Sa 8:30am-noon.) **Internet** access can be found at the **Stadtbücherei** on the Marktpl. on the opposite side of the Rathaus from St. Georg (€0.50 for 15min. Open Tu and Sa 10am-1pm; W and F 10am-1pm and 2-6pm; Th 2-6:30pm), and at **Cafe Radlos** (p. 535). The **post office,** 86720 Nördlingen, is to the right of the train station as you exit. (Open M-F 8:30am-5pm, Sa 9am-11:30am.)

◨ ⬓ ACCOMMODATIONS AND FOOD. Nördlingen does not have a hostel, but there are numerous inexpensive guesthouses in town, clearly marked by "Zimmer frei" signs. You can also stop by the tourist office to find a room. **Gasthof Walfisch ❸,** Hallg. 15, is in the center of town near Marktpl. From the tourist office, head left onto Windg. and take a right on Hallg. The somber hallways and spacious rooms are complemented by the friendly service of the mother-son team that runs the house. (☎/fax 31 07. Singles €20-30; doubles €40-60.) **Drei Mohren Gasthof ❸**, Reimlinger Str. 18, is just inside the town wall near the Reimlinger Tor, one of the many towers that punctuate the town wall. From Marktpl., follow Schäfflesmarkt to Reimlinger Str. (☎31 13; fax 287 59. Singles €20; doubles €40.) **◼Cafe Radios ❸**, Löpsingerstr. 8, serves up everything from traditional Bavarian *Wurst* to Greek, Italian, Turkish and Asian specialties. (☎50 40. Main courses €6-12. **Internet** access is €2 per 30min. Open Th-Tu 10am-1am.) One block away from the Marktpl., **Pizzeria Firenze ❷**, Dreherg. 3, serves cheap and tasty pizza and pasta dishes for €5-7. (Open daily 10am-11pm.)

◻ SIGHTS. Nördlingen's late Gothic **St. Georg Kirche,** which boasts a 90m bell-tower nicknamed "Daniel," is constructed entirely of meteoric rock, making it the only church in the world that is literally heaven-sent. The stately St. Georg was constructed in the 15th century. Every night for the last 500 years, the town watchman has rung atonal bells from atop the tower and called out "So G'sell so!" ("You silly fool!") over the town's red rooftops every 30min. between 10pm and midnight. (Tower open daily Apr.-Oct. 9am-8pm; Nov.-Mar. 9am-5:30pm. €1.60, under 17 €1.10, family €4. Dom open M-F 9:30am-12:30pm and 2-5pm, Sa 9:30am-5pm, Su 11am-5pm.) Look at dioramas and talk with Aksel Rinck, the enthusiastic man-of-the-tower, about the medieval town wall in Nördlingen's **Stadtmauermuseum,** inside the old watch-tower, Löpsinger Tor. (☎91 80. Open Apr.-Oct. daily 10am-4:30pm. €1.50, under 17 €1.) Nördlingen's **Stadtmuseum,** Vordere Gerberg. 1, located in the heart of the old cloth-dyeing quarters, explores the region's culture from the first farming settlements of 6000 BC to the present day. (☎273 82 30. Open Mar.-Nov. Tu-Su 1:30-4:30pm. €3, students €1.50.) In a large, converted barn across from the Stadtmuseum, the exhibitions and multimedia displays of **Rieskrater Museum,** Eugene-Shoemaker-Pl. 1, provides astronomical, geological, and historical information on the Ries meteorite. (☎273 82 20. Open Tu-Su May-Oct. 10am-4:30pm; Nov.-Apr. 10am-noon and 1:30-4:30pm. €3, students €1.50.)

WÜRZBURG ☎0931

Sweeping vistas of the river Main, striking Baroque churches, and the hilltop 13th-century Marienburg fortress form the perfect atmosphere in which to sample the delicious local white wine, which, for the proud Franconians of Würzburg, eclipse any Bavarian fondness for *Bier*. The fortress and the flamboyantly Rococo Residenz, nowadays hosts to museums and nocturnal concerts, are symbols of the past power of Würzburg's prince-bishops. These sovereigns, who governed this part of Franconia from 1168 until 1802, steered the region back to Catholicism even as its citizens longed to adhere to the principles of the Reformation. Würzburg was also never granted the title of free city of the Holy Roman Empire ("freie Reichsstadt"), a privilege which would have freed it from the prince-bishop's influence. Today, the city is known for **Julius-Maximilians-Universität,** which boasts six Nobel Prize winners among its faculty. It was here in 1895 that **Wilhelm Conrad Röntgen** discovered X-rays. The pedestrian zone buzzes with tourists, students, trams and various street vendors. A large portion of the city was destroyed by bombings in the last days of WWII, but most of the historic buildings were restored or rebuilt, making Würzburg a scenic portal on the Romantic and Castle Roads.

BAYERN

◼ TRANSPORTATION

Trains to: **Bamberg** (1hr., 1 per hr., €14); **Frankfurt** (2hr., 2 per hr., €19); **Munich** (3hr., 1 per hr., €15); **Nürnberg** (1hr., 1 per hr., €15); **Rothenburg ob der Tauber** (1hr., 1 per hr., €10).

Buses: Europabus (p. 526) traces the Romantic Road to **Füssen** daily starting at 10am, departing from bus platform #13. The bus station is to the right of the train station.

Public Transportation: Streetcars are the most efficient way around, but large sections outside the downtown are not covered. The **bus** network is comprehensive, but most routes do not run nights and weekends. Ask for **night bus** schedules at the **WSB kiosk** in front of the station. Single fare within the city €1.50; 24hr. ticket €4.10. For a **taxi**, call ☎194 10.

Bike Rental: Fahrrad Station, Bahnhofpl. 4 (☎574 45), to the left of the station as you exit. €10 for the 1st day, €8 per subsequent day. Open Apr.-Oct. Tu-F 9:30am-6:30pm, Sa 9:30am-1:30pm, Su 10am-1pm; Nov.-Mar. closed Su.

Boat Tours: Personenschifffahrt (☎556 33) ferries tourists to Veitschöchheim (one-way 40min.), leaving from **Alter Kranen** (near the Congress Center) at the white kiosk, every hr. 10am-4pm. One-way €5.50, round-trip €8.

Mitfahrzentrale: ☎194 48, in the kiosk to the left of the train station exit. Organizes ride shares, to: **Berlin** (€30), **Frankfurt** (€10), **Munich** (€18), **Stuttgart** (€10), and other cities. Open M-W 10am-4pm, Th-F 10am-6pm, Sa 10am-1pm, Su 11am-1pm.

■✴ 🔃 ORIENTATION AND PRACTICAL INFORMATION

To get to the city's center at the **Marktplatz,** follow Kaiserstr. straight from the station for two blocks, then take a right on Juliuspromenade, and hang a left on **Schönbornstraße,** the main pedestrian and streetcar road; the Markt is a few blocks down and to the right. Streetcars #1, 3, and 5 run from the station to the Markt. The Main River separates the rest of the city from the steep fortressed hills.

Tourist Office: (☎37 23 98) in **Haus zum Falken,** a yellow Rococo building on the Markt-tpl. It provides a free city map, a hotel list, and helps find rooms for free. Open Apr.-Dec. M-F 10am-6pm, Sa 10am-2pm; May-Oct. also Su 10am-2pm; Jan.-Mar. M-F 10am-4pm, Sa 10am-1pm. The **main office,** Am Congress Centrum (☎37 23 35; www.wuerzburg.de), offers the same services. Located in the Palais am Kongresszentrum near the Friedensbrücke, where Röntgenring intersects the Main, accessible by streetcars #2 and 4. Open M-Th 8:30am-5pm, F 8:30am-1pm. If you get into town late, there's a map and hotel information on the board just outside the train station.

Tours: German-language tours of the city depart mid-Apr. to Oct. daily at 10:30am. (€5, students €3.50.) Or rent a cassette (€5) from the tourist office and do your own tour. For nocturnal adventures, join the (German-speaking) **night watchman,** with lantern and spear, on his rounds of the Altstadt. Apr.-Dec. W-Sa 8 and 9pm; Jan.-Mar. F-Sa 8 and 9pm. Meet at the fountain across from the Rathaus. (€3, children free.) **Bus tours** (German) leave the bus station (right leaving the train station) and return 2hr. later. Mid-Apr. to Oct. M-Sa 2pm, Su 10:30am. (€8.50, students €6.30.)

Travel Agency: STA Travel, Zwinger 6. (☎521 76; wuerzburg@statravel.de). Open M-F 9:30am-6pm and Sa 9:30am-1pm.

Bookstore: Hugendubel, Schmalzmarkt 12 (☎01801 48 44 84), offers Harry Potter and other English-language must-reads. Open M-F 9:30am-8pm, Sa 9:30am-10pm.

Pharmacy: Marktpl. 36 (☎32 13 40). Open M-F 8:30am-6:30pm, Sa 8:30am-3pm.

Emergency: Police ☎110. **Fire** ☎112. **Medical Aid** ☎192 22.

Currency Exchange: Sparkasse, Barbarossapl. 2 (☎304 89 10). Open M-W and F 8:30am-4:30pm, Th 8:30am-6:30pm.

Internet cafe: N@tcity, Sanderstr. 27 (☎30 41 94 94; www.netzstatt-wuerzburg.de). €3.50 per hr., students €2.50. Open M-Th 11am-midnight, F-Sa 11am-1am, Su 1pm-midnight.

Post Office: Bahnhofpl. 2, 97070 Würzburg. Open M-F 8am-6pm, Sa 9am-noon.

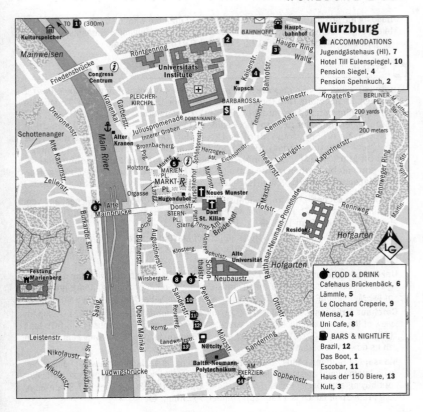

Würzburg

🏠 ACCOMMODATIONS
Jugendgästehaus (HI), 7
Hotel Till Eulenspiegel, 10
Pension Siegel, 4
Pension Spehnkuch, 2

🍴 FOOD & DRINK
Cafehaus Brückenbäck, 6
Lämmle, 5
Le Clochard Creperie, 9
Mensa, 14
Uni Cafe, 8

🍺 BARS & NIGHTLIFE
Brazil, 12
Das Boot, 1
Escobar, 11
Haus der 150 Biere, 13
Kult, 3

🏠 ACCOMMODATIONS AND CAMPING

Many room prices in the city are ridiculous, Würzburg's least expensive beds can be found near the station, around **Kaiserstraße** and **Bahnhofstraße**.

Jugendgästehaus (HI), Burkarderstr. 44 (☎425 90; fax 41 68 62), across the river from downtown. Streetcar #3 (dir.: Heidingsfeld) or 5 (dir.: Heuchelhof-Rottenbauer) to "Löwenbrücke," then backtrack 300m. Follow the Jugendherberge/Kapelle sign down the stairs, turn right, walk through the tunnel, and it's on the left. Enormous villa with great views. Breakfast and sheets included. Check-in 5-10pm. Curfew 1am. €18. ❷

Pension Spehnkuch, Röntgenring 7 (☎547 52; fax 547 60). Turn right after leaving the station and walk 1min. down Röntgenring. Renovated rooms are simple, clean, and conveniently located. Breakfast included. Singles €29; doubles €52; triples €75. ❸

Pension Siegel, Reisgrubeng. 7 (☎529 41; fax 529 67), features a neurotic mural in the stairwell and basic rooms conveniently located just off Bahnhofstr. Breakfast included. Singles €33; doubles €62. ❸

Nichtrauch-Hotel Till Eulenspiegel, Sanderstr. 1a (☎35 58 40). Follow Augustinerstr. away from the Alte Mainbrücke as it become Sanderstr., or take streetcars #1, 3, 4, or 5 to "Neubaustr." Although hardly economical, the rooms in this ivy-covered stucco building are spacious, beautifully decorated, and outfitted with full bathrooms, TVs, and telephones. Fun restaurant downstairs and lots of nearby nightlife. Breakfast included. Singles €63-74; doubles €85-123. Extra bed €30-40 per night. ❺

▐ FOOD

Würzburg's distinctive wines are sold in distinctive bottles, known as *Bocksbeutel* (goat bags; locals claim that they emulate the shape of goats' testicles). To sample them, the **Juliusspital** (Apr.-mid Nov. F 3pm), **Bürgerspital** (Apr.-Oct. Sa 2pm), and the **Staatlicher Hofkeller** next to the Residenz (Mar.-Nov. Sa every hr. 10am-noon and 2-5pm; Su no 5pm tour) all offer 1hr. cellar tours (€5) including a glass of wine. Check with the tourist office for *Kellerführungen*. There is also a farmer's **market** on Marktpl. (M-F 8am-6pm, Sa 8am-4pm), and **Vom Fass**, Eichhornstr. 3, where you can buy wines by the glass (☎404 47 74; www.vomfass.de). For **groceries**, try **Kupsch**, Kaiserstr. 5, near Barbarossapl. (Open M-F 8am-8pm, Sa 8am-6pm.)

Le Clochard Creperie/Bistro, Neubaustr. 20 (☎129 07). Crepes, sandwiches, and vegetarian dishes (€3-7). Free coffee with purchase of a crepe (daily 3-5pm). Open M-Tu 5pm-1am, W-Su 10am-1am. ❷

Lämmle, Marktpl. 5, (☎547 48) located just off Marktpl. A local favorite, this restaurant serves Franconian and Swabian standards in big portions that go well with beer. *Wurst* €5-7. Open daily 4-10pm. ❸

Uni Cafe, Neubaustr. 2 (☎156 72), on the corner of Sanderstr. Just what the name suggests—a relaxed college vibe, trendy music at night, outdoor seating, and a great view of the Marienburg. Lunch €4-6, breakfast €3-5. Open M-Sa 8am-1am, Su 9am-1am. ❷

Cafehaus Brückenbäck, Zellerstr. 2, by the Alte Mainbrücke (☎41 45 45). A superb view of the river Main accentuates salads, sandwiches, and rice dishes (€4-8.50), teas (€3), and cigars (€1-7). Open Tu-W and Su 8am-midnight, Th-Sa 8am-1am. Kitchen shuts down 1hr. before closing. ❷

Mensa, Am Studentenhaus, 1 block from Sanderring, is a sparkling university dining hall with international cuisine for local students and guests, who can pay in cash and without buying any special cards. Entrees €4-6. Open M-Th 7:30am-7pm, F 7:30am-2pm, Sa 11am-2pm. Lunch is 11am-2pm, dinner 5-7:30pm. ❷

◉ SIGHTS

FESTUNG MARIENBERG. This striking fortress has been holding vigil over the Main since the 12th century, when the prince-bishops lived here before the Residenz was built. The footpath to the **Festung** (fortress) starts a short distance from the Medieval **Alte Mainbrücke**, lined with Baroque statues of saints and figures, and built to exalt the prince-bishops' prestige during the Counterreformation. The strenuous climb to the Festung reveals the strategic value of its lofty location. Within the fortress compound you'll find the 11th-century **Marienkirche**, the 40m high **Bergfried** watchtower under which lies the **Hole of Fear** (a dungeon), the **Fürstengarten** rose garden and the 102m deep **Brunnentempel** well. If it weren't for the ancient authenticity of the place, you'd think you were inside a giant toy castle. Artifacts from the lives of the prince-bishops, scale-models of Würzburg at both its ancient splendor and after destruction by WWII bombings, and *objets d'art* cluster in the **Fürstenbaumuseum**. Outside the walls of the main fortress, the long hallways of the **Mainfränkisches Museum**, a former arsenal, are lined with religious statues featuring the expressive wooden sculptures of **Tilman Riemenschneider** (1460-1531), the "Master of Würzburg." Riemenschneider paid dearly for siding with the peasants in their 16th-century revolts: when the insurrection was suppressed, the bishop Julius Echter allegedly had the sculptor's fingers broken, preventing him from working again. Riemenschneider's house is now a restaurant on Franziskanerg., two blocks from Domstr. *(Take bus #9 from the train station to "Festung," or a 30min. walk. Tours in German depart from the courtyard Apr.-Oct. Tu-F 11am, 2, and 3pm. Sa-Su every hr. 10am-4pm, no noon tour. €3, seniors and students €2.50. Fürstenbaumuseum ☎438 38. Open Apr. to mid-Oct. Tu-Su 9am-6pm; mid-Oct. to Mar. Tu-Su 10am-4pm; last entry 30min. before closing. €4, students €3. Mainfränkisches Museum ☎20 59 40. Open Tu-Su Apr.-Oct. 10am-5pm; Nov.-Mar. 10am-4pm. €3, children under 14 free. Pass to both museums €5.)*

RESIDENZ. Johannes Zick's ceiling fresco in the first-floor garden room epitomizes the extravagance of the 18th-century Residenz, the last great symbol of the prince-bishops' power. The work was so bright that it has never needed to be restored; in fact, his use of such extravagant colors got him fired. The Italian painter **Giovanni Tiepolo** replaced him, creating the largest frescoed ceiling in the world, above the grand staircases. Once restoration on Tiepolo's work finishes in 2006, his ceiling of the *Kaisersaal*, which combines painting, sculpture and stucco for stunning depth, will be next for a face-lift. Elsewhere in the Residenz, the **glass room** is a reconstructed masterpiece. The gaudy **Residenzhofkirche**, with its gilded moldings and pink marble, features a balcony with an altar above the main altar: the perfect setting for prince-bishops to take Mass. The university's **Martin-von-Wagner-Museum**, in a wing of the Residenz buzzing with classics students, displays Greek antiquities that belonged to the collector, whom Ludwig commissioned to create the Glyptothek and the Antikensammlung in Munich. A lot of pieces, including early Italian and fleshy Baroque paintings, ended up in the intermediary's house, including his own tacky attempt at Neoclassicism. Behind the complex, the **Hofgarten** is trisected into an Italian amphitheater, a geometric Austrian garden with cone-shaped evergreens, and a faux-wild English garden (all the rage after 1780). *(From the station, walk down Kaiserstr., then Theaterstr. ☎35 51 70. Open Apr. to mid-Oct. 9am-6pm; mid-Oct. to Mar. 10am-4pm. Last entry 30min. before closing. Tours in English depart in summer daily 11am and 3pm, in winter Sa-Su only. €3.50, students and seniors €3. Martin-von-Wagner-Museum's painting gallery open Tu-Sa 9:30am-12:30pm. Greek collection open 2-5pm. The 2 galleries alternate being open Su 9:30am-12:30pm. Both free. Church open the same times as the Residenz. Free. Gardens open dawn-dusk. Free.)*

DOM ST. KILIAN. The 950-year-old Catholic cathedral was rebuilt in the mid-1960s after being obliterated by the Allies in 1945. Reconstruction favored the original Romanesque look, although the vaulted ceilings are Gothic additions, and much of the decor is Baroque. The modern stained glass windows, with their abstract colors, remind visitors of WWII. *(☎321 18 30; www.dom-wuerzburg.de. Open Easter-Oct. M-Sa 10am-5pm, Su 1-6pm; Oct.-Easter M-Sa 10am-noon and 2-5pm, Su 12:30-1:30pm and 2:30-6pm. Free. Tours M-Sa 12:20, Su 12:30 and include the otherwise inaccessible Schönbornkappelle. €2.50, students €1.50. Organ concerts M-Sa at 12:05pm.)*

🎵 🎭 ENTERTAINMENT AND NIGHTLIFE

In summer, Würzburg finds a reason to party almost every weekend, with open-air celebrations that include the city's birthday, the largest African festival in Europe (**Africa-Festival,** May 26-29, 2005), and, above all, the lively **Kiliani-Volksfest** (July 2-18, 2005). Dedicated to the patron saint Kilian, an Irish wandering bishop who died a martyr's death in Würzburg, the Volksfest is held at the Talavera fairgrounds, across the *Friedrichsbrücke* from town, and features carnival rides, game booths, candy stands, and beer tents. To get there, take streetcar #4 to "Talavera." Wednesday is *Familientag*, with all rides half-price. Würzburg's young and beautiful have a good time around Sanderstr., a pedestrian street packed with bars and clubs. The streets near the Marktpl. offer a number of outdoor cafes.

Kult, Landwehrstr. 10, right off Sanderstr. toward the Ludwigsbrücke, is a mellow and alternative *Kneipe* and cafe catering to students and local subculture. (☎531 43. Entrees €4-8. Beer €2.40 for 0.5L. Open M-F 9am-1am, Sa-Su 10am-1am.)

Escobar, Sanderstr. 7, prepares tasty Caribbean cuisine (tapas €3-4.50; entrees €5-9.50) and cocktails in a lively atmosphere filled with the smoke of real Cuban cigars. Monday is all you can eat paella (€6), Thursday is happy hour all night. (Open M-Th 7pm-2am, F-Sa 7pm-3am.)

Brazil, Sanderstr. 7, draws students to its sleek bar and club playing everything from Latin to house. (☎167 17. M all drinks half price, W Latin night, F-Sa top-40. Cover €4. Open M-Sa from 10pm.)

Das Boot, Veithöchheimerstr. 14 (☎593 53; www.das-boot.com), a large fishing ship ancored in the Main. Whatever music floats your vessel, you'll find it here with the wild Würzburg students. Cocktails €5.

The **Haus der 150 Biere,** Bahnhofstr. 22, a shameless neon-sign-and-pinball-machine-laden watering hole, offers 150 different beers from around the world. Every night there's a deal—drink two for the price of one (Tu) or trade on the "Beer Stockmarket" on Wednesday. (☎178 55. Open M-Th 11am-1am, F-Sa 11am-2am, Su 2pm-1am.)

NÜRNBERG (NUREMBERG)   ☎0911

Before the names Berlin or Munich meant anything, Nürnberg was one of the most important cities in the German *Reich.* **Albrecht Dürer,** the foremost German Renaissance painter, was a part of a blossoming of arts here from the 14th to the 16th century. Although the Holy Roman Empire was a loose confederation, and had no capital, the free city of Nürnberg considered itself the unofficial one, holding Imperial Diets at the **Kaiserburg.** Drawing on this tradition, Hitler chose the city for his massive rallies, held each September from 1933 to 1938; it was from here that the 1935 **Racial Purity Laws** were proclaimed. Accordingly, the Allies took aim and by 1945 reduced 90% of the city's historical buildings to rubble. Because of Nürnberg's Nazi ties, the Allies also selected this city to host the war crimes tribunals.

Apart from the **Dutzendteich** rally site and other Nazi relics, the city is famous for its toy fair and **Weihnachtsmarkt** (Nov. 26-Dec. 24, 2004), its sausages and gingerbread, painter **Albrecht Dürer,** and composer **Johann Pachelbel.** Today, the city's Renaissance beauty is visible again thanks to reconstruction, making Nürnberg perfect for exploring Germany's complex legacy and its exciting present. Every other year since the early nineties, the city has given a human rights award as part of the attempt by Nürnbergers to make it the *Stadt der Menschenrechte* (City of Human Rights). See www.menschenrechte.nuernberg.de for more information.

▛ TRANSPORTATION

Flights: The airport, Flughafenstr. 100 (☎937 00) is 7km north of Nürnberg. U2 connects the airport to the city (15min., €1.80).

Trains: To: **Berlin** (5hr., every 2hr., €71); **Frankfurt** (2½hr., 2 per hr., €40); **Munich** (1½hr., 2 per hr., €38); **Prague** (5hr., 2 per day, €44); **Regensburg** (1hr., 1 per hr., €15); **Stuttgart** (2hr., every 2hr., €31); **Würzburg** (1hr., 2 per hr., €15). The **DB Reisezentrum,** located in the central hall of the train station, sells tickets and answers train questions. Open M-F 6am-9pm, Sa-Su 8am-9pm.

Public Transportation: U-Bahn, streetcars, buses, regional trains (R-Bahn), and S-Bahn. Single-ride within the city €1.80. *Kurzstrecke* (short distance) €1.40. 10-stripe *Streifenkarte* €7.80. Day or weekend card €3.60. The *Tagesticket Plus* day card covers 2 adults and 4 children for €5.90. The *Nürnberg Ticket,* available at the tourist office, covers 2 consecutive days of public transportation and entrance to almost all museums, as well as theater and store discounts, for €18.

Nürnberg (Nuremberg)

🏠🏠 ACCOMMODATIONS
Campingpark
  Nürnberg, **25**
Gasthof Schwänlein, **19**
Hotel Garni Probst, **20**
Jugendgästehaus, **2**
Jugend-Hotel
  Nürnberg, **1**
Pension Hannweber, **22**
Pension "Vater Jahn," **21**

🍴 FOOD & DRINK
Bratwursthäusle, **6**
Cafe Kiosk, **9**
Cleopatra, **18**
Enchilada, **7**
Strandcafe Wanner, **24**

Sushi Glas, **17**
Wies'n Biergarten, **13**
Zum Gulden Stern, **16**

🍷 BARS & NIGHTLIFE
Cafe Ruhestörung, **4**
Cafe Treibhaus, **10**
Cartoon, **14**
Casalanca, **23**
Frizz!, **5**
KOMPLEXX, **15**
Mach 1, **11**
Sachs & Söhne, **8**

★ ENTERTAINMENT
Cine Città, **12**
Jazz Studio, **3**

Taxis: Taxizentrale ☎ 194 10 or **City Taxi** ☎ 27 27 70.
Bike Rental: Ride on a Rainbow, Adam-Kraft-Str. 55 (☎ 39 73 37; www.ride-on-a-rainbow.de), northwest of the Altstadt. Take Johannisstr. to Frauenholzstr. and turn right, then another right onto Adam-Kraft-Str. Bikes (not actually rainbow-colored) €6-8 per day. Open M-Tu and Th-F 10am-7pm, W 3-7pm, Sa 10am-3pm.
Mitfahrzentrale: Hummelsteiner Weg 12 (☎ 194 40; www.citytocity.de). 100m from the southern exit of the Hauptbahnhof. Streetcar #4 to "Dutzendteich." Open M-F 9am-6pm, Sa 9am-1:30pm, Su 10am-1pm.

⚡🛈 ORIENTATION AND PRACTICAL INFORMATION

Nürnberg's lively central district lies within the old city wall. From the train station, the main shopping area is across Frauentorgraben down **Königstraße,** which leads through the city walls and down to the river Pegnitz. From the station, follow the "Ausgang City" signs down into the tunnel and the "Altstadt" signs out the other side; you'll end up right on Königstr. **Lorenzerplatz** and the **Hauptmarkt** are just beyond Königstr. and the river, in the Altstadt's pedestrian zone. The **Burg** perches on a hill overlooking the northernmost part of the Altstadt.

TOURIST AND FINANCIAL SERVICES

Tourist Offices: Königstr. 93 (☎233 61 31; www.nuernberg.de). Walk through the tunnel from the train station to the Altstadt and take a right; it will be on your left. The staff books rooms for free and offers English maps and city guides (€3-9), and event schedules. Open M-Sa 9am-7pm. A **branch office** (☎233 61 35) is on the Hauptmarkt near the golden fountain. Open May-Oct. M-Sa 9am-6pm, Su 10am-4pm; Nov.-Apr. M-Sa 9am-6pm; during the Christmas Market M-Sa 9am-7pm, Su 10am-7pm.

Tours: 2½hr. English tours depart from the Hauptmarkt tourist office May-Oct. and Dec. daily at 1pm. €7.50, children under 14 free. A bilingual 2½hr. bus tour leaves from the Hallpl. (Mauthalle) May-Oct. and Dec. daily 9:30am. €11, under 12 €5.50.

Budget Travel: DER Reisebüro, Hauptmarkt 29 (☎20 49 21; www.der.de), on the northwest corner of the Hauptmarkt. Deciphers timetables and gives travel information for a €2.50 fee. Reservations €3. Open M-F 9:30am-6pm, Sa 10am-1pm.

Currency Exchange: Reisebank (☎22 67 78), in the central hall of the train station. 4.5% commission for currency exchange. Traveler's checks €3-6. Open M-Sa 7:30am-7:45pm, Su 8am-12:30pm and 1:15-4pm.

LOCAL SERVICES

Luggage storage: Lockers located in the east wing of the train station on the 1st fl. €1-3 up to 48hr., €2-6 up to 72hr.

Lost and Found: Fundbüro, Siebenkeesstr. 6 (☎431 76 24). Open M-W 9:30am-4pm, Th 9:30am-6pm, F 9:30am-12:30pm. For items lost on trains, go to **DB Fundstelle** (☎219 20 21) in the station. Open M-F 7:30am-7pm, Sa 8-11:30am and 12:15-6pm.

Gay and Lesbian Resources: Fliederlich e.V. SchwulLesbisches Zentrum, Breite G. 76 (☎423 45 70; www.fliederlich.de). Has a cafe and hosts various events throughout the week. Check the monthly magazine *Plärrer* (€2 at newsstands) for gay days at discos and cafes in town. For additional help, gay men can call "Rosa Hilfe" (☎194 46; open W 7-9pm), and lesbian women can call "Lila Hilfe" (☎42 34 57 25; open M 7-9pm).

Laundromat: SB Waschsalon, Tafelfeldstr. 42 (☎598 59 25). Wash €3.50. Dry €0.50 for 12min. Detergent included. Open daily 7am-11pm.

EMERGENCY AND COMMUNICATIONS

Emergency: Police, Theresienstr. 3 (☎110). **Fire** ☎112. **Ambulance** ☎192 22.

Rape Crisis: Frauennotruf, Ludwigspl. 7 (☎28 44 00; www.frauennotruf.info).

Pharmacy: Königstr. 31 (☎22 45 51). Open M-F 8:30am-6:30pm, Sa 9am-4pm.

Hospital: Städtisches Klinikum Nord, Flurstr. 17 (☎39 80). **Medical Assistance,** Keßlerpl. 5 (☎192 92).

Internet Access: Tele Point, Königstorpassage 20, in the underground level of the train station. When you descend, at the city mosaic head left towards the U-Bahn instead of right towards the Königstor exit. €2 per hr. Open M-Sa 9am-11pm, Su 10am-11pm.

Post Office: Bahnhofstr. 2, 90402 Nürnberg. Open M-F 8am-7pm, Sa 9am-2pm.

▐ ACCOMMODATIONS AND CAMPING

You don't have to trek outside the Altstadt walls to hang your hat in an inexpensive pension, but it's best to call ahead in summer.

▓ **Jugendgästehaus (HI)**, Burg 2 (☎230 93 60; fax 23 09 36 11). From the Hauptmarkt, head in the direction of the golden fountain on the far left and bear right on Burgstr. Scurry up to the castle and follow the sign to Burgenstr. (about 20min.). A 15th-century stable and grain store for the imperial castle, the hostel, with Romanesque arches, a dizzying view of the city, and friendly staff, still towers over town. June and July define the phrase "overrun with schoolchildren;" reserve at least 3 wk. in advance. **Internet** €2.40 for 30min. Reception 7am-1am. Curfew 1am. 4- to 6-bed dorms €19.95. ❷

Gasthof Schwänlein, Hintere Sterng. 11 (☎22 51 62; fax 241 90 08). From the station, take the underground passage to Königstr. and make an immediate left on Frauentormauerstr. Follow the town wall and bear right onto Hintere Sterng.; the hotel is 200m down on the left. Small but quiet rooms; aspire to one of the funky toilets. Breakfast included. Reservations by fax or mail only. Singles €26-28, with shower €34, with bathroom €36; doubles €42-43/€46-49/€52-58; triples €67. ❸

Hotel Garni Probst, Luitpoldstr. 9 (☎20 34 33; fax 205 93 36). From the station, follow the underground passage to Königstor past Burger King; turn left on Luitpoldstr. There are some sex shops nearby, but the location is central. A family establishment on the 3rd fl., with oddly shaped rooms. Generous breakfast included. Reception 24hr. Singles €21, with shower €35-40, with bath €41-51; doubles €43, with bath €57-67. ❸

Jugend-Hotel Nürnberg, Rathsbergstr. 300 (☎521 60 92; fax 521 69 54). From the station, take U2 (dir.: Flughafen) to "Ziegelstein," then bus #21 (dir.: Buchenbühl) to "Zum Felsenkeller." Rustic and cheerful with nice grounds, but far from the action. All dorm rooms with bath. Breakfast and sheets included. Reception 8am-10pm. Call ahead if arriving after 5pm. Dorms €19; singles €26.50-29; doubles €42-50. ❶

Pension "Vater Jahn," Jahnstr. 13 (☎44 45 07; fax 431 52 36). From the train station turn left onto Frauentorgraben, then left on Tafelfeldstr. through the underpass. Turn right on Bogenstr. and right again onto Jahnstr. (10min.). Gleaming rooms, some with TV. Breakfast included. Singles €23, with bath €43; doubles €40, with shower €55. Triples available on demand. ❸

Pension Hannweber, Peter-Henlein-Str. 12-14 (☎41 37 70; fax 41 37 75). Same directions as Vater Jahn, except stay on Tafelfeldstr. for one more block, then turn right onto Peter-Henlein. Pension is on left after 4 blocks. Pleasant and clean. Breakfast included. Singles €20-49; doubles €30-65. ❸

Campingpark Nürnberg, Hans-Kalb-Str. 56 (☎981 27 17; www.knaus-campingplatznbg.de), in *Volkspark Dutzendteich*. S2 (dir.: Feucht/Altdorf) to "Frankenstadion." Tent rental available. Reception 8am-1pm and 3-10pm. Open year-round. €5 per person, €3-5 per tent, €8 per site. Electricity and shower included. ❶

▐ FOOD

Nürnberg is famous for its *Rostbratwurst* (small, delectable grilled pork sausage), boiled *Sauere Zipfel* (sausage cooked in sauerkraut), and *Lebkuchen*, a candied gingerbread, traditionally devoured at Christmas. **Edeka**, Hauptmarkt 12 near the Frauenkirche, has cheap groceries. (Open M-F 8:30am-7pm, Sa 8am-3pm.)

Bratwursthäusle, Rathauspl. 1 (☎22 76 95), next to the Sebalduskirche. The most renowned bratwurst joint in Nürnberg serves 6 *Rostbratwürste* for €5.50; other Bavarian specialties €2-6. Beer €3. Open M-Sa 10am-10:30pm (kitchen until 9:30pm). ❷

Enchilada, Obstmarkt 10 (☎244 84 98; www.enchilada.de), behind the Frauenkirche. A popular Mexican restaurant and bar with a variety of vegetarian options and huge entrees for €7-15. Vast selection of cocktails €7-9. Open daily 11am-1am. ❹

Sushi Glas, Kornmarkt 5-7 (☎205 99 01), next to the National Museum. Delicious Japanese specialties and a chic yuppie crowd. If in doubt, order the *Shoshinsha*, a 3-course meal "for beginners" including miso soup, shish kebabs, and 14 sushi rolls (€19). For dessert, the green tea ice cream is superb (€5.20). Standard sushi rolls €5-9. Takeout available. Open M-W noon-11pm, Th-Sa noon-midnight, Su 6-11pm. ❹

THE LOCAL STORY

THE STRANGE CASE OF KASPAR HAUSER

On May 26, 1828, a young man stumbled through the streets of Nürnberg. Dazzled by the sunlight and unable to walk properly, he collapsed into the arms of a passing shoemaker. The stunned boy in peasant clothes was unable to speak, save for one sentence he kept repeating: "Ein Reiter will ich werden, wie mein Vater einer war" (I wish to be a cavalier, as my father was). He would eat only bread and water, and when handed a piece of paper and a quill, wrote the name "Kaspar Hauser." An unsigned letter in his possession requested that he be trained in the service of the king, but failed to explain his condition or origin.

The British Lord Stanhope moved to Germany and made himself Kaspar's protector, taking him from Nürnberg to nearby Ansbach. As Kaspar was taught to speak, it emerged that he had lived from the age of four in a windowless room, with nothing but a small toy horse to play with. His food was placed in the cell when he slept, and he sometimes awoke from an opium sleep to find that his hair and nails has been cut. His only distinct memory was that a man had visited him and taught him to write his name and speak the one sentence he knew.

Though a schoolteacher took Kaspar into his tutelage, the trauma the boy had undergone

Zum Gulden Stern, Zirkelschmiedg. 26 (☎205 92 88; www.bratwurstkueche.de), in the southwestern part of the Altstadt. The oldest bratwurst kitchen in the world roasts sausages over an open fire. 6 *Bratwürste* with sauerkraut served on a metal plate €5.90. Open daily 11am-10pm. ❸

Wies'n Biergarten, Johann Sörgel Weg (☎240 66 88), in the Wöhrder Wiesen. Take U to "Wöhrder Wiesen." This *Biergarten*, with its multicolored umbrellas, is always full of students. On sunny days there is always soccer on the Wöhrder Wiesen, a gigantic grass field. *Maß* €5.40. 6 *Bratwürste* €5.10. Open May-Sept. daily 10am-10pm. ❷

Strandcafe Wanner, Bayernstr. 150 (☎40 22 50; www.strandcafe-wanner.de). S2 to "Dutzendteich." This unique "beach" cafe on the Dutzendteich lake is a combination Asian restaurant, Italian pizzeria, and Bavarian *Biergarten*. The colorful Southeast Asian decor ties it all together. Choose from big satin cushions, straw furniture, or the serviced terrace upstairs. *Maß* €5.70, pizzas €5.50-8, Asian specialties €3-6. Rent a bicycle rickshaw for €5 per hr. to explore the surroundings. Open daily 10am-11pm. ❷

Cafe Kiosk, Bleichstr. 5, (☎26 90 30) just inside the Rosenau. Chill out with families and 20-somethings at this mellow cafe in the pleasant Rosenau park. Perfect for a sunny afternoon away from the commercial and touristed parts of the Altstadt. Entrees €6-7.50. Drinks €2-3. Open daily May-Sept. 10am-10pm. ❸

Cleopatra, Vordere Sterng. 30 (☎200 99 98), offers Egyptian specialties such as the mixed appetizer platter with hummus, veggies, falafel, and pita bread (€6). Lots of vegetarian options €7-9. Hookah €3.50. Belly dancing show F-Sa from 9pm. Take care on the street outside after dark. Open daily 11:30am-2:30pm and 5:30-11:30pm. ❸

🅖 SIGHTS

After WWII, Nürnberg rose like a phoenix from the ashes of Allied bombing. Most churches display empty pedestals where statues were lost to the bombing. From the station, the closest part of the Altstadt is a walled-in area filled with faux-medieval shops; this is the **Handwerkerhof,** a tourist trap disguised as a history lesson. The real sights lie farther up **Königstraße,** in the northwest corner of the Altstadt.

KAISERBURG. Atop the hill, this symbolic structure offers the best vantage point to see the city. The castle, originally erected in the 11th century, was never a *Residenz:* Nürnberg was a free city, ruled by no particular family. Rather, the Kaiserburg, which Holy Roman Emperor **Friedrich Barbarossa** expanded significantly, is known as a *Pfalz* ("palatinate"), a hotel for the Emperor's frequent visits to the city. The original castle was almost completely destroyed in the 14th century, during a war with the **Hohenzollern** family, whose own *Burg* was next door. The aristocratic family left for Brandenburg and ended up ruling Prussia, and the Kaiserburg was rebuilt in 15th- and 16th-century Gothic style. The spartan chambers (furniture, when needed, was borrowed from the homes of the Nürnberg elite) housed every Holy Roman Emperor after Konrad III—it was law that every German *Kaiser* spend at least his first day in office in Nürnberg, a testament to its prominence in the Empire. Massive stone walls (13m tall and 7m thick) surround the castle and the manicured gardens, and a 40m deep well provided water in case of a siege. The castle can only be visited by tour; the tourist office offers one in English. (☎ *22 57 26. Burg open daily Apr.-Sept. 9am-6pm; Oct.-Mar. 10am-4pm. Garden open daily in summer, 8am-8pm. Obligatory German tours every 30min.; last tour Apr.-Sept. 4:30pm; Oct.-Mar. 3:30pm. Admission to both* Burg *and the museum inside €6, students €5.)*

AROUND THE ALTSTADT AND CASTLE

LORENZKIRCHE. Completely destroyed in WWII, the beautiful 13th-century Gothic church has been restored magnificently. Of particular interest is the 20m high **tabernacle,** built by Adam Kraft, whose self-portrait is one of the supports at the base of this stone masterpiece. Veit Stoß's 1517 wooden carving *Engelsgruß* (Annunciation) hangs in front of the altar. *(On Lorenzpl.* ☎ *20 92 87. Open M-Sa 9am-5pm, Su noon-4pm. Free German language tours meet at the entrance in summer M-Sa 11am and 2pm, Su 2pm; in winter M-F 2pm; call ahead for English tours. Suggested donation €1.)*

HAUPTMARKTPLATZ. In 1349, during the great plague, this square, the former Jewish quarter, was witness to a pogrom. In 1352, Karl IV commissioned the small Catholic **Frauenkirche,** whose ornate facade survived WWII, to occupy the place of the destroyed synagogue. Crowds gather at noon to gape at the **Männleinlaufen,** the mechanical clock on the facade, where the seven electors pay homage to the seated Karl IV. The golden **Schöner Brunnen** (Beautiful Fountain) in the corner of the *Platz* resembles a Gothic steeple, composed of 40 carved figures, with Moses and the prophets up top. Hidden within the gate around the fountain is a golden "ring of the journey" (how it got there is a mystery); spinning it supposedly brings good luck. (☎ *20 65 60. Church open M-F 9am-6pm, Sa 10am-6pm, Su 12:30-6pm.)*

SEBALDUSKIRCHE. Across from the Rathaus, Nürnberg's late-Gothic oldest parish church (constructed 1230-1379) became home to a Lutheran congregation in 1525. Once a year, on the feast day of St. Sebaldus,

prevented him from making cognitive progress beyond that of a three year old. He assumed that all objects had human properties: if an apple fell from a tree, Kaspar thought that it was because it had tired of hanging on.

Kaspar's sufferings did not end with his mysterious liberation. He was soon a Europe-wide celebrity, a one-man freak show who never managed to fit in with society. It was not long before people realized that Kaspar bore an uncanny resemblance to the Grand Duke of Baden, who was about to die heirless. Rumors sprang up that Kaspar was his illegitimate son, secreted away to remove him from succession. Soon an attempt was made on the life of the young *idiot savant.* It failed, but a second attack did not; on December 14, 1833, Kaspar Hauser was mortally wounded, and died just three days later. According to rumor, the Duchess of Baden was stricken with sorrow at this news.

In the 1990s, DNA tests using blood from his clothes concluded that Kaspar had no relation to the aristocratic family, but many remain unconvinced, and the mystery surrounding his pitiful existence remains unsolved. His story is still a classic case study in human behavior, and has inspired both a poem by Paul Verlaine and a critically acclaimed movie directed by Werner Herzog.

the saint's remains are taken from their resting spot in the bronze tomb in front of the altar for a parade around town. Famous composer **Johann Pachelbel** (1651-1703), known for his *Canon in D*, was the principal organist here. (☎214 25 00. *Open daily June-Sept. 9:30am-8pm; Mar.-May and Oct.-Dec. 9:30am-6pm; Jan.-Feb. 9:30am-4pm.*)

RATHAUS. Begun in 1340, the Rathaus is now mostly early Baroque with a few Renaissance touches showing through. It held the largest council chamber in central Europe before its destruction by fire in 1945. Beneath the oldest part of the building lurk spooky **Lochgefängnisse** (dungeons) and the medieval torture instruments kept there. (☎231 26 90. *Open Tu-Su 10am-4:30pm. Obligatory tours every 30min.; free English translation brochure available. €2, students €1.*)

FELSENGÄNGE. Constructed following a 1380 decree requiring all restaurants serving beer to brew and store it on location, this 25km web of tunnels and cellars below the Altstadt remains cool year-round. Converted to bomb shelters and sealed off as a caution against gas bombs during WWII, the once well-ventilated tunnels are now damp, deteriorating, and chilly. (*Bergstr. 19, in the Altstadthof.* ☎22 70 66. *1hr. tours descend daily from the statue in Albrecht-Dürer-Pl. at 11am, 1, 3, and 5pm. Tours in German; English translation available. €4, students €3, children under 10 free.*)

RUINS OF THE THIRD REICH

REICHSPARTEITAGSGELÄNDE. The site of the Nazi Party Congress rallies of 1933 to 1938, which drew more than a half million people each year, now hosts a park, a storage area, and the **Nürnberg Symphony Orchestra.** The planned Nazi compound, which Hitler proudly declared "the largest building site in the world," was to become much larger than the city of Nürnberg. The 2km long **Große Straße,** leading across the **Volkspark,** marching grounds for Nazi troops, was also a symbolic link between Hitler and the German *Kaisers,* providing a view of Nazi headquarters at one end and the Kaiserburg at the other. The **Zeppelinwiese,** a field across the Großer Dutzendteich lake from the **Kongresshalle,** contains the **Tribüne,** the massive marble platform from which Hitler addressed more than 100,000 enthralled spectators. Poles spaced intermittently along the desolate field once held enormous banners, made infamous by Leni Riefenstahl's film **Triumph des Willens** ("Triumph of the Will;" p. 70), one of the most striking depictions of the fascist aesthetic.

The Kongresshalle serves an a prime example of Nazi architecture—massive and harsh, mixing Modernist straight lines with Neoclassical pretension, constructed with the intent to make the individual feel small and powerless. The optical illusion created by the outer archways makes people standing under them look much smaller than they actually are. Located at the north end of the Volkspark, this massive structure, intended to host the headquarters of the Party, was begun in 1935, but stalled by the onset of war in 1938. The overwhelming emotional power of Nazi events—injecting strains of Wagnerian theater and Catholic ritual into fascist grandiosity—can be seen in the **Dokumentationszentrum,** located in the North wing of the Kongresshalle. The extensive exhibits, entitled *Faszination und Gewalt* (Fascination and Violence), cover the rise of the *Third Reich,* Nürnberg's role in the growth of Nazism, and the war crimes trials of 1946. Today, the wide steps of the Tribüne are used by skateboarders, who pull their most daring stunts off the podium. The Zeppelin field hosts rock concerts, and the Kongresshalle houses practice halls for the Nürnberg Symphony Orchestra. (*Take S2 (dir.: Feucht/Altdorf) to "Dutzendteich," then take the middle of 3 exits, head down the stairs, and turn left. Walk past the lake on your left, and turn left immediately to reach the museum. Follow the paved path from the museum to reach other sections of the complex.* ☎231 56 66; www.museen.nuernberg.de. *Open M-F 9am-6pm, Sa-Su 10am-6pm. Last admission 5pm. €5, students €2.50. Admission includes audioguides in several languages.*)

JUSTIZGEBÄUDE. On the other side of town, Nazi leaders faced Allied judges during the infamous **Nuremberg war crimes trials,** held in room 600 of the *Justizgebäude.* Soon after the trials, in October 1946, 10 men were hanged for their crimes against humanity. The building is still a courthouse, but on weekends visitors can watch a short film in the courtroom where the trails were held. *(Fürtherstr. 110. Take U1 (dir.: Stadthalle) to "Bärenschanze" and continue on Fürtherstr., walking away from the Altstadt. ☎ 231 54 21. Bilingual tours Sa-Su at 1, 2, 3, and 4pm. €2, students and children €1.)*

🏛 MUSEUMS

GERMANISCHES NATIONALMUSEUM. This gleaming glass building chronicles Germanic art and culture from pre-history to the present, with emphasis on late medieval art, especially Dürer, from the city's golden age. Highlights include Rembrandt's etchings and Cranach's paintings, such as a portrait of Martin Luther. Although the main galleries are closed for restoration until 2008, the exhibit "Faszination Meisterwerk" is on display until late 2005. Prehistory to early history is under renovation until June 2005. Outside the museum's main entrance, the **Straße der Menschenrechte** (Avenue of Human Rights) has 30 white pillars engraved in 50 languages with the text of the United Nations **Universal Declaration of Human Rights** of the 10th of December, 1948. *(Kartäuserg. 1. From the station, take the tunnel to the Königstr. exit. Turn left onto Frauentormauer and right on Kartäuserg. ☎ 133 10. English tours every other Su at 2pm. Open Tu-Su 10am-6pm, W until 9pm. Some sections of the museum close at 5pm. Audioguide €1.50. €5, students and seniors €4. Free W from 6-9pm.)*

JÜDISCHES MUSEUM FRANKEN. Housed in nearby Fürth, once the largest urban Jewish community in southern Germany, this museum chronicles the history and culture of Jews in Franconia, displaying everything from medieval religious manuscripts to everyday artifacts. *(Königstr. 89, Fürth. Take U1 (dir.: Stadthalle) to "Rathaus." ☎ 77 05 77. Open M, W-F, Su 10am-5pm, Tu 10am-8pm. €3, students and seniors €1.50.)*

ALBRECHT-DÜRER-HAUS. In his residence in Nürnberg from 1509 to 1528, Albrect Dürer ran a successful production industry, sending prints across Europe with the help of his wife Agnes. Dürer is also hailed as the first modern artist, due to his interest in self-portrait and his desire to paint naturalistically. This passion would lead to his death of malaria in a Dutch swamp, while on his way to sketch a beached whale. Their life is recreated vividly here, despite the lack of Dürer paintings (most are in Vienna, Munich, and Berlin). Guides dressed as Agnes Dürer lead tours; the audioguide also features her wit. *(Albrecht-Dürer-Str. 39. Uphill from the Sebalduskirche. ☎ 231 25 68. Open Mar.-Oct. Tu-Su 10am-5pm, Th until 8pm; July-Sept. also M 10am-5pm; Nov.-Feb. Tu-F 1-5pm, Sa-Su 10am-5pm. English tours Sa at 2pm; German tours Th at 6 or 6:30pm, Sa 3pm, and Su 11am. €2. Audioguides in several languages also available. Haus €5, students €2.50. Ticket also valid for Stadtmuseum Fembohaus.)*

STADTMUSEUM FEMBOHAUS. Through lively audio plays and other exhibits, Fembohaus introduces you to the ups and downs of Nürnberg's long past and to the building's inhabitants, who were once the most important cartographers in Europe. *(Burgstr. 15. Uphill from the Rathaus. ☎ 231 25 95. Open Tu-Su 10am-5pm, Th until 8pm. €4, reduced €2. Ticket also valid for the Dürerhaus. Not included in the admission price is a multivisual documentary about the city, €4/€2.)*

NICOLAUS-COPERNICUS-PLANETARIUM. Sit back and watch the nighttime sky projected on a concrete dome above you. *(Am Plärrer 41. U-Bahn to "Plärrer." ☎ 929 65 53; www.planetarium-nuernberg.de. Shows W-Th 4 and 7:30pm, 1st and 3rd weekends of the month Sa-Su 2 and 4pm. During school holidays also Tu 2 and 4pm. Children's shows Th 4pm, 1st weekend of every month Sa-Su 2pm. €4.50, students €3, families €11.)*

🎵 🎭 ENTERTAINMENT AND NIGHTLIFE

Whatever your boat is when it comes to nightlife, Nürnberg can float it. The Altstadt is packed with bars and clubs, the best of which can be found just down the hill from the youth hostel and the Kaiserburg. The **Staatstheater Nürnberg** opera house and theater offer last minute tickets to concerts and performances for as little as €8. (Richard-Wagner-Pl. 2-10. ☎34 42 76. 25% reduction for students, 40% 1hr. before performance, 50% with **Nürnberg Card;** p. 540. Box office open M-F 9am-6pm, Sa 9am-1pm.) Every July, Nürnberg holds the **Bardenfest** and **Klassik Open** music festivals, which combine all genres for an event-filled few weekends. Pick up the monthly *Plärrer* (€2) for musical and cultural events and the addresses of bars, discos, and cafes. The €1 *Monatsmagazin*, available at the tourist office, lists concerts, stage productions, and special exhibitions in Nürnberg. Bars and discos also hand out the free guide *Doppelpunkt* (www.doppelpunkt.de).

Cine Città, Gewerbemuseumspl. 3, is near the river on the eastern side of the Altstadt. This shrine to fun packs in 16 bars and cafes, a spectrum of affordable restaurants, 17 German-language cinemas, the biggest IMAX theater in Europe, and a club. (U-Bahn to "Wöhrder Wiese." ☎20 66 60; www.cinecitta.de. Standard movie/IMAX tickets €8 on weekends, €6.70 on weekdays. Open M-Th and Su until 3am, F-Sa until 4am.) **Roxy,** Julius-Loßman-Str. 116, shows mostly recent American releases. (☎480 10 64 for program announcements in English.)

KOMPLEXX, Kohlenhofstr. 1a (☎234 94 12), south of the Altstadt. From the train station, follow Frauentorgraben west, turn left onto Steinbühlerstr., right onto Kohlenhofstr., and left at the light into the parking lot. Head to the left, back toward the abandoned-looking buildings, and then walk right for about 50 yd. This center of vice houses a pool hall, bars and cafes (some with go-go dancing after midnight), and 2 discos (cover €5) with well-known DJs. Leave your Swiss Army knife at home—there are metal detectors at the door. Open W 9:30pm-4am, F-Sa 9:30pm-5am.

Cafe Ruhestörung, Tetzelg. 21 (☎22 19 21). From the Rathaus, head right on Theresienstr., then left on Tetzelg. Mellow and dimly-lit, this place draws a chic older crowd that mixes harmoniously with university students. Outdoor seating. Serves breakfast, sandwiches, salads, and Mediterranean specialties (€2-9). Open M-W 7:30am-1am, Th-F 7:30am-2am, Sa 9am-2am, Su 9am-1am. Kitchen open until 10pm.

Cafe Treibhaus, Karl-Grillenberger-Str. 28 (☎22 30 41), in the western part of the Altstadt, south of Westtor. Metal tables and dim lighting draw a well-heeled, older crowd. Serves snacks (€2-6), salads and pasta (€5-7), and breakfast (€3-9). Their large *Milchkaffee* (€3) raises foam to new heights. Open M-W 8am-1am, Th-F 8am-2am, Sa 9am-2am, Su 9:30am-1am. Kitchen open until 10:30pm.

Casablanca, Brosamerstr. 12, (☎45 48 24) near Kopernikuspl. Take U to Aufseßpl. and exit in the Kopernikuspl. direction. Brosamerstr. is on the right. A fun creperie in the front (☎44 39 47) combines with a cool bar and an art cinema to attract a great crowd at all hours. Get wine for €2-3 to drink during the movie (tickets €6, students €5.50). Creperie open Tu-Sa 7pm-1am, Su 6pm-midnight; bar open daily 7:30pm until late.

Frizz!, Weißgerberg. 37 (☎205 99 85; www.kneipenerlebnis.com), entrance on Maxpl. Sweat to the oldies, 80s, rock and pop. Serves cheap cocktails and a few varieties of *Lammsbräu* wheat beers (€5). M is singles' night; cover €2 for men, free for women. Th is "flirt night" using cell phones; cover €3. Open M and Th 8pm-2am, F-Sa 8pm-4am.

Sachs & Söhne, Hans-Sachs-G. 10 (☎24 13 14). Popular cafe and restaurant, serving Italian specialties (€4-7) in a flower-filled setting. Also open during the day, when sunbathers crowd the chairs on the *Platz* side. Open daily 9am-1am.

Cartoon, An der Sparkasse 6 (☎22 71 70), is a popular gay bar near Lorenzpl. Traditional *Kneipe* interior with a bright, modern twist and a hip 20-something crowd. Beer €3 for 0.4L. Open M-Sa 11am-1am, Su 2pm-1am. The new bar downstairs, **CO2,** serves drinks in a pink and leopard-print room. Open F-Sa 8pm-3am.

Jazz Studio, Panierspl. 27-29, (☎36 42 97; www.jazzstudio.de) on the Burg. Live jazz performances 3-4 evenings per wk.; pick up their brochure in the tourist office for days and times. Tickets €3-18, 20% student discount. No performances late July-Aug.

Mach 1, Kaiserstr. 1-9 (☎20 30 30), in the center of the Altstadt near Fleischbrücke. Th attracts the mellow "Best of the 70s to 90s" crowd; F funk and hip-hop; Sa house. Come here for the "affluent and good-looking" population, not the overpriced drinks (€6 for 0.3L of beer; €5 glass of water). First F in the month is 30+ night. Open Tu from 7pm, Th-F 10pm-4am (cover €4), Sa 10pm-5am (cover €5-10).

BAYREUTH ☎0921

Broad streets, resplendent 18th-century buildings and a large English-style park give Bayreuth an unexpectedly cosmopolitan flair. In the 18th century, the cultivated and ambitious **Margravine Wilhelmine** shaped Bayreuth according to her ideal of enlightened absolutism. In the 19th, **Richard Wagner,** great *Meister* of opera, made it the center of his musical cult. The wealth brought to the city by the legendary *Festspiele* (yearly operatic delirium from July 25 to August 28) is evident in the array of international restaurants and carefully-groomed neighborhoods. WWII obliterated the dark traces of Bayreuth's Nazi interlude, yet spared most of its Italianate architecture. Numerous museums and the still-grandiose traces of the Margravine's reign, both in the city and in the surrounding area.

▐ ▟ TRANSPORTATION AND PRACTICAL INFORMATION

The center of Bayreuth (pronounced "buy-royt," *not* "bay-ruth") is south of the train station, while the **Festspielhaus,** epicenter of all things Wagnerian, is just to the north. To get to the Altstadt, go left out of the train station and follow Bahnhofstr. until it becomes Luitpoldpl., then ends at Kanalstr. One more block in the same direction will place you in the pedestrian zone, stretching from the Markt to Richard-Wagner-Str. The latter will lead you to the Hofgarten, the park flanked by most of the city's museums. South of the *Altstadt* is the university.

Trains: Train station is just north of the Altstadt. To: **Bamberg** (1½hr., 1 per hr., €14.20); **Nürnberg** (1hr., 1-2 per hr., €14.20); **Regensburg** (2½hr., 1 per hr., €15).

Tourist Office: Luitpoldpl. 9 (☎885 88; www.bayreuth-tourismus.de), 4 blocks to the left of the station in the "Reisebüro Bayreuth" building. Books rooms for free, and offers maps, a monthly calendar of events, and 2hr. city **walking tours.** Tours May-Oct. daily 10:30am; Nov.-Apr. Sa only (€4.50, students €2.50). The office sells tickets to Bayreuth entertainment (except the *Festspiele*). Open M-F 9am-6pm, Sa 9:30am-1pm; May-Oct. also Sa until 4pm and Su 10am-1pm. City maps and hotel lists are posted outside the door after hours.

Currency Exchange: Citibank, Maximilianstr. 46. Open M-Tu and Th 9am-1pm and 2-6pm, W and F 9am-1pm and 2-4pm.

Pharmacy: Hof Apotheke, Richard-Wagner-Str. 2 (☎652 10). Get medicine from the people who cured the Margravine's hemorrhoids. Open M-F 8am-4pm, Sa 8am-1pm.

Internet: Available all over town, but mostly at ridiculously steep prices. **Merkur Spielothek,** Maximilianstr. 80-82 (☎507 11 11), charges €3 per hr., if you can make it past the gambling rooms and to the 2nd fl. with your wallet intact. 18+. Open M-Th 7am-2am, F-Sa 7am-3am, Su 10am-2am.

Post Office: Bürgerreutherstr. 1, 95444 Bayreuth (☎78 03 40). To the left as you exit the train station. Open M-F 8am-6:30pm, Sa 8:30am-1pm.

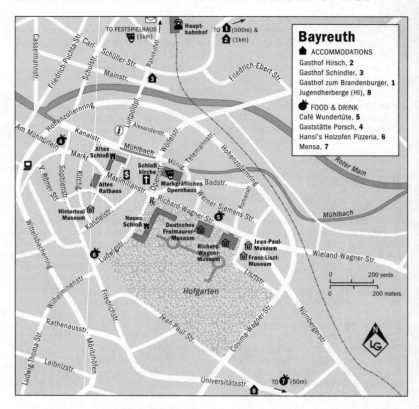

Bayreuth

🏠 ACCOMMODATIONS
Gasthof Hirsch, **2**
Gasthof Schindler, **3**
Gasthof zum Brandenburger, **1**
Jugendherberge (HI), **8**

🍴 FOOD & DRINK
Café Wundertüte, **5**
Gaststätte Porsch, **4**
Hansl's Holzofen Pizzeria, **6**
Mensa, **7**

🏠 ACCOMMODATIONS

If you visit during the **Festspiele,** expect to shell out major cash to stay in Bayreuth: *everybody* raises rates. Any other time, beds are cheap and readily available.

Jugendherberge (HI), Universitätsstr. 28 (☎ 76 43 80; fax 51 28 05). Bayreuth's hostel is outside the city center, past the Hofgarten near the university. Weekdays, take any bus from the station to the Marktpl., and then take bus #4 (dir.: Birken) or bus #6 (dir.: Campus) from the Marktpl. to "Mensa" (€1.50). Or, walk down Ludwigstr. from the city center, take a left onto Friedrichstr., then veer left onto Jean-Paul-Str., which merges with Universitätsstr. (20min.). The hostel is large, but friendly, with snug dorms and strictly observed check-in times. Breakfast and sheets included. Reception 7am-noon and 5-10pm. Check-in 11am-noon, 5-7pm, and 9:30-10pm. Lockout 9:30-11am. Curfew 10pm; ask at the desk for a key. Open Feb. to mid-Dec. €15. ❷

Gasthof Hirsch, St. Georgen 26 (☎ 267 14; fax 85 31 42). A 10min. walk from the station, on a corner building. Exit the back of the station, then turn left onto Brandenburger Str. Bear right when the street divides, and left on St. Georgen, a hilltop which used to house the Margrave's craftsmen. During rehearsal time, the *Gasthof* becomes a hangout for opera workers. Breakfast included. Singles €20-23; doubles €36-45. ❸

BAYERN

Gasthof zum Brandenburger, St. Georgen 9 (☎78 90 60; fax 78 90 62 40). Across from Gasthof Hirsch. Sunny rooms and *Biergarten* out back. Breakfast included. Singles €20-42; doubles €32-72; triples €47-94. ❸

Gasthof Schindler, Bahnhofstr. 9 (☎262 49). A block to the left of the station. Clean rooms and a basement restaurant. Breakfast included. Reception M-Sa 8am-10pm, Su 9am-2pm. Singles €21-26; doubles €44-52; triples €72. ❸

🔆 FOOD

There are plenty of options in Bayreuth, although not all are reasonably priced. **Plus,** Badstr. 10, has cheap groceries. (Open M-F 8:30am-7pm, Sa 8am-3pm.)

Gaststätte Porsch, Maximilianstr. 63 (☎646 49). Enormous portions of Franconian specialties. *Schnitzel* meals €6-9. Beer €1.70 for 0.5L. Open M-Sa from 7:30am. ❸

Hansl's Holzofen Pizzeria, Jean-Paul-Pl. 15 (☎543 44). A cheaper alternative to the local cuisine. Pizza €4-8, salads €3-6. Open daily 10am-10:30pm. ❷

Café Wundertüte, Richard-Wagner-Str. 33 (☎51 47 48). This friendly wood-paneled cafe has a cup of coffee and a slice of raspberry *Torte* with your name on it. Many enticing dishes (€4-7). Open M-Sa 8am-6pm. Hot food 11am-5pm. ❷

Mensa, on the university campus. Take bus #4 (€1.50) from the Marktpl. to "Mensa," then walk past the buildings straight ahead. The *Mensa* is to the right up the steps. Trade the cashier your student ID and €4 for a card, then put money on the card at the *Automaten* in the hall. Buy food and get your €4, plus any balance left on the card, back from the cashier. Cheap meals, including pizzas, for €2-4. Hot entrees noon-2pm and 5-7pm. Coffee and cake 2-4pm for €1.50. Open Mar.-Apr. and Oct. daily 8am-6pm; May-July and Nov.-Feb. M-Th 8am-8:30pm, F 8am-2pm. ❶

👁 SIGHTS

MARKGRÄFLICHES OPERNHAUS. Commissioned in 1744 by the Margravine Wilhelmine, who saw her own operas performed here, this pristine Baroque opera house had the largest stage of any theater in Germany until the *Festspielhaus* was built, and was the reason for Wagner's initial interest in Bayreuth. Note that the ceiling fresco is painted in the wrong direction—a mishap that would not have happened in Paris or London. 40 to 50 shows still take place here each year, but on off-days, the opera house offers a bombastic 25min. multimedia tour featuring the disembodied voice of the Margravine—a very Bayreuth experience. *(Opernstr. 14. ☎759 69 22. Open Apr.-Sept. 9:15am-6pm; Oct.-Mar. 10am-4pm. Shows every 45min. In German (English handout available.) €5, students €4. Combination ticket with Neues Schloß: €7/€6.)*

RICHARD-WAGNER-MUSEUM. *Haus Wahnfried* ("Delusional Peace") was once Wagner's custom-built home. Obliterated in WWII, it now displays an exhaustive documentation of the composer's career. His controversial relationships with Ludwig II, father-in-law Franz Liszt and Nietzsche are all analyzed. Also on display are amusing photos of Wagner's children looking miserable in costumes from his operas. Loud Wagner music thunders throughout the exhibition, which winds chaotically up and down stairs. Exhibits are in German, but luckily there is an English guide booklet (€3). Behind the house are the graves of Wagner, his wife Cosima, and two of their dogs. *(Richard-Wagner-Str. 48. ☎757 28 16. Open Apr.-Oct. M, W, and F-Su 9am-5pm, Tu and Th 9am-8pm; Nov.-Mar. daily 10am-5pm. Music in the drawing room daily at 10am, noon, and 2pm; videos shown at 11am and 3pm. €4.50, students €2.)*

NEUES SCHLOß. When the old palace burned down, **Margravine Wilhelmine,** sister of Frederick the Great, got the chance to put her artistic talents to use in designing a new one. Considered one of Europe's most brilliant and cultured women, Wilhelmine was initially expected to wed the British heir, but in the end her parents forced her to marry the Margrave of Bayreuth. With Hohenzollern flair, the writer, composer, actress and artist attempted to create an "earthly paradise" in what must have seemed to her a provincial cow town. The portrait of Voltaire in her personal chamber commemorates one of the Margravine's most honored acquaintances. The walnut-panelled "palm room" was used by the Margrave for the meetings of the Masonic lodge he founded; Bayreuth was one of the biggest German centers of Freemasonry until the Nazis disbanded the order in 1933. On the ground floor, view Bayreuth porcelain, including solid beer jugs, and a historical exhibit. (☎ 759 69 21. *Open Apr.-Sept. M-W and F-Sa 9am-6pm; Oct.-Mar. daily 10am-4pm. €4, students €3.)*

FESTSPIELHAUS. Wagner's 1872 construction is famed for its acoustics and classical aesthetic. Nonetheless, Wagnerophile Ludwig II could only offer modest funds, resulting in a spartan structure—Wagner fans must endure rigid seats and limited leg room. *(Festspielhügel 2-3. From the train station, go right and up at the end of Siegfried-Wagner-Allee.* ☎ 787 80. *Tours at 10, 10:45am, 2:15, and 3pm. Closed during summer and in Nov. Closed Mon. Call ahead for specifics. €2.50, students, children, and seniors €2.)*

HISTORICAL MUSEUM. Documents the history of the city, including its Enlightenment heyday, and its stint as Hitler's favorite city. Wagner's descendants were early adherents of Nazism, and Hitler had plans for lavish construction in Bayreuth, including a temple to himself over the *Festspielhaus.* Jewish life in Bayreuth, both before and during the Nazi persecution, is documented, in an exhibit developed collaboratively with local schools. *(Kirchpl. 6.* ☎ 764 01 11. *Open July-Aug. daily 10am-5pm; Sept.-June closed M. €1.50, students, children, and seniors €0.50.)*

🎵 **THE WAGNER FESTSPIELE**

For Wagnerians, a visit to Bayreuth is a pilgrimage. Since 1876, every summer from July 25 to August 28, thousands have poured in for the **Bayreuth Festspiele,** held in the **Festspielhaus** that Wagner built for his "music of the future." In 2005, the four Ring Cycle operas will not be performed, but the rest of his repertoire will. Tickets (€12-193, obstructed view €11, no view €6) go on sale during mid-October and sell out immediately. Wagnerophiles write to Bayreuther Festspiele, Postfach 100262, 95402 Bayreuth, well before September and hope for the best.

BAMBERG   ☎ 0951

Once known as the Rome of the north, windy Bamberg really does straddle seven hills, covering the islands at the confluence of the Main-Donau canal and the two arms of the Regnitz river. Bamberg has been powerful and pious since the year 1007, when **Heinrich II** (with his **Queen Kunigunde**) made it a diocese, and the center of the Holy Roman Empire, in an effort to help push Christianity eastward. Crowned with a colossal cathedral and an imperial palace, Bamberg, which escaped WWII unscathed, was once home to luminaries such as Hegel and **E.T.A. Hoffmann** (Romantic author of the story that inspired Tchaikovsky's "Nutcracker" ballet), and today, is a thriving university town. Despite its location in wine-loving Franconia, this UNESCO World Heritage site has more breweries than Munich.

▛ TRANSPORTATION

Trains: The main station is on Ludwigstr. The **Reisezentrum** inside is open M-F 6:10am-7pm, Sa 6:10am-5pm, Su 8am-7pm. Trains run to: **Frankfurt** (3hr., 1 per hr., €29-40); **Munich** (2½-4hr., 1-2 per hr., €15-44); **Nürnberg** (1hr., 3 per hr., €9.40); **Würzburg** (1hr., 1 per hr., €14.20).

Public Transportation: An excellent transportation network centers on the **ZOB** on Promenadestr. off Schönleinspl. To get there, walk down Luitpoldstr. from the train station and take the 2nd right after the bridge, or get on any bus with ZOB on the front. Single ride within the inner zone €1; 4-ride ticket €3. The 2-day *Touristenticket* (€6) offers unlimited travel within the inner zones. Family day cards €8.

Taxis: ☎ 194 10, 150 15, or 345 45.

Bike Rental: Fahrradhaus Griesmann, Kleberstr. 25 (☎ 229 67). From the station, walk straight on Luitpoldstr., right on Heinrichsdamm after the bridge, left at the next bridge, and take the first right on Kleberstr. €5-8 per day. Open M-F 9am-12:30pm and 2-6pm, Sa 9am-1pm.

▛ ORIENTATION

The heart of Bamberg lies on an island between the **Main-Danube** canal and the **Regnitz River** (the Regen and Pegnitz Rivers combined). The winding streets of the Altstadt snake through the island (known as the *Sand*) and across the Regnitz away from the train station. To get to town from the station, walk down Luitpoldstr., cross the canal, and walk straight on Willy-Lessing-Str. until it empties into Schönleinspl. Turn right onto Lange Str. to reach the island section of the pedestrian zone; hang a left off Lange Str. up Obere Brückestr., through the archway of the Rathaus and across the Regnitz to reach the far section of the Altstadt (25-30min.). Or take any bus in front of the station to "ZOB" for a quick ride. The **Bamberg Card,** available at the tourist office or the Deutsche Bahn Service point, is valid for 48hr., and gives free public transportation, a tour of Bamberg, and museum admission (€7.50, additional people €7 each).

▛ PRACTICAL INFORMATION

Tourist Office: Geyerswörthstr. 3 (☎ 297 62 00; www.bamberg.info), on an island in the Regnitz. Follow the directions to Lange Str., above, then follow signs over the footbridge and around the building. The staff books rooms for free and gives out good maps and the free pamphlet *Bamberger*, which lists performances and exhibits. Open May.-Oct. and Dec. M-F 9:30am-6pm, Sa 9:30am-2:30pm, Su 9:30am-2:30pm; Nov. and Jan.-Apr. closed Su. After-hours, a machine outside dispenses a map and hotel list (€1).

Tours: 2hr. city tours in German meet in front of the tourist office Apr.-Oct. M-Sa 10:30am and 2pm, Su 11am; Nov.-Mar. M-Sa 2pm, Su 11am (€5, students €3.50, children under 10 free). Horse-drawn carriage tours of the Altstadt are offered Easter-Oct. Th-Su 1-6pm. Inquire at the tourist office (€8, ages 6-18 €5). Also ask about the 5hr. canoe tour (€25/€15), min. 3 full-price participants.

Currency Exchange: Citibank, Hainstr. 2 (24hr. info ☎ 0180 332 21 11), on Schönleinspl. Open M-W 8:30am-6:30pm, Th-F 9am-6:30pm.

Laundromat: SB Waschsalon (☎ 384 95), on the 2nd fl. of the Atrium mall across from the station. Wash €4. Dry €0.50 per 10min. Open daily 7am-10pm.

BAYERN

Bamberg

♥ **FOOD & DRINK**
Brauerei Greifenklau, **11**
Culinar, **10**
Klein aber Fein, **5**
Mensa, **4**
Spezial-Keller, **12**
★ **NIGHTLIFE**
Blues Bar, **7**
Cafe Abseits, **3**
Calimeros, **8**
Live Club/Haas Sale, **6**

♠♠ **ACCOMMODATIONS**
Bamberger Weissbierhaus, **2**
Campingplatz Insel, **14**
Fässla, **1**
Hotel Hospiz, **9**
Jugendherberge
Wolfsschlucht, **13**

Emergency: ☎ 110. **Police,** Schranne 2 (☎ 912 92 40). **Fire** and **Ambulance** ☎ 112. **Medical Assistance** ☎ 192 22. **Rape Crisis Line** ☎ 582 80.

Pharmacy: Martin Apotheke, Grüner Markt 21 (☎ 221 22). Open M-W and F 8:30am-6pm, Th 8:30am-7pm, Sa 9am-2pm.

Hospital: Klinikum Bamberg, Burger Str. 80 (☎ 50 30). Bus #18 to "Klinikum."

Internet: Tec Cafe, Frauenstr. 5-7 (☎ 20 14 94), M-Th 11am-10pm, F-Sa 11am-midnight, Su 2-10pm. €4.10 per hr. (min. €1). M-F half price noon-2pm.

Post Office: Ludwigstr. 25, 96052 Bamberg, across from the train station. Open M-F 7:30am-6pm, Sa 8am-12:30pm.

⌐ ACCOMMODATIONS AND CAMPING

Cheaper lodgings are near **Luitpoldstraße,** which runs in front of the train station.

Jugendherberge Wolfsschlucht (HI), Oberer Leinritt 70 (☎ 560 02; jh-bamberg@stadt-bamberg.de). Bus #18 (dir.: Burg) from the ZOB to "Rodelbahn" (M-F every 20min., Sa-Su every hr.; €1). Walk downhill and turn left onto Oberer Leinritt just before the river. Bus #18 stops running around 8pm; afterwards, you'll need to take a different bus and a taxi (free with bus ticket) back to the hostel. This former boathouse is far from the city center but has tidy rooms. Breakfast included. Reception 7am-1pm and 5-10pm. Curfew 10pm, but you can get a house key. Reservations strongly recommended in summer. Closed mid-Dec. to mid-Jan. 4- or 6-bed dorms €17.85-19.35; doubles €37. ❷

Bamberger Weissbierhaus, Obere Königstr. 38 (☎/fax 255 03), 10min. from the station. Walk straight from the station on Luitpoldstr. and turn left a block before the river. Spacious, clean rooms with balconies overlook a courtyard and *Biergarten* below. Delectable dinners from €7. Breakfast included. Reception 9am-11pm. Singles €22; doubles €39, with shower €44; triples with shower €57. ❸

Hotel Hospiz, Promenadestr. 3 (☎98 12 60; fax 981 26 66). Central location off Schönleinspl. Walk straight on Luitpoldstr. and double back and to your right when you get to Schönleinspl. Telephones in every room and a generous breakfast. Reception 7am-8pm. Check-out 11am. Phone, fax, or mail reservations. Singles €26, with bath €40; doubles with shower €40, with bath €50; triples €60/€70. ❸

Fässla, Obere Königstr. 19-21 (☎265 16 or 22 998; fax 20 19 89). 10min. from the station. From the train station, walk straight on Luitpoldstr. and turn right before the bridge. Above one of the most popular beer halls in town. Rooms with TVs, phones and full baths. Breakfast included. Singles €34; doubles €52; triples €67. ❹

Campingplatz Insel, Am Campingpl. 1 (☎563 20; campinginsel@web.de). Bus #18 (dir.: Burg) to "Campingpl." Prime riverside locale. Showers and toilets. Wash €2.50. Dry €3. €3.90 per adult, €2.80 per child, €6.70 per campsite. Reception 7:30am-12:30pm and 1-11pm. ❶

🍴 FOOD

Walking around the *Sand*, it sometimes seems that all people do in Bamberg is eat. Austr. is a good place to start, but the hills conceal a couple of wonderful beer gardens. Bamberg boasts many breweries, its most unusual specialty being *Rauchbier* (smoked beer). The daring can try its sharp taste at **Schlenkerla,** Dominikanerstr. 6, *Rauchbier's* traditional home since 1678. (☎560 60. 0.5L €2.05. Open W-M 9:30am-11:30pm.) **Der Beck am Hauptwacheck,** Hauptwachstr. 16, offers scrumptious baked goods. (Open M-F 6:30am-6:30pm, Sa 6:30am-4pm.)

Culinar, Lange Str. 38/40 (☎299 97 00). Deli-style gourmet food. Bakery, butcher, fruit and veggie stand, prepared salads, pastas, hot dishes, a bar, and a sit-down cafe all in one. Big sandwiches €2. Open M-F 8am-6:30pm, Sa 8am-8pm. ❷

Klein aber Fein, Austr. 25. Enjoy huge salads and great sandwiches (€3-5) at one of the small tables crowded out into the street while you meet and greet the university students hanging around the *Mensa* next door. Open daily 10am-1am. ❷

THE LOCAL STORY

ATTENTAT

In a corner of the Bamberg cathedral, a small, overlooked plaque lists the names of five aristocrats, all of whom died between July and October of 1944. The plaque's title reads "In resistance to injustice and dictatorship."

On July 20, 1944, at a meeting in Hitler's secret headquarters in Wolfschanze, Poland, it was apparent to the whole cabinet of Nazi advisors that they would soon face defeat. Claus Schenk, Count of Staufenberg, *Generalstab* of the *Wehrmacht,* entered the room unnoticed with a small suitcase, placed it under the conference table, and left the room.

The suitcase exploded, killing several men and wounding Hitler. Staufenberg, who had been planning the murder for months since becoming disillusioned with the dictator, was executed later that day. His accomplice, Ludwig Freiherr von Leonrod, was put to death a month later. By October, three other nobles were executed for the attack after a show trial.

The *Sprengstoffattentat* is perhaps the most famous of the dozens of failed attempts to kill Hitler. Staufenberg had done his military training in Bamberg and some of his family lived here; it was probably they who commissioned the plaque in the cathedral. Standing beneath a much larger memorial to the soldiers who fell in WWII, this minute piece of metal is a reminder of a small, unhappy story from the worst period Germany has known.

Mensa, Austr. 37, off Obstmarkt, serves very cheap meals (under €3). Show any student ID as you pay. Open M-F 11:30am-2pm. Closed late July to mid-Oct. ❶

Brauerei Greifenklau, Laurenzipl. 20 (☎532 19), unbeknownst to tourists, has been serving its own brew at the top of the Kaulberg since 1719. Head up the Kaulberg road from the Schranne, following Laurenzistr. when it forks off to the right (15min.). Sit in the garden among locals devouring Franconian pork roast with *Kloße* (dumplings). Through the foliage you can see the Altenburg on its hill. Entrees €4-8. Beer €2.10 for 0.5L. Open Tu-Sa 9am-11pm, Su 9:30am-2pm. Kitchen open 11:30am-9:30pm. ❷

Spezial-Keller, Oberer Stephansberg 47, (☎548 87), is Bamberg's best-kept secret. From Judenstr., head past the Stephanskirche up the Stephansberg. Turn left onto Sternwartstr., bear right past the *Gymasium* and turn in right at the gate. Walk all the way along the hedge, then turn left, and the Keller will soon be in view (20min.). This friendly *Biergarten* offers a stunning hilltop view of the city, a playground, and *Rauchbier*. Entrees €4-8, beer €2.10 for 0.5L. Open Tu-Sa from 3pm, Su from 10am. ❷

👁 SIGHTS

DOM. Founded by **Emperor Heinrich II,** the cathedral was consecrated in 1012, burned down twice, and rebuilt in its present-day form in 1237. The most famous object inside, the equestrian statue of the **Bamberger Reiter** (Bamberg Rider), dates to the 13th century and depicts the ideal medieval warrior-king. Just beneath the rider is the tomb of Heinrich II and **Queen Kunigunde,** with their life-size figures on top. Kunigunde walked unhurt over coals to prove her loyalty to her suspicious husband. Both were later canonized. On the left side of the Dom is the **Diözesanmuseum,** with the **Domschatz** and the most beautiful paraments (ritual garments) you will ever see, including Heinrich's star-spangled cloak. *(Across the river and uphill from the Rathaus. Dom ☎50 23 30. Open May-Oct. M-F 9:30am-6pm, Sa 9:30-11:30am and 12:45-6pm, Su 12:30-1:45pm and 2:45-6pm; Nov.-Mar. M-Sa 9:30am-5pm, Su 12:30-1:45pm and 2:45-5pm; Apr. M-F 9:30am-6pm, Sa 9:30am-5pm, Su 12:30-1:45pm and 2:45-5pm. Museum ☎50 23 16. Open Tu-Su 10am-5pm. €3, students and seniors €2, children under 15 free. 1½hr. tours in German of Dom and Domschatz gather Tu-Sa 10:30am at the ticket office in the cloisters. €2.50, students €1.75. Tours of the cathedral leave M-F 2 and 3pm; Sa 10:30am, 1, 2, and 3pm; Su 1 and 3pm. €2, students €1.50. Same meeting place as above, except M meet at the Lady Portal. Organ concerts May-Oct. Sa noon.)*

NEUE RESIDENZ. The largest building in Bamberg, built between 1600 and 1703 to serve as the home of Bamberg's empyrean rulers, the prince-bishops. The dazzling emperor's foyer is borderline kitsch. Porcelain figurines were stolen from the **Chinese Cabinet** in the 1980s; now visitors to the Residenz must be accompanied by a tour guide. One wing is now a museum, whose highlights include some vibrant medieval religious art, Cranach the Elder's famous Lucretia and a comically inaccurate Noah's Ark. Admission includes a tour of the **parade rooms** and entry to the striking **rose garden.** *(Dompl. 8. Opposite the Dom. ☎51 93 90. Open Apr.-Sept. daily 9am-6pm; Oct.-Mar. 10am-4pm. Tours meet Apr.-Oct. daily every 15min., 1 fl. above the cashier's desk. English and French translations available. €4, students and seniors €3.)*

MICHAELSBERG. The former Benedictine monastery of St. Michael is perched atop the hill behind the Dom. It was founded in 1015 and rebuilt in 1610 after a devastating fire. A heavenly herbarium guide to 578 medicinal flowers and herbs was painted on the ceiling by monks with an eye for detail. Behind the main altar, the tomb of local **St. Otto,** keeps its door open to allow pilgrims to visit their favorite saint, who was thought to have curative powers. *(Open daily* *noon-6pm.)* Also see the **Franconian Brewery Museum,** which teaches the fine art of turning hops into *Helles.* The terrace behind the church has a great view of Bamberg. *(Brewery Museum, Michaelsberg 10f. ☎530 16. Open Apr.-Oct. W-Su 1-5pm. €2, students €1.50.)*

ALTES RATHAUS. The old town hall guards the middle of the Regnitz like an anchored ship. Built in the 15th century, the Rathaus was placed to display equal preference to church and state powers on either side of the river. Stone limbs are attached to the frescoes to make the figures seem three-dimensional. **Glanz des Barock** galleries contain the largest collection of porcelain in Europe. *(☎87 18 71. Gallery open Tu-Su 9:30am-4:30pm. €3.50, students and children €2.50.)*

PFAHLPLÄTZCHEN AND KLEIN VENEDIG. Streets between the Rathaus and the Dom are lined with 18th-century Baroque houses, many of which are not yet renovated. The pink house on the corner of Judenstr. is where Hegel edited proofs of *Phenomenology of Spirit.* At the time, unable to find a teaching position, the philosopher worked as editor of the Bamberg newspaper. Just downriver on Am Leinritt, catch the best glimpse of **Klein Venedig,** or "Little Venice." The medieval buildings are former fishermen's houses. Little Venice is also the site of the *Sandkerwa* in August, an event which includes a fisherman's jousting contest.

🎵 🎭 ENTERTAINMENT AND NIGHTLIFE

The third week of August is *Sandkerwa* (*Sandkirchenweih,* originally a celebration of the *Sand* area churches, now a folk festival.) The rest of the year, Bamberg's university and its famous beer make for a lively scene. The Sandstr. is a well-known pub mile, but the Austr. and the Lange Str. also buzz with students.

Live Club, Obere Sandstr. 7, features live acts and a regular club night on M and Sa. The scene changes daily, mixing R&B, hip-hop, or hardcore. (☎50 04 58. Half-price drinks M with €4 cover. Cover €7-34 depending on who's playing. Open M 9pm-1am, Sa 9pm-2am.) One floor up, **Haas Säle,** Obere Sandstr. 7, is a classy open-air terrace with golden stucco, tall palm trees, wooden floors and Hollywood-style swings. (☎51 93 53 29. Beer €2.30 for 0.5L. Open M-F 2pm-2am, Sa-Su 10am-3am.)

Blues Bar, Obere Sandstr. 18, is on the 2nd fl. of the building and hosts funky live folk, blues, and rock F-Sa for a thirty-something crowd. (☎519 11 09. Beer €2.40, cocktails €3-5. No cover. Open Su-F 8pm-2am, Sa 8pm-3am.)

Calimeros, Lange Str. 8, acts as a Tex-Mex restaurant in the evening, later becoming a pub, then a club packed so tight that on good nights everyone dances on the tables. (☎20 11 72. Happy hour Su-Th 5-7:30pm and 11pm-12:30am: caipirinha or margarita €3, pay for 4 get 6. Beer €1 on Th. Open M-Th 10am-2am, F to 3am, Sa to 4am.)

Cafe Abseits, Pödeldorferstr. 39, the oldest student pub, is a local institution that is also great for breakfast (M-Sa until 3pm, Su until 5pm). Features beers that rotate monthly. (☎30 34 22. Take bus #2 to Neuerbstr. Cocktails €3-5, beer €2.20-3.50 for 0.5L. Open daily 9am-1am. Kitchen open until 11:30pm.)

BAYERN

THÜRINGEN (THURINGIA)

Known as the "Green Heart of Germany," the lush hills of Thuringia have provided fertile soil for the nation, from hiking trails of the pristine **Thüringer Wald** to the rich history of Weimar and Jena and the cultural legacy of Luther, Goethe, Schiller, and Wagner. Thuringia holds its own architecturally, with Erfurt's soaring cathedral and Eisenach's stunning **Wartburg** fortress. The historic **Rennsteig Trail** cuts through the southern hills and highlands, and a convenient east-west rail line strings Thuringia's cities together.

HIGHLIGHTS OF THURINGIA

CLIMB THE TOWER of **Eisenach's Wartburg** (p. 577), which once sheltered Luther, and look over J.S. Bach's birthplace and the surrounding forest (p. 578).

CRANE YOUR NECK to take in the majestic cathedral and well-preserved Innenstadt of **Erfurt,** (p. 568) Thuringia's capital, which boasts the region's best nightlife.

LOSE YOURSELF among the ample trails of the gorgeous **Thüringer Wald** (p. 573), from the 6hr. **Goethewanderweg** to the 5-day **Rennsteig.**

TRACE THE FOOTSTEPS of Goethe, Schiller, Hegel, and Novalis in the cultural center of **Weimar** (p. 558) and the university town of **Jena** (p. 566).

WEIMAR ☎ 03643

In its heyday, Weimar attracted such cultural giants as Goethe, Schiller, and **Johann Gottfried von Herder** (grandfather of the Romantics), and the fame of these long-dead men still draws thousands to the city. In 1999, little Weimar was declared the cultural capital of Europe, and during the months leading up to the big celebration the city received a thorough face-lift, making it one of the most renovated cities in the former DDR. The economic perks of being a cultural capital reveal themselves throughout the city. Although Goethe's presence is inescapable, Weimar's importance does not begin and end with the author. As the capital and namesake of the **Weimar Republic,** Germany's attempt at a democratic state after WWI, Weimar has a unique political significance in Germany's recent history. Hitler too was attracted by Weimar's rich culture, and founded the deplorable **Hitler Youth** movement here in 1926. The Bauhaus architectural movement also took root here, and students at the **Bauhaus Universität** continue to bring cultural energy to the city.

⬛ TRANSPORTATION

Situated near the center of Germany, Weimar is easily accessible by both the Dresden-Frankfurt and Berlin-Frankfurt rail lines. Its intelligently designed bus system runs through two nerve centers, the train station and Goethepl.

Trains: To: **Dresden** (2hr., 1 per hr., €30); **Eisenach** (1hr., 2 per hr., €11); **Erfurt** (15min., 4 per hr., €4); **Frankfurt** (3hr., 1 per hr., €40); **Jena** (20min., 2 per hr., €4); **Leipzig** (1½hr., 1 per hr., €21.20).

Public Transportation: Most of Weimar's sights are easy to walk to, but its extensive **bus network** is good for trips to outlying areas. Most buses run until midnight. Single tickets (€1.60) can be bought on board. Book of 7 tickets €6.80; day pass €3.50;

Five Continents. One Home.
Youth Hostels!

Wherever you are travelling: you will find youth hostels everywhere in Germany.
600 youth hostels offer low budget accommodation. For individual stays or attracitive packages, activity holiday or just to relax - youth hostels offer lots of opportunities. There are for example modern city-hostels, medieval castles and little forest houses with nice service, tasty food, pleasant rooms and a relaxing atmosphere, which makes it easy to meet nice people from all over the world.

Visit us at:
www.youth-hostels.de
service@djh.de

www.youth-hostels.d

Die Jugendherbergen

Thüringen (Thuringia)

weekly pass €7.50, students and seniors €5.70. Buy tickets at tourist offices, the main ticket office on Goethepl., or at newsstands with green and yellow "H" signs. Tickets must be validated on the buses.

Taxis: ☎90 36 00 or 90 39 00.

⚡❷ ORIENTATION AND PRACTICAL INFORMATION

A series of open squares strung together by side-streets makes up Weimar's city center, which contains most of its sights. From the train station, Carl-August-Allee stretches downhill past the **Neues Museum** to Karl-Liebknecht-Str., which leads into **Goetheplatz** (15min.). From there, **Theaterplatz** is down Wielandstr. to the left, and the **Marktplatz** is a short walk from Theaterpl. down Schillerstr.

The **Sammelkarte** (€20, students €15) provides free or reduced entry to Weimar's major sights, excluding Goethe's Wohnhaus. The **WeimarCard** (€10) is valid for 72hr. of transportation, free or reduced entry to most sights, and 50% off tours. Purchase cards at tourist offices or at the **Stiftung Weimar Klassik,** Frauentor-str. 4. (☎54 54 01. Open Apr.-Oct. M-F 9am-4:30pm; Nov.-Mar. M-F 9am-4pm.)

Tourist Office: The modern and efficient **Weimar Information,** Markt 10 (☎75 40; www.weimar.de), is on the Markt across from the Rathaus. The staff sells maps (€0.20) and theater tickets, and books rooms for free. **2hr. Walking tours** (in German) leave the

TO BUCHENWALD (8km)

Schopenhauerstr.

Hauptbahnhof

Ettersburgerstr.

Frauenzentrum

Rohlfsstr.

0 200 yards
0 200 meters

Bahnstr.

Fuldaer Str.

Meyerstr.

Brenmerstr.

Brenmestr.

Friedrich-Ebert-Str.

Meyerstr.

Gläserstr.

Schlachthofstr.

Papststr.

Ernst-Koll-Str.

Carl-August-Allee

Carl-von-

Ossietzky-Str.

Röhrstr.

Ernst-Thälmann-Str.

Bockstr.

Eduard-Rosenthal-Str.

Döllstädtstr.

Falkstr.

Fr.-Naumann-Str.

Müllerhartungstr.

RATHENAU-PL.

Am Kirschberg

Friedenssstr.

Asbachstr.

Carl-August-Allee

Neues-Museum-Weimar

Friedensstr.

Jenaer Str.

Ilm River

Weimarhallen-park

Schwanseestr.

K.-Liebknecht-Str.

Rollg

Friedense

Jakobstr.

F.-Freiligrath-Str.

Wagnerg

Brühl

Jakobskirche

Am Jakobskirchhof

Jakobstr.

Gerberstr.

2

Kegelbrücke

Washingtonstr.

Richard-Strauss-Str.

Coudraystr.

G.-Hauptmann-Str.

ROLLPL.

GOETHEPL.

Graben

Laundry

Unter-graben

Marstallstr.

Schloß-museum

Hans-Wahl-Str.

Sternbrücke

Bus Ticket Center

3

Karlstr.

Stadtkirche St. Peter und Paul

HERDER-PL.

Geleitstr.

Eisfe/d

Ritterg

6

BURGPL.

8

Erfurterstr.

Mozartstr.

Heinrich-Heine-Str.

Wielandstr.

Bauhaus-Museum

5

Zeughof

Wittumspalais

Marktstr.

Am Markt

4

Deutsches Nationaltheater

THEATER-PL.

Dingelstedtstr.

7

Windischenstr.

Rathaus

MARKT

i

Cranachhaus

AUGUST-FRÖLICH-PL.

Gropiusstr.

Hummelstr.

9

Schützeng.

Schillers Wohnhaus

Schillerstr.

Frauentorstr.

Puschkinstr.

R

PLATZ DER DEMOKRATIE

Herzogin Anna Amalia Bibliothek

Hegelstr.

Steubenstr.

Schubertstr.

Humboldtstr.

Amalienstr.

Frauenplan

Stiftung Weimar Klassik

Seifeng.

Goethehaus

Ackerwand

WIELAND-PL.

Marienstr.

Goethes Gartenhaus

TO NIETZSCHE ARCHIVE (300m)

Am Poseckschen Garten

10

Geschw.-Scholl-Str.

11

Rudolf-Breitscheid-Str.

Bauhausstr.

Belvederer Allee

Entrance to Park Caves

Franz-Liszt-Haus

GOETHE PARK

Ilm River

(PARK AN DER ILM)

Theo.-Hagen-Weg

Karl-Haußknecht-Str.

Historischer Friedhof (Cemetery)

Berkaerstr.

Haeckelstr.

Ludwig-Feuerbach-Str.

Weimar

🏠 ACCOMMODATIONS
Jugendherberge Am Poseckschen
  Garten, **11**
Jugendherberge Germania, **1**
Hababusch Hostel, **5**

🍴 FOOD & DRINK
ACC, **6**
Crêperie du Palais, **7**
Mensa, **10**
Residenz, **8**

🍺 BARS & NIGHTLIFE
AIDS-Hilfe, **4**
Gerber III, **2**
Studentenclub Kasseturm, **3**
Studentenclub Schützengasse, **9**

office daily at 10am and 2pm; Nov.-Mar. at 11am and 3pm. €6, students €4. The **Weimarer Wald** desk has info on outdoor activities in Thuringia. The office also offers **Internet** access for €2 per hr. Open Apr.-Oct. M-F 9:30am-6pm, Sa-Su 9:30am-3pm; Nov.-Mar. M-F 10am-6pm, Sa-Su 10am-2pm.

Currency Exchange: 4 banks are spread out on Schillerstr. and Frauentorstr., but note that none are open between 4pm F and 8:30am M. All have **24hr. ATMs.**

Women's Resources: Frauenzentrum, Schopenhauerstr. 21 (☎871 16; www.frauenzentrum-weimar.de), offers advice, has a basement *Frauenkulturcafe*, hosts cultural programs, and rents women rooms in a *Frauenpension*. Office open M and F 9am-noon, Tu and Th 2-6pm. Cafe "Lotta" open M-F 1-6pm. Check board outside for schedule.

Laundry: SB-Waschsalon, Graben 47, a few blocks from Goethepl. Wash €3.50. Dry €0.50 per 15min. Open M-Sa 8am-10pm; last wash at 8:30pm.

Pharmacy: Stadt Apotheke, Frauentorstr. 3 (☎20 20 93), just below the Markt. Has a *Notdienst* (emergency service) buzzer. Open M-F 8am-7pm, Sa 9am-2pm.

Internet Access: Roxanne, on the Markt to the left of the tourist office, is a bar, cafe, and record store. €2 per hr. Open M-Sa from 11:30am, Su from 3pm. Another option is the **Stadtbücherei,** Steubenstr. 1. €5 per hr. Open Tu-F 1-8pm, Sa 10am-1pm.

Post Office: Am Goethepl. 99423 Weimar. Open M-F 9am-6:30pm, Sa 9am-noon.

ACCOMMODATIONS

Weimar's youth hostels are clean, hospitable, budget-friendly, and well-located—ideal for student travelers. Private rooms and pensions are available through the tourist office (from €50 for a double).

Hababusch Hostel, Geleitstr. 4 (☎85 07 37; www.uni-weimar.de/yh). From Goethepl., follow Geleitstr.; after a sharp right, there's a statue on your left—the entrance is in the ivied corner behind it. Tired of the wholesome, sterile HI hostels, young Bohemians find an oasis of alternative travel here. Art students with playful tastes run the hostel—check out the bathroom lighting. Guests share meals in the communal atmosphere. Kitchen access. Key deposit €10. Reception 24hr. Dorms €10; singles €15; doubles €24. ❶

Jugendherberge Germania (HI), Carl-August-Allee 13 (☎85 04 90; fax 85 04 91). From the station, walk straight downhill 2min. and it's on your right. This lovely yellow Jugendstil mansion offers clean, modern rooms and is exceptionally convenient. **Free Internet.** Breakfast and sheets included. 2- to 6-bed dorms €20, under 27 €17. ❷

Jugendherberge Am Poseckschen Garten (HI), Humboldtstr. 17 (☎85 07 92; fax 85 07 93), is situated near the city center but fairly distant from the train station. Take bus #8 (dir.: Merketal) to "Am Poseckschen Garten." Turn right onto Am Poseckschen Garten, then left onto Humboldtstr.; the hostel is immediately on your left. A big turn-of-the-century brownstone a few blocks from the city center with 8- to 10-bed rooms. The hostel hosts many school groups, so arrive early. **Internet** access €0.10 per min. Breakfast and sheets included. Lunch or dinner €4.30. Reception daily 6am-12:30am. Lockout 10am-2pm. Curfew 10pm, but you can get a key. €19.50, under 27 €16.50. ❷

FOOD

If a restaurant here has any visible connection to Goethe, it's probably overpriced. Check out **Eisfeld Straße,** leading off Herderpl., where a string of cheaper restaurants serve regional food. For groceries try the **produce market** at the Marktpl. (open M-Sa 7am-5pm), or the **Rewe** supermarkets in the shopping mall on Theaterpl. or on the corner of Frauenplan and Steubenstr. (Open M-F 7am-8pm.)

THÜRINGEN

◪ **Crêperie du Palais,** Am Palais 1 (☎40 15 81). French expats serve crepes and *galettes* large enough to satisfy German appetites, in a cozy interior or on a tree-shaded terrace. €5-8 for a dinner and dessert crepe combo. Open daily 9:30am-midnight. ❸

ACC, Burgpl. 1-2 (☎85 11 61; www.cafe-acc.de). This combination cafe, cultural center, and gallery (upstairs, small donation requested), popular with students, offers daily specials ranging from chicken curry to eggplant for €5, with soup for €6.50. A variety of vegetarian options, salads, and classic *Abendbrote* (plates of cheese and cold cuts) complete the menu, which changes every few weeks. Eat outside with a shaded view of the Schloß or inside the cozy 1st fl. cafe. Open M-F 11am-1am, Sa-Su 10am-1am. ❷

Residenz, Grüner Markt 4 (☎59 408; www.residenz-cafe.de), Weimar's oldest restaurant, offers a taste of Thuringian cuisine at its best, served inside or out front on the porch. Even Gerhard Schröder ate here on a recent visit. Try the *Thüringer Grillplatte* (€10.80) for a taste of 3 local meats with sinus-clearing Thuringian mustard. Also serves vegetarian entrees. Open M-F 8am-1am, Sa-Su 9am-1am. ❸

Mensa: Bauhaus-Universität, Marienstr. 13/15, just across the footpath in front of the Bauhaus building. Also accessible from Park an der Ilm. Join Weimar's artistic community on a terrace in warmer months, or take a coffee break in the **cafeteria** downstairs. A meal in the **Mensa** upstairs runs €4-4.20 (€1.50-2 with student ID). Mensa open daily 11am-2pm. Cafeteria open mid-Oct. to mid-July M-Th 7:30am-7pm, F 7:30am-5pm, Sa 11am-2pm; mid-July to mid-Oct. M-F 7:30am-4pm. The University has a **second cafeteria** in the basement of Coudraystr. 13. Open M-F 7:30am-3pm. ❶

⟳ 🏛 SIGHTS AND MUSEUMS

Weimar will always belong to its poets, whose plays, houses, and gravestones attract pilgrims from around the world. Goethe's hand has left indelible marks, even on Weimar's soil: he landscaped the romantic **Park an der Ilm** that surrounds his quaint **Gartenhaus.** Beyond the relics of Germany's lyrical titans, the **Neues Museum** and **Bauhaus Museum** house surprisingly fresh collections of art, and the **Stadtmuseum** sheds light on Weimar's fascinating and oft-neglected history.

GOETHEHAUS. While countless German towns leap at any excuse to build memorial *Goethehäuser* (Goethe slept here, Goethe tripped on this rock, Goethe stole my wife), this one is the real thing. The **Goethewohnhaus** elegantly presents the immaculate chambers where the genius entertained, wrote, studied, and ultimately died after 50 years in Weimar. Except for the study, which Goethe kept free of distraction, the rooms are jammed with busts, paintings, and sculptures from his 50,000-piece art collection (mostly evoking ancient Greece and Rome), including over 18,000 rocks—not only could the man write, but he knew his geology. The rest of the **Goethe-Nationalmuseum** consists of an exhibit on Weimar's history. *(Frauenplan 1. Open Apr.-Oct. Tu-Su 9am-6pm; Nov.-Mar. Tu-Su 9am-4pm. Expect to wait on summer weekends. €6, students €4.50. Museum exhibit €2.50/€2. Audioguides available.)*

PARK AN DER ILM. Landscaped by Goethe, this sprawling park and the meadows of purple, yellow, and white flowers flanking the Ilm attest to the writer's artistic skill. Note the fake ruins built by the Weimar shooting club, the **Sphinx Grotto** from the late 18th century, and the **Kubus,** a fantastically large black cube used as a theater and movie screen. Perched on the park's far slopes is Goethe's **Gartenhaus,** the poet's first Weimar home and later his retreat from the city. A replica travels around Germany to abate the unquenchable national Goethe-thirst. *(Gartenhaus on Corona-Schöfer-Str. Open Apr. to mid-Oct. M and W-Su 9am-6pm; mid-Oct. to Mar. M and W-Su 9am-4pm. €3, students and seniors €2.)* The **Herzogin Anna Amalia Bibliothek,** Goethe's old intellectual batting cage, is here as well. The impressive Rococo reading room will reopen in 2007 after restoration. *(Pl. der Demokratie 1. Library open daily 10am-5pm.)*

BAUHAUS-MUSEUM. The revolutionary Bauhaus design movement, committed to principles of minimalism and function, followed the turbulent political era of post-WWI Germany. In 1919, Walter Gropius assembled a prodigious group at Weimar's art school, including such future stars as Feininger, Klee, and Kandinsky. Bauhaus highlights are exhibited here; weavings, sculptures, prints, furniture, books, toys, and even tea kettles convey the breadth of the school's philosophy and undertakings. *(Theaterpl., across from the Deutsches Nationaltheater.* ☎ *54 61 61. Open Tu-Su Apr.-Oct. 10am-6pm; Nov.-Mar. 10am-4pm. €3, students and seniors €2.)*

SCHILLERS WOHNHAUS. Sitting a neighborly distance from Goethe's pad, this yellow house was Schiller's home during the last three years of his life after he resigned from academia in Jena. As well as chronicling the poet's life, the museum exhibits the backgrounds to *The Maid of Orleans* and *William Tell*—both written here—and houses original drafts and early editions of his plays. One room displays over 600 medallions and coins imprinted with Schiller's head. *(Schillerstr. 12. Open M and W-Su Apr.-Oct. 9am-6pm; Nov.-Mar. 9am-4pm. €3.50, students €2.50.)*

HISTORISCHER FRIEDHOF. South of the town center, in this overgrown forest cemetery, Goethe and Schiller rest side-by-side in the basement of the **Fürstengruft** (Ducal Vault) with a dozen or so Prussian nobles. Schiller died in an epidemic and was originally buried in a mass grave, but Goethe later combed through the remains until he found Schiller and had him interred here. Skeptics long argued that Goethe had chosen the wrong body, but in the 1960s a team of Russian scientists confirmed the poet's identification. Goethe himself arranged to be buried in an airtight steel case. *(Open daily Mar.-Sept. 8am-9pm; Oct.-Feb. 8am-6pm. Free. Tomb open M and W-Su Apr. to mid-Oct. 9am-1pm and 2-6pm; mid-Oct. to Mar. 10am-1pm and 2-4pm. €2, students and seniors €1.50.)*

SCHLOßMUSEUM. The palace and tower from the former city walls now house three floors of art. The first floor is major Lucas Cranach fest (the painter lived in the Marktpl.); the second is a minor-league collection of religious icons, an impressive assortment of medieval and Renaissance altars, and 19th- and 20th-century German works, including a painting of St. George slaying a docile-looking dragon; and the third includes a sampling of the **Weimarer Malerschule** of the second half of the 19th century, which focuses on simple landscapes and rural life. The palace's most impressive rooms, including the banquet hall, reception rooms, and "poet rooms," are in the east wing. *(Burgpl. 4. To the left of the Marktpl. Open Tu-Su Apr.-Oct. 10am-6pm; Nov.-Mar. 10am-4:30pm. €4, students and seniors €3.50.)*

NEUES MUSEUM WEIMAR. This new museum exhibits the work of modern artists in small but insightful shows that change each year. *(Weimarpl. 5.* ☎ *54 69 63. Open Tu-Su Apr.-Sept. 11am-6pm; Oct.-Mar. 11am-4:30pm. €3, students €2.)*

FRANZ-LISZT-HAUS. After an earlier stint in Weimar, the composer spent his last years here. The instruments and furnishings are supposedly original, but given Liszt's torrid love life, the single bed seems euphemistic. *(Marienstr. 17. Open Apr.-Oct. Tu-Su 10am-1pm and 2-6pm. €2, students €1.50.)*

NIETZSCHE-ARCHIV. Nietzsche lived three quiet years here, suffering from mental and physical illness, before his death in 1900. His sister, who returned from a struggling colony in Paraguay to care for him, archived the philosopher's work after his death, but distorted it during the process. Her totalitarian control over Nietzsche's papers contributed to the Nazi's misappropriation of parts of his philosophy to horrifying ends. On display is a history of the archive, many portraits of the man with his famous mustache, and a library designed by Henry van de Velde. *(Humboldtstr. 36. Open Apr. to mid-Oct. Tu-Su 1-6pm. €2, students and seniors €1.50.)*

THÜRINGEN

OTHER SIGHTS. The cobblestoned **Marktplatz** spreads out beneath the neo-Gothic **Rathaus,** which is closed to the public. Crowds packed the square when Hitler spoke here from the balcony of the **Hotel Elephant** during one of his several visits. Weimar's unique history as the center of German politics after WWI is chronicled in the city's particularly interesting **Stadtmuseum.** *(Karl-Liebknecht-Str. 5-9. ☎90 38 68. Open Tu-Su Apr.-Oct. 10am-6pm; Nov.-Mar. 10am-5pm. €2, students €1, children €0.50.)* The **Stadtkirche St. Peter und Paul** features Cranach the Elder's last triptych altarpiece, which he started shortly before his death. Lucas Cranach the Younger finished the painting and put his dad in it next to Martin Luther. The church is also called the "Herderkirche," in honor of philosopher and linguist **Johann Gottfried von Herder,** who preached here regularly in the 1780s. Amid all the gold, pink, and blue splendor is Cranach's original tomb covering. *(Down Jakobstr. Open M-Sa 10am-noon and 2-4pm, Su after services until noon and 2-3pm. Free.)*

🎵 🍷 ENTERTAINMENT AND NIGHTLIFE

The best resource for theater and music in Weimar is the 🏛Deutsches Nationaltheater, Theaterpl. The theater that got Goethe and Schiller started still presents *Faust* regularly, along with Mozart and Verdi operas and classics from Shakespeare and his contemporaries. It's also the site where the **Weimar Constitution** was signed in 1919. *(☎75 53 34. Box office open M 2-6pm, Tu-Sa 10am-6pm, Su 10am-1pm, and 1hr. before performances.)* Tickets are also available at **Tourist Information,** the only ticket service open from early July to mid-Aug. (Tickets for musical theater events and plays €8-55. 30% student and senior discount.) Weimar's nightlife consists of an eclectic collection of student clubs and cafes. The weekend scene is fueled by energetic students who pack the few discos in town. Check the posters and bulletin boards at the Bauhaus-Universität Mensa (p. 562) for the latest goings-on.

Studentenclub Kasseturm (☎85 16 70; www.kasseturm.de) serves up cheap drinks (shots €1.50-2) in an old medieval tower on Goethepl., opposite the post office. The oldest student club in Germany, with dancing on the top 2 fl. and a relaxed beer cellar below. Student bands take over 1 fl. on Sa. Disco W and F or Sa. Check board outside for weekly schedule. Cover €3, students €2, more for concerts. Open M-Sa from 8pm.

Studentenclub Schützengasse, Schützeng. 2 (☎90 43 23), often has live rock upstairs and a DJ downstairs, with a (slightly) quieter *Biergarten* out back. Disco Tu and Sa. Live bands Tu and F-Sa. Club sponsors a variety of activities from dance classes to jam sessions other nights. Check the board outside for that week's schedule. 18+. Cover €2.50, students €1.50. Open M and W-Th from 7:30pm, Tu and F-Sa from 9pm.

Gerber III, Gerberstr. 3, is a former squatters' house that now shelters an improvised bar covered in graffiti and furnished with randomly positioned couches. The building also has a disco, a climbing wall and a movie theater (€2). Stop by and pick up a *Gerberei* pamphlet for the latest details and disco times. Bar open Tu-Sa from 8pm.

AIDS-Hilfe, Erfurter Str. 17 (☎85 36 36), holds a popular gay cafe. They also host a gay "safer sex" party in the basement on the last F of every month. Men 18+ only. Cover €7.50, €2.50 of which goes to drinks. Open M, W, and F from 8pm.

🗺 DAYTRIP FROM WEIMAR: BUCHENWALD

The best way to reach the camp is by bus #6 from Weimar's train station or from Goethepl. (20min., M-Sa 1 per hr., Su every 2hr.). Check the schedule carefully; some #6 buses go to "Ettersburg" rather than "Gedenkstätte Buchenwald." Buses back to Weimar stop at the KZ-Lager parking lot and at the road by the Glockenturm.

A quarter-million Jews, Gypsies, homosexuals, communists, and political prisoners were incarcerated at the labor camp of Buchenwald during WWII. Buchenwald was not intended as an extermination camp, but over 50,000 prisoners died from malnutrition, harsh treatment by the SS, or medical experiments. Now a memorial to those who suffered here, the compound is a vast gray expanse of gravel with the former location of the prison blocks marked by numbers and crumbling foundations. Some of the remaining buildings around the perimeter can still be visited, including the SS officers' quarters and the crematorium. The uncompromising starkness of the compound and the horror of its history stand in wrenching contrast to the breathtaking Thuringian forests surrounding the site.

Buchenwald's first inmates were German political dissenters, but from 1937 onward, huge numbers of deportees were sent here from Poland, Denmark, Belgium, Norway, and other countries. As the Red Army drew closer to Polish camps, many Jews originally deported to Auschwitz were sent to Buchenwald; most of these prisoners were crowded into the dreaded "small camp," where conditions were even more horrifying than in the other areas. By the end of the war, the camp was the largest in existence, and 95 percent of the prisoners were non-Germans.

Suffering in Buchenwald did not end with liberation: the Soviets used the site as an internment camp from 1945 to 1950 for more than 28,000 Germans thought to be Nazi leaders, war criminals, and opponents of the Communist regime; 10,000 of them died. Now the graves of both victims and perpetrators of Buchenwald's abuses mingle, marked by tall steel posts, in a forest cemetery behind the museum.

The **Nationale Mahnmal und Gedenkstätte Buchenwald** has two principal sights: the **KZ-Lager** and the **Mahnmal.** The former refers to the camp itself, while the latter is a solemn monument overlooking Weimar and the surrounding countryside. The main exhibit of the camp, in the large storehouse building, documents the history of Buchenwald (1937-1945) and the general history of Nazism and German anti-Semitism. An exhibit about the Soviet internment camp is in the basement around the back. Next door, the former disinfection building houses art created by prisoners and artists during and after the war. Many simple tributes are scattered around the camp; the stones of the Jewish memorial at block #22 read: "So that the generation to come might know, the children, yet to be born, that they too may rise and declare to their children." The camp **archives** are open by appointment to anyone looking for records between 1937 and 1945 (archives ☎ 43 01 54, library 43 01 60. Exhibits open May-Sept. Tu-Su 9:45am-6pm; Oct.-Apr. 8:45am-5pm. last entry 45min. before close. Outdoor camp area open daily until sundown.).

The DDR-designed **Mahnmal** (memorial) and **Glockenturm** (bell tower) are 10min. from the camp on the other side of the hilltop. Either go straight up the main road that bisects the two parking lots, or take the footpath uphill from the old Buchenwald Bahnhof and then continue on the main road. The actual memorial is a series of carved blocks depicting stylized scenes of violence. A somber bell tower looms to the left of these blocks, with no marking besides an immense "MCMXLV" (1945) carved on each side. Behind the tower a commanding view of the region unfolds, overseen by the **Plastikgruppe,** a sculpture of ragged, stern-jawed socialist prisoners claiming their freedom. An **information center** near the bus stop at Buchenwald shows a 30min. video with English subtitles on the hour, and has helpful brochures for €0.25, a free walking tour, and audioguides (€3, students €2). Brochures and audio guides are available in nine languages, including English. (☎ 43 00. Open Tu-Su May-Sept. 9am-6pm; Oct.-Apr. 8:30am-4:30pm. A branch next to Weimar's **Tourist Information** on the Marktpl. has more information.)

JENA

☎ 03641

Jena's life is its university. Once undoubtedly the country's finest, the institution proudly points to its illustrious past, especially professor **Friedrich Schiller,** who lectured here in 1789 on the ideals of the French Revolution. His students, Novalis and Hölderlin, joined other literary greats such as Schlegel and Tieck to plant seeds of the German Romantic movement. It was here that philosophers Fichte and Schelling argued for a new concept of intellectual and political freedom, and here, in 1806, that a then-unknown junior philosophy professor named **Georg Wilhelm Friedrich Hegel** wrote the phenomenal *Phenomenology of Spirit.* The 19th century also saw Jena become a world leader in the field of optics: the microscope company **Carl Zeiss** founded continues today as Jenoptik. Jena exudes a bohemian university culture, from off-beat cafes to rock laser shows at the Planetarium.

🖪🔁 TRANSPORTATION AND PRACTICAL INFORMATION

Jena is in the Saale River Valley, 25km east of Weimar by **train** (20min., 2 per hr., €4). Three major train stations serve the town. Trains between Dresden and Erfurt stop at **Bahnhof Jena-West,** a 10min. walk from town, while trains on the Berlin-Munich line and on the Saale line between Saalfeld and Naumburg stop at **Jena**

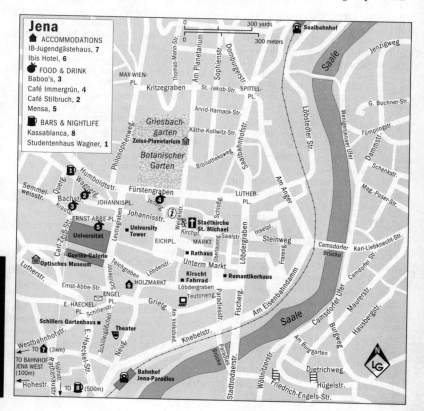

Jena

🏠 ACCOMMODATIONS
IB-Jugendgästehaus, 7
Ibis Hotel, 6

🍴 FOOD & DRINK
Baboo's, 3
Café Immergrün, 4
Café Stilbruch, 2
Mensa, 5

🍸 BARS & NIGHTLIFE
Kassablanca, 8
Studentenhaus Wagner, 1

Saalbahnhof, 15min. north of the center. Most trains from the Saalbahnhof also stop at **Bahnhof Jena-Paradies,** only 5min. from town. Most of the city is connected by a bus and streetcar system whose hub is the "Zentrum" stop on Löbdergraben. (Single ride €1.30; day ticket €3.50.) To get to the town center from Bahnhof Jena-West, head downhill on Westbahnhofstr. until it becomes Schillerstr. Turn left up Schillerstr. to the towering university building. From Saalbahnhof, turn left down Saalbahnhofstr. and take a right on Saalstr., or take bus #15. From Jena-Paradies, turn right on the main road and then bear left up Neug., which leads to Holzmarkt and Löbderstr. Rent **bikes** at **Kirscht Fahrrad,** Löbdergraben 8, near the "Löbdergraben" bus stop. (☎44 15 39. €15 for one day, €5 for each day thereafter. Open M-F 9am-7pm, Sa 9am-4pm.) For a **taxi** call ☎55 66. **Jena Tourist-Information,** Johannisstr. 23 on Eichpl., hands out free maps, leads city **tours** in German (€4), and books private rooms (from €13) for free. (☎80 64 00; www.tourismus.jena.de. Open M-F 10am-6pm, Sa 10am-4pm. Tours M, W, Sa 2pm; Apr.-Oct. also Th 4pm.) The **Goethe-Apotheke** is on Weigelstr. 7, in front of the church; a sign lists **emergency pharmacy** information. (☎45 45 45. Open M-F 8am-8pm, Sa 8am-4pm.) **C.net** Computercafe, Teutoneng 2, has **Internet** access; enter from Grietg. (☎35 73 52. €4 per hr. Open M-Th 1pm-midnight, F 1pm-1am, Sa 11am-1am, Su 11am-midnight). The **post office,** 07743 Jena, is at Engelpl. 8. (Open M-F 9am-6:30pm, Sa 9am-1pm.)

ACCOMMODATIONS AND FOOD

To get to the **IB-Jugendgästehaus ❷,** Am Herrenberge 3, take bus #10, 13, or 40 (dir.: Burgau) to "Zeiss-Werk." Go left as you get off the bus and then right on Mühlenstr. up the hill until it turns into Am Herrenberge (15min.). Or from Bahnhof Jena-West, turn left on Westbahnhofstr. and take a left on Tatzendpromenade. After it becomes Carl-Zeiss-Promenade, take a left on Mühlenstr. (35min.). Removed from the city center, the mammoth IB provides clean rooms, bathrooms, and showers. (☎68 72 30. Breakfast and sheets included. Reception M-F 24hr., Sa 5-8pm, Su from 6pm. 3- and 4-bed rooms €19.50, under 27 €16.50.) The **Ibis Hotel ❹,** Teichgraben 1, although expensive, is especially comfortable and in great location. From Jena-Paradies walk down Neug.; you'll see it on your left (5min.). All rooms have phone, TV and bath. (☎81 30; fax 813 333. Breakfast €9. Reception 24hr. All rooms €49.)

A combination *Imbiß,* cafe, and restaurant, **Baboo's Internationale Spezialitäten ❷,** Johannispl. 12, offers everything from chicken curry (€6.50) and pizza (€1.50) to falafel (€2.50) and *Döner.* (☎42 66 66. Open daily from 10am.) The fresh and friendly self-service **Café Immergrün ❷,** Jenerg. 6, just off Fürstengraben., lined with comfortable couches and modern art, is an unofficial environmental center. Daily vegetarian and meat specials run €2-5. (☎44 73 13. Open M-Sa 11am-1am, Su 10am-midnight.) **Cafe Stilbruch ❸,** Wagnerg. 1-2, offers a large selection of delicious salads, baguettes, and hearty, piping hot *Pfannengerichte* (pan-cooked meals; €6-9). Later in the evening this cafe fills with cocktail patrons. (☎82 71 71. Open M-Th 8:30am-2am, F 8:30am-3am, Sa 9am-3am, Su 9am-2am.) The Markt sells fresh produce (Tu and Th-Sa 8am-noon), and you'll find a **tegut** supermarket in the basement of the Goethe-Galerie. (Open M-Sa 8am-8pm.) Jena's **Mensa ❶** recently moved into a sparkling new location in Ernst-Abbe-Pl., across Leutragraben from the defunct tower. (Full meals €4-4.50, €1.40-1.60 with ISIC. Open M-F 8am-3pm.)

SIGHTS

The **Romantikerhaus,** Unterm Markt 12a, once bubbled with the raw creative energy of the Romantic period. Owned by philosopher and fiery democrat **Johann Fichte** from 1794-99, it later hosted the poetic, philosophical, and musical get-togethers of the Romantics. Rather than reconstruct the house's furnishings, cre-

THÜRINGEN

ative permanent and rotating exhibits teach visitors about the Romantic movement and its origins. (☎44 32 63; www.jena.de/kultur/romantik.htm. Open Tu-Su 10am-1pm and 2-5pm. €3, students and seniors €1.50.) The **Optisches Museum,** Carl-Zeiß-Pl. 12, presents the history of local optics *Wunderkind* **Carl Zeiss** and colleague Ernst Abbe, alongside eyeglasses, telescopes, cameras, microscopes, and optical illusions galore. Be sure to check out the amazingly detailed holograms downstairs. (☎44 31 65. Open Tu-F 10am-4:30pm, Sa 11am-5pm. English audio guide €1. €5, students and seniors €4.) **Schiller's Gartenhaus,** the poet's home on Schillergäßchen, just off Schillerstr, is a museum where the furniture looks, yes, like it could have been used by Schiller. The author used to chat with Goethe in the beautifully-maintained garden. (☎93 11 88. Open Apr.-Oct. Tu-Su 11am-3pm. English brochures available. €2.50, students and seniors €1.30.) The gigantic **university tower** is impossible to miss in Jena's landscape. The ongoing construction on the buildings nearby is intended to cheer up the cylindrical monolith.

The **Stadtkirche St. Michael,** off Eichpl., boasts three treasures: a 13th-century wooden St. Michael, a pulpit from which Luther twice preached, and **Luther's tombstone,** conspicuously not on his grave in Wittenberg. The folks at the Stadtkirche claim the stone was "held up in shipping during a war"—a story that Wittenbergers find hard to swallow. (Open daily 10am-5pm.) Nearby is the **Botanischer Garten,** an early treasure of Jena's medical faculty, renovated by Goethe. (Open daily May 15-Aug. 14 9am-6pm; Sept. 15-May 14 9am-5pm. Last entry 30min. before closing.) The **Zeiss-Planetarium,** Am Planetarium 5, the world's oldest, pleases stargazers and classic rock fans alike with laser shows ranging from children's musicals to the best of Queen. (☎88 54 88; www.planetarium-jena.de. Check the poster on the gate for event times, usually 11am-8pm. Ticket offce open Tu 5:30-9pm, W 7:30-9pm, Th-F 10:30am-noon, and 30min. before all shows. Around €5, students €4.)

🎵🎭 ENTERTAINMENT AND NIGHTLIFE

This university town has plenty going on—keep your eyes open for posters, pick up the *Tipps* guide at the Tourist Information office, or start on **Wagnergasse,** an area popular with students and lined with bars and restaurants. At the end of the strip, set back in a garden, you'll find the **Studentenhaus Wagner,** Wagnerg. 26, headquarters for student culture. The university-sponsored cafe doubles as a venue for plays, readings, live music, and movie screenings. (☎47 21 53. Open M-F 11am-1am, Sa-Su 7:30pm-1am. Cafe open M-Sa from 6pm, Su from 7:30pm.) **Kassablanca,** Felsenkellerstr. 13a, sponsors an array of discos, concerts, and political discussions in a renovated, graffitied train depot. To get there from the center, turn left off Westbahnhofstr. onto Rathenaustr., take a left at the fork onto Hainstr., then turn right on Felsenkellerstr. Climb the hill—the neon-painted trains will be hard to miss on your right. (☎282 60. Cover €2-7. Usually open W-Sa from 8pm.) During **Kulturarena Jena,** a two-month-long festival from early July to mid-August, the area in front of Jena's theater at Engelpl. becomes an open-air performance space. Buy tickets at the tourist office, or join the crowds lining the sidewalks for free. (☎49 26 85, ticket hotline 80 64 06; www.kulturarena.de. €10-18, students €7-16.)

ERFURT ☎ 0361

Street after street of ornate facades line this capital city, the "Thüringisches Rom" (Thuringian Rome). Erfurt benefited from its strategic position on the trade route that connected medieval Europe with the Silk Road; the city's wealthy merchants funded 37 churches and several monasteries, one of which saw Martin Luther's

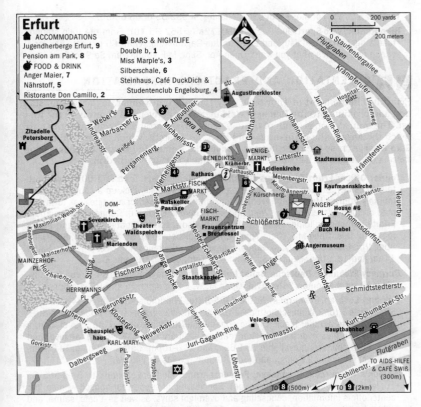

Erfurt

♠ ACCOMMODATIONS
Jugendherberge Erfurt, **9**
Pension am Park, **8**
🍴 FOOD & DRINK
Anger Maier, **7**
Nährstoff, **5**
Ristorante Don Camillo, **2**

🍷 BARS & NIGHTLIFE
Double b, **1**
Miss Marple's, **3**
Silberschale, **6**
Steinhaus, Café DuckDich &
Studentenclub Engelsburg, **4**

formative years as a Augustinian monk. As a capital, Erfurt has a dynamic political history: Napoleon called a meeting of princes here and chatted with Goethe in what is now the **Thüringer Staatskanzlei.** More recently West German Chancellor Willy Brandt met here in 1970 with East German leader Willi Stoph, commencing *Ostpolitik,* the arduous process of East-West reconciliation (p. 59).

▮ TRANSPORTATION

Airport: Flughafen Erfurt (☎ 656 22 22). Take bus #99 or tram 4 to Hauptfriedhof, then bus #91 or 92. Flights to major German airports and European tourist destinations.

Trains: To: **Berlin** (3hr., 1 per hr., €42); **Dresden** (3hr., 2 per hr., €35); **Frankfurt** (2½hr., 1 per hr., €43); **Leipzig** (2hr., 1 per hr., €17); **Weimar** (15min., 4 per hr., €4).

Public Transportation: Buses and **streetcars** run through the pedestrian zones and beyond. Single ticket €1.40, 5 tickets €5.70, *Tageskarte* €3.20. Buy tickets at *Automaten,* stores with *EVAG-Punkt* signs, or on board, then validate them on board. Night streetcars (numbered with an "N" prefix) cover most daytime routes, running every 15-30min. until 1am on weekdays and throughout the night on weekends, except 4-5am. The tourist office sells Erfurt cards (€9.90, valid for 48hr. from time of purchase), good for unlimited transportation, city walking tours, and admission to the city's museums.

THÜRINGEN

Taxis: ☎511 11. For those with bad memories, ☎555 55 or 66 66 66.

Bike Rental: Velo-Sport, Juri-Gagarin-Ring 72a (☎562 35 40). From the train station, take a right on Bahnhofstr. and a left on Juri-Gagarin-Ring. From €5 per day. Ask for a cheap one if that's what you want. Open Apr.-Sept. M-F 10am-7pm, Sa 9am-4pm.

◼️🔼 ORIENTATION AND PRACTICAL INFORMATION

Erfurt lies in the heart of Thuringia, only 15min. from Weimar. Its large train station and proximity to the **Thüringer Wald** make it a convenient gateway to the forest. The train station is south of the city center. Head straight down Bahnhofstr. to reach the **Anger**—the main drag—and then the Altstadt, which is bisected by the **Gera River.** Across the river lies the **Fischmarkt,** dominated by the **Rathaus.** From there, continue on Marktstr. to **Domplatz,** home to Erfurt's cathedral.

Tourist Office: Erfurt Tourismus Gesellschaft, Benediktspl. 1 (☎664 00; www.erfurt-tourismus.de), between the Rathaus and the Krämerbrücke. Pick up a copy of the free monthly *Erfurter Magazin* for event listings and *Takt* or *Fritz* for nightlife. Ask for a free map of Erfurt or the Thüringer Wald and a brochure in English or German to learn about Erfurt's famous buildings (€1.30). The staff also reserves theater tickets and books rooms for free. Open M-F 10am-7pm (Jan.-Mar. closes 6pm), Sa 10am-6pm, Su 10am-4pm. 2hr. **tours** of the city, in German, depart from the office Apr.-Dec. M-F 1pm, Sa-Su 11am and 1pm; Jan.-Mar. Sa-Su 11am and 1pm. €5.50, students €3.

Currency Exchange: Deutsche Bank, from the station, take Bahnhofstr. to Juri-Gagarin-Ring; it's on the corner. **24hr. ATM.** Open M, W, F 9am-4pm, Tu and Th 9am-6pm.

Gay and Lesbian Resources: At the **AIDS-Hilfe,** Windthorststr. 43a (☎346 22 97). Streetcar #3 (dir.: Windischholzhausen) or 6 (dir.: Wiesenhügel) to "Robert-Koch-Str.," then continue another block. On the edge of the Stadtpark behind the train station, a rainbow flag flies over a house that features a library (open W 2-6pm), archive, and cafe. AIDS counseling available Tu 1-6pm and W 6-10pm. **Cafe Swiß** open Tu-F 7pm-midnight (Th under 27 only), and Su 2:30-8pm. Events on Fridays.

Women's Resources: Brennessel Frauenzentrum, Meister-Eckehart-Str. 5 (☎565 65 10; www.frauenzentrum-brennessel.de). Specializing in support for abused women, the center offers information, counseling and overnight stays, as well as a cafe, sauna, and cultural programs. Open M-F 9am-6pm, Th until 9pm. Odd hours mid-June to mid-Aug.

Emergency: Police ☎110. **Fire and Ambulance** ☎112.

Pharmacy: Apollo-Apotheke, Juri-Gagarin-Ring 94 (☎24 11 66). See **Currency Exchange** for directions. Open M-F 7:30am-7pm, Sa 8am-1pm.

Internet: Internet Cafe in the Ratskeller Passage across from the Rathaus with 12 computers. €1.50 per 30min. Happy hour 7-10pm (€2 per hr.). Open M-F 10am-10pm, Sa 1-9pm. **Buch Habel,** Anger 7 (☎59 85 80), on the 2nd fl. €1.50 per 30min. Open M-F 9am-8pm, Sa 9am-4pm.

Post Office: 99084 Erfurt. Open M-F 9am-7pm, Sa 9am-1pm.

🏠 ACCOMMODATIONS

To get to **Jugendherberge Erfurt (HI)** ❷, Hochheimer Str. 12, from the station, take streetcar #5 (dir.: Steigerstr.) to "Steigerstr." Backtrack and turn left onto Hochheimer Str.; the hostel is on the left corner at the first intersection. **Internet** €0.10 per min. Breakfast included. Wheelchair accessible. (☎562 67 05. Check-in after 5pm, desk open from 2pm for reservations. Busy in the summer; call ahead. Dorms with bath €20, under 27 €17. Nonmembers €3.10 extra per night.) **Pension am Park** ❹, Löberwallgraben 22, is along the park behind the train station. From the station, exit to the left and take a left under the bridge on Bahnhofstr. Turn right onto Schillerstr, which leads to Löberwallgraben on the right (10min.). This fastidiously maintained old building features stylish rooms with phone and TV, and use of the kitchen. Breakfast included. (☎/fax 345 33 44. Singles €38; doubles €52.

🍴 FOOD

The region's specialty, *Thüringer Bratwurst*, is sold at stands all over the city (€1-1.50). Check out the many outdoor *Eiscafes*, especially on the Fischmarkt. For **groceries**, try **tegut**, Anger 74/75, next to the Kaufmannskirche. (Open M-F 7:30am-8pm, Sa 7:30am-4pm.) There is also a fresh fruit and vegetable **market** on Dompl. (Open M-Sa 7am-2pm.)

Nährstoff, Futterstr. 18-19 (☎643 18 55), serves fresh *tapas*, from Spanish olives and cheeses to omelettes, chicken in white wine, and calamari (€2.50-9) in a sleek setting. Open daily from 6pm. Kitchen open until midnight. ❷

Anger Maier, Schlößerstr. 8 (☎566 10 58), at the edge of Angerpl. heading toward the Fischmarkt. One of the oldest bars in Erfurt, with a friendly atmosphere and an exceptional *Biergarten*, where guests enjoy shaded tables, a fountain and an extensive menu. Entrees €6-9. English menu upon request. Open M-Sa 9am-1am. ❸

Ristorante Don Camillo, Michaelisstr. 29 (☎260 11 45), has delicious, moderately priced Italian food in a setting worthy of a higher price bracket. Despite the white tablecloths, the expat waitstaff is unpretentious and exceptionally friendly, serving pizzas (€5-8), pastas (from €6), and pricier fish and meat entrees (€10.50-16). Open daily 11:30am-3pm and 5:30-11:30pm. ❸

👁 SIGHTS

MARIENDOM. Seventy 800-year-old steps lead up to the heavenly cathedral that towers over the Dompl. Today it is a Gothic extravaganza, though its 1154 foundation is Romanesque. Fifteen 14th-century stained-glass windows portray Biblical stories and the lives of the saints, a life-size candelabra in the form of a saint is the oldest free-standing piece of bronze artwork in Germany, and a Romanesque sculpture of an enthroned Mary dates back to the 12th century. Opposite of the ornate 17m altar is an 18m baptismal font, connected to the ceiling to symbolize the power of baptism to connect earth to heaven. Out of sight hangs the enormous **Gloriosa bell,** the biggest in medieval Europe, which only rings on important church holidays. Pause a moment by the gigantic **mural** of St. Christophorus, the patron of travelers, who is said to protect them from untimely death. *(Dompl. Open May-Oct. M-F 9am-5pm, Su 1-5pm; Nov.-Apr. M-Sa 10-11:30am and 12:30-4pm, Su 2-4pm. Free.)*

SEVERIKIRCHE. The muted sandstone interior and the Gothic exterior of this church are similar to, and outshone by, the Mariendom, for which it served as a model with its unusual three towers. The enormous Baroque organ screams with flying golden angels, flames, and fake pastel marble, and the 13m high altar is similarly impressive. The sandstone sarcophagus near the entrance supposedly holds the bones of St. Severus, for whom the church is named and who was made a Bishop in the year 284. *(Open May-Oct. M-F 9am-12:30pm and 1:30-5pm, Sa 9-11:30am and 12:30-4:30pm, Su 2-4pm; Nov.-Apr. M-F 10-11:30am and 12:30-4pm, Su 2-4pm. Free.)*

KRÄMERBRÜCKE. The bubbling river Gera provided the *raison d'être* for what is now one of Erfurt's most interesting architectural attractions. The *Krämerbrücke* was built in the 1400s to facilitate the *via regia* (royal road) trade route running from Kiev to Paris. Traders flocked to Erfurt from around the world to

THE CLOISTERS

On July 2nd, 1505, a young Martin Luther was caught in a terrible storm on the road to Erfurt. Fearing for his life, he cried: "Help me St. Anna, I want to become a monk." Although his father had intended for him to be a lawyer, two weeks later Luther entered Erfurt's Augustinian monastery.

A monk's life was difficult: the "morning" bell rang at 2am to summon the Brothers to a cold washing and their prayers; they wouldn't eat until after morning mass at 8am, and then studied until nightfall. Besides the rigorous schedule, extremely cold winters and drafty communal dorm rooms led to many nasty diseases; most monks died before reaching 30. Such misery contrasted sharply to the beautiful surroundings in which the monks lived. The stained glass windows with parrots, lions, and roses that inspired Luther still decorate the church, and Romanesque arcades line the quiet courtyard.

Today, you can stay in one of the cloister's rooms and imagine that you are about to join Luther for morning prayers or a study in the library. Though comfortable beds, hot showers, and modern heating have replaced wooden boards, cold baths, and weak fires, the quiet beauty of the cloister and Erfurt's old city remain. *Augustiner Kloster, Augustinerstr. 10. Streetcar #1 or 5 to "Augustinerstr."* ☎ *57 66 00. Singles €45; doubles €76.)*

pick up *Waid*, the Thuringian-produced blue dye of the Middle Ages. Brewed in urine and reduced to a powder, the blue stuff smelled awful, but also cultivated the fortunes that built all those pretty houses. The bridge still serves a commercial function, lined on both sides with shops that completely block the Gera from view. At the far end of the bridge from the tourist office, the tower of the **Ägidienkirche** is open for those who'd like to climb some rickety stairs for a glimpse of Erfurt's red-roofed houses. *(Tower open Su noon-5pm and sporadically M-Sa. €1.50, students €1.)*

ANGER. Erfurt's wide pedestrian promenade, the *Anger* (German for "meadow"), is one of the most attractive shopping areas in eastern Germany. Fascinating architecture, most of it 19th-century Neo-classical or *Jugendstil*, lines the street. Across from the post office is **House #6,** where Russian **Tsar Alexander I** stayed when he came to Erfurt to meet with Napoleon in 1808. The **Kaufmannskirche,** once the site of business transactions, sits at the end of the Anger behind the post office. The **Angermuseum,** Anger 18, housed in a yellow mansion, displays a small collection of medieval religious art from around Erfurt as well as rotating exhibitions of local contemporary art. *(☎ 562 33 11. Open Tu-Su Apr.-Oct. 10am-6pm; Nov.-Mar. 10am-5pm. €1.50, students €0.75. Special exhibits €4, students €3.)*

AUGUSTINERKLOSTER. Martin Luther spent 10 formative years as a Catholic priest and Augustine monk in this cloister. Over the years, the building has housed a hospital, an orphanage, and various schools. Today, it is home to a small community of nuns and is the meeting place for diverse church groups from around the world. Some of the buildings from the cloister's original construction in 1277 still remain, and tours visit a cell that Luther once called home. *(From the tourist office, cross the Krämerbrücke, turn left on Gotthardstr., and cut left through Kirchg. Tours of the cloister every hr. M-F 10am-5pm, Su 11am. €3.50, students €2.50. With the associated exhibit €5/€4.)* The **library** has one of Germany's most priceless collections, including a number of early bibles with personal notations by Luther himself. When Allied bombs destroyed the library in February 1945, 268 people lost their lives, but the books (hidden elsewhere) were unscathed. *(☎ 576 60 22. Open M 2-6pm, Tu-W 10am-6pm.)*

RATHAUS. The stony neo-Gothic facade of Erfurt's Rathaus belies its more playful interior decorations, which date from the Romantic period. Running along the staircases and hallways of the main entrance, beautiful murals depict fictional and factual events related to Erfurt, such as Faust conjuring up a vision of the cyclops Polyphemus before bewildered and skeptical Erfurt University students. *(Fischmarkt 1. Open M-Tu and Th 8am-6pm, W 8am-4pm, F 8am-2pm, Sa-Su 10am-5pm. Free.)*

OTHER SIGHTS. At the end of the *Anger* towards the Dompl. is the red and white Baroque **Staatskanzlei,** location of a meeting between Goethe and Napoleon, who tried to lecture the poet for writing such gloomy tragedies. Goethe refrained from any retorts about pan-European conquest. Between the *Anger* and Dompl., the lively **Fischmarkt** is bordered by restored guild houses with wild facades. For a view of the city, climb the old walls of the **Zitadelle Petersburg** behind Dompl.

♫ 🎭 ENTERTAINMENT AND NIGHTLIFE

Erfurt's 220,000 citizens maintain an indulgent nightlife. The **Theater Erfurt** puts on regular shows, ranging from operas and ballet to youth theater, at the **Schauspielhaus,** Dalbersweg 2. (Box office, Anger 13, open Tu-F 10am-6pm, Sa 10am-4pm. Student discounts available.) Tickets to these and most other performances in Erfurt can also be purchased at the tourist office. Just off Dompl., the **Theater Waidspeicher** runs a marionette and puppet theater, and holds cabaret shows on weekends. (Box office Dompl. 18. ☎598 29 24; www.waidspeicher.de. Open Tu-F 3-5:30pm, Sa 10am-1pm. Puppet shows €2.50-6, cabaret €4-8.)

The area near Dompl. and the Krämerbrücke between **Michaelisstraße, Marbacher Gasse,** and **Allerheiligenstraße** glows at night with cafes, candlelit restaurants, and bars; **Johannesstraße** also has its share. The **Double b,** Marbacher G. 10, near Dompl., mixes Irish pub with German *Biergarten;* trendy Erfurters show up there for the cordial atmosphere and cheap beers. (☎211 51 22. Open M-F 8am-1am, Sa-Su 9am-1am.) **Silberschale,** Kürschnerg. 3, off Rathausbrücke on the Anger side, has reasonably priced drinks and a delightful back deck with seating right over the shallow Gera. (Open daily 9am-1am, later on weekends.). The laid-back **Miss Marple's,** Michaelisstr. 42, features photos of Agatha Christie's humorous private eye on the walls and an entrance that is a dead ringer for a London phone booth. If you're looking for something to soak up that beer after a long night, check here—the kitchen serves sandwiches and Thüringer specialties (€3.50-9) until 2am. (☎540 33 99. Open daily from 6pm.) The **Studentenclub Engelsburg,** Allerheiligenstr. 20-21, just off Marktstr., a mainstay of the local underground, hosts live bands of many genres from Erfurt and farther afield. While the schedule and cover vary widely (info ☎24 47 70; www.eburg.de), the folks in the **Steinhaus,** a cafe/bar that's part of the same complex, can offer some cheap eats (€2-6) and tell you what's happening. (Open M-F from 2pm and Sa-Su from 11am.) To take a break, head upstairs to **Café DuckDich.** (Open Tu from 8pm and during concerts.) Wanna dance? Erfurt makes it easy, offering a special bus to its two largest discos, **FUN** and **SPOT.** Bus #33 runs from the Anger to the discos and back (every 1-2hr.).

THÜRINGER WALD (THURINGIAN FOREST)

Extending from Eisenach in the northwest to the Saale river in the east, the vast Thüringen Wald is one of Germany's most magnificent landscapes. Because of the forest's proximity to Weimar and Jena, historical university cities that once sheltered many of Germany's foremost intellectuals, it enjoys the unmatched reputation that only poets can bestow. Following Goethe and Schiller's lead, droves of Romantic poets and philosophers found inspiration in the shadows of these trees.

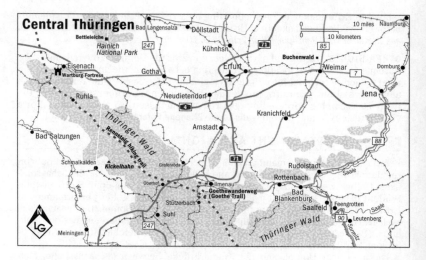

Central Thüringen Bad Langensalza Döllstadt
Bettieleiche ■
Hainich National Park
Kühnhsn
Buchenwald ■
Eisenach
Wartburg Fortress
Gotha
Erfurt
Weimar
Dornburg
Ruhla
Neudietendorf
Jena
Thüringer Wald
Kranichfeld
Bad Salzungen
Rennsteig hiking trail
Arnstadt
Schmalkalden
Kickelhahn
Grafenröda
Rudolstadt
Oberhof
Rottenbach
Ilmenau
Goethewanderweg
(Goethe Trail)
Bad Blankenburg
Saalfeld
Feengrotten
Stützerbach
Suhl
Leutenberg
Meiningen
Thüringer Wald
10 miles Naumburg
10 kilometers

Today, the glory of the forest is more accessible than ever. One of the most popular routes through the region is the 168km long *Rennsteig*. Starting in Hörschel, cutting across a swath of southern Thuringia, and running south into Bavaria, the Rennsteig links gorgeous scenery and traditional villages that are scattered along its path. While history books date the trail to 1330, locals claim that it was first trod upon by prehistoric hunter-gatherers. In the middle of the route, Ilmenau is a good starting point in either direction: take bus #300 (dir.: Suhl) to "Rennsteigkreuzung" (€2). The tourist office in Erfurt (p. 568) or Eisenach (p. 576) sells guides and maps for an extended jaunt. If you're planning a multi-day hike, reserve trail-side huts far in advance. For more information, contact **Fremdenverkehrsband Thüringer Wald,** Postfach 124, 98501 Suhl (☎ 03681 394 50; www.thueringer-wald.com) or **Gästeinformation Brotterode,** Bad-Vilbeler-Pl. 4, 98599 Brotterode (☎ 036840 33 33).

ILMENAU
☎ 03677

The Thüringer Wald's small town of Ilmenau is friendly, bustling, and very proud of its most famous visitor, **Johann Wolfgang von Goethe.** Residents constantly point out that Goethe came to their town a total of 28 times. The author first worked in Ilmenau as a mining minister under the Duke of Weimar, but came back later to seek inspiration from the stunning natural surroundings. The town uses Goethe to lure visitors, vaunting his in-town haunts as well as the 18.5km 🏛**Goethewanderweg** (Goethe Trail), one of the many trails that lead from Ilmenau into the forest.

🚍🚊 **TRANSPORTATION AND PRACTICAL INFORMATION.** Ilmenau can be reached by **bus** or **train** from Erfurt (1hr., 1 per hr., €8.40). The Ilmenau **tourist office** is at Lindenstr. 12. From the station, walk straight up Bahnhofstr. to Wetzlarer Pl. Follow the pedestrian zone until it becomes Lindenstr. (15min.). The staff provides hiking maps and books rooms (from €13) for free. (☎ 20 23 58; www.ilmenau.de. Open M-F 9am-6pm, Sa 9am-1pm.) For **Internet** access try the **City Cyber Cafe,** Kirchpl. 3. (☎ 89 64 00. €4.40 per hr. Open M-F 11am-11pm, Sa-Su 4-11pm.) The **post office,** 98693 Ilmenau, Lindenstr. 1, is along the pedestrian zone before the tourist office. (Open M-F 9am-6pm, Sa 9am-noon.)

THÜRINGEN

█▐ ACCOMMODATIONS AND FOOD. *Jugendherberge Ilmenau (HI)* ❷, Am Stollen 49, is in a drab area far from town, but well located for hikers. Turn left out of the station and then left at August-Bebel-Str., crossing the tracks and veering right on the path along the tracks. After the sharp right curve, cross the bridge on your left and continue until the trail merges with Am Stollen (15min.). Or take bus A (dir.: TU Mensa; €0.90) to "Jugendherberge." (☎88 46 81; fax 88 46 82. Breakfast and sheets included. Reception 4-10pm. Check-out 9:30am. Lock-out 10am-4pm. Curfew 10pm, but you can get a key for a €10 deposit. €18, under 27 €15.) The small **Pension Ulrich** ❷, Corona-Schröter-Str. 5, a 15min. walk from town, will make you feel at home. (☎620 28. Breakfast included. Singles €17; doubles €34.)The **farmer's market** on the Markt sells fresh produce. (Tu and F 8am-6pm.) **Zur Post** ❷, Mühltor 6, on Wetzlarer Pl., serves filling regional dishes like *Thüringer Rostbrätel* (pork roast with potatoes) for €5-8. (☎67 10 27. Open M-F 8:30am-midnight, Sa 11am-1am, Su 11am-midnight. Kitchen closes 11pm.) For groceries, try **Rewe**, in the basement of the *City Kaufhaus* on F.-Hoffmann-Str. in the pedestrian zone. (Open M-F 9am-7pm, Sa 10am-4pm. If the *Kaufhaus* is closed, enter around back.)

▐ THE GOETHEWANDERWEG. The ▐Goethe Trail begins in Ilmenau, up Marktstr. outside the town's **Goethe-Gedenkstätte**, Am Markt 1, a museum that focuses on Goethe's career in Ilmenau and the mining industry he oversaw. (☎20 26 67. Open daily May-Oct. 9am-noon and 1-4:30pm; Nov.-Apr. 10am-noon and 1-4pm. €1, students and seniors €0.50.) The trail is well-marked by a looping *G* monogram, but pay close attention to the signs, since there are numerous trails. The next of many Goethe landmarks is the grave of **Corona Schröter**, the first actress to portray the heroine of Goethe's classical play *Iphigenia in Tauris*. Following the signs out of the graveyard, continue along Erfurterstr. to Neue Marienstr. and head into the hills. Tall pines crowd both sides of the trail as it leads up to the **Schwalbenstein**, an outcropping overlooking the valley where Goethe wrote Act IV of *Iphigenia*. The middle section passes by the **Emmastein**, an outcropping that Goethe drew as an example of the area's rock formations. The trail then leads down into the valley and through the town of Manebach up to a reconstruction of the tiny **Goethehäuschen** (Goethe cottage), where the poet scratched his "Wanderer's Night Song" into the walls; the view may inspire you to similar lyrical heights. On the way to the cottage you'll see the **Hermannstein**, a rock outcropping that supported a castle during the Middle Ages. Take a 200m detour off the trail to the **Kickelhahn**, a summit that provides a stunning panoramic view of the Thuringian forest. Climb up the *Aussichtsturm* (look-out tower) for the full 360° view; on a clear day, you can see all the way to the Harz Mountains. One kilometer farther stands the **Jagdhaus Gabelbach**, the hunting house of Duke Karl August that Goethe frequented in the summer. The refurnished lodge features a display of some of the author's scientific experiments and drawings. (☎20 26 26. Open Apr.-Oct. Sa-Su 10am-5pm; Nov.-Mar. Sa-Su 11am-3pm. €2, students €1.50.) Head down the mountain past a small pond to the *Finsteres Loch*, a picturesque green next to a brook where Duke August's hunting parties, with Goethe in tow, once rested from their long rides. At the end of the trail, **Stützerbach** is a tiny valley town where the local glass-works magnate often hosted the poet. His house is now the **Goethehaus**, but as a nod to the patron there are demonstrations of traditional glass-blowing. (☎036784 502 77. Open Apr.-Oct. Sa-Su 10am-5pm; Nov.-Mar. Sa-Su 11am-3pm. €2, students €1.50.) If you don't want to hike the 6hr. back to Ilmenau, you can take a bus. Go into Stützerbach, turn right onto Bahnhofstr., and then cut to your left through the parking lot in front of the tourist office. Take a right onto Unterstr., which leads over a bridge and to the "Stützerbach, Erholung" bus stop on Schleusingerstr. (M-F about 1 per hr. M-F, Sa-Su 2 per hr. until just before 9pm. €1.50 to Ilmenau.)

THÜRINGEN

Eisenach

▲ ACCOMMODATIONS
Campingplatz am Altenberger See, **5**
Jugendherberge Arthur Becker, **4**

🍴 FOOD & DRINK
BACH Cafe, **3**
Café Moritz, **2**
La Fontana, **1**

EISENACH

☎ 03691

Birthplace of **Johann Sebastian Bach,** residence-in-exile of **Martin Luther,** and site of the famous **Wartburg castle,** Eisenach has basked in a spotlight for almost a millennium. Tourists started visiting the castle as early as the 16th century—mainly to see the black stain that Luther made on the wall of his small room while "fighting the devil with ink." By the 19th century, Wartburg, one of Goethe's favorite spots, had became a national symbol. Eisenach is also the perfect place to start a journey into the Thuringian Forest to the south or the Hainich National Park to the north. Buses run from Eisenach to the heads of various trails (the distance is also bikeable), and the national park, unlike Wartburg, is refreshingly undiscovered.

🔲 🛂 TRANSPORTATION AND PRACTICAL INFORMATION

Trains to: **Erfurt** (50min., 1 per hr., €8); **Göttingen** (2hr., 2 per hr., €22); **Kassel** (1½hr., 2 per hr., €14); **Weimar** (1hr., 2 per hr., €11). Eisenach's **buses** (€0.90 per trip) go to Wartburg. For a **taxi**, call ☎22 02 20. Rent a **bike** at **Fahrrad-Service Helm**, Katharinenstr. 139. (€6-7 per day. Open M-F 9am-6pm, Sa 9am-1pm.) Eisenach's **tourist office**, Markt 2, has information on Wartburg, hands out free maps, offers daily city **tours** (2pm, 1½ hr., €4), and books rooms for free. From the train station, walk on Bahnhofstr. through the arched tunnel and follow it left until you can turn right onto the pedestrian Karlstr. (☎194 33. Open M 10am-6pm, Tu-F 9am-6pm, Sa-Su 10am-2pm.) The **Georgen-Apotheke**, Georgenstr. 18-20, is a centrally located **pharmacy**. (☎74 24 74. Open M-F 7:30am-6:30pm, Sa 8:30am-12:30pm.) **Die Eule**, Karlstr. 3, in the pedestrian zone near the Markt, is a **bookstore** that offers **Internet** access. (☎85 03 88. €3 per 40min. Open M-F 9:30am-7:30pm, Sa 10am-6pm.) The **post office**, 99817 Eisenach, is in the Marktpl. (Open M-F 8:30am-6pm, Sa 8:30am-noon.)

🔏 🗠 ACCOMMODATIONS AND FOOD

Jugendherberge Arthur Becker (HI) ❷, Mariental 24, is in a comfortable old villa far from the center of town, but close to the Schloß. From the train station, take Bahnhofstr. to Wartburger Allee, which runs into Mariental. Pass the pond; the hostel will be on your right (35min.). Or, take bus #3 (dir.: Mariental) to "Liliengrund Parkpl." Recently renovated, the hostel has an elegant dining room and terraces. (☎74 32 59; fax 74 32 60. Breakfast included. Reception 8am-11pm. €18, under 27 €15.) The nearest **camping** is at **Am Altenberger See ❶** in Eckartshausen, with a sauna in view of the lake. From the Eisenach bus station, take bus #31 to "Bad Liebenstein," or #135 to "Bad Salzungen" (Bus M-F 1 per hr., Sa-Su 3 per day. ☎21 56 37. Reception 9am-1pm and 3-9pm. €4 per person, €3 per tent, €1.50 per car.)

The centrally-located **La Fontana ❶**, Georgenstr. 22, serves delicious pizza and pasta (€3) in a central location. (☎74 35 39. Open Su-Th 11:30am-2:30pm and 5-11pm, F-Sa 11:30am-2:30pm and 5-11:30pm.) **Café-Restaurant Moritz ❷**, Bahnhofstr. 7, is known for its Thüringian specialities (€3-9) and sinful ice cream delicacies, served outside on nicer days. (☎905 61. Open May-Oct. M-F 8am-9pm, Sa-Su 10am-9pm; Nov.-Apr. M-F 8am-7pm, Sa-Su 10am-7pm.) Bask in the classical climate of the Bachhaus at nearby **BACH Cafe ❸**, Frauenplan 8. The elegant interior and unadulterated Thüringian menu (entrees €6-10) make it a fitting stop after the museum. (☎21 55 22. Open daily 11am-10pm.) For **groceries** head to the **Edeka** on Johannispl. (Open M-F 7am-7pm, Sa 7am-2pm.)

💿 SIGHTS

🏰 WARTBURG FORTRESS

Tour buses run between the train station and the castle (1 per hr., 9am-5pm, €0.90). Wartburgerallee leads to the foot of the hill, and a number of footpaths lead up the incline. If you weigh 60kg (132 lb.) or less, you can ride a donkey up the last stretch; €3. ☎770 73. Open daily Mar.-Oct. 8:30am-5pm; Nov.-Feb. 9am-3:30pm. Obligatory castle tours (in German) leave every 10min. from "Eingang II." €6.50, students and children €3.50, seniors and the disabled €5.50. Museum and Luther study without tour €3.50, students €2.

The castle high above Eisenach's half-timbered streets lords over the northwestern slope of the rolling Thüringer Wald. It was founded in 1067 by the Franconian **Count Ludwig the Jumper,** who didn't own the land, but covered it with soil from his estate so as to lay claim to it with a clear conscience. By the turn of the 13th century, Wartburg's court was a famed cultural center. Six talented *Minnesänger*, the medieval troubadours who established German choral music, competed here in the *Sängerkrieg* (singers' battle). The musicians had to perform simultaneously and spontaneously for the court. The event was declared a draw, which was lucky since instead of granting a prize to the winner, the court had declared that whoever lost the battle would also lose his life. These events, which inspired Wagner's opera *Tannhäuser*, are depicted in the castle's **Sängersaal.** Another important medieval resident was **St. Elizabeth,** whose charitable deeds are represented in a 20th-century mosaic made from just under four million pieces of glass. After its medieval heyday, Wartburg had to wait a few hundred years before receiving its most important guest, the refugee **Martin Luther,** in 1521. Disguised as a wandering nobleman under the pseudonym Junker Jörg, Luther spent most of his time here translating the Bible and writing anti-Catholic treatises. Due in part to the restorative efforts of Goethe, Wartburg found new life in the 19th century. The castle's **Festsaal** (festival hall) preserves the memory of the 1817 meeting of 500 representatives of university fraternities, who formed Germany's first bourgeois opposition (ruthlessly crushed two years later). A copy of the flag they toasted hangs in the room; its red, gold, and black colors were inspiration for Germany's present flag.

The renovated interior of the castle now matches the Romantic idea of the Middle Ages more closely than historical reality, but the structure itself, including wooden supports, remains remarkably unchanged in the last 850 years. Authentic or not, the Wartburg is sure to enchant. The view from the walls of the courtyard or atop the south tower is spectacular—if you look opposite Eisenach, you can see from the Thüringer Wald all the way across the former East-West border to Hessen. If you arrive later than 10:30am, expect to wait for over an hour to get in. To pass the time, you can hike around the rich woods and grounds for free.

BACHHAUS. Next to an imposing Bach statue on Frauenplan are the recreated Bach family living quarters where Johann Sebastian is thought to have stormed into the world in 1685. Downstairs are period keyboards instruments like a clavichord, a spinet, and a beautifully preserved "house organ" from 1750, about the size of a telephone booth. Roughly every hour, one of the museum's guides plays Bach selections on these instruments and provides historical context in German. English translations available upon request. *(Frauenplan 21. Turn off Wartburgallee down Grimmelg. to reach the house.* ☎ *793 40. Open daily 10am-6pm. €4, students €3.)*

OTHER SIGHTS. Town life centers on the pastel **Markt,** bounded by the tilting pink **Rathaus** and the **Georgenkirche,** an 800-year-old church where Bach family members were organists for 132 years and where J.S. Bach was baptized. The ornate diptych is on the left side of the altar where Martin Luther and **Jan Hus,** a Dutch minister and one of Luther's forerunners in the Reformation, once preached. *(Open M-Sa 10am-12:30pm and 2-5pm, Su 11am-12:30pm and 2-5pm.)* Just up the street from the Markt is the latticed **Lutherhaus,** where Luther spent his school days. *(Lutherpl. 8.* ☎ *298 30. Open daily Apr.-Oct. 9am-5pm; Nov.-Mar. 10am-5pm. €2.50, students €2.)*

HAINICH NATIONAL PARK

Although Germans are no strangers to the well-worn paths of the Thüringer Wald, most are unfamiliar with the richly forested northwestern corner of the woods that is the Hainich National Park. In the time-scale of Germany, Hainich is an infant: it became Germany's thirteenth national park in 1997. The park may be ringed with stunning views of Thüringian farmland, but the moment you venture inside, the outside world couldn't seem farther away. Towering beeches shelter wildcats, bats and wild boars, and cast a rich green light over the forest floor.

✦ ORIENTATION

Hainich is crescent-shaped, its ends pointing south and east. It is accessible from three towns: the spa town **Bad Langensalza** at the eastern tip, **Mühlhausen** in the north, and **Eisenach** (p. 576), west of the southern tip. The quality of the trails around Bad Langensalza and Mühlhausen and their proximity to bus stops make them the best jumping-off points. The park, covering 76km^2, is fairly flat (the highest "mountain," *Alten Berg*, tops out at 494m) and covered in majestic beech forest mixed with ash and maple and draped with exotic orchids. The third of the park that extends west from **Craulaer Kreuz** is a protected zone where human intrusion beyond the hiking paths is prohibited. The eastern section near Weberstadt and the whole southern area of the park were military training camps for Soviet and German armies from 1935 to 1997, but the forest is quickly reclaiming the once ammunition-littered grounds. The largest body of water is the small **Hünenteich** (giant's pond) in the northwest, and the whole north is scattered with swamps.

☐ TRANSPORTATION

Hainich is easy to navigate by car, and all trailheads have free parking. Biking is also a great option; Hainich is a beautiful ride from Bad Langensalza. Take Mühlhauserstr. out of the city and look for a white gravel path on the left as soon as you get out of the residential area. Follow it to the end, take a right, and ride straight to the park (20min.). From there you can bike well-marked trails or follow signs to the Thiemsburg trailhead to lock your bike. Public transportation can be difficult to navigate. **Trains** run to Bad Langensalza from Erfurt (1hr., 2 per hr., €7) and Weimar (1½hr., 1 per hr., €9), and connect from Bad Langensalza to Mühlhausen (15min., 1 per hr., €3.10), where buses run to the park's smaller towns.

During the week, regular **buses** travel near the park from all three towns; some also run on weekends. From the Bad Langensalza bus station, take bus #726 to Thiemsburg (20min.) and Craula (25min.) or #733 to Weberstedt (15min.). From the Mühlhausen bus and train stations, take bus #152 to "Kammerforst, Eichsf.-Str."(20min.) or #153 to Weberstedt (25min.) Bus #30 leaves from Eisenach's bus station to Berka vor dem Hainich (20min.) and Lauterbach (30min.) and goes on to Mühlhausen (4-12 per day, 5am-7pm, €1.50-4.90). Check the schedule carefully for the last bus back—most run until at least 6pm, but some stop as early as 3pm. Bus information is available at tourist and park centers. On weekends, the **WanderBus** travels the perimeter of the park, stopping within walking distance of all trails. Buy your ticket on the bus (€2-4; bikes free). Buses leave five or six times per day from the train and bus stations of Eisenach, Mühlhausen, and Bad Langensalza.

⚑ PRACTICAL INFORMATION

Emergency: Police ☎ 110. **Fire** ☎ 112. Any of the 4 National Park Information Centers (see below) will arrange for emergency assistance in the park.

National Park Information Centers: All 4 centers offer trail maps and information on tours and transportation. The central office in Bad Langensalza is the most informative; those in Kammerforst and Berka vor dem Hainich are at trailhead bus stops. The town information centers in Mühlhausen and Eisenach also have maps and bus information. The national park **website** is www.nationalpark-hainich.de.

Bad Langensalza: Bei der Marktkirche 9 (☎03603 39 07 28; fax 39 07 20). Open M-F 9am-6pm, Sa-Su 10am-3pm.

Berka vor dem Hainich: Hauptstr. 166 (☎036924 418 96). Open Apr.-Oct. M-F 9am-6pm, Sa-Su 9am-4pm; Nov.-Mar. daily 10am-4pm.

HOG WILD

So, you've had your fill of *Schnitzel* and *Wurst*, and you're wondering where it all began? Back before pigs crowded into stalls or rolled around in mud, when the pig was not a symbol of gluttony, when it was more than just a side for eggs, this great animal roamed the wild forests of Germany, striking fear into the hearts of all who crossed its path.

If you have trouble connecting this noble ancestor to your morning *Schinken*, the Hainich National Park can help. The hotel and restaurant **Graues Schloß**, in Mihla near the park, offers a "Wild Boar Weekend" to present the animal in all its glory. Hoping to surprise the boars in their habitat, a guide takes guests into the forest morning and night. Back at the hotel, a film that explores the lives of these porcine princes is shown. Then comes the grand finale; in a moment that separates vegetarians from carnivores, a chef enters and turns the giant pig into a feast. Guests can watch and drool as the meal is made and the master cook reveals his secret boar recipes.

At €135 per person, the weekend is pricier than your average trip into the woods. But if you were on your own, you'd have to hunt the fearsome oinker yourself.

(Hotel and Restaurant "Graues Schloss." Thomas Müntzer Str. 4, Mihla. ☎ 036924 422 72; www.graues-schloss.de.)

Kammerforst: Straße der Einheit (☎ 036028 368 93). Open Apr.-Oct. M-F 9am-6pm, Sa-Su 9am-4pm; Nov.-Mar. daily 10am-4pm.

Behringen: Hauptstr. 97 (☎ 036254 786 40). Open Apr.-Oct. M-F 9am-6pm, Sa-Su 9am-4pm; Nov.-Mar. daily 10am-4pm.

■ **Tours and Events:** Throughout the year, the park organizes guided, German-language hikes and events, ranging from spying on wildcats and boars to celebrating Carnival in the winter forest. (2-8 hr. Times and themes vary widely from week to week; information available at National Park Centers. Tours leave from trailheads around the park. Free; sometimes a small (typically €2.50) contribution is requested to cover costs.)

▓ ACCOMMODATIONS AND FOOD

Camping is prohibited within the park, and there are few facilities on the outskirts. Your best bet is to stay in one of the towns around the park and take day trips—the park center in Bad Langensalza will refer you to rooms in the area. Eisenach (p. 576) and Mühlhausen (p. 581) have hostels; to reserve a private room, contact tourist offices. Craula, 20min. away from Bad Langensalza by bus #726 or the Wander-Bus, has a **Touristische Herberge ❶**, Behringerstr. 81. with 2- to 6-bed rooms close to the park. The hostel is a 35min. walk to "Craulaer Kreuz," a head for three trails, and a 45min. walk to "Thiemsburg," the start of three other trails. (☎ 036254 815 56. Breakfast €2. Sheets €4. €16, under 27 €14.) There are two **Imbiße** in the park: one at the **Thiemsburg** trailhead (open Apr.-Oct. Sa noon-7pm, Su 11am-7pm) and one at the **Ihlefeld** trailhead (open Apr.-Oct. Sa-Su 10am-7pm).

▓ HIKING

Hainich has 13 trails that range from short jaunts to the 32km *Rennstieg*. Clear maps of the park and its trails, available at the park information centers, make mixing and matching trails easy; they are all well-marked with individual symbols and intersect frequently. All trails (except for the *Rennstieg* and *Waagebalken*) are loops that end at their starting points, which are easily accessible by car.

NORTH (NEAR MÜHLHAUSEN)

Betteleichenweg (11.7 km). From the "Kammerforst, Eichsf.-Str." bus stop, continue in the same direction, take your 1st right, and continue straight until you see signs for the trail. Although much of the forest in this area is quite young, the highlight of the loop is the 1000-year-old *Betteleiche* (begging oak), with a time- and weather-worn hole large enough to walk through. The last section winds through the hills near Kammerforst and provides a stunning, sweeping view of Thuringia.

Saugraben (9.5km), via Betteleichenweg from Kammerforst (1.8km). Orchids bloom here in summer, and the end offers a view to the north as far as Mühlhausen.

EAST (NEAR BAD LANGENSALZA)

Rennstieg (32km). From Eigenrieden, west of Mühlhausen, to Behringen. Cuts straight through the national park and continues in forested areas outside the park's official borders. Not to be confused with Rennsteig, to the south.

Sperbersgrund (5.6km), Craula. Follow signs for "Craulaer Kreuz." The lovely Sperbersgrund is one of the few trails in the core zone of the park, a largely untouched area. At the end of the hike, the 400m detour gives a grand view of the Wartburg.

Thiemsburg (3.8km), Thiemsburg. The only trail starting from a bus stop features a wood telephone, a wood organ, and the largest tree in the park (5.45m circumference).

Waagebalken (20km), Weberstedt or Thiemsburg. Running east to west, the Waagebalken is a potpourri of trails, sharing sections of Saugraben, Rennstieg, Betteleichenweg, and Bummelkuppenweg. The full trail begins in Harthaus, near Bad Langensalza.

WEST (NEAR EISENACH)

Bummelkuppenweg (9km), Lauterbach. This trail along the "Hohe Straße," starts with a view of the Werra River, used in the 1800s to haul grain and salt to northern Germany.

Erlebnispfad Silberborn (2.5km), Berka vor dem Hainich. A short walk from the town brings visitors to this little trail full of gadgets—from crank organs that play animal sounds to boxes that emit forest smells—to help kids and adults experience the forest.

MÜHLHAUSEN   ☎ 03601

Just north of Hainich National Park, the bustling town of Mühlhausen began as a Franconian mill in the 8th century and grew into the walled city that is still preserved today. Bach spent two years here as organist, and radical Reformationist **Thomas Müntzer** preached here. With a number of trailheads just short bus rides away, Mühlhausen is a great gateway to the park, and stunning churches and medieval architecture make the city a sight in its own right.

The **tourist office**, Ratsstr. 20, is in the Altstadt, a short walk from the bus and train stations. From the Busbahnhof, walk away from the parking lot up Stättestr., turn right on Steinweg, and take a left on the exceptionally narrow Ratsstr.; from the train station, walk straight up Karl-Marx-Str. to the city wall at Unter der Linde and follow the signs to Steinweg and then to the tourist office. The staff provides hiking maps, city maps (€0.50), leads city tours (Sa-Su 11am, €5), and books rooms (from €13) for free. (☎45 23 35; www.muehlhausen.de. Open M-F 9am-5pm.) The **post office**, 99974 Mühlhausen, is directly across from the Divi-Blasii-Kirche on Johann-Sebastian-Bach-Pl. (Open M-F 9am-6pm, Sa 9am-noon.)

The **Jugendherberge Mühlhausen (HI) ❷**, Auf dem Tonberg 1, offers 2-, 4-, and 6-bed rooms in a beautiful location far from town but convenient for hikers. From the bus or train station take city line #5 or 6 to "Blobach" and follow the signs 500m farther to the Jugendherberge. (☎81 33 18; fax 81 33 20. Sheets included. €15.50, under 27 €12.50.) The bright and friendly **Pension Höfler ❸**, Kuttelg. 23, is located right in the Altstadt and offers a **restaurant ❷** downstairs. (Entrees €1.60-5.60. Open M-Sa 11am-10pm, Su 11am-9pm.) From Steinweg, turn onto Linsenstr. Go two blocks and turn left on Kuttelg. (☎85 67 69; www.pension-hoeffler.de. Breakfast included. Singles €27-30; doubles €44-50.) Around the Obermarkt, near Steinweg, are a variety of fresh produce stands, cheap cafes, and restaurants.

A stroll through the Altstadt reveals numerous churches and medieval buildings. The stunning 800-year-old **Marienkirche**, Bei der Marienkirche, the second largest church in Thuringia, towers over the town. The church now functions as a museum of religious relics and a monument to Thomas Müntzer, a rebel Reforma-

THÜRINGEN

tionist and follower of Luther who instigated a peasant's revolt in 1525 so violent that even Luther disapproved. (Open Tu-Su 11am-4:45pm. €3, students and seniors €2.) The **Divi-Blasii-Kirche**, Johann-Sebastian-Bach-Pl. 4, is also called the *Bach Kirche* in honor of its most famous organist, who played here from 1707 to 1708. The organ Bach used was removed in the 19th century, but a replica was built in the 20th century with the help of **Albert Schweitzer**. (☎44 65 16; fax 44 65 16. Open M-Sa 10am-12:30pm and 1-5pm. Free.) A section of the *Stadtmauer* (city wall) at the **Rabenturm** at the end of Herrenstr. is climbable, as is the 14th-century tower itself. (Open Apr.-Oct. M-Sa 11am-4:45. €3, students and seniors €2.)

BAD LANGENSALZA   ☎03603

Near the eastern tip of Hainich National Park, the walled city of Bad Langensalza boasts a beautiful medieval Altstadt (dating from the 10th-century reign of Otto II), thermal baths and spas, and stunning Japanese gardens. The **tourist office**, Kurpromenade 5, is across the Altstadt from the Bahnhof in the tiny but striking **Frederikenschlösschen** castle. From the train and bus station, walk down Bahnhofstr., turn right on Poststr., and follow the signs around the wall to the *Haus des Gastes*. The staff gives out maps of Hainich National Park and the city, leads city tours (June-Aug. M-Tu and F-Sa 2pm; €2, students and seniors €1.50), and books rooms (from €13) for free. (☎83 44 24; www.bad-langensalza.de. Open M-F 9am-5pm, May-Oct. also Sa-Su 2-5pm.) The **post office**, Bei der Marktkirche 3, 99947 Bad Langensalza, is next to the Marktkirche. (Open 8:30am-6pm, Sa 8:30am-noon.)

Plenty of inexpensive accommodations lurk in and around Bad Langensalza. **Pension "Zur Lohgerberei"** ❷, Lobersg. 2., offers comfy rooms with showers and balconies in the city center. From the train station, walk straight down Bahnhofstr. as it becomes Steinweg and bear left on Langestr. At Wiebeckpl. bear right onto Bergstr., take a quick right onto Unter dem Berge, and veer left onto Lobersg. (☎/fax 84 61 31. Breakfast included. Singles €26-31; doubles and triples €18-21 per person.) Cafes and restaurants line Marktstr. and Jüdeng. and the Korn Markt. The **EDEKA**, Marktstr. 25, sells groceries. (Open M-F 8am-6pm, Sa 8am-noon.)

The streets of the city's Altstadt are lined with churches, shops, fountains, and restored medieval houses. Just outside the *Stadtmauer* is the colorful **Rose Garden**, where dozens of rose varieties grow outside a small museum of scientific exhibits on the beautiful flowers. (Entrance on Vor dem Klagetor. Garden open daily 9am-8pm. Museum open W and Sa-Su 2-5pm. Free.) Next door, the peaceful **Japanese Garden** combines a variety of gardens complete with stepping stones, a waterfall, special benches in a *Trockenlandschaft* (dry landscape), and the requisite bridge over a pond. (Entrance on Kurpromenade. Open daily 9am-8pm. Free.)

SACHSEN-ANHALT (SAXONY-ANHALT)

Saxony-Anhalt seems humble at first glance, but its tranquil grass plains hold cities of international cultural significance. Although Wittenberg and Dessau draw thousands of tourists each year, they remain small enough to preserve a timelessness that harbors traditional German character. The region suffers from the highest unemployment rate in Germany, but it is rapidly rebuilding and modernizing, and majestic cathedral spires now share the skyline with scaffolding and cranes. The *Land* won't disappoint nature enthusiasts, either—Saxony-Anhalt is home to the supposedly witch-haunted Harz Mountains, a skiing and hiking paradise.

HIGHLIGHTS OF SAXONY-ANHALT

RELIVE THE REFORMATION in **Wittenberg** (p. 583), the city where **Martin Luther** posted his **95 Theses** on a church. The city still celebrates its native superstar and has recently been blessed with a **Hundertwasser**-designed high school.

SUBORDINATE FORM TO FUNCTION at the original **Bauhaus,** which imbues the city of **Dessau** (p. 586) with design-school hipness.

WALK IN GOETHE'S FOOTSTEPS to the top of the **Brocken** (p. 596), or visit the half-timbered towns of **Thale** (p. 601) and **Wernigerode** (p. 597), in the allegedly witch-haunted **Harz mountains** (p. 594).

WITTENBERG   ☎ 03491

Wittenberg does its best to keep the memory of **Martin Luther** alive, and in 1938 even went so far as to rename itself **Lutherstadt Wittenberg.** It was here that Luther started the Reformation that irrevocably changed Europe. The city enthusiastically endorses the popular stories of Luther nailing his **95 Theses** to the Schloßkirche in 1517 and burning his papal bull of excommunication in 1520. His scandalous wedding, the final snub to Rome, was so perfectly dramatic that the town reenacts it every June in a three-day festival (see **Luther's Hochzeit,** p. 586). Even in the officially atheistic DDR, many East Germans saw the image of the maverick Luther risking his life to nail up his theses as an emblem of courageous resistance. One of Luther's successors at the Schloßkirche pulpit, **Pastor Friedrich Schorlemmer,** was a key player in the 1989 revolution against the DDR. Since that time, religious pilgrims have returned in full force to Luther's city. Renaissance painter **Lucas Cranach the Elder** also makes his posthumous presence felt in the town in many historical sights: both his paintings of Luther in the Lutherhalle and his world-renowned altar in the St. Marienkirche are not to be missed.

⏻🔁 TRANSPORTATION AND PRACTICAL INFORMATION

Trains: To: **Berlin** (1½hr., every 2hr., €17); **Dessau** (40min., 1 per hr., €6); **Leipzig** (1hr., every 2hr., €9); and **Magdeburg** (2hr., every 2hr., €12). To get to the pedestrian zone from the station, go out of the main building toward the bus stop, turn left through the parking lot and down the street, and follow the curve right. Cross the street and walk straight until the **Lutherhalle** is on your left; the pedestrian zone begins at Collegienstr.

Bikes: Fahrradladen, Coswiger Str. 21 (☎ 40 28 49), rents bikes for €7 per day. Open M-Sa 9am-6pm.

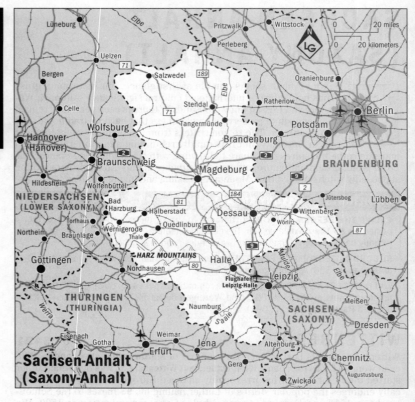

Sachsen-Anhalt (Saxony-Anhalt)

Tourist Office: Schloßpl. 2 (☎ 49 86 10; www.wittenberg.de), at the western end of the pedestrian zone. Provides maps (€0.50) and books rooms. Open Mar.-Oct. M-F 9am-6pm, Sa 10am-3pm, Su 11am-4pm; Nov.-Feb. M-F 10am-4pm, Sa 10am-2pm, Su 11am-3pm. Closed Sa and Su in June. **Tours** in German leave M-F at 2pm and Sa-Su at 11am and 2pm from the Schloßkirche (May-Oct., €6). English and other language tours available at additional cost with advance arrangements. English audio guides €6.

Bank: One of many banks near the Rathaus, **Sparkasse,** Markt 20, has several **ATMs.** Open M-F 8:30am-6pm, Sa 9am-1pm.

Pharmacy: Löwen Apotheke, Collegienstr. 62a. Open M-Tu and Th-F 8am-6:30pm, W 8am-6pm, Sa 9am-noon.

Post Office: 06886 Wittenberg, near the Lutherhalle on the corner of W.-Weber-Str. and Fleischerstr. Open M-F 9am-12:30pm and 2-6pm, Sa 9am-noon.

🛏 ACCOMMODATIONS

🏠**Jugendherberge im Schloß (HI) ❶,** in the castle across the street from the tourist office, has clean rooms with just a touch of Reformation severity. (☎ 40 32 55; fax 40 94 22. **Internet** €6 per hr. Breakfast included. Sheets €3.50. Reception 3-10pm. Lockout 10pm, but keys available for a €5 deposit. Dorms €15, under 27 €12.

Floor space sometimes available for a reduced rate if it's full.) Although not centrally located, **Gästehaus Wolter ❷,** Rheinsdorfer Weg 77, has a truly homey ambience, complete with affectionate family dog, sunny rooms with TVs, and spotless bathrooms. Ride bus #302, 314, or 315 to "Elbedruckerei," walk in the direction of the bus, take the first right, and veer right on Rheinsdorfer Weg. To walk or bike there, take Puschkinstr. north and take Rheinsdorfer Weg at the circle. Or call Frau Wolter, who will happily pick you up from town. (☎41 25 78. Breakfast included. Reception 24hr. Singles €20; doubles €40.)

🌙 FOOD AND ENTERTAINMENT

Budget delights line the Collegienstr.-Schloßstr. strip. Across from alchemist Johann Faust's former home, **Creperie Lorette ❷,** Collegienstr. 70, offers the best of two worlds: French food and German beer. Crepes of every variety are available for €3-9, from the classic Breton egg, ham, and cheese, to fish and vegetable combinations, as well as sweet varieties. (☎40 40 45. Open M-Th 11:30am-8:30pm, F-Sa 11:30am-9:30pm.) Next door, the lively **Irish Harp Pub,** Collegienstr. 71, has Guinness on tap and over 100 brands of whiskey, in addition to live rock or blues on Saturday. (☎41 01 50. Open daily 3pm-3am.) Members of Wittenberg's artsy theater crowd occasionally burst into song or soliloquy at **Vis à Vis ❷,** Sternstr. 14, a cozy alternative establishment somewhat removed from the main tourist district. The staff puts on musical productions, and local bands play on weekends. (☎40 90 09. Entrees €4-8. Open daily 6pm-1am, F-Sa until 2am.)

🄮 SIGHTS

To the chagrin of forward-looking residents, a local politician recently called the city an "open-air museum." Wittenberg, however, truly is the living scene of the Reformation and its leading figure, Martin Luther. Plan your sightseeing around **Collegienstraße,** which is less than 1.5km long and encompasses all the major sights. The ◪**Lutherhalle,** Collegienstr. 54, chronicles the history of the Reformation through letters, texts, art, and artifacts (and signs in English). Some highlights include the original podium where Luther first spoke of his disapproval of Catholic practices and the musty "Luther Room" where a self-important Russian Czar Peter graffitied his name onto the door in 1702. Hundreds of early printed pamphlets, for and against Luther's ideas, show that the Reformation was also a media revolution. Among these is a first-edition copy of Luther's ground-breaking translation of the Bible. (☎420 30. Open daily Apr.-Oct. 9am-6pm; Nov.-Mar. Tu-Su 10am-5pm. €5, students €3.) Turn right from the Lutherhalle and stroll down Lutherstr. to see the oak tree under which Luther allegedly burned a papal bull (a decree of excommunication, not a large Catholic animal).

At the end of Mittelstr., on the Marktpl., is the 725-year-old **Stadtkirche St. Marien,** nicknamed "the Mother of the Reformation." This church is known for its dazzling altar painted by pharmacist and hometown prodigy **Lucas Cranach the Elder.** Stand on the altar where Luther gave his famous "Invocavit" sermon, and take a look at the massive organ dominating the balcony. (Open daily 9am-5pm.) The **Cranachhof,** Markt 4, where Cranach lived most of his life, now holds a museum about the artist; the courtyard hosts lively open-air performances. The **Galerie im Cranach-Haus** showcases modern art exhibitions. (☎420 19 20. Museum and gallery open M-Sa 10am-5pm. €3, students €2.) Wittenberg's elegant **Altes Rathaus,** Markt 26, dominates the Markt with its stately facade. The building is home to an exhibit on modern Biblical graphic art, with works by Beckmann, Picasso, Chagal, Dix, and others. (☎40 11 46. Open Tu-Su 10am-5pm.) Statues of Luther and fellow reformer **Philip Melanchthon** share the plaza

LUTHER'S HOCHZEIT

Eight years after he posted his theses on the doors of Wittenberg's Schloßkirche, Martin Luther scandalously asked for the hand of former nun Katherina von Bora in marriage. Despite the uproar caused by his advanced age (42 years) and his breaking of clerical vows of celibacy, Luther and Katherina wed in 1525.

To the past and present citizens of Wittenberg, this marriage represents a courageous stance against the oppression of the Roman Catholic Church. In 1994, the city declared an annual festival in honor of the marriage, creatively titled *Luther's Hochzeit* (Luther's Wedding). Every year a larger crowd floods the streets of Wittenberg to experience German life 500 years ago. Polkas mingle with sounds of street musicians and minstrels; guilds demonstrate the use of old tools; *Bier* and *Wurst* are consumed in delightfully frightening quantities. The crowds part for frequent parades of revelers dancing behind a Luther and Katherina. At night, the crowds linger to party in the streets to the sound of local bands.

This opulent festival offers a great variety of events in authentic venues from the Reformation. Hotels fill up early, for although this festival remains undiscovered by foreign tourists, it is becoming ever more popular in Germany.

June 10-12, 2005. ☎ 03491 49 86 10; www.wittenberg.de.)

with one of Wittenberg's famous **Jungfernröhrwässer,** 16th-century wells whose waters flow through original wooden pipes (the other is in the Cranachhof).

The **Schloßkirche,** down Schloßstr., is crowned by a sumptuous Baroque cupola, and retains a copy of the complaints that Luther nailed to its doors. These doors are now nail-proof—the originals have been replaced by bronze ones inscribed with the 95 Theses in Latin. Martin Luther is buried in the church, as are philosopher Philip Melanchthon and the Saxon Electors Johann the Steadfast and Friedrich the Wise, whose engraved headstone is a remarkable work of art. The **tower** affords an excellent view of the surrounding countryside, Wittenberg's Altstadt, and the Elbe. (Church open M-Sa 10am-5pm, Su 11:30am-5pm. Free. Tower open M-F noon-4pm, Sa-Su 10am-4pm. €1, students €0.50.)

In 1995, a group of students at the local high school asked architect **Friedensreich Hundertwasser** to redesign their boring, pre-fab school building in his characteristically eccentric style. Using both the students' drawings and his own ideas about the relationship between nature and architecture as inspirations, he built the funkiest high school in Germany. Follow Sternstr. out of the city center (walking in the direction that the Lutherhalle faces) and turn right onto Schillerstr.; the **Hundertwasser-Schule,** Str. der Völkerfreundschaft 130, is the building on the left with the onion dome and trees growing out of it. (Open Apr.-Oct. M-F 1:30-5pm, Sa-Su 10am-5pm. Tours €2, students €1.)

DESSAU ☎ 0340

Founded as a medieval fortress in 1341, Dessau became one of the first German Renaissance settlements, later flourishing under **Princess Henrietta Katharina von Oranien** in the 18th century. Her grandfather, Dessau's famed **Prince Leopold,** introduced a unique marching style into his regiment, creating a model for both the Prussian army and future stereotypes about German militarism. The **Bauhaus** school, renowned for its revolutionary subordination of form to function and its influence on modern architecture, was pioneered in Weimar, but the masters took their ideals and practices to Dessau in 1925, before fleeing into exile as Hitler grew in power. The city has worked diligently over the past 30 years to restore its Bauhaus classics after wartime damage. **Moses Mendelssohn,** one of the greatest German-Jewish philosophers and a fervent proponent of religious tolerance in the 19th century, and composer/playwright **Kurt Weill,** whose works encouraged artistic resistance against Nazism both came from this precocious city.

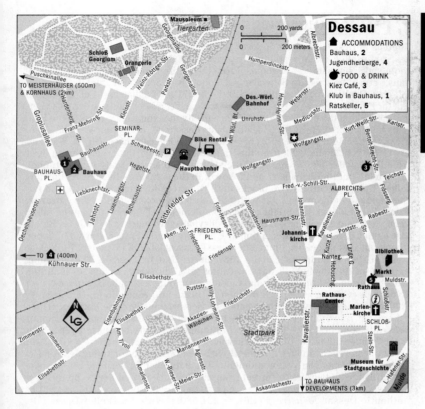

Dessau

⌂ ACCOMMODATIONS
Bauhaus, **2**
Jugendherberge, **4**

🍎 FOOD & DRINK
Kiez Café, **3**
Klub in Bauhaus, **1**
Ratskeller, **5**

TRANSPORTATION AND PRACTICAL INFORMATION

Trains run to: **Berlin** (2hr., 1 per hr., €17); **Leipzig** (1hr., 2 per hr., €9); **Wittenberg** (35min., 1 per hr., €6). Rent **bikes** at the **Mobilitätszentrale** kiosk, left of the train station's main exit. (☎21 33 66. €6 per day. Open M-F 9am-5pm, Sa 9am-2pm. Drop-off until 9pm.) The **tourist office,** Zerbster Str. 2c, finds private rooms for a €3 fee and books hotel and pension rooms for free. Take streetcar #1, 3, or 4 from the train station's main exit to "Hauptpost." The office is behind the huge "Rathaus-Center;" walk toward the center and turn left into Ratsg. When you reach the end, the office will be on your right, across the street. The staff also sells the **Dessau Card** (€8), a three-day ticket that allows one adult and one child unlimited access to all buses and streetcars in Dessau, a number of local discounts, and entry to most sights and museums. (☎204 14 42; www.dessau.de. Open Apr.-Oct. M-F 9am-6pm, Sa 9am-1pm; Nov.-Mar. M-F 9am-5pm, Sa 10am-1pm.) **Tours** depart from the tourist office; English tours are available for groups if arranged in advance. (Apr.-Oct. Sa at 10am. €5, students €4, children free.) For **Internet** access, try the library, Zerbstr. 10; alternatives are scarce. (☎21 32 65. €1 per 30min. Open M-Tu and Th-F 10am-6pm, Sa 10am-1pm.) The **post office,** 06844 Dessau, is at the corner of Friedrichstr. and Kavalierstr. (Open M-F 8am-6:30pm, Sa 8am-12:30pm.)

SACHSEN-ANHALT

⚑ 🏠 ACCOMMODATIONS AND FOOD

Tourists in Dessau have the opportunity to spend a night in the actual ⬛**Bauhaus ❷**, Gropiusallee 38., in aesthetically pleasing singles or doubles, that feature in-room sinks, but shared bathrooms. From the station, take the exit marked "Bauhaus," cross the street to Schwabenstr., follow it to Seminarpl., and veer slightly left onto Bauhausstr. Or, take bus #10, 11, or 471 to "Bauhauspl." Call ahead and ask for Frau Oede or email to make sure you can get a key when you arrive. Otherwise, knock on the door of room 224 and specify that you want a room in the Bauhaus building. (☎650 83 18; oede@bauhaus-dessau.de. Reception M-F 9am-5pm. Flexible check-out 11am. €15-25 per person.) The **Jugendherberge (HI) ❶**, Waldkaterweg 11, is a 25min. walk from the train station through suburban Dessau. Exit from the smaller *Westausgang* of the station, through the underground tunnel, make a left onto Rathenaustr., and follow it to the end; cross the intersection and follow Kühnauer Str. for two blocks until you cross Kiefernweg. About 50m farther, a small path on the right with red and white poles leads to the entrance. Friendly personnel and bright rooms complement a TV room, ping-pong table, giant chess and checkers boards, and a volleyball court outside. (☎61 94 52. Breakfast included. Sheets €3. Reception M-F 8am-3pm and 5-8pm, Sa-Su 4:30-7:30pm. Check-out 10am. Lockout 10pm, but house keys available. €14, under 27 €12.)

Affordable restaurants can be difficult to find in Dessau. The gleaming expanse of the newly built **Rathaus-Center** satisfies every craving for mall life, with bakeries and produce stands inside providing a simple *Bratwurst und Brötchen* (€2), or cheap, German-style pizza and Asian food. (Open M-Sa 9:30am-8pm.) Also try the **street market** on Zerbstr., north of the Rathaus. (Open Tu and Th 7am-5pm.) The tragically hip ⬛**Klub im Bauhaus ❷**, in the Bauhaus school basement, is the ideal spot to indulge in angsty pretense over a light meal. Ponder the plight of the worker over a "poor master omelette" (€3.50), or try the less revolutionary spaghetti with pesto, cheese, or tomatoes for €5. (☎650 84 44. Open daily 9am-midnight.) The **Ratskeller ❸**, Zerbster Str. 4a, conveniently located across the street from the Rathaus-Center, serves up the *Vegetarischer-Teller Dubarry* (€8), a tasty veggie and potato dish, as well as authentic Dessau *Milchreis* (€6). (☎221 52 83. www.Ratskeller-Dessau.de. Open daily 11:30am-midnight.) **Kiez Café ❷**, Bertolt-Brecht-Str. 29a, just off Kurt-Weill-Str., is where the offbeat and artsy congregate for alternative *Kultur*. The cafe features a theater, art-film cinema (€3.50, students €2.50), and art studios. There are so many regulars it's hard to tell who's working there and who's not, but everyone is exceptionally friendly. (☎21 20 32. www.kiez-ev.de. Cafe open M-Th 10pm-1am, F-Sa 10pm-2am, Su 10pm-1am.)

👁 SIGHTS

BAUHAUS. In 1925, the Bauhaus school brought its theory of constructive and artistic unity to this building designed by **Walter Gropius.** Damaged during WWII, the building was reconstructed in 1976 and now houses a graduate institute and an exhibition space for international architecture. The school adorns its walls with the works of legendary alumni Gropius, Klee, Kandinsky, and Brandt. The building is open for self-guided tours and has rotating exhibits on current and past Bauhaus work throughout the complex. *(Gropiusallee 38. Follow directions to the Bauhaus building (p. 588). ☎650 82 51; www.bauhaus-dessau.de. Building and exhibition open daily 10am-6pm; Nov. to mid-Feb. 10am-5pm. 1hr. tours daily 11am and 2pm; extra tours Sa-Su. Call ahead to get a tour of all Bauhaus sights in Dessau. €4, students €3.)*

BAUHAUS MEISTERHÄUSER. In a pine grove along the Ebertalle, the three famous Bauhaus "Master Houses" radiate white, boxy simplicity. Designed by Lyonel Feininger, the first houses the **Kurt-Weill-Zentrum.** Weill is celebrated extensively during the annual Kurt Weill Festival (Feb. 25-Mar. 6, 2005). Restored and refurnished, the houses beautifully demonstrate the striking, no-frills principles of the Bauhaus movement. For the Bauhaus *devoté*, it doesn't get much better than this. *(Ebertallee. Kurt Weill Festival info ☎ 0180 55 64 564; www.kurt-weill.de. Open mid-Feb. to Oct. Tu-Su 10am-6pm; Nov. to mid-Feb. Tu-Su 10am-5pm. €4, students €3. Combination ticket to the Bauhaus exhibition and the Meisterhäuser €8/€5.)*

OTHER BAUHAUS BUILDINGS. To find the other spectacular Bauhaus buildings scattered around town, pick up a copy of *Bauhaus Architecture in Dessau* (€1) or the English-language *Bauhaus* (€0.50) at the tourist office. Walk west along Ebertallee away from the Meisterhäuser; turn right on An der Kienheide, which becomes Elballee, and follow it to the end to reach Carl Fieger's **Kornhaus,** designed as the ultimate party house with a beer hall, cafe, dance floor, and two terraces. Today, the white tablecloths of the waterfront restaurant create a more refined atmosphere; the view of the Elbe from the circular glass dining room is well worth the trip *(☎ 640 41 41. Open daily noon-10pm).* To the south of the city and a bit farther out, two housing developments bear witness to the practical aspirations of the Bauhaus school. While the red brick **Laubenganghäuser** is hard to distinguish from neighboring DDR complexes, the nearby **Mittelring** settlement of orthogonal houses is unique. Only one house now displays its original facade: the city-owned **Moses-Mendelssohn-Zentrum,** Mittelring 38, which includes exhibits about the philosopher's life and work as a Jew in Dessau. *(Streetcar #1 (dir.: Dessau-Süd) to "Damaschkestr." (15min.). ☎ 850 11 99. Open daily 10am-5pm. €2, students €1.)*

NON-BAUHAUS ARCHITECTURE. Dessau also has its share of ornate, old-school architecture as enthralling as Bauhaus is spare. In the 17th-century country estate **Schloß Georgium,** the **Anhaltische Gemäldegalerie** displays a range of lesser-known paintings from the 16th to the 19th centuries along with modern German art. The surrounding gardens transition into woods that extend to the Elbe. *(Puschkinallee 100. From the Bauhaus, turn right on Gropiusallee and right again on Puschkinallee. When you see Kleisstr. on your right, make a left into the park. Go behind the yellow buildings by the street and follow the path to the Schloß. ☎ 61 38 74. Open Tu-Su 10am-5pm. €3, students €2. Gardens open 24hr.)* With its off-beat exhibits on Dessau's history and con-

IN RECENT NEWS

ELBE AND HIGH WATER

Here and there among the towns of the Sächsische Schweiz stand tall wooden poles marked with dates ranging from the 17th century to 2002. These markers although they tower above eye level, are easy to overlook. And even if you do spot one, you'll find no explanation of what it is, for the Germans need no reminder.

These poles are giant rulers that measure water in extraordinary proportions. In August 2002 torrential rains caused the Elbe and Danube rivers to flood and engulf the cities along their banks. Dresden and Wittenberg disappeared under astounding water levels (almost 10m), breaking records set in the 16th century. Huge sections of these cities were evacuated and historical buildings were swamped. When the waters finally receded, the damage was staggering: 12 people killed, 4.2 million affected and €15 billion in damage.

Although most of the effects have since been cleaned up, a few collapsing buildings still attest to the magnitude of the destruction in the smaller towns of the Sächsische Schweiz. Construction sites still remain accompanied by the tall reminders of the water levels. Although most Germans have begun to move on from the experience it's still overwhelming to stand at the base of the huge markers and imagine where the waves once churned.

temporary concerns, the **Museum für Stadtgeschichte** in the Johannbau will satisfy any burning cravings for Dessau esoterica. *(Schloßpl. 3a.* ☎ *220 96 12. Open Tu-Su 10am-5pm.* €2, students €1.)

HALLE   ☎ 0345

Although unemployment is rampant in the former political and industrial capital of Saxony-Anhalt, Halle's university, art school, and first-rate art museum provide an exceptional cultural community. While nearby Leipzig boasts of Bach, Halle has its own musical hero: **Georg Friedrich Händel,** who was born and raised here. The revival of interest in Händel after WWII rejuvenated Halle's artistic community; the music calendar culminates with the yearly **Händel-Festspiele** (June 2-12, 2005; see www.haendelfestspiele.halle.de for more info).

ORIENTATION AND TRANSPORTATION

Halle is divided into several districts; most significant are the DDR-style **Neustadt** and the historic **Altstadt,** separated by the Saale River. The train station, major streetcar terminals, and all sights are in the Altstadt. **Trains** run to **Leipzig** (40min., 3 per hr., €9) and **Naumburg** (40min., 2 per hr., €7). Though most of Halle is easily reached on foot, streetcars also cover the town. (Single ticket €1.75, €2.20 if bought on board; day pass €4). The main street is Große Ulrichstr., which becomes Geiststr. when it leaves the **Marktplatz.**

PRACTICAL INFORMATION

The **tourist office** is in the *StadtCenter Rolltreppe* mall, Große Ulrichstr. 60. From the station, take the E.-Kamieth-Str. exit and walk through the pedestrian tunnel straight onto Leipzigerstr. Head past the **Leipziger Turm** to Marktpl. (15min.) Behind the large tower is Große Ulrichstr.; the tourist office is about 100m down the street. Or, from the station, take streetcar #2 (dir.: Eselmühle) or #5 (dir.: Heide) four stops to "Markt." The office hands out city maps, offers pamphlets on cultural events, and finds rooms for free. (☎ 47 23 30; www.halle-tourist.de. Open M-F 10am-6pm, Sa 10am-2pm.) Tours depart from the tourist office; English tours are available if booked in advance. (M-Sa 2pm, Su 10am. €4.50, students and children €2.50.) You can **exchange money** at the Reisebank in the train station. (Open M-Tu and Th-F 9:30am-12:30pm and 1:30-6pm, W 12:30-6pm.) The **women's agency,** Robert-Franz-Ring 22, holds meetings and lectures, and also offers a hotline, gallery, library, cafe, and monthly parties. (☎ 202 43 31; www.weiberwirtschaft-halle.de. Open to women Tu noon-midnight, W-Th noon-4pm; women and men F noon-midnight.) **Cockbit Bar and Internetcafe,** August-Bebel-Str. 5-7, is between the Markt and the Jugendherberge. (☎ 678 25 88. www.cockbit.de. €3 per hr. Open M-Th 10am-1am, F-Sa 10am-2am, Su 10am-1am.) The **post office,** 06108 Halle, is at the corner of Hansering and Große Steinstr. (Open M-F 8am-6pm, Sa 9am-noon.)

ACCOMMODATIONS AND FOOD

Halle's **Jugendherberge (HI) ❷,** August-Bebel-Str. 48a, is located in a newly restored mansion (built in 1904) just north of the market, in a pleasant student neighborhood. From the station's main entrance, turn left and walk through the tunnel onto Leipzigerstr. Then, take a right onto Hansering, walk through Joliot-Curie-Pl. and take August-Bebel-Str., to the right of the *Opernhaus.* Or take streetcar #7 (dir.: Kröllwitz) to "Puschkinstr." Continue on Geiststr. one block, turn right onto Puschkinstr., and take a right onto August-Bebel-Str. at August-Bebel-Pl. This dignified, well-kept building is in a pleasant student neighborhood a short walk from the city center. Ask for room #7—it has a balcony. (☎202 47 16; fax 202 51 72. Breakfast included. Sheets €3. Reception 7-10am and 5-11pm. Curfew midnight, but you can get a key for a €5 deposit. Dorms €16.50, under 27 €13.50.) Cafes line Leipzigerstr. to the Marktpl., becoming livelier from the Marktpl. up Große Ulrichstr. toward Moritzburg. The Marktpl. hosts a **market** (M-F 10am-6pm, Sa 10am-2pm), and there's an **EDEKA** supermarket on Leipzigerstr. near the train station (open M-F 8am-8pm, Sa 8am-4pm). **Café Nöö ❷**, Große Klausstr. 11, just down Domstr. from the Dom, serves tasty pasta (€4.70-6.50), dramatic breakfasts, and the "Nöö salad": a tortilla bowl filled with turkey, chicken wings, shrimp, egg, and veggies (€6.60). It also offers many vegan and vegetarian options. (☎202 16 51. Open M-Th 8am-1am, F 8am-2am, Sa-Su 10am-2am.) At the **Café & Bar Unikum ❷**, Universitätsring 23, students and locals get together for a drink amid smoke and modern art. Cheap salads, sandwiches, and daily specials (€2-6) make up the menu. (☎202 13 03. Open M-Th 9am-1am, F 9am-2am, Sa 6pm-2am, Su 6pm-1am.) **Zur Apotheke ❷**, Mühlberg 4a, off Mühlg. between the Dom and Moritzburg fortress, suffers from an identity crisis: Thuringian meals (€3-8) in Saxony. (☎50 31 18. Open Su-Th 9am-1am, F-Sa 9am-2am.) **Ökase ❷**, Kleine Ulrichstr. 2, a vegetarian bistro, serves up specials (€2-6) in a chill atmosphere. (Open M-F 10am-7pm.)

🔘 SIGHTS

Central Halle revolves around the **Marktplatz,** bustling with traffic, vegetable stands, and *Eiscafes* (ice cream shops). At its center is the **Roter Turm** bell tower. A number of popular myths surround the tower's name, the most gruesome version stating that after it was built (1418-1506), the blood of the people being executed on the adjoining gallows splattered onto the tower, giving it a grisly tint. Across from the tower is the intricate **Marktkirche "Unsere Lieben Frauen,"** which has a triptych painted by Lucas Cranach's disciples on its altar. The organ on which Händel began his musical studies is above the altar; after a century of silence, organists once again perform concerts on its keys. (Open daily 10am-noon and 3-5pm. Free 30min. organ concerts Tu and Th 4pm.) Just to the right of the church is the unassuming red 16th-century **Marktschlößchen**, Markt 13, which now houses the **Galerie Marktschlößchen,** featuring works of lesser-known contemporary European artists. (☎202 91 41. Open M-F 10am-7pm, Su 10am-6pm. Free.)

An 1859 centennial memorial to composer Georg Friedrich Händel decorates the Marktpl., but the most important Händel shrine is his familial home, the 🔲**Händelhaus,** a short walk from the market down Kleine Klausstr. Through hundreds of manuscripts and composition books and dozens of period instruments, the museum chronicles Händel's life from his 1685 birth in the house to his death in 1758 in London, where he lived for the last 50 years of his life. The museum also displays a beautiful collection of musical instruments from the 16th century onward. (Große Nikolaistr. 5. ☎50 09 00. Open daily 9:30am-5:30pm, Th until 7pm. Free. Cassette tours in English free.) The **Dom** where Händel served as organist is a 5min. walk down Nikolaistr. from Händel's home. This ancient complex, begun in 1271, remains a significant repository of religious relics. Today the church's most treasured offerings are the 17 life-size figures on the church's pillars, dating from the 16th century. (☎202 13 79. Open June-Oct. M-Sa 2-4pm. Restoration in progress, call ahead to confirm hours.) Early summer brings the annual **Händel-Festspiele** (June 2-12), a celebration of the composer's masterful Baroque music. Buy tickets at the *Ticket-Service Roter Turm*, Marktplatz. (☎202 97 71; haendel@halle.de. Open M-F 9am-8pm, Sa 9am-4pm.)

To reach the whitewashed **Moritzburg fortress** from the Dom, head through Dompl. and downhill on Mühlg., then bear right and uphill on Schloßbergstr. The **Staatliche Galerie Moritzburg** occupies most of the 15th-century fortification. This

SACHSEN-ANHALT

art museum, the largest in Saxony-Anhalt, has three galleries that range from Renaissance to contemporary exhibits. Halle's once extensive Expressionist collection—including works by Max Beckmann, Paul Klee, and Oskar Kokoschka—offended Hitler, who drew heavily from this museum to furnish the infamous exhibit of *Entartete Kunst* (Degenerate Art; p. 67) that toured Nazi Germany. Although much of the collection was burned or sold off by the Nazis, the salvaged works remain a monument to artistic freedom. (☎21 25 90. Open Tu 11am-8:30pm, W-Su 10am-6pm; last entry 15min. before closing. €5, students €3. Tu free.)

🎵 🎭 ENTERTAINMENT AND NIGHTLIFE

The *Ticket-Service Roter Turm* sells tickets to most shows in Halle's growing arts scene (open M-F 9am-8pm, Sa 9am-4pm), as does the counter in the **Neues Theater** building. (☎205 02 22. M-Sa 10am-8pm.) The free magazines *Fritz* and *Blitz* list shows, times, and locations. The elegant **Opernhaus Halle,** Universitätsring 24, shows everything from ballet to *Carmen.* (☎511 03 55; www.opernhaus-halle.de. Box office inside. Open M-F 2-6pm. Tickets €4-27, students €3-15.50.) To hear the works of Händel and others, try the **Philharmonisches Staatsorchester Halle,** which plays at the Konzerthalle Ulrichkirche, Kleine Bräuhausstr. 26. (☎221 30 00. Box office open M-Tu and Th 10am-1pm and 3-6pm, W and F 10am-1pm, and 1hr. before shows. Tickets €15 and up, students 30% off.) Completed in 1990, the **Neues Theater,** Große Ulrichstr. 51, features Shakespeare, Molière, Brecht, and local playwrights. (☎20 500; www.nt-schauspiel-halle.de. No performances mid-July to mid-Aug. Box office open M-Sa 10am-8pm and 1hr. before shows. €5-15.50, students €2.50-10.) The **Kleines Thalia Theater,** on Thaliapassage off Geiststr., has avant-garde and children's shows alike. (☎20 40 50; www.thaliatheaterhalle.de. Box office open daily 10am-4pm, and 1hr. before shows. €7, children and students €4. Some shows in the **Grosses Thalia Theater** on Kardinal-Albrecht-Str.)

Turm, Friedemann-Bach-Pl. 5., in the northeast tower of the Moritzburg fortress, hosts the city's *Studentenklub.* The music is a mix of disco, funk, blues, techno, and rock performed by local bands; they also host a jazz festival in July or August. A *Biergarten* and grill are outside. Foreign students with ID (18+) are welcome. (☎202 37 37; www.turm-net.de. Cover €3.50, students €2.50, concerts €8-20. Beer garden open daily by 10pm. Disco open W and F-Sa from 10pm.) If Turm isn't your scene, try the self-conscious **das haus,** along Universitätsring at Scharrenstr. 10. The wood-and-metal decor and delicious pasta (€6-9) complement the cafe's creative drinks (€2-4) or a few beers. (☎472 29 05. Open daily 9am until late.)

NAUMBURG ☎03445

Home to both the local bishop in the Middle Ages and **Friedrich Nietzsche,** Germany's most famous anti-Christian philosopher, in the 19th-century, walled Naumburg has erased almost all traces of its former function as a Red Army post, and most construction sites have disappeared, leaving an energetic and sophisticated atmosphere in their wake. The green spires of Naumburg's famous cathedral, a 13th-century Gothic giant that both enchants with its countless treasures and intimidates with its chilling beauty, are always in view.

🚆 🛈 TRANSPORTATION AND PRACTICAL INFORMATION. Trains to: **Erfurt** (50min., 1-2 per hr., €9); **Halle** (45min., 1-2 per hr., €6.60); **Leipzig** (35min., 1 per 2hr., €8); **Weimar** (35min., 1 per hr., €6.60). To reach town from the train station, bear right on Markgrafenweg and follow it until the end. Take the winding cobblestone road to your left uphill. At the top, a sign points to the Dom; follow it until you see the cathedral's huge towers above the rooftops. From the Dom, it's a short walk down Steinweg and then Herrenweg to the Naumburg Markt, the center of town. The **tourist office**, Markt 6, has free maps, leads city tours, and arranges stays in private rooms (€15-26) for free. (☎20 16 14; www.naumburg.tourismus.de. Open M-F 9am-6pm, Sa 9am-4pm, Su 10am-1pm. Tours last 1½hr. and meet by the cathedral Sa 10:30am and 2pm, Su 10:30am. €2.50, students €2.) For a **taxi** call ☎20 84 44. Head down Marienstr. from the Markt to reach the **post office**, Stephanpl. 6, 06618 Naumburg. (Open M-F 9am-6pm, Sa 9am-noon.)

╓╔ ACCOMMODATIONS AND FOOD. To reach Naumburg's **Jugendgästehaus (HI) ❶**, Am Tennispl. 9, follow Wenzelsstr. from the Marktpl. out of the old walled city to Bürgergartenstr., across and to the right, then follow the signs up the long hill to the hostel (30min.). The surprisingly large (204-bed) hostel is situated in Naumburg's residential outskirts. You can usually have a room to yourself. (☎/fax 70 34 22. Reception daily 7:30am-midnight. 3- to 5-bed dorms €16.50, under 27 €13.50; singles €18/€15; doubles €26/€23.) For something closer to town, **Pension Hentschel ❷**, Lindenhof 16, has clean rooms with bathrooms and showers. (☎20 12 30. Breakfast included. Singles €23; doubles €40.) For a cup of coffee or light meal, try **engelsgasse 3 ❸** (☎20 07 70). To get there, face the Rathaus from the Markt and walk all the way around the building. Built before 1517, this former bakery gained its Rococo facade in the 18th century. Now a cafe, used book store, and art gallery, it has the retro, funky style of renowned modern Leipzig illustrator **Thomas Müller**, whose work covers the walls. Most of the ingredients that go into the salads, omelettes, and pasta dishes (€3.30-7.30) come from small area farms. (Daily lunch specials noon-2:30pm. Open M-F 11am-7pm, Sa 11am-4pm.) Cheap kebabs and other *Imbiß* fare can be found on the way from the station or on streets off the Markt. For a heartier meal, try the *Goulash* with mushrooms and homemade *Knödel* (€8.70) at **Zillestube ❸**, Marieng. 2. (☎20 28 00. Most meals €3-11. Open Tu-F 5pm-midnight, Sa-Su noon-2pm and 5pm-midnight.) Nighthawks hit **Kanzlei** and the **Ratskeller** on the Markt; both serve beer until 1am.

◘ SIGHTS. Beneath its ornate Gothic towers, the huge 13th-century **Naumburger Dom**, Dompl. 16-17, has captivating and unusual details at every corner, from the procession of animals up the railing in the east choir to the 12 statues inside the west choir. The most well-known of these is **Uta**, who stands with her husband **Eckehard II** on the right side; they are widely considered to be the best example of Realism between classical times and the Renaissance. The artist, too humble to carve his name in the cathedral's stone, is remembered today simply as the *Naumburger Meister*—he's left his mark on the Mainz and Merseburg *Doms* as well. Ask for English pamphlets; English tours are available with prior arrangement. (☎23 01 10. Open Apr.-Sept. M-Sa 9am-6pm, Su noon-6pm; Mar. and Oct. M-Sa 9am-5pm, Su noon-5pm; Nov.-Feb. M-Sa 9am-4pm, Su noon-4pm. Tour every hour except noon. Last entry 30min. before closing. €4, students and seniors €3.)

The rest of Naumburg has recovered well from its 45 years as a backwater Red Army post. Its animated Marktpl. hosts a morning **market** (M, W, Sa). Just off the market square is the **Stadtkirche St. Wenzel**. Its rosy interior boasts a Baroque organ tested and approved by J.S. Bach upon its completion in 1746. Climb the 72.5m tower, on the opposite side of the church from the entrance, for a stunning view of the city and surrounding countryside. (☎20 84 01. Open summer M-Sa 10am-noon and 2-5pm, Su only for services; winter M-Sa 10am-4pm, Su noon-4pm. Free tours available with arrangement. Organ concerts May-Oct. W and Sa-Su at noon. €6-8. Other concerts first Sa of the mo. at 5pm, prices vary. Tower €1.50, under 18 €0.75.) It may have been Naumburg's churches that inspired Nietzsche's pious mother to move her family here when her pastor husband died. The **Nietzsche-Haus**, Weingarten 18, off Jakobstr., has a whole room devoted to the philosopher's escapades with the fairer sex. After living here as a child from 1850 to 1858, he returned in 1890 to live with his mother as his health declined. The second floor has a collection of Nietzsche literature for perusal. (☎20 16 38. Open Tu-F 2-5pm, Sa-Su 10am-4pm. €1.50, students €1.) The modern **Stadtmuseum Hohe Lilie,** Markt 18, next to the Rathaus, has exhibits on the history of the town, including a display on the region's beer and a room dedicated to the town's patron, St. Wenzel. Special exhibits are on the top floor. (☎20 06 48. Open daily 10am-5pm. €2, students €1.)

HARZ MOUNTAINS

Heinrich Heine wrote that even Mephistopheles stopped and trembled when he approached the Harz, the devil's dearest mountains. It's easy to see why Heine— and a host of others, including Goethe and Bismarck—were fascinated by these mist-shrouded woods. The region has offered more than inspiration, though; the Harz were Germany's primary mineral source until the 20th century. Since the region straddled the Iron Curtain, both East and West declared much of it off-limits for development during Germany's 50-year division. The effects of that period's shaky economy can still be felt, especially in the East. Now, tourism is rushing in from both sides, but non-Germans have yet to discover this stunning terrain.

📧 TRANSPORTATION. The **Harzerschmalspurbahnen** consist of the **Brockenbahn** winding around the famous peak in the West and the lesser-known **Selketalbahn,** which cuts through the southeast valleys. The Brockenbahn's antique, narrow-gauge railways steam from **Nordhausen** to **Wernigerode,** pass through the unfortunately named towns of **Sorge** and **Elend** (Sorrow and Misery), reach 540m on Drei Annen Hohne, and chug along to the **Brocken,** the Harz's highest peak (1142m). **Trains** run every hr. in summer from 8:30am-8:30pm; some routes only run until 4pm. Schedules are available at most tourist offices, on the web at www.hsb-wr.de, and in the free monthly pamphlet *Brocken Tips.*

Although strenuous, hiking offers a more interesting way to experience this stunning landscape. Torfhaus, Braunlage, Schierke, Elend, and Drei Annen Hohne are all within a day's hike of one another. Three main **hiking** trails criss-cross the area surrounding the Brocken. You can follow in literary footsteps on the **Goetheweg,** a relatively easy and pleasant path (2½hr.) that begins near the Torfhaus bus stop and winds through moors, ancient forests, and high fields. Heinrich Heine walked a longer but more scenic route from Ilsetal outside Ilsenburg, accessible also from Wernigerode by bus #288. The highlights of the **Heineweg** (8½hr.) are the surreal, natural rock formations high up along the path. A less-traveled (and very steep), unnamed path runs from **Schierke.** Plan a unique hiking experience with the *Wanderntips* hiking map, available at any regional tourist office.

📑🔀 ORIENTATION AND PRACTICAL INFORMATION. Hikers and spa-lovers alike rush to these rugged hills. The national park stretches from the northwestern **Oberharz** to the sheltered valleys of the south and **Wernigerode** in the east. Throughout the Harz, historic villages and the natural beauty of the mountains and valleys make for rewarding biking and hiking, while the first snow signals the beginning of the skiing, skating, and tobogganing season. The regional **tourist office** in Goslar (p. 245) and the regional **bus station** in Wernigerode (p. 597) offer a wealth of information for navigating the region. Schedules vary greatly between seasons and some buses only come a few times per day. A bus and rail schedule for the Ostharz is €2, and a similar *Fahrplan* (€1) is available for the buses in the Goslar *Landkreis* (county), which runs all over the *Oberharz.* Sudden, violent rainstorms often blow in quickly. The **Braunlage Wetterstation** gives weather conditions. (☎05520 13 20. Open Apr.-Oct. 5:30am-11pm. Nov.-Mar. call **Schneetelefon** ☎05321 200 24.)

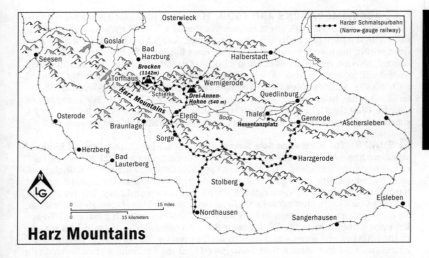

Osterwieck

Goslar

Bad Harzburg

Harzer Schmalspurbahn
(Narrow-gauge railway)

Seesen

Halberstadt

Bode

Torfhaus

*Brocken
(1142m)*

Wernigerode

Schierke

*Drei-Annen-
Hohne (540 m)*

Quedlinburg

Osterode

Elend

Bode

Thale

Gernrode

Aschersleben

Braunlage

Hexentanzplatz

Harz Mountains

Sorge

Herzberg

Bad
Lauterberg

Harzgerode

Stolberg

Eisleben

0   15 miles

0   15 kilometers

Nordhausen

Sangerhausen

Harz Mountains

Spring in the Harz brings the immense regional celebration of **Walpurgisnacht** (April 30). The hedonistic festivities, immortalized by Goethe in his masterpiece *Faust*, center around legendary witches who sweep through the sky on broomsticks to alight on the peak of **Brocken**. The witches dance with the devil until midnight, at which point the "May King" cleans house. *Brocken Tips* lists events and activities in Wernigerode, Goslar, and Quedlinburg. For more on cultural happenings and hiking tips, pick up a free copy of *Harz-Blick* at any Harz tourist office.

BAD HARZBURG ☎ 05322

Perched on the edge of the Harz, a few miles from the Brocken, Bad Harzburg is a popular jumping-off point for hikers bound for glory in the mountains, though older tourists come here to relieve aches at the spa. Its integral role in the local transportation system and cheap rooms make the town a perfect gate to the Harz.

■ ⁊ **TRANSPORTATION AND PRACTICAL INFORMATION. Trains** head to: **Braunschweig** (45min., every 2hr., €5); **Goslar** (10min., every 30min., €2); **Göttingen** (1½hr., every 2hr., €13.50); **Halle** (2hr., every 2hr., €20.40); **Hannover** (1½hr., 2 per hr., €14); **Hildesheim** (1hr., 2 per hr., €9). **Buses** leave every hr. to **Braunlage** (€3.60); **Torfhaus** (€2.40); **Wernigerode** (€3.40). For a **taxi**, call ☎90 00. **Brocken Bike**, Herzog-Wilhelm-Str. 6, rents bikes. (☎92 87 96. €8-15 per day. Open M-Tu and Th-F 10am-6pm, W 10am-4pm, Sa 9am-1pm.) The **tourist office,** Herzog-Wilhelm-Str. 86, is in the Kurzentrum, the town's health center, with a smaller branch outside the Bahnhof. From the train station, walk straight down Herzog-Wilhelm-Str. (15min.). The staff recommends hikes, hands out maps, and books rooms for a €2.50 fee (free if for more than one night). On the second floor is the town **library**, with **Internet** access. (☎753 30; www.bad-harzburg.de. Open M-F 8am-8pm, Sa 9am-4pm, Su 10am-1am. Library open M-Tu and Th-F 10am-1pm and 3-6pm, W 10am-1pm, Sa 10am-noon. Internet €1.50 per 30min.) The **Sparkasse,** Herzog-Wilhelm-Str. 2, has a **24hr. ATM.** The **police station** (☎91 11 10), Herzog-Wilhelm-Str. 47, is between the train station and the tourist office. The **post office,** Herzog-Wilhem-Str. 80, 38667 Bad Harzburg, is across the fountain from the tourist office. (Open M-F 8:30am-12:30pm and 2:30-5:30pm, Sa 9am-noon.)

SACHSEN-ANHALT

⌂❒ ACCOMMODATIONS AND FOOD. Hotels and pensions are in endless supply in Bad Harzburg, with guest houses starting at €10. A *Kurtaxe* applies when staying in the park (typically €3-5); in exchange, you get a *Kurkarte* good for free rides within town and discounts on sights. **Haus Roseneck ❷**, Friederikenstr. 3, is a central pension reminiscent of Oma's house. On the way from the station to the tourist office, turn right on Friederikenstr. (☎49 41. Breakfast included. Shared bath. Singles €20; doubles €40.) The **Bier-Bistro Cinema ❸**, Herzog-Wilhelm-Str. 97 (☎543 36), has home cooking and *Milchreis* pudding (€4-10), in the company of Charlie Chaplin. Cake-and-coffee shops abound on Herzog-Wilhelm-Str., and a **supermarket** is located across the street from the train station's bus stops.

◙ SIGHTS. The **Harzburger Sole-Therme**, Nordhauser Str. 3, provides all kinds of aquatic cures—hot and cold baths (€7.50 per 2½hr.), saunas (€11.50), and a variety of massage therapies. To get to the spa, continue down Herzog-Wilhelm-Str. past the tourist office and follow it as it becomes a pedestrian zone and a smaller path; the spa will be on your right. Bathing suits are mandatory, but rentals are available. (☎753 60. Men's trunks €1.50, women's suit €2.50. Open M-Sa 8am-9pm, Su 8am-7pm; saunarium men only W 8am-1pm, women only Th 8am-3pm.) To see the park without the walk, the **Burgberg-Seilbahn** offers a short (6min.) lift up one of the hills to deep forests and a small castle ruin. (☎753 70. Up €2, down €1.60; round-trip €3.) Purchase a *Wanderntips* (€1) at the Seilbahn station to navigate the trails at the top. A number of trails leave from Kurhausstr., behind the Kurhaus. Follow signs to **Radau Wasserfall** (5km one-way) for a sparkling waterfall by the highway. Cross the highway by the Bergbahn to enter the **Nationalpark Harz** (☎918 90; www.nationalpark-harz.de). In the park, stay on trails and follow signs.

TORFHAUS   ☎05320

Although barely a town, Torfhaus forces visitors to savor the view. Day-trippers park and hike up the most popular path to **Brocken**, the tallest peak in the Harz at 1142m. Since Goethe's ascent in 1777, pilgrims have trekked the **Goetheweg**, the 16km round-trip trail to the summit. To get to the start, walk from the bus stop toward Braunlage and turn left at the yellow "Altenau-8km" sign. At the Brocken summit (2½hr. from Torfhaus), the **Brockenhaus Museum,** inside the former East German *Stasi* building, explains the peak's history, has a virtual flight over the Harz, and sells hiking maps. (Open daily June-Aug. 9:30am-5pm. €4, students €3.) From the top of the Brocken, trails head north toward Bad Harzburg. The **Brockenbahn,** a train that transports less rugged tourists between the Brocken and Wernigerode, runs regularly, but the trip is long. (1hr. €14, round-trip €22.) Torfhaus lies midway between Bad Harzburg and Braunlage. The **Nationalparkhaus Torfhaus,** Torfhaus 21, hands out trail maps. (☎263; www.torfhaus.info. Open daily 9am-5pm; Nov.-Mar. 10am-4pm.) **Ski-Verleih,** near the bus stop, rents downhill and cross-country skis. (☎203. €12-15 per day. Open daily 8:30am-5pm when there's snow.) Walking away from Bad Harzburg, turn right at the "Altenau-8km" sign for the **Jugendherberge (HI) ❶**, Torfhaus 3. (☎242; fax 254. Ski rentals from €5 per day. Reception 12:15-1pm, 4:30-5pm, and 6:15-7pm. Curfew 10pm. €18.10, under 26 €15.40, including *Kurtaxe*.) **Postal code:** 38667.

BRAUNLAGE   ☎05520

The choice location of the small ski village of Braunlage affords it some of the greenest miles of trails and easiest access to Brocken and Wurmburg. Braunlage really shines when snow flies and the ski set invades town; in the summer, vacant chalets offer spa-seekers and hikers plenty of cheap, luxurious overnight options. Braunlage is also a likely bus stop for those traveling across the Harz.

TRANSPORTATION AND PRACTICAL INFORMATION. Buses: 1 per hr. to **Bad Harzburg** (40min., €3.60); **Torfhaus** (20min., €2); **Wernigerode** (1hr., €4.30). Disembark at the "Von-Langen-Str." stop in the center of town. To get to the **tourist office**, Elbingeröder Str. 17, backtrack on Herzog-Wilhelm-Str. and turn right onto Elbingeröder Str. You'll find maps and hiking trail information, an electronic room reservation board, free booking service and a paper brochure with a hotel list. (☎930 70; www.braunlage.de. Open M-F 9am-12:30pm and 2-5pm, Sa 9:30am-noon.) **Post-Apotheke,** Marktstr. 5, is the local pharmacy. (☎930 20. Open M-F 8am-7pm.) The **post office,** 38700 Braunlage, is at Marktstr. 16 and has an **ATM.** (Open M-F 8:30am-noon and 2:30-5pm, Sa 9am-noon.)

ACCOMMODATIONS AND FOOD. Braunlage has a plethora of pensions and vacation homes (from €15). **Parkblick ❷,** Elbingeröder Str. 13, is conveniently located on the way to the tourist office, with spacious, well-furnished rooms and pelt-covered hallways. (☎12 37; fax 29 05. Breakfast included. Singles €20, with shower €25; doubles €40.) For the tireless hiker, the view through the wall of windows in the dining room of Braunlage's **Jugendherberge (HI) ❸,** Von-Langen-Str. 28, provides reason enough to stay here. From the bus stop, follow Von-Langen-Str. uphill and into the woods for 15min. (☎22 38; fax 15 69. Breakfast included. Reception 1-10pm. Under 26 €14.40.) Cheap pizza parlors and traditional German restaurants line Herzog-Wilhelm-Str. **Rhodos ❸,** Elbingeröder Str. 3, whips up Greek dishes and pizzas for €5-10. (☎22 23. Open daily 11:30am-3pm and 5pm-midnight.)

HIKING AND OUTDOOR ACTIVITIES. The **Wurmberg Seilbahn** chairlift is an exhilarating way to approach the hiking paths around Braunlage. The lift to the top (15min.) serves a 3hr. hiking trail to Brocken. Or, get off at the *Mittelstation* to reach the Schierke (2½hr.). Wurmburg (971m) itself is the second-tallest peak in the Harz, topped by a high-tech ski jump used for national competitions. The lift departs from the mountain base in the parking lot behind the ice rink. From the tourist office, turn left, then right on Kurpromenade along the river. (☎999 30. Open May-Oct. daily 9am-4:40pm. €5.50, round-trip €10. To Mittelstation €4.) Rent skis at **Ski-Verleih "Zur Seilbahn,"** Am Grossparkpl., at the Seilbahn station (€15 per day). An ice rink on Harzburger Str. meets the need for winter sports year-round. (☎21 91. Open Tu and Th-F 10am-noon and 2-4pm, W and Sa 10am-noon, 2-4pm, and 8-10pm; Su 10am-noon, 1:30-3:30pm, and 4-6pm. €3. Skate rental €2.50.) The rink also rents **bikes** (€8 per day). After a hike, relax in the pool or sauna at the **Hallen- und Freizeitbad** on Ramsenweg 2. (☎27 88. Open M-W and F-Sa 10am-7pm, Th 10am-9pm, Su 10am-2pm. Sauna €8, pool €5.)

WERNIGERODE   ☎03943

Wernigerode, crowned by one of Germany's most glorious castles, was one of Goethe's hidden haunts, but its central location between the Western and Eastern Harz make this secret too good to keep. The 20th century has only slightly modernized the town. Wernigerode is the junction between the Eastern and Western Harz, and is a transportation hub; the **Brockenbahn** connects it to the Brocken.

TRANSPORTATION AND PRACTICAL INFORMATION. To get to Wernigerode from Magdeburg, change trains at **Halberstadt** (30min., 1 per hr., €4.20); trains also run directly from **Halle** (1¼hr., 1 per 2hr., €16), and **Hannover** (2hr., 1 per hr., €18.60). A bus travels to and from Bad Harzburg (45min., 1 per hr., €3.40). The town has two train stations: **Wernigerode-Westentor** and **Bahnhof Wernigerode.** "Westentor" is the next-to-last stop on the Brockenbahn and bus, and is closer to the city center; cross the rail tracks and go straight, then turn right onto Ringstr.,

SACHSEN-ANHALT

then left and up Westernstr. to the Markt; continuing straight past the Markt onto Breite Str. will bring you to Nikolaipl. and the tourist office. The city bus only stops at "Bahnhof." Call a taxi at ☎ 63 30 53. To get to the Marktpl. and the tourist office from Bahnhof, cross and turn right on Schreiberstr., which becomes Vor der Mauer, and then hang a left on Albert-Bartels-Str.

The **tourist office,** Nicolaipl. 1, books hotels and private rooms (from €20) for free. Insist on a budget room, or ask for a *Prospekt* and make calls yourself. The office also sells a town guide (€1.50) and hands out a less-extensive one, both with a map. (☎ 63 30 35; www.wernigerode.de. Open May-Oct. M-F 9am-7pm, Sa 10am-4pm, Su 10am-3pm; Nov.-Apr. M-F 9am-6pm, Sa 10am-4pm, Su 10am-3pm.) **Tours** depart from the tourist office. (Tu and Sa 10:30am, Th and Sa-Su 2pm; May-Oct. also W 2pm. €2.60.) There is a **Deutsche Bank** near the tourist office, at the corner of Kohlmarkt and Breite Str. (Open M-Tu and Th 8:30am-1pm and 2-6pm, W 8:30am-1pm, F 8:30am-2pm.) The **police** station is at Nikolaipl., across from the pharmacy (☎ 65 30 or **emergency** 110). There is a **pharmacy, Rathaus-Apotheke,** on Nikolaipl. (Open M-F 8am-6:30pm, Sa 9am-1pm.) Exchange currency at the **post office,** Marktstr. 14, 38855 Wernigerode. (Open M-F 9am-6pm, Sa 9am-noon.)

ⁿ⌂ ACCOMMODATIONS AND FOOD. Wernigerode's **Jugendgästehaus (HI) ❶,** Friedrichstr. 53, is refurbished and modern. With your back to the "Westerntor" station, turn left on Ilsenburger Str. and then right onto Friedrichstr. at the big intersection; continue for about 20min., and the hostel will be on your left. Or, from the station, bus #1, 4, or 5 to "Lutherstr." stops right at the hostel. (☎ 60 61 76; www.djh.de. Breakfast included. Sheets €3. Reception noon-9pm. €17.70, under 27 €15.) For cheap food, visit the *Imbiße* that line Breit Str., the Markt, and Nikolaipl. or the **farmer's market** in the Marktpl. pedestrian zone (Tu and Th 10am-5pm). Tucked away on Steingruber Str. off Breite Str., **Gasthaus zur Steingrube ❸** serves *Schnitzel* (€8) and other classics. **Eurogrill ❶,** Westernstr. 6, serves salads and *Döner Kebap* (€2-3) just off the Markt. (☎ 60 55 65. Open daily 10am-11pm.)

◳ SIGHTS. Schloß Wernigerode, originally built around 1110 on its looming perch in the wooded mountains above town, is a lavish monument to the Second Reich. Count Otto zu Stolberg-Wernigerode undertook serious home improvements beginning in the 1860s, resulting in the castle's present Romantic-era glory. The perfectly preserved **Königszimmer** guest suite, where Otto hosted the *Kaiser*, flaunts the Count's wealth with gold-plated wallpaper and other decadent adornments. The flower-trimmed terrace looks out on the Brocken. (☎ 55 30 30. Open May-Oct. daily 10am-6pm; Nov.-Apr. Tu-F 10am-4pm, Sa-Su 10am-6pm. Last entry 30min. before closing. Signs in English and German. €4.50, students €4.) The **Bimmelbahn,** which chugs up to the Schloß, leaves from the intersection of Teichdamm and Klintg. behind the Rathaus. (☎ 60 40 00. May-Oct. daily every 20min. 9:30am-5:50pm; Nov.-Apr. every 45min. 10:30am-5:50pm. €2.50, under 10 €1. Round-trip €4/€2.) Or, walk up the white brick Burgberg road and through the park to the castle (20min.). In the center of the Altstadt, the twin-horned **Rathaus** looms over the marketplace with strikingly sharp slopes and petite wooden figures of saints, virgins, miners, and other archetypes decorating the facade. The **Krummelsche Haus,** Breite Str. 72, the pinnacle of *fachwerk,* is covered with ornate carvings. The **Älteste Haus,** Hinterstr. 48, the oldest house in the city, has survived fires, bombs, and various acts of God since the early 15th century. The **Kleinste Haus,** Kochstr. 43, is 2.95m wide, and the door is only 1.7m high. (Open daily 10am-4pm. €1.) The **Normalste Haus,** Witzestr. 13, has no distinguishing traits.

HALBERSTADT ☎03941

Founded in 804, Halberstadt, the current urban center of the Harz, was a center of Judaism in Germany until WWII. During the 15th and 16th centuries, Christian purists periodically came into power and exiled the Jews from the town, but each time they recovered, to return in greater numbers. As anti-Semitism gained strength in the years before WWII, increasing numbers of Jews emigrated. During *Kristallnacht*, the rest of Halberstadt's Jewish population was driven out. Today, only a fragment has returned. Though 85% of the city was destroyed by Allied bombing and rebuilt in DDR style, many historical buildings have been restored.

TRANSPORTATION AND PRACTICAL INFORMATION. Halberstadt sits in the northeast region of the Harz. **Trains** travel to **Hannover** (2hr., per 2hr., €22); **Magdeburg** (1hr., 1 per hr., €8,10); **Thale** and **Wernigerode** (1hr., 1 per hr., €4.50 daypass good for all Harz). Regular **buses** also service many Harz towns. **Streetcars** run through the city; #1 and 2 go from the Hauptbahnhof into the center (20min.; €0.90, daypass €3). The **tourist office,** Hinter dem Rathause 6, is right off the main pedestrian way behind the Rathaus, next to which is the streetcar and bus stop "Holzmarkt." Free maps and room reservations await. (☎55 18 15; www.halberstadt.de. Open May-Oct. M-F 9am-6pm, Sa 10am-2pm, Su 10am-1pm; Nov.-Apr. M-F 9am-6pm, Sa 10am-1pm.) The **post office,** 38820 Halberstadt, Unter den Zwicken 1-3, is on the corner of Schmiedstr. (☎63 00. Open M-F 8am-6pm, Sa 8am-noon.)

ACCOMMODATIONS AND FOOD. Halberstadt lacks a youth hostel, and most of the cheaper pensions are far from the center of town. **Altstadtpension Ratsmühle ❸,** Hoher Weg 1, is probably your best bet—from the tourist office, go right out the door, then right on the main street, and follow Hoher Weg until it becomes a pedestrian zone; it's on your left, next to the Gerberhaus restaurant sign. Plush rooms come complete with large bathrooms, TVs, and telephones. (☎57 37 90; www.ratsmuehle.de. Breakfast included. Singles €33; doubles €53.) Next door at **Gerberhaus ❸,** you can sip beer (€2) and eat *Klopse* and other traditional plates (€5-8) in the half-timbered loft or the stone-walled cellar. (Open Tu-Th 11am-2pm and 5-11pm, F-Sa until 2am, Su until 10pm.)

SIGHTS. Most of Halberstadt's sights center on the **Domplatz,** across from the Rathaus. In the **Domplatz** itself is the **Dom St. Stephanus,** an impressive but well-worn Gothic structure built in the 13th and 14th centuries on a site occupied by cathedrals since the 9th century. To see the majority of the Dom, including the chapels and the altar area, you'll have to take a guided tour. The **Domschatz** claims the largest collection of art from the Middle Ages held by a German church. (Dom open May-Oct. M-F 10am-5pm, Sa 10am-4:30pm, Su 11am-5:30pm; Nov.-Apr. M-Sa 10am-4pm, Su 11am-4pm. Domschatz same hours but closed Monday. Dom tours May-Oct. Tu-F 10, 11:30am, 2, 3:30pm; Sa 10am and 2pm; Su 11:30am and 2:30pm. Nov.-Apr. Tu-Su 11:30am and 2:30pm. Dom free, Domschatz €2.) In front of the Dom are the **Steine der Erinnerung** (Stones of Remembrance), a somber memorial to Jewish citizens killed in the Holocaust.

The Dom is flanked by museums; the **Stadtisches Museum,** Dompl. 36, displays the city's history, starting with prehistoric cave bears, venturing into swords and Victorian dolls, and finishing with motorcycles and a machine gun. (☎55 14 74. Open Tu-F 9am-5pm, Sa-Su 10am-5pm.) The neighboring **Museum Heineanum,** Dompl. 37, brings together dinosaur skeletons unearthed in Halberstadt with an array of preserved birds, from sparrows to ostriches. (☎55 14 61. Open Tu-F 9am-5pm, Sa-Su 10am-5pm.) Books and letters at the **Gleimhaus,** Dompl. 31, reveal that **Johannes Wilhelm Ludwig Gleim** was not much of a writer, but a trusted friend of heavy-hitting authors of his day, including Goethe and Lessing. (☎687 10. Open May-Oct. Tu-F 9am-5pm, Sa-Su 10am-4pm; Nov.-Apr. Tu-F 10am-4pm, Sa-Su 10am-4pm.) The Stadtisches Museum also sells a combination ticket for all three city museums (€3, children €1.50). Across from the Dom, the 129 spiraling steps of the **Martinitürme** peak at a view of Halberstadt's church towers and distant Brocken. (☎55 19 95. Open May-Aug. Tu-F 9am-5pm, Sa-Su 10am-6pm. €0.75.) An English pamphlet is available at the tourist office to guide you on a walking tour of the city's many Jewish sights, including a beautiful synagogue.

QUEDLINBURG   ☎03946

Quedlinburg's narrow, winding streets are crowded with pastel-painted half-timbered houses, towering churches, and a charming castle on a hill. Today, the city (a UNESCO world cultural treasure since 1994) remains much as **Heinrich (Henry) I** might have seen it in 919 as he waited in the square for the news that he'd been elected emperor, since Allied bombing left Quedlinburg untouched.

⌨⚡ TRANSPORTATION AND PRACTICAL INFORMATION. Trains run 1 per hr. to **Magdeburg** (1½hr., €10) and **Thale** (10min., €1.70). **Buses** depart every hr. from the train station to most Harz towns. **2 Rad Pavillon,** Bahnhofstr. 1b, rents bikes. (☎70 95 07. €6 per day. Open M-F 9:30am-6pm, Sa 9:30am-12:30pm.) Quedlinburg's **tourist office,** Markt 2, books rooms (from €13) for free and provides an invaluable free map. From the station, head down Bahnhofstr. At the end of the street, turn left onto Heiligestr. and follow it as it curves right, becoming Steinbrücke and leading to the Markt. (☎90 56 24 or 90 56 25; www.quedlinburg.de. Open May-Sept. M-F 9am-7pm, Sa 10am-4pm, Su 10am-3pm.) **Tours** leave from the tourist office daily at 10am and 2pm. Exchange money or use the **24hr. ATM** in the **Commerzbank,** Am Markt 6. (Open and W 9am-1pm and 2-4pm, Tu and Th 9am-1pm and 2-6pm, F 9am-1pm.) The **post office,** 06484 Quedlinburg, is at the intersection of Bahnhofstr. and Turnstr. (Open M-F 8:30am-6pm, Sa 8:30am-noon.)

⌨⚡ ACCOMMODATIONS AND FOOD. For a room, look for "Zimmer frei" signs, inquire at the tourist office, or try **Pension Biehl ❸,** Blankenburger Str. 39. Head up Marktstr. from the Markt and turn left onto Marschlingerhof, which becomes Blankenburger Str. This guesthouse offers rooms with sofas, TVs, stereos, and baths in a quiet neighborhood. (☎/fax 70 35 38. Breakfast included. Singles €23; doubles €46.) Quedlinburg's **Jugendherberge ❷,** Neuendorf 28, in the heart of town, sits in a roomy *fachwerk* framework. (☎81 17 03; www.djh-sachsen-anhalt.de. Breakfast included. Sheets €3. Dorms €16.20, under 26 €13.50.)

Culinary delights await on every corner in town. On the way to the castle, grab a local brew in the backyard *Biergarten* of the **Brauhaus Lüdde ❸,** Blasistr. 14. just off the Markt. The circular brewing hall and bar are high-ceilinged and filled with shiny copper brewing kettles. Try the light *Pilsner* (€2) or the nutty *Lüdde-Alt* (€2). Snacks (like sausages) run €4-7 and large meals are €8-14. (☎70 52 06. Open M-Sa 11am-midnight, Su 11am-10pm.) **Wispel Bier-Pub ❶,** on the corner of Weberstr. and Steinweg, offers traditional food at rock-bottom prices, but it's mainly a pub (€1.20-4.10. Open daily 10am-11pm.) Twice a week, local farmers sell their harvest on the **Marktplatz.** (W 7am-5pm, Sa 7am-noon.)

⬛ SIGHTS. The vine-covered 17th-century **Rathaus** overlooks the Markt. A remarkably resilient stone statue of **Roland** guards the stately building, after spending nearly four centuries underground. The statue was buried to punish the people for an attempted insurrection in the mid-14th century, but was retrieved, restored, and returned to its place in the 18th century. Tucked behind the Rathaus, the **Benediktikirche** houses a majestic altar decorated with delicate, gilded angels and rich oil paintings. (Open M-F 11am-4pm.)

The winding roads of **Schloßberg** insulate the **Schloß** complex within a narrow ring of recently restored half-timbered cottages packed snugly together. The 16th-century Renaissance castle overlooks the labyrinthine town below and the Harz Mountains beyond. The **Schloßmuseum** depicts city history from the Paleolithic era to the present. Several rooms are done in 18th-century style, with enough lavish furnishings and rich colors to make the modern visitor feel underdressed. (☎27 30. Open Apr.-Oct. daily 10am-6pm; Nov.-Oct. Su-Th and Sa 10am-4pm. €3, students €2.) Bordered by the castle, **Stiftskirche St. Servatius,** houses the **Domschatz.** Walk across the steps of the altar to view the gilded relics of the **Sükammer,** and then around the crucifix to the shadowy depths of the **crypt.** (☎70 99 00. Open May-Oct. Tu-F 10am-6pm, Sa 10am-4pm, Su noon-6pm; Nov.-Apr. Tu-Sa 10am-4pm, Su noon-4pm.) Loiter in the castle gardens for a the view that includes almost every red roof in the city. (Grounds open May-Oct. 6am-10pm; Nov.-Apr. 6am-8pm.)

Below the entrance to the Schloß, the **Lyonel-Feininger-Galerie,** Finkenherd 5a, displays the watercolors, woodcuts, oil paintings, and comic strips of this influential Modernist painter, all in a beautiful building. (☎22 38. Open Tu-Su Apr.-Oct. 10am-6pm; Nov.-Mar. 10am-5pm. €6, students €3.) Next door, the **Klopstockhaus,** Schloßberg 12, was restored in memory of German Enlightenment writer **Friedrich Gottlieb Klopstock,** Lessing and Goethe's contemporary. Artifacts like Klopstock's letters are interesting for the German-literature fanatic. (☎26 10. Open Tu-Su Apr.-Oct. 10am-5pm; Nov.-Mar. 10am-4pm. €3, students €2.)

THALE   ☎03947

Above the dramatic front of Thale's flowing rivers, jagged cliffs, and splendid mountainside scenery lurks a region of myth and lore—the peaks on either side of the valley are alleged dens of witches, devils, princesses, and flying horses. The town has seen better days, but regains its old popularity every April 30th when visitors on broomsticks coven up at the annual witches' convention.

☞🚆 TRANSPORTATION AND PRACTICAL INFORMATION. Trains run 1 per hr. to: **Halberstadt** (30min.); **Magdeburg** (1½hr.); **Quedlinburg** (15min., €1.60). **Buses** depart to many Harz towns from the bus station next to the train station. (Most every hr., €2-4.) Across from the train station, the **tourist office,** Bahnhofstr. 3, books rooms (€15-30) for free. (☎25 97; www.thale.de. Open May-Oct. M-F 9am-5pm, Sa-Su 9am-3pm; Nov.-Apr. M-F 9am-5pm.) A **Sparkasse** on Bahnhofstr. exchanges money and has a **24hr. ATM.** (Open M and F 8:30am-4pm, Tu and Th 8:30am-5:30pm, W 8:30am-2:30pm.) There is a **police** station on Rudolf-Breitscheidstr. 10. (☎460. Turn left out of the train station, then take a right on Poststr., which becomes Rudolf-Breitscheidstr.) The **post office,** 06502 Thale, Karl-Marx-Str. 16, is a block away from the Sparkasse. (Open M-F 9am-6:30pm, Sa 9am-1pm.)

☞🏠 ACCOMMODATIONS AND FOOD. Thale's **Jugendherberge (HI) ❷,** Bodetal-Waldkater, is situated on Bodetal's famous brook, where good witches are said to roam. Exit the station right, turn left on Parkstr, take the first right, and keep walking along the river on Hubertusstr. The cavernous 2- to 6-bed rooms have river views. (☎28 81; www.djh.de/jugendherbergen/thale. Breakfast included. Sheets €3. Reception 3-6pm and 8-10pm. Dorm beds €16.20, under 26 €13.50.) **Pension Kleiner Waldkater ❹,** next door on Bodetal, is in an 165-year-old brick house. (☎/fax 28 28. Double-as-single €33; doubles €52.) **Hotel Wilder Jäger ❸** is a cheap pension barely 200m from the train station. Turn left out the station and walk to the corner.

(☎61 06 18; fax 772 58 15. Singles €25; doubles €46.) Thale's restaurant offerings are a bit limited; many food stands on Hexentanzpl. offer cheap eats. Beyond the Sparkasse, Karl-Marx-Str. has shops, restaurants, and bakeries.

◨ **SIGHTS.** Legend dates Thale's cultic history back to prehistoric times, when a sorceress named **Watelinde** led pagan rituals that lured impressionable youths down the destructive fast-lane lifestyle of witchery. This heritage is celebrated in the mountaintop tourist zone called **Hexentanzplatz,** which hosts a yearly international witch conference known as **Walpurgisnacht.** Every April 30, the town goes wild when the witches gather to dance. A witch bending over a rock in a provocative pose will likely distort some preconceived ideas of witchery. Don't be disappointed, though, if you find more souvenir vendors than supernatural women. To get to the Hexentanzpl., take the **Kabinenbahn** up the side of the mountain, which departs across the river from the hostel and provides stunning views of the valley below. (☎25 00. daily May-Oct. 9:30am-6pm; Nov.-Apr. 10am-4:30pm. Round-trip €4.50, children €3). Or, take a beautiful 1hr. hike: follow Hubertusstr. past the Jugendherberge and take a left onto the trail by the stone bridge. Once at the Hexentanzpl., follow the signs to the **Walpurgishalle,** a museum commemorating the Harz's history of witchcraft. Displays range from the comical (plastic witches dancing) to the terrifying (an old black mask believed to be used in the original ceremonies). One of two rooms is devoted to the story of Faust and Mephisto, as depicted by large oil paintings. (Open daily 9am-5pm. €2, children €0.50.) Next to the museum is the impressive **Harzer Bergtheater Thale,** a huge outdoor amphitheater, with performances oscillating between the sublime (anything from operas to Goethe's *Faust*) and the infernal (live performances by German *Schlager* stars). Shows run May-September; schedules are available at the tourist office and posted along the path into the theater. (☎23 24. Tickets €8-16; 30% student discount.) The **Roßtrappe,** a rocky peak across the valley from the Hexentanzpl., can be reached by hiking up *Präsidentenweg* and then up Esselsteig; the trail starts upriver from the chairlift station in the valley. Or take the **Sessellift** (chairlift), which departs from the same place as the Kabinenbahn. (☎25 00. Lift open June-Aug. daily 9:30am-6pm; Sept.-May Sa-Su 10am-5:30pm. Round-trip €3, children €2.)

MAGDEBURG ☎0391

Magdeburg has the dubious distinction of having been destroyed in both the Thirty Years' War and WWII. On May 10, 1631, Catholic troops invaded the Protestant city, reducing most of it to rubble. Magdeburg was rebuilt over the rest of the 17th century, only to be demolished in a 1945 Allied bombing. The scars of war are still visible among the concrete apartments erected by the socialist government, but as the capital of Sachsen-Anhalt, Magdeburg has largely escaped post-DDR stagnation. With a fast-paced atmosphere, the self-proclaimed "city with a future" is flourishing with commerce created by reconstruction and the university's vitality.

▐▀ TRANSPORTATION

Trains leave 1 per hr. to: **Berlin** (1½hr., €14.10); **Hannover** (1½hr., €16.20); **Quedlinburg** (40min., €10.70). Magdeburg is conveniently configured for pedestrians. Cutting through the shopping mall in front of the train station will bring you to *Ernst-Reuter-Allee,* which leads directly to **Breiter Weg,** the backbone of the city and the main pedestrian route. Most of the museums and sights are within a block or two of Breiter Weg, mainly between Ernst-Reuter-Allee and Häckelstr. **Streetcars** shuttle between the major attractions. (Single ticket €1.40; day pass €3. Tickets sold at most stops.) For a **taxi,** call ☎73 73 73 or 56 56 56.

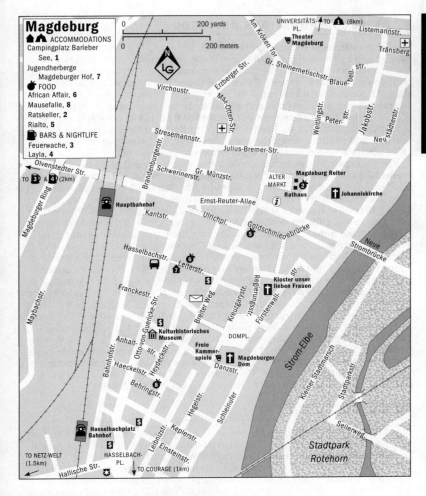

Magdeburg

🏠🏕 ACCOMMODATIONS
Campingplatz Barleber
   See, **1**
Jugendherberge
   Magdeburger Hof, **7**
🍎 FOOD
African Affair, **6**
Mausefalle, **8**
Ratskeller, **2**
Rialto, **5**
🍸 BARS & NIGHTLIFE
Feuerwache, **3**
Layla, **4**

🛈 PRACTICAL INFORMATION

The **tourist office,** Ernest-Reuter-Allee 12 (☎194 33; www.magdeburg-tourist.de), on the big intersection with Breiter Weg, hands out maps, books rooms for free and sells tickets to local events. Pick up a free copy of *Dates* magazine for a schedule of cultural activities and nightlife. (☎540 49 02 03, accommodations service 540 49 03. Office open May-Sept. M-F 10am-7pm, Sa 10am-4pm; Oct.-Apr. M-F 10am-6:30pm, Sa 10am-3pm.) **Tours** leave daily from the office at 11am (€3). **Courage,** Porsestr. 14 (☎/fax 404 80 89), is the local women's center. **Internet** awaits at **Netz-Welt,** Heidestr. 9. Take streetcar #10 (dir.: "Sudenburg") to "Eiskellerpl." Follow Halberstädterstr. and take a left on Heidestr. Or follow Hallischestr. from Hasselbachpl. until it becomes Halberstädterstr. (☎620 17 55. €1.50 per 30min. Open daily noon-2am.) The **post office,** 39104 Magdeburg, is in a late Gothic hulk on Breiter Weg. (Open M-F 9am-7pm, Sa 9am-noon.)

ACCOMMODATIONS AND FOOD

The ▥**Jugendherberge Magdeburger Hof (HI) ❸**, Leiterstr. 10, hides a colorful, futuristic interior and a small cafe on a square bordered by apartment buildings. Follow the streetcar tracks to the right from the train station and left onto Hasselbachstr. until you pass the bus station. Walk up the stairs; the hostel is 30m down on the right. All rooms have baths. (☎532 10 10; www.jugendherberge.de/dh/magdeburg. **Internet** €6 per hr. Breakfast and sheets included. Reception 3-10pm. Dorms €22.70, under 26 €18.) **Campingplatz Barleber See ❶**, is 45min. outside the city center. Take streetcar #10 on Breiter Weg (dir.: Barleber See) to the end (about 30min.), and continue down the main street (August-Bebel-Damm) about 1km. (☎50 32 44. Reception 7am-9pm. Open May-Sept. €6.45 per tent.)

Many inexpensive restaurants crowd the streets around the intersection of **Breiter Weg** and **Einsteinstraße** in **Hasselbachplatz**, the only part of downtown to survive the bombing. Back up Breiter Weg, the **Alter Markt** offers a bounty of cheap food like roasted half-chickens (€2) and fresh fruit. (Open M-F 8am-5pm, Sa 7am-noon.) **Ratskeller ❷**, under the Rathaus in the Alter Markt, sports 18th-century decor and great culinary deals: each weekday features a different *Stammesse* (lunch special) from 11am-3pm, including an entree, starch, and dessert for €4-5. From 3-5pm daily all dishes are available at *Ratsherrenpreise:* half-price plus €1. (Closed until Rathaus renovations conclude in spring 2005. ☎568 23 23. Open M-Sa 11am-11pm, Su 11am-9pm.) Farther down at Breiter Weg 19a, **Rialto ❷** serves hearty portions of Italian food under massive umbrellas along the sidewalk. The complex also includes a separate *Eiscafe* and *Imbiß*. (☎543 34 72. Pasta or pizza €3.50-8. Open daily 11am-midnight.) **Mausefalle ❸**, Breiter Weg 224, at the north end of Hasselbachpl., attracts a young crowd, particularly students. The funky interior and vintage Tom & Jerry posters add character to this hopping hangout. (☎543 01 35. Spaghetti dishes €5-7, salads €6-8. Open M-Th 8:30am-3am, F-Sa 11am-4am, Su 10am-3am.) Right near the hostel, curious tourists and brave locals are drawn into **African Affair ❸**, Leiterstr. 3, where exotic spices garnish exotic species. The menu features dishes (€8-16) made with zebra, ostrich, crocodile, and antelope; try them all during buffet hours (Su noon-3pm and 5-9pm).

SIGHTS

Magdeburg's few dazzling sights seem strangely out of place among the drab facades that dominate the city. The main landmark and city symbol is the sprawling ▥**Magdeburger Dom,** five blocks up Breiter Weg from Hasselbachpl. on Domstr., renowned as the first Gothic church in Germany and the biggest cathedral in East Germany. The hauntingly beautiful towers and cavernous interior house an amazing collection of religious sculptures from the 11th to 13th centuries. Peace can be found in the cathedral's grassy quandrangle just outside the door by the choir. At one end of the cathedral is the low-key grave of Otto I, the second Holy Roman Emperor, who founded the first cathedral on this site in 937. Legend credits the *Kaiser's* spectral guardianship for the preservation of the Dom when Magdeburg was destroyed by Catholics in 1631 and B-17 bombers in 1945. (☎543 24 14. Open summer M-Sa 10am-6pm, Su 11:30am-6pm; winter M-Sa 10am-4pm, Su 11:30am-4pm. Free. Tours M-Sa 2pm, Su 11:30am and 2pm. €3, students €1.50.)

The ancient **Kloster unser lieben Frauen,** Regierungstr. 4/6, is near the Dom among many faceless apartments. This 11th-century nunnery now houses an art exhibition space, concert hall, and cafe. The shift in purpose hasn't compromised the monastic atmosphere—the grounds around the cloister shimmer in sheltered tranquility. The delicate statues in the garden provides the perfect place for a stroll, and the benches among the remains of stone walls are a quiet place to sit. (☎ 56 50 20. Cafe open Tu-Su 10am-6pm. Exhibition hall open Tu-Su 10am-5pm. €2, students and seniors €1.) As you head away from the Dom and cross Breiter Weg on Danzstr., the **Kulturhistorisches Museum,** Otto-von-Güricke-Str. 68-73, will pop up on the left. The museum is a collage of history, science, and modern art; on the first floor are items from Magdeburg's history culminating in chilling Jewish identification papers from WWII and the impersonal DDR exhibit consisting of flags and banners (☎ 540 35 01. Open Tu-Su 10am-5pm. €2, students €1.) The **Johanniskirche,** almost on the Elbe, behind the Alter Markt, once stood as a memorial to the 1945 bombing, which nearly destroyed it. Recently, the church has been rebuilt to its pre-war glory and now holds a variety of temporary exhibitions. (☎ 53 65 00. Open Tu-Su 10am-5pm. €1, exhibitions €2.) Across from the Johanniskirche rises the clock tower of the elegantly proportioned 17th-century **Rathaus.** The **Magdeburger Reiter** (built in 1240), is the oldest free-standing equestrian figure in northern Europe; the original is in the Kulturhistorisches Museum.

🎵 🎭 ENTERTAINMENT AND NIGHTLIFE

Magdeburg has a busy cultural scene. *Dates* and *Stadtpass* provide information about theaters, cinemas, concert halls, clubs, and bars. The **Theater Magdeburg,** Universitätspl. 9, is at the corner of Breiter Weg and Erzberger Str. Its **Großes Haus** hosts big-name operas, ballets, and plays, while the smaller **Podiumbühne** is more experimental. (☎ 540 64 44. Box office open Tu-F 10am-7:30pm, Sa 10am-2pm, and 1hr. before performances. Closed mid-July to early Sept.) The **Freie Kammerspiele,** in front of the Dom, puts a modern twist on the classics. (☎ 540 63 63. Tickets sales M-Th 3-8pm, F-Sa 2-8pm, and 1hr. before curtain. Closed mid-July to early Sept.)

For bars, restaurants, and people-watching, there are a few good areas in Magdeburg: **Hasselbachplatz, Sudenburg,** along Halberstädterstr. and its cross streets (S1 or 10 or bus #53 or 54 to "Eiskellerpl." or "Ambrosiuspl."), and **Diesdorfstraße** (S1 or 6 to "Westring" or "Arndtstr."). Though far from the city center (30min. by foot), Kurt-Schmidt-Str. and Schönebecker Str. offer many clubs as well. Inside an old fire station, the **Feuerwache,** Halberstädterstr. 140, hosts plays, art exhibits, and concerts, and serves as a winter cafe and a summer beer garden. (☎ 60 28 09. Drinks €1.50-3. Open daily 7pm-midnight.) Located south of Diesdorfstr., the candlelit **Layla,** Lessingstr. 66, serves German and Irish beer (and classic rock) to a crowd of easy-going regulars. (☎ 731 70 28. Open daily 10am-2am.)

SACHSEN (SAXONY)

After decades of slow decay, Saxony has fully embraced its history—even the smallest towns have embarked on ambitious reconstruction programs that will shape the region's character for years to come. The castles around Dresden attest to the political power Saxony's electors once wielded, while the socialist monuments and unmistakable cement architecture of Chemnitz bluntly recall life during the DDR. In the eastern part of the *Land*, the rugged forests and sandstone cliffs of the Sächsische Schweiz National Park and the Zittau Mountains are among the most stunning landscapes in Germany, offering an abundance of hiking, kayaking, climbing, and biking opportunities. Saxony is also home to the Sorbs, Germany's only native ethnic minority, whose presence has brought a Slavic influence to many of the region's eastern towns.

HIGHLIGHTS OF SAXONY

CHILL WITH STUDENTS in the trade city of **Leipzig** (p. 640), which harbors an active **university culture** and **cafe scene**.

CLIMB, HIKE, OR SKI the mountainsides of the **Sächsische Schweiz** (p. 622).

EXHAUST YOURSELF amidst the world-class **museums** and grand **Baroque architecture** of **Dresden** (p. 606), before refueling in the throes of an unparalleled **nightlife**.

DRESDEN ☎ 0351

Over the course of two nights in February 1945, Allied firebombs incinerated over three quarters of Dresden and killed between 25,000 and 50,000 civilians. When the fires were finally extinguished a week later, the question facing the city was how best to rebuild. With most of the Altstadt in ruins, the surviving 19th-century Neustadt became Dresden's nerve center: today, it is still an energetic scene for nightlife and alternative culture. The city hopes to have the last remnants of fire damage repaired by 2006, in time for Dresden's 800th anniversary. The resulting architectural atmosphere will be unique: modern buildings like the amazing Volkswagen *Gläserne Manufaktur* (transparent factory) will share space with restored Baroque masterpieces by Pöppelmann and Bährs and the 19th-century Neustadt. In short, the capital of Saxony is always in motion. Both culture fanatics and hardcore partyers will find it intensely vibrant and fascinating for a city its size—backpackers traveling from Berlin to Prague won't want to miss it.

▐ TRANSPORTATION

Flights: Dresden's **airport** (☎ 881 33 60; www.dresden-airport.de) is 9km from the city. S2 runs there from both main train stations. (20min., 2 per hr. 4am-11:30pm, €1.50.)

Trains: Dresden has 2 main train stations: the **Hauptbahnhof** in the Altstadt and **Bahnhof Dresden Neustadt** across the Elbe. Most trains stop at both stations. A 3rd station, **Dresden Mitte**, lies between the two but is rarely used due to its inferior location. The Hauptbahnhof is currently undergoing major renovation expected to last until 2006.

Sachsen (Saxony)

In the meantime, many stores and services will change locations; ask at the **Reisezentrum** or in new service centers for information. For schedules, check the yellow *Abfahrt* posters. Buy tickets from the machines in the main halls of the stations or at the **Reisezentrum** desk. Trains to: **Bautzen** (1hr., 1 per hr., €8.40); **Berlin** (3hr., 1 per hr., €30); **Budapest** (11hr., 1 per hr., €64); **Frankfurt am Main** (5hr., 1 per hr., €70); **Görlitz** (1½hr., 1 per hr., €14.80). Trains to: **Leipzig** (1½hr., 1-2 per hr., €17); **Munich** (7hr., 1 per hr., €79); **Prague** (2½hr., 12 per day, €20); **Warsaw** (8hr., 8 per day, €27); **Zittau** (2hr., 1 per hr., €15).

Ferries: Sächsische Dampfschifffahrt. (☎86 60 90, schedule information ☎866 09 40. Office and information desk open M-W 8:30am-6pm, Th 8am-7pm, F 8am-7:30pm, Sa 8am-8pm, Su 8:30am-6pm.) Ships leave from the Elbe between Augustusbrücke and Carolabrücke in the **Altstadt** for **Seußlitz** in the north and through the **Sächsische Schweiz** to the Czech border town **Děčín** in the south. Ferries to: **Pillnitz** (1½hr., €8.70, round-trip €13.40) and **Meißen** (2hr., €10.70). Day pass €18, children €9.

Mitfahrzentrale: Dr.-Friedrich-Wolf-Str. 2 (☎194 40). On Slesischen Pl., across from Bahnhof Neustadt. Open M-F 9am-8pm, Sa-Su 10am-2pm.

Public Transportation: Most of Dresden is manageable on foot, but **buses** and **streetcars** cover the whole city. Single ride €1.60, 4 or fewer stops €1. Day pass €4; weekly pass €15, children €11.50. Tickets are available from *Fahrkarten* dispensers at major

Dresden Neustadt

ACCOMMODATIONS
Guest House Mezcalero, 4
Hostel Die Boofe, 1
Hostel "Louise 20," 9
Hostel Mondpalast, 15
Lollis Homestay, 8
Pension Raskolnikoff, 16

FOOD & DRINK
Blumenau, 14
Cafe Europa, 2
El Perro Borracho, 7
Planwirtschaft, 10
Raskolnikoff, 17

BARS
Die 100, 5
Brauhaus am Wald-
schlösschen, 18

NIGHTLIFE
BOY's, 6
DownTown &
Groove Station, 11
Flowerpower, 3
Katy's Garage, 12
Scheune, 13

stops, and on the streetcars. For information and maps, go to one of the **Verkehrs-Info** stands in front of the Hauptbahnhof or at Postpl. (both open M-F 8am-7pm, Sa 8am-6pm, Su 9am-6pm), Albertpl. (open M-F 10am-6pm), or Pirnaischer Pl. (open M-F 8am-7pm, Sa 9am-4pm). Most major lines run every hr. after midnight—look for the moon sign marked "*Gute-Nacht-Linie.*" Dresden's **S-Bahn** network reaches from Meißen to the Czech border town Schöna (both €4). Buy S-Bahn tickets from the *Automaten* or at the **Reisezentrum** and validate them in the red machines at the bottom of the stairwells to each track. **Punch your ticket as you board.**

Taxis: ☎21 12 11 or 888 88 88.

Car Rental: Sixt-Budget, An der Frauenkirche 5 (all reservations ☎285 25 12), in the Hilton Hotel (open M-F 7am-7pm, Sa-Su 8am-noon), or the Hauptbahnhof (open M-F 7am-8pm). **Europcar,** Strehlener Str. 5 (all reservations ☎87 73 20), at the Bayerische Str. exit of the Hauptbahnhof (open 24hr.), or at Bahnhof Neustadt, out the Slesischen Pl. exit and up the stairs, then left. (Open M-F 7:30am-6pm, Sa 8am-noon, Su 9-11am.)

Bike Rental: In the Hauptbahnhof near luggage storage (☎461 32 62). €6 per day for a bike that's Deutsche Bahn red. Open daily 6am-10pm.

Hitchhiking: *Let's Go* does not recommend hitchhiking as a safe mode of transportation. Hitchers say they stand in front of the "Autobahn" signs at on-ramps. To get to **Berlin,** take streetcar #3 or 13 to "Liststr.," then bus #81 to "Am Olter." To **Prague, Eisenach,** or **Frankfurt am Main,** take bus #72 or 88 to "Luga," or #76, 85, or 96 to "Lockwitz."

Dresden Altstadt

🏠 ▲ ACCOMMODATIONS
Campingplatz Mockritz, 7
City-Herberge, 4
Ibis Hotel, 5
Jugendgästehaus Dresden (HI), 2
Jugendherberge Dresden Rudi
    Arndt (HI), 6
🍎 FOOD & DRINK
Café Aha, 3
★ NIGHTLIFE
Studentenklub Bärenzwinger, 1

SACHSEN

🔹 ORIENTATION

With a population of a half-million, Dresden crowds the banks of the Elbe river 60km northwest of the Czech border and 200km south of Berlin. The **Elbe** bisects Dresden, with the **Hauptbahnhof** south of the river, on the same bank as the **Altstadt**. The **Neumarkt** and many of Dresden's main tourist attractions, including the amazing Baroque architecture, are centered between the Altmarkt and the Elbe. The area between the Altstadt and the Hauptbahnhof is packed with massive, incongruous corporate shopping developments. North of the river, the **Neustadt,** ironically, is one of the oldest parts of the city, since it weathered the bombings almost completely unscathed. The neighborhoods off of **Albertplatz** pulse with the lively energy of Dresden's young alternative scene. Five immense **bridges**—Marienbrücke, Augustbrücke, Carolabrücke, Albertbrücke, and the "Blue Marvel" Loschwitzbrücke (p. 615)—connect the city's two halves.

⑦ PRACTICAL INFORMATION

Tourist Office: 2 locations: **Prager Str. 2a,** near the Hauptbahnhof (open M-F 10am-6pm, Sa 10am-4pm), and **Theaterpl.** in the Schinkelwache, a small building in front of the Semper Oper. (☎49 19 20; fax 49 19 21 16. Open M-F 10am-6pm, Sa-Su 10am-4pm.) The staff books rooms (€3 fee, rooms €18+) and sells city maps (€0.30). The office sells 2 cards that provide discounts on transportation and museums: the **Dresden City-Card** is valid for 48hr. of transport in the city-zone (€18); the **Dresden Regio-Card** is good for 72hr. in the entire *Oberelbe* region, including Meißen and Sächsiche Schweiz (€29). Call the special city hotlines for general information (☎49 19 21 00), room reservations (☎49 19 22 22), and advance ticket purchases (☎49 19 22 33).

Tours: A variety of companies offer city and specialized tours. Options include ferry tours of the Elbe, sightseeing tours in the Dresden area, and tours for first-time travelers to Germany. Most available in English, many in Chinese, French, Italian, Japanese, and Spanish. Call the city tours hotline (☎49 19 21 40) or ask at the tourist office.

Currency Exchange: ReiseBank, in the main hall of the Hauptbahnhof. €1-3 commission, depending on the amount; 1-1.5% commission for traveler's checks. Western Union money transfer service. Open M-F 8am-7pm, Sa 9am-noon and 12:30-4pm, Su 9am-1pm. Other banks on Prager Str. After hours, the self-service exchange machine in the Hauptbahnhof exchanges at less favorable rates.

Luggage Storage and Lockers: At all train stations. Lockers €1-2 for 24hr.

Bookstore: Das Internationales Buch, Altmarkt 24 (☎65 64 60), in the arcades near Kreuzkirche. Books on travel and Saxony on the 1st fl. English books on the 2nd fl. Open M-F 9:30am-8pm, Sa 9:30am-6pm.

Library: Haupt- und Musikbibliothek, Freiberger Str. 35 (☎864 82 33), in the World Trade Center. From the Hauptbahnhof, bear left and follow Ammonstr. up to Freiberger Str. Lots of info about Saxony and Dresden. Small section of English books on the 1st fl. Open M-F 10am-7pm, Sa 10am-2pm.

Mitwohnzentrale: Dr.-Friedrich-Wolf-Str. 2 (☎194 30). On Slesischen Pl., same building as Mitfahrzentrale. Open M-F 9am-7pm, Sa 10am-2pm.

Gay and Lesbian Organizations: Gerede-Dresdner Lesben, Schwule und alle Anderen, Prießnitzstr. 18 (☎802 22 51, 24hr. hotline 802 22 60). From Albertpl., walk up Bautzner Str. and turn left onto Prießnitzstr. Open M 3-5pm, Tu and Th 10am-noon and 3-5pm, F 10am-noon.

Women's Center: Frauenzentrum "sowieso," Angelikastr. 1 (☎804 14 70). Open M and Th 3-7pm, W and F 9am-1pm. *Frauenkneipe* (women's bar) Th-F from 8pm.

Laundromat: Eco-Express, 2 Königsbrückestr., on Albertpl., has no chairs to sit on while you wait. (Wash €1.90. Dry €0.50. Open M-Sa 6am-11pm) Also try **"Crazy" Waschsalon,** 6 Louisenstr. (Wash €2.50. Dry €0.50 per 10min. Open M-Sa 7am-11pm.)

Emergency: Police ☎110. **Ambulance and Fire:** ☎112.

Pharmacy: Apotheke Prager Straße, Prager Str. 3 (☎490 30 14). Open M-F 8:30am-7pm, Sa 8:30am-4pm. The *Notdienst* sign outside lists current 24hr. pharmacies.

Internet Access: In the bar at **Hostel Mondpalast,** Louisenstr. 77 (☎563 40 50). €3.50 per hr. Open daily 8am-1am. Also in **Groove Station,** Katharinenstr. 11-13. €3 per hr. Open M-Sa from 7pm, Su from 4pm.

Post Office: The **Hauptpostamt,** Königsbrückerstr. 21/29, 01099 Dresden (☎819 13 73), is in the Neustadt. Open M-F 9am-7pm, Sa 10am-1pm. A **branch** in the Altstadt is on Weberg. at the "Altmarkt Galerie." Open daily 9:30am-8pm.

ACCOMMODATIONS AND CAMPING

The Neustadt is home to a number of hostels with late check-out times, close to the nightlife. Quieter hostels and pricier hotels can be found closer to the sights around the Altstadt. Between April and October, reservations are necessary.

Hostel Mondpalast, Louisenstr. 77 (☎563 40 50; www.mondpalast.de). From Bahnhof Neustadt, walk down Antonstr. towards Albertpl. and continue on Bautzner Str. Turn left onto Martin-Luther-Str.; the hostel is at the end of the street. With a guestbook full of rave reviews, this stellar hostel seems to provide all a backpacker could desire: good prices, comfortable beds in spacious rooms, a large kitchen and social dining room, and a bar downstairs. **Internet** €3.50 per hr. Breakfast €4.50. Sheets €1.50. Key deposit €10. Reception 24hr. 10-bed dorms €13.50; 4- to 6-bed dorms €15-16; 3- to 4-bed dorms €16; singles €29, with shower €39; doubles €37/€50. ❷

Hostel "Louise 20," Louisenstr. 20 (☎889 48 94; www.louise20.de). From the Neustadt station take Antonstr. to Albertpl. Turn left on Königsbrückestr. and right on Louisenstr. Above the restaurant Planwirtschaft. A ladder leads to a dorm attic in Dresden's newest hostel. Breakfast €4.50. Sheets €2.50. Key deposit €5. Reception 7am-11pm. Check-out noon. Dorms €10. 5-bed room €15; 3- to 4-bed rooms €16; singles €26; doubles €37. ❶

Lollis Homestay, Goerlitzerstr. 34. (☎81 08 45 58; www.lollishome.de). From Bahnhof Neustadt, walk down Antonstr. toward Albertpl. Turn left on Rothenburgerstr., which becomes Goerlitzerstr. Dresden's smallest, this hostel reproduces all the relaxed feel of a German *Wohngemeinschaft* (shared student flat) with a kitchen and cozy commonroom. **Internet** €0.50 per 10min. Breakfast €3. Sheets €2. Laundry €3. 6-bed rooms €13; singles €27; doubles €36. Ask about weekly and monthly rates in the winter. ❶

Hostel Die Boofe, Hechtstr. 10 (☎801 33 61; www.boofe.de). From Bahnhof Neustadt, take a left and walk parallel to the tracks on Dammweg. Turn left onto Bischofsweg and right onto Hechtstr. A 5min. walk from the Neustadt, this pristinely funky hostel has a restaurant downstairs with specials for guests. Free tie-dyed sheets and a basement sauna (€3 per hr.). **Internet** €1 per hr. Breakfast €4.50. Reception 7am-midnight. Book ahead. 4-bed rooms €15; singles €26; doubles €34, with shower €38. ❷

Pension Raskolnikoff, Böhmische Str. 34 (☎804 57 06; www.raskolnikoff.de). This 6-room pension is squeezed into the same building as the restaurant and gallery of the same name (p. 612). The distinctly relaxed bohemian atmosphere, with fold-out couches and plywood furniture, provides a comfy escape from the hostel scene. Singles €30-35; doubles €40-50; extra person €8. ❸

Guest House Mezcalero, Königsbrückerstr. 64 (☎81 07 70; www.mezcalero.de). From Neustadt station, go straight on Antonstr. and turn left on Königsbrückerstr.; it's 10min. ahead on the right in a quiet courtyard. A spacious Mexican-themed guest house. Breakfast €5. 4- to 6-bed dorms from €15; singles from €30; doubles €50; apartments €25 per person. ❸

City-Herberge, Lingnerallee 3 (☎489 59 00; www.city-herberge.de). From the Hauptbahnhof, walk up St. Petersburger Str. Turn right at Lignerallee. Although housed in an architecturally monstrous apartment complex, this centrally-located hostel is welcoming and has modern hotel-style rooms and a bar downstairs. Shared bathrooms. Breakfast included. Apr.-June, Sept.-Oct., and Dec. singles €36.50; doubles €52. All other times singles €31.50; doubles €46. ❸

Jugendherberge Dresden Rudi Arndt (HI), Hübnerstr. 11 (☎471 06 67; fax 472 89 59). Streetcar #3 (dir.: Coschütz) or 8 (dir.: Südvorstadt) to "Nürnberger Pl." Take Nürnbergerstr. and turn right onto Hübnerstr.; the hostel is at the 1st corner on the right. Or, from the Hauptbahnhof, turn left out of the Bayrische Str. exit, then take your 1st right on Fritz-Löffler-Str. After about 10min. turn right on Nürnbergerstr., then right on Hübner-str. Small rooms with a friendly atmosphere, located in a quiet residential neighborhood. Breakfast included. Laundry €2. Check-in 3pm-1am. Curfew 1am. Reservations recommended. Dorms €18.60, under 27 €16. ❷

Ibis Hotel, Prager Str. (☎48 56 66 61). 3 modern hotel skyscrapers tower over Prager Str., up the street from the Hauptbahnhof and near the Altstadt sights. Simple but comfortable rooms, some with views of Dresden's night skyline. Rooms include TVs, phones, and showers or baths. Breakfast €9. Reception 24hr. Singles from €62; doubles from €74. Apartments (from €80) are a good deal for families. ❹

Jugendgästehaus Dresden (HI), Maternistr. 22 (☎49 26 20; fax 492 62 99). Go out the Prager Str. exit of the Hauptbahnhof and turn left on Ammonstr. (the main road that runs along the tracks) to Rosen Str. (10min.) Turn right, then take a left onto Maternistr. Newly renovated with more than 480 beds, this behemoth houses many school groups in sleek rooms. Wheelchair-accessible. Breakfast and sheets included. Reception 24hr. Check-in after 4pm. Check-out 9:30am. 2- to 4-bed rooms with sinks €20, with private shower €23, under 27 €17.50/€21; singles €8 extra. ❷

Campingplatz Mockritz, Boderitzerstr. 30 (☎471 52 50; www.camping-dresden.de). Bus #76 (dir.: Mockritz) from the Hauptbahnhof to "Campingpl. Mockritz." Only a 10min. ride from Dresden, this family-run spot is surprisingly serene. Reception daily 8-11am and 4-8pm. €4.50 per person, €1.50 per tent. Bungalows €10 per person. ❶

🄵 FOOD

Dresden's increasing tourist population has pushed up food prices. It's difficult to find anything in the Altstadt not targeting tourists; the cheapest eats are at the *Imbiße* stands along **Prager Str.** and around the **Postpl.** The Neustadt area between Albertpl. and Alaunpl. spawns a new bar every few weeks and is home to most of Dresden's quirky, ethnic, vegetarian, and student-friendly restaurants. The free monthly *Spot*, available at the tourist office, details culinary options.

▨ **Café Aha,** Kreuzstr. 7 (☎496 06 73), across the street from the Kreuzkirche. Nestled in a neighborhood full of chains, this maverick restaurant celebrates foods produced by ecologically sound means. Each dish (€3.50-8.40) promotes the idea of "fair trade;" the cafe introduces food from a different developing country each month. Shop downstairs sells international goods at fair trade prices. Often exotic and always delicious. Open daily 10am-midnight. Kitchen closes at 10:30pm, store closes at 6pm. ❷

▨ **Planwirtschaft,** Louisenstr. 20 (☎801 31 87). With decor that harmonizes nature and industry (dried grass hangs next to an antique typewriter), this restaurant offers both traditional German dishes and neo-German cuisine made with ingredients direct from local farms. Inventive soups, fresh salads (€3.50-7), and entrees from stuffed eggplant to roasted lamb and fresh lake fish (€7-13). English menu available. Plentiful breakfast buffet until 3pm (€8.60). Open Su-Th 9am-midnight, F-Sa 9am-1am. ❸

Cafe Europa, Königsbrückerstr. 68 (☎804 48 10; www.cafe-europa-dresden.de). Open 24hr., this self-consciously hip cafe draws a crowd of students and 20-somethings with 120 different warm and cold drinks. Great soups (around €3) and traditional entrees (€6-10) complement the **free Internet** access provided to customers.

El Perro Borracho, Alaunstr. 70, through the passageway and into the courtyard (☎803 67 23). Flowing Spanish wines, *Sekt,* and *sangria* convince Dresdeners to splurge for that vacation in Mallorca. Tasty *tapas,* from calamari to potato *torillas,* and other Spanish specialties. Main courses €6-8. Buffet breakfast 10am-3pm on weekends (€8). Open M-F 11:30am-2am, *tapas* from 6pm; Sa-Su 10am-3am, *tapas* from 3:30pm. ❸

Raskolnikoff, Böhmischestr. 34 (☎804 57 06; http://home.t-online.de/home/raskolnikoff-dresden). A dim Dostoevskian haunt in a ramshackle pre-war brownstone. Savory fare from all 4 corners of the globe (€3-14.50). Locals slide onto wooden benches under low ceilings or the tiki-ringed fountain in back. Open daily 10am-2am. ❸

Blumenau, Louisenstr. 67 (☎802 65 02). One of the most popular, and cheapest, restaurants in the Neustadt. Friendly environment perfect for a morning *Milchkaffee* or evening drink. Entire front open to the street. Menu changes unpredictably. Most dishes €3.10-6.60. Breakfast until 4pm. Extensive mixed drink menu. Open daily 9am-3am. ❷

🔍 SIGHTS

ALTSTADT

Destroyed during WWII and partially rebuilt during Communist times, the Altstadt is, undisputably, one of Europe's major cultural centers. A gigantic restoration effort, slated for completion in 2006, cements Dresden's reputation with each completed project. Most of Dresden's celebrated sights are near the **Theaterplatz.**

ZWINGER. The extravagant collection of **Friedrich August I,** a.k.a. August the Strong, Prince Elector of Saxony and King of Poland, is housed in this magnificent palace, designed by August's senior state architect, **Matthäus Daniel Pöppelmann.** Championed as one of the most successful examples of Baroque design, the palace narrowly escaped destruction in the 1945 bombings. Some of the statues lining the grounds are still charred, but workers are continually sandblasting everything back to aesthetic perfection. The northern wing, a later addition, was designed by **Gottfried Semper,** revolutionary activist and master architect. The palace is now home to Dresden's finest museums (see **Museums,** p. 615). The fountain-filled courtyard, surrounded on all sides by the palace, is free, but the palace interior is only open to museum guests. *(North of Postpl., next to the Semper-Oper.)*

SEMPER-OPER. Dresden's famed opera house, on the Elbe by Augustusbrücke, reverberates with the same opulence as the northern wing of the Zwinger. Painstaking restoration has returned the building to its original state, making it one of Dresden's most prominent attractions. *(Theaterpl. 2. ☎491 14 96; fax 491 14 58. The main entrance lists tour times, usually M-F every 30min. 11am-3pm. €5, students €3.)*

DRESDENER SCHLOß. The residential palace of Saxony's Wettin dynasty of electors and emperors, who adorn the northern wall of the **Fürstenzug** (a mural that uses the full length of the street to illustrate over 900 years of Saxon kings and emperors), was ruined in the Allied firebombing, but restoration is approaching completion. The Schloß houses the large **Kupferstichkabinett,** a collection of all forms of graphic arts from wood cuts to photography. Artists range from Dürer to Rubens to Goya. (Open M and W-Su 10am-6pm. Captions in German and English. €3, students and seniors €2.) In September 2004, the **Grünes Gewölbe** ("Green Vault") returned to its home here to exhibit treasures of the House of Saxony that enliven the palace's history. From a collection of rare medieval chalices to the most lavish Baroque jewels, the vault dazzles the eyes with some of the finest metal and precious stone work in Europe. (☎491 47 14. Check the Schloß or the tourist office for opening hours.) The 100m tall ◪**Hausmannsturm** has a collection of large, sobering photographs of the Altstadt after the February 1945 bombings that, combined with the 360° view of the city from the top, impress upon non-Dresdeners the enormity of the reconstruction project. (Across from the Zwinger on Schloßpl. Open M and W-Su 10am-6pm. Captions in German and English. €2.50, students and seniors €1.50.) The **Katholische Hofkirche** (Catholic court church) hides a beautiful white interior fit for the kings of Saxony who used to frequent it. Originally built in the mid-18th century, the church was destroyed in WWII, but restoration has quickly returned it to its near perfect condition. The organ perched in the balcony miraculously survived the bombing and is the last and largest work of the world-famous organ-builder **Gottfried Silbermann.** *(Open Mar.-Oct. M-Th 9am-5pm; F 1-5pm, Sa 10:30am-4pm; Nov.-Apr. M-Sa until 5pm; Su noon-4pm. Free. Check the board outside the main entrance for tour times, usually M-Th 2pm, F-Sa 1pm.)*

RESURRECTING THE FRAUENKIRCHE

For 200 years the bell-shaped cupola of Dresden's Frauenkirche (Church of Our Lady) was the crowning glory of a stunning sky-line. The Baroque church, completed in 1743, was built by master architect George Bähr as a symbol of strength, community and durability. But the Allied fire-bombing of February 1945 reduced the church to rubble, along with over three-fourths of the surrounding city.

The church lay in ruins for 45 years, until the reunification of Germany brought about the rebuilding of many of Dresden's historical buildings. Reconstruction plans were made in 1990, and the internationally supported work began three years later.

In June 2004, the famous dome once more topped the church. The same golden cross that crowned it 250 years ago was salvaged from the rubble and refurbished—by a British crafts-man whose father flew in the 1945 air raid—and presented to Dresden by Great Britain as a ges-ture of change and reconciliation.

One sixth of the new exterior is composed of stones from the orig-nal church that have been metic-ulously placed in their original positions. Although work on the church will continue through 2005, the completed silhouette of the Frauenkirche is a symbol of healing for many Dresdeners and a sign that the rebirth of a city, and a nation, is almost complete.

BRÜHLSCHE TERRASSE. Running along the river, the Brühlsche Terrasse offers a stunning view of the Elbe or the adjacent Katholische Hofkirche. Alchemist **Johann Friedrich Böttger** was imprisoned in the adjacent palace (the former seat of Saxony's government) by August the Strong until he finally developed the secret recipe for porcelain in 1707. The same **Meissen china** (see **The Search For White Gold,** p. 621) which comprises the Fürstenzug was Böttger's invention, and made for a booming German trade in porcelain. Dresden royalty used to stroll down this grand avenue, still the classiest way to get from the Albertinum to the Schloß.

KREUZKIRCHE. On the Altmarkt, the former Nikolai church became the "Church of the Cross" when it received a splinter of the Holy Cross. A second change came when the first Protestant communion in Dres-den was celebrated here. More difficult transitions fol-lowed: the church was leveled three times: by fire in 1669; in 1760 during the Thirty Years' War; and again in 1897. Thanks to the modern steel supports used to rebuild the church after the last demolition, the Kreuz-kirche survived WWII, despite severe fires that ruined the interior. The current rough plaster interior, origi-nally intended to be temporary, has become a perma-nent reminder of the destruction caused by the war. The tower offers a bird's-eye view of Neumarkt and Altmarkt. *(An der Kreuzkirche 6. ☎ 439 39 20. Church open summer M-Tu and Th-F 10am-5:30pm, W and Sa 10am-4:30pm, Su noon-5:30pm; winter M-Sa 10am-3:30pm, Su noon-4:30pm. Free. Tower closes 30min. before church. €1, children €0.50.)* Although Richard Wagner went to school here, he did not sing in the **Kreuzchor,** a world-class boys' choir founded in the 13th century. *(Concerts Sa 6pm. €4-31, students €3-23.)*

FRAUENKIRCHE. Dresden's most famous silhouette was reduced to rubble by the 1945 bombings. The most complex and expensive project of its kind in Germany, reconstruction of the Frauenkirche began in 1994. The ruin was carefully taken apart and each stone catalogued; the pieces of the puzzle yet to be incorporated are stacked outside the church. Most of the exterior has already lost its veil of scaffolding, and renovations should be fully completed by 2006. *(Neumarkt. ☎ 498 11 31. Tours available every hr. M-F 10am-4pm, also in English; check the small white informa-tion center on Neumarkt for details.)*

NEUSTADT

Across the Elbe, the some of Germany's best-pre-served turn-of-the-century neighborhoods and a handful of Baroque holdouts are home to Dresden's busy cultural scene. A walk down the pedestrian Hauptstr. hits most of the sights and brings you to Albertpl., with its magnificent twin fountains.

GOLDENER REITER. A gold-plated statue of August the Strong stands just across the Augustusbrücke on Haupstr. August's nickname has two sources: his physical strength, which a thumbprint on the Brühlische Terasse supposedly proves (still more miraculous, since it was imprinted after his death), and his remarkable virility—legend has it he fathered 365 children, though the official tally is 15. Newly refurbished, August shines with all his former cocky gallantry.

DREIKÖNIGSKIRCHE. The Church of the Magi, Hauptstr. 23, was designed in 1730 by Matthäus Pöppelmann (of Zwinger fame) but destroyed in 1945. Now the original crumbling altar still stands tall amid the stark white halls of the newly rebuilt (1991) church. Inside, check out the *Dresden Danse Macabre*, a 12.5m Renaissance fresco, or climb up the tower for a view of Dresden. *(Tower open M-Sa 10am-6pm. Su 11:30am-6pm. €1.50, students €1.)*

ELSEWHERE IN DRESDEN

Virtually untouched by the bombings, Dresden's outskirts are rife with spontaneity and local tradition. The banks of the Elbe are perfect for a scenic stroll, and the architecture of the mansions and villas is also well worth a look.

BLAUES WUNDER. A 19th-century suspension bridge connecting Blasewitz and Loschwitz, the *Blaues Wunder* ("Blue Marvel") was the only bridge the Nazis didn't destroy on the eve of the Soviet invasion at the end of WWII. The bridge is a great starting point for romantic summertime walks along the Elbe—the sunny **Körnerplatz,** on the Loschwitz side, is one of Dresden's prettiest squares. North of the square on Schillerstr. 19 is the tiny yellow **Schillerhäuschen,** where Beethoven first heard Schiller's poem *An die Freude* ("Ode to Joy"). He later adapted for the final movement of his *Ninth Symphony*, now the official anthem of the EU. Down Körnerpl. is the ■**Schwebebahn** (overhead railway). The vintage construction is the oldest of its kind in the world and offers stunning views of Dresden and the Elbe. *(Streetcar #12 (dir.: Striesen) or 6 (dir.: Niedersedlitz) to "Schillerpl." Departs every 10min. Open M-Sa noon-midnight, Su noon-6pm. €2, round-trip €3.)*

DIE GLÄSERNE MANUFAKTUR. This nearly transparent €180 million Volkswagen factory was built to make the company's new €90,000 luxury car, the Phaeton. The architecture is bold, with steel cones and glass walls, intended to be a visual metaphor for authenticity; Phaetons in various stages of construction are stacked in plain view. Take the arched pathway that bridges the moat for a closer look, or call ahead for a tour that includes an amazingly realistic virtual test drive. *(Lennestr. 1. ☎89 62 68; www.glaesernemanufaktur.de. Tours M-F every 2hr. 8am-8pm by appointment.)*

FORMER SCHLACHTHOFRINGE (MESSE DRESDEN). Now an industrial-looking convention center, the former "Slaughterhouse Circle" was a POW camp during WWI. Kurt Vonnegut was held here during the bombing of Dresden, inspiring his masterpiece *Slaughterhouse-Five*. Although there is little to see at the Messe, the curious travelers who take bus #82 (dir.: Dresden Messe) to "Ostragehege" will be rewarded by of one of Dresden's architectural oddities: the former cigarette factory Yenidze. Built in 1907, it was modeled after a similar factory in Turkey, and boasts a jewelled, stained-glass dome and candy-striped pink and white facade.

▥ MUSEUMS

After several years of renovations, Dresden's museums are once again ready to stand with the best in Europe. If you are planning on visiting more than one museum in a day, consider investing in a **Tageskarte** (€10, students and seniors €6), which covers one-day admission to the Albertinum museums, the Schloß, most of the **Zwinger** museums, and a number of other sights. The **Dresden Card** (p. 610) also includes free or reduced entrance to many of the major museums.

ZWINGER COMPLEX

■**GEMÄLDEGALERIE ALTE MEISTER.** The Gallery of the Old Masters houses a world-class collection of paintings from 1400 to 1800, predominantly Italian and Dutch. Designed explicitly for the purpose of displaying the collections of August the Strong, these rooms have displayed some of the same paintings for over 200 years. Thanks to the actions of a particularly prudent museum director, these masterpieces were kept hidden and safe during WWII. Cranach the Elder's luminous Adam and Eve paintings, Rubens's Leda and the Swan, and Raphael's Sistine Madonna (with the two pouting angels) are only a few of the treasures covering the gallery's high walls. *(From the Semper-Oper side, walk through the archway, and the gallery entry will be on the right. ☎ 491 46 19. Open daily 10am-6pm. Gallery tours F and Su at 11am and 4pm. €0.50. €6, students and seniors €3.50.)*

■**PORZELLANSAMMLUNG.** With over 20,000 pieces, this museum boasts the largest collection of European porcelain in the world, with a spectacular selection of Meißen china. Exhibits of Korean, Chinese, and Japanese porcelain from the 15-18th centuries are also exceptional. August the Strong invested in intricate religious icons, beautiful centerpieces and a whole menagerie of life-size animals. Regardless of your interest in porcelain, the image of a strong, 250 lb. August cherishing delicate knick-knacks should give you a smile. *(Entry in the archway on Sophienstr. ☎ 491 46 22. Open Tu-Su 10am-6pm. €5, students and seniors €3.)*

RÜSTKAMMER. Rekindle your dreams of chivalric valor with this collection of shiny but deadly toys from the court of the Wettin princes (16th to 18th centuries). Highlights include beautiful silver- and gold-plated suits for man and steed, chain mail, and ivory-inlaid guns. The collection of diminutive armor belonged to Wettin toddlers. *(In the archway across from the Alte Meister. ☎ 491 46 82. Open Tu-Su 10am-6pm. €3, students and seniors €2, covered by admission to the Gemäldegalerie Alte Meister.)*

MATHEMATISCH-PHYSIKALISCHER SALON. Europe's oldest "science museum," these two large rooms host an impressive collection of 16th- to 19th-century scientific instruments, far more stylish than their modern equivalents—ornate compasses, clocks, atlases, and so forth. Also serving as a science laboratory, this salon once set the official time for all of Saxony. *(In the northwest corner of the Zwinger courtyard. ☎ 94 01 46 66. Open Tu-Su 10am-6pm. €3, students €2.)*

ALBERTINUM

Yet another construction project of August the Strong during the first half of the 18th century, this Baroque museum on the banks of the Elbe was designed by the inexhaustible Matthäus Pöppelmann. It was destroyed during WWII, but was quickly rebuilt, and now houses several of Dresden's finest museums.

GEMÄLDEGALERIE NEUE MEISTER. This gallery picks up in the 19th century where the Alte Meister leaves off, with a solid ensemble of German and French Impressionists, including Renoir, Degas, and Monet, and landscapes by hometown hero Caspar David Friedrich. Otto Dix's renowned *War* triptych is here, along with other *Neue Sachlichkeit* (Expressionist) works. *(☎ 491 47 14. Open M and W-Su 10am-6pm. €6, students and seniors €3.50; includes admission to Skupturensammlung.)*

SKULPTURENSAMMLUNG. This immense collection of classical sculpture was rescued from a basement depot during the floods that struck Eastern Europe in 2002. Although several regular exhibition rooms upstairs are filled with the finest pieces, the majority of the collection is piled up for visitors to view in the Albertinum's vaulted cellar. Roman copies are displayed with Baroque plaster and marble completions of Greek fragments. The most prized possession of the museum is an extensive set of sculptured wall sections from a 2000-year-old Assyrian temple. Although the curators have not yet decided how to display the works, they will likely continue to expand exhibit space. *(Included in admission to the Gemäldegalerie.)*

ELSEWHERE IN DRESDEN

DEUTSCHES HYGIENEMUSEUM. Famous for its "Glass Man," a transparent human model with illuminated organs, the world's first public health museum enlightens visitors with exhibits like "Life and Death," "Food and Drink," and "Sexuality." The museum also hosts rotating exhibits, and has materials in English. *(Lingnerpl. 1, enter from Blüherstr. ☎ 48 46 670; www.dhmd.de. Open Tu-Su 10am-6pm. €4, students and seniors €2. Special exhibits €4, students and seniors €2. F after 1pm free.)*

VERKEHRSMUSEUM. Dresden's transport museum rolls through the history of German transportation, from carriages to bullet trains and BMWs. The silver AWE convertible is so slick it will make you cry. *(Augustusstr. 1, beside the Frauenkirche; enter on Jüdenhof. ☎ 864 40. Open Tu-Su 10am-5pm. €3, students and seniors €1.50.)*

STADTMUSEUM. Inside the 18th-century Landhaus, a museum tells the story of the city since its birth in the 13th century. Early history of the *Deutsche Reich* can't compete with the colorful collection of 20th-century memorabilia, including the *Volksgasmask* (People's Gas Mask) and a model 1902 firefighter with a sprinkler helmet. The museum is currently undergoing extensive renovation slated to be finished sometime in mid-2005. Check at the tourist office for more details. *(Wilsdruffer Str. 2, near Pirnaischer Pl. ☎ 65 64 80. Open M-Th and Sa-Su 10am-6pm; May-Sept. W until 8pm. €2, students €1.)*

🎭 ENTERTAINMENT

Dresden has been a focal point of theater, opera, and music for centuries. The **Semper-Oper** is the city's crown jewel, but there are enough smaller theaters available to suit any taste. The tourist office by the Semper-Oper is a great resource for almost all of Dresden's performances, but go directly to the box offices for better deals. Although most theaters take a summer break *(Pause)* from mid-July to early-September, open-air festivals step in to fill the gap. The **Filmnächte am Elbufer** (Film Nights on the bank of the Elbe) festival in July and August offers an enormous movie screen and stage against the illuminated backdrop of the Altstadt. Most shows start at 9 or 9:30pm and cost around €6. (Office at Alaunstr. 62. ☎ 89 93 20; complete schedule at www.filmnaechte-am-elbufer.de, or in brochures available at the tourist office.) Like many palaces in the area, the **Zwinger** hosts classical concerts on summer evenings (shows at 6:30pm, tickets at tourist office).

Sächsische Staatsoper (Semper-Oper), Theaterpl. 2 (☎ 491 17 05; www.semper-oper.de). See opera's finest in the most majestic of settings, newly restored. Call ahead or go to the tourist office for tickets (€3-80, students and seniors up to €5 off). Box office at Schinkelwache open M-F 10am-6pm, Sa 10am-1pm, and 1hr. before shows.

Kulturpalast, Schloßstr. 2, am Altmarkt (☎ 486 66 66; www.kulturpalast-dresden.de). This civic center is home to the **Dresdner Philharmonie** (☎ 486 63 06; www.dresdner-philharmonie.de) and hosts a wide variety of performances. *Ticketcentrale* at Schloßstr. 2. Main entrance open M-F 10am-7pm, Sa 10am-2pm.

Staatsoperette Dresden, Pirnär Landstr. 131 (☎ 20 79 90; www.staatsoperette-dresden.de). Musical theater and operetta from Lerner and Löwe to Sondheim. €4-19. Discounted shows Tu-Th. Ticket office open M 11am-4pm, Tu-Th 10am-7pm, F 11am-7pm, Sa 4-7pm, Su 1hr. before shows.

PEOPLE'S REPUBLIK

Dresden's alternative scene is always rather lively on a typical Friday or Saturday night, but one weekend in mid-June packs thousands of people into the narrow streets between the cafes and clubs of the Neustadt.

This 15-year-old festival, called the *Bunte Republik Neustadt* (colorful republic of the new city), celebrates the joys of loud music, food, and beer. Originally developed in a club right in the middle of the Neustadt, the festival was intended to be a celebration of the growing Neustadt in Dresden after the reunification of East and West Germany. The festival has grown by leaps and bounds each year since. Now attracting bands from all over the country and a few from abroad, the huge party begins around 8pm and continues until at least 4am Friday through Sunday. Though the BRN may appear aimed at the youth who already frequent the Neustadt scene, adults attend and even bring their young children.

The festival is typically held in the second or third weekend of June, but dates aren't officially set until early May. There are no official organizers of the event, but www.bunte-republik-neustadt.net can answer most questions about the festival weekend.

Book rooms in the Neustadt at least a month in advance for festival weeks, but be wary; bands play right outside the popular hostels and will not turn down their volume for early sleepers.

Staatschauspiel puts on classic plays at the **Schauspielhaus,** Theaterstr. 2. (☎49 13 50, box office 491 35 55; www.staatsschauspiel-dresden.de) and smaller, contemporary shows at the **Schloßtheater,** in the Dresdener Schloß (p. 613). Tickets €10-26. Discounts M. Box office (Ostra-Alle 3) open M and W-Th 10am-5pm, Tu 10am-6:30pm, F 10am-3pm, and 1hr. before shows.

Theater Junge Generation, Meißner Landstr. 4 (☎429 12 20; www.tjg-dresden.de). Opera, fairy-tales, a summer theater in the Stallhof of the Dresdner Schloß, and more. Tickets €5-13, 15-50% student discount. Box office, Rundkino Prager Str. Open Tu-F 2-6pm, and 1hr. before shows.

projekttheater dresden, Louisenstr. 47 (☎810 76 10 or 810 76 11; www.projekttheater.de). Cutting-edge, international experimental theater in the heart of the Neustadt. Tickets €11, students €7. Shows 9pm, box office open 8pm.

Die Herkuleskeule, Sternpl. 1 (☎492 55 55; www.herkuleskeule.de). This bitingly political cabaret revels in blasting US culture. Tickets M, Th, Su €8-13, F-Sa €10-15.50. €5.50 student tickets available if there are empty seats 30min. before show. Box office open M-F 1:30-6pm, Sa 10am-noon, and 1hr. before shows.

Die Bühne, Teplitzer Str. 26 in the University (☎46 33 63 51; www.die-bühne.de). This student theater shows contemporary plays, and hosts an excellent English language theater on occasion. Take #11, 72, or 76 to Strehlener Pl. Tickets around €4. Call to reserve tickets; they're sold in the theater.

⬛ NIGHTLIFE

The entire Neustadt seems to spend the day anticipating 10pm. Ten years ago, the area north of Albertpl. was a maze of gray streets lined with tired, crumbling buildings. Now a spontaneous, alternative community has sprung up in the 50 bars and clubs crammed into the square kilometer roughly bounded by Königsbrückerstr., Bischofsweg, Kamenzerstr., and Albertpl. *Kneipen Surfer* (free at Neustadt hostels and restaurants) provides descriptions of every bar. Peruse the back of *SAX* (€3 at the tourist office, or ask to see one at any bar) or check www.dresden-nightlife.de for upcoming concerts and dances. The free monthly *Dresdner,* available in many pubs, also lists nighttime entertainment. For gay and lesbian nightlife, pick up the free *Gegenpol* at the tourist office.

⬛ Brauhaus am Waldschlößchen, am Brauhaus 8b (☎81 19 90; www.waldschloesschen.de). Tram 11 to "Waldschlößchen" or walk 25min. up Bautnitzerstr. With spectacular views overlooking the Elbe and Dresden skyline, this brewery proves Bavaria doesn't have a monopoly on *Bier.*

Shaded terrace attracts crowds of chill Dresdeners of all ages who drink beer by the liter (€4.60), or just want to escape the city on a summer night. A cafeteria and restaurant offer guests the choice between cheap (*Wurst*, noodles, salad €3.50-5) and classic German (entrees €6-12) cuisine. Open 11am-1am.

DownTown, Katharinenstr. 11-13 (☎801 39 23). Constantly packed, DownTown caters to those who want more than conversation. The music is loud, seating rare, and the crowd enthusiastic. The evening begins upstairs at the bar, billiard hall, and tattoo parlor **Groove Station.** Expect to hear pop, Latin, and electronic music. Cover €3.50, students €2.50. Open M-Sa from 7pm, Su from 4pm. Club open Th-Sa 10pm-5am.

Scheune, Alaunstr. 36-40 (☎804 55 32). From Albertpl., walk up Königsbrückerstr. and turn right onto Katharinenstr.; take a left onto Alaunstr. The granddaddy of the Neustadt scene, this huge bar serves as a starting point for many nights out. The building features a small performance space and bar upstairs and a cafe with Indian cuisine downstairs (€6.50-10). Hosts the fantastic *Schaubudensommer* festival for a week every July. Cover varies. Cafe open M-F 5pm-2am, Sa-Su 10am-2am. Club opens at 8pm.

Flowerpower, Eschenstr. 11 (☎804 98 14). From Albertpl., walk up Königsbrückerstr. and take a left on Eschenstr.; it's on the left. Feels like a warehouse turned dorm room, with tapestries, couches, and blacklights. Curtained booths offer extra privacy. Stays lively until 5am for a dedicated crowd of 20-somethings. M is student night, with half-price beer and wine, and F is the "Friday Night Fever" club night. Open daily 8pm-5am.

Die 100, Alaunstr. 100 (☎801 39 57; www.cafe100.de). With over 250 wines on the menu from €2.60 a glass, this *Weinkeller* caters to the thrifty connoisseur. The unpolished, relaxed atmosphere of both the candle-lit interior and the intimate stone courtyard is a perfect escape. Salads and sandwiches €3-4.20. Open daily 5pm-3am.

Katy's Garage, Alaunstr. 42, at the corner of Louisenstr. Guarded by a gigantic stone armadillo, Katy's is one of the area's more energetic venues. Young, edgy Neustadt devotees crowd into the small crimson-colored club for dancing or drinking. Tu hip-hop, W parents night, Th reggae night, F Brit and Indie pop. Cover up to €4. Open from 8pm.

Studentenklub Bärenzwinger, Brühlischer Garten 1 (☎495 14 09), under the garden between the Elbe and the Albertinum. Formerly a part of Dresden's *Festung* (fortress), this subterranean lair attracts a diverse crowd with cheap drinks and student DJs. Beer €1.50, or check boards for specials. Tu and F-Sa usually dance parties. 18+. Cover €3, students €2. Concerts €7-10. Opens Tu and F-Sa 9pm for live shows and dancing.

BOY's, Alaunstr. 80 (☎796 88 24; www.boysdresden.de), just beyond the Kunsthof Passage. A half-naked devil mannequin guards one of Dresden's most popular gay bars, with a small but cozy dance floor. Drinks €2.70-6. Open daily 8pm-3am.

⚡ DAYTRIPS FROM DRESDEN

MORITZBURG

The fastest way is by bus #326, 457, or 458 from Bahnhof-Neustadt to "Moritzburg, Schloß" (25min., €3.20). Return trip from "Moritzburg, Markt" on Marktstr., parallel to Schloßallee. The most scenic route (also the slowest and bumpiest) is the S-Bahn from Dresden to Radebeul-Ost (15min., €3.40), and then the 110-year-old Schmalspurbahn (narrow-gauge railway) from Radebeul-Ost to Moritzburg (30min., €5.20). From the Schmalspurbahn station, follow the crowds up the hill to Schloßallee and take a right. Moritzburg's tourist office is at Schloßallee 3b. ☎035207 85 40; fax 854 20. Open daily Apr.-Oct. 10am-6pm; Nov.-Mar. M-Sa 9am-5pm.

Never one to be bashful about leaving his mark on the Saxon landscape, August the Strong tore down a little palace in 1723 and replaced it with ■**Schloß Moritzburg**, a titanic Baroque hunting lodge. The immense yellow Schloß stands at the end of Schloßallee, Moritzburg's main street, on an island in a beautifully overgrown artificial lake. Two exhibits display the lavish tastes and hunting prowess of August's court; one is devoted entirely to newly reconstructed feather tapestries. (☎ 035207 87 30; www.schloss-moritzburg.de. Open daily Apr.-Oct. 10am-5:30pm; Nov.-Mar. Tu-Su 10am-4pm. Baroque rooms €4.10, students €2.60. Feather room €3.50/€2.50. Combo €6/€4.) A 35min. walk from the Schloß, the smaller **Fasanenschlößchen** was built by the great-grandson of August, Friedrich August III. Facing Schloß Moritzburg, follow Meißner Str. to the end of the lake on your right, then turn right and follow the path for about 15min. Outside, sculptures of moose in tremendous pain greet you at this hunting lodge. The Fasanenschlößchen will be closed for repairs until at least the end of 2004. On a small jetty into the lake, the **Leuchtturm** (lighthouse) once served as a backdrop to the mock sea battles of bored, rich princes. Moritzburg is surrounded by extensive parks and forests criss-crossed by lovely paths, a huge gaming reserve, and the **Sächsisches Langestüt** (Saxon Studfarm), where August the Strong's prolific legacy is honored.

As the meeting place of *Brücke* artists from 1909 to 1911, Moritzburg developed a rich art tradition. After Käthe Kollwitz's home in Berlin was bombed near the end of WWII, Prince Ernst Heinrich offered the artist a place of retreat here. The **Käthe-Kollwitz-Gedenkstätte**, Meißner Str. 7., honors Kollwitz, one of Germany's most significant 20th-century artists, whose art depicts struggling workers, mourning parents, and impoverished children. The museum features a selection of her works, pictures and excerpts from writing that provide insight into the artist's life. (☎ 035207 828 18. Open Apr.-Oct. M-F 11am-5pm, Sa-Su 10am-5pm; Nov.-Mar. M-F noon-4pm, Sa-Su 11am-4pm. €2, students €1.)

PILLNITZ

Take streetcar #1 (dir.: Kleinzschachwitz) or #2 (dir.: Prohlis) to "Comeniuspl.," then jump on bus #83 and continue to Pillnitz (35min., €1.60). Or, the Sächsische Dampf-schifffahrt (p. 607) can get you there by boat. (90min., €8.50, round-trip €13, children half-price.) Head straight through the main garden to the "Alte Wache" tourist office for maps, information, and tours. Open daily May-Oct. 9am-6pm; Nov.-Apr. 10am-4pm.

Among August the Strong's many castles (almost as numerous as his mistresses), the gardens of **Schloß Pillnitz** are the perfect destination for an afternoon picnic or a contemplative stroll. The virile ruler inherited the nearly 300-year-old castle in 1694 and generously passed it on to his mistress the Countess Cosel a few years later. When the Countess got too uppity, August kicked her out and ordered renovations (by none other than Matthäus Pöppelmann) that gave Schloß Pillnitz its distinctive look. August's taste for Chinese style went beyond porcelain—the colorful turrets of the **Bergpalais** and **Wasserpalais**, as well as the castle's banquet hall, imitate Chinese architecture and art. Bordered on one side by the Elbe, the palace sits amidst splendid gardens. In addition to a Baroque courtyard and labyrinth, Pillnitz is home to a diverse arboretum that includes Asian species such as one of the first examples of *Kamilie* brought to Europe, collected by a student of Linnaeus. English and Chinese pavilions complete the regal effect. The residences now house Dresden's **Kunstgewerbemuseum** (the Museum of Decorative Arts), which displays numerous treasures of the Saxon-Polish dynasty. The beautiful furniture, textiles, and porcelain attest to the artistic prowess of Saxon craftmanship from the 15th to 17th centuries. Most visitors, however, spend their time roaming the gardens. Concerts also take place in the garden during the summer; call for info. (☎ 261 32 60. Museum open May-Oct. M and W-Su 10am-6pm. Grounds open daily 5am-nightfall. Bergpalais open Tu-Su, Wasserpalais open M and W-Su. €3, students and seniors €2.)

MEIßEN ☎ 03521

For anyone who takes the 30km trip from Dresden, it is easy to understand why Saxon electors chose to build their home *Schloß* here. The current castle, built on the 1000-year-old foundations of Meißen's first fortress, has occupied the same spot for 500 years. The view from the hilltop onto Meißen, the Elbe, and the surrounding vineyard countryside is magnificent. But the castle has not always served as a residence: in 1710, August the Strong turned it into a factory to produce Meißen's "white gold," **porcelain** that had been developed for the first time, in Europe (see **The Search For White Gold**, p. 621). Today, visitors from around the world flock to this mecca of delicate dishware and the castle it once called home.

☎☒ TRANSPORTATION AND PRACTICAL INFORMATION. Meißen is easily reached from Dresden by **train** (30min., €4.50) or Sächsische Dampfschifffart **ferry** (p. 607). The **tourist office**, Markt 3, is across the Markt from the Frauenkirche. It distributes maps and finds private rooms (€17-26) for free. (☎419 40; fax 41 94 19. Open Apr.-Oct. M-F 10am-6pm, Sa-Su 10am-4pm; Nov.-Mar. M-F 10am-5pm, Sa 10am-3pm.) **City tours** depart from the tourist office daily at 1pm (€4, students €2), and every Wednesday at 7pm a costumed tour guide leads a "Romantic Evening Stroll" through the city (1½-2hr., €5, students and seniors €4). The **post office**, Poststr. 26, 01662 Meißen, is just across the Elbe from the train station. (Open M-F 9am-noon, 2-6pm and Sa 9am-noon.)

☎☒ ACCOMMODATIONS AND FOOD. The **Jugendgästehaus Meißen ❶**, Wilsdrufferstr. 28, is often full. From the station, cross the railroad bridge and follow Oberg. until it meets Plosenweg. Turn left and continue uphill; the hostel is on the left across from the small market (15min.). Or, bus line D runs (2 per hr.) from the train station up the steep hill. If they have space, you'll be in a crowded 5-bed room, but the price is cheap. Besides a great view of the city, the hostel offers a full kitchen and common room complete with TV and billiard table. (☎45 30 65. Breakfast included. Sheets €3. Reception M-F 7am-noon and 4-8pm, Sa-Su 4-8pm. €12.) Another option, up the steps across from the Porzellan Manufaktur, is **Schweizerhaus ❸**, Rauhentalstr. 1. The great location and restaurant downstairs ooze convenience. (☎45 71 62. All rooms with shower. Reception daily until 11pm. Singles €28-39; doubles €36-57.) For food, try **Schönitz ❷**, Neug. 22, for bratwurst (€3-5) or baguettes. Entrees €5-8. (☎45 25 61. Open M-Sa 11am-1am, Su 11am-8pm.) The **Cafe am Dom ❶**, next to the cathedral, has great cakes (€2-4), snacks, and an unbeatable view from a terrace graced with pear trees. (Open daily 10am-6pm.) The farmer's market is on the Markt. (Open Tu-Sa 8am-5pm.) During the last weekend of September, Meißen revels in its annual wine festival.

THE LOCAL STORY

WHITE GOLD: A NEW ALCHEMY

When King August II of Poland (August the Strong) heard in 1701 that famous alchemist Friedrich Böttger had moved to Dresden, the virile king imprisoned him until he could produce gold from cheaper metals. While in jail, Böttger started work on the problem of porcelain production, a process then unknown outside China, along with scholars Pabst von Ohain and Tschirnhaus.

In 1708 Böttger's experiments succeeded, and he produced the first white porcelain in Europe. Two years later, he sent the king a letter formally proclaiming his discovery. To rush the new invention into production, August ordered the Albrechtsburg castle in Meißen emptied to house his new porcelain factory. The king also stationed guards around the castle to keep the technique a secret, and kept Böttger captive for four more years until he had sworn not to reveal the discovery.

The factory remained in Albrechtsburg until 1864 when historians determined that new production techniques would be detrimental to the monument. A new building was built for continued production. The new factory still produces the world-famous Meissen porcelain, no longer an intensely guarded secret: now all who travel to Meißen can watch the intricate art that once so fascinated the powerful August the Strong.

◆ SIGHTS. The narrow, romantic alleyways of the Altstadt climb up to the **Albrechtsburg,** a castle and cathedral overlooking the city, originally the site of Meißen's porcelain factory. From the train station, walk straight onto Bahnhofstr. and follow it over the Elbbrücke. Cross the bridge, continue straight to the Markt and turn right onto Burgstr. ascending till you reach the castle stairs. Or, board the green and white City Bus at the Markt or the station (€2.55, round-trip €3.60). The castle foundations were first built in 929 to protect the area's Sorb population (see **The Absorbing Sorbs,** p. 630). Master architect **Arnold von Westfalen** built the current castle in the 15th century for the ruling brothers Elector Ernst and Duke Albrecht of Wettin. Revolutionary during its time, the castle's design served as an example for similar constructions throughout Germany for the next several hundred years and is considered to have given birth to German *Schloß* design. In the 18th century it served as a porcelain factory and was consequently thoroughly restored. Lavishly decorated with murals (captioned in English) in the 19th century, a number of exquisite vaulted rooms also house an extensive medieval sculpture collection. (☎470 70. Open Mar.-Oct. daily 10am-6pm; Nov.-Feb. 10am-5pm. Last entry 30min. before closing. €3.50, students €2.50.) Next door is the **Meißener Dom,** an early Gothic cathedral that gives visitors their money's worth with four priceless 13th-century statues by the anonymous *Naumburger Meister,* a triptych by Cranach the Elder, and the metal grave coverings of the Wettins. Construction on the cathedral began in 1250, and, amazingly, the stained glass window above the altar dates from the original construction. Tours ascend the open towers of the church and provide an unparalleled view of the town, the Elbe and the countryside. (Open Apr.-Oct. daily 9am-6pm; Nov.-Mar. 10am-4pm. €2, students €1.50. 30min. organ concerts May-Oct. M-Sa at noon. €2.50. Tower tours daily Apr.-Oct. every hr. 1-4pm. €3, students €2.50. Combination Dom and Schloß tickets €4/€2.50.)

Europeans discovered the secret to making porcelain (previously known only in China) at Meißen in 1707. Once more tightly guarded than KGB headquarters, today the glamorous **Staatliche Porzellan-Manufaktur,** Talstr. 9, can be toured by anyone. From the Markt, turn left on Fleischerg., then right on Neug., which becomes Talstr. At the **Schauhalle,** visitors can peruse finished products including a 12 ft. centerpiece made in 1749 for August III. (☎46 82 08. €4.50, students €4.) The real fun is the high-tech tour of the **Schauwerkstatt** (show workshop), in which porcelain artists paint perfectly detailed flowers before your incredulous eyes. (Open daily May-Oct. 9am-6pm; Nov.-Apr. 9am-5pm. €3. English headsets available.) Meißen's Gothic **Rathaus** stands across from the **Frauenkirche;** its 37 porcelain bells are the oldest such carillon in the world and peal a different hymn from a collection of six every 3hr. (Church open May-Oct. daily 10am-noon and 1-4pm.)

SÄCHSISCHE SCHWEIZ NATIONAL PARK (SAXON SWITZERLAND NATIONAL PARK)

Never to be outdone by their southern neighbors, the Germans happily claim the majestic sandstone cliffs and dense forest gorges along the Elbe river as their own "Switzerland." Although archaeologists can trace settlements in the area back to the Bronze Age, the region truly flourished under the auspices of the Saxon electors of the Holy Roman Empire, for whom it served as the perfect destination for hunting expeditions and court festivals. Over the past century, it has become one of the most popular national vacation destinations, but it's virtually unknown outside of Germany. Transportation is excellent, so opportunities for hikers, bikers, and kayakers abound in this exceptional corner of Germany.

THE PARK AT A GLANCE

AREA: 368 km²

CLIMATE: Temperate. Summers 68-86°F (20-30°C).

FEATURES: Sandstone cliffs, table mountains, and river gorges, interspersed with forested areas.

GATEWAYS: Bad Schandau, Königstein, Rathen, Stadt Wehlen.

CAMPING: Most campgrounds are closed Nov.-Mar.

FEES & RESERVATIONS: No entrance or trail fees.

HIGHLIGHTS: Dramatic cliffs and valleys seen from atop the numerous rock formations, particularly stunning from the Bastei lookout point or the Königstein Festung.

TRANSPORTATION

The park is easily accessible by Dresden's S1, which starts in Meißen and runs from the Dresden Hauptbahnhof along the Elbe River. A regular **ferry** service, the **Sächsische Dampfschifffahrt,** also connects the towns along this section of the Elbe. If you plan to explore more than one town in a day, buy a *Tageskarte* (daypass; €9) or a *Familientageskarte* (family daypass; €12) from any *Fahrausweis* machine, located at most train stops. Besides the S-Bahn and buses, these work on many of the ferries in the area. The **Kirnitzschtalbahn,** a historic trolley, travels from Bad Schandau to **Lichtenhainer Wasserfall** (30min.; Apr.-Oct. every 30min. 9:30am-8:30pm; less frequently during winter). The *Wanderwege* (footpaths) coil up the hills into the heart of the park, connecting the towns in the area in a spidery web.

ORIENTATION AND PRACTICAL INFORMATION

The national park is divided into the *vorderer Teil* and the *hinterer Teil* (front and back sections, respectively). The Elbe River, along which most of the region's towns lie, runs from the Czech Republic in the southeast toward Dresden in the northwest, cutting the park in half.

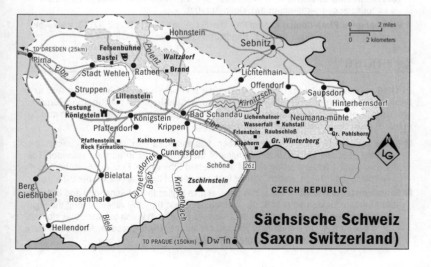

The best source of park information is the **Nationalparkhaus,** Dresdner Str. 2b, 01814 Bad Schandau. In addition to the knowledgeable, English-speaking staff, the house has an exhibit on the park's history, flora, and fauna. (☎ 035022 502 30; fax 502 33. Open daily 9am-8pm.) Visitors can also obtain information from the **Tourismusverband Sächsische Schweiz,** Am Bahnhof 6, Bad Schandau (☎ 035022 495 00; fax 495 33), the **Nationalpark-Verwaltung,** An der Elbe 4, Bad Schandau (☎ 035022 900 60; fax 900 66), or by visiting www.saechsische-schweiz.de, which has extensive information on opportunities for handicapped visitors to the park. The **Sächsische Dampfschifffahrt** offers **boat tours** of the area and other Elbe sights in cooperation with Conti Elbschifffahrts. For more information, contact their Dresden office, Hertha-Lindner-Str. 10 (☎ 0351 86 60 90; www.saechsische-dampfschifffahrt.de). The **emergency number** for fire or ambulance is ☎ 112, for police ☎ 110, and for medical emergency ☎ 115. In case of a mountain emergency, call the **Bergrettungsstationen** (mountain rescue stations) at ☎ 035022 710 71.

ACCOMMODATIONS AND CAMPING

The entire region can be reached on a day-trip from Dresden, but vacationers looking for an extended stay can choose from many types of accommodations within the park. A popular option is the *Ferienwohnung,* a private room or apartment that can be booked through the tourist offices. For hostels and pensions, see individual town listings. The following campgrounds vary widely in services offered and space available, so calling ahead is recommended. Whatever the type of accommodation, reservations are a good idea during the busy summer season, which lasts from April to October.

Campingplatz Königstein, Schandauer Str. 25e, Königstein (☎ 035021 682 24; www.camping-koenigstein.de). Open Apr.-Oct.

Campingplatz Ostrauer Mühle, im Kirnitzschtal, Bad Schandau (☎ 035022 427 42; www.ostrauer-muehle.de). Open year-round.

Campingplatz Thorwaldblick, Schandauer Str. 37, Hinterhermsdorf (☎ 035974 506 48; www.thorwaldblick.de). Open year-round.

Touristencamp Entenfarm, Schandauer Str. 11, Hohnstein (☎ 035975 813 72; www.touristencamp-entenfarm.de). Open Apr.-Oct.

Waldcamping Pirna-Copitz, Äußere Pillnitzer Str., Pirna (☎ 03501 52 37 73; www.waldcamping-pirna.de). Open Apr.-Oct. Handicapped facilities available.

HIKING

HIKING. Hikes of all lengths and difficulty levels are available; only a few are listed here. Trails are well marked, but a map, available at the Nationalparkhaus or any tourist office, is recommended. Be sure to bring your passport if you want to cross over to the nearby Czech Republic.

Basteiaussicht (2½hr.). Starting in Rathen, this easy hike with lots of stairs passes the startling outcrops and dramatic plunges of the Bastei cliffs in all their splendor. The lookout point offers a dizzying view of the forested Elbe valley. Rent boats at the *Amselsee* (blackbird lake), a section of river in the middle of the hike (€2.60 per 30min.).

Schrammsteinaussicht (4½hr.). This popular hike begins in Bad Schandau and includes the *Kipphorn* lookout point (480m), a stone ridge next the Elbe valley. Among the highest spots in the park, this is the perfect vantage point from which to watch that glorious sunrise or sunset. On a clear day, you can see all the way to Dresden. A relatively easy hike except the 30min. ascent to the top of the ridge.

Kuhstall und Raubschloß (3hr.). Begins at the *Lichtenhainer Wasserfall* (thinned-out grove waterfall). Includes the cavernous *Kuhstall* (cowshed) rock formation and the site of the *Raubschloß* (robbers' castle) ruins. (Bus #241 from Bad Schandau or Königstein. Every 2hr., 8am-6:30pm. Or, Kirnitzschtalbahn from Bad Schandau. Every 30min. 9:30am-8:30pm.)

Großer Zschirnstein (4hr.). Begins in Krippen. (S1. Every 30min., 5:30am-10:30pm.) Leads to the *Kohlbornstein* (cabbage spring stone) lookout point (372m), with a view of sandstone rock formations and the neighboring *Böhmische Schweiz* (Bohemian Switzerland) to the east.

Pfaffenstein (3hr.). Begins in Königstein. A moderately difficult hike, with stairs to the *Pfaffenstein* (priest stone) rock formation.

Unterer Affensteinweg (4½hr.). Begins in Bad Schandau. A narrow mountain path with many branches. Includes the *Frienstein* lookout point.

Am Brand (5½-6hr.). Begins in Rathen. Includes the *Brand* (fire) lookout point and the *Waitzdorfer Walls* rock formation. A relatively easy hike except for the climb up the stairs to the lookout point, which takes about 30min.

Höhlen und Hörner (3hr.). Begins in Neumannmühle. (Bus #241 from Bad Schandau or Königstein. Every 2hr., 8am-6:30pm.) Includes the *Großes Pohlshorn* lookout point (379m), known for its silence and view of the forests and rock formations of the *Großen und Kleinen Zschand* area.

▨ OUTDOOR ACTIVITIES

BIKING. The park website (www.saechsische-schweiz.de) suggests bike tours with lengths ranging from 20-70km. The Nationalparkhaus in Bad Schandau (p. 624) can give you information on paths. For bike rental, see Bad Schandau (p. 628), check the park website, or pick up a map at the Dresden Hauptbahnhof (p. 608). Biking in the park is only allowed from 7am-8pm.

Dresden to Schöna (3½hr.). A paved, bike-only path follows the Elbe from Dresden to Schöna. Pick up the path by the docks on the southern side of the Elbe. To avoid riding on streets with car traffic, cross the river with the ferry at Königstein and then again at Bad Schandau. Offers fantastic views of the Elbe and the park's rock formations.

Bad Schandau to Hinterhermsdorf (3hr.). The Elberadweg (Elbe bike path) heads off to the right as soon as you get off the ferry in Bad Schandau. Follow the marked bike paths through the back part of the park to Hinterhermsdorf. Includes the *Lindigtblick* ("pleasing view") lookout point and the *Lichtenhainer Wasserfall*.

CLIMBING. The rock formations and sheer cliff faces of the Sächsische Schweiz make it a natural attraction for rock climbers. Although experienced climbers are permitted to brave the challenging cliffs on their own, it is recommended that visitors first stop by the *Nationalparkhaus*, which can inform climbers about park rules and direct the less experienced toward guides and climbing courses. In the interest of preserving the rock, metal safety devices such as "friends" are forbidden, as are chemical climbing aids such as Magnesia. Some of the most popular climbing regions include *Bielatal* (239m), *Rathener Gebiet* (145m), *Schmilkaer Gebiet* (124m), *Affensteine* (115m), *Großer Zschand* (87m), *Schrammsteingebiet* (80m), and *Brandgebiet* (80m).

WATER SPORTS. Canoeing on the Elbe offers impressive views of the park from below. Some places will take you upriver in a motorboat and let you canoe back. **Kanu-Aktiv-Tours,** Elbpromenade Schadauer Str. 17-19, Königstein (☎035022 507 04; www.kanu-aktiv-tours.de), rents canoes and rubber dinghies for up to 12 people and offers guided water tours. (Boats €22-78 per day. Tours €30-38.) **Spaß Tours,**

Mennicke Str. 29, Stadt Wehlen (☎035024 710 84), rents charter boats for trips anywhere between Bad Schandau and Meißen, and combination rentals that allow you to bike from Wehlen to Bad Schandau and paddle back. (Canoes from €20 per day; family rafts (6 people) €45; large rafts (10 people) €65.)

RATHEN AND STADT WEHLEN ☎035024

Upstream from Dresden, just around the first bend in the Elbe, stand the magnificent sandstone cliffs *Die Bastei* (the bastion), once the favored roaming grounds of the Saxon court. The two towns of **Rathen** and **Stadt Wehlen** frame these cliffs, with Stadt Wehlen closer to Dresden and Rathen on the other side. To get to Wehlen, hop on S1, then look for the *"Fähre"* signs from the Bahnhof (ferry runs daily 5:30am-11:30pm; €0.70, children €0.50). A **tourist office** in the Rathaus on the market finds rooms (from €12.50) for free, and a list of accommodations is posted outside. (☎704 14. Open M-F 9am-noon and 1-6pm, Sa 9am-noon.) Wehlen's best assets are its trails through the Bastei to Rathen, including the favorite paths of **August the Strong,** Elector of Saxony and King of Poland (1694-1733)—look for the *Steinern Tisch*, his mammoth dining table, 3km out of Wehlen.

Huddled around a small stream, the peaceful vacation town of Rathen is just one stop past Stadt Wehlen on the Dresden S-Bahn, but the hike there is a far more beautiful route. However you arrive, Rathen's location on the edge of the national park (p. 622) makes it a great starting point for hikes of any length. Stone pillars towering above the stage make Rathen's **Felsenbühne** one of the most beautiful open-air theaters in Europe. Each summer, Dresdeners make the trip to Rathen for opera, musicals, and theater classics. (Open 9am-5pm. Performances €8-21, students €6-19.) To get to Rathen, take the ferry from the station (Runs daily 5:30am-midnight; one-way €0.70, round-trip €1.30); to reach the Felsenbühne, follow the signs from the ferry landing in town. Tickets and schedules are available from the **Theaterkasse,** on the way to the theater. (☎77 70; www.dresden-theater.de. Open May-Sept. 9am-5pm and evening of performances until 30min. after the show begins. Tickets can also be purchased at the Wehlen and Bad Schandau tourist offices.) A **tourist office** upstairs in the *Gästeamt* gives hiking advice and finds rooms (€12-25) for free. From the landing, follow Zum Grünbar for 5min. and look on the left. (☎704 22; www.kurort-rathen.de. Open Apr.-Oct. M-F 9am-noon and 1-6pm, Sa-Su 9am-1pm; Nov.-Mar. M-F 10am-noon and 1-3pm.)

One good option for accommodations is on the **Burg Altrathen,** a hill above the town that provides beautiful views of the Bastei. To get to the **Gästehaus ❸,** in a castle perched above the Elbe, take a right up the narrow path to the left after the ferry landing, just past the Hotel Erbgericht. (☎76 00; www.burg-altrathen.de. Singles €22-52; doubles €44-104.) Also on a hill is the **Pension Panorama ❷,** which serves as both a bright pink restaurant (entrees €3-11) and guest house. Follow the road from the ferry straight into Rathen and turn right up the slope. (☎/fax 706 69. Open M-W and Sa-Su noon-11pm, F 5-11pm. Singles €20-25; doubles €40-50.)

HOHNSTEIN ☎035975

Set back in the forest, away from the Elbe, the small village of Hohnstein ("high stone" in old Saxon) surveys the valley and forests below it from a tall, stony ridge, and is linked to Rathen by beautiful hikes through one of the national park's most stunning valleys. To get here from Rathen, follow the shorter path through the hills (2hr., trail starts beyond the Amselsee), or the longer, but easier path through the Polenz valley (3hr.). On your way, be sure to stop at the ◪**Hockstein,** an isolated outcropping that provides a spectacular view of the valley below and of Hohnstein across the valley. Follow the signs from Hockstein through the **Wolfsschlucht,** a steep narrow passage between huge rocks. Afterwards, you'll come to **Gauschgrotte,** a valley filled with beautiful green moss and rock formations. In town, the **Museum**

der Geschichte des Burg Hohnstein, housed in the **Naturfreundehaus** (see below), covers the 900-year history of the Burg with exhibits ranging from medieval armor and weapons to anti-fascist resistance in Dresden and the Sächsische Schweiz. An exhibit commemorates **Konrad Hahnewald,** the beloved father of Hohnstein's *Jugendherberge* (now the Naturfreundehaus) and later the first non-Jewish prisoner of the Hohnstein concentration camp. The Burg's tower provides a beautiful panorama of the valley below it and the Hockstein. (☎812 02. Open Apr.-Oct. daily 9am-5pm. €1.50, ages 6-16 €0.50, under 6 and Naturfreundehaus patronsfree.)

As an alternative to hiking, you can reach Hohnstein by taking the S-Bahn to "Pirna" (45min.) and then bus #236 or 237 from the Bahnhof to Hohnstein "Eiche" or "Markt," the most central stop (40min., €3). The **tourist office,** Rathausstr. 10, in the Rathaus, doles out information on the Burg and surrounding trails and finds rooms for free. (☎194 33; fax 868 10. Open M-Tu 9am-noon and 12:30-6pm, W-F 9am-noon and 12:30-5pm, Sa 9am-noon.) The fortress **Naturfreundehaus Burg Hohnstein ❷,** Am Markt 1, doubles as a hostel with multi-bed dorms and smaller rooms designed for families. (☎812 02; fax 812 03. Breakfast and sheets included. Reception open 7:30am-8pm. Check-in 3pm. €18.50, children €12.50.)

KÖNIGSTEIN ☎035021

The next stop on the Dresden S-Bahn's journey into the hills and dales of the Sächsische Schweiz is Königstein. Above the town looms the monumental fortress **Festung Königstein,** its huge walls built right into the stone cliffs that make the Sächsische Schweiz famous. Complete with drawbridges and impenetrable defenses (it was only captured once, in 1402 during a feud over the German throne), this is the castle you dreamed about as a kid. Although it is possible that a Slavic fort already stood in this location as early as AD 600, construction on the fortress in its current form began around 1200. Gradually expanded and modified over the centuries, the oldest buildings that can be seen today date from the 16th century. Then a popular retreat for the kings of Saxony, it was later converted into a notorious state prison and used by the Nazis to stash stolen art. Between 1949 and 1955 it served as a juvenile correction center, but today the complex houses a variety of museums. From the city, it's a 40min. uphill struggle, but the view from atop the fortress's towering walls is worth the sweat. Follow the signs to the well-worn path. (English pamphlets at the information office inside the castle. ☎646 07; www.festung-koenigstein.de. Open daily Apr.-Sept. 9am-8pm, exhibitions 10am-6pm; Oct. 9am-6pm, Nov.-Mar. 9am-5pm. Last entry 30 min. before closing. €5, students and seniors €3.) The double-decker **Festungs Express** buses will schlep you and a crowd of families up to the fortress if you don't want to walk. Rides leave from Reißigerpl., just to the right down Bahnhofstr. from the S-Bahn station. (Apr.-Oct. every 30min. 9am-5pm. €3, children €1; round-trip €4/€1.50. Buy tickets on board.) Paths also lead from the town up to the challenging 415m **Lilienstein,** hiked by August the Strong in 1708. To get there, take the **ferry** (€0.70) and the first right after getting off. Stay on this paved road until you see a sign for "Lilienstein" marked with a blue stripe. The steep 2km hike takes 1½hr. and has striking views of the fortress opposite as well as a panorama of the fields and towns along the Elbe from Stadt Wehlen to Bad Schandau. In the **post office,** 01824 Königstein, the **tourist office,** Schreiberberg 2, books rooms (from €13) and posts a list of vacancies outside. From Reißigerpl., take Hainstr., then turn left on Pirnärstr. and right on Schreiberberg. (☎682 61; fax 688 87. Open Apr.-Oct. M-F 9am-6pm, Sa 9am-noon; Nov.-Mar. M-F 9am-5:30pm, Sa 9-10:30am.)

Königstein's Naturfreundehaus ❸, Halbestadt 13, has clean and comfortable rooms and a dining area that overlooks the Elbe. There's even an enormous chess board out back. To get there, take the ferry across the river and turn right. The hostel is on your right after about 10min. (☎035022 994 80; www.nfh.de. Breakfast included. Reception daily 8am-7:30pm. €25-31.) Fresh fruits and vegetables are

SACHSEN

sold at an open market on Tuesdays and Thursdays in the town's streets, or eat more heartily among antlers and paintings of the Elbe at **Schräger's Gasthaus ❸**, on Kirchg. 1, straight up Hainstr. from Reißigerpl. (Entrees €4.30-8.80.)

BAD SCHANDAU
☎035022

The biggest town in the Sächsische Schweiz, bustling Bad Schandau takes advantage of its location between the two halves of the national park by offering plenty of hiking opportunities. Take the *Kirnitzschtalbahn* trolley car (from the Markt, take Marktstr. straight, turn right on Poststr., and then left on Kirnitzschtalstr.) to the modest but pleasant **Lichtenhain waterfall**, a favorite starting point for 3 and 4hr. hikes on the **Schrammsteine**. (Trolly runs Mar.-Oct. every 30min. 9:30am-8:30pm. €3, round-trip €4.) Bad Schandau is also connected to the rest of Saxony; the **S-Bahn** runs to Dresden (50min., every 30min., €4.50), and **trains** go to Bautzen (2hr., every 2hr., €9) and Prague (2hr., every 2hr., €16). To get to town from the Bad Schandau train station, take the **ferry** (every 30min. 7:50am-9:20pm, €0.70) and walk uphill to the Markt, where you'll find the **tourist office**, Markt 12. The staff finds rooms (€11-25), suggests hikes, and offers city **tours** and trips to the Czech Republic. (☎900 30; fax 900 34; www.bad-schandau.de. Open Apr.-Oct. M-F 9am-7pm, Sa-Su 9am-4pm; Nov.-Apr. M-F 9am-6pm.) Rent a bike at **Rund Um's Fahrradverleih**, Sebnitzer Str. 5. (☎428 83. €7.50-9 per day. Open M-F 9am-6pm, Sa 9am-1pm.) **Spieltreff,** Kirnitzschtalstr. 2, is one of the only places to get **Internet** access in the park. (☎430 20. €6 per hr. Open M-F 10am-11pm, Sa-Su noon-11pm.)

Bad Schandau is more of a family vacation spot than any other town in the area, and for this reason its hotels fill up quickly when the weather is good. In the village Ostrau, the **Jugendherberge Bad Schandau (HI) ❷**, Dorfstr. 14, is a 30min. walk down Rudolf-Sendig-Str. (turn right after Poststr.), then a trip up the elevator (€1.25) in the huge metal tower on your left, or a walk up the path alongside it. At the top take the paved path up to the right and then follow the signs. Heavy pack? Take bus #255 from "Bad Schandau Markt" to "Ostauer Scheibe." Although far from the center of town, it is near the heads of several trails. (☎424 08; www.djh-sachsen.de. Breakfast included. €19.10, under 27 €16.40.) In a town that closes down before 11pm, **Sigl's ❸**, Kirnitzschtalstr. 17, a relaxed bar and bistro, offers food and a wide selection of beers from 5pm until 2am. The restaurant doubles as a **hotel ❸** that's cheaper than those by the ferry dock. (☎407 02; fax 407 87. Apr.-Oct. singles €35; doubles €60-64. Nov.-Mar. €29/€42-48.)

OBERLAUSITZ (UPPER LUSATIA)

Bordering two of Germany's former Warsaw Pact neighbors (Poland and the Czech Republic), Oberlausitz has worked hard to overcome the many years of economic stagnation it experienced prior to reunification, and has met with remarkable success. Many building projects in the area have been devoted to breathing new life into long-neglected architecture and removing overbearing socialist structures. The area around Bautzen exemplifies the successful rejuvenation of this gently hilly, pleasantly rural region on the edge of eastern Germany.

BUDYŠIN (BAUTZEN)
☎03591

Millennium-old Bautzen displays its history on every corner. Perched above the Spree river, ancient towers guard the walled city's architectural treasures, be they Gothic, Baroque, or from the prosperous, industrial *Gründerzeit* (founding time: 1871 to around the turn of the century). Here and there, ruins dating back hundreds of years attest to the ravages of war and time. Before German invasions and fortifications came to Oberlausitz in the 10th century, however, the region was settled by Slavic Sorbs, who continue to live in and around Bautzen, still speaking Sorbian and now on good terms with the former German invaders.

▶ 🛈 TRANSPORTATION AND PRACTICAL INFORMATION

The **train** from Dresden runs twice an hour (1hr., €8.10). To catch a **taxi**, call ☎ 422 22 or 451 51. The **Avis** office at the train station rents cars. To get to the **tourist office**, Hauptmarkt 1, walk from the train station straight through Rathenaupl. and bear left onto Bahnhofstr. Pass the post office on your right and cross the street, bearing left onto Karl-Marx-Str. Turn left on Reichenstr., marked by a tall white tower. Follow Reichenstr. to the Hauptmarkt, the center of Bautzen's Altstadt. The tourist office is on the right of the big yellow Rathaus. The office offers listings of accommodations and books rooms in hotels, pensions, and private homes (€13-40). The staff also offers **city tours** (€4, available in English if you call ahead) and free city maps. (☎ 420 16; www.bautzen.de. Open Mar.-Oct. M-F 9am-5pm, Sa-Su 9am-noon; Nov.-Feb. Tu-F 9am-5pm, Sa-Su 10am-2pm. Tours M-F 2 and 7pm, Sa-Su 11am and 7pm.) To learn more about the Sorbs, visit the **Sorbische Kulturinformation** office, Postpl. 2. The staff has information on cultural events and homestays with the local Sorb population, as well as displays of the winners of the yearly Easter egg contest. (☎ 421 05; www.sorben.com. Open M-F 10am-6pm.) A **pharmacy** is located in the entrance to the Kornmarkt off Karl-Mark-Str. **Glückspitz**, Käthe-Koll-witz-Pl. 1, although not centrally located, is one of the few places in town that offers **Internet access**. (€3 per hr. Open daily from 9am until late.) The **post office**, 02625 Bautzen, is on Postpl. (Open M-F 8am-6pm, Sa 9am-noon.)

▶ 🛈 ACCOMMODATIONS AND FOOD

Built into an ancient defense tower, Bautzen's newly renovated **Jugendherberge (HI) ❷**, Am Zwinger 1, has color-coded 1- to 6- bed rooms, a dining terrace, and a friendly hostel father. From the Hauptmarkt, go up Kornstr. (to the right of the tourist office) and stick with it as it jogs right and turns into Schulerstr.; take a left after you go through the Schülertor, and the hostel will be on your right. (☎ 403 47. Breakfast and linen included. Reception M-F 7am-8pm, Sa-Su 6-8pm. Reservations recommended. €16.50, under 27 €14.90.) Alternatively, treat yourself to **Stephan's Schnitzelstube und Pension ❸**, Schloßstr. 1. From the Hauptmarkt, head uphill with the Rathaus on your right, past Dom St. Petri, and turn left. Stephan's is a light green building a block ahead on the left. This family-run pension is centrally located and has immaculate rooms with private baths, telephones, and TVs. The 4-bed apartment has free laundry facilities. (☎ 475 90; fax 475 91. Breakfast included. Rooms €37, 2 or more people €28 per person.) Stephan's also houses a restaurant that serves traditional German dishes. (Entrees €4-13. Open Su-Th 11:30am-2:30pm and 5:30-10:30pm, F-Sa 11:30am-2:30pm and 5:30pm-midnight.)

The Fleischmarkt, behind the Rathaus, hosts a **market** (Tu and Sa 9am-1pm, Th 9am-6pm). Well-stocked grocery stores line Karl-Marx-Str. above Postpl. (open M-F 8am-6pm, Sa 8am-noon), and the new **Kornmarkt-Center** south of the Kornmarkt has many produce shops and bakeries. (☎ 529 80. Open M-F 9:30am-8pm, Sa 9:30am-6pm.) **Wjelbik ❷**, Kornstr. 7, serves tasty Sorbian dishes in the dimly lit interior of a 600-yr.-old building, complete with authentic decor and real roses on every table. Try the traditional *Sorbische Stulle*, a pork sandwich (€8), or *Sorbische Hochzeitsuppe* (wedding soup; €3), with meatballs and vegetables. (☎ 420 60. Open M-F 11am-3pm and 5-11pm, Sa-Su 11am-11pm.) Four-hundred-year-old recipes (including wild boar) and a great monastic atmosphere make the medieval **Mönchshof ❸**, Burglehn 1., worth a visit. (☎ 49 01 41. Entrees €6-14.75. Reservations recommended. Open M-Sa 11:30am-1am, Su 11:30am-11pm.) To experience the German approach to natural healing, visit **Zur Apotheke ❸**, Schloßstr. 21. The restaurant prepares a wide range of meals rich in herbs (€5-12) and much tastier than the offerings of actual pharmacies. (☎ 48 00 35. Open daily from 11:30am.)

THE ABSORBING SORBS

The Sorbs, Germany's only indigenous ethnic minority, are descended from Slavic tribes that settled the Spreewald and Lusatian mountains during the 6th and 7th centuries. The Sorbian language is similar to Czech and Polish and is divided into two basic dialects: *Niedersorbisch* (Low Sorbian), spoken around Cottbus, and *Obersorbisch* (High Sorbian), spoken near Bautzen. Since the formation of the Sorb nationalist movement in 1848, small *sorbisch*-speaking communities have maintained regional identities.

The Sorbs are famous for intricately dyed Easter eggs and *Osterreiten*, horseback processions that take place every Easter Sunday. January 25 marks the *Vogelhochzeit* (birds' wedding), during which costumed children act as birds grateful for seeds left over from a marriage celebration. All winter, children feed the birds and are rewarded with sweets and cookies during this festival.

The Prussians all but destroyed the Sorbian culture in the 17th and 18th centuries, and the Nazis nearly wiped them out in 1937. Despite post-war laws protecting the Sorbian culture and language, both are in decline: only about 60,000 people still live in Sorbish comminutes. Younger generations are moving to big cities in large numbers, but many communities are working to ensure that children learn Sorbian in school and that their time-honored customs will continue for years to come.

🔍 SIGHTS

SORBISCHES MUSEUM. The museum exhibits in detail the intriguing history and culture of the Sorbs. The varied displays include everything from handwritten translations of the Bible to model houses, painted Easter eggs, modern Sorbian art, *Dudelsacks* (bagpipes) and Sorbian violins. *(Ortenburg 3. On Schloßstr., through the Matthiasturm. ☎ 424 03. Open Apr.-Oct. M-F 10am-5pm, Sa-Su 10am-6pm; Nov.-Mar. M-F 10am-4pm, Sa-Su 10am-5pm. €2.50, students and children €1.50.)*

HAUPTMARKT. This square contains the grand yellow 13th-century **Rathaus**, backed up by the **Fleischmarkt** and the Gothic **Dom St. Petri.** First consecrated in 1221, the elegant Dom became eastern Germany's only *Simultankirche* (simultaneous church) in 1524. Two sets of pews in the church look up at two altars, one Catholic and one Protestant. Each week the church switches not only religions, but also entrances: Catholic week uses a door on the southeast side and during Protestant week a door on the west side opens. Until 1952 this division was made more clear by a 4m high screen down the middle of the church. The 83m tower provides a beautiful view of the city and of the Spree. *(Left from the Reichenturm and down Reichenstr. Open June-Sept. M-Sa 10am-4pm, Su 1-4pm; May and Oct. M-Sa 10am-3pm, Su 1-3pm; Nov.-Apr. M-F 11am-noon. Tower tours Sa at 4pm. Free.)* The **Domstift,** the flashy red-and-gold structure behind the cathedral, houses the Domschatz (cathedral treasury), a collection of jewel-studded gowns, icons, and gold regalia. Ring the bell and ask to see the *Domschatzkammer*. *(Open M-F 10am-noon and 1-4pm. Free.)*

REICHENTURM. The white **Reichenturm** is the leaning tower of Bautzen. Built in 1490 for defense, it now is a full 1.44m from perpendicular. The view from 55m up is marvelous, but you'll have to brave the narrow staircase. *(At the intersection of Kornmarkt and Reichenstr. Open Apr.-Oct. daily 10am-5pm. Last entrance at 4:30pm. Tours €6. Admission €1.20, students €0.90, under 12 €0.60.)* A block away, at the intersection of Wendischer Graben and Wendische Str., you'll find the stone **Wendischer Turm.** A tower built in 1566 that once served as the city's prison, it is attached to the **Alte Kaserne** (old barracks), an elegant building designed by Dresden master **Gottfried Semper** to accommodate 19th-century troops, now serving as an office building.

NIKOLAITURM. Locals claim that the ghostly face above the gate of the Nikolaiturm is a likeness of a former mayor who was bricked into the tower alive as retribution for opening the city to Hussite attackers in the 16th century. *(Follow An der Petrikirche downhill* *from the cathedral, then take a right on Nikolaiporte.)* **St. Nikolai Friedhof** is through the gate and to the left. Since 1745 the graveyard has extended into the eerie ruins of the **Nikolaikirche,** destroyed in 1634 during the Thirty Years' War. The lonely columns and empty window-arches of the church ruins sit up on a hill with an excellent view of the Spree. *(Open daily May-Aug. 7am-8pm; Apr. and Sept. 7am-7pm; Mar. and Oct. 7am-6pm; Feb. and Nov. 8am-5pm; Jan. and Dec. 8am-4pm.)*

AROUND BAUTZEN. Through the **Mühltor** or to the left of the Sorbisches Museum, follow the scenic **Osterweg** and **Reymannweg** paths around the city walls and above the Spree, taking in the views of the 1480 **Mühlbastei** (mill tower), the spire of the 1429 **Michaelskirche,** and the 1558 **Alte Wasserkunst** (old water works), now a technical museum. Climb all the way up for a view over the rooftops of Bautzen. (Museum open daily Apr.-Oct. 10am-5pm; Dec.-Feb. 10am-4pm; Jan. Sa-Su only 10am-4pm. €1.50, students €1.) On the other side of the fortress by the river is the dark, brown-shingled **Hexenhäusel** (witches' cottage). This small wooden structure, the oldest and most famous house in the area, was the only home to survive two devastating fires. The villagers shunned the inhabitants as witches, though the spread of the fire was actually halted by a well inside the house.

ZITTAUER GEBIRGE (ZITTAU MOUNTAINS)

The rocky cliffs of the Zittau Mountains rise in a sliver of Germany wedged between the Czech Republic and Poland. Once a favorite spot of medieval monks, these beehive-shaped mountains are now the conquests of choice for skiers, hikers, and landscape lovers. The sublime surroundings were a fountain of inspiration for Romantic artists like **Ludwig Richter.** Matters have not always been so peaceful, though: in 1491, the region was the scene of the vicious **Bierkrieg** (beer war), when incensed citizens of Görlitz protested Zittau's success as a beer-brewing town by destroying barrels of the brew. Despite unemployment rates of 20% during the past fifteen years, towns like Zittau remain blessed with attractive pedestrian centers that keep the area vibrant and optimistic.

ZITTAU ☎ 03583

At the crossroads of three nations (Poland, the Czech Republic, and Germany) Zittau has served as a trading and cultural center for many centuries. Under the rule of the Bohemian kings, Zittau took on a dominant role in Oberlausitz and was as prominent culturally as Leipzig. Before the 19th century brought machines to the textile industry, Zittau was famous for its weavers, who left behind the magnificent 1472 Lent curtain, the only one of its kind remaining in the world.

▐▛ TRANSPORTATION AND PRACTICAL INFORMATION. Trains roll in from Dresden (1½hr., every 2hr., €15) and Görlitz (1hr., 1 per hr., €5). Get tickets at the Reisezentrum (open M-F 6:45-11:45am and 12:30-4pm, Sa 6:45-11:30am and noon-1:30pm, Su 8:45-11:30am and noon-5:30pm), and note that the Bahnhof hall closes daily at 7:45pm. For a **taxi** call ☎51 25 00 or hail one at Marktpl. The **tourist office,** Markt 1, on the first floor of the Rathaus near the left side entrance, provides free city maps and runs tours of Zittau. From the train station, take Bahnhof Str. down the hill; continue straight on Bautzen Str. until you reach the Hauptmarkt and the yellow Rathaus on your left. (☎75 21 37; www.zittau.de. Open M-F 8am-6pm, Sa 9am-1pm; June-Sept. also Su 1-4pm.) Zittau is a starting point for the 115km **Upper Lusatian Mountain Path;** ask at the tourist office where to pick up the trail. Several grocery stores on the Markt sell fresh fruit and vegetables A **pharmacy, Johannis**

Apotheke, is at Johannisstr. 2. across the Marktpl. from the tourist office. (☎51 21 64. Open M-F 8am-6pm, Sa 8am-noon.) **Computer-Nutzer Laden,** Rosa-Luxembourg-Str. 34, offers **Internet** access. Turn left off Bahnhofstr. onto the Theaterring and follow it until Rosa-Luxembourg-Str. leads off to the left. (€3 per hr. Open Tu-Th 3pm-midnight, F-Su from 3pm.) A **post office,** 02763 Zittau, is at Haberkornpl. 1 and has a **24hr. ATM.** (Open M-F 8am-6:30pm, Sa 9am-noon.)

⌐⌐ ACCOMMODATIONS AND FOOD. There are no HI hostels in Zittau, but the tourist office books rooms (from €20) for free. A good option is **Pension Zwahr ❷,** Theodor-Korselt-Str. 10. From the station take Bahnhofstr. and make a left onto Theodor-Korselt-Str. All the rooms have bathrooms with showers. (☎51 12 50. Singles €20; larger rooms €13 per person.) For German cuisine amid hundreds of old clocks, head to **Seeger Schänke ❸,** Innere Weberstr. 38. (☎51 09 80. Entrees €5.90-12.50. Open daily from 5pm.) The **Savi Café and Bar ❷,** Bautzner Str. 10, serves salads, pasta, traditional dishes (€4-6), and hearty breakfasts in a relaxed, modern atmosphere and offers **Internet** access. (☎70 82 97. Internet €2.40 per hr. Open M-F 9am-midnight, Sa noon-midnight, Su 2:30pm-midnight.) **Filmsiß,** Markt 8, decorated with movie posters and film reels, is a cafe that offers small entrees and cakes (€1.20-7) by day and bar with a very extensive drink list by night. (☎79 47 51. Open Tu-Th noon-11pm, F-Sa noon-1am, Su 2-6pm.)

◙ SIGHTS. The recently-restored ▨**Museum der Kirche zum heiligen Kreuz,** Frauenstr. 23, at the corner of Theatterring and Frauenstr., houses the masterpiece of Zittau's weavers: an extremely rare **Lenten Veil** dating from 1472. With 90 panels displaying scenes from the Old and New Testaments, the gigantic painted curtain was used to shield the clergy and altar from the "unworthy," fasting churchgoers during Lent. The only one of its type in the world, it is also the third largest Lenten Veil in Europe. It was used in the Johanniskirche (see below) until 1672 when it was lost and presumed destroyed. In 1840 it was rediscovered and put on public display until after WWII, when some oblivious Russian soldiers used it as the roof of their open-air sauna—hence the huge steam stain. (Open Tu-Su 10am-noon and 1-5pm. German tours every hr. 10am-3pm. Last entry 30min. before closing. €4, students and seniors €2.) Most of the interesting sights are in the **Altstadt,** around Marktpl. and Johannispl. The **Johanniskirche** shelters an airy interior currently under restoration. Originally built in 1255, the church was destroyed in 1757 by Prussian bombs and rebuilt in Baroque style—the intricate blue and gold ceiling is particularly beautiful. (☎51 09 33; fax 79 59 27. Open M-F 10am-6pm, Sa-Su 10am-4pm.) Climb up its **Aussichtsturm** for a view of the Zittauer Gebirge. (Open M-F noon-6pm. Sa-Su 10am-4pm. €1.50, children €1.) From the church, walk directly down Bautzner Str. to reach the grand **Marktplatz.** The yellow, Renaissance-style **Rathaus** was designed by Prussian architect Friedrich Schinkel in 1843. From the Rathaus, walk up Johannisstr., and follow it as it curves right, ending in Klosterpl. There you'll find the late Gothic **Klosterkirche** and the adjoining **Stadtmuseum,** housed in a former 13th-century Franciscan monastery that is stocked with tourist-friendly medieval torture devices and documenting the art and crafts of the city from the last 500 years. The museum exhibits everything from beautiful furniture and artwork to traditional costumes and religious objects. (☎55 47 90. Open Tu-Su 10am-noon and 1-5pm. €1.50, students €1.)

⚑ OUTDOOR ACTIVITIES. The dramatic Zittau Mountains sit on the German outcropping between Poland and the Czech Republic and offer travelers endless opportunities for exploration amid the volcanic peaks and densely forested valleys. There is a network of over 300km of hiking paths through the mountains. A number of them can be can be reached from Zittau. Otherwise take the ZOJE steam train to the resort towns of **Oybin** or **Jonsdorf,** nestled right in the mountains.

Ask at the Zittau tourist office for times and prices. To find accommodations in these towns call the tourist offices: Oybin ☎035844 733 11; Jonsdorf ☎035844 706 16. Bikers have no shortage of options in the Zittau Mountains. You can rent a bike in Zittau at **Fahrrad Rother,** Ottokarpl. 10 (☎70 23 27) or in Jonsdorf at **Fahrrad Donath,** Zittauer Str. 46 (☎035844 701 71). Trails range from 10-500km in length and traverse the mountains, connecting to trails to Görlitz and the Spreewald.

> **Nießtal-Kloster St. Marienthal** (38km). Begins in Zittau at Martin-Wehnert-Pl. and runs parallel to the Nisa river along the Polish border to Ostritz, then around to Schlegel, south to Hirschfelde, and back to Zittau. Includes the beautiful Kloster St. Marienthal.

> **Schloß Lemberk** (26km). Begins in Jonsdorf and heads to the Czech border, then to Krompach, Hermanice and the Schloß Lemberk; finally around to Petrovice, and back to Jonsdorf by way of the Oybin castle ruins.

SOUTHWESTERN SAXONY

CHEMNITZ ☎0371

For those interested in the history of the East German *Deutsche Demokratische Republik* (DDR), a visit to Chemnitz is a must. As the DDR's center of industry, Chemnitz was taken over by massive new developments on the *Straße der Nationen* (Street of Nations), and was even renamed Karl-Marx Stadt in 1952. As a result, the *Wende* (the "turn" of reunification) has been particularly challenging for Chemnitz, which struggles to rebuild its industry on capitalist terms.

🖿🛂 TRANSPORTATION AND PRACTICAL INFORMATION

Trains run to: **Dresden** (1½hr., 2 per hr., €10.50); **Görlitz** (3½hr., 1 per hr., €26); **Leipzig** (2hr., 2 per hr., €18); **Prague** (4hr., 1 per hr., €36). For a **taxi,** call ☎330 03 33. Although much of Chemnitz is walkable, the city is connected by a system of streetcars and buses, almost all of which stop at "Zentralhalestelle" in the city center. The **bus station** is just a short walk down Georgstr. from the train station. Tickets are available at major stops and on every bus or streetcar. A *Kurzstrecke* ticket (€1) covers up to 4 stops, an *Einzelfahrt* ticket (€1.50) covers all rides within 1hr., and a *Tageskarte* (day pass, €3.20) is valid until 6am the next morning. To get from the train station to the city center, head straight down Georgstr. or Carolastr. After a block, you'll come to Str. der Nationen, the city's north-south axis. Turn left to get to the **tourist office,** Markt 1, in the Rathaus, which finds private rooms (€15-30) for a €5 fee, and has free maps. (☎69 06 80; fax 690 68 30. Open M-F 9am-6pm, Sa 9am-noon.) Check email at **InterNet, cafe +mehr,** Hainstr. 106. (☎401 01 13; www.cafeundmehr.de. €3.60 per hr. Open M-F 10:30am-10pm, Sa 1-10pm, Su 5-10pm.) The **post office,** 09009 Chemnitz, is at the intersection of Rathausstr. and Str. der Nationen. (Open M-F 9am-7pm, Sa 9am-4pm.)

🖿🖸 ACCOMMODATIONS AND FOOD

Pension Art Nouveau ❸, Hainstr. 130, is a 15min. walk from the station. Take an immediate right from Georgstr. onto Mauerstr. and go under the tunnel at the end on the right; turn left out of the tunnel and right immediately on Lessingstr., then left on Hainstr. You'll find clean, pleasant, tastefully furnished rooms: most have private baths, some have kitchens. (☎402 50 72; fax 402 50 73. Singles from €35; doubles €45.) There's always a room at the massive **Hotel Europark ❸,** Schulstr. 38, which has both simple hostel rooms and gorgeous hotel accommodations. From the station take tram #6 (dir.: Altchemnitz) 20min. to "Altchemnitz Center." Facing in the opposite direction of the train, turn left on Zöblitzerstr. The hotel is at the end of the street. (☎ 522 83 41. Reception 7am-3:45pm; information center open 24hr. Hostel: singles €16-21; doubles €28-31. Hotel: singles €33-38; doubles €40-44). The **Jugendherberge (HI) ❷**, Augustusburgerstr. 369, is the cheapest option in Chemnitz, but it's on the extreme edge of town. Tram #5 (dir.: Gablenz) runs from "Brückenstr." to "Pappelhain." Follow the well-marked path for 30min., and take a left on Augustusburgerstr. Many rooms have views of the surrounding farmland. (☎ 713 31. Breakfast and linen included. €17.80, under 27 €15.90.)

For a quick bite, *Imbiße* and a fresh market (Th-Sa mornings) surround the **Rathaus** at the end of Str. der Nationen. Larger appetites can be satisfied at the restaurants on the *Brühl*, a quiet pedestrian zone on the right off Georgstr., or along Str. der Nationen near the Rathaus. Sit in the basement at **Pizzeria Dolomiti ❷**, Str. der Nationen 12, and ponder the irony of the Marx statue glaring at the McDonald's across the street. Enjoy a *Studentenpizza* for €3.40, or pasta for €4.70-6.80. (☎ 676 22 22. Open M-Sa 11am-midnight.) To contemplate the merits of a starving artist's work over a sandwich, make it **Heck-Art ❷**, Mühlenstr. 2. This hybrid gallery, chic bar, and bohemian cafe has a delicious lunch menu (€3-8) and an exhibition space upstairs. (☎ 694 68 18. Open daily noon-midnight.)

ⓒ SIGHTS

Chemnitz's former identity as **Karl-Marx-Stadt** is embodied in the politically charged works of art along the **Straße der Nationen.** Statues of frolicking children or happily scrubbed workers are everywhere, inscribed with cautionary messages like *"Die Partei hat tausend Augen"* (the Party has a thousand eyes). No statue outshines the **head of Karl Marx,** an enormous, angular concrete chunk that's especially intimidating when lit at night. Also along the Str. der Nationen is the quiet **Theaterplatz,** bordered on three sides by large, serene buildings. Straight ahead is the 1992 **opera house,** a product of the early 90s push to build a new Chemnitz. To the right is the **Petrikirche,** first opened in 1888 and continually, painstakingly refurbished since 1992. On the left stands the **Kunstsammlungen Chemnitz,** an art museum that features a sampling of 19th- and 20th-century German art, and a huge collection of paintings and woodcuts by local Expressionist Karl Schmidt-Rotluff. (☎ 488 44 10; www.chemnitz.de/kunstsammlungen. Open Tu-Su noon-7pm. €5, students €2.50.) In a reconstructed castle that was destroyed in the Thirty Years' War, the **Schloßbergmuseum** includes an impressive collection of medieval art and a historical exhibit on the 800-year-old city. (☎ 488 45 20. Open May-Oct. Tu-F 11am-5pm, Sa-Su 11am-6pm; Nov.-Apr. Tu-F 11am-4pm, Sa-Su 11am-5pm. €4, students €2.50.) For a breath of fresh air, walk back to town through **Schloßteich,** a lovely park centered on a lake across from the Schloß, or paddle around the lake itself (boats €3.70-6.40 per hr.). As of October 23, 2004, the **Museum für Naturkunde Chemnitz** will be housed in the **TIETZ,** a shopping complex composed of galleries and cultural venues on Str. der Nationen. Check at the tourist office for hours and prices.

♫ ENTERTAINMENT

The **Theater Chemnitz** dominates Chemnitz's high culture scene with opera, ballet, music, theater, and puppet shows. Tickets are available at the Theater-Service, Käthe-Kollwitz-Str. 7. behind the Theaterpl. museums. (☎ 696 96 96. Open M-F 9am-4:30pm. Tickets €8-36, 50% student discount if there are tickets left right before the show.) Though not known for nightlife, Chemnitz offers more dance venues than any neighboring towns. Shake it at **Fuchsbau,** Carolastr. 8. (☎ 67 17 17; www.fuchsbau.de. Open W, F, Sa from 10pm.) For a more industrial experience, head to **Stadtkeller** on Str. der Nationen just before the Roter Turm. (Cover €5. Hours vary; check the board outside.) **Heck-Art** (p. 634), which functions as a bar as the night progresses, is a little more refined.

NEAR CHEMNITZ: AUGUSTUSBURG ☎037291

A day at the lively **castle** in Augustusburg will help you recover from post-industrial, post-Marx, monochromatic Chemnitz. This princely mountaintop hamlet can be reached by bus #704 (dir.: Augustusburg) or 705 (dir.: Eppendorf) from the Chemnitz *Busbahnhof*. (40min., 6:20am-5:10pm, €3.) The bus stops at the foot of the path to the castle. Trains also travel to Erdmannsdorf, located just down the mountain from Augustusburg (20min., 6am-10pm, €2.40). If you don't make it in time to catch the scenic *Drahtseilbahn* (8min.; 9:15am-5:35pm; €2.10, round-trip €3.10), the castle is a 3km walk uphill. At 1500m above the town, this Renaissance **hunting lodge** of the Saxon electors gives a mesmerizing 360° panorama of the surrounding **Erzgebirge** (Ore Range) mountains—the Czech Republic is even visible on the horizon. At the castle, wander through the spacious courtyards or, to see inside, take a guided tour of the royal playhouse, which leads through the **Brunnenhaus** (well house) and the intimate **Schloßkapelle** (church chapel), the only Renaissance chapel left in Saxony. The altar was painted by Lucas Cranach the Younger, portraying the dour Duke August, his wife Anna, and their 14 pious children. (Tours €2.60, students €1.90.) Also here is a **Motorradmuseum** (motorcycle museum), which documents the history of the motorcycle since its invention in the late 19th century, with everything from early models to BMWs from the 1980s, and racing video games at the end. If you prefer to travel in style, check out the **Kutschenmuseum** (carriage museum); Emperor Leopold II's 1790 carriage is a palace on wheels. The **Museum für Jagdtier- und Vogelkunde des Erzgebirges** (hunting and game museum) features dioramas of local game and ornate weapons. You can also visit the **castle dungeon** to cringe at Medieval torture apparati. (*Schloß* open daily Apr.-Oct. 9am-6pm; Nov.-Mar. 10am-5pm. Each museum €1-3. Day pass for all 4 €6.15, students €4.65.) The eagles and falcons that live at the Schloß swoop and dive in falconry exhibitions. (45min. Tu-Su 11am and 3pm. €5, 14 and under €2.50.) Get dinner (entrees from €7) and a drink in the candlelit **Augustuskeller ❹**, an original castle cellar. (☎207 40. Open Tu-Su 11am-9pm.)

The real treat of a visit to Augustusburg is the 🖫**Jugendherberge (HI) ❷**, inside the castle. Thanks to recent renovations, you'll find immaculate woodwork and spotless washrooms. Best of all, the castle grounds are just out the door and perfect for a stroll as the sun sets. Most rooms have 10-14 beds; singles and 2- and 4-bed rooms are also available. Call in advance as rooms are in high demand. (☎202 56. Breakfast and sheets included. Reception 7am-11pm. Check-in after 3pm. Curfew 10pm but you can get a key. All rooms €17.60, under 27 €14.90.)

OLBERNHAU ☎037360

Known as the "Stadt der sieben Täler" (city of seven valleys), Olbernhau lies nestled on the banks of the river Flöha in the middle of the Erzgebirge. When large deposits of precious metals were discovered here in the 15th century, Olbernhau became an outpost on the **Silver Trail,** a road connecting the area's mining towns from Dresden to Zwickau. Although most of the profits from local mines financed the projects of kings like August the Strong, Olbernhau developed as a thriving trade city, known for its wood and metal handicrafts. Visitors can still gawk at machinery used to form the metals, or watch locals carve their wares. Olbernhau's location on the Flöha also makes it a great starting place for hikes through the wooded landscape of the Erzgebirge mountains.

SACHSEN

▣▨ TRANSPORTATION AND PRACTICAL INFORMATION. Olbernhau can be reached by **bus** from Chemnitz (1½hr.; M-F 1 per hr. 5am-8pm, Sa-Su 1 per 2hr. 6:30am-8pm; €2.40). Rent **bikes** from **Zweirad Sport,** Am Gessingpl. 4, just to the left of the bus station. (☎725 73. €6.50 per day. Open M-F 9am-6pm, Sa 9am-noon.) The **tourist office,** Grünthalerstr. 28 (☎151 35; www.olbernhau.de), is located in the Rathaus. From the bus station, turn right on August-Bebel-Str. The Rathaus will be on your right just before the river. The staff hands out free city maps and a hiking map of the region with marked trail recommendations. (€1. Open M-F 9am-5pm, Th until 6pm, Sa 9am-noon.) Just down the street is the **pharmacy Herz-Apotheke,** Grünthalerstr. 16. (☎725 22; fax 723 03. Open M-F 8:30am-6pm, Sa 8:30am-noon.) The city **library** provides **Internet** access. From the Markt, go through the passageway just to the left of the museum **Haus der Heimat** (p. 636), then turn left again in the parking lot, and the library will be on your right. (☎727 33. €3.20 per hr. Open M 10am-noon, Tu 2-6pm, Th noon-6pm, F 2-6pm.) **Sparkasse,** in the bus station, has **24hr. ATMs.** The **post office,** Bahnhofstr. 1, 09526 Olbernhau, is just down the street from the bus station. (Open M-F 9am-6pm, Sa 9am-noon.)

▨▢ ACCOMMODATIONS AND FOOD. Although there are no hostels in Olbernhau, a number of pensions and Ferienzimmer provide budget accommodations. **Pension Weick ❷,** Töpferg. 18, is a good option. From the bus station, turn right onto August-Bebel-Str. and follow it until it ends just after you cross the river. Turn left on Gerber-G. and bear right onto Töpferg. The pension will be on your right. Rooms have telephones, TVs, and showers and are much cheaper than other options, but be sure to call this pension early—it only has four rooms. (☎752 15. Breakfast included. Singles €20; doubles €38.) Although more expensive, Gästehaus **Zur Wartburg ❸,** Saydaerstr. 1, boasts beautiful rooms with TVs, telephones, and showers and a great location right by the river, near the city center. From the bus station, turn right on August-Bebel-Str. The Gästehaus will be straight ahead after you cross the river. (☎366 66. Breakfast included. Reception M and W-F 11am-11pm, Sa-Su 11am-8pm. Singles €31; doubles €52.)

Bakeries and fresh food stands abound near the Markt and along Grünthalerstr. A number of inexpensive cafes and restaurants are also located in these areas. **Konditorei and Cafe Gleisberg ❶,** Grünthalerstr. 1, right off the Markt, serves up soups and salads (€2-5) in addition to fantastic pastries and cakes (€0.50-3). (☎725 25. Open Tu-F 9:30am-noon and 1-5pm, Sa 9am-11am, Su 2-5pm.) For an elegant meal in a lively location, try **Restaurant Hüttenschänke ❸,** In der Hütte, in the Saigerhütte museum. The restaurant prepares both traditional German fare and inventive dishes. (☎78 70. Entrees €7-15. Open daily 11am-10pm.)

◪ SIGHTS. The 500-year-old **Saigerhütte,** once the center of the copper industry in Saxony, now serves as a museum and demonstration space for the crafts that make the Erzgebirge famous. In the **Althammer,** huge hammers, each weighing over half a ton, still pound sheets of metal to a 0.03mm thickness right before tourists' unbelieving eyes. The complex also houses an open workshop in the foundations of one of the original buildings, a series of old huts where visitors can watch workers spin wool or carve intricate wooden figurines by hand, and a **museum** on the history of the Saigerhütte. (☎733 67. Open Mar.-Oct. Tu-Su 9:30-11:30am and 1-4pm. Tours of the Althammer every 45min. Last tour 4pm. €2, students and seniors €1. Other sections of the complex free.)

Haus der Heimat, Markt 7, Olbernhau's town museum, documents the history of the region and its renowned handicrafts, housing exhibits on toy production, woodcarving, and metalcrafts. (☎721 80. Open Tu-F 10:30am-4:30pm, Sa-Su 12:30-4:30pm. Last entry 4pm. Call tourist office for prices and information on special exhibits.) Scattered throughout the town, many shops sell the wooden handicrafts of Olbernhau.

Watch townspeople carve the products they sell at **Schauwerkstatt,** Neuestr. 19, or peruse shelves of miniatures, nutcrackers, and the region's famous *Räuchermänner* (smoking-men) in the **Kunstgewerbe-Werkstätten,** Sandweg 3.

SEIFFEN ☎037362

Situated in the heart of the Erzgebirge mountains and world-famous for the toys it has produced since 1750, Seiffen draws thousands of tourists every year to its countless stores and workshops. Once a mining town, Seiffen's inhabitants turned to wood-working after its mineral resources dwindled in the middle of the 17th century. Over the years the imagination and inventiveness of Seiffen's toymakers have allowed this small village to flourish, and the toy museum, Seiffen's main attraction, enthralls both young and old with the beautiful, intricate, and sometimes gargantuan toys the town has produced.

⌘🖊 TRANSPORTATION AND PRACTICAL INFORMATION. Seiffen is accessible by **bus #453** from Olbernhau, which stops at both the toy museum and Seiffen Mitte, just a block away from the tourist office (30min; M-F 1 per hr. 6:30am-8pm, Sa 1 per 2hr. 9:50am-8pm, Su 9:50am, 2:50 and 4:25pm; €2.40). Rent **bikes** from **Sportwelt Preußler,** Hauptstr. 199. (☎888 50; www.sportwelt-preussler.de. €7-9 per day. Open M-F 10am-6pm, Sa 10am-1pm.) The **tourist office,** Hauptstr. 95, hands out maps, recommends hikes and books rooms for a €1 fee. From the Seiffen Mitte bus stop, walk downhill about 100m, and the office will be on your left. (☎84 38; www.seiffen.de. Open M-F 9am-5pm, Sa 9am-1pm.) **Sparkasse,** just down the street from the tourist office, has **24hr. ATMs. Geschenkstube,** Bahnhofstr. 8, a handicrafts shop, houses the **post office** and offers **Internet** access. (1st 30min. €2.50, €2 each 30min. thereafter. Open M-F 9am-6pm, Sa 9am-5pm, Su 1-4pm.)

🏠🍴 ACCOMMODATIONS AND FOOD. Due to the large tourist population, inexpensive accommodations are difficult to find in Seiffen. There are, however, a large number of private pensions and *Ferienzimmer,* which tend to be cheaper and can be booked through the tourist office. **Pension Diana ❸,** Steinhübel 21, is located on the edge of town but offers a spectacular view from over 700m. From bus stop "Seiffen Mitte," walk down Hauptstr. and turn right up Bahnhofstr. At the post office, take a right up Glashüttenweg and walk 15min., then turn left on Steinhübelstr. Every room has a TV and shower. (☎82 86; www.diana-pension.de. Breakfast included. Singles €27; doubles €52.) Although expensive, **Hotel Erbgericht ❹,** Hauptstr. 94, occupies an unbeatable

THE HIDDEN DEAL

IN ROYAL FOOTSTEPS

In the 18th century, Saxon Elector and King of Poland August the Strong decided to visit the small villages in the Erzgebirge to watch the locals producing the handicrafts and mining the silver that made the region famous (and made August wealthy).

Today, 250 years later, anyone can follow August's footsteps in the seven-day *Kultur Wandern ohne Gepäck* (cultural hike without luggage). The week begins in Pobershau, passes through Olbernhau, and ends in Seiffen, catching all the important sights in each town. Best of all, hikers never have to carry their luggage; the organizers arrange for it to be waiting in each town when the group arrives.

The whole week costs just €153 for six nights of lodging in private rooms, admission to the sights in every town, and a guide to regale you every step of the way. The hike is a great way to see the charming towns of the Erzgebirge and the stunning (but too often overlooked) landscapes along the way, but if you want this opportunity, be sure to plan ahead; you have to reserve your spot at least six weeks before departure.

(☎037362 84 38; www.seiffen.de. Open M-F 9am-5pm, Sa 9am-1pm. €204 per person to stay in pension doubles; €255 for hotel doubles. Booking service April to October. 5 travelers minimum per hike.)

location right in the middle of town and just down the street from the toy museum. From the bus stop Seiffen Mitte, head downhill on Hauptstr.; the four-star hotel will be on your right after 100m. Every room has a TV, telephone, and shower or bath. Sauna downstairs. (☎77 60; www.erzgebirgshotels.de. Breakfast included. Reception 24hr. Dec. singles €65;doubles €100. Sept.-Nov. €55/85. Apr.-Aug. €50/80. Jan.-Mar. €45/70.) The cheapest accommodation in Seiffen is the **Campingpark Ahornberg Seiffen ❶**, Deutschneudorferstr. 57. From "Seiffen Mitte," head left and downhill on Hauptstr. Turn left on Deutschneudorferstr. Although far from town, the campsite is near several trails and offers a sauna, several volleyball courts, and mini golf. (☎150; www.ahornberg-seiffen.de. June-Aug. and Dec. €4 per person, €4 per tent; tent rental €7-9. 10% discount other months.)

Cafes and restaurants line the entire length of Hauptstr. as it winds through town. **Backerei-Konditorei-Cafe Barthel ❶**, Hauptstr. 85, just down the street from the tourist office, offers delicious pastries (€0.80-3.20), soups and salads (€2-6), and other small dishes. (☎761 14. Open M-Sa 6am-6pm, Su 1-5:30pm.) **Cafe Buntes Haus ❷**, Haupstr. 94, by Hotel Erbgericht, serves delicious regional specialties. (☎77 60. Entrees €4-9.50. Open daily 10am-midnight.)

⬛ SIGHTS. Seiffen's ⬛**Spielzeug Museum** (toy museum), Hauptstr. 73, is without question the biggest attraction in the town. Three floors of toys and exhibitions detail the history of toy production in Seiffen and of the skillful toymakers who made it all possible. See over 5,000 miniatures, nutcrackers, pyramids, chandeliers, and *Räuchermänner* (smoking men) from the past few centuries, including the 4-meter-tall pyramid on the first floor; you can even play with some of them as you go. (☎82 39; www.spielzeugmuseum-seiffen.de. Open daily 9am-5pm. €2.50, students and seniors €2.10, 12 and under €1.30.) The **Freilicht Museum,** Hauptstr. 203, offers insight into the historical processes by which Seiffen's famous arts and crafts were produced. Workers demonstrate traditional carving techniques, and exhibits in the complex's 14 buildings show what life was like in the Erzgebirge between 1850 and 1930. (☎83 88. Open daily 9am-5pm. €2.50, students €2, children €1.) If you'd rather not walk all the way out to the Freilicht museum, you can take Seiffen's **Bimmelbahn** on a tour through the village and the surrounding areas. Beginning at the Spielzeug Museum, the 35min. tram ride highlights the important sights in town and drives to the surrounding villages for a view of the town from above. Hop off at the Freilicht museum, then catch the next tram back to town. (☎86 87; www.bimmelbahn.net. Runs daily every 45min. 10:30am-3:45pm. €2.50, children €1.50.) On the tour, you'll also drive by Seiffen's **Rundkirche,** an octagonal church built in the mid-18th century. Boasting a beautiful blue and white interior, the building contains the altar and chandeliers of its 16th-century predecessor. (Am Reicheltberg, just off Hauptstr. Open daily 1-3pm. Tours daily at noon.) The streets of the town are lined with shops selling local wood handicrafts, particularly nutcrackers, miniatures, pyramids, and *Räuchermänner*. Although the shops along Hauptstr. are the biggest and most convenient, stores away from Hauptstr., up the twisting side roads, have cheaper prices.

ZWICKAU
☎ 0375

Zwickau is best known as the motor city of East Germany. For more than 35 years, the city's *Sachsenring-Auto-Union* produced the DDR's ubiquitous consumer car, the tiny *Trabant*. East Germans used to joke that filling the gas tank of one of the ill-engineered, two-cylinder plastic jalopies doubled its value. Today, Saxony's fourth-largest city emphasizes more genteel distinctions: a thriving theater scene, breathtaking cathedral, and beautiful city center. Composer **Robert Schumann** got his start here, as did a few members of the Brücke painting school (p. 67). But such cultural credits may always be eclipsed by the inexplicably tenacious allure of the *Trabi;* its tinny whine is never out of earshot in Zwickau's narrow streets.

▐▛▐▞ TRANSPORTATION AND PRACTICAL INFORMATION. In the middle of the busy Sachsen-Thüringen rail network, Zwickau is easily reached by **train** from: **Altenburg** (40min., 1 per hr., €7); **Dresden** (2hr., 2 per hr., €18); **Leipzig** (1½hr., 1 per hr., €12). For a **taxi** call ☎ 21 22 22. Zwickau's oldest attractions and most beautiful streets are confined to a circular region in the Altstadt, bounded by a bustling three-lane ring road called **Dr.-Friedrichs-Ring.** The **tourist office**, Hauptstr. 6, is in the center of the circle. From the train station, head left and descend on Bahnhofstr. Continue through the pedestrian tunnel until you reach the large Georgenpl., then turn left on Plauenstr. After you cross Dr.-Friedrichs-Ring, brown signs will guide you towards the Markt and the office, which is just behind a Burger King. From **Zwickau-Zentrum,** the new underground train station, follow Schneebergerstr. into the Markt. The staff hands out free maps, leads city tours, and books rooms (from €17) for free. (☎ 272 59 10; www.kultour-z.de. Open M-F 9am-6:30pm, Sa 10am-4pm.) **Multimedia-Treff,** Bahnhofstr. 1, is packed with kids enjoying the **free Internet** access. (☎ 273 66 63. Open M-Sa 9am-9pm.) A **post office,** Hauptstr. 22, 08056 Zwickau, is just past the tourist office. (Open M-F 9am-6:30pm, Sa 9am-1pm.)

▐▌ FOOD. Cheap dining options can be found along the Hauptmarkt and Innere Schneeberger Str. during the day. The **Restaurant im Historischen Dünnebierhaus ❷**, Neuberinpl. 1, in the back of the building to the left of the theater, offers quality dishes in an elegant setting for surprisingly cheap prices. (Special offers €5.50; regularly €8-10. Open Tu-F 11:30am-2pm and from 5pm, Sa from 5pm, Su from 11am.) For a fresh crepe, filled with anything from goat cheese to forest berries and ice cream (€2.50-8), join younger locals at **egghead ❷**, Peter-Breuer-Str. 34. (☎ 303 33 86. Open daily noon to late.) **Brauhaus Zwickau ❸**, Peter-Breuer-Str. 14, is packed with locals socializing over beer brewed on site, as well as oblivious tourists scarfing down *Schweinhalssteak* (pig's neck steak). (☎ 303 20 32. Entrees €4.50-13. Open daily 10am-midnight.) Much of Zwickau's night scene also takes place along Peter-Breuer-Str. The monthly *Streicher*, free at the tourist office, lists everything from food to bars to shows.

▐▌ SIGHTS. Composer Robert Schumann was born in 1810 in the dusky, yellow, four-story **Robert-Schumann-Haus,** Hauptmarkt 5. Reconstructed in 1956, the house currently holds insightful exhibits on the lives of the composer Robert and his wife Clara Wieck, herself a composer and one of the most accomplished pianists of her day. Musicians perform both Robert and Clara's works monthly from September to May; contact the museum for dates. (☎ 21 52 69; fax 28 11 01. Open Tu-F 10am-5pm, Sa-Su 1-5pm. Call ahead for individualized tours in English, from €15. €4, students and seniors €2. Concerts €10/€7.50.)

The breathtaking Gothic interior of the ▉**Dom St. Marien,** just above the Hauptmarkt, hoards priceless treasures in every corner. Particularly stunning is the large 15th-century gilt "changing altar" from the workshop of Michael Wolgemut that displays eight female figures: Mary surrounded by early Christian martyrs. Years ago, the figures were removed every Christmas from the altar and displayed outside. (Open daily 10am-6pm. 45min. tours every Th 2, 3, 4, and 5pm. Tours of the tower Tu and Th 3pm, Su 6pm. €1.) Just across from the cathedral are the newly restored **Priesterhäuser,** Domhof 5-8, which are among the oldest surviving homes in Germany. Built from 1264-1466, the four houses now host exhibits on the history of Zwickau, church relics, and their own restoration. (☎ 83 45 50; fax 83 45 55. Open Tu-Su 1-6pm. €4, students and seniors €2.)

Rent giant white swan paddleboats on the **Schwanenteich,** a large lake and park stretching along Humboldtstr. (Rentals M-Sa 1-7pm, Su 10am-7pm. Boats €4 per hr., €6 for solar-powered ones.) To get your dose of *Trabi* nostalgia, hit the **August Horch Museum,** Crimmitschauer Str. 36g. From Georgenpl, go north on Humboldt-str. until it becomes Crimmitschauer Str. On display are pre-war Horch eight-cylinder luxury sedans (the company even produced a 12-cylinder behemoth), and, of course, the post-war two-cylinder *Trabants*, with motors that look like they belong in riding lawn-mowers. (The museum should return to Walter-Rathenau-Str. 51. in late 2004. Call ☎ 390 98 95 or the tourist office to be sure. www.trabant.de. Open Tu-Th 9am-5pm, F-Su 10am-5pm. €3, students and seniors €2.)

LEIPZIG   ☎ 0341

Leipzig is the perfect German university city: large enough to have a life outside the limits of academia, yet not so big that the influence of its students is diluted. The resulting fusion creates a youthful and energetic culture within a static, older tradition. Within the ring road keeps that the inner city surprisingly small, Leipzig offers an astounding variety of activities: music lovers, art critics, club fanatics and adventure seekers meet here to satisfy their respective passions. At one time

SACHSEN

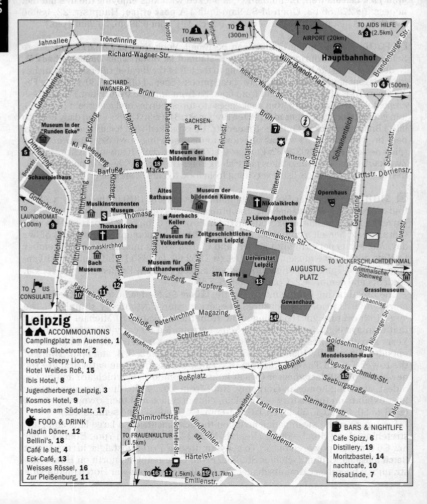

Leipzig

♠ ⛺ ACCOMMODATIONS
Camplingplatz am Auensee, **1**
Central Globetrotter, **2**
Hostel Sleepy Lion, **5**
Hotel Weißes Roß, **15**
Ibis Hotel, **8**
Jugendherberge Leipzig, **3**
Kosmos Hotel, **9**
Pension am Südplatz, **17**

🍴 FOOD & DRINK
Aladin Döner, **12**
Bellini's, **18**
Café le bit, **4**
Eck-Café, **13**
Weisses Rössel, **16**
Zur Pleißenburg, **11**

🍸 BARS & NIGHTLIFE
Cafe Spizz, **6**
Distillery, **19**
Moritzbastei, **14**
nachtcafe, **10**
RosaLinde, **7**

home to Bach, Mendelssohn, Wagner, Nietzsche, Goethe, and Leibniz, the city enjoys an exceptionally rich cultural tradition that boasts world-class museums, churches, and restaurants. Although grounded historically, Leipzig has the momentum for continued change in the decades to come.

▐ TRANSPORTATION

Flights: Flughafen Leipzig-Halle (☎22 40), on Schkeuditzg., is 20km from Leipzig with international service throughout Europe. Outbound trains stop at the airport. (From the train station, 10 min., 2 per hr. 4am-11:30pm, €3.30.)

Trains: To: **Berlin** (2-3hr., 3 per hr., €33); **Dresden** (1½hr., 3 per hr., €25); **Frankfurt** (5hr., 2 per hr., €57); **Munich** (7hr., 3 per hr., €90). Information counter on the platform near track 15, or in the *Reisezentrum* at the entrance of the station.

Public Transportation: Information ☎194 49. Streetcars and buses cover the city; the hub is in front of the Hauptbahnhof. A *Kurzstrecke* ticket covers up to 4 stops (€1.20); a regular ticket covers all rides within 1hr. (€1.50). A day card *(Tageskarte)* is valid until 4am the next day (€4.40). Weekly (€13) and monthly (€38) cards are valid until midnight of the last day. Tickets available from the tourist office, kiosks, and the vending machines at major stops and on some streetcars. Night buses (1 per hr., look for the "N" prefix) take over after midnight. All night buses leave from the Hauptbahnhof.

Taxis: ☎48 84, 710 00, or 42 33. Toll-free ☎0800 800 42 33.

Car Rental: Hertz, Europcar, Sixt-Budget, and **Avis** have counters at the Hauptbahnhof's *Reisezentrum.* Open M-F 7am-9pm, Sa-Su 8am-4pm. More offices at the airport.

Mitfahrzentrale: Goethestr. 7-10 (☎194 40), just past the tourist office. To: **Berlin** (€13); **Dresden** (€8); **Frankfurt** (€23); **Munich** (€24). Open daily 7am-10pm.

Hitchhiking: *Let's Go* does not recommend hitchhiking as a safe mode of transportation. Hitchers going to Dresden and Prague report taking streetcar #3 (dir.: Taucha) to "Portitzer Allee" and continuing on Torgauerstr. to the *Autobahn* interchange. Those going to Berlin take streetcar #8 or 15 (dir.: Miltitz) to "Lindenauer Markt," switch to bus #131, get out at "Dölzig, Holl. Mühle," and walk to the *Autobahn.*

▐ ORIENTATION AND PRACTICAL INFORMATION

Leipzig's **Innenstadt** lies within a ring of about a kilometer in diameter, which encloses most of the sights and nightlife, as well as the university. On its north edge (a 10min. walk from the center of the Markt), the cavernous **Hauptbahnhof,** with a dramatic curved-beam roof and three underground stories of shopping (most stores open M-Sa 9:30am-10pm), is Europe's largest train station, at least until Berlin's new Lehrter Bahnhof opens in 2006. **Augustusplatz** and the university are to the east of the Markt, and the **Thomaskirche** lies to the west.

Tourist Office: Leipzig Information, Richard-Wagner-Str. 1 (☎710 42 30; booking hotline 710 42 55; www.leipzig.de). Walk across Willy-Brandt-Pl. in front of the station, continue across the landscaped area, and turn left at Richard-Wagner-Str. Free maps. They also book rooms for free and sell theater tickets. The **Leipzig Card** is good for free public transport and discounted museums and tours (1-day, until 4am, €5.90; 3-day €11.50). Open M-F 10am-7pm, Sa 10am-4pm, Su 10am-2pm.

Tours: The tourist office leads German and English bus tours daily at 10:30am (2hr.; €12) and 1:30pm (2½hr.; €15, seniors/students €11). Themed walking tours daily, some with English-speaking guides (2hr., €6-8). For information call ☎710 42 80.

Budget Travel: STA Travel (☎211 42 20), in the corner of the university courtyard nearest Universitätsstr. Open M-F 10am-6pm, Sa 10am-1pm.

Consulate: US, Wilhelm-Seyferth-Str. 4 (☎213 84 18). Cross the Innenstadt ring behind the Neues Rathaus and follow Tauchnitzstr. until Wilhelm-Seyferth comes up on the left. The entrance is through Grassistr, the next street to the left. Americans with questions or emergencies may call to make an appointment.

Currency Exchange: Commerzbank, Thomaskirche 22, across the street from the church. Open M and W 9am-4pm, Tu and Th 9am-6pm, F 9am-1pm. Also has **ATMs.**

Women's Resources: Frauenkultur, Windscheidstr. 51 (☎213 00 30; www.frauenkultur.leipzig.w4w.net), is a center for art, meetings, courses, and relaxation. Take streetcar #9, 10, or 11 to "Connewitz, Kreuz," then make a right onto Selneckerstr. and turn right again onto Windscheidstr.—the building is located in first alley on the right. Office open M-F 9am-2pm, frequently later for afternoon events. Often evening women's cafe, but call ahead for the current program.

Gay and Lesbian Resources: AIDS-Hilfe, Ossietzkystr. 18 (☎232 31 27; info@leipzig.aidshilfe.de). Take streetcar #1 (dir.: Schönefeld/Stannebeinpl.) to "Ossietzkystr./Gorkistr." The complex features a popular cafe (open Tu and Th 5-10pm), and distributes the magazine *gegenpol,* which has gay information for all of Saxony. Office open M-Th 10am-6pm, F 10am-1pm. **Rosalinde** (p. 648) offers a variety of activities and support groups for GLBT individuals.

Mitwohnzentrale: ☎194 30, in the same office as the **Mitfahrzentrale** (p. 641). Arranges long-term accommodations. Open 9am-7pm.

Laundromat: Maga Pon, Gottschedstr. 11 (☎993 87 98). Sip espresso (€1.50) while you watch your clothes dry at a hip cafe. Breakfast is served here until 3pm (€2-7). Wash €2.50-3.50. Dry €0.50 per 10min. Open daily from 9am.

Emergency: Police ☎110. **Fire and Ambulance** ☎112.

Pharmacies: Löwen-Apotheke, Grimmaischestr. 19 (☎960 50 27). Open M-F 8am-8pm, Sa 9am-4pm.

Internet Access: Mediacafe Trixon, Härtelstr. 21 (☎212 65 86). Go down Petersteinweg and turn left onto Härtelstr. €2.60 per hr. Open M from noon, Tu-Su from 10am.

Post Office: Augustuspl. 1-4, 04109 Leipzig (☎126 91 15), across from the Opernhaus on Grimmaische Steinweg. Open M-F 9am-8pm, Sa 9am-3pm.

ACCOMMODATIONS AND CAMPING

▨ **Hostel Sleepy Lion,** Käthe-Kollwitz-Str. 3 (☎993 94 80; www.hostel-leipzig.de). A 10min. walk from the station: cross the street and turn right onto Richard-Wagner-Str. At its end, cross the overpass directly ahead and turn left. Follow Gördelerring until Käthe-Kollwitz-Str. branches off to the right. Or, take streetcar #1 (dir.: Lausen) or #14 (dir.: S-Bahnhof Plagwitz) to "Gottschedstr." Operated by young locals and adjacent to the city's nightlife, the Sleepy Lion draws an international crowd. Spacious rooms all have shower and bath. Breakfast €3. **Internet** access €2 per hr. Bike rental €5 per day. Sheets €2. Reception 24hr. 6-8 bed dorms €14-15; singles €28; doubles €40; quads €64. A new branch, called **Central Globetrotter,** Karl-Schumacher-Str. 41 (☎149 89 60), has opened 5min. from the train station. Take the west exit and turn right onto Karl-Schumacher-Str. Shared bathrooms and kitchen for guests. Same services as Sleepy Lion, rooms €1 cheaper. ❷

▨ **Kosmos Hotel,** Gottschedstr. 1 (☎233 44 22; www.kosmos-hotel.de). From the Hauptbahnhof, cross the street and turn right onto Richard-Wagner-Str.; when it ends cut left through the parking lot and then the small park. At the end of the park keep left on Dittrichring and it'll be ahead on the right (12min.). Just downhill from the Thomaskirche, this funky hotel is part of a larger complex including a nightclub and restaurant. Stylishly decorated singles and doubles with themes like "Jungle," "James Dean," and "Dali" come cheaply for the area, but be prepared: Gottschedstr. stays up late. Breakfast €6. Reception 8am-11pm. Dorms €15; singles from €35; doubles from €50, both with private bathrooms. ❸

Hotel Weißes Roß, Auguste-Schmidt-Str. 20 (☎960 59 51). From the station take street-car #11 (dir.: Markkleeberg-Ost), or 10 or 16 (dir.: Lößnig) to "Augustuspl.," and walk down Augustuspl. until it curves to the right, becoming Roßpl. Go through the archway just left of the center of the curving apartment building; the hotel is 100m straight ahead. Attached restaurant serves boisterous locals. Breakfast included. Reception during cafe hours M-F 5-10pm, but call ahead and the manager will let you in. Singles €31, with shower €35; doubles €46/€52. Lower prices when less busy, longer stays negotiable. ❸

Ibis Hotel, Brühl 69 (☎218 60; www.ibishotel.com). From the Hauptbahnhof, cross the street and head a block down Goethestr. Take a right onto the Brühl. If you run out of budget options, the classy Ibis (part of a large chain) is a 2min. walk from the train station. Impeccably clean with reliable service and no surprises. Reception 24hr. May-Aug. any room €49; Jan.-Apr. and Sept.-Dec. €59. ❹

Jugendherberge Leipzig (HI), Volksgartenstr. 24 (☎245 70 11; fax 245 70 12). Take streetcar #1 (dir.: Schönefeld/Stannebeinpl.) to "Löbauer Str." Walk in the direction of the tram and take a left onto Volksgartenstr. Rooms with 2-6 comfortable beds fill this high-rise. Breakfast and sheets included. Reception 2:30-11pm. Curfew 1am; talk to the receptionist if you will be returning later. €21.70, under 27 €19. ❷

Pension am Südplatz, Kochstr. 4 (☎301 96 06). Take streetcar #10 (dir.: Lößnig) or 11 (dir.: Markkleebert-Ost) to "Südplatz." Kochstr. curves off immediately to the right. Clean and cheery rooms right in the middle of Leipzig's hip Südpl. scene. Singles €25, with shower €35; doubles €29/€39. ❷

Campingplatz Am Auensee, Gustav-Esche-Str. 5 (☎465 16 00), by a lake in the nearby suburb of Wahren. From the station, take streetcar #10 (dir.: Wahren) or #11 (dir: Sch-keuditz) to "Wahren." Turn left before the Rathaus onto Linkelstr. and follow the twisting main road (10min.); it will be on your right. Reception daily 7:30am-1pm and 2-9:30pm. €4 per person, €3-5 per tent, €2-6 per car. 2-bed bungalows €20, with shower €35; 3-bed €41. Public showers €0.50. ❶

🗋 FOOD

Leipzig's Innenstadt, especially **Grimmaischestraße,** is well supplied with *Imbiße,* bistros, and bakeries, and has a **market** on Richard-Wagner-Pl., at the end of the Brühl (Tu and F 9am-5pm). Escape downtown crowds with a jaunt to **Karl-Lie-bknecht-Straße,** which is packed with *Döner* stands and well-priced cafes and bars. To get there from the Markt, take Peterstr. to Petersteinweg (15min.), or hop on streetcar #11 (dir.: Markleeberg-Ost) or 10 (dir.: Lößnig) to "Südplatz." Most of the cafes in Leipzig also offer a Sunday brunch buffet.

▨ Bellini's, Markt 3-5, boasts great food in a perfect location. Right in the middle of the bustling Markt, this cafe is usually full in the evenings, with every chair turned toward the street to see the beautiful Altes Rathaus or watch the people walking past. Baguettes (€3) make delicious snacks, and the colorful salads or delicious pasta (€7-9) satisfy cravings for something larger. Open daily from 10am. ❷

Aladin Döner, Burgstr. 12 (☎976 67 07), just south of the Thomaskirche. Making the best *Döner* in town is hard when you've got so much competition, but Aladin Döner is the pick of many locals. Pitas, turkish pizzas, and falafel balance the menu, while a free glass of tea adds a classy touch to the end of a meal. The special "Aladin Döner" comes with fries on top (€3.50). Open daily from 10am. ❷

Zur Pleißenburg, Ratsfreischulstr. 2 (☎960 26 53), just down Burgstr. from the Tho-maskirche. Empty stomach at 4am? Load up on spaghetti (€5) or a hearty *Bauernfrüh-stück* (€4.50) with eggs, ham, and potatoes, at this relaxed hangout set back from the city center. Open daily 9am-5am. ❷

Weisses Rössel, Karl-Liebknecht Str. 64 (☎30 10 92), offers tasty, varied cuisine: pasta dishes and pizza (€7-9) fill a menu with specialties from Thai turkey curry (€8.40) to a true veal *Wiener Schnitzel* (€10). Open M-Sa 6pm to 2am, Su 10am-2am. ❸

BUY ME A BEMME?

With most of Germany overrun by tapas, crepes, bagels, and sushi, Bemme und Bier on Leipzig's Markt has finally found a local answer: the traditional Saxon Bemme, spiffed up for the 21st century. A what? For the uninformed: a *Bemme* is a small piece of dark, whole-grain bread, traditionally covered with fat and pepper. Not too appetizing, perhaps, but Bemme und Bier has spiced them up a bit. You can go with the classics, known to top toasted baguettes: tomato and mozzarella, cucumber and Quark, herbs and fresh cheese. Other sandwich varieties mix and match ham, salami, cheese, and vegetable to any taste. For fish-lovers, there is smoked salmon and even a *Matjes Bemme* with dill honey mustard. For sweet-tooths: sweet peach-cream and, of course, Nutella. What is the best part of the menu, which includes 44 varieties? No matter the topping, each Bemme costs only €0.80. Then there are the deals: a four Bemme meal with two coffees for €4.80; all the healthy Bemmen you can eat for €8.80 (including coffee) from 8-11am. And after 7pm each Monday, the house practically gives away the classic Fettbemmen for 50 cents a pop. In a low-carb world, fat and dark bread might just find its niche.

Bemme und Bier, Markt 4, on the corner of Katharinenstr. ☎ 910 49 80. Open M-Th 8am-10pm, F-Su 8am-midnight.)

Eck-Café, in the courtyard of the university complex across from the Mensa (☎ 973 79 09). Rub elbows with Leipzig University students as they meet for conversation over beer, coffee, and countless cigarettes. Soup €1-1.50; *Wurst* €1-2. Open Oct. to mid-July M-Th 9:30am-5pm, F 10am-2pm. ❶

Café le bit, Rosa-Luxemburg-Str. 36 (☎ 998 20 20), on the right corner at Friedrich-List-Pl. With your back to the station, turn left across Georgring onto Wintergartenstr., which becomes Rosa-Luxemburg-Str. and leads straight there (10min.). Bilingual staff serves great crepes (€1.50-5) to visiting e-mailers in this strangely decorated Internet cafe. **Internet** €1.25 per 30min. Open M-F 9am-3am, Sa-Su 10am-3am. ❷

🔎 SIGHTS

The architecture of Leipzig's Innenstadt is startlingly heterogeneous: on any one street you'll find elegant old townhouses, institutional DDR relics, and gleaming new shopping malls. Leipzig has been on a building spree since 1991 that continues today at a breakneck pace. The heart of the city beats at the Marktpl., a colorful, cobblestoned square guarded by the slanted 16th-century **Altes Rathaus,** with its elegant **clock tower** showing four bright-blue faces. Most of Leipzig's museums and sights are a short walk from the Marktpl.

▨ VÖLKERSCHLACHTDENKMAL. Outside the city ring, this massive pyramid, built in 1913 to look like a Mesopotamian ziggurat, memorializes the 100,000 soldiers who died in the 1813 **Battle of Nations**—a six-day struggle that turned the tide against Napoleon and determined many of Europe's current national boundaries. The inside bears witness to the extreme nationalism of the Wilhemine era that produced it: gigantic stone soldiers lean sadly over their swords and war horses spiral up to the dome. Climb the 364 steps to the top for a fabulous view of Leipzig. *(Streetcar #15 from the Hauptbahnhof (dir.: Meusdorf) to "Völkerschlachtdenkmal" (15min.), then turn right. ☎ 961 85 38; www.voelkerschlachtdenkmal.de. Museum and memorial open daily Apr.-Oct. 10am-6pm; Nov.-Mar. 10am-4pm. €3, students €2. Public tours Tu 2:30pm and Sa 11am. €2, students €1.50. Signs in English.)*

THOMASKIRCHE. Down Thomasg. from the Altes Rathaus is the church where Bach spent the last 27 years of his career as cantor. Elegantly decorated in neo-Gothic style, the church pays simple and fitting homage to the composer. His body was moved in 1950 to a grave beneath the floor in front of the altar. Highlights of the church include a crucifix from Bach's time, an astonishingly beautiful triptych from an anonymous master of the 15th century, and a historical musical instrument collection. The **Thomanerchor,** once directed by Bach, is one of Europe's most prestigious boys' choirs. (☎ *60 28 85; www.thomaskirche.org. Church open daily 9am-6pm. Free. Thomanerchor performances F 6pm, Sa 3pm. €1. Also during Sunday services. Public tours of the tower Sa 11am, noon, 1, 4:15 and 5pm; Su hourly from 2-5pm. €2.)*

NIKOLAIKIRCHE. The 800-year-old Nikolaikirche witnessed the birth of Bach's *St. John Passion* as well as the DDR's peaceful revolution. In 1989, the church became the gathering point for what would become a truly revolutionary political phenomenon. What began as regular Monday meetings at the Nikolaikirche, the only place where the Stasi could not interfere, turned into massive weekly demonstrations *(Montagdemos)*, which eventually contributed to the fall of the DDR. The sandstone facade hides a truly exceptional interior, including alabaster reliefs and towering green columns carved like palm fronds, a nod to a time when the church stood at the intersection of two major trade routes. *(Down Grimmaischestr. from the Altes Rathaus. Church open M-Sa 10am-6pm, Su 9am-6pm. Free.)*

AUERBACHS KELLER. In Goethe's *Faust*, Mephistopheles tricks some drunkards in this 16th-century tavern, before carrying Faust away on an enchanted beer barrel. Check out *Faust* scenes on the walls over a long meal in this elegant, but unpretentious **restaurant** ❹. *(Grimmaischestr. 2-4. Across from the Altes Rathaus, inside the Mädlerpassage. ☎ 21 61 00. Open daily 11:30am-midnight. Entrees €8-19.)*

UNIVERSITÄT LEIPZIG. The former Karl-Marx-Universität, founded in 1409, is on Universitätsstr. Its "sharp tooth" tower, a steel and concrete behemoth, was allegedly designed to resemble a partially open book standing upright. Now owned by a German media company, the tower gleams with recent renovations and is the town's tallest building. Ride the elevator to the 29th floor to see a stunning view of Leipzig and the Völkerschlachtdenkmal from the roof (€1.50).

🏛 MUSEUMS

As part of its effort to restore the city, Leipzig is rebuilding its museums in grand style. By the end of 2004 a new **Museum der Bildenden Künste** will dominate Sachsenpl., and by the end of 2005 a refurbished **Grassimuseum** will reopen on Johannispl. Because some exhibits will be closed during the relocation, call the tourist office or museums themselves if you are planning a trip to Leipzig.

🔲 MUSEUM IN DER "RUNDEN ECKE". The East German *Staatssicherheit,* or *Stasi,* was the largest per capita secret police force in world history. Over 91,000 official employees produced literally miles of paper and mountains of cassettes and photographs in their attempts to keep tabs on suspected "enemies of the state." Because Leipziger citizens occupied the building on December 4, 1989, most of the tools that the *Stasi* used to torment its opponents are preserved and on display, including machines that helped them secretly open and reseal up to 2000 letters per day. The archive, including everything from handwriting samples to reports and samples of human scents, is the largest of its kind in Germany, even after millions of pages were shredded during the final days of the DDR. The museum staff also gives tours of a bunker nearby that contains an exhibit detailing the unrealized plans of the Stasi. *(Dittrichring 24. ☎ 961 24 43; www.runde-ecke-leipzig.de. Tours in German 3pm, for groups in English by appointment, or ask for an English handout in the office. Open daily 10am-6pm. Free. Bunker tours last weekend of every month 1-4pm.)*

MUSEUM DER BILDENDEN KÜNSTE LEIPZIG. Leizpig's art collection includes works by Rubens, Boticelli, Cranach the Elder and the Younger, and an excellent collection of 19th-century German paintings. Currently housed in a pre-war court building, the museum should find its way to a new home on Sachsenpl. by December 2004. A temporary closure during the move is expected. *(Grimmaischestr. 1-7, just behind the Altes Rathaus. ☎ 21 69 90. Open Tu and Th-Su 10am-6pm, W 1-9:30pm. €2.50, students and seniors €1. Special exhibits €4, students €2.)*

JOHANN-SEBASTIAN-BACH-MUSEUM. While the Thomaskirche and the Bach Denkmal across the street serve as fitting monuments to the composer, the Bach Museum's informative exhibits emphasize his role as choir director, teacher, and city musician. The museum also provides important background on the composer's life and work in Leipzig, where he wrote his *Mass in B minor* and both *St. John* and *St. Matthew Passion*. In total he composed over 300 cantatas here. The *Sommersaal* hosts concerts Wednesday at 8pm. *(Thomaskirchhof 16. ☎ 913 72 00. Open daily 10am-5pm. €3, students and seniors €2. Concerts €10/€7.50. Free English audio tours. Public tours F 3pm, Sa 2pm, Su 11am and 3pm. €3.50.)*

MENDELSSOHN-HAUS. This gorgeous house was the residence of composer Felix Mendelssohn-Bartholdy for two of the years that he lived in Leipzig. Mendelssohn led a revival of interest in Bach, conducting many concerts at the Gewandhaus. It was through his urging that the Bach statue outside the Thomaskirche was erected in 1843. Some rooms have been furnished to appear as Mendelssohn knew them, while others hold exhibits on his life and work. Ask for an English translation of exhibit text. *(Goldschmidtstr. 12. Take Augustuspl. away from the Opernhaus toward Roßpl., then a left down Goldschmidtstr. ☎ 127 02 94. Open daily 10am-6pm. €3. Concerts Su at 11am. €10, students €7.)*

ZEITGESCHICHTLICHES FORUM LEIPZIG. Leipzig's Forum of Contemporary History provides a comprehensive and thoughtful look at Germany's history since its division after WWII. Especially powerful are videos of the Berlin Wall's construction and of demonstrators in the angry protests of June 17, 1953 and the more peaceful ones of 1989. Exhibit descriptions are available in English. Special exhibits on the third floor cover contemporary issues in German society. *(Grimmaischestr. 6. ☎ 222 00; www.hdg.de. Open Tu-F 9am-6pm, Sa-Su 10am-6pm. Free.)*

GRASSIMUSEUM. Usually housed under one roof, select displays from three museums are scattered about until their building on Johannispl. is re-opened in late 2005. The **Museum für Völkerkunde** (anthropology museum), above Auerbachs Keller in the Mädlerpassage, displays the dress and customs of peoples from all over the globe. *(☎ 595 82 18. Open Tu-F 10am-6pm, Sa-Su 10am-5pm. €2, students €1.)* Across from the Thomaskirche, the **Musikinstrumenten Museum** holds the world's oldest clavichord and other fragile Renaissance instruments. Most fun of all is the *Klanglabor* ("noise laboratory"), where you can work out your aggressions on the gongs, steel drums, xylophones and even a small pipe organ. *(Thomaskirchhof 20. Open Tu-Su 11am-5pm. €3, students €1.50. Public tours Su 11am. Signs in English.)* The **Museum für Kunsthandwerk** (arts and crafts museum) displays changing exhibits of artists' work in different media—programs indicate what's currently on display. *(Neumarkt 20. Open Tu and Th-Su 10am-6pm, W 10am-8pm. €4, students €3.)*

🎵 ENTERTAINMENT

The patrons that frequent the hip, slightly artsy cafes scattered around Leipzig also support a world-class theater and music scene. Leipzig offers a variety of world-famous musical groups. The first is the **Gewandhaus-Orchester**, a major international orchestra that has been performing since 1843. Some concerts are free, but usually only when a guest orchestra is playing; otherwise, tickets must be purchased at the *Gewandhaus* box office, Augustuspl. 8. *(☎ 127 02 80;*

www.gewandhaus.de. €12-40, students 20% off. Open M-F 10am-6pm, Sa 10am-2pm, and 1hr. before performances.) Leipzig's acclaimed **Opera**, Augustuspl. 12, gives Dresden's *Semperoper* a run for its money. Last minute tickets cost €10; you can then take any empty seat for an additional €5. (☎126 12 61. www.oper-leipzig.de. Phone reservations M-F noon-7pm. Counter open M-F 10am-8pm, Sa 10am-4pm, and 1½hr. before performances. Tickets €12-34, students 30% off.)

The opera house is also an entry point to Leipzig's diverse **theater** scene, hosting the experimental **Kellertheater** (☎126 12 61) in its basement. Renowned for its theater, Leipzig has recently unleashed a wave of experimental plays. The **Schauspielhaus**, Bosestr. 1 just off Dittrichring, produces the classics, including offerings from Euripides, Heiner Müller, Beckett, and Brecht. (☎126 81 68; www.schauspiel-leipzig.de. Tickets €12-36, students €12-29. Box office open M-F 10am-6pm, Sa 10am-1pm, and 1½hr. before performance.) The **cabaret** scene, which features almost exclusively political satire, is centered in the understated **academixer**, Kupfer. 3-5, run by the Leipzig student body, one of the few theaters without summer closings. (☎21 78 78 78; www.academixer.com. Box office open M-Sa 1pm until showtime, Su from 6pm. €9-21. students €6-21.) Also, check out the **Leipziger Pfeffermühle**, Thomaskirchhof 16, in the courtyard of the Bach Museum. (☎960 31 96. kabarett.pfeffermuehle@t-online.de. Open M-F 3-8pm. €15-18, students €10-16.) Leipzig showcases documentaries and short films at its annual late October **film festival** (☎980 39 21 for information, or ask at the tourist office). **naTo**, Karl-Liebknecht-Str. 46 (☎30 39 133), shows indie films in original languages with German subtitles, as does the cinema **"Prager Frühling,"** in the *Haus der Demokratie*, Bernhard-Goering-Str. 152 (☎306 53 33).

🎵 NIGHTLIFE

Free magazines *Fritz* and *Blitz* will fill you in on nightlife, but *Kreuzer* (sold at newsstands, €1.50) puts these to shame with information on concerts and exhaustive film and nightlife listings (make sure you get the monthly version). **Barfußgäßchen**, a street just off the Markt, serves as the see-and-be-seen bar venue for everyone from students to *Schicki-Mickis* (yuppies). In the summer there's only a narrow path to walk between the packed parasol-covered cafe tables. **Café Baum**, the oldest in the city, and **Markt Neun, Zigarre,** and **Varadero** all fill by 10pm. Though crowds dwindle by midnight, the most popular bars stay packed until 3am on a good night. Just across Dittrichring on **Gottschedstraße** and **Bosestraße**, a similar scene takes place in bars such as **Neue Szene, Hemingway,** and the **Milchbar**, but with a slightly younger crowd and the music turned up a notch.

Karl-Liebknecht-Straße hosts Leipzig's newest, most alternative *Szene*. The bars are more spread out, but also more distinctive. Take streetcar #11 (dir.: Markkleeburg-Ost) or 10 (dir.: Lößnig) to "Südplatz." The Irish pub **Killiwilly** at Karl-Liebknecht Str. 44 offers good cheer, while farther south, **Weißes Rössel** (p. 643) is more chill. Early on, the cafe scene seems to rule the night, but Leipzigers are just beginning: local dance clubs are packed throughout the student weekend (which begins, of course, on Wednesday).

🏛 **Moritzbastei**, Universitätsstr. 9 (☎70 25 90, tickets 702 59 58; www.moritzbastei.de), behind the university tower. University students spent 8 years excavating a series of medieval tunnels so they could get their groove on. The result: a huge complex housing a cafe, *Biergarten,* movie theater, multilevel dance floors, and chill bars. Café Barbakan, at the entrance to one of the tunnels, opens daily after 10am. An **open-air movie theater** (screenings June-Aug. M-Sa at 10:30pm, weather permitting) is next to the outdoor terrace and *Biergarten* (open in nice weather M-F 11:30am-midnight, Sa-Su

2pm-midnight). The █**All You Can Dance** disco on W and F blasts pounding music in cavernous rooms with vaulted brick ceilings. Cover €3, students with ID €2; slightly more for concerts (some require advance ticket purchase; office open M-F noon-6pm).

nachtcafe, Markgrafenstr. 10 (www.nachtcafe.com), is Leipzig's hottest club, explaining the uniform of tank-tops. The dramatic 2nd-floor entrance winds around a defunct elevator shaft. Constantly bathed in red light and shaking with at least 3 different kinds of music at a time, nachtcafe leaves few people on the sidelines. Cover €5, F women free. Open W and F-Sa from 10pm. Student party every 2nd M.

Distillery, at the end of Kurt-Eisner-Str. (☎35 59 74 00), near the corner of Lößinger Str. Streetcar #9 (dir.: Markkleeberg-West) to the "K.-Eisner/A.-Hoffman-Str." stop and turn left. A little out of the way, this industrial-yard-turned-disco attracts edgy Leipziger youth with pounding house, techno, and rock. Cover €5-8. Things usually get going after 11pm on weekends. Closed mid-July to Aug.

RosaLinde, Brühl 64-66 (☎484 15 11; www.rosalinde.com). Described by some as the epicenter of Leipzig's gay and lesbian scene, RosaLinde is usually a laid-back bar and cafe, but also holds a *Frauendisco* for women the 1st F of the month at 10pm (€2.50), a "Last Night" party the last Sa of the month at 10pm, and various other events. Drop by early evening to pick up a card listing support groups and special events. Open Tu-Th 5-11pm, F-Sa from 5pm, Su 5pm-11pm.

Cafe Spizz, Markt 9 (☎960 80 43; www.SPIZZ.org). Below this *Barfußgässchen* cafe lies one of the more popular Leipzig clubs. Big jazz names show up occasionally for weekend concerts, while Wednesday "Boogie Nights" jam sessions attract an almost cult-like following. Weekend disco nights entertain a slightly older crowd—the suits head here when they're done with work. W free, disco cover €3, all drinks after cover €1; concerts €10-30. Open W and F-Sa from 10pm.

APPENDIX

CARDINAL NUMBERS

0	1	2	3	4	5	6	7	8	9	10
null	eins	zwei	drei	vier	fünf	sechs	sieben	acht	neun	zehn

11	12	20	30	40	50	60	70	80	90	100
elf	zwölf	zwanzig	dreißig	vierzig	fünfzig	sechzig	siebzig	achtzig	neunzig	hundert

ORDINAL NUMBERS

1st	erste	5th	fünfte	9th	neunte
2nd	zweite	6th	sechste	10th	zehnte
3rd	dritte	7th	siebte	20th	zwanzigste
4th	vierte	8th	achte	100th	hunderte

CLIMATE

Germany's climate is temperate. Rain is common year-round, though it is especially prevalent in summer, when the weather can change with surprising rapidity.

TEMP. (LO/HI), PRECIPITATION	JANUARY			APRIL			JULY			OCTOBER		
	°C	°F	mm	°C	°F	mm	°C	°F	mm	°C	°F	mm
Berlin	-3-1	26-35	48	2-12	37-54	41	13-22	56-73	75	5-13	42-56	51
Frankfurt	-1-3	30-38	45	3-13	39-56	58	13-23	57-75	60	6-13	43-57	55
Hamburg	-1-3	30-38	60	2-11	37-52	45	12-21	55-70	81	6-12	43-55	60
Munich	-4-2	24-36	48	2-11	36-53	71	12-22	54-72	127	4-12	40-55	60

To convert from °C to °F, multiply by 1.8 and add 32. To convert from °F to °C, subtract 32 and multiply by 0.55.

°CELSIUS	-5	0	5	10	15	20	25	30	35	40
°FAHRENHEIT	23	32	41	50	59	68	77	86	95	104

TIME ZONES

Germany uses West European time (abbreviated MEZ in German). Add six hours to Eastern Standard Time and one hour to Greenwich Mean Time. Subtract nine hours from Eastern Australia Time and 11 hours from New Zealand Time. Germany, like the rest of Western Europe, observes Daylight Savings Time, but usually switches over a week before North America.

TELEPHONE CODES

COUNTRY CODES

In Germany, dial 00 to get an international line, then dial the code:

Australia	61		Italy	39
Austria	43		Netherlands	31
Belgium	32		New Zealand	64
Czech Republic	420		Poland	48
Denmark	45		South Africa	27
France	33		Switzerland	41
Hungary	36		United Kingdom	44
Ireland	353		US and Canada	1

CITY CODES

To call between cities in Germany, enter the city code of the town you're calling, followed by the local number. When calling from abroad, drop the first zero of the city code:

Aachen	0241		Schwerin	0385
Bayreuth	0921		Kassel	0561
Berlin	030		Kiel	0431
Bonn	0228		Cologne (Köln)	0221
Braunschweig	0531		Leipzig	0341
Bremen	0421		Lübeck	0451
Dresden	0351		Munich (München)	089
Düsseldorf	0211		Nürnberg	0911
Erfurt	0361		Regensburg	0941
Frankfurt	069		Rostock	0381
Freiburg	0761		Stuttgart	0711
Göttingen	0551		Trier	0651
Hamburg	040		Tübingen	07071
Hannover	0511		Weimar	03643
Heidelberg	06221		Wittenberg	03491
Münster	0251		Würzburg	0931

MEASUREMENTS

Like the rest of the rational world, Germany uses the metric system. Keep this in mind when you see a road sign or any other distance indicator—those are kilometers, not miles, so whatever distance is being described is not as far away as Americans might think. German recipe books use metric measurements (and usually measure ingredients by weight rather than volume). And, unfortunately, gasoline isn't as cheap as it looks to those used to gallons: prices are *per liter*.

MEASUREMENT CONVERSIONS

1 inch (in.) = 2.54cm	1 centimeter (cm) = 0.39 in.
1 foot (ft.) = 0.30m	1 meter (m) = 3.28 ft.
1 yard (yd.) = 0.914m	1 meter (m) = 1.09 yd.
1 mile (mi.) = 1.61km	1 kilometer (km) = 0.62 mi.
1 ounce (oz.) = 28.35g	1 gram (g) = 0.035 oz.
1 pound (lb.) = 0.454kg	1 kilogram (kg) = 2.202 lb.
1 fluid ounce (fl. oz.) = 29.57ml	1 milliliter (ml) = 0.034 fl. oz.
1 gallon (gal.) = 3.785L	1 liter (L) = 0.264 gal.
1 acre (ac.) = 0.405ha	1 hectare (ha) = 2.47 ac.
1 square mile (sq. mi.) = 2.59km^2	1 square kilometer (km^2) = 0.386 sq. mi.

LANGUAGE

"Life is too short to learn German."
—Thomas Love Peacock

Most Germans speak at least rudimentary English, but you will encounter many who do not, especially in parts of Eastern Germany. Before asking someone a question in English, preface your query with a polite *Sprechen Sie English?* (Do you speak English?). Even if your command of German is shaky, most Germans will be delighted when you try to speak to them in their native tongue.

PRONUNCIATION

With only a little bit of effort, you can make yourself easily understood in German. Unlike English, German pronunciation is for the most part consistent with spelling: there are no silent letters.

Consonants are pronounced as in English with the following exceptions: **J:** always pronounced as a Y. **K:** always pronounced, even before an N. **QU:** pronounced KV. **Single S:** pronounced as Z. **V:** pronounced as F. **W:** pronounced as V. **Z:** pronounced as TS. The hissing, aspirant **CH** sound, found in such basic words as *Ich* (I), *nicht* (not), and *sprechen* (to speak), is tricky for untrained English-speaking vocal cords. After A, O, U, or AU, it is pronounced as in Scottish, "loch"; otherwise it sounds like a soft CH, as in "chivalry." If you can't hack it, use an SH sound instead. The consonant combination **SCH,** found at the beginning of many German words, is pronounced SH, as in "shut," while **ST** and **SP** are pronounced "SHT" and "SHP," respectively. **R** after a vowel is pronounced as in English; after a consonant or the beginning of the word, it's a uvular guttural—think a harsher version of the "r" in "rip," pronounced from the back of the throat.

German has one consonant that does not exist in English, **the "ß,"** which is alternately referred to as the *scharfes S* (sharp S) or the *Ess-tset*. It is a shorthand symbol for a **double-S,** and is pronounced just like an English "ss." The letter appears only in lower case and shows up in two of the most important German words for travelers: *Straße*, "street," which is pronounced "SHTRAH-sseh" and abbreviated "Str."; and *Schloß*, "castle," pronounced "SHLOSS." Note that the "ß" is being phased out in an effort to standardize spelling.

German vowels and diphthongs also differ from their English counterparts: **A:** as in "father." **O:** as in "oh." **U:** as in "fondue." **Y:** as in "cool." **AU:** as in "wow." **IE:** as in "thief." **EI:** like the I in "wine." **EU:** like the OI in "boil." An **umlaut** over a letter (e.g., ü) makes the pronunciation longer and more rounded. An umlaut is sometimes replaced by an E following the vowel, so that "schön" becomes "schoen." An **Ä** sounds a lot like the short "e" in "effort," while an **Ö** is pronounced like the "e" in "perm." To make the **Ü** sound, round your lips to say "ooh," keep them in this position, and then try to say "ee" instead. Germans are very forgiving toward foreigners who butcher their mother tongue. There is, however, one important exception—place names. If you learn nothing else in German, learn to pronounce the names of cities properly. Berlin is "bare-LEEN," Hamburg is "HAHM-boorg," Munich (München) is "MEUWN-shen," and Bayreuth is "BUY-royt."

NUMBERS, DATES, AND TIMES

A space or period rather than a comma is used to indicate thousands, so 10,000 is written 10 000 or 10.000. Instead of a decimal point, Germans use a comma, e.g., 3.1415 is written 3,1415. Months and days are written in the reverse of the American manner, e.g., 10.11.92 is November 10. Note that the number in the ones place is pronounced before the number in the tens place; thus "fünfundsiebzig" (FUHNF-oont-ZEEB-tsish; literally "five and seventy") is 75, *not* 57.

The months in German are *Januar, Februar, März, April, Mai, Juni, Juli, August, September, Oktober, November, Dezember*. The days of the week are *Montag, Dienstag, Mittwoch, Donnerstag, Freitag, Samstag/Sonnabend*, and *Sonntag*. Germany uses the 24-hour clock for all official purposes; simply subtract 12 hours from pm times to convert them to their twelve hour equivalents. Thus, *fünfzehn Uhr* (15.00) is 3pm and 20.00 is 8pm. When Germans say "half eight" (*halb acht*), they mean 7:30; "three quarters eight" (*dreiviertel acht*) means 7:45 and "quarter eight" (*viertel acht*) means 7:15.

GERMAN PHRASEBOOK

The following phrasebook is meant to provide only the very rudimentary phrases you will need in your travels. Nothing can replace a full-fledged phrasebook or a pocket-sized English-German dictionary. German features both an informal and formal form of address; in the tables below, the polite form follows the familiar form in parentheses. Note that in German nouns can take any one of three genders; masculine (taking the article **der**; pronounced DARE), feminine (**die**; pronounced DEE) and neuter (**das**; pronounced DAHSS). All plural nouns also take the **die** article, regardless of their gender in the singular.

das Abendessen: dinner
ab/fahren: to depart
die Abfahrt: departure
das Abteil: train compartment
Achtung!: beware!
die Altstadt: old town, historic center
das Amt: bureau, office
an/kommen: to arrive
die Ankunft: arrival
die Apotheke: pharmacy
die Arbeit: work
auf/steigen: to get on
aus/steigen: to get off
der Ausgang: exit
die Auskunft: information
die Ausstellung: exhibit
der Ausweis: ID
das Auto: car
die Autobahn: highway
der Autobus: bus
das Bad: bath, spa
das Bahn: railway

der Bahnhof: train station
der Bahnsteig: train platform
der Berg: mountain, hill
das Bett: bed
die Bibliothek: library
die Bundesrepublik Deutschland (BRD): Federal Republic of Germany (FRG)
das Brot: bread
die Brücke: bridge
der Brunnen: fountain, well
der Bundestag: parliament
die Burg: fortress, castle
der Busbahnhof: bus station
die Damen: ladies (restroom)
das Denkmal: memorial
die Dusche: shower
der Dom: cathedral
das Dorf: village
echt: real
ekelig: disgusting
die Ehefrau: wife
der Ehemann: husband

die Einbahnstraße: one-way street
der Eingang: entrance
ein/steigen: board
der Eintritt: admission
das Essen: food
die Fähre: ferry
der Fahrplan: timetable
das Fahrrad: bicycle
der Fahrschein: train/bus ticket
der Familienname: last name
der Feiertag: holiday
der Fernseher: television
die Festung: fortress
der Flohmarkt: flea market
der Flughafen: airport
das Flugzeug: airplane
der Fluß: river
das Fremdenverkehrsamt: tourist office
das Frühstück: breakfast
die Fußgängerzone: pedestrian zone

das Gasthaus: guest house
die Gaststätte: local bar with restaurant
die Gedenkstätte: memorial
geil: cool OR horny
das Gleis: track
der Hafen: harbor
der Hauptbahnhof: main train station
das Hauptpostamt: main post office
die Herren: Gentlemen
der Hof: court, courtyard
der Imbiß: fast-food stand
die Innenstadt: city center
die Insel: island
das Jugendgästehaus: youth hotel
die Jugendherberge: youth hostel
die Karte: ticket
das Kino: cinema
der Kiosk: newsstand
die Kirche: church
die Kneipe: bar
das Krankenhaus: hospital
das Kreuz: cross, crucifix
die Kunst: art
der Kurort: spa/resort
die Kurtaxe: overnight resort tax
die Kurverwaltung: Kurort tourist office
das Land: German state/province
die Lesbe: lesbian (n.)

der Markt: market
der Marktplatz: market square
die Mauer: wall (freestanding)
das Meer: sea
die Mensa: university cafeteria
die Mitfahrzentrale: rideshare service office
die Mitwohnzentrale: longterm accommodation service
das Münster: cathedral
das Museum: museum
der Notausgang: emergency exit
der Notfall: emergency
der Notruf: emergency hotline
der Paß: passport
die Pension: cheap hotel
der Platz: square, plaza
die Polizei: police
das Postamt: post office
das Privatzimmer: room in a private home
die Quittung: receipt
das Rathaus: town hall
die Rechnung: bill, cheque
das Reisebüro: travel agency
das Reisezentrum: travel office in train stations
die S-Bahn: commuter rail
die Sammlung: collection
die Schatzkammer: treasury
das Schiff: ship
das Schloß: castle

die Schule: school
schwul: gay (adj.)
See: lake
die Speisekarte: menu
die Staatsangehöhrigkeit: nationality
die Stadt: city
der Strand: beach
die Straße: street
die Straßenbahn: streetcar
die Tankstelle: gas/petrol station
der Teich: pond
das Tor: gate
die Toilette: bathroom
der Turm: tower
die U-Bahn: subway
umsteigen: to make a transit connection
die Universität: university
der Veganer/in: vegan
der Vegetarier/in: vegetarian
das Viertel: quarter, district, neighborhood
der Vorname: first name
die Vorsicht: caution
der Wald: forest
WC: bathroom
wandern: to hike
der Wanderweg: hiking trail
der Weg: road, way
die Wurst: sausage
die Zeitung: newspaper
das Zimmer: room
der Zug: train

GREETINGS

ENGLISH	GERMAN	ENGLISH	GERMAN
Hello.	Hallo.	Goodbye.	Tschüß! (informal); Auf Wiedersehen! (formal)
Excuse me./Sorry.	Entschuldigung/ Verzeihung.	My name is...	Ich heiße...
Could you please help me?	Kannst du (Könnten Sie) mir helfen bitte?	What is your name?	Wie heißt du (heißen Sie)?
How old are you?	Wie alt bist du (sind Sie)?	Where are you from?	Woher kommst du (kommen Sie)?
Good morning.	Guten Morgen.	How are you?	Wie geht's (geht es Ihnen)?
Good afternoon.	Guten Tag.	I'm fine.	Es geht mir gut.
Good evening.	Guten Abend.	Do you speak English?	Sprichst du (Sprechen Sie) Englisch?
Good night.	Gute Nacht.	I don't speak German.	Ich spreche kein Deutsch.

USEFUL PHRASES

Thank you (very much).	Danke (schön).	Please.	Bitte.
What?	Was?	I am a university student (male/female).	Ich bin Student (m)/ Studentin (f).
When (what time)?	Wann?	Are there student discounts?	Gibt es Studentenermäßigungen?
Why?	Warum?	No problem.	Kein Problem.

Where is...?	Wo ist...?	I don't understand.	Ich verstehe nicht.
I'm from...	Ich komme aus...	Please speak slowly.	Sprechen Sie bitte langsam.
America/USA	Amerika/den USA	Please repeat.	Bitte wiederholen Sie.
Australia	Australien	Pardon? What was that?	Wie, bitte?
Canada	Kanada	Yes/No	Ja/nein
Great Britain	Großbritannien	Maybe	Vielleicht
Ireland	Irland	I would like...	Ich möchte...
New Zealand	Neuseeland	I'm looking for...	Ich suche...
My (xxx) is broken.	Meine (xxx) ist kaputt!	I need...	Ich brauche...
I'm not feeling well.	Mir ist schlecht.	How much does that cost?	Wieviel kostet das?
I have a headache.	Ich habe Kopfweh.	Where is the phone?	Wo ist das Telefon?
I need a doctor.	Ich brauche einen Arzt.	I don't know.	Ich weiß nicht.
Leave me alone!	Laß mich in Ruhe!	Where is the toilet?	Wo ist die Toilette?
I'll call the police.	Ich rufe die Polizei.	I have potato salad in my Lederhosen.	Ich habe Kartoffelsalat in meinen Lederhosen.
Help!	Hilfe!	What does that mean?	Was bedeutet das?
No, thanks.	Nein, danke.	How do you say that in German?	Wie sagt man das auf Deutsch?
Okay.	Alles klar.	I don't care.	Es ist mir egal.
How's the weather today?	Wie ist das Wetter heute?	Schade.	Too bad.

DIRECTIONS AND TRANSPORTATION

(to the) right	rechts	(to the) left	links
straight ahead	geradeaus	Where is...?	Wo ist...?
next to	neben	opposite	gegenüber
How do I find...?	Wie finde ich...?	It's nearby.	Es ist in der Nähe.
How do I get to...?	Wie komme ich nach...?	Is that far from here?	Ist es weit weg?
one-way	einfach	round-trip	hin und zurück
Where is this train going?	Wohin fährt der Zug?	When does the train leave?	Wann fährt der Zug ab?

ACCOMMODATIONS

Rooms available.	Zimmer frei.	I would like a room...	Ich möchte ein Zimmer...
No vacancies.	besetzt.	...with sink.	...mit Waschbecken.
Are there any vacancies?	Gibt es ein Zimmer frei?	...with shower.	...mit Dusche.
Single room	Einzelzimmer	...with a toilet.	...mit WC.
Double room	Doppelzimmer	...with a bathtub.	...mit Badewanne.
Dormitory-style room	Mehrbettzimmer/ Schlafsaal	nonsmoker	Nichtraucher
Do you have anything cheaper?	Haben Sie etwas billiger?	check out	abmelden

TIMES AND HOURS

open	geöffnet	closed	geschlossen
morning	Morgen	opening hours	Öffnungszeiten
afternoon	Nachmittag	today	heute
night	Nacht	yesterday	gestern

evening	Abend
What time is it?	Wie spät ist es?
It's (seven) o'clock.	Es ist (sieben) Uhr.

tomorrow	morgen
break time, rest day	Ruhepause, Ruhetag
At what time?	Um wieviel Uhr?

FOOD AND RESTAURANT TERMS

bread	Brot
roll	Brötchen
jelly	Marmelade
meat	Fleisch
beef	Rindfleisch
pork	Schweinfleisch
chicken	Huhn
sausage	Wurst
cheese	Käse
fruit	Obst
vegetables	Gemüse
cabbage	Kohl
I would like to order...	Ich hätte gern...
It tastes good.	Es schmeckt gut.
I'm a vegetarian (male/female).	Ich bin Vegetarier (m)/ Vegetarierin (f).
Service included.	Bedienung Inklusiv.
Check, please.	Rechnung, bitte.

water	Wasser
tap water	Leitungswasser
juice	Saft
beer	Bier
wine	Wein
coffee	Kaffee
tea	Tee
soup	Suppe
potatoes	Kartoffeln
milk	Milch
sauce	Soße
french fries	Pommes frites
Another beer, please.	Noch ein Bier, bitte.
It tastes awful.	Es schmeckt widerlich.
I'm a vegan (male/female).	Ich bin Veganer (m)/ Ich bin Veganerin (f).
Tageskarte	Daily special
Give me a nutella sandwich.	Gib (Geben Sie) mir ein Nutellabrötchen.

OPPOSITES ATTRACT

together	zusammen
good	gut
happy	glücklich
big	groß
young	jung
full	voll
warm	warm
safe	sicher, ungefährlich
alive	lebendig
special	besonders
more	mehr
before	vor
pretty	schön

alone	allein/e
bad	schlecht
sad	traurig
small	klein
old	alt
empty	leer
cool	kühl
dangerous	gefährlich
dead	tot
simple	einfach
less	weniger
after	nach
ugly	häßlich

RIDICULOUS(LY) USEFUL PHRASES

Here's looking at you, kid.	Schau mich in die Augen, Kleines.
May I buy you a drink, darling?	Darf ich dir ein Getränk kaufen, Liebling?
Cheers!	Prost!
You're delicious.	Du bist lecker.
That's cool.	Das ist ja geil/crass.

Many thanks for the pleasure ride in your patrol car.	Vielen Dank für den Ausritt in Ihrem Streifenwagen.
I'm hung over.	Ich habe einen Kater.
There is a disturbance in the force.	Es gibt eine Störung in der Kraft.
Inconceivable!	Quatsch!
Hasta la vista, baby.	Bis später, Baby.

APPENDIX

DISTANCES (KM) AND TRAVEL TIMES BY TRAIN

	Aachen	Berlin	Bonn	Bremen	Dresden	D-Dorf	Frankfurt	Freiburg	Hamburg	Hannover	Kassel	Cologne	Leipzig	Munich	Nürnberg	Rostock	Stuttgart
Aachen		642	90	387	649	80	263	541	484	351	307	68	576	650	503	638	450
Berlin	5½hr.		608	390	214	565	564	827	285	285	388	583	192	587	431	219	652
Bonn	1½hr.	5hr.		349	570	78	181	422	450	317	273	26	497	588	399	604	357
Bremen	4hr.	4hr.	3½hr.		488	298	467	700	119	133	281	324	370	745	573	297	657
Dresden.	9hr.	3hr.	8hr.	6hr.		568	471	724	485	371	337	578	124	494	346	474	572
Düssel-dorf	1½hr.	4hr.	45min.	3hr.	7hr.		231	492	423	272	228	41	493	618	449	577	414
Frankfurt	3½hr.	4hr.	2hr.	4hr.	6hr.	3hr.		272	497	362	194	192	398	399	223	651	216
Freiburg	5hr.	6½hr.	4hr.	6hr.	9hr.	4½hr.	2hr.		755	613	454	443	661	340	369	994	179
Hamburg	5hr.	2½hr.	4½hr.	1hr.	5hr.	3hr.	3½hr.	6hr.		163	311	425	377	775	607	184	679
Hannover	4hr.	2hr.	3hr.	1hr.	4½hr.	3hr.	2½hr.	5hr.	1½hr.		176	292	263	640	478	338	565
Kassel	5hr.	3hr.	4hr.	2½hr.	5½hr.	4hr.	2hr.	4hr.	2½hr.	1hr.		248	276	479	304	465	397
Cologne	1hr.	4½hr.	30min.	3hr.	7½hr.	30min.	2½hr.	4hr.	4hr.	3hr.	4hr.		505	579	432	579	379
Leipzig	7hr.	2hr.	6hr.	4hr.	1½hr.	6hr.	3¾hr.	7hr.	4½hr.	3hr.	3½hr.	6hr.		422	274	366	499
Munich	7½hr.	7hr.	5hr.	6hr.	7hr.	6hr.	3½hr.	4½hr.	6hr.	4½hr.	4hr.	5½hr.	6hr.		162	761	221
Nürnberg	6hr.	5hr.	4hr.	4hr.	5hr.	5hr.	2hr.	4½hr.	4½hr.	3hr.	2½hr.	4½hr.	4hr.	2hr.		618	247
Rostock	8hr.	3hr.	8hr.	4hr.	6hr.	7hr.	6hr.	9hr.	2hr.	4hr.	5hr.	7hr.	5½hr.	9hr.	7½hr.		833
Stuttgart	4½hr.	5½hr.	3hr.	5hr.	7hr.	4hr.	1½hr.	2hr.	5½hr.	4hr.	3hr.	3hr.	6hr.	2½hr.	2½hr.	8hr.	

INDEX

MAP INDEX

MAP LEGEND

✚ Hospital	⛟ Gondola	🏠 Hotel/Hostel	P Parking
🚓 Police	✈ Airport	🏕 Camping	**81** Autobahn Number
✉ Post Office	🚌 Bus Station	⛰ Alpine Hut	14 Road Number
ⓘ Tourist Office	🚉 Train Station	🍴 Food & Drink	▬▬ Pedestrian Zone
🅢 Bank	U U-Bahn (Subway)	Internet Cafe	⊓⊓⊓ Stairs
℞ Pharmacy	Ⓢ S-Bahn (Trolley/Surface Rail)	Nightlife	Park
⚑ Embassy/Consulate	⚓ Ferry Landing	★ Entertainment	**Common Map Abbreviations:**
▪ Site or Service	✝ Church	● Sight	Str. & -str. Straße (street)
⚔ Castle	✝ Monastery	🏛 Museum	G. & -g. Gasse (lane)
📕 Library	✡ Synagogue	☕ Theater	Pl. & -pl. Platz (square)
	☪ Mosque	🏔 Mountain	The Let's Go compass always points **N O R T H**.

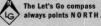